NEW EDITION

Catholicism

OTHER BOOKS BY RICHARD P. MCBRIEN

Caesar's Coin: Religion and Politics in America
Church: The Continuing Quest
Do We Need the Church?
The HarperCollins Encyclopedia of Catholicism (general editor)
Ministry: A Theological, Pastoral Handbook
The Remaking of the Church
Report on the Church: Catholicism After Vatican II

NEW EDITION

Catholicism

Completely Revised
and Updated

Richard P. McBrien

**GEOFFREY
CHAPMAN**

Published in Great Britain by Geoffrey Chapman
A Continuum imprint
The Tower Building, 11 York Road, London ST1 7NX

Copyright © 1981, 1984, 1994 Richard P. McBrien
Study edition first published in Great Britain 1984

Third edition first published in Great Britain 1994
Reprinted 2000

British Library Cataloguing-in-Publication Data
A catalogue entry for this book is available from
the British Library.

Published in the United States by HarperSanFrancisco

Printed in the United States of America

ISBN 0 225 66743 6

CONTENTS

CONTENTS

xiii

FOREWORD

This is the third edition of Father Richard McBrien's *Catholicism,* which in its previous two editions has become a true best-seller with more than one hundred and fifty thousand copies in print. Ninety percent of new books printed in America each year sell only between one and five thousand copies. What makes *Catholicism* so popular?

First, it fills an obvious gap in the English-speaking world. The Church underwent an enormous transformation during and following Vatican Council II. I completed my doctoral studies in theology in 1945 and subsequently taught dogmatic and moral theology. About a decade later (after I ceased teaching) we had, thanks to Vatican Council II, a fresh, challenging, and new view of the Church, the laity, the liturgy, religious freedom, the sacraments, ecumenism, and many other theological aspects of Catholic life. Protestant theology at its best was largely affected, too.

How could one update oneself on all these new vistas? *Catholicism* was the answer for me. During my annual retreat in a small cabin on a lake in northern Wisconsin, the eerie cry of the loons in the background, I spent long hours each night in front of a roaring fire, reading and savoring every word, seeing the contrast of the old and the new in theology, both Catholic and Protestant, clearly and fairly delineated in an extraordinarily clear and competent fashion—no esoteric reasoning, no bombast, no pious piffle, no unintelligible theological jargon. *Catholicism* deals with the deepest Christian mysteries in simple, lucid, and understandable English prose. But even more, in reading *Catholicism,* we see clearly and understand in depth the theological transformations that took place in Vatican Council II, and subsequently.

The growing millions of intelligent and questioning college- and university-educated Catholics in America today are prominent in many fields, but perhaps least educated in the theology of the modern Catholic Church. I am always amazed at the number of young Catholic students who arrive at Notre Dame today, theologically illiterate even though many have attended Catholic high schools and have grown up in Catholic homes. Perhaps their Catholic parents never really understood the theological transformation of Vatican Council II. Even I, as a theologian who followed the council closely, needed the systematic and comparative insights of *Catholicism*. I wish that every one of our students could take the course "Catholicism," taught by Father McBrien each year. Those who do are no longer theologically illiterate Catholics.

The first edition of *Catholicism* was supplemented by a new one-volume edition that incorporated a fair number of changes—clearer or more precise statements that were occasioned by critical readers of the first edition.

This current third edition is also greatly improved. It begins with a brilliant elucidation of "What is Catholicism?"—a new version of what I thought was the best chapter of the first two editions, but unfortunately came at the end of the book. Now it introduces the book and puts all that follows in a clear perspective.

There are several new chapters that complete the total synthesis of Catholicism that follows.

All too few Christians read theological books today, and I believe that is the reason why so many Christians are uninformed, lukewarm, and just plain confused as they face an ever more complicated world. *Catholicism* is a book that any intelligent Anglican, Protestant, Orthodox, or Catholic Christian can and should read with great profit for the mind as well as for the soul.

(Rev.) Theodore M. Hesburgh, C.S.C.
President Emeritus, University of Notre Dame

PREFACE

None of the editions of this book was written with the specialist in mind, although specialists should find the book useful. The reader needs only two resources: intelligence and a basic interest in Catholicism. A formal theological background is not needed, however helpful it might be. Accordingly, words and concepts whose meanings theologians take for granted are defined and explained. The material is presented in an organized and, I should hope, easy-to-follow pattern. Each topic is developed historically, beginning always with the Bible. Summaries are provided after each chapter. The table of contents, the glossary, and the double index provide additional help. There are discussion questions for each chapter, and appendices containing supplementary documentation.

For those who wish to go more deeply into the subject matter of the book or of any section of it, there are reading lists at the end of each chapter. In addition to these suggested readings, there are other basic reference works which the reader might usefully consult:

Catechism of the Catholic Church. Vatican City: Libreria Editrice Vaticana, 1992. (English translation, 1994)

The Christian Faith in the Doctrinal Documents of the Catholic Church. Rev. ed. Joseph Neuner and James Dupuis, eds. New York: Alba House, 1982.

Commentary on the Documents of Vatican II. 5 vols. Herbert Vorgrimler, ed. New York: Herder and Herder, 1967–1969.

Decrees of the Ecumenical Councils. 2 vols. Norman P. Tanner, ed. Washington, D.C.: Georgetown University Press, 1990.

Dictionary of the Ecumenical Movement. Nicholas Lossky, et al., eds. Grand Rapids: William B. Eerdmans Publishing Co., 1991.

The Documents of Vatican II. Walter Abbott and Joseph Gallagher, eds. New York: America Press, 1966.

Encyclopedia of Theology: The Concise Sacramentum Mundi. Karl Rahner, ed. New York: Seabury Press, 1975.

The New Catholic Encyclopedia. 17 vols. New York: McGraw-Hill, 1967–.

The New Dictionary of Theology. Joseph A. Komonchak, Mary Collins, and Dermot A. Lane, eds. Wilmington, Del.: Michael Glazier, 1987.

The New Jerome Biblical Commentary. Raymond E. Brown, Joseph A. Fitzmyer, and Roland E. Murphy, eds. Englewood Cliffs, N.J.: Prentice Hall, 1990.

The Oxford Dictionary of the Christian Church. 2d ed. F. L. Cross and E. A. Livingston, eds. Oxford: Oxford University Press, 1978.

All of the biblical quotations used in this book are from the New Revised Standard Version (see *The New Oxford Annotated Bible With the Apocrypha: An Ecumenical Study Bible,* Bruce M. Metzger and Roland E. Murphy, eds., New York: Oxford University Press, 1991). This new translation has been accepted for Catholic liturgical use in the United States, Canada, and other English-speaking countries. Although the language of this translation—and, indeed, of this book—is gender-inclusive, some expressions will still not satisfy all readers. For example, the NRSV continues to translate the Greek word *basilea* as "kingdom." Consequently, that word continues to be used here, although its alternate, "reign," is also used.

WHY THIS BOOK?

Pope John XXIII was elected to the papacy in 1958. Four years later he convened the Second Vatican Council, and almost everyone would agree that the Catholic Church has not been the same since. On the one hand, Catholicism and the wider community of Christian churches and non-Christian religions have been enriched by the council's renewed, ecumenical vision of the Gospel of Jesus Christ and of the life and mission of the Church in the modern world. On the other hand, the Catholic Church has been torn by conflict between those who have embraced the new with an insufficient understanding and appreciation of the old, and those who have obstinately resisted change in the name of a tradition they only partially grasp. Most Catholics fall somewhere in between—open to renewal and reform, but rooted in their Catholic heritage. Meanwhile, new generations have come along since the council who have not been party to the debate at all. These include thousands, perhaps millions, of younger Catholics who are seeking out those who might bridge the widening gap between the old and the new, the past and the present, the traditional and the contemporary, the pre–Vatican II Church and the post–Vatican II Church. And therein lies the purpose and the driving force of this book.

I remain convinced, nearly fifteen years after the first, two-volume edition of this book appeared in April 1980, that healing and reconciliation are possible because there *is* a fundamental unity between the pre–Vatican II Church and the post–Vatican II Church, the many significant differences notwithstanding. I still intend this book, therefore, as a bridge between the Church of yesterday and the Church of today, and between conservative, traditionally minded Catholics, on the one hand, and progressive, renewal-minded Catholics, on the other, even if some in the former group seem determined to resist and depreciate such an effort. History, I am convinced, provides that bridge, and that is why this book adopts a historical method and approach. The more history we know, the less likely we are to distort the reality of Catholicism by shaping it to our own predispositions or by identifying it with one razor-thin slice of its long and richly diverse history.

I have in mind, for example, the attitude of some younger, progressive Catholics who, through no fault of their own, do not know very much about pre–Vatican II Catholicism. Perhaps they suspect that a retrieval of Catholicism's past would somehow interfere with or reverse its present course. And since they are satisfied with that present course—its ecumenical openness, its spirit of freedom, its concern for justice and human rights, its readiness to change—they prefer to let the past rest in peace, or at least to leave themselves in "good faith" about it.

I have in mind also the attitude of some older, progressive Catholics who once learned a detailed history of Catholicism but who now

xli

remember how narrowly conceived that history was. It was too often an account of consecutive institutional triumphs, of the vanquishing of patently absurd heresies, of relentless and remarkably smooth doctrinal movements from truth to greater truth, but also of a patriarchal Church insensitive to the presence and gifts of women. Events and theological developments surrounding Vatican II discredited that history in their eyes, and they have not been seriously disposed to take it up since.

I have in mind, too, the attitude of those more conservative Catholics, old and young alike, who are satisfied that they know that history well enough, and believe that the Church's present course is, at worst, a betrayal of Catholicism's past, or, at best, an unenlightened dilution of its abiding genius and grandeur. They seek a restoration, to one degree or another, of the pre–Vatican Catholicism they either vaguely remember or never experienced at all.

History is not fully honored by either the progressive or the conservative side, for history both *roots* and *relativizes*. Catholicism did not begin with Vatican II, nor was it set in theological and pastoral cement with the Council of Trent in the sixteenth century and the Baroque period that followed. When taken whole and unrevised, history teaches us that Christian faith and its Catholic expression have assumed many different forms. The tendency of some conservatives is to freeze certain culturally determined forms and equate them with the essence of Catholicism. A criticism of the form becomes an attack upon the Catholic faith itself. The tendency of some progressives is to keep every form so radically open to change that no abiding core or center can easily be discerned.

I have tried in this book and in this new edition to do justice to the true values and legitimate concerns of both sides: the conservative's regard for continuity and stability, and the progressive's regard for development and growth. History provides the major link between the two because it is a reality that is at once absolute and relative. It is *absolute*—and therefore a principle of *permanence*—because it comes from the creative hand of God, is sustained by the providential care of God, and is destined for fulfillment in the final Kingdom, or Reign, of God. But history is also *relative*—and therefore a principle of *change*—because it is the history of humankind, of an unprogrammed interaction between divine grace and human freedom.

Insofar as history is absolute and permanent, we have to come to terms with it. We cannot ignore it or erase it. It defines us. We are who we are because of it. We are historical beings, which means that we do not create ourselves anew, from ground zero, each day. We begin at a point we did not choose and in the midst of a process we did not originate and do not control. On the other hand, history is also relative and changeable. It is even now in process. It is still to be. We are called to become something greater than we are. Tomorrow can be different from today or yesterday. We are to "fill the earth and subdue it" (Genesis 1:28).

POLEMICAL THEOLOGY VERSUS MEDIATING THEOLOGY

This book is not intended as an exercise in polemical theology. I am not arguing points of view peculiar to myself or to a small, maverick school of Catholic theologians. What is presented here is broadly representative of the mainstream of Catholic theology and biblical scholarship as it is practiced throughout the Church today. Indeed, if there is anything original about this work, it is in its fundamental conception and execution. I am responsible for its overall structure, for the selection and synthesizing of its content, and for its integrating themes of sacramentality, mediation, and communion. Beyond that, I have had to rely heavily upon the written work of other theologians and scholars, since neither I nor any other individual could possibly claim expertise in every doctrinal, historical, theological, moral, spiritual, biblical, liturgical, and canonical aspect of Catholicism. One American Catholic biblical scholar, now deceased, once spoke of his own work as so much "shameless borrowing." Many will borrow from this work, in turn. So be it, for it is intended as a resource to be used and disseminated widely.

As far as possible, this is a work of *mediating* theology, one that tries to mediate between the past and the present and between different approaches within the Church. Accordingly, this is not only a book *about* Catholicism but a book written, by intention at least, in the *spirit* of Catholicism as well, i.e., of openness to all truth wherever it is found and of all legitimate interpretations thereof. Given the extraordinarily positive response to the first edition of this book (including a prestigious Christopher Award in 1981 and the Annual Book Award of the College Theology Society), I would dare to suggest that I may have succeeded, however modestly, in fulfilling that original purpose. I hope that this new, thoroughly revised and updated edition will have even greater success in achieving the same end: a more catholic understanding and appreciation of the Catholic tradition.

FROM FIRST EDITION TO NEW EDITION

It is a vast understatement to point out that much has happened in the Catholic Church and in the world beyond it since the first edition of this book appeared in 1980. The fifteen-year pontificate of Paul VI has been followed, thus far, by more than fifteen years of John Paul II. Although some would characterize the present governing spirit of the Church as conservative, even restorationist, many positive developments have occurred in the Church since 1980, not least of which is the emergence of women in positions of pastoral and intellectual leadership. Nowhere has this development been more pronounced than in the fields of theology and biblical studies. The feminist turn in religious scholarship is surely reflected in this new edition of *Catholicism*, although the book hardly does full justice to its scope and significance.

As far as changes in the world are concerned, one need only remind the reader that there was a Soviet Union and a Cold War when *Catholicism* first appeared. The original edition contained a specific discussion of the morality of warfare, with special attention to the threat of nuclear war. That section has been dropped from the new edition, replaced by a section on abortion as a public policy issue. The first edition devoted only one line to abortion!

The world has also changed technologically. When I first composed this book, I did so on a secondhand manual typewriter. The new edition was produced on a personal computer. The gadgetry that we take for granted today was not part of the world of 1980: video cassette machines, modems, cable and interactive television, fax machines, electronic mail, laser discs, pagers, cellular phones, and the like.

xliv

Between the editions, the Committee on Doctrine of the National Conference of Catholic Bishops engaged in a careful and essentially sympathetic review of the text. A statement was issued in 1985 (see *Origins*, 15/9, August 1, 1985, pp. 129, 131–32). In an accompanying press release the committee's chairman, Archbishop John R. Quinn of San Francisco, insisted that "the statement should not be used to call into question Father McBrien's authentic Catholic faith or orthodoxy." Indeed, that statement had characterized the review process as "a model of cooperative ecclesial concern for the integrity of the faith, the pastoral needs of the people, and the scholarly reputation of the author," and it had expressed appreciation for "the effort and motivation...in undertaking the task of presenting a readable compendium of Catholic teaching" and for the clarifications which had already been made in the 1981 Study Edition. (For my detailed response to the statement, see the "1986 Preface to the Study Edition," pp. xxvii–xxxi.)

In preparing this new edition of *Catholicism* I have tried to take into account most of the criticisms and suggestions that I have received over the past thirteen years, as well as my own direct experience in teaching from the book at both undergraduate and graduate levels at the University of Notre Dame. However, individual readers, students, and teachers will be the final judge of those efforts.

Richard P. McBrien
University of Notre Dame
January 1994

ACKNOWLEDGMENTS

Some of those who provided important assistance and encouragement in the writing of the first edition of *Catholicism* were still doing so as I prepared this one. However, I must single out for special thanks Beverly M. Brazauskas, a long-time director of religious education and liturgy in parishes in Connecticut and Indiana, and a publisher's consultant in her field, who read the entire manuscript for clarity, coherence, and typographic errors. She also corrected all the biblical quotations to conform to the New Revised Standard Version, edited the discussion questions, generated various tables within the text, and helped in the preparation of the indexes.

J. Frank Devine, S.J., of the Weston School of Theology in Cambridge, Massachusetts, to whom I paid special and well-deserved recognition for the original edition, continued to offer support and encouragement, but this time from afar. Thomas H. Groome, professor of religious education at Boston College and, in my judgment, the leading scholar in his field, provided invaluable help in the reorganization of the material for this new edition. Appropriately, his suggestions emerged from *praxis*. He, too, has taught from the book ever since it was first published.

Others provided specific assistance for individual sections or chapters of the book. The following current and former colleagues at the University of Notre Dame were particularly generous and constructive with their help: Roger Brooks, now at Connecticut College in New London, (Judaism), Regina A. Coll, C.S.J. (women in the Church), Lawrence S. Cunningham, my successor as department chair (spirituality and contemporary thought), Cornelius F. Delaney (philosophy), Keith J. Egan, of St. Mary's College and Notre Dame (spirituality), Michael J. Himes, now at Boston College (belief and unbelief), Robert A. Krieg, C.S.C. (Christology), Catherine Mowry LaCugna (the mystery of the triune God), John A. Melloh, S.M. (liturgy), and Thomas F. O'Meara, O.P. (grace, ministry, spirituality). Other Notre Dame colleagues offered support through their encouragement and writings: Regis A. Duffy, O.F.M. (liturgy), and Richard A. McCormick, S.J. (moral theology). Charles E. Curran, of Southern Methodist University, was characteristically generous to a fault in offering detailed suggestions and help in the substantial revision of the three chapters on moral theology.

One of my benefactors is now deceased. John F. Whealon, for twenty-two years the Archbishop of Hartford, Connecticut, my home archdiocese, submitted a thirteen-page, single-spaced letter back in September 1982, in which he offered detailed critical commentary on the book. A trained Scripture scholar, he acknowledged that it had taken him many days of work to complete the project, and he expressed the hope that it would "somehow be of help and encouragement" to me and eventually contribute to a text "to which no one can take exception." I took all of his concerns into serious account. I wish he were still alive to read the new edition, even though he might not approve of everything in it. But at least he would have known that his efforts were not in vain.

I am indebted, of course, to the University of Notre Dame for granting the necessary leave to complete this book, to Donna Shearer, my secretary, not only for her assistance with this new edition but also for keeping on top of an even more complex parallel project, a new *Encyclopedia of Catholicism*, to be published soon hereafter by HarperCollins. Thanks are due as well to my editor, John Shopp, and everyone else at HarperSanFrancisco who contributed to the successful completion of this work.

Finally, a very special expression of gratitude is in order for one of the truly great figures in the contemporary Church, Theodore M. Hesburgh, C.S.C., president emeritus of the University of Notre Dame. Not only did he consent to write the Foreword to this new edition (as he had for the 1981 Study Edition), but he has been a source of unswerving support and encouragement over the years. I salute him as a remarkable personification of what Catholicism is all about.

xlviii

Catholicism

INTRODUCTION

*T*HESE first two chapters form an introductory unit to the whole book. Chapter 1 addresses the central question of the work: *What is Catholicism?* It begins with an analysis of the noun "Catholic" and the adjective that is often affixed to it, "Roman." The chapter then situates the reality of Catholicism in the wider context of human, religious, Christian, and ecclesial existence. Finally, it identifies and describes the chief characteristics by which Catholicism can be distinguished from other Christian traditions, especially the principles of *sacramentality, mediation, and communion.* These themes run through the entire work as Catholicism's integrating and defining principles.

Chapter 2 focuses on the foundation of the whole study. Since this is a work of *theology*, rather than of catechesis, and since theology is "faith seeking understanding" (St. Anselm's classic definition), *faith* is the first major topic to be addressed. What does faith mean? What are its dimensions, its characteristics, its sources, its effects, or "outcomes"? By what principles do we "interpret" faith? Are there authoritative sources of faith? If so, what constitutes them as "authoritative"? What connection is there between the faith of an individual before God and the faith of the Church? What role does the Church have in the clarification or even the definition of faith (the question of *doctrine* and *dogma*)? What rules or criteria are to be applied to the interpretation of these church pronouncements? There is a concluding reflection on *discipleship*, which is *the* most important practical outcome of faith.

Other parts of the book—on God, on Jesus Christ, on the Church, on the sacraments, on Christian existence, on spirituality—will bear even more directly and more substantively on the content and practice of Catholic and Christian faith, but these first two chapters lay an essential foundation for the whole work. The first chapter defines the *subject-matter* of the book and its basic *orientation*; the second chapter describes the *method* by which the subject-matter is presented and the orientation developed.

I

What Is Catholicism?

THE MEANING OF THE WORD

Catholicism is a rich and diverse reality. It is a Christian tradition, a way of life, and a community. That is to say, it is comprised of faith, theologies, and doctrines and is characterized by specific liturgical, ethical, and spiritual orientations and behaviors; at the same time, it is a people, or cluster of peoples, with a particular history.

The word *Catholic* is derived from the Greek adjective, *katholikos*, meaning "universal," and from the adverbial phrase, *kath' holou*, meaning "on the whole." The term was first used by St. Ignatius of Antioch (d. c. 107) in his *Letter to the Smyrnæans:* "Where the bishop is to be seen, there let all his people be; just as wherever Jesus Christ is present, we have the catholic Church" (n. 8). Ever since the Reformation, the word has commonly been used in opposition to *Protestant*, but its real opposite is *sectarian*, which pertains to a part of the Church that has separated itself off from the worldwide Church and, to some extent, from the world itself.

Thus, St. Augustine (d. 430) contrasted the separatist and sectarian movements of his time, especially Donatism in North Africa, with the Catholic Church that is both universal and orthodox in its faith. In his letter to Honoratus, a Donatist bishop, he wrote: "Do you happen to know why it should be that Christ should lose his inheritance, which is spread over the whole world, and should suddenly be found surviving only in the Africans, and not in all of them? The Catholic

3

Church exists indeed in Africa, since God willed and ordained that it should exist throughout the whole world. Whereas your party, which is called the party of Donatus, does not exist in all those places in which the writings of the apostles, their discourse, and their actions have been current" (*Epistle 49*, n. 3).

St. Cyril of Jerusalem (d. 386) was even more explicit: "The Church is called 'Catholic' because it extends through all the world... because it teaches universally and without omission all the doctrines which ought to come to human knowledge...because it brings under the sway of true religion all classes of people, rulers and subjects, learned and ignorant; and because it universally treats and cures every type of sin...and possesses in itself every kind of virtue which can be named...and spiritual gifts of every kind" (*Catechetical Lectures*, 18, n. 23).

The word *Catholic* was incorporated into the creeds along with the other notes of the Church: one, holy, and apostolic. It appears in the Creed of Cyril of Jerusalem, the Creed of Epiphanius (d. 403), and in the Nicene-Constantinopolitan Creed (381) that is still recited in the liturgy today.

But the use of the word *Catholic* became divisive after the East-West Schism of the eleventh century and the Protestant Reformation of the sixteenth century. The West claimed for itself the title *Catholic Church*, while the East, which severed the bond of communion with Rome, appropriated the name *Holy Orthodox Church*. After the ruptures of the Reformation those in communion with Rome retained the adjective *Catholic*, while the churches that broke with the papacy were called *Protestant*. However, some today insist that the adjective *Catholic* applies also to many other Christians who regard themselves as evangelical, reformed, and Catholic alike. Indeed, the Second Vatican Council (1962–1965) broadened the notion of catholicity to include churches outside the Catholic Church (*Dogmatic Constitution on the Church*, n. 8), and spoke of them as possessing varying "degrees" of catholicity (*Decree on Ecumenism*, n. 3).

Catholic or Roman Catholic?

There is another, still unresolved, aspect to the controversy, however. Are Catholics who are in communion with Rome *Roman* Catholics or just plain Catholics? Some inside as well as outside the Catholic Church think it ecumenically insensitive to drop the adjective Roman because so many Anglican, Orthodox, Protestant, and Oriental Christians also regard themselves as Catholic. But other Catholics object to the use of the adjective *Roman* on ecclesiological grounds. For such Catholics *Roman* tends to confuse rather than define the reality of Catholicism.

The history of the Church begins with Jesus' gathering of his disciples and with the postresurrection commissioning of Peter to be the chief shepherd and foundation of the Church—but in Jerusalem, not in Rome. Therefore, it is not the *Roman* primacy that gives Catholicism one of its distinctive marks of identity within the family of Christian churches, but the *Petrine* primacy. The adjective *Roman* applies more properly to the diocese, or see, of Rome than to the worldwide Church which is in union with the Bishop of Rome. Indeed, it strikes some Catholics as contradictory to call the Church Catholic and Roman at one and the same time.

Eastern-rite Catholics who are in union with Rome (sometimes pejoratively called *Uniates*) also find the adjective *Roman* objectionable. They prefer to speak of their churches as Catholic and then to distinguish particular ecclesial traditions within the Catholic communion. In addition to the Latin, or Roman, tradition, there are seven other non-Latin, non-Roman ecclesial traditions: Armenian, Byzantine, Coptic, Ethiopian, East Syrian (Chaldean), West Syrian, and Maronite. Each of these is a Catholic church in communion with the Bishop of Rome; none of these is a *Roman* Catholic church. Catholicism, therefore, is neither narrowly Roman nor narrowly Western. It is universal in the fullest sense of the word.

It should be evident from the title of this book (*Catholicism* rather than *Roman Catholicism*) which argument the author finds more compelling. To choose one side, however, is not necessarily to reject the other. One can apply the term *Catholic* to the community of churches in union with Rome without precluding its wider application to Anglicans, Orthodox, Protestants, and Oriental Christians. At the same time, Catholics can reject the adjective Roman without lapsing into ecclesiastical triumphalism. What is important is that each side explain and support the reasons for the position taken.

THE CONTEXT OF CATHOLICISM

Catholicism is not a reality that stands by itself. The word *Catholic* is not only a noun but an adjective. As an adjective it is a qualification of *Christian*, just as *Christian* is a qualification of *religious*, and *religious* is a qualification of *human*. Thus, Catholicism refers to a community of persons (the human dimension), who believe in God and shape their lives according to that belief (the religious dimension), who believe that God to be triune, and Jesus Christ to be the Son of God and the redeemer of humankind (the Christian dimension), who express and celebrate that belief in the Eucharist and who recognize the Bishop of Rome to be "the perpetual and visible source and foundation of the unity of the bishops and of the multitude of the faithful" [*Dogmatic Constitution on the Church*, n. 23] (the ecclesial dimension). To be Catholic, therefore, is to be a kind of human being, a kind of religious person, and a kind of Christian belonging to a specific eucharistic faith-community within the worldwide, or ecumenical, Body of Christ.

To be Catholic is, before all else, to be *human*. Catholicism is an understanding, affirmation, and expression of human existence before it is a corporate conviction about the pope, or the seven sacraments, or even about Jesus Christ and redemption. The first theological questions we ask ourselves are, "Who am I?" and "Who are we?" Every other theological question comes back to these. We cannot understand God, or Jesus Christ, or the Church, or anything else unless and until we come to terms with the question of ourselves. (The wider human context of Catholicism is treated in Part One, chapters 3–5. Its distinctively Catholic moral and spiritual outcomes are treated in Parts Six and Seven, chapters 25–31.)

But Catholicism is more than a corporate understanding, affirmation, and expression of what it means to be human. Catholicism answers the question of meaning in terms of ultimacy. With the Lutheran martyr Dietrich Bonhoeffer (d. 1945), Catholicism affirms that there is more to life than meets the eye, that there is "a beyond in our midst" (*Letters and Papers from Prison*). With Paul Tillich (d. 1965), one of the most prominent and influential Protestant theologians in the twentieth century, Catholicism affirms that there is a "ground of being" which is Being itself (*Systematic Theology*). With St. Thomas

Aquinas (d. 1274), Catholicism affirms that all reality is rooted in the creative, loving power of that which is most real (*ens realissimum*). Catholicism answers the question of meaning in terms of the reality of God. In brief, Catholicism is a *religious* perspective, and not simply a philosophical or anthropological one. Catholicism offers an understanding of God, and that understanding is the foundation and context for its understanding of creation, redemption, incarnation, grace, the Church, moral responsibility, eternal life, and each of the other great mysteries and doctrines of Christian faith. The doctrine of the triune God is what Christian and Catholic faith is all about. (The wider religious context of Catholicism is treated in Part Two, chapters 6, 7, and 10.)

But Catholicism is not some undifferentiated religious view. It is a form of *Christian* faith, alongside Protestantism, Anglicanism, Orthodoxy, and Oriental Christianity. Catholicism's understanding of and commitment to God is radically shaped by its understanding of and commitment to Jesus Christ. For the Christian the ultimate dimension of human experience is a triune God: a God who creates and sustains us and who identifies with our historical condition, and a God who empowers us to live according to the vocation to which we have been called. More specifically, the God of Christians is the God of Jesus Christ. (The wider Christian context of Catholicism is treated in Part Two, chapters 8–9, and Part Three, chapters 11–15.)

However, just as Jesus Christ gives access to God, so, for Catholicism, the Church gives access to Jesus Christ. Catholicism has an *ecclesial* dimension. But the Church is composed of many churches. The Church universal is the communion of local, or individual, churches (denominations, dioceses, patriarchates). Thus, the noun *church* is always modified: the Catholic Church, the Baptist Church, the Orthodox Church, the Lutheran Church, and so forth. Moreover, even these modifiers can themselves be modified: the Maronite Catholic Church, the Southern Baptist Church, the Russian Orthodox Church, the Lutheran Church/Missouri Synod, and so forth.

There are many churches, but one Body of Christ. For Catholicism, however, within the community of churches there is one Church that alone fully embodies and manifests all of the institutional elements that are necessary for the integrity of the whole Body, in particular the Eucharist and the Petrine ministry. In Catholic doctrine that one Church is the Catholic Church. As ecumenical as the Second Vatican Council was, it did not retreat from this traditional Catholic conviction: "They are fully incorporated into the society of the Church who, possessing the Spirit of Christ, accept its entire system and all the means of salvation given to it, and through union with its visible structure are joined to Christ, who rules it through the Supreme Pontiff and the bishops. This joining is effected by the bonds of professed faith, of the sacraments, of ecclesiastical government, and of communion" (*Dogmatic Constitution on the Church*, n. 14). (The wider ecclesial context of Catholicism is treated in Part Four, chapters 16–20, and Part Five, chapters 21–24).

THE SPIRIT OF CATHOLICISM

Before the Second Vatican Council most people inside and outside the Catholic Church had no apparent difficulty locating the line that separated Catholics from other Christians. Sometimes their answers were truly superficial. Thus, Catholics didn't eat meat on Friday, or Catholics don't practice birth control. The most common answer had to do with the papacy. It was said that Catholics are different from non-Catholic Christians because Catholics believe in the authority of the pope.

Even liberal or progressive Catholics accepted that answer. In the most influential book published just prior to the council, a young Swiss theologian, Hans Küng, wrote that "the chief difficulty in the way of reunion lies in the two different concepts of the Church, and especially of the concrete organizational structure of the Church.... Ultimately all questions about the concrete organizational structure of the Church are crystallized in the question of *ecclesiastical office*.... But the heart of the matter of ecclesiastical office, the great stone of stumbling, is the Petrine office. The question 'Do we need a Pope?' is the key question for reunion" (*The Council and Reunion*, London: Sheed & Ward, 1961, pp. 188–89, 193).

Since the council, however, that traditional line of distinction has been blurred considerably. The Lutheran–Roman Catholic Consultation in the United States, for example, achieved a remarkable measure of consensus on the questions of papal primacy and papal infallibility (see *Papal Primacy and the Universal Church: Lutherans and*

Catholics in Dialogue V, Paul Empie and T. Austin Murphy, eds., Minneapolis: Augsburg Publishing House, 1974; and "Teaching Authority and Infallibility in the Church," *Theological Studies* 40 [March 1979] 113–66). Furthermore, it has become increasingly evident that there are sometimes sharper divisions *within* the Catholic Church than there are between some Catholics and some Protestants. One has only to examine the content and orientation of two national Catholic newspapers in the United States to appreciate the point: *The Wanderer* on the right and the *National Catholic Reporter* on the left.

Therefore, a more theologically fruitful approach to the question of Catholic distinctiveness would seem to lie in the direction of identifying and describing various characteristics of Catholicism, each of which Catholicism shares with one or another Christian church or tradition. But no other church or tradition possesses these characteristics in quite the same way as Catholicism. In other words, there is a particular *configuration* of characteristics within Catholicism that is not duplicated anywhere else in the community of Christian churches. This configuration of characteristics is expressed in Catholicism's systematic theology; its body of doctrines; its liturgical life, especially the Eucharist; its variety of spiritualities; its religious congregations and lay apostolates; its official teachings on justice, peace, and human rights; its exercise of collegiality; and, to be sure, its Petrine ministry.

Catholicism is distinguished from other Christian churches and traditions especially in its understanding of, and practical commitment to, the principles of sacramentality, mediation, and communion. Differences between Catholic and non-Catholic (especially Protestant) approaches become clearer when measured according to these three principles.

Sacramentality

In its classical Augustinian meaning a sacrament is a visible sign of an invisible grace (namely, the divine presence). In his opening address before the second session of the Second Vatican Council in 1963, Pope Paul VI provided a more contemporary definition: "a reality imbued with the hidden presence of God." A sacramental perspective is one that "sees" the divine in the human, the infinite in the finite, the spiritual in the material, the transcendent in the immanent, the eternal in the historical. For Catholicism, therefore, all reality is sacred.

Over against this sacramental vision is the view, confirmed by memories of past excesses in the sacramental vision, that God is so "totally other" that the divine reality can never be identified with the human, the transcendent with the immanent, the eternal with the historical, and so forth. The abiding Protestant fear is that Catholics will take the sacramental principle to the point of idolatry.

The Catholic sacramental vision "sees" God in all things (St. Ignatius Loyola): other people, communities, movements, events, places, objects, the environment, the world at large, the whole cosmos. The visible, the tangible, the finite, the historical—all these are actual or potential carriers of the divine presence. Indeed, for Catholicism it is only in and through these material realities that we can encounter the invisible God. The great sacrament of our encounter with God, and of God's encounter with us, is Jesus Christ. The Church, in turn, is the fundamental sacrament of our encounter with Christ, and of Christ with us. And the sacraments, in turn, are the signs and instruments by which that ecclesial encounter with Christ is expressed, celebrated, and made effective for the glory of God and the salvation of all.

Catholicism, therefore, insists that grace (the divine presence) actually enters into and transforms nature (human life in its fullest context). The dichotomy between nature and grace is eliminated. Human existence is already graced existence. There is no merely natural end of human existence, with a supernatural end imposed from above. Human existence in its natural, historical condition is radically oriented toward God. The history of the world is, at the same time, the history of salvation.

This means that, for Catholicism, authentic human progress and the struggle for justice and peace is an integral part of the movement toward the final reign of God (see Vatican II, *Pastoral Constitution on the Church in the Modern World*, n. 39). The Catholic tradition, unlike the Lutheran, for example, has espoused no doctrine of the Two Kingdoms. The vast body of Catholic social teachings, from Pope Leo XIII in 1891 to the present, is as characteristic of Catholic Christianity as any element can be. In virtue of the sacramental principle, Catholicism affirms that God is indeed present to all human life and history.

To be engaged in the transformation of the world is to be collabora-
tively engaged in God's own transforming activity. Our human work
becomes a form of collaboration with God's creative work, as Pope
John Paul II put it in his 1981 encyclical, *Laborem Exercens*.

For Catholicism the world is essentially good, though fallen,
because it comes from the creative hand of God, is redeemed, sustained, and nurtured by God, and is destined for the final perfection
of the reign of God at history's end. That world has been redeemed by
God in Jesus Christ, and experiences healing and unity through the
abiding presence of the Holy Spirit, the "first fruits" of the final reign,
or kingdom, of God.

Mediation

A second principle—really a corollary of the first—is that of mediation. A sacrament not only signifies (as Protestants have historically
emphasized); it also *causes* what it signifies. That is, God is not only
present as an object of faith in the sacramental action; God actually
achieves something in and through that action. Thus created realities
not only contain, reflect, or embody the presence of God, they make
that presence spiritually effective for those who avail themselves of
these sacred realities. Encounter with God does not occur solely in
the inwardness of conscience or in the inner recesses of consciousness. Catholicism holds, on the contrary, that the encounter with
God is a mediated experience rooted in the historical, and affirmed as
real by the critical judgment that God is truly present and active here
or there, in this event or that, in this person or that, in this object
or that.

Again, the Protestant raises a word of caution. Just as the principle of sacramentality edges close to the brink of idolatry, so the
principle of mediation moves one along the path toward magic. Just
as there has been evidence of idolatry in some Catholic piety, so there
has been evidence of a magical view of the divine-human encounter
in certain forms of Catholic devotional life. Some Catholics have
assumed, for example, that if a certain practice were performed a
given number of times or on a given number of days in an unbroken
sequence (like the nine First Fridays), their salvation would be guaranteed. A magical view, of course, is not a solely Catholic problem,

but it is an inherent risk in Catholicism's constant stress on the principle of mediation.

Catholicism's commitment to the principle of mediation is evident especially in the importance it has always placed on the ordained ministry of the priest. God's dealings with us are not arbitrary or haphazard. God is present to all and works on behalf of all, but there are also moments and actions wherein God's presence is specially focused. The function of the priest as mediator is not to limit the encounter between God and the human person, but to focus it more clearly for the sake of the person and ultimately for the sake of the community of faith.

The principle of mediation also explains Catholicism's historic emphasis on the place of Mary, the mother of Jesus Christ. Catholicism affirms the role of Mary in salvation on the same ground that it affirms the role of Jesus Christ—without equating the two. God is present in, and redemptively at work through, the humanity of Jesus. This is the principle of mediation in its classic expression. Catholicism understands that the invisible, spiritual God is present and active on our spiritual behalf through the visible and the material, and that these are made holy and spiritually effective by reason of that divine presence. Catholicism, therefore, readily engages in the veneration (not worship) of Mary and asks her to intercede for us, not because Catholicism perceives Mary as some kind of goddess or supercreature or rival of the Lord himself, but because she is a symbol, image, and instrument of God. It is the God who is present in her and who fills her whole being that is the real object of Catholicism's veneration. Her importance, like that of the other saints, is rooted in the fact that she is a "sacrament" of the divine. And sacraments both signify and cause grace.

Communion

Third, Catholicism affirms the principle of communion: Our way to God and God's way to us is not only a mediated, but also a communal, way. Even when the divine-human encounter is most personal and individual, it is still communal, in that the encounter is made possible by the mediation of a community of faith. Thus there is not simply an individual personal relationship with God or with Jesus Christ that is established and sustained by meditative reflection on Sacred Scripture, for the Bible is the Church's book and the testimony of the Church's original faith. For Catholicism there is no relationship with God, however profound or intense, that dispenses entirely with the communal context of every relationship with God.

And this is why, for Catholicism, the mystery of the Church has always had so significant a place in its theology, doctrine, pastoral practice, moral vision, and devotional life. Catholicism has always emphasized the place of the Church as the sacrament of Christ, mediating salvation through sacraments, ministries, and other institutional elements, and as the Communion of Saints and the People of God. It is here, at the point of Catholicism's understanding of itself as Church, that we come to the heart of the distinctively Catholic understanding and practice of Christian faith. For it is here, in Catholic ecclesiology, that we find the most vivid convergence of the three principles of sacramentality, mediation, and communion.

The Protestant again raises a word of caution. If we emphasize too much the principle of communion, we can endanger the freedom of the individual believer. If sacramentality can lead to idolatry, and mediation to magic, the principle of communion can lead to a collectivism that suppresses individuality, and an authoritarianism that suppresses freedom of thought and of action. One can find many instances in history where this Protestant concern has been justified. Church members have been burned at the stake, literally and figuratively, for articulating opinions at variance with those of the Church's ruling authorities.

But stress upon the individual also has its inherent weakness, just as there are inherent weaknesses in the historic Protestant insistences on the otherness of God (over against the Catholic sacramental principle) and on the immediacy of the divine-human encounter (over against the Catholic principle of mediation). In recent years, in fact, some important Protestant theologians have come to acknowledge these inherent problems in Protestantism itself and the corresponding truth of the Catholic sacramental vision. Paul Tillich's *The Protestant Era* (Chicago: University of Chicago Press, 1948) and Langdon Gilkey's *Catholicism Confronts Modernity: A Protestant View* (New York: Seabury Press, 1975, pp. 1–60) are two cases in point.

For Gilkey, Catholicism manifests "a remarkable sense of humanity and grace in the communal life of Catholics.... Consequently the love of life, the appreciation of the body in the senses, of joy and celebration, the tolerance of the sinner, these natural, worldly, and 'human' virtues are far more clearly and universally embodied in Catholics and Catholic life than in Protestants and Protestantism." The Catholic principle of symbol or sacramentality, Gilkey suggests, "may provide the best entrance into a new synthesis of the Christian tradition with the vitalities as well as the relativities of contemporary existence" (pp. 17–18, 20–22).

Other Catholic Principles

Sacramentality, mediation, and communion are not the only principles or themes one might select to describe and explain the distinctive reality of Catholicism, although these three principles are implied in all others.

1. *Tradition*. Catholicism is a tradition that places great emphasis *on* tradition. It recognizes that the Bible itself is the product of tradition (or, more precisely, of many traditions). Before there were written texts the faith was handed on through proclamation, catechesis, worship, and personal example. For Catholicism, God speaks through means such as these, not only through words but through deeds as well. History in general and the history of the Church in particular are carriers of this divine revelation. Catholicism, therefore, not only reads its Sacred Scripture, but also its own corporate life and experience. As Pope John XXIII (d. 1963) once said, history itself is a teacher.

2. *Reason*. Catholicism also respects and emphasizes the role of reason in the understanding and expression of Christian faith. For Catholicism all created reality is graced, including the intellect. Though fallen, it is redeemed. Though tainted by sin, it is permeated and elevated by grace. That is why philosophy, apologetics, and so-called natural theology have occupied so important a place in Catholic thought. For Catholicism it is never sufficient merely to repeat the words of Sacred Scripture or even of official doctrinal pronouncements. The critical faculties must also be applied to the data of faith if

14

we are to understand it and appropriate it and then put it into practice. Accordingly, the First Vatican Council (1869–1870) not only rejected rationalism (the belief that reason alone could grasp the mysteries of faith), but also Fideism (the belief that an uncritical faith, apart from reason, is sufficient to grasp God's revelation).

3. *Analogy.* Catholicism's use of reason is also analogical. Indeed, some have spoken of a "Catholic imagination" as distinctively analogical (David Tracy, *The Analogical Imagination: Christian Theology and the Culture of Pluralism*, New York: Crossroad, 1981). It pertains to a way of thinking about God and of understanding the divine-human encounter that seeks always to find "similarity-in-difference," in contrast to a more typically Protestant way of thinking that is dialectical— emphasizing always what is unique in God and, therefore, the radical dissimilarities that exist between the divine and the human. For Catholicism we come to a knowledge of God through our knowledge of the created world, and especially of the humanity of Jesus, who is the "primary analogue," and through an understanding of our own human experience. Because the reality of God is mediated through such visible signs as these, the Catholic analogical imagination is essentially sacramental.

4. *Universality.* As its very name suggests, Catholicism is characterized, finally, by its universality, that is, a radical openness to all truth and to every value. It is comprehensive and all-embracing toward the totality of Christian experience and tradition, in all the theological, doctrinal, spiritual, liturgical, canonical, institutional, and social richness and diversity of that experience and tradition. It is neither a sect nor a schismatic entity, although sectarianism and schism are not unknown to it. Nor is it inextricably linked with the culture of a particular nation or region of the world. Catholicism is, in principle, as Asian as it is European, as Slavic as it is Latin, as Mexican or Nigerian as it is Irish or Polish.

There is no list of Catholic "Fathers" or Catholic "Mothers" which does not include the great theological and spiritual writers of the period *before* as well as after the division of East and West and the divisions within the West. Ignatius of Antioch and Gregory of Nyssa are as much Catholic Fathers as are Augustine or Thomas Aquinas.

15

Thecla and Brigid of Kildaire are as much Catholic Mothers as are Catherine of Siena or Teresa of Ávila.

Nor are there schools of theology which Catholicism excludes, variations in their inherent strengths and weaknesses notwithstanding. Catholicism continues to read Irenæus of Lyons and Clement of Alexandria, Athanasius and Cyril of Jerusalem, Gregory of Nazianzen and Augustine, Anselm of Canterbury and Bernard of Clairvaux, Abelard and Hugh of St. Victor, Thomas Aquinas and Bonaventure, Robert Bellarmine and Johann Adam Möhler, Karl Rahner and Hans Urs von Balthasar.

Nor are there spiritualities which Catholicism excludes, their variations again notwithstanding. Catholicism is open to *The Cloud of Unknowing* and the *Introduction to the Devout Life*, to Francis and Clare of Assisi and to Bernard of Clairvaux, to Hildegard of Bingen and Julian of Norwich, to Ignatius Loyola and John of the Cross, to Abbot Marmion and Thomas Merton.

Nor are there doctrinal streams and mighty rivers that Catholicism closes off. Catholics are as guided by the Council of Nicea as by Vatican I, by Chalcedon as by Lateran IV, by Trent as by Vatican II. They read Gregory the Great as well as Paul VI, Clement of Rome as well as Leo XIII, Pius XII as well as John XXIII.

Catholicism is characterized, therefore, by a both/and rather than an either/or approach. It is not nature *or* grace, but graced nature; not reason *or* faith, but reason illumined by faith; not law *or* Gospel, but law inspired by the Gospel; not Scripture *or* tradition, but normative tradition within Scripture; not faith *or* works, but faith issuing in works and works as expressions of faith; not authority *or* freedom, but authority in the service of freedom; not unity *or* diversity, but unity in diversity. In a word, Catholicism is *catholic*.

SUMMARY

1. Catholicism is a Christian tradition, a way of life, and a community.

2. The word *Catholic*, derived from the Greek, means "universal." Its opposite is sectarian rather than Protestant.

3. Many non-Catholic Christians insist on the use of the adjective *Roman* to describe the Church that is in union with Rome, because they also regard themselves as Catholic. But there are Eastern-rite churches that are in union

with Rome, and yet are not of the Roman, or Latin, rite. Therefore, the adjective *Roman* would pertain only to a portion of the Church that is in union with Rome, albeit the largest portion by far.

4. Catholicism is, first of all, a way of being human, then a way of being religious, and then a way of being Christian. Catholicism can only be understood within this wider context.

5. Catholicism is characterized by three principles: sacramentality, mediation, and communion. The special configuration of these three principles within Catholicism constitutes its distinctiveness. It is a tradition that sees God in all things (sacramentality), using the human, the material, and the finite (mediation), to bring about the unity of humankind (communion).

6. Other distinctively Catholic principles include its emphasis on tradition, its regard for reason, its analogical imagination, and its universality, including a both/and rather than an either/or approach to Christian faith and practice.

SUGGESTED READINGS

Adam, Karl. *The Spirit of Catholicism.* Garden City, N.Y.: Image Books, 1954.

Cunningham, Lawrence. *The Catholic Faith: An Introduction.* New York: Paulist Press, 1987.

Delaney, John J., ed. *Why Catholic?* New York: Doubleday, 1979.

Dillenberger, John, and Claude Welch. *Protestant Christianity: Interpreted Through Its Development.* 2d ed. New York: Macmillan, 1988.

Dulles, Avery. *The Catholicity of the Church.* Oxford: Clarendon Press, 1985.

Gilkey, Langdon. *Catholicism Confronts Modernity: A Protestant View.* New York: Seabury Press, 1975, chapter 1.

Happel, Stephen, and David Tracy. *A Catholic Vision.* Philadelphia: Fortress Press, 1984.

Haughton, Rosemary. *The Catholic Thing.* Springfield, Ill.: Templegate Publishers, 1979.

Hellwig, Monika K. *Understanding Catholicism.* New York: Paulist Press, 1981.

Lossky, Vladimir. *The Mystical Theology of the Eastern Church.* London: Clarke, 1957.

Lubac, Henri de. *Catholicism: A Study of the Corporate Destiny of Mankind.* New York: Sheed & Ward, 1958.

Marty, Martin E. *Protestantism.* New York: Holt, Rinehart and Winston, 1972.

Sykes, Stephen, and John E. Booty, eds. *The Study of Anglicanism.* Philadelphia: SPCK/Fortress Press, 1988.

17

I I

Faith and Its Outcomes: Theology, Doctrine, Discipleship

INTRODUCTION

Christian faith is that gift of God by which we freely accept God's self-communication in Christ. Catholicism is a communal, ritual, moral, spiritual, and intellectual expression of Christian faith. According to a common pre–Vatican II understanding, Catholicism is the definitive and normative expression of Christian faith. All other expressions are, at best, partial and imperfect; at worst, they are distorted and false. The Second Vatican Council's *Decree on Ecumenism* took a more positive approach, acknowledging that the separated churches and communities have "significance and importance in the mystery of salvation" and that the "Spirit of Christ has not refrained from using them as means of salvation..." (n. 3).

Whatever the precise relationship between Christian and Catholic faith, there is general agreement across denominational lines that faith is utterly fundamental for the Christian life on earth and for eternal life hereafter. Indeed, the Council of Trent referred to it as the "beginning of human salvation" (*Decree on Justification*, session VI, chap. 8). It is the principle of life for the righteous (Romans 1:17;

19

Galatians 3:11; Philippians 3:9–10) and, with Baptism, it makes us new creatures in Christ (2 Corinthians 5:17), who is its central object (Galatians 2:20).

Just as human life is a process of self-knowledge achieved through critical reflection on one's ordinary human experiences, so Christian life is a process of self-knowledge achieved through critical reflection on one's human and religious experiences, or, more precisely, on one's human experiences seen in their religious depths.

Critical reflection on faith is what is known as *theology*. According to the classic definition of St. Anselm of Canterbury (d. 1109), theology is "faith seeking understanding" (*fides quærens intellectum*). But theology is not the only outcome of faith. In the face of perceived threats to the purity and integrity of the faith or to the unity of the faith-community, the pastoral leadership of the Church on occasion chooses among competing theologies to formulate normative rules that might guide the Church's preaching, catechesis, and formal teaching. These normative rules are called *doctrines* (literally, "teachings"). Doctrines that are promulgated with the highest solemnity, that is, as definitive rules of faith, are called *dogmas* (literally, "what is right"). All dogmas are doctrines, but not all doctrines are dogmas.

But neither Christianity in general nor Catholicism in particular is merely an intellectual expression of faith. Two other major outcomes of faith are worship (sacramental life) and moral behavior. The ancient axiom, *lex orandi, lex credendi* (literally, "the law of praying [is] the law of believing"), indicates that worship is an outcome of faith parallel with theology. The latter is "faith seeking understanding"; the former is "faith seeking ritual expression." Faith also generates moral behavior. The believer is a doer. More precisely, the believer is engaged in a lifelong process of learning how to act in accordance with the faith that has been proclaimed and received. That learning process is known as *discipleship*. Since the whole Christian life is one of discipleship, and since worship is the "summit" and the "source" of that life (Vatican II, *Constitution on the Sacred Liturgy*, n. 10), discipleship embraces both worship and moral behavior. It is, along with theology and doctrine, a major outcome of faith; indeed, it is the primary and decisive outcome of faith (see, for example, Matthew 7:21 and 1 John 4:20).

Unfortunately, many Catholics have difficulty discerning and understanding the crucial differences that exist among these various elements, and especially among *faith*, *theology*, and *doctrine*. As a consequence, they tend to collapse the distinctions between faith and theology, on the one hand, and theology and doctrine, on the other. When some insist that we teach "the faith" rather than theology, they seem to assume that faith is available to us in some nontheological state—that it is possible, in other words, to isolate the former from the latter as one might separate two chemicals in a laboratory experiment. But every statement about faith, indeed every *thought* about faith, is already theological. The question, therefore, is not *whether* faith can be expressed without recourse to theology, but rather *what kind* of theology is best suited to its expression at this time in history and within this particular culture.

Neither are theology and doctrine to be identified. Theology is critical reflection on the faith; doctrine is an official teaching about it. Doctrine always depends upon, and is expressive of, some theology. Nevertheless, one cannot argue back from doctrine to theology and conclude that the theology embodied in the doctrine enjoys the same official status as the doctrine itself. There are many official teachings (for example, on the Real Presence of Christ in the Eucharist or on the ministerial priesthood) that can be embraced without necessarily accepting their underlying biblical, historical, philosophical, and theological arguments and assumptions.

METHOD

The distinctions among faith, theology, doctrine, and discipleship are especially important for understanding the method employed in this book and for grasping the meaning and practical consequences of Christian faith generally. A faith that one never thinks about or consciously expresses, whether in words or in actions, is in effect no faith at all. A person who had such faith would be like an individual who purchased a winning multimillion-dollar lottery ticket, but never bothered to look at it and so never redeemed it. Until the ticket's expiration date is reached, is the person a multimillionaire? In principle, yes. In actuality, no. Although the person would have the resource within his or her possession to become a multimillionaire, that individual could not purchase a Rolls Royce or a vacation home in Florida without first retrieving the lottery ticket and turning it in for cash.

Faith is a gift of God, but, like the winning lottery ticket in the example above, unless the gift is accepted and the "package" is opened, it is of no real value to the intended receiver. It is as if it doesn't even exist. Accordingly, only a faith that is thought about (via theology) and acted upon (via discipleship) is a living faith. But thinking about and acting upon faith require conscious and sustained effort.

The purpose of this book, therefore, is not simply to educate its readers *about* Catholicism. It is to help Catholics and other Christians as well to *think theologically*, that is, to think for themselves about the meaning and practical implications of their faith. The book invites the reader to do that within a Catholic perspective that incorporates the "mind of the Church." But it is not the "mind of the Church" as hierarchy only, but of the *whole* Church, that is, of the whole People of God.

The critical appropriation of one's faith is essential to its maturation. If the "unexamined life is not worth living" (Plato), neither is the unexamined faith. But the critical appropriation of one's faith is also essential to the ongoing renewal of the Church. Within Catholicism there has been a progressive movement, since Vatican II, away from a faith that is passive and childlike to one that is active and adult, and from a style of handing on a faith that is controlling and paternalistic to a style that seeks "to rouse faith in [others] and to confirm them in faith, not to exert coercion upon them" (*Declaration on Religious Freedom*, n. 11).

This book will serve its primary purpose, therefore, if it first provides those who do not know the tradition well with a comprehensive view and critical grasp of that tradition; and, second, if it persuades those who *do* know the tradition that the task of critical appropriation and assimilation is never finished, and that the tradition is best preserved not by repeating it routinely, but by freshly rethinking and reapplying it in every new age and circumstance, and indeed in the face of every new crisis of growth or decline.

But if readers are to grasp the *content* of this substantial book, they must grasp its *method* as well. The method is one that David

Tracy has called "critical correlation," which is a modification of Paul Tillich's well-known "method of correlation" (see Tillich's *Systematic Theology*, vol. 1, Chicago: University of Chicago Press, 1951, pp. 67–73). The correlation is between the Christian message (Scripture, doctrines, creeds, nonbiblical texts, events, images, persons, rituals) and the human situation. For Tillich, the method of correlation "makes an analysis of the human situation out of which the existential questions arise, and it demonstrates that the symbols used in the Christian message are the answers to these questions" (p. 70). Tracy reminds us, however, that these two realities—the Christian message and the human situation—have to be creatively reinterpreted. We cannot simply repeat, or accept at face value, what we find in the one or the other. We must "critically interpret the tradition mediating the [Christ-]event ... [and we] must critically interpret the situation in the light of the event" (*The Analogical Imagination: Christian Theology and the Culture of Pluralism*, New York: Crossroad, 1981, p. 405). This establishes a pattern, or method, of "mutually critical correlations between interpretations of situation and event as each reality influences (confronts, correlates, informs, transforms) the understanding of the other" (p. 406).

Following the "method of critical correlation" that is generally accepted and employed by mainline Catholic theologians today, this book attends critically to both poles of the dialectic. On the one hand, it seeks to provide a critical appropriation of the Christian message, drawing upon the findings of contemporary biblical, theological, and historical scholarship; on the other hand, the book seeks to provide a critical appropriation of the human situation, of the kind of developments listed in Vatican II's *Pastoral Constitution on the Church in the Modern World*, nn. 4–10 (see especially chapter 3 of this book).

The correlation of the Christian message and the human situation in a mutual conversation, or dialogue, has but a single intention: to draw out of our critical reflection upon Christian faith (which is theology) the outcomes of "right belief" (orthodoxy), "right practice" (orthopraxis), and "right worship." The latter two, as indicated above, are folded into the one overarching concept of "discipleship."

For the Catholic, all of the above must be guided by, and done in dialogue with, the living faith as understood, proclaimed, taught, celebrated, and practiced by the Church. Indeed, it is this communal, ecclesial faith that makes the Bible a life-giving text and the postbiblical tradition a life-giving carrier of the Christian message. The Bible is more than a collection of historical books to be studied by scholars and exegetes. It is the primary source and expression of the Church's worship, preaching, catechesis, teaching, and spirituality. So too, tradition is more than a collection of texts, events, and objects. It is the process and story by which the Church lives its faith down through the centuries.

As an interpreter of the Christian message, the Catholic theologian is "internally related" to the Church. "That relationship usually takes the form of an internalized sense of responsibility to the church, indeed a sense of real loyalty to the church community and its traditions and an internalizing of the plausibility structures and the ethical and religious imperatives of the tradition" (Tracy, p. 25).

Here again the "method of critical correlation" is engaged. The Catholic theologian, on the one hand, gives faithful but critical attention to the official teachings of the Church (what is proposed, whether definitively or not, by the hierarchical magisterium), and, on the other hand, accords careful but critical attention to the findings of other theologians, biblical scholars, and academic interpreters of the Christian message.

It is not the case that we have two separate and independent sources of Catholic truth: the official (or hierarchical) magisterium and the theologians. Nor is it the case that Catholics, or the readers of this book, are free to choose whatever they like, as if from one column or the other on a Chinese menu. The method is "critical," but it is also and always "correlative." As Vatican II's *Dogmatic Constitution on Divine Revelation* reminds us, "sacred tradition, Sacred Scripture, and the teaching authority of the Church ... are so linked and joined together that one cannot stand without the others ..." (n. 10). What ultimately holds them all together is the Holy Spirit; what immediately holds them all together is the *sensus fidelium*, the sense of faith that the People of God share among themselves: "The body of the faithful as a whole, anointed as they are by the Holy One (see 1 John 2:20, 27), cannot err in matters of belief. Thanks to a supernatural sense of the faith which characterizes the People as a whole, it manifests this unerring quality when ... it shows universal agreement in matters of faith and morals" (*Dogmatic Constitution on the*

24

Church, n. 12). This was, of course, a favorite theme of the nineteenth-century English convert from Anglicanism to Catholicism, Cardinal John Henry Newman (d. 1890) in his *On Consulting the Faithful in Matters of Doctrine* (1859; reprinted by Sheed & Ward, 1985).

This chapter began with a brief description of the problem created by the failure to understand the differences among faith, theology, doctrine, and discipleship. What follows is a more detailed discussion of each of these elements. Faith, of course, is the fundamental reality. Without it, there would be no theology, no doctrines, and no discipleship. To be sure, faith itself depends upon revelation, but we shall take that up later, in chapter 7. (There is also additional consideration of faith as a theological virtue in chapter 26.)

FAITH

Old Testament Notions of Faith

The Hebrew verb *'amān* (meaning "to be firm" or "to be solid," and therefore "to be true") is the Old Testament equivalent of the New Testament Greek word *pisteuein*. The Hiphil (or causative stem) of the Hebrew *'amān*, meaning "to accept something as true," always indicates a personal relationship. Thus, our acceptance of something as true is really the acceptance of the person who proposes it for belief. The Israelites accepted Moses as their leader on the basis of their trust in him personally. They accepted him as one designated by God.

The Hebrew noun *ᵉmûnah* means "solidity" or "firmness" (see Exodus 17:12), and this solidity or firmness, in turn, offers security (Isaiah 33:6). God offers security because of God's own fidelity (Psalm 36:6) to the divine promises and the Covenant with Israel. God's fidelity is, in turn, grounded in love and mercy (*ḥesed*). Because God is faithful (*neᵉ'mān*), one must believe God's word and accept God's commands (Deuteronomy 9:23; Psalm 119:66). Thus, Abraham believed Yahweh when the Lord promised him numerous descendants.

The Book of Isaiah offers certain peculiar features regarding the reality of faith. The notion of faith implies an acceptance of the power and will of God to deliver Judah from political crisis, and the acceptance is demonstrated by abstinence from all political and military action. To do otherwise is to fail to trust Yahweh. One who believes has no worry (Isaiah 28:16). The scope of faith is unlimited; it demands *total commitment to Yahweh.*

The intellectual quality of faith is more prominent in chapters 40–66 of Second, or Deutero, Isaiah (so called because modern biblical scholars hold that this part of the book did not have the same authorship as the first thirty-nine chapters). The Israelites are the witnesses of the true God to the extent that they draw other nations to know, believe, and understand that Yahweh is their Lord (Isaiah 43:10). But even this faith is not purely intellectual. "Knowing" God, in this sense, is not speculative knowledge. Rather it is the experience of God through God's revealed word and saving deeds. The more common way of describing the faith relationship with Yahweh in the Old Testament is through the notion of hearing rather than believing, and the hearing must lead to acceptance and obedience.

The foundation stone of Old Testament faith is God, the One to whom the world and all living things owe their created existence and upon whom everything depends for survival and well-being (see Genesis 1–2, Exodus 3, e.g.). Old Testament faith expresses itself in repentance, obedience, and trust. (See, for example, the story of Noah in Genesis 6:9,22; 7:5, and that of Abraham in Genesis 22:1–18.) In the Old Testament the response of faith is, therefore, primarily a moral response, i.e., one of trust and obedience rather than of belief.

Old Testament faith is essentially related to the Covenant (see Deuteronomy 6:17; 7:11), and humankind's response entails the keeping of the Commandments. Consequently, Old Testament faith is also basically corporate rather than individual (see the Psalms). It is related to the fear of the Lord, but not fear in the commonsense meaning of the word. Fear of the Lord means rather a willingness and a readiness to do the will of God, and this, in turn, generates a genuine feeling of security and trust (Job 4:6). But there can be no compromises. Old Testament faith makes an exclusive demand upon Israel (Exodus 20:3; Deuteronomy 5:7). God tolerates no idolatry.

Finally, in the period after the Exile, i.e., after the Edict of Cyrus in 538 B.C., faithfulness to the Law is the expression of faith (see especially Daniel and Judith).

New Testament Notions of Faith

Synoptics

In the Synoptics (the Gospels of Matthew, Mark, and Luke, called *Synoptics* because, when they are looked at side by side, similarities of structure and content immediately appear), Jesus demanded faith (Matthew 9:28; Mark 4:40; Luke 8:25), praised faith when he discovered it (Matthew 8:10; Luke 7:9), and declared its saving power (Matthew 9:22; Mark 5:34; Luke 8:48). In the Synoptic Gospels the act of faith is directed to God the Father and to Jesus himself. Faith is, first of all, trust in God (Mark 5:34,36; 9:23; 11:22–23; Luke 17:6), but it is also directed toward Jesus; i.e., it is the acceptance of Jesus as the one he claimed himself to be (Mark 8:27–30,38). Behind all of Jesus' utterances about faith there lies that sense of his special relationship to God as Father (Mark 8:38; 9:37 = Matthew 10:40; Mark 12:1–11, 35–37; Matthew 10:32–33; 11:27–30; 16:17–19).

Acts of the Apostles

Faith is the acceptance of the message of the Gospel (Acts of the Apostles 8:13–14), and the "believers" are those who accept the preaching of the Apostles and join the Christian community. The object of belief is the apostolic preaching, and this belief is centered on Jesus as the Risen Lord (5:14; 9:42; 11:17; 15:11). "Therefore let the entire house of Israel know with certainty that God has made him both Lord and Messiah, this Jesus whom you crucified" (2:36). Belief in the Lordship of Christ is at the core of the apostolic preaching and, therefore, at the heart of faith itself.

Acceptance of Jesus as Lord is expressed through repentance, and this is sacramentally demonstrated in Baptism, to which there is attached the guarantee of forgiveness and the renewal by the Holy Spirit: "Peter said to them, 'Repent, and be baptized every one of you in the name of Jesus Christ so that your sins may be forgiven; and you will receive the gift of the Holy Spirit' " (2:38). (For the relationship between faith and Baptism, a point to which we shall return in the discussion of the Church and the sacraments in Parts Four and Five, see also Acts of the Apostles 10:43; 18:8; 20:21.)

In early Christianity faith requires a break from the past and from other religious allegiances. But it is especially a break from sin. It is belief in God's word as personified in Christ, and so faith necessarily involves a personal relationship with Christ. In the Acts of the Apostles, faith is not simply a subjective attitude; it also embodies objective content ("The word of God continued to spread...and a great many of the priests became obedient to the faith"—6:7; elsewhere in the New Testament, see Jude 20; Romans 1:5; 4:14; 10:8; Galatians 1:23; Ephesians 4:5; 1 Timothy 1:19; 3:9; 4:6). Finally, the faith of early Christianity is directed not only toward the saving events of the past but also toward the future and toward the saving power of the Risen Lord even now (Acts of the Apostles 2:17–21; 3:18–21).

The Pauline Literature

For Paul, justification is achieved through faith and Baptism. The connection between justice and faith was taken over by Paul from Genesis 15:6 ("Abraham believed God, and it was reckoned to him as righteousness"—Romans 4:3). Faith, then, is the key to reconciliation with God and liberation from sin. One must simply confess one's own helplessness and make oneself open to divine grace (Ephesians 2:8–9). Faith is the principle of life for the righteous (Romans 1:17; Galatians 3:11; Philippians 3:9–10), and, in conjunction with Baptism, effects a new creation (2 Corinthians 5:17). The central object of faith is Christ (Galatians 2:20), but for Paul it is not only a matter of faith in Christ but more especially of faith in the preached word (Romans 10:8). Indeed, faith comes through preaching (Romans 10:13–15).

Paul summarizes the content of the preaching in various ways. Essentially the preaching proclaims that God was in Christ reconciling the world to God (2 Corinthians 5:19; Colossians 1:12–20), that Jesus is Lord, and that God has raised him from the dead so that through his resurrection he might communicate new life to those who believe and are baptized: "If you confess with your lips that Jesus is Lord and believe in your heart that God raised him from the dead, you will be saved" (Romans 10:9). And this same text indicates that faith is not simply interior but must be expressed and confessed. There is, in fact, a good summary of the confession of faith in 1 Timothy 3:16: "Without any doubt, the mystery of our religion is

28

great: 'He was revealed in the flesh, vindicated in the Spirit, seen by the angels, proclaimed among the Gentiles, believed in throughout the world, taken up into glory.' " So with Paul, as with the Acts of Apostles, faith looks not only to the past but also to the future (1 Thessalonians 4:14), and even though faith grants a measure of assurance and confidence, it still retains a degree of obscurity (2 Corinthians 5:7).

Faith, according to Paul, is also obedience (Romans 1:5; 16:26), demanding total surrender to Christ. And it is not accomplished in a single act. Faith must grow (2 Corinthians 10:15). So, too, it can become weak and die (1 Thessalonians 3:10; Romans 14:1). And the principle of growth is always *love*. "For in Christ Jesus neither circumcision nor uncircumcision counts for anything; the only thing that counts is faith working through love" (Galatians 5:6). But for Paul only the interior illumination of the Holy Spirit enables us to grasp through faith the mystery of Christ's death and resurrection (1 Corinthians 2:2–16; 12:3; Ephesians 1:17–18; 3:14–17; Colossians 2:2). The believer passes from ignorance of God to the knowledge and love of God through the action of the Spirit (Galatians 4:8–9; Ephesians 4:18; 5:8; 2 Corinthians 4:6). Everything is oriented toward union with God through Christ and in the Holy Spirit (Romans 8:11,19–23, 29; 1 Corinthians 6:15–20; 2 Corinthians 5:8; Philippians 1:19–23; 3:19–21; 1 Thessalonians 4:17).

The Johannine Literature

The Johannine theology of faith is similar to the Pauline, except that John places greater stress on faith as knowledge. To believe in Christ is to know him. The object of faith is more explicit in John: that Jesus came from God (John 16:30), that he is the Holy One of God (6:69), that he is the Messiah (11:27). Jesus is the object of faith, and since Jesus is one with the Father, faith in Jesus is faith in the Father (5:19–27; 12:44,49; 14:1,6–11; 16:27–30; 1 John 2:23).

This knowledge, however, is not assimilated independently of the power and presence of the Holy Spirit. Faith is impossible without the interior "attraction" of grace, by which we are taught to know Christ (John 14:15–23; 15:15,26; 16:13), and by which we share in Christ's own filial knowledge of God (John 6:44–46,57). The believer, therefore, already possesses eternal life (John 3:16–17,36; 5:24; 1 John 3:15; 5:12–13), which consists of knowing Christ (John 17:3) and which tends ultimately to the vision of God (John 17:24,26; 1 John 3:1–2).

What is perhaps unique in the Johannine writings is that faith is placed in the words of Jesus (John 2:22; 5:47; 8:45) as well as in the words of the Apostles or in the apostolic preaching (17:20). In fact, throughout the Fourth Gospel and the First Epistle, the role of the witnesses of faith is emphasized: John the Baptist (1:29–35), God's own witness as guarantor of the faith (1 John 5:7–12), Christ and the Holy Spirit, and even the Christian saints (John 14:12–14). Faith involves the acceptance of the witness, and this, in turn, raises the question of the sign that accompanies the witness. For according to the Johannine presentation, faith arises under the impact of signs (John 1:14; 4:50–54; 8:30; 10:42; 11:45–47; 12:9–11). In the Synoptics, for example, Jesus performs a miracle in response to faith. In John, miracles are employed to evoke faith (17:6–8).

Faith brings life (3:36); unbelief brings condemnation (3:18–20). For John, the greatest tragedy is the sin of unbelief (1:10–11; 16:9). And like Paul, John insists that the work of faith is love of neighbor (1 John 3:23).

Other New Testament Sources

In the Epistle to the Hebrews (especially chapter 11) faith is the solid reality of *hope*, the conviction about the invisible world. It is Jesus who initiates and consummates faith (Hebrews 12:2). One must believe in God, and believe that God creates and rewards the just (11:6). The Letter of James speaks of faith in terms which undeniably are far different from Paul's. It seems that James thought that Paul's views on freedom from the law needed further clarification, if not correction. James insists that faith does not exempt one from all of the obligations of the law. Faith without works is dead. But the works proposed by James are not the works of the law. They are charity to the needy (James 2:15–17), assistance to those in danger (2:25), and so forth. The works of the law mentioned in 2:8–11 are love of one's neighbor and the prohibition of adultery and murder.

In the Pastoral Epistles (1 and 2 Timothy, and Titus), Jude, and the Book of Revelation (Apocalypse), the notion of belief becomes more concrete as the Church itself gradually develops. Faith is a mystery imparted to Christians (1 Timothy 3:9) and is something to be preserved (2 Timothy 4:7; Revelation 14:12).

Early Christian Writers

The term *Fathers of the Church* traditionally embraces all ancient Christian writers down to Gregory the Great (d. 604) or Isidore of Seville (d. 636) in the West, and John of Damascus (d. c. 749) in the East. The term, however, should not be taken in a gender-exclusive way. Christian women have from the beginning witnessed to the faith in every conceivable way: by proclamation, catechesis, teaching, and martyrdom itself. The lack of a comparable list of "Catholic Mothers" may be a defect of contemporary cultures or of historical scholarship. (See Patricia Wilson-Kastner, et al., *A Lost Tradition: Women Writers of the Early Church,* Lanham, Md.: University Press of America, 1981.)

The earliest of the writers, known as the Apostolic Fathers, identified faith with the acceptance of the Christian message or with the knowledge of God and of Christ. The first step toward a certain formulation of faith as assent given to revealed truths was made by St. Justin (d. 165). The believer is one who assents to certain truths and who knows them as truths. St. Irenæus (d. c. 200) spoke more of the object of faith than of the act itself. For Irenæus, the Church proposes the object of faith and the believer accepts it as true and thus comes to a knowledge of the truth. It was Clement of Alexandria (d. 215) who referred to faith as a passing from darkness to the light of knowledge, whose object is God revealed to us in Christ. The knowledge of faith suffices for salvation, but there is given an even higher form of knowledge (*gnosis*) which one can achieve through faith. It was the heresy of *Gnosticism* which distorted this concept of faith as knowledge, making it accessible only to an elite few. Later Fathers, such as Origen (d. 254), St. Cyril of Jerusalem (d. 386), St. Athanasius (d. 373), St. John Chrysostom (d. 407), St. Cyril of Alexandria (d. 444), St. John of Damascus (d. c. 749), and others also wrote of faith in this vein, as assent to doctrines proposed for our belief by the Church.

31

None of these Fathers, however, developed so impressive a theology of faith as St. Augustine (d. 430). For him the act of faith is essentially the assent given to the revelation (see especially his *Commentary on St. John's Gospel*). The knowledge of faith progresses toward the wise understanding of mysteries, but this knowledge remains obscure in comparison with the fullness of the Beatific Vision (i.e., the final, unobstructed, unmediated, "face-to-face" experience of God in heaven, to which Paul refers in 1 Corinthians 13:12).

The Fathers of the Church insisted that faith involves knowledge and assent, and they were always clear about the authority underlying both. From the beginning they employed the simple biblical formula, "Believe in God." Thus, God is the motive or ground of belief, according to the writings of Irenæus, Clement of Alexandria, Ambrose (d. 397), John Chrysostom, and others. Augustine taught that faith cannot be supported by internal evidence. Faith is not the product of reasoning but is founded upon the authority of a witness. Finally, the divine testimony is always worthy of faith because God is infallibly all-knowing and truthful.

The object of such faith is the mystery of Christ. For Augustine the whole mystery proclaimed by Sacred Scripture is the mystery of Christ. All of revelation has its central unity in Christ, to whom it is ordered and in whom it is consummated once and for all.

But faith is not something we merit. According to Augustine, it is always a free gift of God. By the same token, we are free to accept or reject it. This was the consensus of theological opinion among the Fathers at least until the outbreak of the semi-Pelagian controversy in the fifth century. *Semi-Pelagianism*, a variation of Pelagianism, to which we shall refer again in chapter 5, held that grace is not necessary for the beginning of faith (*initium fidei*). Only after we have freely chosen to pursue a life of faith does the grace of God enter in to support our journey to salvation. Against this false teaching Augustine insisted on the complete gratuity of the entire process of justification and salvation. The initial act of faith which is the foundation of the whole supernatural life and the beginning of justification is itself a free gift of God and something totally unmerited by us.

The heart of the Augustinian position is this: We are freely saved, but salvation is ultimately the effect of God's own goodness and mercy (*ḥesed*); therefore, salvation is gratuitous and so is the beginning of salvation, which is faith. Subsequent patristic writings, influenced so much by Augustine's works, concentrated their attention on such key New Testament texts as John 6:44–46,65 ("No one can come to me unless drawn by the Father who sent me ...") and Ephesians 2:8 ("You have been saved through faith, and this is not your own doing; it is the gift of God—not the result of works ...").

But even if faith is entirely the gift of God, the Fathers taught that it also involved some element of human cooperation. Accordingly, one can only believe if there seems to be some basis or reason for believing. Some of the earliest Fathers (e.g., Justin) tried to show the truth of the Christian message by pointing out the various ways in which Christ fulfilled the prophecies of the Old Testament. The Greek Fathers (Origen, Basil, [d. 379], John Chrysostom, and others) and Latin Fathers (Ambrose, Jerome, [d. 420], and especially Augustine) pointed as well to miracles and prophecies. It is important to note, however, that these Fathers—and Augustine in particular—were not arguing that one could establish the credibility of faith on the basis of reason or evidence. On the contrary, for Augustine the internal truth of the mysteries of faith can never be demonstrated. But the availability of such signs as miracles and prophecies does show that our faith is not without some support and credibility, even within the created and visible order of reality.

Second Council of Orange (529)

This is one of many references in this book to official teachings of the Catholic Church, whether of councils or of popes. Unlike many seminary and college textbooks in use before and even during the Second Vatican Council, *Catholicism* presents conciliar and papal teachings within the historical context in which they were formulated and promulgated. We readily acknowledge today that we can no longer adopt a fundamentalistic approach to the interpretation of Sacred Scripture by reading the sacred texts apart from their setting within the particular biblical book and the particular situation in which and for which they were written (the so-called *Sitz im Leben*, "situation in life"). This is clear from such official documents as Pope Pius XII's 1943 encyclical *Divino Afflante Spiritu*, the 1964 Instruction of the Pontifical Biblical Commission, and the 1965 *Dogmatic*

Constitution on Divine Revelation of Vatican II. Neither, then, can we adopt what has been called a "nonhistorical orthodoxy" in our approach to the official texts of church documents.

The Second Council of Orange, a local council held in southern France and acting under the direct influence of Augustine's theology, condemned semi-Pelagianism. Two years later Pope Boniface II (d. 532) confirmed the council's decision. "He is an adversary of the apostolic teaching," the central decree reads, "who says that the increase of faith as well as the beginning of faith and the very desire of faith ... inheres in us naturally and not by a gift of grace" (the council cites Philippians 1:6,29 and Ephesians 2:8).

This may be one of the most important, and least known, teachings of the Catholic Church, one more frequently acknowledged in the breach than in the observance. Through much of the twentieth century Catholic *apologetics* (i.e., the systematic attempt to show the reasonableness of faith and to refute, at the same time, the principal objections raised against Christian belief) has proceeded on the unstated assumption that reason alone can demonstrate the truth of Christian faith, and that grace is necessary only to make such reasoned "faith" a saving faith. The argument was constructed as follows: (1) The Bible is a historical document. Those who are purported to be its authors can be shown to be such. The events and persons about whom they write can be shown to be real events and persons, on the basis of independent historical evidence. (2) The Bible tells the story of Jesus Christ, who claimed to be divine and who proved his claim by his miracles and especially by the primary miracle of the resurrection. (3) The Bible also tells how Jesus founded a Church and invested it with full authority to teach, rule, and sanctify. (4) The Catholic Church alone can trace its history back to the time of the apostles and to the Lord himself. *Therefore* ...

If the truth of Catholic faith is so clear, why do so many continue to reject it or remain indifferent to it? Because (so the argument goes) they are either too lazy to examine the evidence fully and carefully, or because, having examined the evidence and having recognized its truth, they find it too difficult to change their lives in order to conform with the truth they now perceive.

It is as if the nonbeliever were completely free, even without God's grace, to begin the process of examining the evidence and then to accept or reject it. But the Second Council of Orange (and Augustine before that) insisted that even the beginning of faith (*initium fidei*) is a gift of God. If God calls all to salvation (1 Timothy 2:1–6, the classical text) and if salvation is impossible without faith (a Pauline teaching later officially ratified by the Council of Trent in the sixteenth century), there must be saving faith that is not explicitly centered on Christ. But even that faith must be a free gift of God. Accordingly, God calls some people to salvation through communities, institutions, and agencies other than the Church. (We shall return to this point in our consideration of the Church in Part Four.)

Thomas Aquinas

No theologian in the entire history of the Church has had such a decisive impact on Catholic thought and the shaping of the Catholic tradition as St. Thomas Aquinas. His *Summa Theologiæ* is the most comprehensive synthesis (that is what the word *summa* means) of the biblical, patristic, and medieval understandings of the Christian faith, and has significantly shaped the interpretation and articulation of that faith ever since. Aquinas was accorded special theological status by Pope Leo XIII's encyclical *Aeterni Patris* (1879).

For Aquinas the act of faith is essentially an act of the intellect, but not just any act of the intellect. It is *thinking with assent*. What do we believe? God. Why do we believe? On the authority of the God who reveals. For what purpose do we believe? That we might be united forever with God in heaven (*Summa Theologiæ*, II-II, qq. 1–7). Even now faith gives us access to the unseen, but real, world of grace.

Our grasp of God, however, is never the end product of scientific reasoning and demonstration. Whatever arguments we employ either show only that faith is at least not impossible or absurd, or else they are arguments which are themselves drawn from sources (especially Sacred Scripture) whose divine authority is, in turn, accepted on faith. In any case, faith is not information cut off from reality. "Our faith," Aquinas wrote, "does not end in propositions but in the realities themselves" (*Summa Theologiæ*, II-II, q. 1, a. 2, ad. 2).

Thus, even though Aquinas emphasized the intellectual dimension of faith, he never lost sight of faith's close relationship with hope and charity, and therefore with the will as well as the intellect. Faith is directed to the good as well as to the true: "Now faith is the assurance of things hoped for" (Hebrews 11:1). Without hope, faith has no direction or goal. Without charity, faith is simply dead (II-II, q. 4).

For Aquinas, faith is essentially and absolutely supernatural. Its source is God; its motive is God; its goal is God. If there are certain external signs of the truth of faith (e.g., miracles and prophecies), they are without force in the absence of the internal cause of belief, which is the Holy Spirit (II-II, q. 6). Unless the grace of the Spirit is present, elevating the intellect above its own limited natural capacities, we cannot truly believe in God.

Council of Trent (1545–1563)

Just as Augustine influenced the decrees of the Second Council of Orange, so did Aquinas influence those of Trent, a major ecumenical council held in northern Italy in the immediate aftermath of the Protestant Reformation and for the purpose of confronting, however belatedly, the crisis created by the Reformation.

The Council of Trent's decrees on faith were formulated against the Protestant, and especially Lutheran, notion of trusting faith (*fides fiducialis*). Recently, Catholic theologians such as Karl Rahner (d. 1984) and Hans Küng have argued that the differences between Trent and the Reformers on this question were more verbal than substantive, but that was not the perception at the time, nor for centuries thereafter.

The council's teachings on faith are to be found in the *Decree on Justification*, which was formulated during one of the most important sessions of the council, the sixth, lasting from June 21, 1546, until January 13, 1547. It described justification as "a passing from the state in which man is born a son of the first Adam, to the state of grace and adoption as sons of God through the second Adam, Jesus Christ our Savior." The process of justification begins with God's grace through Jesus Christ. This call to justification is completely unmerited. We remain free to reject it, but apart from divine grace we could not take one step toward justification and salvation (a clear echo of the teaching of the Second Council of Orange).

Trent also insisted on the objective content of faith. Faith is not exclusively fiducial, as Luther implied, but includes also some assent to revealed truths. Furthermore, in the spirit of the Epistle of James, faith without works is dead. Faith is not a saving faith apart from hope and charity.

Finally, Trent clarified the meaning of the statement: The sinner is gratuitously justified by faith. "We may be said to be justified freely, in the sense that nothing that precedes justification, neither faith nor works, merits the grace of justification; ... otherwise ... grace is no longer grace."

In summary: Without furnishing a formal definition of faith, the Council of Trent taught that faith is *strictly supernatural* and at the same time a *free* act; taught that faith is *necessary for justification and salvation*, and not simply a matter of intellectual acceptance of truths; and taught that faith *can coexist with sin*, contrary to the position of some sixteenth-century Protestants.

First Vatican Council (1869–1870)

Whereas Protestantism had posed the primary challenge at Trent, it was *Rationalism* (the belief that nothing should be accepted as true unless reason can perceive it to be true) and, to a lesser extent, *Fideism* (the belief that reason is of no value at all in the understanding of Christian truth) and *Traditionalism* (the belief that one must rely upon faith alone as communicated in the traditions of the Church) which provided the stimulus for Vatican I's teachings on this question.

On April 24, 1870, Vatican I promulgated its doctrine on faith in the Dogmatic Constitution *Dei Filius* (the first two Latin words of the document, which mean literally "the Son of God"). *Against Rationalism,* the council taught that our belief in revealed truth is "not because its intrinsic truth is seen with the light of reason, but because of the authority of God who reveals them," and that saving faith is impossible without "the enlightenment and inspiration of the Holy Spirit... ." *Against Fideism and Traditionalism,* the council taught that the "submission of faith" must be "consonant with reason," and that is why God provided various signs, especially miracles and prophecies, whereby the revelation itself might be recognized as being of divine origin. The assent of faith, therefore, is "by no means a blind impulse."

Beyond that, the council also widened the Scholastic notion of faith, which focused so much on its intellectual aspect. Vatican I spoke of the act of faith as one by which we offer ourselves to God in "free obedience." The council also repeated the teaching of Trent on the essential link between faith and justification and on the priority of faith in the supernatural order.

The force of the council's arguments, therefore, was more strongly placed against Rationalism than against Fideism—so much so, in fact, that one bishop suggested that the council add a note to canon 6 to the effect that the council did not intend to deter the faithful from at least examining the motives of credibility. It is perhaps all the more surprising that Catholic apologetics after Vatican I continued on a somewhat rationalistic course, leaving Catholics with the impression that good arguments make conversion to the Church inevitable, except for those persons too indifferent to consider them or too perverse to accept their moral consequences. Nothing could be farther from the teaching of Vatican I, or indeed of the entire Catholic tradition.

Second Vatican Council (1962–1965)

Despite what is occasionally said uncritically and without historical perspective, the Second Vatican Council did not revolutionize or set aside the Catholic tradition as we knew it before 1962. Vatican II's teaching on faith, for example, is basically consistent with the record we have been tracing and examining thus far.

For the council, faith is essentially supernatural: "The grace of God and the interior help of the Holy Spirit must precede and assist . . ." (*Dogmatic Constitution on Divine Revelation*, n. 5). It requires assent to revealed truth but also a giving of oneself to God as well in an "obedience of faith." Its supernatural character notwithstanding, there are signs and wonders which can lead us to faith under the impulse always of divine grace.

Nevertheless, there are at least two new emphases in Vatican II's teaching on faith. Both were prompted by a new awareness of, and appreciation for, pluralism. *First*, the council recognizes that the freedom of the act of faith means just that. Faith is a free gift of God, and ours is a free response to that gift. Neither God's hand nor ours

38

can be forced. In a world of increasingly diverse religious and nonreligious convictions, we must learn to respect the consciences and the motives of those who do not, or cannot, accept Christian faith (*Declaration on Religious Freedom*, n. 2). No one is to be penalized, socially or politically, for his or her convictions about religious matters.

The *second* new emphasis is similar to the first. Just as the Church has grown to respect diversity in the human community at large, so has it grown to respect diversity within the Body of Christ itself. The *Dogmatic Constitution on the Church* (n. 15) and the *Decree on Ecumenism* (n. 3) both acknowledge that Christian faith exists outside the Catholic Church, that it is a justifying faith, and that it relates one not only to Christ but to the Church as well.

Faith: Summary Points

1. Although faith is personal knowledge of God in Christ, that acceptance and knowledge are always achieved and activated within a given community of faith, whether the Church as we know it or some other religious body, and beyond that within the whole human family.

2. This knowledge of God is not merely knowledge in the cognitive or intellectual sense (*fides quæ*), although it *is* that, too. It is a knowledge which implies trust and a total commitment of the self to God, a commitment of heart as well as of mind (*fides qua*).

3. Faith is not just the knowledge of God in general, but the knowledge of God which comes through the reception and acceptance of God's word. In the Christian sense, faith is the acceptance of God's Word-made-flesh in Jesus Christ, and then of the preaching of that Word by the Apostles and the Church.

4. The acceptance of God's word in Christ and in the Church demands not only intellectual assent but also obedience—obedience to the Commandments and to the New Law of the Gospel, which calls us to work for social and political liberation as well as personal transformation of the individual. It is a faith, in other words, that "does justice," to cite the theme of the Thirty-Second General Congregation of the Society of Jesus (December 1974–March 1975).

5. If there is to be genuine obedience, there must be some acknowledgement of past failures, a conversion (*metanoia*, or change of mind), and repentance.

6. Faith always remains free. The "evidence" for faith is never overwhelming. There are signs and witnesses. But these are only external and never finally persuasive in themselves. The only motive of faith that ultimately counts is internal: the presence of the Holy Spirit.

7. On the other hand, faith and reason are not absolutely separate. Even if one does not "reason to" faith, faith must always be "consonant with reason" (Vatican I).

8. Faith is a matter of the highest human importance, because without it we cannot be justified or saved. But since God wishes the salvation of all persons, faith must be available in principle even to those outside the Church. Such faith has sometimes been described as *implicit*, to distinguish it from the baptized Christian's *explicit* faith in Jesus Christ.

THEOLOGY

Theology and Faith

If faith is personal knowledge of God, that knowledge is always sacramental. That is, our faith-perception of God is mediated by our experience of created realities: persons, events, objects. Unalloyed faith does not exist. Nowhere can we discover and isolate "pure faith." A real, living faith exists always in some cognitive, reflective state. Which is to say that we are not even conscious of our faith except theologically. We cannot express it, in word or in action, independently of theology.

Theology comes into play at that very moment when the person of faith becomes intellectually conscious of his or her faith. From the very beginning, faith exists in a theologically interpreted state. Indeed, it is a redundancy to put it that way: "theologically interpreted." For the interpretation of one's faith is theology itself.

Theology is, as St. Anselm of Canterbury defined it some nine centuries ago, "faith seeking understanding" (*fides quærens intellectum*). More specifically, theology is that process by which we bring our knowledge and understanding of God to the level of reflection and expression. Theology is the articulation, in a more or less systematic manner, of the experience of God within human experience.

Theology, in the broad sense of the word, may emerge in many forms: a painting, a piece of music, a dance, a cathedral, a bodily posture, or, in its more recognizable form, in spoken or written words. But none of these forms can ever do justice to the reality they strive to express. All theology is limited and imperfect, because its object, God, is ineffable and utterly mysterious.

If theology is "faith seeking understanding," there can be no theology without faith. Theology is not the interpretation of someone else's faith, but of one's own, or of one's own community of faith.

Theology is not simply talk *about* God, or *about* Christ, or *about* the Bible, or even *about* faith. Theology happens only when there is an effort to come to a better, clearer, more critical understanding of one's own faith *in* God and *in* Christ, as that faith has become available to the inquirer *in* the Bible, *in* the Church, or in some other sector of human experience.

When "theology" is done without faith, it isn't theology at all. It is a *philosophy of religion*. The theologian reflects on his or her own faith-commitment and that of his or her faith-community; the philosopher of religion reflects on the faith-commitment of others. The injunction of Augustine, *Crede ut intelligas* ("Believe that you might understand") makes no sense to the nonbeliever. We do not go to theology for our faith. Theology is there to give us a greater understanding of what we already believe.

Theology and Doctrine

On the other hand, theology has an important critical function to perform. It does not simply take what is believed or taught and try to put the best face possible on it. Theology has the responsibility of measuring what is believed and what is taught against established *criteria*.

1. Is the belief or teaching rooted in, or at least consistent with, the Bible?

2. Has the belief or teaching been expressed and defended, at least in substance, by the authoritative witnesses of the early Church?

3. Has the Church officially proposed this belief or teaching in council or through some other magisterial forum?

4. Conversely, has the official Church ever rejected this belief or teaching in whole or in part, directly or indirectly?

5. Is the belief or teaching consistent with other official teachings of the Church on related matters of faith?

6. Is the belief or teaching consistent with the present consensus of theologians on this or related matters of faith?

7. Is the belief or teaching consistent with contemporary scientific knowledge (that is, with what we know about the "human situation")?

8. Is the belief or teaching consistent with our corporate experience of faith within the Church (the *sensus fidelium*)?

Theology retains its critical function even in the face of official teachings (doctrines, dogmas, and disciplinary decrees). Theology still must ask if the official teaching is consistent with the Bible, the teaching of the ancient witnesses of the Church, previous official pronouncements, other recent or contemporary official pronouncements, the present consensus of theologians, the findings of other sciences, and finally the experience of Christians themselves. When theologians find themselves at some critical distance from the official teaching, their posture is often referred to as *dissent*. (For a discussion of dissent, see, for example, Ladislas Örsy, *The Church: Learning and Teaching*, Wilmington, Del.: Michael Glazier, 1987, and *Moral Theology No. 6: Dissent in the Church*, Charles E. Curran and Richard A. McCormick, eds., New York: Paulist Press, 1988.)

This critical process occurs not only after a teaching has been made official, but also beforehand. *The formulation of a doctrine is itself a work of theology.* Before a belief or teaching is officially adopted and proposed for wider acceptance in the Church, a decision has to be made about its truth and the appropriateness of commending it to the larger community at this time and in this form. Such a decision cannot be made apart from the theological criteria outlined above. Insofar as a particular belief or teaching is elevated to the official status of a doctrine, it is regarded as consistent with the biblical message, the writings of the early witnesses of the Church, and other ecclesiastical pronouncements of past and present, and it presumably represents the best fruits of contemporary theology and related sciences. Finally, it is not only consistent with the present experiences of Christians, but its promulgation will, in fact, enhance and enrich that experience.

Accordingly, the question is not *whether* theology will exercise a critical function in the formulation and subsequent reflection upon doctrine, but rather *which* theology will and *how* will it do so. Sometimes it is not clear for decades, even centuries, if the Church has employed the best theology and mode of expression in its doctrinal pronouncements.

Origin and Development of Theology

Theology is as old as self-conscious faith in God. As soon as human beings began thinking about the ultimate meaning of life, about their relationship to the whole cosmos, about the ultimate purpose and direction of human history (although the notion of "history" as such is a relatively modern development), about the experience of the holy and the sacred, they were beginning to do theology. Theology precedes not only Christianity but even Judaism as well.

The Apostles

Christian theology, however, begins with the Apostles. It developed for two reasons: (1) because the Apostles had to reconcile for themselves the message of Jesus Christ with their own religious experience as Jews; and (2) because the Apostles had to preach the "Good News" that Jesus had bequeathed to them, and this meant interpreting and translating the Gospel for diverse communities and cultures.

Why are there, for example, *four* Gospels in the New Testament? If the Gospels are nothing more than objective accounts of what Jesus said and did, why the need for four? Why not only one? The answer is that the Gospels are more than historical narratives or biographies. They are, first and foremost, *testimonies of faith:* the faith of the evangelist himself and the faith of the community with which he was associated. Each Gospel is an interpretation of the significance of Jesus Christ, directed to different audiences (e.g., Luke's is Gentile, Matthew's is Jewish). As such, each is a work of *theology*. Indeed, the whole of the New Testament is theological to one degree or another.

But New Testament theology is more *catechetical* than speculative (with the obvious exceptions of the Fourth Gospel and some of the Pauline letters). Theology became more deliberately *systematic* as the first serious intellectual challenges were raised against Christian faith. There developed in the second and third centuries an *apologetical* theology. The Apologists (e.g., Justin, Clement of Alexandria, Origen, Irenæus) tried to speak to the cultured in their own language. Technical theological terms were created. Specific theological problems were defined. In the struggle against Gnosticism, for example, the continuity between Old Testament and New Testament had to be established and clarified. In the controversy over the necessity of rebaptizing those who had left the Church and later returned, a theology of the Church (ecclesiology) began to take shape. The need to distinguish inspired from noninspired literature forced the question of the canon of Sacred Scripture ("canon" = the list of books accepted by the Church as inspired and, therefore, as part of the Bible).

Neoplatonism; Roman Juridical Thought

With the Edict of Constantine in 313 the Church acquired legal status, and its theology began to show the marks of the Church's new situation: It was strongly influenced by Neoplatonism, the last of the great Græco-Roman philosophies, and by Roman juridical thought. Given this combination, reality was increasingly perceived in hierarchical terms, with God as the remote, otherworldly, "Supreme Being." It was within this intellectual framework that some of the great theological issues of the times were faced: the inner life of the Trinity, the divine-human status of Christ, and the necessity and effects of grace. Terms and concepts taken over from contemporary Greek culture were employed against *Arianism* in the formulation of the doctrine that in Christ there is one divine person (*hypostasis*), with two natures (singular, *physis*), the one human and the other divine.

44

Those natures are united, without confusion or division, in the one divine person, i.e., hypostatically. (Arianism had taught that Christ was more than a human person but less than God.) Similar concepts were applied to the Trinity: circumincession, procession, generation, spiration. And these, in turn, were incorporated into official teachings and creeds of the Church of the fifth century: the *Council of Chalcedon* (451) and the *Athanasian Creed*.

Monasteries

As circumstances changed, so too did the character of Catholic theology. With the dissolution of the Roman Empire in 476 and the breakdown of traditional social and political institutions, intellectual and cultural leadership within the Church passed from the great bishop-theologians (Augustine, Athanasius, Basil, Gregory of Nyssa, [d. 394], Gregory Nazianzen, [d. 390]) to the monasteries and to such monastic theologians as Anselm of Canterbury, who began as an abbot and later became an archbishop, Bernard of Clairvaux (d. 1153), Hugh of St. Victor (d. 1142), Bonaventure (d. 1274), and others. Theology assumed a *devotional* character consistent with its new monastic environment.

Universities

Indeed, those who had been formed in the spiritual theology of the monasteries found it most difficult to accept, much less adapt to, the new theology coming out of the universities, as represented by Albert the Great, Thomas Aquinas, and their intellectual disciples who were known as the Schoolmen, or Scholastics (thus, the term *Scholasticism*). It was Anselm who provided the bridge between the two approaches: the one emphasizing the sufficiency of faith as expressed in Sacred Scripture, and the other insisting on the need for critical reflection on that faith, using not only Sacred Scripture, but the writings of the early Christian witnesses, theologians, and philosophers, even non-Christian philosophers such as Aristotle.

Theology, Anselm argued, is "faith seeking understanding." Although there were clear differences among the Schoolmen, one could also distinguish a certain common mentality in their approach

45

to theology. All agreed on the power of reason to come to some basic, albeit imperfect, understanding of the mysteries of faith and to construct some overarching synthesis of the whole Christian doctrinal system (thus, Thomas's own *Summa Theologiæ*). The pessimism of Augustinianism, with its emphasis on the depravity of the human condition and the corresponding weakness of human powers, such as reason, gave way to a new intellectual optimism. Things were seen to have natures of their own which do not consist simply of their reference to God. We come to a knowledge of God and of our faith, therefore, not only through direct spiritual illumination but more usually through our sense experience of the visible and the concrete. To this end we are aided by the use of *analogy*, a way of explaining the meaning of one reality by showing its similarity to another (e.g., God is not a "father" in the strict sense of the word, but God's relationship to us is *like* that of a parent to children). But the Schoolmen also agreed on the authority of the Bible as a kind of textbook from which proofs could legitimately and necessarily be drawn. Reason, in other words, was not without guides and limits.

The Scholastic position was embraced neither immediately nor universally. Resistance continued from those still suspicious of the powers of reason. Parallel approaches were also developed, e.g., by John Duns Scotus (d. 1308). And inevitably others took the new emphasis on reason to apparent extremes, as may have been the case with Nominalism, which tended to reduce theology to a kind of word game. The theologian is a manipulator of terms and concepts, none of which can lead us to, much less put us in touch with, the reality of God. The movement, identified in large part with William of Ockham (d. 1347), is regarded as the forerunner of such modern philosophical schools as Logical Positivism, which also denies the possibility of getting beyond words to the reality of things in themselves.

Scholastic theology had certain inherent *weaknesses* as well as strengths. *First,* it relied too heavily on reason and logic. The Bible and the writings of the early Christian witnesses very often took second place to Aristotle and Scholastic colleagues. *Second,* theological questions were regularly studied apart from their historical context. The Bible was read not, as we insist today, according to its original setting and literary meaning, but rather as if it were simply a collection of independent sayings or principles which could be used

46

independently of one another to support particular theological and even philosophical arguments. *Third,* Scholastic theology tended to invent distinctions and subdistinctions unnecessarily ("How many angels can dance on the head of a pin?" is a caricature, of course, but it suggests the kind of useless subtlety that occasionally surfaced at the time). *Finally,* Scholastic theology too quickly constructed systems of thought and then elevated these systems to the status of self-contained authorities. Theology became for many a matter of competition between or among systems and schools.

Seminaries; Religious Orders

As controversy followed controversy and subtlety piled upon subtlety, the role of the universities as centers of theological thought declined, and they were replaced by seminaries and the schools of religious orders. Manuals of theology bore the words *dogmatic-scholastic* in their titles, thus expressing the intention to wed the positive, historical element with the speculative, rational element. The format and structure of these new seminary textbooks were the same as those used by future priests in Catholic seminaries up to, and in some cases beyond, the Second Vatican Council.

First, the thesis was given (e.g., "The Church is the Body of Christ"). This was followed by the *status quæstionis* ("state of the question"), in which various current opinions on the thesis were presented. Next came the proofs: from the Bible, the Fathers and doctors of the Church, and the official teachings of the Church. There were additional arguments of much less weight, drawn from theological reason and from "convenience" (e.g., "It is *fitting* that God should have done such-and-such; but God is all powerful and *could have done* such-and-such; therefore, God *did* such-and-such"). The defense of the thesis concluded with various corollaries, or *scholia*, which applied the thesis to some related minor questions.

Episcopal theology of the earliest Christian centuries had been concerned with a defense of the faith against nonbelievers and heretics; *monastic* theology, with its spiritual and devotional implications; and *university* theology, with giving the whole body of Christian faith some coherent, logical unity and structure. *Seminary* theology, on the other hand, was concerned primarily with preparing future priests

47

for the service of the Church as preachers, teachers, and confessors. From the end of the seventeenth century until the first half of the twentieth century, Catholic theology focused its attention on questions that would likely confront the priest in the course of his ministry. And because the priest is an official of the Church, it was important that he should have access to, and then communicate, the official teaching of the Church rather than his own private opinions. Accordingly, the emphasis was always on the authoritative sources by which a given thesis was shown to be true. Reverence for the Bible notwithstanding, the primary authority was always the official teaching of the Church, i.e., papal statements, conciliar declarations, and Vatican decrees.

Nineteenth-Century Developments

The seeds of yet another major theological transformation (indeed, one in which we still find ourselves) were already being sown in the late eighteenth and early nineteenth centuries. The outstanding theologian of this period was Johann Adam Möhler (d. 1838), who recovered a sense of theological development, a sense of history, and a sense of the Christian message as an organic whole rather than as a collection of theses. He rejected the rationalistic spirit of much contemporary Catholic thought and reunited dogmatic and moral theology. In 1879 Pope Leo XIII's encyclical *Aeterni Patris* sounded the call to reconnect Catholic theology with its own best tradition: Thomas Aquinas in particular, but also Augustine, Bonaventure, and others. Unfortunately, much of the restoration assumed a diffident, defensive, and frequently hostile attitude to the new intellectual trends of its own time. But the idea of genuine historical development continued to gain strength. Cardinal John Henry Newman constructed his own celebrated theory of doctrinal development, linking it with the faith of the community itself down through the centuries. Another major contributor to the new historical and holistic approach to Catholic faith was Matthias Scheeben (d. 1888).

Modernist Crisis

The Modernist Crisis of the late nineteenth and early twentieth centuries, however, interrupted the course of this new historical and integrated approach to Catholic theology. From today's perspective the interruption was only temporary, but *temporary* meant that it spanned the entire theological careers of many twentieth-century scholars and the entire intellectual formation period of the overwhelming majority of priests ordained in the twentieth century. Like most movements and systems in the history of the Church, Modernism is more nuanced and more complex than it first appears, either to its devoted defenders or to its tenacious critics. One might suggest, at the risk of oversimplification, that the Modernists (Alfred Loisy [d. 1940], and others) took the new nineteenth-century emphasis on history and opposition to abstractionism too far to the left.

Like the Nominalism of the post-Scholastic era, Modernism held that there can be no real continuity between dogmas and the reality they presume to describe. Dogmas have a negative function at best. They warn against false notions. They are above all practical. A dogma is a rule of conduct more than a rule of faith. Thus, to say that "Jesus is risen" means that we must regard him as we would have done before his death, or as we would a contemporary.

It is fair to say that the Modernists, in their commendable effort to bring some historical realism to the interpretation of Christian faith, may have adopted too uncritically certain common notions of history abroad during the nineteenth century, along with that century's "dogmatic" and ideological rejection of values (including the supernatural) that cannot readily be observed and tested apart from a study of concrete persons and events. Modernism, therefore, began, as all such movements do, with a partial truth and inflated it into a comprehensive, and therefore radically flawed, system of thought. This system tended to deny the capacity of the human mind to grasp and express the supernatural in ways that are open to objective examination, in accord with objective criteria of truth and appropriateness.

Because it was so vehemently condemned by Pope Pius X (d. 1914) in his encyclical *Pascendi* (1907) and then made the subject of a negative oath that every future priest, bishop, and professor of religious sciences had to take from 1910 until 1967, Modernism stalled the progress which Catholic theology had been making under the impact of such scholars as Möhler, Scheeben, and Newman. It would not be until the Second Vatican Council (1962–1965) that Catholic theologians would feel free once again to depart from the traditional textbook approach and study theological questions in their wider historical and even ecumenical contexts. In the meantime, there were several fits and starts.

Twentieth-Century Renewal

Even as the atmosphere in all Catholic seminaries and religious houses remained tense and their intellectual spirit exceedingly cautious, there were all the while signs of extraordinary renewal: the biblical work of Marie-Joseph LaGrange, O.P. (d. 1938), later endorsed, for all practical purposes, by Pope Pius XII's encyclical on biblical studies, *Divino Afflante Spiritu* (1943); the ecumenical and ecclesiological work of Yves Congar, O.P., later confirmed by Vatican II's *Dogmatic Constitution on the Church* and its *Decree on Ecumenism;* and the philosophical and systematic work of Karl Rahner, S.J., recognized generally as the twentieth century's leading Catholic theologian.

Each of these scholars and many others had been condemned, or at least severely restricted, at some point in their careers by Vatican authorities who appealed to the sorts of guidelines laid down in Pope Pius XII's encyclical *Humani Generis* (1950). This document rejected what it called "the new theology" as it had been developing on the Continent just after the Second World War. This "new theology" was linked with Modernism because of its presumed downplaying of the supernatural order and of the official teaching authority of the Church. But a few of the practitioners of the "new theology," unlike their putative predecessors in the Modernist movement, came eventually to enjoy the approval even of the official Church itself. They served as experts (*periti*) at the Second Vatican Council, or as members of the new Theological Commission established by Pope Paul VI (d. 1978), and some continued to fill important and influential positions in seminaries and universities, on editorial boards of theological journals, and as consultants to diocesan, regional, national, and international bodies. Two became cardinals: Henri de Lubac (d. 1991) and Jean Daniélou (d. 1974).

Divisions of Theology

Theology and Its Faith-Communities

There are different kinds of theology. The interpretation of faith differs on the basis of the faith-community in which, and for which, that interpretation occurs. Thus, there is Christian theology, and within that, Catholic theology, Protestant theology, Anglican theology, Orthodox theology, and so forth. Then, of course, there are Jewish theology, Muslim theology, and as many other kinds of theology as there are religious traditions. Every self-conscious attempt to come to a better understanding of what one believes about God, about the ultimate meaning of life, about our hopes for the future, and about our sense of moral obligation to others, is a work of theology at one level or another.

The Content of Theology

There are differences even *within* Christian and Catholic theology. Theology differs according to content. There is *dogmatic theology*, which interprets faith as it has been expressed in official teachings of the Church (since not every official teaching is a dogma, this theology should more accurately have been called *doctrinal* rather than dogmatic). There is *moral theology*, which interprets the impact of faith on our attitudes, motives, values, and behavior. The division between doctrinal and moral theology was never a happy one. The latter was separated from the former in the sixteenth century for the convenience of priest-confessors, as we shall see in chapter 25.

There is also *spiritual* or *ascetical theology*, which focuses on the inner transformation effected by the presence of faith and grace (the Holy Spirit) in the human mind and heart. There is *pastoral theology*, which seeks to understand and work out the implications of faith for the actual situation of the Church, specifically for preaching, ministry of various kinds, counseling, and the like. And there is *liturgical theology* (closely linked, and sometimes equated, with *sacramental theology*), which interprets the meaning of faith as expressed in the rituals and sacramental life of the Church.

Methods of Theology

Catholic theology also differs according to its various methods. There is *positive* or *historical theology*, which seeks to understand and interpret the faith as that faith has been articulated already in some principal historical source, such as the Bible, the writings of the early witnesses of the Church, the ecumenical councils, or the great theological controversies of past centuries. *Biblical theology*, therefore, is a subdivision of historical theology. It attempts to come to an understanding of the faith as expressed and communicated in the pages of Sacred Scripture. Until the twelfth century Catholic theology was, for the most part, biblical theology. *Patristic theology* (a term less in favor today because of its gender-exclusive overtones) is also a kind of historical theology. It attempts the same task as biblical theology, but in reference to the writings of the early witnesses of the Church rather than the Bible. *Doctrinal theology* can also be viewed as a subdivision of historical theology insofar as the quest for understanding takes the form of an examination of official teachings of the Church in their historical evolution.

On the other hand, theology may be *speculative* rather than historical; such theology seeks an understanding of the faith in light of the best of contemporary knowledge and experience and without limiting the historical inquiry to any given source, such as the Bible or doctrines.

Finally, there is *systematic theology*, which embraces every kind of theology mentioned thus far. It is comprehensive in its method. It seeks to understand and articulate the Christian whole by examining each of its parts in relation to one another and to the whole. Anglican theologian John Macquarrie has called it a work of "architectonic" reason (*Principles of Christian Theology*, 2d ed., New York: Scribners, 1977, p. 16). Some schools of theology refer to it as *constructive theology*. This book, in fact, is an attempt at a systematic theology.

Catholics have often confused *doctrinal* or *dogmatic theology* with the whole of Christian theology, as if theology were always and only our critical (and sometimes not so critical) reflection on, and defense of, the official teachings of the Church. Protestants, on the other hand, have sometimes confused *biblical theology* with the whole of Christian theology, as if theology were always and only our critical (and sometimes not so critical) reflection on the biblical message.

But if all theology were biblical theology, then there could not have been any theology at all before the Bible was written. But if there were no theology before the Bible, how did the Bible get written? The very process by which the Bible came into being is itself a theological process. For the same reason, if all theology were doctrinal or dogmatic, so that there can be no real theology without doctrines to understand, explain, and defend, how could there have been any theology at all before the first doctrinal pronouncement was issued? And if there were no theology before doctrine, how did doctrine even begin to exist? For doctrines are beliefs and teachings that have received official approval. And beliefs and teachings, in turn, are expressions of faith. But expressions of faith emerge from a process known as theology, which is the interpretation of faith.

Bernard Lonergan, S.J. (d. 1984), who devoted much of his theological work to the question of method, also introduced the notion of theology's *functional specialties;* namely, research, interpretation, history, dialectic, foundations, doctrines, systematics, and communications. (For a summary of each, see his *Method in Theology,* New York: Herder & Herder, 1972, pp. 127–33.)

Theological Perspectives

Theologies may also be distinguished according to their various perspectives. *Liberal theology* (uppercase *L*) is not the same as *liberal theology* (lowercase *l*). The former refers to a specific movement in Protestant theology, beginning in the nineteenth century and continuing, with considerably diminished force, to the present. Like Catholic Modernism, Protestant Liberal theology tends to "reduce" the supernatural content of faith to its least common denominator and, for all practical purposes, eliminates that supernatural content entirely from consideration. Lowercase liberal theology refers to a progressive *style* of theology. The adjective *liberal* is entirely relative in its meaning. Thus, it may be regarded as "liberal" to favor the ordination of women. But some on the liberal left may consider support for the ordination of *anyone* as hopelessly "reactionary."

There is also *orthodox theology* and *conservative theology*. Orthodox theology is the interpretation of faith which confines the process of interpretation to sources generated by the Church itself: the Bible, or the early witnesses of the Church, or doctrinal pronouncements and creeds. Orthodox theology may also be known as *confessional theology* (more of a Protestant term, since it refers to the confessions of faith adopted by the Church not only outside but also inside the Protestant Reformation). Conservative theology, on the other hand, refers to a *style* of doing theology, a style that is cautious in the face of proposed change. Again, it is a highly relative term. There are also variations on the orthodox theme. Within Protestantism there is *neoorthodoxy*, associated with the names of Karl Barth (d. 1968) and Reinhold Niebuhr (d. 1971), which challenged Liberalism to reconnect itself with the long-standing themes of Reformation thought on the sinfulness of humankind and the need for the redemptive grace of God.

Other approaches to theology include *radical theology*, which usually refers to the "death-of-God" movement of the mid–1960s; *secular theology*, another mid–1960s movement, which emphasized the this-worldly character of Christian existence and the Church's abiding responsibility to transform the world; *Latin American liberation theology*, which stresses the motif of liberation from economic and cultural oppression and reinterprets the sources of Christianity in accordance with that motif; *feminist theology*, which reinterprets the traditional symbols of the Christian tradition in the light of the experience of women; *black theology*, which stresses the motif of liberation from racial oppression and reinterprets the traditional Christian symbols in the light of the experience of African-Americans and other people of color; *political theology*, which insists on the connection between theory and practice and, therefore, suggests that every statement about God and salvation must be translatable into a statement about the human condition in its total social and political situation; *existential theology*, at the other side of the spectrum from political theology, which emphasizes the individual believer as the *locus* for God's saving activity so that all theological reflection is reflection about one's own personhood and the meaning of one's own human existence; and *process theology*, developed against the presumably static tradi-

54

tional theology of the mainstream churches, which understands God and all reality as in a constant "process" of change and movement forward—nothing is fixed or immutable.

The Audiences, or Publics, of Theology

The content, agenda, and style of theology is affected, finally, by the audiences, or publics, to which it is addressed. According to David Tracy, theology has three publics: *society, the academy,* and *the Church* (*The Analogical Imagination,* chapter 1). When theology addresses *society,* it must attend to all three realms: the technoeconomic, the political, and the cultural. It must be concerned about issues of public policy and their relationship to the Christian message. In accordance with the method of "critical correlation," a theology addressed to society must demonstrate a critical understanding of the public order as well as a critical understanding of the Christian message, and then bring both to bear on one another in a dialogical, mutually corrective, and enriching way. When theology addresses *the academy,* it must do so in a manner that is as rigorously scientific as any of the other disciplines to be found in the academy. And when theology addresses *the Church* (the primary audience, or public, of this book), it must attend to the full spectrum of the Church's pastoral needs: preaching, catechesis, worship, teaching, spiritual formation, and moral action, both personal and social.

No one theologian can attend to all three publics equally. Some theologians, like Reinhold Niebuhr, have had society as their primary audience. Others, like David Tracy himself, have the academy as their primary audience. Most have the Church as their primary audience. Of this last group, those in moral theology and ecclesiology often include society alongside the Church.

Theology: Summary Points

1. *Not all interpretations of faith are theological.* Theology happens when there is an interpretation of one's own faith. Apart from that faith, the exploration of faith is a philosophy of religion rather than a theology.

2. On the other hand, theology has an important *critical function* to perform. It must ask if the various expressions of faith (beliefs, teachings, worship, moral behaviors) are *true*, or at least *appropriate*, to the Christian tradition. Do they conform with Sacred Scripture, the writings of the early witnesses of the Church, the Church's official creeds and teachings, the consensus of the faithful, and contemporary scientific knowledge?

3. *Theology is as old as self-conscious faith in God.* Christian theology began with the awareness that God was present and redemptively active in Christ on our behalf (2 Corinthians 5:19). The Apostles and Evangelists were the first Christian theologians. The Apologists were the first to systematize theology.

4. Almost from the beginning Christian theology has drawn from contemporary thought-forms and culture to express, explain, and even to defend the faith: from contemporary Greek philosophy during the controversies of the fourth and fifth centuries, from Aristotelianism during the Middle Ages, and from modern philosophy in the present age.

5. Theology also changed its character as it has moved from one *pastoral need* to another and from one *environment* to another: The theology done by the great bishops of the fourth and fifth centuries was different from the theology of the monasteries around the end of the first Christian millennium, and that theology differed, in turn, from the medieval theology of the universities, and that from the seminary theology of the seventeenth and eighteenth centuries, and that from the historical and ecumenical theology of today, done again in universities, but more distinctively in the public forum, i.e., through books, articles, and lectures.

6. *There are as many kinds of theology as there are religious faiths.* Theology also differs according to *content* (doctrinal, liturgical, etc.), *method* (historical, speculative, etc.), *perspective* (liberationist, feminist, etc.), and *audience* (society, academy, Church).

7. In the end, *Christian theology is a more or less systematic effort to come to intellectual terms with, and then to express, our experience (knowledge) of God in Christ.* In doing so, theology looks both to the human situation and to the Christian message. It seeks to understand the one in the light of the other, and to maintain a critical conversation/dialogue between them, reflecting on the human situation in light of the Christian message, and on the Christian message in light of the human situation.

Religious Education

Although religious education has more to do with communication than it does with speculation, it would be a grave oversimplification to suggest that religious education is merely the delivery system for a faith-community's beliefs. Religious education is more than the process of communicating what has been grasped by theology and officially adopted by the Church. The religious educator is at once theologian and educator, for *the field of religious education is located at the point where theology and education intersect.* On the one hand, the religious educator must himself or herself critically investigate and understand what is to be communicated and, on the other hand, must attend to the methods, context, and effects of the communicative process.

The aim of religious education is to help people discern, respond to, and be transformed by the presence of God in their lives, and to work for the continuing transformation of the world in the light of this perception of God. *Christian* religious education focuses on Jesus Christ as the great sign or sacrament of God's presence in human history and, more specifically, in the Church which is the People of God and the Body of Christ. Christian religious education, or simply "Christian education," is concerned, therefore, not only with the transformation of the individual and of the world in the light of Christ, but with the transformation of the Church, which is the primary context for our experience of God as Creator, as Redeemer, and as Reconciler.

Just as there are many different forms of belief, so there are several different forms of religious education. There are at least as many different kinds of religious education as there are religious traditions. Christian education, too, can be divided along denominational lines: Lutheran education, Baptist education, Catholic education, etc. And Christian education can also be divided according to specific purposes. *Catechesis,* for example, introduces the new or potential member of the Church, whether a child or an adult, to the whole of the Christian proclamation. The purpose of catechesis is, as the Greek word from which it is derived suggests, the "echoing" of the Christian Gospel in a way that is at once pastoral and systematic. Catechesis, therefore, is not the same as *preaching*, which is yet another form of religious or Christian education. Catechesis is systematic in intent and method (whether it employs the question-and-answer format or not); preaching is not. Catechesis seeks to echo the Christian message in a way that provides the new or potential member of the Church with a sense of the interrelatedness of Christian mysteries or doctrines and of their relative centrality and importance. All catechists and preachers, however, are Christian educators, but not all Christian educators are catechists and preachers.

Much the same can be said of still other forms of religious or Christian education. The *teaching of theology* is clearly a form of religious education, but it differs from catechesis in that it is directed primarily at those who are already mature members of the Church, and it differs from preaching in that it is scientific, appealing immediately to critical reason rather than to a conversion of the mind and heart. So, too, Christian *praxis* is a form of religious education. It is at the same time critical reflection on action already taken, and action that is taken after critical reflection. *Praxis* involves the coming together of theory and practice to produce something different from each.

EXPRESSIONS OF FAITH

Dimensions of the Question

There are expressions of faith which have been accepted by the community at large as having authoritative, even normative and binding, force for every member of the Church. At one unique level we have the Bible. At another level, we have doctrines and dogmas (nondefinitive and definitive official teachings respectively). At a third, we have liturgies and sacraments (which St. Thomas Aquinas called "signs of faith"). At a fourth, we have catechisms. In every instance faith is the generating source (God's revelation, to which faith is a response, is, of course, the ultimate source), and theology is the means by which the expression of faith is realized.

The Bible

Canonicity

The word *bible* is derived from Latin and Greek words (*biblia*) which mean "books." The Bible is a *collection of books* rather than a single literary composition. The books of the Bible are called "sacred" because they are regarded as inspired by God and are not simply the product of ordinary human creativity and effort, although they are that as well. They are considered "canonical" because they are on the list, or *canon* (Greek, "norm," "standard") of books which the Church officially regards as inspired and normative for faith.

In the early history of the Church there was no fixed and closed canon. In fact, the New Testament authors themselves sometimes referred to apocryphal (deuterocanonical) writings in much the same way as to other biblical books. The Gnostic Marcion (d. c. 160) rejected the whole of the Old Testament and some of the New Testament; even some of the Church's major figures, like Origen, Athanasius, Jerome, and Augustine differed on the list of inspired books. The canon was not definitively and solemnly determined until the Council of Trent did so in 1546.

Canonicity is no longer a divisive issue among the churches, and questions of the precise authorship of New Testament books is a matter of free discussion among Catholic scholars.

The Two Testaments

The Bible is divided into Old Testament, or Hebrew Scriptures, and New Testament. The former is centered on the old covenant of Sinai; the latter is centered on the new covenant of Jesus Christ. One of the earliest heresies, *Marcionism* (see previous section), denied the revelatory character of the Old Testament. In its rejection of Marcionism, the Church has insisted from the earliest days on the essential continuity between the two testaments. There is no basis at all, in other words, for the once common belief that the Old Testament is the law of fear and the New Testament, the law of love. The call to mercy and love (*hesed*) is at the core of Jewish faith as it is of Christian faith. The two testaments have a common theological focus: the *reign of God,* i.e., the rule, or dominion, of God that is already present in the world and is destined to be realized in all of its perfection at the end of human history when God will be "all in all" (1 Corinthians 15:28).

Inspiration

Because the Bible is believed to be inspired by God, it has an authority equaled by no other written source. It is, in the theological sense, the *norma normans non normata* (the norm which is the standard for all other norms but is not itself subject to a higher norm).

Inspiration signifies in general the divine origin of the Bible. Already in the Old Testament there was the conviction that certain books are sacred because they are inspired by God. This belief was carried over into the New Testament, where the Old Testament is cited some 350 times in such a way as to show that Jesus and the New Testament writers shared the conviction that the Old Testament was indeed inspired by God. "All Scripture is inspired by God and is useful for teaching ..." (2 Timothy 3:16). The New Testament itself does not claim inspiration, but the Fathers of the Church from the very beginning included the New Testament with the Old Testament in the inspired corpus of books.

Under pressure from the Enlightenment and after the First Vatican Council's formal definition, the question of inspiration became a theological issue during the nineteenth century. Subsequently, a vigorous debate developed, not over the *fact* of inspiration but over its *manner.* In 1893 Pope Leo XIII issued an encyclical, *Providentissimus Deus,* in which he declared that "God so moved the inspired writers by His supernatural operation that He incited them to write, and assisted them in their writing so that they correctly conceived, accurately wrote down and truthfully expressed all that He intended and only what He intended; and only thus can God be the author of the Bible." The teaching of Vatican I and Leo XIII is reaffirmed at Vatican II in its *Dogmatic Constitution on Divine Revelation:* "Sacred Scripture is the word of God inasmuch as it is consigned to writing under the inspiration of the divine Spirit" (n. 9; see also n. 11).

The doctrine implies that (1) the entirety of the canonical Scriptures comes from God in a way that is distinctive from the fact that all things have been created by God or that gifted poets are said to be "inspired"; (2) those who actually wrote the Scriptures did so in a truly human fashion, i.e., they retained their freedom, their personalities, their strengths, and their weaknesses; (3) Sacred Scripture is the foundation of the faith of Israel and of the Church; and (4) the truth to which the Scriptures attest is given for the salvation of humankind.

Inerrancy

Closely linked with the belief about inspiration is the belief about inerrancy. If the Bible is of God, it cannot be in error since God is the author of truth, not lies. A consensus of biblical scholars and theologians favors the following principles: (1) The words of the Bible are true only in the sense in which the human authors conveyed them. Therefore, we must determine how they thought, what influenced them, and so forth. (2) The human authors were not necessarily without error. Many of their personal opinions and even convictions may have been wrong. But inerrancy means that these opinions and convictions did not affect the message itself. (3) Inerrancy does not rule out the use of common literary devices, such as poetry, figures of speech, paradox, approximation, compressed narratives, inexact quotations, folklore, legend, song. (4) The human authors were Oriental, not Western. They did not think metaphysically or according to the rules of Scholastic logic. (5) Insofar as the principle of inerrancy applies, it applies to those essential religious affirmations which are made for the sake of salvation. Therefore, "the books of Scripture must be acknowledged as teaching firmly, faithfully, and without error that truth which God wanted put into the sacred writings for the sake of our salvation" (Vatican II, *Dogmatic Constitution on Divine Revelation,* n. 11).

The conciliar teaching, explicitly cited in *The Catechism of the Catholic Church* (1992), reflects the earlier teaching of Popes Leo XIII (*Providentissimus Deus* [1893]) and Pius XII (*Divino Afflante Spiritu* [1943]).

Scripture and Tradition

But how do we know that the Bible is inspired and immune from error in those matters which pertain to our salvation? This is not an easy question to answer. As mentioned above, the New Testament makes no claim about itself. The Catholic Church has always maintained that there is no other criterion except its own traditions, and that these, in turn, are vehicles of divine revelation. The inspiration of the Bible has been believed from the beginning and, beyond that, has been the subject of an official definition by the Church. Even as we try to understand its meaning in the light of modern notions of authorship, of history, and of psychology and the sociology of knowledge, we recognize that the fact of inspiration is a given. One cannot be true to the Catholic and Christian faith without affirming at the same time the inspired, and therefore finally normative and authoritative, character of the Bible.

But what about the authority of tradition? Does not the Catholic Church teach that there are two separate sources of divine revelation, Sacred Scripture and Tradition, and that the latter is more authoritative than the former? The simplest answer is "No." It is true, on the other hand, that the Council of Trent did speak of two sources of revelation, one written and the other unwritten. And it is also true that many Catholic theologians interpreted the Council of Trent to mean that Scripture and Tradition are two separate streams of revelation and that one (Tradition) is the final measure of the other (Scripture).

Indeed, it seemed for a time that this position was about to be endorsed at the Second Vatican Council, but Pope John XXIII (d. 1963) in November 1962 returned the draft of the *Dogmatic Constitution on Divine Revelation* to the Theological Committee of the council. When the document returned, it spoke not of two separate and independent sources of divine revelation but of a single divine revelation expressed and available in different forms: "It is clear that sacred tradition, sacred Scripture, and the teaching authority of the Church, in accord with God's most wise design, are so linked and joined together that one cannot stand without the others, and that all together and each in its own way under the action of the one Holy Spirit contribute effectively to the salvation of souls" (n. 10; see also n. 9).

A more accurate formulation of the Scripture/Tradition relationship than the usual explanation offered before Vatican II would underscore the principle that *Scripture is itself a product of Tradition*. It is not as if you first have Scripture and then you have Tradition (which is, among other things, the Church's subsequent reflection on Scripture). Tradition comes *before* and *during*, and not just *after*, the writing of Sacred Scripture. In fact, careful study of the various books of the Bible, including the Gospels themselves, discloses several layers of tradition from which the individual books have emerged and taken final form. Those traditions may be oral (preaching), liturgical (prayer formulae), narrative (recollection of important events, especially Jesus' passion), and so forth.

In the wider meaning of the word, *tradition* refers to *the whole process by which the Church "hands on"* (the literal meaning of the word *tradition*) *its faith to each new generation*. This handing on occurs through preaching, catechesis, teaching, devotions, gestures (e.g., the sign of the cross), doctrines, and indeed the Bible itself. In the narrow meaning of the term, tradition refers to *the content of the Church's postapostolic teaching*. The Second Vatican Council opted for the wider meaning of the term: "The Church, in its teaching, life, and worship, perpetuates and hands on to all generations all that it is itself, all that it believes" (*Dogmatic Constitution on Divine Revelation*, n. 8). The Church's tradition is its lived and living faith.

One final distinction: There is Tradition (uppercase) and tradition(s) (lowercase). Tradition (uppercase) is the living and lived faith of the Church; traditions (lowercase) are customary ways of doing or expressing matters related to faith. If a tradition cannot be rejected or lost without essential distortion of the Gospel, it is part of Tradition itself. If a tradition is not essential (i.e., if it does not appear, for example, in the New Testament, or if it is not clearly taught as essential to Christian faith), then it is subject to change or even to elimination. It is not part of the Tradition of the Church.

It is a perennial temptation for Catholics to confuse traditions (e.g., obligatory celibacy for priests of the Roman rite) with Tradition: on the conservative side of the spectrum, to make a nonessential tradition a matter of orthodoxy; or, on the liberal side, to treat a matter essential to faith (e.g., the Real Presence of Christ in the Eucharist) as if it were nonessential and therefore dispensable. The process of sorting out Tradition and traditions is ongoing, and involves the official teaching authority of the Church, the scholarly authority of theologians, and the lived experience and wisdom of the Christian community itself.

63

Doctrine/Dogma

Definition of Terms

A belief or teaching that receives the official approval of the Church, whether through a pronouncement of an ecumenical council (literally, a council drawn from "the whole wide world"), a pope, or a body of bishops in union with the pope (as at an international synod or at a regional council, i.e., representative of segments of the Church universal), is called a *doctrine*. A doctrine that is taught definitively and with the fullest solemnity, i.e., so that its formal rejection is heresy, is called a *dogma* (literally, "what seems right"). The promulgation of doctrines and dogmas is the prerogative and responsibility of the pope alone, acting as earthly head of the Church; the pope and bishops acting together in ecumenical council or international synod; or a body of bishops, subject to the (at least implicit) ratification of the pope—e.g., as in the case of the publication of a national catechism or of pastoral letters. With the increased activity of national episcopal conferences since Vatican II, there has been some debate about their actual teaching authority. Some argue that such bodies have no *mandatum docendi* ("mandate to teach"), but the consensus of theologians and of many bishops is that the teaching authority of episcopal conferences is rooted in the historical practice of the early Church, when conciliar and synodal forms of governance and teaching were more common. This model was never lost in the East.

New Testament Origins

One finds official teachings already in the New Testament. Paul, for example, uses the verb form of the word *tradition* in 1 Corinthians 11:23 (the words of eucharistic institution) and again in 1 Corinthians 15:3–5: "For I *handed on* to you as of first importance what I in turn had received: that Christ died for our sins in accordance with the scriptures; and that he was buried, and that he was raised on the third day in accordance with the Scriptures, and that he appeared to Cephas, then to the twelve" (my emphasis). The clear suggestion is that Paul is using fixed formulae for these recitals, i.e., expressions of belief which had received the official approval of the Church and were widely accepted as normative statements of Christian faith.

Dogma and Its Development

It was not until the eighteenth century, however, that the term *dogma* acquired its present meaning, namely, a teaching (doctrine) which the Church explicitly propounds as revealed by God. The notion was formally adopted by the First Vatican Council and in the Church's Code of Canon Law (see canons 747, 1; 749–51). According to Vatican I, a dogma must meet the following conditions: (1) It must be contained in Sacred Scripture or in the postbiblical Tradition of the Church, and as such considered part of God's revelation. (2) It must be explicitly proposed by the Church as a divinely revealed object of belief. (3) This must be done either in a solemn decree or in the Church's ordinary, universal teaching. Such teachings are "irreformable," i.e., they are not subject to review by a higher authority in the Church. Regarding the second condition, the Code of Canon Law is explicit: "No doctrine is understood to be infallibly defined unless it is clearly established as such" (canon 749, 3).

The determination of what constitutes a dogma is always a theological problem. Surprising though it may seem to many, *there is no agreed-upon list of dogmas in the Church*. One must examine an individual doctrine to see if, in fact, it meets the necessary criteria. In the final accounting, the dogmatic teaching must be *received* by the Church at large and accepted as an accurate, appropriate, and unerring expression of its faith. (This last criterion, "reception," has only recently been recovered as part of authentic Catholic tradition.)

Magisterium

A solemn decree could have only one of two sources: an ecumenical council whose head is always the pope, or the pope speaking as earthly head of the universal Church but apart from a council. *Ordinary, universal teaching* may be communicated in a papal encyclical, a synodal declaration, a decree of a Vatican congregation with the approval of the pope, or an ecumenical council. In the *widest* sense of the term, *teaching authority belongs to the whole Church*. The Second Vatican Council taught that the whole People of God participates through Baptism in the threefold mission of Christ as prophet, priest, and king (*Dogmatic Constitution on the Church*, n. 30). In the *more restricted* sense, magisterium applies to *particular groups of teachers whose authority is grounded in their office* (as in the case of the pope and the other bishops) *or in their scholarly competence* (as in the case of theologians). The charism of teaching, after all, is not linked exclusively with the office of bishop in the New Testament (see Romans 12:6–8 and 1 Corinthians 12:28–31). In the Middle Ages Thomas Aquinas distinguished between the magisterium of the cathedral chair, i.e., the teaching authority of the bishop, and the magisterium of the professorial chair, i.e., the teaching authority of the theologian. In the *strictest* sense of all, however, the term *magisterium* has been applied exclusively to *the teaching authority of the pope and the other bishops*. This is known as the *hierarchical magisterium*.

There is a greater respect today for the historical context of dogmatic pronouncements. Fundamentalism in the interpretation of dogma is no less objectionable than fundamentalism in the interpretation of Sacred Scripture. *Mysterium Ecclesiæ*, a 1973 declaration of the Congregation for the Doctrine of the Faith (formerly the Holy Office, and, before that, the Inquisition), acknowledged in principle the historical conditioning of dogma (see the appendix for pertinent excerpts).

Not only do the mysteries of faith transcend the powers of the human intellect, the document declared, but the very expressions of revelation are historically conditioned and therefore their meaning is not always self-evident to those in some other historical setting. The meaning of dogmatic language may change from one historical period to another. The truth itself may be expressed incompletely (even if not falsely). The original dogmatic teaching may have been directed at specific questions or certain errors, and these may not be the same questions or errors at issue in some later period of the Church's history. Furthermore, the dogmatic formulae themselves inevitably bear the marks of the philosophical and theological universe in which they were first constructed. The formulae may not always be the most suitable for every time and place. Indeed, they must sometimes give way to new expressions which present the same meaning more clearly and more completely. At the same time, of course, *Mysterium Ecclesiæ* rejects the Modernist notion that a dogma can never express Christian truth in a determinate way.

Liturgy and Catechisms

Basically the same principles apply to the liturgy and catechisms. Creeds, prayers, and other formulae of worship are expressions of faith that are officially approved and proposed for general acceptance and use. They, too, are always subject to theological scrutiny according to the criteria already enumerated. The same is true of catechisms and other instruments of Christian education. Insofar as they reproduce dogmatic formulae, they assume the authority of the formulae. Insofar as they express doctrine, the doctrine is no more and no less authoritative in the catechism than it is in its original setting. Insofar as the catechism or educational instrument expresses theological opinions, those opinions are as strong or as weak as the arguments which support them. That applies to *The Catechism of the Catholic Church*, promulgated by Pope John Paul II in October 1992 and published in English in 1994, and it applies, of course, to this book as well.

It is precisely through our eucharistic and sacramental celebrations, on the one hand, and through the religious education and catechetical processes, on the other, that the vast majority of Catholics and interested non-Catholics come into contact with the faith and teachings of the Church.

Discipleship

The word *disciple* means "to walk behind, to follow." In the New Testament one became a disciple only when called by Jesus himself (e.g., Mark 1:17; 2:14). In Mark 10:17–27 the rich young man expresses a desire to follow Jesus, but when the actual call from Jesus is given, with its stringently sacrificial terms, he goes away sadly. According to Luke 9:57–62, several others came to Jesus with the intention of becoming his disciples, but they held back, still bound to their pasts. For Jesus, discipleship demanded a total break with the past. Those who accepted his call immediately left their families, their property, and their occupations (e.g., Mark 1:16–20; 2:14).

To become a disciple, therefore, was to enter into a lifelong relationship with Jesus (Mark 3:14) and even to share in his suffering and death (Mark 10:39; 8:34). The disciples had common meals with

67

Jesus and one another, lived from a common fund, and followed prescribed forms of prayer (Luke 11:1–13). Accordingly, discipleship was not only a process of learning, but of shaping one's whole life around that of the Master without reservation. It drew one into Jesus' own mission (Mark 1:17; 3:14; Matthew 10:5–42), where the disciple was to act as Jesus himself: with compassion, humility, generosity, and suffering service of others (Mark 9:33–50; 10:42–45). The characteristic mark of that discipleship was, and is, always love (John 13:34–35), in particular love for one another.

After the death and resurrection of Jesus, discipleship took on a new, more ecclesial meaning. Since Jesus is no longer physically available, he becomes present where two or three are gathered in his name (Matthew 18:20). Indeed, with the outpouring of the Holy Spirit at Pentecost, the presence of Jesus has been universalized. One can follow him now, in the company of other believers, by word, worship, witness, and service without having to go to Galilee or Jerusalem or anywhere else. The Church itself became known as "the community of the disciples" (Acts of the Apostles 6:2), and Christianity as an entire way of life by which one expresses his or her faith in Jesus (Acts of the Apostles 9:2; 22:4), who is himself the Way (John 14:6). Indeed, in many later New Testament texts the term *disciple* became practically synonymous with *Christian*.

Consequently, discipleship encompasses whatever is intrinsic to the Christian life, including worship and moral behavior. *The* outcome of faith, *par excellence*, is discipleship.

SUMMARY

1. Faith is that gift of God by which we freely accept God's self-communication in Christ. Catholicism is a communal, ritual, moral, and intellectual expression of Christian faith.

2. Faith has different "outcomes." *Theology* is critical reflection on faith, or "faith seeking understanding." *Doctrines* (official teachings) are normative rules of faith that guide the Church's preaching, catechesis, and formal teaching. *Dogmas* are doctrines that are promulgated with the highest solemnity, that is, as definitive rules of faith. *Discipleship* is the principal outcome of faith, embracing the whole Christian life: worship and moral behavior alike.

3. The method by which the faith is articulated and interpreted herein and in mainstream Catholic theology is called "critical correlation." The correlation

is between the Christian message (Scripture, doctrines, creeds, nonbiblical texts, events, images, persons, rituals) and the human situation. The method makes a critical analysis of the human situation out of which the existential questions arise, and it attempts to show that the critically appropriated symbols used in the Christian message are the answers to these questions.

4. In the Old Testament *faith* is rooted in God's fidelity to the divine promises and to the Covenant with Israel. Faith is not so much a matter of believing as of hearing: hearing the word of God and accepting it with trust and obedience.

5. In the New Testament faith is acceptance of Jesus and his message, and later of the apostolic preaching, centered on the Risen Lord. It is the principle of life for the righteous. As such, it is a living, growing reality, not a once-and-for-all act. One comes to "know" Christ ultimately through the grace of the Holy Spirit, but more immediately through signs.

6. For the early Christian witnesses (Fathers of the Church) faith is saving knowledge given to all through revelation, as well as the assent to that revelation. Faith is always a free gift, to be accepted or rejected.

7. The pre–Vatican II Catholic theology of faith was most influenced by St. Thomas Aquinas, the Council of Trent, and the First Vatican Council. It is essentially an act of the intellect, "thinking with assent." It is at once supernatural, free, and necessary for salvation. Although it is never the end product of reasoning, faith is always "consonant" with reason.

8. The Second Vatican Council insisted that faith must always be free from coercion, and that it is to be found outside the Catholic Church and even outside Christianity itself.

9. *Theology* is the process by which we bring our knowledge and understanding of God to the level of reflection and expression. Theology is the articulation, in a more or less systematic manner, of the experience of God within human experience.

10. If theology is "faith seeking understanding," there can be no theology without faith. When "theology" is done without faith, it is a philosophy of religion.

11. Theology is as old as self-conscious faith in God. *Christian* theology, however, begins with the Apostles. But New Testament theology is more *catechetical* than speculative. Theology became more deliberately *systematic* as the first serious intellectual challenges were raised against Christian faith.

12. Theology developed and changed as its environments changed: within bishops' houses, its concerns were primarily pastoral; in monasteries, it became more literary and ascetical; in universities, more speculative; in seminaries, more narrowly clerical.

13. Theologies differ by faith-communities (Christian theology, Jewish theology, etc.), by content (doctrinal, spiritual, pastoral, liturgical, etc.), by method (historical, systematic, etc.), by perspective (liberationist, feminist, etc.), and by audience, or public (academy, society, Church).

14. Because *the Bible* is believed to be inspired by God, it is a privileged expression of faith and a uniquely authoritative source for the interpretation of faith.

15. The Bible is the product of tradition—indeed, of many traditions. In the *wider meaning* of the term, *Tradition* refers to the whole process of "handing on" the faith from Christian generation to Christian generation, through preaching, catechesis, teaching, devotions, gestures, doctrines, and the Bible itself. In the *strict sense* of the term, *Tradition* refers to the content of the Church's postapostolic teaching, written and unwritten alike.

16. Tradition (uppercase) is the living and lived faith of the Church; traditions (lowercase) are customary ways of acting or expressing matters related to faith which are not essential to that faith.

17. A *doctrine* is an official teaching of the Church; a *dogma* is a doctrine taught definitively, i.e., with the highest solemnity, and as such is protected by the Holy Spirit from fundamental error.

18. Insofar as dogmas are human expressions of belief, they are subject to the same limitations of language, style, structure, and even appropriateness as any human expression. There is no list of dogmas to which Catholic theologians or even pastoral leaders would agree. The determination of the dogmatic status of a doctrine is almost always a judgment call.

19. The official teachings of the Church are communicated by an authoritative teaching body known as the *magisterium*. In the *widest sense* of the term, magisterium applies to *the whole People of God,* whose authority is rooted in Baptism and Confirmation; in the *narrower sense,* to *the hierarchy and the theologians,* whose authority is rooted in pastoral office and scholarly competence, respectively. And in its *narrowest sense,* magisterium refers to *the hierarchy alone.*

20. Creeds, prayers, and other formulae of *worship* are expressions of faith that are officially approved and proposed for general acceptance and use. They, too, are always subject to theological scrutiny according to the criteria already enumerated. The same is true of catechisms and other instruments of Christian education.

21. *The* outcome of faith, *par excellence,* is *discipleship.* It encompasses whatever is intrinsic to the Christian life, including worship and moral behavior.

SUGGESTED READINGS

Brown, Raymond E. *Biblical Exegesis and Church Doctrine.* New York: Paulist Press, 1985.

Congar, Yves. *A History of Theology.* New York: Doubleday, 1968.

Dulles, Avery. *The Craft of Theology: From Symbol to System.* New York: Crossroad, 1992.

_____. *The Survival of Dogma.* New York: Doubleday, 1971.

Ferm, Deane W., ed. *Third World Liberation Theologies: A Reader.* Maryknoll, N.Y.: Orbis Books, 1986.

Haight, Roger. *Dynamics of Theology.* New York: Paulist Press, 1990.

Kelly, Tony. *An Expanding Theology: Faith in a World of Connections.* Newtown NSW (Australia): E. J. Dwyer, 1993.

Küng, Hans. *Theology for the Third Millennium.* New York: Doubleday, 1988.

La Cugna, Catherine Mowry, ed. *Freeing Theology: The Essentials of Theology in Feminist Perspective.* San Francisco: HarperSan Francisco, 1993.

Moran, Gabriel. *Scripture and Tradition: A Survey of the Controversy.* New York: Herder & Herder, 1963.

O'Collins, Gerald. *Fundamental Theology.* New York: Paulist Press, 1981.

_____. *Retrieving Fundamental Theology: Three Styles of Contemporary Theology.* New York: Paulist Press, 1993.

Pontifical Biblical Commission. *The Interpretation of the Bible in the Church.* Origins 23/29 (January 6, 1994), pp. 497, 499-524.

Rahner, Karl. *Foundations of Christian Faith: An Introduction to the Idea of Christianity.* New York: Seabury Press, 1978, chapters 1–4.

Ratzinger, Joseph. *Principles of Catholic Theology: Building Stones for a Fundamental Theology.* San Francisco: Ignatius Press, 1987.

Schneiders, Sandra M. *The Revelatory Text: Interpreting the New Testament as Sacred Scripture.* San Francisco: HarperCollins, 1991.

Sullivan, Francis A. *Magisterium: Teaching Authority in the Catholic Church.* New York: Paulist Press, 1983.

PART ONE

Human Existence

THE first theological question we ask ourselves is "Who am I?" or "Who are we?" It is precisely in our attempt to come to terms with the meaning of our own lives that we raise the question of God, of Christ, of Church, and of Christian moral behavior.

We raise the question of *God* because we seek the deepest and surest foundation of meaning that we can find.

We raise the question of *Christ* because we seek some concrete, personal, historical expression of that foundation of meaning. Christ is our way of getting in touch with God.

We raise the question of the *Church* because we seek some institutional and communitarian expression of Christ as the personification of ultimate meaning. The Church is our way of getting in touch with Christ.

And we raise the question of *Christian existence* because we seek some experiential verification of the meaning we embrace. Christian living is the way we express our relationship with the Church, with Christ, and ultimately with God.

But we start with the question of ourselves, with the question of *human existence*. It is, after all, *we* who have come to a belief in God, in Christ as the Word of God, and in the Church as the Body of Christ. It is *we* who seek to find meaning and order in our lives and in our world. Since all theological questions *begin* with us, as the ones who raise the questions in the first place, theology cannot afford to take for granted the *questioner* if it really hopes to understand both the questions we ask and the answers we have been fashioning in response.

Accordingly, chapter 3 offers a *description* of the human situation today, a situation which poses particular kinds of questions and demands particular kinds of answers. We live in a so-called *modern world*. (The word *modern* is used here in its conventional sense, and not by way of contrast with what some philosophers and theologians call the "postmodern" world.) In what does *modernity* consist, and how does it affect our self-understanding?

Chapter 4 explores the range of answers which have emerged in the modern world. Under the umbrella term of *anthropology*, the chapter considers in sequence the

74

understandings of human existence which have been developed in the natural and social sciences, in philosophy, in theology, and in the official teachings of the Catholic Church.

Chapter 5 actually attempts a coherent *theology of human existence* (or theological anthropology) by examining the biblical, doctrinal, and theological meaning of the human person, and specifically an understanding of *nature, grace,* and *Original Sin.*

A theological anthropology sums up the whole of theology, for in our understanding of human existence we progressively articulate our understanding of God, of Christ, of redemption, of Church, of the moral and spiritual life. No aspect of theology is untouched by our anthropology. Therefore, no theology can begin without immediate attention to the question of human existence.

Nonspecialist readers (the majority, for whom this book is written) should be advised that chapters 4 and 5 are particularly difficult because of the complexity and multidisciplinary nature of the material. The fact that the material is also highly compressed compounds the problem. But the issues addressed in these two chapters are utterly basic, and one hopes that whatever extra energy and patience are expended in working through the material will have been worth the effort.

I I I

The Human Condition Today

"THE SIGNS OF THE TIMES"

Like most ecclesiastical declarations emanating from the Vatican (the tiny independent state which is home to the Catholic Church's central administrative offices), the documents of the Second Vatican Council are known by the first two words in the original Latin text. Thus, the *Dogmatic Constitution on the Church* is called *Lumen gentium* ("Light of Nations") and the *Dogmatic Constitution on Divine Revelation* is called *Dei verbum* ("The Word of God"). But the conciliar documents are also identified by their general titles (the other designation given in the preceding examples).

The general title for the council's only "pastoral" constitution is of particular significance. Known on the one hand as *Gaudium et spes* ("Joy and Hope"), it is also commonly cited as the *Pastoral Constitution on the Church in the Modern World*. The preposition *in* is exceedingly important. The constitution is not about the Church *and* the modern world, but about the Church *in* the modern world. The former construction would have emphasized the separation of the Church from the world, as if the Church were somehow different from, even at odds with, the human community at large. The title that was adopted

77

emphasizes the integration of Church and world. The Church is not the non-world. The Church is not something completely apart from the world. Rather, the Church is in the world, and the world is in the Church.

Even here, in so seemingly trivial a matter, one can perhaps appreciate a basic difference in the traditional theological approaches of Catholicism and much of Protestantism. As mentioned in chapter 2, Protestantism tends to emphasize the *dialectical*. Affirmation is set against negation, "Yes" against "No," the divine against the human, the Church against the world. Catholicism, on the other hand, emphasizes the *analogical*. Realities are more similar than dissimilar. The Church and the world are more alike than different. In the words of the Pastoral Constitution: "In their proper spheres, the political community and the Church are mutually independent and self-governing. Yet, by a different title, each serves the personal and social vocation of the same human beings" (n. 76).

The Pastoral Constitution itself emerged from the deliberate collaboration of two of the most important Catholic leaders in the twentieth century, Pope John XXIII and Cardinal Leo-Jozef Suenens, Archbishop of Malines-Brussels in Belgium. On Christmas day, 1961, Pope John formally convoked the council in a constitution entitled *Humanae Salutis* ("Of Human Salvation"). The document used the phrase "signs of the times" (which had been previously limited, by reason of its biblical origins, to the frightening events that are to precede the end of the world) in an entirely optimistic sense. Pope John would employ the term in the same positive manner more than a year later in his encyclical *Pacem in Terris* ("Peace on Earth"). Developments are occurring in human history, he said, which the Christian ought not necessarily shrink from, fear, or resist. They are perhaps instruments of divine revelation. God may be summoning us to recognize new challenges and to devise new ways of meeting these challenges. God may be calling us to conversion in its deepest meaning, a change of mind and of heart (Mark 1:15).

"Indeed," the pope wrote, "we make ours the recommendation of Jesus that one should know how to distinguish the 'signs of the times' (Matthew 16:4), and we seem to see now, in the midst of so much darkness, a few indications which augur well for the fate of the Church and of humanity."

78

Soon after the pope's official convocation of Vatican II, Cardinal Suenens issued a pastoral letter for the Catholics of his archdiocese on the state of the Church and the opportunities open to it. Pope John saw the letter and advised Suenens that it represented his own views exactly. The influence of the Suenens letter on the pope's opening speech to the council on October 11, 1962, was pronounced. Pope John dismissed the worries of those "prophets of gloom, who are always forecasting disaster, as if the end of the world were at hand." Divine Providence, he declared, is "leading us to a new order of human relations" in accordance with "God's superior and inscrutable designs." This new order is one founded on unity: the unity of the entire Church and of all humankind. The council, therefore, must be attentive to both kinds of unity. Its focus cannot be exclusively on the inner life of the Church.

Less than two months later, on December 4, 1962, Cardinal Suenens addressed the council as its first session (of four) moved toward adjournment. We need to do more, he urged his brother bishops, than examine the mystery of the Church as it is in itself (*ad intra*). We must also reflect on its relationship with the world at large (*ad extra*). Indeed, he proposed this as the basis for a restructuring of the council's agenda. Commentators have interpreted Cardinal Suenens's speech to have been a crucial turning point in the history of the council, and certainly for the genesis of the *Pastoral Constitution on the Church in the Modern World*. He had submitted an advance copy of his text to the pope, whose health was now a matter of serious and widespread concern (he died the following June). The cardinal was called to the Vatican by Archbishop Angelo Dell'Acqua, of the Secretariat of State's office, and informed that "Pope John fully approved [the] text. Indeed he had read it in bed and had added a few remarks of his own, writing them in the margin in Italian" (L.J. Suenens, *Memories and Hopes*, Dublin: Veritas, 1992, p. 87). The speech received the unanimous endorsement of the council, and in an address the next day Cardinal Montini of Milan (who would succeed Pope John to the papacy as Paul VI) gave his own full support to Suenens's proposal.

And so a unique kind of ecclesiastical document was produced, a "pastoral constitution," in which the Church is said to have the "duty of scrutinizing the signs of the times and of interpreting them in the light of the Gospel.... We must therefore recognize and understand the world in which we live, its expectations, its longings, and its often dramatic characteristics" (n. 4).

Again, the approach was thoroughly and distinctively Catholic. It bore a view of the world as having come from the creative hand of God, as having been redeemed and renewed by Jesus Christ and the Holy Spirit, as embodying now the presence and activity of God (manifested in the "signs of the times"), and as being destined for eternal glory. Theologically, the Pastoral Constitution called for a "method of correlation," that is, "of scrutinizing the signs of the times and of interpreting them in the light of the gospel" (n. 4).

But what are the principal characteristics of the modern world? What is the present human condition, of which the Church is an integral part and for which it has an abiding missionary responsibility?

THE MODERN WORLD

First, a word about the adjective *modern* and the notion of "modernity." Both words are used here and throughout the book in their conventional senses, and not as some contemporary philosophers and theologians use them, that is, by way of contrast with "postmodern" and "postmodernity." *Modern* consciousness, they insist, pins all its hopes on *rational* consciousness, as manifested especially in the eighteenth-century Enlightenment. *Postmodern* consciousness, on the other hand, suspects the optimism concealed in Western notions of reason. Among the great pioneers of postmodernity (discussed in chapter 4) are Kierkegaard, Darwin, Marx, Freud, and especially Nietzsche. All challenged, in different ways, the illusion that reality is utterly manageable if only reason is free to act upon it. (See David Tracy, *Plurality and Ambiguity: Hermeneutics, Religion, Hope,* San Francisco: Harper & Row, 1987.)

A World of Change

It has been pointed out that if the last fifty thousand years of human existence are divided into lifetimes of approximately sixty-two years each, there have been about 800 lifetimes. Of these 800, 650 were spent in caves. Only during the last 70 lifetimes has it been possible to communicate through the written word, and only during the last 6 lifetimes has the human community had access to the printed word. Only during the last 4 lifetimes have we been able to measure time precisely, and only in the last 2 have we had the use of an electric motor. And within the same lifetime, our own, we have seen part of the world pass successively from agriculture as the primary form of human labor, to the manual labor of factories, and then to the so-called white-collar labor of salespersons, administrators, educators, communicators, engineers, computer specialists, and so forth.

In the meantime the world's population has experienced explosive, almost incomprehensible, growth over the past century. More than one hundred years ago only four cities had populations of a million or more. By 1900 there were 19; by 1960, 141. Just over ten years later the urban population had doubled again. By 1990 there were 351 cities with million-plus populations, including 140 in Asia, 53 in Europe, and 43 in North America.

The same kind of accelerated change has occurred in the area of transportation. In the year 6000 B.C. the camel caravan provided the fastest transportation over long distances: about eight miles per hour (what a moderately quick jogger covers in about the same time). It was not until about 1600 B.C. that, with the invention of the chariot, the speed of travel increased from eight to twenty miles per hour. This "record" was to stand for several thousand years. The first steam locomotive, introduced in 1825, reached a speed of only thirteen miles per hour, and the great sailing ships of the same period were half again as slow. Not until the nineteenth century, with improvements in the steam engine, did we attain speeds of 100 miles per hour. And it had taken the human race thousands upon thousands, even millions, of years to do it. What is perhaps more remarkable is that it then took only fifty-eight years to quadruple that limit, so that by 1938 planes were breaking the 400-MPH. figure. In another twenty-five years even that seemed modest, as the new jets doubled the mark. And then by the 1960s rockets approached speeds of 4,000 miles per hour, and astronauts in space capsules were circling the earth at 18,000 miles per hour. The next frontier was the moon, and then the planets. In 1989, for example, *Voyager 2* of the U.S. space program streaked past the planet Neptune and one of its moons, Triton, sending back computer-enhanced photographs of stunning clarity. Launched twelve years earlier and moving at some 38,000 miles per hour, *Voyager 2* was only 4½ minutes off schedule as it passed over the second farthest planet from the sun.

The whole dizzying process has generated what social commentator Alvin Toffler has called "future shock...the shattering stress and disorientation that we induce in individuals by subjecting them to too much change in too short a time" (*Future Shock*, p. 4). The precise impact of this phenomenon remains a matter of debate among sociologists.

The Elements of Change

The fact that the world has undergone major change in recent decades is beyond dispute. And the process of change continues. What follows is a limited outline of the elements and causes of change, offered with the hope that it might serve as a useful framework for our subsequent theological reflection on the meaning of human existence, the mystery of God, the person and redemptive work of Jesus Christ, and the nature and mission of the Church in the modern world.

Science and Technology—Mobility and Communications

It is generally agreed that the so-called *modern period* of world history begins around 1500. Not coincidentally, it is just about the time of the disintegration of Christian unity in the West and of the rise of critical reasoning and skepticism. For whatever social, economic, political, cultural, philosophical, and religious reasons, our world has been decisively shaped by the development of science and technology. *Science* understands the way things work; *technology* applies science to practical problems. Together both have generated the kinds of extraordinary (and extraordinarily rapid) changes to which we have referred. The two most significant developments have been in the areas of *transportation* and *communications*.

82

The automobile and the jet airplane have given the average person in economically advanced countries a *mobility* of the most unprecedented kind. The world of direct human experience is no longer geographically confined. We can meet people, talk with them, hear their points of view, argue with them, learn from them, teach them, influence them, be influenced by them on a scale unthinkable for those whose means of transportation were limited to the horse, the sailing ship, or their own two legs.

But neither are our human contacts limited any longer to the directly personal. Because of the correlative revolution in *communications* we have immediate access to one another through satellite, standard and cable television, radio, standard and cellular telephones (with speed dialing, call-waiting, and similar features), fax machine, electronic mail, pager, and modem, and mediated access through films, newspapers, magazines, paperback books, audio and video tapes, compact and laser discs, answering machines, and voice mail. Ideas and opinions have countless outlets, and they circulate more freely than ever before in human history. The modern person is a person in constant *dialogue* with others. And through that dialogue he or she is conscious more than ever before of human *interdependence* and of the challenge of building and sustaining human *unity*.

Material and Educational Growth

If increased mobility and communications are the most significant effects of the scientific and technological revolutions, those effects have become, in turn, instruments of acceleration for the same scientific and technological revolutions which produced them. Mobility and communications are two of the principal factors in material and educational growth.

Unlike those who lived before us—fifty years or, indeed, fifty *thousand* years ago—most people in the economically and politically advanced countries of the world can take for granted those *material goods* that were once the constant preoccupation and anxious concern of every man, woman, and child: adequate food, safe and comfortable shelter, sufficient clothing, basic medicines, productive work, and opportunities for leisure. We have created what some philosophers have called a "metacosmos"—something over and above the natural order of things given initially by God. We have taken the raw material of the world (*cosmos*) and given it an order and a shape beyond (*meta*) what was there originally.

Communications make it possible for us to know where and how our material needs can be met, and *mobility* makes it possible either to gain direct access to material goods or to have others deliver them to us.

Educational progress is another major by-product of the scientific and technological revolutions. We are no longer limited in our choice of religious beliefs, because we are exposed to a whole range of them. We are no longer limited in our choice of lifestyles and values, because we are brought in touch with a wide spectrum of them. We are no longer limited to our own commonsense wisdom or that of a small circle of family, relatives, and friends to make sense of human existence, because we are linked in a multimedia way with the greatest minds and greatest discoveries of present and past alike.

Education is liberating in that it frees us from illusions, from decision-making based on insufficient or erroneous information, from boredom, from dependence on the sensate and the tangible, from limited choice of occupation and recreation, and especially from the assumption that things cannot be other than they are. Because education is liberating, politically and religiously repressive regimes always limit access to it, lest the uninformed and the powerless begin questioning the *status quo*.

To summarize: Communications make it possible to expand our narrow individual universe of human experience by putting us in touch with persons, institutions, and scientific findings that widen our range of choice and our opportunities for growth; *mobility* makes it possible for us to reach people and institutions, and to be reached by them, in turn, for our mutual enrichment.

Ambivalence of Progress

But material and educational progress is not without ambiguity and ambivalence. As a minority of the world's population is lifted to the heights of material satisfaction, the gap between the relatively few rich and the many poor is sharpened. We discern more clearly not only the problems left unattended by this rapid progress, but also the many new problems such progress creates: the proliferation of nuclear weapons, international conflicts, civil wars, economic crises, ecological disasters (e.g., massive oil spills), pollution, contamination of the food supply, of water, and of the atmosphere (e.g., the earth's ozone layer), faulty and dangerous manufactured products, high tech and violent crime of all varieties, and the crowding out of spiritual values.

Educational growth discloses the same kind of gaps and contradictions. It helps us to understand our dignity and uniqueness as human persons, as well as the meaning and responsibilities of personal and political freedom. Even as it expands the range of possibilities open to personal choice, education also exposes the countlessly subtle and sometimes blatant assaults upon that choice through manipulation by certain kinds of advertising, through outright deception by officials in government, business, or even religion, and through psychic and social conditioning. The popularity of books during the 1970s and 1980s summoning individuals to greater self-assertiveness (looking out for number one, pulling your own strings, being your own best friend) was itself an indication of many people's desire to regain control of their own lives.

Education also expands our economic, political, social, and religious horizons, disclosing that their corresponding structures and patterns need not be as they are or have been—indeed that they are unfairly weighted in favor of one group or against another. The whole affirmative-action movement on behalf of women and ethnic and racial minorities was a direct outgrowth of this perception. No movement has had so great an impact on contemporary consciousness as feminism. Since the publication of Betty Friedan's *The Feminine Mystique* in 1963, feminism has progressively reshaped the way we understand, articulate, and structure human relationships within the family, the business world, government, the academy, the military, and the Church. Feminism has affected our understanding of God, of Christ, of the Church, of Christian morality, and of spirituality, as we shall see in subsequent chapters.

But there have been *countertrends* as well. Even as we perceive anew the reality of our interdependence as human persons and as nations (globalization), we find ourselves living in an age of increasingly bitter racial and ethnic conflicts, of criminal brutality, and of growing pressures against the integrity of families and of local communities. "The development of technology and the development of contemporary civilization," Pope John Paul II wrote in his first encyclical *Redemptor Hominis* ("Redeemer of Humankind") in 1979, "demand a proportional development of morals and ethics. For the present, this last development seems unfortunately to be always left behind" (n. 15).

Religion and Change

We live in a time of accelerated change, of "future shock." The principal moving forces behind that change have been science and technology; their primary products have been material and educational growth. And mobility and communications have made those products widely available.

Religion has not escaped the effects of such change, both good and bad. The Second Vatican Council's *Pastoral Constitution on the Church in the Modern World* acknowledged this (n. 7). There has been an extraordinarily significant change in attitudes and structures. Many traditional values have been called into question, especially by the young, who feel less responsible to the past because they have had little, if anything, to do with its shaping and direction. They want a more direct and effective hand in the development of policies for the present and for the future, and particularly of those decisions which have an immediate impact on their own lives. Other challenges to traditional religious values have come from women, from racial minorities, and from the poor and oppressed. For them, religion too often validates rather than critiques unjust structures, systems, and patterns of behavior.

Education, the 1971 World Synod of Bishops declared, "demands a renewal of heart, a renewal based on the recognition of sin in its individual and social manifestations." It awakens "a critical sense" leading us "to reflect on the society in which we live and on its values, ... to awaken consciences to a knowledge of the concrete situation and in a call to secure a total improvement; by these means [i.e., by education] the transformation of the world has already begun" (*Iustitia in mundo* [*Justice in the World*], III, para. 13).

These new conditions in the world today have had an effect, therefore, on religion as well, and on a scale not limited to the experience of the young, or women, or racial minorities, or the poor and the powerless: "On the one hand a more critical ability to distinguish religion from a magical view of the world and from the superstitions which still circulate purifies religion and exacts day by day a more personal and explicit adherence to faith. As a result many persons are achieving a more vivid sense of God.

"On the other hand, growing numbers of people are abandoning religion in practice. Unlike former days, the denial of God or of religion, or the abandonment of them, are no longer unusual and individual occurrences" (*Pastoral Constitution*, n. 11).

At first, the scientific and technological revolutions of this century and the major changes they produced seemed to move religion, and especially Christianity, off its accustomed foundations. Belief in a supernatural order was shaken. Many Christians in the mid–1960s shifted from a sacred to a secular perspective in the hope of saving the credibility of the Gospel. Some were influenced in this new course by the prison writings of a young German theologian.

The world has "come of age," Dietrich Bonhoeffer (executed by the Nazis in 1945) asserted in his now-celebrated *Letters and Papers from Prison* (New York: Macmillan, 1962). The world no longer takes the religious premise for granted, he said. It no longer assumes that God is "up there," ready at every moment to intervene in our human affairs, to rescue or to punish. We must learn today that only a "suffering God" can help us, one who allows us to share the pain and agony and risk of creation and to be, like the Son of God, a "man for others."

The challenge for the Church, Bonhoeffer argued, is to find a way to preach the Lordship of Jesus Christ to a world without religion, to present a kind of "religionless Christianity" that not only makes sense but may even be persuasive. By "religionless Christianity" he did not mean a religion without prayer, without worship, without doctrine, without formal institutional structures. He meant rather a Christianity that does not *confuse* the faith itself with these institutions and structures. They are embodiments, expressions, and even carriers of faith, but they are not themselves identical with faith. To be Christian, in other words, is not to perform certain devotional or ascetical practices, but to live in a fully human way, in the service of others, as Jesus lived and served.

The second challenge for the Church, Bonhoeffer maintained, is to find a way to be a servant community in the spirit of Jesus, the Suffering Servant of God. What is to be the place of the Church (literally, "those who are called forth") in a world without religion? Can the Church continue to appeal to humankind as if the world were in some perpetual foxhole, the bullets and mortar shells whizzing overhead? Science and technology have changed the human situation. We no longer ascribe every bolt of lightning and every burst of thunder to divine anger. As we continue to gain a certain measure of mastery over the material world, we are less and less inclined to accept a supernatural explanation of events when a purely scientific explanation seems sufficient.

But that traditional apologetic, Bonhoeffer insisted, was ignoble in any case. The Church cannot rest its preaching of the Gospel and its invitation to Christian faith on the premise that humankind is incapable of governing its daily affairs without regular appeal for divine assistance. God is to be found not on the borders of our life where human powers give out, but at its center. God is indeed the "beyond in the midst of life." It is the Church's peculiar task and challenge in this age to model itself on the servant presence of God in the midst of life, to use whatever resources it has in the service of those most in need.

It is not surprising that Bonhoeffer, though Lutheran, had enormous appeal to Catholics. His approach was at once sacramental and mediational. God has a sacramental presence in the world, and particularly in the neighbor-in-need, and we are called to a life of service on behalf of that neighbor.

Bonhoeffer's fundamentally straightforward insights were taken up in the early and mid–1960s by Anglican bishop-theologian John A. T. Robinson (d. 1983), American Baptist theologian Harvey Cox, and various Protestants who became known as "death-of-God" theologians. In each instance (although with substantially different conclusions) these younger theologians accepted Bonhoeffer's remarkable starting point—that the world has changed dramatically, that it no longer takes the reality of God and the supernatural order for granted (if it ever fully did anyway), and that it sees no necessary connection in any case between religious faith and formal affiliation with a church or synagogue. Bishop Robinson's analysis appeared in a best-selling book, *Honest to God*, published in 1963 (Philadelphia: Westminster Press); Harvey Cox's in a similarly successful work, *The Secular City*, published in 1965 (New York: Macmillan); and the "death-of-God" theologians' in various articles and books, the most important of which was Thomas Altizer's *The Gospel of Christian Atheism*, published in 1966 (Philadelphia: Westminster Press).

All these writers agreed that theology now had to be done according to a secular motif. (The word *secular* is from the Latin *saeculum*, meaning "world.") The Church is in and for the *world*, not above or apart from it. And Christ is a "man for others," not simply God in human form, remote from us and our human concerns. For Robinson and Cox this did not mean the denial of God or of spiritual realities. It meant rather a new way of thinking and speaking about God, a new way of understanding the mission of the Church, and a new style of Christian existence. For the "death-of-God" group, however, it *did* mean the denial of God, the rejection of the Church, and the development of a humanism independently of a traditional belief in the Lordship of Christ.

The Robinson-Cox approach prevailed over the "death-of-God" approach. The theology of Christ, of the Church, and of Christian morality was recast in the light of the changed human condition, with emphasis placed on the "human face" of Jesus, the servanthood of the Church, and the freedom and social responsibility of Christian existence.

However, the Robinson-Cox approach did not prevail over *all* other approaches. With the social and political dislocations of the latter part of the decade, typified in the United States by the anti–Vietnam War protests and the dissolution of President Lyndon Johnson's "Great Society" program for domestic economic reform, Christian activism yielded in some quarters to a new Christian asceticism. There was a withdrawal from social and political involvement into new forms of spirituality represented, for example, in the Catholic Charismatic renewal, a movement begun in the aftermath of Vatican II as a way of better expressing and experiencing the Church as a community of prayer, rooted in the Bible and energized by the power of the Holy Spirit.

By the mid–1970s the pendulum had begun to swing again, this time closer to the center. Theology was increasingly formulated on a "both/and" rather than an "either/or" basis. Jesus Christ is indeed fully human and totally engaged in our worldly concerns, but his humanity and worldly involvement are of significance to us only because he is in the first instance the Son of God and the Lord of history. The Church is indeed called to be a servant community, but its service is of significance because it is in the first instance the Body of Christ. And Christian existence is indeed a life of freedom and social responsibility, but it is a freedom given by the Holy Spirit and a responsibility for the reign of God, that is, the realization of unity through the transforming presence of God's love and justice.

In the 1980s the pendulum swung once more, this time back toward an individualism that emphasized self-fulfillment and self-reliance, in keeping perhaps with a political turn to the right in North America and in Europe, marked by the ascendancy of Prime Minister Margaret Thatcher in Great Britain in 1979 and of President Ronald Reagan in the United States in 1980. The new religious mood was cogently described in Robert Bellah's *Habits of the Heart* (Berkeley: University of California Press, 1985). But no cyclical swing is uniform and undifferentiated. At the same time, there was a new emphasis on multicultural and gender studies, on the problems of the Third World, and on the ecological crisis to such an extent that complaints were sometimes raised against the imposition of a standard of theological and political correctness ("PC").

Although the emphasis on multiculturalism, globalization, feminism, and the ecology continued into the 1990s (see, for example, the annual convention programs of the Catholic Theological Society of America, the American Academy of Religion, and other comparable professional societies in Canada, Great Britain, Ireland, Australia, New Zealand, and elsewhere), theology has also remained focused on the basic doctrinal and ethical questions (the mystery of God, sin and grace, redemption, the Church, Christian morality, and spirituality). New syntheses began to appear in the form of dictionaries and encyclopedias of theology, such as HarperCollins' forthcoming *Encyclopedia of Catholicism* and *The New Dictionary of Theology* (Wilmington, Del.: Michael Glazier, 1987), collections of theological essays, such as *Systematic Theology: Roman Catholic Perspectives*, eds. Francis Schüssler

Fiorenza and John P. Galvin (Minneapolis: Fortress Press, 1991, 2 vols.), and *The Catechism of the Catholic Church* (Eng. trans., 1994).

THE CHURCH IN THE MODERN WORLD

Sociologists have described the modernization process in different ways. Some insist that it happened in spite of, or in the teeth of opposition from, the Church and organized religion generally; others, fewer in number, argue that Christian faith made the scientific and technological revolutions possible in the first place. The former interpretation is linked with Talcott Parsons and his school of disciples; the latter view, with Andrew Greeley and, to some extent, Harvey Cox.

Parsons noted the growth of competing institutions alongside the Church and the family (governmental bureaucracies, business organizations, universities). Productive and economic functions shifted away from the family unit to the new corporations, while the Church yielded many of its legal, economic, and welfare roles to the new state bureaucracies. Greeley has argued, over against this view, that certain uniquely Christian notions led to the conclusion that science is not merely for knowledge but also for action; history is a process rather than a cycle; the universe is purposeful and therefore understandable; the world is a sacrament of God's presence, and we are called by God to collaborate with the divine plan for the world.

Harvey Cox had made a similar point in *The Secular City*. Secularization (i.e., the process of moving away from a religious answer to every human problem and toward the acceptance of human responsibility for the quality of earthly life) is not the enemy of the Gospel. On the contrary, the Bible's own sense of history requires it, beginning with the Lord's command to Adam and Eve to name the animals in the Garden of Eden (Genesis 2:19–20). Unfortunately, humankind has frequently shrunk from the responsibility, starting from the moment when, in the same Garden of Eden, Adam and Eve allowed a serpent to dictate their action (3:1–7).

Whatever the sociological explanation of the modernization process, it is clear that the world has changed markedly over the past few centuries, and has changed even more rapidly over the past several decades. It is evident, too, that science and technology have contributed mightily, not to say decisively, to modernity. Whether science and technology have developed in reaction to the Church and to Christian faith, or whether science and technology have developed because of, and under the inspiration of, the Church and its faith remains a matter of debate.

The principal products of the scientific and technological revolutions, as we have seen, have been material and educational progress. These, in turn, have been supported by advances in transportation and communications. And these, in turn, have accentuated an essential aspect of human existence which was perhaps not sufficiently understood before the so-called modern period—namely, that we are persons in *dialogue,* that we are defined as human beings by dialogue, that we grow and mature by dialogue, that through dialogue we become increasingly aware of our interdependence, and that through our new awareness of interdependence we become increasingly sensitive to our responsibility for the unity of the human race.

Whatever the causes of modernity, the Church need not be threatened by it, because the modernization process only confirms what Christ and the Church have consistently taught: All human beings—of whatever nation, race, gender, or economic status—are brothers and sisters, children of one Creator in heaven, and are called to love one another as God has first loved us (John 15:9–17; 1 John 4:7–21). Modernization has disclosed that we do not, and cannot, live isolated lives, that we can be fully human only insofar as we are open to the other in dialogue and in mutual support. Unfortunately, the principle is still more often honored in the breach than in the practice.

The Second Vatican Council, in the same Pastoral Constitution, appropriately viewed the crisis of modernization as a special opportunity for the Church. In the face of such developments, it said, more and more people are raising the most basic questions about the meaning of life and raising them with a new sharpness and urgency: "What is humanity? What is this sense of sorrow, of evil, of death, which continues to exist despite so much progress? What is the purpose of these victories, purchased at so high a cost? What can we offer to society, what can we expect from it? What follows this earthly life?" (n. 10).

Fundamentalism

But not everyone shares the positive and even optimistic outlook of the council's Pastoral Constitution, *Gaudium et spes* ("Joy and Hope"). Modernity's most determined adversary is fundamentalism, whose face is both Catholic and Protestant, Christian and non-Christian. According to two scholars who have made the most extensive study of worldwide fundamentalism, religious fundamentalisms are "movements that in a direct and self-conscious way fashion a response to modernity" (Martin E. Marty and R. Scott Appleby, *The Glory and the Power: The Fundamentalist Challenge to the Modern World*, Boston: Beacon Press, 1992, p. 10). It is not that fundamentalists reject *all* of the products of modernity. They take full advantage of its remarkable achievements in transportation, communications, medical science, and the like. But they are antagonistic toward the values that seem to accompany these advances. One such value is the superiority of reason over revelation as a means of knowledge; another is the superiority of freedom over an imposed conformity of thought and behavior.

Not until modernity made inroads into religious communities in the late nineteenth and early twentieth centuries did fundamentalism emerge as a major force within the churches, first within Protestantism, more recently within Catholicism, and eventually within Judaism, Islam, Hinduism, and other non-Christian religions. The fundamentalists viewed religious modernists as carriers of the dreaded disease of secular modernism from the outside world. But the religious modernists were regarded as more dangerous than secular modernists because they could manipulate the community's religious symbols and practices from within.

Unlike religious conservatives who are content to keep modernism at arm's length while recommitting themselves to traditional teachings and practices, fundamentalists dig in their heels and fight back. "That is their mark," Marty and Appleby observe. "They want to reclaim a place they feel has been taken from them. They would restore what are presumed or claimed to be old and secure ways retrieved from a world they are losing. Fundamentalists will do what it takes to assure their future in a world of their own defining" (p. 17).

Such a world-building endeavor requires charismatic and authoritarian leadership, as well as a disciplined inner core of staff and a larger group of sympathizers. All follow a rigorous sociomoral code that sets them apart from nonbelievers and from compromisers within the fold. Fundamentalists set boundaries, name and investigate their enemies, seek recruits and converts, and often imitate the very forces they oppose. "Fundamentalism is, in other words, a religious way of being that manifests itself as a strategy by which beleaguered believers attempt to preserve their distinctive identity as a people or group" (p. 34).

Thomas F. O'Meara, O.P., provides a description and critique of Catholic fundamentalism in his *Fundamentalism: A Catholic Perspective* (1990). Catholic fundamentalism, he suggests, is a corruption of Catholic values, especially of sacramentality. It sees the world as evil and dangerous, forgetting that God is its Creator, Redeemer, and Sanctifier. It limits the manifestation of grace to the extraordinary and even the bizarre, forgetting that God is present to ordinary people, in ordinary situations of life. And it limits access to God's grace to a chosen few, the righteous within the larger community of the unrighteous, forgetting that God wishes to save all and has won salvation for all in the redemptive work of Jesus Christ (pp. 80–93).

Catholic fundamentalism has two forms: biblical and doctrinal. Catholic biblical fundamentalism, like Protestant biblical fundamentalism, interprets Scripture "literally" and selectively. But Catholic proof-texts differ from Protestant proof-texts. For Catholics, "You are Peter..." (Matthew 16:18–19) is the hermeneutical prism through which all else in the Bible is to be read. Catholic doctrinal fundamentalism interprets the official teachings of the Church "literally" (which is to say unhistorically) and selectively. Like worldwide fundamentalism, Catholic fundamentalism tends to be militant in style, and more antagonistic to the "enemies within" than to those outside.

The council's Pastoral Constitution urges a different approach. The Church's mission "to shed on the whole world the radiance of the gospel message, and to unify under one Spirit all people of whatever nature, race, or culture" requires that within the Church itself there be "mutual esteem, reverence, and harmony" and a "full recognition of lawful diversity." This imposes upon all members the need for dialogue. "For the bonds which unite the faithful are mightier than anything which divides them. Hence, let there be unity in what is necessary, freedom in what is unsettled, and charity in any case" (n. 92).

SUMMARY

1. The Catholic Church's first official *positive* acknowledgment of modernization (as opposed to the vehemently negative assessments of Pope Pius IX in his *Syllabus of Errors* [1864], for example) came in the Second Vatican Council's *Pastoral Constitution on the Church in the Modern World,* known also by its Latin title, *Gaudium et spes* ("Joy and Hope"), drawn from the first words of the Latin text.

2. The document is significant first for its title: the Church *"in"* rather than *"and"* the modern world. The Church is not against the world or apart from it. The Church is in the world, and the world is in the Church.

3. The document is significant, second, for its positive emphasis on the "signs of the times," i.e., those events of history through which God continues to speak to us and summon us to respond for the sake of the reign of God's love and justice throughout the whole of creation.

4. The document is significant, third, for its distinctively Catholic approach: analogical (emphasizing the similarities between the divine and the human) rather than dialectical (emphasizing the dissimilarities); and its "method of critical correlation," reflecting critically on the mutual relationship between the gospel message and the world to which it is proclaimed and in which it is applied.

5. The world in which the Church lives and for which the Church exists is a world of *change,* at once profound and rapid. The change is evident in the exponential growth of the world's population and in the improvement in the means of transportation and communication.

6. Improvements in *transportation and communications* have been made possible by *science* (understanding how things work) and *technology* (applying science to practical problems). Their principal products have been *material growth* and *educational progress.* The former liberated us from preoccupation with acquiring the basic necessities of life; the latter, from having to accept things as they are. Both have helped to raise human consciousness about racial and gender equality, and also about global interdependence.

7. Material and educational progress have not been unmixed blessings. The former has also produced a nuclear arms race, wars, pollution and various environmental disasters, health hazards in food, and crime of all kinds.

8. *Modernization* has also had a strong impact on religion in general and on Christianity in particular. *Positively,* religion has been increasingly purified of

magical and superstitious overtones; *negatively,* many have abandoned the practice of religion as they have embraced rational and scientific explanations for problems once resolved by formally religious principles.

9. Christian theology responded to the "world come of age" (Bonhoeffer) in the mid–1960s by stressing the secular or worldly aspects of Christian faith: Jesus is a "man for others," the Church is a servant community, and Christian existence is one of freedom and social responsibility (Cox, Robinson).

10. A swing away from Christian activism developed in the late 1960s and early 1970s. This new mood (represented, for example, in the Catholic Charismatic movement) emphasized spontaneity of prayer rooted in the Bible and in an unshakable confidence in the Holy Spirit.

11. The pendulum, however, swung again back toward the center by the mid–1970s. Christian activists increasingly recognized the need for prayer and other traditional spiritual values and practices, while charismatics and others were more inclined to acknowledge the abiding importance of social justice in the life and mission of the Church.

12. In the 1980s the pendulum swung yet again, this time toward an individualism (of the sort described in Robert Bellah's *Habits of the Heart*), in tandem with the political turn to the right in North America and Europe. At the same time, Christian theology began focusing on multiculturalism, globalization, environmentalism, and racial and gender studies. Feminism had an especially pronounced impact on theology and biblical studies.

13. The 1990s, like the 1970s, have seen a swing back toward the center, with the production of new syntheses in the form of dictionaries, encyclopedias, collections, and catechisms. At the same time, there has been a continued emphasis on multiculturalism, globalization, and the like.

14. Whether the modernization process happened in spite of, or over against, the Church and its faith (Parsons and others), or whether it happened because of the Church and its faith (Greeley and others) is a matter of sociological debate. Whatever the case, the Church has adopted an essentially positive, though not uncritical, attitude toward modernity, in the council's *Pastoral Constitution on the Church in the Modern World.*

15. Fundamentalism is modernity's most determined adversary. A worldwide phenomenon, it has both Catholic and Protestant expressions and forms. Catholic fundamentalism is both biblical and doctrinal. It assumes that the truth is one and that there is only one way to understand and express it. The council's approach, by contrast, favors a pluralism that is sustained and enriched through dialogue.

SUGGESTED READINGS

Berger, Peter. *The Heretical Imperative: Contemporary Possibilities of Religious Affirmation*. New York: Doubleday, Anchor, 1979.

Geertz, Clifford. *The Interpretation of Cultures*. New York: Basic Books, 1973.

Gilkey, Langdon. *Catholicism Confronts Modernity: A Protestant View*. New York: Seabury Press, 1975, pp. 1–60.

Greeley, Andrew. "Modernization." *No Bigger Than Necessary*. New York: New American Library, Meridian, 1977, pp. 29–43.

Johnson, Paul. *Modern Times: The World from the Twenties to the Nineties*. New York: HarperCollins, 1991.

Marty, Martin E. *The Modern Schism: Three Paths to the Secular*. New York: Harper & Row, 1969.

Naisbitt, John. *Megatrends: Ten New Directions Transforming Our Lives*. New York: Warner Books, 1982.

_____. *Megatrends 2000: The New Directions for the 1990s*. New York: Morrow, 1990.

O'Meara, Thomas F. *Fundamentalism: A Catholic Perspective*. New York: Paulist Press, 1990.

Sanks, T. Howland, and John A. Coleman, eds. *Reading the Signs of the Times: Resources for Social and Cultural Analysis*. New York: Paulist Press, 1993.

Toffler, Alvin. *Future Shock*. New York: Random House, 1970.

Vatican Council II. "The Church in the Modern World" *(Gaudium et spes)*. *The Documents of Vatican II*. Ed. Walter M. Abbott. New York: America Press, 1966, pp. 199–308.

IV

Understandings of Human Existence

THE QUESTION: WHO ARE WE?

We live in an age of rapid and substantial change. Some believe that the changes have been, for the most part, beneficial to the human community. Others believe that they have been harmful, even destructive. Each side takes its stand on the basis of some (often unstated) understanding of what it means to be human. One cannot, after all, have an opinion about what contributes to human progress unless one first has an opinion about what human beings need, and then identifies those needs in the light of one's perception of the fundamental structure and purpose of the human person and of the larger human community in which the person lives. Similarly, one cannot have an opinion about what impedes human progress unless one also has some antecedent opinion about what makes us "human" in the first place, and about what might threaten the "human" in all of us.

Anthropology is the umbrella term we use to embrace all of the scientific and disciplinary ways in which we raise and try to answer the question, "Who are we?" *Anthropology is our explanation of ourselves.* It means etymologically "the study of man" (*logos* and *anthro-*

pos). More specifically, it is the scientific study of the origin and of the physical, social, and cultural development and behavior of human beings. What makes the anthropological question unique is that we are at once the questioner and the questioned. Consequently, our answers are always inadequate. They can only lead to further questions and further attempts at answers.

Indeed, if we could really get to the bottom of the matter and answer the question of ourselves without remainder, we would at that moment cease to be human. But even to draw that conclusion one has to have some prior understanding of human existence. Implied in that judgment (i.e., that we would cease to be human if we were to answer the question of ourselves finally and forever) is the conviction that freedom and openness to the future are intrinsic to the human condition. If we knew exactly what makes us what we are, what makes us act the way we act and think the way we think, every human thought and action would be programmable to achieve the precisely desired and/or intended effect.

We would marry only those whom our calculations revealed to be completely compatible with us. We would choose as friends only those with similar computerized clearance. We would associate ourselves professionally or occupationally only with those who could work with us most efficiently and effectively and who could best enhance the development of our careers. There would be no more risks, no more taking of chances. Everything and everyone would be plotted on a grid.

Life would no longer be a mystery to be faced and experienced with love, trust, hope, wonder, and not a little anxiety and fear. Decisions would no longer be provoked by crises of any kind. We would not have to choose between compelling alternatives. Motives would be unmistakably clear. Projections would be mathematically established. Our freedom would be the freedom to bow to the evidence, or the freedom to be irrational and deny the undeniable (but even that display of irrationality would have been calculated and anticipated).

As for the future, it would no longer be open. We would know it as we know the present and the past. Only physical and natural disorders (disease, famine, earthquakes, hurricanes, and the like) could disrupt our calculations, and even those would come increasingly under human control to the extent that human weakness, error, or lack of foresight were responsible for them in the first instance.

Even humor would disappear, for it essentially rests on our capacity to see discrepancies (things are not what they seem). The pompous general, in full uniform, slips on a banana peel during a military parade. The neighborhood bully is discovered to be terrified of spiders. An overbearing tightwad loses a ten-dollar bet after boasting loudly that he would be a sure winner. Indeed, there could be no real discrepancies at all. Things would always be as they seemed, for the motives and inner psychic forces governing the action of others would be apparent to all. Nothing would, or could, catch us off guard or by surprise. Laughter, which according to some philosophers is our way of defying the darkness of doubt and ignorance about the future, would be reduced to the sardonic chuckle of one "in the know."

Some, at first glance, might find the prospect of a totally calculable society positively exciting. Most others, it can fairly be assumed, would be frightened and appalled by the thought. In any case, the point remains moot for the time being. The emergence of test-tube babies, computer dating services, various forms of behavior modification and genetic engineering notwithstanding, we are still a long way from that kind of world, intimated in George Orwell's prophetic novel, *Nineteen Eighty-Four* (1949). In the meantime, all of us continue to "make do" with what we have, to make decisions laden with risks, and to place our trust in people we are never fully and finally sure of.

We are, as the German philosopher Friedrich Nietzsche (d. 1900) put it, an "as yet undetermined animal." We can look back in history at the way we have used our freedom and then draw inferences about who we really are, about our motives and our actions. And since that history is not yet finished, our understanding of ourselves is always tentative, subject to revision. Since that history is also multifaceted, our understanding of ourselves is possible only if we use a variety of approaches: biology, ethology, sociology, economics, politics, psychology, literature, philosophy, and theology.

The rest of this chapter will be taken up with a broad range of the views on human existence to be found in some of these disciplines. Given the nature of this book, the major focus remains on theology and doctrine.

The survey that follows is intended simply to provide some wider context for understanding and evaluating the theological and doctrinal material at the end of this chapter and in chapter 5. Of particular, though not exclusive, interest are Freud, Marx, and Nietzsche, whose "hermeneutics of suspicion" has challenged the illusions of Enlightenment consciousness regarding the human person and the human condition: Freud, through the disclosure of the unrecognized motivations of the unconscious; Marx, through the disclosure of the unrecognized motivations of socioeconomic forces; and Nietzsche, through the disclosure of the unrecognized motivation of a will to power empowering our cultural accomplishments (see David Tracy, *The Analogical Imagination*, pp. 346–51). Of equivalent importance is the emergence of *feminist consciousness* in our time, leading us to challenge fundamentally traditional assumptions about the relationship of men and women in the human community, and of the dignity, equality, and role of women in society and in the Church.

A SPECTRUM OF ANSWERS

What follows is obviously only a very broad survey. Each of the fields and each of the major contributors to those fields that are mentioned would merit a full-scale treatment of their own. But that would take us well beyond the purpose or competence of this work. Moreover, some highly pertinent areas are simply not touched, given the limits of space. One such area is that of the arts: literature, theater, films, music, painting, sculpture. Within and through each of these, understandings of human existence are portrayed and expressed. Were it possible, each would deserve special and separate attention. To take but one example, literature, one thinks immediately of the writings of Graham Greene, Flannery O'Connor, Mary Gordon, Walker Percy, François Mauriac, Georges Bernanos, Arthur Koestler, Ignazio Silone, Franz Kafka, James Joyce, John Steinbeck, T. S. Eliot, among modern authors as well as of the great classics such as Shakespeare, Milton, Dostoevsky, Tolstoy, and so many others. And this is only to touch literature. Not films. Not music. Not painting. Not sculpture. There are many blanks for the reader to fill in.

The Natural Sciences

For centuries our self-understanding as human beings had been expressed in terms of the *Ptolemaic world view:* The earth is the center of the whole universe, and we are the center of the earth by the design and will of God. With the *Copernican revolution* the sun displaced the earth as the center, and so we, too, were pushed closer to the margin of the cosmic order. But there endured a tenacious confidence in the powers of reason and in the intellectual faculty as the great line of demarcation between human beings and the rest of life. This conviction, too, would be put to the test in the middle of the nineteenth century.

Darwin

Charles Darwin (d. 1882) was a biologist who, in his early years, was at the same time a believing Christian. He accepted the fixity of species and their special creation as depicted in the book of Genesis. But doubts began to emerge in 1835 when he visited the Galápagos Archipelago, where he noticed that very small differences were present in the so-called species inhabiting separate islands. His original doubts were only reinforced by additional observations of flora, fauna, and geological formations at widely separated points of the globe. All living things, he tentatively concluded, have developed from a few extremely simple forms, through a gradual process of descent with modification. He developed a theory of natural selection to account for the process, and especially for the adaptations of living things to their often hostile environments. His findings were published in *The Origin of the Species* (1859).

At first there was strong opposition to his views from biologists themselves. They insisted that directly observed phenomena must somehow be brought under general laws. But before long all scientific opposition collapsed under the weight of arguments of the kind and force marshaled in a later work, *The Descent of Man*, published in 1871. The field of battle was left entirely to his newly aroused enemies in the ranks of Christianity.

Darwin himself was a modest man, not given to polemics. His public image as an enemy of the Bible and the Church was as much caused by the activities of T. H. Huxley ("Darwin's bulldog"), who delighted in crossing swords with theologians, as by his own scientific hypotheses. But Darwin himself eventually grew away from his traditional faith. He concluded that "the whole subject is beyond the scope of man's intellect.... The mystery of the beginning of all things is insoluble for us; and I for one must be content to remain an Agnostic."

Nonetheless, he was buried with full national honors beside Isaac Newton at Westminster Abbey, and eulogies on him were preached there and at St. Paul's Cathedral, London. By the time of his death, many Christians had already come to terms with the theory of evolution, finding it not incompatible with Christian faith. Even the highly conservative papacy did not place any of Darwin's books on the Index of Forbidden Books, nor was evolution mentioned in Pius IX's *Syllabus of Errors* (1864). The first reservations were expressed in *The Catholic Encyclopedia* (1909), but on scientific, not theological, grounds. So long as Darwin's theory was not used to explain the nature and origin of the human soul, the theory was regarded as a reasonable, albeit unproven, hypothesis.

The immediate challenge of Darwin's theory was not in the area of theological anthropology but in Scripture studies. The theory of evolution would undermine a literal interpretation of the biblical account of creation and the putative length of human history. But even here Darwin was not the only, or the major, "enemy of orthodoxy." Well before the publication of Darwin's *Origin of the Species* in 1859, geologist James Hutton's *Theory of the Earth* (1759) and geologist Charles Lyell's *Principles of Geology* (1830–1833) had already argued the case that the earth was much older than biblical literalists assumed.

Darwin, however, was not completely pleased with the early support his theory received within the Christian church (for example, the book by biologist and convert to Catholicism, St. George Jackson Mivart, *On the Genesis of Species* [1871]). His Christian supporters tended to read too much into Darwin's theory, leaving room always for divine intervention and governance of the process. These so-called "providential evolutionists" held that if selection did take place in nature, there must be an intelligent agent directing the selection process.

Outside of Christian academic and scholarly circles, however, it was a different story. Catholics in the English-speaking world had not yet enjoyed the benefits of the educational progress described in chapter 3, and the Catholic Church remained extremely suspicious of the new biblical scholarship on the Continent and of inroads of Modernist thinking within Catholicism itself. Although fundamentalism had, by this time, only a Protestant face, the reality (not the name) of fundamentalism was fully in place within the Catholic community as well.

In the early 1920s, therefore, the public battle against Darwinism was fought by Protestants, with the most dramatic instance being the famous Scopes trial (1925) in Dayton, Tennessee, pitting agnostic defense attorney Clarence Darrow against sometime presidential candidate and fundamentalist Christian William Jennings Bryan, who was acting as an aide to the prosecutor. A public school teacher, John Scopes, was indicted for teaching evolution in the classroom. He was found guilty, but later released on a technicality. The law itself was repealed in 1967.

On the one hand, we should not make too much of the so-called "monkey trial." As pointed out at the end of chapter 3, fundamentalism has had a broader agenda than combatting Darwin's theory of evolution. It is a movement in reaction against the whole modernist "assault" upon "traditional" Christian values. On the other hand, antievolutionism, in the form of "scientific creationism," remains high on the Protestant fundamentalist list of educational priorities in the United States. Indeed, such Protestants have been accused of running as "stealth candidates" for local school boards and other public offices, with the hidden intention of forcing the teaching of scientific creationism in the schools on an equal basis with the teaching of evolution.

Unfortunately, this has left many with the impression that the only alternative to Darwin's theory of evolution is the version of creation espoused by the fundamentalists. This assumption has been accorded some superficial support from the Catholic side, in particular because of Pope Pius XII's encyclical *Humani Generis* (1950), which explicitly rejected polygenism in favor of monogenism (the theory that all human beings are literally descended from one set of parents, Adam and Eve).

"It is in no way apparent," the encyclical declared, "how such an opinion can be reconciled with that which the sources of revealed truth and the documents of the teaching authority of the Church propose with regard to Original Sin, which proceeds from sin actually committed by an individual Adam and which through generation is passed on to all and is in everyone as his own" (n. 66). At the same time, the encyclical allowed for the development of a so-called "moderate evolutionism" on the condition that all sides, "those favorable and those unfavorable to evolution, be weighed and judged with the necessary seriousness, moderation and measure and provided that all are prepared to submit to the judgment of the Church to whom Christ has given the mission of interpreting authentically the Sacred Scripture and of defending dogmas of faith" (n. 64). The Church's official position, therefore, is that any scientific explanation of the origin and development of the human species is acceptable so long as it doesn't exclude God from the creative process and, in particular, God's role in the creation of the human soul.

Whatever the final scientific assessment of Darwin's theory of evolution and of natural selection, we cannot easily overestimate the importance of his work. No longer can any serious person reflect on the meaning of human existence as if each one of us lives in an environmental or cosmic vacuum. We are not disembodied spirits. We are bodily creatures, materially linked with the rest of creation, and especially with other living beings. Human reason may indeed set us on a qualitatively different level of reality, but so, too, do our will, our imagination, our emotions, our sexuality, our aesthetical sense, and our total bodiliness.

Meanwhile, other natural scientists have carried Darwin's insights to what some would regard as their logical extreme. Harvard University sociobiologist Edward O. Wilson suggests that "the genes hold culture on a leash. The leash is very long, but inevitably values will be constrained in accordance with their effects on the human gene pool." Nature's first commandment, Wilson argues, is to do what is genetically advantageous. In two of his principal works, *Sociobiology: The New Synthesis* (Cambridge, Mass.: Belknap Press of Harvard University Press, 1975) and *On Human Nature* (Cambridge, Mass.: Harvard University Press, 1978), he advances the thesis that aggression, sexual differences, religious impulses, and even altruism are biologically based products of natural selection (see also his *The Diversity of Life*, Cambridge, Mass.: Belknap Press of Harvard University Press, 1992). But unlike other sociobiologists he does not go so far as to justify either war or male dominance as the inevitable outcome of our biological destiny. On the contrary, we have seen only a small portion of the human behavior that is possible. The cultures which enhance or impede this genetic potential represent only a fraction of what is possible.

Lorenz

Konrad Lorenz, an Austrian ethologist (*ethology* is that branch of biology which focuses primarily on behavior), also pursued a path similar to Darwin's. From early childhood he recorded his observations of waterfowl and noted the impact of environment on their behavior. The essence of his thought is contained in his book *The Evolution and Modification of Behavior* (Chicago: University of Chicago Press, 1965), but he is perhaps best known for his later work, *On Aggression*, published in 1966 (New York: Harcourt, Brace & World). Although he concedes that some behavior is environmentally conditioned (the extreme form of this view is proposed by the psychologist B. F. Skinner [d. 1990]), he holds that other behavior is genetically programmed or "imprinted." Environmental factors, of course, develop what is innately present. But it is never sufficient to change the environment if one is to change behavior. In this he strongly opposes those who seem to argue that society, not the criminal, is responsible for crime.

Every person has what Lorenz calls a nonrational sense of values. This alone, he says, can prevent a retrograde evolution of civilized society because we have managed to eliminate in the meantime all other selective factors in human evolution. Included among these nonrational senses of values is human love. Lorenz argues that the abuse of sex through gross commercialization may be at least as harmful as excessive violence in the media. The destruction of the higher emotions, the disappearance of love (falling in love, being in love), may present more of a danger to the survival of culture than violence as such (see also his *The Waning of Humaneness*, Boston: Little, Brown, 1987).

Accordingly, Lorenz has relatively little enthusiasm for the popularization efforts of such writers as Robert Ardrey (d. 1980), *The Territorial Imperative* (New York: Atheneum, 1966), and even less for Desmond Morris, *The Naked Ape* (New York: McGraw-Hill, 1967). The latter, he insists, treats culture as if it were biologically irrelevant. If one is to call human beings apes, then let them at least be culture-apes or the "ideal conception of all apes." That human beings are naked is irrelevant. We might just as well be furry.

Eiseley

Still other natural scientists interpret human existence in grim and pessimistic terms. *The Firmament of Time* (New York: Atheneum, 1960), by anthropologist Loren Eiseley (d. 1977), speaks of the evolution of the human being as if it were some kind of natural disaster drowning out the ancient sounds of nature "in the cacophony of something which is no longer nature, something instead which is loose and knocking at the world's heart, something demonic and no longer planned—escaped, it may be—spewed out of nature, contending in a final giant's game against its master."

The Social Sciences

Freud

Whereas natural scientists have been interested in the interaction of human behavior and the world outside the person, *psychologists* have been concerned with the interaction of human behavior and the world *inside* the person. But even this statement has to be qualified. It may apply in large measure to the founder of modern psychology, Sigmund Freud (d. 1939), but to a much less extent to those who have followed in his path and/or developed courses of their own, such as Carl Jung (d. 1961) and Erich Fromm (d. 1980).

Freud, like Darwin, made his discoveries about human existence through direct observation. Darwin examined nonhuman life; Freud examined the human. He concluded that human behavior is shaped by unconscious drives and motivations and that these, in turn, have some sexual correlation. Our psychic lives consist in the inner strug-

108

gle of conflicting drives for power and sexual gratification, on the one hand, and the psychic and social inhibitions against the fulfillment of those drives, on the other. One of his earliest works is also perhaps his most original, *The Interpretation of Dreams* (1900). Therein, he proposed the principle of wish fulfillment, the Oedipal complex, and the influence of infantile life in conditioning the human adult.

Strongly influenced by the mechanical materialism of his day, Freud's basic theories were highly quantitative. Even culture he regarded as a quantitative activity in which civilization is more or less determined by the degree or intensity of the repression of instincts. But Freud was no *biological* determinist. He saw that in history the only alternative to having no culture at all and no neuroses is having civilization with the repression and neuroses it necessarily entails. He looked upon the whole process of repression as a result of the social development of humankind. Unfortunately, he was innocent of the major sociological writings of the late nineteenth and early twentieth centuries: those of Karl Marx, Émile Durkheim, and Max Weber. He remained primarily interested in the psychological and physiological, even though he was considerably shaken by the events of the First World War and became noticeably less optimistic and rationalistic about human nature.

Nor was Freud a *psychological* determinist. On the contrary, he was trying to liberate us from those hidden psychic forces which direct our actions. If he had been a determinist, he would not have vested any hope in therapy as a means of changing motivation and behavior by making the person aware of the unconscious forces at work in his or her psychic life.

Freud, of course, will always have a cloud over his head in religious circles. Religion, for him, is the product of *wish fulfillment*. God in heaven replaces the fallible and weak human father. By becoming and remaining religious, a person can prolong the status of a child into adult life. Religion, therefore, perpetuates infantile behavior patterns, especially those having to do with guilt and forgiveness. For that reason, religion is a particularly damaging species of illusion because it militates against our necessary efforts to distinguish always between what is and what we want reality to be.

Freud's skeptical attitude toward religion derived from his training in physiology, neurology, and medicine, all of which are concerned with rigorous objectivity. Religion, he believed, indulged and encouraged narcissism, or self-love, by conferring upon its adherents the illusion that they are special or privileged by virtue of their relation to an all-powerful and all-loving God. Freud concluded that religious belief in an all-powerful God with whom one is intimately connected inhibits rather than encourages new knowledge about reality.

Although generally regarded as the enemy of religion, Freud's work, especially his appreciation of the power of religious symbols, has been received more sympathetically by such major Protestant theologians as Paul Tillich (d. 1965), who likened Freud to a biblical prophet attacking the idolatry of the faithful and the authoritarian manner of their religious leaders (see *The Courage to Be*, New Haven: Yale University Press, 1952). At the same time, Tillich was critical of Freud's skepticism, namely, Freud's view that once the unconscious meaning of a religious myth was uncovered, the religious content of that belief would have to yield to a broader psychological self-understanding.

Jung

One of Freud's colleagues, Carl Jung, tempered Freud's severe attitude toward religion. It was Jung who introduced the distinction between the individual and the *collective unconscious*. The latter originates in those patterns of behavior (archetypes) which are determined by the human race itself and which show themselves in dreams, visions, and fantasies, and are expressed in myths, religious stories, fairy tales, and works of art. Consequently, the many images which abound in human history are more than primitive expressions. They are a necessary and profound expression of a communal experience. And this is especially true of Christianity and its rich symbol system.

Because of his belief that religion is an enduring dimension of human life, Jung's psychological theories have exercised more influence on theology and religious studies than have Freud's, especially among Catholic thinkers like Victor White, O.P. (d. 1960), who introduced Jung to a wider religious audience in his *God and the Unconscious* (Cleveland: World Publishing Co., 1963; copyright 1952). A

110

number of other specialists in the study of religion have also made constructive use of Jung's approach, e.g., Joseph Campbell (d. 1987), Mircea Eliade (d. 1986), and Wendy Doniger (formerly Wendy Doniger O'Flaherty). Campbell's works include *The Hero with a Thousand Faces*, New York: Pantheon Books, 1949; *Myths, Dreams, and Religion*, New York: E. P. Dutton, 1970; *The Power of Myth*, New York: Doubleday, 1988; and *The Transformation of Myths Through Time*, New York: Perennial Library, 1990. Among Eliade's many works, see *The Sacred and the Profane: The Nature of Religion*, New York: Harcourt, Brace, 1959. For Wendy Doniger, see *Women, Androgenes, and Other Mythical Beasts*, Chicago: University of Chicago Press, 1980; and *Dreams, Illusion, and Other Realities*, Chicago: University of Chicago Press, 1984. Finally, Jung's influence has also been expanded by the work of Ira Progoff and his popular intensive journal method of self-understanding (see, for example, his *Depth Psychology and Modern Man*, New York: Julian Press, 1959; *Jung, Synchronicity, and Human Destiny*, New York: Julian Press, 1973; and *Life-Study: Experiencing Creative Lives by the Intensive Journal Method*, New York: Dialogue House Library, 1983).

Fromm

Erich Fromm, a German psychoanalyst, is in the tradition of Freud (in fact he is often referred to as a "neo-Freudian") but, by his own account, wishes to liberate Freud's most important discoveries from his somewhat narrow libido theory. Unlike Freud, Erich Fromm insists that much human behavior is *culturally* rather than biologically conditioned. Culture structures persons to conform to the social mold. We are what we have to be, in accordance with the requirements of the society in which we find ourselves. Depending upon our response to these social exigencies, we can be either productive persons or automatons.

Productive persons, Fromm says, are individuals who are relatively independent of others in producing what they need for themselves as they function in society, not just economically but emotionally and intellectually as well. A productive person has a sense of his or her own authority, and the courage of his or her convictions. This is what authenticity means. Automaton conform-

111

ists, on the other hand, yield to the dictates of others, faithfully obeying every signal designed to control human behavior.

Clearly, Fromm holds, the second kind of individual is the one closer to the norm of humanity. We are indeed freaks of nature in that we represent "the only case of a living organism having awareness of itself." We are beings, therefore, who seek an answer to the question of why we were born and why we are living. But we can progress or regress. We progress by increasing our powers of reason, love, and relatedness to others. We regress by seeking only security. In Fromm's judgment, we seem to be losing the battle, although compelling human figures like Pope John XXIII are encouraging reminders of the deep reservoir of strength still present within the human community. (See his *Art of Loving,* New York: Bantam Books, 1963 [copyright 1956] and *For the Love of Life,* New York: Free Press, 1985.)

Marx

Karl Marx (d. 1883) is, of course, sociologist, economist, and political theorist wrapped up in one. Best known for his *Communist Manifesto* (1847) and *Capital* (1867), Marx, like Darwin, argued that human beings are definable only in relation to other realities. For Darwin, human beings are part of the larger *natural* order. For Marx, they are part of the larger *social* order. "The essence of man is no abstraction inherent in each separate individual," he wrote. "In its reality it is the ensemble of social relations." And Marx, like Freud, insisted that human problems are traceable to conflicts produced by *alienation*. For Freud, the alienation is from one's true self; for Marx, the alienation is from the fruits of one's labors and thus from the industrialized world and from other people. We are distinguished from the rest of the animal kingdom by the way we express our lives: by our work, by our various activities, by our changing of the environment, and especially by our producing our own means of subsistence.

But no individual human being, Marx holds, can sufficiently express himself or herself without benefit of society. Only in society, by joint effort, can we express ourselves in the complex way we do. Human beings, therefore, do not really appear on the historical scene until there is society, for it is only in and through *society*, the collective, that we are who and what we are. It is already there when we are born, and it conditions the kind and quality of lives we lead. The individual is derived from society and, therefore, is secondary and subordinate to it.

However, Marx maintains, if each person is essentially social, then each person should enjoy and share in all of the fruits of social collaboration. But because of the structure of capitalist societies, we are divided into the haves and the have-nots, masters and slaves, capitalists and proletarians. The great mass of humankind is alienated or separated from the products of its labors. Instead of expressing themselves through their labor (as in a work of art), most human beings are forced to sell their products to some entrepreneur in order to survive. Moreover, instead of expressing themselves fully through a variety of activities, they are forced to perform only one monotonous task all day long while someone else performs another (a process Marx called the "division of labor").

The solution to this unhappy state of affairs lies in changing the economic base on which society is built, Marx argues. It is not enough, in other words, to *interpret* the world (as Marx accused the German philosopher Ludwig Feuerbach [d. 1872] of doing), but we must also struggle to *change* it. The way to free human beings from alienation is to destroy its causes: private property and the division of labor. We shall once again enjoy the fruits of our own labors and the labors of our fellow human beings in a society he called "communist." In such a society, each contributes according to ability and receives according to need. When we have all we need, there will be no envy, theft, or other crimes against our fellow human beings. After a brutal experimentation of some seventy years duration, worldwide Communism collapsed under the heavy weight of reality. In November 1989, the Berlin Wall came down, and with it the whole Soviet empire.

Important elements of Marxist theory overlap with economic and sociopolitical theories in the West, where it is widely recognized that social and economic structures have to be changed to achieve justice. The West has also become more fully aware of the impact of economic factors in the history of ideas and on the accumulation of knowledge. And *laissez-faire* liberalism, of the sort Marx himself faced, has been rejected as an unacceptable and ultimately unjust expression of economic values. On the other hand, there was always a clear and sharp conflict between Marxist theory and human freedom: freedom of expression, freedom of worship, freedom of movement, freedom of communication, freedom of thought. The cruel suppression of the uprisings in Hungary (1956) and Czechoslovakia (1968), the harassment of Alexander Solzhenitsyn and other Soviet dissidents, and the human slaughter that followed the Communist "liberation" of Cambodia in 1975 were only a few cases in point. These tragic episodes were, of course, in striking contrast to the largely bloodless revolutions that, at the turn of the decade of the 1990s, toppled Communist regimes in Central and Eastern Europe and in the Soviet Union itself.

There were efforts beginning in the late 1930s to extricate Marxism from its almost obsessive preoccupation with economics and use it instead as an all-embracing critical social theory, with some emphasis on cultural criticism and even psychoanalysis. A noteworthy example is the so-called Frankfurt School of social criticism, composed of such figures as Herbert Marcuse (d. 1979), Jürgen Habermas, and others. They have tended to explain very well what has to be changed in human society to maximize freedom but less well what has to be preserved. The objectives of the change also remain vague. From its very beginning, in fact, this group of theorists has resisted the temptation to develop a coherent philosophical system. It has always functioned instead as a kind of gadfly of other existing systems and points of view. (See, for example, Habermas's *Theory and Practice*, Boston: Beacon Press, 1973.)

Feminist Thought

Few, if any, twentieth-century intellectual and social movements have had a greater practical impact on individuals, society, and religion than feminism has had. Beginning with Betty Friedan's *The Feminine Mystique* in 1963, feminism (called in its earliest manifestation the "women's liberation movement") has mounted a wide-ranging, interdisciplinary critique of the ethos and practice of sexism and gender discrimination, as expressed in patriarchal social, political, cultural, and religious structures and in androcentric thought and language (see, for example, Gerda Lerner, *The Creation of Patriarchy*, New York: Oxford University Press, 1986).

114

The anthropology critiqued by feminist thought assumes that male experience is normative for human experience and that women are complementary and subordinate to men. This philosophy of complementarity extrapolates from bodily differences an inherent dissimilarity in roles: the woman's role is one of childbearing and of domestic service; the man's is public leadership and domestic headship.

Feminism holds that women and men are equal in human dignity. It challenges the androcentric assumption that male experience is normative for all human experience, and androcentrism's accompanying stereotypes—namely, that men are characterized by rationality, autonomy, strength, and initiative, while women are characterized by intuition, nurturing, receptiveness, and compassion. Feminism insists that men and women alike are to embody the full range of human characteristics. This is not to say, however, that all feminist thinkers deny differences rooted in gender (see, for example, Carol Gilligan, *In a Different Voice: Psychological Theory and Women's Development*, Cambridge, Mass.: Harvard University Press, 1982, pp. 25–62). Indeed, there is no one school of feminist thought, whether in psychotherapy, political theory, literary criticism, or theology.

"However," writes theologian Catherine Mowry LaCugna, "feminist theory almost always entails the commitment to promote the full humanity of women and men by critiquing, deconstructing, or reforming institutions or forms of thought that demean human persons" (*God For Us: The Trinity and Christian Life*, San Francisco: HarperCollins, 1991, p. 268).

Philosophy

The classical distinctions among science, philosophy, and theology became blurred in the twentieth century such that the distinctions between philosophy and theology, on the one hand, and between philosophy and science, on the other, are neither static nor sharp. Indeed, not even philosophers themselves agree on the definition of *philosophy* because defining it is a part of philosophy itself and hence varies with the different approaches. The closest one might come to a relatively neutral, descriptive definition is "the attempt to grasp the ultimate meaning of existence," or "the attempt to provide a systematic understanding of the world and the person's place in it."

It is clear, in any case, that simply reiterating the old distinction between philosophy and theology will not do, namely, that philosophy proceeds from reason, while theology proceeds from revelation and faith. Indeed, the old distinction between reason and faith in terms of a single truth is no longer adequate, because it is precisely the very notions of "reason," "faith," and "truth" that are at the heart of contemporary debate in philosophy and theology alike.

According to traditional Catholic theology and doctrine (Vatican I), however, reason itself enters into the process of understanding faith and of identifying criteria and signs of revelation. On the other hand, revelation and grace are universally available, to the philosopher and the theologian alike. No matter how hard he or she might try, the philosopher is inevitably influenced by the faith (Christian or not) which he or she brings to the investigation of a problem. Indeed, the problems themselves are often as much theological as they are philosophical: What does it mean to be human? How are we free? What does happiness consist in? What is justice? What is the measure of truth? How and why are we propelled in the pursuit of truth? Some philosophy, therefore, points itself and its practitioners in the direction of God, and so onto the course marked out by theology itself.

The question of the distinction between philosophy and theology is further complicated by the fact that theology and at least some philosophies claim to be concerned with the whole of reality and, therefore, universal in scope. But the solution offered by the First Vatican Council—that truth comes from the same God and cannot be contradictory—is not sufficient. It is not clear, for example, whether one can be both a philosopher and a theologian at the same time, or whether such a choice has to be made at all. At a deeper level, it is not even clear what the notion of a "single truth" means.

Moreover, in addition to the lack of philosophical consensus on these fundamental notions, philosophy in the twentieth century has given rise to a multiplicity of very different perspectives on the basic questions of the nature of the person and the meaning of human life. The early twentieth century saw the rise of phenomenology (Husserl, Merleau-Ponty), process philosophy (Bergson, Whitehead), existentialism (Kierkegaard, Nietzsche, Heidegger, Sartre,

116

Buber), pragmatism (James, Dewey), logical positivism (the early Wittgenstein, Russell, Carnap), and ordinary language philosophy (the later Wittgenstein, Ryle, Austin).

Among contemporary philosophical currents, there are those philosophies that go under the rubric "Continental," which include neo-Marxism (Habermas, Marcuse), hermeneutics (Gadamer, Ricoeur), and deconstruction (Derrida), while most others in the English-speaking world go under the rubric "analytic" and are quite varied in orientation, with its practitioners drawing heavily on contemporary developments in logic and the philosophy of language, sociobiology, neuroscience, cognitive science, and artificial intelligence in developing an account of human existence.

There are, of course, those who continue to develop the Augustinian-Thomistic tradition, but even here those who are not merely historians of medieval philosophy can be thought of as either "Continental Thomists" or "Analytic Thomists," depending on which tradition they are embedded in. Thus, the differences in those traditions also manifest themselves in the varieties of Thomism. Philosophical pluralism seems to be the order of the day.

Early Twentieth-Century Philosophies

Phenomenology

Phenomenology is concerned chiefly with the person as *knower*, while existentialism is primarily concerned with the human person as a source of freedom and spontaneous activity. The connection, however, between knowing and deciding is very close, and so, too, is the connection between these two philosophical movements.

Husserl

Edmund Husserl (d. 1938) is the founder of modern phenomenology, and the publication of his *Logical Investigations* in 1900 and 1901 marks the beginning of this movement. This work attacked what Husserl called "psychologism," which in its extreme forms is found in behaviorism. Consciousness, Husserl argued, is not fully explainable by analyses of the brain, or by neurological searches for the law of mathematics or art. It has a structure and rules proper to itself. Consciousness is never closed in upon itself, however. It has an intentionality, i.e., it is always conscious of something, of *phenomena.*

Phenomenology studies such phenomena, not as things in themselves (as other sciences do) but as objects of intentionality. But it does not revert to psychologism because phenomenology maintains that there is a fundamental and irreducible duality between consciousness and the world. The two are correlated as the eye is correlated with the field of vision. There can be no field of vision without the eye, and yet the two remain distinct. For the same reason there can be no reality without consciousness. The task of phenomenology is to describe the various regions of reality in the way they appear to consciousness, and to show what activity consciousness must carry out in order to allow such regions of reality to appear.

For Husserl, Heidegger's mentor, we are beings in time. Our past experiences enter into our present consciousness and personality. A material thing like a stone can pass through innumerable events and not be changed at all by them. A human person, on the other hand, is changed by what happens. The past is borne within the person because present consciousness retains what is past. And yet we are never imprisoned by the past. We never entirely lose the possibility of changing or redeeming the past, because the present is also open upon the future.

And what applies to the person as individual applies to the human community as a whole. Human temporality, therefore, is not a passive reality. We are not simply caught up in the flow of time. Through our consciousness we look forward to the future and retain the past. We are thereby empowered to engage in a process of inquiry into who and what we really are.

Merleau-Ponty

Maurice Merleau-Ponty (d. 1961) is in the same philosophical tradition as Husserl. His rallying cry, like Husserl's, is "back to the things," or "back to perception" (see his major work, *The Phenomenology of Perception* [1945, Eng. trans., New York: Humanities Press, 1962]). The human person is essentially a "being-in-the-world." We are *embodied* spirits. Merleau-Ponty's philosophy is a middle way between empiricism and intellectualism, between realism and subjectivism, and between determinism and the Sartrean conception of absolute freedom. We are born into a social situation, he says, which in large part determines how we act and what we see. We are not wholly free to throw off our historically and socially conditioned self. On the other hand, our social situation does not wholly determine our modes of action, any more than the ready-made meanings we encounter in the things around us entirely determine what meanings we shall find in them.

"If one sometimes despairs of philosophy's tendency to fluctuate between absurd extremes, this fluctuation is no accident," John Passmore writes. "[A] 'middle way,' as Merleau-Ponty's philosophy illustrates, is not easy to find or to persist in" (*A Hundred Years of Philosophy*, Harmondsworth, Eng.: Penguin Books, 1970, p. 503).

Existentialism

Existentialism has been characterized as a violent reaction against the view of the human person and the world which is enshrined in Plato's *Republic*. For Plato, "existence" is a distant second to "essence" as a way of being. To see the real world is to see it as an intelligible system of essences. Similarly, for Plato, individuality is a defect. One is defined by one's functions in life and by the various "forms" through which the functions are exercised. In this scheme, no one has to suffer the agony of choice; no one has to commit himself or herself as a person.

Kierkegaard

The Danish Lutheran Søren Kierkegaard (d. 1855) is often regarded as the founder, or protoparent, of modern (perhaps better: *post*modern) existentialist thought, alongside the German moralist Friedrich Nietzsche (d. 1900). Kierkegaard was the first to emphasize the *subject* as a responsible person who must always be ready to stand alone before God without benefit of some social, even ecclesiastical, shield. By stressing individuality and authenticity, Kierkegaard challenged the Hegelian emphasis on the abstract and the universal. Our individuality is bound up with the awareness of our limitations and especially with our awareness of impending death. "Sickness unto death" and "dread" are characteristic of "existential man." But Kierkegaard did not interpret them as Freud had.

In his *Fear and Trembling* (1843) Kierkegaard contrasts the "ethical man" with the "religious man." The former is one who subordinates himself to universal moral imperatives (as Kant would have it); the latter obeys divine commands made directly to him as a person, as Abraham did when he was commanded to slay his son Isaac. For Kierkegaard, Abraham is a model of the responsible individual, who obeys the call of faith without seeking to be justified before anything less than the presence of God. His responsible bond with God is maintained, not by means of the categorical imperative, but by reason of his personal, inward dedication of self to God. In the end, the question of questions for Kierkegaard was, "How can I become a Christian?"

Nietzsche

By contrast, Friedrich Nietzsche begins with the assumption that "God is dead." We must learn to reexamine the human situation in light of this fact. If, for Kierkegaard, the question is, "How can I become a Christian?", for Nietzsche it is, "How am I to live as an atheist?" Both thinkers rejected all abstract philosophy on the grounds that "life is more than logic." And in the same spirit as Kierkegaard but with far different results, Nietzsche also wanted to do away with externally imposed values. We can recover our lost freedom only through internally created values, what he called a "transvaluation of values." In *Thus Spake Zarathustra* (1883) the transcendent no longer has any effective power and is submerged in the evils of the times. Under the circumstances "man" has to deify himself (Nietzsche's superman), while remaining aware of his own impotence in the face of a hostile world. Meaning is not out there, waiting to be perceived and appropriated. It is something we have to create by ourselves. And since this process is carried on by many men and women, the real image of the human person will emerge only through the struggle of various groups in value-creating acts. But, of course, Nietzsche had to assume some of the values that he insisted had to be created.

Heidegger

The existentialist philosopher who has exercised the greatest influence on twentieth-century theology is Martin Heidegger (d. 1976). His *Being and Time* (1927) may be the most significant philosophical book published in the twentieth century. He provides, in fact, a bridge between existentialist thought and phenomenology. If we are to come to an understanding of what it means to be human, Heidegger argues, then we must reflect on what it is that we are and do. This requires some preliminary descriptive steps.

We must first of all look to see what shows itself (*phenomenon*) or lets itself be seen in human existence. The test of such description is to compare it with what we ourselves actually know of existence through our own firsthand participation in it. But it is not a simple matter. Existence is not an object we can set before us and describe from the outside. We ourselves are the existents that are to be described, and self-knowledge is exceedingly difficult. Indeed we all have a tendency to conceal the truth not only from others but even from ourselves. We have to strip away the cover. When we do, we find that selfhood is not ready-made but rather is always on the way and always incomplete at any given moment. We can either attain to authentic selfhood by realizing the possibilities open to us, or we can fall below the standard of authentic human existence.

An analysis of human existence discloses certain tensions or polarities. First, there is the polarity between *existence* and *facticity*, that is, between freedom and finitude. We exist in a world. Our possibilities, therefore, are not unrestricted. They are limited by the concrete situation in which we find ourselves, including all the "givens" of human existence such as intelligence, race, temperament, environment, heredity.

A second polarity exists between *rationality* and *irrationality*. Our minds move toward truth, and at the same time toward untruth, error, and deception. Freud, as we have already noted, helped us see the frightening extent to which our lives are governed by dark and irrational forces.

A third polarity exists between *responsibility* and *impotence*. We recognize what we "ought" to be doing and yet cannot bring ourselves to do what is demanded. In the words of the Epistle to the

Romans: "For I do not do the good I want, but the evil I do not want is what I do. Now if I do what I do not want, it is no longer I that do it, but sin that dwells within me. So I find it to be a law that when I want to do what is good, evil lies close at hand. For I delight in the law of God in my inmost self, but I see in my members another law at war with the law of my mind, making me captive to the law of sin that dwells in my members" (7:19–23).

A fourth polarity exists between *anxiety* and *hope*. In a sense, this polarity sums up all the rest. A life lived in the midst of tensions generated by such polarities as these can never be free from anxiety, i.e., from a sense of the threat of absurdity and negativity. On the other hand, such a life can be lived only on the basis of the hope that life is somehow worthwhile. Anxiety springs from the sense of the radical difference that separates us from the totality of reality, while hope springs from the sense of belonging to that totality and having some affinity with it.

A fifth polarity exists between the *individual* and *society*. Human beings realize themselves and their varied possibilities only in and through interaction with other human beings. *Sexuality* and *language* make this unmistakably clear. Every human being is incomplete insofar as the reproductive function is concerned, and the existence of language shows that we are essentially beings in need of communication with one another.

But it is *death* that sets the framework of human existence. When one becomes aware of the boundary or limit of human existence, then one also has recognized that this is one's *own* existence. If there is no thought of death and if the future is regarded as stretching out indefinitely, then there is no great sense of urgency or responsibility. In the inauthentic mode of existence, death is covered up, forgotten, ignored. We employ euphemisms and treat the whole matter impersonally. We acknowledge that everyone must die, but we somehow manage to put our own death off into the indefinite future.

Authentic existence, however, requires that we come to terms with our own death and recognize it for what it is: the boundary and limit of our own personal existence. We are thus compelled to think of all the possibilities that are open to us this side of death and to try and bring these possibilities into some kind of overarching unity. (Recent discussions of the stages of human development—midlife crisis, etc.—are consistent with Heidegger's perspective.) Death, therefore, is not simply the end of life, but the force that introduces a wholeness and unity into life. (See John Macquarrie, *Principles of Christian Theology*, [2d ed.], New York: Scribners, 1977, pp. 62–68.)

Heidegger's later writings, recalling his origins in metaphysics and Catholic mysticism, focused on the presence of Being in landscape, culture, art, and poetry. This may explain how he could influence the writings of two otherwise disparate Catholic theologians, Karl Rahner (d. 1984) and Hans Urs von Balthasar (d. 1988).

Sartre

For the French philosopher Jean Paul Sartre (d. 1980) "nausea" is the experience through which we come to see the human situation as it is: a mass of solid brute facts. It seems to be a world in which it is impossible to move or to breathe. But if one courageously faces its contingency, one will find that there is room in the world, after all, for oneself. Since we are not called upon to be anything in particular, we need no space. We are free. If we were anything, we would not be free. Our everyday self is derived from our experience of others as subjects. They gaze at us and, in virtue of their gaze, we become persons and acquire a nature. We bear that nature as a burden, but it is always possible to cast it off.

Unlike Heidegger, who treats the experience of Nothing as relatively rare, Sartre regards it as taking in all human experience. But even this experience of Nothing has positive characteristics. In Nothingness there is a "passion for being." It desires to become substantial, even though this ambition is logically impossible. In trying to fulfill this ambition, it sets up an "In-itself which creates contingency," namely, God. But, for Sartre, the idea of God is contradictory. It is impossible to escape contingency. Our "dreadful freedom" is the nearest thing we have to a "real nature," and our "nothingness" is the nearest thing we have to "Being." The idea of God is contradictory because it joins in one entity both Being and Nothingness. We are left alone and lonely, existing only in our free acts, in an obscene, godless world, with no values except those which we ourselves create. (See his *Being and Nothingness* [1943], Eng. trans., New York: Citadel Press, 1964.)

Buber

Martin Buber (d. 1965), the Jewish theologian and philosopher, shifted after the First World War from an individualistic philosophy to one rooted in social experience. He wrote of the paradox inherent in every human dialogue, where each party remains himself or herself even as he or she draws very close to the other. The principal expression of his view is contained in his *I and Thou* (New York: Scribners, 1970; original German edition, 1923). Our relationships, he said, are of two kinds: I-thou and I-it. There is nothing wrong with the latter unless they dominate and eventually suppress the former. The opposite of I-thou dialogue is monologue, which implies selfishness and manipulation. Buber is clearly more positive than Kierkegaard about the value of interpersonal relations with other human beings. In genuine dialogue we accept and affirm others in their personhood. By doing so we nurture the divine spark in them, and thereby actualize God in the world.

Process Philosophy

Whitehead

Alfred North Whitehead (d. 1947) began as a mathematician but turned to philosophy. His mathematical penchant for order, generalization, and systematization, however, never left him. He insisted on the interrelatedness of all reality and on human knowledge's exclusive concern with relatedness. The perceiver is a natural organism reacting to the world around him. But our experience of that world is of durations (events), not of point-instants. Change is otherwise unintelligible. In change the past flows into the present, as durations can but instants cannot. The past remains fixed and determined, however, while the future is open and indeterminate. Because of freedom we can "clutch at novelty" and alter the course of events. Religion, in the meantime, helps us maintain some sense of the importance of our individual experience within the social relationships and flowing experience of life.

One commentator has suggested that no one will ever succeed in writing a short account of Whitehead's work. That is undoubtedly true. It is a very complicated system of thought (see, for example, his

Process and Reality, New York: Free Press, 1978; orig. ed., 1929, which one reviewer has called "baffling").

Bergson

French philosopher Henri Bergson (d. 1941), like Whitehead, was concerned with time. Conceptualized time, he says, is a straight line with moments as its points; experienced time is *duration*, not a succession of moments, and it flows in an indivisible continuity. Its phases "melt into one another and form an organic whole." No harm is done by conceptualization, so long as we do not confuse the conceptual with the real. If one wants to know reality, one must "dive back into the flux" which Plato had always spurned in favor of the immutable.

In his most famous work, *Creative Evolution* (1907; Eng. trans., Lanham, Md.: University Press of America, 1984), he expounded a nonmechanistic portrait of biological evolution, propelled toward higher levels of organization by an inner vital impulse (*élan vital*). He carried over this processive approach to his reflections on morality (see his *The Two Sources of Morality and Religion* [1932; Eng. trans., Garden City, N.Y.: Doubleday, 1954]) where he distinguished between static and dynamic morality. The first is a morality of obligation. Behavior is sanctioned by an ordered community. The second is a morality of attraction, issuing from mystical experience. The vital impulse, which is communicated from God to others through the mystic, generates a dynamic morality guided by a vision of humanity as a whole.

Although he had few disciples, Bergson influenced existentialists who liked his distinction between conventional and higher morality and process theologians who abandoned classical theism to find both divine and human creativity at work in an evolving world. He also had an impact on Catholic philosophy and theology through his student Jacques Maritain (d. 1973) and on Maurice Blondel (d. 1949).

Pragmatism

James

American philosopher William James (d. 1910) was one of those directly influenced by Bergson, particularly the latter's advice to "dive back into the flux." His "radical empiricism" was the result, in which he eliminated the dualistic distinction between thoughts and things. There is only the one world of experience. Things and thoughts are simply points of emphasis within that world.

In his book *Pragmatism* (1907) he restated the traditional empiricist view that a useful concept must be grounded in experience. The pragmatic method consists in interpreting each alternative metaphysical theory "by tracing its respective consequences." At the same time, the theory of free will "pragmatically means *novelties in the world*." Improvement is at least possible. We are promised relief if we do something to make the world a better place in which to live. It is this promise and this encouragement to action that give free will its whole meaning.

Dewey

The American philosopher John Dewey (d. 1952) is in the tradition of Darwin and process philosophy. The leading characteristic of his thought is its evolutionary emphasis. Many of Dewey's criticisms, in fact, are directed against the older traditional metaphysics which stressed the unchanging essence of humankind and of the universe. Human thought, therefore, is not for constructing great cosmic systems of reality but for solving problems in an intelligent and reflective way. There is nothing beyond experience. We have to take reality as we find it and reconstruct our goals in keeping with our situation and our environment. In the meantime, there is no greater mistake than to suppose that a philosopher's reflections on experience are identical with experience itself.

There is, of course, a strong similarity not only between Dewey and Darwin but also between Dewey and Marx. All three hold that it is not enough to theorize about reality; we are called upon to change it. Indeed, it is a fatal mistake to divide theory from practice. A concept without practical consequences has no real meaning. Thus, the term *pragmatism* describes this school of thought. Dewey also used the term *instrumentalism*. Ideas, hypotheses, and theories are only so many tools for attaining concrete goals in life. But if there are no metaphysical principles independent of practical content, there can be no absolute moral norms by which one can determine the good. An ethical relativism follows.

Logical Positivism

The starting point of logical positivism is that the only possible source of knowledge is our sense experience. All genuine propositions are reducible to propositions that report "direct perception" or what is "immediately given in experience." (Although associated with Ludwig Wittgenstein [see below], this doctrine is not found in his *Tractatus*, as inferred by members of the so-called Vienna circle.) If we have no tangible data, we can make no judgments and reach no conclusions. We can deal only with what is there. The leading tenet of logical positivism is the principle of verifiability, namely, that the meaning of a proposition lies in its method of verification. The logical positivists saw it as a way of eliminating as meaningless all references to entities not accessible to observation. Metaphysics, therefore, can be dismissed out of hand as nonsense. Although both the logical positivists of the Vienna circle and Wittgenstein opposed metaphysics, the latter was much less dismissive of it. *If* metaphysical insights could be stated in language, they would be for him true insights and not mere muddles or expressions of feelings.

The sociological counterpart of philosophical positivism is August Comte (d. 1857), who argued that science can be concerned only with facts, not values.

Carnap

The German-American philosopher Rudolf Carnap (d. 1970) is regarded as the founder of logical positivism. He defined philosophy as the "logic of the sciences" and considered it a general language whose only legitimate concern is to describe and criticize the language of the particular sciences. For him philosophical disputes are largely due to the failure to analyze logically the concepts employed. Philosophy must be committed to a basic empiricism supplemented by the methods of modern logic and mathematics.

The Early Wittgenstein

Ludwig Wittgenstein (d. 1951) is the principal, or at least the best known, exponent of philosophical positivism. For him the task of philosophy is not the investigation of facts (which is the task of the exact sciences) but the logical analysis of language-units (words, propositions, speech as a whole) by which we speak of the world. There are only two kinds of meaningful propositions: those about factual relationships stemming from experience and verifiable by experience, and those about purely logical relationships which provide no factual knowledge and hence are valid independently of experience.

Positivism provides little in the way of a philosophy of human existence. Positively, it underlines our responsibility to reality as it is, not as we would like it to be. Negatively, it lacks openness to experience in all its dimensions including the religious and metaphysical, which means that positivism, in spite of its humane intentions, is silent in the face of the great human problems. "And so it is impossible," Wittgenstein writes in his *Tractatus Logico-Philosophicus* (1921; Eng. trans., New York: Humanities Press, 1961) "for there to be propositions of ethics."

According to his theory of knowledge, a proposition and its negation are both possible. Which one is true is accidental. Since everything in the world is accidental, there can be no value in the world. This is so because if anything has value, this fact cannot be accidental. The thing *must* have value. "In the world everything is as it is, and everything happens as it does happen: *in* it no value exists— and if it did, it would have no value" (*Tractatus*, 6.41).

Russell

British philosopher Bertrand Russell (d. 1970) had been Wittgenstein's teacher at Cambridge. For Russell all "sound philosophy" begins with "an analysis of propositions"—a truth, he insisted, that was "too obvious, perhaps, to demand a proof." All philosophical problems, therefore, are "logical," that is, they arise out of the analysis of propositions. His views, first stated in *A Critical Exposition of the Philosophy of Leibniz* (Wolfeboro, N.H.: Longwood Press, 1989; orig.

ed., 1900), were more fully developed in *The Principles of Mathematics* (London: Allen & Unwin, 1937; orig. ed., 1903).

He carried this view over into approach to ethics and religion. Since it is the nature of religious faith to accept a proposition in the absence of, or even in opposition to, evidence, religious faith produces bad habits. A person who does not form his or her beliefs on the basis of evidence in one domain (religion) cannot remain open-minded and scientific in another. Furthermore, when the person of faith is confronted with contrary evidence, that person tries to suppress the criticism and even to persecute the critic.

Russell's views on marriage and human sexuality were also controversial, although they are less radical by today's standards. He saw nothing wrong in sexual relations before marriage, birth control, and the continuation of a marriage when no love is left. He was denounced as "the Devil's minister to men" and as "the mastermind of free love."

Ordinary Language Philosophy

Ordinary language philosophy holds that the language of everyday discourse is perfectly suitable for philosophical purposes and that philosophers get into trouble when they deviate from ordinary language without providing any way to make sense of the deviation. It is found in its strongest form in the later works of Wittgenstein.

The Later Wittgenstein

Wittgenstein essentially repudiated his *Tractatus* in his posthumously published *Philosophical Investigations* (New York: Macmillan, 1953). All or most of the problems in philosophy arise from the fact that philosophers have misused certain key terms such as "know," "see," "free," and "reason." They have departed from the ordinary uses of these terms without putting anything intelligible in their place, and so they have become entangled in endless and insoluble puzzles over whether we can know whether people are thinking and feeling, whether we ever really see physical objects, whether anyone does anything freely, and whether we ever have any reason for supposing that one thing rather than another will happen in the future. The task of the philosopher is that of the therapist; namely, to help us see how we have slipped from sense into nonsense and then to show us how to get back to the ordinary use of these words, on which their intelligibility depends.

Similar views were held by Oxford philosophers Gilbert Ryle and John L. Austin (d. 1960).

Philosophies of Human Existence: A Synthesis

Much of twentieth-century philosophy has been essentially a reaction against classical philosophy (Aristotle, Plato, Aquinas) on the one hand, and Idealism (Hegel) on the other. In modern and especially postmodern philosophy there is an emphasis on the *subject*, on the *changeable*, on the *particular*, and on the *practical*, as opposed to the objective, the unchanging, the universal, and the theoretical. Thus, *Existentialism* stresses the individual's obligation to take responsibility for his or her life, and, along with *Phenomenology, Positivism, Process Thought, Pragmatism*, and more recent currents of thought on the Continent and in the United States, it stresses the individual's obligation to attend to reality and to history as they are, not as we would wish them to be or as we would abstractly conceive them to be. Neither reality nor the history within which human reality is framed is static and unchanging; they are in process, from a past that is fixed, because complete, to a future that is as yet open, undetermined. We are called upon to shape that future by reconstructing our experience and reforming our environment to the extent that consciousness and practicality allow. Human existence, therefore, is not a given to be examined, but a potential in process of realization.

Contemporary Philosophies

Neo-Marxism

Neo-Marxism is a philosophical movement associated with the Frankfurt Institute of Social Research. Its leaders have been of Jewish background, and many fled from Germany to the United States during the Nazi period, where their work continued at the New School of Social Research in New York.

Marcuse

A student of Heidegger and a hero to U.S. student radicals in the 1960s, Herbert Marcuse (d. 1979) was critical of empiricism, positivism, and other philosophies which confined themselves to the realm of fact. He insisted that philosophy must be concerned with the way things ought to be rather than with the way things are. Reason has a "subversive power" to be used to change human conditions. The scientific-technological mentality, however, has created the "one-dimensional man" who is preoccupied with facts and their mastery instead of essences and norms (see his *One-Dimensional Man* [Boston: Beacon Press, 1964]). The technological society is a system of domination, he argued.

Habermas

A more rationalistic thinker than Marcuse, Jürgen Habermas focused his attention on epistemology, i.e., how knowledge is related to and affected by the interests of the knower (see, for example, his *Theory and Practice* [Eng. trans., Boston: Beacon Press, 1973] and *Legitimation Crisis* [Eng. trans., Boston: Beacon Press, 1975]. Like Marcuse, however, Habermas was also critical of empiricism and positivism because their assumptions and presuppositions are, like everyone else's, derived from practical interests in variable historical and social conditions. And like Marcuse, Habermas, too, drew upon Freud in trying to bring knowledge and interest into harmony by a process of self-reflection.

Hermeneutics

Hermeneutics (from the Greek verb "to interpret") is a branch of philosophy that deals with understanding and interpretation. That which is "interpreted" includes language, texts, and works of art.

Gadamer

Hans-Georg Gadamer was also a student of Heidegger, and when his teacher died in 1976 he delivered a significant memorial address entitled, "An Invocation to the Vanished God." He claimed that Heidegger had been silent and ambiguous about God and Christianity only because he felt that, as a philosopher, he lacked the appropriate language to speak of God.

Gadamer held, along with the later Heidegger, that language is not just a human instrument but is constitutive of the world. Our relation to the world, he wrote, is "absolutely and fundamentally linguistic in nature" (*Truth and Method* [New York: Seabury Press, 1975], p. 432). He also shared his mentor's interest in art. Art, he insisted, is a form of knowledge, containing a claim to truth that is different from, but not inferior to, that of science. According to Gadamer, the work of art tells us more about the reality of something than do the bare facts uncovered by empirical investigation, because art shows us the essence or the essential meaning. Interpretation, symbolism, and the use of the imagination, therefore, are as necessary for the exploration of reality as are observation and judgment.

Ricoeur

Paul Ricoeur, a French philosopher in the broad phenomenological-existentialist tradition, has addressed many of the same problems as Gadamer has. It was the question of evil, however, that first aroused his interest in symbolism and interpretation. If persons today are to understand, much less accept, the biblical account of the Fall, he concluded, they have to grasp the ancient insights as embodied in myth and symbol.

Ricoeur held that a "hermeneutic of belief" can only be achieved when one has passed through a "hermeneutic of suspicion," which he identified primarily with Freud (see his *Freud and Philosophy* [New Haven: Yale University Press, 1970]). Suspicions, Ricoeur pointed out, rest on one-sided interpretations that fail to take into account the rich diversity and complexity of language. In religious discourse there are five types: prophetic, narrative, descriptive, wisdom, and hymnic. All five are intertwined in the biblical texts. To disregard that fact is to render impossible any reliable interpretation.

Deconstructionism

Contemporary Continental philosophy is dominated by a spirit termed "deconstruction," whose principal exponent is Jacques Derrida. Primarily skeptical in orientation, it stands as a challenge to more traditional conceptions of value, truth, and the self, and it has been very influential in the areas of literary criticism and political theory. Richard Rorty's *Contingency, Irony, and Solidarity* (Cambridge University Press, 1989) provides a clear introduction to some of its principal themes.

The early Michel Foucault (d. 1993) is commonly associated with these themes, but the later Foucault moved in a more positive vein in his attempt to give an account of how the self gets constructed. The contemporary philosopher informed by the Continental tradition (particularly Hegel) and who has articulated perhaps the most sustained account of the self is Charles Taylor (*Sources of the Self: The Making of the Modern Identity*, Cambridge, Mass.: Harvard University Press, 1989).

Analytic Philosophies

We already pointed out above that most other contemporary philosophers in the English-speaking world fall under the rubric "analytic" and are varied in orientation. Its practitioners draw upon contemporary developments in logic and the philosophy of language, sociobiology (see Wilson, above), neuroscience, cognitive science, and artificial intelligence.

Philosophy of Mind

Probably the most active and productive of these contemporary approaches is the *philosophy of mind*. There are two divergent developments in this area of philosophy that any sophisticated account of the human person must come to grips with, namely, the *biological* wing and the *artificial intelligence* wing.

The former thinks of mental processes, including consciousness, as essentially brain-processes and accordingly engages in a philosophical account of human mentality that is informed by *neurophysiology* and/or *sociobiology*. An example of this strand of thought would be

133

John Searle's *The Rediscovery of the Mind* (Cambridge, Mass.: Massachusetts Institute of Technology Press, 1992). The latter strand conceives of mental processes on the model of a computer program and thus engages in a philosophical account of human mentality informed by recent work in *artificial intelligence* and *cognitive science*. An example of this strand is Daniel Dennett's *Consciousness Explained* (Boston: Little, Brown, 1991).

Both approaches are broadly naturalistic and stand as a challenge to more traditional conceptions of the human person.

Contemporary Thomism

Thomism is as pluralistic in character as is modern and postmodern philosophy. Just as there is no single definition or method of philosophy that would win universal agreement among philosophers, so there is no single definition or method of Thomism that would win universal agreement among Thomists.

Thomists are of two general types: historians of medieval philosophy and contemporary philosophers who, to one degree or another, are strongly influenced by the thought of Aquinas. These contemporary philosophers, in turn, can be subdivided into Continental and Analytic Thomists (see below).

Historians

The historians of medieval philosophy are concerned with the accurate reconstruction and interpretation of the texts and views of the historical Thomas. Thus, it was Etienne Gilson (d. 1978), founder of the Institute of Medieval Studies at the University of Toronto, who discovered that Scholasticism was much more differentiated than had been supposed in the nineteenth century, and many historians of medieval philosophy continue in his tradition. (See his *The Philosophy of St. Thomas Aquinas* [Eng. trans., St. Louis, Mo.: B. Herder, 1924; orig. ed., 1919] and *The Spirit of Medieval Philosophy* [Notre Dame, Ind.: University of Notre Dame Press, 1994; orig. ed., 1932, 2 vols.]).

A twentieth-century Thomist with whom Gilson was often paired in the pre-Vatican II period was Jacques Maritain (d. 1973). He is difficult to categorize, however. He sought to develop the neo-

Scholasticism of the nineteenth century to meet twentieth-century problems. In doing so, he drew upon the Thomism of the great baroque commentators, like Cajetan (d. 1534), John of St. Thomas (d. 1644) and Suarez (d. 1617). Also directly influenced by Bergson (see above), his writings touched on the problem of knowledge, the philosophy of history, morality, and the human person (see especially his *True Humanism* [Eng. trans., New York: Scribners, 1938; orig. ed., 1936]).

Continental Thomists

Transcendental Thomists

Post-Kantian European Thomism, done in the light of both Kant and Hegel, is known as Transcendental Thomism (see below). Its principal philosophical exponent was Joseph Maréchal (d. 1944) and its principal theologian, Karl Rahner. To the extent that Thomism remains an important force in contemporary Catholic theology and especially in its understanding of the human person, it is so through the Transcendental Thomism of Maréchal and others (see Gerald McCool, *Catholic Theology in the Nineteenth Century: The Quest for a Unitary Method*, New York: The Seabury Press, 1977).

Lublin Thomists

The Lublin School of Philosophy is best known through its most famous product, Karol Wojtyla, who was elected to the papacy in 1978 and took the name John Paul II. Under the leadership of Father Mieczyslaw Krapiec, O.P., the Lublin School retained Thomas's realist principles as interpreted by Maritain and Gilson and incorporated within this framework the insights of such existentialists as Gabriel Marcel (d. 1973), Heidegger, Karl Jaspers (d. 1969), and Buber as well as the phenomenology of Max Scheler and Roman Imgarden. Marcel, however, has had a particular influence on this movement: with his emphasis on the I-thou relationship (also found in Buber); the notion of intersubjectivity and disponibility, which together denote a loving relationship between two subjects who cocreate a new entity, a "we"; and the insistence that being is superior to having, that a person can

135

never be owned or used as an object and is always superior to the product or work which he or she performs. The approach is especially evident in Pope John Paul II's writings, including his 1981 encyclical on work, *Laborem Exercens*.

Analytic Thomists

A group of English philosophers defend a broadly Aristotelian-Thomistic perspective in the philosophy of mind. These include Elizabeth Anscombe and her husband, Peter Geach, both influenced by Wittgenstein, and Anthony Kenny, a student of John Austin.

At the same time, there has been a rebirth, mainly in the United States, of the philosophy of religion—equivalent to what was traditionally called natural theology. Alvin Plantinga, professor of philosophy and director of the Center for the Philosophy of Religion at the University of Notre Dame, and Richard Swinburne, of Oxford, are among the more prominent figures in the field. It is important to note, however, that Plantinga himself is not a Thomist. Similar work is being done at University of California at Los Angeles (UCLA) and Syracuse University.

Theology

Phenomenology

Schillebeeckx

A Dutch Catholic theologian, Edward Schillebeeckx, adopts a phenomenological approach to the meaning of existence, consistent with the basic approach he followed earlier in his treatment of the sacraments, in *Christ the Sacrament of Encounter with God* (Eng. trans., New York: Sheed & Ward, 1963; orig. ed., 1960). Rejecting both positivism on the one hand and the classical definition of human nature on the other, Schillebeeckx proposes a theology of human existence based on what he calls "anthropological constants." These constants point in a general way toward lasting human impulses, orientations, and values. Among these constants are the following: (1) the relation of the human person to his or her own bodiliness (a human being *is* and

136

has a body); (2) our coexistence with other persons (the human face is an image of oneself *for others*); (3) our relation to social and institutional structures (they are not something added but are intrinsic to our existence); (4) our relation to space and time; (5) our capacity, even our drive, to imagine an ideal state (*Utopia*) which becomes the impulse of hope for the future.

Since the human condition is inevitably characterized by suffering, all action which seeks to conquer suffering presupposes at least an implicit and vague anticipation of a possible, future universal meaning (the reign of God). We refuse, therefore, to submit to the absolute reign of technocracy (which is itself one of the causes of suffering). Schillebeeckx's original phenomenological approach has been complemented by the liberation approach summarized below in the subsection on theological pragmatism.

Existentialism

Bultmann

The major existentialist theologian of the twentieth century is Rudolf Bultmann (d. 1976), a German Lutheran. It was he who applied the philosophy of Heidegger to the interpretation of the New Testament. And it was he who initiated on the Continent and in the United States a whole school of theological reflection characterized by an emphasis on the faith and consciousness of the individual believer. Nowhere is his approach expressed more simply or more succinctly than in his *Jesus Christ and Mythology* (New York: Scribners, 1958).

"The question of God and the question of myself," he wrote, "are identical." Accordingly, when the Bible tells me about God, he says, it really is addressing me about myself, about the meaning of human existence. For Bultmann, existentialist philosophy offers the most adequate perspective and conceptions for understanding human existence. It does not say to me, "In such and such a way you must exist." It says only, "You must exist" or at least says what it means to exist.

Every person has his or her own history, Bultmann goes on. Always the present comes out of the past and leads to the future. We realize our existence if we are aware that each "now" is the moment of free decision: What is the element in the past to be retained? What is our responsibility toward the future? No one can take another's place, since every one of us must die his or her own death. In our loneliness we realize our existence.

Christian existence (or "eschatological existence") is not a worldly phenomenon but is realized in our new *self-understanding*. I encounter God not in the other nor even in myself but in the divine Word. So focused, in fact, is Bultmann's thought on the individual believer that some critics (e.g., Johannes Metz) have described his theology as "privatized." The sociopolitical dimension is all but lost.

Tillich

Paul Tillich (d. 1965), another German Lutheran existentialist theologian who spent many years lecturing in the United States, stressed the anxiety (*Angst*) of moderns, not as something neurotic or pathological, but as something intrinsic to the human condition. Such anxiety has several sources. First, every person must have *meaning* in life, or the power of self-affirmation and integration is lost. Second, each has to struggle constantly with the burden of *guilt*, whether from specific actions or as a vague, general backdrop. Without some means to deal with guilt, we are led into moral confusion and aimlessness. Finally, there is the underlying *fear of death*, which poses the greatest threat of all to the self. Only by coming to terms with the world can we deal with this anxiety about death.

It is by our participation in God, who is the infinite power to resist the threat of nonbeing, that we acquire fully the "courage to be," even in the face of these three forms of anxiety. Similarly, when we become deeply aware of historical existence as full of ambiguities, we become filled with perplexities and despair. The Christian answer is the notion of the *Kingdom of God*, which is the meaning, fulfillment, and unity of history. Tillich's *Systematic Theology* (Chicago: University of Chicago Press: 1953–1964, 3 vols.) offered an existentialist analysis of humanity and of Jesus, but ended in a process approach toward the reign of God in history.

Niebuhr

Reinhold Niebuhr (d. 1971), an American Protestant theologian, also centered his attention upon the category of *anxiety*. Anxiety arises from our recognition of the limitations and contingencies of our existence and from our imagining a life infinitely better than this one. Such anxiety generates sin because we seek to bring anxiety under control by pretending to have power or knowledge or virtues or special favors from God, and this pretense leads, in turn, to pride, cruelty, and injustice. Or else we seek to escape our anxieties by turning inward and pursuing a life of sensuality.

Though not inevitable, sin is universal and existed even before we became sinners. The condition of sin and anxiety, however, leaves us in a state of despair. We sense ourselves as being at once bound and free. We are bound insofar as we are involved in the flux of time; we are free insofar as we stand outside of time. We are aware of this capacity to stand apart because we know ourselves as object, we can judge ourselves as sinners, and we can survey the past and the future. We also know that nothing actually operating in history can ever sufficiently deliver us from despair, despite our optimistic illusions to the contrary. Only a divine, forgiving, timeless love beyond history, such as has been revealed in Jesus Christ, gives meaning to human life.

Process Thought

Teilhard de Chardin

The most celebrated theological exponent of process thought is Teilhard de Chardin (d. 1955). His influence on recent and contemporary Catholic thinking is difficult to calculate but impossible to deny. Some have suggested, in fact, that his spirit hovers over the Second Vatican Council's *Pastoral Constitution on the Church in the Modern World*, particularly its assertion that "the human race has passed from a rather static concept of reality to a more dynamic, evolutionary one" (n. 5).

Teilhard's basic premise is that all of reality, the whole of the cosmic order, is moving toward a goal (the *Omega Point*), gradually progressing from one state of development to another, each one more unified than the preceding. The highest stage of material development is life. The highest stage in the development of life is human life. With human life, consciousness achieves a level of self-reflection. We not only *know*; we *know that we know*. Human existence, therefore, represents a new and unique order of being. (See *The Phenomenon of Man* [1955; Eng. trans., New York: Harper & Row, 1959] and *The Divine Milieu* [1957; Eng. trans., New York: Harper & Row, 1960].)

Although it may appear that the "cosmic involution" (the movement toward unity) has been halted, this is not true. *Hominization,* or the progressive development of human life to higher and higher levels, continues with even greater vigor than before. We can observe this in the increasingly powerful thrust toward *socialization.* As a result of socialization, humankind is continuing to advance toward the supreme degree of consciousness. The conclusions of physics, biology, and psychology confirm this judgment, Teilhard insists. As a result of humankind's standing on its own feet, life is here and now entering a new era of autonomous control and self-orientation. We are beginning to take over the biological forces which heretofore have determined our growth. The whole evolutionary process is moving constantly toward unification and spiritualization, with the whole cosmic system rising unmistakably toward a critical point of final convergence. We shall have reached such a level of self-consciousness that no further growth will be possible. This he calls the Omega Point.

As a Christian, Teilhard equates the Omega Point with Christ. History, therefore, is in movement toward Christ. But Christ is already present in the world. There is even now a Christic dimension to the cosmic order. The Church, in this schema, is the "reflexively Christified portion of the world," the focal point at which human socialization based on charity occurs. Indeed, this is the whole impulse of creation. "To create is to unite," Teilhard declares. The whole of history is the story of the progressive unification of reality and of the human community in particular.

But an inevitable consequence of creation is *sin* (here, of course, Teilhard's thought runs counter to traditional Catholic doctrine on Original Sin, to which we shall return in chapter 5). Because created reality is multiple, it is essentially subject in its arrangements to the operation of chance, and therefore is "absolutely barred from progressing towards unity without sporadically engendering evil, and that as a matter of statistical necessity."

Just as sin is inevitable, so, too, is *incarnation*. There can be no creation without union of Creator with the created. For in order to create, God must be immersed in the multiple, and is even forced into war with the evil element in the multiple. The coming of Christ— another inevitable requirement and effect of the evolutionary process—maintains the evolutionary effort toward hominization by providing a focus of biological involution (*involution* meaning here again the movement toward unification). In Christ-Omega the universal comes into exact focus and assumes a personal form.

For the person who sees what is happening, who perceives the whole evolutionary process in the light of Christ, everything becomes animate and a fit object for love and worship. *Christian charity*, far from being simply a soothing lotion poured over the world's suffering, is the most complete and the most active agent of hominization.

Theological Positivism

For anyone who has been following the argument very closely thus far, this may seem a curious, if not a dubious, category. How can there be a *positivism* that is at the same time *theological*? Is not positivism a denial of what is not directly observable? And does that not include God above all else? The answer is, "Yes, of course, but...." We are referring here not to positivism in its technical philosophical sense (such as described above), but to positivism as a general method or approach.

Positivism limits the study of a reality to that reality's appearance in a given source or sources. A *theological* positivist is one who equates theology with the study of a given source or sources. Thus, theology is not (as defined in chapter 2) the process of giving expression to our experience of God, but rather the study of *documents* in which the experience of God has been recorded and interpreted (especially the Bible or the official teachings of the Church). The theological positivist understands theology as the study of the Bible (which is really limiting theology to biblical theology) or the study of doctrines and dogmas (which is to limit theology to dogmatics). Theology is either "the testing of Church doctrine and proclamation...by the standard of the Holy Scriptures" (Karl Barth, d. 1968) or is the transmission of the teaching of the Church (the methodological assumption of many Catholic theology textbooks in use prior to Vatican II).

The similarity between Wittgenstein and Barth, for example, is at least superficially apparent in the latter's definition of theology with which he begins his massive, multivolume *Church Dogmatics* (Edinburgh: T. & T. Clark, 1936–1969): Theology is "the scientific test to which the Christian Church puts itself regarding the language about God which is peculiar to it." For Wittgenstein, the task of philosophy is the logical analysis of language-units (words, propositions, etc.) by which we speak of the world. It does not get beyond the language to deal with the reality so described or talked about.

In theological terms, the Word of God in Sacred Scripture is taken as a given. It is simply there. One does not question it or challenge it. One comes to terms with it. For some Catholics, the same attitude prevails regarding the pronouncements of the official magisterium. Our understanding of human existence, therefore, is to be derived totally from the Bible or from the official teachings of the Church. Philosophy, or anthropology in the widest sense, is of no significant account in the inquiry.

Pragmatism: Liberation Theology

The parallel between philosophical and theological pragmatism is the same as the parallel between philosophical and theological positivism. In the strict sense of the terms, there is no theological pragmatism, just as there is no theological positivism. But there are similarities in method and approach. It is those similarities which engage our attention here.

The closest approximation of philosophical pragmatism in contemporary Christian theology is in the *Latin American liberation school.* Its principal exponents are, on the Catholic side, Gustavo Gutiérrez of Peru, Jon Sobrino, S.J., of El Salvador, Leonardo Boff of Brazil, and Juan Luis Segundo of Uruguay, and, on the Protestant side, Hugo Assmann of Brazil. They reject both the traditional Catholic and traditional Protestant approaches to theology, the one emphasizing doctrine and intellectual assent, and the other emphasizing the Bible and trusting faith. Theology is faith seeking understanding, the liber-

142

ation theologians admit, but faith is "the historical *praxis* of liberation."

The Word of God is mediated, they insist, through the cries of the poor and the oppressed. Theology, therefore, can only be a form of *praxis;* i.e., it must always be directed toward the changing of the existing social order. It cannot simply interpret it without reference to the practical consequences of the theory of interpretation. Only by participating in the struggles of the poor and the oppressed, Gutiérrez argues, can we understand the implications of the Gospel message and make it have an impact on history. This, in turn, imposes a specific method on theology, which Juan Luis Segundo calls a "hermeneutic circle." Our interpretation of the Bible changes as the world around us changes.

The similarity not only to pragmatism but to positivism as well should be apparent. For the liberation school, theology's reflection on *praxis* is grounded in the Bible. Theology is essentially the study of the Bible insofar as it can be interpreted according to a liberation motif. That motif is, in turn, communicated through actual participation in the struggle for liberation. There is also a not uncritical affinity, finally, with the Marxist view of human existence.

Liberation theology has been subjected to an initially negative criticism by the Vatican's Congregation for the Doctrine of the Faith (see the *Instruction on Certain Aspects of the "Theology of Liberation,"* *Origins* 14/13 [September 13, 1984], pp. 193, 195–204). Subsequently, at the instigation of the Vatican's Secretariat of State, it received a more positive assessment in an *Instruction on Christian Freedom and Liberation,* which pointed out that "the fight against injustice is meaningless unless it is waged with a view to establishing a new social and political order in conformity with the demands of justice" (see *Origins* 15/44 [April 17, 1986]).

Liberation theology has also been criticized by Third World feminist theologians for its failure to address the concerns of women in the Church and in society. Their works include *With Passion and Compassion: Third World Women Doing Theology,* Virginia Fabella and Mercy Amba Oduyoye, eds., Maryknoll, N.Y.: Orbis Books, 1988; *Mary, Mother of God, Mother of the Poor,* by Ivone Gebara, Maryknoll, N.Y.: Orbis Books, 1989; and *Through Her Eyes: Women's Theology from Latin America,* by Elsa Tamez, Maryknoll, N.Y.: Orbis Books, 1989 (see also Tamez's *Against Machismo*, Oak Park, Ill.: Meyer-Stone Books, 1987).

Feminist Theology

Feminist theology, or theological feminism, is the critique of the androcentric bias in which God is imaged and conceptualized as male, male experience is assumed to be normative for all human experience, women are identified with the carnal and irrational, and are held responsible for the entry of sin into the world. Just as there is a philosophy of complementarity, so is there a theology of complementarity, wherein man is regarded as the head of the woman because man fully images God, while woman images God by virtue of her relationship to man. In accordance with the divine plan, so the argument goes, the woman's vocation is childbearing and domestic service to husband and children.

Feminist theology rejects this notion of a divine plan and insists that the traditional relationship between men and women in the home, in society, and in the Church is not dictated by a preordained order in creation. It follows instead from the order of fallen humanity and fallen creation.

"The project of theological feminism," Catherine Mowry La Cugna writes, "is to recover women's experience and integrate it into theological reflection, to search the tradition for what has contributed to women's subjugation, and to search the tradition also for liberating elements (for example, the ministry of Jesus to outcasts; his self-revelation and post-resurrection appearances to women)" (*God For Us*, p. 267). Anne Carr's *Transforming Grace: Women's Experience and Christian Tradition* (San Francisco: Harper & Row, 1988) represents a major expression of this project.

Theological feminism, therefore, rejects both androcentrism and the patriarchal structures that follow from it in the home, in society, and in the Church. A particular point of contention in feminist theology is the extent to which patriarchy, as the cult of fatherhood, is rooted in the central image of divine fatherhood with Christianity. Among the first Catholic (now post-Christian) theologians to critique this image was Mary Daly (*Beyond God the Father: Toward a Philosophy of Women's Liberation*, Boston: Beacon Press, 1973). Later, more fully developed critiques were done by Rosemary Radford Ruether (*Sexism and God-Talk: Toward a Feminist Theology*, Boston: Beacon Press, 1983) and Elizabeth A. Johnson (*She Who Is: The Mystery of God in Feminist Theological Discourse*, New York: Crossroad, 1992).

Feminist theology has a close counterpart in feminist biblical scholarship, including especially Elisabeth Schüssler Fiorenza's *In Memory of Her: A Feminist Reconstruction of Christian Origins* (New York: Crossroad, 1983).

Transcendental Thomism

Under the influence of Maurice Blondel and of Pierre Rousselot (d. 1915), Joseph Maréchal (d. 1944) began a dialogue with Kantian philosophy. The fifth volume of his magistral work, *Le point de départ de la métaphysique* (1922–1926), was devoted to a face-to-face encounter between St. Thomas Aquinas and Kant. Maréchal concluded that Kant was inconsistent in his own transcendental reflection on the *a priori* conditions of human knowledge. Had he been coherent in the use of his own method, he would have realized that the existence of Unlimited Being is an *a priori* condition of possibility for every object of speculative reason. Instead of bringing him to Idealism, Kant's transcendental method would have brought him to the starting point of what Gerald McCool calls a "realistic metaphysics" (*Catholic Theology in the Nineteenth Century: The Quest for a Unitary Method*, New York: Seabury Press, 1977, p. 256). It was this new line of thought, called Transcendental Thomism, that would influence one of the twentieth century's most important theologians, Karl Rahner, and his many disciples.

Rahner

For Karl Rahner the problem of human existence is not simply one theological question among many others. The question of humanity, he insists, "must be looked upon, rather, as the whole of dogmatic theology." He argues that such a view is entirely consistent with Thomas Aquinas's teaching that God is the formal object of theology. As soon as it is understood that the human person stands alone in the whole of creation as the one being who is absolutely oriented toward

145

God and whose very essence is determined by this orientation, then it becomes clear that a thorough study of the human person necessarily involves the study of God, and vice versa. Whatever we might say about the ultimate meaning of human existence is something said at the same time about God, who is the author, sustainer, and destiny of human existence. And whatever we might say about God, therefore, is something said also about human existence.

Such an anthropology, Rahner suggests, must be a *transcendental* anthropology. The word *transcendental* is not easily defined. It means, literally, "that which is capable of going beyond or above or over something else." The "transcendent," therefore, is that which is actually above, beyond, and over the tangible, the visible, the immediately available. God is *the* Transcendent, in that God is above, beyond, and over everything else. God is the one to whom all reality is oriented. Anthropology is transcendental, therefore, when the human person is seen, not simply as a collection of biological and behavioral responses, but as a being whose meaning is to be found beyond the purely corporeal and beyond the satisfaction of physical, social, psychological, political, economic, and cultural needs. The person is transcendental insofar as the person is oriented beyond himself or herself toward God as the source, sustainer, and final perfection of the person's existence.

If you wish to understand human existence, you must seek to discover the conditions in the human person which make it possible for the person to arrive at knowledge of God, to whom the person is oriented. For Rahner the *a priori* condition (i.e., the condition that must be present before any other if there is to be any knowledge of God at all) is *grace*, which is the presence of God in the knowing subject. In other words, *the human person is capable of transcending himself or herself in the knowledge of God, to whom his or her whole life is oriented, because God is already present in the person as the transcendent force or condition which makes such knowledge possible.*

This *transcendental method* has been at work in theology, Rahner notes, at least since Thomas Aquinas, but it has been given a new and stronger impulse by modern and postmodern philosophy, i.e., the philosophy which has developed *after* Descartes (d. 1650), Kant (d. 1804), and the existentialist movement. Much of this philosophy is deeply un-Christian, insofar as it begins *and ends* with the autonomous personal subject which has closed itself to the experience of God. But this philosophy is also most deeply Christian (more, in fact, than its traditional critics in the Catholic neo-Scholastic philosophy of recent decades have understood) because in the Christian understanding of human existence the human person is not one element in a cosmos of things, subordinated to some abstract, impersonal system of reality based on *things.* On the contrary, the human being is the personal subject upon whose freedom as a subject the fate of the entire cosmos depends.

And indeed this has been the direction much of philosophy has been taking us in recent years. The human person is seen not simply as part of a larger cosmic mosaic, but as the most active agent, under God, in the forward movement of history itself. That is why the principal themes of some of today's philosophy (and correspondingly of some of today's theology) include hope, society, the critique of ideology, freedom, and planning for the future.

And that is why there is also so much emphasis today, in theology as well as in philosophy, on the anthropological dimension of all statements about the ultimate meaning and direction of life and of history. We cannot accept teachings as "truths revealed by God" if they have no apparent connection with our own understanding of ourselves, an understanding derived from our experience as human beings. A proper understanding of the relation between nature and grace would make this clear (a point to which we shall return in chapter 5).

To put the matter more simply (assuming at the same time the obvious risk of *over*simplifying): God is not "a" Being separate from the human person. God is Being itself, permeating the person but transcending the person as well. Because God permeates as well as transcends us, there is no standpoint from which we can "look at" God objectively, in a detached manner, as it were. God is always present within us, even before we begin the process, however tentatively and hesitatingly, of trying to come to terms with God's reality and our knowledge of God.

Accordingly, everything we say about God can be translated into a declaration about our own existence. God is a constitutive dimension of our existence. To talk about God is to talk about ourselves as well. The Word of God is not some message given from some heavenly perch, but rather it *is* God. And this is the distinctiveness of Jesus' preaching, namely, that God is present to us, not as some abstract power, but as the very core of our being (what the Scholastics called "uncreated grace"). God, therefore, enters into the very definition of human existence.

We are alive by a principle that transcends us, over which we have no power, and which summons us to surpass ourselves and frees us to be creative in the shaping and redirection of history. History is not determined by inanimate forces or by causes which already exist. Tomorrow can be different from today because God is present to history through the free human persons who are at history's center. Nowhere is this principle more sharply focused or more effectively realized than in Jesus Christ, who is the Word of God-made-flesh, the point at which the human community becomes fully conscious of itself as human and assumes full responsibility for the shaping of its future under God.

Lonergan

Another way of expressing this in a manner consistent with the basic lines of Transcendental Thomism has been proposed by Bernard Lonergan, author of the widely influential *Insight* (New York: Philosophical Library, 1957) and *Method in Theology* (New York: Herder and Herder, 1972). Lonergan, too, breaks away from the classical philosophical doctrine that the human person is static, unchanging, unaffected by the movement of history and variations in the environment. The human person is, on the contrary, "constituted by meaning."

Take the example of a family. On the one hand, we are convinced that families exist. We talk about them. We think we see them. We feel ourselves part of one or more. And yet no one can really touch a family or even see a family, for that matter. A family is a reality "constituted by meaning." We *interpret* a particular collectively of human beings (a man, a woman, children) to be something *more than* what appears on the purely physical level.

We are living at a time, furthermore, when the family is under severe stress. Scientists and other social commentators distinguish among the so-called traditional family, the nuclear family, the single-parent family, the extended family, the communal family, and so forth. The reality itself changes as the meaning changes. And because meanings change, so, too, can the reality of human existence change.

We human beings, insofar as we are constituted by meaning, are, like the family, not directly available to scientific investigation or to "seeing" and "touching" in the usual sense of those words. We see and touch ourselves and other bodies that have specific characteristics and modes of behavior. But our judgment that we and they are "human" is exactly that, a *judgment*. It is a judgment that follows *understanding*, and that understanding, in turn, follows *insight*.

Such an understanding of the human person as "constituted by meaning" stands in striking contrast to the traditional classical and Scholastic definitions of the human as "rational animal." The "constituted-by-meaning" view is a *dynamic* understanding of the human, seeing the human as open to development and change, whereas the classical definition assumes a *static*, once-and-for-all given nature. Furthermore, the "constituted-by-meaning" view takes the concrete and the historical seriously, whereas the classical view is abstract. Indeed, according to Lonergan, it is precisely our new *historical-mindedness* (the distinctive feature of the modern, as opposed to the classical, mentality) which has allowed us to move beyond the earlier formulation of human existence without rejecting its own measure of truth.

But the newer view also provides a firmer philosophical, and also theological, basis for the notion of *responsible* human existence. The human person as "subject" is one who is conscious, oriented toward interrelationship with others, and capable of becoming something other than he or she presently happens to be (i.e., is capable of becoming "self-constituting"). Through increasing degrees of consciousness—from unconscious sleep to dreaming consciousness to experiential consciousness to intelligent consciousness to rational consciousness and finally to rational self-consciousness—the human person as "subject" arrives at the level of deliberating, evaluating, choosing, and finally acting. The subject is a *doer*, not just a thinker. As a doer, the subject has the potential for self-formation, for effecting changes in others or in the environment.

All the while, the subject is conditioned by the fact that one *is* a human subject: in particular places and times, in particular circumstances shaped by tradition and culture, under the impact of specific historical events, and shaped by one's own free decisions and the free decisions of others. One develops a biography which discloses the self. It is as a "subject," therefore, with all of these historical contingencies, that one *becomes* what one is.

Theologies of Human Existence: A Synthesis

The emphasis on the subject, the changeable, the particular, and the practical that we see in so much of contemporary philosophy is carried over into theology. The theological *existentialism* of Bultmann, Tillich, and Reinhold Niebuhr focuses on the anxiety which characterizes human existence: anxiety in the face of meaninglessness, sin, and death. God alone allows us to overcome the contingency of human existence.

The theological *phenomenology* of Schillebeeckx explores the dimensions of that contingency and suggests that we experience transcendence in the struggle to conquer the suffering which characterizes the human condition. In this regard, Schillebeeckx's position is akin to that of the *liberation theologians,* in that human existence is marked by economic conflict, disparity, and oppression—and the suffering these generate. Theology, therefore, is not reflection on God or human existence as such; it is a form of *praxis,* i.e., of participation in the struggle on behalf of the poor and the oppressed. It is reflection on the human condition as an oppressor-oppressed condition of human relationships and is a formulation of ways in which that condition can be transformed by justice. There is a sense, therefore, in which existentialism and liberation theology are at cross purposes, although there are also important points of convergence: particularly their common rejection of the principle that things are necessarily the way they are and we must accept them and deal with them as they are.

Process theology is not necessarily inconsistent with either of these two approaches. It stresses the dynamic movement of history and the changeability of all reality, including God. Conservative process thinkers might stress the inevitability of the process, whereas others, more in tune with liberation theology, would stress the responsibility of human agents in the direction and construction of history.

Feminist theology critiques androcentrism, wherein male experience is regarded as normative for all human experience, and patriarchy, wherein the Fatherhood of God is taken as the basis for a hierarchical, patriarchal system of governance in the home, society, the political order, and the Church, where men are considered destined by God and the order of creation to occupy the positions of power and dominance.

Transcendental Thomism would seem, at first glance, to be closer to existentialism than to the more politically conscious liberationist approach. But Rahner's insistence on the intimate connection between nature and grace, and between theology and anthropology, provides a foundation for an essential link between the two approaches: the emphasis on the subject (as in Bultmann) and the emphasis on the sociopolitical order (as in liberation theology). Indeed, even within existentialism itself (especially with Reinhold Niebuhr) we have a politically refined sense of social justice. History, for the Transcendental Thomist, is not something to be taken for granted, something inevitable, but something to be shaped and directed by free human persons in whom God, the author of creation, is present as the One who makes the new ever possible, and whose Word, in fact, provides the critique by which the old can be corrected and changed. It is in the context of history, in fact, that we *become* who we are.

Insofar as Transcendental Thomism comprehends and preserves the best that is present in the aforementioned philosophical and theological approaches, it will serve as the integrating principle of the theology of human existence that is developed in chapter 5.

Official Teachings of the Church

Official pronouncements (i.e., by popes, ecumenical councils, and other councils of the Church) have advanced the following points on the meaning and context of human existence:

1. God is the Creator of the whole world, material as well as spiritual, and remains present to it through Providence.

2. All created things, therefore, are good because they come from the creative hand of God. But human persons are the crown of divine creation.

3. The dignity of the human person resides in the person's intimate relationship with God. The human person has a soul. (This is the transcendental dimension of human existence.)

4. We are, at the same time, essentially oriented to other people. Human existence is social existence.

5. The human condition is also characterized by a split. We are plagued by weakness and sin. We experience ourselves as limited creatures, and this generates a sense of anxiety.

6. Nonetheless, we are called by God to master ourselves and our environment, and we are empowered to do so by grace and especially by the grace of Jesus Christ.

7. Death is not the end of human existence. Life is changed, not taken away (to use a line from the Preface of the Mass for the Deceased). We are destined for glory.

These teachings are synthesized from the following sources:

1. The provincial Council of Constantinople (543), which condemned certain positions associated with followers of Origen, namely, that the human body is a degrading place of exile to which preexisting souls have been consigned.

2. The provincial Council of Braga, in Portugal (561), which also rejected the antimatter, antibody teaching borrowed from the Origenists.

3. Pope Innocent III's *Profession of Faith* (1208), prescribed for all those returning to the Church from the heresy of *Albigensianism,* a French offshoot of the ancient heresy of *Manichæism,* which taught that matter is evil, and from *Waldensianism,* another French-based movement which assumed the same dualistic notion of spirit and matter but which had as well an anticlerical dimension directed against the display of worldliness and power in the Church.

4. The Fourth Lateran General Council (1215), which spoke the final word against the Albigensian and Waldensian errors. Its teaching was later adopted by the First Vatican Council (1869–1870).

5. Similar condemnations can be found in the Council of Vienna (1311–1312), the Council of Florence (1442) in its *Decree for the Jacobites,* the Fifth Lateran Council (1513), the *Syllabus of Errors*

promulgated by Pope Pius IX (1864), the First Vatican Council, as mentioned above, and Pope Pius XII's encyclical letter, *Humani Generis* (1950).

6. Nowhere is the official teaching more succinctly expressed—and without the intrusion of polemical intent—than in the *Pastoral Constitution on the Church in the Modern World* (*Gaudium et spes*) of Vatican II (1965). The principal elements of that teaching follow:

a. We are created in the image of God, capable of knowing and loving God and appointed by God to master all of the earth for the sake of God's glory (n. 12; see also Genesis 1:26; Sirach 17:3–10; Psalms 8:5–6).

b. But God did not create us as solitary creatures. We are created male and female, and, therefore, as essentially social beings (n. 12).

c. "The call to grandeur and the depths of misery are both a part of human experience" (n. 13).

d. We cannot, however, despise our bodies nor the created world in which we find ourselves, even though both may be the source of pain and anxiety. For by our interior qualities we outstrip the rest of creation. God is present to our hearts, awaiting our discovery (n. 14).

e. "In fidelity to conscience, Christians are joined with the rest of men and women in the search for truth, and for the genuine solution to the numerous problems which arise in the life of individuals and from social relationships" (n. 16).

f. Only in freedom—not from blind internal impulse nor from mere external pressure—can we direct ourselves toward goodness. But since our freedom has been damaged by sin, only with the help of God's grace can we bring our relationship with God and thereby with the whole creation to full flower (n. 17).

g. In the face of death the riddle of human existence becomes most acute. Technology cannot calm our anxiety about death, for the prolongation of biological life cannot satisfy that desire for a higher life which is inescapably lodged in the human heart (n. 18).

h. "Although the mystery of death utterly beggars the imagination, the Church has been taught by divine revelation, and itself firmly teaches, that the human person has been created by God for a blissful purpose beyond the reach of earthly misery" (n. 18).

7. A similarly positive statement on human dignity and freedom in light of the redemption is set forth in Pope John Paul II's first encyclical, *Redemptor Hominis* (1979).

SUMMARY

1. In a time of rapid and substantial change, the meaning of human existence assumes new and urgent force. Various attempts have been made to answer the question, "Who are we?" These efforts can be subsumed under the generic term *anthropology*.

2. Answers have been proposed by the *natural sciences* and by *Charles Darwin*, in particular. We are creatures linked biologically with the rest of creation. Human existence is not simply given. It is something to be worked out through the process of evolution and adaptation to the environment.

3. If the natural scientists have been concerned with the interaction of human behavior and the world *outside* the person, one of the *social sciences*, *psychology*, has been concerned as well with the interaction of human behavior and the world *inside* the person. This is the special contribution of *Freud*. Human existence is not simply a matter of knowing what to do (intellect) and then deciding to do it (will). There are unconscious drives, forces, and motives that influence, probably even determine, our choices and our behavior.

4. Other social sciences, i.e., *sociology* and *economics*, focus on the social, economic, and political context in which human persons find themselves. *Karl Marx*, like Freud, insisted that human problems are traceable to conflicts produced by alienation. For Freud, the alienation is from one's true self; for Marx, the alienation is from the fruits of one's labors and thus from the industrialized world and from other people. It is only in and through *society* that persons can live as human beings. The collective defines who and what we are.

5. *Feminist* thought presents a wide-ranging, interdisciplinary critique of the ethos and practice of sexism and gender discrimination, as expressed in patriarchal social, political, cultural, and religious structures and in androcentric thought and language.

6. Nineteenth- and twentieth-century *philosophical* understandings of human existence cover a wide range of approaches: the *phenomenological* (Husserl, Merleau-Ponty), the *existentialist* (Kierkegaard, Nietzsche, Heidegger, Sartre, Buber), the *processive* (Whitehead, Bergson), the *pragmatic* (James, Dewey), the *positivistic* (the early Wittgenstein, Russell, Carnap), and *ordinary language philosophy* (the later Wittgenstein, Austin, Ryle). In much of these philosophies there is an emphasis on the *subjective*, the *changeable*, the *particular*, and the *practical*, over against the objective, the unchanging, the universal, and the abstract. Human existence is not a given to be examined, but a potential in process of realization.

7. Among *contemporary philosophical currents* there are those philosophies that go under the rubric "*Continental*" (the *neo-Marxism* of Habermas and Marcuse; the *hermeneutical* approach of Gadamer; and the *deconstructionism* of Derrida). Most others in the English-speaking world go under the rubric "*Analytic*," especially the *philosophy of mind*, with its biological and artificial-intelligence wings. Both are broadly naturalistic.

8. Contemporary *Thomism* is similarly pluralistic. There is, in addition to the historians of medieval philosophy (Gilson), the post-Kantian European Thomism of Maréchal, known as *Transcendental Thomism*; the Thomism of the *Lublin School* (which includes Pope John Paul II); and the Thomism found in some of the analytic philosophy in England (Anscombe, Kenny).

9. There are similar emphases in contemporary *theology*, although one can detect two apparently opposed orientations: the one (*existentialist*) which focuses on the subject and the importance of achieving sufficient self-understanding, and the other (*liberationist*) which focuses on the subject's responsibility to criticize and to change an unjust social order.

10. *Feminist* theology seeks to recover women's experience and integrate it into theological reflection, to search the tradition for what has contributed to women's subjugation and also for its liberating elements. In doing so, it challenges both androcentrism and patriarchy.

11. For *Transcendental Thomism* history is not something to be taken for granted, something inevitable, but something to be shaped and directed by free human persons in whom God is present as the One who makes the new ever possible, and whose Word provides the critique by which the old can be corrected and changed.

12. The *Church* over the centuries has *officially taught* that God is the Creator of the whole world, material as well as spiritual, and that all reality, including the bodily, is good. Our dignity resides in our intimate relationship with God, in spite of which we experience anxiety about the meaning of life, sin, and death. We are called nonetheless to master ourselves and our environ-

ment and are empowered to do so by grace. Death is not the end of life but the beginning of a new phase of life. We are destined for glory.

SUGGESTED READINGS

Baum, Gregory. *Man Becoming*. New York: Herder & Herder, 1970.

Carr, Anne. *Transforming Grace: Women's Experience and Christian Tradition*. San Francisco: Harper & Row, 1988.

Macquarrie, John. *Twentieth-Century Religious Thought*. 4th ed. Philadelphia: Trinity Press International, 1988.

McMullin, Ernan, ed. *Evolution and Creation*. Notre Dame, Ind.: University of Notre Dame Press, 1985.

Pannenberg, Wolfhart. *Anthropology in Theological Perspective*. Philadelphia: Westminster Press, 1975.

Passmore, John. *A Hundred Years of Philosophy*. Baltimore, Md.: Penguin Books, 1968.

Peacocke, Arthur R. *God and the New Biology*. San Francisco: HarperCollins, 1986.

Rahner, Karl. "Theology and Anthropology." In *The Word in History*. Ed. T. P. Burke. New York: Sheed & Ward, 1966, pp. 1–23.

_____. *Foundations of Christian Faith*. New York: Seabury Press, 1978, pp. 24–89.

Ruether, Rosemary Radford. *New Woman, New Earth: Sexist Ideologies and Human Liberation*. New York: Seabury Press, 1975.

Tracy, David. *The Analogical Imagination: Christian Theology and the Culture of Pluralism*. New York: Crossroad, 1981, pp. 339–404.

V

A Theology of Human Existence: Nature, Grace, Original Sin

THE QUESTION

Chapter 4 surveyed a relatively wide range of scientific and disciplinary areas—e.g., biology, psychology, sociology, philosophy. This chapter is more explicitly theological. It offers an actual position on the question of human existence, one that strives to be consistent with the Catholic tradition.

The question of human existence is as fundamental for Christian faith and theology as is the question of God. Indeed, the question of human existence and the question of God are two sides of the same theological coin. Our statements about God and Jesus Christ, about creation and redemption, about life and death, about grace and salvation, about sin and judgment, about the Church and morality, are always in some important measure a reflection of our understanding of human existence and of the human condition.

Thus, if we think of ourselves as utterly without worth, we are saying something about God's own handiwork, about the effectiveness of Jesus Christ's redemptive work on our behalf, about the power and impact of Original Sin, about the value of being a member of the Church and of having access to its sacraments, about the meaningfulness of our lives as Christians, and about the basis of our common hope in the coming of the reign of God.

Correspondingly, if we think of ourselves and others as nothing more than a collection of neurological responses to be conditioned and programmed at will, then that, too, says something about our understanding of a whole network of theological questions, not least of which are the questions of sin and redemption.

The chapter begins with a theological reflection on the human person, derived from the principal biblical, historical, and doctrinal sources of the Catholic tradition. There follows a similar consideration of nature and grace, and, finally, of Original Sin. The basis for the ordering of this latter material will be explained in due course. In their totality, the issues treated in this chapter are usually subsumed under the heading *theological anthropology*.

THE HUMAN PERSON

The human person is an individual creature, distinguished from all other creatures by the gift of freedom, bodily incarnated as male and female and animated by a spiritual principle, traditionally called a soul. The individual human person is at the same time social and historical. That is to say that the person's humanity is constituted by the wider community of human persons, and they, individually and communally, are constituted by history and by the world in which they live. Indeed, human persons are, in a sense, cocreators with God of both the world and its history (*Pastoral Constitution on the Church in the Modern World*, n. 39; see also Pope John Paul II's 1981 encyclical *Laborem Exercens* (*On Human Work*): "The human person is the image of God partly through the mandate received from the Creator to subdue, to dominate, the earth. In carrying out this mandate, the human person reflects the very action of the Creator of the universe" [II, n. 4, para. 2]). Only when the human person is understood in this larger context—not only as an individual, but also as social being, as historical being, and as being-in-the-world—can our theology of human existence hope to be comprehensive and catholic.

158

Biblical Views

Old Testament

In the Old Testament the human person is, before all else, a *creature* of God, formed out of the dust of the ground (Genesis 2:7). The word which designates "man/woman" in the concrete sense is *adam*. The word for "dust" is *adamah*. This etymological connection is crucial. We are not composite beings, made of body and soul as two separate parts (as the medieval Scholastic philosophers had it). Soul and flesh are not contrasted in the Old Testament. Unlike the Greeks, who look upon a human being as an incarnated spirit, the Hebrews regarded the human person as an animated body. We do not *have* a soul and a body; we *are* soul and body.

The hope of salvation, therefore, is expressed in terms of the *resurrection of the body* ("Your dead shall live, their corpses shall rise..."—Isaiah 26:19; see also Daniel 12:2–3, and 2 Maccabees 7:14), and this is taken up and developed in the New Testament ("If the dead are not raised, then Christ has not been raised. If Christ has not been raised, your faith is futile"—1 Corinthians 15:16–17; see the entire fifteenth chapter of 1 Corinthians as well as Mark 12:18–25; John 6:39–40; and Acts of the Apostles 24:15). The idea of the *immortality of the soul*, on the other hand, is *not* developed in the writings of the later Old Testament period nor in the New Testament. The notion of immortality reflects a world view different from the Bible's anthropology. Indeed, it is more akin to Greek philosophy (i.e., the human person as embodied spirit) than to the Hebrew mentality (i.e., the human person as animated body).

Bodiliness is also an important basis of our relationship with one another. Human existence, in the Old Testament, is *coexistence with other persons*. That coexistence is, in turn, founded on our primary relationship with God. Each of us is equally powerless in the face of God's transcendence, and at the same time of equal value before God. We are commanded by God to love our neighbor (yes, even in the *Old Testament*, contrary to a popular misconception): "You shall love your neighbor as yourself" (Leviticus 19:18; see also 19:9–18,34; and 25:35–38). Our responsibility for one another is underlined by the prophets as well: "Take away from me the noise of your songs; I will not listen to the melody of your harps. But let justice roll down like waters, and righteousness like an ever-flowing stream" (Amos 5:23–24; see also 8:4–6, and Isaiah 3:13–15).

Coexistence with, and even interdependence upon, one another is highlighted in a special way in the *sexual relationship*. Created male and female, human persons are most deeply themselves in a relationship of intimate mutual love (Genesis 1:27). "Then the Lord God said: 'It is not good that the man should be alone.'...Therefore a man leaves his father and his mother and clings to his wife, and they become one flesh" (Genesis 2:18,24).

Human existence—at once dependent upon God and interdependent in relationship with others—is, therefore, *responsible existence*. The Lord gave Adam an order, not to eat from the tree of knowledge (Genesis 2:16). Human existence is a life of responsibility to the will of God. Fulfilling that responsibility need not be a matter of fear and drudgery; it can be one of merriment and joy (1 Kings 4:20; Psalm 43:4). Unfortunately, we are not always faithful to God's will. But even in sin we disclose the depths of our being as human persons distinguished, set apart, by our *freedom*.

The Old Testament also sees human existence as *sinful existence*. Although there is no fully developed notion of Original Sin, the human race is presented as sinners whose hearts are filled with pride and are thereby closed to the call of God and the cry of our neighbor (e.g., Genesis 8:21; Psalm 143, Psalm 2). Sin is portrayed as something breaking out in the world and harming not only the individual but history itself (Genesis 3–11). And that consciousness of sin deepens as the history of salvation unfolds. "Can Ethiopians change their skin or leopards their spots? Then also you can do good who are accustomed to evil" (Jeremiah 13:23). But the same prophet assures us of the Lord's forgiving spirit: "The days are surely coming, says the Lord, when I will make a new covenant with the house of Israel and the house of Judah.... I will be their God, and they shall be my people...for I will forgive their iniquity, and remember their sin no more" (Jeremiah 31:31–34).

Human existence, therefore, is or can be *hope-filled existence*. There are hopes for a savior and a time of salvation, for the resurrection of the body and new life, and for the fulfillment of the promises of the new covenant.

New Testament

The New Testament's understanding of human existence is consistent with, and develops from, the Old Testament's. We find there no abstract or speculative "philosophy" of human existence, with detailed distinctions between soul and body, or between intellect and will. As in the Old Testament, human existence is *historical existence*, life emerging from, and shaped by, the concrete experiences of everyday happenings.

Accordingly, *Jesus* does not formulate an abstract doctrine of fraternal charity, replete with rules and conditions. Instead he tells the story of the Good Samaritan and asks, "Which...was a neighbor to the man who fell into the hands of the robbers?" (Luke 10:25–37). All of us, he insists, are sinners, in need of *conversion*, that is, a fundamental change of mind and of heart: "The time is fulfilled, the kingdom of God has come near; repent, and believe in the good news" (Mark 1:15). The reform must be, in fact, radical; we are required even to love our enemies: "But I say to you: Love your enemies and pray for those who persecute you....For if you love those who love you, what reward do you have?...Be perfect, therefore, as your heavenly Father is perfect" (Matthew 5:44–48). Indeed, the challenge in the story of the Good Samaritan is to see that even our enemies can be "good."

In the end, we shall be judged by the quality of our response to those in need, friend and enemy alike: "Just as you did it to one of the least of these who are members of my family... just as you did not do it to one of the least of these, you did not do it to me" (Matthew 25:31–46). Just as Jesus' own existence is an existence in the service of others (Mark 10:45), so must every person's be *a coexistence of service*.

Paul's understanding of human existence is developed in the light of the death and resurrection of Christ. As such, it draws out some of the anthropological implications of Jesus' own preaching. Paul, like Jesus and the Old Testament, refuses to speculate about the philosophical nature and properties of the human person. The body-soul dualism of contemporary Greek thought would have been foreign to him. For him the resurrection in which we all hope will be a *resurrection of the body* (1 Corinthians 15), because the body (*soma*) is intrinsic to the being of the human person (1 Corinthians 15:15–19).

"Body" is not just that through which the spirit acts; it is the whole person (by contrast with *sarx,* which applies to the flesh alone). This notion of the body does not eliminate the traditional idea of the soul. Rather it emphasizes the unity of the human person. Thus, the opposition of spirit and flesh is not of soul against body, but of the whole person as oriented toward God and the whole person as oriented away from God.

But we find ourselves *sinners* in the world, in the hands of alien forces, i.e., the domain of the "flesh" (*sarx*) which is in rebellion against God (Romans 8:6–8, 10:3; 2 Corinthians 10:5). When Paul considers the human person as alienated from himself and from God, he speaks of the person as flesh, as sinner. Flesh must be "put to death" at Baptism (Romans 8:9–13), while body, i.e., the person as a whole, is to be transformed at the resurrection (1 Corinthians 15:44; Philippians 3:21). When the whole person is oriented toward God, it is because of the Spirit of God who "dwells" in us, giving life to our "mortal bodies" (Romans 8:11). If we "live according to the flesh" (*kata sarka*), we will die; "but if by the Spirit you put to death the deeds of the body, you will live" (8:13). Once dead, we are made alive in Christ (Ephesians 2:5; 2 Corinthians 4:16).

But even the new creature in Christ lives in a state of tension, between the "already" of Christ's saving work on our behalf and the "not yet" of its final perfection in the reign of God. By *faith,* and through a life based on faith, we work out our salvation in the midst of this tension: "But now that faith has come, we are no longer subject to a disciplinarian [i.e., the law's]" (Galatians 3:25; see also Romans 3:14; Colossians 2:12,20). In this faith there is no longer any fear of death ("Where, O death, is your victory? Where, O death, is your sting?"—1 Corinthians 15:55), but rather *hope* for the appearance of Christ when we "will be revealed with him in glory" (Colossians 3:4). But over all these virtues, including even faith and hope, we put on *love,* "which binds everything together in perfect harmony" (Colossians 3:14).

For *John,* as well as for Paul, the "world" is prone to evil, not because God created it evil, but because it is populated by men and women who are sinners. Indeed, the world would be lost if it were not for Jesus Christ; by sending the Son, God brings the world to a crisis or turning point, but out of a motive of love (John 3:16–17). God

162

sends the Son not to judge the world but to save it (1 John 4:9,14). Without an act of liberation from on high (John 3), we are imprisoned within a domain of evil. By having faith in Jesus Christ, we receive a fresh possibility of life from a new source. This *new life* is an eschatological existence, i.e., an existence between our situation as it is— imperfect, limited, prone to sin—and the final reign of God as it has been promised to us. In the meantime, we find a new home in the community of the faithful and in the *love of the brothers and sisters* by which we prove our sinlessness (1 John 3:14–18; 4:19–21).

It is not for us to decide whether or not we shall be "born again." On the contrary, no one comes to the Father unless the Father draws that person (John 6:44). But as a believer, the person must abide in Jesus' word and act according to his command (1 John 1:6–7; 2:3–6). The hope that is in all of us for a life completely fulfilled is, for John, to be directed to the *present* rather than to the future. We find the "new life" here and now by faith (1 John 1:2–3; John 17:3). To be human is, in the deepest sense, to live by grace, i.e., by the presence of God in our hearts and in our midst.

Early Christian Writers

There are no real breakthroughs in the writings of the early Christian writers beyond the anthropological perspective of the Bible. What the so-called patristic period contributes is an element of systematization (Tertullian's *De Anima* is the beginning) around certain fundamental principles—e.g., the human person as the *image of God,* and the history of the universe as *the history of divinization and salvation.* These themes are expressed clearly and forcefully in Irenæus's *Adversus Hæreses* (literally, "Against the Heresies" of Gnosticism and other related errors).

At the heart of Irenæus's theology is his theory of *recapitulation,* borrowed from Paul but expanded considerably. Recapitulation, for Irenæus, is the taking up in Christ of all that is or has been from the beginning. God gathers up everything which had been sidetracked by the fall of Adam and Eve and renews, restores, and reorganizes it in Jesus Christ, who becomes the Second Adam. Since the whole human race was lost through the sin of the First Adam, the Son of

163

God had to become a human being in order to bring about the re-creation of humankind. "When he became incarnate and was made man," Irenæus wrote, "he recapitulated in himself the long history of humanity, summing up and giving us salvation in order that we might receive again in Christ Jesus what we had lost in Adam, that is, the image and likeness of God" (III,18,1).

But the tendency to dichotomize remained. In the writings of the Eastern, Greek Fathers (e.g., Gregory of Nyssa) the tension between matter and spirit endured. Human fulfillment is possible because on one side of human nature, the spiritual, the human person stands already on God's side. Our goal is the vision of God after death. This vision comes only after purification and restoration to our original purity. For Western, Latin theology (e.g., Augustine) the tension is between the person as sinner and the merciful God. "Every man is Adam, every man is Christ" (cited by Henri Rondet, *The Grace of Christ*, p. 136). The history of the world, therefore, is seen essentially as the history of the reunification of what was divided rather than "the free history of God in the world" (Rahner).

The Medieval Period

Significant scientific, philosophical, and theological advances in our understanding of human existence did not occur until the eighteenth and especially the nineteenth centuries, with the discoveries of Darwin and Freud, the new social analysis of Marx, and the new focus on the human person as subject in the philosophy of Kant, in Idealism, and in modern psychology.

The medieval view of human existence could not, and did not, do justice to the special character of the person. Little or no attention at all was given to the history of salvation. Human beings do not grow and develop; they simply are, with an unchanging essence.

The medieval distinction between mortal and venial sin, for example, did not even set contemporary theologians to wondering about the basis for such a distinction in human behavior itself. There was still no real theological analysis of such fundamental human experiences as anguish, joy, and death. The world and its history were merely the ready-made scene for the unfolding of each individual human drama. Would the person finally save his or her soul, or not? There was nothing new to be added to the world and its history.If the world and history were not in process, neither were human beings.

And yet there were also some counterindications in medieval theology—evidence of some initial movement toward a genuine anthropology. If reflections on salvation had a nonhistorical cast to them, their strongly individual focus also prepared the way, however unwittingly, for the modern period's subsequent emphasis on the person as subject. Medieval theology stressed the importance of the *Beatific Vision*, i.e., the immediate, unobstructed experience of God after death by the saved individual. Medieval theology provided also for nonsacramental possibilities of salvation, i.e., the so-called *votum sacramenti* (desire for the sacrament). If an individual's basic goodwill could, under some circumstances, replace the need for Baptism, then there must be something of fundamental and enduring importance about the activities and processes of the human mind, will, and subjective consciousness. This assumption was also reflected in medieval theology's remarkably provident teaching on the inviolability of conscience, even when it is in opposition to ecclesiastical law.

Scholastic philosophy, and the theology which flowed from it, provided what proved to be a true basis for the later recognition of genuine subjectivity, in that it noted, as Rahner says, that "anything is or has being in proportion to the degree in which it is subjectivity in possession of itself." Or, in the spirit of Teilhard de Chardin, life moves to higher and higher levels of self-reflection. The highest forms of life not only "know"; we "know that we know." The more conscious we are of ourselves, of our knowing powers, of our powers of decision, of the implications of our thoughts, our judgments, and our actions, the more we are in possession of ourselves. And the more we are in possession of ourselves, the greater is the level of "genuine subjectivity." The point, therefore, is that although medieval theology was not particularly attentive to the subjective side of human existence (on the contrary), there were elements and orientations in medieval thought which already anticipated the modern movement in the direction of subjectivity.

The Modern Period

Because of the scientific, philosophical, and theological developments outlined in chapter 4, the time for an anthropological recasting of all the traditional doctrines is at hand. But the task is as yet uncompleted. Early indications of a trend, however, are evident in the *emergence of historical theology,* in the recognition of *religious pluralism* and of the *universality of God's saving grace,* in the new regard for the *world* as something to be *transformed* by the Church, in the recent renewal of interest in *spirituality* for the individual in his or her personal relationship with God, and in the extraordinary and rapid development of *feminist consciousness.*

The Second Vatican Council did not construct a formal theological anthropology, but there are elements present in the conciliar documents which are consistent with the trends just noted: (1) the insistence on conscience as the guide to truth and to genuine solutions to current problems; (2) the declaration that "only in freedom... can we direct ourselves toward goodness"; (3) the reference to our desire for a higher life, a desire which is "inescapably lodged in the human heart" and which makes it possible for us to transcend our anxiety about death (*Pastoral Constitution on the Church in the Modern World,* nn. 16–18); and (4) the affirmation of the fundamental equality of women and men in the human community (*Pastoral Constitution,* nn. 9 and 29). At the same time, the human person is social, historical, and of the world, with a call from God to collaborate in the creation of history, in the transformation of the world, and even in the coming of the final reign of God (nn. 4–10; 23–39).

Theology of the Human Person:
A Synthesis

The *Bible* views the human person as a creature of God, as animated body. Our *bodiliness* is the basis of our relationship with one another. *Human existence is coexistence.* But such existence is also fraught with as many risks as opportunities. Human existence is at once responsible, sinful, and hope-filled. The focus of its hope is the resurrection of the body, and the ground of that hope is the preaching, ministry, and saving death and resurrection of Jesus Christ, whom we accept in faith and to whom we manifest our fidelity in love. To live according to this dynamic of faith, hope, and love is to enter a new life, to become *a new creature in Christ*. This new life and new creaturehood is, as always, shared with others, in accordance with our social nature and the coexistent character of human existence. The immediate context of the sharing is the community of the faithful, which is the Church.

Until modern times, there was little or no significant development of a theology of human existence beyond that already expressed in the Bible. The *early Christian writers*, especially Irenæus, spoke of the human person as the image of God, and of human history as the history of salvation—a process in which all things are being recapitulated in Christ. The *medieval period*, consistently with the prevailing philosophy of the times, viewed human existence "objectively," i.e., as an unchanging form of created life essentially unaffected by the process and vicissitudes of history. Elements in medieval theology anticipated, to some extent, the modern turn toward the "subjective." Medieval theology's emphasis on the inviolability of conscience is one example to which we referred. On the other hand, it clearly did not anticipate the late-twentieth-century transformation of consciousness regarding the fundamental equality of women and men in the human community. On the contrary, the medieval period is filled with negative and demeaning references to women.

Under the impact of scientific and philosophical developments, *contemporary theology* focuses its attention on the consciousness of the human person, on the person's freedom and responsibility, not only to cocreate himself or herself but to cocreate the world and its history under God, and on the radical equality of women and men in the human community. The Second Vatican Council's insistence on the importance of conscience, freedom, and the innate desire for a higher life reflects this modern shift to the subject. Its emphasis on the social, historical, and worldly dimensions of human existence underscores the human person's responsibility for others, for the world and its history, and ultimately for the coming of the final reign of God. And its affirmation of the fundamental equality of women and men lays the foundation for the formal, *de facto* recognition of that equality in society and in the Church alike (as later called for by the 1971 World Synod of Bishops' document, *Justice in the World*, III, para. 4).

167

NATURE AND GRACE

We are at a methodological juncture here. Should Original Sin be considered before or after a consideration of nature and grace? To one way of thinking, Original Sin should come first, to account for the *weaknesses* of our nature and to underscore thereby our *need* for grace. To another way of thinking, one that is taken here to be more consistent with the Catholic understanding of human nature and grace, grace is not something conferred under some divine "Plan B." Thus, had we not sinned, God would have left us ungraced. But because we did sin, God had to act, and the conferral of grace was the response to our new, unhappy predicament. A second reason for our treating nature and grace *before* Original Sin is that the doctrine of Original Sin is better understood as an expression of the tragic dimension of human existence than as a personal sin committed by Adam and Eve, transmitted down through the centuries by whatever means (Augustine, for example, pointed to sexual intercourse as the carrier!), and "washed away" by the waters of Baptism. If the second reason is also valid, then it seems preferable to lead with the positive concepts of nature and grace rather than with the negative concept of Original Sin.

For those who find the first way of thinking preferable to the second there is nothing to prevent them from inverting the order in their reading and use of this material. They should be reminded, however, that there is more to sin than Original Sin and that the doctrine of Original Sin is only a relatively small part of the overall theology of sin (treated in chapter 26).

Nature

Until this century, the formal concept of "nature" served only as a basis of contrast with "grace" in Catholic theology. "Nature" is a concept, however, which is still almost totally absent from the Eastern Orthodox theology of grace and was, until recently, generally resisted by Protestant theology. One can note a turn, for example, in the works of John Cobb (*God and the World*, Philadelphia: Westminster Press, 1969).

The mainstream Catholic tradition has always been insistent that *the grace of God is given to us, not to make up for something lacking to us as human persons, but as a free gift that elevates us to a new and unmerited level of existence.* Hypothetically, we could have had a *purely natural end.* This would perhaps be something akin to *limbo,* a state of "natural happiness" reserved for those who die in infancy without the grace of Baptism and without, of course, the possibility of having ever expressed even an implicit desire for Baptism (*votum sacramenti*) through free choices which happen to be consistent with the will of God.

The real, historical order, however, is already permeated with grace, so that a state of "pure nature" does not exist. In other words, if grace supposes nature, nature in its own way supposes grace, insofar as the grace of Christ sustains us in our actual existence and orients us toward a supernatural end, eternal union with God. This emphasis on the importance of the natural and of the natural order is historically and theologically characteristic of Catholicism.

Eastern Orthodoxy, on the other hand, has tended to stress the spiritual side of human existence to such an extent that the natural foundation may seem all but lost. Much of *Protestantism,* meantime, so emphasized the depravity of the natural human condition apart from the grace of God that the natural order could only be viewed in thoroughly negative terms.

"Nature," to be sure, is not directly a biblical concept but arises from subsequent theological reflection on the New Testament's (especially John's and Paul's) proclamation of "the grace of God through Christ." *We infer who we are as creatures of God by reflecting on who we have become through Christ.* By the grace of Christ we enter into a new relationship of communion with God, and we are transformed interiorly by the Spirit of Christ.

The early Christian writers, from Irenæus on, understood this participation in the life of God through Christ as a true *divinization.* The Latin Fathers, especially Augustine and Pope Leo the Great (d. 461), adopted this concept and made it the foundation of the whole theology of grace in the medieval period, as is particularly evident in Thomas Aquinas.

But the emphasis is not upon divinization alone, but upon its *gratuitous* character as well. We neither deserved nor needed grace.

We would not have been less than human without it. Although, in fact, God created us and the world in and through Christ, God could have created us without including the communication of grace (or better: God's *self*-communication).

Hence, the theological concept of "nature" means that we are bodily creatures who are intelligible (i.e., whose existence makes sense) and who would have been open to full human growth apart from the grace of divinization. The creation of humankind and of the world is theoretically possible without the incarnation of the Son of God in Jesus Christ. The whole self-communication of God—in creation and in the incarnation—is utterly free. Human existence nondivinized by grace is a possible hypothesis.

"Nature," therefore, is neither a purely positive nor a purely negative concept. It is not *purely positive* because it is a concept one *derives* from reflecting on something higher, namely, grace. It is not a *purely negative* concept because it implies the rationality of the human person and the person's fundamental relationship to God, to other persons, to the world, and to its history apart from grace.

The *theological* concept of nature is different, of course, from the philosophical or the scientific (as we have already seen in chapter 4), because theology views the human person as having *a radical capacity (potentia obedientialis) for the divinizing grace of Christ.* This fundamental aspect of the theological concept of nature is not derived from Darwinian or Freudian experimentation, nor from Marxist analysis, nor even from philosophical reflection, but from inferences drawn from the revelation that we are, in fact, called to a participation in the very life of God through Jesus Christ. (The notion of "revelation," which is so obviously crucial in the preceding sentence, will be addressed in chapter 7.)

It is important to add here that the traditional Catholic emphasis on "nature" is not without its dangers—dangers of which Protestants and Orthodox have been mindful. One might easily be led to the exaggerated view that the purely natural person does, in fact, exist and that grace is something merely "added" to, or superimposed upon, nature. It cannot be denied that the introduction of the concept of nature in the explanation of grace can lead, and has led, to a dualistic vision of human existence in relation to God. God is, on the one hand, our Creator, and, on the other hand, our Savior through

Christ—with a different relationship to the human person in each case. How we are to understand the relationship between nature and grace is a matter to be considered later in this section of the present chapter.

Grace

The word *grace* is used in a variety of ways in this chapter and throughout the book. This is so because *grace has never had a single meaning in Catholic theology or doctrine.* In the most basic sense of the word, *grace* refers to the favor God bestows upon us: the gift of divine life itself. But the term *grace* also refers to the help which God gives us to live holy lives, the indwelling of the Holy Spirit, sacramental grace, Christ's grace of headship over the Church, the grace of union by which the Word is united with Christ's human nature, God's forgiveness, the grace of justification, and even the traditional prayer before meals.

Moreover, the traditional theology of grace, as presented in the approved Latin manuals over the years, has always made various distinctions in its analysis of this fundamental topic: between created and uncreated grace; between efficacious and merely sufficient grace; between actual and habitual, or sanctifying, grace; and between elevating and medicinal grace.

In this chapter and in the book as a whole, the different *meanings* given the term *grace* are a function of the different *contexts* in which the term appears. Therefore, the term should always be interpreted in light of the particular context in which it is used below and throughout the book.

Old Testament

In the Old Testament the Hebrew noun *ḥēn* designates a quality which arouses *favor*. The word appears most frequently in the phrase "to find favor in the eyes of" God or other persons. One who seeks favors throws himself or herself completely on the goodwill of the one from whom the favor is sought. The verb *ḥānan*, "to show favor," designates an attitude which is proper toward the needy, the poor,

171

the widow, the orphan, and so forth. One shows favor by gifts, by assistance, and by refraining from punishment. Yahweh shows favor by giving prosperity (Genesis 33:11), by giving children (Genesis 33:5), by accepting sacrifice (Malachi 1:9). Most frequently Yahweh shows favor by delivering from distress (e.g., Psalms 4:2; 6:3; 9:13–14; 25:16; 26:11; 27:7). As in the central Exodus event, Yahweh delivers Israel from its enemies (2 Kings 13:23; Isaiah 30:18–19; 33:2), even when Israel deserves punishment for its sins. Such favor is also forgiveness (Psalms 41:4,11; 51:3; Isaiah 27:11; Amos 5:15). Yahweh's favor is shown *freely*. It can be given or withheld (Exodus 33:19).

New Testament

In the New Testament the corresponding noun for *grace* is the Greek *charis*, a key word in the Christian message having its own history. The word occurs frequently in the introductory and final greetings of the various epistles, usually accompanied by the word *peace*. Thus: "To all God's beloved in Rome, who are called to be saints: Grace to you and peace from God our Father and the Lord Jesus Christ" (Romans 1:7). The word designates the *goodwill of God*, sometimes in a general sense (e.g., Acts of the Apostles 14:26; 15:40) and most frequently in reference to the saving will of God executed in Jesus Christ and communicated to humankind through Christ. Such grace *justifies* us (Romans 3:24; Titus 3:7). By grace Paul (and others) are called (Galatians 1:15). Grace appears in Christ for our salvation (Titus 2:11). By it Jesus suffered death for all (Hebrews 2:9). Faith and love are fruits of grace (1 Timothy 1:14).

Elsewhere in the New Testament the emphasis is less on the saving will of God and more on *that which is given* (James 4:6; 1 Peter 5:4). The Word is full of grace (John 1:14, 16) and dwells within us (14:23). It is a store to which we have full access through Christ (Romans 5:2). It abounds more than sin (Romans 5:15,20; 6:1). It is given us in Christ (1 Corinthians 1:4). It is within the Christian (2 Corinthians 9:14), and extends to more and more people (2 Corinthians 4:15). The prophets foretold it (1 Peter 1:10). Christians are its heirs (1 Peter 3:7), called to grow in the grace and knowledge of Jesus Christ (2 Peter 3:18).

Sometimes grace stands in opposition to *works*, that is, religious works which lack the power to save (Romans 11:5–6; Ephesians 2:5,8–9; 2 Timothy 1:9). Grace stands also in opposition to the *law* (Acts of the Apostles 15:11; Galatians 2:21; 5:4). The Christian is not under the law but under grace (Romans 6:14–18). Grace is a gift, not something owed (Romans 4:4).

The *Gospel* itself can be called grace, in which the Christian should stand and remain steadfast (1 Peter 5:12; Acts of the Apostles 13:43). It is indeed the Gospel of the grace of God (Acts of the Apostles 20:24), or the word of God's grace (Acts of the Apostles 14:3; 20:32).

Grace is also *the principle of Christian life, action, and mission*. The first martyr, St. Stephen, was full of grace and power (Acts of the Apostles 6:8). Paul's apostolate was an apostleship of grace (Romans 1:5, and other passages). His hearers partake of it (Philippians 1:7). It is the *power* by which the apostle performs his apostolic functions (Romans 12:3; 1 Corinthians 3:10, 15:10; Ephesians 3:7–11). It produces good works (2 Corinthians 8:1). The grace of God, not earthly wisdom, guides our conduct (2 Corinthians 1:12).

Its only appearance in the Synoptic Gospels is in Luke. Grace refers to the heavenly reward, hence to a *salvation that is to come* (6:32–34). In 1:30 and 1:52 the Old Testament use of the word survives. But when Luke employs the term to express his own theological insights, he identifies it with the salvation wrought by God in Christ and after Christ, particularly through the words of the Gospel and the preaching thereof (4:22). On the whole, the terminology which Luke uses is not derived from Paul but reflects a wider tradition which may be pre-Pauline.

One final note regarding the meaning of the word *grace* in the New Testament: The Greek noun *charis* is to be distinguished from the noun *charisma* (a term popularized by the charismatic renewal in postconciliar Catholicism as well as by modern politics, as in the expression, "charismatic candidate"). The *charismata* (plural of *charisma*) are a particular type of spiritual gift which enable the recipient to perform some office or function in the Church. Such offices or functions are enumerated in Romans 12, 1 Corinthians 12, and Ephesians 4.

Early Christian Perspectives

Apostolic Fathers

The Apostolic Fathers (Irenæus and others) and the theologians of the *first two centuries* repeat the doctrine of Sacred Scripture, initially stressing its moral demands and then focusing more sharply on the effect of divinization. The first theological reflections are made on the possibility of losing and then recovering the grace of Baptism (*The Shepherd of Hermas* and Tertullian). *The first major controversy* erupted in the second and third centuries under the impact of *Gnosticism,* a heresy which made salvation both nonuniversal and nonhistorical. Salvation was given instead to a select few, and it consisted of a special knowledge (thus, the term *gnosis*). Its principal opponents were Irenæus, Tertullian, and Hippolytus (d. 235).

"We need not mention how necessary it is to do again the work that Saint Augustine and Saint Thomas once did," Henri Rondet has written. "It is most probable that the genius who could attempt such an enterprise has not yet been born" (*The Grace of Christ,* p. 384).

Greek Fathers

The Greek Fathers (from Origen on) developed a doctrine of grace in keeping with the Trinitarian questions of the period. Because the Spirit is truly God, we are truly *divinized* by the presence of the Spirit, i.e., we participate in divine life; and because we are truly divinized, the Spirit must be divine. It is through the incarnation of the divine *Logos* (word) that the Spirit enters the world. "He became human," Irenæus wrote, "that we might become divine" (*Adversus Hæreses,* IV, 28, 1). The Greek doctrine of grace is optimistic about salvation, therefore, because the Holy Spirit truly dwells within us.

The Eastern tradition drew especially upon the mystical and sacramental symbolism of the Johannine writings and of 2 Peter 1:4 that proclaim Christians to be "participants of the divine nature." As expressed in many of its liturgical texts and rites, the Eastern tradition insisted that our sharing in the divine life comes through participation in the sacraments, particularly Baptism and the Eucharist.

And because Eastern Christians viewed death rather than guilt as the major consequence of sin, many Eastern writers stressed *im-*

174

mortality as one of the special effects of grace. We become like God, that is, incorruptible and immortal.

Western Fathers

The Western Fathers (Augustine, and others) were less interested in the intellectual and cosmic aspects of divinization and more *moralistic* in tendency. They also oriented their theology of grace toward the history of salvation and of the individual because of their struggle against *Pelagianism* (the fifth-century heresy which held that human beings can, without the grace of God, achieve supernatural salvation). Grace is a free gift of God and, because of sin, is necessary for salvation. But there is some trace, even in Augustine, of a denial of the universal salvific will of God. Some are *predestined* to salvation, others to damnation.

To be sure, Augustine's view of grace was also *sacramental* in character. He saw "vestiges of the Trinity" throughout all of creation, an inner desire for God in every human heart, and Baptism as the initiation into the inner life of God. But it was his response to Pelagianism that primarily shaped his theology of grace. He stressed the damage done to human nature by Original Sin and the radical incapacity of the human person to fulfill the will of God without God's grace ("Command what you wish," he wrote in *The Confessions*, "but give what you command" [X, 29]).

It is grace that liberates us from the bondage of sin, illuminates the mind with the true, and opens the will to the good. His views on the necessity and gratuity of grace were incorporated into the official teachings of the Church at the Sixteenth Council of Carthage (418), which condemned Pelagianism, and at the Second Council of Orange (529), which condemned semi-Pelagianism. Augustine's thought also had significant authority and influence over the development of the theology and doctrine of grace in subsequent centuries.

The Medieval Period: Thomas Aquinas

The great age of Scholasticism gave precise formulation to the nature and effects of grace by means of newly appropriated Aristotelian categories and terminology. It was St. Thomas Aquinas who introduced the distinction between "habitual" (*habitus*), or "sanctifying," grace and "actual" grace: The former pertains to the indwelling of the Holy Spirit within the person, and the latter, to the *ad hoc* assistance of God given to a person in the performance of an action. The concept of the strictly supernatural character of salvific grace was slowly elaborated. Grace, it was stressed, is a free, unmerited gift of God, for saint and sinner alike.

Aquinas effectively synthesized the various concepts of grace in both Eastern and Western traditions. But one should not look simply to the few specific sections on grace in the *Summa Theologiae*. The overarching structure of the *Summa* is expressive of the theological principle that everything comes from God and is meant to return to God. On the one hand, Thomas incorporated Augustine's emphasis on grace as healing; on the other, the Eastern emphasis on divinization. Furthermore, he made a distinction between "uncreated grace" (the inner life of the triune God) and "created grace" (the change wrought by the divine presence in the individual human person). True to his integrating and synthesizing method, Aquinas described the function of grace as both the healing of human nature wounded by sin, and as the elevating of human nature to participation in the divine life.

Drawing upon Aristotle's notion of the final goal (*telos*) as determinative of all natures, Aquinas concluded that grace is absolutely necessary to human nature because, without it, the human person cannot achieve her or his end, namely, union with God. Only through the indwelling of the Holy Spirit and the "renovation" of all of our natural human capacities can this end be attained.

It was Aquinas who gave us the axiom, "Grace builds on human nature." Grace elevates and transforms human nature, but human nature retains all of its characteristics, including its weaknesses. Thus, grace cannot make a color-blind person a great painter, or one who is tone-deaf a great singer. Grace presupposes nature; it doesn't replace it.

The Reformation Period

Thomas's theology of grace was distorted in subsequent centuries. In order to preserve the gratuity of grace, theologians like Thomas

Cajetan (d. 1534) introduced the notion of "pure nature," with its own finality. Grace came to be considered totally extrinsic to human nature. Thus, the human person has two separate and distinct final ends: a natural end, which the person can seek through his or her own human efforts, and a supernatural end, which is completely beyond human capacity to attain. This would give rise subsequently to the largely fruitless *De Auxiliis* controversy between Dominicans (Domingo Báñez, d. 1604) and Jesuits (Luis de Molina, d. 1600) in sixteenth-century Spain regarding the precise interplay between human effort and divine assistance (Latin, *auxilium*) in the working out of one's salvation.

With the Reformation in the same century and the emergence of new doctrinal deviations within the Catholic Church (e.g., Jansenism), it was necessary for theologians—and eventually the Council of Trent—to defend the freedom of the human person under grace, the truly inward new creation of the human person by habitual grace, the strictly supernatural character of grace, and the universality of God's saving will. But the aforementioned controversy over precisely *how* we can reconcile human freedom with divine power (the debates between the Molinists and the Banezians) was left undecided in 1607 and remains so even today.

The Counter-Reformation Period

The theology and spirituality of the Counter-Reformation reflected a new consciousness of Catholic universality and especially of the universality of grace. The Church on earth was portrayed as luminous with the presence of God, linked with the rejoicing, festive, and triumphant Church in heaven. It was a time of Catholic renewal, inspired by saints like Ignatius Loyola, Francis Xavier, Philip Neri, and Teresa of Ávila, and of new religious orders like the Society of Jesus, the Capuchins, and the Theatines, as well as lay groups engaged in teaching, prayer, and ministries to the sick and needy.

So, too, the art of the period did not simply affirm what the Protestants had attacked: the Virgin Mary, the saints, the papacy, images, sacraments, works and prayers for the dead. It went beyond that, passing through various metamorphoses into the rococo, in developing an elaborate theology of grace in the human personality, in various expressions of prayer and suffering, in mysticism and martyrdom, in liturgy and contemplation. The baroque Church of the sixteenth and seventeenth centuries was a kind of theater in which dramas of grace were presented: conversions, lives of heroic virtue, degrees of mystical experiences—all viewed as interplays of nature and grace, encounters of grace and personality.

The Modern Period

Between the time of the Reformation and the beginning of the Second Vatican Council in 1962, the Catholic theology of grace, like the theology of the Church and the sacraments, was fashioned largely in reaction against Protestantism. Where the Reformers had emphasized the initiative and sovereignty of God, Catholics emphasized human effort and human responsibility. Where the Reformers drew mainly on Sacred Scripture for their understanding of grace, Catholics drew upon the philosophical and theological categories of medieval Scholasticism. Grace was defined as a quantitative entity: something God gives; something we receive; something we can increase by good works; and something we can decrease by venial sin or lose completely through mortal sin.

Accordingly, the standard pre–Vatican II treatise, *De Gratia,* initially developed in the late eighteenth century, was highly technical in content and tone. It usually began with a treatment of *actual grace* (its gratuity, necessity, divisions, compatibility with freedom, capacity for merit) and *habitual,* or *sanctifying, grace* (necessity, etc.). Actual grace was, in turn, subdivided into *elevating grace,* lifting the human person to the divine level; *healing grace,* remedying our sinful tendencies; *operating grace,* giving us new life in Christ; *cooperating grace,* requiring us to do our part; *sufficient grace,* that which is, in principle, necessary to achieve salvation; and *efficacious grace,* that which insures ultimate salvation. Regarding the last distinction: if a person had "merely" sufficient grace, it would not confer eternal life; only efficacious grace could do that. In giving everyone "sufficient" grace, God wills the salvation of all. But God gives only some "efficacious" grace, insuring their salvation.

Under the impact of the biblical and ecumenical movements and of the philosophical turn away from neo-Scholasticism in the late

178

1940s and into the 1950s, the Catholic theology of grace entered a new historical phase at Vatican II and in the decades thereafter. As we shall see below, it was Karl Rahner especially who reversed the neo-Scholastic categories. Grace is, first and foremost, God's self-communication and presence within and among us. It is part of our historical condition of human existence. It is universally available. And it is intrinsic to ordinary, everyday human experience. Since human existence is social as well as individual, however, grace has a social as well as an individual dimension. Therefore, it has an impact on communities, institutions, and social structures in every sphere of human life.

Official Church Teachings

The major formulations of official Church teachings were drafted in response to the two principal distortions of the nature and effects of grace: *Pelagianism* on the left (because it was too optimistic about human freedom) and *Protestantism* on the right (because it was too pessimistic about human freedom). Against the first tendency toward complete self-reliance, the Church officially affirmed at the *Sixteenth Council of Carthage* (418) and the *Second Council of Orange* (529) the necessity of grace in every person's life, from beginning to end. Against Protestantism, the *Council of Trent's Decree on Justification* (1546–1547) asserted that we are interiorly transformed by the grace of Christ. Because of sanctifying, or habitual, grace, the sinner is no longer an enemy of God, but God's friend. And because of this inner transformation, the human person is now capable of meritorious actions that are at once initiated by God's grace but also fully human. Such merit is really God's crowning of God's own gifts, an expression taken from Augustine.

During the post-Tridentine period, attention was centered on the relationship between human freedom and divine help (*actual* grace), but, as noted above, the issue was never resolved. In the meantime, the biblical and patristic perspectives tended to be pushed to the background. Catholic theology (and Catholic spirituality, too) was so much influenced and shaped by existing controversies, on the one hand, and by the response of the official teaching authority, on the other, that we had, in effect, begun to lose sight of the inner renewal all of us experience through the indwelling of the Holy Spirit and through our concomitant personal union with Christ. The return to the biblical and patristic emphases began under Pope Leo XIII (d. 1903) and reached new levels of emphasis in the Second Vatican Council.

Principal examples of this official teaching follow.

1. Second Council of Orange (529): "If anyone asserts that by his [or her] natural strength he [or she] is able to think as is required or choose anything good pertaining to his [or her] eternal salvation, or to assent to the saving message of the Gospel without the illumination and inspiration of the Holy Spirit..., he [or she] is deceived by the heretical spirit..." (canon 7; see also canons 3–6,8).

2. Council of Trent (1547): "Thus, not only are we considered just, but we are truly called just and we are just, each one receiving within himself [or herself] his [or her] own justice, according to the measure which 'all there are activated by one and the same Spirit, who allots to each one individually just as the Spirit chooses' (1 Corinthians 12:11), and according to each one's personal disposition and cooperation" (*Decree on Justification*, chapter VII).

3. Pope Leo XIII, encyclical letter *Divinum Illud* (1897): "By grace God abides in the just soul as in a temple, in a most intimate and singular manner....Now this wonderful union, which is properly called indwelling...is most certainly produced by the divine presence of the whole Trinity: '...and we will come to them and make our home with them' (John 14:23); nevertheless it is attributed in a particular manner to the Holy Spirit."

4. Second Vatican Council, *Dogmatic Constitution on the Church* (*Lumen gentium*) (1964): "The Spirit dwells in the Church and in the hearts of the faithful as in a temple..." (n. 4).

The Problem of Nature and Grace

"Grace" is essentially *God's self-communication to us, and, secondarily, the effect(s) of that self-communication.* "Nature" refers to *human existence apart from God's self-communication and the divinizing effect(s) of that self-communication.* Theology, however, carries the concept of "nature" one step beyond philosophy or anthropology, namely, to mean human existence without grace but at the same time as radically open to, and capable of receiving, grace (*potentia obedientialis*).

The problem of the relationship between nature and grace is as fundamental a problem as we will ever come upon in all of Christian theology. The nature-grace issue underlies these other relationships: creation and incarnation, reason and faith, law and Gospel, human freedom and divine sovereignty, the history of the world and the history of salvation, human progress and the reign of God, natural law and the law of Christ, humanity and the Church, and so forth.

The problem of nature and grace is focused in the questions: Does grace really change human nature, and if so, how is human freedom preserved? How is the human person able to accept freely the self-communication of God in grace?

The Catholic theological tradition works its way through two extreme positions, to which reference has just been made: the extreme left of *Pelagianism*, which emphasizes so much the self-sufficiency of nature that it effectively submerges the transcendental, supernatural dimension of salvation; and the extreme right of some branches of *Protestantism*, which emphasize so much the self-sufficiency of grace (*sola gratia*) that the dimension of human freedom and cooperation in salvation is effectively submerged. The parenthetical qualification regarding Protestantism is necessary because subsequent historical studies have shown that the positions of Luther, Calvin, and Melanchthon were more nuanced than first appeared.

The Catholic theological tradition is grounded, first of all, in the New Testament's perspective of a Christocentric universe (1 Corinthians 8:6; 15:24–28,44–49; Romans 8:19–23,29,30; Ephesians 1:9–10,19–23; 3:11; Colossians 1:15–20; 3:4; Philippians 3:21; Hebrews 1:2–3; John 1:3; 12:32). All *creation* is oriented toward the *Covenant* between God and the People of God, and the Covenant, in turn, toward the *New Covenant* grounded in the incarnation of the Son of God in Jesus Christ. The human community and the entire world in which the human community exists is oriented toward Christ and is sustained by him. Although *hypothetically* it could have been otherwise, *in fact* it has not been otherwise. There is no creation except in view of Christ. There is no Covenant except in view of Christ. There is no human existence, therefore, except in view of Christ and of our New Covenant in Christ.

This intrinsic orientation of the human person and of the entire human community in Christ radically excludes any dualism, or sharp separation, between nature and grace. Although *in principle* we could know God apart from revelation and apart specifically from the revelation of God in Christ, *in fact* we cannot and do not know God apart from this revelation (Romans 1:18–28; Acts of the Apostles 17:24–27).

Sin is an exercise of human freedom *against* the relationship. Grace, however, is not destroyed by sin. The sinner remains radically open to the possibility of conversion and of forgiveness. If grace were not still available to the sinner, conversion and forgiveness would be impossible. The call of God to conversion and repentance (1 Corinthians 1:9; Galatians 2:20; Romans 8:28–30) would be meaningless unless there were some basis in the human person for responding to the call. Grace supposes even in the sinner the capacity to receive it.

Grace supposes the nature of the human person (the Thomistic axiom cited above). Theologically, nature includes the radical capacity for grace. That radical capacity is called, more technically, a *"supernatural existential."* This "supernatural existential" is *a permanent modification of the human spirit which transforms it from within and orients it toward the God of grace and glory.* This supernatural existential is not grace itself but only *God's offer of grace* which, by so modifying the human spirit, enables it freely to accept or to reject grace. *Every human person has this radical capacity* and many, perhaps most, have actualized it by receiving grace. That does not mean that they are conscious of grace as grace. On the contrary, Rahner argues, "The possibility of experiencing grace and the possibility of experiencing grace *as* grace are not the same thing" (*A Rahner Reader*, p. 185).

If grace supposes nature, so, too, does *nature suppose grace*, to the extent that the grace of Christ orients and sustains us in our very human existence. Catholic theology, from Augustine through Aquinas to the present, has argued, in fact, for a "natural desire" for direct union with God. It is only in the vision of God that the human mind can satisfy fully and definitively its desire to know. No finite reality can satisfy that desire. It is only in the encounter with God, the Absolute, that its deepest spiritual aspirations are fulfilled.

By ourselves, however, we could never go beyond the knowledge of the limited and the created. Such knowledge, on the other hand, is consonant with human existence. We would not thereby be less than human because we could know only the limited and the created. In fact, however, God gives us the radical capacity to transcend the limited and the created. There is now a radical capacity in nature itself, and not merely superadded to nature, by which we are ordained to the knowledge of God. Thus, all dualism between nature and grace is eliminated. There are not in the human person two separate finalities (as Cajetan had stipulated), the one oriented toward the vision of God, and the other oriented toward human fulfillment apart from the vision of God. *Human existence is already graced existence.* There is no merely natural end of human existence. *Human existence in its actual condition is radically oriented toward God.*

This means, too, that the whole universe is oriented to the glory of God (Romans 8:19–23). *The history of the world is, at the same time, the history of salvation.* It means also that authentic human progress in the struggle for justice, peace, freedom, human rights, and so forth, is part of the movement of, and toward, the reign of God (Vatican II, *Pastoral Constitution on the Church in the Modern World, Gaudium et spes*, n. 39).

It means as well that human freedom is never to be conceived totally apart from grace, because it is always modified and qualified by grace; so, too, the grace of God is operative only insofar as it interacts with, and radically transforms, the natural order of the human person. The movement and dynamism of human freedom, on the one hand, and divine sovereignty, on the other, will converge perfectly at the end, in the vision of God and the final realization of God's dominion over all. Each person and all of history will then achieve their definitive meaning.

The foregoing synthesis is derived principally from Karl Rahner's theology. Variations on the same themes are also to be found in other major twentieth-century Catholic theologians, especially Henri de Lubac (d. 1991), in his work *Surnaturel* (1946; see also *The Mystery of the Supernatural* [New York: Herder and Herder, 1967]); Edward Schillebeeckx, in his *Christ: The Experience of Jesus as Lord* (Eng. trans., 1980); Bernard Lonergan (d. 1984), in his *Grace and Freedom: Operative Grace in the Thought of St. Thomas Aquinas* (New York: Herder and

Herder, 1971); and Hans Urs von Balthasar (d. 1988), with a some-what wider variation from Rahner than the others, in such works as *A Theological Anthropology* (Eng. trans., New York: Sheed & Ward, 1967) and a chapter on nature-and-grace in *The Theology of Karl Barth* (Eng. trans., New York: Holt, Rinehart and Winston, 1971).

Latin American liberation theologians, such as Leonardo Boff (*Liberating Grace*, Eng. trans., 1979) and Juan Luis Segundo (*Grace and the Human Condition*, Eng. trans., Maryknoll, N.Y.: Orbis Books, 1973), view grace as the liberating power and presence of God in the context of social and political injustice and oppression. Feminist theologians, like Anne Carr (see *Transforming Grace*, 1988) situate grace in psychological categories that are descriptive of the experience of conversion for women and in social terms of criticizing patriarchal systems and structures. Even more recent theological efforts, stimulated by a dialogue with the natural sciences and the environmental movement, are focusing more directly on the cosmos as the wider context for a theology of grace, emphasizing God's relationship with, and presence to, all forms of life on earth, in this universe, and beyond into the whole of the created order. One thinks here of the work of Thomas Berry (for example, *Befriending the Earth: Theology of Reconciliation Between Humans and the Earth*, Mystic, Conn.: Twenty-Third Publications, 1991). A similar approach is taken, but within an explicitly Christological framework, by Australian Catholic theologian Denis Edwards (*Jesus and the Cosmos*, New York: Paulist Press, 1991).

ORIGINAL SIN

Original Sin is the state or condition in which, because of the sin of Adam and Eve, all human persons are born. The term has two references: the initial, "originating" sin of Adam and Eve (*peccatum originale originans*), and the subsequent "originated" universality of human sin (*peccatum originale originatum*).

Misunderstandings of the Doctrine

There are three common misunderstandings of Original Sin. The *first* rejects the doctrine on the assumption that it denies human freedom and therefore exempts us from responsibility for the condition of the world and of human relationships. With the right technology, politics, and education, we can and must strive to overcome social and individual evils.

The *second* accepts the doctrine implicitly, but under a different name. Original Sin is equated with the absurdity of human existence, about which we can do nothing. We are radically and thoroughly flawed. This is the view of a pessimistic existentialism, usually identified with Sartre.

The *third* misunderstanding equates Original Sin with personal sin—a personal sin which somehow is imposed on our otherwise innocent shoulders. Such a view of Original Sin forces us to accept it, or write it off, simply as a "mystery" or to reject the doctrine as an intrinsic contradiction. How can one be really guilty of a sin that someone else committed, without our knowledge or approval?

Theologians today would probably agree with the philosopher Paul Ricoeur, who refers to the doctrine as a rationalized myth about the mystery of evil. Few of us, if any, doubt the reality of evil, in its individual, social, historical, natural, and cosmic dimensions. The doctrine of Original Sin is a way of naming and "explaining" that reality.

(In the historical references that follow, including the New Testament, Original Sin is attributed to Adam alone, not to Adam and Eve. In two biblical texts where the sin is explicitly ascribed to Eve, by name or as the "woman," the references are clearly demeaning to her as a woman [Sirach 25:24–25; 1 Timothy 2:14–15]. To be sure, Original Sin *is* attributable to both. Ignoring Eve's coequal role is a reflection of the premodern rejection of the fundamental equality of women and men in the human community. The documentary material, however, cannot be changed after the fact in order to make it conform to our own contemporary consciousness.)

Biblical Notion

Old Testament

The Old Testament has no formal concept of Original Sin. Clearly it is aware of sin and especially of its corrupting effects (Genesis 6:12). But

Genesis 2:8–3:24 (the account of the first sin of Adam and Eve) should not be read apart from chapters 4–11. Genesis 3 is only an introduction to what amounts to a series of anecdotes intended to show how sin, once admitted into the world, spreads everywhere, bringing death and destruction in its wake.

New Testament

In the New Testament, and especially in *Paul*, we find the substance of a doctrine of Original Sin (1 Corinthians 15:21–23, and Romans 5:12–21). In the latter passage Paul speaks of Original Sin by first drawing a parallel (v. 18) between Adam and Christ. Because of Adam we are sinners without the Spirit (v. 19), but because of Christ, whose Spirit is active within us (Romans 8:9–11), we are sought by God's saving will and are, therefore, in a state of objective redemption. And both these effects—the one from Adam's sin and the other from Christ's saving work—are antecedent to human freedom and personal decision. What *we* do is to ratify the deed of Adam by personal sin (v. 12) or the deed of Christ by faith.

Paul does not, nor can he, explain *how* this is so, how it is that we are affected by the sin of Adam without any personal decision. He insists only *that* it is so, and he argues from the universality of *death*. Because we all die, we are all implicated in sin, since death is the effect of sin. This sense of our corporate involvement in sin cannot be separated from the biblical belief in the solidarity of the human community and in its notion of corporate personality, sometimes linked with the Suffering Servant of God in Isaiah 40–55.

But since, for Paul, death is the effect of sin, death (the death of Christ) can also be the instrument of its destruction. It is by dying to sin with Christ that we are liberated from it (Romans 6:1–23). Through Christ's death comes new life. In dying with Christ we rise also with him (1 Corinthians 15:3,17; Galatians 1:4). Our dying and rising with Christ does not eliminate the enduring conflict between the spirit and the flesh, but we can achieve the final victory through Christ and the Spirit (Romans 8:1–17).

Although the later doctrine of Original Sin has been read back into Paul's Letter to the Romans, neither biblical scholar nor theologian would agree that it is, in fact, there. Paul's intention was simply to assert that we are all sinners and that we share in a situation that has been universal from the beginning. His real focus is not on Original Sin, but on Christ as our Savior.

Postbiblical Developments

Early Christian Writers; Augustine

The biblical teaching on Original Sin, which is exceedingly brief, was not developed until Augustine. References to Christ's redemptive work in writers like Clement of Rome (d. c. 96) and Ignatius of Antioch (d. c. 107) yield only glancing allusions to the source of evil from which we have been redeemed. The Greek Fathers (Irenæus, Basil, Gregory of Nyssa, et al.) were too much involved in opposing the heresies of Gnosticism and Manichaeism (both of which insisted that all matter is evil) to lay stress on such a doctrine. They were trying to show, on the contrary, how the Incarnation elevated and transformed the whole created order. Others, like Justin (d. c. 165) and John Chrysostom (d. 407) denied that we bear the guilt for Adam's sin. We are culpable only insofar as we willingly imitate our first parents in sinning. Adam's sin is a model or prototype.

The situation was just the opposite for Augustine. He faced not those who rejected the goodness of nature but those who glorified nature to excess, i.e., the Pelagians. Augustine portrayed Original Sin (a term he coined) as a situation in which the whole human race finds itself (*massa damnata*), but from which only some individuals are rescued by an utterly gratuitous act of God's mercy. Although God desires the salvation of all in Christ, only those who are justified by faith and Baptism are actually saved. (Pelagius had denied that infant Baptism imparted forgiveness of sin, since infants could not be guilty of sin.)

Augustine linked Original Sin with *concupiscence* (i.e., the human person's *spontaneous desire* for material or sensual satisfaction). It is an effect of Original Sin and is transmitted through sexual intercourse, that is, by the libido in the parents' love by which a person first comes into existence. To the extent that concupiscence infects every human act, all of our deeds are in some sense sinful. Augustine did not suggest that every such deed is a *new* sin, but he never worked out

187

the intrinsic difference between original and personal sin because, for him, the consequences of both kinds of sin are the same in the next world.

Augustine's view had been partially anticipated by earlier Latin writers, beginning with Tertullian (d. c. 200) who tended to see a direct and corrupting connection between Adam's sin and our subsequent human condition, and he spoke of the propensity to sin that is sown in each soul through the parent. Cyprian of Carthage (d. c. 250) was the first to argue that infants are baptized because of the "contagion of death" inherited from Adam. This severe view was continued in the West by Ambrose (d. 397) and Ambrosiaster (late fourth century), but it reached its fullest and most enduring form in Augustine.

Middle Ages; Aquinas

In the Middle Ages, from Anselm of Canterbury (d. 1109) onward, the essence of Original Sin was increasingly equated with the *lack of sanctifying grace* (medieval theology's new term for the divine indwelling) brought about by Adam's actual sin. Concupiscence now appeared simply as a consequence of Original Sin (Aquinas). Thus, it became possible to explain how Baptism blotted out Original Sin without at the same time canceling all of its effects, including concupiscence and death.

For Thomas Aquinas, grace comes to the human person, first, to vivify human life for the journey to the special destiny of the Christian life, and, second, as a remedy for Original Sin. But the theological counterpart to grace is not sin, but human nature. Original Sin is presented as an "illness" which, though it weakens and injures human nature, does not render human nature ugly or radically perverse.

The Council of Trent

The Council of Trent (sixth session, 1547) agreed with the Protestant Reformers that Original Sin, caused by Adam's sin, affects all (except Mary) and that it is really overcome by justification. But *against* the Reformers, who tended to follow Augustine's more pessimistic line,

Trent insisted that Original Sin does not consist in concupiscence itself, since this remains even in the justified. Rather, Original Sin is the lack of original righteousness (justice) and holiness.

Post-Tridentine theology tried to answer the obvious difficulties associated with the traditional doctrine of Original Sin—e.g., How is it possible to translate blame from Adam and Eve to ourselves?

Contemporary Theologians

Contemporary theologians (especially Rahner) reject the notion that Original Sin is simply the sinful act of the first man or is a matter of collective guilt, since both of these views lead to contradictions and are not required by the doctrine of Original Sin in any case.

Sin is a mystery because grace itself is a mystery. Just as the self-communication of God is antecedent to our free decision or any evidence of our worthiness (*ante prævisa merita*) and qualifies and conditions our moral lives, so there is a lack of holiness which is also antecedent to our personal decision and which also qualifies and conditions our moral lives. Because the mystery of Original Sin is subordinate to the mystery of grace, it appears in the Bible only after our divinization by the Spirit is explicitly grasped (as in Paul).

Contemporary theologians also reject the notion (suggested by Augustine and others) that Original Sin is more pervasive and more universal than is redemption, since everyone is affected by Original Sin but some are not effectively touched by the cross and resurrection of Christ. On the contrary, although Original Sin and (objective) redemption are two constitutive components of the human situation in which the power of sin is strong and pervasive, the power of grace and of the universal salvific will of God are even stronger and more pervasive.

A *positive* statement of contemporary theology (especially Rahner) comprises the following principles:

1. All human beings are offered grace and redemption *through Christ*, and not simply insofar as they are human beings or members of the human community. This grace is given us as the *forgiveness of sins*. Indeed, Jesus himself thought of his own death on the cross as an expiatory death "for all."

2. God wills that all should have grace. Thus, if it is not present, this must be because of some guilt freely incurred (otherwise it contradicts God's will). Yet the absence of grace (a condition incurred freely by sin) is also against God's will, even when the individual is not at all responsible for its absence. This lack of grace, which ought not to be, has in an *analogous* sense the character of sin: It is very much *like* sin, in that it is contrary to the will of God, but it is at the same time *unlike* sin, in that it does not involve a free decision against God's will. But God remains attached to us in spite of the sin of Adam and Eve. God bestows grace freely now, not in view of Adam, but in view of Christ. As children of Adam and Eve, we do not have grace. As sons and daughters of God in Christ, we do.

3. The lack of grace is an inner condition of each one of us in that we are all human, but it is also *situational*. We are born into a "situation" in which, because of the sin of Adam and Eve, grace is not at our disposal in the manner and measure which God intended. Accordingly, we now have to make our decision about salvation under the impact of both *concupiscence* and *death*, each of which is an effect of Original Sin. For that reason, and in spite of the work of Christ on our behalf, all of us are still directly affected by Original Sin in our daily lives. We are, to that extent, "wounded" or weakened in our natural powers.

4. On the other hand, this does *not* mean that death and concupiscence are totally unnatural, that we would not have experienced them were it not for the sin of Adam and Eve. They are indications of the as-yet-incomplete victory of grace. And they have been part of human history from the beginning.

5. Our human situation in the face of a free moral decision is always *dialectically* determined: We are in Original Sin through Adam and Eve and at the same time are oriented toward Christ and the God of our salvation. Either we freely ratify our state of Original Sin by personal sin, or we freely ratify our redeemed condition by faith, hope, and love. Our situation is one in which our decision to ratify is always qualified by concupiscence and death, on the one hand, and by the fact of our having been redeemed, on the other. Our moral standing before God, however, is always and finally determined by our free choice, weakened though it be.

6. The doctrine of Original Sin indicates, beyond what has already been stated in the preceding points, (a) that grace is given historically, and not as a necessity of human existence; (b) that it comes from Christ and in view of the merits of Christ (therefore, was available even before the Word became flesh), and not from Adam and Eve at the beginning of history; (c) that the goal of history today, in light of Christ's redemptive work on our behalf, is greater than it was at the beginning of history; (d) that our situation of death, concupiscence, and other experiences of human limitation cannot simply be abolished in history, because they were present from the beginning; and (e) that our efforts to overcome the effects of Original Sin (injustice, war, etc.) constitute a duty that cannot be completed in this world and, therefore, a duty that engages us for the entirety of human history.

Official Teachings of the Church

Sixteenth Council of Carthage

The Sixteenth Council of Carthage (418), a gathering of two hundred bishops, condemned the errors of the British monk *Pelagius,* who reduced the sin of Adam and Eve to one of bad example and insisted that grace is not absolutely necessary for salvation. The canons (or principal doctrinal formulations) of the council were later approved by Pope Zosimus (d. 418).

Indiculus

The *Indiculus* (between 435 and 442), a summary of the doctrine of grace, was composed probably by Prosper of Aquitaine (d. 460), a disciple of Augustine and the strongest opponent of *semi-Pelagianism,* which held that none of us requires grace at the beginning but that God grants it as needed later. This document subsequently received papal approval and was used as the standard exposition on grace by the end of the fifth century.

Second Council of Orange

The Second Council of Orange (529) finally settled the matter against the *semi-Pelagians*. This local council accepted the teachings of Cæsarius of Arles (d. 542), another of Augustine's disciples, plus material from Prosper of Aquitaine. Pope Boniface II (d. 532) approved Orange's action.

Council of Trent

The Council of Trent (sixth session, 1547), *Decree on Justification*, said: We have lost innocence through the sin of Adam, and have inherited not only death but also sin. Nevertheless, we are redeemed by Christ interiorly and not just by a divine decree which leaves us unchanged within. Although we still suffer from the effects of Original Sin, God's justice inheres in us (see especially chapter 16 of the decree). The *Decree on Original Sin* of 1546 restated the teachings of the councils of Carthage and Orange: The consequences of the sin of Adam and Eve were transmitted to all human beings by propagation, not by imitation; all human beings are born into a state of sin and guilt, i.e., of spiritual death, which only the redemptive work of Christ, mediated by Baptism, can remit; and, against Luther, concupiscence, which stems from sin and remains after Baptism, is not properly sin in itself.

Humani Generis

Pope Pius XII's encyclical letter *Humani Generis* (1950) insisted on the truly gratuitous character of the supernatural order (i.e., God was not *required* to create us for glory) and on the importance of our common descent from one pair of parents (monogenism).

SYNTHESIS: A THEOLOGY OF HUMAN EXISTENCE

It is obvious by now that theology does not follow the same clear lines of direction that one might find in such disciplines as accounting, law, chemistry, or the statistical sides of political science and economics. Like the humanities, theology is concerned with the question of human existence. But human existence can only be studied by human beings. We ourselves raise the question *about* ourselves. We have already noted in chapter 4 that there is no standpoint from which we can "look at" God objectively, as detached observers. This is so because God permeates as well as transcends us. For the same reason, there is no standpoint from which we can "look at" ourselves objectively, as detached observers. We are at once the subject and the object of the inquiry. Consequently, our answers to the question of human existence will always be inadequate. They lead to further questions and to further attempts at better answers.

The Christian "standpoint" is inevitably qualified by the conviction that God is real, that the real God is available to us, and that the real, available God is a principle of consciousness, knowledge, and moral action within each one of us. This is so even for those who do not explicitly advert to God's presence as well as for those who explicitly reject the possibility of a divine source and principle of human existence.

We are persons who are self-aware (i.e., we not only *know*; we *know that we know*, and we know ourselves *as knowers*). *We are beings in possession of ourselves as subjects.* And this is the case even before we have had an opportunity to reflect on our existence from various disciplinary points of view.

The knowledge that we have of ourselves before any of us has had an opportunity for systematic investigation and reflection is called *a priori* knowledge (as opposed to *a posteriori* knowledge, i.e., the knowledge of objects which is disclosed to us through study and examination). For the Christian, and indeed for every religious person, our *a priori* knowledge of ourselves as persons includes the light of faith as (what Rahner calls) a "supernatural existential." In other words, *God is present in us from the beginning as the principle and the power of self-knowledge.* We are, "from the very circumstance of [our] origin, ... already invited to converse with God" (*Pastoral Constitution on the Church in the Modern World,* n. 19). We do not come to the knowledge of God by a step-by-step investigation of data, arguments, and evidence. Rather, *our knowledge of God begins at the very moment when we become really conscious of ourselves as personal subjects,* as human beings, with all that this implies.

The Christian knows herself or himself as a creature, and a limited, flawed creature at that (Original Sin). But *the Christian also knows herself or himself as a person addressed by God in history, as a person touched and transformed by God's presence (grace) in Christ (redemption).* What the Christian hears about herself or himself from the corpus of religious doctrines, especially in Sacred Scripture, the Christian recognizes as something of what she or he already knows about herself or himself in faith. *In the presence of some authentic statement about the meaning of human existence, the human person recognizes its truth almost spontaneously.* Aquinas called this "knowledge by connaturality." It "rings true," as it were, in light of ordinary human self-awareness and experience. What is proposed is seen as consonant with what is immediately experienced in the act of self-consciousness.

Grace makes possible human nature's capacity for the connatural reception of God's self-communication in the Word (Christ, Scripture, preaching). *Hypothetically,* human nature could exist without the capacity for God. *Historically,* human nature has the capacity and cannot be without that capacity. However, human nature is open to, but cannot absolutely demand, God's self-communication in grace. Grace remains always *grace* ("gift," "favor"). We have no title to grace, and yet, given the actual historical order and the will of God, we are not fully human without it.

Theological anthropology includes in principle all of the rest of theology, i.e., each of the other major doctrinal elements of Christian faith, and especially the mystery of God. Christology, however, is the recapitulation of theological anthropology. It is only in Christ that we come to a full understanding of who we are as human beings and of our final destiny beyond this world and its history.

SUMMARY

1. Although an individual creature, the *human person* is constituted by social relationships with other persons, by history, and by the world in which she or he lives. Indeed, the human person is, in a sense, a *cocreator* of the world with God.

2. The *Old Testament* understands the *human person* primarily as a *creature* who *is* a *body* (and does not simply *have* a body) and whose hope of salvation is expressed in terms of the *resurrection of the body.* Bodiliness implies *coexistence* with other "bodies," especially in *sexual* relationships. That coexistence must be *responsible,* but because human freedom can be abused, human

existence is also *sinful*. In spite of the spread of sin, human existence is *hope*-filled.

3. The *New Testament* also understands human existence as *historical*. It is limited existence, qualified by sin. *Jesus* calls us all to *conversion* and *repentance,* to a working out of our salvation through a change in our relationships with others. *Paul,* too, speaks of the *bodily* condition of human existence and of our common hope in the resurrection of the body, a hope based on the saving work of Christ and the power of the Holy Spirit. For *John,* to be human is to live by *grace,* i.e., by the presence of God in our hearts and in our midst. Our sinful selves and our sinful world would be lost if it were not for Christ and the *new life* that he brought us and that we enjoy even now.

4. The *early Christian writers* made no real breakthroughs in our understanding of human existence. There was some strong emphasis on the human person as the *image of God* and on human history as the *history of divinization and salvation* (Irenæus, and others). It is Christ who *recapitulates* within himself all that is human in the individual and in history. But a tendency to *dichotomize* between matter and spirit perdures.

5. The *medieval period* focused principally on the person as *object*, a creature among creatures: lower than the angels, higher than the animal kingdom. "Man" was an unchanging essence, unchanged by environment and by history. But at least the beginnings of a turn to the *subject* can be found here, e.g., in medieval theology's concession that one could receive the grace of Baptism by *desire*, a subjective rather than objective principle.

6. Under the impact of scientific, philosophical, and theological developments outlined in chapter 4, a fundamental shift in our understanding of human existence has occurred in the so-called *modern period*. Emphasis is placed on our self-awareness as persons, on our freedom and responsibility, and on the fundamental equality of women and men in the human community. This new direction in thought is reflected to some discernible extent in the Second Vatican Council's *Pastoral Constitution on the Church in the Modern World*.

7. *Nature* refers to the human condition apart from grace, but with the radical capacity to receive grace. *Pure nature* is a *hypothetical* concept. It refers not only to human existence apart from grace, but to human existence without the radical capacity to receive grace as well (known as the *potentia obedientialis* in medieval Scholastic theology, and as the "supernatural existential" in modern Transcendental Thomist theology).

8. *Grace supposes nature,* but *nature* in its own way *also supposes grace,* insofar as the grace of Christ sustains us in our actual, historical existence and orients us toward our one supernatural end, eternal life in the final reign of God.

9. Nature is not directly a biblical concept. It is one that is inferred from subsequent reflection on the New Testament's proclamation of the new order of grace in Christ. We infer who we are as *creatures* of God by reflecting on who we have become through the grace of Christ.

10. The concept of "nature" also underlines the essentially *gratuitous* character of God's self-communication. We are bodily creatures who are fully intelligible and fully open to human growth apart from grace. *In historical fact,* however, we have been given the radical capacity for grace, and therefore *the fullness of our growth is linked inextricably with our growth in the grace of Christ as well.*

11. The concept of *nature* is not without dangers. Its use easily leads one to a *dualistic* understanding of human existence, as if grace were something merely *added* to, or superimposed upon, nature.

12. The reality of *grace*, on the other hand, is fully and deliberately expressed in the Bible. In the *Old Testament* it means literally a "favor," and has to do with our attitude toward the needy and with the experience of liberation from distress and from sin.

13. In the *New Testament* the word for grace, *charis*, becomes a key word in the Christian message, designating the *goodwill of God*, expressed in Christ and producing such *effects* as justification, faith, love, and new life. Grace stands in opposition to *works* and *law*, which cannot of themselves save us. *Salvation* is a free gift, not owed us because of our performance of works or our observance of laws.

14. The *doctrine* of grace developed systematically under the impact of certain major heresies: *Gnosticism*, which challenged the *universality* of grace and of salvation; *Pelagianism*, which challenged the *necessity* of grace for salvation; and historic *Protestantism*, which challenged the *effectiveness* of grace in transforming us interiorly. Major opposition to each of these views was mounted by *Irenæus, Augustine,* and the *Council of Trent.*

15. The *Eastern* tradition viewed grace as *divinization;* the *Western* tradition was more *moralistic*, viewing grace as liberation from the bondage of sin, as having a *healing* function. *Aquinas* synthesized the two traditions, viewing grace as both healing and divinizing.

16. This Thomistic balance was disrupted in subsequent centuries through the introduction of the concept of "pure nature," making grace extrinsic to nature, and by the fruitless controversies (*De Auxiliis*) regarding the relationship between freedom and grace.

17. The Catholic theological tract *De Gratia*, in place from the time of the Reformation until Vatican II, was fashioned against Protestantism. As such it emphasized the quantitative aspects of grace, as well as the process by which it is gained, lost, increased, and diminished. After Vatican II grace was

viewed primarily as God's self-communication, as historical, as universally available, as part of ordinary human existence, personal and social alike.

18. The official Catholic doctrine of grace is contained in the teachings of the Sixteenth Council of Carthage (418), the Second Council of Orange (529), and the Council of Trent's (1546–1547) *Decree on Justification*. Grace is necessary in every person's life from beginning to end. Because it interiorly transforms us, we are capable of actions that are meritorious in God's eyes.

19. With regard to the relationship between nature and grace, the *Catholic theological tradition* avoids two extreme positions: the one which emphasizes nature so strongly that it effectively diminishes the significance of grace, and the other which emphasizes grace so much that it effectively suppresses nature.

20. The Catholic theological tradition is rooted in the New Testament's perspective of a *Christocentric* universe, where all creation is oriented toward the covenant between God and humanity in Christ.

21. Although, *hypothetically*, we could know God apart from the "supernatural existential" (i.e., the radical capacity for grace which God gives us from the beginning), *in fact* we do not know God apart from that *a priori* condition.

22. This *"supernatural existential"* is not grace itself, but only God's offer of grace. It is an offer given to every person. *Grace, therefore, supposes nature, i.e., the radical capacity to receive grace. But nature also supposes grace. There is a kind of "natural desire" for direct union with God.* It is only in that union that we can finally and fully satisfy our desire to know and to become what we sense we are called to become.

23. The *whole universe, too, is oriented by grace to the reign of God. The history of the world is, at the same time, the history of salvation.* Therefore, grace transforms not only persons but the whole created order (Romans 8:19–23).

24. Contemporary theologies of grace, so much influenced by Karl Rahner, also have *liberationist, feminist, and ecological* dimensions.

25. Our understanding of the relationship between nature and grace, however, must also contend with the reality of *sin*, both *personal* and *Original*. Original Sin is the state or condition in which, because of the sin of Adam and Eve, all human persons are born.

26. The *Old Testament* has no formal concept of Original Sin, although it is surely aware of sin and of its widespread corrupting effects.

27. The *New Testament*, and especially *Paul*, develops the notion of "original" sin by drawing a parallel between the sin of Adam and the saving work of Christ (Romans 5:12–21). *We either ratify the sin of Adam and make it our own by personal sin, or we ratify the work of Christ and make it our own by faith.* Just exactly *how* we are affected by the sin of Adam, Paul cannot say. *That* we are affected

by the sin of Adam is clear from the fact that we all *die*, and death, he perceives, is a consequence of sin. Only by dying with Christ can we overcome the destructive effects of sin.

28. This biblical teaching remained undeveloped until *Augustine*. Faced with those who exaggerated the goodness of nature (Pelagianism), he stressed the sinful and wounded condition of every person. He insisted that while everyone is affected by sin, not everyone is rescued from it in fact. A certain theological disposition toward *predestinationism* followed from such an emphasis. Augustine also linked Original Sin with *concupiscence* so strongly that he suggested that the sin (and one of its principal effects, concupiscence) was transmitted in the sexual union of our parents.

29. By the *Middle Ages*, and especially with *Aquinas*, concupiscence was viewed simply as a consequence of Original Sin, and the sin itself as simply *the lack of sanctifying grace*. Thus, by Baptism the sin is completely blotted out (sanctifying grace is bestowed), although the effects of sin remain.

30. *Contemporary theologians*, especially *Rahner*, reject the notion that Original Sin is simply the sin of the first human being or is a matter of collective guilt. These views, they hold, cannot be sustained biblically or theologically. They also reject the Augustinian notion that Original Sin is more pervasive and universal than is grace.

31. Positively, contemporary theologians argue that (1) every human person is *offered* grace; (2) the *absence* of grace follows from some *guilt* freely incurred by the *person*; (3) the absence of grace also follows from the human *situation* itself in which the *effects* of Original Sin weaken our capacity to decide in favor of salvation; (4) death and concupiscence, however, are not totally unnatural, since history begins at the point where neither is absent; (5) our human situation, therefore, is *dialectically* determined; i.e., we are, at the same time, wounded by the effects of sin and oriented toward Christ and the God of our salvation; and (6) all of our efforts to overcome the effects of Original Sin constitute a duty that cannot be completed in this world, and, therefore, a duty that is never done.

32. The *official teachings of the Church* insist on the reality of Original Sin, on the absolute necessity of grace for salvation, and on the interior effects of such grace: the Sixteenth Council of Carthage (418), the *Indiculus* (435–442), the Second Council of Orange (529), the Council of Trent (1547), and Pope Pius XII's encyclical *Humani Generis* (1950).

33. The difficulty in constructing a theological anthropology is rooted in the inescapable fact that we are at once the investigators and the ones investigated. *We cannot achieve a standpoint from which a pure, unobstructed, completely objective understanding of human existence is possible.*

198

34. Nevertheless, there is in every one of us a radical capacity to know ourselves as persons in the light of the reality of God, and to know God as the ultimate object of our every striving toward human growth and fulfillment. *Hypothetically*, human nature could exist without the capacity for grace; *in fact*, however, we do not exist without it.

35. It is only in Christ that we come to a full understanding of who we are as human beings and of our final destiny beyond this world and its history.

SUGGESTED READINGS

Boff, Leonardo. *Liberating Grace*. Maryknoll, N.Y.: Orbis Books, 1979.

Carr, Anne. *Transforming Grace: Christian Tradition and Women's Experience*. San Francisco: HarperCollins, 1988.

Daly, Gabriel. *Creation and Redemption*. Wilmington, Del.: Michael Glazier, 1989.

Dreyer, Elizabeth. *Manifestations of Grace*. Wilmington, Del.: Michael Glazier, 1990.

Duffy, Stephen J. *The Graced Horizon: Nature and Grace in Modern Catholic Thought*. Collegeville, Minn.: The Liturgical Press, 1992.

Haight, Roger. *The Experience and Language of Grace*. New York: Paulist Press, 1979.

Macquarrie, John. *Principles of Christian Theology*. 2d rev. ed. New York: Scribners, 1977, chapter 3.

Rahner, Karl. *Foundations of Christian Faith*. New York: Seabury Press, 1978, chapters 1–5.

_____. *Hominisation: The Evolutionary Origin of Man as a Theological Problem*. New York: Herder & Herder, 1965.

_____. *A Rahner Reader*. Ed. Gerald A. McCool. New York: Seabury Press, 1975, chapters 1–4,9.

Ricoeur, Paul. *The Symbolism of Evil*. Boston: Beacon Press, 1969.

Rondet, Henri. *Original Sin: The Patristic and Theological Background*. New York: Alba House, 1972.

_____. *The Grace of Christ: A Brief History of the Theology of Grace*. Westminster, Md.: Newman Press, 1967.

Schillebeeckx, Edward. *Christ: The Experience of Jesus as Lord*. New York: Seabury Press, 1980.

PART TWO

God

WE move now from the question of human existence to the question of God because the reality of God enters into the very definition of what it means to be human.

But if God is so fundamental and so central to human existence, why is it that many of us reject or practically ignore the reality of God? Why is it so difficult to *believe* in God? Why do any of us, Christian or non-Christian, believe in God at all (chapter 6)?

Belief in God must arise from some experience of God, clear or obscure. How, when, where, and under what circumstances is the reality of God made available to us? Are there recognizable signs of God's self-communication, or *revelation?* What is it that is communicated (chapter 7)?

At the core of the Christian religion is the doctrine of the *triune God*. How has the doctrine of the *Trinity* developed, from its biblical origins to the present day? What are its principal elements? What place and importance does it hold in the total exposition and practice of the Christian faith (chapter 8)?

How does the triune God relate to us in history? What is *divine Providence?* Does God intervene *miraculously* in our lives and in human history? What of the *problem of evil?* Does *prayer* have an affect on God? What of the *language* we use to speak to, and of, God? What does it mean to speak of God as a *Person* or as *Father* (chapter 9)?

What is to be said of *other religions?* To what extent, if at all, are non-Christian religions signs and instruments of God's saving love toward the whole human family? Does Christianity have a unique and special place in salvation history (chapter 10)?

Every theological question is a variation on the *one* theological question: the God-question. In the final accounting, the mystery and doctrine of the Trinity means that the God who created us, who sustains us, who will judge us, and who will give us eternal life is not a God infinitely removed from us (the Father), but a God of absolute closeness, a God who is communicated truly in the flesh, in history, within our human family (the Son), and a God who is present in the spiritual depths of our being and in the core of our unfolding human history as the source of enlightenment and of community (the Holy Spirit).

The doctrine of the triune God is at the heart and center of Christian faith.

V I

Belief and Unbelief: The Search for God

THE PROBLEM

The reality of God enters into the very definition of what it means to be human. Human existence is qualified from the beginning by the God-given radical capacity ("supernatural existential," *potentia obedientialis*) to get beyond ourselves and to reach out toward that which transcends us, the Absolute, and toward that which raises us to a new level of existence, a sharing in the life of the Absolute (grace). The question of God, in other words, is implied in the question of human existence. And the opposite holds true as well. As soon as we raise the problem of God, we are confronted with the problem of human existence.

But if the divine is so central to the existence of human persons, why do so many of us reject or ignore the reality of God? How is it that our radical capacity for grace is not universally actualized? In short, why are there unbelievers as well as believers?

The problem of unbelief is complicated by the fact that *unbelief is always relative*. Unbelief is a negative concept. It presupposes something positive which it negates. From the point of view of religious faith (whether Christian, Jewish, or Moslem, for example), unbelief is a denial or at least an avoidance of God. But from another point of view, these religious traditions themselves may be forms of unbelief. To the ideological Marxist, religious faith may be a refusal to believe in the dialectical historical process or the classless society. To the positivist, religious faith may represent a stubborn refusal to believe in the conclusions of scientific experimentation.

The term *unbelief* is being used in this chapter to mean *the denial or at least disregard of the reality of God* (whether God is named "ultimate concern," the Transcendent, the Absolute, the "beyond in our midst," the ultimate dimension of secular experience, Being, or whatever else). There are, of course, different *kinds* and different *degrees* of unbelief. There are also different *sources*.

According to the Second Vatican Council, *atheism* (which we are equating here with unbelief) has many forms. The *Pastoral Constitution on the Church in the Modern World* summarizes these: *classical atheism,* or the outright denial of God; *agnosticism,* or the refusal to decide whether to believe in God or not (a decision wherein one effectively decides *not* to believe in God); *positivism* (which rejects all reality which cannot be verified by scientific testing); an excessive *humanism* (which exaggerates the human capacity to control the universe through technology and the exercise of reason and free will); the rejection of *false notions* of God which the atheist assumes to be official doctrine; the transfer of ultimate concern from God (the Transcendent) to material things (the totally immanent); and the transfer of blame for social evil from individual, institutional, environmental forces to God as the One who thwarts the struggle for *liberation* by shifting our attention from this world to the next.

"Undeniably," the Pastoral Constitution declares, "those who willfully shut out God from their hearts and try to dodge religious questions are not following the dictates of their consciences. Hence they are not free of blame." But then the council proceeds to an extraordinary admission: "Yet believers themselves frequently bear some responsibility for this situation.... To the extent that they neglect their own training in the faith, or teach erroneous doctrine, or are deficient in their religious, moral, or social life, they must be said to conceal rather than reveal the authentic face of God and religion" (n. 19).

Some major *sociologists of religion* would agree with the main lines of the council's explanation, but their analyses are more broadly based. Thus, at a 1969 symposium in Rome, cosponsored by the Vatican's Secretariat for Non-Believers (now called the Pontifical Council for Dialogue with Non-Believers), sociologist Robert Bellah noted that the phenomenon of unbelief was limited to relatively small groups of intellectuals and cultural elites until the eighteenth century. With the expansion of these classes (especially through education and the concomitant rise in literacy) in the nineteenth century, a new spirit spread to a larger public: a fuller appreciation for the dignity of the individual and the importance of free inquiry, on the one hand, and a reaction against authority (or at least authoritarianism), on the other. This was accompanied, as we already noted in chapters 4 and 5, by a shift in *philosophical* emphasis from the objective to the *subjective* orders. Belief became less an imposed system than a matter of personal decision.

So widespread was this change that many nineteenth-century rationalists and positivists predicted the demise of religion. But that never happened. Why not? Because the antireligious forces made the same mistake that many religious people have committed: They confused religious belief with *cognitive* belief. Thus, with the collapse of cognitive belief, religious belief as such was sure to follow.

The large portion of religious people had never regarded cognitive, intellectualized belief as essential to their religious lives. What they embraced instead was an *embodied* truth, transmitted not through definitions and logical demonstrations, but through narratives, images, and rituals. This insight is fully consistent with the Pastoral Constitution's insistence that "the witness of a living and mature faith... penetrating the believer's entire life... activating him [or her] toward justice and love..." is even more important in overcoming unbelief than is "a proper presentation of the Church's teaching" (n. 21).

Faith, according to Bellah and other sociologists, is deeply embedded in our existential situation and is part of the very structure of human experience—an insight which Bellah correctly attributes to Blaise Pascal (d. 1662) and Søren Kierkegaard (d. 1855), and which we might also link with Karl Rahner and Bernard Lonergan as well. Religion, therefore, is not "a matter of objective-cognitive assertion which might conflict with science, but a symbolic form within which one comes to terms with one's fate" (see *The Culture of Unbelief,*

p. 46). Faith, consequently, is an *inner* reality, and the belief which follows from faith is inner-directed. But that does not mean that faith and belief are purely private. Such faith and such belief relate us to others, to the total human community, and indeed to the whole universe—bringing us even to the point of sacrificing our lives for others.

How widespread is the opposite, unbelief? Again, it depends on how you define it. In one sense at least, everyone is a believer; everyone believes in something important. And insofar as people express their belief, they are "religious." In the context of the United States, for example, such beliefs may issue forth in what Bellah has called "civil religion." It is the linking of one's search for personal authenticity with a sense of national identity and national purpose. The Peace Corps, established during the presidency of John F. Kennedy (d. 1963), would be one major instance of it. It had something of the character of a secular monastic order, complete with a vow of poverty and a heroic devotion to the service of others.

But if you take belief to mean some *explicit* affirmation of the reality of God, then unbelief is considerably more prevalent, and certainly more in evidence than in previous centuries—again, because of advances in education generally, in literacy and communications particularly, and because of the contemporary philosophical shift to the "subject."

And that is why the obverse side of the problem of God is the problem of the unbelieving person. Indeed, the problem of God—of belief and unbelief—becomes a problem only when it is concretely stated in such terms. According to the Bible and to the kind of philosophical theology represented by Transcendental Thomism, the presence of God is integral to the very structure of our historical existence. Therefore, the person who does not "fear God" (in the biblical sense of responding obediently to the presence and call of God) somehow does not exist, and that person's nature is somehow less than, or other than, human. On the other hand, the unbeliever *does* exist. He or she is there. And that is the problem. We shall not, in this chapter or anywhere else in this relatively ambitious book, solve that problem. There are some things that we can do no more than accept as part of our historical situation (a "given" of reality) and deal with as intelligently and as constructively as possible.

The problem of belief and unbelief, therefore, is not primarily the problem of communicating the correct information about God so that everyone will be able to know it, and in knowing it perceive at once its truth. Nor is it simply a problem of laziness or bad will on the part of those to whom the information is directed. Rather, *the problem of belief and unbelief is,* once again, *the problem of human existence.* Is human existence finally and ultimately worthwhile? Is it meaningful? Is it purposeful? Is it intelligible? Is it directed to some end beyond itself? Or is it simply "full of sound and fury, signifying nothing"? And the problem of human existence is but the other side of the *problem of God.* For the question of the intelligibility, purposefulness, and worth-whileness of human existence is always answered, positively or negatively, in terms of God or some verbal surrogate for God.

TRADITIONAL ARGUMENTS FOR BELIEF

Augustine

Catholicism has worked out of two different philosophical traditions: the Platonic and the Aristotelian. The impact of Platonic philosophy took a distinctive turn with Augustine (d. 430). God is truth itself, he said. As the sun is the source of light by which our eyes see the visible world, so God is the source of illumination of the mind by which it sees eternal truths. Truth draws the mind to itself, but the mind is distracted by the sinful will, which draws it down toward inferior things. Only when the will is healed by the grace of Christ can the mind attain to truth. It is the restlessness of the human heart that points us in the direction of God ("Our hearts are restless until they rest in You"). To find God, one must look inward. Anselm of Canterbury's (d. 1109) ontological argument (that God is "a being than which nothing greater can be conceived") is the most thoroughgoing expression of this approach.

Aquinas

With Thomas Aquinas (d. 1274) the Aristotelian tradition enters Catholic philosophy and theology. The path of knowledge, and the path to God, begins not from within but from without, from sense experience. We infer from what is known in the visible, material world what is unknown in the invisible, spiritual world. Thus, he proposed "five ways" to prove the existence of God, all based on observation of the way things are and work in the external world: the argument from *motion* (there must be a Prime Mover), the argument from *causality* (every effect must have a cause), the argument from *necessity*, or *contingency* (all beings are possible, but one must be necessary if there are to be any beings at all), the argument from gradation, or *exemplarity* (our ideas of more or less, of better or worse, presuppose some standard of perfection), and the argument from *design* (the consistent and coherent operation of the whole universe demands some intelligent and purposeful designer) [see *Summa Theologiæ*, I, q. 3, a. 3]. No one argument actually "proves" the existence of God. They are simply ways in which one who already believes can make sense of her or his belief in God.

Pascal

Blaise Pascal (d. 1662) acknowledged that there is no clear evidence for the existence of God. What we confront is "the presence of a hidden God." God is or is not? Which is it? The game is on. If one gambles that God is not, that person has nothing to gain and everything to lose should God exist. If, on the other hand, one wagers that God exists, that person has everything to gain and nothing to lose. It is only in our knowledge of Jesus Christ that we have access to God. Apart from Christ "all communication with God has been cut off."

Newman

Kant had effectively killed the ontological argument, the other arguments were all boiled down to the argument from design, and that was killed by Darwin's theory that adaptations emerge randomly and are selected naturally because of their usefulness in the struggle for survival. The effective end of the traditional "proofs" meant that a different kind of apologetics was needed.

Accordingly, Augustine's way of immanence reappeared in Cardinal John Henry Newman (d. 1890). For Newman, what pointed toward God from within the subject was the experience of being obliged by one's conscience. This was not a naive argument that God inscribed moral laws on the heart. Rather it was Newman's attempt to analyze why, having arrived at a conclusion about what one ought to do, that one experienced one's conclusion as an "ought," i.e., as obliging one in some way. Newman recognized that this did not constitute a "proof" as such. But, as he argued at length in *An Essay in Aid of a Grammar of Assent* (New York: Oxford University Press, 1984; orig. ed., 1870), we do not assent to most positions because of a conclusive syllogistic proof, but because of "emerging probabilities" which support it. In that perspective, the apologetics of conscience seemed very persuasive.

One finds this view also in Maurice Blondel's (d. 1949) "method of immanence" and in the writings of Bernard Lonergan (d. 1984), who was so much influenced by the *Grammar of Assent*.

THE NINETEENTH-CENTURY DEBATE ABOUT GOD AND RELIGION

Outside the Church, the nineteenth century marks a very important stage in the criticism of Christian faith and practice. The first stage of the Enlightenment critique (e.g., the Deists, Voltaire [d. 1778]) mocked Christianity as superstitious and recommended natural religion as a rational substitute. The second stage (Diderot [d. 1784], d'Alembert [d. 1783], Hume [d. 1776]) held that natural religion up to scorn, in effect attacking all religion, regardless of type. The attack was based on the assumption that religion was, at root, a mistake in reason, a logical error. It dismissed religion as silly.

Feuerbach, Marx, Nietzsche, and Freud all made a much graver charge, however. For them, religion is not an object of mockery, but a danger. Religion is not silly; it is harmful. For Marx, it is a kind of "opiate." For Freud, an illusion. For Nietzsche, a repression. Thus, atheism moves from reviling religious belief as unenlightened foolishness to assaulting it as a destructive obstacle to human freedom and progress.

What enters the debate about God and religion in the nineteenth century is a sense of moral obligation in atheism. Hume could be amused by religion; Feuerbach or Nietzsche could only be outraged by it. One must not only be an unbeliever; one must be an active opponent of religious belief. One might say that the Enlightenment offered an intellectual critique of religion; the nineteenth century leveled a moral indictment of it.

Nietzsche

Nowhere is this clearer than in Friedrich Nietzsche, where the key issue is drawn in the famous parable of the madman in *Die fröhliche Wissenschaft* ("The Joyous Science" [1882]), unhappily translated as *The Gay Science*. This may well be the most famous passage in all of Nietzsche's writings. It is the first time that he makes the proclamation that "god is dead." The following points are worth noting:

1. The madman comes seeking God in the marketplace and makes his proclamation of God's death when those in the marketplace mock him. He claims that the people in the marketplace and he have killed God, but they refuse to recognize the implications of their deed.

The location in the marketplace is important. Nietzsche loathed the commercial world of the nineteenth century. He saw that in the social Darwinist, "dog-eat-dog," survival-of-the-fittest marketplace of uninhibited capitalism the idea of God was irrelevant. This is why the people in the marketplace have "killed God." But the nineteenth-century bourgeoisie were incapable of facing up to the full nature of this deed. They tried to preserve the Judeo-Christian ethic without the metaphysics which undergirded it. Nietzsche regarded this as a contemptible evasion of the frightening consequences of the death of God.

2. Nietzsche's sweeping images for these consequences—"wiping away the horizon," "unchaining the earth from the sun," random movement in empty space without any orientation, "no up or down, no back or forth," endless plunging into a vacuum—are designed to give a heady sense of the full horror of facing a world in which the idea of God is dead. The horror is that maintaining the Christian ethic is simply a prejudice, a form of intellectual laziness, possibly an evasion of the too frightening fact of an amoral universe.

3. The madman concludes that he has come too soon (a frequent image in Nietzsche) and that people are not yet ready to hear that

212

God is dead. But he was convinced that inevitably the modern European would have to face the brutal fact whether she or he liked it or not.

4. Living in a godless universe is more than we can bear. To confront the amorality of the universe is beyond human endurance. That is why one has to be *more than* human. And so, in his next book, *Thus Spake Zarathustra* (1883–1891), he proclaims the more-than-human, the Superman. Only the Superman can live in the world without the illusion of God.

SOME CONTEMPORARY VIEWS OF THE PROBLEM

For most of the major figures engaged in the contemporary discussion of God, the usual "proofs" for the existence of God are dead. (A notable exception would be Alvin Plantinga, a Calvinist Scholastic philosopher at the University of Notre Dame.) Other pathways, more in keeping with Newman and Blondel, are being followed.

Küng

Swiss theologian Hans Küng, professor at the University of Tübingen in Germany, discusses the problem of belief and unbelief in *On Being a Christian* (Eng. trans., New York: Doubleday, 1976). "In order to answer the question of God," he insists, "it must be assumed that man accepts in principle his own existence and reality as a whole..." (p. 70). Our attitude to reality, if we are ever to reach God, has to be one of fundamental *trust* and *confidence*. Not that such trust automatically eliminates uncertainty of every kind. Reality is there as a fact, and yet it remains always enigmatic, without any clearly visible support or purpose. The challenge is to find some kind of satisfactory answer, and in this quest the believer is in competition with the unbeliever. Which one can more convincingly interpret the basic human experiences?

Even someone who does not think that God exists could at least agree with the hypothesis that *if* God existed, a fundamental solution to the problem of human existence would be provided. God would be seen as the ultimate reason for all that is, as reality's ultimate support, ultimate goal, and ultimate core. Threats of death, meaninglessness, rejection, and nothingness would be overcome. But we cannot proceed from the *hypothesis* of God to the *reality* of God.

Besides, it is also possible to formulate the *opposite* hypothesis: that God does *not* exist. One must concede that it is indeed possible to deny the reality of God. Atheism (or unbelief in its most explicit form) cannot be refuted on the face of it. There is more than enough *uncertainty* about reality to justify, or at least explain, why someone might decide to deny the reality of God. On the other hand, atheism is also incapable of positively excluding the alternative. If it is possible to deny God, it is also possible to affirm God. Just as atheism rests on a *decision* about the ultimate meaning (or meaninglessness) of reality, so, too, does belief. Just as there is enough *uncertainty* about reality to explain, and perhaps even justify, unbelief, so too there is enough *clarity* in reality to explain, and perhaps even justify, belief.

And so the terms of the problems become clear. *If* God is, God is the answer to our most fundamental questions about reality and about human existence. *That* God is cannot be proved or demonstrated or otherwise established beyond all reasonable doubt. It can ultimately be accepted only in a *confidence* founded on reality itself. Since the "evidence" is so uncertain, it cannot be imposed upon us conclusively. There remains room for human freedom. We are free to decide: to affirm the fundamental worthwhileness of reality and of human existence, or to deny it. Each path is fraught with risks. The decision not to decide (agnosticism) is itself a decision against the intelligibility and purposefulness of reality. It is a vote of no confidence, and *confidence* is what belief and unbelief are really all about.

Lonergan

Although Bernard Lonergan (d. 1984) might not disagree with Küng's analysis of the problem, he proceeds from a more explicitly philosophical starting point than Küng does. That starting point is his approach to human understanding and the structures of consciousness. Religion, he says, is based on the drive to understand. The "question of God is implicit in all our questioning," he writes (*Method in Theology*, New York: Herder and Herder, 1972, p. 105). Even when all the goods of health, education, security, and wealth are in our

214

possession, we still hunger to know who we are. And we infer from this hunger to know that there is some intelligent source of this hunger.

"There lies within [our] horizon a region for the divine, a shrine for ultimate holiness," he continues. "It cannot be ignored. The atheist may pronounce it empty. The agnostic may urge that he finds his investigation has been inconclusive. The contemporary humanist will refuse to allow the question to arise. But their negations presuppose the spark in our clod, our native orientation to the divine" (p. 103).

How, then, does belief differ from unbelief? The believer is attentive to the data of his or her own consciousness, and the unbeliever is not, or at least interprets the data differently. Since no one has ever seen God (John 1:18), one stands always before a silent and invisible God. One "sees," and another does not "see." Being irreligious is like being tone-deaf or color-blind. At least that is how the believer looks at it. But perhaps the believer perceives what is not there. The believer, therefore, can never be certain that his or her belief is accurate and true.

On the other hand, it is in believing that reality assumes intelligibility. "People in love," he writes, "have not reasoned themselves into being in love. The apologist's task is to aid others in integrating God's gift with the rest of their living" (p. 123).

Baum

Following not Lonergan but the French philosopher and theologian Maurice Blondel (d. 1949), Canadian theologian Gregory Baum pursues a similar line of analysis. Belief is not a matter of accepting as true certain elements of some unlikely story about God, but a matter of interpreting human experience in a particular way.

Blondel had named his approach "the method of immanence." The Christian message reveals the hidden (supernatural) dynamism present in human life everywhere. The message is not foreign to life; it explains what has been going on in life and where it is leading us.

In his book *Faith and Doctrine* (1969), Baum carries Blondel's apologetical approach one step further. He identifies the elements of ordinary human experience which contribute to a believing as opposed to an unbelieving response. He calls them "depth experiences," i.e., ordinary human experiences that are memorable, that are the source of many decisions, and that tend to unify human life. Those depth experiences may be specifically religious, or they may be secular. In the final accounting, however, they are all religious in that they ultimately put us in touch with God.

The specifically *religious* experiences are the experience of the holy and the experience of contingency. The so-called *secular* depth experiences are the experience of friendship, encounter, conscience, truth, human solidarity, and compassionate protest.

The religious literature of the world abounds in testimonies to the experience of the *holy*. It is what William James (d. 1910) described in his *The Varieties of Religious Experience* (Cambridge, Mass.: Harvard University Press, 1985; orig. ed., 1902) as a "sense of reality, a feeling of objective presence, a perception of what we may call 'something there,' more deep and more general than any of the special and particular 'senses' by which the current psychology supposes existent realities to be originally revealed." Rudolf Otto (d. 1937), another major analyst of religious experience, insisted in fact that the sense of the sacred or of the transcendent is a purely *a priori* category. It is not something derived from sense experience, he argued in his classic work, *The Idea of the Holy* (New York: Oxford University Press, 1958; orig. ed., 1917). The experience of the sacred is rooted instead in "an original and underivable capacity of the mind implanted in the 'pure reason' independently of all perception." (The similarity to Rahner's notion of the "supernatural existential" is fairly clear.)

The experience of *contingency* is our feeling of radical dependency, our sense of limitation, even of insignificance, and our concomitant sense of insecurity. At the same time we are profoundly aware that we belong to another who is vast, strong, caring, eternally reliable, that we are part of a larger unity which has meaning and in the context of which we find the strength to face life. It is an experience alluded to many times by Jesus himself (the parables of the lilies of the field and the birds of the air, for example) and systematically developed in the works of the great nineteenth-century Protestant theologian Friedrich Schleiermacher (d. 1834).

The experience of *friendship* gives us a new kind of self-possession. We become reconciled with ourselves as we are accepted by another. And since we become more ourselves, we have more energy available for the mission of life. Closely related to the experience of friendship is the experience of *encounter* (as in a teacher-student relationship) that profoundly changes and shapes our lives. The Jewish philosopher and theologian Martin Buber (d. 1965) is one of the principal systematizers of encounter experiences.

Conscience, too, is a depth experience. It is the experience of moral responsibility. We realize the call to transcend ourselves and our own self-interest and to act on behalf of others. In so doing we sense that we are acting in accordance with what is deepest in us and thus opening ourselves to reality and to life as it is and as it is meant to be. As we saw above, a thinker who has assigned to conscience a central place in Christian theology is Cardinal John Henry Newman (d. 1890).

Truth is another depth experience. At certain moments in our lives, whether in conversation, research, or reading, our resistance to truth is overcome and we experience a conversion of the mind to a higher level of consciousness. We suddenly see the picture. And because we see, we are able to plan and redirect our lives differently, make decisions in a new way, and enter more deeply into personal unity. St. Augustine stands out among those who have understood life as a series of conversions to truth, as has Bernard Lonergan.

The experience of *human solidarity* makes us aware of the unity of the human family and its common destination to growth and reconciliation. The experience transcends our ideologies and even shatters them. We realize our interdependence. We share in the joys and sufferings of people everywhere. We recognize the deathly, inhuman character of prejudice, hatred, and discrimination. Baum names Pope John XXIII as one in whom this experience bore astounding fruits. One could add the work of Methodist theologian James Fowler, who, building on the developmental theories of Lawrence Kohlberg (d. 1987), speaks of the sixth stage of faith-development as "universalizing faith."

Connected with the sense of human solidarity is yet another depth experience, that of *compassionate protest.* It is the experience of those who become deeply disturbed by the misery in life, who are burdened by the presence of injustice, exploitation, and war. They identify with those who have no hope in this world. Such persons

217

speak out as prophets, as accusers, as critics, even at the risk of their reputations, their physical safety, and their lives. Martin Luther King, Jr. (d. 1968), personifies this experience. And so, too, perhaps do some of the theologians of liberation in Latin America.

Depth experiences such as these bring us in touch with reality at its deepest level, and in so doing they bring us in touch with ourselves. Or to put the matter differently, as we reflect on the content and meaning of our human experiences, we begin to see that there is more to life than meets the eye, that there is an intelligibility (to use the Lonerganian term) which grounds, explains, and directs all that is. *To believe means to affirm the intelligibility of reality.* Or, in Baum's terms, *to believe means to recognize the significance of our depth experiences.* These experiences put us in touch with the God who is immanent to human life. They explain our lives and give them direction.

Berger

A sociologist of religion in the Lutheran tradition, Peter Berger has developed an apologetic similar to Baum's. He, too, argues for an anthropological starting point in his *A Rumor of Angels: Modern Society and the Rediscovery of the Supernatural* (New York: Doubleday, 1969, pp. 61–94). What is there, if anything, in ordinary human experience which gives rise to belief in transcendental reality? What Baum called "depth experiences" Berger calls "signals of transcendence." He defines them as "phenomena that are to be found within the domain of our 'natural' reality but that appear to point beyond that reality" (pp. 65–66). As such, they express essential aspects of our being. They are not the same as Jung's archetypes, because they are not unconscious and do not have to be excavated from the depths of the mind. They belong to ordinary, everyday experience.

Berger identifies five: our propensity for order, our engagement in play, our unquenchable spirit of hope, our sense of outrage at what is thoroughly evil, and our sense of humor.

Our propensity for *order*, Berger argues, on the side of philosopher of history Eric Voegelin, is grounded in a faith or trust that ultimately all reality is "in order." This transcendent order is of such a character that we can trust ourselves and our destiny to it. Human love—parent for child, man for woman—defies death. Death cannot annihilate the reality and fruits of love. There is an order which banishes chaos and which will bring everything to a unity at the end. And belief in God vindicates that order.

Play also mediates transcendence. When one is playing, one is on a different time, no longer measured by the standard units of the larger society but by the peculiar ones of the game itself. In the "serious" world it may be Tuesday, 11:00 A.M., March 5, 1999. But in the universe of play it may be the second inning, the fourth round, the fifth match, or two minutes before the end of the half. The time structure of the playful universe takes on its own specific quality, a kind of eternity. Religion—belief in God—is the final vindication of childhood and of joy, and of all the playful gestures that replicate these.

Even the Marxist philosopher Ernst Bloch (d. 1977) has argued that our being cannot be understood adequately except in connection with our unquenchable propensity to *hope* for the future. We realize ourselves in projects, as we seek to overcome the difficulties and the limitations of the here and now. The artist, in failing health, strives to finish her creative work. A man risks his life to save another. Herein, we have a kind of depreciation or even denial of the reality of death. And it is precisely in the face of the death of others, and especially of those we love, that our rejection of death asserts itself most loudly. It is here, above all, that everything we are calls out for a hope that will refute the empirical fact. So deeply rooted is this attitude that one might conclude it is part of the very essence of human existence. Belief in God vindicates the gestures in which hope and courage are embodied.

The argument from *damnation* or *outrage* is the other side of the argument from hope. Some evils (e.g., the Nazi war crimes) are so obscene that we are convinced they cry to heaven for vengeance. And we are equally convinced they *will* be condemned and punished. Belief in God validates our deeply rooted conviction in a retribution that is more than human.

Finally, there is the argument from *humor*. By laughing, we transcend the present, the given, what is. We see discrepancies. The neighborhood bully is in deathly fear of spiders. A fastidious writer makes an egregious mistake in grammar. So we see that our imprisonment in the conditions of the present is not final. Things are not always what they seem. They can be other. Belief in God vindicates our laughter.

Rahner

For Karl Rahner (d. 1984), the experience of God is an experience of transcendence, of reality that is above and beyond and beneath the reality that we see and taste and smell and feel. Among the pre-eminent experiences of transcendence are a fear that threatens everything, a surpassing joy, a sense of absolute responsibility, faithfulness, or love, an unconditional hope beyond all hopelessness, a restlessness in the quest for truth.

In all these situations, Rahner argues, "God, as the condition which makes all this possible, is already experienced and accepted, even if this is not expressly and objectively formulated. This is true even if the word 'God' is never heard and is never used as the term for the direction and goal of the transcendental experiences known in this way" (*The Practice of Faith: A Handbook of Contemporary Spirituality* [Eng. trans., New York: Crossroad, 1983], p. 58).

Lash

English theologian Nicholas Lash argues that the whole notion of religious experience has been miscast, most influentially by William James. James seeks to isolate religious experience as a particular kind of experience, presumably the experience of a particular object (God) or kind of object (the Holy). Lash counters this by claiming that religious experience is an ingredient of all experience, that it is a way of experiencing everything, not an experience of one type of thing (see *Easter in Ordinary: Reflections on Human Experience and the Knowledge of God*, Notre Dame, Ind.: University of Notre Dame Press, 1990; orig. ed., 1988).

Earlier Jesuit theologian Michael Buckley had shown that modern atheism grows out of theology's surrendering its task of reflecting on God to philosophy in the seventeenth and eighteenth centuries (*At the Origins of Modern Atheism* [New Haven: Yale University Press, 1987]). Philosophy, in various ways, attempted to found its own treatment of God on arguments, each of which was called into question by philosophical critics, as we saw above. What was lost was any experiential claim regarding religion. That situation began to change with Newman and continues to change with the various authors in this section of the chapter, from Küng to Lash.

OFFICIAL TEACHINGS OF THE CHURCH

The preceding apologetical approaches do not seem to be inconsistent with the official teachings of the First Vatican Council and are certainly not inconsistent with those of the Second Vatican Council. The former council declared that "God, the beginning and end of all things, can be known with certainty from the things that were created through the natural light of human reason, for 'ever since the creation of the world his eternal power and divine nature, invisible though they are, have been understood and seen through the things he has made' (Romans 1:20)..." (*Dogmatic Constitution on the Catholic Faith*, chapter 2).

Nor is the First Vatican Council's teaching a denial of the necessity of grace. The same council insists on the necessity of faith for salvation, and faith is always the work of grace (chapter 3 of the Constitution). Furthermore, we have already argued, with Rahner and others, that human reason does not exist in a historical vacuum. Our history is the history of salvation. Our reason, indeed our whole consciousness, has been radically modified by God's offer of grace. There is no such order of reality as a purely natural order. Likewise there is no such reason as a purely natural reason. Hypothetically, that could have been the case. But in fact it is not. Thus, when Vatican I argues that we can know God through the power of human reason alone, that teaching is not necessarily inconsistent with the view that all of our knowledge of God is, in the first instance, made possible by God, by the offer of grace, by the "supernatural existential."

The Second Vatican Council, we pointed out earlier in this chapter, acknowledges that there are many reasons for unbelief, at least one of which is the failure of the Church to live up to its own teaching. If the Church is to persuade the world of the reality of God, it will not be done simply through a more effective communication of doctrine.

It will happen chiefly through its putting the Gospel into practice (*Pastoral Constitution on the Church in the Modern World*, n. 21).

The council also seems to be pursuing the same theological course outlined above. The Church knows "that its message is in harmony with the most secret desires of the human heart.... Far from diminishing the human person, its message brings to human development light, life, and freedom.... 'Thou has made us for Thyself, O Lord, and our hearts are restless till they rest in Thee' (*Confessions* of St. Augustine)" (n. 21). For that reason we must be prepared always to enter into dialogue with one another, believers and unbelievers alike, in order to learn from one another's human experiences and to assist one another in the interpretation of those experiences (nn. 21 and 23).

What is to be said, finally, of the abiding presence of *unbelief* in the world? According to Vatican II (the *Pastoral Constitution*, nn. 19–22; the *Dogmatic Constitution on the Church*, n. 16; and the *Decree on the Church's Missionary Activity*, n. 7), not every instance of positive atheism, i.e., explicit rejection of God, is to be regarded as the result and the expression of personal sin. Even the atheist can be justified and receive salvation if he or she acts in accordance with his or her conscience. Over against the earlier teaching of the textbooks, the council assumes that it is possible for a normal adult to hold an explicit atheism for a long period of time, even to life's end, without this implying moral blame on the part of the unbeliever.

The council also seems to rule out the notion that those who die without explicit faith in God but who live good lives are destined for some form of natural happiness alone. The council, in the *Decree on the Church's Missionary Activity*, implicitly affirms the thesis that the natural order is already graced and that there can be no purely and distinctly natural end of human existence. Even the so-called nonbelievers can reach a saving faith without having accepted the explicit preaching of the Gospel.

CONCLUSION

Belief and unbelief are two sides of the same human coin. They represent different interpretations of the mystery of human existence. *The believer interprets reality and human existence as finally worth-*

222

while, intelligible, and purposeful. The unbeliever interprets reality and human existence as finally without intelligibility or purpose and, therefore, without ultimate worth. *Neither belief nor unbelief can be established or disproved by arguments alone.* The believer sees what the unbeliever does not see. Still, the believer's perception is not arbitrary. There are dimensions of human experience which cannot be explained fully apart from the God-hypothesis—call them "depth experiences," "signals of transcendence," or whatever else. This does not mean that the case for belief is clearly the stronger of the two, but only that *the case for belief is not without warrants.*

Michael Novak, a disciple of Lonergan, expressed the problem movingly in his *Belief and Unbelief* (p. 24), notwithstanding the gender-exclusive language of the time in which he wrote:

> The believer need not forgive God for the suffering of this world; like Job, he may accuse God to his face. But he does not cease to remain faithful to the conscience which cautions him not, finally, to be dismayed. Belief in God, he knows, could be an empty illusion, even a crime against his own humanity. He knows the stakes. If he is faithful to his conscience and thinks clearly concerning what he is about, he has no place in his heart for complacency or that sweet pseudoreligious 'peace' that sickens honest men. His belief is not unsteady—quite the contrary—though he knows that the thread supporting it, however firmly, is so slender that in the night it cannot by any means be seen. This commitment to conscience keeps him faithful, and his daily experience may make his commitment as plausible as Sartre's experience made his, but there is no final way short of death of proving who is right. Each man has but a single life, during which his choice may go either way. That choice affects many things in his life, but one thing it does not affect: his reliance on his own conscience (formed, no doubt, in friendship with other men) as his sole concern and comfort.

> No one has seen God.

SUMMARY

1. The *problem* of belief and unbelief is focused in these questions: If God is so central to human existence, why do so many apparently reject or ignore God? How is it that their radical capacity for grace is not actualized? Moreover, "unbelief" is a relative concept. "Unbelief" in relation to whom or

what? In this chapter the term refers to the denial or at least the disregard of the reality of God.

2. There are different *sources* or reasons for unbelief: a refusal to decide (*agnosticism*), a rejection of all scientifically unverifiable reality (*positivism*), an exaggeration of the human capacity to control the universe (excessive *humanism*), *false notions* of God, substitution of material goods for God (*materialism*), transfer of blame for social evil from human and institutional failure to the stunting effects of religious faith.

3. The *Second Vatican Council* acknowledged that the failure of believers to live up to their beliefs is one of the chief causes of unbelief.

4. *Sociologists of religion* attribute the growth of unbelief to the expansion of the naturally critical intellectual classes through *education*, the rise in *literacy*, and a *philosophical shift* to the *subject*. Belief becomes more a matter of personal decision and less a matter of socially imposed doctrine.

5. The collapse of belief in the nineteenth century, however, did not bring with it the collapse of religion because the sort of belief that collapsed was *cognitive* belief, not religious belief (in God). That noncognitive belief is deeply embedded in our existential situation and is part of the very structure of human experience.

6. For that reason, some would argue that pure unbelief does not exist. Everyone believes in something important insofar as everyone is in quest of personal authenticity. If, on the other hand, belief is understood to mean explicit acknowledgment of the reality of God, then there is as much unbelief around as there are people and institutions which say, or imply, that they prescind completely from the reality of God.

7. In the end, the problem of belief and unbelief is at once the problem of God and the problem of human existence, for reasons which we have already spelled out in Part One. Belief in God is belief in the worthwhileness, the intelligibility, and the purposefulness of human existence.

8. Traditional arguments for belief include those of *Augustine* (the restlessness of the human heart), *Aquinas* (the "five ways"), *Pascal* (the "wager"), and *Newman* (conscience).

9. The basis for the contemporary discussion about belief and unbelief was laid in the nineteenth century, with the direct, morally based attack upon belief in God by Feuerbach, Marx, Nietzsche, and Freud. Nietzsche's critique is particularly severe.

10. Contemporary Catholic approaches attempt to unify belief in God and the affirmation of human existence. *Hans Küng* admits that neither belief nor unbelief can be finally proved, but the hypothesis of God answers more questions about the meaning and purpose of reality and of human existence

than does unbelief. To believe is to approach reality with *confidence*. *Bernard Lonergan* argues that belief follows from reflection on the structures of our own consciousness and the process of human understanding. Our unrestricted desire to know implies some intelligent source of this hunger for understanding. *Gregory Baum*, following Maurice Blondel, adopts a method of immanence. Belief in God explains and gives direction to our deepest human experiences. God is present to life as the source of life's meaning and as the principle of life's movement. *Peter Berger* has a similar approach. He calls the "depth experiences" of Baum "signals of transcendence." For *Karl Rahner* the experience of God is the experience of transcendence. And for *Nicholas Lash* religious experience has to do with the way we experience everything rather than an experience of one type of thing.

11. The *First Vatican Council* taught that we can come to the knowledge of God through natural reason alone. This teaching is not inconsistent with our present understanding of the relationship of nature and grace (see chapter 5). Since this is already a graced order of existence, reason does not operate in a historical vacuum. God is already present to it, elevating it to a higher order of existence. It is *graced reason* which, according to Vatican I, can know God as the beginning and end of all things.

12. The *Second Vatican Council* insists, furthermore, that the Church's message is in harmony with the most secret desires of the human heart. There is a correlation, in other words, between belief in God and self-knowledge, which is exactly the point contemporary theologians are making. It is erroneous, therefore, to assume, as our earlier textbooks did, that all those who explicitly reject or ignore God are culpable and subject to damnation. Even the unbeliever can attain a saving faith implied in his or her commitment in conscience to those values and activities which are reflections of divine reality.

SUGGESTED READINGS

Baum, Gregory. "A Modern Apologetics." *Faith and Doctrine: A Contemporary View*. New York: Newman Press, 1969, pp. 51–90.

Burrell, David. *Knowing the Unknowable God*. Notre Dame, Ind.: University of Notre Dame Press, 1986.

Caporale, Rocco, and Antonio Grumelli, eds. *The Culture of Unbelief*. Berkeley: University of California Press, 1971.

Gilkey, Langdon. *Naming the Whirlwind: The Renewal of God-Language*. Indianapolis: Bobbs-Merrill, 1969.

Haught, John. *What is God? How to Think About the Divine*. New York: Paulist Press, 1986.

Kasper, Walter. *The God of Jesus Christ*. New York: Crossroad, 1984.

Küng, Hans. *Does God Exist? An Answer for Today*. New York: Doubleday, 1980.

Marty, Martin. *Varieties of Unbelief*. New York: Doubleday, Anchor Books, 1966.

Novak, Michael. *Belief and Unbelief: A Philosophy of Self-Knowledge*. New York: Macmillan, 1965.

Shea, John. *Stories of God: An Unauthorized Biography*. Chicago: Thomas More, 1978.

VII

Revelation: God's Self-Disclosure to Us

QUESTIONS

The Bible itself points out that "no one has ever seen God" (John 1:18). And yet we talk *about* God and *in the name* of God all the time. From where do we derive our "information" about God? How does God communicate with us? Under what conditions and circumstances does such communication occur? How can we be sure that we have, in fact, been "in touch with" God rather than with our own wish-projections and imaginings, as Freud contended? Does God communicate with others besides ourselves? Or is God hidden, by deliberate design, from great segments of the human family?

Is the *form* of divine self-disclosure verbal, dramatic, mystical, historical, social, political, natural, cosmic, or what? *What* is communicated or disclosed? Is it facts about God and the "other world"? Is it God's own self? Would we have "known" that which is revealed even if it were not revealed? If God does indeed reveal, why is it that so many people seem either indifferent to, or ignorant of, divine revelation? Or is it perhaps very difficult to pick up God's "signals of transcendence"?

The questions generated by the problem of revelation, therefore, are the same as the questions generated by the problem of belief and unbelief, touched upon in chapter 6. In this chapter we are addressing the same questions, but from a more deliberately biblical, historical, doctrinal, and theological point of view.

BIBLICAL NOTIONS OF REVELATION

Old Testament

Divine revelation in word and deed is central to the Old Testament: "The deeds wrought by God in the history of salvation manifest and confirm the teaching and realities signified by the words, while the words proclaim the deeds and clarify the mystery contained in them" (Vatican II, *Dogmatic Constitution on Divine Revelation*, n. 2). At the heart of the faith of Israel are the conviction and affirmation that God has intervened in history, modifying the course of Israel's historical experience and the lives of individuals within Israel.

Although the Old Testament does not use the technical term *revelation* to describe this process, the expression "word of Yahweh" seems to come closest in meaning. Even in the case of the *theophanies* (e.g., Yahweh's appearance in human form to Abraham to announce the birth of Isaac and the destruction of Sodom, Genesis 18:1–33), it is not the fact of *seeing* God that is primary in importance but rather the fact of *hearing* God's word, as manifested in the events of history.

Early creedal statements (Deuteronomy 6:20–25; 26:5–10; Joshua 24:2–13), hymns (Exodus 15:1–18), psalms (Psalms 78, 105, 106), and narrative accounts (Joshua to Kings) affirm God's self-disclosure in history. God is also revealed in the glory of nature (Psalms 8, 104) and in religious experience, especially in a liturgical setting (Psalms 18:6; 48:9).

Theophanies and Oracles

The earliest stage of revelation in the Old Testament is characterized by the predominance of theophanies and oracles. Yahweh appears in order to conclude an alliance and changes the name of Abram to Abraham (Genesis 17:1–22; for other appearances to Isaac and Jacob see Genesis 26:2; 32:25–31; 35:9). It is impossible, however, to determine precisely the nature of such manifestations. At times they are presented as if they were external visions, and at other times as internal ones. In general, the Old Testament reflected its own Oriental milieu. That is to say that the Bible employs techniques that were characteristic of its cultural environment: e.g., divination, dreams, omens. These were, of course, purified of their polytheistic or magical connotations.

Before a war or the conclusion of a treaty, Israel would "consult" God through its seers and especially its priests (1 Samuel 14:36; 22:15). Israel acknowledged that God could be revealed in dreams (Genesis 20:3; 28:12–15; 37:5–10; 1 Samuel 28:6; 1 Kings 3:5–14). Joseph excelled in the interpretation of dreams (Genesis 40–41). Gradually Israel began to distinguish between dreams by which God truly communicated with the prophets (Numbers 12:6; Deuteronomy 13:2) and those of the professional seers (Jeremiah 23:25–32; Isaiah 28:7–13).

Sinai Covenant

The Sinai Covenant is a decisive movement in the history of revelation, but it can be appreciated only in the light of the entire history of salvation. Through the Covenant, Yahweh became head of the nation and delivered Israel from Egypt. In return, Yahweh exacted a pledge of fidelity to the Law (Exodus 20:1–17) or to the "ten commandments" (Exodus 34:28). The Law discloses the divine will. Obedience brings blessings; transgression brings malediction. The whole destiny and subsequent history of Israel was now tied inextricably to the will of God as manifested in the event by which Israel was liberated from the bondage of Egypt. The prophets never ceased to apply to the events of their own day the implications of the Sinai Covenant. Whatever legislation followed was considered a prolongation of the Decalogue, or Ten Commandments.

Prophecy

The phenomenon of prophecy also enters into the Old Testament's basic notion of revelation. *Moses* is the prototype of the prophets (Deuteronomy 34:10–12; 18:15,18), but it is only with *Samuel* that prophecy becomes a frequent occurrence in the history of Israel (1

Samuel 3:1–21). *Amos, Hosea, Micah, Isaiah,* the prophets who preceded the Exile (which lasted from the destruction of Jerusalem by the Babylonians in 587 B.C. to the Edict of Cyrus in 538 B.C.), conceived themselves as guardians and defenders of the moral order prescribed by the Covenant. Their preaching is always a call to justice, to fidelity, to the service of the all-powerful God. But because of Israel's frequent infidelity to the Covenant, the divine word uttered by the prophets more often than not brought condemnations and warnings of punishment (Amos 4:1; 5:1; 7:10–11; Hosea 8:7, 14; 13:15; Micah 6–7; Isaiah 1:10–20; 16:13–14; 28:13; 30:12–13; 37:22; 39:5,7).

Jeremiah occupies a particularly important place here because he attempted, as the others did not, to determine the criteria by which the authentic word of God could be recognized: (1) the fulfillment of the word of the prophet, i.e., what the prophet says will happen, happens (Jeremiah 28:9; 32:6–8; Deuteronomy 18:21–22); (2) the prophecy's fidelity to Yahweh and to the traditional religion (Jeremiah 23:13–32); and (3) the often heroic witness of the prophet himself (1:4–6; 26:12–15). For Jeremiah the word of Yahweh is always superior to himself and to everything else. Yahweh places the word in his mouth as if it were a material object (1:9). At times it provides delicious nourishment (15:16); at other times, it is a source of torment (20:9,14). Through the word, Israel is summoned to fidelity to the Law and the Covenant. It is a word of independent and irresistible dynamism and force: "Is not my word like fire, says the Lord, and like a hammer that breaks a rock in pieces?" (23:29).

Deuteronomy

With the book of Deuteronomy the two currents, legal and prophetic, converge. The connection between *Law (Torah)* and *Covenant* is emphasized more than ever. The history of Israel is the history of its fidelities and infidelities to both. If Israel wishes to live, it must put into practice every word of the Law (Deuteronomy 29:28), for this Law from God is the source of all life (32:47). Deuteronomy also enlarged upon the meaning of the "word of Yahweh" already given in Exodus. It no longer applies only to the Ten Commandments but to every clause of the Covenant (28:69), i.e., to the whole corpus of moral, civil, religious, and criminal laws. It placed everything under the heading of the Mosaic Law (28:69; 30:14; 32:47). The word of the Law is something to be interiorized: "No, the word is very near to you; it is in your mouth and in your heart for you to observe" (30:14). The Law consists precisely in this: "You will seek the Lord, your God, and you will find him if you search after him with all your whole heart and soul" (4:29).

Historical Literature

Parallel to the prophetic and deuteronomic currents is the historical literature (Joshua, Judges, Samuel, Kings), which places the word of God in an even more thoroughly historical context. Hereafter, Israel would never think of its religion apart from the category of *history*. It is the word of God which makes history and renders it intelligible. Throughout the long history of the kings, the words of Yahweh penetrate the course of events and express their religious significance (e.g., 1 Kings 2:41; 3:11–14; 6:11–13; 2 Kings 9:7–10; 21:10–15).

A particularly significant text is the *prophecy of Nathan* (2 Samuel 7) which provides the foundation for royal messianism. By reason of this prophecy the dynasty of David became directly and forever allied to Yahweh (2 Samuel 7:16; 23:5). This prophecy, furthermore, is the point of departure for a theology, elaborated by the prophets, which is eminently one of *promise*, turned always toward the *future*, in contrast to the theology built on the Sinai Covenant, whose demands are meant to apply to the present moment.

Exile

At the time of the Exile, the prophetic word, without ceasing to be a living word, became increasingly a *written* word. The word confided to *Ezekiel* is inscribed on a scroll which the prophet had to assimilate before he could preach its contents (Ezekiel 3:1–3). It remains always a word of *judgment*. Ezekiel repeats the refrain that Yahweh does acts of judgment in order that Israel might know that their God is Yahweh, that it is Yahweh who acts, and that Yahweh is holy (6:14; 7:9, 27; 11:12; 12:20; 13:23). Ezekiel meantime attempts to form a new Israel during its period of Exile. His word is also a word of *comfort* and *hope* (33:1–9). But it is never enough simply to hear the word; one

231

must live it (33:32). In Deutero-Isaiah (Isaiah 40–55) the word is boldly personified as a dynamic reality which creates history itself. It dominates history (45:19; 48:16). "So shall my word be that goes out from my mouth; it shall not return to me empty, but it shall accomplish that which I purpose, and succeed in the thing for which I sent it" (55:11).

Wisdom Literature

Yahweh is revealed, finally, in the *wise conduct of the faithful of Israel*. The wise person is the one who fulfills the Law of God (Sirach 15:1; 19:20; 24:23; Ecclesiastes 12:13), for all *wisdom* comes from God (Proverbs 2:6). The wisdom of God is manifested in the works of God and is communicated to those who love God (Sirach 1:8–10; Wisdom 9:2; Job 28:12–27). Wisdom comes forth from the mouth of God from the very beginning of the world (Sirach 24:3–31). Thus, wisdom is itself identified with the word of God. It is at once creative and revealing (Wisdom 7–9).

Indeed, *creation* itself discloses the reality of God. The whole created order gives echo to the word of the One who named its creatures, and these created beings manifest the divine presence, majesty, and wisdom (Psalm 19:2–5; Job 26:7–13; Proverbs 8:23–31; Sirach 42:15–25, 43; Wisdom 13:1–9).

Apocalyptic Literature

In the postexilic period (after 539 B.C.) a distinct genre of literature develops, which contemporary biblical scholars call "apocalyptic" (the Greek word for revelation is *apocalypsis*, "uncovering"). It is marked by an emphasis on the hidden plan of God which explains the historical suffering of a people. This plan is revealed to a specific prophet or seer (e.g., Daniel 7:15–16; 1 *Enoch* 1:1–2; 37:1–5), with assurance that God is on the side of the persecuted (Daniel 7:23–27) and with hope for future vindication through a final cataclysmic judgment (Daniel 8:18–27; 12:1–13).

New Testament

The major themes of the Old Testament—creation, history, prophecy, law, wisdom, apocalypse—are recapitulated in the New Testament in the person of Jesus Christ: "Long ago God spoke to our
ancestors in many and various ways by the prophets, but in these last
days he has spoken to us by a Son, whom he appointed heir of all
things, through whom he also created the worlds. He is the reflection
of God's glory and the exact imprint of God's very being, and he
sustains all things by his powerful word" (Hebrews 1:1–3). *Christ is
the summit and fullness of revelation.*

God is revealed in word (John 3:34; 6:63,68), in history (Acts of
the Apostles 7:2–53), and in religious experience (2 Corinthians 12:1–
9)—all centered in Jesus Christ (1 John 1:1–2). It is Jesus who reveals
God's nature and purpose (Acts of the Apostles 2:22–36) and who is
God's preeminent word (John 1:1–18).

Apocalyptic motifs are also strong in Mark 13 (and parallels) and
in portions of Paul (1 Thessalonians 4:13–5:11; 1 Corinthians 15:35–58)
and in the Book of Revelation itself (the Apocalypse).

Synoptics

In the Synoptic tradition (Matthew, Mark, and Luke) Christ is the one
who reveals insofar as he proclaims the Good News of the Reign of
God and teaches the word of God with authority (Mark 1:14–15;
Matthew 23:10, 5:21–7:29; 24:35). His *authority* to reveal is based on his
sonship. As Son, he knows the secrets of his Father: "No one knows
the Son except the Father, and no one knows the Father except the
Son and anyone to whom the Son chooses to reveal him" (Matthew
11:27; see also Luke 10:22). The Apostles, in turn, have been commissioned by Christ to pass on what they have heard from him and what
they have seen in him (Mark 3:14). They are to preach the Gospel and
invite men and women to accept it in faith (Mark 16:15–16).

The essential *content* of the revelation is the *salvation* that is being
offered to humankind under the form of the Reign of God, which is
announced and definitively realized by Christ (Mark 1:15). The time
is fulfilled. The reconciling power of God (which is what the symbol
"Reign of God" means) is in our midst. Be open to it. Let it transform

your consciousness and your behavior. Christ reveals the Reign of God, therefore, in his word, in his works, and in his presence.

Acts of the Apostles

The Acts of the Apostles describe the apostolic activity as in continuity with the action of Christ. The Apostles have heard Christ speak, preach, and teach, and they have received a commission to give witness to his resurrection and his work (Acts of the Apostles 1:1,22; 10:39), to preach and to teach what he prescribed and taught (2:42). Their function, therefore, is that of *witnesses* and *heralds*. They preach and teach what they have seen and received (e.g., 8:5; 9:20), namely, the word of God (15:35; 18:11), the word of Christ (18:25), and the word about Christ (28:31). More specifically, they proclaim the Good News of salvation through Christ (10:36; 13:26; 20:21), that Jesus is risen (2:32), and that he is the Messiah, the Lord, and the Savior.

Paul

For Paul revelation is the *free and gracious action of God by which God offers us salvation in and through Christ* (Romans 16:25–27; Colossians 1:26). The mystery that revelation communicates is God's plan of recapitulating all things in Christ (Ephesians 1:8–10). Because it *is* a mystery (i.e., because the invisible is manifested through the visible but remains all the while invisible), what is disclosed or unveiled (the root meaning of the word *revelation*) remains all the while hidden (1 Corinthians 2:7). Nonetheless, certain witnesses have "seen" it— namely, the Apostles and the prophets (Ephesians 3:5), and it is concretely realized in the Church (Ephesians 3:8–11).

But nowhere is revelation more fully personified or embodied than in Jesus Christ (Romans 8:3; Galatians 4:4; Philippians 2:7). The Epistles look forward as well to an *eschatological* revelation, i.e., the final and complete manifestation of God. When Jesus comes again, God will be revealed more clearly than in the incarnation itself (1 Corinthians 1:7; 2 Thessalonians 1:7; 1 Peter 1:7, 13). So, too, will the glory of the Christian be revealed (Romans 8:18–21; 1 Peter 1:5; 4:13; 5:1).

Paul also seems to speak of what theologians once called "natural revelation" (although, in light of our earlier reflections on nature and grace and on the historical impossibility of a state of pure nature, "natural revelation" must be only a hypothetical, if not entirely meaningless, concept). In the Old Testament, Yahweh is manifested through *nature* (e.g., Wisdom 13:1–9); so also for Paul: "Ever since the creation of the world his eternal power and divine nature, invisible though they are, have been understood and seen through the things he has made" (Romans 1:20).

And he speaks, finally, of "private" revelations to himself (2 Corinthians 12:1–7; Galatians 2:2) and expects that other Christians will experience revelations which will give them a deeper understanding of the Gospel (Ephesians 1:17; Philippians 3:15). These personal revelations are *mystical insights* which are given to the individual alone.

John

John conceives revelation as the *Word of God-made-flesh* (John 1:1–18). This Word is manifested in creation itself (1:3), through the Law and the prophets (1:11), and finally through the incarnation. The whole life of Christ gives testimony to the Creator, and this testimony is perfect in its content and in its expression (17:4,6,26). He is the Word of God (1:1–2) and the Son of the Father (1:18). What he has seen and heard of the Father he communicates to us (8:38; 8:26,40). The Word is acceptable to us because the Father gives testimony regarding the Son: in the works of Christ by which he is acknowledged as the Son, sent by the Father (5:36; 10:25) and through the interior action of the Father by which he draws us to Christ (6:44–46).

In the Johannine theology of revelation, *Christ is both God revealing* (1:18; 4:23) *and God revealed* (1:1; 14:5–6). For John, the Word of God appears in the flesh (3:6; 1 John 1:1–2). It is both light and life (John 9:5; 8:12; 12:46; 17:3). Whoever sees Jesus Christ, therefore, sees the Father (14:10–11). The Holy Spirit will complete the revelation of Jesus and insure the accuracy of the apostolic teaching (14:26; 16:13)—an emphasis no doubt prompted by the rise of pseudorevelation and pseudoprophecy in the primitive Church.

Methodological Note

We cannot forget here what we acknowledged in chapter 6. Belief cannot be demonstrated beyond all reasonable doubt, nor can belief be positively disproved. And the same limitations hold true for unbelief. What, then, are we to say about the biblical views of revelation just summarized? *First,* the Bible does not prove the *fact* of revelation. The Bible only testifies to its own belief that God is a living God and that the living God has been disclosed to us in various ways at various times and nowhere more fully than in Jesus Christ. *Second,* the Bible presents an *interpretation* of history. It *infers* from the experience of Israel and the early Church that God was active in our corporate and individual lives through the Law, the prophets, the wisdom of Israel, and supremely through Christ. But such a view is always an inference. The presence and saving action of God in Christ, or anywhere else, was not self-evident. It was possible for someone to "look" and yet not "see."

What we have in the Bible, therefore, is an understanding of revelation which follows from certain *presumed* experiences of God but is not necessarily revelation itself. The Bible reports various revelatory experiences along with its *interpretation* of those experiences.

To return to the schema in chapter 2: (1) our experience of God, generated by God's self-disclosure (*revelation*), is recognized and accepted as an experience of God in Christ (*faith*); (2) from within a community of faith, we reflect on the nature and meaning of that experience and articulate what we have reflected upon (*theology*); (3) we are drawn more deeply into that experience of God through the community's teachings (*doctrine*) and worship (*liturgy*), and through our own personal and communal living out of faith (*discipleship*); and, finally, (4) we reflect further on the ways in which that original experience of God has occurred in history and in our lives (*theology of revelation*).

What we have been doing thus far in this chapter is working at that fourth level, namely, trying to identify and synthesize the Bible's understanding not of revelation as such but of the meaning of the *notion* or *concept* of revelation.

Because revelation did not emerge as a major, separate theological question until after the Enlightenment in the eighteenth century,

what follows immediately in this chapter is very schematically presented. There is relatively little historical data from which to draw
upon.

NOTIONS OF REVELATION IN EARLY CHRISTIANITY

Apostolic Fathers

For the Apostolic Fathers (Clement of Rome, d. c. 96; Polycarp, d. c.
155; Ignatius of Antioch, d. c. 107), revelation is the "Good News" of
salvation. Christ is its supreme herald and embodiment. The Apostles are its messengers, just as were the prophets before them, and
the Church receives and transmits their teaching.

Ignatius of Antioch, following John and Paul, insisted that the
Word of God was manifested first of all in creation (*Epistle to the
Ephesians* 15:1) and then in the Old Testament through the prophets
(*Epistle to the Magnesians* 9:1–2; *Epistle to the Philadelphians* 5:2). All of
these earlier manifestations of the Word pointed to, and culminated
in, the supreme manifestation of the Word in Christ. Jesus Christ is
the one and only Master, and he alone can provide the knowledge
of the Father (*Epistle to the Ephesians* 15:1; 17:2; *Epistle to the Magnesians* 9:1).

Ignatius's writings frequently lashed out against heretics and
false doctrines (Judaism, Gnosticism, Marcionism). The triple criteria
of true doctrine for him were Christ, the Apostles, and the Church as
represented in the bishop and his presbyterate (priests). Fidelity to
the Church in the person of the bishop insures fidelity to Christ
(*Epistle to the Smyrneans* 8:1).

Apologists

The Apologists (Justin, and others) shared the same understanding of
revelation, but they were inclined to focus more sharply on its *philosophical* aspects. Because they wrote for, and in dialogue with, the
contemporary intellectual community, they wanted to show that the
Logos (truth) which all philosophers lovingly pursued was embodied
in the *Logos*-made-flesh, Jesus Christ. Christians are his pupils and
disciples, members of his school.

237

Irenæus's view is especially significant. He stressed the dynamic and historical character of revelation, underlining its movement, its progress, and its profound unity. He saw the Word of God in creation, in the theophanies of the patriarchal period, in the Law, the prophets, Christ, the Apostles, and the Church. For Irenæus, revelation is a movement from God to God: from Trinity to the Beatific Vision (our unmediated experience of God in heaven). Christ is at the center of the movement. *Revelation is the epiphany or manifestation of God in Christ.*

Over against Marcionism, Irenæus argued that it is in Christ that the two Testaments are joined: The Old Testament proclaims Christ-announced; the New Testament proclaims Christ-in-fact. Revelation is the teaching of the Son of God, the Gospel message, the apostolic tradition, the faith of the Church, the Christian mystery, the truth, the rule of salvation, the norm of life, Christ himself. Revelation, therefore, is not a human doctrine but a gift of love, which invites the response of faith and leads to eternal life.

Early Greek Writers

Among the early Greek writers there were two major schools: the *Alexandrians* and the *Cappadocians*. The *Alexandrians* (Clement, Origen, Athanasius, Cyril) developed an understanding of revelation very similar to the Apologists'. For *Clement,* Christ is the answer to our quest for truth. But true knowledge can be obtained only through charity, the life to which the *Logos*-made-flesh calls us. Christ reveals the Father and the mysteries of eternal life. The Apostles share in his teaching authority and are commissioned to preach the Gospel to the whole world. They have transmitted to the Church the deposit of faith which they have received and preserved intact.

The *Cappadocians* (Basil, Gregory of Nyssa, Gregory Nazianzen) were engaged primarily in repelling the Trinitarian and Christological heresies (especially a form of late or neo-Arianism, as represented by Eunomius [d. 394], an Anomean), but in the process they also indirectly developed a theology of revelation. According to them, we have two means of access to the Father: visible creation and the teaching of faith. Understanding of the divine mysteries comes only through Christ, under the illuminating force of the Holy Spirit. Christ is the Word-in-person who witnesses to, and instructs us in, the divine mysteries. The Apostles have the mission to proclaim the mystery as the Good News.

Early Latin Writers

The early Latin writers (Tertullian, Cyprian, Augustine) were on the whole less speculative than the Greeks in their treatment of revelation. *Augustine*'s theology of revelation, developed in his commentary on the Fourth Gospel and in his *De Gratia Christi* (*On the Grace of Christ*), is closely linked with his doctrine of *illumination*, which centers on God as the light of truth. Revelation is understood, therefore, more as an *inner light by which we are able to believe* than as that which is proposed for belief.

The one Word of God is at once invisible (the illumination and inspiration of the Spirit) and visible (Christ). In Christ we have God revealing and God revealed. The prophets and the Apostles participate in the light of Christ and give witness to what they have seen and heard. That apostolic witness and word are contained in Sacred Scripture and in the proclamation of the Church. Here below we walk in faith, but our faith aspires to the vision of God.

Augustine's teaching dominated the remainder of the early Christian period in the West. Revelation continues to be understood as any kind of divine illumination. Only in the high Scholasticism of the thirteenth century does the term revelation become restricted to "supernatural knowledge" and eventually to the content of Church doctrine.

MEDIEVAL NOTIONS OF REVELATION

The Augustinian tradition is especially strong in the theology of *Bonaventure*, who also identified revelation with the illuminative action of God or with the subjective illumination which results from God's action. Bonaventure did not clearly distinguish between the notion of revelation and that of inspiration, often confusing the two. On the other hand, Bonaventure did understand the mystery of revelation in its larger historical and processive context: relating it first to the Trinity, then to the history of salvation, to the disclosure of God in the natural order, to contemplation, and, finally, to the Beatific Vision.

The cognitive emphasis emerges particularly in *Thomas Aquinas*. Revelation for him is that *saving act by which God furnishes us with the truths which are necessary for our salvation*. Revelation occurs in history, moving us toward a greater and greater understanding of the revealed truths. The sacred deposit of these truths is built up gradually from the time of the patriarchs and prophets in the Old Testament to the time of the Apostles. The incarnation marks the fullness and consummation of revelation.

Although Aquinas acknowledged that revelation had no other purpose than to proclaim the Good News of salvation, he was interested primarily in the process by which the recipient and bearer of revelation (especially the prophet) assimilated the revelation and handed it on. He portrayed such a process as essentially *cognitive*. Thanks to a special illumination from God, the prophet judges with certitude and without error the various objects presented and seizes the truth which God intends to communicate. The majority of humankind does not have such direct access to revelation. It is always mediated through preaching, and this preaching, in turn, has been authenticated by the miracles and other signs which God provides (*Summa Contra Gentiles*, bk. 3, ch. 154). Revelation, however, does not achieve its perfection until the Beatific Vision (bk. 4, ch. 1).

The opening of Part II-II of his *Summa Theologiæ* is where Aquinas provides his fullest discussion of the *content* of revelation. What is it that we discover in and through revelation? It is "the First Truth insofar as it is manifested in Sacred Scripture and in the doctrine of the Church" (q. 5, a. 3). How is the "First Truth" made known? Through statements or propositions which are presented to the human mind for acceptance or rejection (q. 1, a. 2). The principal expressions of revelation are contained in the articles of the Church's creeds (q. 1, aa. 6–9).

Aquinas follows Augustine to the extent that, like Augustine, he insists on the absolute necessity of an interior illumination from God which elevates the mind to perceive and accept what God reveals. But unlike Augustine, he does not identify this interior divine illumination with revelation itself. For Aquinas and his school, revelation assumes a more *objective* character.

It is always important, of course, to view Aquinas's theology of revelation in the context of his whole system of philosophical and theological thought. For Aquinas, all knowledge is achieved only in the act of *judgment*. Revelation, which is the highest type of *knowledge*, implies the reception of some data and a light by which to pronounce judgment on the data's truth or falsity. This is the case with "natural knowledge"; so, too, is it the case with "supernatural knowledge." Truths are proposed to the mind, and we *assent* to those truths. In revelation, divine truths are proposed through preaching and are authenticated by miracles. We give supernatural assent to those truths under the light of faith (q. 173, a. 2).

And thus, for Aquinas, reason is an ascending movement of the mind from creatures to God, while revelation is a descending action by which the divine truth enters the human mind by a free communication. Revelation, in turn, has two stages: In this life we accept the divine truth of God's word in faith; in the next life we see God face to face, without the need for faith.

For many centuries this was to be the standard Catholic view on the relation between faith and reason.

THE COUNCIL OF TRENT

The Council of Trent (1545–1563) has no explicit teaching on revelation as such. It develops its position indirectly, by what it says about the *sources* of revelation and by what it says about *faith*. The Gospel, which is "the source of all saving truth and rule of conduct," is contained "in the written and unwritten traditions which have come down to us, having been received by the Apostles from the mouth of Christ himself, or from the Apostles by the dictation of the Holy Spirit, and have been transmitted as it were from hand to hand . . . and preserved in continuous succession in the Catholic Church" (*Decree on Sacred Books and on Traditions to Be Received*, Session IV, 1546).

This teaching was set against the newly emerging *Protestant* view that the Word of God is available in Sacred Scripture alone (*sola Scriptura*), and that the Bible is self-authenticating and self-interpreting by the power of the Holy Spirit.

We saw already in the chapter on faith (chapter 2) that this council opposed also the Protestant, and especially Lutheran, emphasis on *trusting* (fiducial) faith. "Adults are awakened for that justice," the council declares in its *Decree on Justification* (Session VI, 1547), "when, awakened and assisted by divine grace, they conceive faith from hearing (cf. Romans 10:17) and are freely led to God, *believing to be true what has been divinely revealed and promised...*" (my italics).

FROM TRENT TO VATICAN I

Influenced by the new rationalistic climate of the day, both Catholic and Protestant theologians moved in the sixteenth and seventeenth centuries in the direction of a new and more rigid Scholasticism, and the formal debate about revelation began.

The post-Tridentine Scholastics (Suarez, d. 1617, and de Lugo, d. 1660) stressed the *objective* character of revelation. God reveals through legates or intermediaries. Revelation is some static reality which one receives from others. And with increasing attacks on the whole concept of revelation, the defenders of traditional Christian faith became more, not less, inflexible on the issue.

The names of the opposition include some of the most important figures in the history of philosophy: Benedict Spinoza (d. 1677), who argued that revelation can add nothing to our knowledge that has not already been attained by reason; John Locke (d. 1704), for whom revelation makes available truths which are knowable to reason alone but which the great bulk of humankind is nonetheless ignorant about; Immanuel Kant (d. 1804), for whom the knowledge of God is impossible for speculative or theoretical reason but is accessible to practical reason alone, i.e., the voice of conscience; Georg Hegel (d. 1831), for whom revelation is the necessary self-generation of Absolute Spirit through the dialectic of historical process rather than the free intervention of a personal and gracious God in history; and Ludwig Feuerbach (d. 1872), for whom the idea of God is nothing more than a human projection.

Under the impact of both Rationalism (Spinoza, Locke, et al.) and Idealism (Kant, Hegel, et al.), Catholic theologians began to grapple anew with the problem of revelation. Some of the early efforts failed because they imbibed too much of the errors they hoped to correct. Thus, we had Catholic *semi-Rationalists* (Georg Hermes, d. 1831; Anton Günther, d. 1863; and Jacob Frohschammer, d. 1893), who accepted revelation as valid but who maintained at the same time that reason could also independently establish all the truths of revelation. At the other extreme, we had Catholic *Fideism* (Louis Bautain, d. 1867), which underrated the powers of reason, and Catholic *Traditionalism* (Louis de Bonald, d. 1840; Félicité de Lamennais, d. 1854; and Augustin Bonnetty, d. 1879), a particular form of Fideism which held that God made a general revelation at the beginning of time and that the human race has been "living off" this general revelation ever since.

Mainstream Catholic attempts at coming to terms with the new spirit of Rationalism and Idealism, but without falling into semi-Rationalism on the left or Fideism and Traditionalism on the right, were fashioned by certain Jesuit theologians at the Roman College (now the Pontifical Gregorian University), Giovanni Perrone (d. 1876) and Johannes Franzelin (d. 1886), the Tübingen theologian Johannes Adam Möhler (d. 1838), England's John Henry Newman (d. 1890), and the German scholar Matthias Scheeben (d. 1888).

Scheeben, with commendable theological balance, emphasized both the external (historical) and internal (supernatural) dimensions of revelation, which culminates in Christ as the fullness of all revelation. Christ is at once the sign and reality of God's revealing presence. Scheeben also distinguished among three different levels or forms of revelation: revelation of *nature (revelatio naturæ)*: God is manifested through the works of creation; revelation of *grace (revelatio gratiæ)*: God is manifested through the divine word expressed by the prophets, Christ, the Apostles, and the Church; and revelation of *glory (revelatio gloriæ)*: God is fully manifested in direct vision at the end. Revelation in all three senses is destined for the totality of humankind.

THE FIRST VATICAN COUNCIL

The teaching of Vatican I (1869–1870) had both a negative and a positive side. *Negatively,* the council's teaching was formulated against *Rationalism* (which proclaimed the complete autonomy of human reason), *Materialism* (which denied immaterial and spiritual reality), *Pantheism* (which spoke of everything as being not only a manifestation of God but identical with God), *semi-Rationalism* (which accepted the fact of revelation but affirmed the power of reason to apprehend the truths of revelation without divine assistance), *Fideism* (which accorded no significant role at all to reason), and *Traditionalism* (a form of Fideism).

Positively, the council taught that revelation can include truths of the *natural order* and that there are *mysteries* (truths of faith which are entirely beyond the natural powers of reason to apprehend) which can and have been revealed. Revelation comes implicitly through the natural order of created things, and explicitly through the teachings of Christ, the prophets, the Apostles, and the Church.

What is revealed is God and the eternal decrees of the divine will. The content is accepted on the authority of God, with the help of divine grace, not on the basis of rational argument.

The whole human race is the recipient of revelation. There are some truths we could have grasped apart from revelation, but only with the greatest difficulty. There are others which we could never have grasped apart from revelation. Accordingly, revelation is *morally necessary* for the majority of humankind to come to a knowledge of religious truths of the natural order (e.g., the immortality of the soul); and it is *absolutely necessary* for all with regard to truths of the supernatural order (e.g., the Trinity). The Church's task is faithfully to guard and officially—and sometimes infallibly—interpret the revelation entrusted to it by Christ and the Apostles. On the other hand, the assent of faith is not blind or arbitrary. It must be "consonant with reason."

The doctrine of Vatican I must be understood, of course, against the background of the period. Its *Dogmatic Constitution on the Catholic Faith* was intended not as a full statement on the meaning of revelation but as an answer to the various philosophical and theological systems which were threatening the integrity of the faith. Vatican I's

244

teaching on revelation is less concrete and less historical than was Trent's, and certainly more abstract. What it lacks in biblical and personalist tones (something to be contributed by Vatican II) it compensates for in its remarkable conceptual clarity.

MODERNISM AND EARLY-TWENTIETH-CENTURY CATHOLIC THOUGHT

But the Vatican Council's clarity did not hold for a group of theologians within the Catholic Church who were still trying to meet the Liberal enemy halfway. The movement was called *Modernism* because its adherents sought to adapt Catholicism to what was valid in modern thought, even at the risk of introducing some discontinuity between new forms of belief and the Church's past teachings. They challenged traditional Catholicism with their scientific approach to Sacred Scripture, their repudiation of classical metaphysics, and their call to the laity to become politically active independently of the hierarchy. The principal Modernists were Alfred Loisy (d. 1940), George Tyrrell (d. 1909), and Edouard Le Roy (d. 1954).

Drawing from the Liberal Protestant writings of the late nineteenth century, they identified revelation with a universal human experience—an ever-evolving personal knowledge of God attained in the ordinary course of life. Accordingly, they downplayed both the dogmatic content of revelation and its supernatural origin and process of communication.

Although more an intellectual orientation than a formal system of thought, Modernism was condemned in three separate ecclesiastical documents: the decree *Lamentabili* of the Holy Office (1907), the encyclical letter *Pascendi* of Pope Pius X (1907), and the *Oath Against Modernism* (1910). Over against Modernism, these documents declared that (1) revelation has a transcendental as well as immanent character; (2) it proceeds from a special intervention on the part of God; (3) it has a doctrinal aspect; and (4) it is a free gift of God, and not something demanded by, or already present in, the human person. Because the synthesis created especially by the encyclical *Pascendi* did not exist as such in the minds or writings of any of the Modernist authors, they felt that they had been seriously misunderstood and misrepresented.

By present theological standards, these anti-Modernist documents seem excessively narrow in perspective. They tended to settle the issues on a purely disciplinary basis—removing Modernists from teaching positions, censoring writings, and encouraging spying on alleged dissidents through the notorious *Sodalium Pianum*, later suppressed by Pope Benedict XV—instead of trying to provide some good, solid answers to the various difficulties with which the Modernists were struggling. It is clear today that the Church could concede many points to the Modernists without at the same time undermining the traditional notion of revelation or indeed of the whole supernatural order.

The most constructive Catholic response to Modernism was formulated by Maurice Blondel (d. 1949), who, as we have already seen, anticipated the work of such theologians as Karl Rahner and Gregory Baum. He rejected both the excessive immanentism of Modernism (which excluded any transcendental dimension) and the excessive extrinsicism of the anti-Modernist documents (which tended to portray revelation as something coming totally from outside). Blondel called his mediating position the "method of immanence." An analysis of human action, he suggested, shows a dynamism which moves us toward a goal lying beyond our power to achieve it, but which, if it were offered as a supernatural gift, would be a genuine fulfillment of the human. The Transcendental Thomist movement of the early twentieth century (Joseph Maréchal [d. 1944], Henri Bouillard, and others) was itself directly indebted to Blondel.

THE SECOND VATICAN COUNCIL

The Second Vatican Council, in its *Dogmatic Constitution on Divine Revelation* (1965), reaffirms the various elements of the doctrine of revelation as proposed by earlier councils and in earlier official papal documents. It is Vatican II's *perspective* which differs from that of these other teachings.

1. It views revelation essentially as God's self-communication, a loving and totally gratuitous invitation to enter a dialogue of friendship (nn. 2–4,14,17).

2. It places the problem and mystery of revelation in the context of the history of salvation (nn. 3,4,6,7,14,15,17,21).

3. It views revelation not simply as divine speech, or as the communication of specific truths, but as something comprising both word and deed: "This plan of revelation is realized by deeds and words having an inner unity: the deeds wrought by God in the history of salvation manifest and confirm the teaching and realities signified by the words, while the words proclaim the deeds and clarify the mystery contained in them" (n. 2).

4. The "word" (*dabar*, the Hebrew root) is dynamic, and not merely conceptual: "God... through the word creates all things and keeps them in existence" (n. 3).

5. It speaks of revelation as the divine "mystery" (singular) disclosed in Christ, i.e., as God's final plan of salvation for all human beings (n. 2), rather than as a cluster of "mysteries" (plural), as Vatican I spoke of it.

6. Revelation is both cosmic and historical; i.e., it is communicated through the works of creation and in the course of the history of Israel, of Christ, and of the early Church (nn. 3–4).

7. Christ reveals, not only through his words and teachings, but also through his redemptive work itself and especially through his passion, death, resurrection, and glorification (n. 4).

8. The deposit of faith is not simply a static entity; there is true growth of understanding on the part of the Church: "For, as the centuries succeed one another, the Church constantly moves forward toward the fullness of divine truth until the words of God reach their complete fulfillment in it" (n. 8). Indeed, God continues to speak to us in the present (nn. 8, 25).

9. Although the Church authentically interprets the word of God, the teaching office is "not above the word of God, but serves it, teaching only what has been handed on, listening to it devoutly, guarding it scrupulously and explaining it faithfully in accord with a divine commission and with the help of the Holy Spirit..." (n. 10).

10. There is a much stronger and more general emphasis on the place of Sacred Scripture in the Church ("all the preaching of the Church must be nourished and ruled by [it]" [n. 21]).

The council also recognized that the knowledge of God is to be found in other religions (*Dogmatic Constitution on the Church*, n. 16; *Decree on the Church's Missionary Activity*, n. 3; *Declaration on the Relationship of the Church to Non-Christian Religions*, n. 2); that God continues to speak to us and summon us to mission through the "signs of the times," which are to be interpreted in the light of the Gospel (*Pastoral Constitution on the Church in the Modern World*, n. 4); and that theologians, along with the bishops, have a special responsibility to discern the voices of the times (n. 44) and fashion a new language in order to communicate more adequately the essential truths of revelation (n. 62).

While Vatican II subtracts nothing from the earlier official teachings, it does add a new and fuller theological dimension more in keeping with advances in twentieth-century biblical studies and Catholic theology.

POST–VATICAN II TEACHINGS

Since the council, official documents and ecumenical dialogues in which the Catholic Church has been engaged have developed further teaching and theological reflection on two major themes. The first concerns the way in which such fundamental and universal experiences as that of human suffering can be regarded as expressions of God's word and saving activity. This theme is developed in Pope John Paul II's encyclicals *Dives in Misericordia* (1980) and *Salvifici Doloris* (1984). The second theme concerns the role of non-Christian religions as alternate ways of revelation and salvation. This theme is developed in Pope Paul VI's apostolic exhortation, *Evangelii Nuntiandi* (1975) and Pope John Paul II's encyclicals *Redemptor Hominis* (1979) and *Dominum et Vivificantem* (1986), and also in interfaith dialogues and much recent theological writing.

We turn now to an outline of the contemporary Catholic theological terrain.

CONTEMPORARY THEOLOGICAL VIEWS OF REVELATION

Contemporary theological positions fall into at least four general categories: (1) those which continue to emphasize the *objective* and/or *cognitive* aspect of revelation; (2) those which work primarily out of *subjective* and/or *personalist* categories; (3) those which *combine* elements of both; and (4) feminist views of revelation in the Bible.

Revelation As Objective and/or Cognitive

Although the purely *cognitive* understanding of revelation was the common notion of revelation in textbooks of Catholic theology throughout most of the twentieth century, it is no longer seriously proposed. Even relatively conservative approaches such as John Hardon's *The Catholic Catechism* (Garden City, N.Y.: Doubleday, 1975), the joint effort known as *The Teaching of Christ* (Huntington, Ind.: Our Sunday Visitor Press, 1976), edited by Ronald Lawler, Donald Wuerl, and Thomas Lawler, and *The Catechism of the Catholic Church* (various co-publishers, 1994; orig. ed., 1992) reflect the broader biblical, historical, and personalist perspective of the Second Vatican Council, even as they continue to underline the objective character of revelation and the assent aspect of faith.

The so-called objective emphasis continues today in more surprising places: in *Wolfhart Pannenberg*, a German Lutheran theologian, in particular. God is made known indirectly, through those mighty acts by which divine sovereignty over history is exhibited and exercised. Indeed, one of Pannenberg's principal works is entitled simply *Revelation as History* (New York: Macmillan, 1968). Pannenberg contends that revelation in history can be recognized by anyone, even without faith. In effect, he falls back into Rationalism or at least semi-Rationalism.

A modification of the revelation-as-history approach is offered by Catholic theologian *Edward Schillebeeckx* in his *Revelation and Theology*, vol. 1 (New York: Sheed & Ward, 1967). God is revealed in history, but the word of God in both Old and New Testaments is necessary to illuminate and clarify the revelatory character of those historical events. This is a compromise position which bears striking resemblance to Vatican II's *Dogmatic Constitution on Divine Revelation*, summarized above.

Another variation is advanced by those in the *liberation theology*. God is disclosed in the historical *praxis* of liberation. It is the situation, and our passionate and reflective involvement in it, which mediates the Word of God. Today that Word is mediated through the cries of the poor and the oppressed. According to *Gustavo Gutiérrez*, the liberation school's principal exponent, "History is the scene of the revelation God makes of the mystery of his person. His word reaches us in the measure of our involvement in the evolution of history" ("Faith As Freedom," *Horizons* 2/1, Spring 1975, p. 32). The Word of God is distorted and alienating unless one is committed to change for the sake of the Kingdom. Such a commitment to liberation gives rise to a new way of being human and of believing, of living and thinking the faith, of being called together as Church. Revelation, therefore, happens when we recognize and accept God's summons to us to participate in the historical struggle for liberation.

Revelation As Subjective and/or Personal

If the preceding theories of revelation define revelation almost entirely from the viewpoint of God, others focus on the believing subject—in keeping with the fundamental orientation of contemporary philosophy. It is an approach strongly proposed on the Protestant side by *Rudolf Bultmann*. Revelation happens when our eyes are opened to the possibilities of authentic human existence and when we begin to respond to the transforming power of the Word of God. Preaching summons us to decision. In the dynamic of the preaching and of the decision which the preaching evokes we have the event of revelation.

A similarly subjective emphasis is given on the Catholic side by *Karl Rahner*, following in the philosophical tradition of Transcendental Thomism and, at least partially, in that of Heideggerian existentialism. The call of grace (the "supernatural existential" to which we referred in chapters 4 and 5) renders us restless for God. God is present to every one of us and is offered in grace to whoever is freely open to the divine presence. For Rahner, revelation is either transcendental or predicamental.

Transcendental revelation is the change of horizon or worldview which the presence of God effects in the person. *Predicamental* revelation is what is given in historical events and formal teachings (Bible, doctrines, etc.). But predicamental revelation is always secondary to transcendental revelation. Once grace has been given and accepted into the inner life of the person (transcendental revelation), it inevitably tends toward expression in the believer's ideas, beliefs, and moral action (predicamental revelation).

Christ is the high point of both kinds of revelation. He is one in whom God is fully present, and he is at the same time the fullest expression of that presence in history. In Rahner's words, Christ is *"at once God himself as communicated, the human acceptance of this communication and the final historical manifestation of this offer and acceptance"* ("Revelation," *The Concise Sacramentum Mundi*, New York: Seabury Press, 1975, p. 1462; italics are Rahner's).

Variations on the subjective/personalist approach to revelation from within the Catholic tradition are provided by Gregory Baum in *Man Becoming* (New York: Herder and Herder, 1970) and Gabriel Moran in *The Present Revelation* (1972).

"Mediating" Views of Revelation

Without denying that theologians like Rahner embrace both sides of the objective/subjective dialectic, one might also note other efforts in contemporary theology to achieve a self-described mediating position between the two poles. It is a position characteristically adopted by Catholic theologian *Avery Dulles* (see his *Models of Revelation* [1983]). Revelation and faith dialogically interact so that the believer responds creatively to the self-manifestation of God, not simply in the depths of his or her own subjectivity, but in the cosmos and in history. Revelation, therefore, is neither an external datum that imposes itself on any alert and open-minded observer (Pannenberg) nor a free expression of one's own subjectivity (Bultmann), but a disciplined response that unfolds under the aegis of faith within a community and a tradition.

Dulles and others who seem to follow this "mediating" position are themselves in the tradition of Rahner, but they assert that they place greater emphasis on Rahner's concept of predicamental revelation (revelation as externally expressed) than Rahner himself does. Transcendental revelation, Dulles insists, never exists except in dialectical combination with its predicamental counterpart. There is no such thing as revelation in general, just as there is no faith in general, nor religion in general. Revelation occurs, and is expressed, within a given historical situation, community, and tradition. In that sense, there is a Christian revelation, a Moslem revelation, an Islamic revelation, a Hindu revelation.

Dulles's position is a self-described "symbolic" approach to revelation (*Models of Revelation*, pp. 131–54). A symbol is that through which we get a glimpse of something else. It is a sign so full of meaning that it can only be evoked gradually, indirectly, metaphorically. The events of revelation (the Exodus, theophanies, prophecies, etc.) are "symbols fraught with a meaning deeper than clear concepts or propositional language can convey." Each symbol contains "a whole range of interlocking meanings that cannot be spelled out adequately in objective conceptual discourse." A revelation that begins with symbolic communication gradually generates a whole series of reflections and interpretations that explain its meaning. Thus, the metaphor of the Good Shepherd can be reexpressed to say that Jesus takes care of his followers as a faithful shepherd takes care of his sheep. While doctrines set limits to the kind of significance that can be found in the Christian symbols, doctrines are not revelation itself. They live off the power of the symbols.

"The true content of revelation," Dulles writes, "is the divinely intended and humanly perceived significance of the events and words. By participation in the community of faith the individual believer can have reliable access to the revelatory meaning of the signs and symbols through which God's self-disclosure has taken place and through which God's salvific designs have been made known" ("Faith and Revelation," *Systematic Theology: Roman Catholic Perspectives*, F. Schüssler Fiorenza and J. Galvin, eds., vol. 1, pp. 97–98).

Feminist Views of Revelation in the Bible

Feminist biblical scholars and theologians, most of whom are Catholics, including Elisabeth Schüssler Fiorenza (*In Memory of Her: A Feminist Theological Reconstruction of Christian Origins* [1983, especially pp. 3–40]), Sandra M. Schneiders (*The Revelatory Text: Interpreting the*

252

New Testament as Sacred Scripture [1991], especially chapter 7, pp. 180–99), and Rosemary Radford Ruether (*Religion and Sexism: Images of Women in the Jewish and Christian Traditions* [New York: Simon and Schuster, 1974]), expose the androcentric and patriarchal character of the biblical texts, of the cultures that produced them, and of the kinds of interpretation that have been given them in subsequent centuries. Most typologies of feminist interpretation divide current scholarship into three hermeneutical approaches: revisionist, reconstructionist, and liberationist. Some add symbolic, and some use the term *deconstructionist* for reconstructionist. However, as feminist scholars continue to interact, these classifications are breaking down.

Revisionist interpretation retells the biblical stories in ways that emphasize the roles and contributions of women that had previously been ignored or obscured by androcentric interpretation. Thus, the story of Martha and Mary (Luke 10:38–42) portrays Mary as a disciple following the same path of learning as Jesus' male disciples, rather than as a safely traditional contemplative.

Reconstructionist (or *deconstructionist*) interpretation exposes more directly the patriarchal and androcentric bias behind the texts and subsequent interpretations thereof. For example, Abraham was prevented by God from sacrificing his only son (Genesis 22), while Jephthah was not prevented by God from sacrificing his only daughter (Judges 11:30–40).

Symbolic interpretation develops the positive significance of female figures, e.g., Eve as the mother of all the living (Genesis 3:20), the woman clothed with the sun (Revelation 12:1–6), and the Church and the new Jerusalem as bride (Ephesians 5:25–27; Revelation 21:2).

Liberationist interpretation calls attention to strong female figures in the Bible, who were empowered by God and who, in turn, empowered others, e.g., Deborah (Judges 4–5), Judith, and Esther as saviors of the people; and the Samaritan woman and Mary Magdalene as disciples who witness to the Lord (John 4:39–42; 20:18). It also brands oppressive texts as nonrevelatory, because of the abusive ways they have been used throughout history to exploit and control women. Thus, 1 Timothy 2:11–16 urges that a woman should "learn in silence with all submissiveness" and that no woman is to be permitted "to teach or to have authority over men." They are to "keep silent." The text even argues that it was not Adam who was deceived but "the woman [Eve] was deceived and became a transgressor. Yet woman will be saved through bearing children, if she continues in faith and love and holiness, with modesty."

TOWARD A THEOLOGY OF REVELATION

Some Theological Elements: Creation, History, Prophecy, Mystery

Like every major part of the Christian theological network of doctrines, revelation can only be comprehended in terms of its relationship with other doctrines and symbols of Christian faith. Thus, our notion of revelation is impacted by our understanding of God, of human existence, of Christ, of Church, of grace, of nature, of history. Indeed, one can point to any major component of the Christian doctrinal system and legitimately suggest that all of theology is embodied and/or implied therein, whether it be the theology of human existence, of history, of Jesus Christ, or indeed of revelation itself.

A complete synthesis of the theology of revelation, therefore, would demand some substantive reference to each and all of the other major doctrines. This is impractical, and unnecessary in any case, since this whole book is itself an attempt at a comprehensive and systematic statement of the whole Catholic tradition. What is included in the synthesis which follows, therefore, are only those important doctrinal elements which are not formally treated elsewhere in this book. *Human existence* has already been examined in Part One. We are at this point engaged in the task of developing a theology of *God*. Our attention will soon turn to the questions of *Jesus Christ* and the *Church*. Accordingly, we shall limit ourselves here to a consideration of the relationship between revelation and *creation, history, prophecy,* and *mystery*.

Creation

It must be said, first of all, that creation has to do with more than the beginning of all reality. Even if we were to assume that the world has always existed coeternally with God, the question of creation would still present itself. Creation, in other words, has to do also with the *lasting relationship between God and reality*, and between God and us in particular. (There will, of course, be a further discussion of this relationship in chapter 9 in connection with the question of *Providence*.)

The doctrine of God, and the doctrine of revelation as well, presupposes a doctrine of creation. How would we know that there *is* a God unless God were somehow available to us? And how can God be available to us except through the created order? And how can we even begin to express our understanding of God except in terms of our perceived relationship with God? That relationship is a creaturely relationship. God is the source and sustainer of our very being.

The doctrine of creation is also intimately allied with the question of *nature*, to which we have already addressed ourselves in chapter 5. "Nature" is that which is. The nature of a being is what it is, as distinguished from other beings. In terms of human existence, "pure nature" is what we are apart from our call to divinization, apart even from our radical capacity to hear and to respond to that call (the "supernatural existential" or *potentia obedientialis*, again). But pure human nature does not exist. We are, from the beginning, open to divine grace.

In terms of the whole created order, "nature" means "being" (our word *nature* is derived from the Greek *physis*, which means not only "being" but also "becoming"). Thus, in the Heideggerian sense, nature is "the process of arising, of emerging from the hidden" (*An Introduction to Metaphysics*, pp. 13–15, 17). Every created being stands between nothing and being and is at various degrees of proximity to the one or to the other. We humans are both distinct from nature (we alone know that we know) and at one with nature in that we, too, are part of the whole created order.

Matter is not evil, as some of the earliest heresies (Gnosticism, Manichaeism) insisted. It comes from the creative hand of God, in one and the same creative act by which God brought forth spiritual realities: "God saw everything that he had made, and indeed, it was very good" (Genesis 1:31).

Among those spiritual realities are *angels*. The word itself is derived from the Greek *angelos*, which, in turn, is the translation of the Hebrew *mal'ak*, which means "messenger." The existence of angels is of theological relevance here for two reasons: (1) angels remind us that there is more to the created order than what we actually see, feel, hear, and taste; and (2) all such spiritual forces other than God are less than God; i.e., they, like us, are part of the *created* order and are not themselves rivals of God in the production of good or the insertion of evil into the world. (The official teaching *that* angels exist as *creatures* of God is given by the Fourth Lateran Council in 1215 and by the First Vatican Council in 1869–1870.)

In the Bible, angels function as their name suggests—as *messengers* of God (2 Samuel 14:17; 2 Kings 19:35; Exodus 14:19; and in the Book of Revelation generally). Jesus speaks often of angels (e.g., Luke 12:8–9), the angel Gabriel announces the births of John the Baptist (1:11–20) and of Jesus (1:26–38), an angel assists Jesus in his agony in Gethsemane (22:43), another angel removes the stone from the tomb of Jesus (Matthew 28:2–3), an angel also announces the message of the resurrection to the women who came to the tomb (28:1–7), and angels are part of the heavenly court at the Last Judgment (13:34–41; 25:31–46).

Since they are intelligent creatures with freedom, angels have the capacity to reject God, as we do. Those angels which have rejected God are portrayed as demons in league with Satan (1 Corinthians 15:24; Ephesians 2:2). In other words, not every "signal" from the world of the numinous necessarily bears a "message" from God. The world of the numinous is as ambiguous and as fraught with sin as is the world of the tangible.

In later centuries speculation about angels was perhaps more influenced by contemporary philosophy (especially Platonic) than by the Bible. Such speculations gave rise to theories about the hierarchy of angels, with names devised for every level. In later medieval thought, particularly with Aquinas, speculation on the nature of angels provided an occasion to reflect on the nature of human thinking and action. The famous argument over the number of angels that can dance on the head of a pin was intended only as a logical exercise and not as a serious question.

Creation, we must repeat, is already an *act of grace*. It is an act of *divine self-giving*. The being of God is poured out so that there might be beings who can share in the divine being. The supreme act of self-giving occurs in the incarnation when God is so identified with a

256

created reality (the humanity of Christ) that God and the created reality are uniquely one. (We shall return to the theology of the incarnation in Part Three.) Indeed, the whole of the creative process is directed toward, and therefore culminates in, the union of the divine and the human in Jesus Christ.

If there were no creation, we could not know God, because there would be no one there to know God. If there were no creation, there would be no *nature*, for nature is the product of creation. Nature arises from the creative act which itself moves from nothing to being. Creation also makes *history* possible, not just in the sense that there must be reality before there can be history, but in the deeper sense that reality must be in movement before there can be history. And creation is a continuous process of movement toward higher and higher levels of being. It is within that progressive movement of history that God "speaks" to us.

Creation, in fact, is considered to be the first chapter in the history of salvation. Creation as ongoing reality underlies the whole of the saving process. God is disclosed not only by the emerging of reality from nothing, but by its continuation and dynamic movement "before our eyes," as it were. We take a look at reality as it is and see how marvelously structured and ordered it is (natural scientists should appreciate this even more than theologians and philosophers do). That does not in itself "prove" the existence of God, but it certainly makes it easier to attribute purposeful intelligence to reality than to ascribe its structure and order to chance. "For from the greatness and beauty of created things comes a corresponding perception of their Creator" (Wisdom 13:5).

It is the *Church's official teaching* that God created the whole world, spiritual as well as material realities (against all forms of dualism, Gnosticism and Manichaeism especially); that the world is distinct from God (against Pantheism); that God created the world in freedom, to manifest divine goodness and glory. All created things, therefore, are good. Indeed, they have their own rightful autonomy and are not simply means to some spiritual end.

This teaching is contained in the documents of the Fourth Lateran Council (1215), the Council of Florence's *Decree for the Jacobites* (1442), the First Vatican Council's *Dogmatic Constitution on the Catholic Faith* (1870), the encyclical letter of Pope Pius XII, *Humani Generis*

(1950), and the Second Vatican Council's *Pastoral Constitution on the Church in the Modern World* (1965). The last document is especially important because it underscores the autonomy of the created order and draws out the principal practical implication of such autonomy, namely, "if methodical research in any branch of learning is carried out in a truly scientific manner..., it will never really conflict with the faith, because both secular things and the realities of faith derive from the same God..." (n. 36).

For the same reason, we might add here, if we discover God through the created order, we need not underestimate the revelatory character of that discovery by referring to it as "natural" revelation (and, therefore, not truly revelation in the strict theological or doctrinal sense). On the contrary, there is only one Creator, who is available to us in a variety of ways and under a variety of forms. Just as there is no such reality as "pure nature," neither is there any such reality as "natural revelation." All revelation, whether through created things or through the prophets, Christ, the Apostles, and the Church, is derived from the same God.

An *ecological* note: The doctrine of creation is especially pertinent today to the ecological crisis. It reminds us of our responsibility of stewardship and of the reverence and awe we should have for the gift of God's own handiwork. Some, however, have pointed to the Genesis account of creation as the reason for our exploitation of the environment. It is alleged that Christians took it (e.g., Genesis 1:26–28) to mean that God gave us a kind of blank check to do with the created order as we will. Recent theologies of creation have sought to refute that charge, stressing the immanence of God, and particularly of the Holy Spirit, in creation, thereby undercutting the dualism of God and nature that characterized the Western Christian tradition for so long (see Jürgen Moltmann, *God in Creation: A New Theology of Creation and the Spirit of God*, San Francisco: Harper & Row, 1985).

History

For the Christian, history is not simply the place or context wherein God communicates eternal truths to humankind. History is itself the creative act of God through which God is manifested and continues to

258

be manifested to us. The climactic moment of history is always the event of Jesus Christ.

Because God is disclosed in and through creative acts, and because these creative acts (to which we respond and with which we cooperate) constitute history, we come to a knowledge of God as we reflect on the principal events of human history and our own personal history. Israel did this before us, fixing its attention constantly on the Exodus in particular (Deuteronomy 6:20–25; Judges 6:8,13; Isaiah 10:26; Jeremiah 2:6; Ezekiel 20:5–6; Psalms 78:12–16; 105:23–38, and other passages too numerous to list). We do so as Christians by reflecting not only on the mighty acts of God in the Old Testament period, but also by reflecting on the supreme creative act of God in Christ, and other "signs of the times" which continue to characterize the world of human experience and history. Nowhere is this perspective more fully developed in the Bible than in the Gospel of Luke and the Acts of the Apostles.

The question whether there are two histories or one, i.e., whether there is a history of salvation alongside of, or even emerging from within, the history of humankind, has been debated since the seeds of a separate theology of *salvation history* were planted in the work of Irenæus. Irenæus's basic understanding reappeared in Augustine's *City of God*. Other formulations were constructed by Joachim of Flora (d. 1202), who spoke of the three ages of history corresponding to the work of each of the Persons of the Blessed Trinity.

But not until the seventeenth century did these notions receive explicit development, in the work of Johannes Cocceius (d. 1669), a Calvinist who contrasted the covenant of grace with the covenant of works. The covenant of grace is recounted in Sacred Scripture, with all historical events therein leading up to, and proceeding from, Jesus Christ. Cocceius was the forerunner of the theological movement of the nineteenth century, in which a formal school of salvation history thought (*Heilsgeschichte*) emerged in the writings of a group of scholars at Erlangen University in Germany: Johann Hofmann (d. 1877) and Martin Kahler (d. 1912), in particular. The Erlangen school, in turn, provided a basis for twentieth-century developments in the work of Old Testament scholar Gerhard von Rad (d. 1971) and Lutheran theologian Oscar Cullmann, who is responsible, more than anyone else, for the full-scale construction of a salvation-history perspective, especially in his *Christ and Time* (Philadelphia: Westminster Press, 1946; rev. ed., 1964).

The salvation-history perspective is clearly assumed by the Second Vatican Council in its *Dogmatic Constitution on the Church* (nn. 2–4, 9) and also in its *Dogmatic Constitution on Divine Revelation* (nn. 2–4). When it is set over against the dogmatically existentialist views of Rudolf Bultmann, against whom Cullmann waged so many theological battles over this issue, the salvation-history approach is strongly persuasive. Whereas Bultmann and others tend toward the ancient heresy of Marcionism, which denied the revelatory character of the Old Testament (it was completely replaced by the New, they argued), Cullmann, von Rad, and others insisted on the essential connection between the two Testaments and on their coequal status as revelatory documents, linked together by Jesus Christ, toward whom the one leads and from whom the other proceeds.

But to the extent that the salvation-history approach tends to introduce a dualism of nature and grace, of the profane and the sacred, to that same extent is it less acceptable as a theological tool. History—whatever the adjective placed before the noun—is from the creative hand of God. Insofar as God is knowable through creation and through the creative events which constitute history, God is knowable through history—the whole history of the world, the whole history of humankind, our own personal histories, and not simply the history of Israel, of Jesus Christ, and of the Church. For the history of which the Bible speaks will be radically transformed (1 Corinthians 15:35–58) and God will be "all in all" (15:28).

Only death remains in history as its "last enemy" (15:26), but history itself is bound for glory, not death. This has been revealed definitively in the incarnation and especially in the resurrection of Jesus Christ (1 Peter 1:3–4; 2 Corinthians 4:14; Philippians 3:10; 2 Timothy 2:11; John 11:25; 6:39–44,54; 1 Corinthians 15).

Prophecy

The prophet is one who, literally, is called to *speak on behalf of another*, in this case on behalf of *God* (Hebrew, *nābi'*). The prophet, as opposed to the institutional figure, stands apart from his or her own society, as critic and judge. The prophet proclaims a message which makes demands. Insofar as the prophet claims to speak on behalf of God, the prophet is the bearer of revelation as well as its interpreter. What he or she speaks is the word of God. The word of God comes to the prophet, not for the prophet's own good, but for the community's.

Accordingly, prophecy is not primarily a matter of predicting the future (that is the function of an oracle or clairvoyant). But insofar as the prophet offers an interpretation of events and discusses the consequences of one form of action or another, or of a failure to act, the prophet is indeed concerned with the future.

There are many prophetic voices in the *Old Testament:* Samuel, Gad, Nathan, Elijah, Elisha, Abraham, Aaron, Miriam, Isaiah, Ezekiel, Jeremiah, Amos, Hosea, Micah, et al. None, of course, is greater than Moses. There are also "false prophets" (Isaiah 3:1–3; Jeremiah 5:31; Ezekiel 13:1–23, e.g.). The true prophet is one who speaks on behalf of God in spite of the great difficulty and severe personal risk (Jeremiah 1:7; 6:11; 20:9; Amos 3:8).

The *New Testament* is insistent that God spoke through the prophets (Matthew 1:20; 2:15; Luke 1:70; Acts of the Apostles 3:18,21; Romans 1:2). John the Baptist was accepted as a prophet, but there is some question whether or not Jesus understood himself as a prophet. In one sense, of course, *Jesus* had to be the supreme prophet, for who could speak on behalf of God more clearly or with more authority? And yet Jesus speaks, unlike the prophets, on *his own* authority.

That there were prophets in the *early Church* is attested to by a number of passages (Acts of the Apostles 11:27; 21:10–11; 13:1–3; 1 Corinthians 13:2; 14:3–5, 24–25; Ephesians 3:5, e.g.). Prophets are listed among the officers of the Church (Romans 12:6; 1 Corinthians 12:10, 28–29; Ephesians 2:20; 3:5; 4:11).

Since revelation is given for all and not for the few, prophecy can be found outside of Israel and the Church. And since revelation is not limited to a particular time in history but occurs within the total historical process itself, prophecy cannot be regarded as if it were completed. God continues to be disclosed through events (the "signs of the times") and through persons who embody the divine presence and who speak boldly on behalf of the God who is present to them.

The *signs* of true prophecy are never so clear that all persons of goodwill must agree on who is or is not a prophet. What are some *criteria* by which to judge one who claims to be, or is regarded as, a prophet? (1) The prophet will claim to speak on behalf of God, particularly on behalf of the Reign of God. (2) The prophetic word will ultimately work for the unity of the Church and of the human family. A prophetic word that destroys unity is antecedently suspect. (3) A prophetic word uttered by someone who does not live by that word is totally without credibility. (4) A prophetic word that is so unusual that it bears no visible connection with ordinary life is also situated on the borders of credibility. Prophecy is never for display, or for the aggrandizement of the "prophet." (5) Prophecy is never so garbled that it cannot be communicated to more than a few. It is always public and community-oriented. Otherwise, we have lapsed into Gnosticism once again.

Formal *teachings of the Church* on prophecy are exceedingly sparse. The most explicit is given by the First Vatican Council's *Dogmatic Constitution on the Catholic Faith,* in which prophecies are linked with miracles as "exterior proofs of [God's] revelation... joined to the interior helps of the Holy Spirit." If, for example, we could accept the late Pope John XXIII as a prophet in the true sense of the word, then his word, his ministry, and the example of his whole life would make it easier for us—and indeed for many outside the Church—to believe that God is real and that the real God was disclosed to us in this kind, jovial, and pastorally courageous priest.

Mystery

At the opening of the second session of the Second Vatican Council in 1963, Pope Paul VI spoke of the Church as a mystery, that is, "a reality imbued with the hidden presence of God." No definition of the word *mystery* can easily improve upon this one. Because God is totally other than we are, because God is totally of the spiritual order, because God, therefore, is not visible to our bodily senses, our experience of God is always *mediated*. We experience the reality of God through our experience of created things, or particular persons, or particular events, or through a psychic sense of divine presence (mysticism). Consequently, every contact with God is mysterious, or sacramental. The *hidden* God imbues a visible reality. In grasping that visible reality we grasp the hidden God.

262

All revelation, therefore, is mysterious, or *sacramental*, in character. (*Sacramental* is understood here in its Augustinian sense, as a "visible sign of an invisible reality.") God is disclosed mediately, not immediately. We may indeed come to a true knowledge of God, but that knowledge is always mediated. To use Bernard Lonergan's expression, we know the world as "mediated by meaning." For Avery Dulles, revelation is mediated by *symbols*. Thus, Jesus did not primarily bring new truths to us, new "information" about the other world. He illuminated reality in new ways, disclosing new meanings.

But revelation is always for salvation. Mystery refers in the first instance, therefore, to God's saving plan for human history (Colossians 1:1–2:6; Ephesians 1–3). But it also refers to the infinite incomprehensibility of God. God always remains ineffable and beyond comprehension. The Lord dwells "in unapproachable light, whom no one has ever seen or can see" (1 Timothy 6:16). Many of the early Christian writers referred to the darkness on the mountain into which Moses entered when he went to speak with God. And Thomas Aquinas had to write that our "utmost knowledge of God is to know that we do not know" God (*De Potentia*, 7,5, *ad* 14). The Protestant Reformers' theology of the cross (*theologia crucis*) included a protest against the tendency to domesticate God by making God a topic among topics in our theological and philosophical systems.

In the nineteenth century, as we have already seen, the Catholic Church confronted two essentially opposed positions: the one which denied the possibility of any knowledge of God apart from revelation in the narrow sense of the word (some form of direct communication from God), and the other which insisted that everything we know about God we know through reason alone. The First Vatican Council rejected both Fideism on the right and Rationalism on the left. In contemporary theological terms, Vatican I insisted that God is knowable through the created order (history, events, persons, prophecies) and yet always remains hidden and incomprehensible. Our knowledge of God, therefore, is always sacramental, at the level of mystery and symbol.

Since we are persons whose openness to God is without limit because God is without limit, our progress in knowledge and freedom can keep advancing to higher and higher levels, closer and closer to the reality that is God. But it is only because God is already somehow available in the tangible, the visible, the finite, the worldly, the personal, the historical, that we can continue to press for the fullest grasp of God. Indeed, our radical capacity for God (which God has implanted in us as part of our historical human nature) makes possible our knowledge and our freedom.

Christ is a mystery insofar as he is the great sacrament and symbol of God's presence to us and of our response to that presence (Ephesians 1:9–10). The Church, too, is a mystery, and for similar reasons (Ephesians 5:32). The sacraments and the truths (symbols) of faith are mysteries of which the Apostles are stewards (1 Corinthians 4:1). The Christian message, therefore, has an all-embracing, comprehensive unity. It is not simply a collection of truths placed side by side, to be believed as they are proposed. The Christian message is about one mystery, the mystery of God, who is revealed sacramentally: in the order of nature, through historical events, through charismatic figures (prophets), through Jesus Christ, who is the great mystery, through the Apostles, through the early Church, and indeed through all those events, objects, and persons which constitute and profoundly shape human experience and human history.

We are never certain, of course, *that* God is present to us in a special way in this or that person or event. We can never be certain either of *what* God calls us to do through particular persons or events. God remains at the same time veiled and unveiled. We cannot escape the realm of ambiguity. The challenge of belief and unbelief confronts us relentlessly. Some "see" and others do not. As suggested in chapter 6, there are no absolute proofs for or against belief, for or against unbelief. On the other hand, belief is not without reason. And therein lies the question of mystery. And therein, too, lies one of the distinguishing characteristics of Catholic theology and of the Catholic tradition: its commitment to the principle of *sacramentality*.

Synthesis: Toward a Theology of Revelation

Revelation is the self-communication of God. It is a process which God initiates and which we recognize and accept because of our radical capacity to be open to the presence and action of God in our history and in our personal lives. *God is disclosed always sacramentally,* mysteri-

264

ously, symbolically. Revelation, or the "unveiling" of God, occurs in nature itself, in historical events, through the words and activities of special individuals (prophets, Apostles, et al.), of special communities (the Church in particular), and supremely in and through Jesus Christ, who is at once God-revealing and God-revealed. All of history, and therefore all of revelation, is oriented toward the Christ-event as history's center and core.

But how do we avoid the two extremes of Modernism on the left and a decadent neo-Scholasticism on the right, i.e., the Modernist view that God is so thoroughly immanent to the world that revelation constitutes nothing more than ordinary human experience and ordinary human knowledge, and the neo-Scholastic view that makes of revelation the transmission of certain truths from one party to another (prophet to Israel, Christ to Apostles, Apostles to Church, Church to members and to the world at large)? To answer this question we must draw again upon our understanding of human existence and of nature-and-grace in particular.

Revelation is God's self-communication, and as self-communication it has a history. The communication is supernatural (i.e., not due to human nature or to human history in its hypothetically "pure" state) and available in principle to every person. Revelation is transcendent (i.e., beyond the material, created order), but it is always and only operative in history, including personal history. If it were not operative in this way, we could not know it, because we are historical persons and the historical and the personal are the only context we have for the quest for knowledge, love, and the exercise of freedom. Revelation, therefore, is always *mediated*, and always mediated *historically* and *personally*. In other words, we never experience God directly, not even in a so-called mystical experience. We only experience God sacramentally, that is, in and through something or someone other than God and other than ourselves, but through which God is self-communicated.

Revelation has *two aspects. First*, it is the *process* by which God is communicated to us. *Second*, it is the *product* or *symbol* of this communication, since God's self-communication is always mediated. That product or symbol might be a person (thus, Christ is revelation), or it might be a conceptual formulation (the Bible, a dogma of the Church). The mediating product or symbol of God's self-

265

communication is revelatory in that it brings about and witnesses to the individual's or community's experience of God. *Christ* always remains the supreme moment of revelation, both as process and as product or symbol, because in Christ alone God's self-communication totally transforms the mediator, so that *the mediator and the mediated are one and the same.* Christ is not only our "go-between" with God. He is also "very God of very God," to cite one of the ancient creeds. Christ is at once the one who mediates for us and the divine reality which is mediated to us.

There is no sharp separation, therefore, between the history of the world and the history of revelation, just as there is no sharp separation between the history of the world and the history of salvation. In other words saving revelation is available within the ordinary fabric of human existence. Here again, the Catholic principle of *sacramentality* is at work. "Nor does divine Providence deny the help necessary for salvation to those who, without blame on their part, have not yet arrived at an explicit knowledge of God, but who strive to live a good life, thanks to divine grace" (Vatican II, *Dogmatic Constitution on the Church,* n. 16). But salvation is impossible without faith (Hebrews 11:6; Council of Trent; First Vatican Council), and faith is impossible without revelation, since faith is personal acceptance of God's self-communication.

The Church's official teachings and the New Testament's own conviction about the universality of salvation (1 Timothy 2:4; 4:10) assume, but do not formally articulate, a theological position, namely, that every human being has the capacity for elevation by grace in the very depths of consciousness. Even when that capacity for grace is not adverted to, it is present and operative as a fundamental orientation to God. *Thus, every human person is already radically open to divine revelation in the very core of her or his being, in that God is present to every person as the offer of grace.*

But more than that is given in revelation. The "more than" is what we profess in the articles of the Creed: the saving activities of God in Israel, in Christ, and in the Church. The "more than" is also given in the various persons and events of history as well as in the natural created order itself.

Revelation over and above that which is given to every person in the core of the person's consciousness, and apart from Christ himself and the infallible teaching of the Church, is inevitably mixed with error, distortion, misinterpretation, and exaggeration. Indeed, those who try to work out a theology of revelation on an extrinsicist basis alone (i.e., revelation seen as the communication of certain truths from on high) must eventually come to terms with the interior, transcendental side of revelation. Like the proverbial tree falling with no one within earshot, there is no revelation unless there is someone to receive it as such in faith. A person, an event, a natural phenomenon is perceived as mysterious or sacramental, i.e., as bearing and mediating the presence of God, only insofar as it actualizes our innate capacity for God. It is known by what Aquinas called "knowledge by connaturality."

The Modernist, therefore, was wrong to ignore or reject the inevitable historical expressions of God's inner presence to every human being. And the extrinsicist was wrong to limit revelation to what occurs outside the person and outside human consciousness.

It is not enough, however, to say that revelation is always mediated. There are at least two levels of mediation: the *person* or the *event* which mediates (the symbol), and the *interpretation* of what is mediated. Only in "the unsurpassable power of the Christ-symbol" (Dulles) do we have what is mediated and an interpretation of what is mediated in one and the same person.

The Exodus event, for example, mediates the presence of God. The prophets mediate what has been mediated: They interpret what has happened, and they call it an act of saving revelation. So, too, the dogmas of the Church do not themselves mediate the presence of God. They interpret what has been mediated. In some cases, they interpret the interpretations of what has been mediated. And in still other cases, they may interpret the interpretations of interpretations of what has been mediated (e.g., Vatican II may definitively interpret Trent, which was definitively interpreting Paul, who was trying to interpret Jesus Christ). *Christ remains always the one mediator who definitively interprets all other mediators and mediating events.* The Church, as the continuation of Christ in history, participates in Christ's work of mediation. *The Church is the definitive interpreter of Christ, the Mediator.*

SPECIAL QUESTIONS: PRIVATE REVELATION AND THE CLOSING OF REVELATION

Private revelation is, by exclusion, whatever is not available to the general community, be it the Church or any other segment of the human family. Private revelation is, in principle, possible at all times. Indeed, even public revelation is given to specific individuals such as prophets or Apostles. To speak, therefore, of *"the closing of revelation"* with the death of the last Apostle means only that the Christ-event, which is the definitive and normative self-communication of God by which all other communications are to be measured and tested, has already happened.

An analogy might be helpful. Christ is like a *master key. In princi-ple,* our knowledge of God in Christ is totally adequate: There is nothing to be discovered about God (about God's mercy, love, fidel-ity, justice, etc.) which has not already been disclosed through Christ. *In fact,* however, many (indeed most) who know God through Christ do not know God as fully as they might. Other persons who do not know God through Christ might know God more fully nonethe-less. They may not have access to Christ, the master key, but they have keys of their own, some of which open many doors and some of which open a few or only a single door. But these persons do have some measure of access. *In principle,* it is better to have the master key than a key that opens only some doors. *In fact,* however, the revela-tion of God in Christ does not insure a fuller measure of knowledge of, or love for, God on the part of those who receive it. Others who have access to God's self-communication apart from explicit faith in Christ may exceed their Christian brothers and sisters in both knowl-edge and love. (The obvious question "Why, then, be a Christian?" will be addressed more directly in chapter 19.)

God continues to be disclosed not only to individuals but also to communities and to the world at large in the same way as before: through natural phenomena, through historical events, through pro-phetic figures, through the lives of truly holy people, through the "signs of the times." On the other hand, the more private those disclosures, the less subject they are to critical scrutiny and testing and the more prone they are to distortion, illusion, projection, and misinterpretation. Some private revelations have, of course, attracted public interest and some measure of public acceptance: e.g., those to Joan of Arc, Margaret Mary Alacoque (the nine First Fridays), and the appearances of the Blessed Virgin Mary at Lourdes and Fatima. Others are clearly bizarre and are quickly condemned even by ordinarily cautious ecclesiastical officials, although such "revelations" (almost always from the Blessed Virgin Mary) often continue to attract a following.

In any case, private revelations have to be tested if they are to influence the Church. What *criteria* can the Church, at the universal and local levels, apply to the claim that one has received a revelation from God directly or through Mary? (1) Is the revelation consistent with the public revelation of Sacred Scripture and of the official interpretations of that revelation by the Church, officially and through the leading witnesses of faith and its theologians? (2) Does the private revelation work toward building up the Body of Christ and the human family, or is it finally divisive? (3) Does the private revelation contribute to our knowledge of God and of our human responsibilities, or is it merely concerned with the unusual and the bizarre ("The Blessed Mother has ordered all nuns to wear their religious habits once again and all lay women to wear blue berets")? (4) Are the bearers of the private revelation themselves good examples and witnesses of integral Christian and human existence, or are they finally odd, eccentric, and difficult to deal with? (5) Is the devotional practice arising from the alleged private revelation approved by the local bishop, who has responsibility for the faith and good order of the diocese?

Private revelations, even if authentic, are never binding on other members of the Church. They bind only those to whom they have been directly given, and those who believe in them and freely choose to be bound by them. No Catholic, for example, is required to believe even in private revelations associated with Marian apparitions that have been approved by the Church for devotional purposes, e.g., Lourdes and Fatima. At the same time, Catholics have every reason and right to be skeptical of alleged private revelations that have not been approved by the Church or, what is worse, have been specifically disapproved.

SUMMARY

1. The "problem" of revelation is the same as the "problem" of belief and unbelief. How do we come to "know" God? With whom does God communicate? How does such communication occur? What is communicated? Why do so many apparently miss God's signals?

2. Central to Israel's faith is the conviction that *God has intervened in history*, taking a personal interest in the fortunes of Israel and ultimately of the whole of humankind. God's communications take many forms: created objects, theophanies, oracles, dreams, prophecies, laws, wise sayings, historical events, and particularly the Covenant with Moses and the Exodus from Egyptian bondage. The *Covenant/Exodus theme* runs throughout the *Old Testament* and shapes Israel's fundamental understanding of God and of the "word" of God.

3. All of the Old Testament themes are recapitulated in the *New Testament* but are now focused in *Jesus Christ,* through whom God has spoken the final word (Hebrews 1:1–3). Jesus reveals the Reign of God and is himself the "Word made flesh" (John 1:1–18). The Apostles and the early Church are witnesses and heralds of Christ, and look forward to the day when the "unveiling" of God (the literal meaning of the word revelation) will be completed with the Second Coming of the Lord.

4. For the *early Christian writers* revelation is simply the Good News of salvation. Christ is its supreme herald and embodiment, and the prophets, Apostles, and Church are its messengers.

5. The Augustinian tradition dominates Catholic theology until the thirteenth century, when there is a turn, in the writings of *Thomas Aquinas,* toward the *cognitive* or *intellectual* side of revelation. Revelation is the *truth* that God communicates through the prophets, Christ, the Apostles, and the Church. Revelation, therefore, is the highest form of *knowledge.*

6. The *Council of Trent,* over against the Protestant notion of trusting faith, insisted on the *objective* character of what has been revealed and to what we must assent in faith.

7. After Trent, i.e., in the *sixteenth and seventeenth centuries,* Catholic theology and contemporary secular thought move in diametrically opposed directions: The former becomes rigidly neo-Scholastic and the latter, rationalistic. The issue of revelation as such becomes for the first time an object of theological discussion and speculation.

8. In the *nineteenth century,* Catholic theology covered the spectrum from the *semi-Rationalists* (Hermes, Günther, Frohschammer) to the *Fideists* (Bautain and others). Both were rejected by *Vatican I.* Middle positions were developed by Möhler, Scheeben, and Cardinal Newman.

9. According to *Vatican I*, revelation comes through the natural order of created things and also through the mediation of the prophets, Christ, the Apostles, and the Church.

10. The Rationalist spirit reemerges in *Modernism* (Loisy, Tyrrell, LeRoy), which tries to adapt Catholic thought once again to contemporary philosophy and biblical scholarship. Its emphasis was on the natural rather than the supernatural, and on the subjective rather than the objective. Although condemned by *Pope Pius X*, its legitimate concerns and questions were carried forward in a more balanced manner by *Maurice Blondel*, who himself anticipated the development of Transcendental Thomism and the work of such present-day theologians as *Karl Rahner* and *Gregory Baum*.

11. The *Second Vatican Council* returns to a more biblical, personalist, historical, cosmic, and ecumenical understanding of revelation as opposed to the highly conceptual approach of Vatican I. Revelation is the divine "mystery" disclosed in Christ, rather than simply a cluster of "mysteries" to be believed on faith. It comprises both word and deed, is not static but dynamic, communicates not conceptual truths but God and the will of God, and continues even in the present.

12. *Post–Vatican II teachings*, especially in the encyclicals of *Pope John Paul II*, focus on human suffering and other universal human experiences as expressions of the word and saving activity of God, and on the presence of revelation and salvation in non-Christian religions.

13. In *contemporary theology* four basic approaches are identifiable: those which continue to emphasize the objective and cognitive aspect of revelation (Pannenberg, Schillebeeckx, Gutiérrez), those which stress the subjective and personalist aspect (Bultmann, Rahner), those which try to mediate between the two (Dulles), and feminist interpretations of revelation in the Bible (Schüssler Fiorenza, Schneiders, Ruether).

14. Revelation would be impossible without *creation*. The creative act is already revelation, the self-communication of God. *"Nature"* is what arises from the creative act. It is through nature that God continues to be disclosed in a progressive movement through the Christ of history to the Second Coming of Christ.

15. God is the Creator of material and spiritual realities alike. The latter includes *angels*, or "messengers" of God, who are spoken of in Sacred Scripture and whose existence is affirmed by the teachings of the Church (Lateran IV and Vatican I).

16. It is the *Church's official teaching*, therefore, that God created the whole world, spiritual as well as material realities (against all forms of dualism, Gnosticism and Manichaeism especially); that the world is distinct from God (against Pantheism); that God created the world in freedom, to manifest

divine goodness and glory. Consequently, all created things are good, have their own rightful autonomy, and are not simply means to some spiritual end.

17. Because God is disclosed in and through creative acts, and because these creative acts constitute *history*, including *personal history*, we come to a knowledge of God as we reflect on the principal events of human history and our own personal history, as Israel and other individuals did before us.

18. *Prophecy* is the act of speaking on behalf of God. The prophet is less the instrument of revelation than the interpreter of revelation.

19. Our experience of God is always *mediated*. This means that all revelation is *mysterious, sacramental,* or *symbolic* in character. God, the invisible One, is known always and only through what is visible. Insofar as any visible reality contains and communicates the presence of God, it can be called a *mystery*. Christ, therefore, is the great mystery. The Church, too, is a mystery. God remains at the same time hidden and disclosed. The presence of God is never so clear that belief is inevitable, nor ever so obscure that belief is impossible.

20. Revelation is both the *process* by which God is disclosed and is one or another of the *products*, or *symbols*, of that process (the Bible, a dogma of the Church, e.g.). Christ alone is at once the reality communicated and the fundamental sign of the reality.

21. A *balanced* theology of revelation has to avoid the *extremes* of Modernism on the left and extrinsicism on the right. Revelation has its origin and foundation *outside* the human subject, but if it happens at all, it happens *within* the consciousness of the human subject.

22. Revelation is *available in principle to everyone*. All are called to salvation, but salvation is impossible without faith, and faith, in turn, is impossible without revelation.

23. Revelation is *closed* only in the sense that the Christ-event has already happened. Revelation *continues,* on the other hand, in that God is a living God and remains available to us. But God will not fundamentally alter nor revoke the self-communication that has already occurred in Christ.

24. Claims of a private revelation, often associated with an alleged Marian apparition, are not binding on anyone other than the person(s) to whom the revelation is given, even if the apparition(s) and subsequent devotion(s) have been approved by the Church.

SUGGESTED READINGS

Dulles, Avery. *Revelation Theology.* New York: Herder and Herder, 1969.
_____. *Models of Revelation.* Garden City, N.Y.: Doubleday, 1983.

Fiorenza, Elisabeth Schüssler. *In Memory of Her: A Feminist Theological Reconstruction of Christian Origins*. New York: Crossroad, 1983.

Latourelle, René. *Theology of Revelation*. New York: Alba House, 1966.

Moran, Gabriel. *The Present Revelation: In Quest of Religious Foundations*. New York: Herder and Herder, 1972.

Niebuhr, H. Richard. *The Meaning of Revelation*. New York: Macmillan, 1962.

Rahner, Karl. "The History of Salvation and Revelation." *Foundations of Christian Faith*. New York: Seabury Press, 1978, pp. 138–75.

Schneiders, Sandra M. *The Revelatory Text: Interpreting the New Testament as Sacred Scripture*. San Francisco: HarperCollins, 1991.

Shorter, Aylward. *Revelation and its Interpretation*. London: Geoffrey Chapman, 1983.

Vatican Council II. *Dogmatic Constitution on Divine Revelation (Dei verbum)*, 1965.

VIII

The Triune God

THE PROBLEM OF THE ONE AND THE TRIUNE

Nothing in this chapter rescinds what has already been stipulated, namely, that the reality of God can neither be proved nor disproved by rational arguments alone. The judgment that God has been revealed in a particular person, event, or mystical experience is always precisely that—a judgment, however reasonable and informed it might be. Indeed, as we shall see in chapter 10, there are many religions rather than one because, among other things, "no one has ever seen or can see" God (1 Timothy 6:16). We can never be absolutely certain that we have had an experience of God, or whether we have correctly perceived, interpreted, and expressed that experience. Since God can become available to us only in some bodily or sacramental way, the self-communication of God will always be conditioned by the historical situation of the person or community to which God is disclosed. Revelation is received, in other words, according to the mode of the receiver. And that is why we must also carry forward here what has already been proposed in the section on human existence, for the God-question is in actuality the reverse side of the question of human existence.

What follows in this chapter is a statement and description—historically, theologically, and doctrinally developed—of the uniquely Christian experience of God. Because Christians are no less human, no less historically situated than others, the Christian perception, interpretation, and expression of the experience of God in faith is also, in principle, subject to ambiguity, error, and distortion. On the other hand, it is the *distinctively Christian conviction* that God has been disclosed so clearly and so definitively in Jesus of Nazareth that there is no possibility of *fundamental* error in the perception, interpretation, or formal doctrinal expression of the experience of God in faith. Fundamental distortion is possible only in *secondary* matters of belief. *Ambiguity*, however, is always possible because of the ineffable character of God and the inherent limitations of language.

But this distinctively Christian conviction raises a major problem for theology: If God is one, how is it that Sacred Scripture and the Church's creeds affirm a pluralism within God, that in God there is Father, Son, and Holy Spirit? *The Christian confession of the Lordship of Jesus is inextricably linked with the Christian belief in the Trinity,* for Jesus' place in saving history makes sense only insofar as he has been sent by the Father and, together with the Father, sends the Holy Spirit to heal, to renew, and to reconcile all that has been wounded by sin. The Christian understanding of God, in other words, cannot be expressed fully, let alone explained, apart from the doctrine of the Trinity and the person and work of Jesus Christ. (Part Three of the book will be devoted exclusively to Christology.) "It is impossible to believe explicitly in the mystery of Christ," Thomas Aquinas wrote, "without faith in the Trinity, for the mystery of Christ includes that the Son of God took flesh, that He renewed the world through the grace of the Holy Spirit, and, again, that He was conceived by the Holy Spirit" (*Summa Theologiæ*, II-II, q. 2, a. 8).

The present chapter takes care not to separate the "one God" (as in the traditional pre–Vatican II theological tract, *De Deo Uno*) from the "triune God" (as in the tract, *De Deo Trino*). To distinguish the "one God" from the "triune God," even for purposes of theological analysis, is to distort radically the distinctively Christian understanding of God. For the Christian, there is only one God, and that one God is triune.

Chapter 9 will be reserved for the discussion of specific questions related to the mystery and doctrine of God, namely, providence, miracles, evil, prayer, personhood, and God-language, particularly as it relates to the Fatherhood of God.

THE PLACE OF THE DOCTRINE OF THE TRIUNE GOD

Because the mystery of the Trinity is at once fundamental and central to Christian theology, the doctrine can be placed either at the beginning or at the end of a comprehensive statement of Christian faith. At the *beginning*, it anticipates the exploration of the whole theological terrain and provides the inquirer with a view of what is to come. At the *end*, it summarizes and synthesizes what has preceded it and provides the inquirer with a substantial review.

A third possibility occurs, however, and it is the one pursued in this book. The doctrine of the Trinity is placed somewhere nearer to the middle, consistent with the process of human discovery operative in the individual consciousness and in human history. The doctrine of the Trinity presupposes some awareness of God and of God's active and gracious presence in Jesus Christ. That awareness, in turn, presupposes some experience of the Transcendent Other as the generator of this awareness. But the judgment that we have indeed had an experience of God also presupposes some understanding of what it means to be human and of the limits of ordinary human experience, for the experience of God is, by definition, that which carries us to and beyond the limits of ordinary, everyday, "objective," empirically verifiable experience.

Accordingly, the doctrine of the Trinity appears in this book as a focal or integrating principle. This doctrine is the way Christians systematically account for the deepest meaning of human existence and systematically express their experience of the ultimate source of that meaning, which is the triune God, disclosed through Jesus Christ and abidingly active as the instrument of reconciliation and unification in the Holy Spirit.

If the doctrine of the Trinity *presupposes* a theology of human existence and of revelation, and even a Christology, it also *implies* a theology of Christ, as it does a theology of the Church and of Christian discipleship and morality. Thus, our discussion of the Trinity both sums up what we have been doing thus far and sets the agenda for the more explicitly Christological, ecclesiological, moral, and spiritual discussions that follow.

Because of the peculiar doctrinal relationship between the mystery of the Trinity and the mystery of Christ, one might persuasively argue that the Trinity ought to be treated systematically *after*, rather than before, Christology. But in a sense, we are doing that. The present chapter provides a synthesis of the whole Christian doctrine of God. As suggested above, the formal doctrine of the Trinity developed under the pressure of confronting the apparent contradiction between the Church's consistent affirmation of monotheism and its simultaneous confession of faith in the Lordship of Jesus. In that sense, Christology generates the doctrine of the Trinity and must be presupposed by it.

On the other hand, Christianity has not been immune from a certain *Christomonism*, a kind of "unitarianism" of the Second Person, in which God as Creator and Judge and God as Reconciler and Sanctifier are effectively replaced by the God who is at our side in the service of the neighbor as the "man for others" (as in the death-of-God theology of the 1960s). Christomonism has also diminished our understanding of the Church and of the Christian life. How else explain the relatively recent extraordinary rediscovery of the presence and power of the Holy Spirit by the West, if not as an acute reaction to the practical exclusion of the Spirit from Latin Christian consciousness, devotion, and even theology?

There *is* a sense in which our exposition of the doctrine of the Trinity follows rather than precedes Christology, since the basic elements of a Christology are presented in this chapter as *antecedents* to the doctrine of the Trinity. But there is another sense in which a Christology cannot fully be developed except within the larger context of trinitarian doctrine if we are not to lapse into Christomonism. Indeed, the uniqueness of Christ is rooted in his consubstantial union with God the Father. An understanding of that uniqueness must, in turn, presuppose an understanding of God as *triune*.

THE GOD OF THE BIBLE

Old Testament

Given the intimate relationship between Judaism and Christianity, represented by the unity of the two biblical Testaments, a historical unfolding of the Christian understanding of God must begin with the Old Testament.

It is by now almost an axiom of theology that the People of God in the Old Testament were not interested in philosophical speculation. Their view and grasp of reality tended to be earthy and concrete. This principle applies especially to their understanding of God. The medieval distinction between essence and existence, for example, would have been totally foreign to the Hebrew mind. Their God was a living God, known to them through the name *Yahweh* given to Moses and his descendants (Exodus 3:13–15). For the Israelites Yahweh is present and active wherever the name of Yahweh is known, recognized, and invoked. To call upon Yahweh is to summon Yahweh. Yahweh's name is glorious (Psalm 72:19), great (1 Kings 8:42), awful (Deuteronomy 28:58), exalted (Psalm 148:13). The name is also the source of deliverance (Psalm 54:3) and exaltation (Psalms 33:21; 89:25). Yahweh's name is at once supportive (Psalm 124:8) and trustworthy (Psalm 33:21; Isaiah 50:10). To know Yahweh's name is to know Yahweh (Isaiah 52:6; 64:1). And so it was crucial to the success of Moses' mission that he should discover the name of God:

> But Moses said to God, "If I come to the Israelites and say to them, 'The God of your ancestors has sent me to you,' and they ask me, 'What is his name?' what shall I say to them?" God said to Moses, "I AM WHO I AM." He said further, "Thus you shall say to the Israelites, 'I AM has sent me to you.'" God also said to Moses, "Thus you shall say to the Israelites, 'The LORD, the God of your ancestors, the God of Abraham, the God of Isaac, the God of Jacob, has sent me to you':
>
> This is my name forever, and this my title for all generations. (Exodus 3:13–15)

What the name *Yahweh* actually means is difficult to determine. There is no unanimity among scholars regarding its derivation. There seems to be general agreement, however, that the name has some etymological connection with the archaic form of the verb "to be" (*hawāh*). The distinguished biblical archaeologist W. F. Albright (d. 1971) links the name with the causative form and suggests that it is only the first word of the entire name, *yahweh-'aser-yihweh*, "He who brings into being whatever comes into being." The name would, therefore, signify the creative power of God. Still others have suggested that the name means "I am who I will be," thereby revealing a

God in process, one who summons us to collaborate in the building of the future.

Whatever the precise linguistic source, the name *Yahweh* clearly distinguished the God of Israel from every other claimant to the divine title (the other gods, or *Elohim*). Yahweh alone is the creator. Yahweh alone is the revealer. Yahweh alone governs history and humankind. Yahweh alone judges and saves. Yahweh alone possesses a dominion which is as wide as creation itself. Yahweh alone is a living God (Joshua 3:10; 1 Samuel 17:26,36; 2 Kings 19:4,16; Psalms 42:3; 84:3; Isaiah 37:4,17; Jeremiah 10:10; Hosea 2:1). Yahweh alone gives life (Job 12:10; Deuteronomy 32:39; 1 Samuel 2:6; Psalm 133:3). Indeed, life is given to those who keep the divine commandments (Deuteronomy 30:15–20). One lives by heeding the word of Yahweh (Isaiah 55:3; Ezekiel 20:11,13,21).

Because the Old Testament is pre-Christian, it does not provide any trinitarian understanding of God. This is not to say that the Old Testament's understanding of God is utterly *inconsistent* with the subsequent trinitarian development of the Christian era. The God of the Old Testament is a living God, intimately involved in the history of the people of Israel, sending forth a word through the prophets and the "signs of the times"—a word so identified with its source that it is called the very word of Yahweh. While it would be theologically unjustifiable to suggest some "foreshadowing" of the Trinity in the Old Testament, the personification of certain divine forces or modalities (the "word," the "wisdom," and the "spirit" of God) which are distinct from God and yet not simply intermediate powers between God and the world provides perhaps a certain prelude to the Christian understanding of God as triune.

New Testament

As we shall point out in chapter 10 on the religions of the world, monotheism is not peculiar to Judaism alone, nor finally to Christianity. What is *original* about the Christian understanding of God is its *identification of God with Jesus of Nazareth*. The revelation of God in Jesus Christ does not occur merely in the prophetic word he uttered, as was the case with the Old Testament prophets. Rather, God is communicated in the very person of Christ. There is an identity between God and Jesus Christ. The Prologue of John's Gospel makes this as clear as does any passage in the New Testament:

> There was a man sent from God, whose name was John. He came as a witness to testify to the light, so that all might believe through him. He himself was not the light, but he came to testify to the light. The true light, which enlightens everyone, was coming into the world.
>
> He was in the world, and the world came into being through him; yet the world did not know him. He came to what was his own, and his people did not accept him. But to all who received him, who believed in his name, he gave power to become children of God. . . .
>
> And the Word became flesh and lived among us, and we have seen his glory, the glory as of a father's only Son, full of grace and truth. (John 1:6–12,14)

There is a kind of parallel "prologue" in the Epistle to the Hebrews:

> Long ago God spoke to our ancestors in many and various ways by the prophets, but in these last days he has spoken to us by his Son, whom he appointed heir of all things, through whom he also created the worlds. He is the reflection of God's glory and the exact imprint of God's very being, and he sustains all things by his powerful word. (1:1–3)

In Jesus, therefore, the reality of God is manifested in visible, personal form. And yet the New Testament generally reserves the Greek title *ho theos* ("God") to the Father of Jesus Christ. Jesus is the *Son* of God. We said "generally," because the title "God" *is* bestowed on Jesus here and there, e.g., in the opening verse of John's Gospel ("and the Word was God") and in the Apostle Thomas's confession of faith upon seeing the risen Lord ("My Lord and my God"—John 20:28). Furthermore, the "glory of our great God and Savior" which is to appear can be the glory of no other than Jesus (Titus 2:13), and Jesus identifies himself with the Father (John 10:30).

In Jesus Christ not only is the Word made flesh, but all of the saving attributes of Yahweh in the Old Testament are actualized. God pardons through Christ (Ephesians 4:32) and reconciles the world through him (2 Corinthians 5:19). God gives the Spirit through the

Son (John 15:26; 16:7). The Christian belongs to Christ, and Christ belongs to God (1 Corinthians 3:23).

The God who acts in and through Jesus Christ and the Holy Spirit is a forgiving God (Matthew 6:14; Mark 11:25; Luke 15:1–32), a merciful God (Luke 1:72,78; 6:36; 2 Corinthians 1:3; Ephesians 2:4; 1 Timothy 1:2; Titus 3:5; 1 Peter 1:3), a kind God (Matthew 19:17; Luke 11:13; 18:19; James 1:5), a loving God (John 3:16; 16:27; Romans 5:5; 8:37,39; Ephesians 2:4; 2 Thessalonians 2:16; Titus 3:4), a faithful God (1 Corinthians 1:9; 2 Thessalonians 3:3), a patient God (Romans 15:5), the God of all grace (Acts of the Apostles 20:24; Romans 5:15; 1 Corinthians 1:4; 3:10; 15:10; 2 Corinthians 1:12; Ephesians 3:2,7), the God of hope (Romans 15:13), the God of peace (Romans 15:33; 16:20; 1 Corinthians 1:3; 2 Corinthians 1:2; Galatians 1:3; Ephesians 1:2; Philippians 4:9), the God of comfort (Romans 15:5; 2 Corinthians 1:3–4; 2 Thessalonians 2:16), the God of salvation (Luke 1:47; 1 Timothy 1:1; 2:3; 4:10; Titus 2:11; 2 Peter 3:9), a compassionate God who desires the salvation of all (Matthew 18:14; 1 Timothy 2:3,4; 4:10; Titus 2:11; 2 Peter 3:9).

Even if it is evident that the doctrine of the Trinity is *not* in the Old Testament, it does not follow, by some process of elimination, that the doctrine of the Trinity *is* clearly and unequivocally in the New Testament. The New Testament speaks simply of "God," the same God who was at work in the Old Testament: the God of Abraham, of Isaac, and of Jacob. The New Testament writers do not even ordinarily speak of Jesus as "God" (except in the rarest of cases, e.g., the Prologue of John's Gospel), since this would be for them an identification of Jesus with the Father. On the other hand, the New Testament recognizes the divinity of the Son. Where the Son appears as preexistent, he is in the realm of the divine (John 1:1; Philippians 2:6–11). He is the presence of the kingdom (Matthew 12:28; Luke 11:20), has lordship over the Sabbath (Mark 2:23–28; 3:1–6), and possesses the fullness of the Spirit (Luke 4:18).

But the New Testament does not specify the terms of the relationship between Father and Son, nor among Father and Son and Holy Spirit. It assumes only that there *is* some relationship (Matthew 11:27; John 1:1; 8:38; 10:38; 1 Corinthians 2:10). The Father "sends" the Son and the Spirit (John 14:16,26; 17:3; Galatians 4:6) and gives the Spirit through the Son (John 15:26; 16:7). Many other texts focus more explicitly on the Father-Son relationship (e.g., Mark 12:1–12; John 1:1, 14; 2 Corinthians 4:4; Hebrews 1:3). But none of these texts individually nor all of them together express a theology of the Trinity as such. They refer to the impact of God upon the Church. They have to do with the actions of God in the world outside of the inner life of God, i.e., with the "economic Trinity" (Father, Son, and Holy Spirit as they are experienced in the history of salvation) as opposed to the "immanent Trinity" (Father, Son, and Holy Spirit as they exist and interrelate within God). It took three or four hundred years before the Church began to make the proper distinctions, to go beyond the formulations of the Bible and the creeds alone, and to see how the "economic Trinity" and the "immanent Trinity" are one and the same, that the God who is with us is who God is.

The God whom we *experience* as triune *is* triune. But we cannot read back into the New Testament, much less into the Old Testament, the trinitarian theology and doctrine which slowly and often unevenly developed over the course of some fifteen centuries.

THE GOD OF THE EARLY CHRISTIAN WRITERS

The main question facing the Church in the immediately postbiblical period concerned the relationship of the Son to God the Almighty (*Pantokrator*). Statements about the Spirit tended to appear as a consequence of Christological statements. The Spirit was regarded as a synonym for God. But that could be not true of the Son, since the Son had specific roles and was perceived to have a distinctive identity apart from the Almighty. Is the Son subordinate to the Father and, therefore, not "true God of true God" (Council of Nicea [325]), or is he "consubstantial" (*homoousios*) with the Father, "true God of true God" indeed?

Consequently, the trinitarian theology of the early Christian writers had its starting point in their reflection on the history of salvation, i.e., on soteriology, or the theology of redemption. The coequal divinity of Christ was of the highest urgency, not because doctrinal purity had to be preserved but rather because our salvation was at stake. If Christ is not truly divine, then he is a creature like us and has no special standing before God. We are still in our sins.

283

The basic unity of the early Christian approach notwithstanding, there is also a discernible difference between the theology of the Greek writers and the theology of the Latin writers. The *Greeks* were oriented toward the *"economic* Trinity"; the *Latins,* toward the *"immanent* Trinity."

The Apostolic Fathers

The doctrine of the "one God," the Father and Creator of all things, was a fundamental premise of the Church's faith from the very beginning. Inherited from Judaism, *monotheism* provided Christianity's first line of defense against pagan polytheism, Marcionite dualism (reality comes from the hands of two opposite but equal forces, the one good, the other evil), and various other contemporary heresies. And yet Christian theology was still in an exceedingly undeveloped state in this earliest of its historical periods.

What is to be gleaned from the Apostolic Fathers of the first century of the Christian era is relatively meager indeed. The fourth bishop of Rome, *Clement of Rome* (d. 100), in urging the Christians of Corinth to end their quarrels, divisions, schisms, and other internal hostilities, declared: "Do we not have one God and one Christ and one Spirit of grace, a Spirit that was poured out upon us?" (*Letter to the Corinthians,* 42). The identity of Father, Son, and Spirit with God and their distinctiveness, one from the other, are also suggested by *Ignatius of Antioch* in his *Letter to the Ephesians:* "You consider yourselves stones of the Father's temple, prepared for the edifice of God the Father, to be taken aloft by the hoisting engine of Jesus Christ, that is, the Cross, while the Holy Spirit serves you as a rope; your faith is your spiritual windlass and your love the road which leads up to God" (para. 9).

The Apologists

Although his writings are not without some ambiguity because of his Platonist philosophical background, *Justin* insists that "we worship and adore" the Father, the Son, and the prophetic Spirit, and that our faith is fixed on Jesus Christ as "the only proper Son who has been begotten by God, being His Word and first-begotten..." (*First Apology*, chapters 6 and 23). The generation of the Son is conditioned by, and is a product of, the Father's will. But this does not suggest any separation between the Father and the Son. On the contrary, Justin, like the other Apologists, never tired of trying to safeguard the *oneness* of God.

No theologian, however, summed up so authoritatively the thought of the second century as *Irenæus*. He approached the mystery of God from two directions: the God who is, and the God who is manifested in the economy of salvation. What is disclosed in history (namely, the trinitarian pluralism of God) was actually there from all eternity. And over against Marcionite dualism and Gnosticism, Irenæus declared that "there is only one God, the Creator—He who is above every Principality, and Power, and Dominion, and Virtue; He is Father, He is God, He the Founder, He the Maker, He the Creator.... He is the Father of our Lord Jesus Christ: through His Word, who is His Son, through Him He is revealed and manifested to all to whom He is revealed; for those [only] know Him to whom the Son has revealed Him" (*Against Heresies*, II, 30). And not only is God the Creator of all things; God is their provident sustainer as well, ruling with goodness, mercy, patience, wisdom, and justice (III,25).

Third-Century Writers

The doctrinal preoccupation of the Church's earliest theologians had been, until now, the oneness and unity of God. As challenges to the oneness of God subsided, they turned their attention to the plural manifestation of God in creation, in redemption, and in reconciliation (known as "economic Trinitarianism"—*economic* because it refers to the measurable "household" activities of God in the world of our experience, i.e., in our "household," as opposed to the unobservable, and therefore unmeasurable, activities within the inner or *immanent* life of God). But this deliberately Trinitarian shift in the understanding of God generated its own set of problems and questions: Principally, how is the ancient doctrine of God as *Pantokrator* ("the Almighty") to be maintained if we are to confess that Jesus Christ is equal to the Father as *Pantokrator*?

Tertullian tried to resolve the problem through the use of analogies, the one biological, the other anthropological. First, the Father and the Son are parts of the same organism, but the organism itself is undivided and its power is one. Second, the Father and the Son, although distinct from each other, are in complete harmony of mind and will. Neither analogy solved the problem. Both are at the level of imagination, while the problem is at the level of thought. (See his *Apology* and his *Against Praxeas*.)

Origen (d. 254), the greatest of the third-century theologians and certainly one of the most gifted theologians of all time, approached the problem at a higher level. Borrowing from contemporary Platonist philosophy, Origen insisted that there is only one God, but that there is also the Logos which emanates from the One and participates in the One as the image of the divine Goodness. The Father is *the* God (only of the Father does Origen use the definite article). The Logos is not *the* God; the Logos is simply God, and is so by emanation and participation in a Platonist sense. The Logos is a God "of the second order." As such, the Logos is a diminished deity, since in the Platonist scheme emanation involves some measure of degradation of being. (See his *Principles, Against Celsus,* and *Commentary on John*.)

Unfortunately, Origen's solution did not do justice to the actual faith of the Church, namely, that the Logos is God in an undiminished divine sense. The best philosophical instrument at his disposal, Platonism, simply could not supply an answer. Origen's attempt, however, paved the way for the forthright, although finally heretical, solution of *Arius* (d. 336), a priest of Alexandria, who argued that the Logos is a creature of God, even though a perfect creature. He came to be out of nothing. "There was when he was not."

Dionysius of Rome (d. 268), twenty-sixth bishop of Rome, provides yet another indication of the mind of leading contemporary theologians on the developing Trinitarian problem. By the time of his pontificate, there were already three clearly distinguishable heresies on the scene: *Sabellianism* (also known as *Modalism*), which taught that God is one person who appears in three different roles according to three different functions: Father, Son, and Spirit; *Subordinationism,* which recognized the trinity of Persons, but made the Son less than the Father and the Spirit less than the Son; and *Tritheism,* which so emphasized the distinction of Persons that there were now three gods instead of one.

Dionysius called a synod in Rome, and in a letter to the bishop of Alexandria, also named Dionysius, about whom there had been some rumors of unorthodox teaching, he insisted that all three points of view mentioned above were wrong. Positively, we must hold: (1) there is one *Pantokrator;* (2) Jesus Christ is the Lord; i.e., he is the *Pantokrator;* and (3) Christ, the *Pantokrator,* is the Son, and as such is distinct from the Father who is *the* God, the *Pantokrator.*

The bishop of Rome, of course, did not solve the problem, but like most authoritative interventions his at least clarified the limits of the discussion and underlined the principles of orthodoxy which are to be maintained, whatever the proposed explanation or solution.

FOURTH-CENTURY THEOLOGICAL AND DOCTRINAL DEVELOPMENTS

Arianism

In every period of the Church's history, theologians have confronted mysteries of faith in one of three ways: first, they in effect eliminate the mystery and reduce everything to what reason can grasp (the Liberal or Rationalist approach); second, they throw up their hands and insist that the mystery is so impenetrable that we should ask no further questions of it (the Fideist or antiintellectual approach); or third, they acknowledge that the mystery never can be resolved, but they press ahead nonetheless, hoping at least to clarify the problem and reach some greater measure of understanding (the mainstream, orthodox approach).

Arius pursued the first course. How can we preserve the oneness of God without denying the preeminence of the Son over the entire created universe? Simple enough. The Son, despite his exalted status in the economy of salvation, is a creature like us. He is no more a mystery than you or I. Arius reasoned that if both the Father and the Son are said to be unbegotten, then it must also be said that there are two separate Gods. But this would contradict monotheism, which Arius wanted to uphold in fidelity to ancient Jewish belief. He maintained, therefore, that only the Father is unbegotten, hence truly

God, and that the Father created the Son. Hence, Arius's catechetical slogan: "There once was when he [the Son] was not."

That is not to say, however, that Arius's attempt at a solution to the mystery of God was simply frivolous in its origins and arbitrary or irresponsible in its conclusions. Indeed, he insisted that the Son possessed a dignity superior to every human creature. But given the nature of human intelligence, it was inevitable that someone would eventually ask the questions of how and why. We move always from *description* (the way things look to us) to *definition* (the way things are in themselves). The Bible describes the creative, redemptive, and sanctifying activities of God: Father, Son, and Holy Spirit. How are these Persons really related to one another, and in particular the Son to the Father? Can we really safeguard the oneness of God if we insist at the same time on the complete equality of the Son with the Father?

On the other hand, the Arian controversy was more than an intellectual debate. At stake was the very practical matter of our salvation in Christ, to which the same Sacred Scriptures clearly attest. If the Son is not God, fully the *Pantokrator*, wholly situated within the divine reality on an equal footing with the Father, then he is not our Savior and we are not saved. For if the Son is a creature like us, he has no special standing before the Creator against whom we creatures have sinned. His act of reparation on our behalf has no ultimate effect.

Council of Nicea

It was the Council of Nicea, summoned in 325 by the Emperor Constantine in the hope of restoring unity to the Church, that gave a definitive answer to the Arian question. "We believe in one God the Father, the *Pantokrator* ('the Almighty'), Maker of all things visible and invisible; and in one Lord Jesus Christ, the Son of God, begotten out of the Father, the Only begotten." Thus far, the affirmation of faith is entirely traditional, fully consistent with earlier creeds and with the biblical formulae as well. But then the council comes to the heart of the Arian controversy: "The only begotten generated from the Father, that is, from the being of the Father, God from God, Light from Light, true God from true God...." Thus, the Son does not emanate from the Father's *will*, as a creature, but out of the Father's *substance,* by a unique mode of origination radically different from the creative act. The Son, therefore, is "begotten, not made." He is not the perfect creature outside the divine order. He is begotten within the divine order and he remains within it. His being is untouched by createdness. Finally, he is "one in being (*homoousios*) with the Father."

The Council of Nicea, therefore, did not simply describe the nature of the begetting of the Son; it defined it. The Son is from the Father in a singular, unshared way, begotten as Son, not made as a creature. This is what "one in being," or "consubstantial" (*homoousios*), means. That is what the Son is. "A passage has been made," John Courtney Murray, S.J. (d. 1967), wrote, "from a conception of what the Son is-to-us to a conception of what the Son, Christ, is-in-himself. The transition is from a mode of understanding that is descriptive, relational, interpersonal, historical-existential, to a mode of understanding that is definite, explanatory, absolute, ontological. The alteration in the mode of understanding does not change the sense of the affirmation, but it does make the Nicene affirmation new in its form" (*The Problem of God,* p. 46).

It soon became clear, however, that Nicea's *homoousios* did not definitively clarify the relationship between God and Christ. A more satisfactory way had to be found to speak of the equality between God and Christ, Father and Son, without compromising the real distinction between Father and Son. It remained for subsequent fourth-century theologians to work it out (see Catherine Mowry LaCugna, *God for Us: The Trinity and Christian Life,* p. 37).

The Aftermath of the Council

Opposition to the Nicene creed came from both extremes: not only from the Arians on the left but also from the conservative party on the right, those who gathered around Eusebius of Cæsarea (d. c. 340), who is also generally regarded as the first serious Church historian. This party wanted to say no more than Sacred Scripture seemed to be saying, namely, that the Son is "like" (*homoios*) in all things to the Father. The same position appears in the formula of the Synod of Constantinople in 361. *Homoousios,* they insisted, is not a biblical word; therefore, the Nicene formula cannot be a formula of faith.

The deeper issue, of course, was the *development of doctrine*. The Eusebians, like many traditionalists down through the centuries, refused to acknowledge the possibility, not to say the appropriateness, of progress in doctrinal understanding. They were at heart fundamentalists, biblical positivists. The Eusebians' affection for their particular reconstruction of the past (*archaism*) would give rise to the opposite tendency, i.e., the notion that no affirmation of faith can ever be final (*modernism*).

The Nicene formula avoids both extremes. It rejects archaism by transposing the biblical affirmations concerning the Son into a new mode of understanding, but always consistent with the biblical. And it also rejects modernism because the notion "consubstantial" (*homoousios*) sets a final limit in the understanding of faith. There can, and must, be further growth in our understanding of this mystery, but the direction and dimensions of that growth are forever conditioned by the finality of the Nicene formula. And the Nicene formula, in turn, provides a charter and a precedent for the later councils of Ephesus (431) and Chalcedon (451), which also had to transcend the biblical formulae and attempt an expression of the internal makeup of Christ in the philosophical categories of nature and person. (We shall be returning to the Christological debates and doctrines in greater detail in Part Three.)

Through the efforts of Athanasius and Hilary of Poitiers (d. 367), the Eusebians (the so-called *homoiousian* party) were eventually reconciled with the orthodox *homoousians*. Hilary contended in his *On the Councils* that both sides were right and had an obligation to recognize the essentially orthodox concerns of the other side. Since the Nicenes acknowledged the distinction of persons within God, they could not really deny the *homoiousian* principle. The *homoiousians*, for their part, had to allow unity of substance (*homoousios*) if they believed seriously in the perfect likeness of substance.

At the Council of Alexandria in 362 the reconciliation was sealed. With Athanasius in the conciliar chair, the assembly legitimated the "three *hypostases* (persons)" formula of the Eusebian party, provided it merely expresses the separate subsistence of the three Persons in the Trinity. From this emerged a new orthodox formula: "one *ousia* (being, substance), three *hypostases* (persons)."

The distinction underscored for the Greek writers the truth that God (*theos*, the Father, the Almighty) has come to us through the Son and the Spirit. God is revealed through the Son, and through the Son God reaches us in the Holy Spirit. Therefore, our "contact" with God, or more properly God's "contact" with us, is *historically definite* (through the Son) and *immediate* (in the Spirit), contrary to the various heresies of the day—e.g., Modalism, Sabellianism, Arianism.

The Greeks were content, however, to define the relation between the one divine being, or nature, and the three *hypostases* (not quite "persons" in the present sense of the word) in terms of traditional philosophical categories. The concrete character of these *hypostases* was then deduced from their function in the history of salvation.

The Cappadocians

There remained the problem of the relationship between the Holy Spirit and the Father, and between the Holy Spirit and the Son. Since Origen's day theological reflection had not kept pace with the considerable devotional practice centered on the Holy Spirit. Under the impact of denials of the divinity of the Spirit (a group of Egyptian Christians, for example, argued that the Spirit was a creature brought into existence out of nothing), the specifically theological task of articulating the divine equality of the Spirit with the Father and the Son was begun by Athanasius and taken up even more systematically by three major theologians and pastoral leaders of the Church, known together as the Cappadocians: Basil (d. 379), his brother Gregory of Nyssa (d. 394), and his friend Gregory of Nazianzus (d. 390).

It was *Basil* who urged that the Spirit must be accorded the same glory, honor, and worship as the Father and the Son; *Gregory of Nyssa* who emphasized the oneness of nature shared by the three Persons of the Trinity; and *Gregory of Nazianzus* who insisted that the Spirit, like the Son, is consubstantial, or one in being, with the Father. (This point would be developed even more fully by Cyril of Alexandria, d. 444, in his *Thesaurus on the Holy and Consubstantial Trinity.*)

For *Basil* the Spirit issues from God not by way of generation (as in the case of the Son) but "as from the breath of [God's] mouth"; for *Gregory of Nazianzus* the Spirit simply "proceeds" from the Father, as John's Gospel has it; but for *Gregory of Nyssa* the Spirit is "out of God" and is "of Christ." The Father is uncaused, and the Son and the Spirit are caused. The Son is directly produced by the Father, while the Spirit proceeds from the Father through the Son, but without any trace of subordinationism (i.e., the heresy that the three Persons of the Trinity are somehow unequal).

The essence of the Cappadocian doctrine of God (as expressed in Basil's *On the Holy Spirit*, Gregory of Nyssa's *Letter #38, On the Holy Spirit: Against the Followers of Macedonius* and *On "Not Three Gods,"* and Gregory of Nazianzus's *The Fifth Theological Oration*) is that the one God exists simultaneously in three ways of being or *hypostases*. Each of the divine *hypostases*, or Persons, is the *ousia* or essence of God; these Persons are distinguished from one another only by their relationships to one another, and those relationships are determined, in turn, by their origins. Thus, the Father is different from the Son in that the Father is unbegotten, while the Son is begotten by a process of generation; the Son is different from the Spirit in that the Son is generated while the Spirit proceeds from the Father [through the Son].

Gregory of Nazianzus's expression of the mystery is fully representative of the Cappadocian position:

> But the difference of manifestation, ... or rather of their mutual relations to one another, has caused the difference of their Names. For indeed it is not some deficiency in the Son which prevents His being Father (for Sonship is not a deficiency), and yet He is not Father. According to this line of argument there must be some deficiency in the Father, in respect of His not being Son. For the Father is not Son, and yet this is not due to either deficiency or subjection of Essence; but the very fact of being Unbegotten or Begotten or Proceeding has given the name of Father to the First, of the Son to the Second, and of the Third, Him of whom we are speaking, of the Holy Spirit, that the distinction of the Three Persons may be preserved in the one nature and dignity of God. For neither is the Son Father, for the Father is One, but He is what the Father is; nor is the Spirit Son because He is of God, for the Only begotten is One, but He is what the Son is. The Three are One in God, and the One Three in properties. ... (*The Fifth Theological Oration*)

The whole Greek theological approach to the mystery of the triune God would later be summed up by *John of Damascus* (d. c. 749) in his *The Source of Knowledge*, part III, "On the Orthodox Faith."

The Councils of Constantinople (381) and of Rome (382)

This post-Nicene theology received official endorsement at two councils, the one ecumenical and the other provincial. The First Council of Constantinople (May–July 381) was called by the Emperors Theodosius (d. 395) and Gratian (d. 383), the one ruling the East, the other the West. All the bishops attending the council were from the East. Of the 186 bishops present, 36 were considered "heretical." The remaining 150 bishops reaffirmed the faith of Nicea.

Against *Arianism* it taught the equality of Christ with God; against *Apollinarianism* it recognized the full humanity of Christ; against the *Pneumatomachians* and the *Macedonians*, who denied the divinity of the Holy Spirit, it held the consubstantiality (oneness-in-being) and the coeternity of the Spirit with the Father and the Son. From this council there eventually emerged the *Nicene-Constantinopolitan Creed* (its use gradually spread through East and West from the late fifth century, but it was not adopted in Rome until 1014). The bishops of Constantinople had not themselves composed the creed. They accepted one that was already available (probably the Baptismal Creed of Jerusalem, perhaps introduced at the council by Cyril of Jerusalem) and which they deemed entirely consistent with the doctrinal formulations of Nicea. The creed is recited today in every Sunday Mass throughout the Catholic world (see the appendix for the full text).

Pope Damasus (d. 384) did not participate in the Council of Constantinople, and there is no historical evidence that he officially accepted its decisions. The following year, however, he summoned a provincial council in Rome, which issued a set of anathemas or condemnations against those who held false teachings about the Father, Son, and Holy Spirit. The collection of condemnations was subsequently known as the *Tome of Pope Damasus I*. Positively, the Council of Rome taught that there is one God of three divine, co-

293

equal, coeternal Persons, each distinct from the other, but not so distinct that we have three separate gods.

AUGUSTINE

There was no comparably sophisticated theology in the Latin West until Augustine, although important contributions had already been made by Irenæus, Tertullian, Hilary, and others. Influenced by the writings of the neo-Platonist convert to the Church, Victorinus (d. c. 380), Augustine accepted without question the doctrine that there is one God in whom Father, Son, and Holy Spirit are at once distinct and consubstantial (or "coessential," as he preferred).

Significantly, nowhere does Augustine try to prove this doctrine. He accepts it as a datum of revelation which, in his view, Scripture proclaims almost on every page. His concern is not with proof but with understanding, which is consistent with his fundamental notion of theology as belief seeking understanding (*Credo ut intelligam*, "I believe in order that I might understand").

Unlike his Greek counterparts, Augustine does not begin with the three Persons as they function in history for our salvation and then work backwards, so to speak, to the unity of God. He begins rather with the one divine nature itself and tries to understand how the three Persons share in that nature without dividing it. Subordinationism of every kind is rejected. Whatever is affirmed of God is affirmed equally of each of the Persons (*On the Trinity*, bk. 5, ch. 9). "Not only is the Father not greater than the Son in respect of divinity, but Father and Son together are not greater than the Holy Spirit, and no single person of the Three is less than the Trinity itself" (8,1). Thus, we are not speaking here of three separate individuals as we would of three separate human beings. There are not three wills, but one. There are not three sources of divine action, but one.

Against the obvious objection that Augustine is destroying the several roles of the three Persons (and, therefore, is lapsing into Modalism), he argued that, even though it was the Son and not the Father who was born, suffered, and died, the Father cooperated fully with the Son in bringing about the incarnation, the passion, and the resurrection. It is fitting, however, for the Son to have been manifested and made visible in those events, since each of the divine

Persons possesses the divine nature in a particular manner and since, in the external operation of God, roles which are *appropriate* to a particular Person in view of that Person's origin within God are fittingly attributed to that Person. And yet all three Persons are always fully involved as one in every external action.

One of Augustine's original contributions to the Christian doctrine of God (and his most effective rebuttal of the charge of Modalism) was his notion of what Thomas Aquinas would later refer to as real or *subsistent relations*. Anticipating the teaching of Anselm (d. 1109) and then of the Council of Florence (1442) that in the Trinity all things are one except what is differentiated by reason of an opposition of relations (e.g., the Father, who is *unbegotten*, is not the Son, who is *begotten*), Augustine opposed the Arian notion that distinctions within God are either substantial (in which case there are three separate gods) or accidental (in which case God is not purely simple).

Whatever the Father, the Son, or the Holy Spirit are, they are in relation to one or both of the others (see *On the Trinity*, bks. 5–7). Threeness in God, therefore, is not rooted in threeness of substance or threeness of accidents but in threeness of *relations:* of begetting, of being begotten, and of proceeding.

What is perhaps Augustine's most original contribution to Trinitarian theology, however, is his use of *analogies* drawn from *human consciousness* to explain the inner life of God. In every process of perception, he points out, there are three distinct elements: the external object, the mind's sensible representation of the object, and the act of focusing the mind. When the external object is removed, we rise to an even higher trinitarian level, superior to the first because the process occurs entirely now within the mind and is therefore "of one and the same substance," namely, the memory impression, the internal memory image, and the focusing of the will.

In his *On the Trinity* Augustine elaborates the analogy at length in three successive stages, with the following resulting trinities: (1) the mind, its knowledge of itself, and its love of itself, (9, 2–8); (2) memory, or the mind's latent knowledge of itself, understanding, and love of itself (10, 17–19); and (3) the mind as remembering, knowing, and loving God (14, 11–end). Augustine regarded the last of the three analogies as the most satisfactory. It is only when the mind has focused itself on its Creator with all its powers of remembering, understanding, and loving that the image it bears of God can be fully restored. "Since these three, the memory, the understanding, and the will, are, therefore, not three lives but one life, not three minds but one mind, it follows that they are certainly not three substances, but one substance" (10, 11).

Augustine himself was realistic about the limitations of this analogical approach. Analogies, as the saying goes, always limp. They tell us how things are *like* other things, but they warn us at the same time that the things being compared are also *unlike* one another. Thus, the operations of human consciousness are by no means identical with the inner operations of the Trinity. Remembering, understanding, and loving are three separate faculties of the human mind. In God there are no distinct faculties. God is absolutely one. Furthermore, in the human mind these three faculties operate independently. In God every act and operation is indivisible (15, 43). Furthermore, why are there only two processions and only three Persons?

We are left, in the end, with the mystery: Scripture and Christian doctrine portray God as acting in three Persons, but Scripture and Christian doctrine also insist firmly and unequivocally on the oneness of God.

The importance and usefulness of the Augustinian approach notwithstanding, it obscured the connection between the "immanent Trinity" and the "economic Trinity" and made of the doctrine, at least in much of the Western Church, a matter of abstract speculation alone, of no real pastoral importance, having no place in the pulpit, for example, except perhaps once a year on Trinity Sunday.

Nevertheless, Augustine's influence on subsequent Christian belief and theology is, to be sure, enormous. Apart from Boethius (d. c. 525), who bequeathed the definition of *person* as "an individual substance of a rational nature," no one competes with him for theological impact on later centuries. But the more immediate effect of his approach was also considerable. The so-called *Athanasian Creed (Quicumque)* of the late fifth century clearly bore the stamp of Augustinian thought. Falsely attributed to St. Athanasius, the creedal formula has stood ever since as the Western Church's classical statement of Trinitarian faith.

Augustine's influence was also operative in the deliberations of the Eleventh Council of Toledo (675), which drew upon the *Quicumque* creed as well as Augustine's writings for the construction of its own profession of faith, in which it declares that God is both One and Three.

ANSELM

Although no complete history of the Christian understanding of God can ignore the watershed figure of *John Scotus Erigena* (d. 877), the most famous scholar and teacher of his day and one of the last who tried to reconcile ancient Greek philosophy with the faith (see his *On the Division of Nature,* in which he seems to propose a pantheistic notion of God), our attention turns here to Anselm of Canterbury, the single most important theologian between Augustine and Aquinas.

Anselm's contribution to the Christian understanding of God is at least threefold: the so-called ontological argument for God's existence; the debt-satisfaction theory of atonement; and the principle that in God everything is one except for the opposition of relationships among the three Persons. Only the last seems to have survived subsequent critical analysis. On the first point, Anselm insisted that God is "a being than which nothing greater can be conceived." But, he said, if such a being exists only in the mind or in the realm of understanding, "the very being, than which nothing greater can be conceived, is one, than which a greater can be conceived. Hence, there is no doubt that there exists a being, than which nothing greater can be conceived, and it exists both in the understanding and in reality" (*Proslogium,* ch. 2). The argument was later rejected by Aquinas and Kant alike. What may be true in the order of the mind is not necessarily real in the order of objective reality.

On the second point, Anselm argued that the sin of Adam could be forgiven only if sufficient satisfaction for the sin were offered to the Father. But only a divine person could adequately resolve the debt incurred by human sin. Therefore, God had to become human if we were to be restored to God's friendship. (We shall return to this theory of atonement in Part Three on Christology.)

On the third point, Anselm argued, following in the tradition of Augustine, that God is absolutely one except for the pluralism of

297

persons created by the opposition of relationships among them. The Father, Son, and Holy Spirit are one God, except insofar as the Father is unbegotten and the Son is begotten, and insofar as the Spirit proceeds whereas the Father and the Son spirate (see his *On the Procession of the Holy Spirit*, chapter 1). This principle is the theological basis for the doctrine of the *mutual indwelling of the three divine Persons*: The Father is always in the Son and the Holy Spirit; the Son is always in the Father and the Spirit; the Spirit is always in the Father and the Son. The mutual indwelling is also known as *circumincession*, or *perichoresis*. The Council of Florence (1442) adopted the principle in its *Decree for the Jacobites*: "The Father alone begot the Son out of His substance; the Son alone was begotten from the Father alone; the Holy Spirit alone proceeds from both Father and Son. These three persons are one God and not three gods, for the three are one substance, one essence, one nature, one God, one infinity, one eternity, and everything [in them] is one where there is no opposition of relationship."

In the final accounting, Anselm believed that the mystery of the triune God is "so sublime" that it "transcends all the vision of the human intellect. And for that reason I think it best to refrain from the attempt to explain how this thing is." It is enough for Anselm to be secure in the knowledge *that* God is, and that what we *do* know of God is "without contradiction of any other reason" (*Monologium*, ch. 64). For theology itself is "faith seeking understanding" (*fides quærens intellectum*).

LATERAN COUNCIL IV

When a new pope is elected, one of his first official acts is to take possession of the Lateran Basilica, the cathedral church of the diocese of Rome. It is as bishop of Rome, of course, that the pope serves as earthly head of the Catholic Church. The Lateran has also been the scene of five general or ecumenical councils. It was the fourth such council of the Lateran, during the pontificate of Innocent III (d. 1216), which produced a profession of Trinitarian faith as well as a formal doctrinal statement on the reality of the triune God.

The council confessed that "there is only one true God … Father, Son, and Holy Spirit: three persons indeed but one essence, substance, or wholly simple nature: ... the Father generating, the Son being born, the Holy Spirit proceeding; consubstantial, coequal, coomnipotent, and coeternal; one origin of all things: the Creator of all things visible and invisible, spiritual and corporal." This creedal affirmation was directed explicitly against *Albigensianism,* one of the most serious heresies in the history of the Church.

Indeed, Philip Hughes (d. 1967), one of the best-known English-speaking church historians of the twentieth century, regarded the seventeen years (1181–1198) that separated Pope Innocent III from Pope Alexander III as "the most critical period of the Middle Ages.... Of all the dangers that threatened, the greatest of all was the revival of Manichaeism which, beginning a hundred years before this, had by now made its own all the south of France (Provence) and much of northern Italy" (*A Popular History of the Catholic Church,* New York: Doubleday Image, 1949, p. 115).

The sect was called Albigenses after the city of Albi, Provence. Its theological position was that matter is evil, that it comes from some source other than the true God. Because matter is evil, we must abstain from food, from marriage, and especially from conception. The sect was well organized and was extraordinarily successful in gathering adherents from the cultured nobility and from the wealthy merchant class.

At first the pope tried to combat the heresy with persuasion and preaching, but when those failed, he adopted more aggressive measures: One was the calling of the Fourth Lateran Council, and another was the establishment of the Inquisition to root out this heresy and others. (For an excellent case study of how the Church went about this task, see Emmanuel LeRoy Ladurie's *Montaillou: The Promised Land of Error,* New York: Braziller, 1978.)

The council taught that God is the author of both matter and spirit and that Christ is fully God, with a human as well as a divine nature. In its second document, the council addressed itself to a bitter dispute between *Joachim of Flora* (d. 1202) and *Peter the Lombard* (d. 1160). The dispute was a kind of microcosm of the historic difference between the Eastern and Western approaches to the mystery of the Trinity. The Eastern approach, as noted earlier, was centered on the saving activity of the three Persons in history. The Western approach, with its roots principally in Augustine, was centered on the one divine nature which subsists as Father, Son, and Holy Spirit. Peter the Lombard had systematized this latter approach in his *Sentences*, making the divine essence the center of his speculation. Joachim attacked Peter, accusing him of producing a fourth Person, the "divine essence."

The council defended Peter against the accusation that he had produced a *quaternity*, and sanctioned the doctrine which became the basis of the Trinitarian theology of most Scholastics thereafter: "In God there is only Trinity, not a quaternity, because each of the Persons is that reality, viz., that divine substance, essence, or nature which alone is the beginning of all things, apart from which nothing else can be found. This reality is neither generating nor generated, nor proceeding, but it is the Father who generates, the Son who is generated and the Holy Spirit who proceeds, so that there be distinctions between the persons but unity in nature. Hence, though 'the Father is one person (*alius*), the Son another person, and the Holy Spirit another person, yet there is not another reality (*aliud*),' but what the Father is, this very same reality is also the Son, this the Holy Spirit, so that in orthodox Catholic faith we believe them to be of one substance."

MEDIEVAL SCHOLASTICISM

Augustine's impact on medieval Scholasticism was enormous, and it was only to be reinforced, not essentially modified, by Thomas Aquinas. Another type of trinitarian theology, more in keeping with the Greek approach and stressing the psychology of love rather than of understanding, was promoted by *Richard of St. Victor* (d. c. 1173), *Alexander of Hales* (d. 1245), and *Bonaventure* (d. 1274).

In his *On the Trinity*, Richard, unlike Augustine, begins with person rather than nature, looking to the unselfish love of human *friendship* as the reflection of the unselfish love of divine friendship (since we are, after all, made in the image of God). In God there is one infinite love and three infinite lovers: lover produces beloved, and lover and beloved are the productive principle of an equal cobeloved. *Alexander of Hales* explains the divine processions through the principle that "goodness diffuses itself." The inner life of the Trinity is characterized by perfect charity. In *Bonaventure* we find this same emphasis on "pure goodness" and "mutual love" as principles under-lying the dynamism and plurality of the inner life of God (see his *Commentaries on the Four Books of Sentences*).

Perhaps because they were less precise than the Augustinian and Thomistic expositions, the so-called Franciscan contributions to trini-tarian theology did not succeed in establishing themselves. Attempts at some constructive synthesis of these two approaches are only recently being made, so long has the theology of the Trinity been under the influence of Scholasticism and later of neo-Scholasticism.

THOMAS AQUINAS

Aquinas's understanding of God is too precise and detailed to sum-marize in so brief a space as this. Its major components, however, are twofold: (1) the identification of essence and existence in God; i.e., God's essence is "to be"; and (2) the participation of the created order in the Being of God, who is the First Cause of all that is.

For the first, he rests his case on the Exodus text (3:14) wherein Yahweh "responds" to Moses' question: "I am who I am." For Aqui-nas, this is the most suitable name for God (*Summa Theologiæ*, I, q. 13, a. 11). "Everything," he writes, "exists because it has being. A thing whose essence is not its being, consequently, is not through its essence but by participation in something, namely, being itself. But that which is through participation in something cannot be the first being, because prior to it is the being in which it participates in order to be. But God is the first being, with nothing prior to Him. His essence is, therefore, His being" (*Summa Contra Gentiles*, I, 22).

From this follows the principle that every created reality partici-pates in the Being of God. God is perpetually and immediately pres-ent to the world of beings, for God is Being itself, the condition for the existence of any beings at all (*Summa Theologiæ*, I, q. 8; q. 104). Unlike the God of *Deism*, who creates the world in the beginning and then allows it to work on its own thereafter (much like the clockmaker's relation to the clock), the God of Aquinas is at once transcendent and immanent to the world (*Summa Contra Gentiles*, II, 21; III, 67–68).

But God's intimate involvement in the created universe does not thereby destroy the integrity of free agents. "God works in things in such a manner that things have their proper operation." Otherwise, "the operative powers which are seen to exist in things would be bestowed on things to no purpose, if things produced nothing through them. Indeed, all created things would seem, in a way, to be purposeless, if they lacked an operation proper to them, since the purpose of everything is its operation" (*Summa Theologiæ*, I, q. 105, a. 5).

Aquinas's understanding of the Being and action of God is consistent with his famous "five ways" to prove the existence of God: the argument from *motion* (there must be a prime mover), the argument from *causality* (every effect must have a cause), the argument from *necessity* (all beings are possible, but one must be necessary if there are to be any beings at all), the argument from gradation or *exemplarity* (our ideas of more or less, of better or worse, presuppose some standard of perfection), and the argument from *design* (the consistent and coherent operation of the whole universe demands some intelligent and purposeful designer) [see *Summa Theologiæ*, I, q. 3, a. 3].

These arguments were not original with Aquinas. He was largely indebted to Plato, Aristotle, Avicenna, Augustine, and especially the Jewish philosopher Moses Maimonides. All of the arguments are reducible to one: the argument from causality. No one argument "proves" the existence of God. They are simply ways in which the believer can begin to "make sense" of his or her belief in God after the fact. (We touched already upon this problem in chapter 6.)

Insofar as God ordains all things to their goal, God is *provident*; i.e., God "foresees" and insures what is necessary for the fulfillment of the end of the world and all that is in it (*Summa Theologiæ*, I, q. 22, a. 1). The human being, as the creature endowed with reason, "is under God's providence in the special sense of sharing in providence inasmuch as he is provident with regard to himself and other things" (I-II, q. 91, a. 2). This sharing of the rational creature in the reason of God (I-II, q. 19, a. 4) is called the "natural law" (q. 91, a. 2). Alongside the natural law is the new law of the Gospel and of the Holy Spirit which is imparted to those who believe in Christ (q. 106, a. 1). There can be only one goal, God, of both the created and the recreated universe, i.e., of the order of nature and the order of grace (I, q. 103, a. 2).

Finally, with regard specifically to the doctrine of the Trinity, Aquinas completed the psychological explanation of the relations of Persons which Augustine initiated and Anselm developed. He was the first to argue that there are two distinct processions (generation and spiration) because a spiritual being has two operations: intellection and volition. These processions produce, in turn, four real relations: paternity, filiation, spiration, and procession, but only three of them are really distinct from one another by reason of their mutual opposition: paternity, filiation, and (passive) spiration (I, q. 28, aa. 1–4). And so there are three Persons, and only three, in God (I, qq. 27–43).

Other important medieval theologians, like *Duns Scotus* (d. 1308), agreed with the conclusion but not with the argument. Anticipating the Greek Orthodox position, Scotus argued that not only opposite relations but also disparate relations (e.g., passive generation and active spiration) distinguished divine persons. Therefore, it was not necessary that the Spirit proceed also from the Son (see *Commentary on the Sentences*, I, d. 11, q. 2).

COUNCIL OF LYONS II; COUNCIL OF FLORENCE

What these two ecumenical councils had in common was their concern for the split between the Eastern and Western Churches, by now already two centuries old. Both tried to effect some kind of reconciliation, but neither succeeded for very long. Insofar as the schism involved divergent understandings of God, and of the Trinity in particular, the conciliar texts are of interest to us here.

Lyons II (1274) adopted as its own a so-called *Profession of Faith of Michael Palæologus*. It was taken from a letter written by the Byzantine Emperor Michael VIII Palæologus (d. c. 1282), in which the emperor merely reproduced, without modification, the text of a profession of faith proposed to him by Pope Clement IV (d. 1268) as early as 1267. Clement believed this to be required of the Greeks if reunion was to occur. Insofar as Michael desired reunion, he himself subscribed to it.

Not surprisingly, the text reflects the Latin approach to the doctrine of the Trinity: It begins with the oneness of the divine nature and then proceeds to the trinity of Persons, with the Holy Spirit proceeding from the Father *and* the Son (not *through* the Son, as the Greeks would have it). In another document, the *Constitution on the Holy Trinity and the Catholic Faith*, the council explains the Latin doctrine on the origin of the Holy Spirit, insisting, against its Eastern detractors, that the origin of the Holy Spirit from the Father *and* the Son does not imply a double principle in God.

The *Council of Florence's* (1438–1440) teaching on God is contained in two documents: the *Decree for the Greeks* (1439) and the *Decree for the Jacobites* (1442). In the former, the council explains the procession of the Holy Spirit from Father *and* Son, but allows also for the formula cherished by the East, namely, procession from the Father *through* the Son, with the understanding, however, that the Son, just as fully as the Father, is the "cause" or "principle" of the subsistence of the Holy Spirit. The *Decree of Union* was signed by both groups, but when the Greeks returned to Constantinople, public opinion forced them to repudiate it. The Churches remain separated to this day.

Representatives of the Syrian Jacobite Church came to Rome afterwards and engaged in similar negotiations leading to a consensus statement, in this case the *Decree for the Jacobites*, important for its emphasis on the concept of *circumincession*, or *perichoresis*, namely, that each Person is always present to the other two Persons: "The Father is wholly in the Son and wholly in the Holy Spirit; the Son is wholly in the Father and wholly in the Holy Spirit; the Holy Spirit is wholly in the Father and wholly in the Son." The Decree is also significant for its articulation of the principle that in the Trinity all things are one except what is opposed by the opposition of relations.

PROTESTANTISM AND THE COUNCIL OF TRENT

The Council of Trent's (1545–1563) doctrinal formulations on God cannot be understood apart from the theology of the Reformers. For *Martin Luther* (d. 1546) the difficulty is not with the immanent Trinity (i.e., the Trinity from the viewpoint of the inner life of God) but with the economic Trinity (i.e., the Trinity from the viewpoint of the action of God in the world, and specifically in the lives of human beings). Luther believes in, and confesses, the mystery of the Blessed Trinity. But he cannot accept the Catholic principle that God desires the salvation of all, that God is essentially a gracious God, and that God wills us to cooperate freely with divine grace in the working out of our salvation.

For Luther, on the contrary, we can do nothing on our own (*sola gratia*). God has mercy on whomever God wills (Romans 9:18). God "wills that [God's] power should be magnified in [our] perdition" (*Lectures on Romans,* chapter 8). But Luther also insists that the true God says "I have no pleasure in the death of the wicked, but that the wicked turn from their ways and live" (see Ezekiel 33:11). "God is the same sort of God to all people that [God] was to David, namely, one who forgives sins and has mercy upon all who ask for mercy and acknowledge their sins" *(Lectures on Psalms, On Psalm 51:1).*

In *Bondage of the Will,* however, Luther stresses God's foreknowledge and omnipotence so much that practically no room is left for our free response. In Christ, of course, we have access to the Father's will and heart. If God be for us in Christ, who or what can be against us (Romans 8:31)? (See his commentary on the First Commandment in *The Large Catechism.*)

John Calvin (d. 1564), the other great Reformer, carries the doctrine of predestination even further. Taking Romans 9:13 literally, he concludes that God loves some and hates others: "It is just as Scripture says, 'I have loved Jacob, but I have hated Esau.' " On the other hand, Calvin acknowledges in his *Institutes of the Christian Religion* that "God has destined all things for our good and salvation.... Nothing that is needful for our welfare will ever be lacking to us" (chapter 14).

And yet "By God's bidding... salvation is freely offered to some while others are barred from access to it.... He does not indiscriminately adopt all into the hope of salvation but gives to some what he denies to others" (bk. III, ch. 21). Salvation is owed to no one; therefore, God does no one an injustice by denying it to anyone. Furthermore, if God cannot punish, how is his mercy to be made manifest (chapter 23)?

The Reformers' attitude toward God's salvific intentions underscores again one of the principal historic differences between Protestant and Catholic theology and spirituality. The former tradition, as we suggested in the earlier discussion of the problem of nature and grace in chapters 4 and 5, has tended to emphasize the radical unworthiness of the person, even after God's redemptive activity on our behalf. The Catholic tradition, on the other hand, insists that God not only makes a declaration of our worthiness for salvation, but actually transforms us and makes us new creatures in Christ and the Holy Spirit.

305

God offers this inner transformation to every person, without exception. No one is excluded beforehand. Only a free act of the will, rejecting the divine offer of grace, can impede God's saving designs. The alternate view—predestination to hell as well as to heaven—has been described by the Anglican theologian John Macquarrie as a "fantastic exaggeration of the divine initiative into a fatalism [which] is repugnant not merely because it dehumanizes man but also because it presents us with a God who is not worthy to be worshipped" (*Principles of Christian Theology*, p. 341).

The *Council of Trent's Decree on Justification* teaches that "all people" have been called to the status of adopted sons and daughters of God in Christ (chapter 2), but that they can freely reject the grace of adoption (chapter 5). Insofar as we do open ourselves to the divine presence, it is because our hearts have been touched through the illumination of the Holy Spirit (ibid.).

The process of passing from the condition of sin as a child of the first Adam to a condition of adopted sonship and daughtership in Christ is called *justification* (chapter 4). Justification "is not only a remission of sins but also the sanctification and renewal of the inward person through the voluntary reception of the grace and the gifts whereby an unjust person becomes just" (chapter 7). God wills the salvation of all, and God will achieve that purpose "unless human beings themselves fail in [God's] grace" (chapter 13). Indeed, the council's sixth canon explicitly anathematizes, or condemns, those who say "that it is not in human power to make our ways evil, but that God produces the evil works just as [God] produces the good ones, not only by allowing them but properly and directly, so that Judas' betrayal is no less God's work than Paul's vocation."

PASCAL

Blaise Pascal (d. 1662), mathematician, scientist, and spiritual writer, perhaps best known for his unique apologetical argument on behalf of belief in God (see chapter 6), provides a relatively balanced understanding of the God of faith. Christianity, he declares, teaches us twin truths about this God: "that there is a God whom human beings can reach, and that there is a corruption in their nature which renders them unworthy of [God]." It is crucial that we keep both truths before us. "Knowledge of one alone causes either the pride of philosophers who have known God but not their misery, or the despair of atheists who know their misery but not their Redeemer."

It is only in our knowledge of Jesus Christ that we grasp both truths at once, namely, that we have access to God and that we are creatures in need of forgiveness and reconciliation. The Christians' God, therefore, is like the God of Abraham, of Isaac, and of Jacob, "a God of love and consolation, a God who fills the soul and heart of those whom [God] has purchased, a God who makes them deeply conscious of their misery and of [God's] infinite mercy; who makes [a] home in their heart, filling it with humility, joy, confidence, and love; who renders them incapable of any other object than [God]" (ibid.). This God is always a "hidden God," but there is an escape from our blindness through Jesus Christ, "apart from Whom all communication with God has been cut off ..." (#246).

A fuller statement of Pascal's importance in the history of the Church and of Christian theology generally would require a more complete description of the cultural and ecclesiastical situation in seventeenth-century France, of the development of *Gallicanism* (a movement of French nationalism which, among other things, insisted on the autonomy of the local Church over against Rome and the papacy), of *Jansenism* (with which Pascal was once associated at Port-Royale), and of various other contemporary spiritual movements associated with the names of Fénelon (d. 1715), Bossuet (d. 1704), and others.

FIRST VATICAN COUNCIL AND ITS ANTECEDENTS

Kant

Immanuel Kant (d. 1804) in his *Critique of Pure Reason* rejected the traditional arguments on behalf of the existence of God, having been awakened from his own "dogmatic slumber" by David Hume's (d. 1776) analysis of causality. Since God is by definition in a totally different order, God's "objective reality cannot indeed be proved, but also cannot be disproved, by merely speculative reasoning" (section 7). Since God operates in the moral order, it is there that God is to be apprehended, if at all. Insofar as we all seek the highest good, we must be able to presuppose that the quest is possible in the first place.

"Granted that the pure moral law inexorably binds every man as a command (not as a rule of prudence), the righteous man may say: I will that there be a God, that my existence in this world be also an existence in a pure world of the understanding outside the system of natural connection, and finally that my duration be endless" (*Critique of Practical Reason,* section 8, New York: Macmillan, 1993; orig. ed., 1788). Since our idea of the highest good in the world leads to the postulation of a higher, moral, most holy, and omnipotent Being which alone can unite our quest for happiness with our obedience to duty, morality thus leads ineluctably to religion. God becomes the powerful moral Lawgiver whose will is the final end of creation and of all human activity (*Religion Within the Limits of Reason Alone,* Preface to the first edition, New York: Harper, 1960; orig. ed., 1793).

We feel ourselves at once impelled to seek the highest good, even duty-bound to seek it, but powerless on our own to reach it. We discover ourselves to be living in an ethical commonwealth under the governance of a moral Ruler who is creator, guardian, and administrator. The Lawgiver's beneficence, however, is limited by human cooperation with the holy law. To say that "God is love" means that God approves us insofar as we obey the law. To speak of a *triune* God, however, is to exceed the limits of reason alone, for we cannot grasp God as God actually is but can only grasp God insofar as God is for us as moral beings (bk. III).

Hegel

Georg W. F. Hegel (d. 1831), on the other hand, did posit the reality of the Trinity, but he grounded the reality of the Trinity on a purely philosophical basis. Central to his whole system (expressed most fully in his *Phenomenology of Spirit,* Oxford: Clarendon Press, 1977; orig. ed., 1806) is the insight that all reality develops *dialectically,* moving through contradictions to a resolution thereof; *thesis* (initial knowledge), *antithesis* (contradiction), and *synthesis* (unification).

The reality of God proceeds in the same way. The Absolute Spirit, which is God, posits its own opposite other, Matter, and resolves the difference in an eternal return to itself. The Father is

Being-in-and-for-itself; the Son is the Other, the finite particulariza-
tion of the universal; the Spirit is the singleness, the unity of the
universal and the particular. The Trinity provides the paradigm for
what occurs in all of reality, which moves inexorably through dialectical processes of universality and particularity, and of identity and
distinction. Everything is moving finally to the Kingdom of the Spirit,
where alone God becomes personal (see *Lectures on the Philosophy of
Religion, Part III*, Berkeley: University of California Press, 1984).

Once again, only a fuller historical, philosophical, and theological discussion can begin to do justice to the extraordinary impact
which both Kant and Hegel have made upon, and continue to make
upon, Christian thought, not to say secular thought—e.g.,
Marxism—Kant in the realms of ethics and fundamental theology,
and Hegel in the realm of systematic theology. Indeed, the influence
of Hegel upon much of recent and present-day German theology, of
both Catholic and Protestant varieties, cannot easily be overesti-
mated. It is particularly strong in Rahner, Metz, Pannenberg, and
Moltmann. The impact of Kant on the revision of our traditional
notions of our knowledge of God in revelation and faith and of our
apprehension of truth generally is also broadly ecumenical. There is
no serious theologian working in the area of fundamental theology
who has not been affected by the Kantian revolution. On the other
hand, Kant's influence in moral theology or Christian ethics has
tended to be restricted for the most part to Protestantism.

Schleiermacher

Friedrich Schleiermacher (d. 1834) carried forward the now traditional
Protestant insistence on the inability of the human mind to grasp the
reality of God—a position consistent, of course, with classical Protestantism's understanding of the relationship between nature and
grace. Schleiermacher taught that faith is essentially our feeling of
absolute dependence. If we find God at all, we find God in our
consciousness. Since the Trinity does not emerge from an analysis of
human consciousness, it cannot be regarded as a primary datum of
Christian faith (see his *The Christian Faith*, where the Trinity is relegated to an appendix).

It is perhaps fair to say that Schleiermacher is the principal forerunner of Liberal Protestantism of the nineteenth and early twentieth centuries. Together with *Adolf von Harnack* (d. 1930), who rejected the doctrine of the Trinity as an unacceptable Hellenization of the essential Christian message, he is one of the principal targets of the neoorthodox revival initiated by Karl Barth around the time of the First World War. For Barth, the Trinity is utterly fundamental and central to God's revelation in Jesus Christ (see the "Prolegomena" of Barth's *Church Dogmatics*).

Kierkegaard

Søren Kierkegaard (d. 1855) constructed a position at odds with both Hegel and Schleiermacher. Against Hegel, Kierkegaard argued that "an infinitely qualitative difference" separates us from God, that we are not in fact absorbed into the universal Spirit but retain our individual selfhood before God. Indeed, so strongly did Kierkegaard insist upon the importance of the individual's responsibility before God that he is generally regarded as a kind of protoparent of modern (or *post*modern) existentialism.

For Kierkegaard God is utterly transcendent, without any need at all for us. On the contrary, it is we who need God if we are to become authentic persons. We are called to an interior conversion of the heart so that we become fixed entirely on the will of God. Against the liberalism represented by Schleiermacher, Kierkegaard argues that "the fundamental error of modern times ... lies in the fact that the yawning abyss of quality between God and humanity has been removed.... Before God [the human person] is nothing (*Journals*, #712). Furthermore, Kierkegaard retains the doctrine of the Trinity as central to Christian faith.

Kierkegaard's impact upon Karl Barth, especially in the latter's development of the notion of God as "wholly Other," is exceedingly profound. Through Barth, Kierkegaard would have a part in shaping the direction of neoorthodox, neo-Reformation Protestant thought in the early and mid-twentieth century, with its emphasis on the transcendence of God and our personal relationship with God, and its corresponding caution regarding the sociopolitical dimensions of the Christian faith.

310

Vatican I

The First Vatican Council (1869–1870) confronted these and other approaches to the question of God: materialism, rationalism, pantheism, and the like. In its *Dogmatic Constitution on the Catholic Faith*, the council taught that "there is one God, true and living, Creator and Lord of heaven and earth, mighty, eternal, immense, incomprehensible, infinite in [divine] intellect and will and in all perfection. As [God] is one unique and spiritual substance, entirely simple and unchangeable, we must proclaim [God] distinct from the world in existence and essence... ineffably exalted above all things that exist or can be conceived apart from [God]." All contrary positions are explicitly anathematized.

TWENTIETH-CENTURY UNDERSTANDINGS OF GOD

A complete survey of pre–Vatican II understandings of God within the Christian community would require a comprehensive outline of twentieth-century theology. John Macquarrie has attempted something like this in his *Twentieth-Century Religious Thought*, 4th ed. (Philadelphia: Trinity Press International, 1988), and John Cobb has produced a similar work, although more limited in scope, in *Living Options in Protestant Theology* (Philadelphia: Westminster Press, 1962). The reader already has had the barest framework for such an outline in chapters 2 and 4 of this book: In chapter 2 there is a descriptive listing of various kinds of contemporary theology, and in chapter 4 there are sketches of various contemporary understandings of human existence. What follows here is a brief survey of the various theological approaches insofar as they embody a particular understanding of God.

First, there are *liberal* and *neoliberal* theologies which tend to reduce the supernatural content of faith to its lowest common denominator. The emphasis in the divine/human relationship is always on the human, particularly in its social and political dimensions. A formal doctrine of the Trinity is marginal to the liberal schema. In this regard, liberal theology draws upon Schleiermacher (from within the Church) and upon Feuerbach and Nietzsche (from outside the

Church). Liberalism in theology is primarily, although no longer exclusively, a Protestant phenomenon.

Second, there are *orthodox* and *neoorthodox* theologies. Both are also known as *confessional* theology. On the Catholic side, this theology stresses the otherness, the unchangeability, and the providential power of God manifested in and through Jesus Christ and the Holy Spirit. On the Protestant side, this theology stresses divine judgment and the wholly otherness of God. But given the historic emphases on justification-as-transformation in Catholicism and on justification-as-declaration in Protestantism, the otherness of God tends to be more strongly stressed in Protestantism than in Catholicism, while the sacramental availability of God in our ordinary everyday lives tends to be more strongly stressed in Catholicism than in Protestantism.

Third, there is *radical* or *"death-of-God"* theology which, in the spirit of Feuerbach, Hegel, and Nietzsche, insists that the transcendent God is dead, that transcendence itself has collapsed into total immanence, that what we call divine or supernatural is just another way of describing the human and the natural. This was a mid–1960s exaggeration of the liberal and neoliberal reductionist understandings of God which have persisted throughout the twentieth century.

Fourth, there is *secular* theology, another 1960s development, which, like liberal and neoliberal theologies, emphasizes the this-worldly character of God and of Christian faith, but without setting aside the content of the Christian tradition. On the contrary, a strong insistence on the social and political dimensions of Christianity is portrayed as consistent with, even demanded by, the principles of the Old and New Testaments and of postbiblical Christian doctrine: God calls us to a life of responsibility in and for the world through the servant Christ ("man for others") and the reconciling Holy Spirit. Indeed, it is in experiencing the "gracious neighbor" that we experience the "gracious God" (John A. T. Robinson [d. 1983]).

Fifth, there are *Latin American liberation* and *black* theologies which also bear a general resemblance to liberal and neoliberal theologies insofar as they stress the social and political dimensions of the faith, but also resemble orthodox and neoorthodox theology insofar as they stress the biblical notion of God as judge and liberator from sin. The God of liberation and black theologies is a God whose primary, if not sole, passion is the freeing of the oppressed from the bondage of economic, racial, or social exploitation. Although rooted in pre–Vatican II insights, Latin American liberation and black theologies are in large measure a postconciliar phenomenon.

Sixth, there is *political* theology, a more comprehensive category than liberation theology, in which God, and more specifically the Reign of God, is seen as the critical principle by which all human, social, and political realities are judged. God is the limit against which all of our notions of justice, humaneness, peace, love, and so forth are finally measured.

Seventh, there is *feminist* theology, which is a critique of the androcentric bias of theology in which the image and concept of God are male, and the patriarchal understanding of society and of social relationships that follows upon this androcentric theology. Although there are differences among schools of feminist thought, a particular point of contention in feminist theology is the extent to which patriarchy, as the cult of fatherhood, has been generated by the central image of divine fatherhood within Christianity.

Eighth, there is *existentialist* theology, which emphasizes the individual believer as the place where God's saving activity occurs in its most concentrated and even in its normative form. Consistently with the position outlined by Kierkegaard in the nineteenth century and subsequently developed by Tillich, Bultmann, and others in the twentieth century, existentialist theology understands God as the source of authentic human personhood. To be exposed to the Word of God is to be open to the principle of conversion and growth. God is not "a" being, but Being itself. God is, more precisely, "holy Being," i.e., Being which *lets be* (Macquarrie). Except for Macquarrie, a formal doctrinal understanding of the Trinity tends to be either obscured by or less than central to contemporary existentialist theology.

Ninth, there is *process* theology, which clearly owes much of its inspiration to the Hegelian understanding of reality but, more immediately, to such twentieth-century theologians and philosophers as Whitehead and Teilhard de Chardin. God is always in a state of flux, moving forward, cocreating history with us. God is neither static nor fixed. God is a dipolar God, in process of becoming other than what God is now, a process which involves a dialectical relationship between all that is meant by "God" and all that is meant by "world." God is at once absolute (as the one whose *existence* depends on no other being) and relative (as the one whose *actuality* is relative to all other beings). Indeed, God alone is relative to all other beings. God alone affects and is affected by all others (Charles Hartshorne). History is moving inexorably toward the Omega Point, when the Kingdom of God will have been brought to perfection (Teilhard de Chardin).

Tenth, there is *creationist* theology, stimulated by a dialogue with the natural sciences and the environmental movement, which focuses on God's relationship with, and presence to, all forms of life on earth, in this universe, and beyond into the whole of the created order.

Eleventh, there is *Transcendental Thomism*, most notably represented by Karl Rahner, which understands God as *the* Transcendent, above, beyond, and over everything else. God is the one to whom all reality is oriented, by a principle which is itself interior to all of reality. That principle is God. God is the "supernatural existential" which makes possible the knowledge of, and the movement toward, the Absolute. In the completion of that movement, both individually and corporately, we find our human perfection. God, therefore, is not "a" Being separate from the human person, but is Being itself, at once permeating and transcending the person. Because God permeates as well as transcends us, there is no standpoint from which we can get a "look at" God objectively.

God is so fully constitutive of our human existence that almost everything we say about God can be translated into a declaration about our own existence as well. This is not to reduce all God-talk to philosophy, but simply to highlight the intimate connection between theology and anthropology in Transcendental Thomism. God is present to history in Jesus Christ and in a special way in the Church, where the human community has become explicitly conscious of itself in its ultimate relationship with God. The similarities with the Hegelian scheme are apparent, but so, too, are the differences.

There are various combinations of the above categories of thought, some of which possess a measure of internal consistency and coherence while others are arbitrarily or uncritically eclectic.

SECOND VATICAN COUNCIL

The council did not set out to produce a full-scale theology of God. Insofar as it developed a more or less coherent theology of anything, it was a theology of the Church, as we shall see in Part Four. The council's understanding of God has to be inferred from what it says about other questions: the salvific value of non-Christian religions, the nature of the Church and its mission in the world.

The council's overriding concern was for unity, not only the unity of the Church but of the whole human race. "For all people comprise a single community, and have a single origin, since God made the whole human race dwell over the entire face of the earth (cf. Acts of the Apostles 17:26). One also is their final goal: God. [God's] providence, [God's] manifestations of goodness, and [God's] saving designs extend to all people (cf. Wisdom 8:1; Acts of the Apostles 14:17; Romans 2:6–7; 1 Timothy 2:4) against the day when the elect will be united in that Holy City ablaze with the splendor of God, where the nations will walk in [God's] light (cf. Revelation 21:23 f.)" (*Declaration on the Relationship of the Church to Non-Christian Religions,* n. 1).

"The Church knows that only God ... meets the deepest longings of the human heart, which is never fully satisfied by what this world has to offer," the *Pastoral Constitution on the Church in the Modern World* declares. Thus, "only God, who created human beings to [God's] own image and ransomed human beings from sin, provides a fully adequate answer" to the various questions about human existence. "This [God] does through what [God] has revealed in Christ [the] Son, who became human. Whoever follows after Christ, the perfect human being, becomes himself or herself more of a human person" (n. 41).

The theology of God and the theology of human existence converge at the point of the theology of Christ. What does most to reveal God's presence in the world is "the brotherly and sisterly charity of the faithful who are united in spirit as they work together for the faith of the gospel and who prove themselves a sign of unity" (n. 21). This community of faith, the Church, is itself the product of trinitarian action. The Church is called forth by the Father to carry forward the work of the Son with the sanctifying power of the Holy Spirit (*Dog-*

matic Constitution of the Church, nn. 2–4). "Thus, the Church shines forth as 'a people made one with the unity of the Father, the Son, and the Holy Spirit'" (n. 4). (The quotation is derived from Saints Cyprian, Augustine, and John of Damascus.)

The call to unity is theologically grounded on the mystery of the Trinity itself. There is "a certain likeness between the union of the divine Persons, and in the union of God's sons and daughters in truth and charity" (*Pastoral Constitution on the Church in the Modern World,* n. 24).

THE TRINITY: A DOCTRINAL SYNTHESIS

The Trinity As Absolute Mystery

The Trinity is an *absolute mystery* in the sense that we do not understand it even after it has been revealed. It is a *mystery* in that it is "hidden in God [and] cannot be known unless revealed by God." It is an *absolute* mystery in that it remains forever such. This is the teaching of the First Vatican Council's *Dogmatic Constitution on the Catholic Faith* (1870). The concept of "mystery," however, is left undetermined by the council. A mystery is at least something which clearly transcends the capacity of our ordinary rational and conceptual powers and exceeds, beyond all human imagination, the range and resources of our everyday knowledge. (For a fuller discussion of the notion of "mystery," see chapter 7.)

God As Triune

That (as opposed to *how*) God is triune is the clear and consistent teaching of the official magisterium of the Church. The Council of Nicea (325) testifies to the Church's official faith in "one God, the Father almighty... and in one Lord Jesus Christ, the Son of God... and in the Holy Spirit." The Council of Constantinople (381) confirmed the faith of Nicea and gave us the so-called Nicene-Constantinopolitan Creed which Catholics and other Christians recite each week at the Eucharist. The teaching of Constantinople was verified the following year at a provincial council in Rome from which appeared *The Tome of Pope Damasus* (d. 384), which declared that there is one God of three, coequal, coeternal Persons, each distinct from the other, but not to the point where we have three separate gods.

Against the heretical assault of Albigensianism, which regarded all matter as evil and therefore was led logically to the denial of the incarnation, the Fourth Lateran Council (1215) confessed that "there is only one true God ... Father, Son, and Holy Spirit: three persons indeed but one essence, substance, or wholly simple nature...." And against certain charges made against Peter the Lombard, the council also taught that "in God there is only Trinity, not a quaternity...." In response to the great schism of East and West the Second Council of Lyons (1274) and the Council of Florence (1438–1440) both reaffirmed the doctrine of the Trinity, by now almost taking it for granted, and concentrated instead on the ecumenically sensitive matter of the procession of the Holy Spirit from the Father (*and? through?*) the Son.

Thereafter the doctrine, indeed the *dogma*, of the Trinity is assumed by official church sources rather than intrinsically developed and formally restated. A minor exception would be Pope Paul VI's profession of faith, "Credo of the People of God" (1968) which begins with the words "We believe in one God, Father, Son, and Holy Spirit...." It is restated in a more formal way in *The Catechism of the Catholic Church* (1992).

God the Father

These same confessions of faith in the Trinity are at once confessions of faith in the divinity of each of the three Persons of the Trinity and, at the same time, in the oneness of God. From Nicea (325) to Pope Paul VI (1968) professions of faith regularly begin with the words, "We believe in one God...." God the Father is the Lord of salvation history and Creator of all that is. The Father is "unbegotten" but acts, and can only act, in the unity of the Son and the Holy Spirit. The Father generates the Son, and with the Son sends forth the Holy Spirit.

Although not an ecumenical council, the Eleventh Council of Toledo (675) in Spain, attended by only seventeen bishops, gave the Church a profession of trinitarian faith that was cherished and revered for many centuries thereafter. Its profession of faith in God the

317

Father is as succinct and doctrinally precise a formulation as one might discover anywhere in the entire history of the Church:

> And we profess that the Father is not begotten, not created, but unbegotten. For He Himself, from whom the Son has received His birth and the Holy Spirit His procession, has His origin from no one. He is therefore the source and origin of the whole Godhead. He Himself is the Father of His own essence, who in an ineffable way has begotten the Son from His ineffable substance. Yet He did not beget something different from what He Himself is: God has begotten God, light has begotten light. From Him, therefore, is "all fatherhood in heaven and on earth." (Cf. Ephesians 3:15)

God the Son

The Son is begotten by the Father and not made out of nothing, like a creature (as the Arian heresy asserted). The Son is of the same substance with the Father. Thus, the Son is coequal in divinity and coeternal with the Father. It is through the Son as the Word, or *Logos*, of the Father that the Father is expressed in salvation history and within the inner life of the Trinity as well. Because the Son is consubstantial (*homoousios*) with the Father, his Sonship is not simply like that of any other son or daughter of God in the conventional sense of the expression, "We're all God's children." Within the human family, of Jesus Christ alone can it be said that he is of the same substance with the Father. In the words of Nicea:

> We believe ... in one Lord Jesus Christ, the Son of God, the only begotten generated from the Father, that is, from the being (*ousia*) of the Father, God from God, Light from Light, true God from true God, begotten, not made, one in being (*homoousios*) with the Father, through whom all things were made, those in heaven and those on earth. For us and for our salvation He came down, and became flesh, was made human, suffered, and rose again on the third day. He ascended to the heavens and shall come again to judge the living and the dead.

God the Holy Spirit

The Holy Spirit is the Father's gift through the Son. It is through the Spirit that the Father is communicated to us with immediacy, and it is

318

through the Spirit that we are able to accept the self-communication of the Father. As the self-communication of God, the Holy Spirit is God given in love and with the reconciling and renewing power of that love. The Spirit has the same essence as the Father, and yet is distinct from the Father and the Son. The Spirit proceeds from the Father through the Son (despite the bitter East-West dispute on this point, the Council of Florence *did* allow for the preposition *through* as a legitimate alternative to the preferred conjunction *and*).

The procession is not a begetting, since this would lead to the supposition that there are two Sons, nor is the Spirit merely a mode in which the Son communicates himself to us. The Spirit originates from the Father and the Son and has a distinct relationship to the Father and the Son which accounts for the Spirit's distinct hypostatic existence within the inner life of God and the Spirit's distinct salvific mission in history (without prejudice to the principle of the mutual indwelling of the three Persons, each one in the others).

From the First Council of Constantinople:

> We believe... in the Holy Spirit, the Lord and giver of life, who proceeds from the Father [and the Son], who together with the Father and the Son is worshipped and glorified, who has spoken through the prophets. [And] in one Holy Catholic and apostolic Church. We acknowledge one baptism for the forgiveness of sins. We expect the resurrection of the dead and the life of the world to come.

Two observations: First, the words *and the Son* (*Filioque*) were added later in Spain in the sixth century, and from there the usage spread to Gaul and Germany. It was eventually introduced into the Roman liturgy by Pope Benedict VIII (d. 1024). The Greeks ignored the *Filioque* and denied the Western Church's right to make any addition to the ancient creed of Constantinople. Second, the realities of the Church, the forgiveness of sins, the resurrection of the dead, and the life of the world to come are a constitutive part of our affirmation of the Holy Spirit because these are directly attributed to the Spirit's role in salvation history, again without prejudice to the principle of the mutual indwelling of the three Persons (circumincession).

Processions, Relations, Persons, and Nature

From the point of view of our "discovery" of the triune character of God, we first experience the divine *processions,* or missions (we experience the Spirit who has been *sent* by the Father and/through the Son, and we experience the Son as the one *sent* by the Father). The processions, in turn, suggest *relations* between and among *persons* (or distinct *hypostases*) which nonetheless participate coequally, coeternally, and consubstantially in the *nature* of God, namely, the *divinity.* The official teachings of the Roman Catholic Church (the adjective *Roman* is used deliberately here to distinguish the teachings from similarly "official" teachings formulated over the centuries in the East) provide no final definitions of any of these key doctrinal terms. They do, however, provide certain fundamental dogmatic principles regarding these terms:

1. There are two *processions* and only two processions in God: generation and spiration.

2. There are four *relations* (paternity, filiation, active spiration, passive spiration), but only three *subsistent relations,* i.e., three relations which are mutually opposed and, therefore, distinct from one another (without, however, being distinct from the very Being of God): paternity, filiation, and passive spiration. Active spiration (which involves Father and Son) is not opposed to either paternity or filiation, and, thus, does not constitute a fourth subsistent relation.

3. In God all things are one except what is opposed by the opposition of relations. Those relations which are opposed and therefore distinct one from the other are called, as noted above, subsistent relations, or *hypostases.* They give rise, in turn, to the trinity of *Persons* within God: Father, Son, and Holy Spirit.

4. Because of the unity of the divine essence, of the processions and of the relative oppositions, which constitute the Persons, there is a *mutual indwelling* (circumincession) of the Persons, one in the other two, the other two in the one, so that the Son is for all eternity in the Father, and the Father from all eternity in the Son, and so on.

These teachings are set forth explicitly, but not exclusively, in the Council of Florence's *Decree for the Greeks* (1439) and *Decree for the Jacobites* (1442).

We must take care, of course, not to confuse the terminology of the early Christian writers and of the ecumenical councils of the past with specific meanings associated with those same words today. This is especially true of the term *person*. It is a notion which for many today is still inextricably linked with *consciousness*. A person is an individual center and subject of consciousness. However, new currents of thought have arisen in science, philosophy, and psychology that emphasize the social and especially the *relational* character of personhood. Feuerbach, Hegel, and others had argued in the eighteenth and nineteenth centuries that persons exist only in relation. In the twentieth century a variety of postcritical movements (described in chapter 4) transcended the dualism and individualism of the Cartesian tradition by giving priority to interaction and participation as modes of being and knowing. The embodied "self" who exists in the world is fundamentally relational.

But there exists in God only one power, one will, one self-presence, one activity, one beatitude, and so forth. Insofar as the individual Persons can even be described as "self-conscious" (which at best is an analogical attribution), it is a self-consciousness which derives from the one divine essence and is common to the divine Persons. This axiom, however, deals only with the efficient causality of God. It does not affect the truth that the *Logos* or Son alone became human, or the theory of uncreated grace in which each of the three divine Persons has a special relation to us. To say otherwise would reduce the doctrine of the Trinity to mere words and the Christian understanding of God to an unqualified monotheism.

THE TRINITY: A THEOLOGICAL SYNTHESIS

For too many Christians, the doctrine of the Trinity is only a matter of intellectual curiosity, on the one hand, or a somewhat arbitrary test of faith, on the other. It is as if Jesus at some point in his teaching ministry called the disciples aside and said, "By the way, there *is* just one more thing you should know. In God there are three divine

Persons: Father, Son, and Holy Spirit. And yet there is still only one God. It's quite important that you believe what I'm telling you. Your readiness and willingness to believe will be a sign of your faith in me and in my word and mission."

Accordingly, the mystery and doctrine of the Trinity is often relegated to an entirely marginal place in the total Christian schema. Karl Rahner once suggested that, as far as many Church members are concerned, the doctrine could be erased completely from the Christian treasury of faith and that many spiritual writings, sermons, pious exercises, and even theological treatises could remain in place with little more than minor verbal adjustments.

A proper theological and pastoral understanding of the Trinity depends upon our perception of the identity between the so-called economic Trinity and the so-called immanent Trinity. The two did, in effect, become separated in pre–Vatican II theology and catechesis, and the former (the "economic Trinity") was practically forgotten. Accordingly, the doctrine of the Trinity was received as if it were merely an arcane description of the inner life of God—a life that we cannot observe at first hand, in any case. In that view, it has to do with a network of divine relationships which concerns only God and not ourselves, except insofar as Christ asks us to believe his "revelation" about such a mystery as a sign of our faith in him and in his total message and mission.

But that, in fact, is not the way the mystery of the Trinity was revealed to us. Nowhere do we find the Lord calling his disciples aside, and "revealing" the Trinity as if it were this week's catechetical lesson. On the contrary, the Church gradually and painstakingly came to certain conclusions about the inner reality of God on the basis of its experience of God within its own human experience and within human history. In other words, the Church began to wonder theologically and doctrinally whether there is more to God than traditional monotheism suggests, or whether, at the other extreme, there might be three gods, or two, or perhaps a small community of unequal gods.

The Church came to the knowledge of God as triune as it progressively reflected on its experience of the triuneness of God's dealings with us in history. And then the Church concluded that the God whom we experience as triune in history (the "economic Trinity") must also be triune in essence, i.e., within the inner life of God (the "immanent Trinity").

In traditional categories, the revelation of the economic Trinity *is* the revelation of the immanent Trinity. We did not first "hear about" the immanent Trinity and then search for signs of its activity in our lives. In that case the revelation of the immanent Trinity would have been a merely verbal, highly abstract communication. Rather, our "understanding" of the immanent Trinity came about precisely as a result of our reflection on the very practical, saving activities of the triune God in our lives. This is so because "God's way of being in relationship *with us*—which is God's personhood—is a perfect expression of God's being as God. In God alone is there full correspondence between personhood and being, between *hypostasis* and *ousia*. God for us is who God is as God" (LaCugna, pp. 304–305). Therefore, *the doctrine of the Trinity* is not a speculative doctrine alone. It is *the way we express our most fundamental relationships with the God of our salvation as well as God's relationships with us.*

Those of us reflecting on the mystery of the Trinity today do so because the doctrine is already there, as a given of our Christian experience, consciousness, and faith. In the primitive Christian community—the disciples, the Apostles, the evangelists, the first faithful members of the Church—the seeds of the doctrine were also "given." But not by the New Testament, since it did not yet exist. And not by creedal statements, although some of these were already circulating and some few found their way into the New Testament.

The earliest Christians were "alerted" to the trinitarian dimension of divine salvation by Christ, first of all, and then by the preaching of the Apostles, and then by attentiveness to their own unusual experience of the triune God (e.g., at Pentecost) in this most unusual period in the history of the Church. But having conceded all of that, the mystery of the Trinity remains precisely that: a mystery, and absolute mystery at that.

If the self-communication of God in Jesus Christ, the Son, and in the Holy Spirit is really the self-communication of *God*, then these self-communications must be attributed to God as God is. "God for us is who God is as God."

The divine self-communication, therefore, has two basic modes: of truth (the *Logos*, or Word) and of love (the Spirit). As *truth*, the self-communication takes place in history, through a particular person. As *love*, it brings about the openness of human beings to the presence of God in Christ and makes possible our acceptance of that divine presence. Without being simply identical, these two forms of divine self-communication constitute together the one divine self-communication which manifests itself in truth and love. And yet there is a real distinction between the two forms of self-communication (or processions, or missions): In the one, the Father is expressed as truth; in the other, the Father is received and accepted in love.

One of the most obvious difficulties with the doctrine of the Trinity arises from the Church's use of the word *person* to identify the various terms of the divine relationships. We take it to be a theologically nonnegotiable matter as well. There is simply no other way of talking about the triune God except in terms of the "one God and the three divine Persons." And yet the New Testament does not use the term *person*. Indeed, it was introduced only very gradually into ecclesiastical language.

And even when the Church passed beyond the biblical formulations, its theologians and official magisterium did not immediately fasten upon the term *person* (*prosopon*). The initial preference was for *hypostasis*. *Hypostasis* can be predicated of any being, not merely of rational beings. It applies to whatever exists in itself.

Persona, on the other hand, always meant the *intellectual* subsistent. Moreover, a particular contemporary notion of "person" further complicates the problem, since that contemporary notion is so much tied in with the idea of a separate and independent subject or center of consciousnesses. Applying that concept of "person" without any modification to the doctrine of Trinity would leave us with three consciousnesses, three free wills, eventually three gods.

Where does that leave us? Can we simply reject the traditional formula first proposed by the Council of Alexandria (362), "one substance, three persons"? We cannot erase history, nor are we really in a position today to produce a better formula which could be universally intelligible, acceptable, and binding on the whole Church.

At least we can, with renewed determination, follow the pattern given from the beginning by the New Testament itself. We can speak of the Trinity always in the context of salvation history, using the names of Father, Son, and Holy Spirit, without forgetting that one God is spoken of throughout. We can also speak of three distinct ways of God's being present in the history of salvation and three different ways of God's own being as God.

The word *ways* has its strengths and weaknesses, to be sure. One of its strengths is that it can help us to see that the Persons are there as in relation to one another and that where the relationships are different, one from the other, we have put our finger, so to speak, on what constitutes difference in God. Father, Son, and Holy Spirit are one and the same God, but subsisting in different ways.

It is only with respect to the ways of *subsistence* that the number three can be applied to God. A way of subsisting is *distinct* from another way of subsisting by its relation of opposition, and is *real* by virtue of its identity with the divine being. Who subsists in such a way is truly God.

But there is an obvious risk in the use of the word *ways*. It is a short step indeed from that term to Modalism, which effectively denies the reality of the Trinity, economic or immanent. We have to be particularly attentive to the reminder of Bernard J. F. Lonergan that a subsistent is *that which is*, whereas a mode of being is *a way in which it is*. Thus, in God paternity is not a mode of being; it is God the Father. There are three in God to whom we can say "You" (*Divinarum Personarum Conceptionem Analogicam*, Rome: Gregorian University, 1957, pp. 172–75).

Finally, what of the so-called *psychological explanation* of the doctrine of the Trinity, the one proposed by Augustine and further developed by Thomas Aquinas? It uses the pattern of the human mind and an analysis of human consciousness in attempting to illustrate the two immanent processions of generation and spiration within the inner life of God. Although it is not the official teaching of the Church, at least not directly, the approach can still be helpful. "It appears all the more legitimate in the light of a metaphysical anthropology which demonstrates that there are only two fundamental acts of spiritual existence, knowledge and love. The obvious thing is to regard these basic acts as paralleled in the two divine processions" (Karl Rahner, "Trinity," *The Concise Sacramentum Mundi*, p. 1764).

On the other hand, the psychological approach is not without its own difficulties. There is some measure of circular reasoning involved. The approach "postulates *from* the doctrine of the Trinity a model of human knowledge and love, which either remains questionable, or about which it is not clear that it can be more than a *model* of human knowledge precisely as *finite*. And this model it applies again to God. In other words, we are not told why in God knowledge and love demand a *processio ad modum operati* (as Word or as 'the beloved in the lover')" (Rahner, *The Trinity*, pp. 117–18). And without such a procession there is no real trinity of ways of subsistence.

What the mystery and doctrine of the Trinity mean, when all is said and done, is that "God lives as the mystery of love among persons. If we are created in the image of this God, and if our destiny is to live forever with this God and with God's beloved creatures," then our Christian vocation is to create those forms and structures of life in the "household," or dwelling place of God and of God's creatures together, that best enable us to live as Christ lived, to show forth the Spirit of God, and ultimately to be deified (Catherine Mowry LaCugna, *God For Us*, p. 378).

The God who created us, who sustains us, who will judge us, and who will give us eternal life is not a God infinitely removed from us. Our God is a God of absolute proximity, a God who is communicated truly in the flesh, in history, within our human family, and a God who is present in the spiritual depths of our existence as well as in the core of our unfolding human history, as the source of enlightenment and community.

The mystery and doctrine of the Trinity is the beginning, the end, *and* the center of all Christian theology.

SUMMARY

1. The *distinctively Christian conviction about God* is that God has become incarnate in Jesus of Nazareth, and that God is triune. God is Father, Son, and Holy Spirit.

2. If God is one, how is it that Jesus is also divine, and how is it, further, that God is triune? These are the questions which largely shaped the history of Christian theology in the first four or five centuries.

3. The Christian understanding of God has its roots in the *Old Testament*, where God (Yahweh) is a living God, i.e., is present and active in the history of Israel, is the Lord of all humankind, the giver of all life. However, there is no "foreshadowing" of the doctrine of the Trinity in the Old Testament.

4. Neither is there a formal doctrine of the Trinity in the *New Testament*. Nevertheless, it identifies Jesus with God (especially the Prologue of John's Gospel), indicating that all the saving attributes of the God of the Old Testament are actualized anew in Christ. It also ascribes an important salvific role to the Holy Spirit, but without specifying the relationships among the Father, Christ, and the Spirit.

5. Over against pagan polytheism, the earliest *Apostolic Fathers and apologists* stressed the doctrine of the one God, creator and sustainer of all things.

6. In the *third century*, emphasis shifted from the oneness of God to the triune pluralism of God, when the Church could no longer avoid the difficult questions posed by the apparent discrepancy between its uncompromising monotheism, on the one hand, and the clear testimony of Sacred Scripture and of its liturgical and prayer life that God is Father, Son, and Holy Spirit.

7. This fundamental confession of faith in the Trinity did not first emerge from philosophical speculation about the inner life of God (the so-called "immanent Trinity") but from a response to the activity of God in the world (the so-called "economic Trinity").

8. One of the earliest attempts at a solution to the problem of the-one-and-the-three proved unorthodox, namely, the *Arian* solution, which made Christ something more than human but less than God the Almighty (*Pantokrator*). The implications were serious: If Christ is a creature like us, he has no special standing before God, and we are still in our sins.

9. The *Council of Nicea* (325) gave a formal answer to Arius. The Son does not "emanate" from the Father's will, as a creature. The Son is "begotten, not made." He is "of the same substance" (*homoousios*) as the Father. For the first time, the Church moved officially from biblical to speculative categories to define its faith.

10. This transition did not occur without opposition. The Eusebians (followers of Eusebius of Cæsarea) preferred to say no more than what Scripture seemed to be saying, namely, that the Son is "like" (*homoiousios*) the Father. Through the efforts of Athanasius and Hilary of Poitiers, the *homoousian* and *homoiousian* parties were reconciled. The agreement was sealed at the *Council of Alexandria* (362), from which emerged a new orthodox formula: "one substance, three Persons."

11. Attention shifted in the *fourth century* to the question of the Holy Spirit's relation to the Father and the Son. It was the so-called *Cappadocian* theologians (Basil, Gregory of Nyssa, and Gregory of Nazianzus) who established the coequal divinity of the Spirit with the Father and the Son, without prejudice to the oneness of substance in God.

12. By the end of the fourth century the Church was in a position to synthesize and officially express its newly systematized trinitarian faith in creedal

327

form. The *First Council of Constantinople* (381) endorsed the so-called *Nicene-Constantinopolitan Creed*, which is recited each week in the Catholic Eucharist.

13. *Augustine* approached the mystery of the Trinity from a different starting point. Instead of beginning with the saving activity of the three Persons in salvation history (as the Greek Fathers did) and working back to the unity of God, Augustine began with the one divine nature and tried to understand how the three Persons share in that nature without dividing it.

14. Threeness in God, he said, is rooted in threeness of *relations:* of begetting, of being begotten, and of proceeding. His use of analogies drawn from *human consciousness* to explain this inner life of the Trinity (remembering, understanding, loving) was perhaps his most original contribution to trinitarian theology. He also anticipated the teaching of the Council of Florence in the Middle Ages that everything in God is one except what is differentiated by the opposition of relations; i.e., the Father and the Son are one God, except insofar as the Father begets and the Son is begotten, and so on.

15. *Anselm* carried forward the Augustinian principle that God is absolutely one except for the opposition of relations between and among the three Persons. This, in turn, provided the theological basis for the principle of the mutual indwelling (circumincession, *perichoresis*) of the three divine Persons: The Father is always in the Son and the Holy Spirit; the Son is always in the Father and the Spirit; and the Spirit is always in the Father and the Son.

16. The *Fourth Lateran Council* (1215) repudiated *Albigensianism*, one of the most dangerous errors ever to attack the Church because of its rejection of the intrinsic goodness of created matter. The council taught that God is the author of both matter and spirit, and that Christ is fully God, with a human as well as a divine nature. The council also produced a doctrinal formulation on the Trinity which became the basis of most of Scholastic theology.

17. During the period of medieval Scholasticism, so strongly shaped by Aquinas, there were certain "minority reports" being written, namely, by the Franciscan school represented by *Richard of St. Victor, Alexander of Hales,* and *Bonaventure,* who were closer to the approach of the Greek Fathers. Their contributions to trinitarian theology, however, did not attract a very wide constituency until recently.

18. *Thomas Aquinas* insisted on the identity of essence and existence in God (God's essence is "to be") and on the participation of the created order in the Being of God, Who is the First Cause of all that is. Insofar as God ordains all things toward their goal, God is a provident God. And insofar as there is only one goal for all reality—created and recreated alike—the order of nature and the order of grace are radically one. Aquinas also followed the Augustinian approach to the mystery of the Trinity, employing similar psychological explanations of the relations between and among the three Persons.

19. The *Second Council of Lyons* (1274) reflected the Latin approach in stressing the procession of the Spirit from the Father *and* the Son (*Filioque*). The *Council of Florence* (1438–1440) reaffirmed the Latin approach, but allowed also for the Greek approach, namely, that the Holy Spirit proceeds from the Father *through* the Son (*per Filium*). For the Greeks the *Filioque* implied a double principle in God; for the Latins the *per Filium* implied a subordination of Son to Father. Neither side intended what the other side thought was implied, and much of the controversy was, in fact, unnecessary.

20. The *Council of Florence* also enshrined the principle that *in God all things are one except what is differentiated by the opposition of relations between and among the Persons.*

21. Insofar as the *Council of Trent* (1545–1563) addressed itself directly to the problem of God, it did so in reaction against the insistence of the major Reformers (*Luther* and *Calvin* in particular) that God deliberately and explicitly excludes some people from salvation (predestination to reprobation). The Catholic tradition, articulated at Trent, argues that God not only makes a *declaration* of our worthiness for salvation but actually *transforms* us from within by the indwelling of the Holy Spirit and offers this transformation to every person, without exception. Only a free act of the will on our part can negate God's universal salvific will.

22. The Christian understanding of God tended to zigzag in the post-Reformation period between Trent and Vatican I (1869–1870), engaging major Protestant philosophers and theologians like Hegel and Schleiermacher.

23. The *First Vatican Council* (1869–1870) rejected some of these positions (rationalism, pantheism, and the like), insisting on the uniqueness and the difference of God from the world.

24. The *Second Vatican Council* (1962–1965) taught that since God is the origin of all that is, the human race is called to unity. The Church is called to be a sacrament of God in the world, a sign of the same unity which is to be found in the Trinity.

25. *Official teachings of the Church* on the Trinity have advanced the following principles: (1) The Trinity is an *absolute mystery;* i.e., it transcends our ordinary human capacity for understanding even after we know it as revealed; (2) God is triune: Father, Son, and Holy Spirit, coequal and coeternal, and yet each distinct one from the other, but not to the point where we have three gods; (3) the Father alone is unbegotten, begets or generates the Son, and sends forth or spirates the Holy Spirit (with or through the Son); (4) the Son is begotten by the Father, but not as a creature (Arianism); he is of the same substance as the Father, "true God of true God" (Nicea); (5) the Holy Spirit proceeds from the Father (and or through) the Son and has a distinct salvific

mission in history: creating the community of faith (Church), forgiving sins, giving new life, etc.

26. There are two *processions*, or missions, in God: generation and spiration; i.e., both the Son and the Holy Spirit are "sent."

27. The processions, in turn, are the basis of the *relations* between and among the Persons or *hypostases* (which do not mean exactly the same, since *persons* are *rational hypostases*). There are four relations: paternity, filiation, active spiration, and passive spiration. But there are only three *subsistent relations*: paternity, filiation, and passive spiration. Active spiration is not really distinct from paternity or from filiation, since there is no opposition of relations between them.

28. These subsistent relations are relatively opposed one to another, and thus are *hypostases* or Persons (again, the two terms are not exactly identical). The *hypostases* or Persons have names: Father, Son, and Holy Spirit.

29. Although there are three Persons, there is only one divine nature or essence. Because of the unity of essence, there is a *mutual indwelling* of the Persons, i.e., of one in the other. This is also called *circumincession*, or *perichoresis*.

30. Such teachings as these are to be found throughout the history of the Church, particularly in the first fifteen centuries, but they are comprehensively proclaimed by the *Council of Florence* (1438–1442).

31. Despite this abundant corpus of official teachings on the mystery of the Trinity, many *fundamental difficulties* remain, especially the ambiguity that continues to revolve around the notion of *person*, a term the New Testament does not use. One contemporary understanding of a person as an independent center or subject of consciousness does not apply to the Trinity. But a more common contemporary understanding of *person-as-relational* does.

32. There is an identity between the *economic Trinity* and the *immanent Trinity*. The God who is with us, active on our behalf in salvation history, is who God is. It is not the immanent Trinity which is first revealed, but the economic Trinity.

33. God relates to us in three distinct *ways* of being present to our history: as Father, as Son, and as Holy Spirit; as Creator, as Redeemer, and as Sanctifier.

34. The triune God who created us, who sustains us, who will judge us, and who will give us eternal life is not infinitely removed from us, but is absolutely close to us, communicated in the flesh and present in our hearts, our consciousness, and our history as the source of enlightenment and community.

SUGGESTED READINGS

Araya, Victorio. *God of the Poor: The Mystery of God in Latin American Liberation Theology*. Maryknoll, N.Y.: Orbis Books, 1988.

Boff, Leonardo. *Trinity and Society*. Maryknoll, N.Y.: Orbis Books, 1988.

Cone, James. *God of the Oppressed*. New York: Seabury Press, 1975.

Congar, Yves. *I Believe in the Holy Spirit*. 3 vols. New York: Seabury Press, 1983.

Gutiérrez, Gustavo. *The God of Life*. Maryknoll, N.Y.: Orbis Books, 1991.

Hill, William. *The Three-Personed God*. Washington, D.C.: University Press of America, 1983.

Jüngel, Eberhard. *God as the Mystery of the World*. Grand Rapids, Mich.: Eerdmans, 1983.

Kasper, Walter. *The God of Jesus Christ*. New York: Crossroad, 1984.

Kelly, J. N. D. *Early Christian Creeds*. 3d ed. New York: Longman, 1972.

_____. *Early Christian Doctrines*. New York: Harper & Row, 1965.

Küng, Hans. *On Being a Christian*. New York: Doubleday, 1976, pp. 57–88; 214–65; 295–318.

LaCugna, Catherine Mowry. *God For Us: The Trinity and Christian Life*. San Francisco: HarperCollins, 1991.

Lonergan, Bernard J. F. *The Way to Nicea: The Dialectical Development of Trinitarian Theology*. Philadelphia: Westminster Press, 1976.

McFague, Sallie. *Models of God: Theology for an Ecological, Nuclear Age*. Philadelphia: Fortress Press, 1987.

Moltmann, Jürgen. *The Trinity and the Kingdom*. New York: Harper & Row, 1981.

Murray, John Courtney. *The Problem of God: Yesterday and Today*. New Haven: Yale University Press, 1964.

Peters, Ted. *God as Trinity: Relationality and Temporality in Divine Life*. Louisville: Westminster/John Knox Press, 1993.

Rahner, Karl. *A Rahner Reader*. Ed. Gerald A. McCool. New York: Seabury Press, 1975, pp. 132–144.

_____. *The Trinity*. New York: Herder & Herder, 1970.

Rusch, William, ed. *The Trinitarian Controversy*. Philadelphia: Fortress Press, 1980.

IX

God: Special Questions

This chapter presents for separate consideration some special questions related to the Christian understanding of God: divine providence, miracles, evil, prayer, the personhood of God, the Fatherhood of God, and God-language in general.

DIVINE PROVIDENCE

The Concept

The question of divine providence is exceedingly difficult because it is at once comprehensive and complicated. It is comprehensive because it sums up God's relationship to the world and to all of history. It is complicated because it raises the problem of the interaction between divine sovereignty and human freedom. The former can never satisfactorily be described, and the latter can never satisfactorily be explained. With the question of Providence, therefore, we come as close to the heart of the problem of God as we possibly can. And the closer we come, the more deafening the silence.

Providence, first of all, refers literally to God's "foresight." It has to do with the way God shapes and directs human history and creation itself, and cares for all creatures and especially all of humanity. Providence is not an exclusively Christian concept, nor even an exclusively religious concept. There are many *secular notions* of "Providence." We find the term first used in the fifth century B.C. and especially in Stoic philosophy. There is a cosmic harmony in the universe insured by some nonpersonal divinity or divinized rationality. Leibniz invoked a similar notion of a preestablished rational harmony. The Enlightenment's concept of inevitable progress in history is a secular variant of the Christian understanding of Providence, and so too are the Hegelian notion of world-reason and the Marxist interpretation of the dialectical movement of history.

Providence in the Bible

The term appears only in the later part of the *Old Testament*, and then under Hellenistic influences (Job 10:12; Wisdom 6:7; 14:3; 17:2). But more important than the term itself is the concept it represents. The Old Testament clearly portrays Yahweh as a powerful, wise, merciful, and caring God. Creation, the election of Israel, the Exodus—all of these and more are manifestations of God's abiding concern for the world and especially for the Chosen People (Exodus 16:1–36; 17:1–7; Numbers 11:4–35; 20:2–13). History is itself the arena of God's saving action (Psalms 9:2; 26:7; 40:6; 71:17; 72:18; Isaiah 9:5; 28:29; 29:14).

The story of Jonah illustrates how God's care even extends to the animal world (Jonah 4:11). But it is especially evident in narratives about holy men and women: e.g., Elijah is fed miraculously by ravens (1 Kings 17:6); Solomon ends up on the throne in spite of his low ranking and the morally tainted circumstances leading up to his conception and birth; Joseph attains the highest distinction in Egypt and succeeds in saving his family in spite of the hostility of his brothers (Genesis 37–50). In the last instance, the providential point is made explicitly: "Even though you intended to do harm to me, God intended it for good, in order to preserve a numerous people, as he is doing today" (50:20).

The *New Testament* also attests to a basic faith in God's loving regard for the world, but now it is linked explicitly with faith in Christ as the great sign of God's love and concern. Jesus admonishes his listeners for their inordinate anxiety about material needs. "Look at the birds of the air; . . . consider the lilies of the field, how they grow;... your heavenly Father knows that you need all these things" (Matthew 6:26–34; see also 10:29–31). There are other New Testament passages which speak of God's plan or predetermined purpose (Romans 8:29–30; Ephesians 1:5,11), especially in the New Testament's understanding of *salvation history*. God's purpose has been manifested in the death and resurrection of Christ (Acts of the Apostles 2:22–24). Indeed, even the villains of the piece—Herod and Pontius Pilate, with the Gentiles and the peoples of Israel—are seen as instruments of the divine intervention: They "do whatever your hand and your plan had predestined to take place" (Acts of the Apostles 4:28). The salvation-history perspective is more fully developed in Ephesians 1:3–14, where Christ is identified as the centerpiece of the divine plan "to gather up all things in him, things in heaven and things on earth" (v. 10). We were chosen in him by God "who accomplishes all things according to his counsel and will." And all of this has been "sealed with the Holy Spirit" who is "the pledge of our inheritance toward redemption of God's own people, to the praise of his glory."

Postbiblical Reflections and Official Teachings

The conviction of faith in a provident God has been held consistently within the Church from the beginning. It is central, of course, to Irenæus's theology of history (e.g., *Against Heresies*, chapter 25), to Augustine's polemic against the Pelagians, who insisted too strongly on the power of unaided human freedom, and to Thomas Aquinas's "sacred doctrine" about God (*Summa Theologiæ*, I, q. 22, where providence is described as the ordering of creation to its end as this order preexists in the mind of God). Thomas maintained that, although God eternally sees and infallibly knows all things as present, human freedom is not compromised (*Summa Theologiæ*, I, q. 14, a. 13).

It is, as well, the straightforward teaching of the First Vatican Council's *Dogmatic Constitution on the Catholic Faith* (chapter 1): "God protects and governs by [divine] Providence all things which [God] has made...." Finally, the Second Vatican Council urges us to discern in the "signs of the times" evidence of "God's presence and purpose" (*Pastoral Constitution on the Church in the Modern World*, n. 11).

Theological Meaning

Christian *faith* in the reality of Providence is not in doubt. Christian *understanding* of Providence is another matter entirely. Once again, we are confronted with the relationship of nature and grace. Some Catholic solutions have tended to overemphasize divine power at the apparent expense of human responsibility and freedom. We become mere actors in a play written wholly by God, with an ending already precisely determined regardless of our flubbing our lines and missing our cues. We need not trouble ourselves, therefore, about this world's injustices. God will take care of everything in the end.

At the other extreme, some solutions have tried so hard to uphold the enduring value of human effort that God becomes little more than a play's producer, backing it with money and influence but depending utterly upon the ability of the actors, director, designers, stagecrew, and the like for its eventual success. Thus, if we do not overcome injustice in the world by our political efforts, the injustice will simply swallow us up in the end, and history will have failed.

Still others have attempted a compromise position, assigning divine and human activity on a fifty-fifty basis (we are completely free in our actions, but God must simultaneously *concur* with our free decisions and invest them with efficacy).

The later medieval, post-Tridentine theological debates *de auxiliis* ("concerning helps") were not so much about the broad issue of Providence as about the narrower, although related, question of *actual grace.* They were essentially fruitless controversies. The Church never took an official stand on behalf of either party, the Banezians or the Molinists, because both took for granted that every act of free consent was itself from God's grace (anything less than that would have been Pelagian, and thus unorthodox).

Karl Rahner's view is representative of the Catholic theological and doctrinal tradition as it is understood today: We begin from where we are. We profess a faith and practice a religion which comprises prayer for God's intervention, miracles, an understanding of history as saving history, persons invested with sacred authority, an inspired book which comes from God, ritual acts which mediate the presence of God, and so forth. On the other hand, our theological starting point seems to say that "God is everywhere insofar as [God]

336

grounds everything, and [God] is nowhere insofar as everything that is grounded is created, and everything which appears in this way within the world of our experience is different from God, separated by an absolute chasm between God and what is not God" (*Foundations of Christian Faith*, p. 82).

Rahner follows the Thomistic principle that God works through *secondary*, or *instrumental*, *causes*; i.e., God is the ultimate cause, but not just one cause among many. God-as-cause is in the world as a totality, but not in any particular things within the world. That is, God does not "intervene" in the world in the sense that God acts now here and now there; now in this event, now in that; now in this person, now in that. God "intervenes" in the sense that *God is always there*. The world is fundamentally and radically open to God. "Consequently, every real intervention of God in his world, although it is free and cannot be deduced, is always only the becoming historical and becoming concrete of that 'intervention' in which God as the transcendental ground of the world has from the outset [been] embedded . . . in this world as its self-communicating ground" (p. 87).

And so we come back to the fundamental problem for the Christian understanding of God: How can God be God, i.e., totally other, and at the same time be in the world, e.g., in Christ, in the Church, in the sacraments? We can exaggerate the first at the expense of the second, and vice versa.

With the hope of avoiding both extremes, Rahner offers an example. We get a "good idea." It seems to come "out of the blue." We can interpret it in a purely physiological and psychological way and conclude that it is not in any sense an intervention of God. Or we can experience ourselves as a subject radically open to God (i.e., as a "transcendental subject"). At the moment we accept that experience, the "good idea" becomes a part of that total network of historical and worldly relationships whose meaning and unity are given by God. In that sense, the "good idea" is an "inspiration" from God.

Rahner writes: "Of course it could be objected against this that in this way everything can be regarded as a special providence, as an intervention of God, presupposing only that I accept the concrete constellation of my life and of the world in such a way that it becomes a positive, salvific concretization of my transcendental relationship to God in freedom. But against this objection we can simply ask the counterquestion: Why, then, may this not be the case?" (p. 89). He continues: "Because the subject's response in freedom is itself really and truly for the subject himself [or herself] something given to him [or her], without it losing thereby the character of the subject's own responsible and accountable action, a good decision along with everything which it presupposes as its mediation correctly has the character of an intervention of God, even though this takes place in and through human freedom, and hence can be explained functionally to the degree that the history of freedom can be explained, namely, insofar as it is based on elements objectified in time and space" (ibid.).

There is never, therefore, a salvific act of God on our behalf which is not also and always a salvific act of our own. Our actions are truly free, and they are at the same time grounded in the grace or presence of God. We can never even begin to have anything to do with God or to approach God without already being moved by God's grace. On the other hand, this movement toward salvation never takes place without our involvement and our freedom.

To be sure, we have not solved the problem of nature and grace, of divine sovereignty and human freedom, or of Providence as such. But we have at least identified the problem as it is, and taken note of the limits within which all attempted solutions must be developed. No explanation of Providence satisfies the biblical, theological, and doctrinal traditions of the Church if it takes history out of God's hands (Pelagianism, Deism, e.g.). And no explanation suffices which takes history out of human hands (extreme Augustinianism and Calvinism). God is present to every person and to history itself as an inner principle which makes forward movement possible without sacrifice of freedom. Precisely *how* that is done, we do not know. We can, like Rahner and others, propose answers based on specific philosophical premises. But these are always explanations "after the fact," so to speak. Theology does not produce the given, but reflects upon it. Theology does not make "possible" the given, but reflects on the terms of its "possibility." Theology, in the end, is not faith. It is faith seeking understanding.

MIRACLES

Spectrum of Views

Few theological questions are treated so unsatisfactorily as the question of miracles. Discussion moves from one extreme to the other: from the extreme right, where miracles are simply accepted in a fundamentalistic sense (they happened in exactly the way they are described in the Bible or by the people in postbiblical times—e.g., the appearances of the Blessed Virgin Mary at Lourdes, France), to the extreme left, where miracles are rejected in principle because they are presumed to be disruptions of the inflexible laws of nature and of physics.

In between there are also other sorts of inadequate explanations. We are assured that the *fact* of miracles is not important, only their *significance*. Or we are reminded, following the Rahnerian approach outlined above, that God is already everywhere as the principle of free action and, therefore, whatever happens, happens through the grace of God; in that sense everything is a miracle.

Miracles in the Bible

There is no word as such for "miracle" in the Bible. It speaks only of "signs," "wonders," "portents," "works of power," or simply "works." There are three major clusters of miracles in the Bible. The most important in the Old Testament are those acts by which Yahweh delivered Israel from Egypt and led Israel to Canaan (the Exodus). A second set appears in the Elijah-Elisha stories which present the confrontation between Yahwism and Baalism. The third major set consists of the miracles of Jesus and his earliest disciples which are linked with the inbreaking of the reign of God. Paul, for example, claims as a firsthand witness that he and others worked miracles (Galatians 3:5; 1 Corinthians 12:9–10; 2 Corinthians 12:12; Romans 15:18–19). Their authenticity, however, depends, as with Paul, on whether they serve to proclaim "the good news of Christ" (Romans 15:19).

Most miracles in the *Old Testament* are sagas or legends celebrating Israel's origin and its heroes and heroines. New Testament miracles are usually grouped into the overarching category of "miracle stories" and then subdivided into exorcisms, healings, epiphanies (divine manifestations), rescue miracles (from danger), gift miracles (extraordinary provisions), and rule miracles (reinforcement of religious rules).

New Testament authors use miracle stories to make a religious point. For example, Mark counterbalances miracle stories in the first half of his gospel with the cross in the second half, thus teaching that Jesus' true identity as the Son of God is recognized at the cross. And the seven "signs" in the first half of John's gospel are placed alongside related discourses as events which reveal Jesus' true identity. For example, the cure of the blind man was not done primarily to restore the man's sight, but to bring him to spiritual insight and to reveal Jesus as the "light of the world" (9:5).

When Jesus refers to his miracles as *erga*, "works" (John 5:36), it shows that he regarded the miracles as an integral part of the work given him by the Father (5:17; 14:10), as well as a continuation of the "works" of God in the Old Testament, like creation (Genesis 2:2) and the Exodus (Exodus 34:10; Psalm 66:5).

Biblical and Theological Criteria

Regarding the reality of the miracles of Jesus in the New Testament, these criteria may be helpful:

1. *Miracles were as important to the ministry of Jesus as his preaching.* They express the saving *power* of God shown in Jesus' healing, feeding the hungry, curing the sick, even raising the dead. Indeed, when the disciples of John the Baptist came out to the desert to ask Jesus if he was the One who was promised, Jesus told them to go back and tell John what they had seen and heard: "The blind receive their sight, the lame walk, the lepers are cleansed, the deaf hear, dead are raised, the poor have good news brought to them" (Luke 7:22).

2. *Miracles are linked with faith.* "If I am not doing the works of my Father, then do not believe me" (John 10:37; see also 15:24). On the other hand, it is possible to be present at the performance of a miracle and not see it as a miracle at all (notice, e.g., the inability or refusal of many to believe in Jesus even after the multiplication of the loaves and fishes—John 6:26). Indeed, it happened that Jesus "could do no deed of power" in his home country, where he was "amazed at their unbelief." Instead "he went among the villages teaching" (Mark 6:5–6).

3. *The miracle stories are meant to evoke faith, but not all of the stories are on the same plane.* The fundamentalist forgets that the biblical accounts are not eyewitness reports, nor scientifically tested documentation, nor historical, medical, or psychological records. They are rather unsophisticated popular narratives, entirely at the service of the proclamation of the Lordship of Jesus. Recent biblical scholarship discloses that there are many different levels at work in the various accounts: Some are patterned after Old Testament models; others follow the narrative styles common to Jewish and Hellenistic stories; others are simply collected accounts (redactional summaries) of the evangelists which give the impression of a continuous and wide-spread miracle-working activity on the part of Jesus.

4. *But certain events apparently did take place, and they were taken, by friend and foe alike, as marvelous in their own right.* The sick were cured, for example. Jesus' enemies did not challenge the fact of the cure but the propriety of curing on the Sabbath.

5. *In the accounts of several of the miracles, too many details are given which have too little interest to have been invented and yet which are so human and true to life that they suggest the presence of an eyewitness.* The cure of the possessed boy is a case in point (Mark 9:14–29).

Unanswered Questions

We are left, in the end, with more questions than answers. Did Jesus really walk on water to calm the waves during a sudden storm, or was the story constructed after the fact as a sign that God hears our prayers for help in times of distress? Were those "possessed by the devil" simply suffering from temporary mental illness, or did the impact of Jesus' kindly personality perhaps effect a momentary re-mission of a more serious emotional problem? Did the story of the coin in the fish's mouth simply answer Jesus' request to catch a fish in order to pay the temple tax? Did other stories, such as the raising of Jairus's daughter from the dead, simply anticipate the resurrection of

Christ in order to present Jesus as the Lord of life and death (keeping in mind, all the while, that when the Gospels were written, they were removed from the historical Jesus by a few decades)?

At the very least, something significant and impressive occurred in the life and ministry of Jesus, over and above his preaching and teaching. He had an impact upon people—the sick, the troubled, the bereaved—in a way that clearly set him apart from his contemporaries. Indeed, he himself pointed to his good works as moments in which the power of God operated in him and through him.

Teachings of the Church

That Jesus performed miracles as signs of revelation is certainly the belief of the New Testament Church and of the official Church of the postbiblical period. The First Vatican Council teaches this in its *Dogmatic Constitution on the Catholic Faith* (chapter 3), where miracles and prophecies are identified as external demonstrations (*argumenta*) that are joined with the internal help of the Holy Spirit to establish the truth of divine revelation. And the Second Vatican Council acknowledges the existence of miracles at least in passing in its *Dogmatic Constitution on the Church:* "The miracles of Jesus also confirm that the kingdom has already arrived on earth..." (n. 5).

Just *what* those miracles were, from a scientific, empirically verifiable, objective point of view (i.e., apart from faith), is difficult to say. We can at least exclude the too simple solutions of the extreme left and the extreme right, and reject the practical avoidance of the problem in some of present-day theology.

Miracles are manifestations of the power of God and as such are consistent with divine Providence. They were central to Jesus' ministry. They enter into the formation of our own faith. Beyond that, many questions remain open.

EVIL

Spectrum of Views

We move from a very difficult problem to a nearly impossible one: *the mystery of evil,* both physical and moral. Again, simple answers abound. At the extreme left, God is portrayed as not involved at all in evil because God is not much involved in good either. At the extreme right, God is directly and immediately implicated in evil. God deliberately, almost callously, inflicts suffering and pain upon us in order to teach us a lesson or gain some unknown greater good. And in the middle, we have the usual traditional explanations that God does not cause evil; God only permits it. Or that evil is nothing in itself; it is simply the absence of good.

For many, of course, the very existence of physical and moral evil (natural disasters, the terminal illness of a young child, the sudden death of a father or a mother, a brutal murder, an act of terrorism, Auschwitz) is the single most persuasive argument *against* the existence of God, or at least against the existence of the God of Christianity. They cannot readily explain, on the other hand, how there can also be so much goodness and heroic charity in a world *without God*.

In the preceding discussion of miracles, we noted that it is easier to accept the *meaning* of miracles than it is to accept the *fact* of their existence. In the case of evil, just the reverse is true: It is easier to accept the *fact* of evil than it is to understand its *meaning*.

Evil in the Bible

In the *Old Testament* evil is equated with immorality and unfaithfulness to the Covenant (Judges 2:11–15; 2 Samuel 12:9–10; 1 Kings 2:44). Its origin is in the human heart (Proverbs 6:14; 21:10; Ecclesiastes 8:11), and is expressed in various ways: as idolatry and apostasy (Deuteronomy 4:25; 1 Kings 11:6), disobedience to divine commandments (1 Samuel 15:9), false prophecy (Deuteronomy 13:5), murder (2 Samuel 12:9), false witness (Deuteronomy 19:18–19), adultery and fornication (Deuteronomy 22:21–24), stealing (Genesis 44:4; Deuteronomy 24:7), and so forth. Humankind brings evils upon itself (Deuteronomy 31:17–18; Isaiah 3:9), but God can lead us out of evil (Jeremiah 15:21) or, as an act of mercy (Exodus 32:14) or in response to the repentance of the unfaithful (Jeremiah 18:8; 26:3,13,19; Jonah 3:10; 4:2), can retract the intention to inflict evil. In the end, the existence of evil transcends human understanding (Job 42:2–3).

Evil, like a miracle, is *power*. But unlike a miracle, it is a power *against* life, not for it. So intense and so focused may this power be

343

that it can be personified as *Satan* (from the Hebrew word *sātān*, which means "adversary").

The *New Testament* carried over the general Jewish teaching about evil spirits and the devil. He is the evil one (Matthew 13:19), the enemy (Luke 10:19), the father of lies (John 8:44), etc. He is especially opposed to Jesus Christ, and his enmity reaches a fever pitch in the passion (Luke 22:3,31; John 13:27; 1 Corinthians 2:8), but therein the devil is also finally defeated (1 Corinthians 2:8; John 12:31; Revelation 12:7–12). This opposition continues, however, in the history of the Church until it is overcome once and for all at the end (Revelation 20:2–3,8,10).

Teachings of the Church

Again, *that* there is evil in the world is obvious. That such evil is often massively collective (the Holocaust, for example) and at the same time very personalized is also evident. *What* this evil is in its core is not so clear. To the extent that the Church has addressed itself officially to the question, the official magisterium has affirmed the existence of the devil and of evil spirits, has acknowledged their negative effect on the course of history, and has insisted that they, like all of creation (material and spiritual), come under the sovereignty of God. Contrary to the impression one might gain from some recent novels and films, evil spirits do not control us to the point of suppressing human freedom and responsibility (see, for example, the Council of Trent's *Decree on Original Sin*).

If it is clear *that* evil exists, it is also clear that God wars against it and that we are called to participate with God in the struggle against evil in every form: social injustice, oppression, infidelity, dishonesty, e.g. "Caught in this conflict, humanity is obliged to wrestle constantly if it is to cling to what is good" (Vatican II, *Pastoral Constitution on the Church in the Modern World*, n. 37). Indeed, God sent the Son to save us from "the power of darkness and of Satan" (*Decree on the Church's Missionary Activity*, n. 3).

Theological Criteria

The fact of evil is undeniable, but why is there evil at all? If it is any comfort, the reader should be assured that he or she has not missed the definitive explanation somewhere along the line. None of the greatest minds of human history, whether Christian or not, has devised a compelling answer. Nor are we about to do so here, succeeding where all others have failed. We can only identify some of the principal options we have in response to evil, and especially to innocent suffering, and then try to decide which is the most intelligent and which conforms best to Christian faith.

First, we can rebel and revolt, shaking an angry fist if not at the real God then at some conventional idea of God. This is the way of Ivan Karamazov in Dostoevsky's *The Brothers Karamazov* and of Albert Camus in his *Rebel*. Second, we can try to bear up stoically, tight-lipped, avoiding the question "Why?" We simply accept what we can neither understand nor change. Or, third, we can stand with *Job*, placing our complete trust in God even in the face of the incomprehensible, and with *Jesus*, from whom we have received the "good news" that God wishes to deliver us from all evil, and indeed that suffering itself can be as redemptive for us individually as it was for all humankind in the passion and death of Christ.

But even Jesus did not *explain* suffering. He endured it, an innocent Lamb in the sight of God (1 Peter 1:19). But in the resurrection his suffering and death acquired meaning beyond themselves. Such meaning is not always, nor even often, apparent. Christ teaches us that suffering *can* have a meaning, or can *acquire* a meaning. We can learn from it. We can be ennobled by it. We can grow through it. For the God who encounters us in suffering is a God who knows suffering from the inside, as it were, in Jesus Christ.

God is literally a *sympathetic* ("suffering with") God. The reality of evil and suffering notwithstanding, God is a God of mercy, of forgiveness, of compassion for all. Furthermore, God has promised the eternal life to those of us who remain steadfast and faithful even in the midst of evil and suffering, a kingdom where God "will wipe every tear from [our] eyes. Death will be no more; mourning and crying and pain will be no more, for the first things have passed away" (Revelation 21:4).

In the end, the problem of moral evil and of innocent suffering reveals as well as conceals the God of love. For if it were not for our faith in God as a God of justice and mercy, of love and peace, of truth and loyalty, we would not recognize the reality of evil in all its depths; nor, what is more important, would we be impelled to do something about it, risking even our lives for the good of others. (Indeed, many who deny God do evil and call it good.) Corruption in government, for example, would not bother us very much, and certainly we would do very little about it, if we did not have at the same time a highly refined sense of moral and political idealism. For some, corruption mocks and negates the ideals (the reaction of the cynic). For others, corruption makes the ideals even more urgently attractive and worthwhile.

But the fact of moral evil and of innocent suffering remains. We can do nothing about evil in general (i.e., we cannot completely eliminate it from the world) and relatively little about it in the concrete (as our everyday experience attests). But what *is* under our control is the manner in which we respond to what is so frequently inevitable. We are *free,* and our freedom is, in turn, a condition which makes some forms of moral evil possible.

Will our free response be one of rebellion and passivity, or will it be a response of trust and renewed growth? Apart from faith in God, the problem of evil (which presumably *destroys* faith in God!) is unresolvable. And apart from faith in Christ and in the redemptive value of his passion and death, evil and innocent suffering can have no positive meaning at all.

The Church insists on the meaning of miracles, and sometimes stammers a bit regarding their factuality. In the case of evil, however, the Church joins the rest of humankind in acknowledging evil's wretched factuality, but it shares with others the agony of interpretation. Nevertheless, it does not stammer here. The Church's faith and trust are as forthright as Job's, built as they are upon the rock of Christ, and strengthened as they are by the power of the Holy Spirit. In the Christian vision of reality, resurrection follows the cross.

PRAYER

What follows here is exceedingly limited in purpose and scope. It does not purport to be a complete theological statement on the nature and place of prayer in Catholic life and devotion. (That is reserved for later discussion in Part Seven.) This particular section of the chapter has to do only with the question of prayer as it applies to the enduring problem of the relationship between divine sovereignty and human freedom. Therefore, prayer is treated here simply as an aspect of the problem of nature and grace, and of its several corollaries, including two topics discussed above, namely, divine providence and evil.

The Problem

Can we change the course of events through prayer? Can we alter God's will and so receive some blessing that otherwise might pass us by? Can we fend off some evil occurrence by specifically imploring God to save us from it?

The problem of prayer is difficult because it is a component of the difficult problems of Providence and of evil. Prayer has to do with the interaction between divine sovereignty and human freedom. Just as we can distort the meaning of Providence by exaggerating the one over the other, so we can distort the meaning of prayer by seeing it, on the one hand, as a method of manipulating the mind and heart of God, or, on the other hand, as a completely useless activity, no more sublime or mysterious than autosuggestion or the power of positive thinking.

Prayer in the Bible

In the *Old Testament* prayer is an ongoing dialogue between Yahweh and Israel, based on the Covenant that God had made with Israel (Deuteronomy 4:31). For the Israelites, Yahweh alone has the power to save them from their enemies, as has been demonstrated so decisively in the deliverance from bondage in Egypt (Exodus 32), and they do not hesitate to make a claim upon that power in times of need. It was surely Israel's belief that they *could* change the mind of

347

God and influence the course of historical events (e.g., Psalms 124–126,129).

The *New Testament* presents prayer in both negative and positive lights. Negatively, Jesus condemns the hypocrisy of long prayers by those who ignore the needs of others or inflict harm upon them (Mark 12:40; Luke 20:47). Positively, he speaks of prayer as a dialogue between a loving parent and child (Matthew 6:9–13; 7:7–11; Luke 11:9–13), and assures us that our prayers will be heard and answered (John 15:7,17; 16:26). He offers a model of prayer in his thanksgiving to his Father in an hour of failure (Matthew 11:25; Luke 10:21).

Theological Meaning

Prayer is a *response* to God's initiation of dialogue with us. It is an act by which we accept ourselves as subjects radically open to the presence of God. Prayer is a conscious, deliberate coming to terms with our actual situation before God, a "raising of our hearts and minds to God," as the traditional definition puts it. When we explicitly advert to that relationship, we are praying. Every action we perform as a way of expressing our sense of that relationship with God is a prayer. Every act whereby we sacrifice our own personal interests for a higher moral or spiritual purpose because of our explicit faith in God is a prayer.

Prayer is, therefore, always an act of faith and of hope, which is fulfilled in our surrender to the love of God. In prayers of *praise* and *thanksgiving*, we give more explicit and deliberate form to our sense of the majesty and sovereignty of God and of our own place within the total scheme of reality. In prayers of *contrition*, we acknowledge our failure to respect this fundamental relationship with God and deliberately open ourselves anew to God's abiding presence within us, a presence which makes it possible for us to become someone other than we are, someone better than we are. In prayers of *petition*, we explicitly come to terms with our needs and those of other people. We make ourselves ever more sensitive to our obligations to do whatever is possible to fulfill those needs, whether for ourselves or for others. And insofar as those prayers of petition are public (as in the Eucharist), we put other members of the community on notice and draw them into the process of identifying and meeting needs, and they, in turn, enlarge our own horizons and make us more fully aware of the plight of others besides ourselves and our loved ones.

But does prayer of petition reverse or alter the divine will? Can anything we say or do in prayer change God's mind? In one sense, the answer is "No." If God already knows our needs before we express them, our prayers cannot represent for God an unforeseen request. In another sense, however, the answer is "Yes." Our prayers are already, from the beginning, an integral component of God's providential care for human history and our own personal history. If God sees everything in an eternal "instant," then God has already "factored in" our prayer in determining and guiding the course of our human and personal histories.

In the end, however, the problem is beyond resolution. We cannot finally understand the effect of prayer, on God, on human history, or on ourselves, because those effects are folded into the mystery of the divine-human relationship: nature and grace, Providence, evil, and the like. We are left with the well-known Ignatian formula: "Work as if everything depended upon you, but pray as if everything depended upon God."

GOD AS PERSON

Is God "a person"? We are not asking here the question of the Trinity, whether there are three Persons in the one God. We raise instead the question whether God is a separate Being among beings. Putting the question that way, the answer is "Of course not. God is not *a* person because God is not any one thing or being."

But if the noun person is taken *analogically*, the answer has to be different. Does the reality we name "God" have qualities which we also attribute to persons? Yes, insofar as we understand persons as centers of intelligence, love, compassion, graciousness, fidelity, and especially the *capacity for relationship*.

What we mean by the noun *God* certainly must comprehend such qualities as these. In other words, it is better to attribute "personality" to God than to look upon God as some impersonal, unconscious cosmic force. That is not the God of the Old and New Testaments, nor of Christian tradition, nor of ordinary Christian experience. Nevertheless, we must always remember that the attribution of personality to God is always analogical; i.e., God is *like* a person, but God is also very much *unlike* a person. In the end, the revelation of God in the person of Jesus Christ tips the balance in favor of attributing personality to God. Nowhere is God's love, compassion, fidelity, and capacity for relationship with us more fully expressed than in Jesus Christ himself.

GOD AS FATHER

Jesus and the Fatherhood of God

If Jesus were still with us in his earthly, historical existence today, would he be speaking of his relationship to God as one of Son and Father and of our relationship to God as one of children and Father? Or would the raising of our consciousness about sexuality and the oppressive character of androcentric language and thought patterns have also affected Jesus' preaching and teaching? The question is entirely speculative, of course, but it seems reasonable to suppose that, in light of our contemporary consciousness, Jesus would have modified substantially his references to God.

During his own lifetime, certainly, Jesus assumed a strongly countercultural posture. For example, he mingled freely with women and emphasized their fundamental human equality before God. He included women among his disciples and appeared first to a woman after the resurrection. Even the most vigorous exponents of a feminist point of view today have always exempted Jesus from their criticisms of institutional Christianity.

Nevertheless, the facts are that Jesus did live at a particular time, in a particular place, among particular people, within a particular social, cultural, economic, and political context. He was at once a product of, and a prophet to, his own age. But granting the historically conditioned character of Jesus' references to the Fatherhood of God, we must still come to terms with the *transhistorical* meaning of those references. Even if, by contrast, Jesus had spoken of God as our Mother (as the late Pope John Paul I did in one of his informal addresses), he would still have had the same essential message to communicate about God.

What is the message implied in the Fatherhood of God? That God is a loving and caring God (Matthew 6:5–8, 26–34; 7:11; 10:29–31; 18:14; Luke 11:13), that God's love must inspire us to love even our enemies (Matthew 5:48), that God is likewise a forgiving God, even a model of forgiveness (Matthew 6:14–15; 18:35; Mark 11:25). Nowhere is this more movingly expressed than in the parable of the prodigal son, also known as the parable of the forgiving father (Luke 15:11–32).

Furthermore, Jesus' references to his own relationship with his Father in heaven simply underscore the intimacy of Jesus with God (whether God is spoken of as Father or as Mother, as Husband or Wife, as Brother or as Sister). Jesus' will and God's are one (Matthew 26:39–43; Mark 14:35–39; Luke 22:41–42; 23:34,46). God is the source of Jesus' power and authority (John 1:14,18; 16:15). To know Jesus is to know God (John 14:7–9) because Jesus and God are one (John 10:30). Jesus is in God, and God is in Jesus (John 10:38; 14:10). Whatever Jesus teaches, he has learned from God (John 8:28–38).Whatever Jesus does, he does as the work of God (John 10:32; 14:10). No one comes to God except through Jesus (John 14:6), but God is greater than the historical Jesus (John 14:28). Jesus sends his disciples forth with the same fullness of power with which he was sent (John 20:21).

In each of the preceding texts from the New Testament it is actually *Father* and not the more generic noun *God* that is used. But the fact that we can so easily substitute *God* for *Father*—and not even notice it—suggests that it is not the *Fatherhood* of God that is important to Jesus but the *Godhood* of the Father.

Theological Reflection

As several Catholic theologians have pointed out, over the course of time the Fatherhood of God became "hopelessly entangled with a patriarchal understanding of it" (Catherine Mowry LaCugna, *God For Us*, p. 393). The idea of a divine monarchy was projected onto the political world, as a justification for earthly monarchy, and onto society itself, as a justification for all kinds of hierarchy and domination—religious, moral, and sexual, as well as political. Just as the divine monarch is immutable, impassible, and self-sufficient, so the patriarch, the *pater familias,* is the unquestioned authority, the one who rules the household as if everything in it, including the women, is his property, to do with as he wills.

"When the root metaphor for the divine in Christian discourse is patriarchal...," Elizabeth A. Johnson writes, "it inevitably sustains men's dominance over women" (*She Who Is: The Mystery of God in Feminist Theological Discourse,* p. 38). Indeed, she characterizes it as a form of idolatry, i.e., employing a representation of the divine in such a way that its symbolic and evocative character is lost from view. The image, rather than disclosing reality, is mistaken for the reality itself. If God is, literally, a Father, there are real consequences in the order of human existence, and particularly in the relationships of men and women and in the place of women in society and in the Church.

The doctrine of the Trinity itself had emerged within a patriarchal and imperialist culture, in which it was simply taken for granted that the male is the active principle in the production of life, and the female the passive principle. Males, therefore, are to hold the superior place in all social arrangements, while the female is to be marginal and submissive.

By contrast, the Cappadocians (fifth century) had urged the Church to think of the Fatherhood of God not as self-sufficiency or as the incapacity to share authority with others (this was Eunomius's position, namely, that God could not share divine being [*ousia*] with the Son), but relationally, as "relation-to-another-who-is-equal" (LaCugna). Gregory of Nazianzus, for example, mocked those who concluded that God is male because God is called Father. After all, he said, God's fatherhood of the Son has nothing to do with marriage, pregnancy, midwifery, or the danger of miscarriage.

In effect, the Cappadocians formulated an understanding of God that contained a germ of a nonpatriarchal orthodoxy, but subsequent doctrinal developments tended to obscure it. Fortunately, that "germ" is now in full flowering.

GOD-LANGUAGE

The feminist critique of Christian theology and worship holds that the *exclusive, literal, and patriarchal* use of masculine language and images for God borders on the idolatrous. That critique rests on the cardinal axiom that God transcends *all* words, concepts, and images.

In spite of the rich diversity of images and metaphors for God in the Bible, prevailing Christian language names God exclusively in male terms, forgetting or marginalizing the rest. And when those images *are* used, as in the case of God the *Father*, they are taken literally, as if God had all the properties and characteristics of a human father. Finally, the paradigm for the symbol of God emerges from a world in which men rule within a patriarchal system.

"Feminist theological analysis makes clear that exclusive, literal, patriarchal speech about God has a twofold negative effect," Elizabeth A. Johnson points out. "In stereotyping and then banning female reality as suitable metaphor for God, such speech justifies the dominance of men while denigrating the human dignity of women. Simultaneously this discourse so reduces divine mystery to the single, reified metaphor of the ruling man that the symbol itself loses its religious significance and ability to point to ultimate truth. It becomes, in a word, an idol" (*She Who Is*, p. 36).

These two effects inseparably damage the *imago Dei* in us and distort our knowledge of the Creator in whose image we are made. "Inauthenthic ways of treating other human beings," Johnson continues, "go hand-in-hand with falsifications of the idea of God." In sum, an exclusive, literal, patriarchal language about God is both oppressive and idolatrous.

Johnson proposes three strategies for speaking of God anew, liberated from a language that is at once oppressive and idolatrous. First, given the long history of the term *God* in Christian theology and worship, the word should continue to be used, but "pointed in new directions through association with metaphors and values arising from women's experience" (p. 43). Second, because the exclusive use of the word *God* would run the risk of suppressing many of the most prized characteristics of God's relationship to the world, such as fidelity, compassion, and liberating love, it is appropriate to speak of God in personal symbols. But to counteract the persistent and corrosive dominance of male symbolism for God, those personal symbols must be reflective of, and emerge from, the actual experience of women. Third, those symbols should not simply ascribe feminine qualities to God or disclose a feminine dimension in God.

God-language must express the fullness of female humanity as well as of male humanity and of the world of nature, "in equivalent ways" (p. 47).

Although God transcends sex and gender, God is the Creator of both male and female in the divine image and is the source of the perfection of both. Therefore, either can equally well be used as metaphor to point to divine mystery. For example, in each of the parallel parables of the shepherd looking for his lost sheep and the homemaker looking for her lost coin (Luke 15:4–10), the central figure vigorously seeks what is lost and rejoices with others when it is found. Neither story discloses anything about God that the other hides. Using traditional men's and women's work, both parables direct the hearer to God's redeeming action with the use of images that are equivalently male and female. The woman with the coin is no less an image of God than is the shepherd with the sheep. But the use of such equivalent language invalidates traditional stereotyping wherein the major work of redemption in the world is done by men, while women are excluded or marginalized.

Only if the full reality of women as well as men enters into the symbolization of God, Johnson argues, can "the idolatrous fixation on one image be broken and the truth of the mystery of God, in tandem with the liberation of all human beings and the whole earth, emerge for our time" (p. 56).

Catherine Mowry LaCugna cautions, however, against abandoning traditional God-language altogether in favor of *functional* God-language: Creator for Father, Redeemer for Son, and Sanctifier, or Sustainer, for Holy Spirit. Functional language, following the Augustinian model, "appropriates" certain activities to the Persons, which only reinforces thinking of the Divine Persons as discrete individuals. Furthermore, a functional approach also draws us away from the central claim of trinitarian doctrine—that God *as God* is triune mystery.

LaCugna also cautions against speaking of the Holy Spirit as feminine to counterbalance the masculine pronouns for Father and Son. But feminine imagery for God doesn't establish that God has feminine aspects any more than masculine imagery establishes masculine aspects. The practice also implies that God is indeed primarily masculine, but with a feminine side.

354

In sum, trinitarian God-language need not be inherently sexist and patriarchal. On the contrary, "trinitarian doctrine articulates a vision of God in which there is neither hierarchy nor inequality, only relationships based on love, mutuality, self-giving and self-receiving, freedom, and communion. These values are the leitmotif of theological feminism."

"In sharp contrast to the unitarian God who is the first choice of some Christian feminists," LaCugna concludes, "the God who exists as an eternal communion (*koinonia*) of love is a surer foundation for authentic *koinonia* of the body of Christ in which 'there is neither Jew nor Gentile, slave nor free, male nor female' (Galatians 3:28; Colossians 3:11)" ("The Trinitarian Mystery of God," in *Systematic Theology: Roman Catholic Perspectives*, vol. 1, Francis Schüssler Fiorenza and John P. Galvin, eds., Minneapolis: Fortress Press, 1991, pp. 183–84).

SUMMARY

1. *Providence* is, literally, God's "foresight" in relation to the created order and to history. Both Old and New Testaments present God as a provident, caring, concerned, powerful God. History is God's history as well as ours. It is salvation history. God's plan and design is centered on Christ, and the sending of the Holy Spirit is the "first payment" against the full redemption offered in Christ.

2. Belief in Providence has been consistent throughout the entire postbiblical history of the Church, but there have been *different understandings* of that belief, some stressing the divine power at the apparent expense of human freedom, and vice versa.

3. Transcendental Thomism, as represented by Karl Rahner, notes with Thomas Aquinas that God works through *secondary causes*. On the one hand, God is there from the beginning and the world is radically open to the presence of God from its beginning. On the other hand, our actions remain completely free, but they are at the same time grounded in the grace or presence of God. Precisely how this is the case we do not know. We can only exclude clearly unsatisfactory solutions which diminish the sovereignty of God or human freedom.

4. *Miracles* pose yet another difficult problem, a variation really on the question of Providence. It is easier to determine the *significance* of miracles than their *factuality*. What is clear, however, is that (1) miracles were important to the ministry of Jesus; (2) they were challenges to faith; (3) they vary considerably in the way they are "reported" in the New Testament; (4) the

factuality of some of them was not challenged, even by the enemies of Jesus; and (5) some "reports" of miracles are too detailed and too true to life simply to be dismissed.

5. Two *extreme views* are to be excluded: the one which rejects miracles of any kind as a matter of principle, and the other which accepts the reality of miracles in an uncritical, fundamentalistic way. Miracles, in the end, are manifestations of the presence and power of God and are consistent with the doctrine of Providence. Beyond that, many questions remain open.

6. *Evil*, like a miracle, is *power*. But unlike a miracle, evil is a power against life, not for it. The triumph of Christ over evil will be made manifest finally and perfectly when the Reign of God appears in all its fullness.

7. The *problem of evil* is the reverse of the problem of miracles. We have a problem with the factuality of miracles, but not at all with the *factuality* of evil. We find it relatively easy to offer explanations of the meaning of miracles, but we find it very difficult to find *meaning* in evil.

8. Human response to evil may take three forms: (1) rebellion, (2) resignation, or (3) trust and hope. The third course is that of *Job* in the Old Testament and of *Jesus Christ* in the New Testament. Because of Christ, suffering is redemptive. Our God is literally a sympathetic ("suffering with") God. God wars against evil and seeks our collaboration in the struggle against the powers of darkness.

9. *Prayer* is a conscious, deliberate acknowledgment of, and coming to terms with, our actual situation before God. Through prayer we accept our relationship with God and become more fully aware of the implications of that relationship. Our understanding of prayer, however, cannot be prejudicial to the sovereignty of God, on the one hand, or to human freedom and responsibility, on the other.

10. Is God "a *person*"? No and yes. No, because God is not *an* anything. God is not even *a* Being. Yes, in an *analogical* sense. God is *like* a person in that God is loving, caring, compassionate, faithful, forgiving, and capable of relationship. Nowhere are these personal characteristics more fully expressed than in Jesus Christ.

11. God is also *Father*, but not in the gender-exclusive sense. God transcends gender. God is neither male nor female. God is loving, caring, forgiving, etc. It is the Godhood of the Father that counts, not the Fatherhood of God.

12. The *feminist critique* of *God-language* is threefold: it is exclusive, literal, and patriarchal. It employs exclusively male imagery, interprets metaphors like "Father" literally, and promotes social relationships wherein males dominate females. Accordingly, androcentric language for God is both oppressive and idolatrous. God-language must be open to the experience of women and to the use of symbols that reflect and embody that experience, without denying

the capacity of "equivalent" male symbols and images to express the reality of God.

SUGGESTED READINGS

Boff, Leonardo, and Virgilio Elizondo, eds. *1492–1992: The Voice of the Victims*. Philadelphia: Trinity Press International, 1990.

Johnson, Elizabeth A. *She Who Is: The Mystery of God in a Feminist Theological Discourse*. New York: Crossroad, 1992.

Kee, Howard C. *Medicine, Miracle, and Magic in New Testament Times*. New York: Cambridge University Press, 1986.

LaCugna, Catherine Mowry. *God For Us: The Trinity and Christian Life*. San Francisco: HarperCollins, 1991.

Lewis, C. S. *The Problem of Pain*. New York: Macmillan, 1945.

McFague, Sallie. *Models of God: Theology for an Ecological, Nuclear Age*. Philadelphia: Fortress Press, 1987.

Monden, Louis. *Signs and Wonders: A Study of the Miraculous Element in Religion*. New York: Desclee, 1966.

Ricoeur, Paul. *The Symbolism of Evil*. Boston: Beacon Press, 1967.

Ruether, Rosemary Radford. *Sexism and God-Talk: Toward a Feminist Theology*. Boston: Beacon Press, 1983.

Schneiders, Sandra. *Women and the Word: The Gender of God in the New Testament and the Spirituality of Women*. New York: Paulist Press, 1986.

X

Religion and Its Varieties

THE QUESTION

There is always a debate about the meaning of the word *religion*. With the growth of many small sects, cults, and movements in the United States, even governmental agencies like the Internal Revenue Service are hard-pressed to decide which group can legally be classified as a religion for tax-exemption purposes, and which cannot. Etymology helps us only a little bit.

Religion is derived from the Latin noun *religio,* but it is not clear which of three verbs the noun is most closely allied with: *relegere* ("to turn to constantly" or "to observe conscientiously"); *religari* ("to bind oneself [back]"); and *reeligere* ("to choose again"). Each verb, to be sure, points to three possible religious attitudes, but in the final accounting a purely etymological probe does not resolve the ambiguity.

Let us assume for the moment, however, that religion has something to do with our perception of, and response to, the reality *God.* Why is it, then, that we have not one religion but many? And of the many, why is it that sociologically marginal, even bizarre, types abound?

And what of the mainstream religions, the so-called major world religions? Does their very existence, not to mention their numerical strength, undermine Christianity's traditional claim to uniqueness and supremacy? If we are to regard them as more or less legitimate signs and instruments of God's saving grace (as does the Second Vatican Council's *Declaration on the Relationship of the Church to Non-Christian Religions*), does not that imply they have received divine revelation of some kind and have interpreted it with at least some measure of clarity?

Under what circumstances and through what forms of mediation do the non-Christian religions encounter God in revelation? According to what criteria do they interpret their revelation experience(s) accurately and adhere to them faithfully?

And what of Judaism? Undoubtedly, the Church's relationship with Judaism is different from its relationship with all other non-Christian religions. Christianity emerges from Judaism. Jesus was himself a Jew. The Church accepts the Old Testament, or Hebrew Scriptures, as just as much the Word of God as the New Testament. Indeed, the Church condemned the heresy of Marcionism early in its history, and has never retreated from that doctrinal insistence on the fundamental unity of the two Testaments. Has Judaism now been superseded completely? Are Jews no longer the People of God? Does Christianity have anything still to learn from Judaism?

And what of the general relationship between religion—*any* religion—and the society in which it finds itself? Is religion, of its very nature, inimical to human welfare? Is religion the enemy of freedom, of rationality, of political responsibility? Why have so many regarded religion in this light? Are recent trends in the direction of greater religious involvement in the social and political processes of history consistent with, or opposed to, religion's essential purposes and functions?

And what, finally, of the general relationship between religion and institutionalism? Is religion, of its very nature, so private and so spiritual that it can and must avoid structural expression? Can one be "religious," in other words, without belonging to, and actively participating in, a specific religious group? Can there be such a thing, literally, as a "religionless Christianity" (Dietrich Bonhoeffer)?

THE NOTION OF RELIGION

Defining Religion

The very attempt to define religion is itself problematical. One brings already an idea of religion to the task—an idea that does not correspond with its various manifestations over the course of human history and over the face of the earth. In primitive societies, for example, what the West calls religious is so integral a part of ordinary life that it is never experienced or thought of as separable or distinguishable from all else. For Hinduism, for example, everything that is, in a real sense, is divine. Therefore, almost everything can be and is given a religious significance by one sect or another. In all forms of Buddhism the existence of a transcendent creator-deity is denied in favor of an indefinable, nonpersonal, absolute source or dimension that can be experienced as the depth of human inwardness.

Over the centuries the notion of religion has been defined in the West in more ways than can be categorized—philosophically, anthropologically, psychologically, sociologically, phenomenologically, culturally, and theologically. It would seem that the best definition would try to incorporate elements from all rather than from only one or two of these disciplines. But that has not been the case, for the most part.

Some have restricted themselves to an abstractly *philosophical* approach. They have prescinded from all the particularities of the various religions and have tried instead to identify the pure essence of religion as such. Others have taken a purely *phenomenological* approach, searching for certain visible characteristics common to each of the world's religions. Still others have adopted a narrowly *theological* approach, insisting that there is, and can be, only one true religion, Christianity.

Others have isolated the *psychological* dimension of religious experience (the feeling of absolute dependence; the experience of the holy) and limited the nature and scope of religion accordingly. Some indeed make of religion a mere projection of human wishes, a phenomenon that emerges at the point where human beings can no longer bear their sense of dependence, their anxieties, or even their poverty.

Still others have defined religion *functionally,* locating it at the intersection of *sociology and culture.* Religion is a "given" of the human situation, something to be observed and studied in its total structural composition and defined in terms of its role in meeting social needs and shaping culture.

If one proposes to define a reality so highly differentiated and complex as religion, no single method will suffice. Thus, religion requires a *philosophical* analysis which is concerned with the nature of things, with principles, with theories and laws that transcend the particular and the specific but, at the same time, help to illumine and explain them.

But that philosophical analysis must also be *phenomenologically* developed. Not even in the most narrow medieval philosophies were essences plucked from thin air. All inquiry after truth begins with sense experience. One must first take a look at what is out there before coming to a conclusion about what it is of its essence. So too with religion. If we hope to define religion as it is and not simply as it might be in one or another philosopher's mind, then we would have to take account of religion in all of its varieties—a nearly impossible task.

That very phenomenological exploration will disclose the obviously social and cultural dimensions of religion, its impact on interpersonal relationships, social, political, and economic institutions, art, music, architecture, and the like. Accordingly, no attempt at a definition of religion that is at once philosophical and phenomenological will lack an explicitly *sociological* dimension.

But a closer look at the social aspects of religion will reveal that its varied social expressions are only a reflection of the conversion of mind and heart—for good or for ill—that has occurred in a religion's individual adherents. Religion clearly meets a deeply rooted human need to find meaning in life, as well as the corresponding social need to find a community which shares and sustains that meaning. And so the *psychological* dimension is indispensable to any useful and comprehensive definition of religion.

In the end, however, a definition of religion must also be *theological* unless we are to sever all connection between religion and revelation, or between religion and God. Most people, in fact, who would describe themselves as religious or who would be identified as reli-

gious according to standard philosophical, sociological, and psychological categories, attest to their own firm conviction that God is on
the "other side" of their religious relationship and that somehow God
has managed to reach across the "infinitely qualitative distance"
(Kierkegaard) between the divine and the human through an act (or
acts) of self-communication known as revelation.

The earliest theologians of the Church (e.g., Justin, Tertullian,
Irenæus, Clement of Alexandria, Origen) emphasized the link
between the *Logos* (truth) of contemporary Greek philosophy and
the *Logos*-made-flesh of Christian faith. Whenever human thoughts
and actions are determined by, and directed toward, the *Logos*, we are
at least at the threshold of religion. But for these writers, as for
Augustine later, there were not *many* religions, but only *one*, just
as there are not many *Logoi*, but only one *Logos*. And since the
Son of God is coeternal with the Father, the *Logos* whom the philosophers and others sought even before the coming of Christ was the
same *Logos* who became flesh *in* Christ. The one true religion, therefore, "has been expressed outwardly and carried on under one set
of names and signs in times past and [under] another set now;
it was more secret then and more open now; ... yet it is one and the
same true religion.... The saving grace of this religion, the only
true one, through which alone true salvation is truly promised, has
never been refused to anyone who was worthy of it..." (Augustine,
Letter #102).

For *Thomas Aquinas*, too, the knowledge of God is possible for
every person, because it arises from the recognition of the effects of
God's action in the world. Such knowledge is one of the "preambles
of faith" (i.e., those truths which can be known apart from the explicit
teaching of Christ and the Church and which are a necessary foundation for Christian faith itself).

For Aquinas, religion is one of the "potential parts" of the virtue
of *justice*, in that religion bears many of the characteristics of justice
but at the same time falls short of the full meaning of the virtue. The
essence of justice consists in rendering to another his or her due.
When one has been rendered what is due, equality has been established or restored. But there can be no equality between God and
ourselves. Therefore, religion will always be something like the virtue
of justice but is not exactly the same.

Thomas agrees that a purely etymological exploration will not finally disclose the meaning of religion. It is simply not clear from which verb the noun is derived. But no matter, because each of the possible sources is consistent with the view that religion "denotes properly a relation to God" (*Summa Theologiæ*, II-II, q. 81, a. 1).

Is religion for God's benefit or our own? "We pay God honor and reverence, not for [God's] sake (because [God] is full of glory...), but for our own sake, because by the very fact that we revere and honor God, our mind is subjected to [God]; wherein its perfection consists, since a thing is perfected by being subjected to its superior..." (a. 7).

The Thomistic and earlier patristic perspectives were themselves linked together by the *Transcendental Thomists* and others in this century. Because we are alive by a principle which transcends us, we are not merely *capable* of reaching beyond ourselves to God, which is what an act of religion is all about. We are actually *summoned* to do so. And this is also the position adopted by the *Second Vatican Council*, namely, that we are "at once impelled by nature and also bound by a moral obligation to seek the truth, especially religious truth" (*Declaration on Religious Freedom*, n. 2).

Religion, therefore, has to do with the whole of human existence, and not merely with some special sector of it. God's presence touches the whole person in the totality of the person's relationships not only with God but with all other persons, and with the whole cosmic order as well. *Religion is the whole complexus of attitudes, convictions, emotions, gestures, rituals, beliefs, and institutions by which we come to terms with, and express, our most fundamental relationship with Reality (God and the created order, perceived as coming forth from God's creative hand).*

That relationship is disclosed by a process we have called *revelation*. Religion, therefore, is our (more or less) structured response to revelation. The word *Reality* has been capitalized in the definition to insure that religion will not be confused with any "philosophy of life." In the act of religion we deliberately reach out toward God. We perceive God in the persons, events, and things we see, that is to say, sacramentally. Religion presupposes and flows from *faith*. One is not religious who does not think there is more to reality than meets the eye. The religious person believes himself or herself to be in touch with another dimension, with "the beyond in the midst of life" (Bonhoeffer).

This does not mean, however, that every person of faith is also religious. It is possible to have only *implicit* faith in God. Even those who think of themselves as atheists might be, in the depths of their existence, persons of faith. Such persons might be rejecting false notions of God, as the Second Vatican Council admitted. In any case, they can be oriented to God, without realizing it, through their firm commitment to love, justice, and other values. It is not *explicit* faith in God which saves, but only that faith, explicit *or* implicit, that issues forth in obedience to God's will (Matthew 7:21; see also the Parable of the Sheep and the Goats in Matthew 25:31–46). On the other hand, the actions of a person with *implicit* faith only cannot be called religious except in the widest sense of the word. We understand religion here as an individual, social, and institutional manifestation of some *explicit* faith in God.

Characteristics of Religion

1. The most basic characteristic of religion is its sense of the *holy* or the *sacred*. For the sociologist Émile Durkheim (d. 1917) the sacred, unlike the secular or the profane, has no utilitarian purpose at all. It is something revered for its own sake. It elicits from us what the phenomenologist of religion G. van der Leeuw (d. 1950) has called *awe*. Religious rites are not performed to achieve something so much as to express an attitude. Awe, in other words, develops into *observance*.

Other characteristics of the sacred, for Durkheim, are its being perceived as a *power* or *force*, its *ambiguity*, its *invisible* or *spiritual* quality, its *noncognitive* dimension, its *supportive* or *strength-giving* nature, and the *demands* it makes upon believers and worshipers. (See *The Elementary Forms of the Religious Life*, New York: Free Press, 1965; orig. ed., 1915.)

Rudolf Otto (d. 1937) has also analyzed what he calls *The Idea of the Holy* (1917), referring to it as the "numinous," i.e., as something beyond rational and ethical conceptions. It embodies a mystery that is above all creatures, something hidden and esoteric, which we can experience in feelings. The holy is the *mysterium tremendum et fascinosum* (a mystery which at the same time overwhelms and fascinates

365

us). It is "wholly other" (which is how the Protestant theologian Karl Barth also referred to God), quite beyond the sphere of the usual, the intelligible, and the familiar. The experience of the holy, according to Otto, arouses a feeling of unworthiness in the believer.

2. Religion not only has to do with the impact of the holy upon us but with our *response* to the holy as well. Religion necessarily includes *faith*, whether explicit or implicit. The content of that faith may differ from religion to religion, and there will even be sharp differences of interpretation within the same religion, but there can be no religion in the Christian sense of the term without some self-consciousness and reflective awareness of the holy, the sacred, the ultimate, of God.

3. In most instances religion gives rise to *beliefs* of various kinds: some popular, some official (doctrines, creeds). And the more sophisticated the religion, the more likely the emergence of a *theological* tradition, even of *systematic* theology.

4. Religion is also expressed in various *actions: moral behavior* consistent with beliefs, and *liturgy*, or the ritualization of beliefs.

5. Religion also can generate a *community* of shared perceptions, meanings, and values. Each such community has at least some rudimentary *structure*.

The connection between the original religious inspiration and the community it eventually generates is worth noting here. The foundational religious experience is *charismatic* in nature. Max Weber (d. 1920) defines *charisma* as "a certain quality of an individual personality by virtue of which [the person] is set apart from ordinary [persons] and treated as endowed with supernatural, superhuman, or at least specifically exceptional powers or qualities. These are such as are not accessible to the ordinary person, but are regarded as of divine origin or as exemplary, and on the basis of them the individual concerned is treated as a leader" (*The Theory of Social and Economic Organization*, Glencoe, Ill.: Free Press, 1957, pp. 358–59). The three chief characteristics of a charisma are that it is unusual, spontaneous, and creative.

A second stage is reached when the charisma is "routinized." Pure charisma can only exist in the act of originating. When the leader dies, his or her disciples face a crisis. Are they to disband, or continue? If they decide to continue, then the charismatic element will somehow have to share the stage with the institutional and the structural. Otherwise, there can be no permanence to the charisma. There has to be stability of thought, of practice, and of organization.

Every religious group that hopes to endure, even those groups which describe themselves today as "charismatic," assumes stable organizational forms. No group is completely charismatic if it agrees to meet at a certain time, in a certain place, to engage in certain activities, however spontaneous those activities turn out to be. The holding of national meetings, of conventions, the publication of magazines, the circulation of newsletters—all of these represent a routinization of the original charismatic impulse, even for self-described "charismatic" groups.

The routinization process becomes a serious problem only when the organizational interests overtake the charismatic or even replace them. A religious community must constantly reflect on its original purposes, the values of its founder, the convictions about God and human life which originally set the community apart. It must take care that each of its institutional forms and patterns of behavior facilitates rather than impedes those basic purposes. The challenge to a religious community that would remain faithful to its original charisma is not to find ways to *de*institutionalize itself but to *re*institutionalize itself according to its abiding faith. A religious community without any institutional forms at all, on the other hand, is a religious community which has a tenuous hold on social existence. By their very nature, charisms die out unless they are somehow routinized, i.e., unless they find adequate institutional expression.

Criticisms of Religion

The very notion of religion can be, and has been, criticized from within as well as from without. *From within,* religion has been characterized as the product of human effort to assert itself against God. But in revelation it is God who takes the initiative. We are simply overtaken by the revelation and accept it as God's word. Anything beyond this, any attempt to "deal with" God from our side, places religion above revelation. This particular critical view of religion is identified with Karl Barth and, to some similar extent, with Emil

Brunner (d. 1966), both of whom insisted on the exclusivity of Christian revelation and, therefore, the intrinsic error of every other kind of "religion."

Religion has also been criticized from within by Paul Tillich and Dietrich Bonhoeffer, who rejected the Christian tendency to make religion a separate compartment of life. Many centuries earlier, of course, we had internal criticisms of religion-in-practice by the *prophets* of Israel. The history of the Church is also replete with examples of reformist movements: e.g., the reform of spirituality, of monasteries, of clerical lifestyles, of ecclesiastical authority, of canon law, of the liturgy, of seminaries. Significantly, Christianity itself suffered its most severe division in an event known as the Reformation.

Religion is also subject to criticism *from without*. It is perceived as a projection of the human spirit. For Ludwig Feuerbach, God is the highest projection of our selves in the objective order. A similar position is taken by John Dewey. For Freud religion is an illusion, a regression to the helplessness and insecurity of childhood, the product of wish fulfillment. For Marx it is the opiate of the people, numbing their capacity for outrage at the gross inequities of the economic order. Others, like Albert Camus, insist that religion is not the *only* response to a limit situation, one in which all of our most basic values are put to the test. In his novel *The Stranger* Camus writes of a man condemned to die the next day, achieving a sense of serenity in the face of an impersonal and indifferent cosmos.

There is, finally, a criticism of religion which defies easy categorization. It is neither the criticism of a nonbeliever, nor that of the internal reformer. It is rather the antireligious critique of those who may insist that they believe in God, perhaps even in Jesus Christ, but who deny the necessity of any ordered, structured, and institutionalized expression of their faith and belief. It is a kind of religious *individualism* which in the United States has been identified with names like Anne Hutchinson, Thomas Paine, Thomas Jefferson, Ralph Waldo Emerson, Henry David Thoreau, and Walt Whitman. Its present-day variants have been described in *Habits of the Heart: Individualism and Commitment in American Life,* by Robert Bellah, et al. (Berkeley: University of California Press, 1985).

Types of Religion

Taking as our starting point the principle that God is at once transcendent and immanent, "the beyond in our midst," religions can be differentiated from one another on the basis of the relative stress they place on the transcendent or the immanent nature of God. The division, of course, is based on a Christian perspective. It is in the central Christian doctrine of the incarnation that God is revealed as *both* transcendent and immanent: the Word was made flesh.

We can discern, therefore, two basic types of religions: those which stress the transcendence of God, and those which stress immanence. Within each type there are degrees of emphasis. Thus, a religion in the transcendence series may stress the otherness of God so much that God's relationship with the world of beings is all but lost, as in *Deism*. A religion in the immanence series, on the other hand, may stress the worldliness of God so much that God's relationship with the world of beings becomes one of complete identity, as in *Pantheism*.

Religions in the *transcendence series* are interested in history and eschatology, their worship tends to be objective and highly verbal, they have a sense of ethical demands following from their faith in God, and they have some measure of rational reflection on that faith (theology). Religions in the *immanence series*, on the other hand, tend toward a timeless, ahistorical understanding, their worship is more elaborately ritualistic, their personal goals are not so much obedience to God's will as absorption into God, and they favor mystical experience over rational reflection.

Among religions in the transcendence series are Judaism, Islam, and Confucianism. Among religions in the immanence series are Buddhism and Hinduism. When pushed to their ultimate extremes, religions in the transcendence series lapse into atheism; religions in the immanence series lapse into fetishism, of which "black magic" is a form. In the first extreme, God is pushed so far beyond the reality of this world that the divine disappears altogether. In the second extreme, God is so identified with the reality of this world that this world's goods take on the character of the divine itself. (See John Macquarrie, *Principles of Christian Theology,* 2d. rev. ed., pp. 161–70.)

THE NON-CHRISTIAN RELIGIONS

Religions of the Past

Egypt, Canaan

In ancient Egypt (c. 2778–2263 B.C.) the king was worshiped. Later, when divinity was transferred from the royal throne to the Sun (*Re*), the king was regarded as the son of the Sun-God. Later still, during the period of the Middle Kingdom (2052–1786 B.C.), monotheism came more fully to the front. *Amon* was the supreme God, not only during the Middle Kingdom but during the New Kingdom as well (1580–1085 B.C.). Perhaps the most distinctive feature of ancient Egyptian religion was its preoccupation with the afterlife, a belief most visibly manifested in the construction of the pyramids and the laying in of ample provisions for the entombed king to use in the next life.

Another important religion of the ancient East (important because it was part of the religious scene at the time when Israel took possession of the land) was that of the Canaanites. Myth and ritual in Ugarit (present-day northern Syria) centered on the effort to secure the *fertility* of nature. The supreme God, *El*, was nonetheless surpassed in power by *Baal*, who displayed his might in the thunderstorm and the bestowal of fertility.

Ancient Greece

For the ancient Greeks there were many gods (polytheism), "higher powers" possessing all of the Greek ideals of beauty, wisdom, and power. The gods alone are immortal. *Zeus* is the father of the gods and, as such, is supreme. He reigns with the other gods on Mount Olympus, from which point he takes in all reality, including the future. Hence he is a great source of oracles. One of Zeus's two brothers is *Hades*, lord of the underworld; the other is *Poseidon*, whose palace is in the depths of the sea; *Apollo* is the son of Zeus, always appearing in the prime of youth. He has the power of healing and forgiveness. Among his many functions, he is the source of justice, law, and order in the State, and is the god of wisdom as well. *Dionysius*, on the other hand, inspires wild enthusiasm and frenzy in his followers, and he himself celebrates his feasts among satyrs and beasts. Greek sacrificial rites, centered on the sacrificial meal, had one primary purpose: fellowship. The central place of worship was the temple, where the images of the gods were kept, and the temple was served, in turn, by a priesthood.

Ancient Rome

Triads of gods headed the pantheon of ancient Rome: first *Jupiter, Mars,* and *Quirinus,* and then Jupiter, *Juno,* and *Minerva.* Jupiter dwelt on mountaintops, was the source of storms, and gave warriors strength in battle. He prized loyalty and justice. Mars was the god of war, and Quirinus was very much like him. Juno, Jupiter's wife, was the guardian of marriage, as Zeus's sister *Hera* had been in Greece, and other parallels with the ancient Greek gods were obvious (Minerva = Athena, Neptune = Poseidon, Venus = Aphrodite, Mercury = Hermes, e.g.). Just as in Greece, the most important religious act was the sacrifice. The gifts were animals or corn, and there were set prayers and rituals. The high priest of the Roman State was called the *Pontifex Maximus,* a title assumed eventually by the pope and only recently disavowed by Popes John Paul I (d. 1978) and John Paul II. The Vestal Virgins were women priests. Piety (reverent devotion) was the key to a correct relationship with the gods, and on the human level it required the honoring of obligations between persons and especially the obligation of love for one's parents. Worship of the emperor was a later development.

Mayans, Aztecs, Incas

Other ancient and now defunct religions were to be found in the Orient and in certain parts of Europe. In what is present-day Latin America there were the Mayans (focused, it seems, on the rain-god *Chac*), the Aztecs (with their human sacrifices), and the Incas (with their sun and moon gods, *Inti* and *Mama Quilla*). As usual, the temple was the place of worship and contained a golden disc representing the sun; it also contained the mummies of dead kings. There was a well-organized priesthood and, as with the other religions of Central and South America, there was a belief in survival after death.

Religions of the Present

What follows here are the barest of summaries. Christians can only begin to imagine how a work of this sort, written from, let us say, a Muslim perspective, might summarize all of Christianity in a few paragraphs. For fuller summaries of each religion, consult the Suggested Readings at the end of this chapter, particularly the sixteen-volume *Encyclopedia of Religion* (1987).

Zoroastrianism

Zoroastrianism, the ancient religion of Iran (Persia), has been preserved to the present in the form of the preaching and teaching of its prophet *Zarathustra* (Hellenized as *Zoroaster*), who lived sometime between 1000 and 600 B.C. It is a religion marked by dualism (the struggle between good and evil) and eschatology (the individual is rewarded or punished after death, depending on his or her behavior in this life). Both principles are said to have influenced Judaism, Islam, and Christianity.

Hinduism

Hinduism, one of India's ancient religions and followed today by about 70 percent of India's roughly 700,000,000 people, is obscure in its origins—an obscurity linked undoubtedly with a certain sense of timelessness in Indian history itself. What we do know of its earliest period comes from the sacred book of the *Veda* ("knowledge"), which tells of magical cults and priestly powers. The priests (Brahmans) gradually became supreme, and their wisdom is reflected in the *Upanishads* (*Upa*, "near"; *ni-shad*, "sitting down"). The title of these texts indicates the position of the pupil in receiving the sacred knowledge imparted by the teacher.

Unlike the Veda, the Upanishads are pessimistic in outlook. The sadness of life is reflected in the belief in a cycle of rebirths which is the necessary consequence of each person's *karma* or "work" of good or evil deeds in life. Salvation is possible only through mystical absorption in the knowledge of the one true reality, the Absolute, *brahman*, the ultimate source and goal of all existence. *Brahman* causes all existence and all beings to emanate from itself and is the self (*atman*) of all living beings.

Although Hinduism has no doctrine of God, *brahman* may also be conceived of as a personal "high god" (usually as Vishnu, the preserver, or Shiva, the destroyer). Of the various forms in which Vishnu appears on earth (*avatāra*, "descent"), that of *Krishna* has great importance. It is as Krishna that Vishnu appears in the *Bhagavad-Gita* (*The Song of the Majestic*). Here he proclaims religious and moral truths. Along with the Sermon on the Mount, the *Bhagavad-Gita* was Gandhi's (d. 1948) favorite reading.

The core of Hinduist ethics is the belief in the unity of all life and its correlative respect for life and a feeling of close identity with all living beings. It is also an intensely ascetical and meditative religion, as in the practice of *yoga*.

Buddhism

Buddhism, also Indian in origin, is derived from the title *Buddha*, which means "enlightened one." *Siddhārtha Gautama* (d. 480 B.C.) was the first Buddha. A member of a princely line who encountered human misery during his frequent trips from his father's palace, he eventually chose to live like a beggar-monk, a homeless ascetic. He is said to have received the *bodhi* ("enlightenment") one night while sitting under a fig tree. He proclaimed the revelation in a sermon. The content is called *dharma*, the doctrine of Buddhism. It teaches that we can break out of the grim cycle of rebirths and attain *Nirvana* ("dissolution") by following the "middle way," avoiding both total, hedonistic absorption in the world and excessive self-torment. *Nirvana* implies the overcoming of all desires and gives salvation according to one's deeds.

At first the movement was limited to male monks; then nuns were allowed in, and finally laypersons. There were inevitably strict and less strict observances. *Hinayana* Buddhism allowed entry into *Nirvana* through monasticism alone. *Mahayana* Buddhism, in which laypersons were prominent, holds that salvation is open to all who faithfully revere the many earlier Buddhas and the Buddhas yet to come. It is this latter form of Buddhism which is to be found in *Tibet*, where the *lamas*, and especially the *Dalai Lama* and the *Panchen Lama*, are regarded as reincarnations of a Buddha.

Taoism

Taoism, an ancient Chinese religion, is derived from the term *tao*, which means "the way." The *tao* comprises a male, active principle (*yang*) and a female, passive principle (*yin*), representing heaven and earth. We must all live in harmony with the order of the universe as determined by the *tao*. Wisdom consists in knowing the will of heaven. One of the principal exponents of *Taoism* was Cung-fu-tse (d. 479 B.C.), whose name was Latinized by the Jesuit missionaries of the seventeenth century as *Confucius*. Confucius collected the ancient writings and added his own interpretations, which had an ethical bent to them. His naturalistic ethics centered on *jen* ("humaneness," "benevolence"). The right order of the *tao* is maintained by the rites (*li*) performed by the emperor, who is the Son of Heaven. Rome strictly forbade the Jesuit missionaries, however, from equating "heaven" or the "supreme ruler" with God.

Shintoism

Shintoism, an ancient Japanese religion, also focuses on the way (*to*) of numinous beings (*shin*). It is essentially a polytheistic religion with a simple worship of nature. Eventually it was amalgamated with Buddhism, which was introduced into Japan in the sixth century A.D. Entrance into paradise is insured for those who trust in the grace of Buddha. Buddhist doctrine is assimilated through meditation on the *Lotus of the Good Religion (Hokkekyo)*. The practice of meditation remains central in the many schools of *Zen Buddhism* which reached Japan from China.

Islam

Islam, an ancient Arabic religion, means literally "total surrender to the will of Allah." Its origins lie with its Prophet *Mohammed* (d. 632), who experienced a call from Allah to proclaim monotheism. He began to preach in Mecca, laying emphasis on judgment, the resurrection on the last day, and faith in Allah as the one God. Encountering hostility from the Meccan aristocracy, Mohammed moved to Yathrib. The flight was known as his *hegira* ("abandonment of kindred"), and with it the Moslem era begins.

Yathrib's name was changed to Medina, and it was here that Mohammed broke with Judaism, orienting his prayers now to Mecca rather than Jerusalem. He saw his task as reviving the monotheism of Abraham. His early disciples recorded or memorized his teachings, and after his death they were collected into the *Koran*, composed of 114 chapters (*sura*) divided into verses (*ayat*). There is no logical or chronological order to them. There *is* a division between the Meccan and the Medinese *suras:* The Meccan convey the traditional emphases on Allah as creator and judge, on the resurrection, and on hell, while the Medinese contain authoritative directives. Successors of Mohammed are known as *caliphs*, who are responsible for the temporal interests of the community.

In Islam Allah is eternal, simple, omnipotent, supreme over all. There is no distinction between the spiritual and the temporal. Whatever Allah does is completely just. Whatever happens, Allah causes. We freely choose between good and evil, and Allah creates the human act which corresponds with the choice. Allah has sent prophets to speak in his name (Abraham, Moses, Jesus, and lastly Mohammed). He is the creator of angels, devils, and even the *jinn* (genies). There is a future life (paradise and hell).

Allah will forgive all sins except apostasy. The faithful are urged to care for the needy, orphans, pilgrims, prisoners, and the like. They are to pray, be loyal to contractual obligations, and be resigned to misfortunes. The "pillars of Islam" are prayer (recited five times each day), profession of faith, alms, fasting, and pilgrimage to Mecca at least once in one's lifetime. *Sari*, the religious law of Islam, is derived from the Koran, the *sunna* (Mohammed's own example), analogy (*qiyas*) and prudent judgments (*ra'y*), and the common opinion of the learned or the customary practice of the people (Islam's principle of flexibility).

In the eighth century Islam suffered a division between the *Ṣufī* and the more orthodox *Sunnites*. The word *sūf* means "wool" and refers to the coarse wool garments which the ascetics wore in imitation of the Christian monks. For the Sunnites, to love Allah is simply to worship and obey Allah according to established rules. For the Ṣufī, *union* with Allah is possible—a teaching that was detestable to the Sunnites, who insisted there can be no equality and therefore no reciprocity between Allah and ourselves. By the ninth century Sufism was flourishing, and it remains at the base of Moslem ethics today.

Christians at first regarded Islam as a heretical movement within Judaism (the view of St. John Damascene, for example). Later, after the Moslem penetration of the West and the West's penetration of the East in the Crusades, extensive dialogue followed contact. Evidence of the dialogue can be found in various writings, especially Thomas Aquinas's *Summa Contra Gentiles*. The dialogue, however, was to cease (and not to reopen until the post–Vatican II period) with the wars against the Turks beginning in the late sixteenth century and the final downfall of the Ottoman Empire in 1918.

Judaism

Judaism has its origins in the formation of the Twelve Tribes of Israel, which some Old Testament scholars have identified with the covenant of Shechem described in Joshua 24. Other scholars insist that the Israel which worshiped Yahweh existed before Shechem, and that the Shechem covenant enlarged but did not create Israel. More immediately, Judaism emerges from the period when the exiles returned from Babylon in the sixth century B.C. Most of these exiles were recruited from the tribe of Judah (see Ezra 1–2). They saw themselves as the purified "remnant of Israel," i.e., as that portion of the Twelve Tribes which had survived the catastrophe of captivity and submitted to it as the judgment of God upon their guilt (see especially Ezra 6:13–18).

Among the *principal characteristics* of Judaism are its sense of the Covenant, the land, history, and the Kingdom of God.

1. The most fundamental conviction of the Jewish people has always been that they are a people of the *Covenant:* Yahweh is the God of Israel, and Israel the people of Yahweh (Exodus 19:4–6; Joshua 24). God is present among the people of Israel as a powerful God (Isaiah 45:14). The promises of descendants to the patriarchs are to be under-

stood in the light of this Covenant (Genesis 13:16; 15:5; 26:4,24; 28:14; 32:13, e.g.).

The God of the Covenant, however, is not the object of systematic theological reflection, as in Christianity. The God of Israel is a holy God who calls the people of Israel to be a holy people, their distinction (or holiness) being marked by their adherence to the divine commands (or Torah) linked with the Covenant: the observance of the Sabbath and feast days, the recital of prayers, the keeping of purity laws, circumcision, the maintenance of ancient Jewish tradition, the hope of salvation. These biblical laws were developed to their zenith by the sages of early rabbinic Judaism in the first six centuries of the common era.

Throughout Jewish history, into the present age, the holy God of Israel is ever a God of mercy and justice, concerned with the people, giving them instruction and reproof, inspiring them to right conduct, and through the guidance of divine law inhibiting their impulses to infidelity. As in Islam, even the most ordinary and profane activities of everyday life are to be transformed into opportunities for sanctification under the sovereignty of God, who is always present and whose presence becomes increasingly effective in its power.

2. A second major characteristic of Judaism is its *respect and reverence for Jewish history*. Judaism finds courage to live through the hardships of the present by recalling and reflecting upon the glories of the past, God's promises to the patriarchs, and the gift of law that binds God and the Jews (Genesis 24:7; 50:24; Exodus 13:5,11; Numbers 14:16; Deuteronomy 4:31; 6:23, e.g.). Of particular note is the role of the Exodus from Egypt and revelation of law at Sinai, a chain of events that underlies both biblical and contemporary rabbinic Jewish worship. The past as such, and through the literary genre of *Midrash* (contemporizing biblical interpretation), serves as a model for Jewish life throughout all time.

3. There is also Judaism's close relationship to *the land* of Israel as promised by the God of the Covenant. The claim to the promised land has never been abandoned by Jews even to the present day, with the establishment of the State of Israel in 1948: "Keep, then, this entire commandment that I am commanding you today, so that you may have strength to go in and occupy the land that you are crossing

over to occupy, and so that you may live long in the land that the Lord swore to your ancestors to give them and to their descendants, a land flowing with milk and honey" (Deuteronomy 11:8–9).

4. Finally, there is the conviction of faith which sums up and incorporates all of the others, namely, belief in the coming of the *Kingdom of God*. Sometimes, the notion of God's kingship is exceedingly nationalistic, as in the time of the Maccabees (170 B.C.–A.D. 70) or in the rebellion led by Bar Kochba (A.D. 132–135). At other times, the hope of a Messiah to deliver the Jews from captivity into salvation is more universal in outlook. Here the messianic age is envisioned as a joyful and faithful living with God, in accord with the divine will for all humankind.

One should not confuse Judaism's hope in salvation, however, with the traditional Christian hope in eternal life for each person. Judaism's generally optimistic sense of what we can accomplish in this life with God's help (Psalms 8; Zechariah 1:3; Malachi 3:7) has no corresponding sense of any individual call to happiness in some life beyond. It is the people of Israel that will survive and prosper, and not any particular person within it.

The *source* of Judaism is the *Torah* (literally, "instruction"), which is the most general word for law in Judaism. The Torah has both a written and an oral form. The written Torah is the *Tanakh* (Hebrew Bible), consisting of twenty-four books. The oral Torah is to be found above all in rabbinical literature, especially the *Mishnah* (literally, "tradition," "repetition"), which is a codification and clarification of biblical law and subsequent traditions. The Mishnah is the core of a larger collection of rabbinical opinions known as the *Talmud* ("teaching"). Talmudic interpretation ranges from philological to practical, but in any case seeks to train its readers in abstract thinking and the application of enduring principles of law to ever-changing circumstances. A corpus of biblical interpretations known as *Midrash* ("searching") complements the Talmud, integrating both the ethical-legal (*halakhah*) and narrative-homiletical (*haggadah*).

Judaism, like all of the great religions of the world, has endured change throughout history. The Old Testament provides a full and rich account of Israel's and of Judaism's historical experiences before the coming of Christ. After the destruction of the Temple at Jerusalem in A.D. 70. Judaism entered a new period of religious life. The leaders of the Israelite community sought continuity within the study and practice of Torah in an age without a temple, without political independence, and in a newly pluralistic situation, surrounded by other peoples and other religions, especially Christianity and Gnosticism.

It was in the exchange between Judaism and Greek philosophy that the first stirrings of Jewish "systematic theology" occurred, and in the medieval period Jewish thought assumed an Islamic cast, when Jewish Neoplatonism and Aristotelianism appeared on the scene. Among the great philosopher-theologians of the period are Jehudah Halevi (d. 1140), who insisted on the superiority of revelation over reason, and Moses Maimonides (d. 1204), who insisted on the essential conformity between revelation and reason (philosophy) and on the necessity of the latter to apprehend the former. Just as there had been a strong Catholic reaction against Thomas Aquinas for his vigorous use of reason in the understanding of faith, so sometimes was there a vehement protest against Maimonides from within contemporary Judaism.

In other circles (and nearly universally today), however, Maimonides is viewed as one of the greatest legal and philosophic minds of the entire Jewish tradition. Still, the Halevian attitude of reserve toward the pretensions of reason remained vital until the middle of the eighteenth century, when a sharply rationalistic orientation reasserted itself in the writings of Moses Mendelssohn (d. 1786). This orientation set the stage for the insightful theology of Hermann Cohen (d. 1918), Franz Rosenzweig (d. 1929), and Martin Buber (d. 1965). At the same time, and in response to the rapidly changing modern world, Judaism developed the Reform, Orthodox, Conservative, and Reconstructionist movements found in our own day and age.

CHRISTIANITY AND THE OTHER RELIGIONS

As pointed out in chapter 3, the world today is marked in an unprecedented way by the experience of *pluralism* and *diversity*. We are more aware than ever before of the diversity which characterizes the human community. Just as Copernicus helped us see that our earth is not at the center of the universe, and Darwin helped us see that our species did not spring up independently of other lifeforms, so our belated recognition of pluralism and diversity helps us see that the world is filled with "heresies," i.e., selective perceptions of reality and selective apprehensions of truth. In such a world, even the Christian faith appears "heretical." (See Paul J. Griffiths, ed., *Christianity Through Non-Christian Eyes* [1990].)

Why, then, are there many religions rather than one? Just as God is in principle available to every person in grace (Rahner's "supernatural existential") and to every people (since we are essentially social), so also religion, as the (more or less) structured response to the self-communication of God, is available in principle to every person and people. But since "no one has ever seen God" (John 1:18), we can never be absolutely certain that we have had an actual experience of God or that we have correctly perceived, interpreted, and expressed that experience.

Furthermore, God can become available to us only on terms consistent with our bodily existence, i.e., sacramentally. Every experience of God or, from the other side, every self-disclosure of God, is inevitably conditioned by the situation of the person or community to which God has been communicated. That sacramental experience of God is at once mediated and communal. Those communities are differentiated by time, place, culture, history, language, temperament, and social and economic conditions.

Revelation, therefore, is always received according to the mode of the receiver, to cite a familiar Thomistic principle ("*Quodenim recipitur in aliquo recipitur in eo secundum modum recipientis,*" *Summa Theologiæ,* I, q. 79, a. 6). Since religion is our (more or less) structured response to the reception of God in revelation, our response will be shaped by that mode of reception. Indeed, the Son of God became incarnate in a particular time and place, in a particular cultural and religious situation, in a particular person of a particular family, nation, and ethnic community.

When one scans the spectrum of religions, past and present, as we have already sketchily done above, one begins to appreciate the striking similarities between Christianity and the other great religions of the world: their common sense of the supreme majesty of God, their ethical codes, their rites of worship, their priesthoods, their call to repentance, conversion, and reform. Suddenly for many Christians the old skepticism toward the non-Christian religions ("How can anyone seriously believe in them?") is bent back toward Christianity itself ("Why should we think that we're any better than any other religion?"). This can give rise to an attitude of *religious indifferentism*, wherein all religions are regarded as equally valid.

On the opposite side, other Christians hold fast to a position, known as *exclusivism*, which contends that there is no salvation apart from Christ and the Church (*"extra ecclesiam nulla salus"*). Even though the Catholic Church itself has in recent decades conceded that non-Christians (and, *a fortiori*, non-Catholic Christians) can be saved by an implicit faith in Christ or by an implicit desire for membership in the Church, the exclusivists urgently call for renewed efforts at "evangelization" understood not in the broad and comprehensive manner of Pope Paul VI's 1975 Apostolic Exhortation *Evangelii Nuntiandi* ("On the Evangelization of the Modern World")—the proclamation of the word, the celebration of the sacraments, the offering of corporate witness to Christ, and participation in the struggle for justice and peace (nn. 27–29,41)—but only in the narrower sense of "making converts" or of bringing "fallen away" Catholics back to the Church.

The first group may have collapsed the questions of exclusiveness and uniqueness. They fail to recognize that the Christian faith can be a compellingly *unique* expression of divine revelation in Jesus Christ without at the same time being the *exclusive* sign and instrument of revelation. The second group seems to believe that the present state of Christian missions can be changed simply through the application of more aggressive techniques or through the commissioning of greater numbers of dedicated missionaries. But decisions were rendered by the Catholic Church some centuries ago which have had the practical effect of closing off whole countries, even whole continents, to the effective presence of Christianity. One thinks, for example, of the initially successful sixteenth-century mission to China under the leadership of Jesuit Father Matteo Ricci (d. 1610) that was aborted when Rome rejected the development of native rites and opposed other cultural adaptations.

Beyond that, the other great world religions are intricately enmeshed in the social, political, ethnic, and cultural elements of their geographical settings: Islam with the Arab world (though Islam also

381

exists outside that world), Judaism with a specific people, Hinduism and Buddhism with Asian culture, Taoism and Shintoism with Oriental culture. From the Christian perspective, there seems to be a relative permanency to the present condition of religious pluralism and diversity. Less than one percent of the people of China and Japan are Christian, and only two percent of the people of India. We are, in the words of the French Dominican theologian Yves Congar, "a small church in a large world." This is a fact that we can either wring our hands over or respond to in pastorally realistic and constructive ways.

The Second Vatican Council's approach to other religions has been strikingly positive: "The Catholic Church rejects nothing which is true and holy in these religions. It looks with sincere respect upon those ways of conduct and of life, those rules and teachings which, though differing in many particulars from what it holds and sets forth, nevertheless often reflect a ray of that Truth which enlightens all people. Indeed, it proclaims and must ever proclaim Christ, 'the way, the truth, and the life' (John 14:6), in whom everyone finds the fullness of religious life, and in whom God has reconciled all things . . . (cf. 2 Corinthians 5:18–19)" (*Declaration on the Relationship of the Church to Non-Christian Religions*, n. 2).

Theologians who reject both indifferentism on the one extreme and exclusivism on the other have tried to come to terms with the challenge of religious pluralism and diversity in a similarly positive and constructive fashion. There are various approaches, three of which are given here:

First, there is the view that there is still but one true religion and that insofar as other "religions" embody authentic values and even saving grace, they do so as "anonymously Christian" communities. All grace is grace in Christ, who is the one Mediator (1 Timothy 2:5). Therefore, all recipients of grace are at least in principle new creatures in Christ, people whose lives are governed implicitly or virtually by the new life in Christ that is at work within them. This is a position identified especially with Karl Rahner.

A *second* view acknowledges the salvific value in each of the non-Christian religions and underscores, as the preceding view does, the universality of revelation and of grace. It does not speak of the other religions as "anonymously Christian," but instead implicitly regards them as lesser, relative, and extraordinary means of salvation. This position is to be found in the teaching of the Second Vatican Council and of a perhaps declining number of Catholic theologians today.

These first two positions are also known as *inclusivist*, because they seek to "include" non-Christian communities in the fulfillment of the divine plan of salvation that God established in Christ and through the Church.

Without prejudice to the uniqueness and truth of Christian faith (a crucially important qualification), a *third* view affirms the intrinsic religious value of the other great religions of the world and, going beyond the second view, insists on the necessity and worthwhileness of *dialogue* with them. These other religions are not only to be tolerated or even respected; they are to be perceived as having something to teach us, not only about themselves and their own "doctrines," but also about God, about human life, about Christ, that is, about *our own* doctrines. In this third view, these other religions are not regarded, however benignly, as merely deficient expressions of Christianity or secondary instruments of salvation in Christ.

This third view is at least implied in the Second Vatican Council's call for dialogue with non-Christian religions (e.g., *Decree on the Church's Missionary Activity*, n. 34; *Declaration on Christian Education*, n. 11) and in the subsequent establishment by the Vatican of the Pontifical Council for Interreligious Dialogue. Catholic theologians who are identified with this approach include Hans Küng, Heinz Robert Schlette, Raimundo Panikkar, Gavin D'Costa, Joseph DiNoia, and others, as represented, for example, in *Christian Uniqueness Reconsidered: The Myth of a Pluralistic Theology of Religions*, Gavin D'Costa, ed. (1990). This third view is to be distinguished, however, from one described in the D'Costa volume as a "lazy pluralism," as represented in *The Myth of Christian Uniqueness: Toward a Pluralistic Theology of Religions*, John Hick and Paul F. Knitter, eds. (1987).

Each of these three views, their differences among themselves notwithstanding, respects the uniqueness and truth of Christianity, and, in varying degrees, the intrinsic religious and salvific value of non-Christian religions.

We are left, then, with fashioning an agenda for dialogue: to encourage other religions to bring out what is best and deepest in their own traditions and to encourage them along the course of self-criticism and renewal. But since dialogue is by definition a two-way process, the call to self-criticism and renewal applies equally to the Church. It should be led to appreciate anew its own traditions, to discover and learn from the traditions of the other religions, and "to do justice to the distinctive claims advanced by the adherents of traditions with whom dialogue is envisaged" (J. A. DiNoia, *The Diversity of Religions: A Christian Perspective* [1992], p. 163).

Christianity in dialogue with other religions will not shrink from emphasizing its own uniqueness, but dialogue will make it increasingly open to the religious richness and intrinsic salvific value of the other great traditions as well.

Because of the historically unique relationship between Christianity and *Judaism*, the latter offers a special opportunity for dialogue. Jesus was himself a Jew, of a Jewish family. His preaching was directed first of all to the Jewish people, and his earliest disciples were Jewish. The Old Testament was the Bible of the early Christian community and remains an integral and coequal part of Sacred Scripture for Christians today. The Gospel presupposed the Law and the prophets. In spite of the fact that Judaism and Christianity had so much in common, they were at odds with each other from the beginning. The anti-Jewish polemic in John's Gospel has been noted by New Testament scholars, and the second-century rabbinical prayer (*Shemoneh 'Esreh*), recited daily, includes a curse against "heretics and Nazarenes."

The postbiblical history of Christian-Jewish relations has been, until very recently indeed, a record of hostility, alienation, and atrocities. Jews were slaughtered during the Crusades and exiled from their homes in England, France, Spain, and Portugal in the fourteenth and fifteenth centuries. Talmuds were burned beginning in the twelfth century, and Passion Plays and Blood Libel (the notion that Jews ritually murder Christians) proliferated in the fourteenth century. But, of course, no episode affecting the Jews has had a more profound effect on the Christian conscience than the Holocaust (*Shoah*), the Nazi extermination of six million Jews at the time of the Second World War. "After Auschwitz there can be no more excuses," Hans Küng has written. "Christendom cannot avoid a clear admission of its guilt" (*On Being a Christian*, p. 169).

Because the persecution of Jews has too often been explained, even defended, on the basis of Jewish involvement in the crucifixion of Jesus, the Second Vatican Council clearly and unequivocally condemned such thinking: "What happened in His passion cannot be blamed upon all the Jews then living, without distinction, nor upon the Jews of today. Although the Church is the new people of God, the Jews should not be presented as repudiated or cursed by God, as if such views followed from the holy Scriptures.... Moreover, mindful of its common patrimony with the Jews, and motivated by the gospel's spiritual love and by no political considerations, [the Church] deplores the hatred, persecutions, and displays of anti-Semitism directed against the Jews at any time and from any source" (*Declaration on the Relationship of the Church to Non-Christian Religions*, n. 4).

Is there any sense, furthermore, in which the Jews can still be regarded, from the Christian perspective, as part of the People of God? Yes, insofar as they are "the people to whom the covenants and the promises were given and from whom Christ was born according to the flesh (cf. Romans 9:4–5). On account of their fathers, this people remains most dear to God, for God does not repent of the gifts [God] makes nor of the calls [God] issues (cf. Romans 11:28–29)" (*Dogmatic Constitution on the Church*, n. 16). And at the end of history the Jewish people will join with us and all others to address the Lord "in a pure voice and 'serve him with one accord' (Zephaniah 3:9; cf. Isaiah 66:23; Psalms 65:3; Romans 11:11–32)" (*Declaration on the Relationship of the Church to Non-Christian Religions*, n. 4).

OFFICIAL CATHOLIC TEACHING ON RELIGIOUS PLURALISM

Since the fact of religious pluralism and diversity has struck the consciousness of the Church only recently, especially since the Second World War, the official teachings of the Catholic Church before Vatican II are of a considerably different orientation from those of the council itself and thereafter. There are four historical stages in the development of this teaching.

In the first stage the Church's attitude toward other religions was primarily negative. It was taken for granted that they cannot lead to salvation. Positively, the Church was teaching that Jesus Christ is the only Mediator between God and humankind, in keeping with 1 Timothy 2:5: "For there is one God; there is also one mediator between God and humankind, Christ Jesus, himself human, who gave himself as a ransom for all."

The second stage occurred in the medieval period when the Church felt threatened by the continued presence of distinct Jewish communities in the West and by Moslem military aggressiveness. For the first time, the official Church issued pronouncements on the subject, and these were generally negative.

A third stage developed in the nineteenth century when the enemy was no religion in particular but Liberalism and its egalitarian philosophy that one religion is as good (or as bad) as another. Indifferentism is condemned.

A fourth stage has only recently emerged under the impact of the recognition of pluralism and diversity. The centerpiece of this stage is the Second Vatican Council's 1965 *Declaration on the Relationship of the Church to Non-Christian Religions* (*Nostra Aetate*).

The official doctrine of the Church may be summarized as follows: All religions are related somehow to the Christian economy of salvation; apart from this relationship they have no salvific power; yet their adherents can find salvation, even though their religions are not on an equal footing with Christianity. These other religions contain many authentic values, although they also are mixed with error, and hence need to be purified. But they do contain elements of the supreme truth and seeds of God's word, and divine grace works in them. They deal, therefore, with the one God and with ultimate questions about human existence. Accordingly, we must support true religious freedom, tolerance, and respect. Our relations with other religious bodies should be characterized by acceptance, collaboration, and dialogue. Christians can learn from the values of other religious traditions. And there should be charity in any case.

Examples of these teachings follow: The Second General Council of Nicea (787) insists that only those Jews who sincerely wish to convert to Christianity should be received into the Church. Otherwise, they should be allowed to "be Hebrews openly, according to their own religion" (canon 8).

Pope Gregory VII's letter to Anzir, Moslem King of Mauritania (1076), acknowledges that Christians and Moslems worship the same

God: "for we believe and confess one God, although in different ways, and praise and worship [God] daily as the creator of all ages and the ruler of this world."

The Council of Florence, *Decree for the Jacobites* (1442), refers for the first time in an official document to non-Christians as "pagans." Earlier that designation had been reserved to schismatics and heretics. On the other hand, the document does not deny the presence of grace beyond the borders of the Church. It also affirms that Christian freedom makes all human customs lawful if the faith is intact and edification attended to. The key negative teaching, however, is contained in this declaration: "[The Holy Roman Church]... firmly believes, professes and preaches that 'no one remaining outside the Catholic Church, not only pagans,' but Jews, heretics, or schismatics, can become partakers of eternal life; but they will go to the 'eternal fire prepared for the devil and his angels' (Matthew 25:41), unless before the end of their life they are received into it."

Religious indifferentism was explicitly condemned in the following: Leo XII's encyclical letter *Ubi Primum* (1824), Gregory XVI's encyclical letter *Mirari Vos Arbitramur* (1832), Pius IX's encyclical letter *Qui Pluribus* (1846), his allocution *Singulari Quadam* (1854), his encyclical letter *Quanto Conficiamur Moerore* (1863), and his *Syllabus of Errors* (1864). On the other hand, *Singulari Quadam* acknowledges that individuals outside the Church may simply be in ignorance of the truth through no fault of their own and so "are not subject to any guilt in this matter before the eyes of the Lord." Furthermore, his *Quanto Conficiamur* reminds us that we should bear no enmity against those outside the Church. "On the contrary, if they are poor or sick or afflicted by any other evils, let the children of the Church endeavor to succor and help them with all the services of Christian love."

Pope Leo XIII marks another shift in the Church's official teaching, a shift which anticipates the later doctrine of Vatican II on religious freedom. In his encyclical letter *Immortale Dei* (1885) he recognizes that a government may, for the sake of a greater good or of avoiding some evil, "tolerate in practice and by custom" various other forms of worship. Furthermore, "nobody [is to] be forced to join the Catholic faith against his [or her] will...."

In the First Plenary Council of India (1950), held in Bangalore, convoked by a papal legate, Cardinal Gilroy, and approved by Pope

387

Pius XII in 1951, indifferentism is once again rejected, but for the first time in an official document of the Catholic Church a clearly positive statement is made regarding the spiritual values of the world religions. "We acknowledge indeed that there is truth and goodness outside the Christian religion, for God has not left the nations without a witness to [God], and the human soul is naturally drawn toward the one true God.... But the inadequacy of all non-Christian religions is principally derived from this, that, Christ being constituted the one Mediator between God and [humankind], there is no salvation by any other name."

The teaching of the Second Vatican Council on the subject is contained in the *Dogmatic Constitution on the Church* (1964), the *Declaration on the Relationship of the Church to Non-Christian Religions* (1965), the *Decree on the Church's Missionary Activity* (1965), and the *Pastoral Constitution on the Church in the Modern World* (1965).

The council's teaching can be summarized as follows: The council stresses what unites us with other people rather than what divides us (*Declaration on the Relationship of the Church to Non-Christian Religions*, n. 1). It mentions other religions with respect: Hinduism, Buddhism, Islam, Judaism, and the primitive religions (*Decree on the Church's Missionary Activity*, n. 10; *Declaration on the Relationship of the Church to Non-Christian Religions*, nn. 2–4; *Dogmatic Constitution on the Church*, n. 16). They provide not only human answers to life's problems but also precious religious values (*Pastoral Constitution on the Church in the Modern World*, n. 12). They represent goodness intrinsic to the human heart which finds expression in rites and symbols, and are a true preparation for the Gospel (*Dogmatic Constitution on the Church*, n. 16; *Decree on the Church's Missionary Activity*, n. 9). They also contain treasures of ascetical and contemplative life (*Decree on the Church's Missionary Activity*, nn. 15,18). Thus, their faith is a response to the voice and self-communication of God (*Pastoral Constitution on the Church in the Modern World*, nn. 36,22).

Indeed, the Holy Spirit was at work in the world even before Christ (*Decree on the Church's Missionary Activity*, n. 4). Religious traditions outside the Church have their place in God's saving design (*Decree on the Church's Missionary Activity*, n. 3), with values that are intimately related to the divine mystery (*Dogmatic Constitution on the Church*, n. 16; *Declaration on the Relationship of the Church to Non-*

Christian Religions, n. 2). The Church, therefore, must adopt a wholly new attitude toward non-Christian religions (*Declaration on the Relationship of the Church to Non-Christian Religions*, nn. 1–5). We are to reject nothing of the truth and holiness we find in them (*Declaration on the Relationship of the Church to Non-Christian Religions*, n. 2) and should respect even those doctrinal elements which differ from our own because they may also contain a ray of truth (*Declaration on the Relationship of the Church to Non-Christian Religions*, n. 2; *Pastoral Constitution on the Church in the Modern World*, n. 57). We must learn to appreciate the riches of the gifts of God to all the peoples of the world (*Decree on the Church's Missionary Activity*, nn. 11,18).

While the right to freedom from coercion in civil society is inviolable, our moral duty toward the one Church of Christ remains untouched (*Declaration on Religious Freedom*, nn. 1–4). We must oppose every form of discrimination based on creed as well as on sex and race (*Declaration on the Relationship of the Church to Non-Christian Religions*, n. 5). We must be open to all forms of dialogue, imbued with the spirit of justice and love, and must engage in a common search for moral and spiritual enrichment (*Pastoral Constitution on the Church in the Modern World*, n. 92; *Decree on the Church's Missionary Activity*, nn. 11,12,16,18,34; *Declaration on the Relationship of the Church to Non-Christian Religions*, nn. 2,3,5). This will require discernment, but it is part of the Church's task and can be done without compromise of its faith in Christ (*Dogmatic Constitution on the Church*, nn. 16,17; *Decree on the Church's Missionary Activity*, n. 9; *Declaration on the Relationship of the Church to Non-Christian Religions*, nn. 2,5; *Pastoral Constitution on the Church in the Modern World*, n. 28).

Pope Paul VI's encyclical letter *Ecclesiam Suam* (1964) insists, on the one hand, that "there is one true religion, the Christian religion, and that we hope that all who seek God and adore Him, will come to acknowledge this.... Yet we do, nevertheless, acknowledge with respect the spiritual and moral values of various non-Christian religions, for we desire to join with them in promoting and defending common ideals in the spheres of religious liberty, human [solidarity], teaching and education, social welfare and civil order. On these great ideals that we share with them, we can have dialogue, and we shall not fail to offer opportunities for it whenever, in genuine mutual respect, our offer would be received with good will." The same spirit permeates Pope Paul's letter *Africarum Terrarum* (1967) to the hierarchy and the peoples of Africa.

Pope John Paul II's encyclical *Redemptoris Missio* (1991), although stressing the abiding urgency of missionary evangelization, also commends the path of interreligious dialogue as "a part of the Church's evangelizing mission" (n. 55). Without abandoning its own principles or lapsing into a false irenicism, the Church must enter into dialogue with other religions for the mutual enrichment of the respective religious communities. "Dialogue," he writes, "leads to inner purification and conversion, which, if pursued with docility to the Holy Spirit, will be spiritually fruitful" (n. 56).

SUMMARY

1. Religion is very difficult to define. In fact, there is no single definition agreed upon by all, even within the religious sciences themselves. It is not even clear from which word or words the term *religion* is derived.

2. We have *defined religion* here as the whole complexus of attitudes, convictions, emotions, gestures, rituals, beliefs, and institutions by which we come to terms with, and express, our most fundamental relationship with Reality (God and the created order, perceived as coming forth from God's creative hand).

3. That relationship is disclosed by a process we have called *revelation*. Religion, therefore, is our (more or less) structured response to revelation.

4. Although the early Christian writers stressed the truth of the Christian religion, they also acknowledged that the saving grace of the Christian faith has never been refused to anyone who was worthy of it (Augustine). It is possible for every person to know God by seeing evidences of God in the created world (Aquinas). Insofar as religion is our response to God's presence, religion is in principle available to every person. And insofar as God *is* present to every person, we are not only capable of reaching beyond ourselves to God; we are actually summoned to do so (Rahner, Vatican II).

5. But not every person of faith is religious. *Implicit faith* is sufficient for salvation but insufficient for religion. Religion is an individual, social, and institutional manifestation of some *explicit* faith in God.

6. Among the *characteristics* of religion are these: (1) a sense of the *holy* or the sacred (a totally other power or force which at once overwhelms and fascinates us); (2) some self-conscious response to the experience of the holy, i.e., *faith*; (3) the articulation of that response in the form of *beliefs*; (4) *moral behavior* and *ritual* consistent with the perception of the holy; and (5) the

emergence of a *community* of shared perceptions, meanings, and values, with at least some rudimentary *structure*.

7. In most religions there is an intrinsic tension between *charism* and *institution*.

8. Religion's *critics* are both inside and outside organized religion.

9. For Christianity God is at once transcendent (beyond the world of created reality) and immanent (within the world). Other religions seem to differ from Christianity to the extent that they stress transcendence more than immanence, or vice versa.

10. Among the non-Christian religions, the *ancient religions* have run the gamut from polytheism to monotheism. All have some sense of divinity, some practice of worship, some form of priesthood, and some sense of moral obligation flowing from their relationship to the divinity or divinities. Followers of some religions believed in life after death.

11. *Religions of the present* include: *Zoroastrianism, Hinduism, Buddhism, Taoism, Shintoism, Islam,* and *Judaism*.

12. There has always been a plurality of religions in the world, but the recognition of *pluralism* and *diversity* is a peculiar phenomenon of modern times. Why are there many religions rather than one alone? Because God is available to all peoples, widely *differentiated* as they are by time, by geography, by culture, by language, by temperament, by social and economic conditions, etc. Revelation is received according to the mode of the receiver, and the response to revelation (religion) is necessarily shaped by that mode of reception.

13. Among the responses to religious pluralism and diversity are these: *exclusivism, indifferentism,* the theory of *"anonymous Christianity,"* the view that other religions are *extraordinary means of salvation,* and a *dialogical* approach.

14. *Judaism* always has a special relationship with Christianity, for obvious historical and theological reasons. The Jews are still to be regarded as part of the People of God insofar as the Covenant and the promises were given them, Christ was born of them, God has not withdrawn the divine gifts from them, and they, like all Christians, are called to the final Kingdom.

15. The *official teaching* of the Catholic Church on the question of non-Christian religions has passed through various stages. In the beginning the attitude was basically negative, since Christ was perceived as the one Mediator between God and us; in the medieval period negative teachings were formulated under the impact of the threat of continued Jewish presence in the West and of Moslem military aggressiveness; in the nineteenth century the enemy was religious indifferentism, and emphasis was placed on the

uniqueness and superiority of Christianity; but with the recognition of pluralism and the changing consciousness of the Church represented by Vatican
II, the official teachings moved in a more positive direction.

16. Present official teaching acknowledges the religious and salvific value of
non-Christian religions (without prejudice to the unique place of Christianity
in the economy of salvation) and calls for religious liberty for all and dialogue
among all.

SUGGESTED READINGS

D'Costa, Gavin, ed. *Christian Uniqueness Reconsidered: The Myth of a Pluralistic Theology of Religions*. Maryknoll, N.Y.: Orbis Books, 1990.

DiNoia, J. A. *The Diversity of Religions: A Christian Perspective*. Washington D.C.: The Catholic University of America Press, 1992.

Dupuis, Jacques. *Jesus Christ at the Encounter of World Religions*. Maryknoll, N.Y.: Orbis Books, 1991.

Earhart, H. Byron. *Religious Traditions of the World*. San Francisco: HarperCollins, 1993.

Eliade, Mircea, et al., eds. *The Encyclopedia of Religion*. 16 vols. New York: Macmillan, 1987.

Griffiths, Paul J., ed. *Christianity Through Non-Christian Eyes*. Maryknoll, N.Y.: Orbis Books, 1990.

Haught, John F. *What Is Religion? An Introduction*. New York: Paulist Press, 1990.

Hick, John, and Paul F. Knitter, eds. *The Myth of Christian Uniqueness: Toward a Pluralistic Theology of Religions*. Maryknoll, N.Y.: Orbis Books, 1987.

Hillman, Eugene. *Many Paths*. Maryknoll, N.Y.: Orbis Books, 1989.

James, William. *The Varieties of Religious Experience*. New York: New American Library, Mentor, 1958.

John Paul II, Pope. *Redemptoris Missio. Origins*, vol. 20, no. 34 (January 31, 1991), pp. 541, 543–568.

Küng, Hans. *Christianity and the World Religions: Paths of Dialogue with Islam, Hinduism, and Buddhism*. Garden City, N.Y.: Doubleday, 1986.

Macquarrie, John. "Religion and Religions." *Principles of Christian Theology*. 2d rev. ed. New York: Scribners, 1977, pp. 149–73.

Mendes-Flohr, Paul. *Contemporary Jewish Religious Thought: Original Essays on Critical Concepts, Movements, and Beliefs*. New York: Scribners, 1987.

Otto, Rudolf. *The Idea of the Holy*. Baltimore: Penguin Books, 1959.

Paden, William. *Religious Worlds: The Comparative Study of Religions*. Boston: Beacon Press, 1988.

Rahner, Karl. "History of the World and Salvation-History" and "Christianity and the Non-Christian Religions." In *Theological Investigations*, vol. 5. Baltimore: Helicon, 1966, pp. 97–134.

Schlette, Heinz. *Towards a Theology of Religions.* New York: Herder and Herder, 1966.

Seltzer, Robert. *Jewish People, Jewish Thought: The Jewish Experience in History.* New York: Macmillan, 1980.

Smith, Huston. *The World's Religions.* San Francisco: HarperCollins, 1991.

Sullivan, Francis A. *Salvation Outside the Church? Tracing the History of the Catholic Response.* New York: Paulist Press, 1992.

PART THREE

Jesus Christ

WHAT is distinctively Christian about the Church's faith is its understanding of God as triune. But it is only because we first knew God in Jesus Christ that we came to know God as triune. Thus, it is equally true that the distinctively Christian element in Christian faith is the confession of the Lordship of Jesus. Christianity alone identifies Jesus of Nazareth with God. Jesus Christ is "true God of true God." He is of one substance with the Father.

A separate section on the mystery of Jesus Christ, therefore, requires little justification. Christian theology, not to say Catholic theology, is centered on him. Our understanding of, and response to, the triune God is a function of our understanding of, and response to, Jesus Christ.

Why then is there not also a separate section on the Holy Spirit, if the Christian God is a triune God? First, because the preoccupation of the New Testament is with God the Almighty and with Jesus Christ, who comes among us to manifest and to do the Father's will: to proclaim and practice and hasten the coming of the Kingdom of God. Second, because the Holy Spirit is never an object of that proclamation, whether of Jesus or of the Church. Rather, the Holy Spirit is the power through which that proclamation is uttered and fulfilled.

On the other hand, the Holy Spirit is at issue in every major theological discussion: the divinization of humankind by grace, the renewing and reconciling presence of God in history, the mystery of the Church, the celebration of the sacraments, the exercise of Christian witness.

"The Holy Spirit cannot become a formula, a dogma apart," the Greek Orthodox theologian Nikos Nissiotis writes. "Pneumatology is the heart of Christian theology, it touches all aspects of faith in Christ. It is a commentary on the acts of the revealed triune God, the life of the Church, and of the man who prays and is regenerated.... Orthodox pneumatology does not allow the doctrine of the Holy Spirit to become a separate chapter of dogmatic theology" (cited by Patrick Corcoran, *Irish Theological Quarterly*, vol. 39/3, July 1972, p. 277).

In this Part on Jesus Christ we examine first how he is understood, interpreted, and accepted today—whether as teacher, holy man, liberator, brother, etc.—and how he variously relates with contemporary culture (chapter 11).

The heart of the matter, of course, is the New Testament. We would know practically nothing about Jesus Christ (apart from the barest of biographical details) if it were not for the testimony of the Church preserved in the pages of the New Testament. And here we are confronted with the central problem of connecting the Jesus of history and the Christ of faith. Does the Church's testimony about Jesus conform with what Jesus thought, said, and did? What was the significance of his life and death? Did he redeem us? Did he rise from the dead (chapter 12)?

But the New Testament record was open to various interpretations, and the missionary needs of the early Church required it to communicate the Gospel across cultural lines. The supposedly straightforward, uncomplicated message of the Bible had to be reinterpreted, recast, reformulated. And it was: by the early writers of the Church, by the early ecumenical councils, and by the theologians of the Middle Ages. The story of that process is not easily reviewed, but the Church's present and future understanding of the meaning and mission of Jesus Christ is forever shaped by that story and by its dogmatic residue (chapter 13).

The discussion about the mystery of Jesus Christ has been, in a sense, reopened in the twentieth century for various reasons, including the shift from an uncritical to a critical reading of the New Testament and from a static to an evolutionary understanding of human existence. Consequently, there has been a fresh outpouring of Christological writings, the first such outpouring since the medieval period. Who are the principal contributors? How consistent are their contributions with the biblical and dogmatic traditions (chapter 14)?

Christology can be abstract unless it is always related to soteriology. In other words, we are ever concerned about the nature and person of Jesus Christ because we are ever concerned about his effectiveness in bringing about our salvation. If he is not truly God, then he could not *save* us. If he is not truly a human being, then he could not save *us*. If divinity and humanity are not united in a single person, then *he* could not save us. Certain practical questions help focus the central dogmatic issues: The questions of the virginal conception of Jesus and his sinlessness help focus the truth of his divinity, and the questions of his knowledge, or consciousness, and sexuality help focus the truth of his humanity (chapter 15).

Although the mystery of Jesus Christ is not the most fundamental doctrine of Christian faith (it is rooted, after all, in the mystery of the triune God), it is unquestionably at the heart of Christian faith. And so, too, is Part Three, in relation to the rest of the book.

XI

Christ and Contemporary Culture

THE JESUS OF HISTORY AND THE CHRIST OF FAITH

What is distinctively Christian about the Church's faith is its understanding of God as *triune* and of *Jesus Christ* as "true God from true God" (Nicene-Constantinopolitan Creed). Indeed, it is because we first knew God in the *Logos*, the Word that is Jesus Christ, that we came also to know God as triune.

Who is this Jesus whom we proclaim as "God from God" and Lord of history? How do we know him? On what basis do we connect the Jesus of our faith, our worship, our prayers, and our devotions with the Jesus who lived in Palestine some two thousand years ago? How do we know that we are really teaching and preaching as Jesus did? Does our present understanding of Christian faith accurately reflect the intentions and consciousness of the Lord himself? Is the Church truly faithful to the mission God has given it in Christ and in the Holy Spirit? Is the Church as Christ meant it to be?

Such questions as these arise because of the apparent gap that exists between the so-called "Jesus of history" and the "Christ of faith." The distinction between the names *Jesus* and *Christ* is an important one. "Christ" is not Jesus' last name. "Jesus" (literally,

"Yahweh is salvation") is the name given him at birth. Insofar as he lived at a particular time, in a particular place, with particular parents, was engaged in a particular occupation, associated himself with particular persons, established a particular reputation among his contemporaries, and died a particular death, in a particular place, at a particular time, under particular circumstances, this "Jesus" is a *historical fact*.

But insofar as some of his contemporaries reacted to him in a particular way and estimated his significance in a particular fashion, and insofar as subsequent generations have readily affirmed with Paul that "God... reconciled us to himself through Christ" (2 Corinthians 5:18), this man "born of a woman" (Galatians 4:4), this "carpenter's son" (Matthew 13:55) bears *a meaning which transcends the historical fact* of his existence, although never disconnected from it. This "Jesus of Nazareth" is the "Christ" (literally, the "anointed one") who has been promised and whom we now accept in faith.

Jesus, therefore, is a matter of historical record; *Christ* is a matter of meaning or of interpretation, an interpretation that we call "faith." To affirm the historicity of Jesus without affirming his Christhood is to take Jesus as a human being and no more, the greatness of his humanity notwithstanding. To affirm his Christhood, on the other hand, without identifying the historical Jesus with the Christ is to make of "Christ" a cosmic idea, an abstraction, a universal principle alone.

Neither affirmation is true to the Christian faith. Christians confess that Jesus *is* the Christ. He is indeed *Jesus Christ,* and he is "the same yesterday and today and forever" (Hebrews 13:8). But the Jesus Christ of the New Testament, of the creeds, of the dogmatic formulae, of the liturgy, and of the living faith of the whole Church is not always recognizable in the world about us, and sometimes not even in the Church itself.

Too often the Christ of our personal faith bears little resemblance to the Jesus of history or to the Christ of the Church's faith. We make of Jesus Christ what *we* would like him to be for us. Consequently, he no longer challenges us from the outside to conform to him, but rather we project on him all that we are or would like to be. The affirmation of the Lordship of Jesus becomes, then, a form of *self-affirmation*.

400

But it has always been so, as Jaroslav Pelikan has reminded us in his *Jesus Through the Centuries: His Place in the History of Culture* (1985). The "most conspicuous feature" of the history of images of Jesus through the centuries "is not sameness but kaleidoscopic variety." Thus, "it has been characteristic of each age of history to depict Jesus in accordance with its own character" (p. 2). Our age is no different in that respect.

JESUS CHRIST TODAY

There has been an extraordinary resurgence of interest in, even enthusiasm for, Jesus in recent years. One recalls that he made the cover of *Time* magazine twice in one year (June 21 and October 25, 1971), at the high point of the so-called Jesus movement. We have had the "Jesus People," even "Jews for Jesus." He was celebrated on Broadway and in film: *Jesus Christ Superstar* and *Godspell*. Bumper stickers advertised his name: "Honk if you love Jesus," "Jesus is the Answer," and "Jesus is Lord." The revival of Evangelical Christianity and the growth of the charismatic movement in the Catholic Church ran almost a parallel course to Jesus' sudden popularity in the "outside world."

But *which* Jesus was it who won the hearts of a new generation of young people and inspired the spiritual rebirth of young and middle-aged alike, including even a president of the United States (Jimmy Carter)? And which Jesus was it who continued to be taught, and honored, and appealed to in the official churches? Which Jesus was preached from the pulpits? Which Jesus was the centerpiece of the catechisms and college textbooks? Which Jesus was the norm of conscience? Which Jesus set the example for a truly human and truly Christian life?

One can detect at least five such Jesuses:

Jesus, Teacher: For many Christians, especially Catholics, Jesus Christ is perceived primarily as a teacher, as one sent by the Father to communicate certain truths that we must accept if we are to achieve the spiritual end for which God created us. Those who see Jesus primarily as a teacher tend to emphasize, sometimes to the point of exaggeration and distortion, the doctrinal side of Christianity, the teaching role of the bishops (*magisterium*), the virtues of docility and obedience, and the impropriety of dissent.

Even if this view of Jesus is partial and one-sided, there is much truth in it, for Jesus was indeed a teacher. This was a title, in fact, given him more frequently than any other. He was regarded as a teacher (Matthew 10:24; Luke 20:21; John 3:2). He gathered a group of disciples and acted as their rabbi, or teacher (Matthew 8:18–22; 21:1–11; 26:17–19; Mark 4:35–41; 11:1–11, e.g.). He was asked the type of questions a teacher would be asked (Matthew 22:36; Luke 10:25). His place for teaching was often the synagogue (Matthew 4:23; 9:35; 13:54; Mark 6:2; Luke 4:15,31; 6:6). He taught "with power" and as one having authority (Matthew 7:29; Mark 1:22; 11:18). His teaching was that of the one who sent him (John 7:16), and Jesus taught whatever he himself was taught by the Father (John 8:28).

Not surprisingly, the early Church continued the ministry of teaching in fidelity to its charge from the Lord. Teachers appeared among the lists of officers in the Church (1 Corinthians 12:28; Ephesians 4:11), and teaching was regarded as part of the office of Apostles (1 Timothy 2:7; 2 Timothy 3:10) and of the bishop (2 Timothy 4:2). With the death of the last of the Apostles, the Church was particularly concerned that the apostolic traditions be preserved and that whatever was taught should be "sound teaching" (1 Timothy 1:10; 2 Timothy 4:3; Titus 1:9, 2:1). The ultimate object of the Church's teaching, then as now, was the same as it was in Jesus' own teaching: the kingdom of God (Mark 1:15). But after the resurrection of Christ, the Church increasingly saw Christ as the personification of the kingdom, and so the Church's teaching centered more and more on Christ himself (Ephesians 4:21).

Jesus, Ruler, Judge, and King: Others have distorted the reality of Jesus by exaggerating his function as *ruler*, or shepherd, and as *judge*. How else explain why so many Christian leaders over the centuries adopted the lifestyles of the rich and powerful, governed their communities in severe, authoritarian ways, and gloried in the pomp and circumstance of ecclesiastical titles and ceremonies? And how else explain, even today, the readiness of many ordinary Catholics to identify "the Church" with its hierarchy, especially the pope, and to invest them with almost limitless authority and jurisdiction?

402

And yet Jesus was indeed a *ruler*, or shepherd, and a *judge*. But he is the shepherd who leaves the ninety-nine to search out for the one stray, and whose rejoicing over its recovery is beyond measure (Matthew 18:12–14; Luke 15:3–7). He is, in fact, the good shepherd (John 10:1–6,10–16) and the door of the sheepfold (10:7–9). He is concerned with the unity of the flock (an echo of Ezekiel 34:11–22).

The title of *shepherd* was applied to ministers of the church as well. Pastors (etymologically, "shepherds") are included on the lists of officers (Ephesians 4:11). The elders are addressed as shepherds of the flock (Acts of the Apostles 20:28; 1 Peter 5:2–4). Peter is given the distinctive ministry of shepherd (John 21:15–17).

Jesus is also accorded the title *king* in Matthew 2:2, where his royal character is the key to understanding the entire narrative, whose purpose is to present the true kingship of Jesus as free of external pomp. Jesus simply accepts the designation in his conversation with Pilate (Matthew 27:11; Mark 15:2; Luke 23:3). The longer version of the dialogue (John 18:33–39) makes even clearer the unworldly character of the kingship of Jesus. Indeed, the kingship of Jesus is mentioned only once in the postresurrection period (1 Corinthians 15:24–26) and the reference there is eschatological. Jesus will be king only after the conquest of all his enemies.

The title of *judge* is also sparingly applied to Jesus. On the last day Jesus will come "to judge the living and the dead" (2 Timothy 4:1). But Jesus' role as judge is at best paradoxical in John's Gospel. On the one hand, we are assured that God did not send the Son to judge the world but to save it (John 3:17), and Jesus himself says the same thing (John 12:47). Yet he also says that he has come into the world for judgment (John 9:39). Some biblical scholars explain the apparent discrepancy by noting that the *believer* is not judged, whereas the *unbeliever* is already judged by his or her very unbelief (3:18; 5:24). Jesus is the judge in the sense that he becomes the standard by which the world will, in a sense, judge itself.

Meanwhile, the disciples are warned that they themselves should not judge others (Matthew 7:1; Luke 6:37). Those who are merciless will be judged mercilessly (James 2:13).

Jesus, Holy Man of God: The Jesus of certain types of holy cards, songs, prayers, and devotional literature is often a Jesus almost totally removed from ordinary human life. Various iconic representa-

403

tions, for example, portray an otherworldly Jesus, his expressionless facial features distorted to emphasize that his true home and his true concerns are somewhere else. He is a Jesus without interest in challenging and changing unjust and oppressive social, political, economic, or religious institutions and structures. His mission is exclusively "spiritual," and so must ours be.

Jesus is, to be sure, a *holy man of God*. But holiness is not an otherworldliness which denies the radical goodness of the created order. Holiness is *wholeness* (see, for example, Josef Goldbrunner's book of that title, *Holiness Is Wholeness*, Notre Dame, Ind.: University of Notre Dame Press, 1964). The holy person is the one who is fully what God created that person to be, and who has been recreated in the Holy Spirit.

Holiness, in its deepest biblical meaning, is simply the life of God. God alone is holy: "There is no Holy One like the Lord, no one besides you; there is no Rock like our God" (1 Samuel 2:2). God's name (which is equivalent to God's "person") is holy (Leviticus 20:3; 22:2; Ezekiel 20:39; 36:20). Persons, places, even seasons become holy by being touched with the divine presence (see, e.g., Deuteronomy 26:15; Exodus 3:5; 28:41; Psalm 46:5; Leviticus 25:12; Isaiah 65:5; Haggai 2:12).

Where the holiness of God is mentioned in the New Testament, the Old Testament roots are clear, as in the Lord's Prayer ("hallowed be your name"—Matthew 6:9; Luke 11:2) and in 1 John 2:20, for example. Jesus, too, is called the holy one of God (Mark 1:24; Luke 1:35; 4:34; John 6:69; Acts of the Apostles 3:14; Revelation 3:7) and the holy servant of God (Acts of the Apostles 4:27, 30).

It is to the Church and its members that the term is more frequently applied. The Church is a temple holy to the Lord (Ephesians 2:21), made so by the indwelling of the Spirit (1 Corinthians 3:17). We are to lead "lives of holiness and godliness" (2 Peter 3:11). Just as the holiness of Jesus was the principle of his life of servanthood (Mark 10:45), so the holiness of the Church and of the Christian is for the sake of Christian discipleship. And that discipleship, as we shall point out in the next image, has a social and political dimension.

Jesus, Liberator: Jesus is the one who came into the world to preach the Gospel to the poor and to liberate the oppressed. He is indeed "the Liberator of the poor and the wretched of the land," and in that sense he may even be described as "black" (James Cone, *God of the Oppressed*, New York: Seabury Press, 1975, pp. 2, 133–37). Others have perceived him as "red," or "gay," or "feminist." Today, as in his own lifetime, Jesus is to be found in "bad company" (see Adolf Holl, *Jesus in Bad Company*, New York: Holt, Rinehart and Winston, 1973).

But this is not to say that Jesus' whole life and work were that of a political revolutionary. His message of the Kingdom of God was directed not only against the existing order but against the Zealots as well, the political revolutionaries of his own day. "My kingdom is not from this world" (John 18:36).

That Jesus identified with the poor and the oppressed of his own day is without question, however. He himself belonged to the lower class and made it clear that wealth is an obstacle to entrance into the Kingdom of God (Matthew 19:16–30; Mark 10:17–31; Luke 18:18–30). He appeals to Isaiah 61:1 in responding to the Pharisees regarding his mission, a mission which includes preaching the good news to the poor (Matthew 11:5, Luke 4:18). He praises Zacchæus for his generosity to the poor (Luke 19:1–10). And even if we cannot be certain that Jesus ascribed to himself the title "Suffering Servant of God" (with its roots in the Servant Songs of Deutero-Isaiah, chapters 40–55), it is clear that the early Church so interpreted his mission (Acts of the Apostles 3:13,26; 4:27,30).

The words of the baptism of Jesus (Matthew 3:17; Mark 1:11; Luke 3:22) are almost an exact quotation from Isaiah 42:1. The various descriptions of the passion are probably a development of the idea of the Servant as well (Matthew 26:28; Mark 14:24; Luke 22:20). Jesus took the form of a slave on our behalf (Philippians 2:5–11). He touches lepers (Mark 1:40–41), feeds the hungry (Mark 6:34–44), converses frequently with women (Mark 7:24–30; John 4:4–30), has women in his company (Luke 8:1–3), cures on the Sabbath (Luke 13:10–17), defends an adulteress (John 8:1–11), condemns the hypocrisy of religious officials (Matthew 23:1–36), blesses those who are poor, hungry, mournful, persecuted, who seek peace (Matthew 5:1–12), places love of neighbor on par with the love of God (Mark 12:28–31), and insists that our response to our neighbor in need will be God's standard of judgment on the last day (Matthew 25:31–46).

Jesus, Our Brother: Others are satisfied to describe Jesus as a human being who inspires us to treat one another as brothers and sisters. The great message of Christianity, as summed up by the Protestant historian Adolf Harnack (d. 1930), consists in "the fatherhood of God and the brotherhood of man." Jesus discloses to us what "brotherhood" is all about. This is, in part at least, the romanticized Jesus of *Jesus Christ Superstar* and *Godspell*. He is the symbol of joy and true life, a victimized figure who is nonetheless universally admired. "He's a man—he's just a man. He's not a king—he's just the same as anyone I know" (*Jesus Christ Superstar*).

Brotherhood (and sisterhood as well) is important to the New Testament conception of the Christian life. That is undeniable. Christians are called brothers about 160 times, and Jesus himself said that one who does the will of the Father is his (Jesus') own brother—and sister and mother (Matthew 12:50; Mark 3:35; Luke 8:31). But a Christology which goes no farther than to say that Jesus is our brother who calls us to a life of brotherhood and sisterhood fails to do justice to the Church's doctrinal tradition. Purely humanistic interpretations of Jesus recall a question the late Anglican Archbishop William Temple (d. 1944) put to their adherents: "Why any man should have troubled to crucify the Christ of Liberal Protestantism has always been a mystery" (*Readings in St. John's Gospel*, New York: Macmillan, 1942, p. xxix).

CHRIST AND CULTURE

Each of these "Jesuses," taken alone, represents a selective reading of the historical record, filtered through the prism of one's own experience and culture. *Culture* is understood here as "the totality of socially transmitted behavior patterns, arts, beliefs, institutions, and all other products of human work and thought characteristic of a community or population" (*The American Heritage Dictionary*, 2d college ed.). It includes both the "high culture" that poets, philosophers, and artists create, but also the popular culture of politics, of economic and social life, and of ordinary people.

Jesus himself is in *relationship* to culture. In a classic study, Protestant theologian H. Richard Niebuhr (d. 1962) identifies five such relationships: Christ *against* culture; Christ *of* culture; Christ *above* culture; Christ and culture *in paradox;* and Christ as *transformer* of culture (see *Christ and Culture* [1951]).

406

Christ Against Culture

A more contemporary version of this model would be Christ as *countercultural*. Although it cannot simply be conceded that this was the original attitude of the Christian community toward the world, it surely was an answer which appeared very early in the history of the Church. The First Letter of John counsels the faithful against loving the world, for the world is under the power of evil, full of lies, hatred, murder, and lust. It is a dying world, destined to pass away (1:6, 2:8–9,11,15,17; 3:8,11–15; 5:4–5,19). The same negative orientation is to be found in the writings of Tertullian (*Apology* and *On Idolatry*), and later was significantly present in the monastic movement of the Catholic Church and in the sectarian movement within Protestantism (the Mennonites and the Quakers, for example).

The witness of radical Christianity is a perennial gift to the whole Church. Jesus alone is Lord. We cannot compromise our faith with the kingdoms of this world. On the other hand, the Christ-against-culture position denies in action what it affirms in word. The radical Christian uses the very language, thought patterns, scientific understandings, sociological analyses, and so forth which are themselves expressions of culture. Even the writer of 1 John used the terms of the Gnostic philosophy to which he objected. Tertullian was a Roman to the core. And monasticism actually *contributed* to the advancement of culture. At the edges of the radical position, furthermore, is at least a touch of the Manichaean heresy, which rejects the goodness of matter. But nature has been elevated by grace. God is present to the creation. Indeed, God became incarnate.

The Christ of Culture

The opposite extreme is completely at home with culture. There is no tension at all between Christ and the world. Jesus came not to challenge the world or to pronounce a judgment upon it but to bless and embrace it. In the earliest period this seemed to have been the position adopted by the *Judaizers*, i.e., those who sought to maintain loyalty to Christ without abandoning any important element of their Jewish traditions, and by the *Gnostics*. In more recent times, the Christ-of-culture approach is identified most closely with what Niebuhr calls the "culture-Protestantism" of the nineteenth and early twentieth centuries, of Friedrich Schleiermacher, Albrecht Ritschl (d. 1889), Harnack, and Walter Rauschenbusch (d. 1918), father of the Social Gospel movement in American Protestantism. The Kingdom of God for them was, for the most part, the realization of human "brotherhood" in this world. We are all God's children. The Lord calls us to accept and love one another as brothers and sisters.

There is something to be said about the Christ-of-culture view, just as there is something to respect in the Christ-against-culture stance. Earlier generations of non-Christians were not only impressed with the constancy and uncompromising behavior of the young Church; they were also attracted by the harmony of the Christian message with the moral and religious philosophy of their best teachers and by the agreement of Christian conduct with that of their most popular heroes. Furthermore, the word of God *is* expressed in culturally diverse ways. The coherence of Christ with culture is rooted in the incarnational principle itself. Jesus is relevant to every time, place, and people.

But the Christ-of-culture perspective is also too selective in its reading of the New Testament. Jesus does, in fact, stand over against the world, as the Christ-against-culture position convincingly argues. Sin is in the world—everywhere. Education alone will not produce justice or goodness or peace. The oppressed, once liberated from their oppression, too often become, in turn, the oppressors of others. Jesus' kingdom is not of this world (John 18:36).

Christ Above Culture

This approach and the next two share the conviction that nature, on which all culture is founded, is good and rightly ordered by the Creator—indeed, that it has been re-created by Christ and the Holy Spirit. These three positions also recognize the universality and radical character of sin. Culture is possible because of grace, i.e., God's presence; and grace is expressed sacramentally, in cultural forms. Nonetheless, there are three variations within this centrist point of view: *synthesists, dualists,* and *conversionists.*

The *synthesist* ("Christ above culture") confesses a Lord who is both of this world and of the other. Jesus is both God and a human being, one person with two natures, divine and human. As a human being, Jesus is very much *of* culture. As God, he is very much *above* culture. As a human being *and* God, he is at once *of* culture and *above* it.

This motif runs through the New Testament. Indeed, New Testament faith is a radically incarnational one. Christ insists, for example, that he has not come to abolish the Law and the Prophets, but to fulfill them (Matthew 5:17–19), that we should render to Caesar the things that are Caesar's and to God the things that are God's (Matthew 22:21). Justin Martyr and Clement of Alexandria were among the principal patristic synthesizers, but Thomas Aquinas and the Catholic theological tradition generally have been particularly strong representatives of this approach.

The position is attractive because it is consistent with our abiding human quest for achieving balance and for unity, a unity grounded in the unity of the triune God. We shy away from single-minded, extreme positions. But some have worried that the synthesist view leads to a cultural conservatism. God is perceived by the synthesists to have been embodied very well in a particular culture; therefore, that culture (identified with "Christian civilization") should be preserved at all costs. But no culture is perfect. Does a synthesist approach take sufficient account of the radical evil which is everywhere present, or of the multiplicity of cultural ways in which Christian faith can be expressed?

Christ and Culture in Paradox

The *dualist* view is identified especially with Paul and Luther. We dwell now in an "earthly tent," Paul reminds us. But when it is destroyed, as inevitably it will be, we shall have "a building from God, a house not made with hands, eternal in the heavens. For in this tent we groan, longing to be clothed with our heavenly dwelling" (2 Corinthians 5:1–2).

For Luther there are two kingdoms, the one of God and the other of the world. God's kingdom is a kingdom of grace and mercy, but the kingdom of the world is a kingdom of wrath and severity. We cannot confuse the two, thereby putting wrath into God's kingdom or mercy into the world's, as the fanatics do. And yet the two kingdoms are closely related, and the Christian must affirm both in a single act of obedience to the one God of mercy and wrath, not as a divided soul with a double allegiance and duty. Living between time and eternity, between wrath and mercy, we find life at once tragic and joyful. There is no solution to this until the Kingdom of God comes in all its perfection at the end (see his *Treatise on Good Works*, for example, in *Three Treatises*, Philadelphia: Fortress Press, 1970). A twentieth-century variation on the Lutheran position has been expressed by Reinhold Niebuhr, especially in his *Moral Man and Immoral Society* (New York: Scribners, 1932).

The strengths of the dualist position are reasonably clear. Sin exists not only in the individual but in communities, in institutions, in laws. On the other hand, such dualism has also led Christians to a certain disdain for law and even toward the same kind of cultural conservatism we detected in the preceding view. The dualists seem to rest content with the quality of political and economic life. For the dualist, laws, institutions, the state are only restraining forces, without positive purpose and impact. All of our work in the temporal order, therefore, is transitory. However important cultural duties might be for us, the Christian's heart is simply not in them.

Christ the Transformer of Culture

This model emphasizes the participation of the Word in creation itself and of the Creator in the incarnation of the Son and in the redemption wrought through the Son's work. God brings order out of chaos in the act of creation, and Christ brings new order out of the chaos of sin in the act of redemption. History, therefore, is the dramatic interaction between God and humankind. It is the story of God's mighty deeds and of our response to them. We live "between the times." The future is already being realized in the present. The Kingdom of God is even now.

This *conversionist* motif is most clearly indicated in the Fourth Gospel, especially in its Prologue (1:1–18). "For God so loved the world that he gave his only Son, so that everyone who believes in him may not perish but may have eternal life. Indeed, God did not send the Son into the world to condemn the world, but in order that the world might be saved through him" (3:16–17). John's sacramental

410

vision, particularly his emphasis on the Eucharist and Baptism, stresses the conversion of ordinary elements and symbols into signs and instruments of God's redeeming and sanctifying presence. Christ is the one who transforms human actions. Indeed, when Christ is lifted up, he will draw all to himself (1:29; 3:14–17; 12:32,47).

The same conversionist motif can be found in Augustine's classic work, *The City of God*, and in his *Confessions*. Christ transforms culture in that he redirects, reinvigorates, and regenerates human life as expressed in human works which are at once perverted and corrupted by sin although of a radically good and holy nature. Whatever exists is good. Jesus Christ has come to heal and to renew what sin has tarnished.

Calvin, unlike Luther and more like Augustine, also saw a positive role for social and political institutions. God's sovereignty must be made manifest in the whole network of human relationships, even in the public domain.

Christ and Culture: A Synthesis

In the end, of course, there is no fundamental opposition between Christ and culture. The work of culture is the work of grace, and the power of grace is expressed in culture (as the *synthesists* hold). And yet we live as if in two worlds simultaneously: in *this* world, but not completely *of* it (as the *dualists* remind us). But if the world we live in is destined for the Kingdom of God, we are called to collaborate with God in its ongoing re-creation and renewal (as the *conversionist* position states). Meanwhile, the witness of the radicals helps to sharpen our sense that the Kingdom is not *of* this world, and the witness of the harmonizers or cultural Christians encourages us to commend the eternal message of Christ to those who might otherwise ignore it.

Who is the Christ of contemporary culture, then? He is all of these Christs, yet no one of them alone. But if he is to be the Christ of *history* and of Christian *faith* as well as the *contemporary* Christ, each of our modern versions of Jesus must be measured against the standards of the biblical texts and the Church's subsequent interpretations of those texts.

"One of the strange features of Christianity," Jesuit biblical scholar George MacRae (d. 1985), former Stillman Professor of Roman

Catholic Studies at Harvard Divinity School, once observed, "is that its adherents are so often dissatisfied with the Jesus whom tradition has bequeathed to them. New theories about Jesus, new discoveries that present him in a different light, whatever their historical plausibility, never lack an eager reception among the curious. And it was always so—that is what we sometimes fail to recognize" (*Commonweal*, vol. 99, January 25, 1974, p. 417).

MacRae noted that Paul himself was frequently preoccupied with rejecting divergent images of Jesus and cites, by way of example, a passage in 2 Corinthians (11:3–4):

> But I am afraid that as the serpent deceived Eve by its cunning, your thoughts will be led astray from a sincere and pure devotion to Christ. For if someone comes and proclaims another Jesus than the one we proclaimed, or if you receive a different spirit from the one you received, or a different gospel from the one you accepted, you submit to it readily enough.

We move in chapter 12 to a fuller discussion of those New Testament texts and of the Church's faith that is embodied and expressed therein.

SUMMARY

1. Christianity alone proclaims that God is triune and that Jesus of Nazareth is "true God from true God." But is the Christ of *faith* the same as the Jesus of *history*? Is the Christ of *our* faith the Christ of the Church's faith as well?

2. Popular views of Jesus Christ, both within and without the Church, range from one end of the theological spectrum to the other. Some see Jesus principally as a *teacher*; others perceive him as *ruler, judge,* and *king*; others know Jesus as the *holy man of God*; still others view Jesus as a *liberator* or revolutionary; finally, some see Jesus as their *brother*.

3. There are five models which describe the relationship between Christ and culture. (1) Christ *against* culture; (2) the Christ *of* culture; (3) the Christ who is *above* culture; (4) Christ and culture *in paradox*; and (5) Christ the *transformer* of culture.

4. The work of culture is the work of grace, and the power of grace is expressed in culture (as the *synthesists* hold). And yet we live in this world of culture while not being completely of it (as the *dualists* declare). But this world is itself destined for the Kingdom of God, and we are called to facilitate

its movement toward the Kingdom (as the *conversionists* insist). All the while, the radicals ("Christ against culture") remind us that the Kingdom ultimately is not of this world, and the harmonizers or cultural Christians ("Christ of culture") encourage us to commend the eternal message of Christ to those who might otherwise ignore it.

5. The Christ of contemporary culture is all of these Christs, yet no one of them alone. The standard against which any of these Christs is to be measured is the Christian tradition itself.

SUGGESTED READINGS

Bammel, Ernst, and C. F. D. Moule, eds. *Jesus and the Politics of His Day.* Cambridge: Cambridge University Press, 1984.

Boff, Leonardo. *Jesus Christ Liberator: A Critical Christology for Our Time.* Maryknoll, N.Y.: Orbis Books, 1978.

Cullmann, Oscar. *Jesus and the Revolutionaries.* New York: Harper & Row, 1970.

Frei, Hans. *The Identity of Jesus Christ: The Hermeneutical Basis of Dogmatic Theology.* Philadelphia: Fortress Press, 1975.

Macquarrie, John. *Jesus Christ in Modern Thought.* London: SCM Press, 1990.

Niebuhr, H. Richard. *Christ and Culture.* New York: Harper & Row, 1951.

Pelikan, Jaroslav. *Jesus Through the Centuries: His Place in the History of Culture.* New Haven: Yale University Press, 1985; New York: Harper & Row, 1987 (paper ed.).

Sobrino, Jon. *Jesus in Latin America.* Maryknoll, N.Y.: Orbis Books, 1987.

XII

The Christ of the New Testament

THE JESUS OF HISTORY AND THE CHRIST OF FAITH

Jesus of Nazareth really lived. No one seriously questions that fact today. He was born at a particular time, in a particular place, of a particular family, and he passed through various stages of human development just like anyone else. He engaged in particular public activities. His words and actions had a particular impact, on particular people, under particular circumstances. And he died at a particular time, in a particular manner, at a particular place, in the presence of particular people.

But there is more to this Jesus than that. Indeed, he is called Jesus *Christ* and not simply Jesus *of Nazareth* because a special significance has been attached to the otherwise bare historical facts of his existence some two thousand years ago. This special significance was attached to the life and death of Jesus of Nazareth even during the first century of Christianity, immediately after his death by crucifixion at the hands of the local Roman government and at the instigation of the local religious establishment.

Thus, it was very early asserted that this Jesus of Nazareth, who "was crucified under Pontius Pilate, suffered, and was buried," did not remain in the state of death but rose from the dead "on the third day." Furthermore, that he is now "seated at the right hand of the Father," and that "he shall come again in glory to judge the living and the dead" and that his Kingdom shall have "no end." This is so because Jesus is Lord; he is "true God from true God,... one in being with the Father."

The question arises: Was the Christ whom the Church confessed in faith, both within the New Testament and beyond it, the same Jesus of Nazareth whose sheer historical facticity no one seriously challenges? In other words, *Did the primitive and postbiblical Church create a Christ who is divine from a Jesus who was purely human?* And what of Jesus himself? How did he estimate his own significance? Were the words and claims which the New Testament places on the lips of the carpenter's son really the words and claims of Jesus, or were they the words and claims of the Church read back into the life and ministry of Jesus? In other words, *What connection, if any, can we establish between the Church's evaluation of Jesus and Jesus' own evaluation of himself?*

It is, once again, the problem of the Jesus of history and the Christ of faith.

THE SOURCES AND THEIR INTERPRETATION

Non-Christian Sources

The few non-Christian sources for the life of Jesus provide us with very little information. They do confirm the argument, however, that from the earliest days it never occurred even to the bitterest enemies of Christianity that the historical existence of Jesus should be challenged. Tacitus (d. c. 116) reported that Jesus was condemned to death by Pontius Pilate under Tiberius (*Annals* 15,4). Suetonius (d. c. 120) wrote of a certain "Chrestus" who caused disturbances in Rome (*Claudius* 25,4). Pliny the Younger (d. c. 110) acknowledged in a letter to Trajan that Christ was revered as a God (*Epistola* 10,96). Josephus the historian (d. c. 93) referred to James as the brother of Jesus who is called the Christ (*Antiquities,* 20,200). The Talmud references and the apocryphal gospels (e.g., the Gospel of Thomas) likewise add nothing to our knowledge of Jesus. Again, at best this non-Christian material provides independent evidence for the actual existence of Jesus.

New Testament

The most important source for the life of Jesus, therefore, remains the New Testament itself, and the four Gospels in particular. But when one dips into the Gospels, one finds that they do not present history as we generally understand that word today. In other words, they would not stand up alongside a lengthy obituary essay in the *New York Times* as a work of objective reporting and interpretation. They provide us instead with a testimony of faith. *Their purpose is not to reconstruct the life of Jesus in every chronologically accurate detail, but to illustrate the eternal significance of Jesus through selected examples of his preaching, his activities, and the impact of both upon his contemporaries.*

The Gospels were written by men of faith for women and men of faith. They are the product of subsequent reflection on the life of Jesus—a process that required anywhere from thirty-five to sixty years. They are complex documents because of their peculiar purpose, because of the diversity of their origin and the audiences to which they were initially addressed, and because of the various stages of development they passed through before reaching the form in which we have them.

Stages of Development

There are at least *three stages of development* culminating in the actual writing of the Gospels: (1) the original words and deeds of Jesus; (2) the oral proclamation of the Apostles and disciples (catechesis, narratives, testimonies, hymns, doxologies, and prayers); and (3) the writings themselves. These are specified as such by the Instruction of the Pontifical Biblical Commission, *The Historical Truth of the Gospels*, 1964. (An excerpt is given in the appendix. The full text and a commentary by Joseph Fitzmyer appear in *Theological Studies*, vol. 25, 1964, pp. 386–408.)

Depending upon one's point of view, one might expand the number of stages to five, for example: (1) the period of direct contact and communication between Jesus and the disciples and others; (2) the emergence of an oral tradition following the resurrection, a period in which there were no significant writings because the expectation of the Second Coming or return of Christ was intense and vivid; (3) the hardening of the oral tradition into the shape of accepted doctrine communicated through letters (Epistles), which were written for specific occasions and audiences and not for posterity; (4) the writing of the Gospels as soon as it became clear that the Lord was not about to return very soon, a period in which the first generation of Christians was dying out and a new generation, with no direct contact with, or memories of, Jesus was coming on the scene; (5) the completion of the New Testament canon (official collection of books accepted by the Church as inspired) with the composition of the pastoral Epistles (Timothy and Titus) and 2 Peter, a period in which the Church is newly conscious of itself as a society, still threatened from without and from within.

Layers of Tradition

How many stages of development there were is a matter of choice, but *the fact of development is beyond question today*. Indeed, we cannot easily overestimate the significance of the Pontifical Biblical Commission's Instruction of 1964 on the historicity of the Gospels. The Commission calmly and openly admits that we do not have in the written Gospels the words and deeds of Jesus as exactly and as completely as they were first uttered or performed, nor do we even have the full and exact record of what was communicated orally between the death and resurrection, on the one hand, and the actual composition of the Gospels, on the other. What we have, rather, is *the finally edited version* given by the evangelists.

The *first layer* of tradition is made accessible through *historical criticism*. Historical criticism is a relatively late development in the history of Christian theology and of biblical interpretation. Until the Enlightenment of the eighteenth century it was generally assumed that the Gospels gave a clear and reliable account of the life of Jesus, that there was no discrepancy at all between the faith of the primitive Church and the facts upon which that faith was built.

Herman Reimarus (d. 1768), a German professor of oriental languages, was the first to challenge this assumption with the rallying cry "Back from the Christ of dogma to the real Jesus." The immediate reaction to Reimarus's thesis was strongly negative. Many different versions of the "life of Jesus" appeared, as if in rebuttal of Reimarus. But the differences among the several "lives" of Jesus were glaringly obvious. As we pointed out in chapter 11, many authors portrayed Jesus as they would like him to have been rather than Jesus as the early Church knew him to be. The biographical confusion generated an attitude of fundamental skepticism about the whole project.

Albert Schweitzer (d. 1965) slammed the door once and for all on Liberal efforts at reconstructing the life of Jesus with his own *The Quest of the Historical Jesus*, published right at the turn of the century. The historical Jesus, it now seemed, could not be recovered scientifically from the New Testament documents. But this, too, proved to be an overreaction, and since Schweitzer's time there has, in fact, been a steady return of confidence in the scholar's and the Church's capacity to get behind the testimonies of faith and identity at least the basic historical foundation of Jesus' life and ministry. (See, for example, Edward Schillebeeckx's *Jesus: An Experiment in Christology* [1979] and John Meier's *A Marginal Jew: Rethinking the Historical Jesus* [1991].)

The *second layer* of tradition is discovered through a method known as *form criticism*. This method was developed in Germany between the two world wars and was concerned primarily with the formation of the Gospel tradition which occurred through catechesis and liturgical expressions, roughly between A.D. 35 and 60. It is essentially a means of analyzing typical features of biblical texts (hymns, acclamations, confessions, sermons, instructional material, editorial remarks, descriptive narratives, sayings of Jesus, dialogues, Old Testament allusions and quotations, etc.) in order to relate them to their original "situation-in-life." It was the development of form criticism which brought out the fact that a long period of *oral* tradition preceded any writing of the New Testament.

The *third layer* of tradition is examined through the method of *redaction criticism*, whose origin is in the mid–1950s. Redaction criticism tries to discover the dominant ideas which governed the final editing of the Gospels as we have them today (e.g., What was the "peculiar purpose" of each evangelist mentioned by the Biblical

Commission's 1964 Instruction?). Just as form criticism discloses the existence of an *oral* tradition prior to the formulation of the New Testament, so redaction criticism stresses the antecedent existence of both oral and written traditions from which the New Testament authors worked, and which they creatively transformed to suit their particular theological and catechetical intentions.

Different Cultures

Furthermore, there are different cultures at work in the production of the New Testament, and these, in turn, generate distinctive theological viewpoints regarding the meaning of Jesus. These are the cultures of the Palestinian communities of Aramaic/Hebrew-speaking Jewish Christians, of the Syrian communities of Greek-speaking Jewish Christians, of the communities of Asia Minor and Greece with their Greek-speaking Gentile Christians, and finally of the particular communities influenced by major individual Christians like Paul and John. One might also classify these cultures more broadly as Palestinian, Jewish-Hellenistic, and Hellenistic-Gentile.

Only in the past century has biblical scholarship acquired the linguistic and historical data necessary for even recognizing such theological and cultural diversity within New Testament Christianity. Previous scholarship, for example, had known Aramaic, the language which Jesus apparently spoke. But the only forms of Aramaic which it had at its disposal came from several centuries before Jesus (Imperial Aramaic) or from several centuries after Jesus (Syriac and Talmudic Aramaic). "To reconstruct the language of Jesus from such evidence," Catholic biblical scholar Raymond Brown writes, "was not unlike trying to reconstruct Shakespearian English from Chaucer and the *New York Times*" (*Horizons*, vol. 1, 1974, p. 43). The situation improved over the past one hundred years through such discoveries as the Dead Sea Scrolls in 1947. (For a thorough summary of their contents and significance, see John J. Collins, "Dead Sea Scrolls," *The Anchor Bible Dictionary*, vol. 2, New York: Doubleday, 1992, pp. 85–101. See also Joseph Fitzmyer's *Responses to 101 Questions on the Dead Sea Scrolls*, New York: Paulist Press, 1992.)

Sayings of Jesus

In spite of the plurality of stages, layers, forms, and so forth, biblical scholars have reached a consensus regarding criteria for establishing authentic sayings of the historical Jesus: (1) Sayings which contain Aramaicisms characteristic of the Palestine of Jesus' day are more likely to have their origin in Jesus. (2) The shorter or shortest of two or three different accounts of the same incident is probably the one closer or closest to the source, since authors tend to expand and explain. (3) Sayings or principles attributed to Jesus which are contrary to the developing traditions of the early Church, and which would even have been a source of embarrassment for it, are usually more authentic than those which clearly give support to current attitudes. (4) The same is true of elements in the message of Jesus which make a break with the accepted traditions and customs of Judaism (although this criterion must be used with caution since we are ill-informed about popular Jewish-Aramaic religious practices and vocabulary in early first-century Galilee). (5) Words and deeds which are attested to by many different sources probably have a strong historical basis. (6) Negatively, sayings which reflect the faith, practices, and situation of the postresurrection Church cannot be taken always at face value. All of these criteria must be taken together and used in a mutually self-correcting way.

Interpretations of the Sources

Until the eighteenth century, there was no New Testament problem. Christians of every major denomination assumed that the Christ of the New Testament and the Jesus of history were exactly one and the same. But once the assumption was challenged, Christians began dividing over the question of the relationship between the Christ of faith and the Jesus of history, i.e., between the Church's interpretation of Jesus and Jesus' own self-understanding.

Those positions move all the way from the conservative right, which posits a real relationship between Jesus' self-evaluation and the New Testament Church's Christology, to the liberal left, which denies any real relationship or continuity between the two. Those positions are also distinguished by their scholarly or nonscholarly

421

bases of support. *Scholarly* conservatism and *scholarly* liberalism are expressed by reputable scholars who have produced a body of articles that meet the publishing standards of the professional biblical journals or whose books have been reviewed favorably in such journals. It is not enough, therefore, that a point of view be expressed and defended by someone holding a biblical degree or a teaching position in biblical studies. *Nonscholarly* conservatism and *nonscholarly* liberalism are the product of those who either hold no biblical degrees and/or no teaching positions in biblical studies or who have not published a body of articles in serious professional journals or books which have been reviewed favorably in such journals. The distinction is important for making sense of such comments as "Scripture scholars are divided over this question."

What follows is a summary, with some modifications, of Catholic biblical scholar Raymond Brown's schematization of twentieth-century views on the Christology of the New Testament.

Nonscholarly Conservatism

This view *identifies* the Christology of the New Testament with Jesus' own self-evaluation. Even though the Gospels were written some thirty to sixty years after the ministry of Jesus, this conservative position maintains that there had been *no significant Christological development* in that time. Thus, when Jesus accepted Peter's confession that Jesus was indeed the Messiah, the Son of the living God (Matthew 16:13–20), that acceptance reflects the self-understanding of Jesus—despite the fact that Peter's confession and Jesus' reaction are very different in the *earlier* Gospel of Mark (8:27–30). And if in the Gospel of John, Jesus speaks as a preexistent divine figure (8:58; 17:5), he must have actually spoken that way during his lifetime—despite the fact that there is no indication of this in the three synoptic Gospels.

This view was first held defensively (i.e., over against the views of the scholars of the major Protestant denominations) by Protestant fundamentalists and other less-than-fundamentalist Christians, particularly in various mainline Reformation churches of the U.S. South. Catholics generally also held this position, but not defensively. After the condemnations of Modernism there was strict supervision over

Catholic biblical studies from 1910 until Pope Pius XII's encyclical *Divino Afflante Spiritu* in 1943. Before 1943, the nonscholarly conservative position was the only view taught, accepted, and preached in the Catholic Church; it was simply taken for granted. Once the principles of modern biblical criticism were approved by Rome and assimilated by Catholic scholars, however, some Catholics did become exceedingly defensive about the traditional approach.

In light of the fact that the Gospels do not provide a literal account of what Jesus said and did, and in light of the evidence for development in the production of the New Testament, the nonscholarly conservatives should have asked, "How much development?" Instead they asked, "How do we know that any of it is true?" And rather than risk the loss of faith itself, they simply rejected the whole network of scholarly premises, even those formally and explicitly endorsed by the pope in the encyclical of 1943 and by the Pontifical Biblical Commission's Instruction of 1964.

Nonscholarly Liberalism

As on a political spectrum (Stalin at the extreme left, Hitler at the extreme right), the extremes of biblical interpretation touch. If the nonscholarly conservative asked the wrong question ("How do I know any of it is true?"), so too did the nonscholarly liberal. The only difference is in the answers given. The conservative rejects the scholarship in order to "save" the Christ of faith. The nonscholarly liberal rejects the Christ of faith in order to "save" her or his favorite notion of the Jesus of history.

The nonscholarly liberal concludes that there is no continuity at all between the Christology of the New Testament and Jesus' self-evaluation. He was nothing more than an ordinary man, except that he was more brilliant, more charismatic, more of a revolutionary, or take your pick. It is not finally important that Jesus was or was not the Son of God. It is what he taught us about life that counts, and what he taught us is that we have to love one another.

Although nonscholarly liberalism began as a Protestant phenomenon, enjoying wide popularity during the early decades of the twentieth century before it was effectively challenged by scholars and by declining membership rolls, it made a belated entrance into

Catholicism as a reaction to the exaggerated dogmatism of the pre–Vatican II period.

Scholarly Liberalism

Scholarly liberalism, unlike its nonscholarly counterpart, does not dismiss the Christology of the New Testament as unimportant, nor does it deny that the New Testament writers claimed far more than that Christianity was a "way of life." On the other hand, scholarly liberalism shares with its nonscholarly cousin the conviction that the Christology of the New Testament is a mistaken evaluation of Jesus which does not stand in real continuity with the self-evaluation of Jesus. For the liberals, New Testament Christology is a *creation* of the early Church.

Unquestionably, modern biblical studies owe a great debt of gratitude to the previous work of the liberal scholars. They were the ones, after all, who first challenged the nonscholarly conservatism which dominated all Christian churches until the eighteenth century. It was the liberals who discerned developmental patterns in the New Testament and who laid the groundwork for many of our present principles of biblical interpretation. Perhaps the best example of this scholarly liberalism in terms of both method and content was Wilhelm Bousset (d. 1920), whose book *Kyrios Christos* was first published in German in 1913 and in English translation in 1970 (Nashville: Abingdon).

For the scholarly liberals the historical Jesus was a preacher of stark ethical demand who challenged the religious institutions and who cut through the false ideas of his time. If the early Church had not turned him into the heavenly Son of Man, the Lord and Judge of the world, or indeed the Son of God, his ideals and insights might otherwise have been lost. But now that the crutch of New Testament Christology is no longer necessary (Christ's place in history and in our collective memories is secure), it can be discarded.

Bultmannian Existentialism

World War I undercut the optimism of liberal theology, and of liberal biblical scholarship as well. The war created a need for a God who saves us in Jesus, rather than for a Jesus who taught us how to live and, in effect, to save ourselves. In theology the antiliberal movement was headed by Karl Barth. In the area of biblical studies it was led by Rudolf Bultmann.

Some mistakenly place Bultmann in the liberal camp because so many of his views were regarded as radical when he first proposed them. Yet his New Testament theology is a rejection of pre–World War I liberalism. Without discarding the legitimate methodological achievements of liberalism, Bultmann nevertheless denied the liberal thesis that New Testament Christology was a creation of the early Church. (See *Jesus Christ and Mythology*, New York: Scribners, 1958.)

That is not to say that Bultmann's own view is clear and unequivocal. Brown regards it "difficult to characterize exactly" and suggests that "in some of his writing at least he is agnostic about the self-evaluation of Jesus" (*Horizons* article, p. 45). But Bultmann definitely did not think that the Christology of the New Testament distorted the import of Jesus, as the liberals maintained. Rather, there is a *functional equivalence* between the Church's Christological proclamation and Jesus' own proclamation of the Kingdom.

It is in this functional equivalence that Bultmann's existentialist philosophy can be found at work (see chapter 4, where Bultmann's existentialist philosophy is mentioned in the context of various theologies of human existence). If we are to escape from the vicious circle of futile existence, it will only be through the saving action of God in Jesus. We are called upon to accept this action of God. Where Jesus preached the Kingdom, the Church preached Jesus. Functionally, this preaching was equivalent. Dispensing, therefore, with the Church's proclamation would be to dispense with the challenge that is at the core of Christianity, a challenge that is primarily based on what God has done for us, rather than what we can do for ourselves.

Moderate Conservatism

Just as Bultmann's position was somewhat to the right of the scholarly liberals, so most contemporary biblical scholarship is somewhat to the right of Bultmann. This does not ignore the fact that Catholic scholarship has moved decidedly to the left since the 1940s, but it has moved "to the left" in relation to the nonscholarly conservatism which controlled Catholic theology and biblical studies beforehand.

This moderate conservatism posits a discernible *continuity* between the self-evaluation of Jesus and the Christology of the early Church. Nonetheless, there is some difference of opinion within the moderate conservative group. On one side, there are those for whom the Church's Christology is *explicit* in Jesus' self-evaluation, and, on the other, those for whom the Church's Christology is only *implicit* in Jesus' self-understanding. Neither side, however, holds that Jesus applied to himself or accepted the so-called "higher" titles of later New Testament Christology, e.g., *Lord, Son of God,* or *God.* Both sides regard the application of these titles to have been the result of later Christian reflection on the mystery of Christ. Where the two sides differ, therefore, is on the matter of the so-called "lower" titles that were known to the Jews from the Old Testament or intertestamental writings—e.g., *Messiah, Prophet, Servant of God,* or *Son of Man.*

The *explicit* school was popular in the 1950s and early 1960s and is still respectable today. Among its adherents are such Protestant scholars as Oscar Cullmann, C. H. Dodd (d. 1973), Joachim Jeremias, and Vincent Taylor (d. 1968). Most Catholic scholars writing on the subject in the 1960s were in the same camp.

In the 1970s, however, in Protestant and Catholic writing alike, the *implicit* school gained acceptance. According to this approach, Jesus did not express his self-understanding in terms of titles or accept titles attributed to him by others. Rather he conveyed what he was by speaking with unique authority and by acting with unique power. This view of Jesus' attitude does not necessarily detract from his greatness. If Jesus did not find the title *Messiah* acceptable, for example, it may mean only that the title simply did not match his uniqueness. The Church was able to call him "Messiah" successfully only after it reinterpreted the title to match Jesus' greatness. Thus, the ultimate tribute to Jesus may have been that every term or title in the theological vocabulary of Israel had to be reshaped by his followers to do justice to him, including even the title *God* itself.

Even the Second Vatican Council, as early as 1965, anticipated this shift: "Jesus perfected revelation by fulfilling it through His whole work of making Himself present and manifesting Himself: through His words and deeds, His signs and wonders, but especially through His death and glorious resurrection from the dead and final sending of the Spirit of truth" (*Dogmatic Constitution on Divine Revelation*, n. 4). Among the scholars holding to the *implicit* opinion are, on the Reformation side of the line, F. Hahn, Reginald Fuller, Norman Perrin (d. 1977), some of the post-Bultmannians in Germany, and Catholic authors of the 1970s such as Bruce Vawter (d. 1986) and Raymond Brown (it would seem).

Biblical scholarship will probably continue to move back and forth between these two moderately conservative positions. But regardless of whether one detects explicit or implicit Christology in the self-evaluation of Jesus, the line of *continuity* between his self-understanding and the early Church's subsequent proclamation is more firmly secure than was ever thought possible earlier in the twentieth century. (For a summary, see the chart on page 460.)

WHERE FROM HERE? THE QUESTION OF METHOD

From this point we can proceed in one of two directions. We can adopt the more traditional approach and take up the life and teachings of Jesus, beginning with the Gospel accounts. Thereafter, we would present the early Church's estimation of Jesus. But there are problems with this alternative. The fact is that the New Testament contains no biography of Jesus written during his lifetime nor even shortly after his death. What we have, as noted earlier, are testimonies of faith, constituted from fragments of the oral and written traditions which developed after Jesus' death and resurrection. It is Jesus *as he was remembered* by the earliest Christians and *as he was experienced* in their communities of faith whom we meet in the Gospels.

A second course is open to us, one that *begins* with the faith of the Church as expressed in the New Testament and moves from there to the message, mission, and person of Jesus as the source of that faith. The faith of the Church is centered on the *resurrection* of Jesus from the dead. The *kerygma*, or proclamation, is by definition a testimony to the resurrection, the earliest witness to which is given in Paul's First Letter to the Corinthians (15:3–8), written sometime in the year 56 or 57. Paul is obviously incorporating a creedal formula that he had previously been taught:

> For I handed on to you as of first importance
> what I in turn had received:
> that Christ died for our sins
> in accordance with the scriptures,
> and that he was buried,
> and that he was raised on the third day
> in accordance with the scriptures,
> and that he appeared to Cephas,
> then to the twelve.
> Then he appeared to more than five hundred brothers and sisters at
> one time, most of whom are still alive, although some have
> died.
> Then he appeared to James,
> then to all the apostles.
> Last of all, . . . he appeared also to me.

Paul explicitly states that he is drawing on tradition, and certain internal evidence suggests this—e.g., the stylized structure of the passage and the use of such terms as *the twelve*, which is not an expression he uses otherwise. Clearly, he had some ready-made text at hand. And this would have been an entirely normal practice in the composition of the various books of the New Testament. Authors like Paul would draw upon existing liturgical formulations, as Paul had done earlier in the same letter when he quoted from a traditional eucharistic prayer (1 Corinthians 11:23–26).

We begin, therefore, where the New Testament begins, not with the nativity scene in Bethlehem but with the Church's proclamation of the risen Christ.

THE RESURRECTION

Its Meaning and Importance

The resurrection has been understood poorly. We refer here not only to the question of its facticity (whether it was a bodily, historical happening) but to the question of its place and significance in the whole Christ-event and in the mystery of salvation. For pre–Vatican II Catholic theology the resurrection had long been viewed in apologetical terms, that is, as simply the strongest possible corroboration of

Jesus' messianic claims. It had no importance in itself in the work of redemption. We were redeemed by the cross, and by the cross alone.

Contemporary theology, in keeping with the results of modern New Testament studies, more commonly understands the resurrection as central to, not simply confirmatory of, Christian faith, and as the beginning, not the end, of the story.

Three men died on crosses in occupied Palestine sometime during the fourth decade of the Christian era. The executions were relatively routine. And so, too, was the mode of execution. Without question the Roman authorities regarded all three as troublemakers, disturbers of the Roman peace. Over the head of one of them, however, the Romans affixed a sign "The King of the Jews," obviously in a spirit of derision and contempt. If we could return to Calvary on that first Good Friday, that is all we would have seen: three men being put to death by crucifixion. And yet one of the three, the one they called "King of the Jews," would not be swallowed up forever by his death.

At some point soon after his death, his closest followers would become convinced that he had, in fact, risen from the dead and that he lived again in their midst in a new and more powerful way than before. On the basis of their experience of the resurrection, these disciples would see the life and death of Jesus in a whole new light. They would reinterpret everything that he had said and done, recalling and reconstructing it all to the best of their ability. The message of the New Testament was always the message of the resurrection:

> You that are Israelites, listen to what I have to say: Jesus of Nazareth, a man attested to you by God with deeds of power, wonders, and signs that God did through him among you, as you yourselves know—this man, handed over to you according to the definite plan and foreknowledge of God, you crucified and killed by the hands of those outside the law. But God raised him up, having freed him from death, because it was impossible for him to be held in its power....
>
> This Jesus God raised up, and of that all of us are witnesses....
>
> Therefore let the entire house of Israel know with certainty that God has made him both Lord and Messiah, this Jesus whom you crucified (Acts of the Apostles 2:22–24,32,36).

Paul was even more explicit about the centrality and utterly crucial importance of the resurrection for Christian faith: "And if Christ has not been raised, then our proclamation has been in vain and your faith has been in vain" (1 Corinthians 15:14).

The ambiguity that surrounded the life and death of Jesus now disappears. Under the impact of the resurrection everything falls into place. For the first time the Apostles look upon the figure of Jesus with confidence and self-assurance. His relationship with the Father, the Almighty, is now clearer than ever before. Jesus is without doubt the Christ, the Anointed One, of God. He is the Son of Man, the Suffering Servant, the Son of God, the Lord, the Son of David, the Word.

At first such titles as these were *functional;* i.e., they described what Jesus had done. Then they became *confessional;* i.e., they were used in prayer and worship. They specified what it meant to be a Christian, i.e., one who confesses that Jesus is Lord. And eventually the titles were to assume a *metaphysical* and *theological* character; i.e., they would become intellectual tools to probe the inner reality of Jesus Christ: his person, his natures, and their relationships.

It was because of the early Church's faith in the resurrection that it came to acknowledge the *divinity* of Jesus. And once the Church acknowledged the divinity of Jesus, it began laying the foundations for the doctrine of the *incarnation,* which sees Jesus as the Word made flesh (John 1:14). From the doctrine of the incarnation the Church was led ineluctably to the *preexistence* of Jesus (John 1:1; Philippians 2:5–9) and to the question of his relationship to the whole of *creation* and to the *history of salvation* (Colossians 1:15–20; Romans 8:19–22; Ephesians 1:9–10,22,23). He is indeed the "first fruits" (1 Corinthians 15:20) of the "new creation" (2 Corinthians 5:17), which is the *Kingdom of God.*

Varieties of Interpretation Within the
New Testament

As noted earlier in this chapter, there are different cultures at work in the production of the New Testament, and these, in turn, generate distinctive theological viewpoints regarding the meaning of Jesus. In each case, however, it is the Easter experience which provides the foundation for Christology.

Palestinian Community

In the Palestinian community, the closest to the events of the life, death, and resurrection of Jesus, there is a keen sense of the *imminence* of the Second Coming of Jesus. Jesus is identified as the *Son of Man* (Acts of the Apostles 7:55–56), who will return in power and glory—an identification which has apparent roots in Jesus' own sayings about the Son of Man (Mark 8:38; Luke 12:8–10). The return of Jesus as the Son of Man is the final act of vindication for all that Jesus said and did during his lifetime. Indeed, this hope shaped the liturgy of the Palestinian Church. At the center of its eucharistic worship is the *Maranatha* prayer, "Our Lord, come!" (1 Corinthians 16:22), "Come, Lord Jesus!" (Revelation 22:20).

More important and certainly more central to the Palestinian Christology was its confession of Jesus as *the Messiah* (Acts of the Apostles 3:20), or the *Christ* (literally, "the anointed"). And because Jesus is the Messiah, he is also seen as the *Son of David* (Revelation 3:7; 5:5) and the *Son of God* (Luke 1:32), who will appear at the Second Coming, or *Parousia*. This explains, too, why such stress is placed in Matthew and Luke on the genealogies (Matthew 1:1–17; Luke 3:23–38). It was necessary that Jesus be able to trace his ancestry all the way back to David, for it had to be a descendant of the house of David who would inaugurate the messianic era (Mark 11:10).

The *Son of God* title, on the other hand, expressed the closeness between Jesus and God, but not necessarily his divinity, as many might think. In the Old Testament, for example, various individuals and groups are called sons of God (e.g., Exodus 4:22–23; Hosea 11:1; Isaiah 1:2; Jeremiah 3:19). Subsequently, the title came to have messianic significance, but it was not until the much later Hellenistic stage that the title signified divinity.

Among other titles applied to Jesus by the Palestinian community were *Prophet* (Acts of the Apostles 3:22–24) and *Servant* (3:26), fused as the Mosaic prophet-servant of Yahweh. But the *Christ* title remained the focal point for all the rest.

431

Jewish-Hellenistic Community

The Jewish-Hellenistic community, composed of Greek-speaking Jewish converts to Christianity, had to translate such Palestinian categories into intelligible Hellenistic ones. The delay of the *Parousia* seemed to require a major theological shift away from emphasis on the Second Coming of Jesus in the future to the *present exalted state* of Jesus. Thus, Jesus is the one who is *already* Lord (*Kyrios*) and Christ (Acts of the Apostles 2:36), for he is even now "exalted at the right hand of God" (2:33). Indeed, that becomes the central confession of faith: "Jesus Christ is Lord" (Philippians 2:11; see also Acts of the Apostles 11:20; 16:31). It is in the name of the "Lord Jesus" that Christians are baptized (Acts of the Apostles 8:16; 19:5). In using the title *Lord*, the Greek-speaking Jews were attributing divine status to Jesus, for it was a title employed in the Greek Old Testament (the *Septuagint*) to translate the Hebrew equivalent for Yahweh. And so the various Palestinian titles are recast in the light of this new and distinctive emphasis on the exaltation of Jesus: Christ, Son of Man, Son of David, Son of God (Acts of the Apostles 2:36; 11:17; Romans 1:3–4). At an even later stage, the Jewish-Hellenistic Church projects these titles back into the earthly life of Jesus as well.

Hellenistic-Gentile Community

The final stage of Christological development occurs within the Hellenistic-Gentile community, under the impact of the missionary activity of the Pauline and Johannine schools of theology. The Church now fully accommodates itself to the conceptual categories of the Greek world. The classic expression of this Christology is contained in the great hymn of Philippians 2:5–11, complete with the three-deckered Hellenistic cosmology: heaven, earth, and the underworld (v. 10). Correspondingly, there is a threefold division of Jesus' existence: his preexistence (v. 6), his becoming flesh in the incarnation (vv. 7–8), and his exaltation following his death and resurrection (vv. 9–11). Variations on this threefold pattern can be found in Colossians 1:15–20 and the Prologue of John's Gospel (1:1–14).

Furthermore, what was only hinted at in the early stages of Jewish-Hellenistic Christology is fully developed in Hellenistic-

Gentile Christology: The earthly life of Jesus is itself already an exalted form of existence, although veiled. In the synoptic Gospels we have evidence of this in the infancy narratives, the accounts of Jesus' baptism by John, and the Transfiguration (e.g., Luke 1:5–2:52; 3:21–22; 9:28–36). In John's Gospel, of course, this so-called "high Christology" is full-blown.

And there is a correlative reinterpretation of the titles as employed by the earlier Christologies. The *Son of Man* is portrayed as "the One who descended" from heaven (John 3:13), and when he ascends, it will be "to where he was before" (6:62). The title *Christ* becomes, for all practical purposes, a proper name for Jesus. *Son of God* takes on a higher meaning than it once enjoyed in the Old Testament, and *Lord* becomes entirely central. Thus, for the Hellenistic-Gentile Church God is even now present exercising lordship over the universe in and through Jesus Christ, who is the risen and exalted Lord.

Its Redemptive Effects

The resurrection is a saving event because it is not until Jesus has received the fullness of life which is properly his as Son of God and Son of Man that his redemptive work is complete. He is the firstborn of those who rise (Colossians 1:18). Jesus "was handed over to death for our trespasses and raised for our justification" (Romans 4:25). Those of us who die and are buried with him will also rise with him to new life (6:3–11). He was in fact raised from the dead "in order that we may bear fruit for God" (7:4). To be "in Christ" who is risen is to be "a new creation" (2 Corinthians 5:17). We have been born anew "into a living hope through the resurrection of Jesus Christ from the dead" (1 Peter 1:3). Indeed, the Spirit cannot be given until Jesus has been raised and glorified (John 7:39; 16:7), and the first thing the risen Lord does when he appears to the disciples behind locked doors is to breathe the Holy Spirit upon them (20:19–23). Our very bodies are given life through the Spirit which now possesses us (Romans 8:11).

The resurrection, therefore, is the principle of our own new being. The Father who raised Jesus will also raise us (2 Corinthians 4:14). Those who die with Christ will live with him (2 Timothy 2:11). Jesus is the resurrection and the life. Those who believe in him will be raised on the last day (John 11:25–26; 6:39–44,54; see also Philippians 3:20–21; Revelation 21:1–22:5). Nowhere is this theme more fully elaborated than in 1 Corinthians 15: "If Christ has not been raised, your faith is futile and you are still in your sins. Then those also who have died in Christ have perished" (vv. 17–18). But Christ was raised. And just as "death came through a human being," so "the resurrection of the dead has also come through a human being; for as all die in Adam, so all will be made alive in Christ" (vv. 21–22).

Its Historicity

Did It Happen?

Something happened after the death of Jesus. The tomb was found empty on Easter morning, many claimed to have seen the risen Jesus, and many more were marvelously transformed by the event and its aftermath. Certainly from the very earliest days of Christianity, Jesus' followers were convinced that he had indeed been raised from the dead—and this in spite of the fact that the disciples didn't expect it to happen (e.g., Luke 24:13–35).

The Pauline confession to which we referred earlier (1 Corinthians 15:3–8) has its origins at least as early as A.D. 35, the year of Paul's own conversion to Christ. The construction of these verses reflects an Aramaic or Hebrew background, which tends to confirm the hypothesis that it comes from a very primitive tradition indeed. Paul does not use the details of his own experience of the risen Lord to prove the truth of Christian belief in the resurrection. The proof is to be found in the transformation of Paul's life from persecutor of Christians to Apostle (Galatians 1:13–17; 1 Corinthians 15:8–10).

What Happened?

The problem, of course, is that no one actually saw the resurrection. We have no eyewitnesses. To the extent that we know anything about it at all, we know it through its effects. Is it a historical event, therefore? The answer has to be "No" if by *historical* one means an event that could have been photographed as it was occurring or that a disinterested person could have observed happening.

There is no indication in the New Testament record that the early Church believed the resurrection to have been in the very same category of history as the crucifixion, for example. Even the enemies of Jesus could see what was taking place on Calvary. On the contrary, Jesus is said to have entered an entirely new mode of life, a spiritual existence in which he becomes the source of "freedom" and "glory" for "all of us" (2 Corinthians 3:17; 1 Corinthians 15:44-45). If Jesus had simply resumed the kind of bodily existence he had before his death, then he would not have been the risen Lord. On the contrary, for him there could be no return to the realm of ordinary space and time. His history was over. He had moved into the final and definitive state of existence and would never die again (unlike, for example, Lazarus, whom Jesus had raised from the dead).

And yet to concede that the resurrection was not a historical event in our ordinary sense of historical event (something open to scientific investigation and verifiable by neutral witnesses) does not mean that the resurrection was not a *real* event for Jesus with *historical implications* for others.

Behind the apostolic confession of faith in the risen Lord lies the experience of having witnessed him at some time and in some way. The disciples were convinced that they had indeed seen him, so that *for them* the appearances *are* historical. And it would have been very difficult from a purely psychological point of view to synchronize such a wide range of individual experiences of the risen Lord unless there was some basis in reality for them. Furthermore, the appearances are not to people in general, but to particular individuals, in particular places, at particular times.

Nonetheless, it would seem better to speak of the resurrection as *transhistorical*, or *metahistorical*, rather than *unhistorical*. The average person will translate *unhistorical* simply to mean that it never happened at all. It is transhistorical, or metahistorical, in the sense that it refers to an event that took place on the other side of death and, therefore, which lies beyond the confines of space and time. Similarly, the reality of the risen Lord is also a reality which transcends history as we know it. By the resurrection Jesus enters a completely new universe of being, the end-time of history, beyond the control of history and beyond the reach of historians.

To Whom Did It Happen?

Was the resurrection truly something that happened *to Jesus?* Some have argued that it did not happen to Jesus but to his disciples. In other words, the mystery of the resurrection means that the early Church and in particular the Apostles and disciples were suddenly enlightened regarding the meaning of Jesus' life and death. The resurrection was an evolution of their consciousness as they gradually began to understand what Jesus was all about, much as many Americans might have been inspired to work diligently in the cause of civil rights following the assassination of Martin Luther King, Jr. (d. 1968).

The question of the *bodiliness* of the resurrection, therefore, is a very important one. If it *was* a bodily occurrence, then it was something that *did* happen to Jesus, and not just to his disciples. It was a sovereign act of God the Father glorifying Jesus of Nazareth and making him the source of new life for all of us.

The bodily element is clear in the description of some of the postresurrection appearances of Jesus to his disciples. The evangelists speak of touching (John 20:27), eating (Luke 24:41–43), and conversing (John 21:15–22). This drives home the underlying unity between the Jesus of history and the risen Lord. It also counteracts the Greek tendency to spiritualize everything, to make of the resurrection, therefore, an abstract, noncorporeal event. The physical emphasis also challenges certain Gnostic interpretations of Jesus that were already beginning to appear in the second half of the first century.

On the other hand, there had to be something radically different about Jesus' "bodiliness" following the resurrection. The resurrection, after all, was not the resuscitation of a corpse. The disciples, for example, sometimes did not recognize him as he stood before them (Luke 24:16; John 20:14; 21:4), and some even doubted that it was he (Matthew 28:17; Luke 24:41). The risen Jesus is portrayed as coming and going in a manner unlike that of any mortal body (Luke 24:31; John 20:19,26). Mark says explicitly that he appeared "in another form" (Mark 16:12). This contrary emphasis on the difference between Jesus' historical existence and his risen existence safeguards against a too-physical understanding of the resurrection, and stresses

436

the Pauline teaching that Jesus underwent a marvelous *transformation* (1 Corinthians 15:42–44).

Therefore, in trying to determine what really happened and to whom, we have to avoid two extreme answers: one which denies all bodily reality to the resurrection and makes of it something that happened to the disciples alone; and the other which exaggerates the bodily character of the resurrection and makes of it an event that was equally available to the disinterested observer and to the person of faith. The first extreme can be called *subjectivist*; the second, *objectivist*.

The *subjectivist* has to ignore the accounts of the appearances— especially the cases of Paul (e.g., Galatians 1:13–16) and James (1 Corinthians 15:7) who had resisted belief in the resurrection—as well as the empty tomb. He or she has to explain away the extraordinary change and conversion in the lives of a small group of ordinary men and women whose faith had just been shattered by the crucifixion, who had abandoned Jesus on Calvary, and who had apparently begun returning to their everyday lives. Suddenly, they begin to believe in the resurrection, go out and preach it, develop a whole new way of understanding human existence on the basis of it; then even lay down their lives for it. And what is the subjectivist to make, finally, of the whole network of doctrines developed by the Church in direct response to its faith in the resurrection: the doctrine of the Holy Spirit, the Church, the sacraments, eternal life? If the resurrection is not something that really happened to Jesus, then what foundation do the principal doctrines of Christianity have?

The *objectivist*, or fundamentalist, on the other hand, oversimplifies the New Testament and simply ignores the manner in which it was put together. He or she ignores the metaphorical character of New Testament language about the resurrection and the symbolic imagery used by Paul, who describes the risen Jesus in terms of "a spiritual body" and "a life-giving spirit" (1 Corinthians 15:44,45). The objectivist also cannot make sense of the fact that even Jesus' closest disciples did not at first recognize the risen Lord when he appeared to them. Why not, if the resurrection was essentially the resuscitation of the corpse of Jesus?

Who Saw It Happen?

No one actually saw the resurrection happen, as we have already noted. But many claimed to have seen the risen Lord. The Gospels do not agree, however, regarding the places where Jesus *appeared* after the resurrection, nor regarding the persons to whom he appeared. (Compare Mark 16:1–8; Matthew 28; Luke 24; Mark 16:9–20; John 20; and John 21.) It is better not to attempt an artificial harmonization of the accounts, but to accept the discrepancies as inevitable in view of the lateness of the reports, the nature of the events in question, and variations in authorship, audience, and theological purpose.

In spite of these differences there are *common elements* in the accounts of the appearances. *First,* those to whom he appears are in a state of depression or at least keen disappointment (Luke 24:21). *Second,* it is always Jesus who initiates the appearances (John 20:19; Luke 24:15; Matthew 28:9,18). *Third,* Jesus gives some form of greeting—e.g., "Peace be with you" (John 20:19; Matthew 28:9). *Fourth,* a moment of recognition follows (John 21:7; 20:20; Matthew 28:9,17). And, *finally,* Jesus gives a word of command to go forth and make disciples (Matthew 28:19; John 20:21; 21:15–17; Luke 24:46–49).

Regarding the last item: Did Jesus actually *speak* during these appearances? Some Catholics have thought, for example, that Jesus spent forty days after the resurrection instructing the Apostles in theology, ethics, and canon law. There is a self-contradictory character, for example, to the Lucan account of Paul's conversion experience on the road to Damascus (Acts of the Apostles 9:7 and 22:9). In one text the companions of Paul are reported to have heard the voice from heaven, but in the other they did not. Did the risen Lord communicate with the Apostles verbally, or did he communicate intuitively? It is a question that one cannot really answer with certitude. An increasing number of scholars, however, do doubt that the risen Jesus used words.

But some form of communication is said to have taken place. What was it? Raymond Brown's hypothesis, which others support, is as follows: After the crucifixion, the Twelve fled Jerusalem and made their way back to Galilee, thoroughly discouraged by recent events. If, in fact, they had heard of the empty tomb before leaving Jerusalem, their puzzlement and fright must have been only heightened all

438

the more. As Peter returned to his fishing, Jesus appeared to him on the shores of the Sea of Tiberias (John 21:1–14), and faith in the resurrection was born. Subsequently, Jesus appeared to the rest of the Twelve, confirming perhaps the inchoate faith stirred by Peter's report. It was on the occasion of his appearance to the Apostles that he breathed the Holy Spirit upon them and commissioned them to proclaim that the Kingdom of God had come among them in a new and definitive way through what God had accomplished in Jesus.

The Apostles would gradually discover on their own that the proclamation of the Kingdom of God would involve bearing witness to the Lord in word and in deed, baptizing people and forgiving their sins, and forming a new community, a new Israel, the Church. By the time the Gospel narratives themselves were written, all this was already happening. Accordingly, certain words of Jesus were incorporated into the actual commission, as if Jesus himself on that occasion had instructed them in detail.

Two final points about the appearances: In the various accounts, the postresurrectional confession is not "We have seen Jesus" but "We have seen the Lord" (John 20:18,25; 21:7; Luke 24:34). Since *Lord* is a "high" Christological evaluation of Jesus, the evangelists are telling us that the witnesses enjoyed not only the *sight* of Jesus but also and even primarily *insight*. They saw that Jesus had been transformed, that he was now in the realm of God (Acts of the Apostles 2:32, 36). Thus, the appearances involve a sight that is revelatory, i.e., an experience of God within ordinary human experience.

Second, it is striking that *Mary Magdalene* is mentioned in five of the six resurrection narratives in the Gospel tradition: Mark 16:1–8; Matthew 28:1–20; Luke 23:56b–24:53; John 20:1–29; and Mark 16:9–20 (she is not mentioned in John 21:1–23). She is, therefore, a major witness. In these six narratives *Peter* is mentioned by name in four and is spoken of together with Mary Magdalene in three. Peter is *not* mentioned in Matthew 28, the chapter which announces both the resurrection and the postresurrection command to evangelize the world.

This last point does not deny the authority of Peter, nor does it deny that he was the recipient of a postresurrection appearance. But it does show the *complementary roles* of women, Peter, and the other disciples as witnesses to the risen Christ. Among the women, Mary

Magdalene is clearly portrayed in Scripture as having the primary role.

Where Did It Happen?

Jesus was buried in a tomb owned by Joseph of Arimathea, "a respected member of the council" (Mark 15:43). Two days later the tomb was discovered to be empty. Those are the barest details.

Like reports of the appearances, the *empty tomb* accounts are full of inconsistencies and embellishments. (Compare Mark 16:1–8; Matthew 28; Luke 24; and John 20.) It is very curious indeed that in Mark's account the women flee the empty tomb out of fear and astonishment and "said nothing to anyone" about it (Mark 16:8). In Luke's account, when the women inform the Apostles, "these words seemed to them an idle tale, and they did not believe them" (Luke 24:11), although Peter did get up and run out to the tomb to see for himself. But these indicate that *the fact of the empty tomb* proves nothing in itself. It simply raises questions like, "What happened to Jesus' body? Did someone steal it? Did Jesus in fact rise from the dead?"

And yet an empty-tomb tradition did develop, and the nature of the evidence lends a high degree of probability to it. No author, for example, would have used female witnesses in a fabricated story, since women were simply not accepted at the time as witnesses. Furthermore, the early Jewish controversies about the resurrection all supposed that the tomb was empty. The arguments were over the question of how. Some charged that the disciples had stolen the body (Matthew 28:11–15; 27:64). Others said the gardener had taken it away (John 20:13–15). Indeed, if the tomb were still intact, it would have been impossible to propose the story in the first place.

What of the significance of the empty-tomb tradition? At best it is a secondary piece of evidence, second certainly to the appearances. *We do not make an act of faith in the empty tomb but in the resurrection.* There are plenty of empty tombs in the world. The publicity surrounding the King Tutankhamen exhibitions conducted throughout the United States in 1978–1979 only dramatized that fact. He was one of the very few ancient figures whose tombs were discovered with the body and other artifacts still there. Does that mean all of the other Pharaohs rose from the dead?

440

The empty tomb was more important for the first Christians than it is for us today. For them it was yet another safeguard against the Gnostic denial of the bodiliness of Jesus and of his resurrection. In the actual genesis of faith in the resurrection, it was the appearances of the risen Lord that first brought the disciples to believe; this belief, in turn, made sense of the empty tomb. Having seen him, the Apostles now understood the reason why the tomb had been empty. He was raised and then appeared to them (1 Corinthians 15:4–5; Luke 24:34). The first Christians, therefore, proclaimed a bodily resurrection in the sense that they did not think that Jesus' body had corrupted in the tomb. On the other hand, that risen body was now a spiritual body and not simply a resuscitated corpse, as we noted earlier (1 Corinthians 15:42–44).

THE PASSION AND DEATH

Although the doctrine of the cross was not the earliest Christology to emerge from faith in the resurrection but was something developed only by degrees, it is inextricably linked with resurrection faith and is at the same time entirely central to the New Testament's evaluation of the life, message, and mission of Jesus. Already in the primitive creedal formula in 1 Corinthians 15:3–8, there is the confession of faith "that Christ died for our sins."

On the other hand, the connection between the crucifixion and the resurrection had not always been so explicitly drawn. The great Christological hymn of Philippians 2:6–11 is one of the earliest attempts to make sense of the death of Jesus, not as Paul would usually have it, i.e., "for our sins," but as the culmination of Jesus' life of obedient humiliation within the human condition:

> who, though he was in the form of God,
> did not regard equality with God
> as something to be exploited,
>
> but emptied himself,
> taking the form of a slave,
> being born in human likeness.
>
> And being found in human form,
> he humbled himself

and became obedient to the point of death —
even death on a cross.

Therefore God also highly
exalted him
and gave him the name
that is above every name,

so that at the name of Jesus
every knee should bend
in heavens and on earth and
under the earth,
and every tongue should confess
that Jesus Christ is Lord,
to the glory of God the Father.

However we finally interpret this text (regarding, for example, its origin, its proper punctuation, its structure, the Christological model upon which it is based), there is no question that it is a very early Christology indeed (pre–A.D. 56 or 57, when Paul wrote to the Philippians), one that was inspired by the resurrection and pieced together from various available images of Jesus. Yet it did not attempt an interpretation of the death of Jesus, nor did it concern itself with his historical existence. The words *death on a cross* in verse 8c are not part of the original hymn but were added by Paul or by a Pauline editor. The addition was consistent with a growing trend within the early Church to work back from the resurrection experience to the death and life of the one who had been raised.

Indeed, his death makes sense only if the Gospel portrait of the historical Jesus is accepted as basically reliable. To suggest that he was executed only or even primarily because of his political attitudes and behavior toward the Roman government, whether as a Zealot or as a Zealot sympathizer, does not correspond with his preaching against violence, his almost studied indifference to specifically political questions, and his central teaching about love for one's enemies. His problem was primarily with the Jews rather than with the Romans. That is how the Gospels present it, and that is how early Jewish antagonists of Christianity recalled it as well.

He was periodically locked in controversy with the Jewish men of power: the chief priests, the Sadducees, the Pharisees, and their

442

Scribes. Unfortunately, the portrayal of Jewish hostility to Jesus and of direct Jewish involvement in his condemnation and death has allowed many Christians down through the centuries to justify a virulent anti-Semitism ("Christ-killers" and all that). But the counter-reaction has also been unfortunate. In playing down Jewish complicity in the death of Jesus, even transferring it entirely to Roman shoulders, we remove the very basis for the Gospel traditions. In effect, the credibility of the event we seek to explain is undermined, perhaps destroyed completely. If Jesus has been remembered as he was, then his confrontation with the religious as well as the political establishment was practically inevitable. But if that religious confrontation did not exist to the extent it is reported in the New Testament and with the effect it is also reported to have had, then the portrait of Jesus itself is open to question and to challenge.

Jesus functioned as a prophet greater than Moses. He claimed to forgive sin. He initiated a new form of table fellowship between God and humankind. He promised salvation. And he, of course, sharply criticized the religious situation as he found it in contemporary Israel. "For this reason the Jews were seeking all the more to kill him, because he was not only breaking the sabbath, but was also calling God his own Father, thereby making himself equal to God" (John 5:18). "He commits blasphemy!" they charged. "Who can forgive sins except God alone?" (Mark 2:7). When Jesus was asked by the high priest of the Sanhedrin whether or not he considered himself the Messiah, the Son of the Blessed One, Jesus answered, "I am; and 'you will see the Son of Man seated at the right hand of the Power,' and 'coming with clouds of heaven.'" With that the high priest tore his robes and said, "You have heard his blasphemy!" (Mark 14:61–63).

But Jesus had been on a collision course from the beginning of his preaching ministry. He preached the Kingdom of God in a wholly new way, as a reality that has now "come near," demanding repentance and faith (Mark 1:15). "Do you think I have come to bring peace to the earth? No, I tell you, but rather division! . . . father against son and son against father, mother against daughter and daughter against mother..." (Luke 12:51–53; see also Matthew 10:34–36). He had to know, as many prophets before him knew, that his life was at stake because of his preaching and particularly because of his attack upon those doing business in the Temple, after which, "the chief priests and scribes . . . kept looking for a way to kill him" (Mark 11:18).

But did he explicitly connect his death with our redemption? If he did, why did the earliest New Testament Christology not make the same connection? Presumably it would have done so if it had some basis for it in the sayings of Jesus. And yet eventually, within the New Testament, Jesus' death *is* interpreted in redemptive categories, as a work of atonement for our sins. Such a conviction evidently had to develop, not at once but over a period of time, as the life and death of Jesus continued to be contemplated in the light of the resurrection.

But as we noted earlier, resurrection faith first inspired the Church to look forward to the Second Coming, not backward. Only later did it reverse direction and display greater interest in the actual historical existence of Jesus, an interest which produced the Gospels. But where the older Christologies of the Epistles worked out of contemporary thought patterns, the Gospels remained more or less faithful to Old Testament thinking. It was this kind of thinking which accommodated itself most readily to the notion of redemptive sacrifice.

The idea of *vicarious atonement*, i.e., the sufferings of an innocent person having redeeming value for the sins of others, was already well accepted in the Judaism of Jesus' day. The best-known expression of this concept occurs in the Servant songs of Deutero-, or Second, Isaiah (42:1–4; 49:1–6; 50:4–9; 52:13–53:12), where the Servant, probably Israel itself, becomes an instrument of divine salvation through his/its passion and death. Jesus himself is identified with the *Servant of the Lord* in the early Christian proclamation (Acts of the Apostles 3:13,26; 4:27,30) and is taken into the Gospel accounts themselves (Matthew 8:17; 12:18–21; Luke 22:37). The Second Isaian imagery is clearly woven through the passage of 1 Peter 2:22–25:

He committed no sin; and no deceit was found in his mouth.

When he was abused, he did not return abuse,
when he suffered, he did not threaten;
but he entrusted himself to the One who judges justly.

He himself bore our sins in his body on the cross,
so that, free from sins, we might live for righteousness;
by his wounds you have been healed.

444

For you were going astray like sheep,
but now you have returned to the shepherd and guardian of your
souls.

But the Servant role, at first eagerly attributed to Jesus, was later abandoned as being too Jewish and, therefore, not readily understandable within the Gentile world. Other, more flexible Old Testament figures came to the surface, particularly the notion of *ransom* and the associated idea of *redemption*. A Marcan saying (10:45) is taken up by the Gospels (Matthew 20:28), with parallels elsewhere (1 Timothy 2:6) to show that Jesus understood his own mission as giving his life as a ransom for many.

In the New Testament world of commerce, a ransom was the price that had to be paid to buy back a pawned object or to liberate a slave. Thus, Christ is seen as the ransom given to liberate us all from the slavery of sin. But it has been an extraordinary misunderstanding to view this act of ransoming in more than *metaphorical* terms, as if it were some necessary payment demanded by God. On the contrary, "the redemption that is in Christ Jesus" is itself "a gift" of God (Romans 3:24). We have no reason for supposing that the New Testament intended to press the metaphor any farther than did the Old Testament.

We do not pay a ransom to God (Psalm 49:8); it is God who is our redeemer (Psalm 78:35; see also Psalm 19:14; Isaiah 63:5). The metaphor means that forgiveness of sin is not some casual or arbitrary act of God. Sin is truly a bondage leading to death. It "costs" God much to forgive and to deliver us from that bondage. In speaking of the blood of Christ as the "price" he had to pay, the New Testament is trying to emphasize that the risen Lord's life and death somehow served God's salvific purposes in history. *There is no exact "commercial" description of what actually occurred in Jesus' passion and death.*

What does it mean, therefore, to speak of Jesus as having become a "curse" for us, and as having shed his blood in *expiation* of our sins?

First, what does it *not* mean? It does *not* mean that Jesus was accursed of God like the *scapegoat* of the Old Testament (Leviticus 16:20–28), which was burdened with the sins of all the people and then driven away to die in the desert, the abode of the demons. Christ is never likened in New Testament Christology to the scapegoat of the Old Testament. It does *not* mean, therefore, that Jesus was marked out for death by the Father in expiation for offenses against the divine majesty, for neither is there any Old Testament model for such a notion.

What we have is an exercise in Pauline paradox (Galatians 3:13, with a quotation from Deuteronomy 21:22–23). Christ has brought us back from the "curse" of the Law by himself becoming a "curse" for us. As in the case of the word *ransom*, the usage here is *metaphorical*. He mixes proper and improper senses of the same word in order to make a point. The cross is "foolishness to those who are perishing, but to us who are being saved it is the power of God" (1 Corinthians 1:18). "Has not God made foolish the wisdom of the world? For since, in the wisdom of God, the world did not know God through wisdom, God decided, through the foolishness of our proclamation, to save those who believe" (1:20–21).

What of the *blood sacrifices?* When they were employed as a means of atonement, the death of the animal was entirely incidental. Blood in itself was regarded as a purifying and sacred element (Deuteronomy 12:23). Insofar as the shedding of Christ's blood is clearly associated with the establishment of a new covenant (Hebrews 9:12–14; Mark 14:24; Matthew 26:28; Luke 22:20), the allusion is always to the enactment of the Old Covenant on Sinai (Exodus 24), namely, the blood of a *peace offering*, not a sacrifice of expiation. It is not that God was so enraged by the world's sin that a price was to be exacted (the prevalent idea of God among the pagans), but that God "so loved the world that he gave his only Son..." (John 3:16).

Jesus himself seems to have viewed his impending death as the fate of a *prophet* (see Luke 13:34).

In summary, the Church's faith in the saving power of Christ's death emerged from its initial faith in his resurrection, and not from any general sense of need for deliverance from sin or from some wide-ranging exploration of Old Testament texts. *Jesus' death assumes meaning within the context of his resurrection:* "Unless the grain of wheat falls into the earth and dies, it remains just a single grain; but if it dies, it bears much fruit. Those who love their life lose it, and those who hate their life in this world will keep it for eternal life" (John 12:24–25).

446

THE LIFE AND MESSAGE OF JESUS

The Historical Situation

Basic introductions to the New Testament abound. The more one knows about and understands the social, economic, political, and religious situation at the time of Jesus, the more intelligently one will be able to interpret the New Testament's faith in him as well as the import and impact of Jesus' words and deeds upon his contemporaries. We can do no more here than outline that situation in the broadest of strokes. And that may not be particularly unfortunate. On the contrary, the late Protestant New Testament scholar Norman Perrin acknowledged that in his own experience as a teacher, students tend either to skip the introductory material on the Hellenistic, Roman, and Jewish "background" of the New Testament or to forget its content by the time they actually begin dealing with the texts themselves, just when the material is most necessary. So in his book, *The New Testament: An Introduction*, to which we are greatly indebted for the last section of this chapter, Perrin places all this material at the end, in two appendices, and discusses the background materials when and where they are relevant to understanding the texts themselves.

Since 63 B.C. the Jews had been politically subject to Roman power. Although by present standards that power was exercised with some measure of tolerance for national and religious diversity, there was in Jesus' time a widespread expectation of a political messiah. The Jewish party known as the *Zealots* wanted to throw off the yoke of Roman domination, and by violent revolutionary means. Although some latter-day political leftists have tried to portray Jesus as a member of the Zealot party, there is no real evidence that he even took a stand on the political issues of his time. Indeed, the New Testament seldom mentions a political group hostile to him, with the exception of the discussion about taxation (e.g., Matthew 22:15–22). On the other hand, much attention is given his religious controversies with the Pharisees. To be sure, the distinction between the religious and the political was not always clear at this time.

How closely Jesus is to be identified with the *Essenes* is a matter of dispute, although recent scholarship seems to suggest that the points of contact were substantially fewer than was thought soon after the Dead Sea Scrolls were discovered. The Essenes, or Qumran community, were a sect within Judaism which separated itself from regular commerce with the world and established hierarchically structured communities of salvation wherein members could follow the Law of God perfectly until the end of history. Jesus, on the other hand, addressed himself explicitly to the whole nation of Israel and not simply to this "remnant" within the nation.

The Jews of his day were exceedingly jealous of their religious and national traditions, and so, unlike their brothers and sisters living outside of Palestine, they tended, at least in Palestine, to resist the pervasive influence of Greek culture. Jesus, therefore, shows no sign of Hellenistic influence. He probably speaks in Aramaic. His parables are drawn from ordinary Jewish life; his theological arguments, from the Old Testament.

If it were not for the near universality of Hellenistic culture in this ancient world, Christianity might not have spread so rapidly and so widely. In most cities public instruction in the Greek language was available to anyone interested in acquiring it. And, of course, there was a real incentive to do so because people were needed to fill various positions in business and government. For a movement, therefore, that was composed primarily of "the low and despised in the world" (1 Corinthians 1:26–31), it was crucial to communicate its message in spoken and written form far beyond its own particular circle.

Life

We know relatively little about the actual life of Jesus. He was baptized by John the Baptist, and the beginning of his ministry in Galilee was in some way linked with that of the Baptist. His ministry centered on the proclamation of the Kingdom of God, with a sharp edge of challenge to it. His preaching was reinforced by an apparently deserved reputation as an exorcist (Mark 1:27; Luke 4:36). In a world that readily believed in the powers of good and evil, in demons and evil spirits, Jesus was able to help many who thought themselves to be possessed by such forces.

448

One of his fundamental concerns was to bring together a group of respondents to his proclamation of the Kingdom of God, regardless of their gender, status, or background. Central to the life of this group was sharing a common meal that celebrated their unity in their new relationship with God. Jesus, therefore, set himself and his group against the Jewish tendency to permit the fragmentation of the religious community and to engage rather freely in "excommunications" of certain undesirables. He spoke as one having great authority (Mark 1:22; John 7:46; Matthew 5:21–22). He forgave sins (Mark 2:10; Matthew 9:6; Luke 5:24). And he addressed God as Abba, or Father (Mark 14:36).

These activities provoked severe opposition—an opposition which reached a climax during a Passover celebration in Jerusalem when he was arrested, tried by Jewish authorities on a charge of blasphemy, and by the Romans on a charge of sedition, and then crucified. (It should not be forgotten that Jesus was considered a Jewish layman, and that the mortal struggle between himself and his opponents, many of whom were priests, had a strong laity-versus-clergy aspect to it.) Indeed, his decision to go up to Jerusalem and to end his Galilean ministry proved to be the major turning point. He definitively rejected a political mission, even though the hopes of some of his followers were still oriented in this direction to the very end (Luke 19:11; 24:21).

During his lifetime he had chosen from among his followers a small group of disciples who thereafter exhibited in their own activities something of his power and authority.

Message

Proclamation of the Kingdom of God

At the heart and center of Jesus' message of salvation was his proclamation of the coming of the Kingdom of God as a reality open to everyone, including the destitute poor, the sick and the crippled, and tax collectors, sinners, and prostitutes. (The Kingdom, or Reign, of God in the preaching of Jesus is also discussed in chapters 25 and 31.)

Although it is almost impossible to define what Jesus meant by the Kingdom of God, there is general agreement among New

Testament scholars that four sayings concerning it have especially strong claims to authenticity: "The time is fulfilled, and the kingdom of God has come near" (Mark 1:15); "But if it is by the finger of God that I cast out the demons, then the kingdom of God has come to you" (Luke 11:20); "The kingdom of God is not coming with things that can be observed; nor will they say, 'Look, here it is!' or 'There it is!' For, in fact, the kingdom of God is among us" (Luke 17:20–21); and "From the days of John the Baptist until now the kingdom of heaven has suffered violence, and the violent take it by force" (Matthew 11:12). Nor is there any doubt at all that the proclamation of the Kingdom of God is at the very center of the message of Jesus.

To speak of the Kingdom of God is to speak of the exercise of divine power on our behalf. The Kingdom is an apocalyptic symbol referring to God's final act of redemption at the end of the world, and so it is a symbol filled with hope. God, acting as King, visits and redeems his people as a loving father—a father who rejoices over regaining his lost children (e.g., Luke 15:1–32). This is the central theme of Jesus' preaching.

In the light of the four sayings listed above, there is obviously some tension between present and future in Jesus' understanding of the Kingdom. It is at once "in the midst of you" and has "come near"; i.e., it is imminent but still in the future. To the extent that the Kingdom is present, it comes about in the healings and exorcisms (Luke 11:20) and in the endurance of suffering (Matthew 11:12). On the other hand, Luke denies the possibility that the Kingdom comes about through any one experience (17:20–21), such as the prophet Daniel describes, for example (Daniel 11:3–35).

What, then, does Jesus mean when he says that the Kingdom is "in the midst of you"? If he is not speaking of the history of kings, wars, and persecutions, as Daniel was, then he is speaking of the history of the individual and of the individual's experience of reality. But, of course, individual reality is never divorced from its larger social and political context (which is the interpretation Bultmann's thoroughgoing existentialism gives), and so the power of God also realizes itself in our relationships with one another and in the many institutional expressions of those relationships.

The Parables

The inclusive graciousness and goodness of God are spelled out again and again in the parables. The following points seem to be agreed upon by contemporary New Testament scholars:

1. Jesus taught in parables, but the early Church translated many of them into *allegories*. In parables, the whole story counts as a totality; in allegories, each detail is important and has to be interpreted to detect its special meaning. Once the allegory has been deciphered, it can be set aside, for it has achieved its purpose. Not so with a parable, which keeps yielding new meanings. An example of allegory in the New Testament is the interpretation of the parable of the Sower in Mark 4:13-20.

2. Both the allegorizing of the parables and their placement and application within the Gospels are the work of the Church and the evangelists. To interpret a parable of Jesus, therefore, one must first reconstruct it in its original nonallegorical form and then interpret it as a parable in the context of the message of Jesus without reference to its place or function in the Gospels.

3. The fundamental element in a parable is the element of *metaphor*. The Kingdom of God, which is the unknown, is compared to something that is known. Thus, "The Kingdom of God is like..." (see, for example, Matthew 13:44–46).

4. There is in every parable, therefore, a *literal* point (what it means in itself) and a metaphorical point (what it refers to).

5. The purpose of a parable is normally *pedagogical*. But Jesus used parables not only for instruction but also for *proclamation*. An example is provided by the parable of the Good Samaritan (Luke 10:30-36). If the parable were merely exemplary, illustrating by way of example the principle of neighborliness, then it would have been more effective to have the hated Samaritan the injured man and the Israelite the one who gives aid. But the way Jesus tells it, the story in itself focuses attention not on the needs of the injured man but on the deed of the Samaritan, from whom no Jew would expect hospitality (see Luke 9:52–56). Thus, the parable asks the listener to conceive the inconceivable: that the Samaritan is "good." The listener is thereby challenged

451

to reexamine his or her most basic attitudes and values. The parable has become not instruction but *proclamation*.

The parable of the Unjust Steward (Luke 16:1–9) may be even more challenging, for Jesus commends a man who compounds his dishonesty (having cheated his master) by committing additional acts of dishonesty (cutting the debts owed his master so he will have friends after he loses his job). The point of the parable is to admit the presence of an order of reality that challenges all accepted norms of behavior and rules of human relationships. And that is how other parables function as well—i.e., by turning our worlds upside down and challenging us to reconsider our whole perspective on life (e.g., the Rich Man and Lazarus in Luke 16:19–31; the Pharisee and the Publican in Luke 18:10–14; and the Wedding Guest in Luke 14:7–11). That experience of sudden reversal is one experience of the inbreaking Kingdom of God.

But Jesus also used the parables for *instruction*. Examples are the Hidden Treasure and the Pearl (Matthew 13:44–46), the Tower Builder and the King Going to War (Luke 14:28–32), the Friend at Midnight (Luke 11:5–8), and the Unjust Judge (Luke 18:1–8).

The Proverbial Sayings

A proverb is a saying that gives insight into ordinary human situations—e.g., "Prophets are not without honor, except in their hometown, and among their own kin, and in their own house" (Mark 6:4). Sometimes proverbs have an imperative ring to them—e.g., "Do not give what is holy to dogs; and do not throw your pearls before swine or they will trample them under foot and turn and maul you" (Matthew 7:6). Some proverbs are formulated as questions—e.g., "And can any of you by worrying add a single hour to your span of life?" (Matthew 6:27). In general, proverbs are affirmations of faith in God's rule over the world—i.e., faith in the Kingdom of God.

The most radical proverbial sayings of Jesus are the injunction to let the dead bury their own dead (Luke 9:60) and the command to turn the other cheek, to give away one's cloak (the only garment hiding sheer nakedness), and to walk the extra mile (Matthew 5:29–41). Again, they challenge the hearers not to radical obedience but to

radical questioning. They jolt the hearers out of their routine existence and force them to see human existence in a new light. As such,
proverbial sayings are a form of proclamation of the Kingdom of God.

Other proverbial sayings carry forward this technique. Jesus tells
his listeners that the first will be last and the last first (Mark 10:31),
that whoever would save his life must lose it (Mark 8:35), that it is
easier for a camel to get through the eye of a needle than for a rich
man to enter the Kingdom (Mark 10:23–25), and that the one who
exalts himself will be humbled, and vice versa (Luke 14:11). Still other
sayings highlight the element of *conflict:* A kingdom divided against
itself cannot stand (Mark 3:24–26), and no one can plunder the house
of a strong man without first binding him (Mark 3:27).

Finally, there are the *instructional* sayings: No one who puts a
hand to the plough and looks back is fit for the Kingdom (Luke 9:62);
entrance into the Kingdom is by a narrow gate (Matthew 7:13–14);
nothing outside of a person is defiling; only what is inside defiles
(Mark 7:15); one must receive the Kingdom like a child (Mark 10:15);
and we must love our enemies if we are to be perfect (Matthew
5:44–48).

Always it is the Kingdom, or Reign, of God which is being proclaimed.

The Lord's Prayer

The Lucan version (11:2–4) is generally recognized as being close to
the prayer which Jesus actually taught his disciples:

> Father, hallowed be your name.
> Your kingdom come.
>
> Give us each day our daily bread.
>
> And forgive us our sins,
> for we ourselves forgive everyone indebted to us.
> And do not bring us to the time of trial.

The simplicity and brevity of this prayer suggest a very special,
intimate relationship between the petitioner and God. For the person
who can pray the Lord's prayer, the Kingdom has already come. On
the other hand, this prayer also asks that the Kingdom might yet

come. It looks to the future as well as to the present, just as some of the parables challenge Jesus' hearers to look to the future (the Sower in Mark 4:3–9; the Mustard Seed in Mark 4:30–32; the Leaven in Matthew 13:33; and the Seed Growing of Itself in Mark 4:26–29).

It does not follow, however, that Jesus' conception of the future is the same as ours, namely, temporal and historical. On the contrary, Jesus rejected tendencies in first-century Judaism to exaggerate the importance of signs and wonders. Perhaps the future that Jesus spoke of is the future that emerges as the consummation of the present, the fulfillment of what is already available to those who respond to the challenge of his proclamation of the Kingdom of God.

Table Fellowship and Miracles

Jesus also proclaimed the coming of the Kingdom of God, as an inclusive reality open to everyone, through table fellowship and miracles. He delighted in eating *meals* with the religious outcasts of his day, the "tax collectors and sinners," and saw in these meals a joyful anticipation of the heavenly banquet, at which the poor and the socially and religiously marginalized would also have a place. Indeed, his association with the marginalized placed Jesus in a constant state of ritual impurity, in the eyes of the stringently law-observant. He antagonized them even more by insisting that "sinners" (Jews who were considered to have departed from the Covenant) would be admitted to the Kingdom of God, without demanding that they employ the usual mechanism of Jewish repentance and sacrifice.

In keeping with his festive mood, Jesus did not practice voluntary fasting, nor did he ask his disciples to do so (Mark 2:18–20). In his mind, the time of penitential preparation was over. Consequently, Jesus was ridiculed and derided by the more conventionally devout as a "glutton and a drunkard" (Matthew 11:19).

Jesus' *miracles* of healing and exorcisms (see chapter 9) were not simply kind deeds done on behalf of individuals in need; they were concrete ways of proclaiming and bringing about God's triumph over evil in the final hour. The miracles were signs and partial realizations of what would come about fully in the Kingdom of God.

FROM JESUS TO CHRIST

Before making the leap from the New Testament to the postbiblical period of theological and doctrinal reflection on Jesus, the reader should be reminded that there was a continuous development of Christology *within* the New Testament. Its elements include a Second-Coming Christology (Luke and Acts of the Apostles), Resurrection Christology (Acts of the Apostles and Paul), ministry Christology [from the baptism of Jesus to the cross] (the Gospels), boyhood Christology (the Gospels, except Mark, and some Pauline passages), conception Christology (Matthew and Luke), and preexistence Christology (Paul, John, Matthew, Luke).

This New Testament Christology was primarily *functional*, underscoring the role Jesus played in effecting God's salvation for us, but it also reflected much of what Jesus was in himself (*ontological* Christology).

Accordingly, the one who proclaimed the Kingdom of God in his own lifetime became, after his death, the one *proclaimed*. The historical details of this transition are probably lost to us forever. What we have is what we began with in this chapter, namely, the early Church's testimony of faith in the risen Lord. All else in the New Testament flows from that—forward and backward alike.

SUMMARY

1. No one seriously questions that Jesus of Nazareth really lived. What is at issue is whether this same Jesus of history is also the Christ of faith proclaimed by the New Testament.

2. The Gospels, however, do not provide us with the kind of biographical information which we are accustomed to receive from current books and newspapers. They are the finally edited versions of the oral and written proclamation of the early Church regarding Jesus Christ.

3. In order to reconstruct the process of development and come to a greater understanding of what the New Testament proclaims, we must employ *historical criticism* (What is the nature of documents we have in hand?), *form criticism* (What are the various units out of which the Gospels were put together?), and *redaction criticism* (What was the peculiar purpose of each evangelist?).

4. The Gospels are products of different Christian communities with distinctive theological perspectives: *Palestinian*, *Jewish-Hellenistic*, and *Hellenistic-*

Gentile. The first emphasized the imminence of the Second Coming of Jesus and his fulfillment of the role of the Christ, or the Messiah; the second shifted emphasis away from the future to the present exalted state of Jesus, who is now proclaimed as Lord; the third combines present and future with past, dividing Jesus' existence into preexistence, the incarnation, and the exaltation.

5. In *nonscholarly conservatism* the Christology of the New Testament is *identified* with Jesus' self-evaluation. Jesus knew and expressed from the beginning what the Church affirmed of him after the resurrection. *Nonscholarly liberalism* concludes that there is *no continuity* at all between the Christ of faith and the Jesus of history. *Scholarly liberalism* insists that New Testament Christology is a *creation* of the early Church. *Bultmannian existentialism* acknowledges a *functional equivalence* between the early Church's Christology and Jesus' own proclamation of the Kingdom, in that they made the same practical demands upon the hearers. *Moderate conservatism* posits a discernible *continuity* between the Christ of faith and Jesus' self-evaluation. One branch suggests that the Church's Christology was *explicit* in Jesus' self-understanding with regard to the so-called "lower" titles (e.g., Messiah, Prophet, Servant, Son of Man), while another indicates that such titles are at most *implicit* in Jesus' self-evaluation.

6. The *resurrection* of Jesus from the dead is both the *starting point* and the *center* of the early Church's faith in him as the Christ and Lord of history. This is evident in such primitive sources as the creedal formula in 1 Corinthians 15 and in the apostolic proclamation of Peter in the Acts of the Apostles 2.

7. The resurrection is perceived as a saving event in that it is the necessary step by which Jesus receives the *fullness of life* that he is destined to share with us. He is the *firstborn of those who rise* (Colossians 1:18). To be "in Christ" is to be a "new creation" (2 Corinthians 5:17).

8. *Did it happen?* Something happened, although there were no eyewitnesses. The tomb was found empty, many claimed to have seen the risen Jesus, and his followers were marvelously transformed.

9. *What happened?* Jesus entered into an entirely *new mode of existence.* The resurrection was *for Jesus* something *real, although transhistorical, or metahistorical.* It was something *real and historical* from the side of *the disciples,* so profoundly were they affected by it and by the appearances.

10. *To whom did it happen?* The extreme liberal or *subjectivist* answer is that the resurrection was something that happened to the disciples alone; i.e., it is the "miracle" of their sudden and wondrous transformation as they reflected on the meaning of the life and death of Jesus. The extreme conservative or

objectivist solution is that the resurrection was so literally real that a photographer could have captured the event on film had he or she been present.

11. *Who saw it happen?* No one. And yet many claimed to have seen Jesus *after* it happened. The principal witnesses of the risen Lord were the women (especially Mary Magdalene), Peter, and the other disciples.

12. *Where did it happen?* We know only that Jesus was buried in a tomb owned by Joseph of Arimathea and that two days later it was discovered to be empty. At best, the empty-tomb tradition is a *secondary piece of evidence.* We do not make an act of faith in it.

13. The early Church did not at first focus on the redemptive significance of the *crucifixion* and only thereafter view the resurrection as Jesus' reward for suffering death or as the Father's way of proving Jesus' claims about himself. It was the other way around.

14. Did Jesus die "for our sins," or did he die because of his political views and activities? He claimed to forgive sin. He initiated a new form of table fellowship, promised salvation, and sharply criticized the religious and political establishments of his day. In the end, the Jews rejected him and brought about his death because he *blasphemed* and because of his *attack upon the Temple.*

15. Did Jesus explicitly connect his death with our redemption? No. Eventually, however, the connection *is* made by the early Church as it contemplated the meaning and implications of the resurrection.

16. Was the crucifixion an act of *vicarious atonement?* The initial source of this idea was in the Servant songs in Deutero-Isaiah, but the notion was later abandoned as being too Jewish. The notion of *ransom* came to the fore, but in a *metaphorical,* not a commercial, sense. It is not a payment for our sins, but is something God gives to us (Romans 3:24).

17. Did Jesus die in *expiation* for our sins? Not in the sense of his becoming a *scapegoat.* The New Testament never likens him to that. The shedding of Christ's *blood* is not a sacrifice of expiation but, in the biblical sense, a *peace offering.*

18. Jesus was a Jew, but neither a Zealot nor an Essene. His parables are drawn from ordinary Jewish life, his theological arguments are rooted in the Old Testament, and his political interests are minimal.

19. We know very little about his actual *life:* He was baptized by John the Baptist, began his ministry in Galilee, and focused all his preaching and teaching on the Kingdom of God. He had a well-deserved reputation as an exorcist and healer, gathered a group of disciples around him, without regard for gender, status, or background, and celebrated their unity through the sharing of meals. Opposition to him from within Judaism reached a

457

climax during a Passover celebration in Jerusalem, when he was arrested, tried, and crucified.

20. His *message* centered on the *Kingdom of God*. He announced it as something that has "come near" (Mark 1:15).

21. Jesus' message was communicated principally through *parables, proverbial sayings, the Lord's Prayer, table fellowship,* and *miracles*.

22. There is a continuous Christological development *within* the New Testament: from preexistence Christology to Second-Coming Christology. The one who proclaimed the Kingdom in his lifetime is himself proclaimed after his resurrection.

SUGGESTED READINGS

Brown, Raymond. *The Virginal Conception and Bodily Resurrection of Jesus.* New York: Paulist Press, 1973.

_____. " 'Who Do Men Say That I Am?'—Modern Scholarship on Gospel Christology." *Horizons.* Vol. 1 (1974), pp. 35–50.

_____. *The Death of the Messiah: A Commentary on the Passion Narratives in the Four Gospels.* 2 vols. New York: Doubleday, 1994.

Fiorenza, Elisabeth Schüssler. *In Memory of Her: A Feminist Theological Reconstruction of Christian Origins.* New York: Crossroad, 1983.

_____. *But She Said: Feminist Practices of Biblical Interpretation.* Boston: Beacon Press, 1992.

Fitzmyer, Joseph A. *Scripture and Christology: A Statement of the Biblical Commission with a Commentary.* New York: Paulist Press, 1986.

_____. *A Christological Catechism: New Testament Answers.* New York: Paulist Press, 1991.

Frei, Hans. *Scriptural Authority and Narrative Interpretation.* Philadelphia: Fortress Press, 1987.

Fuller, Reginald. *The Foundations of New Testament Christology.* New York: Scribners, 1965.

Fuller, Reginald, and Pheme Perkins. *Who Is This Christ? Gospel Christology and Contemporary Faith.* Philadelphia: Fortress Press, 1983.

Krieg, Robert A. *Story-Shaped Christology: The Role of Narratives in Identifying Jesus Christ.* New York: Paulist Press, 1988.

Lane, Dermot A. *The Reality of Jesus: An Essay in Christology.* New York: Paulist Press, 1975.

_____. *Christ at the Centre: Selected Issues in Christology.* New York: Paulist Press, 1991.

Meier, John. *A Marginal Jew: Rethinking the Historical Jesus.* New York: Doubleday, 1991.

_____. "Jesus," in *The New Jerome Biblical Commentary*. Raymond E. Brown, Joseph A. Fitzmyer, and Roland E. Murphy, eds. Englewood Cliffs, N.J.: Prentice Hall, 1990, pp. 1316–28.

O'Collins, Gerald. *Jesus Risen*. New York: Paulist Press, 1987.

_____. *Interpreting Jesus*. New York: Paulist Press, 1983.

_____. *Interpreting the Resurrection: Examining the Major Problems in the Stories of Jesus' Resurrection*. New York: Paulist Press, 1988.

Perkins, Pheme. *Resurrection: New Testament Witness and Contemporary Reflection*. Garden City, N.Y.: Doubleday, 1984.

Perrin, Norman. *The New Testament: An Introduction*. New York: Harcourt Brace Jovanovich, 1974.

Schillebeeckx, Edward. *Jesus: An Experiment in Christology*. New York: Seabury Press, 1979.

_____. *Christ: The Experience of Jesus as Lord*. New York: Seabury Press, 1980.

Senior, Donald. *Jesus: A Gospel Portrait*. Rev. ed. New York: Paulist Press, 1992.

Vawter, Bruce. *This Man Jesus: An Essay Toward a New Testament Christology*. New York: Doubleday, 1973.

TWENTIETH-CENTURY VIEWS OF THE CHRISTOLOGY OF THE NEW TESTAMENT
(from *Horizons*, vol. 1, 1974, p. 38)

VIEWS WITHIN THE DOMAIN OF SCHOLARSHIP

Nonscholarly Liberalism	*Scholarly Liberalism*	*Bultmannian Existentialism*	*Scholarly Conservatism*	*Nonscholarly Conservatism*
This view regards the Christological question as unimportant, for Christianity is primarily concerned with how one should live. Jesus came to teach a way of life centered on love. It was his followers who first gave any importance to evaluating him.	(Early 1900s) Liberal scholars developed a scientific methodology for detecting precise states of growth in NT Christology. They judged this growth to be a creation, distorting the historical Jesus. Christology was once necessary in order to preserve the memory of Jesus, but now modern scholarship can give us the historical Jesus without Christology, which should be dispensed with.	(1920s through the 1950s) A reaction to liberalism. He further refined scientific methodology, but rejected the liberal judgment on the invalidation of Christology. Bultmann is indefinite and even agnostic on how Jesus evaluated himself. But the NT Christology is functionally equivalent to Jesus' message about the Kingdom, since both are a demand to accept what God has done through Jesus. Christology cannot be dispensed with.	(1960s and 1970s) Most scholars today are less agnostic than Bultmann about the historical Jesus and admit a continuity between the evaluation of Jesus during the ministry and the evaluation of him in the NT. Yet they continue to use with refinement the methodology for detecting growth in NT Christology. The dominating motif is development in continuity. A division exists as to whether to posit an explicit Christology in the ministry of Jesus (he used or accepted some titles: Son of Man, Suffering Servant, Messiah) or an implicit Christology (Jesus did not use or accept Christological titles).	A failure to allow any development from the ministry to the NT. This theory posits that Jesus was Christologically evaluated during his ministry exactly as he is portrayed in the Gospels (which are literal accounts of the ministry).
Liberalism was popular in the Protestantism of the late 1800s and early 1900s. It has revived today in Catholicism as a reaction to the dogmatic strictness of the past.	Exemplified in W. Bousset's *Kyrios Christus* (1913).		Implicit Christology ... Explicit Christology	A view held defensively by fundamentalist Protestants. Also held by Catholics until Church changes in the approach to the Bible began to affect Gospel study in the 1960s.
			Scholars such as Hahn, Fuller, Perrin; some post-Bultmannians; many Catholics of the 1970s. ... Scholars such as Cullmann, Jeremias, Dodd, Taylor; most Catholics of the 1960s.	

XIII

The Christ of Postbiblical Theology and Doctrine

THE QUESTION

Jesus is at the center of Christian faith. But not just the carpenter's son, Jesus of Nazareth; Christians confess that Jesus is the Christ, the Promised One of God, the risen Lord. An understanding of Jesus Christ, therefore, implies and/or presupposes some understanding of a triune God who is fully engaged in our history, indeed of a God who became one of us in order that the whole world, first created through the Word, might be restored fully through the same Word-made-flesh and the Holy Spirit. That is why the chapters on the triune God (chapters 8 and 9) preceded this one.

An understanding of Jesus Christ also implies and/or presupposes some understanding of what it means to be human, for we are a new creation in Christ, called to "maturity, to the measure of the full stature of Christ" (Ephesians 4:13). That is why the chapters on human existence (chapters 4 and 5) also preceded this one.

Christians believe that Jesus Christ has a unique role in our salvation because he is at the same time divine and human. If he were not at once human and divine, how could he have redeemed us? But if he *is* at once human and divine, how is that union to be understood? We inquire into the nature(s) and person of Jesus Christ because who he is *in himself* is the foundation of what he is *for us,* just as the God "who is" is God "for us."

A HISTORICAL AND THEOLOGICAL OVERVIEW

Development in the Church's understanding of faith occurred for various reasons: (1) the naturally inquisitive and probing impulse of the human mind; (2) the challenge of dissident opinions; and (3) the need to communicate the Christian message across cultural lines. Each of these factors was already at work even in the New Testament period. Christological development occurred as the early Church made contact with the wider Hellenistic world around it, and as the heresy of Gnosticism tested the limits of Christian orthodoxy. There was an acceleration of Christological development after the New Testament period as the Church extended its missionary outreach, and as the need increased to translate, clarify, and refine the inherited Jewish categories found in Sacred Scripture.

From the earliest stage of this theological development, the concept of Word, *Logos,* was at the center. For the *Jews,* the Word had been present and operative at creation (Genesis 1), in the utterances of the prophets, and in the Wisdom literature. For the *Greeks,* the Word was identified with reason and with the Truth of the philosophers. If for the Jews the Word was a form of God's presence in *history,* for the Greeks it was an all-pervasive principle of rationality within the *universe.* Christianity united and transformed these two understandings of the Word, as is evident in the Prologue of John's Gospel (1:1–18). By the second century the *Apologists* made the connection even more explicit. Jesus is the key to both history and the universe. The Christ-event is one of unlimited significance because through it the Word itself became flesh.

But exaggerations of the divinity or of the humanity of Jesus soon appeared within the Church itself. For the *Docetists* (from the Greek verb, *dokein,* "to seem, to appear"), the body of Jesus only appeared to be real, and for the *Gnostics* it was at best incidental to our salvation. Over against these views, Ignatius of Antioch insisted that if Jesus was not fully human like us, then he could not have saved us. At the other extreme there were approaches which undermined the divinity in favor of the humanity of Jesus—e.g., the *Adoptionism* of the

Ebionites, a Jewish-Christian sect. Such early Christian pastoral leaders as Irenæus argued that if Jesus is not "of God," then he could not have saved us. Note, again, that it is concern for our *salvation* which inspires these earliest rebuttals of Christological deviation.

Others attempted mediating positions—Tertullian, Origen, Paul of Samasota, Arius—but these proved unsatisfactory because they tended, in divergent ways to be sure, to make of Jesus something more than human but less than God. The Word is of one substance with the Father, but not of the same nature. Or the Word is within God, but lower in rank than the Father. Or the Word is a semidivine creature. Such views fall under, or at least come close to, the general category of *Subordinationism*. It was at the Council of Nicea in 325 that Subordinationism of every kind was rejected. Jesus Christ is "true God of true God... begotten, not made."

In the aftermath of Nicea two major theological schools emerged: one in Alexandria, Egypt, and the other in Antioch, Syria. The *Alexandrian school* was interested principally in preserving the *divinity* of Jesus and focused on the *unity* of the humanity with the Word, while the *Antiochene school* was concerned principally with his *humanity* and so adopted a looser approach to the unity of the human and the divine. Thus, standard histories of Christology refer to the Alexandrian approach as *Logos-sarx* (literally, "Word-flesh"), and the Antiochene as *Logos-anthropos* (literally, "Word–human being"). The former stresses that *the Word* took on flesh; the latter, that the Word became *a human being*.

As this theological and doctrinal history was to unfold, each school of thought would generate extremes. From the Alexandrian school there would be those like Apollinaris (d. 390) who would insist so strongly on the divinity of Jesus, i.e., on the unity of the humanity with the Word, that they would deny him a human soul. And from the Antiochene school there would be those like Nestorius (d. c. 451) who would insist so strongly on the humanity of Jesus, regarding it as a separate and distinct personal entity, that they would deny that Mary was truly the Mother of God.

If one is to make any sense of the otherwise complicated and often confusing history of the controversies and the councils, one has to keep the tensions between these two schools always in mind. The mystery of Jesus Christ has to do with the way in which divinity and

463

humanity come together in one and the same person. Stress the divinity too much, and you run the risk of supplanting his humanity. Stress the humanity too much, and you run the risk of denying his divinity. In either case, not only is orthodoxy lost, but our salvation in Christ as well.

That orthodoxy was first articulated and defended, not without ambiguity, by the Council of Nicea (325), which rejected every solution which made Jesus Christ anything less than divine. Next came the First Council of Constantinople (381), which condemned Apollinaris and, therefore, struck a doctrinal blow for Jesus' humanity. After that, the Council of Ephesus (431), which condemned Nestorius and reinforced the Church's conviction that the one person, Jesus, is "true God of true God" and that Mary, his mother, is not only the mother of Christ but the Mother of God as well (*Theotokos*). There followed the Council of Chalcedon (451), which balanced Nicea's "of one substance with the Father" with its own formula, "of one substance [being] with us as to the humanity, like unto us in all things but sin," thereby achieving some measure of synthesis between the Alexandrian and Antiochene schools. Still another doctrinal statement was provided by the Second Council of Constantinople (553), which to a great extent repeated the definition of Chalcedon, reiterating its condemnation of Nestorianism. Finally, there was the Third Council of Constantinople (680–681), which in fidelity to Chalcedon condemned *Monothelitism* (the view that in Jesus there is only *one will*, the *divine* will). (For a synoptic view of the evolution of Christological doctrine, see the chart on p. 489.)

Since Constantinople III there has been no significant *doctrinal* development to this very day. What we have had are some refinements of concepts and terminology in the Scholastic period, but without the same concern for soteriology as the New Testament, the early Christian writers, and the councils of the Church had. At the risk of oversimplifying, one might suggest that the medieval theologians were more interested in Jesus Christ as he is *in himself* (e.g., his consciousness, his knowledge, his freedom, his sinlessness, the mode of the divine-human union) than as he is *for us*, as our Savior. This same heavily speculative, not to say abstract, approach to Christology has governed the production of post-Tridentine, pre–Vatican II seminary textbooks and catechisms, and accounts in part for neoscholastic Christology's general lack of pastoral usefulness for preaching, religious education, social ministry, and spirituality.

For all practical purposes, it was not until the occasion of the fifteen-hundredth anniversary of the Council of Chalcedon that Catholic theologians, in any concerted way, took a fresh look at their own doctrinal tradition. Not surprisingly, it was Karl Rahner who led the way with a highly influential article, "Chalcedon—End or Beginning?" (which appears in a still-untranslated work, *Das Konzil von Chalkedon*, 3 vols., A. Grillmeier and H. Bacht, eds. Würzburg, 1954). Rahner argued that every conciliar definition is *both* an end and a beginning: an *end* of one phase of a discussion and the settling of certain points of controversy, but the *beginning* of a whole new phase of questioning, leading to deeper insights. Doctrinal formulations must constantly be rethought, not because they are false or radically imperfect, but precisely because they are true and, as such, can yield further truth and shed new light on other, related matters. Indeed, doctrinal pronouncements remain alive only insofar as they are continually elucidated. Consistent with his own theological starting point (i.e., the human person as radically open to the offer of God's grace), Rahner developed an understanding of the incarnation as the unique and supreme instance of the essential completion of human reality. Anthropology is fulfilled in Christology.

EARLY CHRISTIAN PERIOD

Before Nicea

The *earliest Christological heresies* came from opposite extremes: *Docetism* and *Gnosticism* on the right (denying the humanity of Jesus for the sake of the divinity) and *Adoptionism* on the left (denying the divinity of Jesus for the sake of his humanity). Neither extreme, perhaps because they were so obviously extremes, required any kind of official condemnation such as a general council of the Church might render. Certain of the early theologians and pastoral leaders were quick to identify the fundamental errors in these positions, and especially their implications for our salvation.

"There is only one physician," Ignatius of Antioch wrote in his *Letter to the Ephesians*, "both carnal and spiritual, born and unborn.

God became man, true life in death; sprung both from Mary and from God, first subject to suffering and then incapable of it—Jesus Christ our Lord" (n. 7). Ignatius hereby testifies to both the divinity and the humanity of Jesus united in a single person. Against the Docetists and Gnostics, he insists that Jesus is the son of Mary and is subject to suffering.

Later in the same epistle (nn. 18–19) Ignatius speaks of Jesus as the epiphany or manifestation of God. Jesus' purpose is "to mold the 'newness' (Romans 6:4) of eternal life." He is the Word who breaks God's silence in order to destroy death and bring new life. To accomplish this he was "really born and ate and drank, really persecuted by Pontius Pilate, really crucified and died... really rose from the dead" (*Letter to the Trallians*, nn. 9–11). If, however, all of this was "make-believe," then his saving work on our behalf is all for naught, and the Eucharist that we celebrate together is of no account (*Letter to the Smyrnæans*, n. 7).

The Word, or *Logos*, concept is also central for *Justin* as he tries to show the connection between the Greek philosophers' pursuit of Truth and our common human quest for the fullness of life and for salvation. "The Christ who has appeared for us represents the *Logos* principle in its totality, that is both body and *Logos* and soul" (*Second Apology*, nn. 10,13). Only in him is the Word fully present. And yet that particular expression or embodiment of the Word is available in principle to all and for all, just as the Word already contains whatever truth is to be found apart from the particularity of the Christ-event and of Christian faith: "The truths which people in all lands have rightly spoken belong to us Christians.... Indeed, all writers, by means of the engrafted seed of the Word which was implanted in them, had a glimpse of the truth." The same approach is developed several decades later by Clement of Alexandria.

An early indication of what Scholastic theology calls the *communicatio idiomatum* is provided by Bishop Melito of Sardis (d. c. 190), who testifies not only to the divinity and humanity of Jesus but also to their *mutuality:* "He who suspended the earth is suspended; he who fixes the heavens in place is himself fixed in place; he who fastened all things is fastened to the wood;... God is murdered..." (*Homily on the Pasch*).

Since the "communication of the idioms" (the mutual predication of properties) is a matter of some importance in interpreting the later history of Christology, it might be appropriate to explain it now, where it first appears. Because there is only one divine Person, Jesus Christ, who acts through two natures, one divine and one human, we may legitimately predicate, or affirm, of this one person attributes which are both human (e.g., the ability to suffer) and divine (e.g., unlimited knowledge). But even beyond that, one can also predicate of his humanity what is his by virtue of the divinity, and vice versa. Thus by the "communication of idioms," one can say that "Mary's son is all-knowing" or that "God was born of Mary." Rejection of the personal unity of Jesus led Nestorius, for example, to reject the "communication of idioms" with reference to Jesus' birth and the motherhood of Mary. The Council of Ephesus would insist that Mary is the Mother of God, and precisely on the theological principle that she gave birth not to a nature alone but to a person, a *divine* Person. As a consequence of the union by which divinity and humanity are united in one Person, we can predicate of the one Person what is rooted in either nature.

The great third-century theologian Irenæus carried forward the defense of Christological faith against the extremists. The balanced quality of his position is striking. Jesus was human and truly suffered, but he was also "our only true master... the Word of God." More to the point: "Had he not as a human being overcome our adversary, the enemy would not have been justly overcome. Again, had it not been God who bestowed salvation, we should not have it as a secure possession. And if we had not been united to God, we could not have become partakers of immortality. For the mediator between God and humankind had to bring both parties into friendship and concord through his kinship with both; both to present humankind to God, and make God known to humankind" (*Against Heresies* 3.18.6,7). Jesus Christ, therefore, *recapitulates* everything in himself, restoring all reality to fellowship and communion with God.

Irenæus is well in advance of the formulation of a classic Christological principle, one to be fashioned and refined by Athanasius and Gregory of Nazianzus—namely, "What is not taken up [by the Word] is not healed; but what is united with God is also saved."

467

Subsequent efforts at preserving orthodoxy while opening new lines of communication with contemporary non-Christian philosophy led inevitably to some Christological ambiguity. If Jesus Christ was to be believable as the fullness of truth, then his identification with the world of ordinary intellectual experience had to be secure. Accordingly, such theologians as Origen, Tertullian, and Paul of Samasota struggled to find new formulations of the relationship between Jesus and God the Father, concerned as they were both about the intellectual skepticism of their colleagues outside the Church and about the Gnostic and Docetic tendencies of many of their brothers and sisters within the Church. And they were concerned as well with reconciling their faith in one God with their confession of Jesus as Lord. Accordingly, their language at times suggested a *Subordinationist* orientation, i.e., one that made the Son of God less than, or "subordinate to," the Father.

Thus, Origen's *First Principles* speaks of the necessity for some "intermediate instrument" between God and flesh to make their union possible. And there is at least a hint of Nestorianism (the positing of two separate persons in Christ) in his *Commentary on John*, where he distinguishes perhaps too sharply between Christ as the Word and Christ as human, a distinction that is not overcome, according to Origen, until after the exaltation. So "spiritual" is Origen's approach that much of his Christology is open to misinterpretation. This will explain why the official Church reached back beyond Origen to Irenæus to find theological grounding for its teachings on the unity of God and humanity in Jesus Christ.

Tertullian, on the other hand, anticipated by more than two centuries the Christological formulation of the Council of Chalcedon. In his *Against Praxeas* (n. 27) he insists that Jesus, who is truly God and truly human, is at the same time a single subject: "Jesus is one person, God and man." Such union does violence to neither the divinity nor to the humanity: "Flesh does not become spirit nor spirit flesh...." Unfortunately, Tertullian's understanding of the redemptive significance of the incarnation is not so penetrating or balanced. True to his Roman legalistic spirit, he focuses entirely on the cross as the price of our salvation. Jesus came into this world, taking on our humanity, for one purpose only: to suffer the death of the cross. There is no corresponding emphasis on the rest of Jesus' human life, nor on the significance of the Word's taking on our flesh. Jesus stands as our representative, therefore, in a juridical sense alone. It was this legalistic approach that would influence much of Western theology for centuries thereafter.

Paul of Samasota, perhaps in reaction to Origen's tendency to shake Jesus loose from his human roots, seems to have professed some kind of adoptionist Christology. The Father dwells in the human being Jesus, thereby making of him his son. Paul of Samasota's view was condemned by the Synod of Antioch, which declared in 268 that "the divine Word is in [Jesus] what the interior man is in us." But did the synod also mean that Jesus did not have a *human* soul? Precisely that implication would be drawn within the century, and it would create a storm of theological controversy and political conflict.

The Council of Nicea (325)

It was Arius who carried these *Subordinationist* tendencies to their extreme. The Son is a creature, created in time by the Father and then used by the Father in the creation of the world. Thus, Christ was neither God nor a human being. Rather, he was less than God but more than a human being. He was a kind of composite intermediary being, but not the mediator spoken of by Irenæus and others.

Against the Arian view, the Council of Nicea solemnly proclaimed the oneness in being ("consubstantiality") of the Son with the Father. He is "God from God, Light from Light, true God from true God, begotten, not made, one in being (*homoousios*) with the Father.... For us men and for our salvation He came down and became flesh, was made man, suffered, and rose again on the third day."

The First Council of Constantinople
(381)

Its ambiguities still unresolved, the controversy generated by Paul of Samasota and by the Synod of Antioch's response to him surfaced again around 360, almost a century later. Apollinaris of Laodicea, a faithful supporter of Athanasius and a strong defender of the Council of Nicea, made the *denial of the human soul* in Jesus the very heart of his

469

Christology. For Apollinaris the Word is the unique principle of the flesh of Jesus. If Christ also had a human soul, or mind, then the Word would have been *in* a man, as Paul of Samasota seemed to be saying, but the Word itself would not have been made flesh. "How can God become a human being without ceasing to be God except by taking the place of the mind in a human being?" Apollinaris asked.

As a reaction against perduring adoptionist tendencies in the Church, the position of Apollinaris was understandable. But it failed to safeguard the transcendence of the Word and the integrity of Jesus' human nature. And in failing to safeguard the latter in particular, it undermined the effect of Christ's saving activity on our behalf. Accordingly, the position had to be condemned, as it was, by the First Council of Constantinople in 381 and again the next year at a Council of Rome convened by Pope Damasus I (d. 384). The "heresy" of the Apollinarists was censured by name in Canon I of the former council's declarations, and in Canon VII of the latter's, the text of which follows: "We condemn those who say that the Word of God dwelling in human flesh took the place of the rational and spiritual soul, since the Son and the Word of God did not replace the rational and spiritual soul in His body but rather assumed our soul (i.e., a rational and spiritual one) without sin and saved it."

The Council of Ephesus (431)

The controversy which had broken out in Antioch around the year 360 saw the emergence of two distinct and opposed parties. The debate between them was of major moment because it would set the stage for, and shape the terms of, the landmark Christological definitions of both Ephesus and Chalcedon.

On the one side, there were those who regarded the unity of the Word and the human in Christ rather loosely and who were intent upon defending his full humanity. This was the *Antiochene* school, and *Nestorianism* was its extreme expression. On the other side, there were those who tended to exaggerate the unity of Christ to the point where, as in Apollinaris, the human soul was entirely supplanted. They were intent upon defending Christ's divinity. This was the *Alexandrian* school, and *Monophysitism* was its extreme expression.

470

Two of Apollinaris's opponents, Diodore of Tarsus (d. c. 394) and Theodore of Mopsuestia (d. 428), launched their own counter-protest and proclaimed the complete fullness of the humanity of Jesus. But the aggressiveness of their disciple Nestorius (d. 451) provoked resistance from Cyril of Alexandria (d. 444), who, in turn, allowed himself to use Apollinarian expressions. The Council of Ephesus condemned Nestorius.

More specifically: Diodore of Tarsus, like almost every exponent of a heterodox or even heretical point of view, was not intent upon *denying* some aspect of Christological truth. He was concerned rather with *preserving* something which he feared to be in danger of denial from the other side, namely, the transcendence of the Word. Diodore, therefore, did not deliberately set out to divide the human Jesus from the divine Word, but that was the effect of his position that the human being Jesus was son of Mary in the flesh and of God *by grace*, whereas the Word is the Son of God (not of Mary) *by nature*: "The man born of Mary is son by grace; God the Word is Son by nature" (Syriac Fragments 31–32; cited in Carmody and Clarke, *Word and Redeemer*, p. 83).

Theodore, bishop of Mopsuestia, joined forces against the *Logos-sarx*, or Word-flesh, approach of the Alexandrians, namely, the view which emphasizes the drawing of all that is of the flesh into the Word (as against the Antiochene *Logos-anthropos*, or Word–human being, approach which emphasizes the Word's becoming human). It was important for Theodore, and for others of the *Logos-anthropos* school, that Jesus be an agent and model of our liberation from sin and death, and he could be such only to the extent that he was truly one of us and with us. "Therefore it was necessary," Theodore wrote in his *Catechetical Homilies*, "that he should assume not only the body but also the immortal and rational soul; and not only the death of the body... but also that of the soul, which is sin" (n. 5). And so the human being Jesus, body and soul, ascended into heaven beyond Satan's reach. We, too, ascend beyond Satan's power insofar as we participate in the death and resurrection of Jesus. Mary, therefore, *is* the Mother of God, but Theodore seemed to understand the title in a weakened sense, as Diodore had before him. The human being born of Mary is not identically God, but only has God (the Word) dwelling in him.

471

Nestorius, patriarch of Constantinople (until deposed by the Council of Ephesus in 431), carried these views to their extreme. He fully represented the Antiochene insistence on the *Logos-anthropos*, or Word–human being, approach. The Word really and truly *became human*. Accordingly, such expressions as "God has suffered" or "God was nursed at his mother's breast" were offensive to him. They smacked of Arianism and of Apollinarianism, both of which in their own way rejected the full incarnation, or becoming flesh, of the Word.

For Nestorius there are two natures in Christ, one divine and the other human, and each has its own *personal* manifestation. These, in turn, form a third "person of union." The Nestorian position demands, of course, a special understanding of the motherhood of Mary: "If anyone wishes to use this word *theotokos* [literally, "mother of God"] with reference to the humanity which was born, joined to God the Word, and not with reference to the parent, we say that this word is not appropriate for her who gave birth, since a true mother should be of the same essence as what is born of her.... None gives birth to one older than herself" (*Letter to Pope Celestine*, n. 2).

Cyril, bishop of Alexandria, brought the *Logos-sarx*, or Word-flesh, Christology to its peak in this controversy, as Nestorius had brought the opposite *Logos-anthropos*, or Word–human being, Christology to its own logical heights. As a bishop (and most of the participants were pastoral officeholders, not academicians), Cyril was principally concerned with the effects of the debate on our understanding of salvation and, more immediately, of the Eucharist. If the divine and the human are not really and fully united in Jesus Christ but are, as Nestorius would have it, separate and divided, then the flesh of the Word could not be the life-giving instrument of our own divinization—neither in salvation history nor in Holy Communion. In an almost classic expression of the Alexandrian *Logos-sarx* approach, Cyril writes that "the flesh does not bring the Word down to its own level; for divinity can in no wise be diminished. Of itself the flesh is incapable of imparting life..." (*Commentary on John*, n. 4).

Cyril was to address three letters to Nestorius, the *second* of which (written in 430) the Council of Ephesus formally accepted as a statement of orthodox faith. Therein, Cyril explicitly disavowed any Apollinarian interpretation of his position. The Word truly became flesh through a real hypostatic union. The Word *is* truly human, and not merely *in* a human being. Therefore, Mary can be called the Mother of God, and not the Mother of Christ, because "it was not an ordinary man who was first born of the holy virgin, and upon whom afterwards the Word descended, but he himself, united to humanity from the womb, who is said to have undergone fleshly birth, as making his own the birth of his own flesh." Thus, we worship "one Christ and Lord," and not a "human being along with the Word." What was born of Mary was "his rationally animated body to which the Word was hypostatically united."

The Council of Ephesus, convened by the emperor Theodosius II (d. 450), was formally opened by Cyril on June 22, 431, before the arrival of the delegates from Rome, representing Pope Celestine (d. 432). Cyril's second letter to Nestorius was approved by the council Fathers. Nestorius's views were condemned, and Nestorius was deposed as patriarch of Constantinople. When the Roman delegation finally arrived, they ratified in the name of the pope what had already been decided and done.

Neither the council nor the pope's representatives, however, officially accepted the so-called twelve anathematizations, or condemnations, contained in Cyril's *third* letter to Nestorius. Nonetheless, the document was read to the council, and it created a great measure of dissatisfaction among the Eastern bishops, i.e., those close to the Antiochene school of thought. Some of Cyril's language, as we noted earlier, was at least suggestive of an Apollinarian approach, particularly his characterization of the union of the divine and the union in Christ as a "physical" one (third anathema). The council ended with the mutual excommunication of the two great patriarchs of the East, John of Antioch and Cyril of Alexandria.

At the invitation of the emperor Theodosius II, John of Antioch (d. 441) provided a profession of faith to which Cyril was able to subscribe in 433. It expressed better than Cyril had the reality of Christ's distinct human nature, and the distinction between the two natures united in one person. Pope Sixtus III (d. 440) congratulated both parties and by implication accepted the so-called *Formula of Union* (also known as the "Symbol of Union" and the "Edict of Union") between Cyril and the bishops of Antioch. It was chiefly through this formula that the Antiochene school made its contribution to the subsequent development of the Christological dogma at Chalcedon.

Because this formula is so important a bridge between Ephesus and Chalcedon, a relatively generous excerpt is reproduced here.

> We confess therefore our Lord Jesus Christ, the only begotten Son of God, perfect God and perfect human being composed of rational soul and body, begotten before all ages from the Father as to his divinity, and the same in the last days born of the Virgin Mary as to his humanity for us and for our salvation, consubstantial with the Father in divinity and consubstantial with us in humanity. For a union of two natures has taken place; hence we confess one Christ, one Son, one Lord. In accordance with this union without confusion, we profess the holy Virgin to be Mother of God (*theotokos*), for God the Word became flesh and was made human and from the moment of conception united to himself the temple he had taken from her.
>
> As for the words of the gospels and of the apostles concerning the Lord, we know that theologians have considered some as common because they are said of the one person (*prosopon*), while they have distinguished others as applying to the two natures (*physeis*), reserving those which befit God to Christ in his divinity while assigning those which are lowly to Christ in his humanity.

The Council of Chalcedon (451)

The "Formula of Union," however well-intentioned and well-conceived, did not hold the parties permanently together. Cyril's successor as bishop of Alexandria, Dioscorus (d. 454), would interpret some of Cyril's ambiguous formulations too literally. In the heat of struggle against Nestorianism, he tended to understand the hypostatic union as something achieved at the level of nature (*physis*) rather than of person. Thus, the divine and the human come together in Christ in *one divine nature* (Monophysitism). Eutyches (d. c. 454), the aged head of a monastery in Constantinople, carried the position to an even greater extreme, denying that Christ was consubstantial with us. Christ's human nature was completely absorbed by the divine nature.

Eutyches was brought to trial and condemned at a synod in Constantinople in 448. Although temporarily rehabilitated by Dioscorus, Eutyches was also subsequently condemned by Pope Leo the Great (d. 461), to whom he had appealed. In a letter (the *Tome of Leo*) addressed in June 449 to Flavian (d. 449), patriarch of Constantinople, the pope gave the clearest expression to date of the doctrine of the incarnation. In Christ there are two distinct natures united in one person: "The same one who is a genuine human being is also genuinely God, and in this unity there is no deception as long as both lowliness and divine loftiness have their reciprocal spheres.... Each 'form' carries on its proper activities in communion with the other. The Word does what belongs to it, and the flesh carries out what belongs to it" (Norris translation, pp. 149, 150).

With his Augustinian stress on Christ as Mediator and on the saving power of the miracles and mysteries of the life of Christ, the pope clearly linked Christology with soteriology. Because of the union of the divine and human natures in the one divine person, all of the activities of the human Jesus are rooted in, and spring from, the one divine person and are, therefore, of infinitely salvific value. And yet they also remain fully human actions and fully representative of the whole human community, for the Lord was "born in the integral and complete nature of a true human being, entire in what belongs to him and entire in what belongs to us" (Norris, p. 148).

But Pope Leo's letter did not settle the matter once and for all, at least not so far as Dioscorus and Eutyches were concerned. They exercised their considerable local influence and succeeded in having a synod convened at Ephesus in August of 449 at which, under very strong political pressure, the bishops approved Eutyches' doctrine and deposed two of his episcopal opponents. Pope Leo labeled the synod a "robbery" (*latrocinium*), and it is still known today as the "robber synod" of Ephesus. Its proceedings were condemned by a Roman synod which met the very next month. It also asked that the emperor, Theodosius II, convoke a general council in Italy. He refused. It was left to his successor, Marcion (d. 457), to summon the Council of Chalcedon in October 451. With nearly six hundred bishops, including three papal legates and two representatives of Latin Africa, this was by far the largest and most important council of the early Church.

At the first sessions the legality of the "robber synod" of Ephesus was examined and found wanting. Eutyches' doctrine was once again rejected, and Dioscorus was condemned for his part in the synod and for his complicity in bringing such unwarranted pressure to bear on the bishops. But the bishops at Chalcedon were not initially interested in drafting yet another confession of faith. They were satisfied with the formulations of Nicea (325), Constantinople (381), and the *Tome of Leo* (449). The emperor's representatives, however, insisted on something more, and they prevailed. A commission of bishops drafted a schema, but it was so ambiguous about the union of natures in Christ that the papal legates rejected it and threatened to move the council back to Italy. The emperor's delegates sided with the pope's and ordered the bishops to face up to the issue. They would have to choose between Dioscorus and Pope Leo.

A new commission, whose members now also included the Roman delegates and the emperor's, composed a profession of faith which the council accepted. Borrowing freely from Cyril of Alexandria's second letter to Nestorius, the "Formula of Union," and the *Tome of Leo* (the reading of which had elicited cries of "Peter has spoken through the mouth of Leo"), the Chalcedonian symbol of faith repudiated *both* Nestorianism and Monophysitism.

The *Alexandrian* school had clearly triumphed in the central formula, "one and the same Lord Jesus Christ." It is the "one and the same Lord Jesus Christ" who appears and lives in the man Jesus of Nazareth. The *Arians* were once again repudiated for having seen in the incarnation the "proof" that the Son is not truly God; and so, too, were the *Nestorians,* who sacrificed the unity of Jesus Christ in order to "save" the complete humanity.

The *Antiochene* school also triumphed in the formula "the same truly God and truly man composed of rational soul and body... like unto us in all things but sin...." The Antiochenes had fought for these principles against the old *Docetism* and also against certain tendencies in the disciples of *Origen*. Jesus of Nazareth was truly one of us and of our human family, but through the hypostatic union he is, at the same time, the source of our redemption and sanctification.

The older Christologies of Irenæus and Tertullian were also represented in the Chalcedonian definitions. It was Irenæus who provided the formula "one and the same" and who insisted that "had it not been God who bestowed salvation, we should not have it as a secure possession. And if we had not been united to God, we could

476

not have become partakers of immortality." And it was Tertullian's formula, one person in two natures, which the council took over and made its own, although without any detailed elaboration. The "person" is the "who" of the union, namely, the eternal Son of God. The "natures" are the "what" of the union. Accordingly, Jesus Christ is consubstantial with the Father and also substantially one with us.

The definition follows:

> Following, therefore, the holy fathers, we confess one and the same Son, who is our Lord Jesus Christ, and we all agree in teaching that this very same Son is complete in his deity and complete—the very same—in his humanity, truly God and truly a human being, the very same one being composed of a rational soul and a body, coessential (*homoousios*) with the Father as to his deity and coessential with us—the very same one—as to his humanity, being like us in every respect apart from sin [cf. Hebrews 4:15]. As to his deity, he was born from the Father before all ages, but as to his humanity, the very same one was born in the last days from the Virgin Mary, the Mother of God, for our sake and the sake of our salvation: one and the same Christ, Son, Lord, Only Begotten, acknowledged to be unconfusedly, unalterably, undividedly, inseparably in two natures, since the difference of the natures is not destroyed because of the union, but on the contrary, the character of each nature is preserved and comes together in one person and one hypostasis, not divided or torn into two persons but one and the same Son and only begotten God, Logos, Lord Jesus Christ—just as in earlier times the prophets and also the Lord Jesus Christ himself taught us about him, and the symbol of our Fathers transmitted to us. (Norris translation, p. 159)

The Second Council of Constantinople (553)

The solemnity of the conciliar definition notwithstanding, some bishops in Syria and Egypt who were inclined to Monophysitism expressed concern that Chalcedon had contradicted Ephesus (the council that had condemned the opposite heresy of Nestorianism). In 519 some Monophysite monks sought from Pope Hormisdas (d. 523) approval of their own formula, "one of the three [Persons in the Trinity] has suffered in the flesh." They were not satisfied with the pope's response. Several years later the emperor Justinian (d. 565), himself sympathetic to the Monophysite cause, for political rather than theological reasons, asked Pope John II (d. 535) for papal approval of the formula. He gave it, more or less, in a letter to the Senate of Constantinople in 534, but he also reaffirmed the Church's rejection of *both* Nestorianism and Monophysitism.

The controversy continued. A so-called "neo-Chalcedonian" current developed, giving many the hope that somehow the Chalcedonian formula might be reconciled with Monophysitism. The current's supporters urged the condemnation of the first opponents of Monophysitism: Theodoret of Cyr (d. 466), Ibas of Edessa (d. 457), and Theodore of Mopsuestia (d. 428), Nestorius's teacher. All were accused of Nestorian tendencies, and their works were lumped together under the heading of *Three Chapters*. Again, the emperor Justinian, concerned about the politically divisive effects of these disputes, asked a pope, this time Vigilius (d. 555), to take a public stand against these three opponents of Monophysitism. At first the pope refused, insisting that the three were orthodox by Chalcedonian standards. Only after he had been taken by force to Constantinople in 548 did he issue the condemnation. The reaction in the West was severe. Relations between the emperor and the pope were broken off, and Vigilius published a strong anti-Monophysite profession of faith (552).

At Justinian's call the Second Council of Constantinople opened in May of 553, condemned the *Three Chapters*, adopted vehemently anti-Nestorian positions, and embraced the newly popular Monophysite formula, "One of the three has suffered in the flesh." The council never won acceptance in the West, nor did it achieve the union Justinian hoped for in the East. The pope did eventually approve it, but the doctrinal scope of that approval is not entirely clear. It seems to have been restricted to the three canons which were directly concerned with the *Three Chapters* of Theodoret, Ibas, and Theodore. To the extent that the council has any longer term doctrinal significance for Catholic faith, its importance may consist simply in its reaffirmation of the earlier condemnations of Nestorianism. Otherwise, it is not an exceptionally bright moment in the conciliar history of the Church.

The Third Council of Constantinople
(681)

By now Islam, a new and powerful threat to the unity of Christendom, had made its entrance upon the world scene. These internal theological divisions within the Church were a luxury it could afford now even less than before. A new emperor, Heraclius (d. 641), offered his support to Sergius (d. 638), patriarch of Constantinople, in the latter's attempts at some theological reconciliation. Unfortunately, Sergius only succeeded in producing yet another Christological deviation, this one called *Monothelitism* (one will), or *Monenergism* (one action).

In one of those interesting cases of history where a pope seems to have come down on the side of a heretical position, Pope Honorius (d. 638) agreed with Sergius that the expression *one will* could be used, but then Sergius carried it one step further: If one will, then one nature. And so he was back to Monophysitism. It was inevitable that Monothelitism and its companion, Monenergism, would be condemned. The first conciliar blow against Monothelitism was delivered at a nonecumenical Council of the Lateran (649), convoked by Pope Martin I (d. 655) and attended by 105 bishops from Italy and Africa.

The definitive thrust, however, came from the Third Council of Constantinople, convoked by the emperor Constantine IV (d. 685) with the consent of Pope Agatho (d. 681). The council accepted the doctrinal formulation which the pope had previously expressed in a letter to the emperor (March 680), and it condemned Monothelitism and all of its supporters, even chastising the deceased Pope Honorius for his unwitting approval of the heresy. One year later Pope Leo II (d. 683), Pope Agatho's successor, formally approved the council's proceedings.

A portion of the definition follows:

> Believing our lord Jesus Christ, even after his incarnation, to be one of the holy Trinity and our true God, we say that he has two natures shining forth in his one subsistence in which he demonstrated the miracles and the sufferings throughout his entire providential dwelling here, not in appearance but in truth, the difference of the natures being made known in the same one subsistence in that each nature wills and

479

performs the things that are proper to it in a communion with the other; then in accord with this reasoning we hold that two natural wills and principles of action meet in correspondence for the salvation of the human race. (Tanner edition, vol. I, pp. 129–30)

Subsequent Councils

Doctrinal development stopped at this point. To the extent that Christological dogma was touched upon by subsequent councils of the Church, it was always simply a matter of reiterating the teachings of one of these earlier councils—Nicea, Ephesus, and Chalcedon in particular. This is the case with the *Fourth Lateran Council* (1215) in its profession of faith; in the profession of faith given at the *Second Council of Lyons* (1274); in the *Decree for the Jacobites* at the *Council of Florence* (1442); in the *Decree on Justification* at the *Council of Trent* (1547); and in various papal encyclicals and decrees of Roman congregations in more recent years. As we shall see in Part Four, the Second Vatican Council focused its attention principally on the mystery of the Church, not on Christology. Vatican II's Christology, therefore, is to be inferred largely from its ecclesiology.

Synthesis

Against assorted Christological errors—especially Arianism, Nestorianism, and Monophysitism—the official teachings of the Church preserved an essential balance in its understanding of the mystery of Christ, at once God and a human being. The Word of God, who became human, suffered, died, and rose for our salvation, is truly God, of the same substance as the Father (*Nicea*). But he is also fully human, of one nature with us (*Constantinople I* and *Chalcedon*). In spite of the irreducible difference between his divine and his human natures, he is one and the same, the eternal Son of God, who as a human being is born of the Virgin Mary, the Mother of God (*Ephesus, Chalcedon,* and *Constantinople II*). Because he is a human being, he leads a truly human life in all things but sin: a life of truly human actions, of truly human freedom, of truly human consciousness (*Constantinople III*).

MEDIEVAL CHRISTOLOGY

Some Antecedents

Augustine

Augustine died in 430 and therefore had no direct role in any of the major Christological councils. And yet he remains, alongside Thomas Aquinas, as one of the most influential of all Christian theologians. For Augustine, Christ is the *Mediator* between God and humankind. He is the Word incarnate, a teacher of infinite knowledge and wisdom, who leads us to eternity through temporal realities. By identifying completely with our human condition, Jesus Christ shows us how to live and gives all of us hope for life without end. On the other hand, "we would not be redeemed by the one mediator between God and humankind, Jesus Christ himself human (1 Timothy 2:5), if he were not also God" (*Enchiridion*, n. 137). Christ, therefore, is the new head of the human race. We are predestined to glory through him, and we are joined to him even now as members of his Church.

Boethius

Boethius (d. 525) is the one generally credited with refining the meaning of the terms *person* and *nature* as they function in Christological discussion. It was his definition of *person* which carried over into medieval thought and which provided some verbal leverage for clarifying the preceding conciliar doctrines: "an individual substance of a rational nature." The definition was slightly modified by Thomas Aquinas (who spoke of an "incommunicable" substance as well) and especially by Richard of St. Victor (d. 1173), for whom person is "an incommunicable existence of an intellectual nature." Contemporary developments in the theology of the Trinity, reflected, for example, in Catherine Mowry LaCugna's *God for Us*, to which we referred in chapter 8, underscore not the "incommunicability" of the personhood, but its relational character. To be a person is to be in relation to others, to be oriented toward communion with others.

481

Anselm

Anselm of Canterbury's place in the history of Christology is insured by his distinctive *theory of satisfaction*. It is an understanding of redemption, however, which seems to distort rather than illuminate the meaning of Christ's mission, so far does it appear to be from the New Testament's theology of the cross and resurrection (see chapter 12).

According to Anselm's argument, as expressed in Book I of *Cur Deus Homo?* (Why Did God Become Man?), sin disturbed the order of the universe. Some compensation had to be offered to restore what had been disrupted. But we were simply not up to the task. The offense was against an infinite God, and we are finite. Only infinite satisfaction would do, and only God could provide it (chapter V of *Cur Deus Homo?*). But not just God. It had to be one who is at once God and a human being, a God-man. This answered the question: Why did God become a human being? But it did not answer the question: Why did Jesus have to die?

Anselm proposed that satisfaction required more than the incarnation. Jesus had to do something which he as a human being was not otherwise bound to do. Because he was sinless, he was not bound to die. But he endured death nonetheless as a voluntary payment of the debt incurred by our sins, and so he satisfies for those sins (chapters IX–XII).

Anselm's theory is to be understood against the background of the Germanic and early medieval feudal system. There is a bond of honor between feudal lord and vassal. Infringement of the lord's honor is tantamount to an assault upon the whole feudal system. A demand for satisfaction, therefore, is not for the sake of appeasing the lord's personal sense of honor but for the sake of restoring order to the "universe" (feudal system) in which, and therefore against which, the "sin" was committed. The feudal lord cannot simply overlook the offense, because the order of his whole economic and social world is at stake. So, too, with God (chapters XIII–XV).

Aquinas would later modify Anselm's theory, arguing that it was *fitting* for God to act in that way, but it was not *necessary*, as Anselm had insisted (*Summa Theologiæ*, III, q. 1, a. 2). Thus altered, Anselm's theory entered the wider stream of medieval and then postmedieval theology. It was never made an official teaching of the Church, however. Over the years, many Catholics have incorrectly assumed it to be a matter of doctrine, if not even of dogma. Through Calvin and Luther, Protestants, too, ingested the theory in its more severe form (Christ died as our *substitute,* in punishment for sin).

Thomas Aquinas

Aquinas followed in the tradition of Augustine in formulating his own answer to the question at hand: "Why did God become a human being?" The incarnation occurred because "it belongs to the essence of goodness to communicate itself to others... [and] to the essence of the highest goodness to communicate itself in the highest manner to the creature" (III, q.1, a.1). Thus, the incarnation deepens our faith in goodness, strengthens our hope, enkindles charity, sets us an example, divinizes us, turns us from evil, heightens our sense of human dignity, destroys our presumption about grace and salvation, removes our pride, and frees us from sin (q. 1, a. 2). Given the last effect, it was "fitting" that Jesus Christ serve as our Mediator between God and us since in him alone are God and humankind united.

Thomas turned his attention quickly, however, to the *mode of union,* and it is here, in question 2, that he defines and distinguishes the meanings of *nature* and *person. Nature* signifies *what* a thing is, as distinct from some other species of reality. *Person* signifies *who* it is, i.e., an individual substance of a rational nature (Boethius again). "If the human nature is not united to God the Word in person, it is not united to him at all; and thus belief in the incarnation is altogether done away with, and Christian faith wholly overturned" (q. 2, a. 2). He also insists, with Chalcedon, that the union is truly *hypostatic,* against those who would continue to argue that there are two hypostases in the incarnation, the one of God, the other of a human being, while there is but one person, Christ. "Person," Thomas notes, "only adds to hypostasis a determinate nature, i.e., rational" (q. 2, a. 3). To say otherwise is to lapse once more into Nestorianism, thereby destroying the unity of the God–human being and undermining his salvific work on our behalf.

The medieval and Counter-Reformation discussions about the meaning of *person* would demand more effort and space than the purpose of this book requires or allows. It is sufficient simply to note that three discernible schools of opinion developed: the *Thomist* school, represented especially by the Dominican Báñez (d. 1604); the *Scotist* school, represented by Duns Scotus himself (d. 1308); and a mediating *Jesuit* school, represented by Francisco de Suarez (d. 1617). By contrast with the soteriological orientation of the New Testament and the early Christian writers, these schools were preoccupied with the "how" of the union of the divine and the human in Christ. The ensuing debate proved to be as complicated as it was abstract, defying easy synthesis here.

The first (Thomist) school insisted that Christ's human nature participates in the same act of existence by which the Word itself exists. The "act of human existence" is subtracted from it, without loss of human dignity. On the contrary, Christ's human nature receives an even higher dignity in being alive by the same principle of existence by which the Word is alive. The second (Scotist) school preferred to define personality in a negative way, as an incapacity for dependence (conversely, a capacity for independence). In the hypostatic union the power of God brings to fulfillment this capacity for independence by fully orienting the human nature of Christ to God. Finally, the Suarezian (Jesuit) position says, against the Thomists, that nothing is "subtracted" from the human nature of Christ. The two natures are joined by what Suarez called a created mode of union. Against the Scotists, Suarez argued that personality is a positive, not a negative, reality. It is an essentially necessary form in which a nature is manifested. Since the Church has never officially and finally defined its understanding of the mode of union, the question remains open.

Much of the remainder of Thomas's Christology dwells on questions which have to do with the *inner makeup* of Christ: his intellect, his soul, the presence of grace, the virtues, his knowledge, his grasp of the Beatific Vision, his powers, his bodily integrity, his capacity for suffering, the unity of wills, his ability to merit, his subjection to the Father, and so forth. Principal exceptions, beyond the opening statement on the fittingness of the incarnation, are provided by Thomas's discussion of Christ's headship over the Church (q. 8), his role as Mediator (q. 26), and then the sequential treatment of the various mysteries of Christ's life, death, resurrection, and exaltation (qq.

35–59). But these "exceptions" did not govern the Christologies of subsequent centuries. They remained focused on the so-called constitutive questions, i.e., Christ as he is *in himself* rather than *for us*. Christology and soteriology drew farther and farther apart. A parallel development occurred, as we have already seen, in the theology of the Trinity.

Neoscholasticism

Catholic Christology from the medieval period to the middle of the twentieth century (specifically, the fifteen-hundredth anniversary of the Chalcedonian definition) is really a history of commentaries on Thomas Aquinas's *Summa Theologiæ*, retaining all the while the *Summa's* basic structure. One can take up practically any Latin textbook from this vast period and find this to be the case. Thus, the Jesuit Charles Boyer, for many years professor at the Pontifical Gregorian University in Rome, over the years the academic training ground of many Catholic bishops and theologians, patterned his own work almost exactly on the *Summa*. His *De Verbo Incarnato* discusses in sequence the fittingness of the incarnation, the mode of union, the two wills, and the redemptive work. Several other subsidiary questions appear almost exactly where Thomas himself treated them — e.g., the priesthood of Christ, the adorability of the humanity of Christ, the headship of Christ.

On the other hand, Boyer, like many other postmedieval theologians, failed to carry forward some of Thomism's stronger biblical and patristic insights, especially the discussion of the mysteries of Christ's life and the more comprehensive understanding of the redemption. On the latter point, for example, Thomas does not completely limit Christ's saving work to the cross; Boyer and most others do. (Indeed, even Bernard J. F. Lonergan's *De Verbo* text in use at the Gregorian during Vatican II relegated the resurrection to an epilogue.) In this they reflect a Latin tradition which goes back even before the Middle Ages, to the time of Tertullian (d. 220). For them, the resurrection and exaltation are a *reward* for Christ's obedient death and a *proof* in support of his claims to divinity. As we saw in chapter 12, such a view brings us a considerable distance indeed from the theological perspective of the New Testament.

SUMMARY

1. Development in the Church's understanding of Jesus Christ occurred for three reasons: (1) the naturally inquisitive and probing impulse of the human mind; (2) the challenge of dissident opinions; and (3) the need to communicate the Christian message across cultural lines.

2. Distortions of the Church's Christological faith appeared at opposite ends of the theological spectrum. At the *extreme left* there were denials of the divinity in favor of the humanity (*Adoptionism*), and at the extreme right there were denials of the humanity in favor of the divinity (*Gnosticism, Docetism*). These were opposed by such early Church Fathers as *Ignatius of Antioch, Justin, Melito of Sardis*, and *Irenæus*.

3. In their efforts to commend Christian faith to their philosophical contemporaries and, at the same time, to deal effectively with the Gnostic and Docetic threats from within the Church, some of the early Church theologians (*Origen*, in particular) came close to *Subordinationism*, making the Son of God less than, or subordinate to, the Father.

4. It was *Arius*, however, who carried these tendencies to their logical conclusion. The Son is a *creature*, neither God nor a human being, but a composite intermediary being. Against the Arian view the *Council of Nicea* (325) defined the "consubstantiality" of the Son with the Father, teaching that the Son was "begotten, not made."

5. Some pressed the Nicene definition too far in the other direction. *Apollinaris of Laodicea*, a member of the *Alexandrian school*, emphasized so much that the Word is the unique principle of the flesh of Jesus that Jesus was left with *no human soul* at all. Apollinarianism was condemned by the *First Council of Constantinople* (381).

6. By contrast, the *Antiochene school* (*Diodore of Tarsus* and *Theodore of Mopsuestia*) preferred to regard the unity of Christ more loosely in order to protect the integrity of his humanity. Their position was carried forward, to an extreme, by *Nestorius*, who posited two separate persons in Christ. Mary, therefore, is not the Mother of God (*theotokos*) but only the Mother of Christ, the human being. Nestorius was opposed by *Cyril of Alexandria* and then condemned by the *Council of Ephesus* (431).

7. A "*Formula of Union*" was worked out after the Council of Ephesus between Cyril and some of the bishops of Antioch, who still were not satisfied with the results of the council nor with some of Cyril's preconciliar expressions. But the "Formula" did not hold the parties together permanently, and Cyril's views were carried to their own extreme by *Eutyches*, who argued that Christ's human nature was completely absorbed by the divine nature so that we have not only one divine person but also one divine nature (*physis*). Thus,

Monophysitism. The *Council of Chalcedon* (451) condemned Monophysitism and reaffirmed the condemnation of Nestorianism.

8. Monophysitism continued, however, in Syria and Egypt, and charges and countercharges were exchanged. The *Second Council of Constantinople* (553) repeated the earlier condemnations of Nestorianism.

9. Monophysitism reappeared in the next century in slightly altered form. *Sergius*, patriarch of Constantinople, argued that there is only one divine will in Christ (*Monothelitism*). After Sergius carried his position to *its* logical extreme—if only one will, then only one nature—Monothelitism was condemned at the *Third Council of Constantinople* (681).

10. There has been no *doctrinal* development since Constantinople III. Subsequent councils have merely repeated the earlier conciliar definitions whenever they turned their attention to Christological issues: *Lateran IV* (1215), *Lyons II* (1274), *Florence* (1442), *Trent* (1547), and *Vatican II* (1962–1965).

11. Subsequent *theological* development culminated in the medieval synthesis of *Thomas Aquinas*, which held sway in Catholic theological education until the middle of the twentieth century.

12. *Anselm of Canterbury* is best known for his theory of *satisfaction*. Sin disrupted the balance of the universe, and at the same time imposed a debt upon the human race. Only a God-man could restore that balance and make adequate payment of that debt.

13. *Aquinas's* own Christology reflected the concerns and preoccupations of medieval theology. Although he does speak of Christ's headship, his role as Mediator, the fittingness of the incarnation as a manifestation of divine goodness, and of the mysteries of Christ's life, the principal emphasis of Thomas's Christology is on the *inner makeup* of Jesus Christ: the union of natures with the one divine person, the knowledge of Christ, the operation of his wills, his powers, his consciousness, etc. The focus is on Christ as he is *in himself* rather than on Christ as he is *for us*.

14. Postmedieval neoscholastic Christology follows that same pattern, but often without carrying forward Thomas's more comprehensive understanding of the redemption (to include the resurrection and exaltation) and his attention to the mysteries of Christ's life.

15. Pre–Vatican II manuals of theology reflected the neoscholastic synthesis. With the celebration of the fifteen-hundredth anniversary of the Council of Chalcedon in 1951, Catholic Christology began to take a new turn.

SUGGESTED READINGS

Carmody, James, and Thomas Clarke. *Word and Redeemer: Christology in the Fathers*. Glen Rock, N.J.: Paulist Press, 1966.

Grillmeier, Aloys. *Christ in Christian Tradition: From the Apostolic Age to Chalcedon (451)*. New York: Sheed & Ward, 1965.

Kelly, J. N. D. *Early Christian Doctrines*. New York: Harper & Row, 1960.

Neuner, J., and J. Dupuis, eds. "Jesus Christ the Savior." *The Christian Faith in the Doctrinal Documents of the Catholic Church*. Westminster, Md.: Christian Classics, 1975, pp. 135–90.

Norris, Richard A., trans. and ed. *The Christological Controversy*. Philadelphia: Fortress Press, 1980.

Pelikan, Jaroslav. *The Christian Tradition, vols. 1–3: 1. The Emergence of the Catholic Tradition (100–600); 2. The Spirit of Eastern Christendom (600–1700); and 3. The Growth of Medieval Theology (600–1300).* Chicago: University of Chicago Press, 1971, 1974, 1978.

Smulders, Piet. *The Fathers in Christology: The Development of Christological Dogma from the Bible to the Great Councils*. De Pere, Wis.: St. Norbert Abbey Press, 1968.

Tanner, Norman P., ed. *Decrees of the Ecumenical Councils, vol. I (Nicæa I–Lateran V)*. Washington, D.C.: Georgetown University Press, 1990.

THE EVOLUTION OF CHRISTOLOGICAL DOCTRINE

Heretical Left (Exaggerations of the *humanity* of Christ)	*Orthodox Center*	*Heretical Right* (Exaggerations of the *divinity* of Christ)
	Ignatius of Antioch (d. c. 107): If Jesus were not fully human like us, he could not have saved us.	*Docetism* (Christ only "seemed" to be human) *Gnosticism* (The humanity of Christ is only incidental to salvation)
Ebionitism (Jesus is the *adopted* Son of God) *Subordinationism* (The Word is lower in rank than the Father)	*Irenæus of Lyons* (d. c. 200): If Jesus were not "of God," he could not have saved us.	
Arianism (The Son is only the greatest of *creatures*)	*Council of Nicea* (325): Jesus is "*homoousios*," of the same substance, with the Father, "true God from true God."	
School of Antioch *Logos-anthropos* (Word-man) approach: The Word became a *human being.* *Nestorianism* (In Christ there are *two persons*, one divine and one *human*. Mary is the mother of Jesus, not the Mother of God) *Nestorianism* (Theodore of Mopsuestia, et al., *The Three Chapters*)	*Council of Constantinople* (381): Jesus had a *human soul.* *Council of Ephesus* (431): In Christ there is only *one divine person*. Mary is the Mother of God. *Council of Chalcedon* (451): In Christ there are *two natures*, human and divine, united hypostatically in *one divine person*, without confusion, change, division, or separation. *Second Council of Constantinople* (553): Reaffirmed Chalcedon, especially against Nestorianism.	*School of Alexandria* *Logos-sarx* (Word-flesh) approach: The *Word* became flesh. *Apollinarianism* (There is no human soul in Christ) *Monophysitism* (In Christ there is only *one divine nature*. The human nature is absorbed into the divine)
	Third Council of Constantinople (680–681): There are *two wills* in Christ, just as there are two natures.	*Monothelitism* (In Christ, there is only *one divine will*) *Monenergism* (In Christ there is only *one divine energy*, or action)

XIV

The Christ of Contemporary Theology

CATHOLIC CHRISTOLOGY BEFORE 1950

Catholic Christology from the time of Aquinas to the middle of the twentieth century remained essentially the same in structure and in content. The approach taken by the "Spanish Summa" (*Sacræ Theologiæ Summa*, vol. III, Madrid: Library of Christian Authors, 1953) was typical of the textbooks in general use in Catholic seminaries and colleges throughout this period. The material was divided into two main parts: the mystery of the incarnation (Christ as he is in himself), and the redemptive work of Christ (Christ as he is for us). The two "Christs" are brought together by the sin of Adam. If Adam had not sinned, the Word would not have become flesh.

But the discussion immediately turned from the "fittingness" of the incarnation to a metaphysical analysis of the way in which the union of Word and flesh occurred and the conditions under which it was sustained. Herein, the treatment followed the conciliar teaching outlined in chapter 13: The union occurs at the level of person, or hypostasis, not at the level of nature, and so forth. The residual medieval influence was particularly evident in the raising of various subsidiary questions—e.g., whether Christ could have been called a human being or the Christ while he lay in the tomb between Good

Friday and Easter Sunday; the reconciliation of the "sadness" of Christ with his sinlessness; the legitimacy of devotion to the Sacred Heart.

The limitations of early-twentieth-century Catholic Christology, however, were even more apparent in its treatment of the redemption. The exposition was shaped by the medieval focus upon *merit*, i.e., something which is or ought to be accepted by another, for which the one accepting ought to give something in return. By his passion Christ merited all the gifts of grace and of glory for humankind. He rendered more than adequate reparation for sin and, therefore, satisfied the "vindictive justice" of God. The resurrection and exaltation of Christ were mentioned in these Christologies, but their redemptive significance remained unclear. Indeed, what Christ accomplished through his passion was taken as fully sufficient for our salvation.

A marked change in this approach was signaled by the publication of Catholic scholar Francis X. Durwell's *The Resurrection* (New York: Sheed & Ward, 1960). This book argued that the resurrection was the center, not an adjunct, of Christ's redemptive work.

WHY THE CHANGE?

There is a pronounced difference between medieval and neoscholastic Christology and the Christology of the twentieth-century manuals, on the one hand, and the Christologies of contemporary Catholicism (Rahner, Küng, Schillebeeckx, Kasper, et al.), on the other. How to account for this? There are at least six principal reasons: (1) the shift from an uncritical to a critical reading of the *New Testament* (see chapter 12); (2) the shift from a static to an *evolutionary* and *existentialist* understanding of human existence (see chapters 4 and 5); (3) the emergence of a *global consciousness*, with a concomitant sense of the interdependence of nations and of peoples, and the parallel growth and influence of the *ecumenical movement*—interfaith as well as interchurch; (4) the development of *historical* and *political consciousness*, provoked by the Second World War, the Holocaust, colonialism, political repression, the nuclear threat, and the like, and later reflected in *liberation theology;* (5) the rise of *feminist consciousness;* and (6) a new interest in the *Jewishness of Jesus*. These developments, in turn, must be viewed alongside the theological reexamination of the Council of Chalcedon, on the occasion of its fifteen-hundredth anniversary, to which reference was made in chapter 13.

Catholic Christology assumed a new shape, therefore, as it assimilated not only the advances of twentieth-century New Testament scholarship, but also the newly emerging evolutionary, ecumenical, liberationist, feminist, and ethnic consciousness.

CONTEMPORARY CATHOLIC CHRISTOLOGIES

The distinction between Christology "from below" (or "ascending") and Christology "from above" (or "descending") must be clear at the outset because it recurs throughout this chapter. The two terms did not come into general use until after the Second Vatican Council and were explicitly defined by Karl Rahner in a lecture given in Munich in 1971 (see "Two Basic Types of Christology," *Theological Investigations,* *vol. 13*, New York: Seabury Press, 1975, pp. 213–23).

Christology "from below" begins with the Jesus of history, a human being like us in all things except sin, who stands out from the rest of the human race by his proclamation of, and commitment to, the Kingdom, or Reign, of God. His life of dedicated service to others led him to the cross, from which point God raised him up and exalted him. This was the emphasis of the Antiochene School in the age of the Christological debates, as it was of the Synoptic Gospels. It is the dominant approach in Catholic Christology today, and was anticipated before the council by Romano Guardini's (d. 1968) *The Lord* (Chicago: Regnery, 1954; original German ed., 1937) and Karl Adam's (d. 1966) *The Christ of Faith* (New York: Pantheon, 1957; orig. German ed., 1954).

Christology "from above" begins with the preexistent Word of God in heaven, who "comes down" to earth to take on human flesh and to redeem us by dying on the cross, rising from the dead, and returning to enjoy an exalted state as Lord in heaven. This was the emphasis, as the reader may recall, of the Alexandrian School in the age of the great Christological controversies, as it was of the Fourth Gospel and of Paul. It was also the dominant form of Catholic Christology from the medieval period until Vatican II.

Carried too far, a Christology "from below" becomes Nestorian-ism or Adoptionism: Jesus is not really divine, but fulfills a unique role in the history of the human race, calling attention to the demands of God's Kingdom among us. Carried too far, a Christology "from above" becomes Monophysitism or Docetism: Jesus is not really human, but only appears to have taken on our human condition.

Christologies "From Below"

Karl Rahner

Because he is the most important and most influential Catholic theologian of the twentieth century, Karl Rahner's Christology has to be taken with the greatest measure of seriousness. Although expressed in assorted articles in the various volumes of his *Theological Investigations* (see especially "On the Theology of the Incarnation," vol. 4, pp. 105–20, and "Christology Within an Evolutionary View of the World," vol. 5, pp. 157–92), the most comprehensive and systematic statement of Rahner's Christology is available in his *Foundations of Christian Faith* (New York: Seabury Press, 1978, chapter 6, pp. 176–321). The reader must be forewarned: The material is not easy to grasp. But its complexity does not diminish its importance.

Jesus Christ is what is specifically Christian about Christianity, Rahner insists at the outset. This is said without prejudice to the principle that someone who has no concrete, historical contact with the explicit preaching of the Church can nevertheless be justified and saved in virtue of the grace of Christ. The transcendental self-communication of God is available in principle, as an offer of grace, to every person, as we noted in chapter 5. But for the Christian the process of divine self-communication reaches its goal and its climax in Jesus Christ. He or she alone is Christian who explicitly professes in faith and in Baptism that Jesus is the Christ, that he is the decisive and climatic moment in God's transcendental self-communication to humankind.

The basic and decisive point of departure for Christology, he argues, lies in an encounter with the historical Jesus of Nazareth, and hence in an "ascending Christology." At the same time, he warns against placing too much emphasis on this approach. The idea of God coming into our history "from above" also has its power and significance. Both an ascending and a descending Christology have to be taken into account even if, in the light of contemporary evolutionary consciousness, our *starting point* is "from below" rather than "from above."

Rahner's notion of *evolution* is heavily influenced by Hegel. Matter and spirit, Rahner suggests, are intrinsically related to each other. They spring from the same creative act of God, and they have a single goal in the fullness of God's Kingdom. The world and its history are moving, i.e., are in evolution, toward a unity of matter and spirit, which Rahner (like Hegel) conceives as a *becoming* higher. The capacity for becoming something higher is called the capacity for "self-transcendence."

Since the free gift of God's grace, i.e., God's self-communication, was incorporated into the world from the beginning, the history of the world is really also the history of salvation. At the point (or points) where we realize that the direction of history is toward the Kingdom of God, we can speak of the experience of *revelation*. But whether we realize it or not, i.e., whether we are formally and explicitly religious, even Christian or not, does not change what is in fact going on. God is always present to the world and to persons within the world as the principle of self-transcendence. We have the capacity to move beyond ourselves, to become something higher and better than we are, because "the Absolute Beyond" is already in our midst, summoning us forward toward the plenitude of the Kingdom.

There are, of course, other, relative causes at work in the world and in our individual histories. These, too, have to be taken into account when we strive to understand the course and direction of history. We have the human capacity to better ourselves by means of human resources already available to us. But even those mundane resources, or causes, are made possible in the first instance by God.

For Rahner, "The permanent beginning and the absolute guarantee that this ultimate self-transcendence, which is fundamentally unsurpassable, will succeed and has already begun is what we call the 'hypostatic union'" (*Foundations*, p. 181). In other words, the unity of matter and spirit, which is what the movement of history achieves, reaches its climax in the union of Word and flesh in Jesus Christ. With the incarnation, history has entered its "final phase."

The divinization of the world is under way but not yet complete. The further course of this phase and its final result remain "shrouded in mystery."

In light of the mystery of Jesus Christ, therefore, it is clear that the human person is neither purely matter (as the behaviorists believe) nor purely spirit (as the Platonists contend) but a single reality which comprehends both matter and spirit. Indeed, it is only in the human person that both of these elements can be experienced in their real essence and in their unity. The person is *spirit* insofar as he or she is conscious of himself or herself as one who lives in the presence of God and whose whole being is oriented toward God. The person is *matter* insofar as she or he is an individual whose concreteness as an individual is experienced as something inescapably given. Apart from matter the human person cannot experience the world, other persons, or even herself or himself. Indeed, apart from matter the human person cannot even experience the *spiritual* reality that is present in ourselves and in others. Thus, there is a fundamental *reciprocity* between matter and spirit. Together they constitute the world and human persons within the world.

On the other hand, there is an essential difference between matter and spirit. Influenced also by Teilhard de Chardin, Rahner argues that the whole historical process involves a movement from lower to higher, from the simple to the complex, from unconsciousness to consciousness, and from consciousness to self-consciousness. Everything is in a state of *becoming,* and becoming is a process of *self-transcendence,* and self-transcendence is possible because God is present to life as the principle of growth and development.

Human persons, therefore, are the self-transcendence of living matter. Apart from human persons, matter would never have achieved consciousness, much less self-consciousness. The history of the material world is thus intertwined with, even dependent upon, the history of humankind. Through humankind the material world reaches its goal by reaching beyond itself. Because we are not only observers of nature but a part of nature as well, our history is also a history of the active transformation of the material world itself. It is through such free action, arising from the spiritual dimension of the human person, that both we and nature reach our single and common goal.

However, since we act in freedom, both the history of the material world and human history are in a state of guilt and trial. We can reject God's self-communication and refuse to enter this historical movement toward God. But our freedom always remains grounded in the reality of God. The religious person, and the Christian in particular, knows that the history of the world will find its fulfillment in spite of, as well as in and through, human freedom.

The human person, consequently, is not an accident of evolution but a necessary part of it. The world in fact becomes conscious of itself, of its essential unity, and of its purpose and goal by means of humankind. But this coming to consciousness is possible only because God is immediately present to reality in grace. In that sense, the end, or goal, of history is also its beginning. The history of the cosmos from the beginning is always and basically a history of the human spirit, a desire to become conscious of itself and of its ground, who is God.

It is from this *evolutionary perspective,* Rahner argues, that we must understand the place of Jesus Christ. The process of divine self-communication to the world and the process of our free acceptance of that self-communication of God reach a point in history which makes these acts, from God's side and ours, both irrevocable and irreversible. Since the goal of the whole historical movement is present to history from the beginning (as its *final cause,* the Scholastics would say), that event by which movement toward the goal of history becomes irrevocable and irreversible must also be part of that historical process from the beginning. Thus, all of history has a unity, and that unity is focused in the event of Jesus Christ. (The cosmic implications of Rahner's evolutionary Christology are developed in popular form by Australian Catholic theologian Denis Edwards, in his *Jesus and the Cosmos,* New York: Paulist Press, 1991.)

Consequently, the doctrine of the hypostatic union is not a speculative doctrine alone. Jesus is truly a human being; i.e., he is truly part of the earth, truly a moment in this world's biological process of becoming, a human being in human history, for he was "born of a woman" (Galatians 4:4). He, too, has received God's self-communication, and he too accepts it and lives out that acceptance. That principle cannot be stressed too much. The Word *became flesh.* The Word did not simply draw near to flesh, and, therefore, affect the

497

world indirectly, through affecting the spirit of the world, as the Gnostics contended. The Word takes hold of flesh and is expressed in its materiality. It is through the flesh that the Word is present to the world. Spirit and flesh are one in the Word-made-flesh.

Such an understanding of the incarnation, Rahner insists, in no way denies that God could also have created a world without an incarnation. In other words, God could have denied to the self-transcendence of matter that ultimate culmination which takes place in grace and incarnation. For every movement from a lower to a higher stage is always unexpected and unnecessary. Self-transcendence occurs as a kind of leap from one level to the next because it is only the presence of God to life which makes such leaps possible.

And that brings us to the other side of the doctrine of the incarnation. It is *God* who takes on flesh. But not in the sense that God simply enters our history from the outside, moves us a step further along the road to fulfillment, and then leaves us behind. Rather the incarnation is an intrinsic moment in the whole historical process by which grace is communicated to all persons. And because that divine self-communication occurs at a particular time and in a particular person, the self-communication becomes unconditional and irrevocable from God's side, and irrevocable and irreversible from our side, insofar as that divine self-communication is definitively accepted by a human being, Jesus Christ. In Christ, the communication of grace is not only established *by* God; it *is* God. That which is offered is inseparable from the offerer. Here we have a human reality, Jesus of Nazareth, who belongs absolutely to God. And this is what the *hypostatic union* means: *God once-and-for-all, in a specific human individual, is communicated to us, and that communication is absolutely, unequivocally accepted.*

Because of the incarnation, God is in humankind and remains so for all eternity, and humankind is for all eternity the expression of the mystery of God because the *whole* human race has been assumed in the individual human reality of Jesus. For this reason *Christology* is the beginning and the end of *anthropology*. The finite is no longer in opposition to the infinite. Christ is a human being in the most radical way, and his humanity is the most autonomous and the most free not in spite of its being assumed, but because it has been assumed, because it has been created as God's self-expression. The humanity of

498

Christ is not simply the "form" of God's appearance on earth. *God* exists (literally, "stands out from") in Christ. The Church has consistently condemned every heretical attempt to say otherwise, whether Gnosticism, Docetism, Apollinarianism, Monophysitism, or Monothelitism.

Christian faith, therefore, is the acceptance of Jesus Christ as the *ultimate* word of God to humankind. But there are many who in effect have accepted Jesus Christ but do not *explicitly* acknowledge him as God's ultimate word. What of them? Anyone who fully accepts his or her own humanity and the humanity of others has at least *implicitly* accepted Christ because Christ is in all of us and God is in Christ. On the one hand, God accepts us and loves us in the neighbor. And, on the other hand, we accept and love God in the neighbor, as the parable of the Sheep and the Goats (Matthew 25) shows. Just as our love for our neighbor must always take some concrete form in the love of a specific individual, so must our love for God. "Those who say, 'I love God,' and hate their brothers or sisters, are liars; for those who do not love a brother or sister whom they have seen, cannot love God whom they have not seen" (1 John 4:20).

For the same reason, a transcendental Christology (summarized above) requires that the self-communication of God occur in a particular, concrete individual, Jesus Christ. That is why Christology today begins "from below." It does not start by saying "God became a human being" but by saying that in Jesus God's merciful and absolute self-communication to the world is finally accomplished and made present to us. The incarnation must be historical because it must touch historical beings and the total actual history of the world. We can realize our humanity nowhere else except in history.

Jesus of Nazareth understood himself, however incompletely and gradually, to be this savior, and his resurrection established and manifested that he is such. He did not regard himself simply as another prophet, but he made our reaction to him decisive for our entrance into the Kingdom of God. Indeed, Jesus is himself the Kingdom.

Hans Küng

If Karl Rahner is the most important and most influential twentieth-century Catholic theologian, Hans Küng may be the best known and most controversial. His major Christological work, *On Being a Christian* (New York: Doubleday, 1976), was preceded by books on church reform, papal infallibility, priesthood, and other practical topics. In *On Being a Christian* Küng shifts his attention from questions about the movement Jesus initiated to questions about Jesus himself.

The book is less philosophical and less speculative than Rahner's. Although Küng and Rahner share the same "from below" starting point for their Christologies, Küng never ascends so far as Rahner, who establishes an eventual connection between the newer "from below" Christology and the traditional "from above" Christologies of the great councils of the Church and of the medieval theologians. Küng is also much less inclined to see the significance of Jesus in Rahner's larger historical and cosmic terms. Küng's Jesus is a man born to ordinary parents, with brothers and sisters, who grew up to become a wandering, uneducated Jewish layman, supremely indifferent to sacred traditions and institutions. Our knowledge of him comes from the earlier New Testament writings, Mark and the authentic letters of Paul, as interpreted by modern German scholarship. Jesus addresses God as *Abba* (Father), organizes feasts in anticipation of the Kingdom of God, and makes the human person the center of biblical religion. He is condemned for blasphemy and put to death. His followers experience his "new life" as God's *representative* among us and as our representative before God. For Küng, the various New Testament titles given to Jesus are only honorific. There is no preexistence, no incarnation, and no redemption in any traditional sense of the words. Those doctrinal assertions which claim otherwise are the product of Greek speculation.

The main lines of the book's arguments are summarized in the form of twenty theses in a later work, *Signposts for the Future* (New York: Doubleday, 1978, pp. 2–40; see also *The Christian Challenge*, New York: Doubleday, 1979). The Christ of Christian faith, Küng argues, is no other than the historical Jesus of Nazareth (thesis 4). He was not interested in proclaiming himself. He was totally subordinated to God's cause, the Kingdom of God, the direct, unrestricted rule of God over the world. Jesus, therefore, preached the will of God as the one supreme norm of human action. And God's will is none other than humankind's total well-being (thesis 5). It was for the sake of our well-being that Jesus challenged and thereby relativized sacred institutions, law, and cult. In their place he preached love, even of one's enemies. He identified himself with the poor and the wretched of the earth, proclaiming all the while the forgiveness of God (thesis 6).

Because of his words and deeds, Jesus proved a divisive figure. Some hated and feared him; others showed him spontaneous trust and love. Jesus demanded of all a final decision: to direct one's life for God's cause or for our own. In claiming to be above Moses and the prophets and in forgiving sin, Jesus exposed himself to the charge of blasphemy (thesis 7). Indeed, Jesus so identified himself with God's cause that he even addressed God as Father (*Abba*), *his* Father. It became impossible to speak of Jesus without speaking of this God and Father, and it was difficult thereafter to speak of this God and Father without speaking of Jesus. "When it was a question of the *one true God*, the decision of faith was centered not on particular names and titles but on this *Jesus*" (p. 19). The way in which one came to terms with Jesus decided how one stood with God. Jesus acted and spoke in God's name, and for the sake of God he allowed himself to be slain (thesis 8).

Jesus did not simply accept his death. He actively provoked it. He appeared as the personification of sin and as the representative of all sinners. And the God with whom Jesus had identified himself throughout his public life did not identify with Jesus at the end. Jesus was "forsaken." Everything seemed to have been in vain (thesis 9). But Jesus' death was not the end. After his death his followers experienced him as alive. The death of Jesus, like the death of any one of us, is transition to God, retreat into God's hiddenness, into that domain which surpasses all imagination. It is significant, of course, that Küng describes the resurrection as primarily something that happened to the disciples: "There remains the *unanimous testimony of the first believers*, who regarded their faith as based on something that really happened to them..." (p. 21; thesis 10, italics in original).

Therefore, the cause of Jesus continued. His followers were convinced that he was still alive. He became the content of the

Church's own proclamation (thesis 11). But, for Küng, it is not the resurrection which is at the heart of the Christian proclamation, but the crucifixion. It is the great distinctive reality which distinguishes this faith and its Lord from other religious and irreligious faiths and ideologies: the cross in the light of the resurrection, and the resurrection in the shadow of the cross (thesis 12). The crucifixion is "the permanent signature of the living Christ" (*On Being a Christian*, p. 400).

Walter Kasper

Walter Kasper has produced yet another Christology "from below" in his *Jesus the Christ* (New York: Paulist Press, 1976) and *The God of Jesus Christ* (New York: Crossroad, 1984). According to his own introductory account, the first book is indebted to the Catholic Tübingen School, and in particular to the Christological approaches of Karl Adam and Joseph Geiselmann. Their theology focused on a study of the origins of Christianity in Jesus Christ which they knew were accessible only through biblical and ecclesiastical tradition. So, too, does Kasper begin there, with the New Testament, and with the historical Jesus who is proclaimed as the risen Christ.

Kasper develops what he calls a historically determined, universally responsible, and soteriologically determined Christology. It is *historically determined* in that it begins with, and is oriented to, the specific history and unique life and destiny of Jesus Christ. It narrates the story of Jesus of Nazareth and asks: Who is he? What did he want? What was his message and mission? This means that Christology today must deal with problems of modern historical research: the quest for the historical Jesus, the quest for the origins of Easter faith, and the quest for the earliest Christological formulation of belief. These historical questions have to be answered if faith in Christ is to be taken seriously.

Christology must also be *universally responsible*, i.e., philosophically sophisticated. Christology inquires not just into this or that existent, but into existence in general. Christian faith claims that "the ultimate and most profound means of reality as a whole has been revealed only in Jesus Christ, in a unique and at the same time finally valid way" (p. 21). But such an understanding of Christ implies a specific understanding of reality. Thus, there can be no question of playing off an ontological or philosophical Christology (such as the early Christian writers and councils of the Church left us) against a nonontological or functional Christology. We have to do both: to take seriously both the history and the deeper philosophical questions which the history provokes.

Finally, Christology must be *soteriologically determined*. Christology and soteriology form a whole. There are soteriological motives behind all the Christological pronouncements of the early Church. Both the defense of the true divinity and the defense of the true humanity were intended to protect the reality of the redemption. Kasper, therefore, rejects two extremes: the one which subordinates soteriology to Christology (as the medieval theologians and neoscholastics did), and the other which reduces Christology entirely to soteriology, as the Reformers did and as Friedrich Schleiermacher did, arguing from the present experience of redemption back to the Redeemer, and making all Christological propositions an expression of Christian self-consciousness. Schleiermacher's influence, Kasper notes, can be seen in Tillich, Bultmann, and the Bultmannian school of thought. For Kasper, therefore, being and meaning are indissolubly joined. "What is believed can be known only in the exercise of belief. The exercise of belief, however, is meaningless if it is not directed to a something which is to be believed" (pp. 23–24).

The Jesus whom Kasper finally presents is the historical Jesus as mediated to us by conservative New Testament scholarship, in contrast, for example, to the more liberal exegesis upon which Küng relies. Jesus preached the Kingdom of God as "the coming to power in and through human beings of the self-communicating love of God" (p. 86). The Kingdom must be seen, therefore, "in the context of mankind's search for peace, freedom, justice, and life" (p. 73). Through his miracles Jesus showed that in him "God was carrying out his plan, and that God acted in him for the salvation of mankind and the world" (p. 98). That preaching and activity include an "implicit Christology." Jesus went beyond the Law in his teaching. He made no distinction between his word and God's. And he summoned people to make a decision for or against him as the touchstone for their decision for or against the Kingdom of God. His summons to decision and his gathering of disciples underlined his authority and

503

his (and his disciples') break with their past. Jesus, therefore, was reluctant to accept certain titles, not because they exceeded his own claims, but because he was more than those titles could express (p. 103). Jesus understood himself and functioned as our *representative*. He foresaw and accepted his death in that light, even though his disciples did not see the significance of his death until the resurrection.

Unlike Rahner, Kasper does not perceive the incarnation as an integral part of historical evolution. Whether the incarnation happened because of sin, or whether sin happened in order to make the incarnation possible, Kasper says is unanswerable. Whatever the case, the cross and resurrection of Jesus Christ are the climax of God's self-revelation for the salvation of the world. They are that "than which nothing greater can come to be" (p. 192). Insofar as he attempts an answer of his own, Kasper comes close to Anselm's. "The order of the universe (peace and reconciliation among men) is possible only if God himself becomes man, the man for others, and so establishes the beginning of a new human solidarity" (p. 225).

Kasper understands the hypostatic union, in the end, pneumatologically. The Father is self-communicated in love to the Son. It is in the Spirit that this love can be communicated outside the Trinity. The Spirit is also involved in the reverse movement. "The creature filled with God's Spirit becomes in freedom an historical figure through which the Son gives himself to the Father. In this all-consuming dedication to the point of death, the Spirit as it were becomes free; he is released from his particular historical figure, and consequently Jesus' death and resurrection mediate the coming of the Spirit (cf. John 16:7; 20:22). And thus Jesus Christ, who in the Spirit is in person the mediator between God and man, becomes in the Spirit the universal mediator of salvation" (p. 252).

This pneumatological approach is more fully developed in his later book on the Christian doctrine of God, *The God of Jesus Christ*. Therein he stresses the freedom of God and its definitive revelation as self-surrendering love in the cross and resurrection of Jesus. It is a love energized and transmitted by the transformative power of the Spirit, who draws the world into the divine love, as the world's own truest fulfillment.

Edward Schillebeeckx

Edward Schillebeeckx subtitles his 767-page book on *Jesus* "An Experiment in Christology" (New York: Seabury Press, 1979). And it is only the first, and shorter, of two Christological volumes. The sequel (*Christ: The Experience of Jesus as Lord*, New York: Seabury Press, 1980) treats of the Christ of Pauline and Johannine faith, whereas this one presents the historical figure we know as Jesus of Nazareth. So Schillebeeckx, too, constructs a Christology "from below." He is interested in discovering what is "peculiar, unique, about this person Jesus," for it was this Jesus who succeeded in touching off a religious movement that has become a world religion asserting that he, Jesus, is the revelation, in personal form, of God.

"Thus the question of his ultimate identity governs the whole of this enquiry," Schillebeeckx writes. "My purpose is to look for possible evidences in the picture of Jesus reconstructed by historical criticism..." (*Jesus*, p. 34). The volume confines itself, however, to the period of primitive Christianity, "a period that brings us closest to Jesus and is still very reticent over the matter of identifying Jesus of Nazareth, in whom followers of Jesus, after his death, found final and definitive salvation" (p. 35). The subtitle, therefore, is deliberate. The book is a prolegomenon. It clears the ground for the fuller argument.

The presentation is heavily exegetical. The aim is to discover the historical Jesus, and the historical Jesus is available to us only in the pages of the New Testament. Part I addresses the problem of how we get in touch with the historical Jesus. Schillebeeckx's alternative to other quests for the historical Jesus is to examine the actual movements (Christian communities) which Jesus set in motion, and especially their confessions of faith in him, all of which were based on some historical facet of Jesus' life and work.

Part II synthesizes what can be reconstructed: Jesus' message, the rejection, his death, and the response of his disciples after his death. The Easter experience is portrayed as one of receiving forgiveness and grace from a Jesus known to have died, and this experience of forgiveness, in turn, provided the basis for the disciples' coming back together again.

Part III describes and analyzes the growth of the early creeds, each of which was founded on some remembered experience of the historical Jesus. The various Christological titles were expanded and transformed by these historical memories. So we have here again a Christology "from below." It begins with "the encounter with and recollection of Jesus of Nazareth, the prophet of the near approach of God's rule and the praxis of the kingdom of God, who turns our human way of living upside down and thus is able to touch off some explosive situations..." (p. 570). But from the Council of Nicea onwards, Schillebeeckx contends, one particular Christological model ("from above"), the Johannine, developed as the norm of all reflection on Christ. Thus, the history of the Church has never done justice to the possibilities inherent in the Synoptic model, which he presents here.

Part IV of his book is an attempt at a beginning of such a Christology, developed out of a mixture of Thomism, existentialism, and some elements from linguistic philosophy. Here he underlines the universality of Jesus as the definitive salvation from God. Jesus is the parable of God and the paradigm of humanity, the one who realizes that human concerns and God's coincide and that we must realize that we are "of God" even when death seems to contradict this. "Through his historical self-giving, accepted by the Father, Jesus has shown us who God is: a *Deus humanissimus*" (p. 669). But precisely *how* the man Jesus can be for us at the same time the form and aspect of a divine Person, the Son, is in Schillebeeckx's view "a mystery theoretically unfathomable beyond this point."

What we affirm, however, is that what Jesus preached, what he lived and died for, the Kingdom of God, was in the end the person of Jesus Christ himself, the eschatological man, Jesus of Nazareth, who is exalted to the presence of God and who of his plenitude sends us the Spirit of God, to open up "communication" among human beings. "Jesus' being as man is 'God translated' for us. His pro-existence as man is the sacrament among us of the pro-existence or self-giving of God's own being.... The unique universality lies, therefore, in Jesus' eschatological humanity, sacrament of God's universal love for human beings.... Jesus is the firstborn of the kingdom of God. The cause of God as the cause of man is personified in the very person of Jesus Christ" (p. 670).

And this is the sole heart and center of Christianity. Jesus brought no new system or set of doctrines. Rather he came to put the

Kingdom of God into practice. He had the wonderful freedom "to do good" (Mark 3:4). In his dealings with people he liberated them and made them glad. He was a warm companion at table. His eating and drinking with his own and with outcasts brought freedom and salvation. He showed, in other words, that it *is* possible to put the Kingdom into practice in this world, in our history.

Jesus' unique universal significance is, in turn, historically mediated through the Church's own practice of the Kingdom: a work of service, carried out in faith, as we are led by the Spirit of Christ. "Thus it is in the power of Jesus' Spirit that the Church mediates the manner in which God is concerned with all human beings" (p. 672). And, thus, we are invited today to combine the theoretical theology with *orthopraxis* (literally, "right practice") i.e., "the practice of the kingdom of God, without which every theory and every story loses its credibility—certainly in a world calling in its impotence for justice and liberation" (p. 673).

(For a more popular exposition of Schillebeeckx's Christology, see his *God Among Us: The Gospel Proclaimed*, New York: Crossroad, 1983.)

Liberation Theologians

Leonardo Boff

Another set of Christologies "from below" has emerged from the Latin American liberation school of theology. The Brazilian theologian Leonardo Boff, in *Jesus Christ Liberator: A Critical Christology for Our Time* (Maryknoll, N.Y.: Orbis Books, 1978), stresses the historical Jesus over the Christ of faith. The historical Jesus, not the Christ of faith, speaks to our situation today. He did not present himself as the explanation of reality but as an urgent demand for the transformation of that reality (p. 279).

Accordingly, Jesus preached not himself but the Kingdom of God, which is "the realization of a utopia involving complete liberation, a liberation that is also structural and eschatological" (p. 280). The Kingdom is a reality that is at once present and still to be completed in the future. It is to the poor, the suffering, the hungry, and the persecuted that Jesus preaches, because it is they who must directly challenge the justice of the messianic king. Through Jesus, God has sided with them.

Everything about Jesus' words and deeds must be interpreted in this light. He was not merely a reformer but a liberator: "You have heard . . . but I tell you." He preaches a God to whom we have access not primarily through prayer and religious observance but through service to the poor, in whom God lies hidden and anonymous. Jesus establishes fellowship with society's outcasts (Matthew 11:19). He rejects wealth (Luke 19:9) and dominative power (Luke 22:25–28). Jesus' own praxis, in other words, establishes a new way of looking at God and at reality, i.e., through the prism of the struggle for liberation.

The conversion demanded by Jesus is not simply a change of convictions but a change of practice. And it is concerned not just with individuals but with social and political structures as well. "In the conditions of history, then, the kingdom of God does not come unless human beings accept it and enter into the whole process of conversion and liberation" (p. 287).

But Jesus chose to die rather than impose the Kingdom by violence. Indeed, he provoked his death by his call for conversion, his proclamation of a new image of God, his freedom from sacred traditions, his prophetic criticism of those in power. "His preaching and his outlook brought him close to the liberation project of the Zealots" (p. 289). On the other hand, he renounced the political messianism of the Zealots and their confidence in the use of force.

Through the resurrection the life that was hidden in Jesus was unveiled. The resurrection shows that it is not meaningless to die for another, that the murderer will not triumph over his victim. "Thanks to his resurrection, Jesus continues to exist among human beings, giving impetus to their struggle for liberation" (p. 291). Thereafter, to follow Jesus is to "follow through with his work and attain his fulfillment" (p. 292).

In effect, what we think of Christ, how we understand the meaning of the hypostatic union, the resurrection, and so forth is not primary. "Life is more important than reflection" (p. 157). Liberation Christology, therefore, is not so much a contribution to our understanding of the nature and mission of Jesus Christ as it is a way of understanding the meaning and demands of liberation. Liberation

Christology has a prophetic, even messianic task, i.e., to move Christians outside Latin America to hear the painful cry of their oppressed brothers and sisters and to bring justice to those who fight to regain their freedom (p. 295).

Jon Sobrino

A Jesuit theologian from El Salvador, Jon Sobrino has produced a similarly comprehensive Christological statement in his *Christology at the Crossroads* (Maryknoll, N.Y.: Orbis Books, 1978). (There is also a later collection of essays entitled, *Jesus in Latin America*, Maryknoll, N.Y.: Orbis Books, 1987.) *Christology at the Crossroads* is written from the same liberational framework and with the same "from below" starting point: "If the *end* of Christology is to profess that Jesus is the Christ, its *starting point* is the affirmation that this Christ is the Jesus of history" (p. xxi). And this means also giving priority to the praxis of Jesus over his own teaching and over the teaching of the New Testament theologians regarding Jesus' praxis. "Thus the New Testament will be viewed primarily as *history* and only secondarily as *doctrine* concerning the real nature of that history" (p. xxii).

Furthermore, Jesus' past can be recovered in the present only to the extent that it pushes us toward the future. The convergence of these three tenses occurs in the symbol of the Kingdom of God, and that is understood, in turn, in a trinitarian sense. It is the Father who is "the ultimate horizon of human existence and history" (p. xxiv), the Son who practices the Kingdom, and the Holy Spirit who makes possible life in accordance with the example of the Son. "Liberation theology is concentrated in Christology insofar as it reflects on Jesus himself as the way to liberation" (p. 37).

The emphasis remains functional; i.e., what is finally important is what Christ is for us, not what he is in himself. This functional emphasis runs the risk, to be sure, of collapsing completely into functionalism. Sobrino suggests, for example, that if at any point Christ ceased to be of interest to people or to serve as the path to salvation, he "would cease to be the revelation of what human beings are, and hence the revelation of who God is" (p. 388).

The declarations of the Council of Chalcedon, he argues, lack concreteness and historicity. There is no reference to Jesus' own life and the historical situation of his ministry. The most basic difficulty, however, is that Chalcedon seems to assume that we already know "at the very outset who God is and what it means to be human" (p. 329). But only Christ can tell us of God and ourselves.

Accordingly, while he respects the importance of dogmas and of the need to interpret them, he insists that dogmas can have "a true and profound Christian sense" only if they are rooted in the actual life of the believer and of the Church. The "ultimate truth of dogma cannot be separated from the liturgy and the following of Jesus" (pp. 324–25). Orthodoxy must always be linked with orthopraxis and doxology.

(Other Christologies in the Latin American liberation school include Juan Luis Segundo's five-volume *Jesus of Nazareth Yesterday and Today*, especially vol. 2, *The Historical Jesus of the Synoptics*, and vol. 3, *The Humanist Christology of Paul*, Maryknoll, N.Y.: Orbis Books, 1985, 1986, and José Miguez-Bonino, ed., *Faces of Jesus: Latin American Christologies*, Maryknoll, N.Y.: Orbis Books, 1984.)

Feminist Theologians

Much of the foundation for contemporary feminist Christology is provided by feminist biblical scholars. In this regard, the work of Elisabeth Schüssler Fiorenza is of primary importance, especially her ground-breaking book, *In Memory of Her: A Feminist Theological Reconstruction of Christian Origins* (1983). More recent works include her *Bread Not Stone: The Challenge of Feminist Biblical Interpretation* (Boston: Beacon Press, 1986), and *But She Said: Feminist Practices of Biblical Interpretation* (Boston: Beacon Press, 1992).

Anne Carr

In her *Transforming Grace: Christian Tradition and Women's Experience* (San Francisco: HarperCollins, 1988), Anne Carr also proposes a Christology "from below" that is "derived from what the stories of the New Testament reveal about the concrete patterns of the history of Jesus and the early churches" (p. 158). She points out that many women who take the feminist critique of patriarchy, sexism, and androcentrism seriously and who struggle with the Christian sym-

510

bols and their transformation continue to call themselves Christian, pray to Christ, and pray with Christ to God. "Both historically and in the present, the life, death, and resurrection of Jesus of Nazareth, the Christ event, has been, is, life-giving and liberating for women" (p. 160).

The many new images of God offered by Christian feminist theologians suggest that "Jesus Christ is *not* a symbol of patriarchal male supremacy for women but rather and precisely a powerful symbol of its subversion" (ibid.). Indeed, the classical formulation of Chalcedon speaks only of the divinity and humanity of Christ, not his maleness. As the church Fathers insisted, "What was not assumed was not redeemed." Jesus Christ is the source of redemption and grace for all human beings, women as well as men. He proclaims the radical equality of all persons and the universal love of God.

Unfortunately, much of medieval and neoscholastic Christology implicitly denied the principle of inclusiveness, as is evident even in Thomas Aquinas's anthropology, which held that not only is the male the "more noble" sex of the human species, but that women are somehow defective as human beings. For Aquinas, therefore, the incarnation of the Word of God in the male Jesus is not simply a historical, contingent fact. Since the male represents the fullness of God's image, and since, conversely, women cannot represent the "headship" of God either in society or in the Church, it follows that Christ should be male (e.g., *Summa Theologiæ*, I, q. 92, a. 1 and 2; III, suppl., q. 39, a. 1). The symbol of "headship" — good in itself, Carr insists — is one of many that has functioned in a false, ideological, and oppressive way (see pp. 164–65). She cites (and critically transforms) other implicitly subversive images: Jesus as sacrificial victim, his self-surrender on the cross, Jesus as servant, Jesus as son.

But for women who remain committed to Christ and the Church, these traditional symbols and noninclusive interpretations thereof are not the starting point of their faith or their theology. Rather, the starting point is women's "present experience" in the Church — their experience of its communal life, of the sacraments, of the preaching of the Gospel, and of "the corporate and graced awareness of critical Christian feminism" (p. 168).

What women find in the Jesus of the Gospels is a person of "remarkable freedom and openness to women," as evidenced in his inclusion of women among his disciples, his friendship with Mary Magdalene, his positive use of women in his parables, his breaking of taboos in speaking with the Samaritan and Syro-Phoenician women, and the role of women as the first witnesses of the resurrection. "The theological symbols of Christian tradition," Carr writes, "are interpreted today by women within this narrative context that the New Testament stories provide" (p. 169).

Elizabeth Johnson

Elizabeth A. Johnson's Christology is situated in the wider context of a theology of God (see her *She Who Is: The Mystery of God in Feminist Theological Discourse* [New York: Crossroad, 1992], pp. 150–69; and also her more popular work, *Consider Jesus: Waves of Renewal in Christology* [1990]). "Christian faith," she writes, "is grounded on the experience that God who is Spirit, at work in the tragic and beautiful world to vivify and renew all creatures through the gracious power of her indwelling, liberating love, is present yet again through the very particular history of one human being, Jesus of Nazareth" (*She Who Is*, p. 150).

Jesus' maleness poses a central problem for feminist theology — not his maleness as such, but the distorted manner in which it has been interpreted and used in "official androcentric theology and ecclesial praxis" to diminish women. This happens in two ways. First, Jesus' maleness reinforces a patriarchal image of God. If Jesus is a man, and he is the fullness of divine revelation, it must follow that God is also male, or at least that there is some basic affinity between divinity and maleness. Second, Jesus' maleness reinforces an androcentric image of humanity and a dualistic anthropology which stresses the headship of men over women. If God became incarnate in a male, it must be because the male sex is superior or normative — higher in dignity and honor than the female sex. The argument is regularly employed by opponents of women's ordination: Men alone are able to represent Christ as priests.

For Johnson the basic elements of a feminist Christology are rooted in the ministry, death, and resurrection of Jesus and in the Wisdom tradition of Sacred Scripture. Among these elements are the following: (1) Jesus' preaching proclaims justice and peace for all people, women and men alike. He always showed partiality to the marginalized, and these always included women who "at every turn [are] the oppressed of the oppressed" (*Consider Jesus,* p. 108). (2) Jesus' naming God *Abba* subverts the notion of God as a dominating patriarch, because the *Abba* God is compassionate, intimate, and close, inviting us to create communities of mutuality and equality. (3) Jesus called women to be disciples, and these women did not run and hide when Jesus was arrested, but stood by him in his hour of suffering. (4) Jesus was crucified for having preached that all human beings, men and women alike, are called to a life of compassion and self-sacrificial love, thereby challenging at its root the patriarchal ideal of the dominating male. (5) The Spirit of the risen Christ was poured out on all who believe, women as well as men, thereby breaking down all artificial divisions between people. (6) Jesus was identified soon after his resurrection as *Sophia,* or Wisdom, that is, as one who is "revelatory of the liberating graciousness of God imaged as female...." Consequently, "women, as friends of Jesus-Sophia, share equally with men in his saving mission throughout time and can fully represent Christ, being themselves, in the Spirit, other Christs" (*She Who Is,* p. 167).

Christologies "From Above"

Process Theologians

Teilhard de Chardin

Teilhard de Chardin (d. 1955) never produced a systematic Christology. Indeed, he was not primarily a theologian at all but a paleontologist and archaeologist. But because he was a convinced Christian and a priest, he felt a special need to reconcile somehow his work as a natural scientist with his faith and his vocation. He did this, as noted in chapter 4, by placing Christ within an evolutionary framework. (See, for example, *Hymn of the Universe,* New York: Harper & Row, 1965.)

Christ is both the bearer and the goal of the upward movement of the universe toward the divine. Christ is the Omega Point, the focus of union needed by the "noosphere" in order that the noosphere might achieve a creative breakthrough into a new and final state of complexity and convergence. All of history, therefore, is a movement toward Christ, and yet Christ is at the same time already present in the world. His presence gives all of reality a Christic dimension. The Church is that place where the Christification of the universe is explicitly understood and acknowledged. Insofar as the Church practices Christian charity, the Church injects the most active agent of hominization into the world. The world thereby becomes a commonwealth of persons united in selfless love.

This intimate link between Christ and the perfection of the universe Teilhard believed to be justifiable on New Testament grounds, specifically on the basis of the Fourth Gospel and the Epistles to the Colossians and the Ephesians. (For a fuller statement of Teilhard's Christology, see Christopher Mooney, *Teilhard de Chardin and the Mystery of Christ*, New York: Harper & Row, 1965.)

Teilhard's principal contribution to Christology is his insistence on a historically evolutionary framework for understanding the mystery of Christ. That Christology, however, is very much a Christology "from above," an approach more typical of the time in which he wrote. His influence on Karl Rahner has already been noted, but his mystical vision of the ultimate unity of all reality in Christ has found a much wider audience beyond the ranks of theologians. (Teilhard's evolutionary perspective has been developed in popular form, though in a more explicitly Rahnerian, "from below" approach, by Denis Edwards in *Jesus and the Cosmos*.)

Piet Schoonenberg

Dutch Jesuit theologian Piet Schoonenberg follows a similar Christological course in his book, *The Christ: A Study of the God-Man Relationship in the Whole of Creation and in Jesus Christ* (New York: Herder & Herder, 1971), where he addresses the question of the *preexistence* of Christ. The Second Person of the Trinity, he writes, is none other than the human person of Jesus, who came to exist at a specific moment in time. God is initially a single Person, therefore, but as history unfolds God becomes two Persons, and then three. (Kasper has criticized the tendency in Schoonenberg's thought toward suggesting that the immanent Trinity came into existence for the first time in salvation history. See *God of Jesus Christ*, p. 276.)

He presents this in a more nuanced way in a set of "theses on the trinitarian God," the twenty-sixth of which states: "In the salvation history before Christ the distinction between God and the Logos was already present. In the incarnation, however, this distinction became fully interpersonal, a distinction between the Father and the Son. In the same way the Spirit was already working before Christ but became the Paraclete only through Christ, being with and in Christ's church and hence in some personal relation to the Father and the Son" ("Trinity—The Consummated Covenant: Theses on the Doctrine of the Trinitarian God," *Studies in Religion* 5 [1975–1976], p. 114).

Christ is God's ultimate revelation, therefore, and not simply a fortuitous climax to history. In him the fullness of what it is to be human is realized, just because the fullness of God dwells in him.

Christology and World Religions

The reader should refer again to chapter 10 where the relationship of Christianity to other religions is discussed, and where the different views of Catholic theologians on religious pluralism are summarized comparatively. Although several Catholic theologians have written directly on this subject (Hans Küng, Karl Rahner, Paul Knitter, and others), for purposes of economy only Raimundo Panikkar's work is summarized here.

Given the renewed emphasis in Christology on the Jewishness of Jesus, readers should take particular note of the literature in this area. For example, John T. Pawlikowski, *Christ in the Light of the Jewish-Christian Dialogue* (New York: Paulist Press, 1982) and *Jesus and the Theology of Israel* (Wilmington, Del.: Michael Glazier, 1989), Rosemary Radford Ruether, *Faith and Fratricide: The Theological Roots of Anti-Semitism* (New York: Seabury Press, 1974), and Michael B. McGarry, *Christology After Auschwitz* (New York: Paulist Press, 1977).

Raimundo Panikkar

Raimundo Panikkar follows the path of those theologians who insist that we must enter into real dialogue with non-Christian religions rather than seeing them merely as objects of study. In other words, we must enter into the subjectivity of these other traditions. In his *The Unknown Christ of Hinduism: Towards an Ecumenical Christophany* (Maryknoll, N.Y.: Orbis Books, 1981), Panikkar argues that the dialogue must be an existential one, that it must take place in a Christ who does not belong to Christianity alone but to God.

In order to make such a dialogue possible, he calls for a "universal Christology," which makes room not only for different theologies but for different religions as well. He suggests that this "universal Christology" is a form of the *Logos* Christology ("from above") developed by the early Christian writers. There is a shift from the humanity of Christ to the *Logos* who is the center of the universe by reason of his relation to all of humanity. The reason for persisting in calling this link between God and humanity "Christ" is that "it seems to be that, phenomenologically, Christ presents the fundamental characteristics of the mediator between divine and cosmic, eternal and temporal... which other religions call Isvara, Tathagata or even Jahweh, Allah, and so on" (*The Trinity and the Religious Experience of Man*, Maryknoll, N.Y.: Orbis Books, 1973, p. 54).

It is the reality of Christ, as the link between God and humanity, that makes possible the encounter between Christianity and the other religions of the world. But Panikkar makes clear that his "Christ" is not to be identified exclusively with Jesus of Nazareth (*The Trinity*, p. 53). Jesus is simply one of the names for the cosmotheandric principle, although that principle has found a *sui generis* epiphany in Jesus.

This universal Christ is the fulfillment of the aspiration of India as much as of Israel. Therefore, no one should be asked to renounce his or her own religion for the sake of accepting Christ (*The Unknown Christ of Hinduism*, p. 54).

Hans Urs von Balthasar

Hans Urs von Balthasar's (d. 1988) Christology must be viewed within the wider context of his fifteen-volume trilogy (*Herrlichkeit* [The Glory of the Lord], *Theodramatik* [Theo-Drama], and *Theologik* [Theo-Logic], 1961–1987) organized in terms of the transcendentals: "A being *appears*, it has an epiphany; in that it is beautiful and makes us marvel. In appearing it *gives* itself, it delivers itself to us: it is good.

And in giving itself up, it *speaks* itself, it unveils itself: it is true" ("A Résumé of My Thought," in *Hans Urs von Balthasar: His Life and Work*, David L. Schindler, ed., San Francisco: Ignatius Press, 1991, p. 4). It must also be viewed in the context of the Gospel of John which, by contrast with the Synoptics, presents a Christology "from above."

There are three important elements, or moments, in von Balthasar's Christology: the incarnation, the cross, and history. (1) *The Incarnation.* His Christology begins with the historical self-emptying of the eternal Word of God, and this is for him the fundamental affirmation of faith. Jesus Christ is "the image of the invisible God," in whom "all the fullness of God was pleased to dwell" (Colossians 1:15,19). Because God is shown and given in Christ, we know God now not only from the outside, "economically," but also "theologically," from within. (2) *The Cross.* The descending, or self-emptying, of the Word from on high reaches its climax on the cross, which is for von Balthasar the center of Christology. The absoluteness, splendor, and love of God are most clearly revealed there. Christ's obedient, self-giving on the cross reveals the inner life of God, who is eternally self-giving and self-emptying. (3) *History.* Jesus Christ is the unique "concrete" person of history as a whole. The general *logos* of history (all that manifests something of reason, morality, meaning, value, freedom) is integrated and brought to completion in the one *Logos*, who is Christ. He alone gives everything its final meaning. Thus, he is at once the "absolutely unique one" (he alone is *the* way, *the* truth, and *the* life), and the "infinitely integrating one" (all that is truly human finds fulfillment in him, and this includes non-Christian religions, philosophies, and moral systems).

(For pertinent excerpts, see *The von Balthasar Reader*, Medard Kehl and Werner Löser, eds., New York: Crossroad, 1982.)

PROTESTANT CHRISTOLOGIES

Since the central interest of this book is in the Catholic tradition, the description of current and recent Protestant (and Orthodox) Christologies will be abbreviated. Some general introductory remarks, however, are in order: (1) The "from below" approach began at an earlier historical point for Protestants than for Catholics because Protestants were first to feel the impact of biblical criticism. Indeed, until the liberating encyclical of Pope Pius XII, *Divino Afflante Spiritu* (1943), the field of biblical criticism was left almost entirely to Protestants. (2) Protestantism, in its very origins, has been a liberal rather than a conservative modification of historic Catholicism. The "Protestant principle" to which Paul Tillich referred in his book *The Protestant Era* (Chicago: University of Chicago Press, 1948) has rejected attempts to identify the infinite with the finite, whether in sacraments, sacramentals, dogmas, or ministries. He called this attempted identification the temptation to idolatry. Some Protestants, not surprisingly, carried this principle to its logical extreme in Christology. For them, Jesus was a human being like us in all things, perhaps even including sin, except that he was much better than the rest of us. (3) Protestant Christology, however, is not unremittingly liberal. On the contrary, much of Protestant Christology in this century has been developed in reaction against the previous liberal, even reductionist, spirit of the nineteenth- and early twentieth-century theology, just as much of present-day Catholic Christology has been developed in reaction against the ahistorical, metaphysical Christology "from above" which prevailed in the Catholic Church until the middle of the twentieth century.

Rudolf Bultmann

The first sustained challenge to this thoroughly humanistic approach came in our century from Rudolf Bultmann (d. 1976), a German Lutheran. For Bultmann, "we can know almost nothing concerning the life and personality of Jesus" (*Jesus and the Word*, New York: Scribners, 1958, p. 8). What we do know is what the early Church believed him to be, and, secondarily, that he actually existed and was crucified. At the center of Jesus' proclamation is the Kingdom of God, but not as a power outside of ourselves but as a power given to us to be authentically human in our existence. Jesus summons us to a decision to think deeply about our lives, to attend to the limit set to our lives by death, and to assume responsibility for our lives in view of our impending deaths.

Bultmann's *existentialist interpretation* does not commend itself to the more activist interpreters of Jesus Christ—the Latin American liberation school in particular—because it denies our capacity to get back to, much less reconstruct, the Jesus of history. But neither is Bultmann attractive to more conservative interpreters. For Bultmann, *"faith in the resurrection is really the same thing as faith in the saving efficacy of the cross"* ("New Testament and Theology," in *Kerygma and Myth*, Hans Bartsch, ed., New York: Harper & Row, 1961, p. 41; author's italics). It is not something that happened to Jesus. It is something that happened to the disciples. It is also incorrect, according to Bultmann, to speak of Christ as divine. In Christ God speaks to the depths of the human person. The early councils of the Church, therefore, illegitimately Hellenized the primitive faith of the New Testament and turned from an existentialist to a metaphysical interpretation of the Christ-event.

Oscar Cullmann

At odds with Bultmann's approach is that of Oscar Cullmann, another German Lutheran. Where Bultmann placed little confidence in history, Cullmann placed almost total confidence there. What the New Testament presents is not primarily an existentialist interpretation of the Christ-event but a *salvation-history interpretation*. Unlike the Jewish and Greek conceptions of history, Christian historical understanding views history in linear rather than circular terms. History begins with creation and ends with the Second Coming (*parousia*). At the midpoint stands Jesus Christ. Over against the abiding temptation to Docetism, Cullmann insists that redemption occurs in time. It is not an abstraction. The redemptive events which culminate in Jesus Christ are historical events, and not just a mythological process of salvation, as Bultmann proposed. Jesus is the definitive revelation of God's redemptive love for humankind.

But if Cullmann's approach is different from, even opposed to, Bultmann's, so is it different from the more traditional ontological, metaphysical, "from above" approaches which have been common to Catholic theology since the medieval period. Cullmann offers a functional Christology in the sense that we discover who Jesus is by discovering what he has actually done for us in history. This was the approach of the New Testament, he argues. All of the titles of Christ, for example, are in virtue of what Christ does for us, rather than in virtue of what Christ is in himself. Each title signifies a specific function of Christ in salvation history. (See *Christ and Time*, rev. ed., Philadelphia: Westminster Press, 1964, and *The Christology of the New Testament*, rev. ed., Philadelphia: Westminster Press, 1963.)

Cullmann's salvation-history approach had a significant influence on the Second Vatican Council.

Karl Barth

The most direct rebuttal of Liberal Protestantism came from the Swiss Calvinist theologian Karl Barth (d. 1969). Over against both Liberalism and one of Liberalism's notable opponents, Rudolf Bultmann, Barth argued that our knowledge of God does not arise from our knowledge of the human condition but from revelation, i.e., from the Word of God given to us without predisposition, preunderstanding, or pre–anything else. There is only one God, the God of the Gospel, and that God can be known in only one way, through the Word which is Jesus Christ.

Theology, for Barth, is Christology. Christ tells us at once who God is and who we are. Christology frames our theology and our anthropology as well. Furthermore, the Jesus of history and the Christ of faith are one and the same. And the Christ as he is in himself is the same as the Christ as he is for us. He is the reconciling Christ. He is God for us. On the other hand, Jesus is "man totally and unreservedly as we are," uniting to himself and in himself all that is human. Although Barth's Christology tries to work both "from below" and "from above," the emphasis is clearly on the latter. (See *Church Dogmatics*, vol. IV/1, Edinburgh: T. & T. Clark, 1956; for a briefer summation of Barth's basic theological approach, see *Evangelical Theology: An Introduction*, New York: Doubleday, 1963.)

Barth had a profound influence on Hans Urs von Balthasar.

Paul Tillich

A German Lutheran and an existentialist like Bultmann, Paul Tillich (d. 1965) begins his Christology "from below" through an analysis of the human condition. We are beings marked by anxiety, faced as we are by the abiding threat of nonbeing. We are conscious of ourselves

520

as alienated beings, as beings now separated from the ground of all being. It is a separation which implies an original union, a ruptured union which demands to be healed. This awareness leads us to seek "New Being," the Being who gives us "the courage to be." Christianity affirms that Jesus of Nazareth, who has been called the Christ, is the one who brings the new state of things, the New Being (see *Systematic Theology*, vol. 2, Chicago: University of Chicago Press, 1957, p. 97). What is significant about Jesus is "not that essential humanity includes the union of God and man [but] that in one personal life essential manhood has appeared under the conditions of existence without being conquered by them" (p. 94).

Tillich says that it makes no sense at all to speak of Jesus as divine. He argues that "the only thing God cannot do is to cease to be God. But that is just what the assertion that 'God has become man' means" (p. 94). The traditional teaching is to be discarded and replaced with "the assertion that in Jesus as the Christ the eternal unity of God and man has become historical reality" (p. 148). Indeed, there are Adoptionist overtones in Tillich's statement that essential God-manhood means that "there is one man in whom God *found* his image undistorted, and who stands for all mankind—the one, who for this reason, is called the Son or the Christ" (*The Eternal Now*, New York: Scribners, 1963, p. 76; my italics). For Tillich, Christ brings to all of us the hope that the existential anxiety and estrangement which characterizes and mars our situation can be healed and that unity with the ground of our being can be restored.

Dietrich Bonhoeffer

Another German Lutheran theologian, influenced by Harnack on the left and Barth on the right in his years of academic formation, Dietrich Bonhoeffer (d. 1945) marked out a course somewhere between their two approaches. He moved progressively through three phases of theological development: a liberal phase rudely shattered by the First World War, a confessional (Barthian) phase similarly undermined by the rise of Nazism in Germany, and an ecumenical phase prompted by the devastating experience of the Second World War.

Bonhoeffer never produced a formal, systematic Christology, but what we have of his Christology comes from class notes taken by his students in the second, confessional phase (see *Christ the Center*, New York: Harper & Row, 1966). Thus, Jesus is God for us (p. 107). God chose to come among us and to address us in weakness. He reconciled us with God through the crucifixion and rose for our justification. Christ is known to us today in the community of saints. He is present there *pro me* (for me).

Christology and ecclesiology are, therefore, inseparable. Christ is really present only in the Church (*Communio Sanctorum*, New York: Harper & Row, 1964, p. 100). He is disclosed to us there as the new human being, or as new humanity itself (*Act and Being*, New York: Harper & Row, 1963, p. 121).

Jesus, and the God whom he reveals, is not at the borders of life where our human powers give out, but at its very center. And he is there only for others, as "the man for others." In fact, "His 'being there for others' is the experience of transcendence," i.e., the experience of God's transforming presence (*Letters and Papers from Prison*, New York: Macmillan, 1962, pp. 209–10).

With Bonhoeffer the emphasis within Protestant theology shifts once again to "the below" of human experience. But it is not simply a reproduction of the Liberal Protestant approach. He insists in *Christ the Center*, for example, that Jesus is important in what he does *for us* because of who he is *in himself*. Nor is it simply a slightly altered version of the "from below" existentialist analysis of Bultmann and Tillich. Bonhoeffer, on the contrary, laid the foundation for the development of the secular and radical theology of the 1960s. If Jesus is "the man for others," Christian existence must be existence for others, the Church must be a servant Church, and so forth. We meet this Jesus in one another. To use a Catholic phrase, Jesus is sacramentalized in the neighbor.

It is a theme that would be taken up by Bishop John Robinson, on the more conservative wing of secular theology (see *The New Reformation?* Philadelphia: Westminster Press, 1965, and *The Human Face of God*, Philadelphia: Westminster Press, 1973), and by the so-called death-of-God theologians, on the more radical wing of the movement. Robinson would remain closer to the traditional Christology, although with a humanistic and then Teilhardian leaning, while the "death-of-God" theologians, like Thomas Altizer and Paul Van Buren, would press the humanistic tilt very strongly (see Altizer's *The*

Gospel of Christian Atheism, Philadelphia: Westminster Press, 1966, and Van Buren's *The Secular Meaning of the Gospel*, New York: Macmillan, 1963). To believe in Christ is to stand at his side in the service of the neighbor.

Wolfhart Pannenberg

Still another German Lutheran, Wolfhart Pannenberg, provided one of the first modern systematic Christologies in his *Jesus: God and Man* (Philadelphia: Westminster Press, 1968). For several years, in fact, it was the only textbook available on the subject, even for Catholic use. Following in the theological tradition of both Barth and Bonhoeffer, Pannenberg insisted that we can know God "only as he has been revealed in and through Jesus" (p. 19). We do not first know God and then come to a knowledge of Jesus as one with the God of Israel.

The God of Jesus Christ is a God who is revealed in and through *history*. But such revelation takes place not at the beginning of history but at its end. Jesus Christ is the end of history, and therefore it is only in the light of the revelation in Jesus Christ that everything that preceded him in the history of Israel assumes the character of revelation as well, "in the totality of events" (p. 388). Indeed, the end that stands before all of us has actually occurred already in Jesus Christ, in his death and resurrection. The latter is "the actual event of revelation" which establishes the divinity of Jesus and confirms God's self-revelation in him (p. 129).

The resurrection is, for Pannenberg, an utterly historical event. It is not something accessible only through the eyes of faith (p. 99). All of the biblical data regarding the resurrection (the empty tomb, the appearances, etc.) converge so that the assertion that Jesus really rose from the dead is to be presupposed until contrary evidence appears (p. 105). Significantly, Pannenberg pays almost no attention to the cross. Using Hegelian categories (a practice, as we have seen, not at all uncommon among German theologians, Catholic and Protestant alike), Pannenberg locates the identity of Jesus with the Father in Jesus' *dedication* to the Father. And the Father is, in turn, dedicated to the Son (p. 332). Jesus' unity with the Father is not fully given at the incarnation, however. Rather, it is through the process of his life of dedication to the Father that Jesus' existence is integrated with the divine and his identity as Son of God becomes established (pp. 337, 344).

Pannenberg's Christology does not readily fit under either of our two working categories: "from above" or "from below." It may be more accurate to characterize his as a Christology "from ahead." It is an approach peculiar to Pannenberg, and no theologian of substance seems to have taken it up since he first proposed it. (See Alister E. McGrath, *The Making of Modern German Christology: From the Enlightenment to Pannenberg*, Oxford: Basil Blackwell, 1986, pp. 163–80.)

More recent English-language works by Pannenberg include *Systematic Theology*, vol. 1 (Grand Rapids, Mich.: Eerdmans, 1991, esp. chap. 5) and *An Introduction to Systematic Theology* (Grand Rapids, Mich.: Eerdmans, 1991, esp. chap. 4).

Jürgen Moltmann

A German Reformed theologian, Jürgen Moltmann is, among Protestant Christologists, closest to the perspective and interests of the Latin American liberation school. His position is expressed in his influential *Theology of Hope* (New York: Harper & Row, 1967) and, later, in *The Crucified God* (New York: Harper & Row, 1974). In the first book Moltmann's focus was, like Pannenberg's, on the resurrection. Influenced by the Marxist philosopher Ernst Bloch, Moltmann concentrated on the themes of the future and of hope. Even though he left room for a prophetic role for Christian faith and for the Church (see his last chapter on "The Exodus Church"), Moltmann concluded that his approach was still abstract, bearing too little relationship to praxis. The Frankfurt School of social critical theory replaced Bloch as his philosophical inspiration. His thinking came to center on the cross of Jesus, shifting from hope in Christ's future to the following of the historical Jesus.

Christian existence is itself praxis. The following of the crucified God transforms us and our situation. If Christology is to be truly responsible, it must consider the psychic and political implications of its words, images, and symbols. It must be a political theology of the cross. The history of human suffering, focused on Calvary, has to do in the end with justice. Human sympathy is insured only when the murderer does not finally triumph over the victim.

A central question posed by *The Crucified God* is "How can God himself be in one who has been forsaken by God?" (p. 190). His answer: "In the passion of the Son the Father himself suffers the pains of abandonment" (p. 192). The Good News of human hope and liberation is all contained in that proclamation. God is now inseparable from the Godforsaken of the earth. The Church, therefore, is called to identify in the same way with society's outcasts, the oppressed, the poor. "The glory of God," Moltmann insists, "does not shine on the crowns of the mighty, but on the face of the crucified Christ" (p. 327).

A more recent, but less well received work is entitled, *The Way of Jesus Christ: Christology in Messianic Dimensions* (San Francisco: HarperCollins, 1990).

Eberhard Jüngel

Eberhard Jüngel's work is closely linked with that of his Tübingen colleague, Jürgen Moltmann (indeed, Moltmann's recent book, mentioned above, is dedicated to both Jüngel and Hans Küng, another Tübingen colleague). Jüngel's position on the resurrection, for example, is closer to that of Moltmann than to Pannenberg. Through the resurrection, he says, God is disclosed as being identified with the crucified Christ. Faith then recognizes the crucified man, Jesus of Nazareth, as identical with God. It is not clear, however, whether Jüngel is suggesting that God is *identical* with the crucified Jesus, or whether God *"identifies himself"* with the crucified Jesus. Whatever the case, we are dealing here, as in Moltmann, with a theology of the "crucified God."

Drawing heavily upon Martin Luther's *theologia crucis*, he insists that faith in the crucified Jesus Christ leads to the heart of Christian belief. Indeed, the cross is the criterion for correct thinking about God (see his *God as the Mystery of the World: On the Foundation of the Theology of the Crucified One in the Dispute between Theism and Atheism*, Grand Rapids, Mich.: Eerdmans, 1983, p. 184). All of Christian theology is a theology of the cross. The resurrection, therefore, is the revelation of the Lordship of the crucified one. It has its meaning only in relation to the one who was crucified (for Pannenberg the resurrection's mean-

525

ing is independent of the crucifixion, as if the latter were only a necessary precondition for the former).

For Jüngel God's presence in the world is hidden upon the cross. With Dietrich Bonhoeffer, he insists that only a suffering God can help, only a God who is willingly "pushed out of the world." In the end, the cross puts everything to the test.

John B. Cobb

Methodist theologian and Whiteheadian, John B. Cobb, Jr., acknowledges that his earlier Christological efforts were really exercises in Jesusology (*Christ in a Pluralistic Age*, Philadelphia: Westminster Press, 1975). Under the influence not only of process thought but of the writings of Pannenberg and Thomas Altizer, Cobb insists that "Christ" is not just Jesus but any incarnation of the Word of God. Christians, therefore, must be open to the possibility of "radical creative transformation" in light of the insights of other religious traditions. The Christian view must lose itself in other traditions in order to find itself.

The vision remains Whiteheadian from beginning to end. Christ is not so much a person as a process, although Christians name Christ only in "responsible relation" to Jesus. But "Christ" cannot name the process if the process leads to nothing. If there is no hope, then all that is said becomes pointless. The content of that hope is that we shall all transcend our separate individuality to enter "a fuller community with other people and with all things. In this community the tensions between self and Christ decline, and in a final consummation they would disappear. This is the movement of incarnation. Christ is the name of our hope" (p. 258).

ORTHODOX CHRISTOLOGIES

John Meyendorff

Russian Orthodox theologian John Meyendorff (d. 1992) provides a useful statement of Orthodox Christology in his *Christ in Eastern Christian Thought* (Washington: Corpus Books, 1969). It is his firm conviction that Byzantine Christological thought—far from being, as

526

is sometime supposed, a crypto-Monophysitic, Hellenized form of Christianity—is in fact consistent with some of the most fundamental concerns in contemporary theology, the approach of Karl Rahner in particular. What has always been central to the whole Eastern patristic understanding of salvation is the principle that "man is truly man when he participates in God's life. This participation... is not a supernatural gift, but the very core of man's nature" (p. viii). We must realize in ourselves the image and likeness of God, and this participation diminishes in no way our authentically human existence, energy, and will. And so it was with Jesus Christ.

By assuming humanity hypostatically, the *Logos* "becomes" what he was not before, and even "suffers in the flesh." This openness of God to the creature actually "modifies" God's personal existence. Such an understanding of the incarnation, according to Meyendorff, excludes all Docetism or Monophysitism, and it affirms that the salvation of humankind was a matter serious enough to bring the Son of God to the cross (p. 164). This, of course, represents a Christology "from above."

Meyendorff insists, however, that one can begin as well "from below." The notion of *participation* implies not only openness in the divine being but also a dynamic, open, teleological concept of the human. Since Gregory of Nyssa, the destiny of humankind is viewed, in Greek patristic thought, as an ascent in our knowledge of God through greater participation in the divine life itself. It is precisely at this point that post-Chalcedonian Byzantine Christology meets the modern Christological concerns. By basing Christological thinking on anthropology, as Rahner does, one is necessarily led to the other major conclusions of Greek patristics: The human being does not disappear in contact with God but, on the contrary, becomes more truly and more freely human, not only in the human being's similarity to God, but also in what makes the human being radically different from the Creator. "And this is the very meaning of the hypostatic union of divinity and humanity in Christ" (p. 165).

Nestorianism had argued the opposite, insisting on the idea of competition between, and mutual exclusion of, divinity and humanity. A proper understanding of Christ, Meyendorff continues, requires that we consider the *Logos* as the hypostasis, the "uniting unity" and the source of Christ's human existence. And this, in turn, challenges the traditional Scholastic notion of God's absolute immutability. God *became* human. A sound Christology, Meyendorff argues in concert with Rahner, implies "the return to the pre-Augustinian concept of God, where the three hypostases were seen first of all in their personal, irreducible functions, as Father-God, Son-Logos, and the Spirit of God, and not only as expressions of the unique immutable essence" (p. 166). The *being* of God, therefore, cannot simply be identified with the *essence* of God, as has been done in the West ever since Augustine.

Meyendorff is encouraged by the present movement in Western theology, represented in Rahner's work, because it implies not only a return to pre-Augustinian thought but also a return to the basic presuppositions of the Christological thought analyzed throughout Meyendorff's own book. This coincidence shows "the astonishing relevance, for our own time, of the patristic view of the Christian message.... The ecumenical significance of this discovery is incalculable" (p. 166).

John Zizioulas

Greek Orthodox theologian John D. Zizioulas points out that "in the theology of the first three centuries, the approach to the idea of truth through the *logos* failed in two ways in its attempt to link the biblical concept of truth with that of Greek thought: it did not reconcile the Greek concept of being with the ontological otherness of God's being, and it did not fully identify the ontological content of truth with Christology in its historical aspect" (*Being as Communion: Studies in Personhood and the Church*, Crestwood, N.Y.: St. Vladimir's Seminary Press, 1985, p. 93).

The fourth-century Greek Fathers managed a breakthrough, Zizioulas notes, when a clear distinction was established between two terms that were formerly regarded as interchangeable: *participation* and *communion*. Participation is now used only for creatures in their relation to God, and never for God in God's relation to creation. Thus, God and the world cannot be ontologically placed side by side as self-defined entities. Creaturely truth is dependent upon that in which it participates (truth as *communion by participation*), while God is truth as *communion without participation* (p. 94).

There remained the problem of the relationship between truth and history. According to Zizioulas, it was St. Maximus the Confessor (d. 662) who was the first in the history of Christian thought to work out an answer to the question. "The truth of history is identical with that of creation itself, both being oriented towards the future. Perfection is not an original state to which creation is bidden to return, but a *peras* ["end," or "fulfillment"] which summons from ahead" (pp. 95–96). History derives its meaning, therefore, from the end toward which, and *from* which, it is moving.

Christ is the *logos* of creation, and all the *logoi* of created beings are found in him. Both *logos* and *logoi* are inconceivable apart from the "dynamical movement of love," for it is love, not being, that is the "substratum of existence" (p. 97). God knows things not according to their nature, but as realizations of the divine will. God's knowledge is none other than God's love.

And this is where the incarnation comes in. *"The incarnate Christ is so identical to the ultimate will of God's love, that the meaning of created being and the purpose of history are simply the incarnate Christ"* (ibid., italics in original). Thus, the incarnate Christ represents "the ultimate, unceasing will of the ecstatic love of God, who intends to lead created being into communion with [God's] own life, to know [God] and itself within this communion-event" (p. 98). Christ is the one, synthesizing truth that is "at the heart of history, at the ground of creation, and at the end of history," moving everything toward the true being which is true life and true communion.

Since only the Son is incarnate, only the Son *becomes* history. The divine economy *is* the Christ-event. Even Pentecost is part of the Christ-event. The distinctive contribution of the Spirit is "to liberate the Son and the economy from the bondage of history" (p. 130). The Son dies on the cross, and it is the Spirit who raises him from the dead, making of him an eschatological being.

It is the Spirit, the source of communion, who creates the corporate personality of Christ, and it is only because of the Spirit that we can speak of the Church as the Body of Christ. Indeed, the Spirit doesn't simply "animate" the Church which already somehow exists. It makes the Church *be*. It is the very essence of the Church.

CHRISTOLOGICAL CRITERIA

So broad and diverse a sampling of recent and current Christologies is not easily synthesized. They range all the way from the *Christomonism* (Christ *alone* manifests the presence and word of God) of Karl Barth to the *universalism* of Raimundo Panikkar, for whom Jesus of Nazareth is not the only manifestation of the Christ. How does one even begin to evaluate such a wide array of theological positions?

Legitimate differences notwithstanding, some Christological views seem to be more (or less) consistent with the broad Catholic tradition than others. On what basis, however, can we make that judgment? The criteria that follow are not offered as an easy way of identifying unorthodox or even heretical understandings of Jesus Christ. Very few deficient Christologies are expressed so unequivocally as, e.g., "I begin with the premise that it makes no sense at all to speak of Jesus of Nazareth as divine." At the serious academic and scholarly levels, even views which may be *reductively* unorthodox are first proposed as bona fide efforts to explain real difficulties in the mystery of Christ. That could undoubtedly have been said of each of the theologians of the first seven centuries who, in the end, found their explanations condemned by one or more of the great Christological councils.

On the other hand, there *is* an objective and objectifiable Christian and Catholic tradition. It is rooted in the faith, preaching, and *praxis* of the Church as embodied in the New Testament, in the dogmatic formulations of the ecumenical councils, the theological writings of the early Christian theologians, doctors, and pastoral leaders of the Church, the doctrinal assertions of other, nonecumenical councils and of popes, and in the Church's liturgy. In listing criteria by which to differentiate between Christologies which are consistent with this broad tradition from those which are not, it is *not* being suggested here that the content of that tradition is always readily identified and grasped. But the opposite impression also has to be challenged, namely, that, when it comes to expressing our faith in Jesus Christ, one Christian's ideas are as good as another's, that we somehow begin afresh in each generation, taking or leaving what history bequeaths to us or what the Church proclaims, celebrates, and teaches today.

1. The Catholic Christological tradition, synthesized at the *Council of Chalcedon* (451), has three principal *dogmatic* components: (1) *Jesus is divine;* (2) *Jesus is human;* and (3) *the divine and the human are united in one person, Jesus Christ.*

These principles are *not* purely metaphysical. They are primarily *soteriological.* If Jesus is not *at once* divine *and* human, then he did not save us. Both the divinity and the humanity are fully operative and effective in the redemption because they are indeed *united* in one person.

Christological explanations which explicitly or implicitly deny any of these three principles are inconsistent with the Catholic tradition. *Examples:* (1) "Jesus was not an ordinary human being. He was the greatest of human beings. He achieved the highest *degree* of humanity." (2) "Jesus could not have been tainted in the least by ignorance, error, or, dare we say it, sexual appetites. That would be demeaning to the Son of God present in the human body of Jesus." (3) "Jesus is the Christ, to be sure. But there are other expressions of 'the Christ' as well. Indeed, 'the Christ' is a cosmic process carrying the world toward its final perfection, and Jesus is only one of his/its principal carriers and instruments."

2. *The object of Christian faith is not Christology, but Jesus Christ himself. There is no radical separation, therefore, between the Jesus of history and the Christ of faith. Jesus Christ "for us" is who Jesus Christ "is."*

This criterion is an elaboration of the third dogmatic component listed above, namely, that the divine and the human are united in one person, Jesus Christ. No evolutionary or universal Christology is consistent with the Catholic tradition which breaks the unique and definitive connection between Jesus of Nazareth and the Christ of the cosmos. This principle does not, on the other hand, exclude all such Christologies. Karl Rahner's Christology, for example, is one which reflects an evolutionary perspective, yet, by the standards proposed here, his is eminently consistent with the Catholic tradition.

3. *Jesus' life, death, and resurrection are redemptive.*

Jesus' life, death, and resurrection were neither merely exemplary or inspiring, nor (in the case of the resurrection especially) merely divine disruptions of physical and natural laws. This criterion is an elaboration of the first two dogmatic components given in criterion 1 above, namely, that Jesus is divine *and* human. A merely exemplary or motivational explanation effectively denies the first dogmatic principle; a purely interventionist explanation effectively denies the second.

No explanation, from whatever side of the theological spectrum, is consistent with the Catholic tradition if the *redemptive* significance of the life, death, and resurrection of Jesus is denied or ignored. Thus, the resurrection is not to be regarded simply as a proof of Jesus' divinity or a reward from the Father.

4. *Christological explanations which contradict the central affirmations of the Church's liturgy are in violation of the long-standing theological norm: "The rule of prayer is the rule of belief" ("Lex orandi, lex credendi").*

The probable origin of the axiom is the *Indiculus*, composed sometime between 435 and 442 by Prosper of Aquitaine (d. 460), a disciple of Augustine. The axiom is cited throughout the history of the Church, and in such twentieth-century documents as Pope Pius XII's encyclical on the Sacred Liturgy, *Mediator Dei* (1947). Pope Pius XI attributes the formula to Pope Celestine I (d. 432). In any case, it goes back at least to the early fifth century.

(The emphasis on worship, witness, and prayer as necessary components of Christology is especially strong in Frans Jozef van Beeck's *Christ Proclaimed: Christology as Rhetoric*, New York: Paulist Press, 1979.)

5. *Christological explanations which deny or are silent about the social and political implications of Jesus Christ's saving work misunderstand or supplant what was central to Jesus' proclamation and practice, namely, the Kingdom of God.*

The New Testament makes clear that our reaction to Jesus (conversion) and to his proclamation of the Kingdom of God is decisive for our entrance into the Kingdom, because Jesus is the sacrament of God's universal love for all human beings, and we human beings are, in turn, the sacrament of Jesus' presence among us. Thus, love of God and love of neighbor are inextricably connected.

The Kingdom of God, therefore, has to do with the fulfillment of our humanity, of human history, and of the whole cosmos. In that sense, salvation is humanization, and humanization occurs through liberation in the widest meaning conveyed by Romans 8.

6. *Christological explanations which interpret the maleness of Christ in an androcentric way or the headship of Christ in a patriarchal way effectively deny the proclamation and praxis of Jesus regarding the universality of God's love and the openness of the Kingdom to all, women and men alike.*

SUMMARY

1. *Catholic Christology* from the time of Aquinas to the middle of the twentieth century focused principally on the so-called ontological questions (i.e., Who is Christ *in himself?*) and only secondarily on the soteriological questions (i.e., Who is Christ *for us?*).

2. The *change* from the medieval approach to the so-called modern approach occurred for *six principal reasons:* (1) the shift from an uncritical to a critical reading of the *New Testament;* (2) the shift from a static to an *evolutionary and existentialist* understanding of human existence; (3) the emergence of a *global consciousness* and the parallel growth and influence of the *ecumenical movement;* (4) the development of *historical and political consciousness,* as reflected in *liberation theology;* (5) the rise of *feminist consciousness;* and (6) a new interest in the *Jewishness of Jesus.* Change also came about through the theological reexamination of the *Council of Chalcedon,* on the occasion of its fifteen-hundredth anniversary.

3. There are two main Christological approaches: (a) Christology *"from above"* which begins with the preexistent Word of God in heaven (the emphasis of the Fourth Gospel and of Paul, of the School of Alexandria, and of Catholic Christology from the medieval period until Vatican II), and (b) Christology *"from below"* which begins with the Jesus of history (the emphasis of the Synoptic Gospels, of the School of Antioch, and the dominant approach in Catholic Christology today).

4. *Karl Rahner's* Christology is cast in *evolutionary* terms and is a function of his basic theological *method of transcendence.* The whole world is moving in evolution toward becoming something higher than it now is. It is called to self-transcendence.

5. For Rahner the permanent beginning and absolute guarantee of this self-transcendence is the *hypostatic union,* where matter and spirit are climactically united in the union of Word and flesh in Jesus Christ. Ever since that union, *history is in its final phase.*

6. The world becomes conscious of itself through humankind, which alone unites matter and spirit in itself. The world moves forward toward its goal, *the Kingdom of God,* insofar as we actualize our capacity for self-transcendence. Thereby we become more than we are, and more than we could ever be if we were matter alone.

7. From the beginning, *the whole evolutionary process is centered in Jesus Christ* as its final cause. The process towards the Kingdom becomes *irrevocable* and *irreversible* in him. The Word became flesh, thereby taking hold of the world. Christ not only offers grace; he *is* grace. Jesus *is* the *Kingdom* which he proclaims.

8. *Hans Küng*'s Jesus is not the cosmic figure of Rahner's Christology. He is an ordinary historical figure who made an extraordinary impact not only upon his contemporaries but upon much of the human race ever since.

9. Küng's Jesus proclaims *the Kingdom*, but is not himself the Kingdom. Everything (laws, traditions, cult, etc.) is to be subordinated to the Kingdom, i.e., to human well-being. *Salvation is humanization.*

10. Through his death, Jesus appeared as the personification of sin and as the *representative* of all sinners. After his death, his followers experienced him as alive (the resurrection). But it is the crucifixion, not the resurrection, that is for Küng the "permanent signature of the living Christ."

11. *Walter Kasper*'s Christology begins with the specific history of Jesus of Nazareth (therefore, it is *historically determined*), but moves beyond that to philosophical reflection (therefore, it is *universally responsible*). Since all the classical Christological pronouncements were intended to protect the reality of the redemption, his Christology is also *soteriologically determined*.

12. Kasper *differs from Küng*, for example, in that Kasper follows a more conservative school of biblical interpretation and posits an implicit Christology in the thinking of Jesus. Jesus was reluctant to accept titles because he was greater than what those titles could express. Kasper, however, agrees with Küng in seeing Jesus as our *representative* before God.

13. Kasper *differs from Rahner*, who perceives the incarnation as an integral part of historical evolution. Kasper adopts a position closer to *Anselm's*. Thus, God became human to restore order and balance to the universe.

14. What may be distinctive about Kasper's Christology is its *pneumatological* interpretation of the hypostatic union. It is the Holy Spirit who makes possible the movement of the Son outside the Trinity, and it is the Holy Spirit, released from the historical figure of Jesus after his death and resurrection, who makes possible the coming together of all humankind in saving unity.

15. For *Edward Schillebeeckx* the historical Jesus is the parable of God and the paradigm of humanity. He is "the sacrament of God's universal love for human beings...."

16. Jesus brought no new doctrine or religious system, according to Schillebeeckx. Rather he proclaimed and *practiced the Kingdom of God*. He showed that it is possible to put the Kingdom into practice. Jesus' unique universal

significance is, in turn, historically mediated through the Church's own practice of the Kingdom.

17. The Christology of the *Latin American liberation theologians* is represented in the work of *Leonardo Boff* and *Jon Sobrino*. Both stress the historical Jesus over the Christ of faith. Jesus preached not himself but the *Kingdom of God*, the realization of complete liberation. It is to the poor, the suffering, and the oppressed that he preaches, for these are the people who challenge the justice of God. God has sided with them through Jesus. The emphasis is always functional: What is finally important is what Christ is for us, not what Christ is in himself. Orthodoxy is always to be linked with orthopraxy and doxology.

18. *Feminist* Christology, as represented by *Anne Carr* and *Elizabeth Johnson*, is at once a critique of traditional Christology, which is patriarchal, sexist, and androcentric, and a positive reformulation or "transformation" of traditional Christian symbols in the light of feminist consciousness.

19. For *Carr* the Jesus of the New Testament is a person of remarkable freedom and openness to women, as evidenced, for example, by his inclusion of women among his disciples and his positive use of women in his parables.

20. *Johnson* emphasizes, for example, Jesus' preference for the marginalized and oppressed, and especially the identification of Jesus with Wisdom (*Sophia*), who reveals the liberating graciousness of God, imaged as female.

21. There are also Catholic Christologies *"from above."* For *Teilhard de Chardin*, all history is a movement toward Christ, the *Omega Point*, and yet Christ is also already present in and to the world, giving it a Christic (love-oriented) dimension. For *Piet Schoonenberg*, the Second Person of the Trinity is none other than the human person of Jesus, who came to exist at a specific moment in time.

22. *Raimundo Panikkar* proposes a "universal Christology" that is a form of the *Logos* Christology developed by the early Christian writers. The theological emphasis is shifted from the humanity of Christ to the *Logos* who is the center of the universe by reason of his relation to all of humanity. But this "Christ" is a cosmotheandric principle, not to be identified exclusively with Jesus of Nazareth.

23. *Hans Urs von Balthasar*'s Christology has three important elements, or moments: the incarnation, the cross, and history. It begins with the historical self-emptying of the eternal Word of God. That process reaches its climax in the cross, which reveals the inner life of God as eternally self-giving and self-emptying. Jesus Christ is the unique "concrete" person of history as a whole, who alone gives everything its final meaning.

535

24. *Protestant Christologies* have generally been more sympathetic to the "from below" approach and for a longer time because (1) biblical criticism developed first within Protestantism; and (2) Protestantism has characteristically been skeptical of identifying any human reality with the divine. On the other hand, much of twentieth-century Protestant Christology has been developed in reaction against extremely liberal or reductionist tendencies within Protestantism.

25. Thus, *Rudolf Bultmann* challenged Liberalism's assumption that we can know the historical Jesus with confidence. What the New Testament offers us is a philosophy of human existence.

26. *Oscar Cullmann* makes salvation history the context for understanding Jesus Christ. All of the New Testament titles were applied to Jesus in a functional, not an ontological, way. Jesus "for us" is primary, not Jesus as he is "in himself."

27. *Karl Barth* mounted the strongest and most direct assault upon Liberalism, opposing Bultmann at the same time. Jesus is the Word of God. All theology is Christology. There is no other point of access from and to God except through Jesus Christ.

28. For *Paul Tillich*, Christ is the "New Being" who allows us to overcome the anxiety and estrangement which characterize human existence because he conquered both in his own life.

29. For *Dietrich Bonhoeffer*, Jesus is the "man for others." He is Christ "for me." He exists for us today in and through the community of saints.

30. Bonhoeffer's "man for others" Christology laid the foundation for a more thoroughly human interpretation of Jesus in the so-called secular theology of the 1960s: *Bishop John Robinson*, insisting that Jesus is to be discovered in the neighbor and that he shows us the "human face" of God; *Thomas Altizer* and *Paul Van Buren*, making Jesus the model and inspiration of our service of others.

31. For *Wolfhart Pannenberg*, history is the vehicle of divine revelation, but the latter takes place at the *end* of history, in Jesus Christ. It is only in the light of Christ that antecedent events become revelatory. Jesus' divinity is rooted in his complete dedication to the Father, and it is fully and finally established in the resurrection, which is a literally historical event.

32. For *Jürgen Moltmann*, the cross is central. Through the passion and death of Jesus, God actually suffers with us and identifies with the oppressed of the human race. It is only in the practice of the Kingdom of God that we truly follow the way of Christ, a practice which involves the same identification with the outcasts, the poor, and the persecuted of society.

33. *Eberhard Jüngel*, following in the tradition of Luther and Moltmann, places the crucified Christ at the center of all Christian theology. God's

presence in the world is hidden upon the cross. In the end, the cross puts everything to the test.

34. *John Cobb* holds that the Christ is in Jesus, but not exclusively so. It is only in losing itself in other traditions that Christian faith can find itself. What Jesus represented and proclaimed is the common hope of all: full community with other people and with all things.

35. *John Meyendorff* is representative of *Russian Orthodox* thought, with its historical emphasis on our participation in the divine life accomplished through the passion and death of Christ.

36. For *John Zizioulas*, a *Greek Orthodox* theologian, the incarnate Christ is so identical to the ultimate will of God's love, that the meaning of created being and the purpose of history are simply the incarnate Christ. The divine economy *is* the Christ-event.

37. Contemporary Christologies which are consistent with the broad Catholic Christological tradition incorporate the following principles: (1) Jesus is divine; (2) Jesus is human; (3) the divine and the human are united in one person, Jesus Christ; (4) Jesus Christ "for us" is who Jesus Christ "is" (thus, Christology is inherently soteriological); (5) Jesus' life, death, and resurrection are redemptive; (6) *Lex orandi, lex credendi* ("The rule of prayer is the rule of belief"); (7) there are social and political implications to Jesus' proclamation and practice of the Kingdom of God; and (8) androcentric and patriarchal interpretations of Jesus effectively deny his proclamation and praxis regarding the universality of God's love and the openness of the Kingdom to all.

SUGGESTED READINGS

Cook, Michael L. *Responses to 101 Questions about Jesus.* New York: Paulist Press, 1993.

Edwards, Denis. *Jesus and the Cosmos.* New York: Paulist Press, 1991.

Fiorenza, Elisabeth Schüssler. *In Memory of Her: A Feminist Theological Reconstruction of Christian Origins.* New York: Crossroad, 1983.

Johnson, Elizabeth A. *Consider Jesus: Waves of Renewal in Christology.* New York: Crossroad, 1990.

Krieg, Robert A. *Story-Shaped Christology: The Role of Narratives in Identifying Jesus Christ.* New York: Paulist Press, 1988.

Lane, Dermot A. *The Reality of Jesus: An Essay in Christology.* New York: Paulist Press, 1975.

_____. *Christ at the Centre: Selected Issues in Christology.* New York: Paulist Press, 1991.

Macquarrie, John. *Jesus Christ in Modern Thought.* London: SCM Press, 1990.

McDermott, Brian O. *Word Become Flesh: Dimensions of Christology*. Collegeville, Minn.: Liturgical Press, 1993.

O'Collins, Gerald. *What Are They Saying About Jesus?* New York: Paulist
Press, 1977.

_____. *Interpreting Jesus*. New York: Paulist Press, 1983.

Richard, Lucien. *What Are They Saying About Christ and World Religions?* New
York: Paulist Press, 1981.

Sloyan, Gerald S. *Jesus, Redeemer and Divine Lord*. Wilmington, Del.: Michael
Glazier, 1989.

Sobrino, Jon. *Jesus in Latin America*. Maryknoll, N.Y.: Orbis Books, 1987.

XV

Special Questions in Christology

This chapter addresses four specific questions in Christology: the *virginal conception* of Jesus, his *sinlessness*, his *knowledge*, or *consciousness*, and his *sexuality*. The first two underscore the *divinity* of Jesus Christ; the third and fourth, his *humanity*.

THE VIRGINAL CONCEPTION OF JESUS

It is the official teaching and the universal belief of the Church that Jesus was "born of the Virgin Mary," as the Nicene Creed proclaims. The truth and validity of that teaching and belief are not in question here, but biblical scholars and theologians have been asking what that belief might mean and how it might be understood today, in light of developments in New Testament exegesis and our understanding of human existence. It must also be clear at the outset that what is at issue here is the belief that *Jesus was conceived in the womb of a virgin, Mary, without the intervention of a human father (virginitas ante partum)*. The issue is *not* the related belief that Mary remained a virgin during the childbirth (*in partu*) and for the rest of her life (*post partum*). We shall be treating the question of Mary's *in partu* and *post partum* virginity in chapter 30. Our concern in the present chapter is Christological rather than Mariological.

There are five subquestions to be considered: (1) Is the belief in the virginal conception of Jesus truly a belief of the New Testament Church? (2) Is that belief rooted in historical fact? That is, was Jesus actually conceived without a human father? (3) Does the Church officially impose belief in the historicity of the virginal conception of Jesus? (4) Can New Testament scholarship and the official teaching of the Church be reconciled? (5) What does the belief finally mean in relation to Jesus Christ?

Is It a Belief of the New Testament Church?

Belief in the virginal conception of Jesus *is* to be found in the New Testament, and, given the nature of the New Testament, that belief was held by at least some Christian communities of the first century. The references are twofold: Matthew 1:18–25 and Luke 1:26–38, the so-called Infancy Narratives. Both convey two ideas: Jesus' Davidic descent and the Spirit's role in his conception.

Matthew reports that Mary conceived before she and Joseph lived together, that he "had no marital relations with her until she had borne a son; and he named him Jesus" (v. 25). Mary "was found to be with child from the Holy Spirit" (v. 18). "All this took place," Matthew writes, "to fulfill what had been spoken by the Lord through the prophet: 'Look, the virgin shall conceive and bear a son, and they shall name him Emmanuel'" (vv. 22–23).

No one questions the authenticity of the narrative. There is a difference of opinion on whether it is Matthew's own conviction that Jesus was virginally conceived, or whether Matthew was drawing upon a tradition which preceded him. The current weight of scholarship seems to be on the latter side. One major reason for saying so is that the other infancy account, Luke 1:26–38, also speaks of a virginal conception by the power of the Holy Spirit (v. 35). Since this is one of the few points on which they agree, scholars conclude that this tradition antedated both accounts. In fact, this tradition must have been old enough to have developed into narratives of very diverse character and to have circulated in different Christian communities.

The rest of the New Testament (Paul, Mark, the Johannine tradition) is silent about the virginal conception. Biblical exegetes, Catholic and Protestant alike, generally reject the hypothesis that implicit references to the virginal conception are given in Mark 6:3, John 1:13, 6:42, 7:42, and 8:41 (see Raymond E. Brown et al., eds., *Mary in the New Testament: A Collaborative Assessment by Protestant and Roman Catholic Scholars*, p. 289).

Is the Virginal Conception Historical?

This question cannot be answered with a clear "Yes" or a clear "No," at least not on the basis of scientifically controllable evidence from the New Testament.

The arguments *in favor* of historicity are twofold: (1) One searches in vain for exact parallels in non-Jewish religions, societies, and mythologies which might explain how early Christians happened upon the idea of a virginal conception without even a male deity or element to impregnate Mary, because apparent parallels (e.g., the births of Buddha, Krishna, the Pharaohs, et al.) all involved a divine male in some form or other. (2) There were rumors abroad that Jesus was conceived illegitimately. Matthew's account acknowledges this gossip, and it is implied also in Mark 6:3, where Jesus is referred to as the "son of Mary"—an unusual designation unless paternity is uncertain or unknown—and in John 8:41, where the Jews sneer, "We are not illegitimate children...." In early Jewish polemics against the new Christian faith the charge persisted that Jesus was born of an adulterous union since he was obviously not the son of Joseph.

But the arguments *against* historicity are also strong: (1) If Joseph and Mary knew that their son had no human father but was conceived in truth by the Holy Spirit alone, why would they have kept this secret from Jesus? And if they had not kept the secret, why could he not have known and affirmed from the very beginning that he was the Messiah and the unique Son of God? Our consideration of the Christological development of the New Testament (in chapter 12), however, disclosed a movement from a lower to a higher Christology within the New Testament period itself. Jesus may have had only an implicit Christology of his own. (2) The Infancy Narratives themselves, in both structure and content, suggest a nonhistorical rather than historical accounting of the conception of Jesus. The two basic stories are virtually irreconcilable; e.g., compare Matthew 2:14 with Luke 2:39. There is an artificiality in format—e.g., Matthew's genealogy with its three groupings of fourteen generations. There is folklore—e.g., the appearance of angels in dreams, guiding stars, treasures from the East. (3) The rest of the New Testament is completely silent about the virginal conception. (4) How could one have verified the historicity of the virginal conception in the first place? It would have been known to Mary and Joseph alone, and those to whom they told it.

The scales seem to tip in favor of the theory that the belief in the virginal conception of Jesus is the result of what is technically called a *theologoumenon* (literally, "that which is said about God"). A theologoumenon stands between a theological interpretation that is normative for faith (a doctrine or a dogma) and a historically verifiable affirmation. In other words, a theologoumenon is a nondoctrinal theological interpretation that cannot be verified or refuted on the basis of historical evidence, but that can be affirmed because of its close connection with some defined doctrine about God. In the case of the virginal conception of Jesus, the word *theologoumenon* means that the early Church, in the writings of Matthew and Luke, read back into the earthly origins of Jesus a historically unverifiable element that was designed to say something about the significance of Jesus for our salvation: Jesus did not *become* one with God as time went on; *Jesus was one with God from the moment of his conception.*

Does the Church Officially Teach the Historicity of the Virginal Conception?

Creedal and doctrinal references to the virginal conception ("born of the Virgin Mary") can be found in: (1) the Apostles' Creed (date uncertain); (2) the Nicene Creed (325); (3) the Nicene-Constantinopolitan Creed of the First Council of Constantinople (381); (4) the Athanasian Creed (end of fifth century); (5) the Fourth Lateran Council (1215); (6) the Second Council of Lyons (1274); and other less authoritative sources (for those references, see *The Christian Faith in the Doctrinal Documents of the Catholic Church*, J. Neuner and J. Dupuis, eds., Westminster, Md.: Christian Classics, 1975, p. 137).

542

Given the original setting and purpose of those creedal and doctrinal formulations, their primary concern would seem to have been with preserving the unity of the divine and the human in Jesus Christ, rather than with affirming the historicity of his virginal conception. The Church was teaching, against the Gnostics, Docetists, Monophysites, and others, that Jesus was truly human, that he was truly born of a woman. And it was teaching, against the Adoptionists, the Nestorians, and others, that he was truly divine.

Nowhere, however, did the Church define the "how" of Jesus' conception. Clearly, his origin is in God, and the Holy Spirit is directly operative in his conception. But whether the Holy Spirit's involvement positively excluded the cooperation of Joseph is not *explicitly* defined. One can assume, on the other hand, that the early Christian theologians and pastoral leaders of the Church themselves believed the virginal conception to be historical. They simply presupposed it. And until the beginning of the nineteenth century the virginal conception of Jesus, even in this biological sense, was universally believed by Christians.

What happened to change that virtual unanimity of belief? Two of the same factors which generated a change in our understanding of Jesus Christ and of Christian faith itself, namely, a newly critical way of reading the New Testament, and a newly evolutionary way of perceiving human existence and human history.

Can New Testament Scholarship and Official Church Teaching Be Reconciled?

There is no contradiction between the two. Even if it were clear that the official Church had explicitly defined the historicity of the virginal conception of Jesus, it would not follow that such a teaching is contradicted by biblical criticism. New Testament scholarship does not claim that the historicity of the virginal conception can be *disproved* exegetically.

Admittedly, there *is* some measure of discrepancy between the traditional teaching and belief, on the one hand, and the general drift of some contemporary New Testament scholarship, on the other. If all Catholic theologians were somehow to reach agreement on the normative character and binding force of the constant and ordinary magisterium on this important matter, Catholic biblical scholars assure us that they could "live with it" (Joseph Fitzmyer, "The Virginal Conception of Jesus in the New Testament," *Theological Studies*, vol. 34, December 1973, p. 574; the article is reprinted, with a postscript, in *To Advance the Gospel: New Testament Studies*, New York: Crossroad, 1981, pp. 41–78). But such scholars also insist on taking the critical position toward the New Testament text itself which their discipline demands. The Matthæan annunciation scene and possibly the Lucan account assert the virginal conception of Jesus, "but the question as to whether they make of that assertion an affirmation of faith or a theologoumenon is still a vital question," according to Fitzmyer.

It must be stressed, however, that Catholic exegetes and theologians who have been involved in this discussion have not denied the virginal conception of Jesus. They have raised questions about it, as is their responsibility as scholars, and they have been trying to draw the line between "what is of the essence of Catholic faith and what has been uncritically associated with it in pious and unquestioning assumptions." They cannot ascribe to the biblical sources, therefore, what the texts themselves will not allow, nor would the official Church want to base its arguments for the doctrine on an uncritical reading of those texts.

What Is the Meaning of the Belief?

The virginal conception has been understood from the very beginning as a statement about Jesus first, and about Mary only secondarily. Through this belief, the Church clearly taught that Jesus is from God, that he is unique, that in Christ the human race truly has a new beginning, that the salvation he brings transcends this world, and that God works through human instruments, often weak and humble instruments at that, to advance the course of saving history.

If in denying the historicity of the virginal conception, one is also denying such principles as these, then one has indeed moved outside the boundaries of the Christian, and certainly the Catholic, tradition. However, a more traditional understanding of the doctrine remains an integral part of belief and devotion for a great many Catholics.

THE SINLESSNESS OF JESUS

Belief in the sinlessness of Jesus Christ is a direct implication of belief in the hypostatic union, i.e., the belief that the human nature of Jesus Christ is perfectly united with the Second Person of the Trinity. The dogma of the hypostatic union, in turn, is a product of the Church's reflection on the intimacy and communion between Jesus and the Father, to the extent that Jesus spoke of God as "my own dear Father" (*Abba*). Belief in the virginal conception of Jesus establishes the basis of this intimacy in Jesus' origin. He is from God, having been conceived by the power of the Holy Spirit. It is in this context that the question of Jesus' sinlessness must be answered.

There are five subquestions to be considered here also: (1) Is the belief in the sinlessness of Jesus Christ truly a belief of the New Testament Church? (2) Is that belief rooted in historical fact? That is, was Jesus actually without sin throughout his entire lifetime? (3) Does the Church officially teach not only the sinlessness of Christ but his impeccability as well? (4) Can our understanding of the New Testament be reconciled with the official teaching of the Church? (5) What does the belief in the sinlessness of Jesus Christ mean?

Is It a Belief of the
New Testament Church?

Belief in the sinlessness of Christ *is* rooted in the New Testament— more widely, in fact, than belief in the virginal conception. The pertinent texts are John 8:46, 14:30; 2 Corinthians 5:21; 1 Peter 2:22; and Hebrews 4:15. Jesus declared that Satan had no hold on him (John 14:30) and challenged his opponents to convict him of sin if they could (John 8:46). Paul, in very early testimony, proclaims that Jesus "knew no sin . . . that in him we might become the righteousness of God" (2 Corinthians 5:21). "He committed no sin," the author of 1 Peter writes (2:22). Finally, the Epistle to the Hebrews commends Jesus Christ to us as our great high priest "who in every respect has been tested as we are, yet without sin" (4:15).

Significantly, nowhere is it asserted that Jesus could not have sinned, that he was absolutely incapable of sin (*impeccabilitas*). The New Testament declares that, in fact, Jesus did not sin (*impeccantia*).

Indeed, he was genuinely *tempted* to sin (Mark 1:12–13; Luke 4:2–13; Matthew 4:1–11). It was neoscholastic Christology, on the contrary, which concluded the impeccability of Jesus. And since neoscholastic Christology has prevailed in Catholic teaching until the middle of the twentieth century, as we noted in chapters 13 and 14, the understanding of the sinlessness of Christ as impeccability has simply been taken for granted for the past five or six centuries.

Is That Belief Rooted in Historical Fact?

Did Jesus, in fact, never sin? It is a claim which is even more difficult to verify historically than the claim for the virginal conception. It is, for all practical purposes, impossible to verify. No one could have read into the mind and heart of Jesus to detect any sinful attitudes and wishes, even if he had them. And no one could have been with Jesus every moment of the day or night to notice his doing something sinful, even if he had committed a sinful act.

But neither do we have any evidence that Jesus *did* sin. Not even his gravest enemies could make the accusation, and even less make it stick. This is one of the most remarkable aspects of the belief in, and the claim of, the sinlessness of Christ. If the moral gap between Jesus' words and deeds had been apparent to anyone at all, it would have been brought to public attention, so threatening and so revolutionary was his message. Indeed, it would not have taken much to twist the Zacchæus episode (Luke 19:1–10) into one of consorting with the oppressing class. Nor, as John A. T. Robinson has observed, "would most ministers today be able to survive three circumstantial (and, I believe, independent) reports that he had his feet (or head) kissed, scented, and wiped with the hair of a woman, whether or not of doubtful repute" (*The Human Face of God*, p. 98; the references are to Mark 14:3–9; Luke 7:36–50; and John 12:1–8).

Does the Church Officially Teach the Impeccability of Jesus?

The official Church certainly teaches as much as the New Testament does, namely, that Jesus Christ was without sin. In fact, where the

546

Church formulates its belief, it simply repeats biblical expressions, especially the Hebrews text. This is true in the following instances: (1) the Council of Chalcedon (451), which defines that Jesus Christ is "coessential with us—the very same one—as to his humanity, being like us in every respect apart from sin"; (2) the Lateran Council (649), "sin only being excepted"; and (3) the Eleventh Council of Toledo (675), "without sin."

The work of interpretation becomes difficult when moving to the Third Council of Constantinople (681), which condemned *Monothelitism* (in Christ there is only *one will*, and that divine). The council taught that there are two wills, the one human and the other divine, just as there are two natures. The human will, however, is "compliant, it does not resist or oppose but rather submits to the divine and almighty will." On the other hand, the same doctrinal formulation declares that the human will "has not been destroyed by being divinized. It has rather been preserved...."

Although one could reasonably infer from the teaching of Constantinople III that Jesus Christ was incapable of sin, that precise point is not explicitly made. Indeed, one could also reasonably argue that if Jesus were utterly incapable of sinning, his human will was not after all preserved. Rather, it would have become so "compliant" to the divine will as to be indistinguishable from it. But that is precisely the heresy of Monothelitism which the council condemned.

It seems better to conclude that *it is the clear and constant belief and teaching of the Church that Jesus Christ was perfect in his humanity, that he was so completely in union with the Father that he was in fact absolutely without sin.* It is not that Jesus Christ was absolutely *incapable* of sin, but rather that he was *able not to sin* and, in fact, *did not sin.* However, both views—the one favoring impeccability and the one that does not—are within the range of Catholic orthodoxy.

Can the New Testament Witness Be Reconciled with the Official Church's Teaching?

This question, in the light of the preceding, answers itself. The New Testament does not enter the realm of theological speculation. There is no analysis of the operation of Jesus' human will, nor is there any philosophical reflection on the dynamics of human consciousness or of human freedom. But neither is there very much of this in the Church's doctrines, not to say dogmas. On the contrary, where the official Church formulates its teaching, it simply builds on the biblical testimony, relying in particular on the expression from the Epistle to the Hebrews, namely, that Jesus is completely like us in everything except sin. The text does not say—nor does the Church—that Jesus is different because sin is metaphysically impossible for him, but that he is different because, in fact, he was *without sin*.

What Does the Sinlessness of Jesus Christ Mean?

The fact that Jesus Christ is without sin makes him the supreme expression of communion between God and humankind. It is because he is utterly, completely, and perfectly holy in his very humanity that he is able to disclose the divine to us through that same humanity. Jesus Christ, the sinless one, shows us not only the human but the divine. "He is the reflection of God's glory and the exact imprint of God's very being" (Hebrews 1:3).

THE KNOWLEDGE, OR CONSCIOUSNESS, OF JESUS

The question of the knowledge, or consciousness, of Jesus is important for two reasons: (1) Many problems of New Testament interpretation cannot be solved if there is no possibility of development, even error, in the knowledge of Jesus (see the discussion in chapter 12); and (2) Hebrews 4:15 and the Council of Chalcedon assert that Jesus is like us in all things "yet without sin." How much like us is Jesus if he knew exactly what the future held for him, down to the finest detail? We face the future with wonder and hope, and sometimes with fear and dread. Jesus would have experienced none of these human emotions if he knew, with factual certitude, precisely what the Father had in store for him, and especially that the Father would raise him from the dead "on the third day."

At issue in the first two special questions were the origin of Jesus in God (the virginal conception) and the intimate communion of

Jesus with God (the sinlessness of Jesus). Both italicize the *divinity* of Jesus Christ. At issue here, and in the next question, is the *humanity* of Jesus Christ. Is he really one with us—in all things except sin?

There are three subquestions to be considered: (1) Does the New Testament attribute ignorance and even error to Jesus? (2) Does the official Church admit of ignorance and error in the mind of Jesus? (3) Can the New Testament record be reconciled with the official teaching of the Church?

Does the New Testament Attribute Ignorance and Even Error to Jesus?

Although there are indications in the New Testament that the early Church thought Jesus to be in possession of unlimited and infallible knowledge, the weight of the evidence seems to be on the other side.

Indications in Favor of Unlimited Knowledge

Given the development from a low (Jesus-as-human) to a high (Jesus-as-divine) Christology within the New Testament and within the Gospels themselves (e.g., from Mark to John), it is not surprising that the later New Testament material should have suppressed any suggestion of Jesus' ignorance. For example, Matthew 9:20–22 reports the same incident found in Mark 5:25–33, where a woman "afflicted with a hemorrhage for a dozen years" touched Jesus' garment and "healing power had gone out from him." In the earlier Marcan account, however, Jesus does not know who touched him. In Matthew's account, Jesus turns and immediately identifies the woman.

In John's report of the miracle of the loaves, Jesus asks Philip where they could find enough bread to feed such a "large crowd" (John 6:5). But John quickly adds that Jesus "said this to test him, for he himself knew what he was going to do"(v. 6). Later in John 6:64 we are assured by the author of the Fourth Gospel that Jesus knew that some of his disciples would be unfaithful, and Judas in particular (6:71; 13:11).

All of the Gospels attribute to Jesus the ability to know what others are thinking (Mark 2:6–8; Mark 9:33–34; Luke 9:46–47; John

2:24–25; 16:19,30). But it is not always clear whether this reflects Jesus' own keen perception of human nature or whether it is really a form of superhuman knowledge.

Finally, there are several examples where Jesus is portrayed as having knowledge of events taking place somewhere else. In John 1:48–49 he knew that Nathanæl had been under the fig tree. In Mark 11:2 he knew that there would be a colt at the entrance of a nearby village. In Mark 14:13–14 and Luke 22:10 Jesus sends two of his disciples to the city with the instruction that they would come upon a man carrying a water jar and that he would provide a room for them in which to celebrate the Passover feast. But the Old Testament prophets also were believed to have had this kind of knowledge. Thus, Ezekiel had visions of events in Jerusalem although he was still in Babylon (Ezekiel 8; see also 1 Samuel 10:1–8).

Indications Against Unlimited Knowledge

In Mark 5:30–33 (= Luke 8:45–47), to which we referred above, Jesus does not know who in the crowd touched his garment. In Luke 2:46 he asks questions of the teachers of the Law in the Temple. In Luke 2:52 he is described as having "increased in wisdom." Both these texts are significant because they are part of the Lucan Infancy Narrative, where Jesus is presented unequivocally as God's Son from the moment of his conception.

Even in the specifically religious realm Jesus is shown to have been ignorant about certain matters. He reflects the inadequate and sometimes erroneous biblical views of his contemporaries. He cites an Old Testament text which apparently does not exist (John 7:38). He is wrong about the identity of the high priest at the time David entered the house of God and ate the holy bread which only the priests were permitted to eat (Mark 2:26); it was Ahimelech (1 Samuel 21:1–6) and not Abiathar, as Jesus thought. He was in error, too, about the fact that Zechariah, son of Jehoiada, was killed in the Temple (2 Chronicles 24:20–22); it was not Zechariah, son of Barachiah, as Jesus said (Matthew 23:35). And Jesus mistakenly attributed Psalm 110 to David, making it a messianic psalm besides (Mark 12:36), even though there was no expectation of a Messiah at the time it was composed. Jesus also shared the primitive ideas of his contemporaries about demons, confusing demon possession with epilepsy and insanity (Mark 5:4, 9:17–18; Matthew 12:43–45; Luke 11:24–26). He drew upon the same limited religious concepts of his day to describe the afterlife and the end of the world (Mark 9:43–49; 13). There is nothing new, superhuman, or unique about such declarations. Jesus simply employed ideas and imagery that were already current.

We cannot even take at face value his foreknowledge and predictions of his passion, death, and resurrection (Mark 8:31; 9:31; 10:33–34; and parallels). Among other exegetical problems, one has to account for the exceedingly curious attitude of the disciples who, if they had really heard Jesus make such predictions, should not have been taken by such complete surprise by the crucifixion even when it was imminent; nor, of course, should they have been so totally unprepared for the resurrection (Luke 24:19–26).

Much the same can be said of Jesus' predictions of the destruction of the Temple at Jerusalem (Mark 13:2). He insisted, for example, that "not one stone will be left here upon another." And yet they are still there, even today!

The biblical and theological discussions about Jesus' knowledge of the date of the Second Coming (*parousia*) cannot usefully be summarized here. But all those who favor a so-called maximalist position (namely, that Jesus knew everything, and everything about everything) have to contend with the stark assertion: "But about that day or hour no one knows, neither the angels in heaven, nor the Son, but only the Father" (Mark 13:32).

Did Jesus, finally, know himself to be the unique Son of God? It is true that Jesus spoke of God as his Father in such a way as to suggest a special, intimate relationship. But there is no incontrovertible proof that he claimed a unique sonship not open to other persons. "Why do you call me good?" he asks a man who kneels before him to inquire about everlasting life. "No one is good but God alone" (Mark 10:18). And when he teaches his disciples to pray, he instructs them, and all of us, to address God just as he addresses God, as "Father" (Luke 11:2). The Fourth Gospel, of course, clearly shows Jesus claiming to be the Son of God, but that book was written precisely to prove that point (20:31).

The Firm Convictions of Jesus About the Kingdom

To suggest that Jesus did not have unlimited knowledge, that he was ignorant of many things and in error about others, is not to suggest at the same time that Jesus was a man without extraordinary intellectual strength and vision. On the contrary, Jesus displayed an exceedingly novel and courageous degree of *conviction* on the most central matter of all, the Kingdom of God. He was obviously convinced that the reign of God was active even now in his preaching, in his actions, and in his very person. He interpreted it with complete authority.

Six times in the fifth chapter of Matthew he says to his disciples, "You have heard,..." and follows each with the assertion, "What I say to you is..." He puts demands upon others. He forgives sins. He changes the Law of Moses. He violates the Sabbath ordinances. He offends against proprieties—e.g., by eating with sinners. He forbids divorce. He urges us to turn the other cheek, and so forth. All of this implies a unique conviction and, therefore, a unique human consciousness about himself and his relationship to God, a relationship without parallel in the lives of any of the Old Testament prophets. Moreover, there is no indication anywhere in the New Testament that Jesus only gradually developed this particular conviction. On the contrary, as he begins his public ministry, that conviction is at the heart of his proclamation (Mark 1:15).

Does the Official Church Admit of Ignorance and Error in Jesus?

The gap between the New Testament and the official teaching of the Church is greater here than on the first two special questions, the virginal conception and the sinlessness of Jesus. On the other hand, the magisterial sources are less authoritative (nothing approaching an ecumenical council, for example), and their dependence upon the medieval synthesis is even more pronounced.

Medieval Christology had argued, on the basis of the hypostatic union, that no perfection is to be denied Jesus if it was at all possible for him to have had it. Therefore, he not only knew everything, but he knew everything about everything. He had *beatific* knowledge, i.e., God's knowledge of all things; *infused* knowledge, i.e., angelic knowledge requiring no learning effort; and *experimental* knowledge, i.e., what he inescapably encountered within the particularities of his earthly life. An extreme form of the medieval position was expressed by certain seventeenth-century commentators on Thomas Aquinas, known as the *Salmanticenses* (theologians associated with the University of Salamanca, in Spain). In their view, Jesus' knowledge was so unlimited that he could accurately be described as the greatest mathematician, the greatest doctor, the greatest painter, the greatest farmer, the greatest sailor, the greatest philosopher, and so forth.

Not all medieval theology was so narrowly focused. Thomas himself acknowledged that "if there had not been in the soul of Christ some other knowledge besides his divine knowledge, he would not have known anything. Divine knowledge cannot be an act of the human soul of Christ; it belongs to another nature" (*Summa Theologiæ* III, q. 9, a. 1). The official declarations of the postmedieval Church, however, have tended to carry forward the spirit, if not the letter, of the Salmanticenses rather than the frequently more nuanced approach of Thomas.

In 1907 the Holy Office, under the direction of Pope Pius X, issued its anti-Modernist decree *Lamentabili,* in which it rejected certain contemporary assumptions about the knowledge and consciousness of Jesus, namely, that he was in error about "the proximity of the Messianic advent" and that his human knowledge was limited.

In 1918 the same Holy Office, this time under the direction of Pope Benedict XV, categorized certain propositions as being "unsafe" for teaching in Catholic seminaries and universities, namely, the opinion that Christ may not have had the beatific vision during his lifetime, that he would not have known "from the beginning... everything, past, present, and future, that is to say everything which God knows with the 'knowledge of vision.' "

Finally, in 1943 Pope Pius XII declared in an encyclical letter on the Church as the Mystical Body of Christ (*Mystici Corporis*) that Jesus enjoyed the beatific vision "from the time He was received into the womb of the Mother of God." Consequently, "the loving knowledge with which the divine Redeemer has pursued us from the first moment of His incarnation is such as completely to surpass all the searchings of the human mind."

There are also two premedieval pronouncements. The first comes from the *Constitutum* of Pope Vigilius (553), in which certain Nestorian propositions are condemned: "If anyone says that the one Jesus Christ who is both true Son of God and true Son of Man did not know the future or the day of the Last Judgment and that He could know only as much as the divinity dwelling in Him as in another revealed to Him, *anathema sit*."

The second comes from a letter of Pope Gregory the Great to Eulogius (d. 607), Patriarch of Alexandria, in which the pope commends the patriarch for his treatise against the *Agnoetes,* a sect which inverted the Monophysitism of the day by teaching that the divine nature was absorbed into the human. Resting their case on the passage in Mark's Gospel to which we referred above (13:32), the Agnoetes argued that Jesus was ignorant about the Day of Judgment. Gregory affirmed Eulogius's argument that the passage in question applied not to Christ as Head but to Christ as Body, i.e., Christ as Church. What Jesus knew *in* his human nature he did not know *from* his human nature. Because he is one in being with the Father, he has a knowledge which surpasses all others', including even that of the angels. Therefore, no ignorance was present in him, much less error.

Can We Reconcile the New Testament Record and the Teachings of the Church?

No; at least not *these* teachings. But then, what precisely are these teachings excluding, and what authority do they have?

The difficulty with answering the first of these two questions is compounded by the variety of theological universes that are operative in the New Testament, the medieval period, and in contemporary thought. On closer examination, the three universes are not mutually opposed. The medieval position is the "odd one out." The New Testament and present-day theology are in closer harmony, one with another.

The teachings in question reflect certain assumptions about the meaning of knowledge which may be open to challenge today. The teachings assume, first, that God is not involved in human consciousness or in the growth of human knowledge except as a divine supplement. Thus, ordinary human beings (i.e., everyone except Jesus Christ) begin with absolutely nothing (*tabula rasa*) and proceed to accumulate knowledge experimentally, i.e., through human experience. Insofar as ordinary human beings know anything beyond what they can gather through experience, they receive it from God, as a revelation. Revelation, in this conception, is knowledge which is given over and above human knowledge.

The medieval approach to the problem of Jesus' knowledge is merely consistent with the medieval understanding of the relationship between nature and grace and of the meaning of revelation. Those same medieval conceptions of nature-and-grace and of revelation were immediately operative in the anti-Modernist documents and in *Mystici Corporis* (1943).

The medieval understanding of Jesus' knowledge also reflects a pre-Enlightenment concept of history as something essentially static, as if history were simply the record of human actions in the world (e.g., comparable to a jet stream or the wake of a ship) rather than the evolutionary context in which human actions assume their meaning, significance, and direction (e.g., comparable to water as the element in which sea creatures live and develop).

In the modern, as opposed to classical, understanding of history, an exact foreknowledge of all events (such as Christ is supposed to have had) would make truly free human action impossible. Human freedom is not simply the negative absence of constraints but the positive capacity to venture one's own future for something greater. It involves risk-taking, trust, hope, mystery.

Accordingly, to identify the human consciousness of Jesus with the divine consciousness, or to make Jesus' human consciousness something completely directed by the divine consciousness, is to relapse into Monophysitism. This sets clearly one limit to our understanding of Jesus' human consciousness and knowledge.

However, we must continually remind ourselves that we are dealing ultimately with a mystery, which does not readily yield to theological analysis. It may be helpful to distinguish, as some contemporary theologians do, between the *unreflexive consciousness* in the depths of Jesus' being and the *objectifying and verbalizing consciousness* which had a history and which fully shared in the human situation (concepts, ideas, etc.) of Jesus' time, encompassing processes of learning, surprising experiences, crises of self-identity, etc.

In his *unreflexive consciousness* Jesus was aware of himself as a subject in whom God was fully present and as one who was fully present in God. The *immediacy* of this contact with God was unique, based as it is on the hypostatic union, and it explains the extraordinary *conviction* with which Jesus proclaimed and practiced the Kingdom of God. Similarly, his sense that his own relationship with God is something *exemplary* for all other human beings generated the *conviction* that he was himself the personification of the Kingdom which he proclaimed and practiced.

In his *objectifying and verbalizing consciousness* Jesus understood and expressed *less* than the "content" of his unreflexive consciousness. In other words, Jesus, like the rest of us, knew more than he was capable of saying. Through dialogue and personal interaction with others he, like the rest of us, came to a fuller understanding of who he was and what or who he was for. He went to his death knowing at least that it was the fate of a prophet, and he accepted his death in the light of his conviction that God would vindicate what he had said, done, and been. Such a theological explanation does not at all deny that Jesus Christ was, in his very being and from the beginning, the Word made flesh, nor does it deny that through his death and resurrection he fully realized and achieved for us all that God intended to realize and achieve through him.

It is readily admitted that this theological explanation is not the one operative in the magisterial documents under consideration. But is this explanation positively excluded by those documents? And if so, what authority do these documents have?

The *Constitutum* of Pope Vigilius was directed specifically against Nestorian errors. Even if one were to grant *dogmatic* status to the *Constitutum*—and no one can—it does not explicitly exclude the position outlined above (proposed by Rahner, Schoonenberg, and others). The two Holy Office decrees of 1907 and 1918 also have to be interpreted carefully: The first rejected certain Modernist theses but contained no distinct censure of the view outlined above; the second simply called views like it "unsafe." *Mystici Corporis* raises the question of Jesus' knowledge almost in passing. The encyclical is not directed at contemporary Christological aberrations. Insofar as the passage is doctrinally pertinent, it applies more properly to the glorified Savior who now acts as the risen Head of the Body, which is the Church.

Even if one were to grant, however, that these documents do condemn the position presented here, and by Rahner and other Catholic theologians elsewhere, one would still have to raise the question of the authoritative status of such condemnations. On a scale of authoritative value, decrees of Vatican congregations and even papal encyclicals fall well below infallible pronouncements of ecumenical councils. And one might also make a reasonable case that they fall below the doctrinal pronouncements of an international synod of bishops or of a regional council of the Church, i.e., one involving several national churches but not "the whole wide world," which is the literal meaning of the word "ecumenical."

Moreover, the teaching authority of the Church—at whatever level of exercise—is "not above the word of God, but serves it..." (Vatican II, *Dogmatic Constitution on Divine Revelation*, n. 10). The word of God, as proclaimed in the New Testament and as interpreted in the light of present theological principles, calls into question the apparent intent of the magisterial pronouncements on this question of the knowledge of Jesus. Finally, this newer approach is not without precedent even in the patristic period. It was Cyril of Alexandria (d. 444), whose anti-Nestorian writings were officially adopted by the Council of Ephesus (431), who wrote of Jesus Christ: "We have admired his goodness in that for love of us he has not refused to descend to such a low position as to bear all that belongs to our nature, included in which is ignorance" (*Thesaurus on the Holy and Consubstantial Trinity*, thesis 22).

THE SEXUALITY OF JESUS

Here again the issue is the *humanity* of Jesus, but it is posed even more sharply than in the preceding question. Is he really like us in all things except sin, or is he so much an exception to the rule of human existence, indeed of *sexually* human existence, that he can scarcely be *one of us*, let alone the representative of *all of us*?

Our discussion will make its way through four subquestions: (1) How does the New Testament portray the sexuality of Jesus? (2) How has the sexuality of Jesus been understood in the tradition and official teachings of the Church? (3) Can the New Testament record be reconciled with that tradition and those teachings? (4) Can our own contemporary understanding of sexuality be reconciled with either or both: the New Testament and the tradition, on the one hand, and the teachings of the Church, on the other?

How Does the New Testament Portray
the Sexuality of Jesus?

One is struck at once by the almost total silence of the New Testament about the sexuality of Jesus. The New Testament reports that he knew hunger and thirst. He even knew anger, as on the occasion of his driving the money-changers from the Temple (Mark 11:15–17). He was tempted to pride, idolatry, and the desire for power (Matthew 4:1–11). And he endured rejection, betrayal, physical abuse, and finally death itself. But nowhere is he sexually tempted, much less engaged in sexual activity. Was he, in fact, sexless? And if sexless, how was he fully human?

There are a few references to sexual morality which do convey something of Jesus' attitude toward sexuality: "You have heard that it was said, 'You shall not commit adultery.' But I say to you that everyone who looks at a woman with lust has already committed adultery with her in his heart" (Matthew 5:27–28). He accentuates his point: "If your right eye causes you to sin, tear it out and throw it away; . . . if your right hand causes you to sin, cut it off and throw it away; it is better for you to lose one of your members than for your whole body to go into hell" (vv. 29–30).

Jesus moves immediately from adultery to divorce: "But I say to you that anyone who divorces his wife,... causes her to commit adultery; and whoever marries a divorced woman commits adultery" (v. 32). He also tells his audience, "For in the resurrection they neither marry nor are given in marriage, but are like angels in heaven" (Matthew 22:30). (The meaning, force, and applicability of Jesus' ethical teaching will be examined more fully in Part Six on Christian Morality.)

On the other hand, the Gospels also present Jesus as a man known for his conviviality, his readiness to bless matrimonial unions, as one who even refers to the wedding feast as a symbol of the Kingdom of God (Matthew 22:1–14).

But how account for the obvious paucity of material on his sexuality? One plausible explanation is that Jesus deliberately wished to disassociate his proclamation of the Kingdom of God from the standard attitude toward human existence one finds in the other contemporary religions, where sex consistently played a large, if not even central, part. Some idealized sex as a sign of power that had to be replenished from on high; others condemned sex as a pollution to be purged from our lives. Jesus simply refused to sanction the religious status of sex. He is neither Dionysian nor anti-Dionysian.

Interpretations, beyond this one, vary widely. Hugh Montefiore, an Anglican scholar and later a bishop, suggested that Jesus may have had homosexual tendencies ("Jesus the Revelation of God," in *Christ for Us Today*, Norman Pittenger, ed., London: SCM Press, 1968, pp. 108–110). William Phipps, a Protestant theologian, proposed that Jesus was married and that the postresurrection encounter with Mary Magdalene can best be understood in light of his marital relationship with her (*Was Jesus Married?* New York: Harper & Row, 1970).

There are, however, at least three arguments against the suggestion that Jesus was married: (1) The Gospels say nothing at all about a marriage; (2) the antierotic bias of the New Testament churches came very early into Christianity, and it can be supposed that if Jesus had been married, that tendency would have been checked; and, most decisively, (3) when Paul invoked his right to marry a believing woman "as do the other apostles and the brothers of the Lord and Cephas" (1 Corinthians 9:5), why did he not appeal to Jesus' own marriage to support his argument?

How Has the Sexuality of Jesus Been Understood in the Tradition and Teachings of the Church?

In a word, poorly. The influence of idealistic Greek philosophy, and the thought of Plato in particular, has been profound. Plato's true philosopher does not concern himself with sexual pleasure (*Phædo*, 64, 82). Sexual desire is referred to as a diseased aspect of the person-

559

ality (*Republic*, 402–5). The well-balanced person is the one who sublimates his sexual energies in intellectual pursuits (*Republic*, 485). Aristotle is at least as negative. A woman, he noted, is "a mutilated male" (*On the Generation of Animals*, 737a). The male is by nature superior. He commands; the female obeys (*Politics* 1254b, 1260a).

This same spirit was carried forward into the patristic and medieval periods by such men as Gregory of Nyssa and Augustine, for whom the sexual impulse is a sin and a shame (*City of God*, 14:17–18). Indeed, the genital organs are indecent and dishonorable (*partes inhonestæ*, neoscholastic theology would call them). They are the bodily instruments for the transmission of Original Sin (*On Marriage and Concupiscence*, 1:13). The ideal society for Augustine was a society without passion, where male and female would join for reproduction not through the "eager desire of lust, but the normal exercise of the will" (*City of God*, 14:26). The highest ideal, therefore, is consecrated virginity. In his anti-Manichæan writings (e.g., *The Good of Marriage*), however, Augustine presented a more positive estimation of marriage, highlighting the importance of fidelity in the mutual love of the spouses and pointing out that marriage is a sacrament of the future peace and unity of God's people in eternity.

Thomas Aquinas was more moderate, but his views were also influenced by Greek philosophy, especially Aristotelian biology, and by Augustinianism. The celibate life is to be preferred, he argued, because it is "unseared by the heat of sexual desire" (*Summa Theologiæ* II-II, q. 152, a. 1). He quoted with approval Augustine's injunction that sexual contact proper to the married state pulls down the mind from its heights (q. 151, a. 3). Following Augustine's theory on Original Sin, Thomas also argued that Jesus had to be conceived virginally because sin is transmitted by the male seed (III, q. 31, a. 3). Aquinas's attitude toward women was similarly appalling by present standards: The woman is an entirely passive agent in the act of love, and is less than a man on nature's scale (I, q. 99, a. 2; II-II, q. 26, a. 10; III, q. 32, a. 4). At the same time, he argued for the importance of friendship in marriage, which he described as a "partnership of the whole range of domestic activity" (*Summa Contra Gentiles* 3.123.6). Comparably negative attitudes toward sexuality can be found in the major Protestant Reformers: Luther, Zwingli, and Calvin (see W. Phipps, *The Sexuality of Jesus*, New York: Harper & Row, 1973, pp. 95–104).

Not surprisingly, this same attitude found expression in religious art and a counterreaction in secular literature. Mass-produced paintings, statues, and holy cards depicting Jesus in one form or another (the Infant of Prague, the Sacred Heart, e.g.) are unrelievedly sexless. It is an art style called *Kitsch*, something one instantly recognizes but cannot define. "*Kitsch* is weak, save in two respects," Bruno Brinkman, S.J., writes. "It encourages submission and obedience, and it is strong in repressing or infantilizing sex, which is different from sublimating it. It has been unmistakably powerful and popular. We must not forget that in religious houses such statues were for decades the object of regular private, if not community, *cultus* [worship]" ("The Humanity of Christ: Christ and Sexuality," *The Way*, vol. 15, 1975, p. 210). *Kitsch* expresses fear of the human body and of sexuality. It is patently Docetic in tendency. It preaches and teaches a Jesus who is not recognizably human.

This vehemently antisexual bias has brought forth a variety of reactions. The most celebrated is D. H. Lawrence's (d. 1930) short story "The Man Who Died" (reprinted in *Christian Faith and the Contemporary Arts*, Finley Eversole, ed., New York: Vintage Books, 1959). Lawrence makes Jesus' resurrection his awakening to sensual love. On the other side is Nikos Kazantzakis's (d. 1957) *The Last Temptation* (New York: Simon and Schuster, 1960), in which Jesus' spiritual struggle, his final battle with Satan, is defined by his carnal desire for Mary Magdalene, even as he hangs on the cross. But Jesus is shaken out of his dream and overcomes the Devil's power: "The moment he cried ELI ELI and fainted, Temptation had captured him for a split second and led him astray. The joys, marriages, and children were lies... illustrations sent by the Devil" (p. 496). Just as Lawrence had read into Jesus' life his own exceedingly permissive approach to sexuality, so Kazantzakis had projected upon *his* Jesus a mixture of late Western asceticism and Buddhism.

And what of the *official teachings* of the Church? The Church is nearly as silent as the New Testament. The only direct reference is to be found in the documents of the Second Council of Constantinople (553), not one of the more authoritative of the Church's ecumenical councils, as we pointed out in chapter 13. A condemnation of Theodore of Mopsuestia is issued and is subsequently approved by Pope Vigilius. Among Theodore's allegedly Nestorian views is one which holds that "God the Word is one while Christ is another who, disturbed by the passions of the soul and the desires of the flesh, freed himself gradually from inferior inclinations...." The issue at hand was not Jesus' sexuality, but the unity of the two natures in the one divine Word. In any case, it is not a *dogmatic* definition nor, as given there, is it even clearly a *doctrine* of the Church.

Can the New Testament and the Tradition and Teachings of the Church Be Reconciled?

On this precise point, i.e., whether or not Jesus had an active sexual life or was sexually tempted, there is no possibility of contradiction, since the New Testament says nothing about either. The larger question, i.e., whether the patristic and medieval traditions are fundamentally consistent with the whole of the New Testament message and of Christian faith, will be addressed by implication, at least, in the next section.

What Does Our Contemporary Christian Consciousness Disclose About Sexuality in General, and About Jesus' Sexuality in Particular?

It seems entirely consistent with Christian faith in the *humanity* of Jesus Christ that Jesus should have known sexual temptation. Temptation itself is no sin; therefore, it would not violate the previous principle that Jesus was indeed sinless. Moreover, the New Testament does explicitly acknowledge that Jesus was tempted by Satan in the areas of power and worldly acclaim. To accept a Jesus who is at once fully human and yet immune from sexual desires is to stretch not only one's imagination but also one's theological convictions about the incarnation and the fundamental goodness of creation, the human body, and human sexuality.

It would not necessarily follow, however, that Jesus, as a necessary expression of his humanity, actually did engage in sexual activities. Neither would it follow that sexual activity within marriage would have been inconsistent with Jesus' *divinity*. Although it is true of a small minority of the world's population, it is true nonetheless that there are well-integrated, courageous, forceful, responsible, and thoroughly dedicated human beings who do not marry. One has only to point to a random sample of such persons within the past few decades alone: Pope John XXIII (d. 1963); Dag Hammarskjold (d. 1961); Mother Teresa of Calcutta; Father Theodore M. Hesburgh, long-time president of the University of Notre Dame; Archbishop Oscar Arnulfo Romero (d. 1980) and the four women martyrs of El Salvador (Sisters Ita Ford, Dorothy Kazel, and Maura Clarke, and Ms. Jean Donovan [all murdered in 1980]); Sister Thea Bowman (d. 1991); and so many others.

But to think and speak of Jesus as if he—and those just mentioned—were asexual, if not antisexual, not only does an injustice to God's creation of sexuality but may finally undermine the humanity of Jesus as well, and would thereby remove an indispensable basis for our redemption and salvation.

Sexuality is not to be understood in a biological sense alone. Even celibates are sexual beings. The sexual difference between a man and a woman is constitutive of human nature itself, and that constitutive dimension finds expression in the psychological as well as the physiological levels of human existence. Sexuality, therefore, is not something added on to a neutral human nature. It determines a person as man or as woman. The "human person" is neither man alone or woman alone. Man and woman together, in radical equality and dignity, constitute what we mean by the human. The need for communication and complementarity is self-evident.

In sexuality a man and a woman experience their individual insufficiency and their dependence upon each other. And each one depends not just on the other, but on the other as his or her sexual complement. Sexuality, even when fulfilled in marriage, still points beyond itself to its perfect fulfillment in God. In the "already" and the "not yet" experience of fulfillment in sexual union, we come to a certain understanding of the transcendental relationship we have with God.

Jesus was fully a human being, with sexual desires and with an understanding of sexual struggle. But he subordinated (not "suppressed") the *genital* expression of that sexuality in order to leave

563

himself completely free for the proclamation of the Kingdom of God. Freud called this "sublimation." It is not something negative, like "repression." On the contrary, it represents a change in the goal as well as the object of the powerful sexual drive, putting its enormous energies at the service of some other value. This happens when there has been a free choice by which this drive is accepted and redirected. In the absence of a consciously free decision, however, repression occurs and personal maturity is blocked. This leads, in turn, to false attitudes, compensations, and/or an exaggerated quest for power for its own sake, what psychologists refer to as "asexual emotionalization." None of these effects of repression was ever attributed to Jesus. Jesus, the perfect human being, was a sexually integrated human being.

SUMMARY

1. The *virginal conception* of Jesus refers to the belief that *Jesus was conceived in the womb of a virgin, Mary, without the intervention of a human father (virginitas ante partum)*. It does *not* refer to the virginity of Mary during or after the birth of Jesus (*in partu* or *post partum*).

2. Belief in the virginal conception of Jesus *is* to be found in the *New Testament,* specifically in the Infancy Narratives of Matthew and Luke. The rest of the New Testament is silent about it.

3. It cannot be determined, on the basis of the New Testament evidence, whether the virginal conception of Jesus was a *historical fact.* The belief, therefore, may have been a *theologoumenon,* i.e., a nondoctrinal theological interpretation that cannot be verified or refuted on the basis of historical evidence, but that can be affirmed because of its close connection with some defined doctrine about God.

4. The *official Church* presupposes the virginity of Mary ("born of the Virgin Mary"), although its primary concern would seem to have been with preserving the unity of the divine and the human in Jesus Christ, rather than with affirming the historicity of his virginal conception.

5. Belief in the virginal conception means that Jesus is from God, that Jesus is unique, that in him the human race has had a new beginning, that the salvation he brings transcends this world, and that God works through the weakness and even powerlessness of human instruments to advance the course of salvation history.

6. Because Jesus Christ is believed to be "from God," he is also believed to be *without sin.*

7. Belief in the *sinlessness* of Jesus is rooted in the *New Testament*, and especially in Hebrews 4:15. The New Testament affirms only that Jesus was without sin (*impeccantia*), not that he was absolutely incapable of sin (*impeccabilitas*).

8. The sinlessness of Christ cannot be *historically verified*, but neither do we have any historical evidence or even accusations that Jesus *did* sin.

9. The *official Church* teaches at least as much as the New Testament, namely, that Jesus was de facto without sin. Taken comprehensively, the official teaching is that Jesus Christ was perfect in his humanity and so completely in union with the Father that he was absolutely without sin. He may also have been incapable of sin, but he was at least able not to sin and, in fact, did not sin.

10. The belief in the sinlessness of Jesus underscores the more fundamental belief that he is the *supreme expression of communion between God and humankind*, that he is "the reflection of the Father's glory, the exact representation of the Father's being" (Hebrews 1:3).

11. The question of Jesus' *knowledge*, or *consciousness*, is important, first, because unless we can admit to ignorance and perhaps even error in Jesus, certain problems of New Testament interpretation cannot be solved. Second, a Jesus who knows all things, and everything about all things, is not apparently the same human Jesus who the Council of Chalcedon confessed is like us in all things except sin.

12. On the basis of the *New Testament* evidence alone, one finds arguments on both sides of the question. Some texts, reflecting a later, higher Christology, attribute unlimited knowledge to Jesus, while many other texts, reflecting an earlier, lower Christology, reveal both ignorance and error in Jesus.

13. In any case, Jesus displayed a novel and courageous degree of *conviction* about the Kingdom of God, seeing his preaching, his actions, and his very person as signs and instruments of its inbreaking. He spoke with unprecedented *authority*. He put *demands* on others. He *forgave sins*. He *changed the Law of Moses*, and so forth. Indeed, he *began* his public ministry with this conviction already in place (Mark 1:15).

14. The *medieval tradition* and the *twentieth-century decrees of the Holy Office* clearly favor the "unlimited knowledge" side of the argument. In the light of our *present-day understanding* of philosophical and theological issues, however, Jesus would not have been a *free* human being, and therefore would not have really been one like us in all things except sin, if he knew exactly what lay ahead for him.

15. Theologians distinguish between (a) Jesus' *unreflexive consciousness* which was the source of his unshakable conviction about his role in the coming of the reign of God, and (b) his *objectifying and verbalizing consciousness*

which gradually reached the level of clear and precise self-understanding and expression.

16. The few *doctrinal pronouncements* which have addressed the issue of Jesus' knowledge support the view that Jesus did have unlimited knowledge, but it is not clear which Modernist understandings were condemned, and to what extent they were condemned.

17. The issue of Jesus' humanity is posed even more sharply by the question of his *sexuality*. If Jesus was sexless, how was he human?

18. The *New Testament* is silent about the matter, although it reports other basic human emotions, such as anger, hunger, temptations to power.

19. The antisexual *tradition* of the Church on this question has been influenced, in a decidedly negative way, by Greek and especially *Platonic* philosophy, as mediated by *Augustine* and other Fathers.

20. The *official Church* is nearly as silent as the New Testament on Jesus' sexuality. *Constantinople II* (553) alone refers to the matter, but it is in the context of its anti-Nestorian thrust. The issue was not directly the sexuality of Jesus but the unity of the two natures in the one divine Word.

21. It would seem entirely consistent with Christian faith in the *humanity* of Jesus to believe that he knew *sexual desires and sexual temptations*, neither of which are in themselves sinful.

22. One need not, on the other hand, attribute *overt genital sexual activity* to Jesus on the grounds that his humanity could not have been fulfilled without it. *Sublimation* involves a free acceptance of our sexual drives and a free redirection of those drives for other values. *Repression*, on the other hand, leads to false attitudes, compensatory behavior, and inordinate quests for power over others. Jesus was a sexually integrated man.

SUGGESTED READINGS

Brinkman, Bruno. "The Humanity of Christ: Christ and Sexuality." *The Way* 15 (1975), 209–24.
Brown, Raymond E. "How Much Did Jesus Know?" *Jesus, God and Man: Modern Biblical Reflections*. Milwaukee: Bruce, 1967, pp. 39–105.
_____. *The Virginal Conception and Bodily Resurrection of Jesus*. New York: Paulist Press, 1973, pp. 21–68.
_____. *Responses to 101 Questions on the Bible*. New York: Paulist Press, 1990.
Brown, Raymond E., et al., eds. *Mary in the New Testament: A Collaborative Assessment by Protestant and Roman Catholic Scholars*. New York: Paulist Press, 1978.

Driver, Thomas F. "Sexuality and Jesus." *New Theology No. 3.* Eds. Martin Marty and Dean Peerman. New York: Macmillan, 1966, pp. 118–32.

Fitzmyer, Joseph A. *A Christological Catechism: New Testament Answers.* New York: Paulist Press, 1981.

_____. *Scripture and Christology: A Statement of the Biblical Commission with a Commentary.* New York: Paulist Press, 1986.

Malatesta, Edward, ed. *Jesus in Christian Devotion and Contemplation.* St. Meinrad, Ind.: Abbey Press, 1974.

Phipps, William E. *The Sexuality of Jesus: Theological and Literary Perspectives.* New York: Harper & Row, 1973.

Rahner, Karl. "Dogmatic Reflections on the Knowledge and Self-Consciousness of Christ." *Theological Investigations.* Vol. 5. Baltimore: Helicon, 1966, pp. 193–215.

Robinson, John A. T. *The Human Face of God.* Philadelphia: Westminster Press, 1973, pp. 1–98.

Schoonenberg, Piet. *The Christ: A Study of the God-Man Relationship in the Whole of Creation and in Jesus Christ.* New York: Herder & Herder, 1971, pp. 104–52.

PART FOUR

The Church

WE come now to the heart of the distinctively Catholic understanding of Christian faith. Catholics have always more strongly emphasized the role of the Church in mediating salvation than have other Christian traditions. And within the mystery of the Church, Catholics have always stressed the mediating function of certain ministries, structures, and institutional forms. Thus, Catholics in union with the see of Rome have insisted on the importance of the ordained ministries of the bishop, presbyter, and deacon, and the special role of the Bishop of Rome, the pope. Catholics have underlined, too, the essentially sacramental character of Christian existence and have taken care to define precisely the nature, meaning, and number of the sacraments, as well as the conditions under which they are celebrated (see Part Five). Consistently with the historical method of this entire book, Part Four begins with an examination of the origins of the Church and the churches in the New Testament (chapter 16) and traces their development and growth through subsequent centuries (chapter 17). Special emphasis is given the event which, more than any other, has shaped, and continues to shape, contemporary Catholic thought and practice, the Second Vatican Council (chapter 18).

There follows a survey of contemporary ecclesiology and an attempt at a systematic definition of the Church and a description of its mission, with special attention to questions regarding its necessity and its catholicity (chapter 19). Other special questions are examined in chapter 20, the final chapter of Part Four: authority, papacy (primacy and infallibility), ministry, and women in the Church (including the ordination question).

In this book generous attention is given the mystery of the Church, not because it is more important than the mystery of God or of Jesus Christ, but because it is with the mystery of the Church that the distinctively *Catholic* understanding and practice of Christian faith most clearly emerges. The Church is the *sacrament* of the triune God's presence among us; it is the *mediator* of God's salvific activity on our behalf; and it is a *communion* of grace to which all humanity is called in the final Kingdom of God.

XVI

The Church of the New Testament

FROM CHRISTOLOGY TO ECCLESIOLOGY

The interlocking character of Christian doctrine is by now unmistakably clear. Our understanding of Jesus Christ is a function of our understanding of God, and our understanding of God is, in turn, a function, at least correlatively, of our understanding of human existence. Jesus has meaning and value for us because he is no ordinary person; he is "hypostatically" one with the Word of God. And God has meaning and value for us because God is the source, the core, the sustenance, and the destiny of our being as individual human persons and as members of the total human community. God enters into the very definition of our humanity. We are alive by a principle which transcends us.

There is also a connection, therefore, between our understanding of human existence, of God, and of Jesus Christ, on the one hand, and our understanding of the Church, on the other. Or more immediately, our understanding of the nature and mission of the Church depends upon our understanding of the meaning and value of Jesus Christ, who reveals to us at one and the same time who God is and who we are.

This presupposes, of course, that there is some vital link between Jesus Christ and the Church, that the Church somehow issues forth from Christ and is identified with his person and work. It is precisely for the sake of examining and establishing that connection that we turn first to the question of the Church in the New Testament. In keeping with the historical method employed throughout this book, we begin at the beginning and then follow the course of the Church's development down to the present time.

THREE QUESTIONS

The Church exists. No one questions that fact, even though many would differ when it comes to defining what we mean by *Church*. The initial problem is not with the *existence* of the Church but with its origins: (1) When did the Church *begin* to exist? (2) Did Jesus *intend* that the Church should exist? (3) Did the Church remain *faithful* to Jesus' intentions even during the so-called foundational period encompassed by the New Testament writings?

These three questions are reducible to one: *What connection, if any, can we establish between the Church's evaluation of itself and Jesus' evaluation of the Church?* This is only a variation of the question which framed the parallel chapter ("The Christ of the New Testament") in Part Three, namely, the question of the Christ of faith and the Jesus of history.

It requires just as much care and delicacy to answer the question in its ecclesiological form as it did to answer it in its Christological form. The Gospels are the same primary source for both. That source can only be interpreted *developmentally.* The Gospels themselves emerged through a three-stage process: (1) the original words and deeds of Jesus; (2) the oral proclamation of the Apostles and disciples (catechesis, narratives, testimonies, hymns, doxologies, and prayers); and (3) the writings themselves. Insofar as the Gospels report sayings of Jesus on the Church (e.g., Matthew 16:18; 18:17), we have to ask: (1) What did those sayings mean when, and if, spoken by Jesus himself? (2) What did they mean in the earliest stage of the apostolic preaching? (3) What did they mean to the communities which preserved them and to the New Testament author(s) who recorded them?

The writings, in turn, reflect a progressive theological movement as the Gospel is proclaimed and accepted in one setting and then in another: (1) in the *Jewish-Christian* community of Palestine, which was closest to the events of the life, death, and resurrection of Jesus and which was most concerned with establishing the connection between Jesus and the house of David; (2) in the *Jewish-Hellenistic* community, which, in the light of the obvious delay of the Second Coming (*parousia*), stressed the present exalted state of Christ ("Jesus *is* Lord!"); and (3) in the *Hellenistic-Gentile* community, which, under the impact of the missionary activity of the Pauline and Johannine schools of theology, declared that God is even now exercising lordship over the universe in and through Jesus Christ, who is the risen and exalted Lord.

Recognizing such developments in both composition and theological content is one thing; interpreting the finally developed material is another. We should not be surprised, therefore, to discover a diversity of ecclesiological approaches not only *within* the New Testament but also within the present-day body of biblical exegetes and theologians. And since the conclusions of scholars are part of the public domain, a diversity of nonscholarly opinion about the Church is also to be expected.

JESUS AND THE CHURCH: A SPECTRUM OF INTERPRETATIONS

Nonscholarly Conservatism

This view *identifies* the whole of New Testament ecclesiology with Jesus' own evaluation of the Church. Even though the New Testament books were composed over a period of some fifty to eighty years and were addressed to diverse audiences of diverse circumstances, this nonscholarly conservative position maintains that there had been *no significant ecclesiological development* in all of that time. Thus, when Jesus accepted Peter's confession that Jesus was indeed the Messiah and made Peter the rock upon which he would build his Church (Matthew 16:13–20), that acceptance and that designation reflected the self-understanding of Jesus—despite the fact that Peter's confession and Jesus' reaction are very different in the earlier Gospel of Mark (8:27–30). Indeed, the next scene in Mark's Gospel has Jesus reprimanding Peter, "Get behind me, Satan!" (8:33).

According to the nonscholarly conservative view, Jesus left the Twelve Apostles a detailed blueprint for a Church: seven sacraments with precise matter and form, the papacy vested with supreme and universal jurisdiction, the monarchical episcopate, doctrines, liturgies, and laws. Indeed, the whole purpose of his "coming down from heaven" was to pay humanity's "debt" to the Father by his death on the cross and then to leave a Church behind in order to communicate the benefits of that saving act to as many people as possible. This view was commonly held by Catholics until the Second Vatican Council and the application of biblical scholarship to ecclesiology in the 1960s. Traces of it continue to be found in the Catholic Church today, sometimes even among its pastoral leaders.

Nonscholarly conservatism cannot withstand biblical criticism. There is no evidence in the New Testament that Jesus indicated in detail the where, the how, or the when of ecclesial development. Not even the Acts of the Apostles presents this type of continuity. On the contrary, the great advances in ecclesiastical life and organization which are reported there are responses to new and unprecedented challenges. One of the first great crises to confront the Church centered on the question of whether Gentiles might also be admitted to membership in the Christian community (Acts of the Apostles 10:1–11:18). When Peter was compelled to justify his eating with, and then baptizing, uncircumcised persons (namely, the Roman centurion Cornelius, his relatives, and close friends), he appealed not to some specific doctrinal or legal directive of Jesus but to the prompting and instruction of the Holy Spirit (11:12). Thus, if we are to speak of *continuity* in New Testament ecclesiology, it must be in terms of the Spirit of Christ who dwells within the Church, in every circumstance, time, and place. There was no institutional master plan.

But continuity does not mean *uniformity,* as if there were some unbroken line of development within the New Testament period. There are strong differences in outlook found among the various New Testament writers. For example, Matthew's attitude toward the Law (5:18; 23:2–3) is clearly not the same as Paul's in Galatians (chap. 3) and Romans (2–4; 7; 13). And Luke in the Acts of the Apostles makes no attempt to hide the fact that the Hellenistic Christians vehemently objected to the type of ecclesiastical organization which had begun to prevail among the Jewish Christians (15:1–29).

574

Nonscholarly Liberalism

The nonscholarly liberal concludes that there is *no continuity* at all between the Church's self-understanding and Jesus' evaluation of the Church. Jesus came to teach us a way of life centered on love and based on freedom from institutional oppression of every kind. He proclaimed the Kingdom of God, but his followers gave us the Church instead.

Although nonscholarly liberalism began as a Protestant movement, it has made a delayed entrance into Catholicism as a reaction against the ecclesiastical authoritarianism and the dogmatic and ethical fundamentalism of the pre–Vatican II period.

Scholarly Liberalism

Scholarly liberalism, unlike its nonscholarly counterpart, does not dismiss the ecclesiology of the New Testament as nonexistent or unimportant. On the other hand, scholarly liberalism shares with nonscholarly liberalism the conviction that the ecclesiology of the New Testament is a mistaken evaluation of what Jesus intended. For the liberals, New Testament ecclesiology is entirely a creation of the early Church.

The liberals hold that Jesus himself did not intend a Church because he expected the Kingdom of God as imminent: at first within his own lifetime, and then as something that would come about immediately after his death. The disciples, therefore, expected the Second Coming in the very near future. They perceived themselves as the ultimate Messianic Community of the Saints, the elect of the final generation who would soon enter a new form of being in the new æon. With the further delay of the *parousia*, the postapostolic Church abandoned this Pauline view and assumed organizational form of a type that suggested some historical permanence.

This view is expressed in Martin Werner's *The Formation of Christian Dogma* (Boston: Beacon Press, 1957) but goes back to earlier figures like Johannes Weiss, Albert Schweitzer, and Adolf Harnack.

575

Bultmannian Existentialism

Over against the Weiss-Schweitzer-Werner point of view, Rudolf Bultmann argued that Jesus did link entrance into the Kingdom with affiliation with a community, the Jewish people. "Do not be afraid, little flock, for it is your Father's good pleasure to give you the kingdom" (Luke 12:32). For Bultmann, the individual will find deliverance "only because he belongs to the eschatological community, not because of his personality" (*Jesus and the Word*, London: Collins, 1958, p. 41). Furthermore, he rejected the scholarly liberal's assertion that Jesus' expectation of the Kingdom of God led to his enunciating only an interim ethic. Jesus was unconcerned with the human future; he was concerned only with God's. Every person *now* stands under the judgment of God's word and will. This is the hour of decision; this is the *final* hour (p. 96).

On the other hand, Bultmann rejects the sacramentalism of the Fourth Gospel and of Hellenistic Christianity in general. For Jesus, it is not sacramental washings or meals that make a person pure, but only a pure heart, i.e., a good will (Mark 7:15). "The teaching of Jesus and that of the oldest group of his followers contained no trace of any such sacramental conception" (p. 111).

Scholarly Conservatism

Most scholars today admit *continuity within development*. They reject the fundamentalistic assumptions of their nonscholarly cousins who deny development and inflate continuity into identity. They also reject the Liberal's stress on discontinuity to the point where there is no discernible connection at all between what Jesus said and did and what eventually emerged as Church.

This so-called scholarly conservative position has its *Protestant* and *Catholic* wings, but their differences have perhaps had less to do with exegesis than with theological and doctrinal commitments. Catholics are more likely than Protestants to underline the Church's role in mediating salvation. Thus, Catholic biblical scholars such as Rudolf Schnackenburg, Anton Vögtle, and Raymond Brown affirm a stronger sacramental and ministerial character to the New Testament Church than Protestant biblical scholars such as Ernst Käsemann,

Eduard Schweizer, or Hans Conzelmann. For the Catholics, this structure is constitutive or essential to the Church. For the Protestants, it is at best functional and, therefore, not absolutely necessary to the Church's integrity.

Catholic scholars have tended to emphasize *continuity;* Protestant scholars have tended to emphasize *development.* In recent years, however, the Catholic and Protestant wings of the scholarly conservative school have moved closer to each other. Catholics continue to underline continuity, but without prejudice to development. And Protestants continue to underline development, but without prejudice to continuity. An example of this remarkable ecumenical convergence is provided by the joint exegetical and theological study, *Peter in the New Testament* (New York: Paulist Press, 1973), sponsored by the United States Lutheran–Roman Catholic Dialogue.

(The chart on page 606 summarizes the various approaches to the question of Jesus' relationship with, and attitude toward, the Church.)

DID JESUS INTEND TO FOUND A CHURCH?

The answer is "No" if by *found* we mean some direct, explicit, deliberate act by which Jesus established a new religious organization. The answer is "Yes" if by *found* we mean "lay the foundations for" the Church in various indirect ways. In this second case, it is preferable to speak of the Church as having its *origin* in Jesus rather than as having been founded by Jesus.

Jesus Did Not "Found" the Church

The Kingdom of God, Jesus insists, is open in principle to everyone: "I tell you, many will come from east and west and will eat with Abraham and Isaac and Jacob in the kingdom of heaven, while the heirs of the kingdom will be thrown into the outer darkness" (Matthew 8:11–12; see also Luke 13:28–29). But he says at the same time that his mission is not to gather together all of the just and the righteous. Indeed, he instructs his disciples: "Go nowhere among the Gentiles, and enter no town of the Samaritans, but go rather to the lost sheep of the house of Israel" (Matthew 10:5–6). To be sure, his vision of a renewed Israel included the Gentiles *coming* (Matthew 8:11), but that is different from a mission of going out *to* them.

The call of *the Twelve* has to be seen in this light. The Twelve were to represent Jesus' call to all of the twelve tribes of Israel, and they were to serve as rulers and judges "when the Son of Man is seated on the throne of his glory" (Matthew 19:28; Luke 22:30). So, too, the wider circle of disciples were entrusted with the mission to Israel as a whole (Luke 10:1–20).

Although the missionary mandate makes particular demands upon the disciples, Jesus imposes no specific rule of life, nor is membership in the company of his disciples a condition of salvation. On the contrary, "Not everyone who says to me, 'Lord, Lord,' will enter the kingdom of heaven, but only the one who does the will of my Father in heaven" (Matthew 7:21). And the will of the Father is often done without explicit awareness: "Lord, when was it that we saw you hungry and gave you food? . . . Truly I tell you, just as you did it to one of the least of these who are members of my family, you did it to me" (Matthew 25:31–46). Neither the disciples nor those Israelites who were disposed to hear his message and repent were ever organized formally into a religious group.

One should not be surprised, therefore, to find no evidence of a specific act of founding a Church or of gathering together a community of the elect. Had Jesus done this, his gesture would have been interpreted as the founding of a separate synagogue and would have minimized and even destroyed the uniqueness of his proclamation. Indeed, the only time in all of the Gospels where Jesus is reported to have made explicit reference to the founding of the Church is given in Matthew 16:18. Not until Jesus is risen from the dead do the first Christians even speak of a "Church."

Accordingly, "we have no evidence to support the view that Jesus envisioned a lengthy period with a span of centuries before the complete fulfillment of God's plan. To the contrary, the majority of scholars today support the assumption that Jesus expected the end to come soon" (Frederick J. Cwiekowski, *The Beginnings of the Church*, p. 44).

Jesus Laid the Foundations for the Church

First, Jesus did gather disciples around him. They participated in his healing power, which was a sign for Jesus that the Kingdom of God was breaking through: "He sent them out to proclaim the kingdom of God and to heal" (Luke 9:2). On the other hand, the message of the Kingdom which he preached and which he commissioned them to preach was a divisive one. They would be like "sheep in the midst of wolves" (Matthew 10:16). "Brother will betray brother to death, and a father his child, and children will rise against parents and have them put to death; and you will be hated by all because of my name" (10:21–22). Consequently, those Israelites who would accept his proclamation of the Kingdom would inevitably be distinguished from those who rejected it.

Second, he anticipated an interim period between his death and the *parousia*, even though, as we saw in our discussion of Jesus' knowledge in chapter 15, it is difficult to determine just what his understanding of this time period was. He foresaw that Jerusalem would reject the call to salvation and that instead the pagans would be invited to the heavenly banquet as a new People of God, without regard for ethnic origins (Matthew 8:11–12).

Third, the community of disciples did in fact stay together after the rejection of Jesus by the majority of the Jewish people. It is from this perspective that one must understand the Last Supper, with the Lord's injunction: "Do this in remembrance of me" (1 Corinthians 11:24). Likewise the word to Simon Peter suggests that the disciples understood Jesus as having intended them to stay together (Luke 22:31–34). In fact, there never was a churchless period in the New Testament following the resurrection.

DID THE EARLY CHRISTIAN COMMUNITY UNDERSTAND ITSELF AS CHURCH?

The Word *Church*

The Greek word *ekklēsia* originally signified a legislative assembly of citizens. Only those citizens who enjoyed full rights could belong to this assembly, and so the word implies both the dignity of the members and the legality of the assembly. The word, however, had no religious usage. It was adopted by the Septuagint (the Greek version of the Old Testament) to render the Hebrew word *kāhāl*, which, with the Hebrew word *'ēdāh*, signifies the religious assembly of the Israelites. The word appears about one hundred times in the Septuagint, often qualified by the phrase "of the Lord" *(kāhāl yahweh)*.

Because in its earliest phase the young Christian community did not view itself as distinct from Judaism, the Christians simply took over the term to apply to their own gatherings of prayer. *Not until the admission of Gentiles to the community did the distinction between the Church and Judaism become acute.* Thereafter, the word *ekklēsia* applied to the Christian community alone.

The word appears on the lips of Jesus only twice in the *Synoptic Gospels* (Matthew 16:18; 18:17). Of the first, we have already spoken. It does refer to the Church in a larger sense. The second reference (18:17) clearly refers to the local community.

The word occurs twenty-three times in the *Acts of the Apostles*. In no passage does it certainly refer to anything except the local church, and usually the church of Jerusalem, the parent and prototype of the other churches (5:11; 8:1,3). These churches outside of Jerusalem are organized with their own bishops, presbyters, and deacons, and they are founded by the Apostles (e.g., 20:28). Entrance is not by Jewish birth but by rite of Baptism, which quickly became a standard feature of Christian life. And it is God who gathers the people together (20:28 again). The wide use of the term *communion* (*koinonia*) in the New Testament shows that those who were baptized felt strongly that they had much in common. Another self-description was *the Way* (Acts of the Apostles 24:14). But the designation that became most popular was *ekklēsia*, perhaps because it best reflected their sense of continuity with Israel.

The word *ekklēsia* occurs sixty-five times in the *Pauline material* — more frequently, therefore, than anywhere else in the New Testament. In most instances the word signifies a local church. Paul is also the first to use the *plural* form of the word (1 Corinthians 11:16; 14:33; 2 Corinthians 8:18; 12:13; Galatians 1:2,22; Romans 16:4,16; and so forth). Within half a century of development, however, it refers, in *Ephesians* and *Colossians*, to the whole worldwide assembly of Christians. Christ is the head, and the Church is the fullness of his body (Ephesians 1:22–23; Colossians 1:18–20). It is through the Church that the mystery of salvation is revealed (Ephesians 3:10). The relationship between Christ, who is the great sacrament of salvation, and the Church, which is his body, is a great mystery (Ephesians 5:22–32). The figure of the Church as the body of Christ is the basis of Paul's appeal for Christian unity and fellowship (1 Corinthians 12:12–26; Romans 12:4–5). This unity is symbolized by the one bread of the Eucharist (1 Corinthians 10:17).

On the other hand, sometimes the *ekklēsia* is just a small house community (Romans 16:5; Philemon 2), listed alongside larger communities (1 Corinthians 16:19). It often has a specifically liturgical meaning (1 Corinthians 11:18; 14:23,24), and refers also to particular congregations (1 Corinthians 11:18,20,33–34; 14:23). The churches of the New Testament, whether local or universal, are congregations gathered in the name of Jesus Christ. Indeed, they are churches of Jesus Christ (Romans 16:16; 1 Thessalonians 2:14; Galatians 1:22). The Church is the true Israel and the legitimate heir of the Covenant promises (Romans 9–11).

The word *ekklēsia* appears in the *Johannine writings* in 3 John 6, 9, and 10, and twenty times in Revelation, always referring to particular churches. In the Fourth Gospel the Christian community is described as a flock gathered into a sheepfold (10:1–5), and Jesus, as the Good Shepherd. He is also the true vine; his followers, the branches united to him (15:1–8). He commits the flock to Peter (21:15–17) and prays that all of his followers may be one, as he and the Father are one (17:20–21).

In the *other New Testament writings* the word occurs once in James 5:14, where it probably signifies a particular church. There also appears a clearly defined body of followers of Jesus which is called a synagogue (James 2:2).

The Church of the New Testament is no uniform or monolithic reality. It is at once local and universal, but not in the sense that the local church is simply a subdivision of the Church universal, nor that the Church universal is simply the sum total of local churches. Although the precise relationship between the Church universal and the local church(es) is not made clear in the New Testament, it *is* clear that what is excluded in the preceding sentence is excluded also by the

New Testament. There is not a Corinthian division of the Church, for example, but "the church of God that is in Corinth" (1 Corinthians 1:2; see also 2 Corinthians 1:1). On the other hand, the Church universal is a living, integrated organism: "the fullness of him who fills all in all" (Ephesians 1:23).

The early Christian community did, in fact, appropriate to itself the title "Church" in both senses. It knew itself to be the community of Jesus the Messiah, whom God raised to his right hand (Acts of the Apostles 2:32–36; 3:13–15,20–26; 5:30–31; 7:55–56; 9:4–5; 10:37–43; 13:27–31). That the original Jerusalem church traced itself back to Jesus is evident in its maintenance of the circle of the Twelve, listed once again by name (less Judas) in Acts of the Apostles 1:13, and completed at the election of Judas's replacement (1:25–26). The celebration of the Eucharist, in fidelity to the Lord's own command, is yet another crucial link with the company of Jesus' disciples (1 Corinthians 11:23–25).

Thus, a purely individualistic Christianity is unthinkable for the earliest Christians. Belief in Christ and life in Christ are to be found only within the community of believers joined to the Lord. All of the New Testament writers write as members of the one Church of Jesus Christ. There is no fragmentation. All of the particular churches are built on the foundation of the Apostles and prophets, and Christ is always the cornerstone (Ephesians 2:20).

The Coming of the Holy Spirit

The descent of the Holy Spirit upon the Church at *Pentecost* did not inaugurate the Church. It already existed (Acts of the Apostles 1:15). But Pentecost was the moment when the Church was specifically endowed with power from on high (Luke 24:49; Acts of the Apostles 1:18). For the early Church the outpouring of the Spirit upon the Church was an established fact, and the manifestations of the Spirit's gifts were not in doubt (1 Corinthians 12–14). Even in Thessalonica those gifts were perceptible (1 Thessalonians 5:19), and so, too, in the Galatian churches (Galatians 3:2–5) and in Rome (Romans 12:6–8). The Spirit is the gift of God to all who believe and are baptized (Acts of the Apostles 2:38; Galatians 4:6; Romans 5:5). The Spirit is the first fruits of the final Kingdom (1 Thessalonians 4:8; 1 Peter 1:2; Hebrews 6:4; Jude 19–20; 1 John 3:24; 4:13).

The coming of the Holy Spirit makes Christ's community the temple of God (1 Corinthians 3:16; 2 Corinthians 6:16; Ephesians 2:22), a spiritual building where true spiritual sacrifices are offered (1 Peter 2:5) and where true worship in spirit and in truth occurs (John 4:23–24). Through the Spirit all members of the Church have access to the Father and become fellow citizens of heaven with the saints (Ephesians 2:18–19). It is the Spirit who guides the Church in mission (Acts of the Apostles 5:3,9; 8:29,39; 9:31; 10:19; 13:2; 15:28; 16:6–7; 20:23; 21:11) and who speaks to the churches (Revelation 2:7,11,17,19; 3:6,13,22).

The early Church, therefore, did not understand itself simply as another sect within Judaism or even as another religious organization. The Church of the New Testament proclaimed the Gospel "in the Holy Spirit" (1 Thessalonians 1:5). Its message and preaching were given through "a demonstration of the Spirit and of power" (1 Corinthians 2:4). It was a community transformed by the presence of the Spirit, the first fruits of redemption (Romans 8:23; 2 Corinthians 1:22), and sealed with the Spirit (Ephesians 1:13). The Church is a community saved "through the water of rebirth and renewal by the Holy Spirit . . . that, having been justified by his grace, we might become heirs according to the hope of eternal life" (Titus 3:5,7).

HOW DID THE EARLY CHRISTIAN COMMUNITIES EXPRESS THEMSELVES AS CHURCH?

The Original Jerusalem Community

The religious life of the original Jerusalem church is summarized in the Acts of the Apostles 2:43–47; 4:32–35; and 5:12–16. We find apostolic activity, supported by healing and miracles, which, in turn, increased the membership of the community; the sharing of goods among the members; and a rich liturgical and prayer life both in a special meeting place in the Temple and in the houses of members themselves. They gathered for the breaking of the bread (2:46; 20:7,11), clearly the eucharistic meal of 1 Corinthians 11:20 which was the central and common worship of all the Christian churches.

This original Jerusalem community maintained its close links with Judaism: the strong attachment to the Temple (a point clearly opposed by the Hellenists, see Acts of the Apostles 6:13–14; 7), the continuation of Jewish practices, and the voluntary community of goods. The Jerusalem church was not without inner conflict and tension, however. The dispute between the Jewish and Greek members over the care of widows (6:1–6) and, of course, the great debate over the need for circumcision and the observance of Jewish dietary laws (15:1–31) were major cases in point.

The Church at Antioch in Syria

Antioch was at this time the third-largest city in the Roman Empire. The Christian community here was a mixed group: former Jews and former pagans ("Greeks") alike. It was not without its own internal struggles among various types of Jewish Christians and their Gentile converts. In the 40s there were face-to-face disputes among Hellenists and Paul on one side and Peter and men from James on the other. The issue was what the Gospel meant in relation to the Jewish heritage. After the year 70 the church contained conservative and liberal Jewish Christians, and an ever increasing majority of Gentile Christians, closer in their thinking to the liberal Jewish Christians. Matthew, the evangelist at Antioch, sought to hold this mixed group together.

Here, for the first time, the followers of Jesus Christ were called *Christians*. They had regular meetings at which the large congregation was "taught" (Acts of the Apostles 11:26). Prophets and teachers were active here (13:1–3), and the gifts of the Spirit were evident (11:27; 15:32). And it was from this community that Paul and Barnabas were sent to carry the case against the Judaizers at the Council of Jerusalem (15:1–29). Both attested to the marvelous work of God among the Gentiles (15:12). The Council of Jerusalem resolved the crisis with a principle that has remained normative for the Church ever since (if sometimes more in the breach than in the observance): "For it seemed good to the Holy Spirit and to us to impose on you no further burden than these essentials" (15:28).

584

The Church of Corinth

This was a church of predominantly pagan origin whose life is disclosed through the two letters of Paul. What is striking about the church in this busy port city is its charismatic character (1 Corinthians 1:5–7; 12:8–11) and its human weaknesses. The charismatics often created confusion (1 Corinthians 14). Serious disorders arose at the celebration of the Eucharist because of the behavior of the rich (1 Corinthians 11:20–34). Partisan groups attached to particular missionaries emerged (1 Corinthians 1:11; see also 3:4–5, 22). Many sided with opponents of Paul, as his second letter suggests. Pagan vices, especially of a sexual kind, still prevailed (1 Corinthians 5; 6:12–20).

On the other hand, there was also a flourishing church life at Corinth. The apostolic preaching and instruction were sounded in the assemblies (2 Corinthians 3:4–4:6). Worship occupied a central place (1 Corinthians 11:17–34). Baptism and Eucharist were sources of deep religious experience (1 Corinthians 1:13–16; 6:11; 10:1–11,16–22). They understood themselves as the Church of God (1 Corinthians 1:2; 10:32; 11:22; 2 Corinthians 1:1) which honors the Lord (1 Corinthians 1:2,9; 8:6; 10:21; 12:3; 2 Corinthians 3:17–18; 4:5). It was a church in fellowship with the church of Jerusalem (for which the great collection was taken up) and with the other churches (1 Corinthians 1:2; 7:17; 11:16; 16:1,19; 2 Corinthians 1:1; 8:24; 12:13; 13:12).

Unity in Diversity

Despite all local differences among the Jewish-Christian, Jewish-Hellenistic, and Hellenistic-Gentile communities, *common elements* stood out clearly: faith in Jesus as Messiah and Lord; the practice of Baptism and the celebration of the Eucharist; the apostolic preaching and instruction; the high regard for communal love; and the expectation of the coming Kingdom of God. Great freedom was allowed in all other matters—a freedom which, when exercised, manifested the limitations as well as the spiritual grandeur of God's Church.

585

HOW DID THE EARLY CHURCH UNDERSTAND ITS MISSION?

Church and Kingdom of God

Just as Jesus' message and mission are centered on, and framed by, the coming Kingdom of God, so, too, are the Church's. It is indeed what Jesus instructed his disciples to pray for: "your kingdom come" (Luke 11:2; Matthew 6:9). It is the reality signified in the many parables attributed to Jesus. But the Church lives "between the times," i.e., between the decisive inbreaking of the Kingdom of God in Jesus Christ and the final outpouring of the Holy Spirit at the end. As such, the Church is both a Church of glory and a Church of the cross.

It is a *Church of glory* insofar as it has been sanctified from within: Christ "gave himself up for her, in order to make her holy by cleansing her with the washing of water by the word, so as to present the church to himself in splendor, without a spot or wrinkle or anything of the kind" (Ephesians 5:25–27). "For in the one Spirit," Paul writes elsewhere, "we were all baptized into one body—Jews or Greeks, slaves or free—and we were all made to drink of one Spirit" (1 Corinthians 12:13). Indeed, "there is one body and one Spirit, just as you were called to the one hope of your calling" (Ephesians 4:4).

But the Church is also a *Church of the cross.* Although it is to the risen body of Christ that Christians are joined (Romans 7:4), within this age that body continues also to be a *suffering* body. "We are... always carrying in the body the death of Jesus, so that the life of Jesus may also be made visible in our bodies" (2 Corinthians 4:8–10; see also Galatians 6:17; 1 Corinthians 15:31; Romans 8:36). Being joined to the risen Christ means being baptized "into his death.... For if we have been united with him in a death like his, we will certainly be united with him in a resurrection like his" (Romans 6:3–5). We share "in the blood of Christ" (1 Corinthians 10:16), and by our own suffering, joined to his, we complete "what is lacking in Christ's afflictions for the sake of his body, that is, the church" (Colossians 1:24).

The glory that, in one sense, is *already* in the Church, is *not yet* revealed. We are "heirs of God and joint heirs with Christ—if, in fact, we suffer with him so that we may also be glorified with him" (Romans 8:17). The tension between glory and suffering is clearly stated in Philippians: "I wish to know Christ and the power flowing from his resurrection; likewise to know how to share in his sufferings by being formed into the pattern of his death. Thus do I hope that I may arrive at resurrection from the dead" (Philippians 3:10–11). The process is ongoing: "So we do not lose heart. Even though our outer nature is wasting away, our inner nature is being renewed day by day. For this slight momentary affliction is preparing us for an eternal weight of glory beyond all measure" (2 Corinthians 4:16–17). Paul continues, "So if anyone is in Christ, there is a new creation: everything old has passed away; see, everything has become new!" (5:17).

As a Church both of glory and of the cross, *the Church is both a sign and an instrument of the Kingdom of God*. Peter receives the keys of the Kingdom (Matthew 16:19). He and the other Apostles are given the power of binding and loosing, of forgiving and of withholding forgiveness (Matthew 18:18), of sharing in Jesus' own power (Mark 2:10; John 20:23), even over the demons (Mark 3:15; 6:7). This is indeed the deepest meaning of Jesus' authority: to break the rule of Satan (Luke 11:20; Matthew 12:28; Mark 11:28,33) and thereby to establish the Kingdom of God.

After profound and severe internal disputes about whether the Gospel should be proclaimed to the Gentiles and about the conditions under which the Gentiles would accept that Gospel, the Church came to understand itself as having been sent by Christ to make disciples of all nations and to baptize them in the name of the Father, the Son, and the Holy Spirit (Matthew 28:19). This is the grandeur and the burden of the Church. Not all who are called prove worthy of the call (Matthew 22:11–14). Nonetheless Jesus promises to be with the Church for all ages (Matthew 28:20). In the meantime, healings and other signs of renewal will show that the powers of the future age are already present in the Church (Luke 10:17,19; Mark 16:17).

Nowhere is the orientation of the Church toward the Kingdom more explicitly revealed than in the Eucharist, which anticipates the eating and drinking at the Lord's table in the Kingdom (Luke 22:30). "Truly I tell you, I will never again drink of the fruit of the vine until that day when I drink it new in the kingdom of God" (Mark 14:25; see also Matthew 26:29).

Proclamation of the Word

That the Church understood itself as having been commissioned to proclaim the Word of God is beyond any reasonable doubt. To *evangelize*, or to announce the good news of salvation, is a favorite word in Luke, occurring ten times in his Gospel and twenty-five times in the Acts of the Apostles. So, too, does it occur frequently (twenty-one times) in the Pauline material, where he speaks also (sixty times) of "the gospel." The evangelist delivers not his own word but the word of God (1 Thessalonians 2:13). It is a Gospel to be proclaimed throughout the world (Mark 13:10). After Easter it becomes the message of salvation about Jesus crucified and risen (Acts of the Apostles 8:5; 9:20; 1 Corinthians 1:23; 15:12). The preaching itself shows forth "the glory of Christ, who is the image of God" (2 Corinthians 4:4). It has been announced "to every creature under heaven" (Colossians 1:23). It is a message about God's reign.

The proclamation also takes the form of *teaching* (Acts of the Apostles 4:2,18; 5:21,25,28,42; 11:26; 15:35; 18:11; 20:20; 28:31). It takes place publicly in the Temple and in houses (5:42; 20:20). The proclamation applies Sacred Scripture to the daily life of the community as a word of instruction, of encouragement, and of consolation (14:22; 15:30–32; 1 Thessalonians 2:2; 1 Corinthians 14:3,31). It is sometimes *prophetic* (1 Corinthians 14). The prophets are listed even before the teachers (1 Corinthians 12:28; Ephesians 4:11), and the faithful are said to be built on the foundation of the Apostles and the prophets (Ephesians 2:20; 3:5). On the other hand, there were false prophets or pseudoprophets against whom the Church had to act (1 Thessalonians 5:21; 1 Corinthians 12:3; 1 John 4:1–3).

Worship and Sacraments

Baptism

Even Rudolf Bultmann acknowledged that there never was a time in the life of the Church when there was no Baptism. The testimony of Paul is particularly important. In the spring of 56 or 55 or perhaps even 54, he wrote from Ephesus to the Church of Corinth that "in the one Spirit we were all baptized into one body—Jews or Greeks, slaves or free" (1 Corinthians 12:13). This testimony takes us back biographically to about the year 33, just after Jesus' death. Baptism has its roots, therefore, not in the later Hellenistic churches but in the Jewish-Christian Church, and the Gospels themselves point to the prototype, *the baptism of John.*

John's baptism is characterized by eschatological expectation; it involves a call to repentance; it is administered only once; and it does not introduce one into a sect but is demanded for the whole people. Jesus himself was baptized by John (Mark 1:9–11), and because of that the community was convinced that he approved "a baptism of repentance for the forgiveness of sins" (Mark 1:4). The Church baptized not only in memory of John's baptism but also in memory of Jesus.

Easter gave Baptism a completely new meaning. Jesus is now perceived as the risen Lord (Acts of the Apostles 2:36). Salvation is through his death and resurrection. Even though Baptism is still a baptism of repentance for the forgiveness of sins, repentance is seen as a turning to Christ, and the forgiveness of sins occurs on the authority of Christ and by his power. Baptism is administered "in the name of Jesus Christ" (Acts of the Apostles 2:38; 8:16; 10:48; 1 Corinthians 1:13–15; Galatians 3:27; Romans 6:3). By being baptized in the "name" of Jesus, a person becomes subject to him and is committed to his rule and care. The word *name* is a legal concept, signifying authority and competence.

Baptism is a baptism into Jesus' death and resurrection (Colossians 2:11–13; 3:14; Ephesians 2:5). And just as the Holy Spirit is released through the resurrection, so, too, is the Spirit given in a special way at Baptism (Acts of the Apostles 19:2–6; Titus 3:6). But the effect is not automatic. Baptism without faith is empty, and without openness to the Spirit there is no holiness (1 Corinthians 10:1–13; Hebrews 6:4–8; and all of 1 Peter).

In spite of all these textual references, a posture of caution is recommended. New Testament evidence for the development of Baptism is "very meager" and "quite thin" (Cwiekowski, *The Beginnings of the Church,* p. 76).

Eucharist

If the New Testament evidence for the development of Baptism is very thin, it is "even thinner in the case for the beginnings of the community meals within which the eucharist would develop" (ibid.).

Like Baptism, the Eucharist, or Lord's Supper (the term used in the oldest account in 1 Corinthians 11:20), is rooted in the very beginning of the Church. The Last Supper tradition is ancient and is given in four variant versions: 1 Corinthians 11:23–25; Mark 14:22–25; Matthew 26:26–29; and Luke 22:15–20. The Pauline account dates from the years 54–56 and refers to the fact that Paul handed on this tradition to the Corinthians at the beginning of his missionary activity in Corinth (about 49). But Paul also states that this tradition comes directly from the Lord. Peter was still alive and could have repudiated Paul's account if it were inaccurate. Paul himself lived for many years with members of the Jerusalem church (Barnabas, Mark, Silas) and took part in the Lord's Supper in various communities. His account must have agreed with those of eyewitnesses.

The meal that Jesus shared with his Apostles was the last of a long series of daily meals he had with his disciples. For Orientals, shared meals have always signified peace, trust, and community. But Jesus also shared meals with sinners, outcasts, and tax collectors, as a sign that the Reign of God had begun and was open to all and demanded love of all. The *Last Supper*, however, was a special meal. It was either a Passover meal or perhaps a farewell meal on the night before the Passover feast. Whichever it was, it was celebrated with a view to the coming Kingdom of God. Indeed, the Kingdom was the focus of everything Jesus did and said, not only at this meal but in his whole life and ministry.

The structure was obviously taken over from the Jewish ritual meal: the words over the bread, followed by its breaking and sharing, and the blessing over the wine. But now Jesus identifies himself with the bread and wine. It is his body which is broken and his blood which is poured out in atonement for sin and for the establishment of a new Covenant. All four texts agree on this. The Jews regarded every death, but particularly the death of an innocent one, as having the character of atonement. And so Jesus could have easily seen his own

590

innocent suffering in this way, without necessarily linking it to the more fully developed theology of the postresurrection Church.

By distributing the bread and wine as his flesh and blood, Jesus gave his disciples a share in the power of his death to make atonement and to establish a new Covenant. This, too, is a familiar Oriental idea: Eating and drinking communicated divine gifts.

After the resurrection the disciples gathered again and again for these shared meals, but now with the conviction that the risen Christ was in their midst as they gathered in his name (Matthew 18:20). There was joy in their new fellowship: joy over the presence of Christ and joy over the approach of the Kingdom of God (Acts of the Apostles 2:46). It is important to note that the celebration of the Lord's Supper after the death and resurrection of Christ was not an arbitrary act on the part of the Church. The Church was convinced it was following the Lord's own injunction, and indeed it referred to the actions of Jesus at the Last Supper as the pattern and authority for what it did.

The Eucharist, therefore, is a meal of remembrance and thanksgiving, of fellowship, and of anticipation. It looks at once to the past, the present, and the future. "For as often as you eat this bread and drink the cup, you proclaim the Lord's death until he comes!" (1 Corinthians 11:26).

Through the Eucharist, the Church proclaims its faith in the Lordship of Jesus and in the coming of the Kingdom. Through the Eucharist the Church manifests and more fully recognizes and deepens its unity in Christ (1 Corinthians 10:16–17). Through the Eucharist the Church sets a pattern for its own ministry to those in need (1 Corinthians 11:17–34) and exposes itself thereby to judgment (11:34).

(We shall, of course, be returning to the sacraments of the Church in Part Five.)

Mission to All and for All

The Church did not always understand itself as a missionary community, if by *missionary* one means an acceptance of a call to proclaim the Gospel to those outside the Jewish community itself. The first Christians were missionary in the sense that they reached out to the whole people of Israel (Acts of the Apostles 3:11; 4:1; 5:25,40,42), even

591

beyond Jerusalem (9:32–43; Galatians 2:8; 1 Corinthians 9:5). But it was only thereafter that they carried the Gospel to the Gentiles (Matthew 8:11 = Luke 13:28). The transition from the mission to the Jews to the mission to the Gentiles did not occur without serious difficulty, as we have already noted. There was resistance on the part of the Jewish Christians of Jerusalem, including the Apostles. Luke, on the other hand, gives a theological foundation for broadening the mission (Acts of the Apostles 28:25–28) and points to an intervention from God and the authority of Peter as factors in changing the situation (10:1–11:8).

The differences, however, were not irreconcilable. The Jerusalem church still had very close ties with the Jews and Jewish ways of thought and customs (1:6; 10:14), and yet James, the leader of the Jerusalem community, declared himself in agreement with the Pauline approach, which dispensed with the absolute need of circumcision, and with Paul's mission to the Gentiles (Acts of the Apostles 15; Galatians 6:10). Previously, Barnabas, the representative of the Jerusalem church, had approved the conversion of Greeks in Antioch and indeed had accompanied Paul on his first missionary journey (Acts of the Apostles 13–14).

On the other hand, Jerusalem's privileged position is upheld. The mission to "the ends of the earth" begins from Jerusalem (Acts of the Apostles 1:8; Luke 24:47; Romans 9–11). Israel was to be given its last opportunity for repentance through the apostolic preaching (Acts of the Apostles 2:38; 3:19; 5:31; Mark 7:27; Romans 1:16; 2:9). Historically, the Hellenistic Christians, who had a freer and more open attitude toward paganism, were probably the first to proclaim the Gospel to the Gentiles.

Paul sees the conversion of the Gentiles as a mystery of the history of redemption, after which all of Israel will be saved (Romans 11:25). That the Gentiles are co-heirs of Christ and sharers in the promise Paul sees as a matter of recent revelation in the Spirit (Ephesians 3:5–6). Through their incorporation into the Church, "the wisdom of God in its rich variety might now be made known" (3:10).

592

HOW DID THE EARLY CHURCH ORGANIZE
ITSELF FOR MISSION?

First, there is *no uniform order or structure* to the Church of the New Testament. This varied from place to place. It is not clear, for example, how the Twelve function even in the Jerusalem church, and why they seem to recede into the background after Acts of the Apostles 6:2, or why the elders are mentioned with them at the Council of Jerusalem, or what rank and position "the Seven" held (6:3–6). There is no doubt about Peter's special position, but what of the importance of James, the "brother of the Lord," who assumes a position of pastoral leadership in Jerusalem alongside Peter (12:17; 15:13–21; Galatians 1:19; 2:9) and after Peter leaves (Galatians 2:12; Acts of the Apostles 21:18)?

Second, however, there is *some* order and structure which shapes the life and mission of the Church. The Church is never without it. (Raymond Brown is critical of those scholars who, "working more on suspicion than on evidence," paint a picture of a wholly egalitarian "Jesus movement" which only gradually became more "patriarchally authoritative in developing churches" [*The New Jerome Biblical Commentary*, p. 1343].) In this sense, that order is *constitutive* of the Church rather than merely functional. Thus, although Paul recognized the fundamental equality of all who have been baptized to a newness of life in Christ (Galatians 3:28), he also called upon Christians to respect "those who labor among you, and have charge of you in the Lord and admonish you..." (1 Thessalonians 5:12). Indeed, the early Church was a community highly differentiated by reason of charisms and ministries (1 Corinthians 12:4–11).

This is not to say that all authority and missionary responsibility were given to the hierarchical few to be exercised for the sake of the many. On the contrary, the whole congregation was involved in important decisions in this earliest of periods (Acts of the Apostles 15; 1 Corinthians 5). But there were also members who served in some leadership capacity. Local churches were guided by presbyters, and others were appointed as overseers (the original meaning of the word for bishop, *episcopos*; see Acts of the Apostles 20:28). And that is not only Lucan theology. A hierarchically structured community is also at the basis of Paul's listing of the various ministers and ministries in 1

Corinthians 12:28, and he derives these various offices from the Lord himself (Ephesians 4:11). Mention of the Apostles first, and then prophets and teachers, cannot be by chance. There is a sacred order of ministers and pastors who are responsible to their heavenly chief shepherd (1 Peter 5:2–4).

Third, there is *no radical opposition between the charismatic and administrative ministries,* as some Protestant scholars had argued in the past. All of the gifts and charisms have the same source, the Holy Spirit (1 Corinthians 12:11). Some of these gifts are clearly "charismatic" —e.g., the gift of tongues. Others are clearly "administrative" or "institutional" —e.g., teaching and presiding (Romans 12:7–8; Ephesians 4:11–12).

Fourth, *neither is there any radical opposition between the order of the Jerusalem church and the order of the Pauline communities.* Despite his absence from Corinth, Paul decides the cases of the incestuous man (1 Corinthians 5:3–5), gives directives for the divine service (11:17, 33), admonishes and gives concrete prescriptions (7:17; 16:1; Titus 1:5), and gives definite moral guidance (1 Thessalonians 4:11; 2 Thessalonians 3:4,6,10,12). The church of Corinth must have recognized his apostolic authority. Why else would they have submitted certain questions to him for decision (1 Corinthians 7:1, and following chapters)? Nor is the picture presented by the Pastoral Epistles (1 and 2 Timothy, and Titus) improbable for the period of consolidation of the Pauline communities.

Fifth, whatever the office or ministry, it is always for the sake of *service,* never for domination. The model is Jesus, who lays down his life for others (Mark 10:45). The one who humbles himself will be exalted, and vice versa (Luke 14:11; Matthew 23:12). Paul consistently refers to his own office as that of a servant (1 Corinthians 4:1,9–13; 2 Corinthians 4:5,12,15; 6:4–10; Philippians 2:17).

Sixth, the chief ministry in the Church is the *Petrine ministry,* i.e., a ministry for the universal Church. Indeed, even if one were to conclude that Jesus did not say "You are Peter, and on this rock I will build my church..." in July of the year 29 at Cæsarea Philippi, we still have to contend with the clear fact that this tradition, embedded in Matthew 16:18, was maintained somewhere in the first-century Church and represents a Christian evaluation of Peter's position with which every serious Christian must cope.

Peter was one of the first called, and remained prominent there-after among Jesus' disciples. He is the most frequently mentioned disciple in all four Gospels. Even the distant Gentile converts of Paul in Galatia know of Peter. He functioned as the spokesman of the Apostles and is always placed first on lists of Apostles (Matthew 10:2). Indeed, he was probably the first to whom the Lord appeared after the resurrection (1 Corinthians 15:5; Luke 24:34; Mark 16:7). This fact alone may explain the prominence of Peter in the early Church, not all of which is explicable in the light of his role during the life of Jesus. That Peter served as the spokesman of the Apostles after the resurrection is clear in the Acts of the Apostles, but it was never a unilateral or unaccountable sort of role. He is also portrayed as con-sulting with the other Apostles and even being sent by them (Acts of the Apostles 8:14). He and John act almost as a team (3:1–11; 4:1–23; 8:14). It was Peter who took the decisive step in ordering the baptism of the Gentile Cornelius (Acts of the Apostles 10). And although Paul spoke of Peter's ministry as being directed to the circumcised (Gala-tians 2:7), Peter's influence in Gentile areas is obvious (1 Corinthians 1:12; 1 Peter 1:1).

Whatever the minimal facts of Peter's life and ministry, it is also clear that he became a symbol for Christian thought. He is portrayed as having played many different roles in the life of the Church. Modern New Testament scholars speak of a *trajectory* of biblical im-ages of Peter. It begins with Peter as the great Christian *fisherman* (Luke 5; John 21), then as the *shepherd*, or pastor, of the flock (John 21), then as the Christian *martyr* (John 13:36; 1 Peter 5:1), then as the *receiver of special revelation* (Mark 9:2–8, and parallels; 2 Peter 1:16–18; Acts of the Apostles 5:1–11; 10:9–16; 12:7–9), then as the *confessor of the true faith* (Matthew 16:16–17) and as its *guardian* against false teaching (2 Peter 1:20–21; 3:15–16). He is portrayed also as a weak and sinful man, but a *repentant sinner*. He is reproached by Paul (Galatians 2:11–14), misunderstands Jesus (Mark 9:5–6; John 13:6–11; 18:10–11), is rebuked by Jesus (Mark 8:33; Matthew 16:23) and denies Christ (Mark 14:66–72). But he is rehabilitated. The risen Lord appears to him (John 21:15–17), and he becomes again a source of strength to the Church (Luke 22:32).

Other Apostles were also subjects of similar trajectories, but no trajectory outdistanced Peter's, not even the Twelve's or Paul's. This

595

is even implied already in 2 Peter, where the image of Peter is evoked to correct those who are appealing to Paul.

The Subapostolic (After 65) and Postapostolic (after 95/100) Periods

The six points in the preceding section represent a kind of homogenization of texts, leaving aside for the most part the fact of development *within* the texts. This section is by way of a reminder that there *was* development, and that the ecclesiology of the New Testament cannot be understood apart from it.

By the year 65 the three best-known figures of the early Church had died as martyrs: James, Peter, and Paul. Those who assumed positions of pastoral leadership tended to speak in the name of the deceased Apostles (thus, the term *subapostolic*). The ministerial thrust of this period is less missionary (fishing) and more pastoral (shepherding), given the demands of actually caring for the communities founded between the 30s and the 60s.

Another mark of transition was the shift from Jewish to Gentile dominance, parallel to the shift in the majority of the Christian population. The destruction of Jerusalem by the Romans in the year 70 had the side effect of supplanting Jerusalem as the center of the worldwide Christian community. By the late first century it is the church of Rome that speaks to the Christians of North Asia Minor and Corinth (1 Peter 1:1; *1 Clement*) and is preeminent in love (Ignatius of Antioch's letter to the *Romans,* preface). Jews decline as an object of conversion, and become, more ominously, an object of polemics (Revelation 2:9; 3:9). Jewish Christians, in turn, were expelled from the synagogues, in large part because of their implicit affirmation of the divinity of Christ (John 9:22,34; 12:42) over against the historic Jewish confession of the oneness of God (Deuteronomy 6:4).

Christianity now began to appear more clearly as a new religion rather than as a movement, or sect, within Judaism. The titular privileges of Israel were taken over by the Church (1 Peter 2:9–10), and the Eucharist replaced the Jewish sacrifices. But an element of loyalty to the old tradition remained, as reflected in Matthew's Gospel (5:18; 23:2–3) and in James (2:24).

596

After the year 65 church structures also became more regular-ized: *presbyteroi* (elders) were appointed in every town, functioning there as *episkopoi* (bishops, overseers, supervisors). Deacons, too, were part of this structure, but it is not clear how their functions differed from those of the presbyter/bishops. There seemed to have been women deacons (1 Timothy 3:11) and an official class of widows (1 Timothy 5:3–16).

Almost at the same time, however, the *Didache* (15:1–2) was urging Christians to appoint bishops and deacons to take the place of the older charismatic structure of apostles, prophets, and teachers (1 Corinthians 12:28). Itinerant prophets and apostles had become a source of trouble and needed regulating. Eventually a monoepiscopal structure emerged in which each local church was governed by a bishop, and by the end of the second century a tripartite ministerial structure became the norm: bishop, presbyter, deacon.

Another change in the subapostolic and postapostolic period (the latter referring to the period after 95/100) involved a shift from viewing the Church primarily in local terms (the church of a particular city or town, or even a "house church") to that of an idealized universal reality, as the body of Christ and his "fullness" (Ephesians 1:22–23; 2:19–20; 3:9–10; 4:15–16; 5:23–27; Colossians 1:12–13,18,24).

Finally, the role of the Spirit in the life of the Church is empha-sized in the Acts of the Apostles (1:4–5; 2:38; 8:15–17; 9:17; 15:8; 19:5–6), wherein every step the Church takes, from Jerusalem to the end of history, is under the Spirit's guidance. But openness to the Spirit was not without its difficulties and risks, as the bitter disputes that erupted among the Johannine communities would painfully reveal (1 John 1:3; 2:19; 4:1,6).

WHAT IS THE CHURCH OF THE NEW TESTAMENT?

The mystery of the Church, like all else in Christian theology, must be viewed in the larger context of the mystery of the triune God. The three biblical images of the Church listed below underscore the rela-tionship of the Church to each of the three Persons of the Trinity.

People of God

According to Hebrew ways of thinking, the people form a whole, a *corporate personality.* The individual takes on meaning, importance, and even destiny insofar as the individual is involved with the people. Israel understood itself as the people of God, by God's own call (Exodus 19:5; 23:22; Deuteronomy 7:6; 14:2; 26:18). "I will take you as my people, and I will be your God" (Exodus 6:7). The call to people-hood is linked with the *Covenant:* "I will look with favor upon you... and I will maintain my covenant with you.... I will place my dwelling in your midst, and I shall not abhor you. And I will walk among you, and will be your God, and you shall be my people..." (Leviticus 26:9–12). The same connection is to be found in the major prophets (e.g., Jeremiah 32:38–41).

After its rift with Judaism, the early Church came to appropriate this image to itself: "But you are a chosen race, a royal priesthood, a holy nation, God's own people, in order that you may proclaim the mighty acts of him who called you out of darkness into his marvelous light. Once you were not a people, but now you are God's people..." (1 Peter 2:9–10). The allusions to the Old Testament are evident: in particular Isaiah 43:20–21 and Exodus 19:6. The passage suggests that the Church is the new People of God purchased by the redemptive work of Christ.

That fundamental text from the Old Testament, "I will take you as my people, and I will be your God," is cited several times throughout the New Testament and applied to the Church itself, as the new eschatological community. Paul quotes it in 2 Corinthians 6:16 from Ezekiel 37:27 in order to distinguish the Church from the unbelievers. In Hebrews 8:10 it occurs in the lengthy quotation from Jeremiah 31:31–34 to show that this great prophecy has been fulfilled in the new Covenant. And the formula appears finally in Revelation 21:3 in the vision of the future Jerusalem. Indeed, the notion of the Church as the new eschatological People of God is the guiding theme of the Epistle to the Hebrews.

This new People of God, formed out of the remnant of Israel and from many Gentiles, arises out of the love and grace of God: "Once you were not a people, but now you are God's people; once you had not received mercy, but now you have received mercy" (1 Peter 2:10).

598

But, again, it is a "purchased" people, "obtained with the blood of his own Son" (Acts of the Apostles 20:28). God makes a new beginning for the human community in grace. The Church is itself the new People of God (Titus 2:14, where the reference again is to Ezekiel 37:23).

Nowhere is the Church spoken of explicitly as the "new" People of God, but there *is* explicit mention of the *new* Covenant (Luke 22:20; 1 Corinthians 11:25; 2 Corinthians 3:6; Hebrews 8:13; 9:15; 12:24), and that Covenant is connected, at least implicitly, to a new community (Hebrews 8:8–12 cites Jeremiah 31:31–34, where such a link is made). But it is no longer a covenant signed by circumcision, but by faith in Jesus Christ and the "spiritual circumcision" (Colossians 2:11), i.e., Baptism.

As noted above, a tension between the old and new People of God remains, however, and it is most strongly portrayed in Paul, especially in Romans 9–11. Unbelieving Israel is in partnership "with demons" (1 Corinthians 10:20), but believing Israel is "the Israel of God" (Galatians 6:16). God calls us, Jew and Gentile alike. "There is no longer Jew or Greek, there is no longer slave or free, there is no longer male or female; for all of you are one in Christ Jesus. And if you belong to Christ, then you are Abraham's offspring, heirs according to the promise" (Galatians 3:28–29).

But even in the New Testament the new People of God is not identical with the community of the elect. In other words, membership in the Church is no guarantee of participation in the Kingdom of God. There are false prophets in the Church who will be repudiated by the Lord at the end (Matthew 7:22–23). All evildoers will be cast out (13:41–43). On the other side, many who did not belong to the Church will be acknowledged by the Son of Man as his brothers and sisters (25:31–46). "Then he will send out the angels, and gather his elect from the four winds, from the ends of the earth to the ends of heaven" (Mark 13:27). The final test will be a just life. No one will enter the marriage feast without a wedding garment (Matthew 22:11–13).

Body of Christ

If the People-of-God image underlines the Church's intimate connection with Israel and with God's call to a covenant relationship, the Body-of-Christ image underlines the Church's intimate connection with Jesus Christ and with God's call to a communal relationship, one with another in Christ.

The image is, of course, distinctively Pauline, although it bears some affinity with the Johannine allegory of the vine and the branches (John 15:1–8). The Church in the New Testament is the People of God, but a people newly constituted in Christ and with Christ. The two images, therefore, are not mutually opposed. The Church is the People of God insofar as it is the Body of Christ, and it is the Body of Christ insofar as it is the People of God. In principle, both images are rooted in the Old Testament idea of *corporate personality*.

The conception of the Church as Body of Christ is grounded in the union that exists between the Christian and the *risen* body of Christ. Just as the resurrection is central to New Testament Christology, so is it central to New Testament, and especially Pauline, ecclesiology. When the Christian shares in the bread of the Eucharist, he or she becomes one body with Christ (1 Corinthians 10:16–17). Thus, the one who eats or drinks unworthily profanes the body of the Lord (11:27) and eats and drinks unto his or her own condemnation (11:29). It is in one body that Christ has reconciled us to the Father by his death (Ephesians 2:16–17; Colossians 1:22). The Church has become one body, his own, in which the Holy Spirit dwells (Ephesians 4:4). Christians are called one body (Colossians 3:15).

The physical realism of the union between Christ and the Church lies behind the development from the notion of one body "in" Christ (Romans and 1 Corinthians) to one Body "of" Christ (Ephesians and Colossians). But it *is* a development. In Romans 12:4–21 and in 1 Corinthians 12:4–27, for example, the application of the image refers more to the union of Christians with each other than with Christ. It speaks of a diversity of charisms and offices which, despite their multiplicity, do not compromise the fundamental unity of the Church. The members are one because they are baptized by one spirit into one body (1 Corinthians 12:13). They are called not one body "in" Christ but one body "of" Christ (12:27). The same identity is presupposed in 1 Corinthians 6:15: "Do you not know that your bodies are members of Christ?" Indeed, it is because the Christian is really a member of the Body of Christ that she or he can also be called metaphorically a temple of the Holy Spirit (6:19).

The ideas of these earlier letters are presupposed as the Body-of-Christ image is introduced, with seeming abruptness, in Ephesians 1:23 and Colossians 1:24. Christ is now called the head of his Body, the Church (Ephesians 5:23; Colossians 1:18; 2:19). As head of the Church, Christ is the principle of union and growth (Ephesians 4:16; Colossians 2:19). The Body of Christ is something that is to be built up (Ephesians 4:12,16).

With some measure of urgency, the Pauline author of Ephesians pleads with the community to "lead a life worthy of the calling . . . making every effort to maintain the unity of the Spirit in the bond of peace. There is one body and one Spirit" (4:1–4; see also Colossians 3:12–15).

Temple of the Holy Spirit

Because the Church is the Body of Christ, it can also be called the Temple of the Holy Spirit. Here again the *resurrection* is central. The Spirit proceeds from the "Lord of the Spirit," who through his resurrection has become "a life-giving spirit" (1 Corinthians 15:45). There is, of course, a special outpouring of the Spirit at Pentecost, as the fruit of Christ's saving action (Acts of the Apostles 1:8; 2:3–4,38; 4:8,31; 6:8; 9:17; 11:24; 13:52; 19:2). This thought is particularly clear in John where it is asserted that the Spirit could not be given until the Lord had been glorified (7:39; 6:63). The risen and exalted Lord releases the Spirit and with the Spirit builds his Church. The Body of Christ "grows into a holy temple in the Lord; in whom you also are built together spiritually into a dwelling place for God" (Ephesians 2:21–22). Jew and Gentile alike have "access in one Spirit to the Father" (2:18).

Just as Jesus identified himself with the Temple, so the Body of Christ is itself the new Temple (1 Corinthians 3:9, 16–17; 2 Corinthians 6:16; Ephesians 2:19–22). The Church is now the place of God's dwelling. It is, in the theological sense of the word, a *mystery*, i.e., "a reality imbued with the hidden presence of God" (Pope Paul VI, at the opening of the second session of Vatican II, September 1963).

The Spirit is manifested in various ways, witnessing to the presence and activity of God in the Church (Acts of the Apostles 2:3–13; 10:47; 11:17; 15:8). The Spirit teaches the disciples what to say (Luke 12:12), reveals the mysteries of God (Luke 1:41,67; Acts of the Apostles 11:28; 13:9), inspires prophecy (2:18), is the source of wisdom (6:3), faith (6:5; 2 Corinthians 4:13), encouragement (Acts of the Apostles 9:31), joy (13:52), hope (Romans 15:13; 1 Corinthians 14:14–16; 2:4–5; Galatians 3:5), and love (Romans 5:5; Colossians 1:18; Galatians 5:13-26).

The Spirit directs the officers of the Church in important decisions (Acts of the Apostles 13:2; 15:28; 20:28). The Spirit is conferred upon all of the members at Baptism (19:2,6; 2:38–39; 15:8–9; 8:16–18; 9:17; 10:44; 11:16–17) and at the imposition of hands (8:14–17; 19:6). The gifts of the Spirit are for the building up of the Church (1 Corinthians 14:12,26). By her or his union with the Spirit of the risen Christ, the Christian rises in a spiritual body (1 Corinthians 15:35–50). The Christian's and the Church's present possession of the Spirit is a foretaste (Romans 8:23) and a pledge (2 Corinthians 1:22; 5:5) of the salvation, i.e., of the Kingdom of God, that is to come.

SUMMARY

1. The mystery of the Church flows directly from the mystery of Christ. The Church is the Body of Christ and carries forward his mission.

2. Was Jesus' evaluation of the Church identical with the Church's evaluation of itself? As in Christology, there is a spectrum of answers: *nonscholarly conservatism, nonscholarly liberalism, Bultmannian existentialism,* and *scholarly conservatism.*

3. Jesus did *not* intend to found a Church if by *found* we mean some direct, explicit, deliberate act by which he established a new religious organization. He never addresses a select group of people; he imposes no specific rule of life; he makes no connection between membership in his circle with salvation.

4. Jesus *did* found a Church, at least indirectly; i.e., he laid the foundations for it. First, he gathered disciples around him for the proclamation of the Kingdom of God. Second, he anticipated an interim period between his death and the final coming of the Kingdom. Third, at the Last Supper and in

the injunction to Peter, he looked toward the disciples' staying together even after his death.

5. The word *church* is from the Greek *ekklēsia*, which refers in its original political meaning to an assembly of citizens who enjoy full civil rights. It was taken over by the Greek-speaking Jews to translate the Hebrew word *kāhāl*. Not until the admission of Gentiles to the community did the word *ekklēsia* apply to the Church alone, over against Judaism.

6. The Church of the New Testament is at once *local* (even as "house church") and *universal*. The development occurs after the year 65, in the subapostolic period.

7. *There is no individualistic Christianity in the New Testament.* Belief in Christ and life in Christ are to be found only within the community of believers joined to the Lord.

8. The Church did not begin at *Pentecost*. It already existed by that time. Pentecost was the moment when the Church was endowed in a special way with the power of the Holy Spirit.

9. Before the year 65, the Jewish-Christian community of *Jerusalem* maintained close links with Judaism. Its leaders were Jews and Jewish practices were still observed. The propriety of imposing circumcision and Jewish dietary laws on Gentile converts was a major point of conflict. After the year 65, and especially after the destruction of the Temple in 70, the breach between Christianity and Judaism widened.

10. The Jewish-Hellenistic community of *Antioch* embodied some of the same conflicts over the proper relationship of the Church to Judaism. It was here that the followers of Christ were called "Christians" for the first time.

11. The Hellenistic-Gentile community of *Corinth* was marked by the gifts of the Spirit, but they were often sources of division rather than unity.

12. Despite the differences among these three types of churches, certain *common elements* remain: faith in Jesus as Messiah and Lord, the practice of Baptism and the celebration of the Eucharist, the apostolic preaching and instruction, regard for communal love, and the expectation of the Kingdom of God. Freedom was allowed in most other matters.

13. The *mission* of the Church, like the mission of Jesus, centered on the *Kingdom of God*. The Church lives between the promised Kingdom and the fully realized Kingdom.

14. The Church is both *sign* and *instrument* of the Kingdom. It is sent by Christ to proclaim the Kingdom of God, to make disciples of all nations, to baptize them in the triune God, to forgive sins, and to break the power of Satan. The orientation to the Kingdom is explicit in the Eucharist.

15. The mission of the Church, more specifically, includes the *proclamation* of the Word (evangelization), the celebration of the *sacraments*, and *service* to those in need.

16. The mission is *to all* and *for all*. This did not happen without much resistance, even sharp conflict. But eventually the Church understood itself as having a mandate to reach out to the Gentiles, as coheirs of Christ and sharers in the promises given to Israel.

17. There is *no uniform order or structure* in the New Testament Church. On the other hand, all churches had *some* order and structure.

18. There is no radical opposition between the charismatic and administrative ministries. All have the same source, the Holy Spirit, and the same purpose, the building up of the Body of Christ.

19. The chief ministry in the Church is the *Petrine*, a ministry to and for the universal Church. There is a trajectory of images about Peter (fisherman, shepherd, guardian of the faith, etc.) which tend to support the special status he came to enjoy in the New Testament and the postbiblical Church.

20. The subapostolic church (post-65) and the postapostolic church (post-95/100) were churches in transition: from missionary to pastoral ministry, from Jewish to Gentile leadership, from existence as a kind of sect within Judaism to that of a separate religion, from loose structures to more regularized structures, from a localized understanding of Church to one more idealized and universal.

21. The Church of the New Testament is portrayed according to various *images,* the most important of which are three: People of God, Body of Christ, and Temple of the Holy Spirit.

22. The image of *People of God* is linked with the Old Testament notions of *corporate personality* and *covenant:* The Church is founded on a *new Covenant* in Christ.

23. The image of *Body of Christ* denotes that Christians constitute a closely knit community. They are united to the *risen* Christ and therefore to one another "in Christ."

24. The image of the *Temple of the Holy Spirit* indicates that the Church is "a dwelling place for God" (Ephesians 2:21–22). The Spirit is a foretaste and a pledge of the Kingdom that is to come.

SUGGESTED READINGS

Brown, Raymond E. *The Churches the Apostles Left Behind: New Testament Cradles of Catholic Christianity.* New York: Paulist Press, 1985.

_____. *The Community of the Beloved Disciple: The Life, Loves, and Hates of an Individual Church in New Testament Times.* New York: Paulist Press, 1979.

Brown, Raymond E., et al. *Peter in the New Testament: A Collaborative Assessment by Protestant and Roman Catholic Scholars.* New York: Paulist Press, 1973.

Brown, Raymond E., and John P. Meier. *Antioch and Rome.* New York: Paulist Press, 1983.

Brown, Raymond E., Carol Osiek, and Pheme Perkins. "Early Church," in *The New Jerome Biblical Commentary.* Englewood Cliffs, N.J.: Prentice Hall, 1990, pp. 1338–53.

Cwiekowski, Frederick J. *The Beginnings of the Church.* New York: Paulist Press, 1988.

Fiorenza, Elisabeth Schüssler. *In Memory of Her: A Feminist Theological Reconstruction of Christian Origins.* New York: Crossroad, 1983.

Fiorenza, Francis Schüssler. *Foundational Theology: Jesus and the Church.* New York: Crossroad, 1984.

Harrington, Daniel J. *God's People in Christ: New Testament Perspectives on the Church and Judaism.* Philadelphia: Fortress Press, 1980.

Meeks, Wayne. *The First Urban Christians: The Social World of the Apostle Paul.* New Haven: Yale University Press, 1983.

Minear, Paul. *Images of the Church in the New Testament.* Philadelphia: Westminster Press, 1960.

Robinson, John A. T. *The Body: A Study in Pauline Theology.* London: SCM Press, 1952.

Schnackenburg, Rudolf. *The Church in the New Testament.* New York: Herder and Herder, 1965.

Schweizer, Eduard. *Church Order in the New Testament.* London: SCM Press, 1961.

TWENTIETH-CENTURY VIEWS OF THE ECCLESIOLOGY OF THE NEW TESTAMENT

Nonscholarly Liberalism	Scholarly Liberalism	Bultmannian Existentialism	Scholarly Conservatism	Nonscholarly Conservatism
There is no continuity at all between the Church's evaluation of itself and Jesus' evaluation of the Church. Jesus came to teach us a way of life centered on love and based on freedom from institutional oppression. Jesus did not intend to found a Church in any sense. He came only to preach the Kingdom of God.	Because of Jesus' own expectation of the Kingdom as imminent, bringing an end to this world order, he did not intend to found a Church. With the delay of the *parousia* until after the death and resurrection of Jesus, the Church perceived itself as the ultimate Messianic Community of the Saints, the elect of the final generation, Jews and Gentiles alike, who would soon enter a new form of being in the new aeon. With the delay of the *parousia* well beyond the death and resurrection, the postapostolic Church abandoned this Pauline view and assumed an organizational form suggesting some historical permanence.	In reaction to Liberalism, Bultmann insisted that Jesus linked entrance into the Kingdom of God with affiliation with the Jewish people, as the eschatological community. He rejects the Liberal view that Jesus' expectation of the Kingdom as imminent led him to expound only an interim ethic. On the other hand, Jesus never thought of a mission to the Gentiles, nor would he have countenanced the sacramentalism of the Fourth Gospel and of Hellenistic Christianity.	Most scholars today admit a stronger and broader continuity between the Church's self-evaluation and Jesus' evaluation of the Church. Yet they recognize growth and development in the New Testament ecclesiology. But there is continuity in development.	Jesus left the Twelve Apostles a detailed blueprint for a Church: seven sacraments with precise matter and form, the papacy as vested with supreme and universal jurisdiction, the monarchical episcopate, doctrines, liturgies, and laws. The Church's evaluation of itself (as given in Counter-Reformation and pre-Vatican II theology) and Jesus' evaluation of the Church are identical.
Liberalism has emerged within Catholicism in recent years as a reaction against ecclesiastical authoritarianism and doctrinal and moral fundamentalism.	Expressed by Johannes Weiss (1892) and especially in Martin Werner's *The Foundation of Christian Dogma* (1941).		Differences between Catholic and Protestant scholars are more a reflection of theological and doctrinal commitments than of exegetical differences. Catholics emphasize the Church's role in mediating salvation more than the Protestants do, and this accounts for some differences in approach toward questions of sacramental and ministerial order. Recent ecumenical dialogues, however, suggest a growing convergence of views.	A view held by Catholics until the Second Vatican Council and the application of biblical studies to ecclesiology in the 1960s.

XVII

The Church in History

THE QUESTION OF HISTORY

This chapter is deliberately entitled "The Church in History" rather than "The History of the Church." We are not so much interested here in the accumulated past of the Church as in the impact history itself has had upon the Church, and the Church upon history. *The relationship between the Church and history is a theological one.* It has to do with the presence and operation of grace in the world, with the direction and destiny of the world toward the Kingdom of God, and with the role of the Church in proclaiming, celebrating, embodying, and serving the reality of grace and of the Kingdom, as personified in Jesus Christ.

The earliest Christian historians divided history in various ways. Some used the *six world-ages,* analogous to the six days of creation, each world-day the equivalent of one thousand years. "But do not ignore this one fact, beloved, that with the Lord one day is like a thousand years, and a thousand years are like one day" (2 Peter 3:8). The seventh day, the universal Sabbath, would bring the *millennium,* when all those who had died "for their testimony to Jesus and for the word of God" would come "to life and [reign] with Christ a thousand years" (Revelation 20:4–5). *Millenarianism* has always had a sympathetic hearing in the Church, albeit at the fringes rather than at the center of the Christian community: Anabaptists, Adventists, Mormons, Jehovah's Witnesses, and others.

Other historians used the *four world-empires*—Assyrian-Babylonian, Persian, Macedonian, and Roman—by way of interpreting Daniel 2:36–45 and 7:2–27. The fourth of these empires, the Roman, is now Christianized and will last until the end of the world. This explains why so many Christians clung to the Roman "way" well into the Middle Ages.

Still other historians have employed the threefold *Augustinian schema:* before the law (*ante legem*), under the law (*sub lege*), and after the law (*post legem*). There were variations. Some substituted *grace* for *law*, and Joachim of Flora (d. 1202) imposed a trinitarian perspective: the Old Testament as the age of the Father, the New Testament as the age of the Son, and the post–New Testament period as the age of the Holy Spirit. Joachim prophesied that in the year 1260 the Petrine hierarchical Church would be replaced by the new Johannine Church of the Spirit.

Theologically, the Church has had two major historical moments and is now moving into a third. The *first* was its *Jewish* moment. The Christ-event was proclaimed in the beginning within and to Israel. This is the period of Jewish Christianity, centered in Jerusalem. The *second* is, or was, its *culturally determined* moment, when the Church became the Church of Hellenism, of Europe, of the Americas. The *transition* or, perhaps more accurately, the *break* between the first and second moments was signaled by the decision (or series of decisions) to carry the Gospel to the Gentiles without imposing circumcision or other Jewish laws and customs on the new Christians.

As we noted in chapter 16, Jesus did not explicitly anticipate this widening of the mission. When Peter had to justify his baptizing of Cornelius, the Roman centurion, he appealed not to some specific directive of Jesus but to the prompting and instruction of the Holy Spirit (Acts of the Apostles 11:12). Paul made exactly the same appeal (Acts of the Apostles 16:9, 18:9; 20:22; 22:21, passim; see also Ephesians 3:5–6). But if something as "essential" as circumcision could be set aside, what can and must be retained from the Old Testament? Moreover, the Church would also change the Sabbath, move the center from Jerusalem to Rome, and modify various ethical and disciplinary directives. We simply do not have, at this point, a clear theology of explanation for this substantial, perhaps even radical, break between Jewish Christianity and Gentile Christianity.

The *third* moment, whose inauguration was heralded by the Second Vatican Council, is the movement from a Church of cultural confinement (especially European and North American) to a genuine *world Church*. There is as much misunderstanding of, and resistance to, this transition to a world Church as there was to the transition to a Church of the Gentiles in the first century. Today's resistance has ample precedent: in the rites controversy of the seventeenth century (to which brief reference will be made later in this chapter), in the insistence on the Latin language in liturgy and in all official communications, in the imposition of canon (Roman) law on the whole Church, in the enforcement of certain culturally conditioned styles of Christian life (e.g., clerical celibacy), and in the rejection of the religious experiences of non-European cultures.

Given this theological schema, which Karl Rahner initially proposed, the material in this chapter is not so much an outline of the Church's course throughout all of its history thus far as it is an outline of the Church's course in the *second moment* of its still-very-young history. Even within that second moment, i.e., the period of the Church's cultural confinement especially within European culture, there are transitions and breaks to which attention is given here.

THE CHURCH AND HISTORY

If "the Church" is principally a hierarchical society, with the pope at the top of the pyramid and the bishops just below him, then the history of the Church is the history of the popes, of ecumenical councils, of heresies and schisms, of contests with the secular government, and the like. And that is precisely what many (indeed, too many) histories of the Church appear to be.

If, on the other hand, the Church is primarily the People of God—laity, religious, and clergy alike—then its history includes more than papal initiatives, conciliar definitions, and struggles for power, whether from the outside or from within. History has to take into account the lives and achievements of the vast majority of the Church's membership: its laity, its religious, and its so-called lower clergy.

If, furthermore, the Church is the Body of Christ, it must be incarnate in history and affected by history, as Jesus was (see especially chapter 15). It is not like some gust of wind that blows through a house, scattering loose items but without any effect upon itself.

And if the Church is, finally, the Temple of the Holy Spirit, it must be infinitely adaptable to the changing circumstances of history, without compromise of its fundamental identity or without loss of the radical unity given by the Spirit.

Here is raised the issue of classicism versus historical consciousness. The *classicist* perceives the Church as a static, essentially unchanging reality, by divine decree and guidance immune to process. The Church moves through history, but is affected by it only at the most superficial levels. The *historically conscious* approach understands history as a human as well as a divine phenomenon. What occurs is also the result of human passions, human decisions, and human actions. And just as each person is different from the other, so is each event and each culture. But not only are the "events" of history contingent. So, too, are the *interpretations* of those "events." The historian herself or himself is a particular person, of a particular family and nation, of a particular economic and social status, with particular intellectual strengths and limitations, with particular theological and philosophical commitments, with particular associations and experiences.

We cannot define *history*, therefore, as simply the residue or sum total of "what happened." *Data* have to be translated into *facts,* and facts have to be *interpreted* by reason of their *interrelationship* with other facts. But who, apart from God, has access to all the data? And who, apart from God, knows all the facts? And who, apart from God, sees all the facts in their exact interrelationship with one another?

Consequently, history is always written by those with limited data, fewer facts, and faulty perspective. That is why histories of the same reality can differ so markedly, not only in terms of how facts are interpreted, but even in terms of *which facts* are considered.

The history of the Church is reflection on the *mystery* of the Church, i.e., on the active, continuous, and purposive presence of God in the world through the Christian community. God calls and moves the world to the Kingdom of God. The Church is the sign and instrument of that call and movement. The Church itself is called and is in movement toward the Kingdom. The whole process by which the world, and the Church within the world, is moving toward the Kingdom is what we know, theologically, as *history*.

Since the call requires a *free response* (see chapter 5 on the fundamental relationship between nature and grace), history is not only the history of God's interventions in human affairs, as the classicist believes. Furthermore, since both the call and the movement toward the Kingdom are given in *grace,* history is not only the history of contingent human events, as the historicists have contended. (We distinguish here between *historicism* and historical consciousness. Historicism is a form of historical consciousness, but it is not the only form.)

In the end, "history is...the teacher of life," as Pope John XXIII, himself a historian, was always fond of saying. What history teaches us about the Church is that it is a living, changing, ever adaptable organism whose life and structure are never to be identified with any one culture, social system, or period of time. "And everything," Pope John said, "even human differences, leads to the greater good of the Church" (opening speech to the Second Vatican Council, October 11, 1962).

THE CHURCH IN THE GRÆCO-ROMAN PERIOD
(FIRST THROUGH SEVENTH CENTURIES)

The New Testament Period

This comprises at least the first two generations of Christians, and probably carries forward into the middle of the second century. It is marked, first, by the preaching and ministry of Jesus and his impact on his disciples and those beyond the circle of his followers; second, by the preaching and teaching of the disciples and by the prayers and practices of the earliest converts; and, third, by the formation of stable communities, or churches, from which the various New Testament writings emerged. The impact of history upon the Church, and of the Church upon history is particularly evident in this period of foundation and formation (see chapter 16).

Two major turning points confronted the Church. The *first* had to do with the scope of its mission. Was it to be a Church for the Jews alone, or for the Gentiles as well? And if the latter, were the Gentiles to be subject to the traditional laws and customs of Judaism? The *second* turning point, or crisis, had to do with the apparent delay of the Second Coming of Jesus Christ. Many had expected the end of this world and the inauguration of the new age to occur within their own lifetimes. Indeed, one of the principal controversies of modern New Testament scholarship has centered upon the expectations of Jesus himself. Did he expect the coming of the final reign of God within his own lifetime? Was he then compelled to revise his expectation and conclude that his own death was a precondition for its coming? And if so, did his disciples share this assumption? Should the community of Christian faith prepare itself for a long historical life, replete with sacraments, doctrines, moral codes, and the like, or should it pursue a course similar to one adopted early in Thessalonia, of eschewing meaningful labor, abiding structures, and institutions, and contenting itself instead with a period of passive waiting for the imminent end of the world (2 Thessalonians 3:6–15)?

The *first* crisis was resolved once and for all around the years 48 or 49 at what is traditionally known as the Council of Jerusalem (Acts of the Apostles 15:1–35). The mission to the Gentiles, already initiated at Antioch (11:19–26) and dramatized by Peter's baptism of the Roman centurion Cornelius and several of his friends (Acts of the Apostles 10), was formally approved, with the remarkable, even revolutionary, stipulation that circumcision would not be required of converts to the faith (as the *Judaizers* had insisted). As in the resolution of many crises in the history of the Church, the losing side was granted a face-saving concession. Certain Jewish laws would nonetheless have to be observed, such as the prohibition against eating meat with blood still in it or the meat of animals not killed according to Jewish ritual.

The *second* major crisis was not so decisively resolved, although the balance clearly shifted against those who preferred the Thessalonian option. The *parousia*, or Second Coming, could no longer be regarded as imminent. The Church would have to dig in, as it were, for the long course. It would have to be attentive to the building of a full and rich liturgical life as a way of keeping alive not only the memory of what God had accomplished in Jesus Christ but also the hope of future glory, "until he comes" (1 Corinthians 11:26). It would have to see to it that there were competent ministers to carry forward

612

the pastoral work of the Apostles and other disciples, and creeds and codes to specify and clarify the demands of Christian existence in a world of competing possibilities and even of open hostility.

Second and Third Centuries

As the young Church progressively detached itself from Judaism and entered the mainstream of Græco-Roman civilization, it confronted the challenge of communicating the message of Jesus across diverse social, intellectual, and cultural lines. This task fell in the beginning upon the *Apostolic Fathers* (so called because they were themselves pupils of the Apostles) and the *Apologists,* or defenders of the faith. By the end of the century a major theological center was established in *Alexandria,* Egypt. Less than one hundred years later, another such center would be founded in *Antioch,* Syria. The two schools, as we pointed out in chapter 13, would become principal competing forces in the great Christological debates of the fourth and fifth centuries.

A correct understanding of the Gospel was a problem not only for those still outside the Church, but for some inside as well. Already the community, summoned to unity by its Lord (John 17:20–23), was wracked by heresy: principally *Gnosticism* (salvation is through "knowledge" available only to an elite few), *Adoptionism* (Jesus was not truly divine), and *Docetism* (Jesus only "seemed" to be human). It was at least partially in reaction to the challenge of Gnosticism, with its appeal to private sources of revelation, that the Church established the *canon,* or list, of Sacred Scripture as the sole norm of faith and underscored the role of the bishops, standing in *apostolic succession* to the Apostles, as official interpreters or guarantors of the apostolic tradition.

From the latter half of the second century, the bishops began meeting in *synods* to present a common defense against these heresies, now including the *purist* (holier-than-the-Church) extremes: *Manichæism* (material realities, including marriage, are to be renounced), *Montanism* (no sins committed after Baptism can be forgiven) and *Donatism* (a sacrament is not valid if the minister of the sacrament is in the state of mortal sin). The more widespread the heresy, the more broadly based were the synods. Local synods were replaced by provincial synods. It would not be until the beginning of the fourth century that the Church would hold its first *ecumenical* council (literally, a council representing the "whole wide world") at Nicea.

Once Christianity began making an impact upon society, it came to the notice of those completely uninterested in such internal theological disputes. As one Catholic historian has written, "The established state cult of the emperor could hardly be expected to favor a religion founded by an executed criminal" (John P. Dolan, *Catholicism*, p. 11). But more offensive even than the character of its "founder" was Christianity's absolute claims. It was not proposed as just one new religion among many, but as the *true* religion. "In a culture and civilization toward which they had contributed nothing, the Christians, by rejecting the religious pluralism of the Roman state, made themselves public enemies" (Dolan, p. 11).

Until the middle of the second century, however, the *persecution* of Christians was of a local nature with a relatively small number of victims. It is important to remember that all accounts of the persecutions were written by Christians, whose characterizations of the emperors were not entirely disinterested. On the other hand, there would be many instances of severe repression and cruelty in later years, especially in the reigns of Decius (d. 251) and Diocletian (d. 305), with a forty-year period of peace and missionary success in between, under the emperor Gallienus (d. 268).

Fourth Century

The conversion of Constantine (d. 337) in the year 312 marked another great turning point in the interaction of the Church with history. The new emperor pursued a vigorous campaign against pagan practices and lavished money and monuments upon the Church. Roman law was modified to accommodate Christian values, and the clergy were accorded privileged status (which tended to separate them further from the laity). Opinions differ about the long-term effects of this display of imperial favor. For some historians it signaled the beginning of a sort of *Cæsaro-papism* (Caesar is pope), with the Church utterly dependent upon the state and forced eventually to subordinate its spiritual interests to political considerations. Conversions to the faith often had as much to do with social status as with religious conviction. Some sectarian Protestants, who follow the Christ-against-culture model (see chapter 11), refer to this moment as the beginning of "Constantinian Catholicism," that is, an institutional Catholicism in an unholy, mutually advantageous alliance with the state.

For others, the conversion of Constantine provided the Church with extraordinary opportunities for proclaiming the Gospel to all nations and for bringing necessary order into its doctrinal and liturgical life. It also allowed the Church to be less defensive about pagan culture, to learn from it and be enriched by it.

The protest against "Constantinianism" contributed to the rise of the *monastic movement*. Although the roots of monasticism reach back into the pre-Constantinian period, the great monastic exodus from society coincided with the era of Constantine. When the multitudes entered the Church, the monks went into the desert, not as an escape but as an encounter with the demons who inhabited those waterless places. Antony of Egypt (d. 356), generally regarded as the founder of monasticism, had withdrawn into the desert in 285 and remained there for twenty years living a hermit's existence. Only under Antony's contemporary Pachomius (d. 346) did the movement to the desert (the root meaning of the word *hermit*) become communal, according to organized patterns of life.

Monasticism had an almost immediate impact on the Church. Bishops began to be recruited from among those with some monastic training. Athanasius, for example, was a disciple of Antony. According to August Franzen, "The strong missionary impetus, the remarkable development of pastoral care, the effort to Christianize the Roman State, and above all the theological work of the great councils of the 4th to the 7th century are inconceivable without monasticism" ("Church History," *The Concise Sacramentum Mundi*, New York: Seabury Press, 1975, p. 264). On the other hand, when monks were transferred to episcopal sees, they also tended to bring with them some of their monastic mores, particularly celibacy and a certain disdain for ordinary human experiences. The separation between leaders and the general membership of the Church, therefore, was not only on the basis of office and power but also on the basis of spirituality.

615

The Doctrinal Controversies of the Fourth and Fifth Centuries

We have already reviewed in chapters 8 and 13 the history of the doctrinal controversies regarding the Trinity and the mystery of Jesus Christ. All of these occurred in the Greek-speaking East.

Over against pagan polytheism, the Apostolic Fathers and the Apologists had consistently stressed the doctrine of the one God, the Father, the Almighty. In the third century the emphasis shifted to the triune pluralism of God when the Church could no longer avoid the difficult questions posed by the apparent discrepancy between its uncompromising monotheism and the clear testimony of Sacred Scripture and of the Church's liturgical life that Jesus Christ is also Lord, and that upon rising from the dead he gave the Church his Spirit.

One of the earliest attempts at a solution to the problem of the-one-and-the-three proved unorthodox, namely, the *Arian* solution, which made Christ something more than a man but less than God, the Almighty. The implications were serious: If Christ is a creature like us, he has no special standing before God as savior, and we are still in our sins. The first general, or ecumenical, council of the Church was called by the emperor Constantine in 325. Over 250 bishops assembled at *Nicea*, the imperial summer residence. Representation from the West was negligible: five priests. The pope was not present, nor did he send any special legates. Nonetheless, the council gave what the Church has subsequently accepted as the definitive answer to Arius. The Son does not "emanate" from the Father's will, as a creature. The Son is "begotten, not made." He is "of the same substance" (*homoousios*) as the Father. For the first time, the Church moved officially from biblical to speculative categories to define the faith.

This transition did not occur without opposition. Followers of Eusebius of Cæsarea preferred to say no more than what Scripture seemed to be saying, namely, that the Son is "like" (*homoiousios*) the Father. Through the efforts of Athanasius and Hilary of Poitiers, the two sides were reconciled at the Council of Alexandria in 362, from which emerged a new orthodox formula, "one substance, three persons."

Meanwhile, others pressed the Nicene definition too far in the opposite direction. Apollinaris of Laodicea, a member of the Alexandrian School, placed so much emphasis on the Word as the unique principle of life in Jesus Christ that Jesus was left with no human soul at all. *Apollinarianism* was condemned at the First Council of Constantinople in 381. This was also the council that approved the so-called *Nicene-Constantinopolitan Creed*, expressing faith in the fullness of the Blessed Trinity: Father, Son, *and* Holy Spirit. It was the so-called *Cappadocian Fathers* (Basil, Gregory of Nyssa, and Gregory of Nazianzus) who established the coequal divinity of the Spirit with the Father and the Son.

Still another theological approach developed at Antioch. Concerned with the emphasis of the Alexandrians on the divinity of Christ and intent upon preserving the humanity of Jesus, the Antiochenes preferred to regard the relationship between Jesus and the Word more loosely, to the point where Jesus seemed to be divided in two. Thus, Mary was said to be the Mother of Jesus the man but not the Mother of God. This was the position of Nestorius, and of *Nestorianism*. Nestorius was opposed by Cyril of Alexandria and then condemned by the Council of Ephesus in 431.

But Cyril's views were themselves carried to an extreme by Eutyches, a monk in Constantinople, who argued that Christ's human nature was completely absorbed by the divine nature so that we have not only one divine person but also one divine nature (*physis*). Thus, the heresy was known as *Monophysitism*. The Council of Chalcedon in 451 condemned Monophysitism and reaffirmed the earlier condemnation of Nestorianism. The Alexandrians were satisfied with the council's formula, "one and the same Lord Jesus Christ," and the Antiochenes were pleased with the formula, "the same truly God and truly man composed of rational soul and body...like us in all things but sin...."

During this same period theological activity in the Latin West was significantly less pronounced. *Augustine*, of course, was the principal figure and *Pelagianism* the principal heresy. Here the concern was with the doctrines of justification and grace. It was Augustine who led the fight against those who assumed that salvation is the result of human effort alone.

617

The "Barbarian Invasions" and the
Germanization of the Church

By the beginning of the fifth century, the West was also caught up in the great Germanic migrations: the Visigoths in southern France (Gaul) and Spain, the Vandals in North Africa, and the Ostrogoths and Lombards in Italy. Augustine died in 430, while the Vandals were besieging Hippo, his episcopal city. Those migrations were to last for six hundred years and were to come in three waves: the continental Germans in the fifth and sixth centuries, the Saracens in the seventh and eighth centuries, and the Scandinavians and Vikings in the ninth and tenth centuries. Although their disruptive effect on the social, political, and religious scenes was serious enough, it has often been exaggerated.

Most of those who turned to Christianity after entering the Roman Empire turned to Arianism. Many of the conversions were tribal rather than individual and deeply personal. Such was the case of the Frankish tribes under Clovis (d. 511). In many cases, therefore, there was only a superficial appreciation of the doctrinal and moral content of the new religion. Hence, superstitious practices and vestiges of pagan worship remained for many centuries.

The position of women among these tribes was extremely low, much lower, in fact, than in Roman society. Divorce was only gradually abolished. Legal matters were settled by ordeal, either by fire or water or combat rather than by the Roman system of proof substantiated by witnesses. Compensation, a practice whereby money was given to make satisfaction for crimes, was encouraged by the Church since at least it avoided bloodshed. It also proved to be the forerunner of the medieval system of *indulgences*.

The strongly *militaristic* and *feudal* elements in Germanic culture influenced Germanic Christian devotion and spirituality: Christ was the *Heiland*, the most powerful of kings; the place of worship was the *Burg-Gottes*, God's fortress; monks were the warriors of Christ; the profession of faith was regarded as an oath of fidelity to a feudal lord. Since the conversion of the northern lands was largely the work of laymen (Olaf, Erich, Canute), ecclesiastical authority was usually reserved to the warrior chief. The anointing of kings was regarded as a sacramental act.

Unlike the ancient Christian-Roman law which had guarded the independence of the Church, German law held to a more political idea of church office and, therefore, was less concerned with the moral qualifications of the officer, whether a bishop or an abbot of a monastery. By the eighth century, politically controlled churches of this kind far outnumbered those under the authority of the local bishops. With the development of feudalism, the system was solidified, preparing the way for the great *investiture controversy* in the eleventh century between the popes (especially Gregory VII, d. 1085) and the rulers of state, i.e., the struggle about whether ecclesiastical leaders would be appointed by the Church or by the state.

On the other hand, credibly strong ecclesiastical leadership *was* exercised at this time by *Pope Gregory the Great* (d. 604), who inaugurated the mission to the Anglo-Saxons in the British Isles. He also displayed imaginative and resourceful administrative skills in his distribution of church funds: to ransom captives from the Lombards, to charter vessels to bring grain to Rome from the islands, to ship lumber to churches in Egypt or blankets to the monks at Mount Sinai. The emperor at Constantinople did not like this papal usurpation of imperial power, but the pope was, after all, paying the bills. *The rise of the temporal power of the papacy* (in response to a vacuum of civil leadership, following the collapse of the Western Empire) is commonly assigned to the middle of the eighth century, but it had its origins here, during the pontificate of Gregory the Great (590–604).

THE CHURCH AS THE DOMINANT FORCE IN THE WEST
(700–1300)

The Holy Roman Empire

When, in the middle of the eighth century, the exarchate of Ravenna fell to the Lombards and the Eastern emperor proved unable to assist the papacy, Pope Stephen II (d. 752) turned to the Franks. In 754 Pepin (d. 768) was consecrated king and given the title of patriarch of the Romans. The process was completed on Christmas day, 800, with the crowning of *Charlemagne* (d. 814) by Pope Leo III (d. 816) as emperor of the Romans and protector and defender of the papacy. He was to see to it that Roman liturgy and Roman disciplinary practices were introduced and observed throughout his new empire. He appointed all bishops and abbots and presided over all synods. The role of pope receded far into the background. The line between Church and state dissolved.

With the collapse of the Carolingian empire, however, the papacy was plunged into even worse straits. The attacks of the Normans and the Saracens and the absence of any strong personalities among the successors of Leo reduced the papacy to a plaything of the Roman nobility. Throughout the tenth and much of the eleventh centuries the office languished in what historians have called the *sæculum obscurum* (dark age).

Western Monasticism

Eastern monasticism was transferred to the West by St. Martin of Tours (d. 397), who established a monastery near Poitiers in 362. Distinctive shape was given Western monasticism by *St. Benedict* (d. c. 550) in the middle of the sixth century. After a period as a hermit, he established a community at Monte Cassino, imposing a sensible rule with vows of poverty, chastity, obedience, and stability. The purpose of the monastery was to honor God by worship and to benefit the community by prayer. Since the monastery was to be self-sustaining, the monks were required also to work in the fields. Thus, the essence of the Rule of St. Benedict: *Ora et labora* (Pray and work).

The role of the monastery as a center of scholarship developed only gradually. Benedict thought it desirable that his monks be literate enough to read the Bible and the Fathers of the Church. Later, with the Carolingian renaissance, many of the monks were relieved of manual labor and were able to devote themselves to scholarly pursuits. One of the most practical was the copying of the texts of the classics of Western civilization.

Western monasticism, thus transformed, was to play a crucial part in the Gregorian Reform of the late eleventh century. By the ninth century most monks were drawn almost exclusively from the nobility, and the monasteries had become one of the most important social institutions. Monastic schools were the only effective replacements for the municipal schools of the late Roman Empire. In spite of their personal poverty, the monks had vast landholdings and agricultural enterprises that played an important role in the economy and government. After the eighth century the monks became part of the feudal system. Abbots were made vassals of the king.

The Gregorian Reform

By the middle of the eleventh century, however, sufficient social, economic, and political stability had returned to Europe. There appeared an elite who studied philosophy, theology, and law outside of monasteries. Monks had less and less to do with temporal matters, and the impulse to return to the realm of the spiritual became increasingly strong. Men like *Peter Damian* (d. 1072) and *Cardinal Humbert* (d. 1061) were among the leading reformers, carrying their cause even as high as the papal office itself. Not content with purifying the monasteries, they devised a program for the entire Christian world.

Avoiding some extreme proposals, *Pope Gregory VII* (d. 1085) focused his attack upon three evils: simony (the buying and selling of ecclesiastical offices and/or spiritual goods), the alienation of property (the passing of church property into the private hands of a bishop's or a priest's offspring), and lay investiture. Each reform was designed to free the Church from political control and to restore the authority of the pope over the whole Church. Gregory proclaimed in 1075 that the pope held supreme power over all Christian souls. He was the supreme judge, under God alone. All prelates (bishops and abbots) were subject to him, and his powers of absolution and excommunication were absolute.

This *Dictatus Papæ*, alongside the systematic establishment of the Roman Curia as the central organ of church government, gave one of Gregory's successors, *Innocent III* (d. 1216), a unique position of authority and leadership among all the Western nations. This was to find expression in the new Western general, or ecumenical, councils (Lateran I–IV; Lyons I–II) and was supported by the Church's canonists, or lawyers.

621

The Emergence of Canon Law and
the Canonical Mentality

Indeed, this was perhaps the principal, unintended results of the Gregorian Reform: the beginning of the dominance of *canon law* in the medieval Church. Because of the systematizing efforts of the monk *Gratian* (d. c. 1159), a concordance of ecclesiastical laws appeared about the year 1150, entitled *The Concord of Discordant Canons*. Like the *Sentences* of Peter Lombard (d. 1160) which systematized theology as it existed up to that time, this work was to become the basic text of a new branch of theological studies, canon law. *Legal decrees rather than the Gospel became the basis for moral judgments.* Even the *sacraments* assumed a legal cast, and a whole sacramental jurisprudence developed. (Who can administer a sacrament? Who is eligible to receive a sacrament? When? Under what circumstances?) Baptism was portrayed less as a moment of rebirth in Christ than as a juridical act by which a person becomes a member of the Church, with full rights, privileges, and obligations. Matrimony was considered a legal contract whose validity depended upon the absence of any one of a whole list of impediments drawn up by Rome. A knowledge of canon law became the requisite for ecclesiastical advancement, and it remained so until the post–Vatican II period.

By 1234 all former collections of papal decisions were combined and codified by *Pope Gregory IX* (d. 1241) into *The Five Books of Decretals*. The classical *juridical* doctrine of the Church was now clearly established. The Church is a visible, hierarchically structured organization with supreme power vested in the pope. The place of the laity and all religious and lower clergy is to obey the directives of the Church's lawfully constituted authority. Indeed, many rights formerly exercised by bishops and synods were now reserved to the pope. Even the election of a new pope was reserved to cardinals who were themselves appointed by the pope. Bishops meanwhile were obliged to take an oath of obedience to the pope that resembled the feudal oaths binding a vassal to his lord.

The pope was no longer only consecrated. He was crowned with a tiara, a helmet-shaped head covering used originally by the deified rulers of Persia. The coronation rite, so redolent of imperial prerogatives, was used in the conferral of the papacy from that time until

1978, when Pope John Paul I (d. 1978) chose simply to be "installed" into his new "supreme pastoral ministry." Pope John Paul II, who succeeded to the papacy the following month, also refused to be crowned.

The Monastic Renewal

The Gregorian Reform (also known as the *Hildebrandine* Reform, since Gregory VII had been Cardinal Hildebrand before election to the papacy) was not an unqualified success. Emperor Henry IV (d. 1106) sacked the city of Rome, Gregory died a prisoner in Salerno, and the investiture struggle continued for many centuries. On the other hand, simony was effectively prohibited, and celibacy was imposed upon the Latin-rite clergy as a way of dealing with the alienation of property. Concurrently, the same ascetic impulse that worked so powerfully to produce a reform of the central administration of the Church also found a natural outlet in the *renewal of monasticism*.

New orders appeared: Camaldolese (founded by Romuald, d. 1027), Carthusians (Bruno, d. 1101), Cistercians (Robert of Molesme, d. 1111, and Bernard of Clairvaux, d. 1153), and the religious Orders of Chivalry (Knights of Malta, 1099, Templars, 1118, and Teutonic Knights, 1189). The ongoing reform of the clergy was carried forward by the Canons Regular movement: Augustinians and Premonstratensians, or Norbertines, the latter founded by Norbert of Xanten (d. 1134). The laity formed Bible groups, and many dedicated themselves to lives of evangelical poverty. The Crusades, for all the negative results they generated (especially the Fourth Crusade), also released extraordinary religious energy, solidifying the sense of community and widening the horizons of Western Christians through contact with the great Byzantine and Islamic cultures. The development of Western philosophy and theology in the medieval period could not have occurred as it did without this encounter with the East.

Outstanding in all of this movement was St. Bernard of Clairvaux, described as an "admonisher of popes and preacher of Crusades." "If you are to do the work of a prophet," he told the pope, "you will need a hoe rather than a sceptre." Although he believed in the theory of the two swords (namely, that the pope had power not only in the spiritual realm but also in the temporal), he insisted that the temporal power was always to be used for spiritual purposes alone. The pope was a minister, not a lord.

From this point of view, Bernard was a reformer, a progressive by modern standards. But there was another side to him. His approach to spirituality might be summed up in the Latin phrase, *credo ut experiar* (I believe that I might experience), in contrast to Augustine's *credo ut intelligam* (I believe that I might understand) or Anselm's *fides quærens intellectum* (faith seeking understanding). Bernard, therefore, heralded a turn toward subjective, even individualistic, piety that began to surface throughout Europe. His mysticism was founded on the union of Christ and the soul, and his devotional life was focused on the Blessed Virgin, to whom all Cistercian churches were dedicated. The once-popular Catholic formula, *Ad Jesum per Mariam* (To Jesus through Mary), is ascribed to Bernard. And his opposition to the use of dialectics in the study of revelation is also well known.

Theological Renewal

Bernard's attitude notwithstanding, there was a significant turn in the theological posture of the Church at the outset of the second Christian millennium. The early medieval theology of the monastic schools, so closely wedded to the biblical texts, no longer satisfied the increasingly critical minds of the mid-eleventh century. Independent schools appeared which sought new ways of doing theology. Anselm of Canterbury was himself part of this movement. At the beginning of the thirteenth century several such schools in Paris united to form the first *university*. Other universities followed in Bologna, Padua, Naples, Montpellier, Oxford, Cambridge, Salamanca, and Valencia. Not until a century later did a similar development occur in Germany.

There were also new assaults upon orthodoxy, e.g., the Albigensians, or Cathari, and the Waldensians, to which reference has already been made. The *Inquisition* was founded at this time, and in 1252 Pope Innocent IV (d. 1254) authorized the use of *torture* to secure proof of heresy. By all reasonable standards, the Inquisition was one of the shabbiest chapters in the entire history of the Church.

Others found alternate ways of combatting heresy. St. Francis of Assisi (d. 1226) and St. Dominic (d. 1221) founded the *Franciscans* and

624

Dominicans respectively to express, by way of their example of voluntary poverty and their straightforward preaching of the Gospel, what the true faith required. These *new religious movements*, in turn, inspired a *resurgence of theological scholarship*. On the Dominican side: Albert the Great (d. 1280), Thomas Aquinas (d. 1274), and Meister Eckhart (d. 1328). On the Franciscan side: Alexander of Hales (d. 1245), Bonaventure (d. 1274), and Duns Scotus (d. 1308). Perhaps equally important, if not more important, was the *pastoral* orientation of these new *mendicant* (begging) orders. In the older forms of monasticism, people entered religious life for their own spiritual welfare: the glory of God through personal sanctification. But the Franciscans and Dominicans centered their activities in the preaching of the Gospel and the care of souls, i.e., ministry "out in the world."

The East-West Schism

From the time of the Council of Chalcedon (451), when Rome rejected the proposal (canon 28) to grant major jurisdictional powers to Constantinople, relations between the two sees were marked by sporadic tension and conflict. The subsequent controversy over Monothelitism (one divine will in Christ) saw the Roman view triumph over the Constantinopolitan at the Third Council of Constantinople in 680, but even a deceased pope, Honorius, came in for censure (see chapter 13).

The Eastern emperors' attempt to enforce a policy of *iconoclasm* (the abolition of all religious images) in the eighth century widened the gap. The West, which by now no longer understood the Greek language, could not distinguish between *veneration* and *adoration*. Where the Easterners recommended the former, the Westerners thought they meant the latter. And the refusal of the East to send military assistance to the pope in 753 prompted Rome's turning to the Franks, as we have already noted.

The next breach occurred in 858 when the patriarch of Constantinople was deposed by the emperor and replaced by Photius (d. 895), against the wishes of Pope Nicholas I (d. 867). Nicholas sent delegates to Constantinople, who decided in favor of Photius. But then Photius insisted that he did not accept the pope's supremacy, so the pope withdrew his support. After much negotiation, a reconciliation between the patriarchate and the papacy was achieved at a council held in Constantinople in 879. Peace was maintained throughout the tenth century, but it came apart in the middle of the eleventh century and has not been healed even to this day.

Michael Cerularius (d. 1058), patriarch of Constantinople, assumed office in 1043. He brought with him an exceedingly low opinion of the papacy and some measure of ignorance about recent Roman reforms. Because the pope had been insisting that Easterners conform to Latin usage in the West, Michael, in turn, ordered the Latin churches in Constantinople to adopt Greek usages. When they refused, he closed them down and ordered the head of the Bulgarian Church to write to the bishop of Tani in southern Italy, where the Eastern Christians were living, and denounce such Latin customs as the use of unleavened bread in the Eucharist. The letter was to be forwarded thereafter to the pope. It arrived at an inopportune moment. Pope Leo IX (d. 1054) had just been defeated by the Normans and was being held in captivity. His cardinal-secretary, Humbert of Moyenmoutier, also known as Humbert of Silva Candida (d. 1061), with little knowledge of Greek, probably mistranslated some of the letter, thereby exaggerating its offensive tone. Legates were dispatched to Constantinople, Humbert among them.

To compress the story: The legates botched their diplomatic mission, dealing heavy-handedly with the patriarch. On July 16, 1054, they marched into the Church of Santa Sophia just before the afternoon liturgy and laid on the altar a bull excommunicating Michael Cerularius, the emperor, and all their followers, and then departed, ceremoniously shaking the dust from their feet. The general populace, already annoyed at the emperor's concessions to the Latins in their midst, rioted and could be calmed only after a public burning of the bull. A synod condemned the legates, but significantly not the pope. The door was left ajar for still another reconciliation. In the meantime, Pope Leo died, leaving his successor with the option and the opportunity for making peace. Unfortunately, Leo's successors and others in Rome believed Humbert's account of the sorry events, and no peace initiatives were taken.

With the election of Urban II (d. 1099) in 1088, hopes rose. The new pope was a man of good will and calmness. He reopened negotiations with the Byzantine court and lifted an earlier excommunication of the emperor. When the pope called for a crusade at Clermont in 1095, one of his motives was to bring help to Eastern Christians. But the crusade had the opposite effect. Quarrels between the emperor and the crusaders developed over the status of the reconquered city of Antioch. The conduct of the Western knights disgusted the people, and the situation became inflamed when the crusade leader drove the Greek patriarch out of the city and replaced him with a Latin patriarch. Though no one can give an exact date for the beginning of the East-West Schism, it was this Fourth Crusade (1202–1204) which probably drove the last wedge in. In 1203 the crusaders sacked the city of Constantinople, not even sparing the churches. Two later attempts at bringing the two sides back together—at the Council of Lyons in 1276 and at the Council of Florence in 1439—did not have lasting results. The climate began to change for the better, under the impact of Pope John XXIII and the Second Vatican Council. On December 7, 1965, the day before the council adjourned, Pope Paul VI and the ecumenical Patriarch Athenagoras mutually lifted the anathemas of 1054.

THE DISINTEGRATION OF WESTERN CHRISTIAN UNITY AND THE TRANSITION TO A WIDER MISSION (1300–1750)

The unity of the Christian West rested on two universally recognized forces: the papacy and the empire. When the papacy fell from its position of temporal power and the empire was overwhelmed by the growth of national states, the twin supports of "Christendom" buckled and collapsed. The process began in the fourteenth century, continued in the fifteenth, and reached its climax in the Protestant Reformation in the sixteenth century. Not until the middle of the eighteenth century was it arrested.

Church and State in Conflict

With the defeat of the Hohenstaufen emperors after the middle of the thirteenth century, the papacy found itself in mortal conflict with the new dominant powers in France. Philip the Fair (d. 1314) claimed a royal power to tax the Church. *Pope Boniface VIII* (d. 1303) retaliated with a papal bull, or manifesto, entitled *Clericis Laicos*, threatening excommunication upon anyone interfering with the collection of papal revenues. The situation worsened when Philip demanded the degradation of the bishop of Parmiers, a demand that was calculated as an open affront to ecclesiastical authority. Boniface issued another bull, *Unam Sanctam* (1302), asserting papal authority over the French national state. It has been described as the most absolute theocratic doctrine ever formulated:

> We are taught by the evangelical works that there are two swords, the spiritual and the temporal, in the control of the Church. . . . Certainly he who denies that the temporal sword was under the control of Peter, misunderstands the word of the Lord when he said: "Put your sword into the sheath." Therefore, both the spiritual and material sword are under the control of the Church, but the latter is used for the Church and the former by the Church. One is used by the hand of the priest, the other by the hand of the kings and knights at the command and with the permission of the priest. . . . We therefore declare, say, affirm, and announce that for every human creature to be submissive to the Roman pontiff is absolutely necessary for salvation.

Boniface was arrested by Philip at Anagni in September 1303 and died soon thereafter. The action sent shock waves throughout Catholic Europe. Boniface's successors Benedict XI (d. 1304) and Clement V (d. 1314) came increasingly under French influence until the latter moved the papacy in 1309 to *Avignon*, where it remained until 1378. The period was known variously as the Avignon Exile and as the *Babylonian Captivity of the Church*. It was not a time of unrelieved disaster for the Church, however. On the contrary, there was much evidence of renewed interest in missionary activity.

But this was also a period of intensified *financial abuses*, and perhaps more than anything else these prepared the way for the eventual breakup of the Church at the Reformation. Those appointed to ecclesiastical office were expected to pay a benefice tax. There seems to have been a price tag on everything. In 1328, for example, Pope John XXII (d. 1334) announced in a public audience that he had excommunicated, suspended, or interdicted one patriarch, five archbishops, thirty bishops, and forty-six abbots for failure to make their appropriate payments. As the financial burden rested more and more heavily on the so-called upper clergy, they, in turn, were forced to seek ways of supplementing their own income to pay these enormous taxes. The money came somehow from the laity. Both groups, the upper clergy and the laity, developed a contempt for the system of taxation. The laity became increasingly anticlerical, and the clergy increasingly nationalistic.

Conflicts Within the Church

Trouble began brewing as well on the theological front. Two major challenges were pressed against the prevailing ecclesiological and canonical notions of ecclesiastical, and especially papal, authority: one by William of Ockham (d. 1347), an English Franciscan, and the other by Marsilius of Padua (d. 1343), former chancellor of the University of Paris.

William of Ockham accepted the pope's supreme authority over the Church, but only if exercised in a ministerial, not dominational, way, and for the good of the whole Church, not for the temporal power of the papacy or the ecclesiastical bureaucracy. Placing the pope above all law and placing everyone else under his absolute authority is a direct violation of the principle of Christian liberty. Although the pope was now elected by the College of Cardinals, that system could readily be changed since the responsibility rests on the entire body of the faithful.

Marsilius of Padua was even more radical in his opposition. In his *Defensor Pacis* (1324), which some have characterized as the dividing line between medieval and modern notions of political and religious theory, he argued that the Church is a spiritual and sacramental community, united by a common faith and a common celebration of the sacraments. Relying on Aristotle, Marsilius argued that the clergy-laity distinction had been overdrawn. Each cleric and each layperson is a citizen with inherent rights to participate in the affairs of state. Ordination has nothing at all to do with it. The Church should be governed by those closest to the scene: local bishops and priests, rather than the pope. And sanctions such as excommunication should be ignored since coercive power is foreign to the Gospel. The pope is no more than the executor of the wishes of the whole Christian community. Supreme authority rests with a representative

629

council of all Christians. However, despite his apparently democratic leanings, Marsilius seemed to hold that actual power in the governance of the Church should be exercised by the civil ruler.

The Great Western Schism (1378–1417)

The papacy returned to Rome in 1378. In April of that year the College of Cardinals, long since predominantly French in composition, elected the archbishop of Bari, Bartolomeo Prignano, who took the name Urban VI (d. 1389). Within a few months the same electoral body declared their previous decision null and void and proclaimed a new pope, Clement VII (d. 1394). Now the Church had two claimants to the papacy, and schism resulted. To resolve the terrible ambiguity, key churchmen turned to *conciliarism*, a theory originally developed by canonists in the twelfth century and carried forward by Marsilius of Padua in the fourteenth.

According to this theory, the Church is a vast corporation, with some members exercising leadership roles. All power resides ultimately in the whole body of the faithful, but that power is transferred to certain representatives, as in the case of the College of Cardinals in the election of the pope. There are in effect two churches: the Universal Church (the Body of Christ, in the New Testament sense) and the Apostolic Church, the administrative arm of the Universal Church. The latter, however, is always subordinate to the former. The theory was later refined by such theologians as Jean Gerson (d. 1429), who insisted that the pope is subject to the judgment and legislation of a general council, which is the only true representative of the Universal Church.

By 1409 the situation worsened. At a council held in Pisa a third pope was elected, Alexander V (d. 1410). Meanwhile, Benedict XIII (d. 1428) had succeeded Clement VII, and Gregory XII (d. 1415) was in office in the Roman line. By the end of his reign, however, Benedict had no support outside a small Spanish town where he lived, and Gregory had the allegiance only of certain Italian princes. The one who, according to some, had the least claim on the papacy, Alexander V, actually had the widest measure of support. Upon the death of Alexander, the Pisan party elected Baldassare Cossa, who took the name John XXIII. He proved such a poor choice that he alienated most of his original backers. The emperor Sigismund (d. 1437) forced John XXIII to call a new council, which met at *Constance* in November 1414. More than 100,000 people descended upon the city: 185 bishops, 300 theologians and canon lawyers, and vast numbers of priests, monks, laypersons, and politicians. Not only the bishops but also the doctors of theology and law were voting members of the assembly. The dominant figure, however, was the emperor.

Realizing that he was about to be condemned and deposed, John XXIII fled Constance but was arrested and placed under guard while the council continued. On May 29, 1415, John XXIII was formally deposed after a trial, and six days later he accepted his sentence. Meanwhile, the Roman pope, Gregory XII, now eighty-nine years of age, was still holding out at Rimini, where he refused the emperor's invitation to the council. He decided to abdicate, but first sent his representatives to Constance formally convoking the council and then formally announcing his resignation. The third claimant, Benedict XIII, was also condemned, but he refused to accept the judgment and died, as one put it, "excommunicated and excommunicating." On St. Martin's day, November 11, 1417, the conclave, consisting of twenty-three cardinals and five prelates from each of the five nations represented at the council (Italy, France, England, Germany, and Spain), elected a new pope, Martin V (d. 1431). The schism was over.

Conciliarism

Two important pieces of legislation were produced by the Council of Constance, and they have been the subject of much discussion and debate ever since. The one, *Hæc Sancta* (1415), espoused the supremacy of a general council and the collegiality of the bishops; the other, *Frequens*, decreed a kind of parliamentary government for the Church, requiring the calling of general councils at specified intervals. Although the new pope generally approved the decrees insofar as they were truly conciliar and did call a council at Pavia five years later, it was obvious that he and his immediate successors were determined to resist the onslaught of conciliarism in the Church. In fact, Eugene IV (d. 1447) suspended the next general council at Basel and transferred it to Florence in 1431. It was at Basel that conciliarism reached its highest development, inspired undoubtedly by the work

631

of a German priest, Nicholas of Cusa (d. 1464). In a work published during the council entitled *De Concordantia Catholica* (On Catholic Concord), Cusa argued for the supremacy of a general council over the pope. The council, in turn, governs the Church only through the consent of the faithful.

In 1460 Pope Pius II (d. 1464) issued a decree condemning the "deadly poison" of conciliarism and forbidding under pain of excommunication any appeal beyond the pope to a general council. The prohibition was repeated by Popes Sixtus IV (d. 1484) and Julius II (d. 1513). Among the strongest opponents of the pope's negative stance toward general councils were members of the reformed monastic groups, especially the Carthusians. The pope's resistance to the conciliar principle, they argued, was rooted in the Roman Curia's fear of being held to account for centuries of evil practices. That was not the first attack upon the Curia, nor would it be the last, as the history of the Second Vatican Council shows.

The Reformation

The Reformation is the all-embracing term which describes the fragmentation of Western Christianity in the sixteenth century. Like all other major developments in the history of the Church, including even the decision to carry the Gospel to the Gentiles, this one did not occur in a single event and through the efforts of a single person, such as Martin Luther (d. 1546). It was instead an extremely complex process in which religious, intellectual, political, and social forces converged.

Insofar as one can identify specific *causes* of the Reformation, they include the following: (1) the corruption of the Renaissance papacy; (2) the divorce of piety from theology, and of theology from the Bible and the postbiblical tradition of the Church; (3) the aftereffects of the Western Schism; (4) the rise of the national state; (5) the close connection between Western Christianity and Western civilization; and (6) the vision, experiences, and personalities of Luther, Ulrich Zwingli (d. 1531), and John Calvin (d. 1564).

1. The *Renaissance* (literally, "rebirth") of the fifteenth century tried to recapture the literary and artistic achievements of Latin and Greek

632

antiquity. The focus was not upon ideas but upon the aesthetic and the emotional. The movement was, by many accounts, excessive in its celebration of the human. Not only were the works of art of the ancient civilizations brought forward, but so too were the mores and morals of those civilizations. Although there were instances of real, substantial advancements in this period (e.g., the establishment of the Vatican Library by the first of the Renaissance popes, Nicholas V, d. 1455), it was also a period marked by nepotism, simony, military expeditions, financial manipulation, political intrigue, and even murder. The year America was "discovered" by Columbus (1492), the notorious Alexander VI (d. 1503) ascended to the papal throne. The outstanding exception in this line of unworthy popes was Pius II (d. 1464).

2. At the same time Catholic *piety* grew increasingly away from sound theology, and theology, in turn, from its own best tradition. Religious art and spirituality appealed directly, almost blatantly, to the emotions. Emphasis on the sufferings and wounds of Christ in excruciatingly physical detail became commonplace. Statues of Christ with blood dripping down from his crown of thorns appeared everywhere. Attention was riveted on the Last Judgment, not as the day of redemption but as the day of reckoning and of terror.

Catholic *theology* also drifted along an antiintellectual course. In reaction against the excessive abstractions of neoscholasticism, a new style of theology known as *nominalism* rejected all forms of mediation between God and humankind: sacraments, church authority, meritorious deeds, and so forth. Nothing can bridge the gap between God and us except the mercy of God manifested in Christ. Since we are utterly corrupt, justification is exclusively God's work. The rapidity with which this new theological approach spread through Europe—influencing Luther, Calvin, Zwingli, and others—indicates the intensity of dissatisfaction with the status quo of late medieval Catholicism. There was an "alluring simplicity" to the Protestant message, and it caught on almost immediately. And it had its Catholic counterparts—e.g., in the *Imitation of Christ* of Thomas à Kempis (d. 1471).

3. The debilitating effects of the *Great Western Schism* are obvious enough. The pope's ability to function as a symbol and instrument of unity was seriously undermined even within the Church of the West. The *East-West Schism* had weakened the office's credibility and effectiveness one to two centuries earlier.

4. The rise of the *national states* made independence from the influence of the papacy increasingly possible, likely, and then certain. The new slogan was *Rex imperator in regno suo* (The king is emperor in his own kingdom). That political perspective gradually widened to embrace even authority over the Church.

5. The insistence of the Western Church on tying its identity too intimately to *Western civilization* denied the Church a necessary measure of flexibility and adaptability. The papacy, and ecclesiastical authority in general, had taken on an imperial cast. The Church was less the People of God than a hierarchical, indeed an absolutely monarchical, society. Its rulers tried to impose as a matter of faith what we have since come to recognize all too clearly to be only a matter of culturally conditioned political theory and churchcraft. (Compare, for example, Boniface VIII's *Unam Sanctam* with the Second Vatican Council's *Dogmatic Constitution on the Church.*)

6. In the final accounting, no one can ever ignore the direct *impact of personalities* themselves on the course of events, no matter how much we talk of larger social, political, and economic forces. The Reformation took hold in Europe and in the forms it assumed because of the peculiar strengths and weaknesses of specific men: Luther, Calvin, and Zwingli in particular.

Luther was a monk who, like most medieval Christians, took the "last things" very seriously: death, judgment, heaven, and hell. He was tormented by the thought of God's judgment as he reflected on his creatureliness and unworthiness. Traditional modes of mortification and penance did not work for him. He was still without peace. He concluded that he had to relinquish all forms of self-reliance. God alone would save him if only he would trust in God's power and readiness to save him. All other devices of mediation, including *indulgences* (the remission of a temporal punishment in purgatory still due to sins which have already been forgiven), are contrary to the simple, unadorned message of the Gospel. The charging of fees for indulgences brought the matter to a head, and on October 31, 1517,

Luther posted his now famous Ninety-Five Theses on the door of the castle church at Wittenberg. The rest is history.

Zwingli was a Swiss humanist who became vicar of the cathedral at Zurich in 1519, whereupon he announced that he would preach the entire Gospel of Matthew and not only the excerpts available in the liturgy. He would thereby carry the Church back to its simpler, primitive, non-Roman origins. He abolished fast days, removed images, and banned all church music. Zwingli's system of church polity, not surprisingly, was well suited to the city of Zurich, which had a representative government. His ecclesiology was also considerably more democratic, anticlerical, and antiinstitutional than Luther's, who was satisfied to introduce the vernacular into the liturgy and eliminate religious vows and celibacy.

Calvin, a French theologian who left the Catholic Church in 1533, provided Protestantism with its first integrated doctrinal system: *The Institutes of the Christian Religion* (Grand Rapids, Mich.: Eerdmans, 1972; orig. ed., 1536). Calvin was especially noted for his theory of *predestination*. We can do nothing at all about our salvation. God has already determined our destiny. Since the fall of Adam, all of us deserve to be damned. And God indeed allows many to be damned to manifest divine justice. But some are saved to manifest divine grace. There are signs in a person's life by which one can tell if he or she is destined for salvation or reprobation: profession of the true faith, an upright life, and attendance upon the sacrament of the Lord's Supper. The Church, therefore, is the company of the elect.

Calvin's ecclesiology was somewhere between the still essentially "Catholic" Luther on the right and the strongly "Protestant" Zwingli on the left. Where Luther still employed the crucifix (with the figure of Christ upon the cross), and where Zwingli abandoned it altogether, Calvin allowed the cross but without the corpus. Calvinism was to become the most international form of Protestantism.

Other Reformation movements included the *Anabaptists* on the far left (to the left even of Zwingli) and the *Anglicans* on the right (to the right even of Luther). The *Anabaptist* movement is often referred to as the "radical Reformation." They were called *ana*baptists (literally, "baptized again") because they held as invalid the baptism of infants ("dipping in the Romish bath"). For them the Church is a completely voluntary society of convinced believers. Only those who are truly converted and repentant can be baptized.

Anglicanism, on the other hand, is the result of a fusion of nationalism and religious upheaval. The quarrel with Rome was not over doctrine nor even over morality and finances, but over a royal wedding. Pope Clement VII (d. 1534) refused to allow King Henry VIII (d. 1547) to divorce his first wife and take a second. What followed was a moral course of action in search of theological justification. The writings of Marsilius of Padua and others proved useful to this purpose. The state "acquired" the Church, and Henry became in effect his own pope. Even today, the reigning monarch of Great Britain is at the same time the head of the Church of England.

The Counter-Reformation

By the 1530s all of Scandinavia, the British Isles, and much of Germany, Austria, and France had severed the bonds of communion with Rome. In spite of the fact that Luther himself had called for a general council to examine his doctrine, nothing of the sort was done until 1545. The reasons for the delay were for the most part political. The pope as a temporal ruler was caught between the territorial designs of the Hapsburgs, on the one hand, and the king of France, on the other. The threat of conciliarism still hung over Europe. There was a general fear in Rome that should a general council be called, the very office of the papacy might be abolished. Another reason for the delay was the simple failure of the Church's leadership to recognize the seriousness of the Protestant movement, and especially how much opposed it really was to traditional Catholic doctrine. Luther was looked upon at first as a sincere reformer who was merely expressing dissatisfaction with the abuses in contemporary Catholicism.

Not until the election of Paul III (d. 1549) in 1534 did the situation begin to change. Surrounding himself with bona fide reformers, he mandated steps to eliminate the abuses. A call was issued for the reform of the Roman Curia, particularly its financial dealings. When a council finally convened in 1545 in the northern Italian town of Trent, its attendance was skimpy: less than forty bishops, mostly Italian. There was a long debate about the representative character of the assembly, and then about the relative importance of dogmatic over against disciplinary issues. In early 1546 the opposed forces within the council reached a compromise, deciding to deal simultaneously with both matters.

Although its composition was slight in comparison with Chalcedon (about 630 delegates) and Vatican I (about 700), not to mention Vatican II (over 2,000), and although its proceedings were twice suspended (from 1548 to 1551, and again from 1552 to 1561), the *Council of Trent* (1545–1563) is perhaps second only to the Second Vatican Council (1962–1965) in terms of disciplinary decrees and the clarification of Catholic doctrine. Until Vatican II, twentieth-century Catholicism was shaped more by the Council of Trent than by any other historically tangible event or force.

The council definitively articulated Catholic doctrine on the matter of faith and grace against Luther, Zwingli, Calvin, and their followers. Following a middle course between Pelagianism (everything depends on human effort) and Protestantism (everything depends on God), the council insisted that salvation comes from God as a pure gift, but that it requires some measure of human cooperation (see chapter 5). It has been asserted that "had Trent's decree on justification been decreed at the Lateran Council at the beginning of the sixteenth century, the Reformation would not have occurred and the religious unity of the Middle Ages would have endured" (John P. Dolan, *Catholicism*, p. 149).

The council also clearly and decisively defined the meaning and number of the sacraments, especially the Eucharist, thereby confirming a tradition which first emerged about 1150 and achieved conciliar formulation at Florence in 1439. Its decree on marriage, *Tametsi*, required that a wedding be celebrated before a priest and two witnesses, and held as invalid marriages between Catholics and Protestants. The council also created the *Index of Forbidden Books* (not abolished until the pontificate of Paul VI, d. 1978) and established *seminaries* for the training of future priests. Both of these actions, conceived as temporary measures, proved to have lasting effects on the life of the Church: The first kept both the laity and the clergy separated from the major intellectual works of modern times, and the second tended to sharpen the distinction between clergy and laity by encouraging an academic and spiritual formation for priests in isola-

637

tion from the ordinary workday world of the rest of the People of God. Again, those effects have only recently begun to change under the impact of Vatican II.

At the heart of the Catholic Counter-Reformation was the newly established *Society of Jesus*, founded by St. Ignatius of Loyola (d. 1556), a former soldier, and approved by Pope Paul III in 1540. Although it was only one of several new communities in the Church, the Jesuits stand out because of their dedication to various forms of the apostolate, especially the education of the young and of future priests, their sense of solidarity as a community and with the pope, their scholarship and learning, and their rapid expansion, growing as they did to more than 13,000 within fifty years of Ignatius's death. To the extent that the Counter-Reformation succeeded, it did so primarily through the worldwide efforts and missionary imagination of the Society of Jesus.

There was a concurrent resurgence of art, piety, and theology in the so-called *Baroque age* (1550–1750). Baroque neoscholasticism replaced the more obscure pre-Reformation, nominalistic theology. Spanish and Italian theologians like Bellarmine, Soto, Suarez, Cano, and others, distinguished themselves. Suarez (d. 1617) made a particularly strong impact, influencing every branch of theology and philosophy. Theology became exceedingly systematized. The authority of each theological position was precisely identified. Suarezianism had its spiritual effects as well: especially on the Spanish mystics (St. Teresa of Ávila, d. 1582, and St. John of the Cross, d. 1591), who, in turn, influenced French spirituality.

But by and large the post-Tridentine Church continued to emphasize those practices which came under particular attack by the Protestants: veneration of the saints, Marian devotions, and eucharistic adoration. The first and second tended, unwittingly or not, to diminish the role of Christ, and the third, the role of the laity in the Church and at the Eucharist. The liturgy was still the affair of the clergy.

In 1661 Pope Alexander VII (d. 1667) forbade any translation of the missal into the vernacular under pain of excommunication. The antivernacularists wanted instead to preserve the aura of "mystery." Recitation of the rosary at Mass became common, and preaching, when it occurred at all at the Eucharist, was divorced from the biblical readings. The reception of Communion took place after the Mass. The sacrament was primarily to be worshiped rather than taken as spiritual nourishment. Thus, this period saw the spread of eucharistic processions, Forty Hours devotions, and benediction of the Blessed Sacrament. (See Josef Jungmann, *The Mass of the Roman Rite: Its Origins and Development*, vol. 1, New York: Benzinger Brothers, 1951, pp. 146–48.)

The baroque character of the age was also manifest in architecture and in sacred music (the works of J. S. Bach, d. 1750; G. F. Handel, d. 1759; D. Scarlatti, d. 1757; and G. B. Pergolesi, d. 1736; and the growth of polyphonic song). The liturgy became as much a grand spectacle as an act of community worship.

At the same time the seventeenth and eighteenth centuries were marked by religious fervor and holiness. The seventeenth century has been called the century of saints: St. Vincent de Paul (d. 1660), St. Jean Eudes (d. 1680), Jean Jacques Olier (d. 1657), Jacques Bossuet (d. 1704), and others. Of particular importance was St. Francis de Sales (d. 1622), bishop of Geneva, who was considerably ahead of his time as an ecumenist, a pastoral leader, an encourager of the lay apostolate and of lay spirituality. He gave particular expression to the latter in his *Introduction to the Devout Life* (1590). The section on marriage is the very antithesis of the monastic prejudice which characterized so many earlier treatments of the married state.

Jansenism

By the beginning of the seventeenth century, the papacy was as strong as it had been since the thirteenth. But doctrinal controversy continued to hamper the Church's quest for a unified missionary effort. Michael de Bay of Louvain (d. 1589), also known as Michael Baius, considered grace, immortality, and freedom from concupiscence as due to us and given in creation; they were not gifts freely bestowed by God. Thus, by Original Sin we lost not only goods that were "extra" to begin with, but goods that are constitutive of our human condition. Therefore, the wound of Original Sin is radical.

Baianism was less important in itself than in a movement it influenced, namely, *Jansenism*, generated by one of Michael's pupils at Louvain, Cornelius Jansen (d. 1638). Jansen wrote a defense of Baius entitled *Augustinus*, in which he attacked Thomism and the theology of the Jesuits and argued that Augustine, not Thomas, is the true representative of Christianity. The book appeared two years after Jansen's death and evoked a strong reaction. Protestants were pleased. Jansen had laid bare the Pelagianism of Rome. Pope Urban VIII (d. 1644) placed the book on the Index. Jansenism spread nonetheless, especially through France, where it influenced the training of large numbers of priests. It promoted the theory of predestination and a morally rigorous style of Christian life.

Since Original Sin has so radically corrupted human nature, everything purely natural is evil. Grace is given only to the few. Reception of Communion, therefore, is to be experienced only rarely, as an occasional reward for virtue. (Since Jansenism was from the outset an anti-Jesuit movement, its stand on reception of Communion was not surprising in view of the Jesuits' promotion of frequent reception.) Much of pre–Vatican II U.S. Catholicism's obsession with sexual morality and its relatively narrow eucharistic piety (e.g., infrequent reception of Communion and then only after "going to Confession") has been linked, fairly or not, to this Jansenist influence.

Gallicanism

The condemnation of Jansenism by Rome fueled the fires of independence in France. In 1682 the French clergy declared that the pope had only spiritual authority, that he is subject to the decrees of the Council of Constance, and that henceforth all of his pronouncements would have to be approved by the consent of the entire Church. This latter point is especially important because it would be a matter of specific condemnation at the First Vatican Council (1869–1870) when, on the matter of *papal infallibility*, the Church would officially declare that a pope's authoritative teachings are *not* subject to the consent of the entire Church. Some Catholics in the twentieth century interpreted that to mean that the pope has absolute teaching authority, that can in no way require the consent of the Church. But as we shall see when returning to the question of papal infallibility in chapter 20, Vatican I meant here to rule out the juridical necessity of some subsequent formal vote taken by a general council or other representative agency in the Church. Infallible teachings, on the other hand, do require the consent of the Church in the sense that what the pope teaches must really be consistent with the actual faith of the whole Church.

Gallicanism (so called because of its French, or Gallic, origins) persisted in France even beyond the Revolution at the end of the eighteenth century. As transplanted to Germany it was called *Febronianism* or *Josephism* (after the emperor Joseph II, d. 1790).

The Enlightenment

Conditions grew substantially worse as the intellectual atmosphere also changed. It was at this time that the West was to undergo one of the most revolutionary of all movements in Western history. The *Enlightenment* began in the Netherlands and in England in the mid-seventeenth century and reached its high-water mark in French rationalism (Voltaire, d. 1778, et al.). Its fullest philosophical expression occurred in Germany (Leibniz, d. 1716; Lessing, d. 1781; and Kant, d. 1804). It had relatively little effect in southern and eastern Europe.

The Enlightenment was characterized by its confidence in reason, its optimistic view of the world and of human nature, and its celebration of freedom of inquiry. It had a decidedly hostile attitude toward the supernatural, the notion of revelation, and extrinsic authority of every kind. It was chiefly in the Protestant countries that a distinctively Enlightenment Christianity took hold in the form of dogmatic reductionism and an antisacramentalism. The reconciliation of science and culture, on the one hand, and Christianity, on the other, was facilely achieved.

But there was also a Catholic Enlightenment which brought about a renewal of church life as early as the eighteenth century, particularly in the Catholic states of Germany. It took the form of advances in historical and exegetical methods, improvements in the education of the clergy, the struggle against superstition, reform of the liturgy and catechesis, and the promotion of popular education. In many ways, its reforms paved the road for the renewal of the nineteenth century.

In the final accounting, the Enlightenment marks the division between an often precritical, authority-oriented theology and a critical, historically sophisticated, and philosophically mature theology.

641

The fact that much Catholic theology was written *after* the Enlightenment does not mean that all of it was truly a post-Enlightenment theology. On the contrary, much Catholic theology before Vatican II was still largely unaffected by the Enlightenment. At the same time, we need to be reminded that the Enlightenment itself has undergone serious critical reevaluation (as pointed out in chapter 3), particularly regarding its too-optimistic assessment of the powers of reason and its too-sweeping dismissal of spiritual values. (See again David Tracy, *Plurality and Ambiguity* [1987].)

The Missions

The transition from a culturally confined Church to a genuine world Church might have begun also at this time, but it did not. With the discovery of new territories by the Spanish and Portuguese in the early fifteenth century and with the continuing geographical expansions of the sixteenth and seventeenth centuries, the Church had an opportunity to be enriched not only quantitatively but qualitatively as well. But *colonialism* compromised the missionary efforts on the political side, and *controversies over methods* compromised those efforts on the ecclesiastical side. The debate over the Chinese and Malabar rites (1645–1692, 1704) brought the promising Jesuit missions in China and India to an end. Rome insisted on the Latin way. The movement to a world Church would have to wait.

THE CHURCH IN THE INDUSTRIAL AND TECHNOLOGICAL AGE (NINETEENTH AND TWENTIETH CENTURIES)

The French Revolution (1789)

The crisis that precipitated yet another qualitative leap in the Church's historical course was the *French Revolution,* the Enlightenment's political carrier. It brought about the end of the feudal, hierarchical society that had been so much a part of medieval Catholicism. But it tried to do more than that. It tried to destroy Catholicism itself, and not just its organizational structure. The French Revolution's extremism generated a counterreaction among some European intellectuals, who once again turned to the basic principles of Catholicism. The Revolution also destroyed Gallicanism by uprooting the clerical system upon which it had been based. The clergy were forced to look to Rome and the papacy for direction. In a few words, the French Revolution gave the Catholic Church the "grace of destitution." It no longer had much to lose. It was free once again to pursue the mission for which it had existed from the beginning.

Nineteenth-Century Renewal

In France and Germany *Romanticism* extolled Catholicism as the mother of art and the guardian of patriotism. Catholic revival groups as well as new theological schools came into existence. Georg Hermes (d. 1831) in Bonn tried to overcome the new rationalism by using the very concepts of Kant and of Fichte, but he was condemned in 1835 as a semirationalist. Similar efforts were made by A. Günther (d. 1863) and J. Frohschammer (d. 1893), with similar results. More successful theological ventures were undertaken by the *Tübingen school* (J. Möhler, d. 1838, et al.).

The French priest Félicité Lamennais (d. 1854) and the French Dominican preacher Jean Lacordaire (d. 1861) also attempted a reconciliation between Catholic faith and modern freedoms. Thousands who had been alienated from the Church returned to Catholicism. In Italy, Antonio Rosmini's (d. 1855) *The Five Wounds of the Church* called attention to the need for internal ecclesiastical reform and renewal. And in England John Henry Newman (d. 1890) centered his interests on the problems of faith in the modern world, e.g., in his *Grammar of Assent,* and thereby anticipated by many decades the modern theological and philosophical return to the subject, as in the work of Rahner, Lonergan, and Transcendental Thomism. But Newman was not typical of nineteenth-century theology which, for the most part, was *neoscholastic,* and essentially *restorative.*

Nineteenth-Century Reaction

For every authentic attempt to deal constructively with the new intellectual currents there seemed to be as many, if not more, forces moving in the opposite direction. A rigid traditionalism developed in France (going by the names of *Integralism* and *Fideism*), distrustful of all rational reflection in theology and excessively dependent upon papal direction (*Ultramontanism*, literally those who look "beyond the mountains," the Alps, to Rome). The papacy, under Gregory XVI (d. 1846) and Pius IX (d. 1878), set its face against the winds of Liberalism, and nowhere more defiantly than in the latter's *Syllabus of Errors* (1864), where he proclaimed that the pope "cannot and should not be reconciled and come to terms with progress, liberalism, and modern civilization."

At the First Vatican Council Pope Pius IX also secured the dogmatic definition of papal primacy and papal infallibility, but at the same time lost the Papal States (September 1870) and with them his remaining political power. Indeed, the pope became "the prisoner of the Vatican." It was not until the Lateran Treaty of 1929 that the pope's temporal rights to the Vatican territory were acknowledged, and then it was not until 1958 that a pope, John XXIII, made pastoral visitations outside that tiny principality. Paul VI was the first pope in modern times to leave Italy while serving as pope. He did so on several occasions: to visit the Holy Land, India, Latin America, the United States, Australia, and the Philippines. Pope John Paul II continued that practice, traveling to continents and countries all over the globe.

The Social Question

The second phase of the Enlightenment occurred at the economic level. Just as the first phase had disclosed how conditioned our thinking is by extrinsic "authorities" (revealed or otherwise), the second phase disclosed how conditioned our very lives are by extrinsic economic and social forces. With the rapid development of industrialism in the nineteenth century, the condition of the workers worsened. Marxism stepped into the gap. The workers were now alienated not only from the fruits of their labor but from their historic faith as well. Religion, Marx had warned them, was but an opiate, designed to make them forget their oppressive situation. By the time the Church responded at the official level in 1891, especially in Pope

Leo XIII's (d. 1903) encyclical *Rerum Novarum* (On the Condition of Workers), it was for many already too late.

With the accelerated growth in the population, the move to the industrial cities, the increase of literacy, the dissemination of information, and dramatic improvements in health care, especially in the decline of infant mortality, the Church found itself unable to meet the pastoral needs of its people and to reiterate, without provoking dissent, its traditional moral teaching on birth control and divorce. This new human situation was only the forerunner of what has been described more fully in chapter 3.

Modernism

The Church's first reaction to the continued industrial, social, and intellectual upheavals of the late nineteenth century was to pronounce a condemnation upon them. That was done, for the most part, by Pope Pius X (d. 1914). The enemy this time was not Liberalism but Modernism.

Modernism was not a single movement but a complex of movements. It assumed many very different forms: some clearly unorthodox, others clearly orthodox by today's standards. Unfortunately, the distinction was not often recognized or made. The term *Modernism* was applied to all who refused to adopt a strictly conservative standpoint on debatable matters. Indeed, some of the positions eventually taken by the Second Vatican Council would have been characterized as Modernism had they been expressed by individual theologians or church persons in the early twentieth century, and, in fact, that was precisely what sometimes happened.

In its unorthodox form, Modernism was so subjectivist and existentialist as to be antiintellectual. There could be no fixed doctrinal positions. Everything was always in a state of flux. The new methods of interpreting the Bible accentuated this trend. The French biblical exegete Alfred Loisy (d. 1940) insisted that one must study the Bible as any other historical document, without doctrinal or dogmatic presuppositions. The movement found expression in England in the work of the ex-Jesuit George Tyrrell (d. 1909), who insisted that Christ did not present himself as a teacher of orthodoxy and that dogma is just a human effort to put into intellectual terms the divine force working in all of us. Some of his disciples carried the point a step further, coming close to pantheism. In Italy the movement took social and political form, favoring the establishment of society in complete freedom from hierarchical control.

As noted in chapter 7, Modernism was condemned in various documents issued by the authority of Pope Pius X: the Holy Office decree *Lamentabili* (1907), the encyclical *Pascendi* (1907), and the Oath Against Modernism (*Sacrorum Antistitum*, 1909). Although all the clergy were required to take this oath, its imposition produced such a strongly negative reaction in Germany that the German bishops secured an exemption for Catholic university professors.

Much of twentieth-century Catholic theology in the years before Vatican II was written while authors were looking back over their shoulders at the Modernist crisis. Church officials sustained this atmosphere by continuing to equate most deviations from neoscholastic theology with Modernist unorthodoxies. But Modernism in its more sophisticated theological forms was *right* about several important matters: (1) The inner religious experience *is* an essential element of the life of the spirit and, in large measure, generates and supports the act of faith; (2) dogmatic formulae are always inadequate to their object, which is God; (3) revelation is first and foremost for the sake of salvation and the quality of human life rather than for the satisfaction of intellectual curiosity; (4) revelation was only gradually unfolded in the life of the Church, and with many fits and starts; and (5) the Bible, and indeed all the sources of Christian tradition, must be studied according to the most scientifically critical methods at hand.

On the other hand, (1) inner religious experience is not the only way to come to a knowledge of God; (2) dogmatic formulae are not completely devoid of objective content; (3) the development of dogma and of our understanding of revelation is not a completely natural process which can just as easily distort the meaning of the Gospel as illuminate it; and (4) the Bible and other authoritative sources are not just historical documents, but are expressions and products of the Church's collective faith and must also be read and interpreted as such.

The Church's official magisterium may have oversimplified the Modernist position and prematurely condemned it, without really understanding its inner substance and its fundamental truth. But the

Modernists themselves often exaggerated their partial grasp of that truth, uncritically adopted late-nineteenth-century positivist views of history, and individualized theology by tearing it from its broader ecclesial context.

Between the Two World Wars
(1918–1939)

Although Catholic theology and its official interpretation remained conservative in the aftermath of the Modernist crisis, the period between the two World Wars was one of unusual progress on several major fronts, each of which would reach a fuller flowering at the Second Vatican Council in the 1960s:

1. The *liturgical movement* worked to bridge the gap between altar and people by emphasizing the liturgy as an act of communal worship in and through Christ, as the head of the Church, and by recovering the Thomistic principle, affirmed at the Council of Trent, that the sacraments are both signs and causes of grace. As *signs* of grace, they must be intelligible.

2. The *biblical movement* prudently carried forward the work of critical interpretation without provoking additional papal or curial condemnations. Père Marie-Joseph Lagrange (d. 1938) continued his scriptural studies in Jerusalem and trained a corps of scholars who were available for service to the Church when, in 1943, Pope Pius XII issued the so-called Magna Carta of Catholic biblical scholarship, *Divino Afflante Spiritu.*

3. The *social action* movement continued to apply the social teachings of the Church, including Pope Pius XI's major encyclical *Quadragesimo Anno* (Forty Years After [*Rerum Novarum*]) in 1931. In the United States, for example, this movement was centered in the drive for the recognition of labor unionism in American industry.

4. The *lay apostolate* under Pius XI and especially Pius XII sought to involve larger and larger numbers of the laity in the work of the Church ("Catholic Action").

5. The *ecumenical movement*, in spite of the negative tone of Pius XI's encyclical *Mortalium Animos*, on the occasion of the Faith and Order

Conference of 1927 at Lausanne, began attracting the scholarly attention of such major Catholic theologians as Yves Congar in his pioneering work, *Divided Christendom* (1939).

6. The *missionary movement* was now increasingly carried out with a minimum of colonial and European influence. The first native bishops in the new mission territories were consecrated in 1926, and Pius XII furnished the mission countries with their own hierarchies.

7. A *theological renewal* was signaled by the emergence of a theology inspired by the Catholic Church's renewed respect for Thomas Aquinas but not uncritically wedded to his system. Because of the preceding six items, the new theological approach was more biblically, historically, pastorally, socially, and ecumenically oriented. Prominent among the varieties of developing Catholic theologies was Transcendental Thomism, whose principal and most celebrated exponent was the German Jesuit Karl Rahner. The new understanding of the mystery of Church as People of God with a mission to the whole world was anticipated in the writings of the century's most important ecclesiologist, the French Dominican Yves Congar.

The Second World War and Its Aftermath (1940–1962)

The change in official Catholicism is evident in the encyclicals that were produced during this period. The *liturgical movement* was given a major push in Pius XII's *Mystici Corporis* (1943) and *Mediator Dei* (1947), and in the restoration of the Easter Vigil (1951) and the rites of Holy Week (1955). The *biblical movement,* as just noted, received remarkable endorsement in Pius XII's *Divino Afflante Spiritu* (1943)— remarkable certainly in the light of the exceedingly restrictive directives of the Pontifical Biblical Commission at the turn of the century. The *social action movement* and the *lay apostolate* in general were warmly endorsed in John XXIII's *Mater et Magistra* (1961) and later in *Pacem in Terris* (1963) and in Paul VI's *Populorum Progressio* (1967). The *ecumenical movement* had to await the pontificate of John XXIII before it could surface with official blessing. John XXIII established in 1960 the Secretariat for the Promotion of Christian Unity (now the Pontifical Council for Christian Unity) and invited non-

Catholic Christians as official observers at Vatican II. The *missionary movement*, and particularly the need for adaptation and enculturation, was strongly approved in Pius XII's encyclicals *Summi Pontificatus* (1939), *Evangelii Præcones* (1951), and *Fidei Donum* (1957). Finally, the *theological renewal*, after a glaring setback in Pius XII's *Humani Generis* (1950), found itself at the center, not the margin, of the deliberations of the Second Vatican Council.

The next chapter is devoted entirely to that extraordinary event, a moment comparable in historical significance to the early Church's abandonment of circumcision as a condition for membership.

SUMMARY

1. The relationship between the Church and history is a theological one. It has to do with the movement of the world, and of the Church within the world, toward its destiny in the Kingdom of God, and also with the presence of God to the world here and now through the Church.

2. We use here Karl Rahner's schema: the Church of *Jewish Christianity* (a very brief period); the Church of *cultural confinement* (Hellenistic Christianity, European and American Christianity); and the Church of the world, or the period of the *world Church*.

3. The transition, or break, between the first and second periods occurred at the point (or points) at which the Church carried the Gospel to the Gentiles and decided at the same time not to impose circumcision as a condition for membership. The transition, or break, between the second and third periods has only just begun to occur with the Second Vatican Council.

4. *Classicism*, in effect, denies the reality of history as a process as well as the element of human cooperation with the grace of God. *Historicism*, in effect, denies the reality of history as the work of God and as the sign of God's presence in grace. *Historical consciousness* understands history as a process that is grounded in, and sustained and guided by, the grace of God, but which also emerges through human decisions and events according to an often unpredictable pattern.

5. The Church of the *Græco-Roman civilization* (first through seventh centuries) began with the transition from Jewish Christianity to Christianity of and for Gentiles, which occurred within the New Testament period itself. It includes the age of the *Apostolic Fathers* and the *Apologists*, who defended the faith against *Gnosticism*, *Adoptionism*, and *Docetism*.

6. These, in turn, moved the Church to determine its *canon* (list) of Sacred Scripture as the norm of faith and to articulate an understanding of *apostolic*

succession, by which the witness of the Apostles as authoritatively interpreted by the bishops is an additional norm and guarantee of faith.

7. By the latter half of the second century *organizational complexification* occurred: local synods, regional synods, and then, in 325, an ecumenical council (Nicea). This development was in response to continuing challenges to the purity of faith from *Montanism* and *Donatism*.

8. *Persecutions* began also at this time as Christianity increasingly set itself at odds with the religious pluralism of contemporary society.

9. A major event at the beginning of the fourth century was the conversion of the emperor *Constantine* and his edict of 313 granting legal status to Christianity.

10. The *monastic movement* began at this time at least partially in protest against the lessening of Christian fervor in this new atmosphere of legal status.

11. The fourth and fifth centuries were also preoccupied with *dogmatic controversies* in the East about the relationship between the one God and Jesus Christ, and then about the Holy Spirit in relationship to both. *Arianism* was opposed by the *Council of Nicea* in 325; *Apollinarianism* was condemned by the *First Council of Constantinople* in 381; *Nestorianism* was condemned by the *Council of Ephesus* in 431; and *Monophysitism* was rejected by the *Council of Chalcedon* in 451.

12. In the West, meanwhile, the theological challenge came from *Pelagianism* on the issue of nature and grace (salvation is through human effort alone), and its chief opponent was *Augustine*.

13. By the beginning of the fifth century also, German tribes began migrating through Europe without discernible control. This movement has been called the *Barbarian Invasions*. The strongly militaristic and feudal character of Germanic culture was to influence Christian devotion, spirituality, and organizational structure.

14. The tradition of the warrior chief in these tribes led eventually to the great *investiture struggle* between the rulers of state and the popes, especially *Gregory VII* (d. 1085): Shall ecclesiastical leaders be appointed by the Church, or by the state?

15. Meanwhile, a mission to the Anglo-Saxons in the British Isles was inaugurated by *Pope Gregory the Great* (d. 604), who also imaginatively employed undeniably strong financial resources to draw temporal power to the papacy.

16. The Church entered another major historical period at the beginning of the eighth century, when the pope turned to the Franks for help against his enemies. This was the start of the Holy Roman Empire, which reached its

650

climactic moment in the year 800 with the crowning of *Charlemagne*. The line between Church and state disappeared, for all practical purposes.

17. When the Carolingian empire collapsed, however, the papacy was left at the mercy of an essentially corrupt Roman nobility. Throughout the tenth and eleventh centuries the papacy languished in its "dark age."

18. Meanwhile, *monasticism* was imported into the West from the East, reaching its high point in the middle of the sixth century with the founding of Monte Cassino by *St. Benedict*. Western monasticism would became the principal carrier of Western civilization during the early Middle Ages.

19. Some measure of stability returned to Europe by the middle of the eleventh century. Monks returned to their monasteries, and a spirit of renewal and reform prevailed. *Pope Gregory VII* attacked three evils: simony, the alienation of property, and lay investiture. Each reform was designed to liberate the Church from lay control. The powers of the papacy were enormously strengthened, especially in the pontificate of *Innocent III* (1198–1216).

20. *Canon law* was codified to support the new network of papal authority. Legalism replaced theology in the self-understanding of the Church and in its sacramental life, especially concerning marriage. The classical, juridical, papal-hierarchical concept of the Church was firmly established by the middle of the thirteenth century. By now the pope was crowned like an emperor, a practice observed until 1978, when newly elected Pope John Paul I abandoned the coronation rite.

21. Although the Gregorian Reform was not a complete success, there was a renewal of religious life, of the life of the clergy, and even of the Church's central administration. *Bernard of Clairvaux* (d. 1153) was one of the principal instruments of the renewal.

22. With the consolidation of independent schools at the beginning of the thirteenth century, theology moved from the monasteries to the emerging *universities* and assumed the speculative character of university disciplines.

23. New assaults upon orthodoxy came from purist groups: the *Albigensians*, or *Cathari*, and the *Waldensians*. The *Inquisition* was founded at this time to deal with these movements. Others combated the new heresies through preaching, example, and pastoral care: *Francis of Assisi* and *Dominic* in particular, and the mendicant orders they founded. A renewed theological scholarship also grew out of these communities: *Aquinas, Bonaventure, Duns Scotus*, et al.

24. In 1054 the patriarch of Constantinople, *Michael Cerularius*, was heavy-handedly excommunicated by papal legates, but the death blow to East-West unity was dealt by the *Fourth Crusade* (1202–1204) and the sack of Constantinople by Western knights. Thus began the *East-West Schism*.

25. The Church moved into another major period of its history at the beginning of the fourteenth century, a period of disintegration which reached its climax in the *Protestant Reformation* of the sixteenth century.

26. *Events which prepared the way for the Reformation* included: the confrontation between *Pope Boniface VIII* and *Philip the Fair*, leading to the pope's imprisonment and death; the proliferation of serious financial abuses during the papacy's Babylonian Captivity at Avignon, in France (1309–1378); the rise of nationalism and anticlericalism in resentment against papal taxes; the new theological challenges to the canonical justifications of papal power, especially in *Marsilius of Padua*'s advocacy of a conciliar rather than a monarchical concept of the Church (1324); the *Great Western Schism* (1378–1417) with, at one point, three different claimants to the papacy; and the turn to the principle of *conciliarism* to resolve the problem at the *Council of Constance*, which decreed the supremacy of a general council and the collegiality of the bishops.

27. Among the *causes of the Reformation* were (1) the corruption of the Renaissance papacy of the fifteenth century; (2) the divorce of piety from theology, and of theology from the Bible and the early Christian tradition; (3) the debilitating effects of the Great Western Schism; (4) the rise of the national state; (5) the too-close connection between Western Christianity and Western civilization; and (6) the vision, experiences, and personalities of *Luther, Zwingli,* and *Calvin.*

28. The *Reformation* itself took *different forms:* On the *right,* it retained essential Catholic doctrine but changed certain canonical and/or ecclesiological forms (Lutheranism and Anglicanism); on the *left,* it repudiated much Catholic doctrine as well as much of Catholicism's sacramental life (*Zwinglianism* and the *Anabaptist* movement); nearer to the *center,* it modified both doctrine and practice but retained much of the old (*Calvinism*).

29. The Catholic response was belated. When it came, it was vigorous. Known as the *Counter-Reformation,* it began at the *Council of Trent* (1545–1563) and flourished under the leadership of *Pope Paul III* (1534–1549). The council articulated Catholic doctrine on faith and grace, defined the sacraments, created the Index of Forbidden Books, and established seminaries.

30. At the heart of the Catholic Counter-Reformation was the *Society of Jesus* (Jesuits). Spiritual renewal in the form of Spanish mysticism also occurred at this time in the work of *Teresa of Ávila* and *John of the Cross.*

31. But by and large the *post–Tridentine Church* continued to emphasize the practices so vehemently attacked by the Protestants: veneration of the saints, Marian devotions, and eucharistic adoration.

32. By the beginning of the seventeenth century the Church was racked again by doctrinal and moral controversy, this time provoked by *Jansenism,*

which portrayed nature as totally corrupt, promoted a theory of predestination, and developed a moral code that was rigorous and puritanical.

33. *Gallicanism* developed as a result of Rome's efforts to combat and suppress Jansenism, which was largely a French movement. Gallicanism affirmed that the pope lacks supreme authority in the Church. That belongs only to a general council. Therefore, all papal decrees are subject to the consent of the entire Church, as represented in such a council.

34. These internal problems were complicated by the most fundamental external challenge to traditional Christianity, the *Enlightenment*. It displayed enormous (indeed exaggerated) confidence in reason; it had an optimistic view of human nature and the world (inevitable progress); and it celebrated freedom of inquiry. It made inroads particularly in Protestant countries.

35. A counterpart to the Enlightenment occurred within the Catholic Church of the eighteenth century, with advances in scholarship, education of the clergy, reform of the liturgy and catechesis, and so forth.

36. *Missionary expansion* at this time, especially by the Spanish and Portuguese, was marred by colonialism and Romanism. Flexibility and adaptation were not in order. This was the period of the great controversy over the Chinese rites.

37. The *French Revolution* (1789) ended medieval Catholicism once and for all.

38. Catholic reactions to the excesses of the French Revolution included a *romanticist* movement (an attempt at recovering the glories of the Church's past) and a *theological* movement designed to come to terms constructively with the Enlightenment.

39. The nineteenth century does not present a uniform picture. Although *Cardinal Newman*'s interest in the problem of faith anticipated the major theological developments of the twentieth century, the Church also witnessed the spread of *Integralism*, *Fideism*, and *Ultramontanism*, all of which found support in the pontificates of *Gregory XVI* and *Pius IX*, author of the *Syllabus of Errors* (1864), which condemned "progress, liberalism, and modern civilization."

40. The official Church's response to the *social question* was more positive, though belated. *Pope Leo XIII* initiated a series of teachings on behalf of social justice that have remained largely pertinent even to the present day.

41. The Enlightenment continued to pound at the Church's door, but now in the form of *Modernism* at the turn of the twentieth century. Not a single school of thought so much as a cluster of movements, Modernism emphasized the inner religious experience in the genesis of faith, and correspondingly downplayed the role of revelation, of dogma, and of ecclesiastical authority. The reaction of the Pope, *Pius X*, was unmistakably negative.

42. Between the two World Wars, Catholicism lived at once under the impact of the Modernist crisis and under the power of new movements within the Church: liturgical, biblical, social action, lay, ecumenical, missionary, and theological.

43. These movements were to surface, now with official approval, in the years during or just following the Second World War. They were forerunners of the renewal and reforms of the Second Vatican Council.

SUGGESTED READINGS

Bainton, Roland. *Christendom: A Short History of Christianity and Its Impact on Western Civilization.* 2 vols. New York: Harper & Row, 1966.

Barry, Colman. *Readings in Church History.* 3 vols. Westminster, Md.: Newman Press, 1960–1965.

Bausch, William. *Pilgrim Church: A Popular History of Catholic Christianity.* Mystic, Conn.: Twenty-Third Publications, 1989.

Bettenson, Henry, ed. *Documents of the Christian Church.* New York: Oxford University Press, 1967.

Bokenkotter, Thomas. *A Concise History of the Catholic Church.* Revised and expanded edition. New York: Doubleday Image Books, 1990.

Dillenberger, John, and Claude Welch. *Protestant Christianity: Interpreted Through Its Development.* 2d ed. New York: Macmillan, 1988.

Dolan, John P. *Catholicism: An Historical Survey.* Woodbury, N.Y.: Barron's Educational Series, 1968.

Rahner, Karl. "Basic Theological Interpretation of the Second Vatican Council," in *Concern for the Church: Theological Investigations XX.* New York: Crossroad, 1981, pp. 77–89. (Also in *Theological Studies* 40 [1979], 716–27.)

Rogier, Louis J., ed. *The Christian Centuries: A New History of the Catholic Church.* 3 vols. New York: McGraw-Hill, 1964, 1968; New York: Paulist Press, 1978.

Ruether, Rosemary, and Eleanor McLaughlin, eds. *Women of Spirit: Female Leadership in the Jewish and Christian Traditions.* New York: Simon & Shuster, 1979.

XVIII

The Church of the Second Vatican Council

THE SIGNIFICANCE OF VATICAN II

The Second Vatican Council was only the twenty-first general or *ecumenical* council of the Church. To a great extent it was convened, organized, and governed by the same laws and processes which shaped its predecessor, Vatican I (1869–1870), and, to a slightly lesser extent, the Council of Trent (1545–1563). This is not to say, however, that all of the councils have followed the same pattern as Trent, Vatican I, and Vatican II. The eight ancient ecumenical councils of the Byzantine East, for example, were convened not by the Bishop of Rome but by the emperor (although later approved by the pope). In an official statement released on the eve of Vatican II's opening, Pope John XXIII pointed out that "by virtue of the number and variety of those who will participate in its meetings [Vatican II] will be the greatest of the councils held by the Church so far." Why should this have been so?

First, the total number of delegates to this council greatly exceeded the number attending any of the preceding twenty. The largest previous ecumenical council had been Vatican I, with 737 in attendance. Vatican II had more than 2,600 bishops from all over the world (2,908 would have been eligible to attend the first session).

Counting theologians and other experts on hand, the number of participants approached 3,000.

Second, and more significant, this council was not only the largest in number but also the most representative in terms of nations and cultures. Even Vatican I, with its 737 delegates, was dominated by Europeans, including European bishops of missionary lands. But between Vatican I and Vatican II a major change occurred in the composition of the hierarchies of mission countries. In his encyclical letter *Maximum Illud* (1919), Pope Benedict XV insisted on the primary importance of establishing a native clergy and a native hierarchy in mission lands, of the disinterestedness required from foreign missionaries, and of their full adaptation to their adopted country. The same stress on developing a native clergy and native bishops was carried forward in subsequent encyclicals by Popes Pius XI and Pius XII. Consequently, most of the bishops from mission countries in attendance at Vatican II were themselves natives of those lands and products of those cultures. Among eligible bishops, 1,089 were from Europe, 489 from South America, 404 from North America, 374 from Asia, 296 from Africa, 84 from Central America, and 75 from Oceania.

Third, the council was also more representative than earlier councils in terms of non-Catholic and lay observers. With the arrival of three representatives of the Russian Orthodox Church, sixty-three non-Catholic observers were in attendance by the beginning of the second session (1963), an increase of eighteen over the first session. Almost every major Christian church was represented. In addition, eleven laymen were invited to attend the second session. This number was to increase to fifty-two lay auditors by the beginning of the fourth session (1965), twenty-nine of whom were men and twenty-three women, including ten nuns.

Fourth, this was the first ecumenical council to have available to it electric lights, telephones, typewriters, and other modern means of communication and transportation. It was also the first to be covered by newspapers and magazines from all over the world, as well as by radio and television.

Finally, the council was also unique in its intended purpose. Unlike so many councils before it, it was not called to confront a serious attack upon the doctrinal or organizational integrity of the Church. It was not called simply to repeat ancient formulas or to condemn dissidents and heretics. On the contrary, Pope John XXIII, in his opening address of October 11, 1962, said that the council's goal was to eradicate the seeds of discord and promote peace and the unity of all humankind. Insofar as it would attend to doctrine, the council was to keep in mind the basic distinction between the substance of doctrine and the way in which it is presented. The Church must employ, to this end, the best methods of research and the literary forms of modern thought. The council would thereby prepare "the path toward that unity of humankind which is required... in order that the earthly city may be brought to the resemblance of that heavenly city...."

In a word, Vatican II was a council unique in the history of the Church because it was the first really *ecumenical* council. As such, it signaled the Catholic Church's movement from a Church of cultural confinement, particularly of the European variety, to a genuine world Church.

TWENTIETH-CENTURY CATHOLIC THEOLOGY BEFORE VATICAN II

One must be careful about a purely pejorative understanding of the expression "pre–Vatican II theology." There is no uniform preconciliar theology. In the early and mid-twentieth century we find not only the theology of the textbooks or manuals, but also the theology of individual theologians whose work was not yet accepted at official levels but who were, in fact, laying the foundation for the documents of Vatican II. Included among these theologians were Karl Rahner, Yves Congar, Henri de Lubac, Edward Schillebeeckx, Hans Küng, and the American Jesuit John Courtney Murray.

Textbook Theology

Nowhere is the traditional pre-Vatican ecclesiology more faithfully or more responsibly set forth than in Joachim Salaverri's "*De Ecclesia Christi*" ("On the Church of Christ") in the first volume of the so-called Spanish *Summa* (*Sacræ Theologiæ Summa*, 5th ed., Madrid: Library of Christian Authors, 1962). The basic approach is clear in the organization of the material. Salaverri divides his ecclesiology into three main parts, or books. The first is on the "social constitution" of the Church. Here he explains, in chapter 1, Christ's "institution of a hierarchical Church." He suggests that the Church is the visible, earthly, external form of the Kingdom of God and that it is governed by the college of the Apostles, by mandate of the Lord himself. The Apostles were granted the power of teaching, ruling, and sanctifying, with the understanding or proviso that every person would submit himself or herself to this power.

Salaverri argues in his second chapter that the Church is not only a *hierarchical* Church; it is also a *monarchical* Church. This is rooted in Christ's conferral of the primacy on Peter, which the author proves on the basis of an exegesis of the New Testament that is not fully consistent with that of Catholic biblical scholars today (as already suggested in chapter 16 of this book). According to Salaverri, after the resurrection Christ gave Peter "direct and immediate" authority over the universal Church. Peter is, therefore, the Vicar of Christ and the "superior" of the Apostles. The permanence of this monarchical-hierarchical Church is insured through the act of succession: apostolic in the case of the bishops, Petrine in the case of the pope. The papal primacy, Salaverri argues in his tenth thesis, is "universal, ordinary, immediate, truly episcopal, supreme and full, and is subject to no higher judgment on earth." There is, of course, much here that is reminiscent of the papal claims in the Middle Ages, especially as represented in the *Dictatus Papæ* of Gregory VII (1075) and the bull *Unam Sanctam* (1302) of Boniface VIII. Salaverri concludes Book I with the assertion that "the Roman Catholic Church alone is the true Church of Christ" and he "demonstrates" this on the basis of the necessity of a permanent hierarchy and primacy to insure the permanence of the Church as Christ instituted it.

In Book II, Salaverri moves to a thorough discussion of the teaching authority (*magisterium*) of the Church and the sources of that authority. He argues that Christ established in the Apostles a teaching authority that is authentic (i.e., attached to an ecclesiastical office), perpetual, and infallible (immune from error). The pope is infallible when he speaks *ex cathedra* ("from the chair") on matters of faith and morals with the intention of binding the whole Church. The bishops share in this infallibility when they define a dogma of faith in union with the pope either at an ecumenical council or through some other vehicle of common teaching. Doctrinal decrees of the various Vatican administrative offices (the Roman Curia) express the intention of the pope and therefore are to be received with "internal and religious assent of the mind." The source for the Church's official teaching authority is the divine apostolic tradition, including Sacred Scripture, the Fathers of the Church, and theological consensus (especially the opinion of Thomas Aquinas).

In Book III, Salaverri turns finally to the "supernaturality" and "properties" of the Church. But here, too, the discussion is largely in terms of the hierarchical, the organizational, and the juridical. Thus, thesis 23 asserts: "The Church is a perfect and absolutely independent society with full legislative, judicial, and coercive power." When he speaks of the Church as Mystical Body of Christ, the focus is upon conditions for membership. One gains entrance through valid Baptism, and one may subsequently be excluded by heresy, apostasy, schism, or excommunication. The Church, in any case, is necessary for salvation even by "necessity of means." (A distinction was drawn in the older theology between "necessity of means" and "necessity of precept." *Necessity of precept* refers to a condition that "ought" to be fulfilled because the Lord asked us to do so, but it is possible nonetheless to reach a particular end without fulfilling the condition. *Necessity of means* refers to a condition that "ought" to and "must" be fulfilled if the end is to be attained.)

Regarding the properties of the Church, Salaverri proposes that the Roman Catholic Church alone possesses the "notes" of unity, holiness, catholicity, and apostolicity. All other churches, insofar as they lack one or more of these notes, are "false churches." The whole treatise on the Church concludes with the thesis that Christ gave the Apostles and their successors the threefold power of teaching, ruling, and sanctifying, and that this is the primary law for the whole Church.

"Progressive" Theology

One cannot underestimate the important contribution of Catholic biblical scholars during this period, particularly following Pius XII's encyclical *Divino Afflante Spiritu* (1943), which encouraged Catholic scholars to study the Bible in a historically critical manner. However, through no fault of their own, Catholic biblical scholars did not play a significant role at the council. (See, for example, Gerald P. Fogarty, *American Catholic Biblical Scholarship: A History from the Early Republic to Vatican II*, San Francisco: Harper & Row, 1989.)

Yves Congar

The most important ecclesiologist of the twentieth century, Yves Congar perhaps did more than any other single theologian to prepare the way for the Second Vatican Council. The council's major themes are already anticipated in Congar's books. He wrote of the Church as the People of God in his *Mystery of the Temple* (Westminster, Md.: Newman Press, 1962; orig. ed., 1958). Within the People of God the laity are called to full participation in the mission of the Church (*Lay People in the Church*, Westminster, Md.: Newman Press, 1965; orig. ed., 1953). The Church is more than the Roman Catholic Church alone (*Divided Christendom*, London: Geoffrey Bles, 1939; orig. ed., 1937). The mission of the Church is not to grow and multiply but to be a minority in the service of the majority. Like the French Underground during the Second World War, the Church is a small community which prepares the way for the salvation of all in the coming of the Kingdom. The Church exists in itself but not for itself (*The Wide World, My Parish*, Baltimore: Helicon, 1961). This Church, ecumenically conceived, is always in need of reform, even institutional and structural reform, in head as well as in members (*Vraie et fausse réforme dans l'Eglise*, Paris: Editions du Cerf, 1950). This book, whose title means "True and False Reform in the Church," was never translated into English, and in fact was withdrawn from circulation because of its controversial content.

Karl Rahner

Although Rahner's principal theological contributions were not in the area of ecclesiology as such, he too prepared the way for Vatican II with his fundamental notion of the universality of grace (already discussed at length in our earlier chapters on human existence, chapters 4 and 5) and the correlative notion of the *diaspora* Church. In an essay published in 1961 but written earlier than that, "A Theological Interpretation of the Position of Christians in the Modern World" (*Mission and Grace*, London: Sheed & Ward, 1963, pp. 3–55), Rahner notes that some events in the history of salvation "ought not" to be, but are and "must" be so (e.g., the crucifixion, the existence of poverty, etc.). The minority, scattered (*diaspora*) condition of the Church is one of those "musts" of salvation history. This diaspora situation, he argues, is not only permitted by God but positively willed by God. And we must draw our conclusions from this.

It means that the Church is no longer "in possession" and cannot act as if it were. The age of "Christendom" is over. The Church must attract people on the basis of choice, not on the basis of social convention or political pressure. Those who belong to the Church will belong to it as a matter of conviction, not of habit. "Just where is it written that *we* must have the whole 100 per cent? God must have all. . . . Why should we not alter to our use, quite humbly and dispassionately, a saying of St. Augustine's: Many whom God has, the Church does not have; and many whom the Church has, God does not have?" (p. 51).

Edward Schillebeeckx

Another major theological influence before the council was Edward Schillebeeckx's *Christ the Sacrament of Encounter with God*, first published in Dutch in 1960, and translated into English in 1963 (New York: Sheed & Ward).

Schillebeeckx's argument is as follows: Apart from the sacramental principle, there is no basis for contact (encounter) between God and the human community. God is totally spiritual, and we are bodily creatures. Thus, it is only insofar as God adapts to our material condition that God can reach us and we can reach God. The embodiment of the spiritual in the material and the communication of the spiritual through the material is the sacramental principle. Christ is the great sacrament of God, because God addresses us through the humanity of Christ and we respond through that same humanity of Christ. The Church, in turn, is the sacrament of Christ, who otherwise would be removed from our range of daily, bodily existence. The seven sacraments are, finally, the principal ways by which the

Church communicates the reality of Christ and of God, and by which we respond to Christ and to God in worship.

The essence of the Church, therefore, "consists in this, that the final goal of grace achieved by Christ becomes visibly present in the *whole* Church as a visible society" (p. 56). The Church is not only a means of salvation; it is the principal sign, or sacrament, of salvation. It is not only an institution but a community. Indeed, it is an institutionalized community. The important missionary implication is not whether the whole world enters the Church but whether the Church itself gives credible witness to the presence of Christ and of God within the community.

Henri de Lubac

A similarly sacramental perspective was advanced by the French Jesuit Henri de Lubac in his influential work *Catholicism: A Study of the Corporate Destiny of Mankind* (New York: Sheed & Ward, 1950). "Humanity is one, organically one by its divine structure; it is the Church's mission to reveal to men that pristine unity that they have lost, to restore and complete it" (p. 19). The Church, de Lubac insisted, is "not merely that strongly hierarchical and disciplined society whose divine origin has to be maintained.... If Christ is the sacrament of God, the Church is for us the sacrament of Christ..." (p. 29). Indeed, "it is through his union with the community that the Christian is united to Christ" (p. 35).

John Courtney Murray

John Courtney Murray was not formally an ecclesiologist, although his best-known writings touched upon the relationship between Church and state and on the correlative question of religious freedom. Not invited to the first session of the council because of his controversial views on these issues, Murray proved to be the major influence in the composition of the council's *Declaration on Religious Freedom*. His pre–Vatican II contributions were done through scholarly articles in *Theological Studies* in which he subjected certain traditional teachings, especially those of Pope Leo XIII, to historical and theological reinterpretation. He argued not that the Leonine doctrine was false but that it was archaic. It was based on a paternalistic rather than a constitutional concept of political authority. Leo's position was also formulated in the context of the Continental laicist state, and Leo confused society with the state just as they were confused in the philosophies of pagan antiquity. But given developments in Catholic social philosophy and in the political character of much of the world, the Leonine teaching can no longer hold.

Over against this teaching, Murray argued for the four truths which came to be accepted in essence by the council: the dignity of the human person (a principle which pervaded the doctrinal work of Pope Pius XII); our endowment with natural rights and duties (also in Pius XII, but developed by John XXIII in *Pacem in Terris*); the juridical nature of the state, i.e., its primary commitment to the protection of human rights and the facilitation of duties (Pius XII again); and the limitation of the powers of government by a higher order of human and civil rights (Pius XII, as elaborated upon by John XXIII). (See Murray's paper, "The Declaration on Religious Freedom" in *Vatican II: An Interfaith Appraisal*, pp. 565–76, with discussion, pp. 577–85.)

Hans Küng

Hans Küng was only thirty-three when he published his *The Council and Reunion* (London: Sheed & Ward, 1961). It was undoubtedly the single most influential book in the council's preparatory phase because it alerted so many people in the Catholic world to the possibilities for renewal and reform through the medium of Vatican II. For Küng, reunion of the churches depends upon their prior reform, including the reform of the Catholic Church. This is always necessary because the Church consists not only of human beings but of sinful human beings. Although his book is remarkably comprehensive, its basic ecclesiological point is that "the chief difficulty in the way of reunion lies in the two different concepts of the Church, and especially of the concrete organizational structure of the Church" (p. 188). The difference is most sharply focused in the question of ecclesiastical office: its origin, powers, scope of authority, and forms. And the heart of the matter is the Petrine office: "Do we need a pope?" Pope John XXIII, Küng noted, was giving the papacy a whole new style and perhaps in the process eliminating or diminishing many of the historic objections to the office from the Protestant side.

Almost all of the reforms Küng argued for were eventually adopted—e.g., the establishment of episcopal conferences, the abolition of the Index of Forbidden Books, simplification of the liturgy.

POPE JOHN XXIII

It is difficult to exaggerate the role played by Pope John XXIII in the total event known as the Second Vatican Council, even though he was to die between the first and second sessions (1963). When elected in 1958 Pope John insisted that his was a "very humble office of shepherd" and that he intended to pattern his ministry after that of Joseph in the Old Testament story, who greeted the brothers who had once sold him into slavery with the compassionate and forgiving words, "I am your brother, Joseph" (Genesis 45:4). When the new pope took possession of his cathedral church, the Lateran Basilica in Rome, he reminded the congregation that he was not a prince surrounded by the signs of outward power but "a priest, a father, a shepherd." From the beginning he broke the precedent of centuries and visited the sick in the Roman hospitals, the elderly in old age homes, the convicts at Regina Coeli prison. Every day he celebrated what was then known as the dialogue Mass (i.e., with responses from the people). On Holy Thursday he washed the feet of selected members of the congregation, and on Good Friday he walked in the procession of the cross.

This new-style pope first announced the council on January 25, 1959, and officially convoked it on December 25, 1961, with the hope that it would be a demonstration of the vitality of the Church, a means of rebuilding Christian unity, and a catalyst for world peace. In his address at the council's solemn opening on October 11, 1962, the pope revealed again his fundamental spirit of hope and even optimism about the future. He complained openly about some of his advisers who "though burning with zeal, are not endowed with much sense of discretion or measure. In these modern times they can see nothing but prevarication and ruin." He called them "prophets of gloom, who are always forecasting disaster, as though the end of the world were at hand." On the contrary, "Divine Providence is leading us to a new order of human relations...."

To carry out its purposes, the council would have to remain faithful to the "sacred patrimony of truth received from the Fathers. But at the same time it must ever look to the present, to the new conditions and new forms of life introduced into the modern world which have opened new avenues to the Catholic apostolate." But a council was unnecessary at this time, the pope insisted, if the preservation of doctrine were to be its principal aim. "The substance of the ancient doctrine... is one thing, and the way in which it is presented is another." This is not the time for negativism. The Church counteracts errors by "demonstrating the validity of her teaching rather than by condemnations." The council and the Church in council are like Peter who said to the beggar, "I have no silver or gold, but what I have I give you; in the name of Jesus Christ of Nazareth, stand up and walk" (Acts of the Apostles 3:6).

Thus, the Church of Vatican II will spread everywhere the fullness of Christian charity, "than which nothing is more effective in eradicating the seeds of discord, nothing more efficacious in promoting concord, just peace, and the brotherly unity of all." This means that the council must work for the unity of the whole Christian family and for the unity of the whole human family. "The council now beginning rises in the Church like daybreak, a forerunner of most splendid light. It is now only dawn."

POPE PAUL VI

In celebrating the impact of John XXIII on the council, one should not neglect the significant contribution of his successor, Paul VI. It was he who continued the council after John's death, presiding over three of its four sessions and struggling all the while to maintain unity without yielding on renewal and reform. He introduced collegiality in the Church through the establishment of the World Synod of Bishops, advanced the cause of ecumenism, promoted the renewal of the liturgy, and opened the Church to the world, particularly through his opening to the East (*Ostpolitik*) that would prepare the way for a new order of Church-state relationships in Eastern Europe following the downfall of Communism. (See Peter Hebblethwaite, *Paul VI: The First Modern Pope*, 1993.)

THE COUNCIL DOCUMENTS IN GENERAL

There are sixteen council documents in all. Two were produced in the second session (1963): the *Constitution on the Sacred Liturgy* and the *Decree on the Instruments of Social Communication*. Three were produced in the third session (1964): the *Dogmatic Constitution on the Church* (*Lumen gentium*), the *Decree on Ecumenism*, and the *Decree on Eastern Catholic Churches*. Eleven were produced in the fourth and final session (1965): the *Decree on the Bishops' Pastoral Office in the Church*, the *Decree on Priestly Formation*, the *Decree on the Appropriate Renewal of the Religious Life*, the *Declaration on the Relationship of the Church to Non-Christian Religions*, the *Declaration on Christian Education*, the *Dogmatic Constitution on Divine Revelation*, the *Decree on the Apostolate of the Laity*, the *Pastoral Constitution on the Church in the Modern World* (*Gaudium et spes*), the *Decree on the Ministry and Life of Priests*, the *Decree on the Church's Missionary Activity*, and the *Declaration on Religious Freedom*.

Their Authority

These documents are unequal in juridical standing, in content, and in effect. They vary in *juridical standing* in that the dogmatic constitutions are more "authoritative" than decrees and declarations. *Constitutions* touch substantively upon doctrinal matters which pertain to the very essence, or "constitution," of the Church. *Decrees* and *declarations* are directed at practical questions or specific pastoral concerns. As such, they presuppose the doctrine and the theology of the constitutions. Two of the four constitutions (on the Church and on revelation) are called "dogmatic" in that they do indeed touch upon matters which are themselves part of the dogmatic content of Christian faith. One of the constitutions is called "pastoral"—a designation unprecedented in the history of the Church—in that it touches upon the fundamental, "constitutive" relationship of the Church to the world at large. And a fourth constitution, on the sacred liturgy, has no special designation at all. Liturgy is part of the Church's constitutive nature, but it is not part of the dogmatic content of its faith. Rather it is dogma in practice (*Lex orandi, lex credendi* again).

These documents vary also in *content*. Some are substantive— e.g., the *Dogmatic Constitution on the Church*, and others are remarkably thin—e.g., the *Declaration on Christian Education*. Some reflect the progressive theological currents of the preconciliar period—e.g., the *Decree on Ecumenism*, and others reflect the more traditional currents—e.g., the *Decree on the Instruments of Social Communication*.

These documents vary, finally, in their *effect* upon the Church. How a teaching is "received" by the Church is one of the important criteria by which we judge the teaching's authority. It is not enough, in other words, that a document should have issued forth from an ecumenical council. Just as there is a hierarchy of sacraments (Eucharist being the most important, according to the Council of Trent) and a hierarchy even of biblical books (the Epistle to the Romans, for example, is certainly more important than the Epistle to Philemon), so there is a hierarchy of official pronouncements.

Theologians judge the *degree* of any official pronouncement's authority, therefore, by a variety of standards: (1) *What is the nature of the document?* Is it an encyclical? An address to a group of pilgrims to Rome? A disciplinary decree from a Vatican congregation? A declaration of an ecumenical council? A dogmatic constitution of an ecumenical council? (2) *What is the source of the pronouncement?* A pope? An ecumenical council? A synod of bishops? (3) *How representative was the process by which the document was written?* Were all those with competence and a legitimate interest in the question under discussion actually consulted, and did they effectively participate in the formulation of the pronouncement? (4) *Do the concepts and language of the final formulation reflect the current state of the discussion on the topic?* Are the terms of the current debate and the rejected positions clearly understood? (5) *How is the pronouncement received by those with competence on the topic,* either by reason of their academic and scientific qualifications or by reason of their experiential knowledge of the subject? Does the pronouncement, in other words, have any significant impact on the life and thinking of the Church?

According to this norm of *reception*, the following seven documents of Vatican II have emerged in this postconciliar period as among the most important: the *Dogmatic Constitution on the Church*

667

(*Lumen gentium*), the *Pastoral Constitution on the Church in the Modern World* (*Gaudium et spes*), the *Decree on Ecumenism*, the *Constitution on the Sacred Liturgy*, the *Dogmatic Constitution on Divine Revelation*, the *Declaration on Religious Freedom*, and the *Declaration on the Relationship of the Church to Non-Christian Religions*. In other words, most of the significant changes in Catholic thought and practice since Vatican II are more closely linked with the teachings and orientations of these seven documents than the other nine.

Their Relationship to the Church

All of the documents are concerned, in one way or another, with the mystery of the Church:

The Church in General: Nature and Place in History

    Dogmatic Constitution on the Church (*Lumen gentium*)

The Inner Life of the Church

  Proclamation and Teaching

    Dogmatic Constitution on Divine Revelation (*Dei verbum*)

    Declaration on Christian Education (*Gravissimum educationis*)

  Worship

    Constitution on the Sacred Liturgy (*Sacrosanctum Concilium*)

  Ministries and Forms of Christian Existence

    Decree on the Ministry and Life of Priests (*Presbyterorum ordinis*)

    Decree on Priestly Formation (*Optatum totius*)

    Decree on the Bishops' Pastoral Office (*Christus Dominus*)

    Decree on the Appropriate Renewal of Religious Life (*Perfectæ caritatis*)

    Decree on the Apostolate of the Laity (*Apostolicam actuositatem*)

  Interrelationships among Churches

    Decree on Ecumenism (*Unitatis redintegratio*)

    Decree on Eastern Catholic Churches (*Orientalium Ecclesiarum*)

The Church and the World Beyond the Church

  Other Religions

    Declaration on Non-Christian Religions (*Nostra aetate*)

The World at Large

Pastoral Constitution on the Church in the Modern World (*Gaudium et spes*)

Decree on the Church's Missionary Activity (*Ad gentes*)

Declaration on Religious Freedom (*Dignitatis humanæ*)

Decree on the Instruments of Social Communication (*Inter mirifica*)

THE COUNCIL DOCUMENTS IN PARTICULAR

(For more detail, the reader should consult not only the comprehensive and scholarly commentaries on the documents in the Vorgrimler volumes, *Commentary on the Documents of Vatican II*, but also the more accessible and pastorally practical commentaries in the Hastings volume, *Modern Catholicism: Vatican II and After*. Both references are given in full at the end of this chapter. What follows here are only brief, and often inadequate, summaries.)

The Major Documents

Dogmatic Constitution on the Church

The first draft of this document, prepared by the council's Theological Commission in 1962, resembled the standard textbook treatments of the mystery of the Church which were in general use in seminaries, colleges, and universities throughout most of the twentieth century, before Vatican II. The successive drafts (there were four in all) disclose the extraordinary development which occurred in the council's self-understanding. Whereas at the beginning the emphasis was on the institutional, hierarchical, and juridical aspects of the Church, with special importance assigned to the papal office, the finally approved and promulgated constitution speaks of the Church as the People of God and of its authority as collegial in nature and exercise.

According to *Lumen gentium*, the Church is a *mystery* before all else, i.e., "a reality imbued with the hidden presence of God" (Pope Paul VI). It is, to use an almost identical theological term, a *sacrament*, "a visible sign of an invisible grace" (Augustine). "By its relationship with Christ, the Church is a kind of sacrament of intimate union with

God, and of the unity of all humankind, that is, it is a sign and an instrument of such union and unity" (n. 1). The Church is the visible embodiment of the triune God. It is called by the Father (n. 2) to union with and in Christ (n. 3) through the power of the Holy Spirit (n. 4). It is inaugurated by Jesus' preaching of the Kingdom of God, which he also personified and brought into being by his good works. The Church, too, is called to proclaim, embody, and serve the coming Kingdom of God (n. 5). As such, the Church is the pilgrim People of God in movement through history, sharing in Christ's threefold mission as Prophet, Priest, and King (chapter II). The Body of Christ "subsists in" the Catholic Church, which is to say that it is present in its fullness there, but not exclusively. The verb *subsists in* was explicitly chosen to replace the copulative verb *is* in a previous draft (n. 8).

Not until after the council had described the Church as People of God did it direct its attention to the Church's hierarchical structure. An earlier draft of the constitution placed the chapter on the hierarchy before the chapter on the People of God. In one of the most crucial debates waged during the entire council, the point was urged that the chapters should be reversed. To speak of the Church's hierarchy before speaking of the Church as People of God would simply reinforce the textbook tradition that the Church is, first and foremost, a hierarchical institution to which people belong for the sake of certain spiritual benefits. The argument prevailed, and the chapters were reversed. The Church is presented in *Lumen gentium* as the whole People of God (chapter II), which has a certain hierarchical structure to enable the People of God to fulfill its mission in history (chapter III).

The third chapter on the hierarchical structure of the Church, however, is important not only for the position it finally occupies in the dogmatic constitution but also for its content. The governance of the Church is no longer portrayed in purely monarchical terms, as it was in the theology textbooks and in the first draft of *Lumen gentium* itself. Authority is given not just to Peter and his successors but to the whole college of the Apostles and to those who succeed to the apostolic commission: "Together with its head, the Roman Pontiff, and never without its head, the episcopal order is the subject of supreme and full power over the universal Church" (n. 22). This collegial union is especially apparent in an ecumenical council, but it is also manifested "in the mutual relations of the individual bishops with particular churches and with the universal Church. ... In and from such individual churches there comes into being the one and only Catholic Church. For this reason each individual bishop represents his own church, but all of them together in union with the Pope represent the entire Church joined in the bond of peace, love, and unity" (n. 23). The Church, therefore, exists in each legitimate local congregation, as was the case in the New Testament, and also in the communion of all these local congregations (n. 26). The Church is at once local and universal.

The Church is also at once lay, religious, and clerical. The Church is the whole People of God, not just the hierarchy. "Everything which has been said so far concerning the People of God applies equally to the laity, religious, and clergy" (n. 30). Pastors were not intended by Christ to shoulder the whole mission themselves. On the contrary, their task is one of coordination of the gifts, charisms, and ministries which in fact exist within a given local church, to see to it that "all according to their proper roles may cooperate in this common undertaking with one heart" (n. 30). The laity, therefore, do not simply participate in the mission or the ministry of the hierarchy: "The lay apostolate, however, is a participation in the saving mission of the Church itself. Through their baptism and confirmation, all are commissioned to that apostolate by the Lord himself" (n. 33). And because the laity are as much a part of the Church as religious and clergy, and because the Church is called to holiness in order to be a credible sign of Christ to the world, everyone in the Church—laity, religious, and clergy alike—is called to holiness (chapter V). But this is always an imperfect realization. The Church is still on pilgrimage. It "dwells among creatures who groan and travail in pain until now and await the revelation of the sons of God" (n. 48).

In the meantime, Mary is "a preeminent and altogether singular member of the Church, and... the Church's model and excellent exemplar, in faith and charity" (n. 53; also n. 63). She is "a sign of sure hope and solace for the pilgrim People of God" (n. 68). The council comes very close to calling Mary "Mother of the Church," but it was left to Pope Paul VI to do so explicitly in his closing speech at the end of the third session, November 21, 1964.

Pastoral Constitution on the Church in the Modern World

As we pointed out in chapter 3 of this book, the impetus for this unprecedented "pastoral" constitution came from Pope John XXIII and Cardinal Leo-Jozef Suenens of Belgium. With the prior knowledge and approval of the pope, Cardinal Suenens rose at the end of the first session (December 4, 1962) and urged the council to do more than examine the mystery of the Church in itself (*ad intra*). The council must also attend to the Church's relationship with the world at large (*ad extra*). The document *Gaudium et spes* ("Joy and Hope") is the principal result of that important intervention. (It was Pope John Paul II, then a bishop delegate at the council, who suggested the adjective *pastoral* for this unusual constitution.)

The pastoral constitution recapitulates the Church's social teachings as they had developed from Pope Leo XIII's encyclical *Rerum Novarum* (1891), through Pope Pius XI's *Quadragesimo Anno* (1931), and Pope John XXIII's *Mater et Magistra* (1961) and *Pacem in Terris* (1963). But it correlates this teaching with intellectual and scientific developments outside the Church as well: "The Church has always had the duty of scrutinizing the signs of the times and of interpreting them in the light of the gospel" (n. 4). The ecclesiological theme is sounded at the outset: The Church exists not alongside the world but within the world, and not in domination over the world but as its servant. "Inspired by no earthly ambition, the Church seeks but a solitary goal: to carry forward the work of Christ himself under the lead of the befriending Spirit. And Christ entered this world to give witness to the truth, to rescue and not to sit in judgment, to serve and not to be served" (n. 3). (The reader is referred again to chapters 3 and 6 of this book, where some attention was already devoted to this conciliar document.)

Even though the Church will not fully attain its saving and eschatological purpose except in the age to come, the Church is called even now "to form the family of God's children during the present history of the human race..." (n. 40). The Church is "at once a visible assembly and a spiritual community [and] goes forward together with humanity and experiences the same earthly lot which the world does" (n. 40). In trying to imbue the world and its history with deeper meaning and importance, "the Church believes it can contribute greatly toward making the family of humankind and its history more human" (n. 40). On the other hand, the Church is not a political party. It has "no proper mission in the political, economic, or social order" (n. 42). Nor is the Church bound to any "particular form of human culture, nor to any political, economic, or social system" (n. 42).

The pastoral constitution nevertheless recognizes and underlines the connection between religious faith and temporal activities. It characterizes the split between the two realms as "among the more serious errors of our age.... Therefore, let there be no false opposition between professional and social activities on the one part, and religious life on the other. The Christian who neglects his or her temporal duties neglects his or her duties toward one's neighbor and even God, and jeopardizes his or her eternal salvation" (n. 43). Although the Church has a proper role to play even in the political order, it must be one of cooperation, not domination. In any case, the Church should receive no favors or privileges from civil authority, especially when they compromise the Church's capacity for credible prophetic witness (n. 76).

The document acknowledges that the dichotomy between faith and action can occur within the Church as well as outside it, and the council calls upon Christians to close the gap between message and performance wherever it exists. In all, "the Church has a single intention: that God's kingdom may come, and that the salvation of the whole human race may come to pass" (n. 45). The Church is in fact the universal sacrament of salvation. It is the sign of that fellowship "which allows honest dialogue and invigorates it" (n. 92). This means that life inside the Church must be governed always by the principle "Let there be unity in what is necessary, freedom in what is unsettled, and charity in any case" (n. 92). Insofar as the Church offers a credible witness to the truth, it will arouse the world to a "lively hope" in the coming of the Kingdom of God (n. 93).

Decree on Ecumenism

The quest for Christian unity is a missionary responsibility, for the Church is called to be a sacrament of Christ and of the unity of the triune God who is present within the Church (n. 2). The decree is remarkable for a variety of reasons: It describes the ecumenical movement as one of seeking the *restoration* of Christian unity rather than as a *return* of non-Catholics to the already existing unity of the Catholic Church; it acknowledges the ecclesial reality of other Christian communities, which share the same Sacred Scriptures, the same life of grace, the same faith, hope, and charity, the same gifts of the Holy Spirit, the same Baptism, and many other common elements which constitute the Church; and it admits, finally, that both sides were to blame for the divisions that ruptured the Church at the time of the Reformation (nn. 3,20–23).

The immediate path to unity is through reform and renewal (n. 6). "There can be no ecumenism worthy of the name without a change of heart" (n. 7). This change of heart (which the council links with "spiritual ecumenism") may express itself at times even in joint celebration of the Eucharist. Although it is not simply a means of unity to be employed indiscriminately, eucharistic sharing may at times be necessary for the gaining of the grace of unity (n. 8). In the meantime, ecumenism also requires theological collaboration, dialogue, and joint study, as well as cooperation in social action (nn. 9–12).

Constitution on the Sacred Liturgy

This document is based on the ecclesiological assumption that the liturgy is "the outstanding means by which the faithful can express in their lives, and manifest to others, the mystery of Christ and the real nature of the true Church" (n. 2). It underscores the Church's mission to be a sign, or sacrament, of Christ and of God's presence in and for the world. The Church is called to proclaim the Gospel not only in word but also in ritual: in the sacraments and in the Eucharist particularly (n. 6).

Through the liturgy the Church continues Christ's worship of the Father, which Christ achieved principally by the paschal mystery of his passion, death, resurrection, and exaltation to the right hand of God (n. 5). Through our participation in that same worship, we have a foretaste of the heavenly liturgy that is to come (n. 8). Although the liturgy does not exhaust the entire activity of the Church (n. 9), it can be described as "the summit toward which the activity of the Church is directed; at the same time it is the source from which all her power flows" (n. 10).

Because the Church is the whole People of God, everyone must be encouraged to participate actively in the celebration of the Eucharist and the other sacraments (nn. 26,28,29,31,47–55). But this is impossible if the liturgy, which is a world of signs and symbols, is not intelligible to those who participate in it (n. 21). And so this principle must govern the reform and renewal of the Church's liturgical life: If the sign is to cause the grace it signifies (as the Council of Trent declared), then the sign must be understandable. Otherwise it is not a sign at all, and, if not a sign, it cannot cause the grace for which it exists. That is why the language of the Eucharist and the other sacraments is once again the language of the people, and that is why the rites or ceremonies have been restructured and simplified since Vatican II. The latter process has been guided by the principles that there should be "legitimate variations and adaptations to different groups" and that there be no "rigid uniformity in matters which do not involve the faith or the good of the whole community" (nn. 37–38).

Dogmatic Constitution on Divine Revelation

The Church is commissioned to preach the Gospel to the whole of creation. What the Church is called upon to proclaim today it draws from Sacred Scripture and from the tradition "which comes from the apostles...with the help of the Holy Spirit. For there is a growth in the understanding of the realities and the words which have been handed down.... The Church constantly moves forward toward the fullness of divine truth until the words of God reach their complete fulfillment..." (n. 8). The teaching office of the Church interprets the word of God as it is communicated in Scripture and in the successive interpretations of the Scriptures (tradition). "This teaching office is not above the word of God, but serves it.... It is clear, therefore, that sacred tradition, sacred Scripture, and the teaching authority of the Church...are so linked and joined together that one cannot stand without the others, and that all together and each in its own way

675

under the action of the one Holy Spirit contribute effectively to the salvation of souls" (n. 10).

Declaration on Religious Freedom

This document was at first to be a chapter of the *Decree on Ecumenism,* and later an appendix of that same decree. Finally, it was given independent status as a declaration of the council. Although it is hardly a milestone in the history of the world (the principle of religious liberty had long since been recognized and defended by others inside and outside the Church), the declaration was a major event in the history of the Catholic Church and of the Second Vatican Council. It was by far the most controversial document produced by the council, because it raised in a special way the underlying question of *doctrinal development.* In light of so many seemingly unequivocal condemnations of the principle of religious freedom in earlier papal documents, how could the Church now turn around and endorse the principle? The distance between Pope Pius IX's *Syllabus of Errors* (1864) and Vatican II's *Declaration on Religious Freedom* (1965) is more than chronological. They inhabit two different theological universes.

This declaration ends the so-called double standard by which the Church demands freedom for itself when in a minority position but refuses to grant freedom to other religions when they are in the minority. The council declares as a matter of principle that the dignity of the human person and the freedom of the act of faith demand that everyone should be immune from coercion of every kind, private or public, in matters pertaining to the profession of a particular religious faith (n. 2). No one can be compelled to accept the Christian faith, nor can anyone be penalized in any way for not being a Christian (n. 9). The supreme model is Jesus himself and, after him, the example of the early Church (n. 11).

Declaration on the Relationship of the Church to Non-Christian Religions

This document, too, was originally planned as a chapter in the *Decree on Ecumenism.* It was also to be concerned principally with the Jews. Its vision, however, is considerably broader than that. It acknowledges, first of all, that the whole human community comes from the creative hand of the one God, and that variations in religious faith and expression are a reflection of the diversity that characterizes humankind itself. "The Catholic Church rejects nothing which is true and holy in these religions.... [They] often reflect a ray of that Truth which enlightens all persons" (n. 2). And so the Church encourages dialogue and collaboration with the followers of other religions in order to promote common spiritual and moral values.

The declaration recounts the many basic elements the Church has in common with the Jews. Since there is such a close union between Christians and Jews, we must pursue the way of mutual understanding and respect. Specifically, we must eschew the notion that Jews can be blamed as a race for the death of Jesus. Furthermore, the Jews are not repudiated or accursed by God (n. 4). Every form of persecution is to be condemned, and so, too, every kind of discrimination based on race, color, condition of life, or religion (n. 5).

The Other Documents

The following eight decrees and one declaration have not been unimportant in the life of the Church, but their teaching is usually implied already in one or more of the so-called major documents. Even if the individual documents might not be considered "major," the issues treated in each *are* of major importance: missionary activity, the lay apostolate, Eastern Catholic churches, bishops, priests, religious life, education, and communications.

Decree on the Church's Missionary Activity

This document presupposes the dogmatic constitution *Lumen gentium* and the pastoral constitution *Gaudium et spes*. It differs from both of them in that they speak of the "mission" of the Church in its total sense of preaching the Gospel in word, sacrament, witness, and service to the whole human community, Christians and non-Christians alike, whereas the *Decree on the Church's Missionary Activity* is concerned with one important aspect of that total mission, namely, "evangelization and the planting of the Church among those peoples and groups where it has not yet taken root" (n. 6). The distinction is between the "mission of the Church" and "the missions."

The decree does not restrict its vision to the de-Christianized West. The Gospel is to penetrate Asia, Africa, and Oceania as well. But wherever missionaries go, they are not to impose an alien cultural reality from outside. They are to recognize and preserve "whatever truth and grace are to be found among the nations, as a sort of secret presence of God.... And so, whatever good is found to be sown in the hearts and minds of men and women, or in the rites and cultures peculiar to various peoples, is not lost" (n. 9). This pastoral principle is rooted in the theological principle of the incarnation (n. 10). Finally, "the whole Church is missionary, and the work of evangelization is a basic duty of the People of God..." (n. 35).

Decree on the Apostolate of the Laity

This document also presupposes what is contained in *Lumen gentium* and *Gaudium et spes*. Moreover, its subject matter is treated in various other pronouncements of the council—e.g., the aforementioned *Decree on the Church's Missionary Activity*. This decree makes clear, as the *Dogmatic Constitution on the Church* (*Lumen gentium*) also made clear, that the laity are full members of the People of God and, as such, share directly in the mission of the Church, not simply by leave of the hierarchy but "from their union with Christ their Head. Incorporated into Christ's Mystical Body through baptism and strengthened by the power of the Holy Spirit through confirmation, they are assigned to the apostolate by the Lord himself" (n. 3). This apostolate is located principally, but not exclusively, in the temporal order: the world of family, culture, economic affairs, the arts and professions, political institutions, and so forth (n. 6).

Decree on Eastern Catholic Churches

This decree is really a complement to the *Decree on Ecumenism*. It relates to the seven non-Latin, non-Roman Eastern Catholic ecclesial traditions (i.e., those Eastern churches in union with Rome as distinguished from those Eastern Orthodox churches which are still separate from Rome ever since the East-West Schism at the turn of the thirteenth century): Armenian, Byzantine, Coptic, Ethiopian, East Syrian (Chaldean), West Syrian, and Maronite. Each of these is a Catholic church in communion with the Bishop of Rome; none of these is a *Roman* Catholic church. Catholicism, to repeat what was said in chapter 1 of this book, is neither narrowly Roman nor narrowly Western. It is universal in the fullest sense of the word.

These churches, which have also been known by the pejorative term, *Uniate* churches, have been sources of much friction between Rome and the Orthodox world because they were originally conceived as "substitutes" for, rather than as "bridges" to, the Orthodox East, and as such have always been resented by the latter.

Although the decree proclaims the equality of the Eastern and Western traditions of Christianity (n. 3) as well as the importance of preserving the spiritual heritage of the Eastern churches (n. 5), the decree itself is still very much a Latin text about the Eastern tradition (nn. 7–23). It clearly manifests, however, an ardent desire for reconciliation with the separated churches of the East and opens the door from Rome's side to common eucharistic sharing (nn. 24–29).

One of the most significant features of this document is its affirmation that the Eastern Catholic communities are distinct *churches*, not just "rites" (n. 2), and that they also have the "rights and privileges...which existed in the time of union between East and West" (n. 9).

Decree on the Bishops' Pastoral Office in the Church

In its earlier stages this document reflected the preconciliar ecclesiology which tended to make bishops entirely subordinate to the pope and the Curia and to make the office of bishop more a jurisdictional than a sacramental reality. The finally approved decree, however, reflects the teaching of *Lumen gentium* on collegiality. Thus, bishops exercise their episcopal office "received through episcopal consecration" (n. 3). They exercise that office at three levels: over their own dioceses, or "particular churches"; in collaboration with other bishops on a regional or national level (episcopal conferences); and as a worldwide body in union with the pope (college of bishops).

Bishops, therefore, are not simply delegates or vicars of the pope in a diocese, as an exceedingly hierarchical model of the Church once proposed. They are "the proper, ordinary, and immediate pastors" of their own dioceses (n. 11). That pastoral office, which includes preaching the Gospel, presiding at worship, and ministering to those in need, must always be exercised in the mode of a servant (n. 16). The bishop must carry out his episcopal, or supervisory, duties in a manner that encourages communication and integration among the various apostolates (n. 17). Indeed, the decree contains a kind of job description and list of qualifications for the office of bishop (nn. 11–21).

Decree on the Ministry and Life of Priests

This decree emerged as a separate document because many bishops at the council thought there was too little said about priests in the *Dogmatic Constitution on the Church.* The essence of the decree's teaching follows: "Established in the priestly order by ordination, all priests are united among themselves in an intimate sacramental brotherhood. In a special way they form one presbytery in a diocese to whose service they are committed under their own bishop." Whether they are in parish work, teaching, or some other special activity, priests are "united in the single goal of building up Christ's Body" (n. 8). This work includes the proclamation of the Gospel, the celebration of the Eucharist and other sacraments, governance of a community, and ministering to those in need (nn. 4–6).

Decree on Priestly Formation

For four centuries the training of Catholic priests had been shaped by the directives of the Council of Trent, which was itself originally a reform council. Prior to Trent, priests were ordained with little or no theological or spiritual formation. But eventually the reforms of Trent developed into rigid rules, and seminaries tended to become increasingly isolated from the world around them. The essence of the present-day reform, encouraged in such large measure by Vatican II, is the impulse to combine the theological and the spiritual with the pastoral, and thereby to allow seminary training to be adapted to the particular social and cultural circumstances in which priestly service will be rendered. Such a reform required some measure of decentralization of authority, so that national churches could also have a direct hand in determining what is required for effective priestly service. Therefore, the decree proposes the principle of adaptation (n. 1) and insists on a close connection of seminary formation with pastoral realities (n. 4). Meanwhile, theological studies should be biblical, ecumenical, historical, and personally formative (nn. 16–17). Special attention must be given to the relationship between theory and practice (n. 21). Continuing education programs for the clergy are also of great importance (n. 22).

Decree on the Appropriate Renewal of the Religious Life

Religious life refers to a corporate form of Christian existence in which members of the Church gather together in common pursuit of the evangelical counsels: poverty, chastity, and obedience (see Matthew 19:10–12,21). We have already referred to the origins and growth of religious life in chapter 17. Renewal of such a life depends on two principles: "(1) a continuous return to the sources of all Christian life and to the original inspiration behind a given community and (2) an adjustment of the community to the changed conditions of the times" (n. 2). Such communities must always see themselves as part of the Church and as participants in its mission, whatever their composition, structure, and apostolate. "But inasmuch as the religious life which is committed to apostolic works takes on many forms, a necessary diversity will have to distinguish its path to a suitable renewal, and members of the various communities will have to be sustained in living for Christ's service by means which are proper and fitting for themselves" (n. 8). Indeed, a cloistered lifestyle is incompatible with full dedication to apostolic work (n. 16).

The decree also called upon religious to "give a kind of corporate witness to their own poverty. Let them willingly contribute something from their own resources to the other needs of the Church, and to the support of the poor..." (n. 13). In any case, religious communities should "avoid every appearance of luxury, of excessive wealth, and accumulation of possessions" (ibid.), abolish all class distinctions among their members (n. 15), and involve all members in the renewal process (n. 4). Significantly, the decree does not repeat the teaching of the Council of Trent that the religious state is superior to marriage. It also encouraged the work of conferences of major superiors, and underscored their need to collaborate with religious leaders in other countries and with their own national episcopal conference (n. 23).

There was also a more conservative tone and spirit to the decree which was recognized and embraced by religious men and women devoted to the preservation of traditional forms of religious life, e.g., traditional religious clothing (habits), traditional places of residence (convents and other religious houses), and traditional modes of exercising authority (more directive than collegial or participative). One such organization was known as *Consortium Perfectæ Caritatis*, taking its name from the Latin title of the decree.

Declaration on Christian Education

This declaration is different from most of the other council documents in that it deals only with a few fundamental principles and leaves further development to the postconciliar process, particularly in the various conferences of bishops. The focus is on the education of the young as it occurs in the home, the school, and the church. Emphasis is placed most strongly on schooling. Insofar as the declaration does reflect something of the spirit of the council itself, it insists that education must be broadly humane, in keeping with advances in all of the sciences, and with a concern for nurturing personal maturity and social responsibility (nn. 1–2).

Decree on the Instruments of Social Communication

This decree was one of the first two documents approved by Vatican II, on December 4, 1963, at the end of the first session. That may explain why it is so clearly out of touch with the theological and pastoral character of the council as a whole. It is indeed, alongside the aforementioned *Declaration on Christian Education*, one of the two weakest documents produced by Vatican II. The language employed in the opening paragraphs is typical of the spirit which informs the decree: "As a Mother, the Church welcomes and watches such inventions with special concern.... Such would be the press, the cinema, radio, television, and similar media, which can be properly classified as instruments of social communication" (n. 1). "Mother Church...is also aware that men and women can employ these gifts against the mind of the divine Benefactor, and abuse them to their own undoing. In fact the Church grieves with a motherly sorrow at the damage far too often inflicted on society by the perverse use of these media" (n. 2).

THE ECCLESIOLOGY OF VATICAN II

The council's distinctive understanding of the nature and mission of the Church is a reflection and embodiment of the following theological and pastoral principles:

1. *The Church is, first and foremost, a mystery or sacrament*, i.e., "a reality imbued with the hidden presence of God" (Pope Paul VI). This principle, articulated in the first chapter of *Lumen gentium*, was corrective of the unduly strong pre–Vatican II emphasis on the Church as *institution* and *organization*. It also laid the foundation for the postconciliar process of renewal and reform.

2. *The Church is the whole People of God.* This principle, expressed in the second chapter of *Lumen gentium*, was corrective of the unduly strong pre–Vatican II emphasis on the Church as *hierarchical* institution, which tended to make the study of the Church more akin to "hierarchology" than to "ecclesiology."

3. *The whole People of God—laity, religious, and clergy alike—is called to participate in the mission of Christ as Prophet, Priest, and King.* This principle, presented in the fourth chapter of *Lumen gentium* (especially nn. 30,33) and reaffirmed in the *Decree on the Apostolate of the Laity,* corrects the pre–Vatican II notion of *Catholic Action,* wherein the lay apostolate is essentially a participation in the mission of the hierarchy.

4. *The mission of the People of God includes service (diakonia) to human needs in the social, political, and economic orders as well as the preaching of*

the Word and the celebration of the sacraments. This principle is especially set forth in *Gaudium et spes* and is reiterated in more abbreviated form in such documents as the *Decree on the Apostolate of the Laity*, the *Decree on Ecumenism*, the *Decree on Bishops' Pastoral Office in the Church*, the *Decree on the Ministry and Life of Priests*, and the *Decree on the Church's Missionary Activity*. The principle supplants the pre–Vatican II notion of *preevangelization*, wherein such service is, or may be, a necessary preparation for the preaching of the Gospel (evangelization) but is not itself essential to the Church's mission as are the preaching of the Gospel and the celebration of the sacraments.

5. *This Church,* so composed and with such a mission, *is realized and expressed at the local as well as the universal level. The Church is a communion of churches, structurally expressed in the collegiality of the bishops.* This principle, always emphasized in the East, is articulated especially in *Lumen gentium* (n. 26), and is also expressed in the *Decree on the Bishops' Pastoral Office in the Church*, the *Decree on the Church's Missionary Activity*, the *Decree on Eastern Catholic Churches*, and the *Decree on the Ministry and Life of Priests*. The principle corrects a common pre–Vatican II notion that the Church is, for all practical purposes, always to be understood as the Church universal, centralized in the Vatican under the supreme authority of the pope, with each diocese considered only as an administrative division of the Church universal, and each parish, in turn, an administrative subdivision of the diocese.

6. (a) *This Church,* at once local and universal, *embraces more than the Catholic Church. It is the whole Body of Christ: Catholics, Orthodox, Anglicans, Protestants, and Oriental Christians alike.* (b) *Nor is the Catholic Church is to be identified solely with the Roman Catholic Church.* The first principle is to be found in the *Decree of Ecumenism* and in the *Dogmatic Constitution on the Church (Lumen gentium)*. It modifies the pre–Vatican II concept that the Catholic Church alone is the one, true Church, and that the other Christian communities (never called "churches" before Vatican II) are somehow "related" to the Church but are not real members of it. This is not to say, however, that all churches are equal. The second principle is to be found in the *Decree on Eastern Catholic Churches*, wherein the Eastern communities are regarded as more than "rites," but as "churches" within the Catholic communion of churches.

684

7. *The mission of the whole Church includes:* (a) *the proclamation of the Word of God, both internally and externally;* (b) *the celebration of the sacraments, especially the Eucharist;* (c) *the witnessing to the Gospel through a life of discipleship;* and (d) *the rendering of service to those in need, both inside and outside the Church.* This multiple principle is grounded (a) in the *Dogmatic Constitution on Divine Revelation* and the *Decree on the Church's Missionary Activity;* (b) in the *Constitution on the Sacred Liturgy;* (c) in the *Pastoral Constitution on the Church in the Modern World*, the fifth chapter of the *Dogmatic Constitution on the Church* ("The Call of the Whole Church to Holiness"), the *Decree on the Bishops' Pastoral Office in the Church*, the *Decree on the Ministry and Life of Priests*, the *Decree on the Church's Missionary Activity*, and the *Decree on the Appropriate Renewal of the Religious Life;* and (d) for the service aspect of mission, in the same documents. This multiple missionary principle expands upon a narrower view of mission in pre–Vatican II ecclesiology, namely, one that tended to restrict the mission to *the preaching of the Word and the celebration of the sacraments*, and one which perhaps paid too little attention to the missionary responsibility of corporate witnessing to the Gospel. Because the Church itself is a *sacrament*, it is an essential part of its mission to practice what it preaches.

8. *All authority in the Church is to be exercised as a service and in a collegial manner.* The principle is particularly proposed in *Lumen gentium* (chapter III) and is reaffirmed in such other documents as the decrees on bishops, priests, and religious life. The principle is intended to transform the exercise of authority from one of domination and unilateral decision-making, as generally prevailed in the pre–Vatican II period.

9. (a) *Religious truth is also to be found outside the Body of Christ and should be respected wherever it is discovered.* (b) *No one is ever to be coerced to embrace either the Christian or the Catholic faith.* This dual principle is set forth in the *Declaration on the Relationship of the Church to Non-Christian Religions* and in the *Declaration on Religious Freedom*. It replaces a too narrow understanding of revelation, of the availability of divine grace, and of the universal salvific will. It also contradicts the pre-Vatican formula, "Error has no rights."

10. *The nature and mission of the Church are always to be understood in relationship and in subordination to the Kingdom of God.* The Church is an

685

eschatological community. This principle is expressed in article 5 of *Lumen gentium* and again in article 45 of *Gaudium et spes*. It replaces what was perhaps the most fundamental pre–Vatican II ecclesiologi- cal misunderstanding, namely, that the Church is *identical* with the Kingdom of God. Rather, the Church is "at the same time holy and always in need of being purified, and incessantly pursues the path of penance and renewal" (*Lumen gentium*, n. 8).

SUMMARY

1. The Second Vatican Council was the largest and most representative council in the Church's history, with its bishops drawn from every major continent and culture. With this council, the Church began its movement from a Church of cultural confinement to a genuine world Church.

2. Twentieth-century *ecclesiology before Vatican II* was of two kinds: *textbook* ecclesiology, which stressed the institutional, juridical, and hierarchical as- pects of the Church, and *"progressive"* ecclesiology, which understood the Church as the whole People of God, always in need of renewal and reform.

3. The single most influential personality associated with the event of Vati- can II was *Pope John XXIII*, who convened the council and set its tone by the style he himself adopted as pope, namely, that of a servant-shepherd. The council, he insisted, was not for condemnations but for updating the Church for the sake of its own spiritual vitality, Christian unity, and world peace.

4. There were *sixteen council documents* of varying authority, content, and effects. The most authoritative in the *juridical sense* were the four *constitutions:* on the Church, on the Church in the modern world, on revelation, and on the sacred liturgy. The most authoritative in terms of their *reception* in and by the Church have been the four constitutions, plus the *Decree on Ecu- menism*, the *Declaration on Religious Freedom*, and the *Declaration on the Rela- tionship of the Church to Non-Christian Religions*.

5. The major documents in summary form are

   a. *Dogmatic Constitution on the Church:* The Church is a mystery, or sacra- ment, the whole People of God, in whose service the hierarchy is placed. The authority of pope and bishops is to be exercised as a service and in a collegial mode. Bishops are not simply the vicars of the pope, and the laity participate fully and directly in the Church's mission.

   b. *Pastoral Constitution on the Church in the Modern World:* The Church must read the signs of the times and interpret them in the light of the Gospel. The Church does not exist alongside or apart from the world; the Church is part of the world, and its mission is to serve the whole human family.

c. *Decree on Ecumenism:* Christian unity is a matter of restoration, not of a return to Rome; other Christian communities are churches within the Body of Christ; and both sides were to blame for the divisions of the Church.

d. *Constitution on the Sacred Liturgy:* The Church proclaims the Gospel not only in word but also in sacrament, or by sacred signs. Since the whole People of God is involved in this worship, the signs must be intelligible.

e. *Dogmatic Constitution on Divine Revelation:* The Word of God is communicated through Sacred Scripture, sacred tradition, and the teaching authority of the Church, all linked together and guided by the Holy Spirit. The sacred realities are always open in principle to a growth in understanding.

f. *Declaration on Religious Freedom:* No one is to be forced in any way to embrace the Christian or the Catholic faith. This principle is rooted in human dignity and the freedom of the act of faith.

g. *Declaration on the Relationship of the Church to Non-Christian Religions:* God speaks also through other religions, so we should engage in dialogue and other collaborative efforts with them. The Jews have a special relationship to the Church. They cannot be blamed as a people for the death of Jesus.

6. The other documents in summary form are

a. *Decree on the Church's Missionary Activity:* The Gospel is to be preached also and always to non-Christians, but not as a culturally alien reality. Evangelization is an obligation for every member of the Church.

b. *Decree on the Apostolate of the Laity:* The laity participates in the whole mission of the Church, but especially in the temporal order.

c. *Decree on Eastern Catholic Churches:* The Eastern Catholic churches can be a bridge to the Orthodox East. The integrity of Eastern traditions of liturgy, spirituality, and discipline is to be restored and respected.

d. *Decree on the Bishops' Pastoral Office in the Church:* Bishops are the pastors of their own local churches, collaborate with other bishops through episcopal conferences, and with the pope and all other bishops through the episcopal college. Authority is always for service.

e. *Decree on the Ministry and Life of Priests:* Priests are members of a presbyterium in union with a bishop, and with him serve the building up of Christ's body.

f. *Decree on Priestly Formation:* There must be a closer connection between seminary training and the pastoral situation.

g. *Decree on the Appropriate Renewal of the Religious Life:* The renewal of religious life must be based on the Gospel, the original purposes of the community, and the changed conditions of the times.

h. *Declaration on Christian Education:* Education must be broadly humane and up-to-date, with a concern for personal maturity and social responsibility.

i. *Decree on the Instruments of Social Communication:* The Church must be vigilant toward the media because of the ever-present danger of their abuse, but must also use the media where opportune.

7. The *distinctive ecclesiology* of Vatican II is based on the following principles:

a. The Church is a mystery, or sacrament, and not primarily an institution or organization.

b. The Church is the whole People of God, not just the hierarchy.

c. The whole People of God participates in the mission of Christ, and not just in the mission of the hierarchy.

d. The mission of the Church includes service to those in need, and not just the preaching of the Gospel or the celebration of the sacraments.

e. The Church is a communion of churches. It is truly present at the local level as well as at the universal level. A diocese or parish is not just an administrative division of the Church universal.

f. The Church includes Orthodox, Anglicans, Protestants, and Oriental Christians as well as Catholics. The Catholic Church includes the Eastern Catholic churches as well as Roman Catholics.

g. The mission of the Church includes the proclamation of the Word, the celebration of the sacraments, the witnessing to the Gospel individually and institutionally, and the rendering of service to those in need.

h. All authority is for service, not domination.

i. Religious truth is to be found outside the Church as well. No one is to be coerced to embrace the Christian or the Catholic faith.

j. The Church is always for the sake of the Kingdom of God and is not itself the Kingdom.

SUGGESTED READINGS

Abbott, Walter, and Joseph Gallagher, eds. *The Documents of Vatican II.* New York: America Press, 1966.

Alberigo, Giuseppe, Jean-Pierre Jossua, and Joseph A. Komonchak, eds. *The Reception of Vatican II.* Washington, D.C.: The Catholic University of America Press, 1987.

Anderson, Floyd, ed. *Council Daybook: Sessions 1 and 2*. Washington, D.C.: National Catholic Welfare Conference, 1965; *Session 3* (1965); and *Session 4* (1966).

Hastings, Adrian, ed. *Modern Catholicism: Vatican II and After*. New York: Oxford University Press, 1991.

Hebblethwaite, Peter. *Pope John XXIII: Shepherd of the Modern World*. New York: Doubleday, 1985.

_____. *Paul VI: The First Modern Pope*. New York: Paulist Press, 1993.

Lindbeck, George. *The Future of Roman Catholic Theology: Vatican II—Catalyst for Change*. Philadelphia: Fortress Press, 1970.

Miller, John H., ed. *Vatican II: An Interfaith Appraisal*. Notre Dame, Ind.: University of Notre Dame Press, 1966.

O'Malley, John W. *Tradition and Transition: Historical Perspectives on Vatican II*. Wilmington, Del.: Michael Glazier, 1989.

Outler, Albert. *Methodist Observer at Vatican II*. Westminster, Md.: Newman Press, 1967.

Pawley, Bernard C., ed. *The Second Vatican Council: Studies by Eight Anglican Observers*. New York: Oxford University Press, 1967.

Rynne, Xavier. *Vatican Council II*. New York: Farrar, Straus and Giroux, 1968.

Stacpoole, Alberic, ed. *Vatican II Revisited: By Those Who Were There*. Minneapolis, Minn.: Winston Press, 1986; London: Geoffrey Chapman, 1986.

Vorgrimler, Herbert, ed. *Commentary on the Documents of Vatican II*. 5 vols. New York: Herder and Herder, 1967–1969.

XIX

The Church in Contemporary Theology and Doctrine

As noted in chapter 18, many of the progressive features of the Second Vatican Council were anticipated in the work of theologians writing *before* Vatican II. Some of these theologians continued to exercise leadership in the postconciliar period as well. The spirit of the council has also been reflected in official ecclesiastical statements, in pastoral developments of various kinds, in ecumenical dialogues, and in the work of individual Protestant and Orthodox theologians. We have perhaps reached a point in the evolution of post–Vatican II ecclesiology where a working consensus has nearly been achieved among theologians and in ecumenical dialogues on the question of the nature and mission of the Church.

ECCLESIOLOGY SINCE VATICAN II

Just as in the case of Christology, one can speak of an ecclesiology "from above" and an ecclesiology "from below." The former emphasizes the nature of the Church as a *communion* in grace with the triune God. "The church is, as it were, the icon of the trinitarian fellowship

691

of Father, Son and Holy Spirit" (Walter Kasper, *Theology and Church,* New York: Crossroad, 1989, p. 152). One finds a similar emphasis in Joseph Ratzinger and in Hans Urs von Balthasar, as well as in the *Catechism of the Catholic Church* (1992), which reflects the ecclesiology of the latter two theologians. Each would insist that the basis for this ecclesiology "from above" is the Second Vatican Council itself. By contrast, the latter ("from below") approach emphasizes the nature of the Church as an earthly community of human beings who, though transformed by the grace of God and the enduring presence of the Holy Spirit, have a mission in and for the world that includes, in addition to the preaching of the Word and the celebration of the sacraments, the struggle on behalf of justice, peace, and human rights. Most contemporary ecclesiology falls into the latter category.

Catholic Ecclesiology

Karl Rahner

Rahner's understanding of the Church is consistent with his fundamental approach to the theology of *grace*. The Church is the sacrament of God's universal saving activity on our behalf. It is "the historically real and actual presence of the eschatologically victorious mercy of God," or "the sign of the grace of God definitively triumphant in the world in Christ" (*The Church and the Sacraments,* London: Nelson, 1963, pp. 14, 18). The Church is not itself the Kingdom of God. "It is the sacrament of the Kingdom of God in the eschatological phase of sacred history which began with Christ, the phase which brings about the kingdom of God" ("Church and World," *The Concise Sacramentum Mundi,* New York: Seabury Press, 1975, p. 239).

The relationship of Church and world is a function of the relationship of Church and Kingdom, or Reign of God. The Kingdom, which is the redemptive presence of God, is not purely otherworldly, spiritual, metahistorical. It is also this-worldly, concrete, and historical. Accordingly, the Church must understand its mission in a way that falls between two extremes: *integrism,* which regards everything in the world as evil or worthless unless and until it is somehow "integrated" with Christianity, and *esotericism,* which regards everything in the world, apart from Christianity, as unrelated to salvation, and therefore to be shunned. Provided that the spirit of detachment from the world, of penance, contemplation, and renunciation remains alive in the Church, there need be no mistrust of the Church's present and recent course in announcing the unity of the love of God and love of neighbor (i.e., we manifest our love of God precisely in and through our love for others), in taking up the cause of the poor and the oppressed, in speaking and acting on behalf of human rights and freedom, and in opening dialogue with the rest of humankind.

Rahner insists that we can never forget that we are sinners, not only we ourselves as individuals but also as a society which creates or tolerates inhuman social conditions and institutions. "The danger of debasing Christianity by confining the struggle with sin to the wholly private sphere is imminent and menacing," because so much sin has been institutionalized and has become part of our taken-for-granted world (*The Shape of the Church to Come*, New York: Seabury Press, 1974, p. 124). If the Church avoids the task of challenging institutionalized sin, it will be regarded as a "merely conservative power, devoted to the defence [sic] of things as they are" (p. 125). On the other hand, if the Church is to be outwardly credible, it must allow its commitment to justice and freedom to become more effective in its internal life as well.

The Church of the future will be an open Church, ecumenical from its very roots, democratized, and especially declericalized. It will be "a world Church, in which the churches of Africa, South America and even Asia, will really be autonomous elements with their own specific character and their own importance in the whole Church" (*Concern for the Church*, p. 110). This will effect over time a more basic structural change in the Church, specifically in the way the local churches relate to the central authority in the Vatican. Is it not time, he asks, "to begin a theological reflection about whether the seat of the primacy in the Church will have to remain in Rome in the future, when the real centers of power and authority will no longer lie in the older Europe?" (pp. 126–27).

Edward Schillebeeckx

Sacramentality is also the key to Edward Schillebeeckx's understanding of the nature and mission of the Church. The key idea which inspired the fundamental change of emphasis at Vatican II, he argues, is that of the Church as the *sacramentum mundi* ("sacrament of the world"). In this context *world* means fellowship, community, or other-oriented existence. It is a way of being human in the world, i.e., of being in dialogue with one's fellow human beings (*God the Future of Man*, New York: 1968, p. 123). The Church is committed to the coming Kingdom of God, but it is not yet in possession of the Kingdom. The Church is still on the way, in history, searching tentatively for solutions to the problems of human existence. Its message is not "This is precisely how the world can be fully humanized," but rather "Humanity is possible." The task of humanization, in other words, "is not a labor of Sisyphus" (p. 156). The hope of the final Kingdom, where all things will be brought to perfection, stimulates the Church never to rest satisfied with what has already been achieved in this world. The promised future has not yet been given. Therefore, nothing that now exists is beyond prophetic criticism. On the other hand, "The Church's critical function is not that of an outsider, pursuing a parallel path, but rather that of one who is critically involved in the building of the world and the progress of the nations" (p. 161).

Schillebeeckx's post–Vatican II turn in the direction of a more socially and politically active and critical function for the Church is consistent with his retrieval and use of sociocritical theory (see his *The Understanding of Faith*, New York: Sheed & Ward, 1974) and with his more recent work in Christology, referred to in chapter 14. The third volume in his trilogy, beginning with *Jesus* and *Christ*, is at least partially on the Church, although it is not the ecclesiological tract he had originally intended to write. Because of the persistence of a pre-Vatican mentality in the Church and the polarization it generates, he felt that he had to search once again for the kernel of the Gospel and Christian faith. The book is entitled *Church: The Human Story of God* (New York: Crossroad, 1990).

The book critiques the traditional axiom "No salvation outside the Church," because the saving grace of Christ (discussed so thoroughly in the *Christ* book) cannot be confined to the visible boundaries of a hierarchically structured Church. Indeed, he rejects the ecclesiocentric orientation of traditional ecclesiology and calls for a *negative* ecclesiology that says less and less about the Church. Humanity, he argues, is numinous; it is the primary symbol of the divine. The Church is only epiphenomenal, that is, secondary. "God is absolute," he writes, "but no particular religion is absolute" (p. 166).

Schillebeeckx's notion of mission remains solidly liberational in approach: "To bring the gospel to all the needy in the world, not only through words but through solidarity in action and thus through a praxis of liberation is the very nature of Christianity" (p. 185).

He argues in the final chapter for a democratic rule in the Church, free of authoritarian structures, and open to the Spirit who inspires all, without regard for canonical status.

Hans Küng

Hans Küng's major postconciliar work on the Church is entitled simply *The Church* (New York: Sheed & Ward, 1968). It is a significant book in that it is the first major volume in ecclesiology which attends at some length to the subordinate relationship of the Church to the Kingdom of God. Standard Catholic textbooks, as we noted in chapter 18, usually identified the two. The Church, for Küng, is first and foremost a historical reality. It is the pilgrim People of God. As such, its essential reality is embodied in changeable forms. Adaptation occurred even within the New Testament period itself. The Church emerged not from the direct mandate of Jesus but as a product of his preaching of the Kingdom of God. The Church's own mission is similarly oriented toward the coming Kingdom.

It is here perhaps that Küng's close contacts with the churches of the Reformation, especially Lutheranism, shape his theology in a manner that not all recognize to be unmistakably Catholic. Specifically, Küng insists very strongly on the discontinuity between Church and Kingdom. The Church does not bring about the Kingdom but is "its voice, its announcer, its *herald*. God alone can bring his reign; the Church is devoted entirely to its service" (p. 96).

On the other hand, Küng does not want to dissociate completely the Church from the Kingdom. It is the anticipatory sign of the Kingdom. The Church is also the Body of Christ and the Creation of the Holy Spirit, as well as the pilgrim People of God. It is a community constituted by Baptism and the Lord's Supper, and it exists at

695

both local and universal levels. A local church is not merely a section of the universal Church, nor is the universal Church merely an accumulation of local churches. Each local church is a manifestation of the Body of Christ in that place, and the Church universal is a dynamic communion of local churches, something more than the sum total of those churches.

A persistent emphasis in Küng's post–Vatican II books and essays on the Church is the need for ongoing institutional reform. The Church is a credible proclaimer and witness of the Kingdom only if it also follows the way of Jesus as a provisional, serving, guilty, and determined Church. It must be a community marked not only by faith, hope, and charity, but also by truthfulness and freedom (*On Being a Christian*, New York: Doubleday, 1976, pp. 481–84). All authority in the Church must always be ultimately in the service of the Kingdom and immediately in the service of the Church itself. We should speak, as the New Testament did, of service (ministries) rather than of offices. The Petrine ministry (papacy), as important as it is, cannot be the sole criterion of orthodoxy or for identifying what and where the Church is (pp. 829–42). The dividing line between Catholic and Protestant is less sharp than we have traditionally thought. For Küng, the names represent basic attitudes. *Catholic* expresses a preference for the whole, for continuity, and for universality; *Protestant* embraces a concern for the Gospel (Sacred Scripture) and for constant reform. These two attitudes are not necessarily mutually exclusive at all.

In more recent years (and perhaps because of his difficulties with the Vatican, involving the withdrawal of his license to teach as a Catholic theologian in 1979) Küng has broadened his ecclesiological horizons, devoting less attention to internal and even traditional ecumenical issues and more to the dialogue of the Church with non-Christian religions (see, for example, *Christianity and the World Religions: Paths of Dialogue with Islam, Hinduism, and Buddhism*, Garden City, N.Y.: Doubleday, 1986).

Avery Dulles

Avery Dulles, one of the leading Catholic theologians in the United States, has made his initial contributions to post–Vatican II ecclesiol-

rest of the hierarchy), but he embodies and testifies to the faith of his own community, of which he himself is an integral part.

(The communion motif was adopted by the Anglican–Roman Catholic International Commission [ARCIC II] in its agreed statement of 1991, "The Church as Communion." See *Origins*, April 11, 1991.)

Liberation Theology

Gustavo Gutiérrez

The principal theologian of the Latin American liberation school, Gustavo Gutiérrez, of Peru, embraces the Second Vatican Council's sacramental perspective. The Church's existence is not for itself but for others. On the one hand, the Church rescues the world from anonymity and enables it to know the ultimate meaning of its historical future. On the other hand, the Church must listen to the world and be evangelized by it. As the universal sacrament of salvation, the Church must signify in its own structures the salvation it announces. "As a sign of the liberation of man and history, the Church itself in its concrete existence ought to be a place of liberation.... The break with an unjust social order and the search for new ecclesial structures... have their basis in this ecclesiological perspective" (*A Theology of Liberation*, Maryknoll, N.Y.: Orbis Books, 1972, p. 261).

Although the "primary task of the Church...is to celebrate with joy the salvific action of the Lord in history" (p. 265), the Church must reflect on and live the Gospel in light of the situation in which it finds itself. Thus, in Latin America the Church must take a clear stand against social injustice and in favor of the revolutionary process which seeks to abolish that injustice and build a more human order. The first step is to recognize how much the Church itself is tied to that unjust system. The Church must truly announce the good news of the Kingdom which "reveals, without any evasions, what is at the root of social injustice: the rupture of the brotherhood which is based on our sonship before the Father..." (p. 269). And the Church must also make its own members aware of their oppressed condition, to affirm their humanity, and to motivate them to take responsibility for the quality of their lives ("The oppressed themselves should be the agents of their own pastoral activity"). "Universal love is that which in solidarity with the oppressed seeks also to liberate the oppressors from their own power, from their ambition, and from their selfishness" (p. 275). In the meantime, the unity of the Church cannot be achieved apart from the unity of the world. "In a radically divided world, the function of the ecclesial community is to struggle against the profound causes of the division among men. It is only this commitment that can make of it an authentic sign of unity" (p. 278).

Although concern for the internal reform of the Church was not originally prominent in liberation theology, already in his classic work, *A Theology of Liberation* (Maryknoll, N.Y.: Orbis Books, 1973; orig. ed., 1971), Gutiérrez linked the struggle for justice outside the Church with a concern for internal structural reform, and grounded the link theologically in the sacramentality of the Church. It "should signify in its own internal structures the salvation whose fulfillment it announces." Therefore, the Church itself must be "a place of liberation" (p. 261).

Leonardo Boff

Brazilian theologian Leonard Boff proposes yet another model of the Church, sacrament of the Holy Spirit, in his *Church: Charism and Power: Liberation Theology and the Institutional Church* (New York: Crossroad, 1985; paper, 1992). He argues that the traditional incarnational ecclesiology (the Church as the continuation of Christ, or as one with Christ) is too narrow because it fails to take into account the decisive event of the resurrection. Through the resurrection Jesus entered an entirely new Spirit-filled existence, giving him a "global relationship to all reality" (p. 145).

Ecclesiology must be rooted in Christology, to be sure, but both must be rooted, in turn, in pneumatology. The Church must be defined in terms of energy, charism, and the progress of the world because "the wind blows where it chooses" (John 3:7) and "where the Spirit of the Lord is, there is freedom" (2 Corinthians 3:17). "The Church must be thought of not so much as beginning with the risen Christ, now in the form of the Spirit, but rather as beginning with the Holy Spirit, as the force and means by which the Lord remains present in history and so continues his work of inaugurating a new world" (p. 150). Therefore, the Church has the same boundaries as the risen Christ, and these are cosmic in nature. No one is outside the Church because no one is outside the reality of God and the risen Christ. Everything in the Church—dogmas, rituals, liturgy, canon law, hierarchical structures—has to be measured against the standard of the Holy Spirit. If they inhibit the work of the risen Christ acting through the Spirit, they must be reformed, replaced, or discarded. The life and structure of the Church is essentially charismatic, and charisms are open to everyone, not just to priests and bishops (p. 159).

Because the book focused so sharply on the institutional pathologies and dysfunctional aspects of the Church, Boff was silenced for a time by the Vatican and only later (in 1992) left his Franciscan order and the priesthood.

Feminist Theology

Although no full-scale feminist ecclesiologies have emerged to date (in the way that feminist Christologies, feminist theologies of God, and feminist spiritualities have), the general lines of feminist thought on the Church are clear enough. Again, most, if not all, Catholic feminist reflection on the Church is rooted in feminist biblical studies.

Elisabeth Schüssler Fiorenza

Elisabeth Schüssler Fiorenza's work has been more influential than any other on the development of feminist Christologies, theologies of God, spiritualities, and ecclesiologies. All the themes and emphases that one finds therein are already developed in her groundbreaking work, In Memory of Her (New York: Crossroad, 1983): the inclusiveness of Jesus preaching and practice of the Kingdom of God (pp. 118–30), the heavy weight of the patriarchalization of the Church, its ministries, and its offices (pp. 288–315), the emergence of a discipleship of equals (pp. 140–54) and of women as "paradigms of true discipleship" (pp. 315–33).

Although the post-Pauline and post-Petrine writers seek to limit women's leadership roles in the Church to roles which are culturally and religiously acceptable, she concludes, the writers of Mark and John "have made it impossible for the Christian church to forget the invitation of Jesus to follow him on the way to the cross. Therefore, whenever the gospel is preached and heard, promulgated and read, what the women have done is not totally forgotten because the Gospel story remembers that the discipleship and apostolic leadership of women are integral parts of Jesus' 'alternative' praxis of *agape* and service" (p. 334).

Various essays by Schüssler Fiorenza on the Church and related topics have been collected into a single volume, *Discipleship of Equals: A Critical Feminist Ekklesia-logy of Liberation*, New York: Crossroad, 1993.

Rosemary Radford Ruether

Rosemary Radford Ruether views the Church as essentially a Spirit-filled community in which all the members are radically equal and have the capacity and the call to minister to one another, without benefit of social hierarchies—male over female, father over children, lord over servant, clergy over laity. Such a church is an exodus community (in contrast with a community in exile), called to abandon the established social order and its religious agents of sacralization and to witness to an alternative social order demanded by obedience to God (*Women-Church: Theology and Practice of Feminist Liturgical Communities*, San Francisco: Harper & Row, 1985, pp. 22–23).

Women-Church is a feminist countercultural movement in which "women collectively have claimed to be church and have claimed the tradition of the exodus community as a community of liberation from patriarchy" (p. 57). The movement, however, need not be permanent if, as one hopes, there is a "development of a new cohumanity of men and women liberated from patriarchy" wherein "men begin to critique their own dehumanization by patriarchy and form their critical culture of liberation from it in a way that truly complements the feminist exodus and allows the formation of real dialogue" (p. 61). In the meantime, Women-Church "must take responsibility for a more radical reappropriation of ministry from clericalism" (p. 86)—especially in the matters of liturgy, church administration, theological education, and social praxis.

ogy in his *The Dimensions of the Church* (Westminster, Md.: Newman Press, 1967) and *Models of the Church* (New York: Doubleday, 1974; expanded ed., 1987). The former book, subtitled *A Postconciliar Reflection*, notes that the council moved beyond Robert Bellarmine's (d. 1621) highly institutional notion of church as "a group of men bound together by the profession of the same Christian faith and by the communion of the same sacraments, under the rule of the legitimate pastors, and especially of the one vicar of Christ on earth, the Roman pontiff" (cited, p. 4). Indeed, the great weakness of Bellarmine's view is that it omits "precisely what makes the Church the Church, namely, the communion of minds and hearts through sharing in the same divine life" (p. 5). The council's understanding of the Church as People of God and as sacrament carried our ecclesiology forward, Dulles suggests, and its refusal to identify the Church of Christ exclusively with the Catholic Church broadened that ecclesiology's base (p. 10).

A fuller expression of Dulles's theology of the Church was presented in his widely read and influential *Models of the Church*. Here he insists that the mystery of the Church is too rich and diverse to be confined to any single theological category. It is not just an institution, or a mystical communion, or a sacrament, or a herald, or a servant. It is all these. The *institutional model* makes it clear that the Church must be a structured community, including pastoral officers bearing authority to direct and guide it, to preside over worship, to determine the limits of dissent, and to represent the community in an official way. The *community model* makes it evident that the Church must be united to God by grace, and that its members must be united to one another in Christ. The *sacramental model* reminds us, especially in the community's prayer and worship, that the Church must be a sign of the continuing vitality of Christ's grace and of our hope for the redemption he promises. The *kerygmatic,* or *herald, model* underlines the Church's abiding call to herald the Gospel and to summon people to faith in Jesus as Lord and Savior. The *servant model* stresses the importance of the Church's contribution to transforming the world and impregnating human society with the values of the Kingdom of God.

Taken in isolation, however, each model can distort the reality of the Church, Dulles warns. Thus, the institutional model can exagger-

697

ate the importance of structures, of official authority, of obedience to rules. The community model can generate an unhealthy spirit of enthusiasm, leading to false expectations and impossible demands. The sacramental model can lead to a sterile aestheticism and to an almost narcissistic self-contemplation. The kerygmatic model can exaggerate the importance of merely verbal faith at the expense of social action. And the servant model can lead to an uncritical acceptance of secular values and a completely this-worldly view of salvation.

In the original edition of the book, Dulles expressed a clear preference for the sacramental model. However, in the expanded edition of 1987, his preference shifts to a sixth model, *community of disciples,* which he regards as a "variant of the communion model" (p. 206). (For a brief discussion of discipleship, see again chapter 2 of this book.) Although Dulles is least disposed to the institutional model (p. 187), some subsequent writings would suggest that his spirit of caution is more directly focused on the servant model than on the institutional. This is clear in his *The Resilient Church* (New York: Doubleday, 1977, pp. 9–27).

His more recent works on the Church include *The Catholicity of the Church* (Oxford: Clarendon Press, 1985) and *The Reshaping of Catholicism: Current Challenges in the Theology of the Church* (San Francisco: Harper & Row, 1988). Catholicity, he writes in the former book, is characterized by the rubrics of breadth, length, depth, and height. It is broadly inclusive, not bound to any single culture, and, therefore, opposed to every kind of sectarianism or religious individualism (breadth). It is in communion with every generation and, therefore, cannot limit itself to any one historical period, including even the apostolic age (length). It permeates human nature and culture and is open to truth and value wherever they might be found (depth). But its universal unity is from above, via a participation in the life of the triune God (height).

Johannes Metz

Metz is best known for introducing the concept of "political theology," i.e., a theology which relates theory and practice, measuring all reality in the light of the promised Kingdom of God. And because the Kingdom has not yet come in all its perfection, there is nothing, including the Church, which escapes the critical gaze of political theology (see *Theology of the World*, New York: Herder and Herder, 1969, pp. 107–40).

The Church itself is not exempt from criticism, because the Church is also part of the world. "For it is *that world* which attempts to live from the promised future of God, and to call *that world* in question which understands itself only in terms of itself and its possibilities.... The Church is the eschatological community and the exodus community.... The Church is not the goal of her own strivings; this goal is the Kingdom of God" (p. 94). The Church has a hope and witnesses to a hope, but its hope is not in itself. The hope is in the Kingdom as the world's future. The Church is the universal sacrament of hope for the salvation of the whole world. It is precisely because of this that the Church must be "the liberating and critical force of this one society" (p. 96). Hope is living for the other.

Gregory Baum

Canadian theologian Gregory Baum recapitulates the central themes already contained in these other theologies, especially Rahner's. The distinctive mission of the Church today is one of dialogue. Proclamation includes listening and learning. It is a way of becoming more aware of the ambiguity of the Church's own situation in the world and of entering more deeply into what is God's will for us. Indeed, it was dialogue with the secular world that taught the Church to cherish religious liberty, pluralism, critical interpretation of texts, etc., as religious values (*Faith and Doctrine*, New York: Newman Press, 1969).

But dialogue is not simply a missionary tactic imposed by circumstances. Dialogue is imperative because God's saving presence is everywhere. Ecclesiology studies the manner in which salvation comes to everyone, and hence it has to do with human life in community. In that sense, ecclesiology may be regarded as "the theological study of human society" (*Man Becoming*, New York: Herder and Herder, 1970, p. 69), a position close to Schillebeeckx's in his own *Church* book.

The Church, Baum writes, is people insofar as they are touched by grace. That grace offers and creates community. Such community is the Church, which comes into being "whenever and wherever people become friends through God's presence to them" (*The Credibility of the Church Today*, New York: Herder and Herder, 1968, p. 47).

This is not to say, however, that the Church has no specific character of its own. "The universality of grace does not obliterate the distinction between Church and humanity. The Christian Church is the community in which Jesus Christ, in whom God reveals himself unconditionally and definitively, is proclaimed and celebrated" (p. 48). The mission of such a Church is a movement of humanization. It serves humankind "to help the redemptive presence of God...triumph in terms of unity, reconciliation, social justice, and peace" (p. 198).

Jean Tillard

Perhaps best known for his work on the papacy (*The Bishop of Rome*, Wilmington, Del.: Michael Glazier, 1983), Jean-M. R. Tillard advances the theology of communion in his *Church of Churches: The Ecclesiology of Communion* (Collegeville, Minn.: Liturgical Press, 1992). He holds that communion, or *koinonia*, is at the heart of Vatican II's ecclesiology and provides the basis for ecumenical agreements about the nature of the Church and the structure of ministry.

Although securely grounded in patristic and Orthodox theology, it is a line of thought that has only recently reemerged in Catholic writings on the Church. Two other Dominicans, Jerome Hamer and Yves Congar, were among the first to recover it in the 1960s, followed in the next decade by theologians such as Ferdinand Klostermann and Ludwig Hertling. But it is Tillard who has provided the fullest development to date.

The ecclesiology of communion has both a vertical and a horizontal dimension. The Church is a communion in grace with the triune God, and it is at the same time a communion of all the faithful. The horizontal dimension is destined for perfection in the vertical.

For Tillard an ecclesiology of communion rescues the notion of teaching authority from any unduly juridical and hierarchical understanding. The whole Church, represented in the communion of all the local churches, is the bearer of God's word, and not just the pope and the other bishops. Accordingly, the local bishop does not stand above or apart from his own local church (alongside the pope and the rest of the hierarchy), but he embodies and testifies to the faith of his own community, of which he himself is an integral part.

(The communion motif was adopted by the Anglican–Roman Catholic International Commission [ARCIC II] in its agreed statement of 1991, "The Church as Communion." See *Origins*, April 11, 1991.)

Liberation Theology

Gustavo Gutiérrez

The principal theologian of the Latin American liberation school, Gustavo Gutiérrez, of Peru, embraces the Second Vatican Council's sacramental perspective. The Church's existence is not for itself but for others. On the one hand, the Church rescues the world from anonymity and enables it to know the ultimate meaning of its historical future. On the other hand, the Church must listen to the world and be evangelized by it. As the universal sacrament of salvation, the Church must signify in its own structures the salvation it announces. "As a sign of the liberation of man and history, the Church itself in its concrete existence ought to be a place of liberation.... The break with an unjust social order and the search for new ecclesial structures... have their basis in this ecclesiological perspective" (*A Theology of Liberation*, Maryknoll, N.Y.: Orbis Books, 1972, p. 261).

Although the "primary task of the Church... is to celebrate with joy the salvific action of the Lord in history" (p. 265), the Church must reflect on and live the Gospel in light of the situation in which it finds itself. Thus, in Latin America the Church must take a clear stand against social injustice and in favor of the revolutionary process which seeks to abolish that injustice and build a more human order. The first step is to recognize how much the Church itself is tied to that unjust system. The Church must truly announce the good news of the Kingdom which "reveals, without any evasions, what is at the root of social injustice: the rupture of the brotherhood which is based on our sonship before the Father..." (p. 269). And the Church must also make its own members aware of their oppressed condition, to affirm their humanity, and to motivate them to take responsibility for the quality of their lives ("The oppressed themselves should be the agents of their own pastoral activity"). "Universal love is that which in solidarity with the oppressed seeks also to liberate the oppressors from their own power, from their ambition, and from their selfishness" (p. 275). In the meantime, the unity of the Church cannot be achieved apart from the unity of the world. "In a radically divided world, the function of the ecclesial community is to struggle against the profound causes of the division among men. It is only this commitment that can make of it an authentic sign of unity" (p. 278).

Although concern for the internal reform of the Church was not originally prominent in liberation theology, already in his classic work, *A Theology of Liberation* (Maryknoll, N.Y.: Orbis Books, 1973; orig. ed., 1971), Gutiérrez linked the struggle for justice outside the Church with a concern for internal structural reform, and grounded the link theologically in the sacramentality of the Church. It "should signify in its own internal structures the salvation whose fulfillment it announces." Therefore, the Church itself must be "a place of liberation" (p. 261).

Leonardo Boff

Brazilian theologian Leonard Boff proposes yet another model of the Church, sacrament of the Holy Spirit, in his *Church: Charism and Power: Liberation Theology and the Institutional Church* (New York: Crossroad, 1985; paper, 1992). He argues that the traditional incarnational ecclesiology (the Church as the continuation of Christ, or as one with Christ) is too narrow because it fails to take into account the decisive event of the resurrection. Through the resurrection Jesus entered an entirely new Spirit-filled existence, giving him a "global relationship to all reality" (p. 145).

Ecclesiology must be rooted in Christology, to be sure, but both must be rooted, in turn, in pneumatology. The Church must be defined in terms of energy, charism, and the progress of the world because "the wind blows where it chooses" (John 3:7) and "where the Spirit of the Lord is, there is freedom" (2 Corinthians 3:17). "The Church must be thought of not so much as beginning with the risen Christ, now in the form of the Spirit, but rather as beginning with the Holy Spirit, as the force and means by which the Lord remains present in history and so continues his work of inaugurating a new world" (p. 150). Therefore, the Church has the same boundaries as

702

the risen Christ, and these are cosmic in nature. No one is outside the Church because no one is outside the reality of God and the risen Christ. Everything in the Church—dogmas, rituals, liturgy, canon law, hierarchical structures—has to be measured against the standard of the Holy Spirit. If they inhibit the work of the risen Christ acting through the Spirit, they must be reformed, replaced, or discarded. The life and structure of the Church is essentially charismatic, and charisms are open to everyone, not just to priests and bishops (p. 159).

Because the book focused so sharply on the institutional patholo-gies and dysfunctional aspects of the Church, Boff was silenced for a time by the Vatican and only later (in 1992) left his Franciscan order and the priesthood.

Feminist Theology

Although no full-scale feminist ecclesiologies have emerged to date (in the way that feminist Christologies, feminist theologies of God, and feminist spiritualities have), the general lines of feminist thought on the Church are clear enough. Again, most, if not all, Catholic feminist reflection on the Church is rooted in feminist biblical studies.

Elisabeth Schüssler Fiorenza

Elisabeth Schüssler Fiorenza's work has been more influential than any other on the development of feminist Christologies, theologies of God, spiritualities, and ecclesiologies. All the themes and emphases that one finds therein are already developed in her groundbreaking work, *In Memory of Her* (New York: Crossroad, 1983): the inclusive-ness of Jesus preaching and practice of the Kingdom of God (pp. 118–30), the heavy weight of the patriarchalization of the Church, its ministries, and its offices (pp. 288–315), the emergence of a disciple-ship of equals (pp. 140–54) and of women as "paradigms of true discipleship" (pp. 315–33).

Although the post-Pauline and post-Petrine writers seek to limit women's leadership roles in the Church to roles which are culturally and religiously acceptable, she concludes, the writers of Mark and John "have made it impossible for the Christian church to forget the

703

invitation of Jesus to follow him on the way to the cross. Therefore, whenever the gospel is preached and heard, promulgated and read, what the women have done is not totally forgotten because the Gospel story remembers that the discipleship and apostolic leadership of women are integral parts of Jesus' 'alternative' praxis of *agape* and service" (p. 334).

Various essays by Schüssler Fiorenza on the Church and related topics have been collected into a single volume, *Discipleship of Equals: A Critical Feminist Ekklesia-logy of Liberation*, New York: Crossroad, 1993.

Rosemary Radford Ruether

Rosemary Radford Ruether views the Church as essentially a Spirit-filled community in which all the members are radically equal and have the capacity and the call to minister to one another, without benefit of social hierarchies—male over female, father over children, lord over servant, clergy over laity. Such a church is an exodus community (in contrast with a community in exile), called to abandon the established social order and its religious agents of sacralization and to witness to an alternative social order demanded by obedience to God (*Women-Church: Theology and Practice of Feminist Liturgical Communities*, San Francisco: Harper & Row, 1985, pp. 22–23).

Women-Church is a feminist countercultural movement in which "women collectively have claimed to be church and have claimed the tradition of the exodus community as a community of liberation from patriarchy" (p. 57). The movement, however, need not be permanent if, as one hopes, there is a "development of a new cohumanity of men and women liberated from patriarchy" wherein "men begin to critique their own dehumanization by patriarchy and form their critical culture of liberation from it in a way that truly complements the feminist exodus and allows the formation of real dialogue" (p. 61). In the meantime, Women-Church "must take responsibility for a more radical reappropriation of ministry from clericalism" (p. 86)—especially in the matters of liturgy, church administration, theological education, and social praxis.

Anne Carr

The Church, Anne Carr writes, is "the gift of the Spirit, born of the life, death, and resurrection of Jesus." It is the "enduring sign of Jesus' twofold solidarity with God and with humankind that is meant to be the sacrament... of the salvation of the whole world...." (*Transforming Grace*, San Francisco: HarperCollins, 1988, p. 194). But this one church of Christ has a pluralism of manifestations. "In this context," she continues, "the scholarly recovery of the 'lost' history of women in the early Christian communities is significant" (p. 195). She cites Elisabeth Schüssler Fiorenza's work as "especially suggestive about the character of the earliest Christian churches as radically egalitarian, inclusive of marginal people (women and slaves), and counter-culture" (ibid.).

The mission of the Church is one of service to people, especially the poor, the oppressed, and the marginalized. Although structures of authority are necessary for this mission, those structures are always subordinate to it and are to be judged by their capacity to enable the Church to fulfill the mission. Feminist theology rejects a "patriarchal model of the church in which the focus on authority and obedience is one of coercive power that suggests distrust of the members who are envisioned more as children than as responsible adults" (p. 199). Therefore, Christian feminist women are deeply involved in the transition from a patriarchal to an egalitarian model of the Church.

Ecclesiology "From Above"

One twentieth-century, "from above" ecclesiologist not listed below because his work has never been translated into English is Heribert Mühlen. His major work is *Una Mystica Persona* (3d ed.; Munich: Schöningh, 1968) wherein he defines the Church as "one person [the Holy Spirit] in many persons [Christ and us]."

Hans Urs von Balthasar

Hans Urs von Balthasar offers a classic "from above" ecclesiology. The Church is a "communion of saints" created and sanctified by the Holy Spirit. There is, of course, a horizontal dimension to the Church in which the members care for one another, but the horizontal dimension is impossible without the vertical (John 1:16; Colossians 1:19; Ephesians 1:23). The latter is "a continually overflowing richness on which all the poor may draw; it is also called the treasure of the church" (*The Von Balthasar Reader*, M. Kehl and W. Löser, eds., New York: Crossroad, 1982, p. 230). The preferred biblical image of the Church for von Balthasar is Bride of Christ. Christ is head of the Church and the Church is subject to him. Indeed, it owes its whole existence to him "who brought it forth out of his own fullness; only then can there be any talk of the church as 'bride'" (p. 232).

But there are not two churches: the one real and empirical, the other the communion of saints. It is simultaneously both the spotless Bride of Christ and an imperfect reality that is subject to criticism and correction. All that is really important to the Church, however, is prior to any of its members and any of their failings; namely, Baptism, Eucharist, reconciliation, Holy Scripture, and so forth (p. 254). "The external organization of the church at which so many take offense is really nothing other than the representation of the vitality and capacity for life of that great organic body possessed and animated by the present Christ" (pp. 258–59).

The Church receives its "original generating power" only from "God's initiative in the Christ-event," creating a community rooted in "the living personal presence of the Trinity, articulated in their life of brother-sister love and a communion which is both sacramental and existential. Wherever in the world such a community exists is where the liberation of the world is beginning to take place" (p. 312). The contrast between this understanding of liberation and the one articulated, for example, in Latin American liberation theology illustrates a principal difference between an ecclesiology constructed "from above" and another "from below."

Protestant Ecclesiology

Jürgen Moltmann

For Moltmann, a Reformed (or Calvinist) Protestant, the Church is "the community of those who on the ground of the resurrection of Christ wait for the kingdom of God and whose life is determined by this expectation" (*Theology of Hope*, New York: Harper & Row, 1967, p. 326). The Church is the body of the crucified and risen Lord "only where in specific acts of service it is obedient to its mission to the world.... It is nothing in itself, but all that it is, it is in existing for others. It is the Church of God where it is a Church for the world" (p. 327). The Church's service of the world and of humanity is not such that it strives to keep everything as it is; its service is rather for the sake of helping the world and humankind transform themselves and become what they are promised to be. "For this reason 'Church for the world' can mean nothing else but 'Church for the kingdom of God' and the renewing of the world" (p. 328). The Church's mission is reconciliation with God, forgiveness of sins, peace. The salvation it proclaims is not merely salvation of the soul but also "the realization of the eschatological *hope of justice*, the *humanizing* of man, the *socializing* of humanity, *peace* for all creation" (p. 329).

Following an approach similar to Metz's, and having also in mind the classic Marxist critique of the Church, Moltmann insists that "mission means not merely propagation of faith and hope, but also historic transformation of life" (p. 330). Christian hope calls everything in question by measuring everything against the future Kingdom. The hope of resurrection, therefore, brings about a new understanding of the world as not yet finished. Our world is a world of unfinished possibilities. "To disclose to it the horizon of the future of the crucified Christ is the task of the Christian Church" (p. 338).

The same themes are carried forward, but with more deliberate attention to the place and role of the Holy Spirit, in Moltmann's later work, *The Church in the Power of the Spirit* (New York: Harper & Row, 1977). The Church is, before all else, the Church of Jesus Christ. "Every statement about the church will be a statement about Christ. Every statement about Christ also implies a statement about the church; yet the statement about Christ is not exhausted by the statement about the church because it also goes further, being directed towards the messianic kingdom which the church serves" (p. 6). The Church's mission "embraces all activities that serve to liberate man from his slavery in the presence of the coming God, slavery which extends from economic necessity to Godforsakenness" (p. 10). It is an ecumenical Church; the whole Church is present in each church. Therefore, the concerns of one are the concerns of all others, and vice versa. So, too, the Church is a political Church, committed to, and ever engaged in, the struggle for liberation.

Wolfhart Pannenberg

Wolfhart Pannenberg, a German Lutheran, also places the Church in the context of the coming Kingdom of God. It is an eschatological community, "a community of high expectation and hope" (*Theology and the Kingdom of God*, Philadelphia: Westminster Press, 1969, p. 74). It is true to its vocation "only as it anticipates and represents the destiny of all mankind, the goal of history." Protestantism, Pannenberg suggests, has focused too much on the piety and salvation of Church members themselves ("the congregation of saints wherein the gospel is rightly preached and the sacraments rightly celebrated"). The doctrine of the Church begins not with the Church but with the Kingdom of God, "the utterly concrete reality of justice and love" (p. 79).

The mission of the Church is to proclaim the universal significance of Jesus, to be a community through which contemporary men and women can participate in the hope for the ultimate fulfillment of humanity, to witness to the limitations of any given society, to stir the imagination for social action, and to inspire the visions of social change (pp. 83–85). But in the end it is the Kingdom of *God*. The Church's function is always and only "preliminary."

George Lindbeck

An American Lutheran, George Lindbeck stresses the sacramental character of the Church. The Church's "essence" is "to be a sacramental sign or witness to God's saving work in all that it is and does. It exercises this witnessing or missionary function in its *diakonia* or secular service of the world..., its *leitourgia* or worship of God..., and its *koinonia* or communal unity expressed both interpersonally and in institutional structures...and in common faith and dogma" (*The Future of Roman Catholic Theology*, Philadelphia: Fortress Press, 1970, p. 5). Apart from this mission to be a sacramental sign and anticipation of the Kingdom of God, there is nothing which differentiates the Church from the rest of humankind (p. 27).

Orthodox Ecclesiology

John Zizioulas

John Zizioulas recapitulates in his own work (*Being as Communion: Studies in Personhood and the Church*, 1985, pp. 123–42 passim) the main lines of Orthodox ecclesiology: the equal importance of the local church with the universal Church whose simultaneity is expressed in the one Eucharist; conciliarity as an expression of the Church as communion—a communion of many local churches which together are constitutive of the one, universal Church; the inextricable link between the bishop and the local church, in such wise that neither can exist without the other; and the churches as reflections (iconic representations) of the Kingdom of God, poised between the already and the not yet. "It is not in history that the ecclesial institutions find their certainty (their validity) but in constant dependence on the Holy Spirit" (p. 138).

Ecumenical Ecclesiology

In addition to the theological work done by individual theologians, the post–Vatican II period has also witnessed the production of a new form of theological communication: consensus statements of bilateral, trilateral, or multilateral groups composed of theologians and pastoral leaders from various Christian traditions. In the United States alone remarkable progress has been recorded since the council on such specific questions as the Eucharist, ministry, even the papacy. A measure of consensus on the general topic of the Church and its mission has also been achieved by such bilateral consultations as the Presbyterian-Reformed–Roman Catholic, the Orthodox–Roman Catholic, the United Methodist–Roman Catholic, the Lutheran–Roman Catholic, and the Anglican–Roman Catholic. The last may usefully represent the others as an example of the nature and degree of ecclesiological consensus. (For a recent compilation of documents, see *Building Unity: Ecumenical Dialogues with Roman Catholic Participation in the United States*, Joseph A. Burgess and Jeffrey Gros, eds., New York: Paulist Press, 1989.)

In its "Agreed Statement on the Purpose of the Church" (*Documents on Anglican-Roman Catholic Relations III*, Washington, D.C.: United States Catholic Conference, 1976, pp. 1–11), the Anglican/ Roman Catholic Consultation in the U.S.A. defines the Church as "that community of persons called by the Holy Spirit to continue Christ's saving work of reconciliation. As Christ proclaimed the Kingdom, so the Church serves the Kingdom..." (p. 2). This mission is carried out in various ways: by the proclamation of the Good News, in the context of the fellowship of believers, in the witness of individual members and in its own structures and agencies, and in its service to those in need. The mission, therefore, is threefold: proclamation, worship, and service.

The proclamation must also be a word of challenge, at times even of confrontation. "The imperative of evangelism... has many dimensions" (p. 6). The Eucharist is the summit and source of the Church's mission, for it "testifies to the dependence of all people upon God and it affirms God's action for humanity in the death and resurrection of Jesus Christ, in the promise of the gift of the Spirit, and in our ultimate destiny of union with the Father" (p. 6). But the witness of worship is "only fully complete when it results in a commitment to service" (p. 7). The contemporary reexamination of mission has emphasized the call of the Church to be an agent and forerunner of God's Kingdom of justice and peace. "Human liberation, we agree, is that aspect of the Church's mission of service which is most challenging for our time" (p. 8).

The statement concludes: "We, as Roman Catholics and Episcopalians charged by our churches to explore the possibility that there is a fundamental unity between us, find that we are in substantial agreement about the purpose or mission of the Church as we have set it forth above. We have uncovered no essential points on which we differ" (p. 9).

The findings of the U.S. dialogue are consistent with those of the international bilateral, the Anglican–Roman Catholic International Commission (ARCIC), the first of which met between 1970 and 1981. It submitted a Final Report in 1982 (excerpts in *Origins*, April 15, 1982) that was critically reviewed by the Vatican in late 1991 (*Origins*, December 19, 1991, including a reply to the Vatican by George Carey, Archbishop of Canterbury). By contrast, the 1988 Lambeth Conference of Anglican bishops found the Final Report "consonant in substance with the faith of Anglicans" and "a sufficient basis for taking the next step forwards towards the reconciliation of our churches grounded in agreement in faith."

In conjunction with Pope John Paul II's visit to England in 1982, he and Archbishop Robert Runcie established a second commission to study remaining outstanding differences between the two communions. ARCIC II began its work in 1983 and issued a first report, "Salvation and the Church" in 1987, and a second in 1991 on "The Church as Communion." By 1989, when Archbishop Runcie paid an official visit to the pope, it was clear that the question of the ordination of women had emerged as a major stumbling block. The Church of England subsequently approved women's ordination in 1992, under the leadership of the new Archbishop of Canterbury, George L. Carey.

The Ecclesiology of Official Church Documents

The 1971 Synod of Bishops

A world synod of bishops, although only a consultative body at present, is second only to an ecumenical council in collegial representation and authority. It is an entirely modern phenomenon, a direct outgrowth of the Second Vatican Council, designed to give structure to the council's desire to draw the bishops of the world into the ongoing governance and direction of the Church. The 1971 synod issued two statements, one on *The Ministerial Priesthood* and the other on *Justice in the World* (Washington, D.C.: United States Catholic Conference, 1972).

The latter document is of major ecclesiological significance because (1) it is the only Vatican document, in one hundred years of Catholic social teachings, which applies the social teachings of the Church to the Church itself; and (2) it stated, more explicitly than any other comparable document, that the social apostolate of the Church is a "constitutive dimension" of the Church's mission.

The first has to do with the *witness* of the Church. "While the Church is bound to give witness to justice, it recognizes that anyone who ventures to speak to people about justice must first be just in their eyes. Hence we must undertake an examination of the modes of acting and of the possessions and life style found within the Church itself" (III, para. 2, p. 44). Although the document does not explicitly ground the assertion in the principle of *sacramentality*, that is its theological basis. Because the Church is called to be a sign as well as an instrument of salvation, it has a missionary mandate to practice what it preaches about justice.

The second concerns the *scope* of the Church's *mission*, which includes not only the preaching of the Gospel and the celebration of the sacraments, but also what was once subsumed under the term "social apostolate." "Action on behalf of justice and participation in the transformation of the world fully appear to us as a *constitutive* dimension of the preaching of the Gospel, or, in other words, of the Church's mission for the redemption of the human race and its liberation from every oppressive situation" (Intro., para. 6, p. 34; my italics). Indeed, everything the Church says and does has to be touched by this overriding concern for justice: the exercise of ministry, education, liturgy, etc. And everything is, in turn, placed in the context of the coming Kingdom of God, a kingdom of justice and love, a kingdom rooted in "the radical transformation of the world in the Paschal Mystery of the Lord . . ." (IV, para. 3, p. 52).

The 1985 Extraordinary Synod of Bishops

Pope John Paul II convened an Extraordinary Synod of Bishops in late 1985 to commemorate the twentieth anniversary of the close of the Second Vatican Council. Its Final Report recapitulated the principal ecclesiological themes found in previous Catholic social teachings: the Church as sacrament of salvation of the world, its need to interpret the "signs of the times" (including "hunger, oppression, injustice and war, sufferings, terrorism, and other forms of violence of every sort") in the light of the Gospel, its need for dialogue with non-Catholic Christians, non-Christians, and nonbelievers, its preferential option for the poor, and its need to put aside any false and useless opposition between the Church's spiritual mission and its service to the world (II, D., paras. 1–6).

712

Papal Statements

Ecclesiam Suam (*His Church*, 1964): Pope Paul VI's inaugural encyclical stressed the fundamental need for *dialogue*. Although the encyclical is not precisely postconciliar, the council had already established clear ecclesiological lines, and the encyclical itself reflects them. The Church is called to dialogue with humankind at various levels. The pope sketches four concentric circles: The first and widest comprises all people, with whom dialogue must be initiated and sustained on each of the great problems of the world; the second circle embraces all religious people; the third, all Christians; and the fourth, all Catholics.

Populorum Progressio (*On the Development of Peoples*, 1967): This encyclical, so strong in its insistence on the social and political character of the Church's mission, is generally credited with inspiring the growth of Latin American liberation theology and of shaping the remarkable documents of the Second Latin American Bishops' Conference, which met in Medellin, Colombia, in 1968. The pope points immediately to the teachings of the Second Vatican Council on the Church's responsibility to the world at large and especially to those in need, and ultimately to the example of Jesus himself, who preached the Gospel to the poor as a sign of his mission (n. 12).

Octagesima Adveniens (*A Call to Action*, 1971): This "Apostolic Letter" to Cardinal Maurice Roy, President of the Council of the Laity and of the Pontifical Commission, Justice and Peace, recapitulates the social doctrine of the Catholic Church from *Rerum Novarum* (1891), whose eightieth (*octagesima*) anniversary provided the occasion for the document. The Church is called "to enlighten minds in order to assist them to discover the truth and to find the right path to follow amid the different teachings that call for their attention; and secondly to take part in action and to spread, with a real care for service and effectiveness, the energies of the Gospel" (n. 48).

Evangelii Nuntiandi (*On Evangelization in the Modern World*, 1975): This is technically an "Apostolic Exhortation" on the occasion of the 1974 World Synod of Bishops in Rome. The document, which various commentators regard as the most impressive in Paul VI's fifteen-year pontificate, links the mission of the Church with Jesus' proclamation of the Kingdom of God, as "liberation from everything that oppresses

713

humanity, but which is above all liberation from sin and the Evil One..." (n. 9). Just as Jesus accomplished this proclamation in works as well as in word, so is the Church called to be a servant as well as a herald of the Gospel. "Evangelization would not be complete if it did not take account of the unceasing interplay of the Gospel and of humanity's concrete life, both personal and social" (n. 29). Thus, "the Church strives always to insert the Christian struggle for liberation into the universal plan of salvation which [the Church] itself proclaims" (n. 38). The principle of sacramentality is also affirmed when it insists that "the first means of evangelization is the witness of an authentically Christian life... the witness of poverty and detachment, of freedom in the face of the powers of this world, in short, the witness of sanctity" (n. 41).

Redemptor Hominis (*Redeemer of Humankind*, 1979): This inaugural encyclical of Pope John Paul II is primarily concerned with human dignity, rooted in the saving work of Christ. It says that the Church must be a constant champion of human dignity, consistent with the teachings of the Second Vatican Council and especially of its *Declaration on Religious Freedom* (n. 10). Where the encyclical touched the mystery of the Church more directly, it tended to favor a transcendental ecclesiology ("from above"), emphasizing the spiritual and eschatological dimensions of the Church's existence rather than its servanthood and its sociopolitical role in the world (see n. 18). A passing reference to the Church as a "community of disciples" (n. 21) inspired Avery Dulles to develop that as a sixth model of the Church.

Laborem Exercens (*On Human Work*, 1981), written on the ninetieth anniversary of Leo XIII's *Rerum Novarum*, was the first of Pope John Paul II's three major social encyclicals. The Church, he pointed out, does not have precise answers to all the problems of the world, but it *is* expected to provide a moral framework within which these problems should be addressed, namely, "to call attention to the dignity and rights of those who work, to condemn situations in which that dignity and those rights are violated, and to help to guide... [technological, political, and economic] changes so as to ensure authentic progress by humanity and society" (n. 1, para. 4; see also n. 24, para. 3).

Sollicitudo Rei Socialis (*On the Social Concern of the Church*, 1988) is the most explicitly ecclesiological of John Paul II's social encyclicals.

Written on the occasion of the twentieth anniversary of Paul VI's *Populorum Progressio*, it reiterated and embraced several of the latter's ecclesiological themes regarding the role of the Church as advocate and agent of justice and on behalf of the poor (n. 39). Following Paul VI's *Evangelii Nuntiandi*, he wrote, "The teaching and spreading of its social doctrine are part of the Church's evangelizing mission" (n. 41). He also echoed Paul VI's insistence in *Populorum Progressio* on the global character of the social teachings as well as the Church's preferential option for the poor (n. 42).

    Centesimus Annus (*The Hundredth Year*, 1991), written on the hundredth anniversary of *Rerum Novarum*, repeats the point that the social teachings pertain to the Church's evangelizing mission and are "an essential part of the Christian message" (n. 5; see also n. 54). But, again, the Church has no specific programs to propose. Instead, it offers its social teachings as "an indispensable and ideal orientation..." (n. 43). But the social message of the Gospel "must not be considered a theory, but above all else a basis and motivation for action" (n. 57). At the center of the message is always the dignity of the human person (n. 53; also nn. 47, 54–56), a point the pope had made already in his first encyclical, *Redemptor Hominis*. It also reaffirmed the Church's preferential option for the poor (nn. 11 and 57) and the importance of the Church's own witness to its social teachings (n. 57).

Catechism of the Catholic Church

The *Catechism of the Catholic Church* (1992) recapitulates and weaves together various pertinent texts from the documents of the Second Vatican Council. The Catechism's ecclesiology is, like von Balthasar's, "from above." The Church is born from the side of Christ on the cross, "from Christ's heart pierced at his death" (n. 766). Here below the Church lives "in exile" from its true home in heaven (n. 769). In the meantime, it "inhabits" history, but also transcends it. Indeed, the Church's "first purpose is to be the sacrament of the intimate union of human beings with God" (n. 775). In articulating the Church's mission, the Catechism makes no mention of the broader social mission described in the council's *Pastoral Constitution on the Church in the Modern World*. Instead, the mission is one of evangelizing those who have not heard the Gospel and of enabling all people "to share in the communion between the Father and the Son in their Spirit of love" (n. 850).

Bishops' Statements

(Because of the large number of episcopal conferences throughout the world, what follows here is exceedingly limited—in this case, to the United States and Latin America. Readers in Canada, Ireland, the United Kingdom, Australia, New Zealand, and various countries in Europe, Africa, and Asia should take the comparable statements of their own bishops into account.)

The Church in the Present-Day Transformation of Latin America in the Light of the Council (Second General Conference of Latin American Bishops, Medellín, Colombia, 1968): Inspired by the Second Vatican Council and by *Populorum Progressio,* the so-called Medellín documents describe the Church as an instrument of liberation, an agent of social justice, a defender of the poor and the oppressed. This understanding of the Church's mission must penetrate every major area of Church life: education, youth ministry, the family, catechesis, and so forth. "No earthly ambition impels the Church, only its wish to be the humble servant of all people" (XIV, 18).

Message to the People of God (Third General Conference of Latin American Bishops, Puebla, Mexico, 1979): The same sense of integration characterizes the work and final message to the people of Latin America in this Third General Conference as in the preceding one: Christ assumed humanity and its real conditions, except for sin. Therefore, the Church must be concerned with the whole person, with the matter of human rights, economic justice, the use of power and force, and so forth. Given the importance of Marian piety in the Church of Latin America, the Final Document reserved a large place for Mary as Mother and Model of the Church (nn. 282–303).

"Political Responsibility" (Administrative Board, United States Catholic Conference, 1976): "Christians believe," the statement declares, "that Jesus' commandment to love one's neighbor should extend beyond individual relationships to infuse and transform all human relations from the family to the entire human community." The bishops cite a classic text, Luke 4:18: "He has anointed me to

716

bring good news to the poor. He has sent me to proclaim release to the captives, and recovery of sight to the blind, and let the oppressed go free." The call to feed the hungry, clothe the naked, care for the sick and the afflicted, comfort the victims of injustice (Matthew 25) requires more than individual acts of charity. We must understand and act upon "the broader dimensions of poverty, hunger and injustice which necessarily involve the institutions and structures of economy, society and politics." The U.S. bishops have issued similar documents, with only slight variations in the texts, before each of the U.S. presidential election campaigns since 1976.

Sharing the Light of Faith: National Catechetical Directory for Catholics of the United States (Washington, D.C.: United States Catholic Conference, 1979): The ecclesiology of this document is essentially that of the Second Vatican Council. The Church is described first as a mystery, and then as People of God, servant, sign of the Kingdom, pilgrim, and hierarchical society. The Kingdom is understood also as a Kingdom of justice, love, and peace, as well as of holiness and grace, and authority is to be exercised collegially and in the spirit of service. The interpretation of the four marks of the Church (one, holy, catholic, apostolic) differs in emphasis from the pre–Vatican II textbooks. Catholicity, for example, means that "the gospel message is capable of being integrated with all cultures. It corresponds to all that is authentically human" (p. 40). Apostolicity is not portrayed in a purely *chronological* sense—i.e., that the Catholic Church's bishops can trace their episcopal orders all the way back, in an unbroken chain, to the Apostles, but in a *dynamic* sense as well—i.e., as "the continuing fidelity to Christ's loving and saving work and message, to ministry and service inspired by the evangelical vision and teaching of the original apostles" (p. 41).

"The Challenge of Peace" (Pastoral Letter, U.S. Catholic Bishops, 1981) is of ecclesiological significance because of its underlying *methodological* assumptions, namely, (1) its insistence that not every statement in the letter is of equal authority (n. 9); (2) the distinction it makes between binding principles and their applications, the latter involving "prudential judgments" which are "based on specific circumstances which can change or which can be interpreted differently by people of good will" (ibid.); and (3) its recognition of the different, and often overlapping, audiences for church teachings, demanding appropriate modifications of teaching styles (n. 17). The ecclesiological model it adopts is that of "community of disciples" (drawing from John Paul II's *Redemptor Hominis* and Avery Dulles). It must be a witnessing community in a world "increasingly estranged from Christian values" (n. 277).

"Economic Justice for All: Catholic Social Teaching and the U.S. Economy" (Pastoral Letter, U.S. Catholic Bishops, 1986) reiterated the main ecclesiological themes of "The Challenge of Peace": the Church as a community of disciples (nn. 45–47) and its mission as one of solidarity with the poor (n. 55). On the other hand, this second pastoral letter contains a remarkably extensive recapitulation of the 1971 World Synod's *Justice in the World* with its insistence that the Church must practice what it preaches: *"All the moral principles that govern the just operation of any economic endeavor apply to the church and its agencies and institutions; indeed the church should be exemplary"* (n. 347; italics in the original). This means recognizing the right of church employees to form unions (n. 353), combatting discrimination against women (ibid.), and having an abiding concern for the image it projects through its properties, investments, and the like (nn. 354–55). Although rooted in the principle of sacramentality, the text does not appeal to it in order to ground the argument.

THE NATURE OF THE CHURCH: TOWARD A DEFINITION

(The reader should be advised that what follows here is neither a synthesis of contemporary theological reflection on the Church nor of current official teaching on the subject. Both have already been summarized in the preceding pages of this chapter. The remaining material of the chapter represents the author's attempt to pull the preceding together and apply it to questions regarding the nature, mission, necessity, and catholicity of the Church.)

Models of the Church

The word *model* has, first, an *evaluative* meaning—e.g., "She is a model teacher" or "He is a model student," in which the term conveys some notion of excellence. A model is an exemplar of some value. The word may also be used in a more *neutral,* or *descriptive,* sense—e.g., "model home" or a "fashion model." A model can also be a *philosophical* category, describing a fundamental perspective or way of understanding some complex reality. It may in that instance be either evaluative or neutral. The word *model* is employed here in the philosophical, or perspectival sense, and in its neutral, rather than evaluative, sense.

There are at least three dominant models of, or ways of perceiving, the Church, and they are presented below not in order of importance but in the chronological sequence in which they have entered the recent history of the Catholic Church.

Institution

This model perceives the Church *primarily* (which is not to say exclusively or exhaustively) as a hierarchically structured, visible society, or organization, which mediates salvation to its individual members through the preaching and teaching of the Word and the administration of the sacraments. This was, of course, the dominant model in Roman Catholicism (as distinct from Eastern Catholic traditions) before Vatican II, and it inspired the first draft of the council's *Dogmatic Constitution of the Church*. Perhaps the most sophisticated expression of this model is contained in Joachim Salaverri's tract *De Ecclesia Christi* in the so-called *Spanish Summa* (summarized in chapter 18).

Strengths

This model was and remains attractive because it affords a strong sense of ecclesiastical *identity* (the Church is a specific, visible, clearly defined reality, rooted in the will of God, the mandate of Jesus Christ, and the power of the Holy Spirit); it gives the members a sense of their *place* and *role* within the Church, even if it be a subordinate one (some have clearly defined authority, others do not); and it is attentive to historical *continuity* (the Church has definite origins and has passed through specific points of development in which its identity was further clarified and determined, and both of these—origins and points of passage—connect the Church of the present with the Church of the past).

Weaknesses

On the other hand, the institutional model tended, *first*, to exaggerate the hierarchical or societal aspect of the Church at the expense of the communitarian. That indeed was the point of the debate at Vatican II over the placement of chapters II and III in *Lumen gentium*. Is the Church first the People of God with a particular structure, or is it a hierarchical reality which happens to provide spiritual benefits to a particular people? *Second,* the institutional model may have also exaggerated the role and importance of the ordained, and especially of bishops, at the expense of the missionary responsibility of the entire community of the baptized. Thus, the mode of decision-making was monarchical and/or oligarchical rather than collegial or democratic. *Third,* the institutional model tended to limit the scope of the Church to the Catholic Church, at the expense of the Christian and ecclesial reality of the other churches (Orthodox, Anglican, Protestant, and Oriental Christian). *Fourth,* this model tended to limit the scope of the Church's mission to the preaching of the Word and the celebration of the sacraments, at the expense of the Church's broader social and political responsibilities. *Finally,* this model tended to identify the Church with the Kingdom of God on earth, at the expense of the abiding need for renewal and reform not just of its individual members but of the whole Church, structures and persons, head and members.

Community

This model perceives the Church primarily as a community, or a people, whose principal task is the promotion and sustaining of personal growth through interpersonal relationships. This model was at least partially embraced by Vatican II in its central teaching on the Church as the People of God. It is an understanding of the Church proposed at the beginning of the 1960s by Edward Schillebeeckx in his *Christ the Sacrament of Encounter with God* and at more popular levels by Catholic authors with a psychological orientation—e.g., Eugene Kennedy and Henri Nouwen. It is a model that was warmly endorsed by those favoring a theology of festivity and fantasy in the late 1960s and early 1970s—e.g., Harvey Cox in *The Feast of Fools* (New

720

York: Macmillan, 1969). This was also the dominant model in the early years of the Catholic Charismatic movement, and it is consistent with a late-twentieth-century emphasis in American culture on personal growth and development (the so-called human potential movement).

However, in more recent years, the community model has taken on broader dimensions. Thus, the Church is not only a community of persons in the above sense, but also a *communion* of grace, uniting all its members in Christ and drawing all its members into the communion of the triune God. In addition, the community model has been incorporated into a separate model of the Church known as "the community of disciples," whose orientation is not so much interpersonal as it is focused on following in the way of Christ.

Strengths

First, the community model emphasizes the reality of the Church as a people and the responsibility of the Church to provide a context for human growth in Christ. Specifically, this model avoids some of the problems associated with the institutional model and conforms better than the institutional model to the biblical, patristic, and Vatican II stress on the Church as the People of God. *Second,* this model stresses the responsibility of the Church not only to make certain spiritual benefits available to its members, as in the sacraments, but to contribute positively to the human growth of its members. *Third,* this model underlines the Church's abiding missionary responsibility to be a sign of Christ's presence by the mutual love shown within the community of his disciples.

Weaknesses

On the other hand, the community model, *first,* is not always clear in identifying those elements which make such a community distinctive. What makes the Christian community different from other communities? *Second,* this model tends to concentrate on the value of the individual's growth at the expense of the social and political responsibilities of the whole community and at the expense of the community's abiding commitment to the renewal and institutional reform of

721

the Church itself. Viewing the community model through the prism of *communio* or "community of disciples" would tend to diminish the force of the first weakness, since the relationship with Christ and/or the triune God gives it a distinctively Christian identity. The second risk, however, remains.

Change-Agent

This model, also known as the servant model, perceives the Church primarily as an instrument of social change whose task is the wise and courageous allocation of its own moral and material resources for the sake of the coming of the Kingdom of God among humankind—a Kingdom of justice and peace as well as of holiness and grace. It is a model supported by Vatican II's *Pastoral Constitution on the Church in the Modern World*, the 1971 Synod of Bishops' *Justice in the World*, and similar official documents of the Catholic Church. It is also articulated in recent theological writings on the Church—e.g., those of Metz, Moltmann, Schillebeeckx, and Gutiérrez.

Strengths

The change-agent, or servant, model properly emphasizes the social and political responsibilities of the Church, insisting that the Kingdom of God is indeed a Kingdom of justice, peace, and freedom. Furthermore, this model underscores the principle that *diakonia*, which includes service in the sociopolitical order, is as essential, or constitutive, to the mission of the Church as are the proclamation of the Word and the celebration of the sacraments.

Weaknesses

First, this model, too, is not always clear in identifying those elements which make such an agent of social change distinctive. Why belong to the Church if one can work more effectively for justice and peace outside of it? *Second*, some of those who have emphasized the servant model have also tended to identify the Church with the Kingdom of God, as the institutional model's proponents have sometimes done. Thus, wherever God, or the Spirit of God, is redemptively present as

722

the source of justice and reconciliation, there is the Church. But since the redemptive presence of God is the Kingdom of God, such an assertion effectively identifies the Kingdom with the Church.

These aren't the only models of the Church one can propose. Avery Dulles offers others, including herald, sacrament, and community of disciples. Others might wish to add teacher and learner, empowerer and enabler, provider for those in need, and advocate.

A balanced theology of the Church would have to incorporate the distinctive strengths of all these models without equating the whole mystery of the Church with any one particular perspective.

Definition of Church

The Church is the whole body, or congregation, of persons who are called by God the Father to acknowledge the Lordship of Jesus, the Son, in word, in sacrament, in witness, and in service, and, through the power of the Holy Spirit, to collaborate with Jesus' historic mission for the sake of the Kingdom of God.

The definition embraces all Christians: Catholics, Orthodox, Anglicans, Protestants, and Oriental Christians. Thus, although the noun *church* is singular, it is always to be understood at the same time as having a pluralistic character. There is "the Church" and there are "the churches." Again, this is not to say that *all* churches fully satisfy the criteria implied in the definition.

But the distinction between the Church and the churches is not only ecumenical. There is also the distinction between the Church as "Church universal" and the church as "local church." *Church* refers at once to the whole Body of Christ and the whole People of God, as well as to the congregation of Christians in a particular place (a parish, a diocese, e.g.). Indeed, the Church universal is itself a *communion of local churches.*

When does a group of persons at a local level become a church? When the following theological and pastoral conditions are verified: (1) a corporate confession of the Lordship of Jesus; (2) ratification of that confession of faith in Baptism, the Eucharist, and other sacraments; (3) regular nourishment on the biblical word of God as a force that convokes and sustains the community of faith; (4) a sense of communion (*koinonia*) within the group—i.e., a common awareness of the call to become a community; (5) an acceptance of the Gospel of Jesus Christ as the conscious motivation for one's values and ethical commitment (therefore, to become not just a community, but a community of *disciples*); and (6) the existence and exercise of certain formal ministries designed to assist the community in remaining faithful to its mission and providing order, coherence, and stability to its internal life so that it really can be a sacrament of Christ and of the Kingdom. For the Catholic Church this last item also implies union with the pope and the college of bishops, who are themselves related by succession to Peter and the other Apostles.

Each of these ecclesial elements is a matter of degree. On the other hand, the noun *church* is not applicable to a particular group except where all of these elements are present, to one degree or another. Thus, we always have to distinguish between movements and associations within the Church (even within a local church), and "the Church" itself (whether universal or local).

The definition and brief explanation presuppose, of course, all that has gone before, in this chapter and in chapters 16–18.

THE MISSION OF THE CHURCH

The mission of the Church is focused, as is Jesus' mission, on the *Kingdom of God*. By *Kingdom of God* is meant *the redemptive presence of God actualized through the power of God's renewing and reconciling Spirit.* Literally, the Kingdom of God is the reign, or rule, of God. The Kingdom happens whenever and wherever the will of God is fulfilled, for God rules where God's will is at work. And since God's will is applicable to the cosmos, to nature, to objects, to history, to institutions, to groups as well as to individuals, the Kingdom of God is as broad and as overarching as the claims and scope of the divine will itself.

More precisely, one might argue that the Kingdom of God is indistinguishable from God as such. The Kingdom is not something other than God. The Kingdom *of* God *is* God insofar as God is redemptively present and active in our midst through the power of the Holy Spirit. The Kingdom is the divine redemptive presence, reconciling, renewing, healing, and liberating.

724

The mission of the Church is unintelligible apart from the Kingdom of God. The Church is called, *first,* to proclaim in word and in sacrament the definitive arrival of the Kingdom in Jesus of Nazareth; *second,* to offer itself as a test case or sign of its own proclamation—i.e., to be a people transformed by the Spirit into a community of faith, hope, love, freedom, and truthfulness; and *third,* to enable and facilitate the coming of the reign of God through service within the community of faith and in the world at large.

Each of these three missionary responsibilities generates, or is the foundation of, one of the three generic models of Church given above. The call of the Church to proclaim the Gospel in word and in sacrament in an organized and authorized manner is consistent with the concerns of the *institutional* model. The call of the Church to proclaim the Gospel by the quality of its own life is consistent with the concerns of the *community* model. And the call of the Church to proclaim and apply the Gospel through the struggle for social justice, peace, and human rights is consistent with the concerns of the *change-agent,* or *servant,* model.

The Mission of the Church

Missionary Responsibility	*Corresponding Model*
Proclamation/praxis of the Gospel in *word* and in *worship,* in an *organized* and *authorized* manner.	*Institution*
Proclamation/praxis of the Gospel by the *quality* of the *Church's own life.*	*Community*
Proclamation/praxis of the Gospel by *application* of the Gospel to the struggle for *social justice, peace,* and *human rights.*	*Change-agent (Servant)*

Proclamation in Word and Worship

The Church is that segment of humankind which hopes in the future of the world because of its fundamental faith in the unique significance of the life, death, and resurrection of Jesus of Nazareth, and in the abiding power of the Holy Spirit. Its first task is to keep alive the memory of Jesus Christ in word and in sacrament, to call attention to his and the Spirit's continued active presence in history, and to profess its hope in his and the Spirit's totally new, creative manifestation in the future Kingdom.

Whatever changes in form and structure this Church assumes in the years ahead, it will always be that community which explicitly and publicly identifies Jesus Christ as the focal point of the whole historical process. The Church will not only announce this in word (preaching, catechesis, teaching), but it will celebrate that faith in sacrament. Through the *Eucharist* in particular the Church gives thanksgiving to God for the confirmation and validation of God's promises of reconciliation and peace in Jesus Christ (2 Corinthians 1:20). Through the Eucharist the Church keeps alive Christ's memory in order to make clear that he is indeed the hinge of history, that he is the supreme measure of all that is good and human. And finally, through the Eucharist the Church fixes the eyes of the world on the future, where the world's ultimate meaning and destiny reside.

The Church, therefore, is a community of *faith* in the significance of what has already happened in and through Jesus Christ; it is a community of *love* as an expression of the effects of that Christ-event; and it is a community of *hope* in the power of the God of Jesus Christ to re-create all things anew in Christ and the Holy Spirit. The celebration of the Eucharist is the "summit and source" of the Church's mission, to use the terms of Vatican II.

But the Church is not commissioned to proclaim the Kingdom of God in an uncritical or naive manner. The Church can never equate any earthly reality, including itself, with the Kingdom of God. The Pauline appeal that we "not be conformed to this world" (Romans 12:2) means that we should never forget the relative character of everything this side of the final Kingdom. The Church, therefore, proclaims the Gospel with a consciousness of sin in the world and in its own household as well. Its proclamation is always prophetic.

Prophecy means, literally, *speaking on behalf of God*. A prophetic Church is a Church that speaks always on behalf of God, measuring everything against the promised Kingdom of God. The Church's preaching, however, is effective and credible to the extent that the Church itself has been converted by it. And this leads to the second missionary task.

Signification, or Witnessing

The Church must also be a sign of what God *is* actually doing in history and of what the human community *should* be doing in response to God's saving action. Women and men should be able to look upon this Christian community and thereby take courage with regard to the future course of history. They should be filled with confidence in the core of reality—affirming its intelligibility and its worthwhileness—because the ordinary women and men who belong to this community and maintain close affiliation with that core of reality are constantly being transformed by the Spirit of love, justice, intelligence, compassion, fortitude, and so forth. The Church has the responsibility, therefore, to be so open itself to Jesus, the reconciling Word of God, and to the reconciling power of the Spirit that the Church becomes the unmistakably clear sign of Jesus' and the Spirit's presence in the world. The Church must be a community marked by faith, hope, love, freedom, and truthfulness, that is, by authentic *discipleship*, not only in its official proclamations but in its lifestyle as well.

But the Church cannot be a sacrament of God's Kingdom unless the Kingdom exists somehow within the community. A sacrament is both sign and reality. The two are distinct but inseparable. Thus, *the Church is not itself the Kingdom of God*, yet *the Church must be inseparable from the Kingdom*. If indeed the Church were in no way imbued with the hidden presence of God, its preaching would have no force and its service no lasting effect. The Church would not be a mystery, or sacrament, at all.

But insofar as the Kingdom *is* present within the Church, that fact imposes upon the Church the missionary obligation to make the Kingdom's presence visible and effective for others. It means that the Church must *be* what it is; it must practice what it preaches. It means, too, that the Church must continually renew and reform itself in fidelity to the Gospel. Accordingly, the question of institutional or structural renewal and reform is always an important one.

The issues that have been on the Church's agenda in the post–Vatican II years—e.g., the ordination and equality of women, the selection of bishops, coresponsibility for decision-making at all levels of church life, the limits of papal and episcopal authority—may not be the issues on tomorrow's agenda. But the underlying challenge will always be there: How can the Church best express in form and structure the inner reality which it embodies? The question is a missionary question, because the Church is called to be a sign as well as an instrument of the Gospel and of the Kingdom of God.

It would be illogical, therefore, to argue that the Church should be a vigorous agent of liberation and yet be, at the same time, indifferent to the processes by which the Church selects its leadership or reaches important decisions regarding the allocation of its limited human and material resources. If the Church is called to be a sacrament of Christ, then how it organizes itself for mission and how it practices the virtue of justice within as well as without the community of faith become matters of profound practical consequence.

Service: The Basis and Limits of the Church's Involvement in the Public Forum

Because the Kingdom of God is also a Kingdom of justice, peace, and freedom, and because the Church exists for the sake of the Kingdom, the Church's mission must also include responsibility for humanization in its fullest sense. The Church's activities on behalf of social justice or human rights are not merely preparatory to the real mission of the Church, as the notion of "preevangelization" had it before Vatican II. Apart from the official church documents already cited (*Gaudium et spes,* the synodal document *Justice in the World,* and various papal statements, including especially John Paul II's *Sollicitudo Rei Socialis* and *Centesimus Annus*), the Church's involvement in the social and political orders is justified on the basis of the social and institutional character of sin itself. Since the Church is called to combat sin of every kind, the Church has responsibility in all areas where sin appears. More positively, the Church is called to uphold and practice virtue. Justice is one of the cardinal, or "hinge," virtues (along with prudence, fortitude, and temperance), and social justice is one of the principal kinds of justice (alongside commutative, distributive, and legal justice). Therefore, the Church's commitment to, and involvement in, the struggle for social justice, peace, and human rights is an essential, or "constitutive," part of its mission.

728

The Church has "the right to pass moral judgments, even on matters touching the political order," the council's *Pastoral Constitution on the Church in the Modern World* declares, "whenever basic personal rights or the salvation of souls make such judgments necessary" (n. 76).

On the other hand, there are *limits* to the Church's involvement in the public forum. The Church's intervention in the social and political orders must always be responsible, never arbitrary, particularly in the light of the Church's limited resources. Accordingly, such intervention must be governed by the following criteria: (1) The issue must be clearly *justice-related*. (2) The ecclesiastical body or bodies should have the *competence* to deal with the issue. (3) There should be *sufficient resources* within the particular church(es) to deal with the problem effectively. (4) The issue should have a *prior claim* over other justice-related problems which compete for the Church's attention and limited resources. (5) The Church should always make its case on the basis of persuasive *arguments*, and, therefore, it should neither expect nor accept any special *privileges* conferred by the civil authorities (*Gaudium et spes*, n. 76). (6) The Church should never cast its lot with any political party, movement, or regime, nor support or oppose partisan political officeholders or candidates for office. (7) The *form* of ecclesiastical action should not unnecessarily or unduly polarize the Church itself, since the Church is always called to be a sign of the Gospel and of the Kingdom of God. A diversity of viewpoints is to be expected and tolerated, so that agreement with the specific form of social or political action selected by the church(es) should not become itself a test of authentic Christian faith and commitment. This is not to say, on the other hand, that the mere risk of *conflict* within the Church should discourage such intervention. Conflict is essential to growth. But *excessive* conflict can be corrosive and finally destructive of the unity of the Church itself.

THE NECESSITY OF THE CHURCH

Do we need the Church? We have already indicated what we mean by *Church*. The question here is, what do we mean by *need*? The need may be *psychological* (the need for meaning), *sociological* (the need for a community of shared meaning), or *theological* (the need for direction in life, and ultimately the need for salvation). The question of the necessity of the Church takes in all three levels of meaning.

Who has the need? *First,* every human being, insofar as he or she needs to find some meaning for life and some sense of community of shared meaning, has at least a fundamental openness to religion of some kind. *Second,* the world at large needs religious communities that testify to values which otherwise might be forgotten and lost, to the detriment of the human community itself. *Third,* insofar as Jesus Christ is the Lord of history and the Savior of all humankind, the world at large also needs a particular religious community which testifies to the significance of Jesus Christ and which somehow carries forward his saving work on behalf of all, members and nonmembers alike. *Finally,* individuals who are convinced in faith of the Lordship of Jesus need a community where this fundamental conviction can be shared in word, in ritual, and in communal living, and through which it can be applied to the world at large for the sake of the world's salvation.

Accordingly, (1) the Church is necessary *for the world* as a sacrament, an efficacious sign and instrument of God's redemptive activity in Jesus Christ, leading toward the final Kingdom of God. The necessity of the Church *for the world* is a *historically contingent* necessity; i.e., *hypothetically* the Kingdom of God could come about without the Church or even without Jesus, but *in fact* it does not and will not. (2) The Church is necessary *for those individuals* who are in fact called by God to acknowledge the Lordship of Jesus and to collaborate with him in the coming of the Kingdom of God. The necessity of the Church *for the individual* is similarly *contingent,* but contingent this time on the call of God to belong to *this* community rather than to another. Personal salvation, in other words, is not inextricably linked with one's membership or nonmembership in the Church. It is existence within the Kingdom of God, not within the Church, that finally determines our relationship with God and our reception of salvation. It is not the one who says, "Lord, Lord!" who will enter the Kingdom, but "only the one who does the will of [the] Father in heaven" (Matthew 7:21). Where is it said, Rahner asked, that we must have the whole 100 percent?

730

THE NECESSITY OF THE CATHOLIC CHURCH

What is different about the Catholic Church? (We are speaking here of the whole communion of Catholic churches in union with the see of Rome, not only of the *Roman* Catholic Church. Regarding that relationship, see again chapter 1.) If the Church is necessary to the world and to individuals within the world, is the *Catholic* Church also necessary to the Body of Christ as a whole and to individuals inside and outside the Body of Christ?

One must distinguish between what is *characteristic* of Catholicism and what is *distinctive* about it. What is characteristic may also be found in different shape or form in other churches, but what is distinctive will be found in Catholicism alone.

What is *characteristically* Catholic? *First*, the conviction that *grace* is finally triumphant over sin, not only as the declaration of God that we are just but through a real interior transformation by the power of the Holy Spirit. Thus, the world and humankind are not fundamentally evil and dangerous, because God is their Creator, Redeemer, and Sanctifier. *Second*, the conviction that the presence of grace is not limited to the extraordinary and even the bizarre, because God is present to *ordinary* people, in *ordinary* situations of life. *Third*, the conviction that access to God's grace is *not limited* to a chosen few, the righteous within the larger community of the unrighteous, because God wishes to save *all* and has won salvation for *all* in the redemptive work of Jesus Christ. *Fourth*, the sense of *tradition*, of *doctrine*, and of the importance of maintaining *continuity* not only with the Church's origins but with its principal points of passage from its beginnings to the present. *Fifth*, the sense of *peoplehood*, of *community*, and of *church*. *Sixth*, the sense of *sacramentality* and its correlative sense of the importance of *mediation*. God is present to us through signs and symbols, and the presence of God is effective for us through these same visible signs and symbols.

What is *distinctively* Catholic? Here the answer given earlier by Hans Küng in his *Council and Reunion* still applies: The ecumenical question is the question of ecclesiastical office, and of the Petrine ministry in particular. It is true that Catholic ecclesiology posits a collegial understanding of the Church—i.e., that it is a communion of churches. But so too do the Orthodox traditions. But Catholicism

731

alone insists on the role of the Petrine minister, the pope, as the "perpetual and visible source and foundation of the unity of the bishops and of the multitude of the faithful" (*Dogmatic Constitution on the Church*, n. 23).

One may become, be, and/or remain a Catholic for any number of reasons which have something to do with what is *characteristic* about Catholicism but nothing to do with what is *distinctive* about it. But that fact does not negate Catholicism's distinctive *ecclesiological* feature, namely, the importance it accords to the place and function of the Petrine ministry exercised by the Bishop of Rome.

This is not to say, however, that belief in the Petrine ministry is the *only* distinctive feature of Catholicism. Although the Catholic Church is not alone among Christian churches in affirming the triumph of grace over sin, its ordinariness and its universality, is not alone in its sense of tradition and doctrine, in its commitment to the principles of sacramentality and mediation, or in its emphasis on the peoplehood of the Church, one can argue that there is within Catholicism a particular *configuration* of such values as these—a configuration which one does not discover elsewhere in the Body of Christ. (See again chapter 1.)

It is with this distinction in mind between what is characteristic and what is distinctive about Catholicism that we must confront the question: Do we need the Catholic Church?

For one thing, the Catholic Church is a part, and a very large and significant part indeed, of the whole Body of Christ. Therefore, the Catholic Church is necessary *for the world* for the same reason that the Church as a whole is necessary for the world, namely, as a sacrament of Jesus Christ and of the Kingdom of God.

Second, the Catholic Church is necessary *for the whole Body of Christ* because the Catholic Church alone has all the institutional elements which are necessary for the integrity of the Body of Christ (e.g., the Petrine ministry, the seven sacraments) as well as the many characteristic values which serve to enrich the rest of the churches (e.g., its regard for community, its confidence in God's grace as transformative, as ordinary, and as universal, its sacramental perspective, its spiritualities, its coherently systematic approach to the Christian theological and doctrinal tradition).

Finally, the Catholic Church is necessary *for the individual* who is called to the Church as such and who is, beyond that call to confess the Lordship of Jesus, persuaded that the fullness of ecclesial union with Christ requires participation in that church within the Body of Christ, whose unity is expressed not only through faith and its sacraments, but also through the ministry of the Petrine minister, the pope, who stands in the midst of the Church as the "source and foundation" of the unity of the communion of churches.

In light of the teaching of the Second Vatican Council, especially the *Decree on Ecumenism* and the *Declaration on the Relationship of the Church to Non-Christian Religions*, a common pre–Vatican II answer to the question of the Catholic Church's necessity—namely, that the Catholic Church alone is the "one, true Church of Christ," outside of which authentic religious truth does not exist and salvation can be attained only with the greatest difficulty—is subject to some qualification. This position is to be tested against the following theological principles: God is present as an offer of grace to every human being; revelation is available apart from the Church; and within the Church itself there are many churches which, to one degree or another, "are brought into a certain, though imperfect, communion with the Catholic Church...are incorporated into Christ...have a right to be honored by the title of Christian, and are properly regarded as brothers and sisters in the Lord by the sons and daughters of the Catholic Church" (*Decree on Ecumenism*, n. 3). The *Decree on Ecumenism* complements the teaching of the *Dogmatic Constitution on the Church* that the Church of Christ "subsists in" the Catholic Church, which gives it a certain normative status in relation to the other churches.

SUMMARY

1. Ecclesiology *"from above"* views the Church as a *communion in grace*, whose origin is the inner, communal life of the Trinity. This is the approach of *von Balthasar* and *Zizioulas*. Ecclesiology *"from below"* emphasizes the nature of the Church as a *community of human beings* who, although transformed by grace, have an earthly mission to fulfill—one that includes the liberation of the world from injustice and oppression. It is the approach generally adopted in contemporary ecclesiology.

2. Catholic ecclesiology since Vatican II has developed the basic theological insights of the council itself. The greatest emphasis, first, is on the *sacramentality* of the Church ("the universal sacrament of salvation"). This emphasis is seen especially in *Rahner, Schillebeeckx, Dulles, Gutiérrez, and Tillard.* Second, there is a stress on the subordination of the Church to the *Kingdom of God* and a wider understanding of the Kingdom to include the coming of peace, justice, and freedom (*Rahner, Schillebeeckx, Küng, Dulles, Metz, Baum, Gutiérrez, Boff, Ruether, Carr*). Third, there is renewed attention to the need for ongoing institutional reform as a way of fulfilling the Church's sacramental mission (*Rahner, Küng, Gutiérrez, Boff, Ruether, Carr*). Finally, because of the universal availability of grace, all the foregoing theologians stress the abiding need for dialogue with others and for collaboration in the task of humanizing the world.

3. A sampling of *Protestant and Orthodox ecclesiology* since Vatican II suggests a new or renewed emphasis also on the *sacramentality* of the Church (*Lindbeck, Zizioulas*) and a movement away from the traditional Protestant notion of the Church as the "congregation of saints wherein the gospel is rightly preached and the sacraments rightly celebrated" (*Pannenberg, Moltmann*). There is an insistence, too, on the subordination of the Church to the *Kingdom of God* and on the Church's correlative responsibility to participate in the struggle for liberation, social justice, and humanization (*Moltmann, Pannenberg, Lindbeck*).

4. Similar convergences have been noted in recent *ecumenical dialogues*—e.g., in the Anglican–Roman Catholic dialogues at both international and national levels.

5. *Official documents* of the Catholic Church have also reaffirmed the principal teachings of the Second Vatican Council, focusing particularly on the Church's responsibility for social justice and liberation, e.g., *Justice in the World* (1971 Synod of Bishops, *Populorum Progressio* (Pope Paul VI, 1967), *Octagesima Adveniens* (Paul VI, 1971), *Evangelii Nuntiandi* (Paul VI, 1975), *Laborem Exercens* (John Paul II, 1981), *Sollicitudo Rei Socialis* (John Paul II, 1988), *Centesimus Annus* (John Paul II, 1991), the Medellín and Puebla statements of the Latin American Bishops Conference, and two pastoral letters from the National Conference of Catholic Bishops in the United States ("The Challenge of Peace," 1983, and "Economic Justice for All," 1987). An exception is the *Catechism of the Catholic Church* (1992).

6. There are at least three basic perspectives (models) in ecclesiology today: Church as *institution*, as *community*, and as *change-agent*, or *servant*. The first was the dominant perspective in the pre–Vatican II period (Church as a hierarchically structured, visible society, as a means of salvation, through word and sacrament); the second was encouraged by the council itself (Church as people, fellowship, communion); and the third was impelled by

the activist concerns of the 1960s and a renewed appreciation of the Church's social doctrine (Church as agent of social change, instrument of liberation, etc.). A balanced theology of the Church must be open to the values in all three.

7. *Definition:* The Church is the whole body, or congregation, of persons who are called by God the Father to acknowledge the Lordship of Jesus, the Son, in word, in sacrament, in witness, and in service, and, through the power of the Holy Spirit, to collaborate with Jesus' historic mission for the sake of the Kingdom of God.

8. The definition embraces Catholics, Orthodox, Anglicans, Protestants, and Oriental Christians alike, and applies at once to the Church universal and to the local church. The Church is, in fact, a communion of churches. This is not to say that all churches fully satisfy the criteria implied in the definition.

9. Church comes into being where there is (1) a confession of Jesus as Lord, (2) sacramental ratification of that faith, (3) openness to the biblical Word of God, (4) a sense of fellowship, (5) a readiness to apply the Gospel to life (discipleship), and (6) some ministerial structure to ensure stability and direction to the community.

10. The *mission* of the Church is directed to the *Kingdom of God*, which is the redemptive presence of God actualized through the power of God's renewing and reconciling Spirit. The mission is threefold: *proclamation* in word and worship, *signification*, or witnessing, and *service*.

11. *Proclamation* focuses on the significance of Jesus Christ and is principally expressed in the *Eucharist.* That proclamation, whether in word or sacrament, is always *prophetic,* measuring everything against the standard of the coming Kingdom of God.

12. *Signification* emphasizes the sacramentality of the Church. The Church is called to be a sign, or witness, of what it proclaims and of what it embodies (mystery). Accordingly, the Church must engage in continuing institutional renewal and reform.

13. *Service* even in the sociopolitical order is required by the social and institutional character of sin, and by the Church's obligation to practice and uphold virtue, including social justice.

14. *Intervention* in the public forum must meet the following criteria: (1) justice-related issue, (2) competence of the Church to deal with it, (3) sufficient resources within the Church to deal with it effectively, (4) priority of this issue over other issues, (5) the availability of good arguments to support the intervention, (6) independence from all partisan political interests and influence, and (7) a form of action that is not unnecessarily or unduly polarizing.

15. The Church is *necessary* insofar as it helps answer the quest for meaning (the psychological need), for a community of shared meaning (the sociological need), and for guidance and example in the pursuit of salvation (the theological need). This need is in principle incumbent on every human being and on the world at large, but specifically upon those individuals who come to believe in the Lordship of Jesus.

16. The Church is a *sacrament for the world*, to disclose what God is doing for all. Its necessity for the world is *historically contingent;* i.e., the Kingdom hypothetically could come about without the Church or even without Jesus, but *in fact* it will not come about without them.

17. The Church is necessary for those *individuals* who are called by God to confess Jesus as Lord, but that necessity is also *contingent* on the call of God to this community (the Church) rather than to some other community.

18. Catholicism *characteristically* emphasizes the universal triumph of grace over sin as a transforming presence, for ordinary people in ordinary situations; tradition, doctrine, and continuity; peoplehood, community, and church; and especially the principles of sacramentality and mediation. Catholicism is *distinctive* in its conviction regarding the fundamental importance of the Petrine ministry to the life and mission of the Church and in its comprehensive (catholic) grasp of the preceding characteristics.

19. Catholicism is as *necessary* for the *world* as the whole Church is necessary, namely, as a sign and instrument (*sacrament*) of the world's salvation. It is necessary for the whole *Body of Christ* because Catholicism alone has all the institutional elements necessary for the integrity of the Body of Christ as well as the many characteristically Catholic values which enrich and enhance the life and mission of the whole People of God. Finally, Catholicism is necessary for the *individual* who is called not only to confess the Lordship of Jesus but also to enter into explicit union with that communion of churches whose visible center of unity is the Petrine minister within the college of bishops.

20. This understanding of the necessity of Catholicism differs from the common pre–Vatican II understanding of the Catholic Church as the "one, true Church of Christ." The deeper theological reasons for the shift in understanding are the renewed appreciation of the universal availability of grace and revelation, and the recognition that the Church (i.e., the whole Body of Christ) is composed of many churches, some of which are not in communion with the Bishop of Rome. The Catholic Church, however, retains a certain normative status in relation to the other churches.

SUGGESTED READINGS

Boff, Leonardo. *Church: Charism and Power: Liberation Theology and the Institutional Church.* New York: Crossroad, 1985.

Dulles, Avery. *Models of the Church.* Expanded ed. Garden City, N.Y.: Image Books, 1987.

_____. "A Half Century of Ecclesiology." *Theological Studies* 50 (September 1989) 419–42.

Hillman, Eugene. *Toward an African Christianity: Inculturation Applied.* New York: Paulist Press, 1993.

Kennedy, Eugene C. *Tomorrow's Catholics/Yesterday's Church: The Two Cultures of American Catholicism.* New York: Harper & Row, 1988.

Küng, Hans. *On Being a Christian.* New York: Doubleday, 1976.

McBrien, Richard P. *Do We Need the Church?* New York: Harper & Row, 1969.

_____. *Church: The Continuing Quest.* New York: Newman Press, 1970.

_____. *The Remaking of the Church: An Agenda for Reform.* New York: Harper & Row, 1973.

_____. "On Being a Catholic." *Why Catholic?* Ed. John Delaney. New York: Doubleday, 1979, pp. 115–36.

Rahner, Karl. *Concern for the Church: Theological Investigations XX.* New York: Crossroad, 1981.

Ruether, Rosemary Radford. *Women-Church: Theology and Practice of Feminist Religious Communities.* San Francisco: Harper & Row, 1985.

Schillebeeckx, Edward. *Church: The Human Story of God.* New York: Crossroad, 1990.

Schineller, Peter, et al. *Why the Church?* New York: Paulist Press, 1977.

Sullivan, Francis A. *The Church We Believe In: One, Holy, Catholic and Apostolic.* New York: Paulist Press, 1988.

XX

Special Questions in Ecclesiology

This chapter addresses four "special questions" in contemporary ecclesiology: *authority, papacy, ministry,* and *women in the Church.*

AUTHORITY

General Philosophical and Theological Considerations

The word *authority* is derived from the Latin, *auctor* ("author"), or from *augere* ("to cause to grow, to increase, to enlarge). It may be *de iure* or *de facto* authority. Authority is *de iure* (i.e., by right or by law) when it is attached to, or supported by the power of, an office. A police officer has *de iure* authority. Authority is *de facto* (in fact, i.e., the way it really is) when it is actually obeyed and, therefore, achieves its intended effect. A political columnist who influences governmental policy has *de facto* authority. It is not only possible but ideal that those who legitimately hold and exercise *de iure* authority should also possess *de facto* authority. Thus, the police officer who enforces the law should also be perceived as a law-abiding citizen himself or herself and therefore worthy of one's respect as well as one's obedience. Finally, the word *authority* is also applied to inanimate objects—

e.g., books (especially the Bible), institutions, codes of law, symbols. But if such authority exists, it resides in the person or persons who stand(s) behind these objects.

Ultimately, all authority is rooted in God, who is the *Author* of all that is. "Let every person be subject to the governing authorities; for there is no authority except from God, and those authorities that exist have been instituted by God" (Romans 13:1).

Biblical Notions

Old Testament

God is the Author, or source, of all creation. Our own authority over nature comes from God (Genesis 1:28), as does the authority of parents over children (Leviticus 19:3). Even as society becomes more complex, the same principle holds. It is God who confers on Hazæl the government of Damascus (1 Kings 19:15; 2 Kings 8:9–13), and on Nebuchadnezzar the government of the entire Orient (Jeremiah 27:6).

But the authority entrusted by God is never absolute. The law regulates the exercise of authority by listing the rights of slaves (Exodus 21:1–6,26–27; Deuteronomy 15:12–18; Sirach 33:30). Even the father's authority over his children must look to their good education (Proverbs 23:13–14; Sirach 7:23–24; 30:1). Those holding political power must take care not to deify themselves and thereby blaspheme against the God who alone is absolute Author of all life (Daniel 11:36; 7:3–8,19–25). Such pretensions will meet with destruction 7:11–12,26).

This is true also of authority entrusted to religious leaders, such as Moses, the prophets, and the priests (Exodus 19:6), and of the ancients who assist Moses (Exodus 18:21–26; Numbers 11:24–25). All who hold authority exercise it in the name of God. Conflicts are inevitable—e.g., Saul with Samuel (1 Samuel 13:7–15; 15), Ahab with Elijah (1 Kings 21:17–24), and many kings with their prophets. Religious authority can be abused. The power of the Israelite royalty ends in the tragedy of exile. After the exile, Israel is more openly accepting of God's authority. It is from God that Cyrus and his successors have received the empire (Isaiah 45:1–6). But there is also a new attitude toward *de iure* authority—an attitude which appeals to divine vengeance and, in the end, to revolt when the pagan nation turns persecutor (Judith; 1 Maccabees 2:15–28).

New Testament

Authority (*exousia*) is ascribed also to Jesus (John 17:2; 5:27; Revelation 12:10). He preaches with authority (Mark 1:22 and parallels). He has the power to forgive sins (Matthew 9:6–8; Mark 2:5–10). He is lord of the sabbath (Mark 2:23–28 and parallels). He casts out demons and works cures (Mark 1:27; Matthew 12:27–28; Luke 11:19–20). He interprets the law, as the rabbis did, but with definite authority (Matthew 7:28–29). In Matthew he is depicted as speaking in his own name, unlike the teachers of old: "But I say to you..." (Matthew 5:21–48). Indeed, so "authoritative" is Jesus' manner that he is specifically confronted with the question "By what authority are you doing these things? Who gave you this authority to do them?" (Mark 11:28). The New Testament, therefore, sees the authority of Jesus as something central to his ministry. Here was "something greater than the temple" (Matthew 12:6), greater than Jonah and Solomon (Matthew 12:41–42), and different from the power of "this world" (John 18:36).

After his death and resurrection, the authority of Jesus is perceived anew. He is declared risen and enthroned at the right hand of God (Acts of the Apostles 2:34–36). He is the Lord (Philippians 2:9–11), the son of God "with power" (Romans 1:4). To him "all authority in heaven and on earth" is given (Matthew 28:18). All creation is subject to him (Philippians 2:10), and he will sit upon God's judgment seat (2 Corinthians 5:10) to judge the living and the dead (Acts of the Apostles 10:42). Past, present, and future are under the authority of Christ, in whom all God's promises are affirmed (2 Corinthians 1:20).

On the other hand, Jesus exercises his authority in the manner of a servant (Mark 10:45; Luke 22:27). It is precisely because he did not cling to divinity that he became Lord of all (Philippians 2:5–11). And so he charges his disciples to follow his example: "The kings of the Gentiles lord it over them.... But not so with you; rather the greatest

741

among you must become like the youngest, and the leader like one who serves [*diakonos*]" (Luke 22:25–26; John 13:14–15). His kingdom, after all, is not of this world (John 18:36). Therefore, his disciples are not to be engaged in any struggles for power or preferment among themselves (Matthew 20:20–28; Mark 10:35–45).

The absolute power which Jesus claims in Matthew 28:18 is not transferred to his disciples. Not even Peter receives absolute authority. In Acts of the Apostles 1–12, where his leadership is most clearly portrayed, decisions are made by "the Twelve" or "the apostles" or "the church," and not by Peter. His action in Acts of the Apostles 10 is reviewed by "the circumcised believers" (11:1–18). His devious behavior at Antioch elicits an open rebuke from Paul (Galatians 2:11–14). Nor are the apostles the sole participants in Jesus' authority. There are also prophets, teachers, wonder-workers, evangelists, presbyters, and others (1 Corinthians 12:28; Ephesians 4:11). Paul himself is criticized by some of the Corinthians harshly and unjustly. He responds to the criticisms with warmth, and never suggests that he is above criticism because of his status.

The Spirit is, in fact, given to the whole Church and not exclusively to the leaders of the Church (1 Corinthians 12:1–28; Romans 12:3–8). There is a diversity of gifts and charisms, and all must work together as one for the good of the whole. The power which Christian authority has is grounded in the Holy Spirit, and the Holy Spirit is available to all. Indeed, no one can even profess that Jesus is Lord except in the Holy Spirit (1 Corinthians 12:3). Therefore, authority in the Church is always of a unique kind, not simply another form of standard social or political authority. It is a power existing within the Body of Christ, not just within another human organization. Authority as a function of the Body of Christ is a new concept of authority, just as the Body of Christ is a new concept of society. Authority is an operation of the Holy Spirit, but it is only one operation.

And what specifically of *teaching authority?* "Teacher" was a common category, which applied even to the Scribes. Teaching involved commentary on the Sacred Scriptures (i.e., the Old Testament), but the texts were accommodated to whatever point a teacher wanted to make. Jesus himself was a teacher, and was so regarded. He was preoccupied with proclaiming the reign of God, but his teaching filled out his preaching and explained the nature of the Kingdom and its demands. The people were amazed by Jesus' teaching because, unlike the Scribes, he taught with authority.

On the other hand, the entire New Testament conceives the Gospel as a *way of life*. Only in Matthew are the Apostles *commissioned* to teach, which helps explain why interpreters refer to Matthew as the most Jewish of the Gospels. The Apostles did teach, however. The object of their teaching was Christ (Acts of the Apostles 5:42), the word of the Lord (15:35), the word of God (18:11). In Colossians the object is the person and the mission of Christ; in 2 Thessalonians it is the Second Coming of Christ. When teaching is enumerated among the gifts, it is listed after revelation, knowledge, and prophecy (1 Corinthians 14:6).

At Antioch there were prophets and teachers (Acts of the Apostles 13:1). Teachers are listed with other officers of the Church (Romans 12:7; 1 Corinthians 12:28; and Ephesians 4:11). Their function seemed to have been to explain the person and mission of Jesus Christ and the demands of discipleship in light of the Old Testament. The teachers were not an elite group, like the Scribes, nor was teaching limited to certain persons. As the Church grew and its organizational structure became more complex, concerns were expressed about deviations and unsound teaching (1 Timothy 1:3–7; 6:2–5; 2 Timothy 4:3–4; Titus 1:9–14; 3:9). The sure foundation of sound doctrine is the Old Testament (1 Timothy 4:11–16; 2 Timothy 3:14–17).

But in the New Testament, teaching was simply not one of the primary functions of the Church. That distinction belonged to the proclamation of the Gospel, the announcement of the good news of the Kingdom of God. Teaching was an important subsidiary function, done by people whom today we would call theologians and religious educators. It was the explanation of the Gospel; it was not the Gospel itself. The teaching was not the word which saves. Just as proclamation and teaching are not the same, neither are faith and doctrine. Teaching interprets faith; it is not itself faith. (See again the discussion of teaching authority in chapter 2.)

Postbiblical Developments

Postapostolic Period to the Third Century

The insistence upon authority is strong in Clement of Rome, Ignatius of Antioch, Irenæus, and Cyprian. They, and others at this time, link its religious and spiritual significance with its juridical status, i.e., its status as authority of presiding over a community and regulating its life. Clement writes to correct the church of Corinth in which presbyters responsible for church government have been deposed by a faction of young upstarts. His letter, in stressing traditional authority, offers the first evidence of a joining together of the memories of Peter and Paul. The letter also sets forth the idea of a succession of authority: from God to Christ to the Apostles to the bishops and the deacons and then to their successors. Ignatius's assertions, in fact, are so vigorous in this regard that Protestant critics formerly doubted the authenticity of his letters, so outrageously "Catholic" were they. By being subject to their bishop, he wrote, the Magnesians or the Trallians are subject to God or to Jesus Christ (*Magnesians* III,1–2; *Trallians* II,1). Irenæus, in his fight against Gnosticism, insisted on the primacy of the bishops' teaching as a sure guide to Christian truth, while Clement of Alexandria and Origen argued that the teachers are, in a way, part of the apostolic succession and that the Church need not look only to the hierarchical magisterium for pure apostolic doctrine. Tertullian (d. 225), in fact, tended to reduce the role of bishops to a purely disciplinary function.

In the next century (and into the fourth) the onslaught of new heresies solidified the magisterial standing of the bishops. Indeed, most of the principal theologians were themselves bishops. There is not only a bishop of Rome concerned about unity, Victor I (d. 198), but also an important bishop in Africa, Cyprian, who insisted, "The bishop is in the Church, and the Church in the bishop."

But the Church is always the whole community, and not just the hierarchy. "I have made it a rule," Cyprian writes elsewhere, "ever since the beginning of my episcopate, to make no decision merely on the strength of my own personal opinion without consulting you [the priests and the deacons] and without the approbation of the people" (*Letters* 14:4). In fact, the whole Church community took part in the election of bishops and the choice of ministers. Even though the early Church already possessed a firm canonical structure, it also wanted to be ready for any movement prompted by the Holy Spirit. And so the intervention of the laity was welcomed as a matter of principle. But the Church also regarded the bishop as possessed of the gifts of the Spirit in a preeminent way. *It was because of the apparent presence of these gifts that one was chosen a bishop in the first place.*

Fourth to Eleventh Centuries

With the *Edict of Constantine* (313) the situation changed markedly. Bishops and presbyters, especially in large urban dioceses, were now invested with civil authority and accorded a status similar to that of state officials. (Centuries later, bishops of dioceses which had been isolated originally in missionary areas where the Germanic tribes had been evangelized, little by little became prince-bishops.) Monasticism developed, as pointed out in chapter 17, partly in reaction to this new worldly favor. In monasticism it was possible for a charismatic or spiritual authority to continue to exist, and monastic leaders came to enjoy a kind of independent authority in the Church over the ordinary hierarchical authority. This was especially true in the East. From the beginning of the eighth century, and as a result of the Monothelite controversy and the iconoclast crisis during which the monks became the defenders of orthodoxy, there was a real transfer of spiritual direction and of the exercise of ecclesiastical authority from the hierarchical priesthood to the monks. It was clear that they were truly men of God. A similar, though less pronounced, development occurred in the West, where saints and abbots developed their own spheres of influence.

This is not to say that there was a fundamental opposition between monastic and hierarchical authority at that time. Many of the bishops were, or had been, monks, or at least men trained in monasteries—e.g., Basil, John Chrysostom, Augustine, Martin, Patrick, Isidore of Seville, Gregory the Great. From St. Augustine of Canterbury's time (d. 604 or 605) until the twelfth century, all archbishops of Canterbury were monks. The connection between the episcopal ministry and the monastic ideal was also evident in the oldest sections of the Latin ritual of ordination, which state the

745

duties, not the powers, of bishops—e.g., assiduous study of Sacred Scripture, prayer, fasting, hospitality, almsgiving, listening, edification of the people by word and through the liturgy. The bishop was to represent the moral ideal of authority, for *genuine authority is moral authority*.

The Church was perceived as more than a juridical organization with rules, regulations, and officials to administer them. It was more fundamentally a body of men and women praying, fasting, doing penance, asking for grace, engaging in spiritual combat to become more like Christ. It was important, therefore, that the bishop and indeed the pope be themselves credible examples of Christian existence. "*Vobis sum episcopus, vobiscum Christianus*" ("For you I am a bishop; with you I am a Christian"), St. Augustine of Hippo wrote (*Sermon* 340:1). It is out of this same period (fourth and fifth centuries) that the celebrated formula emerged: *Qui præfuturus est omnibus, ab omnibus eligatur* ("He who would be the head of all should be chosen by all"). The formula is that of Pope Celestine I (d. 432), and it occurs again in the councils of Orleans (549) and Paris (557) and in the *Decretals of Gratian* (c. 1140).

The Middle Ages

The reform of the Church begun by Pope Leo IX (d. 1054) and continued by Gregory VII (d. 1081) represents a turning point in the history of authority. The reform was aimed not only at the renewal of the Church but also at its liberation from the control of lay princes and other political figures. To do this, Gregory claimed for the Church the completely autonomous and sovereign system of rights proper to a self-contained, spiritual society, and an authority which covered not only the whole Church but kings and their kingdoms as well. To support his argument Gregory ordered the Church's scholars and jurists to comb the archives and uncover every scrap of precedent for his view. Canon law was born, and the foundation was laid for the kind of exaggerated papal claims to be made by Innocent III (d. 1216) and Boniface VIII (d. 1303).

Even the episcopal title *Vicar of Christ*, later claimed by the emperor and eventually by the pope alone (supplanting the more traditional *Vicar of Peter*), was transformed from an essentially *sacramental* image (Christ and the saints are working through this servant) to a largely *juridical* one (the pope possesses powers given him by Christ). And so a *legalism* was introduced, and it radically changed the originally spiritual notion that obedience to God's representative is obedience to God. The presence of grace in the representative was no longer crucial. Episcopal authority was no longer *moral* authority but *jurisdiction*, and it was bestowed even before the sacrament was conferred. The bestowal of grace was secondary. And so the idea developed that a priest "governs" his parish, bishops "govern" their dioceses and "judge" in all matters, and the pope rules as a "sovereign" — indeed, is the "Sovereign Pontiff."

A countermovement developed. Charges were now hurled at the Church's leaders, especially from the spiritual movements of the twelfth century, and later from Franciscanism and from the Hussite movement. Each was saying in effect that the Church, and the pope in particular, had obscured the Gospel with pomp, that it was becoming more the Church of Constantine than of the Apostles. "All this, as well as the claims to prestige and riches, goes back to Constantine, not to Peter," St. Bernard (d. 1153) wrote to Pope Eugenius III (d. 1153).

The new juridicism notwithstanding, Catholic theology preserved many elements of the ancient ecclesiology, at least until the death of the two greatest doctors of the thirteenth century, Thomas and Bonaventure. In Thomas, for example, the idea of the Church as the congregation of the faithful is still very much alive. Authority is not merely juridical. It is linked with spiritual gifts and with the achievement of the perfection of Christian charity. Matthew 16:19 is interpreted as referring principally to Peter's confession of faith. The theology of the new law as formulated in the *Summa Theologiæ* I-II, q. 106, is completely evangelical. It is a law of love and service, not of fear and slavishness.

In the later Middle Ages, ecumenical councils such as Constance (1414–1418) and general councils such as Basle (1431–1439) included theologians in their ranks, but with the Protestant Reformation the juridical and clerical character of councils and of the magisterium generally was underscored. Teaching became less a matter of insight and enlightenment and more a matter of the imposition of approved formulae. The Church divided according to those who taught (and presumably no longer had to learn) and those who learned (and presumably had nothing to do with teaching). That hard and fast distinction between the teaching Church (*ecclesia docens*) and the learning Church (*ecclesia discens*) has only recently begun to disappear.

"It is a fact," Yves Congar has pointed out, "that the authority of prelates of every degree was never insisted on so much as in the fourteenth and fifteenth centuries. The thunderclap of 31 October 1517 [the day Luther posted his 95 theses against indulgences on the door of the church at Wittenberg] was only the first of a violent storm" (in *Problems of Authority*, John M. Todd, ed., p. 143).

The Council of Trent to the Twentieth Century

The Reformation questioned authority not only in its corrupted forms but in principle. In reaction the Council of Trent (1545–1547, 1551–1552, 1562–1563) insisted even more strongly on the authority of the hierarchy, so much so that the ecclesiology which developed after Trent was more akin to a *hierarchology*. The pope was now regarded as a "universal bishop." Each Catholic was directly under the pope and subservient to him, even more than to the individual Catholic's own bishop. The shift of all significant power to Rome occurred at an accelerated pace. Ecclesiastical authority became increasingly centralized. And people were asked to obey because of the status and office of the legislator, not because he and his decrees were obviously prompted by the Spirit. The definition of papal primacy at Vatican I was the culmination of this development.

This understanding of authority prevailed until the Second Vatican Council. Indeed, it could be argued that the so-called Pian popes (Pius IX, Pius X, Pius XI, and Pius XII) were among the most administratively powerful in all of church history. Pope Pius XII's *Humani Generis* (1950), for example, insisted that even papal encyclicals, although they do not engage the fullness of the pope's teaching authority, demand both external and internal assent. "And when the Roman Pontiffs carefully pronounce on some subject which has hitherto been controverted, it must be clear to everybody that, in the

748

mind and intention of the Pontiffs concerned, this subject can no longer be regarded as a matter of free debate among theologians."

Vatican II

Although the Second Vatican Council continued to teach that the pope and the bishops exercise supreme authority over the Church, it says that this authority is always to be exercised as a service and in a collegial manner. Indeed, several conciliar documents speak approvingly of *episcopal conferences* and of their important pastoral function. (For a thorough discussion of these functions, including that of teaching, see *The Nature and Future of Episcopal Conferences*, Hervé Legrand, et al., eds., Washington, D.C.: The Catholic University of America Press, 1988, and *Episcopal Conferences: Historical, Canonical, and Theological Studies*, Thomas J. Reese, ed., Washington, D.C.: Georgetown University Press, 1989.) Furthermore, authority is to be used only for the edification ("building up") of their flocks (*Dogmatic Constitution on the Church*, n. 27). Pastors, too, are not intended to shoulder alone the whole saving mission of the Church. They must collaborate with their brothers and sisters, including the laity, that all might work together as one for the good of the whole (n. 30). The principle of authority-as-service is reaffirmed in other conciliar documents as well: in the *Decree on the Bishops' Pastoral Office in the Church*, the *Decree on the Ministry and Life of Priests*, and the *Decree on the Appropriate Renewal of the Religious Life*.

Ecumenical Developments

Postconciliar ecumenical statements on the question of authority have come from the Anglican–Roman Catholic International Commission and the Lutheran–Catholic Dialogue in the United States. The Anglican–Roman Catholic document is entitled "An Agreed Statement on Authority in the Church" and is also known as *The Venice Statement* (Washington, D.C.: United States Catholic Conference, 1977). The authority with which it is concerned is the authority of Christ, which is activated by the Holy Spirit to create community with God and with all persons. Of interest is the response to *The Venice Statement* by the Anglican–Roman Catholic Consultation in the

749

U.S.A., which criticized their international counterparts for concentrating too much on the authority of the pope and bishops and too little on the authority of the whole Church, laity and clergy alike. (See "Authority in the Church: Vital Ecumenical Issue," *Origins* 7/30, January 12, 1978, pp. 474–76.)

The Lutheran–Catholic Dialogue touched upon the question of the teaching authority of the Church in connection with its study of papal infallibility. All Christian authority is rooted in Christ and the Gospel, which is a word of power from God (Romans 1:16). It is proclaimed by various witnesses who share in the authority of Christ.

The Church and Authority

All authority has its origin in God, who alone is the Author of all life. God's authority is at once creative and unitive. Jesus Christ's mission was to re-create and reunite what had been wounded by sin. He proclaimed the good news that the power (authority) of re-creation and reunion was about to be released anew in the Holy Spirit and that it would eventually bring all things together at the end in the Kingdom of God.

The Church shares in the authority of Christ and in the power of the Holy Spirit. Its authority is for the same purpose: to proclaim the Gospel of the Kingdom of God and to manifest and release the power of the Holy Spirit to re-create and reunite the whole human community. The Church is itself the sacrament of community.

Because the Church is the whole People of God, authority resides in the community as a whole, although it is exercised in various ways, by various persons, for the good of the whole. Wherever and whenever authority is exercised, it is exercised in the manner of Jesus, who was among us as one who serves (Mark 10:45). Authority that is detached from holiness is not real Christian authority. Authority which seeks to coerce places itself above the grace of the Holy Spirit, and so is not real Christian authority either. Since the Church comes into being through the free response of individuals to the call of God in Jesus Christ by the grace of the Holy Spirit, authority should be exercised only in a way that respects the freedom of the act of faith and the voluntary character of membership in the Church (see again Vatican II's *Declaration on Religious Freedom*).

750

· PAPACY

The papacy is a matter of central importance in the Catholic tradition. Belief in the Petrine ministry as exercised by the Bishop of Rome distinguishes Catholicism from all of the other great Christian traditions. The two principal doctrines pertaining to the Petrine office concern the primacy of the pope over the whole Church and the gift of infallibility which he enjoys when he solemnly speaks as earthly head of the Church on matters of faith and morals.

Consideration of both these doctrinal issues follows. The reader who wishes to press beyond the schematic presentations of this section of the chapter is advised to consult the more detailed material in the following volumes: *Papal Primacy and the Universal Church, Lutherans and Catholics in Dialogue V*, Paul Empie and T. Austin Murphy, eds. (Minneapolis: Augsburg Publishing House, 1974); *Peter in the New Testament*, Raymond E. Brown, Karl P. Donfried, John Reumann, eds. (Minneapolis: Augsburg Publishing House, 1973); "Teaching Authority and Infallibility in the Church," *Theological Studies* 40 (March 1979), 113–66; J.-M. R. Tillard, *The Bishop of Rome* (Wilmington, Del.: Michael Glazier, 1983); Patrick Granfield, *The Limits of the Papacy: Authority and Autonomy in the Church* (New York: Crossroad, 1987); and Robert B. Eno, *The Rise of the Papacy* (Wilmington, Del.: Michael Glazier, 1990).

Papal Primacy

The Issue

The Church is the sacrament of the unity which God wills for all humankind in Christ through the Holy Spirit. But the fact is that the Church is divided. There are Catholic Christians and Lutheran Christians and Presbyterian Christians and Pentecostal Christians, and so forth. Ironically, a particular ministry within the Catholic Church which exists precisely for the purpose of symbolizing and helping to realize the unity of the whole Church is also a great obstacle to that unity. Recent ecumenical discussions of the papacy, therefore, are of highest importance. Separated Christians already embrace and accept realities which serve the unity of the Church as a whole:

751

Baptism, the Sacred Scriptures, liturgies, creeds, confessions of faith, ecumenical councils.

The Lutheran–Catholic Dialogue relates these various means of unifying the Church to the "Petrine function," i.e., a particular form of ministry exercised by a person, officeholder, or local church with reference to the Church as a whole. This Petrine function "serves to promote or preserve the oneness of the church by symbolizing unity, and by facilitating communication, mutual assistance or correction, and collaboration in the church's mission" (*Papal Primacy*, n. 4, p. 12). The function is called Petrine because that is the kind of role the apostle Peter fulfilled among Jesus' original disciples. Among the companions of Jesus, Peter is given the greatest prominence in the New Testament accounts of the Church's origins. He is spoken of in relation to the founding of the Church (Matthew 16:18), strengthening the brethren (Luke 22:32), and feeding the sheep of Christ (John 21:15–17). He is a prominent figure in some of the Pauline letters, in the Acts of the Apostles, and in two of the so-called Catholic Epistles (1 and 2 Peter)—all of which suggests that he was associated with a wide-ranging ministry. The subsequent history of the Church portrayed him as a pastor of the universal Church. Indeed, "the single most notable representative of this [Petrine] Ministry toward the church universal...has been the bishop of Rome" (n. 5, p. 12).

But at least three areas of controversy have marked the discussion of the ministry of the Bishop of Rome: historical, theological, and canonical. Catholics and other Christians have differed about the meaning and implications of Peter's role in the New Testament Church. *Historically*, Catholics have insisted that it was a function of leadership conferred by Jesus himself and that it has been passed down through the centuries, while non-Catholic Christians have tended to minimize the significance of Peter in the New Testament and have clearly rejected the notion of a succession in pastoral authority from Peter to the bishops of Rome. *Theologically*, Catholics have argued that the papacy is of divine law, i.e., that it exists by the will of Christ, while non-Catholic Christians have insisted that it is of human origin only. *Canonically*, Catholics have looked upon the legal power of the pope as supreme, full, ordinary, and immediate (Vatican I), i.e., not subject to any higher human jurisdiction, while other

Christians have viewed such claims as leading to intolerable abuses of power.

History

New Testament

Peter was a figure of central importance among the disciples of the Lord. He was the first called, served as spokesman for the other Apostles, and may have been the first to whom the Lord appeared after the resurrection (that is the tradition of Paul and Luke, but Mary Magdalene, not Peter, is the primary witness in the tradition of Matthew, John, and the Marcan appendix). Nevertheless, the terms *primacy* and *jurisdiction* are probably best avoided when describing Peter's role in the New Testament. They are postbiblical, indeed canonical, terms.

As noted in chapter 16, the Church of the New Testament is both the church in and of a particular place (e.g., Corinth, Antioch, Jerusalem) and the Church universal (the Body of Christ, as in Ephesians). Although it is not unmistakably clear how Peter relates to the Church universal, it *is* sufficiently clear that he *does* relate to the Church universal in certain significant ways. He is listed first among the Twelve (Mark 3:16–19; Matthew 10:1–4; Luke 6:12–16) and is frequently their spokesman (Mark 8:29; Matthew 18:21; Luke 12:41; John 6:67–69); he is the first apostolic witness of the risen Jesus (1 Corinthians 15:5; Luke 24:34); he is prominent in the original Jerusalem community and is well known to many other churches (Acts of the Apostles 1:15–26; 2:14–40; 3:1–26; 4:8; 5:1–11,29; 8:18–25; 9:32–43; 10:5; 12:17; 1 Peter 2:11; 5:13). His activities after the Council of Jerusalem are not reported, but there is increasing agreement that Peter did go to Rome and was martyred there. Whether he actually served the church of Rome as bishop cannot be known through evidence at hand. And from the New Testament record *alone*, we have no basis for positing a line of succession from Peter through subsequent bishops of Rome.

For the Catholic tradition, the classic primacy texts are Matthew 16:13–19; Luke 22:31–32; John 21:15–19. The fact that Jesus' naming of Peter as the rock occurs in different contexts in the three Gospels does raise a question about the original setting of the incident. We cannot be sure whether this naming occurred during Jesus' ministry or after the resurrection, with subsequent "retrojection" into the accounts of Jesus' earthly ministry. As for the conferral of the power of the *keys,* this suggests an imposing measure of authority, given the symbolism of the keys. And yet special authority *over others* is not clearly attested. Rather, in the Acts of the Apostles Peter is presented as consulting with the Apostles and even being sent by them (8:14). He and John act almost as a team (3:1–11; 4:1–22; 8:14).

On the other hand, there is a discernible "trajectory" of images relating to Peter and his ministry. He is portrayed as the fisherman (Luke 5:10; John 21:1–14), as the shepherd of the sheep of Christ (John 21:15–17), as an elder who addresses other elders (1 Peter 5:1), as proclaimer of faith in Jesus the Son of God (Matthew 16:16–17), as receiver of a special revelation (Acts of the Apostles 1:9–16), as one who can correct others for doctrinal misunderstanding (2 Peter 3:15–16), and as the rock on which the Church is to be built (Matthew 16:18).

The question, therefore, to be posed on the basis of an investigation of the New Testament is whether the subsequent, postbiblical development of the Petrine office is, in fact, consistent with the thrust of the New Testament. The Catholic Church says "Yes." Some other Christian churches are beginning to say "Perhaps."

Second Century to Middle Ages

The trajectory of biblical images of Peter did continue in the life of the early Church, and those images were enriched by additional ones: missionary preacher, great visionary, destroyer of heretics, receiver of the new law, gatekeeper of heaven, helmsman of the ship of the Church, coteacher and comartyr with Paul. At the same time, the early Church was in the process of accommodating itself to the culture of the Græco-Roman world, particularly the patterns of organization and administration prevailing in areas of its missionary activity. The Church adopted the organizational grid of the Roman Empire: localities, dioceses, provinces. It also identified its own center with the empire's, Rome. Moreover, there was attached to this city the tradition that Peter had founded the church there and that he and Paul were buried there.

In the controversy with Gnosticism, defenders of orthodoxy appealed to the faith of episcopal sees founded by the Apostles, and especially to the faith of the Roman church which was so closely associated with Peter and Paul alike. During the first five centuries the church of Rome gradually assumed preeminence among the churches. It intervened in the life of distant churches, took sides in theological controversies, was consulted by other bishops on doctrinal and moral questions, and sent delegates to distant councils. The church of Rome came to be regarded as a kind of final or supreme court of appeal as well as focus of unity for the worldwide communion of churches. The correlation between Peter and the bishop of Rome became fully explicit in the term of Pope Leo I (d. 461), who insisted that Peter continue to speak to the whole Church through the bishop of Rome. (Indeed, it was from the end of the fourth century that the most traditional papal title, *Vicar of Peter*, became commonly accepted by popes themselves.) It was also Leo who decisively intervened in the great Christological controversies and whose letter to Flavian of Constantinople in 449 provided the basis for the definitive formulation of faith two years later at the Council of Chalcedon (see chapter 13).

The Middle Ages

In order to protect the Church at large and the papacy in particular against continuing encroachments by lay powers, Gregory VII and Innocent III, relying on such documents as the *False Decretals* of Pseudo-Isidore (c. 847–852) claimed monarchical status for their office, in accordance with contemporary secular models of government. Boniface VIII carried the claim even further, insisting on absolute power over the whole world, temporal as well as religious. (Pope Gelasius I [d. 496] had originally opened the way to the theology of the "two powers.")

After the East-West Schism, begun in the late eleventh century and finalized by the turn of the thirteenth century, the shape of the papacy changed considerably. Only one patriarchate remained in the West, that of the pope, and his patriarchal leadership came to be entirely absorbed by the power of the papacy. Western Christianity became what some Orthodox describe as a papal church, that is, a church in which the members' relation to the see of Rome is so predominant that it swallows up the relation to the local bishop. The traditional vision of the Church of God as a "communion of local churches" was in danger of being entirely absorbed into the vision of a "universal Church under a universal primate." It was also during this period (the pontificate of Eugene III [1145–1153]) when title *Vicar of Christ*, originally an episcopal title, became identified exclusively with the Bishop of Rome. Innocent III (1198–1216) appealed to the title as the basis of his universal power, even over temporal authorities. The more traditional title (since the end of the fourth century) had been *Vicar of Peter.*

In the high Middle Ages such prominent theologians as Thomas and Bonaventure stressed the powers of the Roman see, and over against both Conciliarism and Protestantism Scholastic theologians and canonists reaffirmed the monarchical structure of ecclesiastical government. This view received official endorsement in the Council of Florence's *Decree of Union for the Greek and Latin Churches* (1439) in terms very much like those of Vatican I in the nineteenth century.

Post-Tridentine Developments to the Twentieth Century

Great defenders of papal authority like Robert Bellarmine (d. 1621) diffused the theory that the title *Vicar of Peter* was incorrect and that the Bishop of Rome has to be called *Vicar of Christ*, because the pope acts in the place of Christ, with all the power that corresponds with this function. This abiding inclination of the official theologians and canonists to assert papal prerogatives was accentuated by the rise of nationalism (e.g., Gallicanism), the intellectual challenges of the Enlightenment, and the new liberalism of the nineteenth century. Vatican I (1869–1870) was the culmination of this development, although its teachings on the papacy appear moderate in comparison with some of the medieval and Counter-Reformation views.

In its *Dogmatic Constitution on the Church of Christ* (*Pastor Aeternus*, "Eternal Pastor"), the council declared that "the primacy of jurisdiction over the whole Church was immediately and directly promised to and conferred upon the blessed apostle Peter by Christ the Lord."

The primacy is passed on to whoever "succeeds Peter in this Chair, according to the institution of Christ Himself...." This power is full and supreme over the whole Church not only in matters that pertain to faith and morals but also in matters that pertain to the discipline and government of the Church throughout the whole world. This power is ordinary and immediate over each and every church and over each and every shepherd and faithful.

However, the council also stressed the fact that the Bishop of Rome is not the bishop of any other local church. Indeed, the subsequent correspondence between Pius IX and the German bishops (1875), provoked by the invention of the German Chancellor Bismarck, underscored this point very clearly. The papacy is not an absolute monarchy under whom the bishops are simply vassals of the pope.

Vatican I's teaching was reiterated by Pope Leo XIII in his encyclical *Satis Cognitum* (1896), in the Holy Office's decree *Lamentabili* under Pius X (1907), in Pius XII's *Mystici Corporis* (1943), in the Holy Office's letter to Cardinal Cushing on the Leonard Feeney case (1949), and in Pius XII's *Humani Generis* (1950).

Vatican II

With the Second Vatican Council the papacy is viewed in increasingly communal and collegial terms. The pope exercises supreme authority over the Church, but the bishops also share in that authority. To be sure, the supreme authority vested in the college of bishops cannot be exercised without the consent of the pope. "This college, insofar as it is composed of many, expresses the variety and universality of the People of God, but insofar as it is assembled under one head, it expresses the unity of the flock of Christ" (*Dogmatic Constitution on the Church*, n. 22). The pope still has "full, supreme, and universal power over the Church," but the bishops are no longer perceived as simply the pope's vicars or delegates. They receive from the Lord "the mission to teach all nations and to preach the gospel to every creature" (n. 24). They govern their diocese not as "vicars of the Roman Pontiff, for they exercise an authority which is proper to them..." (n. 27).

Finally, whatever authority the pope and the bishops enjoy, it is always to be exercised within a communion of local churches through the faithful preaching of the Gospel, the administration of the sacraments, and loving service. They collaborate thereby in the work of the Holy Spirit, which is the work of unity: in the confession of faith, in the common celebration of divine worship, and in the loving harmony of the family of God (*Decree on Ecumenism*, n. 2). Their teaching authority, too, is subordinate to a higher principle. "This teaching office is not above the word of God, but serves it..." (*Dogmatic Constitution on Divine Revelation*, n. 10).

Ecumenical Statements

In addition to the Lutheran–Catholic Dialogue on the issue of papal primacy (mentioned above), the Orthodox/Roman Catholic Consultation in the United States released a statement on primacy and conciliarity in 1989, in which it was agreed that the roles of primacy and of synods are "mutually dependent and mutually limiting." Synods are "the faithful community's chief expression of the 'care of all the churches,' which is central to every bishop's pastoral responsibility." (See *Origins* 19/29 [December 21, 1989], pp. 469, 471–72.)

The Church and Papal Primacy

The Church is at once local and universal. The Body of Christ truly exists in particular locales (*Dogmatic Constitution on the Church*, n. 26) and is also the Church universal. It is indeed a *communion* of churches. Insofar as the Church is a communion of churches, the papal office serves the unity of the Church as "the perpetual and visible source of and foundation of the unity of the bishops and of the multitude of the faithful" (n. 23). The pope's primacy is a primacy of service, in service of unity. Insofar as the Church is a communion of *churches*, the papal office must respect the legitimate diversity of these churches (n. 23), a collegial mode of decision-making (n. 23), and the time-honored Catholic social principle of subsidiarity, which holds that nothing is to be done by a higher group, agency, or level of authority that can be done better or as well by a lower group, agency, or level of authority. (See J.-M. R. Tillard, *Church of Churches: The*

Ecclesiology of Communion, Collegeville, Minn.: Liturgical Press, 1992, chap. 4.)

The Church, whether local or universal, is the People of God. The Spirit is given to all. All share in principle in the total mission of the Church: prophetic, priestly, and kingly. The hierarchy, including the pope, exists to serve the rest of the Church in the exercise of that Spirit-rooted mission. The primacy is precisely for that purpose.

Papal Infallibility

The Issue

Infallibility literally means "immunity from error." In theological terms it is a charism of the Holy Spirit which protects the Church from error when it solemnly defines a matter of faith or morals. It is a *negative* gift; i.e., it guarantees that a particular teaching is *not* wrong. Infallibility does not ensure that a particular teaching is an *adequate* expression of a truth of faith or morals or even an *appropriate* formulation of that truth. *Papal infallibility* is a dimension of the *Church's* infallibility, not vice versa. The pope's infallibility is the same infallibility as that "with which the divine Redeemer willed His Church to be endowed" (*Dogmatic Constitution on the Church*, n. 25).

Papal *infallibility* is conceptually distinct from papal *primacy*. There is no reason in principle why the pope would have to possess the charism of infallibility in order to function as the chief shepherd of the Church. Conversely, infallibility could in principle be vested in persons who do not hold the supreme pastoral office in the Church. In other words, primacy of itself does not require infallibility, nor does infallibility necessarily presume primacy. The Catholic tradition, however, does insist on the correlation of the two terms: *primacy* and *infallibility*. They do, *in fact*, require one another.

Papal infallibility is related to several larger questions: the authority of the Gospel and of the Church, the indefectibility of the Church, and the certitude of Christian faith. Between the First Vatican Council, which defined papal infallibility, and the Second Vatican Council, which placed it in its wider context, the issue of papal infallibility was often discussed in very narrow terms. In the popular mind and even in some of the theology textbooks it was thought that all papal statements were somehow protected by infallibility. Consequently, the faithful Catholic had to receive all papal pronouncements "as if" they were infallible. Encyclicals were sometimes interpreted as infallibly conveying true doctrine even when they did not meet the specific conditions laid down by Vatican I for infallible definitions. Pope Pius XII's *Humani Generis* (1950) may have unintentionally given some currency to this view by stressing the definitive character of papal teaching even in encyclicals. But this has not been the exclusive tendency of the conservative wing of the Church alone. Hans Küng's *Infallible? An Inquiry* (New York: Doubleday, 1971) argued that the birth control encyclical *Humanæ Vitæ* (1968) was infallible by traditional standards, but then he attacked the dogma of infallibility because the encyclical's teaching on birth control was, for Küng, obviously wrong (p. 71).

The issue of infallibility is also affected by a new understanding of authority abroad in the world because of a variety of factors, some of which were discussed earlier in chapters 3 and 6. Simply stated, the modern world is a world of pluralism, diversity, and the necessity of choice. Sociologist Peter Berger, for example, describes modern consciousness as living under the impact of this need to make our own choices (the word *heresy* is derived from a Greek word meaning "a choice"). He calls this modern phenomenon *The Heretical Imperative* (New York: Doubleday, 1979). We are no longer governed by fate, he argues, nor do we defer automatically to higher authority.

What possible meaning can the claim of immunity from error have in such a world and in light of modern experience? Does it make sense any longer for the Church to press the point that it and its official representatives (the pope, an ecumenical council, the body of bishops in union with the pope) are, in fact, guaranteed this charism of immunity from error when solemnly teaching about the faith and its moral demands? These are the kinds of questions which theologians have to address, even as they remain essentially faithful to the definitive teaching of the Church.

History

New Testament

The basis for our modern concept of infallibility is linked with such New Testament concepts as the authority of Jesus in proclaiming the Kingdom of God, the transmission of that authority in some measure to the Apostles, the authority of the Gospel itself, the authority of various witnesses to the Gospel ("Whoever listens to you listens to me"—Luke 10:16), the concern for sound doctrine, especially in the Pastoral Epistles, and the conviction that the Spirit has been given to the Church as a guide to all truth (John 16:13). This is not to suggest, of course, that our modern concept of infallibility appears precisely as such in the New Testament.

Postbiblical Developments

A complete history of the development of the notion of infallibility has yet to be written, even though important special studies are now available (e.g., Brian Tierney, *Origins of Papal Infallibility*, Leiden: Brill, 1972). What is clear is that the concern for the faithful transmission of the Gospel did not diminish after the New Testament period. In the late-second-century struggle against Gnosticism, the Fathers of the Church linked the reliable handing on of the apostolic teaching with the faith of the episcopal sees founded by the Apostles themselves. By the middle of the third century, special importance was being accorded the faith of the church of Rome, which by tradition was regarded as having been founded by Peter himself. Some Roman emperors included the faith of the bishop of Rome in the official norm of orthodoxy, and the biblical image of the Church "without spot or wrinkle" (Ephesians 5:27) began to be applied to the church of Rome. Rome became *the* apostolic see. According to the *Formula of Pope Hormisdas* (d. 523), written in the year 515, "the catholic religion has always been preserved immaculate" in Rome. This conviction persisted into the Middle Ages and found expression in such influential documents as the Pseudo-Isidorian *Decretals*, in statements by various popes and theologians, and in assorted collections of canon law.

But this postbiblical development was neither unilateral nor unequivocal. There were challenges to such claims both in the East and

761

the West. Eastern Christians regarded Rome as only one of several apostolic sees to which protection of the faith had been entrusted. But the faithfulness of such popes as Liberius (d. 366), Vigilius (d. 555), and Honorius (d. 638) was questioned. Certain Western metropolitans (archbishops) even in the early Middle Ages were sometimes wont to contradict papal decisions. Prophetic voices were raised from the eleventh century on—almost five hundred years before the Protestant Reformation—against the style and practice of the papal ministry. Moreover, it was readily admitted by some theologians and canonists that individual popes in the past had been in error on specific points of doctrine, and some classical canonists have reckoned with the possibility that the pope could deviate from the faith (see Brian Tierney, *Foundations of Conciliar Theory*, Cambridge: Cambridge University Press, 1955, pp. 57–67).

Nonetheless, the formula "Rome has never erred" survived, and in the course of time it came to be understood as meaning that Rome "cannot" err. Roman bishops from the fourth century on regarded their confirmation of conciliar actions as an indispensable sign of authoritative teaching, even though their own doctrinal decisions needed to be accepted by secular authorities, councils, and fellow bishops in order to be enforced. But with the growing practice of making appeals to Rome, the bishop of Rome came to be regarded as the court of final appeal, the last word. The legal maxim "The first see is judged by no one" appeared initially in the sixth century and was later interpreted to mean that the pope's teaching authority is supreme. This was restated in the era of the Gregorian Reform, and Thomas Aquinas would describe the pope as one whose judgments in matters of faith must be followed because he represents the universal Church which "cannot err" (*Quodlibet* IX, q. 7, a. 16).

According to Brian Tierney's study (to which reference was made above), the term *infallibility* was first applied to the pope's teaching authority by a fourteenth-century theologian, Guido Terreni (d. 1344). Use of the word was occasioned by a controversy over poverty in the Franciscan order during the late thirteenth and early fourteenth centuries. Advocates of a rigorist position employed "infallibility" to defend the binding authority of statements by earlier popes against the decisions of their successors. Under the impact of the Reformation, the concept of infallibility quickly gained wider theological currency, especially among such Counter-Reformation theologians as Robert Bellarmine (d. 1621), Francisco de Suarez (d. 1617), and Thomas Stapleton (d. 1598). It was appealed to in the condemnations of Jansenism and Gallicanism in the seventeenth and eighteenth centuries and received solemn approbation in the dogma of Vatican I in 1870. The teaching was reaffirmed by Vatican II, but was placed in the larger setting of the infallibility of the whole Church and the collegiality of bishops with the pope.

Ecumenical Convergences

The Lutheran–Catholic Dialogue of 1978 noted, among others, the following points of convergence: (1) The Bible is normative for all of the Church's proclamation and teaching. (2) The apostolic tradition in which the Word of God is transmitted is interpreted with the assistance of creeds, liturgies, confessions, doctrines, structural forms of government, and patterns of devotion and service. (3) The Holy Spirit remains with the Church until the end of time and will not allow it to deviate fundamentally from the truth of the Gospel, from its mission, or from its life of faith (= *indefectibility*). (4) The Church expresses its faith and fulfills its mission especially in the ministry of word and sacrament, supervised and coordinated by specific ministries and structures, including the ministry of bishops and the bishop of Rome. (5) Their ministries include overseeing the Church's proclamation and, when necessary, the reformulation of doctrine in fidelity to Sacred Scripture. (6) Harmony between the teaching of these ministers and the acceptance of that teaching by the faithful constitutes a sign of the fidelity of that teaching to the Gospel. (7) No doctrinal definition, however, adequately expresses the truth of the Gospel, given the inevitable cultural and historical limitations of language and concepts.

The two sides agreed that the differences which still exist between them are perhaps more verbal than substantive. Catholics are now more attentive to the excesses and even abuses of papal authority and are committed to the principle that the Church is the whole People of God, subject always to the Word of God in Sacred Scripture. Lutherans are now more conscious of the intent of the dogma of infallibility, namely, to preserve the Church in fidelity to the Gospel.

763

Thus, "in the new context, each side finds itself compelled to recognize that the other seeks to be faithful to the gospel" (n. 42).

At the Seventh Assembly of the World Council of Churches at Canberra, Australia (1991), it was said by Orthodox and Protestant representatives alike that now it is no longer the presence of the papacy but its absence from the World Council of Churches (except Faith and Order) which is the main problem of the ecumenical movement.

Theological Clarifications

1. Vatican I defined certain conditions for the exercise of the infallibility with which the pope is empowered. He is empowered with infallibility only when he is in the act of defining a doctrine of faith or morals, speaking as head of the Church (*ex cathedra*, "from the chair"), with the clear intention of binding the whole Church.

2. Infallibility is not a personal prerogative of the pope. He is empowered with the charism of infallibility only when he is in the act of defining a dogma of faith. It can be said, without exaggeration, that a pope who never defined a dogma of faith was never infallible. That would apply to such recent popes as John XXIII, Paul VI, John Paul I, and John Paul II. (Contrary to popular belief, the canonization of a saint does not meet Vatican I's conditions for an infallible teaching.)

3. To say that the definitions of the pope are "irreformable by themselves (*ex sese*) and not by reason of the agreement of the Church (*non autem ex consensu ecclesiæ*)" does not mean that the pope is above the Church. That phrase was added to the council's definition in order to exclude the tendency of some Gallicans and Conciliarists to regard approval by the bishops as necessary in order to give infallibility to any papal definition. Thus, the term *consensus* at Vatican I is to be understood in the juridical sense of official approval and not in the more general sense of agreement or acceptance by the Church as a whole, which, according to Bishop Vincenz Gasser (d. 1879), the definition's author and official interpreter, can never be lacking.

4. A similar difficulty arises with the notion of "irreformability." It does not mean that infallible teachings are immune from change. On the contrary, as formulations written in human language, they are

always historically conditioned and therefore subject to revision. According to *Mysterium Ecclesiæ* (Congregation for the Doctrine of the Faith, 1973), doctrinal definitions are affected by the limited context of human knowledge in the situation in which they are framed, by the specific concerns that motivated the definitions, by the changeable conceptions (or thought categories) of a given epoch, and by "the expressive power of the language used at a certain point of time."

5. If there is any reasonable doubt about the Church's or the pope's intention to engage the charism of infallibility, then the definition in question is not to be regarded as infallible. "No doctrine is understood to be infallibly defined unless it is clearly established as such" (*Code of Canon Law*, can. 749, 3).

6. Infallibility does not apply to noninfallible, or nondefinitive, statements—a truism, to be sure. Although the *Dogmatic Constitution on the Church* (n. 25) restates and carries forward Pope Pius XII's teaching in *Humani Generis*, i.e., that Catholics owe "religious allegiance of the will and intellect" even to noninfallible teachings of the pope, it is significant that the council did not reassert the doctrine of *Humani Generis* forbidding further public discussion of matters settled by the pope, even though this doctrine appeared in the preliminary draft of November 10, 1962.

7. Vatican II also made it clear that the infallibility of the pope and bishops must always be related to the faith of the whole Church, that there must always be close, collegial cooperation between pope and bishops in the process of definition, that the assent of the Church can never be wanting to an authentic definition, that the Church is always a pilgrim Church, subject to sin and weakness, that there is a hierarchy of truths in the Christian deposit of faith, and that the doctrine of Vatican II on papal infallibility is not itself the last word on the subject.

The Church and Infallibility

The Church is concerned with the truth of the Gospel, not for its speculative but for its *saving* value. The truth is to be put into action, just as Jesus practiced as well as proclaimed the Kingdom of God. Infallibility is of significance to the Church insofar as the Church is called to proclaim the Gospel faithfully and to be a sign of that Gospel through its unity of both life and faith. Insofar as infallibility attends to the fidelity of the proclamation and the unity of the Church which proclaims the Kingdom of God, it is and will always remain a matter of much theological and pastoral importance. Disengaged from exaggerations of papal authority and placed in the wider context of collegiality and the nature of the Church as the People of God, the dogma of infallibility is much less an ecumenical problem than it once was.

MINISTRY

The Issue

From the time of the Council of Trent, and largely in reaction to Protestantism's stress on the "priesthood of all believers," the Catholic Church tended to restrict the notion of ministry to the ordained (bishops, priests, and deacons) and to those steps taken in preparation for ordination (lector, acolyte, exorcist). But today, especially in the light of the Second Vatican Council and postconciliar pastoral developments, ministry has taken on a broader and richer meaning for Catholics, one no longer restricted to the ordained. (The ordained ministries of bishop, presbyter, and deacon will be given specific treatment in chapter 24, in relation to the sacrament of Holy Order.)

History

No completely satisfactory history of the development of ministry and of ministries yet exists. One may consult Bernard Cooke's *Ministry to Word and Sacraments: History and Theology* (Philadelphia: Fortress Press, 1976), Yves Congar's *Lay People in the Church* (Westminster, Md.: Newman Press, 1965), Edward Schillebeeckx's *The Church with a Human Face: A New and Expanded Theology of Ministry* (New York: Crossroad, 1985), and Kenan B. Osborne's *Ministry: Lay Ministry in the Roman Catholic Church: Its History and Theology* (1993). What emerges from these studies is the recognition, already noted in the preceding chapters, of (1) a broad diversity of ministries in the history of the Church, as well as of (2) a relatively wide diversity of modes in which various ministries have been exercised.

New Testament

The word *ministry* means "service." Jesus himself gave an example of service (Mark 10:45). The apostolate itself is seen as a ministry (Acts of the Apostles 1:17,25). The call of Paul to the apostolate (Romans 1:1) is also a call to a ministry (1 Timothy 1:12; 2 Corinthians 4:1), which Paul tries to fulfill worthily (Acts of the Apostles 20:24). He understands himself as a minister of God (2 Corinthians 6:3–4) and of Christ (11:23), in the service of the Spirit (3:6–9), of reconciliation (5:18) of the Gospel (Colossians 1:23; Ephesians 3:7), and of the Church (Colossians 1:25).

But the word *diakonia* ("service") is applied beyond the apostolate. It refers also to certain material services necessary to the community, such as serving at table (Acts of the Apostles 6:1–4) and the collection for the poor at Jerusalem (11:29; 12:25; Romans 15:31; 1 Corinthians 16:15; 2 Corinthians 8:4; 9:1,12–13). A ministry is entrusted to Archippus (Colossians 4:17) and to Timothy (2 Timothy 4:5), and the title *minister* is given to Apollos as to Paul (1 Corinthians 3:5), to Timothy (1 Thessalonians 3:2; 1 Timothy 4:6), to Phoebe (Romans 16:1), to Tychichus (Colossians 4:7; Ephesians 6:21), and to Epaphras (Colossians 1:7). There was, in fact, a diversity of ministries (1 Corinthians 12:4–11; Romans 12:6–8) and a diversity of charisms in view of the work of ministry (Ephesians 4:11–16). Every ministry was to be used under the influence of the Holy Spirit (Romans 12:7) as a mandate received from God (1 Peter 4:11).

According to contemporary biblical scholars (for example, James G. D. Dunn, *Unity and Diversity in the New Testament*), ministry in the New Testament went through at least three stages: (1) *pre-Easter discipleship,* in which ministry was centered exclusively in Jesus himself; (2) *first-generation Christianity,* with two diverging patterns of ministry: (a) *charismatic,* as in the original Jerusalem community and later in Corinth, and (b) *structured,* based on the synagogue model (elders, prophets, preachers); and (3) *second-generation Christianity,* where the patterns became both intermingled, as in Acts of the Apostles, and more divergent, as in the Pastoral Epistles, on the one hand, and the Johannine books, on the other.

Ministry in the earliest years of the Church, therefore, was of two kinds: (1) ministry that flowed from the missionary enterprise and

767

involved apostles, prophets, and teachers; and (2) ministry that consisted of the residential care of local communities—presbyters, primarily in the Jewish-Christian communities, and bishops and deacons in the Gentile-Christian communities. There is an integration of these two kinds of ministry in the Pastoral Epistles, but even there the precise relationship between bishops and deacons, on the one hand, and the presbyters, on the other, is not clear. The watchwords are always pluralism, diversity, and variety.

The Early Centuries

The Letter of Polycarp (d. c. 155), bishop of Smyrna, to the Christian community of Philippi is addressed to the "presbyters and deacons," the leaders of the local church. There are no bishops. *Episcope*, "oversight" or "supervision," was performed by the presbyters. Neither is there any mention of bishops in the *Didache*, one of the most ancient and authoritative documents of the Church. We never find the singular word for supervisor (*episcopos*). Only the function (*episcope*) is mentioned, and that is applied to the whole body of presbyters. Alongside the presbyters are the older charismatic leaders, prophets and teachers.

Judging from the letters of Ignatius of Antioch, however, the single bishop evidently became the pivotal figure in the local church, having authority over the local presbytery (council of elders) and the deacons, and jurisdiction over the administration of the sacraments. But historians and theologians don't know how this development occurred. In any case, ministry became canonically and liturgically institutionalized by the first half of the third century. The *Traditio Apostolica* of Hippolytus (d. 235), which influenced centuries of liturgical tradition, is the first major witness of the practice of ordination.

As the Church spread beyond town limits, presbyters assumed episcopal and sacerdotal responsibilities over smaller communities. From that point on presbyters began to be known also as priests. As a result the difference between bishops and the so-called country priests became blurred.

The Middle Ages

A division between clergy and laity widened during the Middle Ages when theologians and canonists divided the Church into two separate states: the *ordo clericorum* and the *ordo laicorum*. The latter was composed of men and women of the world, those given to the flesh. The former was composed of those devoted to the spiritual realm, responsible for the governance of the Church. The division was influenced also by a Neoplatonist view of the world, which defined reality as gradational and hierarchical, consisting of lower and higher forms. The clergy were at the higher end, with the pope at the very top, and the laity were at the bottom.

Toward the end of the eleventh century another important distinction was made between the power of *orders* and the power of *jurisdiction*. Canon lawyers distinguished between the power of orders, which is the priestly power to celebrate the Eucharist and forgive sins, and the power of jurisdiction, which is the authority to exercise those priestly powers on behalf of a diocese, a parish, or a religious community. This distinction separated priestly power, communicated in ordination, from *ministry*, or service to the People of God in a particular place.

The Council of Trent to the Twentieth Century

The Council of Trent's approach to ministry, particularly the ordained ministry of the priesthood, was fashioned out of at least three different developments: (1) the interference of the lay nobility in the appointment of bishops and pastors, (2) the Reformers' critique of the ordained priesthood, and (3) feudalism's emphasis on a hierarchical system of authority and privilege. The Council of Trent reacted against the first two factors by emphasizing the ordained priesthood over against the priesthood of all the faithful, but absorbed the third factor by reinforcing the pyramidal structure of pope, bishops, priests, deacons, and laity. In the absence of a balanced ecclesiology and a sound theology of ministry, the Council of Trent simply reinforced the conventional legalistic teachings of the day, including the distinction between the power of ordination and the power of juris-diction.

This view of the priesthood was passed on within the Catholic Church without criticism or essential change all the way into the middle of the twentieth century. The term *ministry* became identified more and more with Protestantism.

Vatican II

The Second Vatican Council sought to reinstate the notion of ministry as service rather than ecclesiastical status. *Ministry* is no longer a word to be applied only to the ordained. There is "a variety of ministries" in the Church (*Dogmatic Constitution on the Church*, n. 18; *Decree on Ecumenism*, n. 2).

Moreover, the Church itself is no longer to be identified exclu-sively nor even primarily with the hierarchy. The Church is the whole People of God (*Dogmatic Constitution on the Church*, chapter II). All share, by Baptism, in the threefold ministry of Jesus Christ as prophet, priest, and king. "Everything which has been said so far concerning the People of God applies equally to the laity, religious, and clergy." Indeed the lay apostolate is "a participation in the saving mission of the Church itself" (*Dogmatic Constitution on the Church*, nn. 30, 31).

Even though there are still some occasional references to the "sacred power" of the ordained priest, the medieval distinction be-tween the power of orders and the power of jurisdiction is aban-doned. Whatever "power" the minister has is always in the service of the People of God, of which the minister is also a member. The council also recognized the liturgical ministries of servers, lectors, commentators, choir (*Constitution on the Sacred Liturgy*, n. 29), and that of catechists (*Decree on the Church's Missionary Activity*, n. 17).

But the Second Vatican Council's teaching is not without some ambiguity. For example, it insists that, although all the faithful partic-ipate in the priesthood of Christ by Baptism and Confirmation (*Decree on the Apostolate of the Laity*, n. 3), there is nonetheless a difference not only "in degree" but "in essence" between "the common priesthood of the faithful and the ministerial or hierarchical priesthood" (*Dogmat-ic Constitution on the Church*, n. 10).

The faithful exercise their priesthood by joining in the offering of the Eucharist, by receiving the sacraments, by offering prayer and thanksgiving, by the witness through a holy life, and by practicing self-denial and active charity. The ordained priest, "by the sacred power he enjoys, molds and rules the priestly people" and acts "in the person of Christ" as he "brings about the Eucharistic Sacrifice, and offers it to God in the name of all the people" (*Dogmatic Constitution on the Church*, n. 10).

In the final accounting, however, Vatican II recovered the notion of ministry as service rather than as an ecclesiastical status. Whatever "sacred power" the ordained possess and exercise, it is always for the sake of the life and mission of the whole People of God, all of whom, by Baptism and Confirmation, participate in the one priesthood of Christ: "Pastors also know that they themselves were not meant by Christ to shoulder alone the entire mission of the Church toward the world. On the contrary, they understand that it is their noble duty so to shepherd the faithful and recognize their services and charismatic gifts that all according to their proper role may cooperate in this common undertaking with one heart" (*Dogmatic Constitution on the Church*, n. 30).

Ministeria Quædam

Pope Paul VI's apostolic letter *Ministeria Quædam* (1972) set aside the Council of Trent's notion that all ministries below priesthood are simply steps toward the priesthood, and restored lay ministries to the Latin Church, to be conferred not by ordination but by installation. The apostolic letter established two lay ministries, those of lector and acolyte, and left open the possibility of the creation of others.

Ecumenical Discussions

Although several of the ecumenical consultations have addressed themselves to the question of ordained ministry, especially of bishops and presbyters (priests), none has as yet dealt with the specific question of nonordained ministries, except in relation to the general ministry of the whole Church. The Lutheran-Catholic Dialogue, for example, does acknowledge the existence of such ministries (citing 1 Corinthians 12, Romans 12, and Ephesians 4), but its own study was deliberately limited to valid ministry in relation to the Eucharist. Even the Presbyterian-Reformed–Roman Catholic Consultation, which has a broadly inclusive understanding of ministry, had not attended directly to the existence of formal, nonordained ministries.

The Church and Ministry

Each *ministry* within the Church is a function of the *mission* of the Church: word, worship, witness, and service. Every Christian is called to ministry in the wide sense (Mark 10:45) as a call and an empowerment to serve others in Christ and because of Christ, but not every Christian is called to ministry in a formal sense, i.e., as a service *designated* by the Church to assist, in the name of the church, in the fulfillment of its mission. On the other hand, the lay apostolate is not simply a participation in the ministry of the hierarchy, but rather is "a participation in the saving mission of the Church itself," commissioned by the Lord himself in Baptism and Confirmation (*Dogmatic Constitution on the Church*, n. 33). The ordained ministries of presbyter and bishop exist not to dominate these other ministries, but to integrate and coordinate them (*Dogmatic Constitution on the Church*, n. 30; *Decree on the Bishops' Pastoral Office in the Church*, n. 17).

WOMEN IN THE CHURCH

The Issue

"In accordance with the venerable tradition of the Church" (*Ministeria Quædam*, n. 7), women are excluded from officially designated ministries in the Catholic Church today, even from the newly reconstituted lay ministries of acolyte and lector (although canons 228–30 allow for "lay persons," as distinct from "lay men," to fulfill various functions attached to these and other ministries). On the other hand, the recovery of an understanding of the Church as the whole People of God, women and men alike, has led many to question that traditional policy. This ecclesiological development is parallel with an even broader development outside the Church, i.e., a growing recognition of the equality of women and men and of the innumerable ways in which that equality has been denied and thwarted in society. Thus, there is pressure on the Catholic Church from outside, but more intensely from inside, to revise its canon law and pastoral practice, and to admit qualified women to ministry at every level.

History

New Testament

We have evidence of at least two designated ministries exercised by women in the New Testament: *widows* and *deaconesses*. The prestige and functional roles of the female minister, however, seemed to have varied from area to area. Women ministers who gave service within the community are mentioned as early as the year 58 in reference to Phoebe in Romans 16, where she is described as "a deacon of the church at Cenchreæ." In the context of a discussion of the qualifications of various ministers, 1 Timothy 3:11 notes that "the women, similarly, should be serious, not slanderous gossips. They should be temperate and entirely trustworthy." The widowhood, on the other hand, seems to have been confined throughout its existence to those who were in fact widows. 1 Timothy declares, "Let a widow be put on the list if she is not less than sixty years old and has been married only once; she must be well attested for her good works" (5:9–10). The widows were to give themselves to a ministry of prayer, but they may have had other duties including helping to raise children, giving hospitality, caring for the sick, and conducting pastoral visits.

Postbiblical Developments

The earliest description of the duties of deaconesses is given in the *Didascalia Apostolorum* (The Teachings of the Apostles), written as a kind of rulebook for a community in Syria in the early third century. Deaconesses are to be sent to minister to other women, to anoint them in Baptism, to instruct them, to visit the sick, and to minister to those in need. A deaconess was ordained by the laying on of hands in the presence of the presbyters, deacons, and other deaconesses. The same Syrian document presents widows as respected intercessors who pray over the sick and lay hands on them. As with all women, including the deaconesses, they were not to teach. The details of the position of widows are not so important as the fact that they eventually developed into a class of senior women within the Church, analogous to the presbyters. They were sometimes linked together with bishops, presbyters, and deacons as "ecclesiastical dignitaries" (Origen, *Homily on Luke 17*), and at other times considered as part of the clergy (Tertullian, *On Monogamy* 11:1,4; 12:1). The fifth-century *Testament of Our Lord,* written also in Syria, provides an ordination prayer and specifies that there should be thirteen widows who sit in front during the celebration of the Eucharist immediately behind the presbyters, on the left side of the bishop. Widows at this time frequently performed the functions of the deaconess, assisting at the baptism of women. They led prayer services and generally exercised leadership over women members of a community.

The growth of the Church's membership and its spread from the cities and towns to smaller towns and villages during the latter part of the third and early fourth centuries brought about rapid organizational changes, as we have noted in chapter 19. Presbyters were now regularly delegated to preside over the Eucharist in place of the bishop and soon were established as permanent pastors in the outlying congregations. The deacon, who was originally an assistant to the bishop, either moved up with the bishop in the larger diocesan structure or stayed behind in a local community as assistant to the presbyter. In both instances the importance of the diaconate was lessened. The deacon's administrative duties were gradually taken over by the presbyters, and deacons in parishes lost prestige.

Meanwhile, the political situation outside the Church exerted additional pressure that led to further organizational change. The loosely knit structure of the first three centuries was not adequate in the face of the manipulation of the Church by the imperial power. Greater centralization seemed required, and the Church simply took over the organizational forms already available in the political realm. Diocesan bishops became like city magistrates. Bishops of provincial capitals were metropolitans, with authority over other bishops in their province. They were the counterparts of the provincial governors. The new ecclesial structure became more and more vertical. Lower offices were now regarded as probationary stepping-stones to higher offices. The line between clergy and laity developed, popular election of bishops disappeared, women were forbidden to go to the altar, and eventually lay men as well were excluded from the sanctuary. The office of deaconess was ordered suppressed by the councils of Epaon (517) and Orleans (533) in the West, but it survived for a longer time in the East, although women were absorbed into the monastic life rather than designated for pastoral ministry.

1960 to the Present

Without prejudice to the fact that women have exercised positions of leadership and influence in the history of the Church (see, for example, *Women of Spirit: Female Leadership in the Jewish and Christian Traditions*, Rosemary Ruether and Eleanor McLaughlin, eds., New York: Simon & Schuster, 1979), it has not been until the thoroughly contemporary phenomenon of the women's liberation movement and of the subsequent development of feminist biblical studies and feminist theology that a new awareness of the place of women in the Church began to emerge. That movement, we cannot forget, began only in the early 1960s, and in many parts of the world has not yet begun. Its impact was already evident in the remarkable encyclical letter of Pope John XXIII, *Pacem in Terris* (1963), which notes that "women are becoming ever more conscious of their human dignity" and are demanding rights "befitting a human person both in domestic and in public life." He called this development one of three "distinctive characteristics" of the present day.

The Second Vatican Council's *Pastoral Constitution on the Church in the Modern World* recognized the "new social relationships between men and women" (n. 8) and noted that women are demanding equality with men in law and in fact (n. 9). Pope Paul VI's birth control encyclical *Humanæ Vitæ* made the same observation (n. 2). In 1971 he issued a "Call to Action" (*Octagesima Adveniens*) in which he referred to the struggle to end discrimination against women in many countries (n. 13). Later that same year *Justice in the World*, of the 1971 Synod of Bishops, urged that "women should have their own share of responsibility and participation in the community life of society and likewise of the Church."

In 1972 Pope Paul VI issued an apostolic letter, as we noted above, in which he explicitly excluded women even from the new lay ministries of lector and acolyte (*Ministeria Quædam*), but in 1976 the Pontifical Biblical Commission reported that it could find no support for the exclusion of women from the ordained priesthood on the basis of the biblical evidence alone. "The Bible does not contain a ready answer to the question of the role of women in the Church or in society" ("Can Women Be Priests?" *Origins* 6/6, July 1, 1976, pp. 92–96). This latter document is of major importance, and merits separate study. The reader should also consult the "Consensus Statement from the Symposium on Women and Church Law," sponsored by the Canon Law Society of America, and published in *Sexism and Church Law*, James Coriden, ed. (New York: Paulist Press, 1977, pp. 150–60).

The 1987 Synod of Bishops condemned discrimination against women, and so, too, did Pope John Paul II in a subsequent apostolic exhortation on the laity, *Christifideles Laici* (1989). However, the pope also reaffirmed the Church's traditional exclusion of women from ordained ministries and emphasized their dual roles as mothers and preservers of the "moral dimension of culture" (n. 51). In a papal letter released the previous year, *Mulieris Dignitatem* (On the Dignity and Vocation of Women), he emphasized the equality of men and women as human beings created in God's image, but again stressed motherhood, alongside virginity, "as two particular dimensions of the female personality" (n. 17). The woman discovers herself, he writes, "in conceiving and giving birth to a child" (n. 18). Finally, in showing a preference for the biblical image of the Church as the Bride of Christ, he points out that the symbol of the bridegroom is masculine, and as such "represents the human aspect of the divine love which God has for Israel, for the church and for all people.... Precisely because Christ's divine love is the love of a bridegroom, it is the model and pattern of all human love, men's love in particular" (n. 25). Accordingly, only men can preside at the Eucharist because only men can represent Christ the bridegroom (n. 26).

The Ordination of Women

Arguments in Favor

Positive arguments have been offered in the past by committees of learned societies (e.g., Canon Law Society of America, Catholic Theological Society of America), national associations (e.g., Leadership Conference of Women Religious), various ecumenical consultations (e.g., Presbyterian-Reformed–Roman Catholic Consultation, "Women in the Church," in *Journal of Ecumenical Studies* 9, 1972, pp. 235–41), and the works of individual scholars (e.g., Karl Rahner and feminist theologians generally). Some of these arguments are:

1. The exclusion of women from priesthood violates human dignity and the baptismal mandate to participate in the mission of the Church according to one's qualifications, opportunities, and vocation.

2. Women have in fact served as deaconesses in the early Church (1 Timothy 3:8–13; 5:2; Romans 16:1, where Phoebe is named as a deacon).

3. There is nothing in Sacred Scripture which positively excludes the ordination of women.

4. Arguments against the ordination of women are deficient:

   a. To say the tradition of the Church is against it assumes that we are already in the adulthood of the Church. But if the Church is still alive in the year 20,000, the latter part of the twentieth century will look like the "early Church" to those in the two hundred and first century.

   b. Women are equal to men in human dignity and before God. The exclusion of women on the basis of gender assumes a radical inferiority of women and, therefore, a basic incapacity, if not unworthiness, to act on behalf of the Church in the presence of God.

   c. Jesus, in fact, called no one to *ordained priesthood* (as distinguished from discipleship and the apostolate).

5. Women today fulfill most of the designated ministries in the Church: as pastoral associates, directors of liturgy, youth ministers, ministers to the sick and the elderly, lectors, eucharistic minis-

ters, music ministers, ministers of hospitality, even parish administrators. They clearly have the capacity to fulfill the ordained ministries as well.

6. The needs of the Church have reached a critical stage, given the large numbers of communities all over the globe, even in countries like the United States, where the Eucharist cannot be celebrated because of the lack of ordained presiders. The Eucharist is essential to the life of the Church; the rules of eligibility for ordination are only peripheral. The need to maintain the former clearly outweighs the desire to preserve the latter.

Arguments Against

Negative arguments have been expressed in such Vatican documents as the 1976 *Declaration on the Question of the Admission of Women to the Ministerial Priesthood* from the Sacred Congregation for the Doctrine of the Faith, the statement of the U.S. Catholic bishops, *Theological Reflections on the Ordination of Women* (1972), certain ecumenical consultations (e.g., Catholic-Orthodox, "Bishops and Presbyters," *Origins* 6/9, August 12, 1976, pp. 142–43), and the works of individual theologians.

1. The constant tradition of the Church is opposed to ordination of women to priesthood.

2. Jesus did not call women, not even his mother, to priesthood.

3. The ordained priest must act in the name of Christ, the bridegroom, and, therefore, must be able to represent him physically as well as spiritually. The Orthodox refer to this as "iconic" representation.

4. No one has a right to ordination.

5. It is not clear that the women who were called deaconesses in the New Testament were ordained or whether their ordination was sacramental.

(For a fuller discussion of these and similar arguments, both for and against, see the *Research Report: Women in Church and Society*, New York: Catholic Theological Society of America, 1978.)

The Church and Women

Whatever position one takes on the ordination question, recognition of the full Christian and human equality of women with men is essential if the Church is to be perceived, and to function, as the whole People of God. The Church must always be faithful to the example of Jesus Christ, whose sacrament it is. In striking contrast to the contemporary usages of the Jewish world, Jesus surrounded himself with women who followed him and served him (Luke 8:2–3; 10:38–42). It was the women who were charged with announcing the resurrection to the "disciples and Peter" (Mark 16:7).

The whole purpose of creation and of redemption is the unity of all in God, and the Church is called to be a sign and instrument of the unity of God and humankind, and of the unity of humankind itself (*Dogmatic Constitution on the Church*, n. 1). Therefore, the missionary responsibility of the Church is to attest to the full human and Christian dignity of women not only by word but also by example. The sacramental principle, always central to Catholicism, is here again of utmost importance.

SUMMARY

1. *Authority*, from the Latin word *auctor* ("author"), has to do with the capacity to influence the thinking and/or behavior of others. It may be associated with an office (*de iure* authority) or with certain intrinsic qualities which evoke respect and which lead to persuasion (*de facto* authority). God is the ultimate authority, or Author, of all that is.

2. In the *Old Testament* authority is exercised by human agents, but it is never absolute. In the *New Testament*, Jesus provides the model for its exercise. He is one who serves. He uses his power to forgive sins, to heal, and thereby to proclaim the Kingdom of God. He shares his authority with his disciples.

3. *Teaching* authority, while important, is always secondary to the proclamation and practice of the Kingdom. Teaching explains the Gospel; it is not itself the Gospel. Teaching interprets faith; it is not itself the faith.

4. In the *second and third centuries* authority is identified with those who preside over the Christian churches, especially the bishops and presbyters. But the Spirit is perceived to have been given to the whole community, although in a special way to *bishops*. Only those in whom the gifts of the Spirit were discernible were elected bishops in the first place.

5. In subsequent centuries (*fourth to eleventh*) authority becomes confused with *political* authority, especially in the aftermath of the Edict of Constantine. Monasticism grows in reaction to the exercise of worldly authority. The only genuine authority, in the monastic view, is *moral authority*.

6. With the Gregorian Reform (*eleventh century*), in response to lay encroachments against the Church, the papacy claims *monarchical* authority. Papal authority becomes juridicized and exaggerated, especially under Innocent III and Boniface VIII.

7. Against the excesses of the Reformation, the Council of Trent (*sixteenth century*) insists even more strongly on the hierarchical authority of the Church. The pope becomes the Church's "universal bishop," the "Sovereign Pontiff." Authority is centralized in Rome.

8. This trend culminates in the definition of papal primacy at Vatican I (*nineteenth century*) and is carried forward in the encyclicals of Pope Pius XII (*twentieth century*).

9. Vatican II (*1962–1965*) stresses the notion of authority as *service* and insists that it must be exercised always in a *collegial* mode.

10. The *papacy* is an exercise of the *Petrine function*, i.e., a particular form of ministry to the Church as a whole.

11. The *New Testament* does not call Peter the first pope. On the other hand, he exercises a unique role in the early Church. No single text "proves" this. Rather, there is a pattern or *trajectory of images* (e.g., fisherman, shepherd) which suggest that the postbiblical development is indeed consistent with the thrust of the New Testament.

12. The bishop of Rome becomes increasingly important in the *early centuries* of the Church in resolving serious doctrinal controversies. He sends delegates to councils and is appealed to as a court of last resort. The correlation between Peter and the bishop of Rome becomes fully explicit in Leo I (d. 461).

13. *Primacy* becomes an increasingly juridical concept under the impact of the threats posed by the encroachment of lay political power, Conciliarism, Protestantism, nationalism, the Enlightenment, and nineteenth-century liberalism. The doctrine of papal primacy was formulated by Vatican I.

14. Vatican II restores a collegial and spiritual understanding of papal primacy. Supreme authority is vested in the pope and the bishops, forming together a single college. The authority is always for the faithful preaching of the Gospel, the administration of the sacraments, and loving service.

15. The Church is a communion of churches. The papacy exists to serve the *unity* of that communion of churches, but it must always respect the *legitimate diversity* of those churches, *collegiality* in decision-making, and the principle of *subsidiarity*, not appropriating to itself decisions which are better reached at lower levels.

16. *Infallibility* means literally "immunity from error." It is concerned with the faithful transmission of the Gospel, the indefectibility of the Church, and the certitude of faith.

17. The concept of infallibility does not appear in the *New Testament*, although the concern for sound doctrine does. There was, however, a growing conviction in the *early centuries* of the Church that Rome, and the bishop of Rome in particular, was a reliable touchstone of orthodoxy. And yet popes were conceded to have erred in matters of faith.

18. The term *infallibility* was first applied to papal teaching authority during the course of a *fourteenth-century* dispute about Franciscan poverty. The concept was taken up and accentuated by the Counter-Reformation theologians, in the controversy with Jansenism and Gallicanism, and then made the subject of a dogmatic definition at Vatican I.

19. *Vatican I* taught that the pope is infallible only when he is in the act of defining a doctrine of faith and morals, as earthly head of the universal Church, with the clear intention of binding the whole Church. His teachings are not subject to some subsequent vote on the part of the bishops, as the Gallicans had insisted.

20. *Vatican II* insisted that papal infallibility must always be related to the faith of the whole Church, whose assent can never be lacking.

21. In the *New Testament* ministry means service. There is a diversity of ministries, and this diversity continues through the history of the Church.

22. From the *Council of Trent* until the middle of the twentieth century there was a sharp division between clergy and laity, with formal ministerial functions reserved to the clergy. *Vatican II* expanded the concept to include lay ministers such as lector, acolyte, and catechist.

23. Ministry is always for the sake of mission. In principle, ministry is open to all. By Christian ministry is meant *a service rendered to others in Christ and because of Christ*. A *designated* ministry is one that is rendered in the name of the Church and to assist in the fulfillment of its mission.

24. *Women* are presently excluded from all formal ministries in the Catholic Church, although not from their functions. In the *New Testament* and in the first five or six centuries of the Church's history, however, women served as *deaconesses* and as *widows* (the latter was also a special office, not simply a civil fact).

25. With the growth of the Church, an increase in its organizational complexity, and its adoption of political and societal models from contemporary Græco-Roman life, the so-called lower ministries were absorbed upward, becoming stepping-stones to higher ecclesiastical office. Deaconesses were suppressed in the sixth century, and the office of widow disappeared.

26. The women's liberation movement in the 1960s and feminist theology of the 1980s and 1990s encouraged a new attitude toward the place of women in the Church. This positive change was reflected in Pope John XXIII's encyclical *Pacem in Terris* and was reinforced by Vatican II's *Gaudium et spes*. Nonetheless, resistance to women in formal ministries, especially the presbyterate, continues, and Pope Paul VI's *Ministeria Quædam* opens the ministries of lector and acolyte to men only.

27. Those who *favor* ordination of women to the priesthood point to the injustice of the present exclusion based on gender alone, the tradition of deaconesses in the early Church, the absence of any evidence against it in the New Testament, and the present critical needs of the Church.

28. Those who *oppose* ordination of women point to the constant tradition of the Church and the necessity of the priest's physical as well as spiritual resemblance to Christ.

SUGGESTED READINGS

Brown, Raymond, et al. *Peter in the New Testament*. Minneapolis: Augsburg Publishing House, 1973.

Chittister, Joan. *Women, Ministry and Church*. New York: Paulist Press, 1983.

Coll, Regina A. *Christianity and Feminism in Conversation*. Mystic, Conn.: Twenty-Third Publications, 1994.

Congar, Yves. *Power and Poverty in the Church*. Baltimore: Helicon, 1964.

Coriden, James, ed. *Sexism and Church Law: Equal Rights and Affirmative Action*. New York: Paulist Press, 1977.

Dolan, Jay P., et al. *Transforming Parish Ministry: The Changing Roles of Catholic Clergy, Laity, and Women Religious*. New York: Crossroad, 1989.

Dunn, James G. D. *Unity and Diversity in the New Testament: An Inquiry into the Character of Earliest Christianity*. Philadelphia: Westminster Press, 1977.

Empie, Paul C., et al., eds. *Papal Primacy and the Universal Church: Lutherans and Catholics in Dialogue V*. Minneapolis: Augsburg Publishing House, 1974.

Lawler, Michael G. *A Theology of Ministry*. Kansas City, Mo.: Sheed & Ward, 1990.

McBrien, Richard P. *Ministry: A Theological, Pastoral Handbook*. San Francisco: Harper & Row, 1987.

McKenzie, John L. *Authority in the Church*. New York: Sheed & Ward, 1966.

O'Meara, Thomas F. *Theology of Ministry*. New York: Paulist Press, 1983.

Osborne, Kenan R. *Ministry: Lay Ministry in the Roman Catholic Church: Its History and Theology*. New York: Paulist Press, 1993.

Tillard, Jean-M. R. *The Bishop of Rome*. Wilmington, Del.: Michael Glazier, 1983.

Todd, John M., ed. *Problems of Authority*. Baltimore: Helicon Press, 1962.

PART FIVE

The Sacraments

FEW things are more characteristic of Catholicism than its sacramental life, which is centered on the seven sacraments, and on the Eucharist in particular. If nothing else, Catholicism is a sacramental faith-tradition.

Traditionally, the sacraments were treated within, and almost as an appendage to, Christology. According to traditional Catholic theology, sacraments are acts of Christ. With the renewal of Catholic theology, and especially of ecclesiology, in the twentieth century, the sacraments came to be treated more often as part of the mystery of the Church. According to this approach, sacraments are acts of the Church. If the Church itself is a sacrament, it must act sacramentally. And so it does through the seven sacraments.

Today the emphasis seems to be moving back to a more centrist, or mediating, approach. The sacraments have both a Christological and an ecclesiological dimension. They are acts of Christ in the Church; they are acts of the Church through which Christ continues to act on our behalf.

In order to underscore the fundamental importance of the sacraments in the life and mission of the Church, they are accorded a separate part of this book. The reader, however, should remember that the sacraments cannot be treated in isolation from the mysteries of Christ and the Church. They can only be understood and fully appreciated within the larger contexts of Christology and ecclesiology.

Moreover, the sacraments cannot be studied in isolation from one another. They are not seven separate sacraments. They are closely interrelated. Thus, the sacraments of Baptism, Confirmation, and Eucharist are all part of a single process of Christian initiation. The sacraments of Penance, or Reconciliation, and Anointing of the Sick are sacraments of forgiveness and healing—ministerial functions that are inextricably related to one another. And the sacraments of Matrimony and Holy Order are sacraments of vocation and commitment. In Matrimony the Christian community is built up and manifested at its most natural, familial level. In Holy Order the Christian community is provided structure and direction for the exercise of its mission.

Part Five begins with a consideration of general principles of sacramental theology, that is, the nature of the sacraments, their effects, their institution, their number, and so forth.

Here again, the three major characteristics of Catholicism— sacramentality, mediation, and communion—are fully engaged. The sacraments, as signs of grace, express and realize the sacramental nature of the Church; as causes of grace, they mediate the saving presence of God; and they are both signs and causes of our communion with one another and with God.

XXI

The Sacraments in General

THE PLACE OF SACRAMENTAL THEOLOGY

The major theological, pastoral, and even aesthetical characteristic of Catholicism is its commitment to the principle of *sacramentality*. Catholicism has never hesitated to affirm the "mysterious" dimension of all reality: the cosmos, nature, history, events, persons, objects, rituals, words. (Indeed, there is no word for *sacrament* in the New Testament. *Mysterion* is the closest to it.) Everything is, in principle, capable of embodying and communicating the divine. There is no finite instrument that God cannot put to use. On the other hand, we humans have nothing else apart from finite instruments to express our own response to God's self-communication. Just as the divine reaches us through the finite, so we reach the divine through the finite. The point at which this "divine commerce" occurs is the point of *sacramental encounter*. For Christians, *the* point of a sacramental encounter with God is the *humanity* of Jesus Christ, the primordial, or primal, sacrament.

Catholicism has also historically emphasized the notion of peoplehood and of church as a *mediating* principle. God's relationship to us and our relationship to God are not exclusively, nor even primarily, individual and personal. They are corporate and communal. "In Adam's fall, we sinned all." If indeed our relationship with God were not primarily corporate and communal, rather than individual and personal, the doctrines of Original Sin and of redemption would make no sense. But the principle of human solidarity is not only a theological principle. It is also firmly grounded in modern social science (e.g., Max Scheler, Alfred Schutz, Émile Durkheim, George Herbert Mead, Georges Gurvitch) and, beyond that, in the contemporary human experience of *interdependence* (see again chapter 3).

Those points of encounter between God and humankind, therefore, are never simply "transactions" between the divine and *this* person, although they are also clearly that as well. God touches all of humankind, and the human community as a whole responds to its experience of the divine through a sacramental mode. The word *sacramental* is being used here in its *widest* sense, of course. It applies to *any finite reality through which the divine is perceived to be disclosed and communicated, and through which our human response to the divine assumes some measure of shape, form, and structure.* (We cannot go into any detail regarding this wider understanding and manifestation of sacramentality. The interested reader should consult the works of Mircea Eliade—e.g., *Patterns in Comparative Religion,* New York: Sheed & Ward, 1958, and *Myths, Rites, Symbols: A Mircea Eliade Reader,* W. C. Beane and W. G. Doty, eds., New York: Harper & Row, 1976.)

Taken in the more *specific* sense as *those finite realities through which God is communicated to the Church and through which the Church responds to God's self-communication,* sacraments are directly ecclesiological in character. This is not to say that sacraments are not also linked closely with theological anthropology, with Christology, with eschatology, or with Christian moral life. But their immediate context is the Church. The Church is the *fundamental sacrament* of God's promise and deliverance of the Kingdom of God in Jesus Christ. It is the "universal sacrament of salvation" (*Dogmatic Constitution on the Church,* n. 48).

The sacraments, i.e., those seven specific actions which the Church has defined to be sacraments (Eucharist, Baptism, Confirmation, Reconciliation, Anointing of the Sick, Marriage, and Holy Order), are acts of God, to be sure. They are acts of Christ, to be sure. But they are immediately *acts of the Church.* They are expressions of the nature and mission of the Church. The sacraments are not simply actions which the Church performs, or means by which the Church makes grace available. They are "representative of the deepest concentration of sacramentality latent in all church activity" (Edward

Kilmartin, *Christian Liturgy I: Theology*, Kansas City, Mo.: Sheed & Ward, 1988, p. 280). They are privileged moments when the Church manifests itself as Church.

Correspondingly, those who receive the sacraments are not only related anew to God or to Christ. The sacraments immediately relate the recipient to the Church. The *lasting effect* of the sacrament (the *res et sacramentum,* to be explained in due course) is one of *relationship with the Church.* Thus, the sacrament of Penance (Reconciliation) has as its immediate purpose and effect not the restoration of friendship with God but reconciliation with the Church. The penitent who has committed a serious sin but who has made an act of perfect contrition (which restores union with God) is still required to seek forgiveness in the sacrament, because that serious sin compromises the mission of the Church to be a holy people, a sacrament of Christ and of the Kingdom of God. It is not just God who is "offended" by the sin. The Church, too, has been violated. Its sacramentality has been tarnished. The sinner also has to "make up" with the Church.

Of course, the sacraments and sacramental theology are at the same time closely connected with Christology, with which they have usually been linked in the past. It is Christ who is encountered in the sacraments. It is Christ who acts in the sacraments. It is Christ's worship of the Father that is expressed in the sacraments. Indeed, the seven sacraments find their fullest expression and even definition only in him: *He* is the baptized one and the confirmed one; *he* is the really present one; *he* is the reconciler; *he* is the priest; *he* is the lover; *he* is the healer. Thus, it is not as if Jesus Christ is another sacrament *alongside* the seven sacraments. *He* is *the* sacrament; the seven sacraments are manifestations of his presence and saving activity on our behalf.

On the other hand, a too-close connection between sacramental theology and Christology has led historically to an exaggeration of such questions as the "institution" of the sacraments by Christ and the power of the sacraments to "channel" the grace of Christ, earned on Calvary, to the individual recipient, even when that individual is a seven-day-old infant.

Doing sacramental theology solely as part of Christology rather than as part of ecclesiology as well tends to ignore the sacramental principle itself. We do not encounter Christ directly, but in the

Church, which is his Body. Although it is Jesus Christ who is present and active in every sacramental celebration, it is the Church which makes that celebration available and which mediates his presence and saving action.

GENERAL PRINCIPLES

Signs, or Symbols, of Faith

It is not an exaggeration to suggest that Catholic sacramental theology and practice, from the time of the Reformation until the full flowering of the liturgical renewal at the Second Vatican Council, concentrated too much on the *causality* of the sacraments and too little on their role as *signs*. Accordingly, it seemed to make little difference if the congregation failed to grasp the meaning of the words and rituals of the Eucharist and the other sacraments, so long as the sacraments were validly administered by an authorized minister using the prescribed matter and form, to a properly disposed recipient (i.e., someone not placing an obstacle in the way, such as lack of faith or serious sin). But it was the clear teaching of the Council of Trent (*Decree on the Sacraments*, Session VII, 1547), and before that of Thomas Aquinas (*Summa Theologiæ* III, qq. 60–65), that *sacraments cause grace insofar as they signify it*. Indeed, the twentieth-century renewal of sacramental theology is essentially a rediscovery of that Thomistic perspective.

Before the time of Aquinas, moreover, the emphasis had been on the sign. It was Augustine who gave the first technical definition of a sacrament as a sign of grace ("a visible sign of invisible grace"). The priority of sign over cause continued until the Scholastic revival of the twelfth century. Its thinking was climaxed and balanced by Thomas, who added the notion of *efficacious* sign of grace; i.e., the sacraments *cause* what they signify. Thomas's own great contribution lay in his exposition of *how* the sacraments cause grace.

Although Thomas himself was exceedingly well balanced in his understanding of the relationship between sign and cause, postmedieval theology was not. The sign aspect of sacraments receded from the center of ecclesial consciousness. The sacraments were perceived as instruments of grace, producing their spiritual effects by the very performance of the ritual according to the prescribed manner (*ex opere operato*, "from the work worked").

Thomas devoted his entire first question in sacramental theology (III, q. 60) to the sign, and it is a motif that runs through his whole treatment of the sacraments. The purpose of a sign, he insisted, is to instruct, to call to mind the reality that it signifies. In using the sign, we, from our side, express our faith in the unseen reality hidden underneath the sign. Sacraments, then, are signs which proclaim *faith*.

Second, sacraments are signs which express *worship*. Through the sacraments we participate ritually, i.e., through signs, in Christ's own worship of the Father. The Lord's Supper, or Eucharist, is linked from the beginning with the Passover meal, at which Israel gratefully (eucharistically) relived its deliverance from the bondage of Egypt and prayed for the coming of the Messiah. The early Church spoke of Christ as its Passover who had been sacrificed (1 Corinthians 5:7) and related its own fellowship meals to Christ's sacrificial action (1 Corinthians 10:16–17).

Third, sacraments are signs of the *unity of the Church*. The faith that is expressed in each sacrament is the faith *of* the Church and the faith mediated to the individual *by* the Church. Insofar as the celebrants (recipients, ministers, congregation) of a sacrament have a common faith in what they do and in whom they encounter through what they do, the sacrament is also a sign of the Church's faith and of its unity.

Fourth, sacraments are signs of *Christ's presence*, and ultimately of God the Father's. Since Christ is neither God alone nor a human being alone, but the Word-made-flesh, the human actions of Christ which are memorialized and represented in the sacraments, especially in the Eucharist, are not confined to the actual time in which they were first expressed (e.g., at the Last Supper, on a particular occasion, in a particular room, during a particular moment in human history). Because Christ himself is also a sacrament, indeed the *primordial* sacrament (or sacrament of the "first order"), God is present in and through him. And since God transcends time as well as space, the saving presence and action of God in Christ is mediated every time the sacrament is celebrated. The risen Lord lives now, at this moment. His presence is signified in every sacrament.

Causes of Grace

The traditional (i.e., post-Tridentine, pre–Vatican II) explanation of sacramental causality stressed the teaching of Trent's canon 6: "If anyone says that the sacraments of the New Law do not contain the grace which they signify, or that they do not confer that grace on those who place no obstacles in the way . . . let him be anathema." Neither the merit (holiness) of the minister nor that of the recipient is causally involved, except in a negative way (i.e., the recipient must not put an obstacle in the way).

What the Council of Trent was trying to safeguard was the basic truth that the grace of the sacraments is caused not by human forces but by God acting in and through Christ and the Church. We do not merit saving grace; it is a pure gift of God. The phrase *non ponentibus obicem* ("for those not placing an obstacle") was taken from Augustine, who had used it to support the argument that infants receive the grace of Baptism because they are clearly not capable of placing any moral obstacle to it. Trent applied the principle across the sacramental board: *It is not the personal merit of the recipient that causes the grace received.* On the other hand, God does not force the human will.

Its balance and good intentions notwithstanding, the teaching of the council was more often misunderstood than understood. Many Catholics came to believe that the graces of the sacraments were theirs if only they placed no obstacle, i.e., were not in mortal sin. The measure of preparation, the intensity of faith, the awareness of the sign's meaning—none of these counted in the end. So long as there is no moral obstacle, the sacrament "works."

Thomas Aquinas, on the other hand, never used the phrase *not placing an obstacle.* He refers always to the sign of the sacrament as serving to dispose one more perfectly for receiving sacramental graces (*ex opere operantis,* "from the work of the worker"). He calls for an interior conversion to God, for a personal encounter between the Christian and Christ. Rarely does he speak of "valid reception" of the sacrament. He emphasizes instead the "right disposition" which is worthy of a Christian: faith and devotion.

In fact, this Thomistic stress on the right disposition is so much a part of authentic Catholic tradition that a major twentieth-century theologian, Karl Rahner, argued that there is always an element of uncertainty about the effect of the sacrament. "With the sacrament a person knows just as little as he does with his merely 'subjective' actions performed in faith, whether it has really given him God's grace. Just as little and just as much" (*The Church and the Sacraments*, p. 25). The popular notion has been just the opposite, of course. The belief has prevailed among Catholics that they are always more certain that their sins have been forgiven in the sacrament of Penance than are Protestants and others who have to rely solely on the precarious path of personal contrition. "Falsely, therefore, do some accuse Catholic writers as if they maintained that the sacrament of penance confers grace without any good disposition on the part of those receiving it; this is something which the Church of God never taught or accepted" (Trent, *Doctrine on the Sacrament of Penance*, chapter IV, Session XIV, 1551).

But this is looking at the matter from the point of view of the individual who is free and, therefore, has no certain knowledge that his or her own life will end victoriously in the Kingdom of God. On the other hand, it is the faith and hope of the Church as a whole that the world has been redeemed and that history itself will reach final salvation because of what God has already revealed and achieved in Christ. At least to this extent, the individual is assured that the grace of salvation is present and available in and through this sign (*ex opere operato*). We also know that each one of us remains free to give a "Yes" or a "No" (and this is the *opus operantis*).

The sacraments do not cause grace magically. They are free acts of God, and they are free acts of ours. They "work" only to the extent that we bring faith and devotion to them. "Sacraments are nothing but God's efficacious word to man, the word in which God offers himself to man and thereby liberates man's freedom to accept God's self-communication by his own act" (Karl Rahner, *Foundations of Christian Faith*, New York: Seabury Press, 1978, p. 415).

Effects of Sacraments

The sacraments do not *cause* grace, in the sense that the redemptive grace of God in Jesus Christ is otherwise unavailable. The offer of grace is already present to the individual, to the Church, and to the human community at large in God's original self-communication, as noted in chapter 5. The sacraments shape and focus that communication of grace so that the divine presence may be effective for this individual or for this group insofar as they are members of the Church and responsible for its mission.

Thus, everybody does not strictly "need" Baptism to become a child of God and an heir of heaven. Every human person, by reason of birth and of God's universal offer of grace, is already called to be a child of God and an heir of heaven. Catholics are not required to believe that unbaptized infants go to limbo, a state of "natural happiness" but without the vision and company of God. We do not "need" the sacrament of Holy Order to minister to others. Every person, by reason of his or her graced humanity, is called and empowered to minister to others. We do not "need" the sacrament of Matrimony to commit ourselves to another for life. And so on. *The sacraments signify, celebrate, and effect what God is, in a sense, already doing everywhere and for all.* But the sacraments also mandate and equip specific members of the human community, i.e., disciples of Jesus Christ, to be the corporate sign and instrument of God's presence and saving activity in Christ.

Thus, in every sacrament there is, in addition to the sign or ritual (*sacramentum tantum,* "the sign alone") and the grace, or immediate effect (*res tantum,* "the reality alone"), the lasting effect (*res et sacramentum*). It is that which is signified by the *sacramentum tantum* (the rite) and, in turn, disposes the recipient to grace (the *res tantum*). Why did this distinction arise in sacramental theology? As a way of dealing with one of the major medieval challenges to the Real Presence of Christ in the Eucharist.

According to Augustine, "A good person receives the sacrament and reality of the sacrament, but a bad person receives only the sacrament and not the reality" (*Commentary on John,* 26, 11). What Augustine had in mind by *reality* was the grace of the sacrament. Berengar of Tours (d. 1088) accepted the reality of the sacrament, i.e., the grace of union with Christ, but he denied that Christ's true body was present in the Eucharist. For him there were only two elements in the sacrament: the external sign, or symbol, and the ultimate effect, the grace. Theologians did not agree upon a third eucharistic element for almost a century. Not until Hugh of St. Victor (d. 1142) and Peter Lombard (d. 1160) did the concept of the *res et sacramentum* finally emerge. The bread and wine (*sacramentum tantum*) signify the body and blood of Christ (*res et sacramentum*); the body and blood of Christ, in turn, are the basis for union with Christ (*res tantum*) insofar as the body and blood are received worthily. But whether they are received worthily or not, the body and blood of Christ are really present because they have been signified and made present by the *sacramentum tantum* (the rite of the Eucharist).

Only gradually was the triple distinction applied to all of the sacraments, and only more recently, in the closing decades of the nineteenth century, was the *res et sacramentum* understood in a consistently ecclesiological sense, namely, in Matthias Scheeben's (d. 1888) *The Mysteries of Christianity*. For Scheeben, the *res et sacramentum* of the Eucharist is not just the risen body of the Lord, but the whole Christ, the Church.

By tradition the Church does not repeat three sacraments: Baptism, Confirmation, and Order. They are received only once. The *res et sacramentum* for those three sacraments is also called the *character*. The term was taken over from pagan antiquity, where it referred to the seal by which a soldier or a slave might be identified as belonging to the service of the emperor or an owner. When used by Christians like Tertullian and Augustine, the term was intended to apply to the sacramental rite alone. It was the rite of sealing by which a person became a Christian for life, even if he or she were to lapse into heresy or schism. Only later, in the medieval period, did the word *character* become identified with the *res et sacramentum*, i.e., the lasting effect which is distinguishable from the rite itself as well as from the grace produced by the sacrament. The term *character* does not refer to an indelible mark on the soul, as some catechisms had it. It is simply the word used to describe the permanent effect of three sacraments: Baptism, Confirmation, and Holy Order. These sacraments are not, in fact, administered more than once to the same person during the course of her or his lifetime. Therefore, they must produce some effect that is permanent (= "the character").

The *res et sacramentum* of *Baptism* and *Confirmation* is membership in the Church and responsibility for its mission. For *Holy Order* it is the abiding responsibility for pastoral service to the Church. For the non-character sacraments, explanations vary: *Matrimony* (the bond of union between man and woman, symbolizing the union of Christ and the Church), *Penance* (reconciliation with the Church), *Anointing of the Sick* (a healing of the separation between the individual and the Church created not by sin but by sickness), and the *Eucharist* (the real presence of Christ). In each instance, the *res et sacramentum* is signified by the rite itself (*sacramentum tantum*) and disposes the recipient(s) for the grace that is appropriate to the special relationship with the Church which is called for in this particular sacrament.

Intention of Minister and Recipient

The Minister

The sacraments do not achieve their intended effect if certain conditions are not fulfilled on the part of the minister of the sacrament and on the part of the recipient. The sacraments are acts of the Church. *The minister represents the Church and acts in its name.* Since everything the Church does, it does as the Body of Christ, the minister of a sacrament also acts in the name of Christ. On the other hand, the sacramental act is not automatic in its effect. The minister must voluntarily carry out the intention of the Church. He or she must intend what the Church intends. This does not mean, however, that the minister must also be a person of profound faith or even of moral probity, although both of these are eminently desirable. But if those qualities were demanded of each minister in every instance, the Church would never know when and to what extent its sacraments were properly celebrated and administered.

It is precisely because the sacraments are acts of the Church, and not simply acts of personal devotion, that the role of the minister is so important. There has been much controversy in the history of Catholic theology over this question of the minister's intention. Is it possible, for example, for a Jewish nurse to baptize validly a dying person who wishes to be baptized? The standard answer has been "Yes, so long as she intends to do what the Church intends." The theological problem with this approach is that it tends to conceive of the sacraments as indispensable means of achieving some spiritual effect. But they are not any more "indispensable" than the Church itself. People can be saved without Baptism (unless they know themselves to be called to the Church and deliberately reject the call), and in extraordinary cases people can even enter the Church without Baptism (as in the case of the dying person who wishes to be associated with the Body of Christ in some explicit way but is physically incapable of passing through the normal rite of initiation). Indeed, a catechumen is already in some real sense a part of the Church even before receiving Baptism itself.

It is the official teaching of the Catholic Church that the minister must have at least "the intention of doing what the Church does" (Council of Florence, *Decree for the Armenians*, 1439; and also Council of Trent, *Decree on the Sacraments*, canon 11). The validity of the sacrament is independent of the worthiness of the minister (condemnation of John Wycliffe by the Council of Constance, 1415; Council of Trent, op. cit., canon 12). But not every member of the Church is qualified to administer every sacrament (Council of Trent, canon 10: "If anyone says that all Christians have the power [to preach] the word and to administer all the sacraments, *anathema sit*").

The Recipient

The *fruitful reception* of the sacraments (in contradistinction to their valid celebration) depends, as noted earlier, on the *disposition* of the recipient. Again, the sacraments are not magic. Sacraments are acts of the Church. The reception of sacraments draws one more fully into the life and mission of the Church. A sacrament can have no ecclesiological impact if the intended recipient has no faith in it or in the reality it symbolizes, or if he or she is morally unprepared for it.

What of a person who receives Baptism, Confirmation, or Holy Order in a state of mortal sin? The traditional answer would have it that the sacrament is validly received but that the grace is not communicated unless and until perfect contrition occurs. The answer is still correct in principle, but the case presupposes that "mortal sin" is relatively common even among active members of the Church who frequent the sacraments and who would be deemed fit candidates for one of the character sacraments. However, mortal sin involves a fundamental rejection of God and the reorientation of one's whole life away from all that is good and just. It is not something that most people "commit" frequently. Certainly it will be rare, even nonexistent, in the life of a sincere and active member of the Church. Furthermore, this assumption that mortal sin may often obstruct the grace of a character sacrament also seems to forget the principle reaffirmed by the Second Vatican Council's *Dogmatic Constitution on the Sacred Liturgy:* "[The sacraments] do indeed impart grace, but, in addition, the very act of celebrating them most effectively disposes the faithful to receive this grace in a fruitful manner, to worship God duly, and to practice charity" (n. 59).

This raises, finally, the question of the *baptism of infants,* since we have here the case of persons who are manifestly incapable of being "disposed" for a fruitful reception of a sacrament. Two extremes are to be avoided: one which assumes that the primary purpose of Baptism is the "washing away of Original Sin" so that the baptism of infants is a matter of highest priority no matter what the circumstances; the other which assumes that sacraments are only for adults and that life in the Church is within reach only of adults or of mature young people.

The practice of the Church is consistent with ordinary human experience. Just as one enters a family by birth and is really a part of that family even though for a long period of time there is no real capacity for giving human love but only for receiving it, so one may be brought into the family of the Church before he or she is capable of understanding its significance or of expressing the love that marks this community as the Body of Christ and the Temple of the Holy Spirit. In the case of infants, the intention is expressed not by the child but by those who bring the child for Baptism—e.g., parents, sponsors, relatives, and friends (*Summa Theologiæ,* III, q. 68, art. 9). There is a coresponsibility here that is also not foreign to sacraments even for adults. One thinks, for example, of the role of sponsors and of one's family and friends at Confirmation, of the witnesses and one's family and friends at Marriage, of one's loved ones and others at the Anointing of the Sick.

Institution of the Sacraments

Were the sacraments "instituted" by Christ? Here again, the question is to be answered in its larger ecclesiological context. Just as the Church was not "founded" by Christ in the sense that he immediately and directly established a new religion, with specific organizational structure, doctrines, moral codes, and so forth (see chapter 16), nei-ther do the sacraments issue from some precise mandate of the Lord. On the other hand, the Church does have its origin in Jesus Christ, especially in his proclamation of the Kingdom of God and the call to discipleship; and the sacraments, in turn, have their origin in the Church.

The question is also to be answered in terms of Christology. If one adopts exclusively a Christology "from above" (as in the Johan-nine writings), then, of course, every possibility is open. The omni-scient *Logos* came down from heaven with his program and mission already fixed. He intended the Church as we know it, with the full sacramental life as exists in it. But if one starts instead with the historical Jesus (Christology "from below"), it becomes historically improbable that Jesus would have explicitly determined more than the Synoptic Gospels indicate. *Jesus willed the sacraments to the same degree and extent as he willed the Church.*

The rapidity with which Catholic theology, under the impact of recent developments in ecclesiology, in Christology, and in biblical studies, is moving away from the standard textbook treatments of the institution and the number of sacraments is very remarkable. In 1960 the Dutch theologian Edward Schillebeeckx argued in his important and influential work, *Christ the Sacrament of Encounter with God*, that "Christ...must himself have established the sevenfold direction of grace..." (p. 116).

Just three years later Karl Rahner was beginning to move beyond that cautious view, arguing that "the institution of a sacrament can... follow simply from the fact that Christ founded the Church with its sacramental nature" (*The Church and the Sacraments*, p. 41).

And then in a later book (published originally in German in 1976), Rahner questioned even the possibility of tracing Baptism back to the words of Jesus, leaving the Lord's Supper as the only sacra-ment directly instituted by Christ ("Do this in remembrance of me," Luke 22:19; 1 Corinthians 11:24). Rahner continues to link the "insti-tution" of the sacraments with the "founding" of the Church, in an analogous way. The Church is in its essence sacramental, i.e., "the irreversible presence of God's salvific offer in Christ. This sacramen-tality is interpreted by the church in the seven sacraments, just as the church developed its own essence in its constitution. From this perspective, an individual Christian can accept without hesitation and live out this seven-fold sacramental order as it in fact exists" (*Foundations of Christian Faith*, p. 413).

The Number of Sacraments

What is essential is not the number seven, but the affirmation that there are certain ritual actions through which the saving presence and activity of God, on the one hand, and the sacramental nature of the Church, on the other, are visibly and effectively engaged. Even according to the most stringent interpretation of the teaching of the Council of Trent that there are seven sacraments, one could say that there are nine, taking diaconate and the episcopate as separate sacramental stages of the sacrament of Holy Order. Or one could say there are only six, considering Baptism and Confirmation as one sacrament. Or one could say that there are eight, combining Baptism and Confirmation but expanding Holy Order from one sacramental order to three.

It was and always is up to the Church to determine whether certain acts flowing from its nature as a sacrament of universal salvation are fundamentally and unconditionally a realization and expression of that nature. Before the number seven was finally settled upon during the medieval period (at Lyons II in 1274, at Florence in 1439, and at Trent in 1547), the Church lived through its entire first millennium and then some without ever having settled upon even a final definition of *sacrament*, let alone their precise number. On the contrary, there were literally hundreds of sacred rites (what we call today "sacramentals") which were simply referred to as "sacraments." These included Sacred Scripture, the mysteries of faith, cultic rites, and even allegory and typology.

Today *sacramentals* are understood as sacred signs which bear a resemblance to the sacraments. Insofar as the sacramentals cause grace, they do so not *ex opere operato*, primarily through the power of the rite itself, but *ex opere operantis*, primarily through the faith and devotion of those who are using, receiving, or celebrating the sacramental. Examples of sacramentals are baptismal water, holy oils, blessed ashes, candles, palms, crucifixes, statues, and medals.

SUMMARY

1. Catholicism is characterized by its commitment to the *principle of sacramentality*, namely, the conviction that everything is capable of embodying and communicating the divine, that all reality has a "mysterious" dimension insofar as it is imbued with the hidden presence of God.

2. Just as God reaches us through the finite and the visible, so we reach God through the finite and the visible. The point at which this occurs is the point of *sacramental encounter*. For Christians, *the* point of sacramental encounter with God is the *humanity* of *Jesus Christ*.

3. For Catholics especially, the *Church* also plays an important sacramental, or *mediating*, role in salvation history. Just as Christ is the sacrament of encounter with God, so the Church is the sacrament of encounter with Christ, and, ultimately, with God.

4. In its *widest sense*, the word *sacrament* applies to any finite reality through which the divine is perceived to be disclosed and communicated, and through which our human response to the divine assumes some measure of shape, form, and structure.

5. In a *more specific sense*, sacraments are those finite realities through which God is communicated to the Church and through which the Church responds to God's self-communication.

6. Since the medieval period, the sacraments have been understood primarily as *causes of grace*. Their function as *signs of faith* was subordinated to concerns about causality. For *St. Thomas Aquinas*, however, sacraments cause grace insofar as they signify it. If they are not intelligible and effective *signs*, or *symbols*, then they are not effective *causes*.

7. Sacraments, therefore, are (1) signs of *faith*, (2) acts of *worship*, (3) signs of the *unity of the Church*, and (4) signs of *Christ's presence*.

8. The *Council of Trent* taught that the sacraments also *cause* grace for those who place no obstacle to it. It is not the personal merit of the recipient that causes the grace received. At the same time, God does not force the human will.

9. *St. Thomas* insisted on the "right disposition" of the recipient—i.e., interior conversion, faith, devotion. The "fruitfulness" (as opposed to the mere "validity") of the sacrament depends on this.

10. Sacraments do not cause grace in the sense that grace is otherwise unavailable. The offer of grace is already present to the world in God's original self-communication. The sacraments signify, celebrate, and effect what God is, in a sense, already doing everywhere and for all.

11. In every sacrament there is the sign or ritual (*sacramentum tantum*), the fruit, or immediate effect (*res tantum*), and the lasting effect (*res et sacramentum*).

12. The distinction arose as a way of dealing with the challenge posed by *Berengar of Tours*, who acknowledged that the Eucharist is a sign of and causes the grace of union with Christ (*res tantum*) but who denied the real presence of Christ in the sacrament. Theologians insisted that it is still the body and blood of Christ, even if it does not cause grace in this particular recipient.

13. Those sacraments which, by tradition, the Church does not repeat are known as "character" sacraments. The term *character* conveys the notion of a "sealing" of the Christian, either as a member of the Church (*Baptism-Confirmation*) or in its service (*Holy Order*).

14. The lasting effects of the non-character sacraments are the bond of union between a man and a woman (*Matrimony*), a healing of the separation between an individual and the Church caused by sin (*Reconciliation*), a healing of the separation of an individual and the Church caused by sickness (*Anointing of the Sick*), and the real presence of Christ (*Eucharist*).

15. The *minister* of the sacrament acts in the name of the Church and therefore must intend to do what the Church wishes to be done (Councils of Florence and Trent). But the validity of the sacrament does not depend on the holiness of the minister (Councils of Constance and Trent). Not every member of the Church is qualified to administer every sacrament (Council of Trent).

16. The *recipient* must be disposed properly (faith, conversion, devotion). If not, "the very act of celebrating" the sacrament may produce the proper disposition (Vatican II).

17. *Infant baptism* is the exception rather than the rule of sacramental reception. Two extremes are to be avoided in explaining it: the one which assumes that Original Sin cannot be "removed" without Baptism, and the other which assumes that sacraments are only for adults or for mature young people. The community's "intention" supplies for the infant's, and it is the community which nurtures the baptized member's faith.

18. The sacraments were "*instituted*" by Christ in the same way that the Church was "instituted" by Christ. They have their origin in Jesus' proclamation of the Kingdom of God and in his call to discipleship. Jesus willed the sacraments to the same degree and extent as he willed the Church.

19. By definition of the Councils of Lyons II, Florence, and Trent, the Catholic Church recognizes *seven* signs as sacraments in the fullest sense: Baptism, Confirmation, Eucharist, Penance (Reconciliation), Anointing of the Sick, Matrimony, and Holy Order. The number seven, however, is not

absolute. Baptism and Confirmation might be taken as one sacrament, or the sacrament of Holy Order as three (diaconate, priesthood, episcopate).

20. *Sacramentals* (e.g., holy water, crucifixes) are sacred signs which bear a resemblance to the sacraments. They cause grace *ex opere operantis*.

SUGGESTED READINGS

Bausch, William. *A New Look at the Sacraments*. Mystic, Conn.: Twenty-Third Publications, 1983.

Cooke, Bernard. *Sacraments and Sacramentality*. Mystic, Conn.: Twenty-Third Publications, 1983.

Duffy, Regis A. "Sacraments in General," in *Systematic Theology: Roman Catholic Perspectives, Vol. II*. Francis Schüssler Fiorenza and John P. Galvin, eds. Minneapolis: Fortress Press, 1991, pp. 183–210.

_____. *Real Presence: Worship, Sacraments, and Commitment*. San Francisco: Harper & Row, 1982.

Ganoczy, Alexandre. *An Introduction to Catholic Sacramental Theology*. New York: Paulist Press, 1984.

Martos, Joseph. *The Catholic Sacraments*. Wilmington, Del.: Michael Glazier, 1983.

_____. *Doors to the Sacred: A Historical Introduction to Sacraments in the Catholic Church*. Expanded ed. Tarrytown, N.Y.: Triumph Books, 1991.

Osborne, Kenan B. *Sacramental Theology: A General Introduction*. New York: Paulist Press, 1988.

Rahner, Karl. *The Church and the Sacraments*. New York: Herder & Herder, 1963.

Schanz, John P. *Introduction to the Sacraments*. New York: Pueblo Publishing Co., 1983.

Schillebeeckx, Edward. *Christ the Sacrament of Encounter with God*. New York: Sheed & Ward, 1963.

Semmelroth, Otto. *Church and Sacrament*. Notre Dame, Ind.: Fides, 1965.

XXII

The Sacraments of Initiation: Baptism, Confirmation, and Eucharist

THE RITE OF INITIATION

Most Christians are baptized shortly after birth, but Confirmation and Eucharist are postponed for several years. The usual practice is not the ideal, however. The norm, as set down in the new *Rite of Christian Initiation,* is that a person should receive all three sacraments during the annual celebration of the Easter Vigil, following a suitable period of formation known as the *catechumenate.* But even when the norm cannot be observed, i.e., when Baptism is not followed immediately by Confirmation, or when the sequence of Confirmation and Eucharist is reversed, the ritual still calls for some postbaptismal anointing to replace Confirmation, and at Confirmation itself, the Baptism is renewed and reaffirmed and the Confirmation rite leads to eucharistic Communion.

The doctrine of Christian initiation is summed up in the "General Introduction" to the rite in the revised Roman Ritual:

1. Through the sacraments of Christian initiation men and women are freed from the power of darkness. With Christ they die, are

buried, and rise again. They receive the Spirit of adoption which makes them God's sons and daughters and, with the entire people of God, they celebrate the memorial of the Lord's death and resurrection.

2. Through baptism men and women are incorporated into Christ. They are formed into God's people, and they obtain forgiveness of all their sins. They are raised from their natural human condition to the dignity of adopted children. They become a new creation through water and the Holy Spirit. Hence they are called, and are indeed, the children of God.

Signed with the gift of the Spirit in confirmation, Christians more perfectly become the image of their Lord and are filled with the Holy Spirit. They bear witness to him before all the world and eagerly work for the building up of the body of Christ.

Finally they come to the table of the eucharist, to eat the flesh and drink the blood of the Son of Man so that they may have eternal life and show forth the unity of God's people. By offering themselves with Christ, they share in his universal sacrifice: the entire community of the redeemed is offered to God by their high priest. They pray for a greater outpouring of the Holy Spirit so that the whole human race may be brought into the unity of God's family.

Thus the three sacraments of Christian initiation closely combine to bring the faithful to the full stature of Christ and to enable them to carry out the mission of the entire people of God in the Church and in the world. (*The Rites of the Catholic Church*, New York: Pueblo Publishing Co., 1976, pp. 3–4.)

It is clear from this "General Introduction" and from the introductions to the other separate rites, including the baptism of children and confirmation by bishops, that *the premier rite is that of full initiation of adults*. All the other initiatory rites are to be understood in the context of this *Rite of Christian Initiation of Adults* (RCIA), and their various details often refer back to the full rite of adult initiation as the governing norm of them all.

This represents a major shift in theological and pastoral understanding from the sacramental theology and liturgical practice of the pre–Vatican II Church and those of the post–Vatican II Church. In the pre–Vatican II period, many theological explanations of the sacraments began with the baptism of infants (for example, Bernard Leem-ing, *Principles of Sacramental Theology*, Westminster, Md.: Newman Press, 1956, chap. 2), as if to underline the principle that the sacra-ments really do confer grace *ex opere operato*, by the power of Christ alone and not by the faith of the recipient (as some Protestants had insisted). Adult baptisms were essentially modifications of the rite of infant baptism (in much the same way as adult religious education was regarded as the exception, and the religious education of youth the norm).

A second major change suggested by the new rites, especially of adult initiation, is the explicit recognition that *the sacraments are closely related one to another*. Baptism is not simply the "ticket" which gives one entrance into the Church's sacred grounds, nor is Confirmation the first moment when the Holy Spirit is conferred (see *The Rites*, n. 34, p. 30). Baptism, Confirmation, and the Eucharist together consti-tute a single process of initiation. One is not simply handed a mem-bership card. One is fully introduced into the Spirit-filled life of the community which is God's people and Christ's body.

Third, the sacraments are seen less as means of personal sanctifi-cation and more as *empowerments* "to carry out the mission of the entire people of God in the Church and in the world." The broader ecclesial vision is sharpened by the directive that the rite of Christian initiation should normally occur during the Easter Vigil which "speaks" about initiation in terms of the evangelization of the cos-mos: fire, wind, wax, bees, light and darkness, water, oil, nakedness, bread, wine, aromas, words, and gestures. The full paschal sweep of God's intentions and accomplishments in Jesus Christ is sketched out. All of the other sacraments and sacramentals find their meaning and purpose only within this salvation-history context.

Finally, therefore, with the restoration of the catechumenate (the process of pastoral formation of candidates for entrance into the Church), the point is reinforced that membership in the Church is not simply for individual salvation but for participation in the saving work of God, in Christ, through the Church. One does not assume this *missionary responsibility* lightly. The Church, both universal and local, has to take care that those who present themselves for member-ship understand that missionary responsibility and are properly equipped to fulfill it. All must share in the candidate's growth in faith:

the community at large, relatives, friends, the sponsors, catechists, the bishop or his delegate, priests, and deacons. "The initiation of catechumens takes place step by step in the midst of the community of the faithful. Together with the catechumens, the faithful reflect upon the value of the paschal mystery, renew their own conversion, and by their example lead the catechumens to obey the Holy Spirit more generously" (Introduction, n. 4, pp. 20–21).

It is important to note, however, that the catechumenate does *not* apply to those who are seeking entrance into the Catholic Church from some other Christian community. Eastern Orthodox Christians need only make a simple profession of faith, but only after recourse to Rome may they enter the Latin rite. In other cases the admission to the Catholic Church consists of the profession of faith, ordinarily with the Catholic community as a part of the eucharistic celebration, followed by Confirmation (if the person has not already been confirmed in his or her own church), and climaxed by eucharistic Communion for the first time within the Catholic community. No abjuration of heresy is required, as in the past, nor is the candidate to be absolved from any penalty of excommunication. Conditional baptism ("If you are not already baptized, I baptize you...") is not permitted "unless there is reasonable doubt about the fact or validity of the baptism already received. If after serious investigation it seems necessary—because of such reasonable doubt—to confer baptism conditionally, the minister should carefully explain beforehand the reasons..., and he should administer it in the private form" (*Directory on Ecumenism,* 1967).

BAPTISM

New Testament Origins

Pre-Christian Ablutions and Baptisms

There were already many different kinds of ritual acts in Judaism, including those practiced by the Qumran sect, or Essenes. There were purification rites associated with food preparation and diet, and there were initiatory rites associated with water. This practice of *proselyte baptism* (by which Gentiles became Jews) seems to have developed with the expansion of Judaism outside Palestine. It had three phases: instruction concerning Judaism's persecuted condition and the commandments of the Law, circumcision for males, and a water bath for all. The central element of this ritual process was circumcision, by which solidarity was established with the holy nation of kings and priests (Exodus 19:6). Gradually, the water bath began to absorb the initiatory aspects of circumcision, and finally displaced it altogether. By the Christian era, therefore, proselyte baptism had assumed an increasingly initiatory rather than purificatory character.

This is not to suggest that Christian baptism was derived from proselyte baptism. What evidence there is leads us to conclude, on the contrary, that Christian baptism was patterned after the baptism of Jesus by John the Baptist in the Jordan river. There is no hint of a death-resurrection theme, no initiatory motif, no notion of admission to a new community. The emphasis is instead upon repentance as a preparation for messianic work. John's baptism was also a baptism in water. It would give way to another baptism in water and the Holy Spirit (Matthew 3:11; Luke 3:16). John himself regarded his baptism as a temporary rite. In submitting to it, Jesus established his solidarity with those who were the objects of John's preaching, the faithful remnant of Israel.

Baptism in Transition: From Judaism to Christianity

The Fourth Gospel says at one point that Jesus himself baptized, and at another that he did not but authorized his disciples to do so (John 3:22–23; 4:1–4). In any case, baptism continued to be practiced outside Jesus' circle, and it eventually widened the rift between his disciples and the followers of John. These pre-paschal baptisms were no longer Jewish, but neither were they as yet fully Christian. Not until the gathering at Pentecost is the outpouring of the Holy Spirit associated with baptism (Acts of the Apostles 2:1–39). There can be little doubt that the Pentecost occurrence influenced the ways in which the evangelists later interpreted the baptism of Jesus by John and the subsequent initiatory practice of the Church. Both water baptism and the outpouring of the Spirit are necessary as a follow-up to the proclamation of Jesus' resurrection and exaltation. Thus, the normal sequence:

proclamation of the Gospel, conversion in faith, water bath, and postbaptismal teaching, fellowship in the Spirit, breaking of the bread, and prayers (Acts of the Apostles 2:42).

Baptism in the New Testament Churches

The relatively sparse data from the Synoptics, the Acts of the Apostles, and the Fourth Gospel are summarized in the preceding paragraph. More detail is provided by non-canonical writings (i.e., writings which were written at the same time as the New Testament but which were not subsequently included on the list, or canon, of inspired books): in the *Didache* (literally, "The Teaching," composed about the year 100), in the *Apology* of Justin, and later in Tertullian and the *Apostolic Tradition* (c. 200) of Hippolytus (d. c. 236). The last describes a demanding system, normally lasting three years, of evangelization, moral formation, and gradual insertion of the candidates into the liturgical life of the community. After a final period of examination and intense prayer and fasting, the catechumens were initiated with the oil of exorcism, the profession of faith, water baptism by immersion, a postbaptismal imposition of hands, and anointing by the bishop. With the large influx of converts in the fourth century, however, the catechumenal process was not always able to prepare candidates in the same demanding fashion.

The *theology* of Baptism is developed later, in the Pauline corpus, in 1 John, and in 1 Peter. Baptism incorporates us into the death, burial, and resurrection of Jesus (Colossians 2:12; Ephesians 2:1–6; Philippians 3:10–11), and into the body of Christ (1 Corinthians 12:12–14,27). The baptismal event and the Christ-event are, for all practical purposes, identical. It is a baptism of repentance (Acts of the Apostles 2:38) and an expression of belief in the Good News (8:37). Baptism purifies (Ephesians 5:26), cleansing our hearts from an evil conscience (Hebrews 10:22). We become "dead to sin and alive to God in Christ Jesus" (Romans 6:11). And what does it require of us? We must lead a wholly different kind of life, "not under law but under grace" (6:12–23). Indeed, the Christian moral life is a living out of the paschal mystery that our baptism celebrates (2 Corinthians 4:10). For Paul, therefore, the initiation event is a process of total identification with

Christ. (See also the discussion of Baptism in the New Testament in chapter 16.)

Postbaptismal Controversies

Donatism and the Holiness Issue

Named after Donatus (d. 347), a false claimant to the episcopal chair at Carthage, Donatism was an early rigoristic movement (much like Jansenism in the postmedieval period) which maintained that church membership was restricted to those who are free from sin. Sacraments administered by priests in sin were regarded as invalid. Those who left the Church and then reentered must be rebaptized. Rome's answer was that Baptism should not be readministered; a solemn laying on of hands would suffice. This difference in practice led to an open conflict between Cyprian (d. 258), bishop of Carthage, and Pope Stephen I (d. 257). The two agreed that Baptism could not be repeated. The question was whether or not heretics could validly baptize to begin with. Eventually Roman law prevailed, and the principle (to which we referred in chapter 21) was established that the personal holiness of the minister is not required for the efficacy of the sacrament.

Pelagianism and Infant Baptism

Since Pelagianism (see chapter 5) affirmed that we can attain salvation by our own efforts because we are naturally good, and since, in effect, Pelagianism denied the reality of Original Sin, it denied at the same time the necessity and even the propriety of infant baptism. *Augustine* mounted the principal counterattack, arguing in his treatise *On Baptism* (I, 24, 34) that we must be in sacramental communion with Christ's redemptive act if we are to reach the Kingdom of God and salvation. Indeed, he cited the actual practice of infant baptism as a theological argument to prove the reality of Original Sin as antecedent to any personal sin. (Ironically, Augustine's argument was reversed in later centuries by those who insisted that infant baptism is necessary to take away Original Sin.)

811

On the other hand, Augustine also inveighed against a purely mechanical concept of the sacrament. Without faith there is no sacrament. Thus, against the Donatists he argued that Christ, and not the sinful priest, is the true minister of Baptism; against the Pelagians, that Baptism is necessary for salvation; he also insisted that the fruitfulness of the sacrament depends on the dispositions of the recipient, i.e., the recipient's faith and love.

Thus, by the late fourth and early fifth centuries the theology of Baptism reached a certain level of maturity, weaving together various strands of New Testament and classic patristic theologies. What once happened to Christ now happens to us in Baptism. We are reborn to a new life, and we are given the Holy Spirit as an empowerment to live in Christ and in his body, the Church. However, the catechumenate also went into decline between the fourth and sixth centuries, losing its character as a step taken in faith. By the Middle Ages it no longer existed, for all practical purposes. (For a fuller treatment of the history of the rite of initiation, see J. D. C. Fisher, *Christian Initiation: Baptism in the Medieval West,* London: S.P.C.K., 1970, and Leonel Mitchell, *Baptismal Anointing,* London: S.P.C.K., 1966. Some of this material is summarized in *Made, Not Born,* pp. 50–98, cited in the Suggested Readings at the end of this chapter.)

Reformation and Contemporary Debates

Infant baptism was among the most contested issues of the sixteenth-century debates on the sacrament. The Reformers asked how infant baptism could be justified since the recipient obviously had no faith. The discussions were aggravated by the Anabaptist movement, which practiced a "believer's baptism" and insisted on a *re*-baptism ("ana"-baptism) of those baptized as infants. On the other hand, both Luther and Calvin opposed the Anabaptists. Luther pointed out that infants do not resist the power of God's grace. By baptism they are brought into a believing church where Word and sacrament are rightly preached and celebrated. Calvin appealed to the Holy Spirit as the nurturer of the beginnings of faith and repentance even in infants. Since baptism is a sign of the Covenant, infants receiving this sacrament also partake of the Covenant promise and community. He also cited Paul's teaching that the infants of believers are already sanctified (1 Corinthians 7:14).

The issue flared again as an intra-Protestant controversy in the twentieth century, with Karl Barth opposing the practice on grounds similar to those of the Anabaptists (see *The Teaching of the Church Regarding Baptism*, London: SCM Press, 1948), and he, in turn, being opposed by Oscar Cullmann (*Baptism in the New Testament*, London: SCM Press, 1950) and Heinrich Schlier, a Protestant exegete who later converted to Catholicism. Both appealed to Romans 6:1–11 where Paul insists that Jesus' death and resurrection free us from sin and grant new life to "all of us who have been baptized into Christ Jesus" (v. 3).

The so-called Lima Document of the World Council of Churches acknowledges both forms of baptism: infant and believer's. In both cases the initiative of God in Christ is asserted as the crucial unifying belief. (*Baptism, Eucharist and Ministry*, Faith and Order Paper No. 111, Geneva: World Council of Churches, 1982).

The Doctrine of Baptism

The theological development is summed up in the *Council of Trent*'s canons on the sacrament of Baptism (Session VII, 1547): that Baptism is valid even if administered by heretics, that it is necessary for salvation, that it imposes obligations to live a holy life, that its grace can be lost through serious sin, that it can never be repeated, that it can be administered to infants and children, etc. The *Second Vatican Council*'s *Dogmatic Constitution on the Church* notes that Baptism incorporates us into the Church, orients us to the worship of God, and gives us a rebirth as sons and daughters of God (n. 11). The council also insisted that initiation is our entrance into the paschal mystery (n. 7), calls us to witness as a priestly, apostolic, and holy people (*Decree on the Apostolate of the Laity*, nn. 11, 2, 3), and is a bond of unity and a source of potentially full unity among the divided Christian communities (*Decree on Ecumenism*, n. 22).

The conciliar retrieval of the classical tradition on initiation bore pastoral fruit in the restoration of the catechumenal process in 1972 (to which we referred earlier in this chapter). The four stages or periods are: (1) the pre-catechumenate, in which there is initial evan-

gelization; (2) the catechumenate, in which there is continued evangelization and catechesis; (3) the period of immediate preparation for
and reception of the sacraments of initiation; and (4) the postinitiation
catechesis (*mystagogia*) and more active participation in the mission of
the community.

"Baptism of Desire"

The Church has always taught that Baptism is necessary for salvation. On the other hand, we have seen in chapters 5 and 7 (and also in
chapter 10 on the question of religious pluralism) that the offer of
grace and revelation is universally available. Accordingly, the doctrine that Baptism is necessary for salvation can mean that for those
called explicitly to the Church, Baptism is necessary for their salvation (see again chapter 19 on the necessity of the Church). In other
words, if we are convinced in conscience that Jesus is Lord and
Savior, we are obliged to seek admission to his Church, for there is no
other place that we can go where the Lordship of Jesus is proclaimed
and celebrated, and where we can collaborate in his historic mission
for the sake of the Kingdom of God.

This understanding of the necessity of Baptism for salvation has
also been known as "Baptism of desire." A widely held position,
taught by Thomas Aquinas, was that prior to Christ it was sufficient
to believe in God and in providence. This was tantamount to *implicit*
faith in Christ. After the coming of Christ, however, *explicit* faith was
necessary. It was generally assumed in the Middle Ages, we must
never forget, that the world as a whole had already been evangelized.
This is long before the geographical discoveries and the development
of modern means of transportation and communication described in
chapter 3. After the discoveries of America and the Far East, the
question of human salvation was posed with much greater urgency.
Some theologians taught that people across the sea who had not yet
been evangelized were like those who were alive before the coming of
Christ. They, too, could be saved by implicit faith. These theologians
were convinced of two principles: Christ is the one mediator of
salvation, and every person is touched somehow by the grace of
Christ.

This general understanding of a "Baptism of desire" received its most formal expression in the so-called Boston Letter sent by the Holy Office (now called the Congregation for the Doctrine of Faith) to Cardinal Richard Cushing (d. 1970) in 1949. A controversy had developed in the Archdiocese of Boston, Massachusetts, because of the literal interpretation given the principle "Outside the [Catholic] Church, no salvation" by Father Leonard Feeney, S.J. (d. 1978). According to the letter, it is Catholic doctrine that "it is not always required that a person be incorporated in reality (*reapse*) as a member of the Church, but it is required that the person belong to it at least in desire and longing (*voto et desiderio*). It is not always necessary that this desire be explicit. . . . God also accepts an implicit desire, so called because it is contained in the good disposition of soul by which a person wants his or her will to be conformed to God's will." This teaching is reaffirmed by Vatican II's *Dogmatic Constitution on the Church*, n. 16 (see also n. 9). (See Gregory Baum, "Baptism of Desire," *The Concise Sacramentum Mundi*, New York: Seabury Press, 1975, pp. 75–78.)

The Rite of Baptism

Ideally the rite of Baptism is celebrated during the Easter Vigil. When not, the celebration should be filled with the Easter Spirit. The rite itself begins with an instruction by the celebrant, followed by a litany, blessing of the water, renunciation of Satan, anointing with the oil of catechumens, profession of faith, the pouring of the water, and the invocation of the Trinity ("[Name of the baptized], I baptize you in the name of the Father, and of the Son, and of the Holy Spirit"), anointing, clothing with the white garment, and presentation of the lighted candle.

Jesus, the Church, and Baptism

The sacraments not only signify and communicate grace for the recipient. They also disclose something fundamental about the *Church* which celebrates them. Thus, Baptism incorporates one into the Church, associates one with the death and resurrection of Christ unto new life, effects a forgiveness of sins, and orients one to the worship of God and the wider mission of the Church. In baptizing, the Church reveals itself to itself and to the rest of the world primarily as a *community*, the Body of Christ, and only secondarily as an institution; the Church identifies itself with the sufferings and death of Christ and so points the way to a share in his resurrection and glorification; it shows itself a forgiving community and, at the same time, a community in need of forgiveness; and its whole life is directed to the glory of God which is achieved in and through the humanization of the world. The Church which baptizes and is baptized has been given "a new birth by water and the Holy Spirit" and as such is a "holy people... [anointed] with the chrism of salvation" just as "Christ was anointed Priest, Prophet, and King" unto "everlasting life" (*Rite of Baptism*).

But the sacraments also disclose something fundamental about *Jesus*. He, too, is baptized (Mark 1:4–11). But his submission to John's baptism was not an expression of sinfulness but of his union with sinful humanity (John 1:32–34). His baptism, like ours, inaugurates him into a mission for the sake of community: immediately, his own community of disciples, but, ultimately, the whole human community (also Matthew 3:13–17; Luke 3:21–22). And he commands his disciples to baptize (Mark 16:15–16). Christian baptism is a participation in Jesus' baptism, and an initiation into his mission.

CONFIRMATION

History

There is no separate rite of Confirmation in the New Testament. Where the Spirit is given, the Spirit is given in connection with Baptism.

The East has never separated Baptism and Confirmation (chrismation). Theologically, the East has viewed them as essentially a single sacrament and, juridically, the East has always regarded the presbyter as the legitimate minister of Baptism and the postbaptismal rites (including anointing).

In the West, however, the postbaptismal rites (including the anointing) were reserved to the bishop. At least two developments eventually led to the separation of Baptism and Confirmation: (a) the sense of urgency about the now universal practice of infant baptism (a development linked with Augustine's elaboration of the doctrine of Original Sin against the Pelagians), and (b) the unavailability of bishops to attend immediately to the postbaptismal rites in the cases of the emergency baptism of catechumens and because of the growth of the Church in rural and outlying areas. The bishop now came to those who had already been baptized sometime earlier. Here, too, we have the starting point for the later episcopal visitations, mainly for Confirmation (the word appears for the first time during this period). The prerogative of the bishops as ministers of the postbaptismal rites in the West did not presuppose, but in fact created, two independent sacraments.

At first, the separation of the two rites was regarded as abnormal and less than ideal. Consequently, efforts were made to administer the postbaptismal rites as soon as possible after Baptism, including the baptism of infants, as was the practice in the East. It was not until the thirteenth century that opposition to the separation of rites began to relax and official allowance was made for the concrete pastoral situation. A provincial council at Cologne in 1280, for example, postponed Confirmation until at least the age of seven. A minimum instead of a maximum age was now imposed. Adults continued to follow the older tradition and received the postbaptismal rites immediately after Baptism. Originally, these rites were relatively simple, as in the baptismal anointing today. From the ninth century on, however, a second anointing which had been known only in Rome was expanded to a self-contained "rite of confirmation."

It was only in the high Middle Ages that a specific theology of Confirmation was developed in order to justify, *after the fact*, the now autonomous rite carried out only by the bishop. The notion emerged that Confirmation provides a *gratia ad robur* ("grace for strength"), the armor of the soldier of Christ. The False Decretals of Gratian, which formed the basis of all medieval law, treated Confirmation as a greater sacrament even than Baptism. Peter Lombard, whose *Sentences* influenced much of medieval theology, including Aquinas, followed the same line and described Confirmation as the gift of the Spirit "for strengthening" (*ad robur*) in contrast with baptismal grace, which is "for forgiveness" (*ad remissionem*). Even though this distinction had no basis in Sacred Scripture, the liturgy, or the Fathers of the Church, it was retained in the theology textbooks until the present time (see, for example, *Sharing the Light of Faith, National Catechetical Directory for Catholics of the United States,* p. 68). The distinction was definitively established by the Council of Florence in its *Decree for the Armenians* in 1439, and was confirmed without further reflection by the Council of Trent against Luther. Always the difference between the two ordinary ministers of the sacrament is emphasized: the presbyter for Baptism, the bishop for Confirmation.

Throughout this period the practice of receiving Confirmation prior to the reception of first Eucharist continued. It was Pope Pius X in the 1910 decree *Quam Singulari* who placed first confession prior to first Eucharist, both to be received at the age of reason (approximately seven). Confirmation was delayed to a later age, setting the stage for a catechesis that stressed Confirmation as the sacrament of maturity, making one a "soldier of Christ," and so forth. Pastorally, the sacrament would later assume the character of a graduation exercise from formal religious instruction.

The Second Vatican Council called for a revision of the sacraments of initiation (*Constitution on the Sacred Liturgy,* nn. 64–71) and eventually of the rite of Confirmation itself, which was promulgated in 1971.

Today the rite of Confirmation is often administered, even in the West, by presbyters rather than bishops, since the ideal time for the celebration of the full rite of initiation is at the Easter Vigil. It is presumed that the local bishop will preside on that occasion at his cathedral church.

The Rite of Confirmation

The celebration of the sacrament follows the presentation of the lighted candle in the baptismal part of the rite of initiation. The presider reminds the newly baptized that they are to "share in the outpouring of the Holy Spirit." After a prayer for the sevenfold gift of the Holy Spirit, the presider, with the laying on of the hand, anoints the forehead of the candidate with chrism in the sign of the cross, saying: "Be sealed with the Gift of the Holy Spirit."

The revised rite (1971) for children baptized as infants stipulates that Confirmation be postponed until the age of reason, unless an episcopal conference chooses a "more appropriate" age. Ordinarily Confirmation should take place within the Eucharist to express the fundamental connection of the sacraments.

The ideal liturgical order remains Baptism-Confirmation-Eucharist, although some religious educators, appealing to the practice of the Church for most of its history, argue that there are good developmental reasons for spreading them over a period of years.

Theological Reflection

Baptism and Confirmation could be considered, in light of their origins and history, *one sacrament*. Confirmation, which comprises the postbaptismal rites of anointing, the laying on of hands, and the words "Be sealed with the Gift of the Holy Spirit," is a *ratification*, or sealing, of Baptism. For those who were baptized as infants, Confirmation provides an opportunity to ratify freely and deliberately what was done for them at Baptism. It helps to focus their minds and the minds of the whole community on the essentially *missionary* dimensions of the baptismal commitment.

Jesus, the Church, and Confirmation

As a continuation and/or ratification of the Christian's baptismal commitment, Confirmation expresses the essentially missionary character of the *Church* and its nature as the Temple of the Holy Spirit. It is a community called to manifest "the spirit of wisdom and understanding, the spirit of right judgment and courage, the spirit of knowledge and reverence . . . the spirit of wonder and awe in [God's] presence" (*Rite of Confirmation*). It is not only a sacred, grace-bearing sign for the good of the recipient, therefore, but it is also a principal moment when the Church reveals itself to itself and to the rest of the world as a particular kind of community, filled with the Holy Spirit and committed to the Spirit's release for the transformation of the whole of creation.

The sacrament also reveals *Jesus* as the one who receives and sends the Holy Spirit, as the one, therefore, who is confirmed in his mission and who confirms us in ours.

EUCHARIST

Introduction

Our reflections on the Eucharist are framed by two basic doctrinal principles: the one enunciated by the Council of Trent and the other by the Second Vatican Council. Trent taught that the Eucharist is not simply one of the sacraments but is preeminent among them because Christ is present in the Eucharist even before the sacrament is used (*Decree on the Most Holy Eucharist,* chapter III, Session XIII, 1551); Vatican II declared that "the Liturgy..., most of all in the divine sacrifice of the Eucharist, is the outstanding means whereby the faithful can express in their lives, and manifest to others, the mystery of Christ and the real nature of the true Church" (*Constitution on the Sacred Liturgy,* n. 2). The Eucharist is indeed "the source and summit of the entire Christian life" (n. 11).

Biblical Origins

The term *eucharist* is derived from the Greek word which means "thanksgiving." Jesus himself "gave thanks" at the Last Supper (Luke 22:19; 1 Corinthians 11:24; Mark 14:23; Matthew 26:27). The more strongly Semitic flavor of Mark's account has led some biblical interpreters to conclude that its wording is even closer to the original than Paul's. The differences between the Marcan and Pauline accounts are too great for us to assume a common Greek source. On the other hand, there is sufficient measure of agreement between them to assume a common Aramaic source. The essential kernel of the various reports, however, is clearly part of a unanimous tradition in the New Testament churches.

The *meal* which is the object of these reports was only the last in a long series of daily meals which Jesus shared with his disciples. In the Oriental world of his day, a shared meal was always a sign of peace, trust, and communality. Jesus, of course, proclaimed the Kingdom by sharing meals with outcasts, tax-collectors, and the like. But this last meal was special. According to the Synoptics it was a ritual Passover meal, a festive farewell meal. Whether it was a Passover meal or not (John says otherwise), it had the same basic structure: the words over the bread, its breaking and sharing; the words over the wine, and its sharing. But Jesus identified the bread and wine with his own body and blood. And sensing his own impending death, he speaks of himself as a sacrifice. Just as the unleavened bread is broken, so will his body be broken. And just as the wine is poured out, so will his blood. All four texts agree that Jesus' death is an atonement and establishes a new Covenant. The Jews, in fact, regarded every death of an innocent person as an atoning death, and Jesus saw his own death in this light.

There are connections here also with the Old Testament: first, with the idea of the sacrifice of the old Covenant in Exodus 24:8,11 and of the new Covenant in Jeremiah 31:31–34; and, second, with the idea of the atoning sufferings of the servant of God in Isaiah 53:12. Thus, the New Testament interprets the death of Jesus as an atoning death which establishes a new Covenant in his blood and brings redemption to all. By distributing the bread and wine, his body and blood, Jesus was indicating that his disciples were to share in his sacrifice and in the power of his atoning death. This, too, is a familiar idea in Oriental thinking: that eating and drinking communicate divine gifts.

With the resurrection the disciples now see the Last Supper and their own subsequent meals together in a new light. They eat and drink with the assurance that Christ will make good his promise to be present among those who are gathered in his name (Matthew 18:20). The new fellowship is now characterized by eschatological joy, a fundamental confidence in the coming of the Kingdom (Acts of the Apostles 2:46).

There are, of course, arguments among New Testament scholars and theologians of various Christian churches regarding the precise meaning and implications of Jesus' words at the Last Supper. For one tradition (Paul and Luke) it was essentially a cultic service. For another (John) it was essentially a farewell meal with a commandment to love one another as he had loved them, with no mention of a meal ritual or a memorial command. It is sufficient for our purpose to note that there is an undeniable continuity between what happened at the Last Supper and what the disciples did together at meals after the resurrection. There is no other explanation for the fact that the disciples repeated this meal and that later communities always referred to the actions of Jesus at the Last Supper to explain and justify what they did at the eucharistic table. The post-Easter Church was convinced that it was doing what Jesus intended it to do when he said: "Do this in remembrance of me" (1 Corinthians 11:24–25).

As an act of remembrance (*anamnesis*) the Eucharist not only recalls to mind what Jesus did but also effectively makes it present again. Thus, Paul affirms the bodily presence of Jesus: "The cup of blessing that we bless, is it not a sharing in the blood of Christ? The bread that we break, is it not a sharing in the body of Christ?" (1 Corinthians 10:16). Indeed, those who eat and drink unworthily "will be answerable for the body and blood of the Lord" (11:27). Because we partake of the same bread, "we who are many are one body" (10:17).

The Lord's Supper establishes and celebrates the communion that exists not only between the Church and Christ but also within the Church—i.e., not only "with Christ" but also "in Christ." And it is a communion that looks always not only to the past—i.e., to the Last Supper and to the redemptive events that followed it—but also to the future, "until he comes" (11:26). Jesus himself had said that he would not drink again of the fruit of the vine until that day when he would drink it new in the Kingdom of God (Mark 14:25; Matthew 26:29; Luke 22:18). Christ's presence in the Eucharist, therefore, is the presence not only of the crucified and risen one, but also the presence of one who is yet to come.

On the other hand, that presence comes about not through some magical formula, but through the proclamatory words of faith. John places a clear warning at the end of Jesus' words about the bread of life: "It is the spirit that gives life; the flesh is useless. The words that I have spoken to you are spirit and life" (John 6:63). The word is ultimately effective, however, only if it is creative of a sense of community. Where there is no fellowship, where there are divisions, where there is insensitivity to those in need, there is no real community and the Lord's Supper brings judgment, not grace (1 Corinthians

11:17–34). What is proclaimed must be lived (11:26). (See also the discussion of the Eucharist in the New Testament in chapter 16.)

History of the Eucharist

General Structure

As we have just seen, the Eucharist, or Lord's Supper, was celebrated in the beginning as a *meal*. (The term *Mass* is derived from the Latin word *missa*, which meant "dismissal," the closing blessing at any ecclesiastical celebration. The term was eventually applied only to the Eucharist.) During the second and third centuries the meal disappeared. The prayer of thanksgiving (formerly known as the "canon" and now once again called the "Eucharistic Prayer") became the central feature of the rite. It was during this prayer that the bread and wine were consecrated, after which the people responded "Amen" to ratify what had been said and done. Communion followed.

The same introductory prayers that are recited today ("The Lord be with you." "And also with you." "Lift up your hearts." "We lift them up to the Lord." "Let us give thanks to the Lord our God." "It is right to give him thanks and praise.") are to be found in the account of Justin about the year 150 and in a text put forward as a model by Hippolytus about 215. Though the details of the service were left to the discretion of the presider, especially the phrasing of some of the prayers (another practice recently restored), the whole Christian world must have celebrated the Eucharist in much this form until well into the fourth century.

In the earliest centuries, too, the Eucharist was celebrated every Sunday, but on few other occasions. Daily Mass was not the rule. The Eucharist was attended by the whole Christian community of the neighborhood, early in the morning (now that it was separated from the supper meal at the end of the day) and before work (since Sunday was still an ordinary workday). Part of the traditional synagogue service survived and was incorporated into these liturgies. The memoirs of the Apostles or the writings of the prophets were read, and these were followed by a sermon from the president of the assembly and a prayer for the general needs of the community.

There are also various indications of an Offertory procession (also since restored) as early as the third century. This ceremony in which bread and wine and other gifts were brought forward to the altar may have been a conscious reaction against Gnosticism, which denied the goodness of matter.

As the Church was liberated from persecution and spread more easily through the empire, cultural diversification set into the liturgy. The entrance rite was expanded to include prayers at the foot of the altar (since eliminated and now incorporated into the introductory greetings and penitential rite). Readings from Scripture, however, formed the core of the early part of the Mass in every celebration, and hence this part of the liturgy was simply called, as it is today, the liturgy of the word. Responses were developed for each reading— songs which survive today in the form of psalm verses and the alleluia. Much solemnity attended the reading of the Gospel: e.g., candles and incense. There followed the recitation of the creed, except in non-Roman rites, where the creed occurred just before the Eucharist Prayer itself. After the creed came the intercessory prayers (as we have them again today), then the preparation of the gifts (the prayers which are still recited silently over the gifts were not introduced until the ninth century). Finally, the Eucharist itself.

Eucharistic Prayer

For many centuries the canon, or Eucharistic Prayer, was recited in the West in an undertone not audible to the congregation. Today it is once again proclaimed aloud. In the East it was always proclaimed in that manner. The admonition "Do this in remembrance of me" was followed, in all liturgies, by the *anamnesis:* "We remember, we do this to commemorate you." The prayer ends, as it did from Hippolytus's day, with the solemn doxology: "Through him, with him, in him, in the unity of the Holy Spirit, all glory and honor is yours, almighty Father, forever and ever." After Communion there was the blessing (*missa*), and the sacred vessels were cleansed after the liturgy itself.

This basic, straightforward structure was progressively interrupted by the insertion of a variety of petitions for the living and dead, and then by the *epiclesis,* or solemn invocation of the Holy Spirit. Even the breaking of bread came to be embroidered with

824

prayers. The canon was rendered inaudible by the Carolingian liturgists, who wished to make it a sort of sanctuary which the priest alone could enter. To compensate for this, the elevation of the host and chalice after the consecration was introduced in the thirteenth century so that the whole congregation could look upon and adore the sacrament. It was only at the close of the canon that the priest resumed contact with the people. (In the pre–Vatican II Latin Mass, the *"Nobis quoque peccatoribus"* toward the end of the canon and the *"per omnia sæcula sæculorum"* just before the *Pater Noster,* or Our Father, were the only audible sounds made by the celebrant following the recitation of the preface.)

Congregational Participation

By the seventeenth century frequent Communion had fallen into disrepute, partly through the influence of Jansenism. Not until the early years of the twentieth century was frequent Communion encouraged again, by Pope Pius X. As recently as 1960 most people were still not making responses at Mass. What responses there were the "altar boy," or server, made in their name. The "dialogue Mass" was introduced in the late 1950s just before the Second Vatican Council, but the Latin language was still used. During the Romanticist eighteenth century, choirs had begun to supplant the congregation, singing elaborate polyphonic renditions of the various parts of the Mass: *Kyrie* ("Lord have mercy"), *Gloria, Credo, Sanctus* ("Holy, Holy"), and *Agnus Dei* ("Lamb of God"). As a concession, the congregation was encouraged to sing vernacular hymns not taken from the Eucharist itself, but this was stopped in the twentieth century.

Private Masses

The practice of private Masses, i.e., Masses celebrated by a priest without a congregation, appeared about the sixth century, chiefly in the form of votive Masses, or Masses for the necessities of the faithful. The Mass was perceived increasingly as an act of petition, something to be performed to receive some particular benefit from God, or it was often regarded as a rite, however complicated, to produce hosts for the tabernacle. And since private Masses became so frequent, they were also regarded eventually as the norm rather than the exception. The Second Vatican Council, however, declared the communal celebration preferable to individual and quasiprivate celebrations (*Constitution on the Sacred Liturgy*, n. 27).

Eucharistic Doctrines

Catholic eucharistic doctrine has been focused on two issues: the sacrificial nature of the Mass and the real presence of Christ in the consecrated elements of bread and wine. The major components of official Catholic teaching in recent decades are to be founded in four documents: Vatican II's *Constitution on the Sacred Liturgy* (1963), Pope Paul VI's encyclical *Mysterium Fidei* (1965), the instruction *Eucharisticum Mysterium* of the Sacred Congregation of Rites (1967), and the Holy Thursday letter *Dominicæ Cenæ* of Pope John Paul II (1980). The two papal letters are closer in orientation to the Council of Trent than to Vatican II, because of their emphasis on the sacrifice of the Mass and the role of the priest in offering the sacrifice.

It is official Catholic teaching (Council of Trent) that the Mass is a true *sacrifice*, not only of praise and thanksgiving and of commemoration but also of expiation for the living and the dead, without diminishing the value of the sacrifice of Calvary. Christ is the same victim and priest in the Eucharist as he was on the cross, although the mode of offering is different at Mass. The sacrifice of the cross was a bloody sacrifice; the sacrifice of the Mass is unbloody. Nonetheless, the fruits of the latter sacrifice are the same as those of the former. The sacrifice of the Mass, Trent declared, is "properly offered not only for the sins, penalties, satisfactions, and other needs of the faithful who are living but also for the departed in Christ who are not yet fully cleansed" (*Decree on the Mass*, chapter II).

It is also official Catholic teaching that Christ is *really present* in the consecrated elements of bread and wine. By the Middle Ages the real presence of Christ was being reduced by many (especially Berengar of Tours, d. 1088) to a merely spiritual presence, in reaction to a crudely physical notion (represented, for example, in the belief that if one were to scratch the consecrated host, it would bleed). For the first time in the history of Catholic doctrine, the Fourth Lateran Council (1215) spoke of *transubstantiation*, i.e., the belief that the substance of bread and wine is changed into the body and blood of Christ. This teaching was reaffirmed and made more precise by the Council of Constance (1415) and the Council of Trent (1551). Zwingli and Calvin, however, denied transubstantiation completely, while Luther held to *consubstantiation*, i.e., the belief that the bread and wine become the body and blood of Christ but that they remain also bread and wine.

The traditional medieval teaching on the real presence was repeated in Pope Paul VI's *Mysterium Fidei* (1965), an encyclical written against the views of certain Dutch Catholic theologians who were attempting to explain the real presence without employing the Scholastic concept of transubstantiation. A mere "transignification or transfinalization," he insisted, is not sufficient to explain the real presence. Rather, the consecrated elements bear not only a new meaning (transignification) and a new purpose (transfinalization) but a new substantial, or ontic, reality as well (transubstantiation). The pope also reaffirmed the teaching that the real presence continues after Mass, and he defended eucharistic adoration and private Masses.

The *scope* of Christ's presence has been subject to controversy as well. According to the same medieval doctrine of transubstantiation, the whole Christ is present under each form, the consecrated bread and the consecrated wine. For that reason, Trent insisted, it is unnecessary to receive the Eucharist under both species as John Hus (d. 1415) and his disciples in Bohemia had argued. (The practice of Communion under both kinds has been reintroduced into the Roman Catholic Church following Vatican II.) But if Christ is present under each form, that is not to say that he is present *only* there.

The Second Vatican Council has taught that the presence of Christ in the Eucharist is not confined to the consecrated elements of bread and wine. Christ is present, first, in the community which has assembled for worship. Second, he is present in the person of the minister who presides in his name. Third, he is present in the biblical word which is proclaimed. Finally, he is present in a uniquely sacramental way in the sacred species themselves (*Constitution on the Sacred Liturgy*, n. 7).

The real presence of Christ in the sacred species comes about through the ordained priest, who "confects" the Eucharist (Lateran Council IV). The power of the priest to consecrate the bread and wine is not dependent upon his personal holiness (Council of Constance). Under the impact of the twentieth-century renewal, this traditional Catholic emphasis on the role of the ordained priest was broadened to include the participation of all the faithful who are present at the celebration of the Eucharist. Both Pope Pius XII's *Mediator Dei* (1947) and Vatican II's *Constitution on the Sacred Liturgy* insisted that the faithful participate not merely through the priest but along with him (*Constitution*, n. 48). This is not to say, however, that their function is the same as the priest's.

For an ecological and cosmic understanding of the eucharistic presence of Christ, see Tony Kelly, *An Expanding Theology: Faith in a World of Connections* (Newtown, NSW, Australia: E. J. Dwyer, 1993), pp. 169–80.

Intercommunion

The term *intercommunion* (also known as *communicatio in sacris*, "communication in sacred realities") refers to this full *eucharistic sharing* (also known as "*eucharistic hospitality*") between and among separated Christians. It describes the reception of Holy Communion by a single separated Christian in a church other than his or her own, or it refers to the future possibility of full church-to-church reciprocity in the celebration and reception of the Eucharist.

The principle is endorsed by Vatican II: "As for common worship (*communicatio in sacris*), however, it may not be regarded as a means to be used indiscriminately for the restoration of unity among Christians. Such worship depends chiefly on two principles: it should signify the unity of the Church; it should provide a sharing in the means of grace. The fact that it should signify unity generally rules out common worship. Yet the gaining of a needed grace sometimes commends it" (*Decree on Ecumenism*, n. 8).

Implementation of this principle was left to the Secretariat for Promoting Christian Unity (now the Pontifical Council for Christian Unity). This Vatican agency issued an *Ecumenical Directory* in 1967 and released a special instruction on intercommunion in 1972. The conditions under which intercommunion is allowed by these two documents are these: (1) Admission to the Eucharist is confined to particular cases of those Christians who have a faith in the sacrament in conformity with that of the Catholic Church. (2) Such Christians must experience a serious spiritual need for the eucharistic sustenance. (3) They must be unable for a prolonged period to have recourse to a minister of their own community. (4) They must ask for the sacrament of their own accord. (5) They must have proper dispositions and lead lives worthy of a Christian.

Even if these conditions are fulfilled, "It will be a pastoral responsibility to see that the admission of these other Christians to communion does not endanger or disturb the faith of Catholics." These "rules" do not apply to Orthodox Christians, who, "though separated from us, have true sacraments, above all, because of apostolic succession, the priesthood and the eucharist, which unite them to us by close ties, so that the risk of obscuring the relation between eucharistic communion and ecclesial communion is somewhat reduced."

The revised Code of Canon Law (1983) stipulates that: "Whenever necessity requires or genuine spiritual advantage suggests and provided that the danger of error or indifferentism is avoided, it is lawful for the faithful for whom it is physically or morally impossible to approach a Catholic minister, to receive the sacraments of penance, Eucharist, and anointing of the sick from non-Catholic ministers in whose churches these sacraments are valid" (canon 844, par. 2).

Ecumenical Consensus Today

It was once assumed that Catholics alone (with the usual exception of the Orthodox) believed in the sacrificial nature of the Eucharist. The ecumenical dialogues and consultations at both international and national levels since 1965 have almost completely undermined that common assumption. The sacrificial nature of the Eucharist is affirmed in varying degrees by the Anglican–Roman Catholic, Orthodox-Catholic, Lutheran-Catholic, and Presbyterian-Reformed– Catholic consultations, and in a 1970 consensus statement of a study commission of the National Council of Churches in the United States.

With regard to the real presence, the consensus is even wider and stronger. Every consultation in which Catholics have been involved affirms some measure of basic agreement on the real presence of Christ in the Eucharist, e.g., with Lutherans, Presbyterians and Reformed, Disciples of Christ, Anglicans, and Orthodox. The Lutherans, for example, do not even reject everything implied in the medieval term *transubstantiation*, but they shy away from it because it is "misleading."

On the Eucharist in general and intercommunion in particular, see Geoffrey Wainwright's articles, "Eucharist" and "Intercommunion," in *Dictionary of the Ecumenical Movement*, Nicholas Lossky, et al., eds. (Grand Rapids, Mich.: William B. Eerdmans Publishing Co., 1991), pp. 374–77, 518–20.

Jesus, the Church, and the Eucharist

The first effect of the Eucharist is a more profound incorporation into the unity of the *Church*. St. Thomas himself regarded the Eucharist as the sacrament of the Church's unity (*Summa Theologiæ*, III, q. 82, a. 2). According to Karl Rahner, the Church is "most manifest and in the most intensive form, it attains the highest actuality of its own nature, when it celebrates the eucharist" (*The Church and the Sacraments*, p. 84). The Church at the Eucharist is a structured community, a community listening to the word of God, a community in continuity with the preaching, ministry, death, and resurrection of its Lord, a community looking forward to the coming of the Kingdom, a community conscious of its sinfulness and repentant of its sins, a community convinced of the power of God's grace, a community ready to serve others, i.e., to carry out "the breaking of the bread" beyond the Church, and a community here and now open to the presence of the Lord and his Spirit.

Through the Eucharist, *Jesus* invites us to a table fellowship that is an anticipation of the heavenly banquet itself, one that is open to everyone: outcasts, tax-collectors, and anyone else marginalized by respectable society. In celebrating the Eucharist we take on the mind and heart of Jesus himself, opening ourselves, as he did, to everyone without exception and committing ourselves to the creation of a world where no one is excluded from the table. When Jesus said, "Do this in memory of me," he was asking us not only to repeat the celebration of the Eucharist but also to fulfill the missionary mandate implied in the celebration.

SUMMARY

1. The *rite of Christian initiation* includes three sacraments: Baptism, Confirmation, and Eucharist. It follows a suitable period of formation known as the *catechumenate*. The initiation of *adults* is the pastoral norm, not the exception. The new rite underscores the *unity among the sacraments,* their close relationship with the *mission of the Church,* and the *responsibility of the local church* to share in the candidate's growth in faith.

2. Those entering the Catholic Church from some other Christian church do not become catechumens, nor are they rebaptized, nor do they abjure "heresy." They are already members of the Body of Christ.

3. The sacrament of *Baptism* is not without pre-Christian origins—i.e., the purification and initiation rites of Judaism, and the baptism of John the Baptist.

4. The New Testament data on the *practice of Baptism* even in the postresurrection period are sparse. The *theology of Baptism,* however, is developed in Paul, 1 John, and 1 Peter. Baptism incorporates us into the death, burial, and resurrection of Jesus, and into the body of Christ.

5. Against *Donatism* and *Pelagianism, Augustine* insisted that Christ, not the sinful priest, is the true minister of Baptism, and that, because Baptism is necessary for salvation, infants can and ought to be baptized.

6. The principal Reformers, *Luther* and *Calvin,* supported the practice of infant baptism, but it was opposed by the *Anabaptists,* who insisted that the only valid baptism is believer's baptism. Their position was taken up in the twentieth century by Protestant theologians like *Karl Barth,* who was opposed, in turn, by *Oscar Cullmann.*

7. The major elements of the Catholic theological tradition on Baptism were gathered up and definitively taught by the *Council of Trent.* An even wider ecclesiological vision, however, was provided by *Vatican II,* which emphasized our incorporation into the Church and our call to worship.

8. *"Baptism of desire,"* tantamount to *implicit faith* in Christ, was adopted by the Holy Office in 1949 in its response to the so-called Feeney case in Boston, Massachusetts, where the principle "Outside the [Catholic] Church, no salvation" had been pushed to extremes.

9. *Confirmation* is also a sacrament, but it may be considered as part of the sacrament of Baptism. There is no separate rite of Confirmation in the New Testament.

10. The *separation of the rites* of Baptism and Confirmation in the West occurred because the postbaptismal rites (= Confirmation) were reserved for bishops, and bishops were often unavailable when Baptism was administered. An elaboration of this separate rite of Confirmation began in the ninth

century, and it was only in the high Middle Ages that a specific theology of Confirmation developed. The distinction was ratified by the Councils of Florence and Trent.

11. Both Baptism and Confirmation underscore the *missionary* dimension of Jesus' ministry and of the role of the Church in the world.

12. The *Eucharist* is the preeminent sacrament because Christ is present in it even before it is used. It is also the "source and summit" of the entire Christian life.

13. The term *eucharist* means "thanksgiving." It has its origins in the meal which Jesus celebrated with his disciples, known as the *Last Supper*, at which he directed them to "do this in remembrance" of him.

14. At this meal Jesus identified himself with the bread and wine ("This is my body..."). He also ate and drank with his disciples with the knowledge that his own death was imminent. Consistently with Jewish consciousness, he perceived innocent death as *atoning* death.

15. The disciples and the early Church came to interpret this meal as establishing a new Covenant in the blood of Christ for the redemption of all, and so they continued the practice of shared meals after the death and resurrection.

16. The Eucharist became an act of remembrance (*anamnesis*) of what Christ had done, an act of fellowship and communion not only "with Christ" but also "in Christ," and an act of eschatological anticipation.

17. By the second and third centuries the meal aspect of the Eucharist had disappeared. The prayer of thanksgiving (canon, Eucharistic Prayer), introduced by readings and followed by Holy Communion, became central. At first the Eucharist was celebrated only on Sundays.

18. As the persecutions lifted and the Church moved more freely throughout the empire, the Eucharist assumed many different cultural forms. The rite became more elaborate. In some cases, there were distortions of its original purpose. For example, the congregation no longer participated actively, the canon was recited quietly by the celebrant, frequent Communion declined, private Masses for special intentions multiplied. The liturgical reforms mandated by Vatican II restored the Eucharist to its original purpose and structure.

19. The *real presence* of Christ became a doctrinal preoccupation of the medieval Church because it had been challenged, in particular by Berengar of Tours. Lateran IV, Constance, and Trent all definitively affirmed the doctrine, especially against the Reformers. And Trent also affirmed the doctrine of the *sacrificial* nature of the Eucharist and its *expiatory* value.

20. Vatican II's *Constitution on the Sacred Liturgy* insisted on the active participation of all the faithful not merely through the priest but along with him. It

also noted that Christ is present at the Eucharist not only in the consecrated elements of bread and wine, but also in the community, the word, and the minister.

21. *Intercommunion* refers to full eucharistic sharing between and/or among separated Christians. It is also known as *communicatio in sacris* ("communication in sacred realities").

22. There is a remarkable *ecumenical convergence* today on such previously controverted questions as the sacrificial nature of the Eucharist and the real presence of Christ in the Eucharist.

23. The first *effect* of the Eucharist is *a more profound incorporation into the Church*. The Church is most manifest and most fully itself in the Eucharist, where the Church is visible as a structured community, listening to the word of God, breaking bread and sharing the cup "until he comes."

24. In celebrating the Eucharist we take on the mind and heart of Jesus himself, opening ourselves, as he did, to everyone without exception and committing ourselves to the creation of a world where no one is excluded from the table.

SUGGESTED READINGS

Austin, Gerard. *The Rite of Confirmation: Anointing with the Spirit.* New York: Pueblo Publishing Co., 1985.

Duffy, Regis. *On Becoming Catholic: The Challenge of Christian Initiation.* San Francisco: Harper & Row, 1984.

Foley, Edward. *From Age to Age: How Christians Celebrated the Eucharist.* Chicago: Liturgy Training Publications, 1991.

Jungmann, Josef. *The Mass: An Historical, Theological, and Pastoral Survey.* Collegeville, Minn.: Liturgical Press, 1976.

Kavanagh, Aidan. *The Shape of Baptism: The Rite of Christian Initiation.* New York: Pueblo Publishing Co., 1978.

_____. *Confirmation: Origins and Reform.* New York: Pueblo Publishing Co., 1988.

Léon-Dufour, Xavier. *Sharing the Eucharistic Bread: The Witness of the New Testament.* New York: Paulist Press, 1987.

The Murphy Center for Liturgical Research. *Made, Not Born: New Perspectives on Christian Initiation and the Catechumenate.* Notre Dame, Ind.: University of Notre Dame Press, 1976.

Osborne, Kenan. *The Christian Sacraments of Initiation.* New York: Paulist Press, 1988.

Power, David N. *The Eucharistic Mystery: Revitalizing the Tradition.* New York: Crossroad, 1992.

Reumann, John. *The Supper of the Lord: The New Testament, Ecumenical Dialogues, and Faith and Order on Eucharist.* Philadelphia: Fortress Press, 1985.

Rite of Christian Initiation of Adults: Study Edition. Chicago: Liturgy Training Publications, 1988.

Schillebeeckx, Edward. *The Eucharist.* New York: Sheed & Ward, 1968.

Schmemann, Alexander. *The Eucharist: Sacrament of the Kingdom.* Crestwood, N.Y.: St. Vladimir's Seminary Press, 1987.

Searle, Mark, ed. *Baptism and Confirmation.* Vol. 2 of *Alternative Futures for Worship.* Collegeville, Minn.: Liturgical Press, 1987.

Thurian, Max, and Geoffrey Wainwright, eds. *Baptism and Eucharist: Ecumenical Convergences.* Grand Rapids, Mich.: Eerdmans, 1983.

Turner, Paul. *Confirmation: The Baby in Solomon's Court.* New York: Paulist Press, 1993.

XXIII

The Sacraments of Healing: Penance and Anointing of the Sick

INTRODUCTION

We are initiated into the Christian community by Baptism-Confirmation and the Eucharist, but initiation is only the beginning of a *process*. We are not already fully mature in Christ by the mere fact of having been baptized, anointed, and invited to share the Lord's Supper. We are human. Hence we are prone to sin and vulnerable to illness, physical incapacity, and finally death. And yet the call to Christian existence is a call to perfection: "Be perfect, therefore, as your heavenly Father is perfect" (Matthew 5:48). It is God's will that we be sanctified (1 Thessalonians 4:3; Ephesians 1:4), that we become as saints (Ephesians 5:3). We are to love God with all our mind and all our strength, and our neighbor as ourselves (Mark 12:30). Jesus' proclamation of the Kingdom of God, which shaped his own ministry as well as the mission of the Church, is a call to conversion: "The time is fulfilled, and the kingdom of God has come near; repent, and believe in the good news" (Mark 1:15).

Two sacraments are celebrated by the Church as a sign and instrument of God's and of Christ's abiding *healing* power. The sacrament of *Penance,* or *Reconciliation,* is for those whose bond with the Church, and ultimately with God and Christ, has been weakened or even severed by sin. The sacrament of the *Anointing of the Sick* (formerly called *Extreme Unction*) is for those whose bond with God and the Church has been weakened by illness or physical incapacity. In either case, the purpose of the sacrament is to heal and to restore the morally and/or physically sick member to full communion with the Church so that once again he or she can participate in its life and mission.

Beyond that, Jesus is disclosed in these sacraments as one who heals and forgives, and the Church is disclosed as a healing and forgiving community, as the sacrament of the healing and forgiving Lord. The Church is also the penitent Church, ever bathing the feet of Christ with its tears and hearing his words, "Neither do I condemn you" (John 8:11). And because of its unshakable confidence in the triumph of God's mercy and grace in Christ, when night falls the Church holds high the lamp of hope and reveals itself as the *universal* sacrament of salvation, the community which gives up on no one and no situation, no matter how seemingly hopeless.

PENANCE/RECONCILIATION

History

New Testament Period

The text to which Catholic doctrine has traditionally appealed in asserting the sacramentality and divine origin of Penance is John 20:22–23, which records one of Jesus' postresurrection appearances: "Receive the Holy Spirit. If you forgive the sins of any, they are forgiven them; if you retain the sins of any, they are retained" (see also Matthew 16:19; 18:18). By itself, the text does not "prove" that Jesus instituted the sacrament of Penance as we know it today or that he conferred the power to forgive sins only on the Apostles, their successors, and their chosen delegates. We have no basis even for concluding that these are the "very words" of Jesus, given the different approach to history in the Fourth Gospel, over against the Synoptics.

836

On the other hand, the text *is* entirely consistent with Jesus' abiding concern about sin and his readiness to forgive and to heal (e.g., Matthew 9:2–8; Mark 2:5–12; Luke 5:20–26). In all three reports of Jesus' cure of the paralytic at Capernaum there is mention of the forgiveness of sins. The forgiveness of sins is also prominent in the preaching of the Apostles (Acts of the Apostles 2:38; 5:31; 10:43; 13:38; 26:18). Accordingly, even though John does not tell us how or by whom this power was exercised in the community for whom he wrote, the very fact that he mentions it shows that it was exercised.

The pastoral strategy of the New Testament churches seems to have been one of compassion, correction, and challenge. Mutual correction and forgiveness form part of the fabric of community life (Matthew 5:23–24; James 5:16), but compassion is balanced against an awareness of the effect of sin on the life and mission of the Church itself. In some few cases, a form of excommunication seems to have been practiced (1 Corinthians 5:3–5; 1 Timothy 1:19–20).

Second and Third Centuries

The material for this period is scant. What evidence there is suggests that Penance was available for the baptized. *The Shepherd of Hermas* (ca. 150), an important para-scriptural document, takes for granted the practice of postbaptismal forgiveness, but only once in a lifetime. The community would pray at the deathbed of one who fell into a publicly known serious sin a second time, but the sinner would be denied the sacraments. The first to deny the Church's and the bishop's right to forgive those guilty of serious sins were the *Montanists* and the *Novatians*, both arguing that certain sins (e.g., apostasy, murder, adultery) were outside the Church's powers.

Fourth, Fifth, and Sixth Centuries

The rigorists were condemned by the *Council of Nicea* (325), which explicitly directed that the dying are to be reconciled and given *Viaticum* (the term used for Holy Communion for those at the point of death—i.e., "on the way," *via*, to heaven).

During this period Penance was public in character and came to be known as "Canonical Penance" because local councils devoted a number of canons, or juridical decisions, to regulating its practice. Canonical Penance was administered only once in a lifetime, since Baptism was normally received late in life and was seen as calling for a deep conversion, neither easily nor frequently set aside. The Church demanded proof of reconversion before restoring the grace of Baptism through Penance.

Canonical Penance was always reserved for serious sins, e.g., apostasy, murder, heresy, adultery. These were matters of common, public knowledge. The offender would receive a form of liturgical excommunication and was forced to leave the celebration of the Eucharist at the Offertory, along with the catechumens. For less serious offenses there were other forms of penance: almsgiving, fasts, charity to the poor and the sick, and prayers.

Public penance required the sinner's demonstrating a change of heart, presenting himself or herself before the bishop and the local community, and joining the local group of penitents. Then, after a suitable period of probation (the length of which varied substantially from region to region and from sin to sin), he or she would be readmitted to the Christian community by a rite known as the "reconciliation of the penitent." In the West, more often than in the East, an additional penance was sometimes imposed, namely, lifelong celibacy. This led to the breakup of marriages and provoked intense resistance from the laity, who began to postpone the sacrament until they were near death. It became effectively the sacrament of the dying.

As the needs of the people and the circumstances of the Church changed, private penance became more the rule and so, too, the actual "confession" of sins. By the end of the sixth century Canonical Penance came to be known simply as *Confession*. (The once-in-a-lifetime, public rite of Penance officially ended in the West with the Fourth Lateran Council's decree in 1215 that all the baptized must confess their sins and receive Holy Communion at least once a year.)

Seventh to Eleventh Centuries

This period is marked by a pronounced Celtic influence as the missionary efforts of the Church reached into the British Isles, far removed from the influence of Rome and from all of Europe. (The Irish monks themselves were to bring this Celtic influence to bear upon the Continent in the late sixth and early seventh centuries.) Since the liturgical life of the Celtic church was monastically oriented, private penance became normative for priests and religious, and under their direction it spread among the laity as well. It was imposed even for trivial offenses and became increasingly divorced from the larger community of faith. In fact, a person could be restored to the Eucharist even before completing the penance. If the penance were deemed too onerous, the penitent could ask for a *commutation* to a lighter penalty. It was also possible to substitute the payment of a sum of money instead of performing the actual penance. This practice was known as *redemption*.

Furthermore, Penance was administered by priests as well as the bishop. In order to help the priests in the selection of appropriate penances, a codification of penitential practices was developed, the so-called penitential books (*libri poenitentiales*). These were lists of every kind of sin, with the exact type of penance attached. The minister of the sacrament was no longer the healer and the reconciler. He was now the *judge*. A formula of absolution was also developed at this time.

Eleventh to Fourteenth Centuries

Four principal changes occur in this period. Penance becomes satisfaction, confession, contrition, and absolution. In the ancient Church the emphasis was on the *reconciliation* of the sinner with the Church and ultimately with God. Now the emphasis shifts to the doing of a penance, or the making of *satisfaction*, for sin. When this became too strenuous, the practices of commutation and redemption were introduced.

Second, *confession* of sins originally served the purpose of ensuring that adequate satisfaction was being imposed, but gradually confession came to be considered as having its own efficacy, its own power to reconcile the sinner. Thus, we find at this time the development of arguments urging the necessity of confessing to a priest.

Third, in the writings of Abelard (d. 1142) and Peter Lombard there was a shift to *contrition*, i.e., the conversion of heart. The sinner, if truly contrite, was already forgiven even before confession. So

839

pronounced was this new stress on contrition that the purist Albigensians and Waldensians denied any efficacy whatsoever to confession to a priest, a view condemned by the Fourth Lateran Council in 1215.

All orthodox theologians and canonists came to the defense of the role of the priest, and this led to a fourth shift: to *absolution* by a priest. Since absolution was *not* part of the practice and teaching of Penance in the early Church, there was some dispute among the medieval authors about its place in the sacrament. By the time of Thomas Aquinas, however, absolution came to be regarded as essential, along with confession and contrition.

From the Middle Ages to Vatican II

Thomas's theology was endorsed in the Council of Florence's *Decree for the Armenians* (1439): (1) Penance is a sacrament; (2) it consists of contrition of the heart (including the resolution not to sin in the future), oral confession to the priest, satisfaction (e.g., prayer, fasting, almsgiving), and absolution by the priest; and (3) the effect of the sacrament is the forgiveness of sins.

The Reformers, and Luther in particular, rejected this teaching. Although Luther accepted the sacramentality of Penance, he believed there was an abiding danger of regarding the works of the penitent as more important than faith in God's mercy. He also rejected the reservation of the power of forgiveness to priests. The first official reaction to Luther's views came in a bull of Pope Leo X (d. 1521), *Exsurge Domine* (1520). Calvin also accepted private confession and absolution as a means of arousing faith and confidence in God's mercy, but he denied its sacramentality.

The definitive response to the Reformers came from the *Council of Trent* (*Doctrine on the Sacrament of Penance,* Session XIV, 1551). It taught that Penance is a sacrament instituted by Christ; that it is distinct from Baptism; that the three acts of the penitent are contrition, confession of all serious sins in number and kind, and satisfaction; that absolution is reserved to priests alone; and that the priest must have jurisdiction, since absolution is a juridical act.

However, in the council's earlier *Decree on Justification* (1547) it taught that God's grace is absolutely gratuitous, that we do nothing to gain it. Good works, including the act of contrition, the confession of sins, priestly absolution, and penance after confession, are to be viewed within this framework.

Vatican II

The Second Vatican Council called for a revision of the rite and formulae for the sacrament of Penance "so that they more clearly express both the nature and effect of the sacrament" (*Constitution on the Sacred Liturgy*, n. 72). The sacrament's purpose, the council's *Dogmatic Constitution on the Church* declares, is to "obtain pardon from the mercy of God" and to be "reconciled with the Church whom [sinners] have wounded by their sin, and who, by its charity, its example and its prayer, collaborates in their conversion" (n. 11).

The New Rite of Penance

The new rite of Penance was based on criteria proposed by Vatican II's *Constitution on the Sacred Liturgy:* (1) the rite should clearly express both the nature and the effect of the sacrament; (2) the role of the church community must be emphasized; (3) the reading of the Word of God should be central; (4) a public form of worship should predominate over a private form; and (5) the rite should be short and clear, free from useless repetitions and not requiring extensive explanation.

There are four forms of the new rite: individual, communal with individual confession and absolution, communal with general absolution, and an abbreviated emergency ritual when death is imminent. The rite for the first three forms includes the following: a prayer of welcome, a reading of Sacred Scripture (which is optional), a reflection on the Word of God, confession of sins with an expression of sorrow, a prayer of absolution, and a prayer of praise and dismissal.

Although not on a par with the new Rite of Christian Initiation of Adults (to which we referred in chapter 22), the new Rite of Penance does bring out the ecclesial dimension of the sacrament more fully than does the traditional (i.e., post-Tridentine) practice of private confession. In the new rite, the effect of the sacrament is identified as reconciliation with God and with the Church. The minister functions more as a healer than as a judge. Emphasis is placed on conversion inspired by the Church's proclamation of God's word. And communal celebration of the sacrament is provided for and encouraged.

Contemporary Theological and Pastoral Issues

Theologians, religious educators, liturgists, and other pastoral ministers continue to discuss several issues: the frequency of confession, the age of first confession, the use of general absolution, and the need to confess privately to a priest. Because the new rite takes more time and care, many believe that an emphasis on frequent confession might encourage a curtailing of key prayer-elements in the new rite. They are also skeptical about the pastoral wisdom of requiring very young children to receive the sacrament of Penance before they are ready and also to make it a precondition for the reception of first Eucharist, as required by present church discipline. Third, various episcopal conferences differ regarding the use of general absolution, and some church leaders, contrary to the spirit of the new rite and the intention of the council, seem to want to make the first form of Penance (individual-to-priest) normative. Finally, pastoral ministers and others wonder why, if general absolution is conferred and one's mortal sins are already forgiven, one should still have to confess privately to a priest.

Jesus, the Church, and Penance

In its celebration of the sacrament of Penance, the *Church* reveals itself as the sacrament of God's mercy in the world, but also as a sinful community, still "on the way" to the perfection of the Kingdom. Those who sin and who must avail themselves of the sacrament are just as much "the Church" as are those who, in the name of the Church, act to reconcile the sinner with God and the Church. The Church knows what it is both to forgive and to be forgiven, mindful always of the Lord's own prayer, "And forgive us our sins, for we ourselves forgive everyone indebted to us" (Luke 11:4).

A Church which cannot admit its sin is not the Church of Christ. A Church which cannot forgive the sins of others against itself is not

842

the Church of Christ. *How* the liturgical process of conversion, repentance, and forgiveness is to be structured is always of less importance than *the fact that* it goes on continually within the Church.

And it goes on continually within the Church because the Church's model is always *Jesus* himself, who is the reconciler, the healer, and the forgiver of sins *par excellence*. The sacrament of Reconciliation does what Jesus does.

ANOINTING OF THE SICK

History

New Testament

Apart from James 5:14 there is no mention of *Anointing* as a sacred rite in the New Testament. The pertinent text is as follows: "Are any among you sick? They should call for the elders of the church and have them pray over them, anointing them with oil in the name of the Lord." It continues: "The prayer of faith will save the sick, and the Lord will raise them up; and anyone who has committed sins will be forgiven. Therefore, confess your sins to one another, and pray for one another, so that you may be healed" (5:15–16).

The "elders" or "presbyters" are those appointed and ordained by Apostles or disciples of Apostles (Acts of the Apostles 14:23; Titus 1:5). The presbyters are described by James as having extraordinary spiritual gifts which enable them to heal the sick. Sickness, it must be noted, was attributed to sin, as in the Old Testament and contemporary Judaism, and so it posed a problem for the early Church. At the sickbed it is the task of the presbyter to pray for the sick person and to anoint him or her with oil in the name of the Lord. The oil is regarded as a vital substance, a restorative. There is nothing magical implied, however. It is not the oil but the prayers to the Lord which provide the hope of recovery and the forgiveness of sins. (The recommendation that Christians declare their sins "to one another" is not without relevance to our previous discussion of the sacrament of Penance.)

Although James 5:14 by itself does not "prove" the sacramentality of the Anointing of the Sick, it does indicate that there was such a practice in the early Church, that it required the presence of some leader of the community, that it involved prayers, anointing, and the forgiveness of sins, and that its purpose was the restoration of the sick member not only to physical health but also to spiritual health within the community of faith.

Second Century to the Middle Ages

There is, for all practical purposes, no evidence in the early centuries for the actual rite of Anointing. Since it was not a public liturgical act like the rite of initiation, it was passed over in the liturgical books. Just as lay Christians brought home the Eucharist from the Sunday celebration for Communion during the week, so they also brought home blessed oil for use as needed. The bishop or other members of the local clergy undoubtedly visited the sick and may well have been the ministers of Anointing. For the most part, however, the laity seem to have been the ordinary ministers of the sacrament. As Penance was delayed until the imminence of death, the Anointing, too, was delayed, since it was reserved to those in full communion with the Church. As Anointing was delayed, it became part of a continuous rite alongside Penance and Viaticum—all administered by a priest.

The first documentary item for the sacrament is provided by a letter of *Pope Innocent I* (d. 417) to Decentius, bishop of Gubbio, in which certain practical points are clarified regarding the administration of the rite of Anointing. It links the Anointing with the text of James and notes that the oil is blessed by the bishop and applied to the sick person by the bishop or a priest. This letter became a basic source for the late Roman and early medieval period, inasmuch as it was incorporated into the most important canonical collections and thus became the starting point for theological discussion of the sacrament.

In the first part of the eighth century Bede the Venerable (d. 735), author of the earliest extant commentary on the Epistle of James, states that it has been the custom of the Church from apostolic times for presbyters to anoint the sick with consecrated oil and to pray for their healing. Nowhere in the early tradition does one find mention of the Anointing as a sacrament of *preparation for death*. Where mention *is* made of a "sacrament of the dying," the reference is always to the Eucharist, administered as Viaticum.

The Early Medieval Period

With the Carolingian Reform at the beginning of the ninth century—i.e., the effort guided by the emperor Charlemagne to impose Roman liturgy and Roman disciplinary practices throughout his new Holy Roman Empire—Anointing becomes established among the "last rites." By the middle of the twelfth century the association between Anointing and dying was so taken for granted that it came to be called *sacramentum exeuntium* ("the sacrament of the departing") or in the words of Peter Lombard, *extrema unctio* ("last anointing").

By the close of the twelfth century Extreme Unction was in fact appropriating to itself the function and effects previously associated with Viaticum. Thus, Anointing became more and more a sacrament of the dying, although its original purpose was to be a remedy against sickness, with the real hope of recovery. Even in the early medieval period the Church did not require that a sickness be terminal before the sacrament could be administered.

Thirteenth and Fourteenth Centuries

In this period the doctrine of the seven sacraments came to its full development, and Anointing of the Sick was counted among them. It was understood as the sacrament of spiritual help for the time of grave illness unto death. Restoration to bodily health was regarded as a subordinate and conditional effect only. Theologians began to exaggerate the sacrament's spiritual powers: The Franciscan school argued that all venial (i.e., nonserious) sins were forgiven as well as serious sins, and the Dominican school argued that the sacrament removed even the consequences of sin and anything which lessened a soul's capacity for the life of glory in heaven. To die immediately after Extreme Unction, in other words, guaranteed an unimpeded journey to God.

Fifteenth and Sixteenth Centuries

This theological understanding of the sacrament as a sacrament for the dying was endorsed by the Council of Florence's *Decree for the Armenians* (1439), which declared that the sacrament could "not be

845

given except to a sick person whose life is feared for." The Council of Trent's *Doctrine on the Sacrament of Extreme Unction* (1551) was formulated as a complement to the council's teaching on the sacrament of Penance. It defined the Anointing of the Sick as a true sacrament.

The first draft of its doctrinal formulation, however, had directed that the sacrament be given "only to those who are in their final struggle and who have come to grips with death and who are about to go forth to the Lord." The final draft introduced important modifications, declaring that "this anointing is to be used for the sick, particularly for those who are so dangerously ill as to seem at the point of departing this life." It speaks of the sacrament's effects as purification from sin as well as from the effects of sin, comfort and strength of soul, the arousal of confidence in God's mercy, readiness to bear the difficulties and trials of illness, and even health of body, where expedient for the welfare of the soul.

Trent's teaching is remarkable not only for what it contains about the spiritual, psychological, and bodily effects of the sacrament but also for what it omits about the sacrament as a last rite. The council thereby struck at the root of a growing abuse which delayed the sacrament until the very last moment of life.

Twentieth Century

The Tridentine doctrine shaped the theological, canonical, and pastoral understanding and practice of this sacrament for centuries thereafter. In the twentieth century some tentative advances were suggested. Theologians and liturgists alike suggested that, insofar as this is a sacrament of the dying, it is essentially an "anointing for glory." Others, however, pointed out that the prayers of the ritual made no mention of death, and that the sacrament was really a sacrament of the sick. The "last sacrament" is not the Anointing, but Viaticum. Indeed, it was only in the middle of the twelfth century, these theologians argued, that the stress on preparation for death had emerged.

Vatican II

The Second Vatican Council endorsed this second line of thought, recommending that the sacrament be called the Anointing of the Sick rather than Extreme Unction and noting explicitly that it "is not a sacrament reserved for those who are at the point of death," but for those who begin to be in some danger of death "from sickness or old age" (*Constitution on the Sacred Liturgy*, n. 73). Indeed, the *last* sacrament to be administered to the dying is Viaticum (n. 68). The *Dogmatic Constitution on the Church* places the sacrament in its larger ecclesial context: "In the holy anointing of the sick with the prayer of the priest, the whole Church recommends the sick to the Lord, who suffered and has been glorified, asking him to give them relief and salvation. It goes further and calls upon them to associate themselves freely with the passion and death of Christ, and in this way to make their contribution to the good of God's people" (n. 11).

The New Rite of Anointing and Pastoral Care of the Sick

The new rite acknowledges that sickness prevents us from fulfilling our role in human society and in the Church. On the other hand, the sick person participates in the redemptive sufferings of Christ and provides the Church with a reminder of higher things and of the limitations of human life. Indeed, Pope Paul VI's apostolic constitution promulgating the new rite in 1972 pointed out that the sick are also anointed for ministry: to become models of faithful and hope-filled association with Christ in his passion and death.

The ritual elements include a greeting, words to those present, a penitential rite (Scripture, litany), the priest's laying on of hands, blessing of oil, prayer of thanksgiving, the anointing of the forehead and hands with oil with the words, "Through this holy anointing may the Lord in his love and mercy help you with the grace of the Holy Spirit;" and "May the Lord who frees you from sin save you and raise you up." There is a prayer after anointing, the Lord's Prayer, Communion, and a blessing.

The rite presupposes earlier visits to the sick person, including Communion calls, and some direct dealing with the sick person's sense of isolation and with the concerns of family and others inti-mately affected by the illness.

Jesus, the Church, and the Anointing of the Sick

The Church's concern for the sick is in fidelity to Christ's command to visit the sick and is consistent with a wholistic understanding of salvation as reaching the total person. The *Church* discloses itself in this sacrament as the community of those who are on pilgrimage to the Kingdom of God, with eschatological faith and hope. The Church is a sacrament of Christ the healer, the one who saves us in our human wholeness, body as well as soul. It is at the same time a community always in need of healing, a community subject to physi-cal as well as spiritual reverses.

A Church which is not interested in healing and in the total health of the whole human person and of the human community at large is not the Church of Christ. A Church which abandons those who, by certain of the world's standards, are no longer of practical use is not the Church of Christ. Nor is that Church truly the Church of Christ if it turns its back on the sick whom society scorns or rejects: the drug addict, the alcoholic, the victim of AIDS. The Church which anoints the sick is the Church of the "Lord Jesus Christ, [who] shared in our human nature to heal the sick and save all humankind" (Prayer After Anointing).

As in all the sacraments, it is *Jesus* who is revealed and who ministers. In the Anointing of the Sick he is revealed as a healer of body as well as of soul, and as one who ministers to the sick and the dying and who energizes their faith in the Kingdom of God and stirs their hope in eternal life.

SUMMARY

1. Jesus is disclosed in the sacraments of *Penance* and *Anointing of the Sick* as one who forgives and heals, and the Church is disclosed as a forgiving and healing community.

2. The *forgiveness of sins*, often linked with the healing of the sick, was an abiding feature of Jesus' own ministry and later of the preaching and ministry of the Apostles.

3. In the *earliest centuries* of the Church's history, Penance (also known as "Canonical Penance") was administered no more than once after Baptism, and then only for the gravest public sins—e.g., apostasy, murder, adultery. There was no private confession of sins to a priest. The bishop was the minister of the sacrament.

4. In the late sixth and early seventh centuries the character of Penance changed under the influence of the *Irish monks*, who encouraged the practice of private penance for the laity, even for relatively minor offenses. As the relationship between sins and penances became more complicated, special books were published to help the confessor decide which penance to impose for which sins.

5. By the *Middle Ages* the sacrament of Penance has four separate components: satisfaction (the doing of a penance), confession, contrition, and absolution by a priest. The *Council of Trent* made these definitive, declaring that all grave sins had to be confessed to a priest in kind and number. The priest acted as a judge, and the confessional was his tribunal.

6. *Vatican II* mandated a change in the rite of Penance to bring out its *ecclesial* dimension, as a way of reconciling with the Church.

7. Through this sacrament of Penance the *Church* reveals itself not only as a reconciler of sinners, but also as a community always in need of reconciliation. And through it *Jesus* continues to forgive, heal, and reconcile us to one another and to God.

8. Apart from James 5:14 there is no mention of Anointing as a sacred rite in the New Testament. Although the text does not "prove" the institution of the sacrament of the *Anointing of the Sick*, it does indicate that such a practice existed in the early Church.

9. The first documentary evidence for the administration of this sacrament in the postbiblical period is provided in a letter of Pope Innocent I (d. 417). From the beginning it was not regarded as *the last sacrament*. That function was served by *Viaticum*, one's last Communion. With the Romanization of the Church under Charlemagne, the sacrament of Anointing became "Extreme Unction," the sacrament of the dying.

10. Its sacramentality was taught by the Councils of *Florence* and *Trent*. *Vatican II* restored the primitive emphasis on the anointing of the sick rather than on the last anointing of the dying.

11. The *Church* discloses itself in this sacrament of Anointing as a healing community always on the way to the Kingdom of God and always itself in

need of healing. *Jesus,* too, is revealed and acts as a healer, not only of the soul but also of the body.

SUGGESTED READINGS

Ahlstrom, Michael, Peter Gilmour, and Robert Tuzik. *A Companion to Pastoral Care of the Sick.* Chicago: Liturgy Training Publications, 1990.

Dallen, James. *The Reconciling Community: The Rite of Penance.* New York: Pueblo Publishing Co., 1986.

Duffy, Regis. *A Roman Catholic Theology of Pastoral Care.* Philadelphia: Fortress Press, 1983.

Favazza, Joseph A. *The Order of Penitents: Historical Roots and Pastoral Future.* Collegeville, Minn.: Liturgical Press, 1988.

Fink, Peter, ed. *Anointing of the Sick.* Vol. 7 of *Alternative Futures for Worship.* Collegeville, Minn.: Liturgical Press, 1987.

Gula, Richard. *To Walk Together Again: The Sacrament of Reconciliation.* New York: Paulist Press, 1984.

Gusmer, Charles. *And You Visited Me: Sacramental Ministry to the Sick and Dying.* New York: Pueblo Publishing Co., 1984.

John Paul II, Pope. *Reconciliatio et Poenitentia* (Apostolic Exhortation on Reconciliation and Penance). *Origins* 14/27 (December 20, 1984).

Kennedy, Robert J., ed. *Reconciliation: The Continuing Agenda.* Collegeville, Minn.: Liturgical Press, 1987.

Osborne, Kenan. *Reconciliation and Justification.* New York: Paulist Press, 1990.

Poschmann, Bernard. *Penance and the Anointing of the Sick.* New York: Herder & Herder, 1964.

Rahner, Karl. "Penance." *Encyclopedia of Theology: The Concise Sacramentum Mundi.* New York: Seabury Press, 1975, pp. 1187–1204.

———. *On the Theology of Death.* New York: Herder & Herder, 1961.

XXIV

The Sacraments of Vocation and Commitment: Matrimony and Holy Order

INTRODUCTION

All Christians are initiated into the Church through the same essential process, but not all Christians are called to live as Christians in the same mode of existence. Most are called to live in intimate union with another in marriage. Some others are called to a life of service of the Christian community itself, specifically through a ministry which attends directly to the order and mission of the Church. So fundamental are both the call to married life and the call to pastoral leadership of the Church that each of these calls and its corresponding commitment is celebrated as a sacrament: the one, the sacrament of *Matrimony;* the other, the sacrament of *Holy Order.*

Like all the sacraments, both these sacraments are directed to the nature and mission of the Church. In Matrimony the Christian community is itself built up and manifested at its most natural, familial level. The union of Christ and his Church is symbolized (Ephesians 5:22–32). In Holy Order the Christian community is provided structure and direction for the exercise of its mission. These are the sacraments of *vocation* and of *commitment.* The Church is revealed in them as a community called forth (the root meaning of the word *church*, *ekklesia*) and committed to a life of mutual love and service.

MATRIMONY

History

Old Testament

The Church's understanding of the sacredness of marriage is rooted in the *creation* narrative in Genesis. "The Lord God said: 'It is not good that the man should be alone.'... Therefore a man leaves his father and his mother and clings to his wife, and they become one flesh" (2:18,24). The Lord blesses their union and orders them to "be fruitful and multiply" (1:28). Marriage functions primarily in the Old Testament, however, as an institution for the preservation of the husband's clan. That is why children, especially sons, are regarded as a blessing and a gift from God (Genesis 24:60; Psalm 127:3) and why childlessness is a disgrace and a chastisement (Genesis 30:1–6; 1 Samuel 1:6–11).

The highest honor paid to marriage in the Old Testament is the application to it of the symbol of the *Covenant* between Yahweh and Israel (Hosea 2; Isaiah 54:4–5; Jeremiah 2:2; 3:20). Hosea interpreted his own marriage to Gomer as a representation of the covenantal union between God and Israel. Gomer left Hosea for other lovers just as Israel had abandoned its God for other gods. As Hosea waited faithfully for Gomer's return and took her back without recrimination, so God waited for Israel and welcomed her back.

Images of marriage and marital love can also be found elsewhere in the prophetic traditions, the Song of Songs, the story of Tobit, the Book of Proverbs, the Wisdom of the Son of Sirach, and Qoheleth.

New Testament

Jesus deepens the Hebrew concept of marriage, insisting on the oneness that exists between the man and the woman. The woman is not to be cast aside at will. He speaks, therefore, against divorce, so strongly in fact that the one who marries a divorced woman commits

852

adultery (Matthew 5:31–32; 19:3–12). But the early Church adds an "exceptive clause" as a softening of Jesus' demands: "except on the ground of unchastity (*porneias*)" (5:32). Catholic exegetes differ about the precise meaning of *porneias*. According to one interpretation, the clause does not contain a real exception since it does not refer to divorce but to separation without remarriage in the case of an adulterous wife, who in Israelite law would be stoned. But the text does not use the word for adultery. A more accepted solution is that the text does not contain a real exception to the prohibition against divorce because *porneia* (equivalent to the Hebrew word for prostitution) refers to an incestuous union due to marriage within forbidden degrees of kinship (Leviticus 18:6–18). Such a union would not be a true marriage at all and would not require a divorce but a decree of nullity or annulment (see Acts of the Apostles 15:20,29).

Jesus consistently regards marriage as a state in life proper to this age; in heaven there will be no marrying (Mark 12:25). All of the concerns of marriage must yield to the claims of the Second Coming (Luke 14:20; see also Matthew 24:38–39; Luke 17:27). As always with Jesus, everything is to be seen in light of the Kingdom of God.

But the New Testament's view of marriage is ambivalent. Paul in 1 Corinthians affirms the early Christian missionary ideal whereby those who were carrying the Gospel to others were asked to leave spouse and family behind for the sake of Jesus and the Kingdom of God (Mark 10:29; Luke 18:29). Paul wishes that the faithful would renounce marriage in favor of virginity because he thinks the Lord will soon return and because he worries about the risk of distraction in the meantime (7:32–35). He reduces marriage to something of secondary importance in view of the Second Coming. Whereas the creation narrative cautions that it is not good for man to be alone, Paul insists that "it is well for a man not to touch a woman" (7:1). But he does not go so far as to condemn marriage. There are several passages in fact in the New Testament where the messianic period is described as a wedding feast (Matthew 9:15; 25:1–13; Mark 2:19; John 3:29).

The deutero-Pauline and pastoral epistles contain a third tradition, that of the household codes, so named because they regulated the behavior of the household. These epistles, unlike the early Christian ascetical approach and Paul's commendation of the unmarried state, affirm the importance of marriage and of family. The pastoral epistles, in fact, insist that bishops should be successful in marriage and family life before their election to office (1 Timothy 3:3–5).

In Ephesians marriage is portrayed as a symbol of Christ's union with his Church (5:21–33). The union of man and woman in marriage is not only compared with the union of Christ with the Church; it is actually based on the union of Christ with the Church. When husbands love their wives as their own flesh, they are only doing what Christ does with the Church.

Feminist interpreters, like Elisabeth Schüssler Fiorenza, suggest that the stress on the husband/wife, Christ/Church parallel was not for the sake of reinforcing the patriarchal order of relationships within the home and within society, but had an apologetical purpose. Given the charge that Christians were disruptive of the social order, the household codes of the later books of the New Testament were designed to show that Christians were not, in fact, opposed to the Roman sociocultural order.

Second to Fifth Centuries

The New Testament's ambivalence toward marriage continues beyond the apostolic age. Marriage is viewed more and more as the justification of the use of sex which has been infected by sin (a "lawful remedy for concupiscence," the neoscholastic textbooks would call it). This trend reached its fullest development in *Augustine*, who influenced the Church on this subject more profoundly than any other single individual did. Augustine (as we noted in chapter 15 in connection with our discussion of the sexuality of Jesus) linked sexuality with animality. The purpose of marriage is none other than the begetting of children. Indeed, our sexual desires are nothing more than the unfortunate effects of Original Sin. Every child is literally born of his or her parents' "sin" because procreation is possible only with the seductive aid of physical lust. But it is a tolerable "sin" because God wills that we should be fruitful and multiply, and it provides a legitimate way of keeping "perverse desire within its proper bounds."

But there was also a more positive and generally neglected aspect of Augustine's approach to marriage, particularly in his writings against the Manichæans with whom he had once been sympathetic.

In his *The Good of Marriage* he taught that marriage has three values: fidelity, offspring, and sacrament. *Fidelity* is the faithfulness inherent in the mutual love of the spouses. It pertains to sexual love, but is not limited to that. Fidelity also involves a commitment of love and trust. The *offspring* are to be accepted in love, nurtured with affection, and educated in the Christian faith. Marriage, finally, is also a *sacrament*, signifying on earth the future unity of God's people in heaven. This applies in a particular way to the marriage of a bishop, which constitutes a sign of the fundamental unity and peace of the eschatological city.

In spite of the numerous anti-body passages in the early Christian writers, they never went so far as to deny the basic value and sanctity of marriage as upheld, for example, in 1 Timothy 4:1–5 ("For everything created by God is good; and nothing is to be rejected...").

Middle Ages to Vatican II

Discussion of marriage continued along an ambivalent course into the medieval period. Abelard acknowledged its sacramentality but insisted that it did not "avail unto salvation.... For to bring home a wife is not meritorious for salvation, but it is allowed for salvation's sake because of incontinence." The goodness of marriage meanwhile was affirmed against the Cathari, the Waldensians, and the Albigensians, the medieval counterparts of the Manichæans. In 1184 the Council of Verona under Pope Lucius II condemned the Cathari. In 1208, in the Profession of Faith prescribed by Pope Innocent III, marriage was accounted a true sacrament. That teaching was reaffirmed in 1274 by the Second Council of Lyons, in the Council of Florence's *Decree for the Armenians* (1439), and then, most definitively, at the Council of Trent (*Doctrine on the Sacrament of Matrimony*, Session XXIV, 1563). Trent required that Catholic marriages take place in the presence of a priest, especially to curb the widespread practice of clandestine marriages.

The Protestant Reformers upheld the sacredness of marriage in the order of creation, but they denied that marriage belonged to the order of grace as a sacrament. They also rejected the Church's authority over marriage, and approved the practice of divorce as a lesser of two evils. Trent affirmed the opposite position in each instance.

Among the council's more "historically conditioned" canons is the tenth: "If anyone says that the married state surpasses that of virginity or celibacy, and that it is not better and happier to remain in virginity or celibacy than to be united in matrimony, *anathema sit*."

The Tridentine perspective remained normative for Catholic theology, canon law, and pastoral practice until the Second Vatican Council. Meanwhile, Trent's teaching was vigorously reaffirmed by Pope Leo XIII in *Arcanum Divinæ Sapientiæ* in 1880 and by Pope Pius XI in *Casti Connubii* in 1930, which set forth as marriage's primary purpose the propagation of life, calling the "mutual faithfulness of husband and wife" the "second blessing" of marriage.

Vatican II

As happened with so many other theological and pastoral questions, the Catholic Church's perspective on marriage was significantly modified by the Second Vatican Council. In contrast with previous official pronouncements and conventional theological and canonical insights, the council adopts a remarkably personalistic standpoint. It no longer uses the traditional term *contract* to describe the marriage bond. Instead, the council speaks of the "marriage covenant" which is sealed by an "irrevocable personal consent" (*Pastoral Constitution on the Church in the Modern World*, n. 48).

Second, neither does the council continue to employ the old distinction between primary and secondary ends in which the begetting of children is always more important than the mutual love of husband and wife. "Hence, *while not making the other ends of marriage of less value*, the true practice of conjugal love, and the whole nature of family life resulting from it, tend to dispose the spouses to cooperate courageously with the love of the Creator and Savior who through them day by day expands and enriches His own family" (n. 50, italics mine).

Third, the sacrament of marriage is not something added to the marriage union established through mutual human love. "Authentic married love is taken up into divine love and is ruled and enriched by the redemptive power of Christ and the salvific action of the Church..." (n. 48). This new emphasis in the theology of marriage is consistent with the claims of contemporary sociology that this is the first age in which people marry and remain in marriage because they love each other. And so there is this stress on the mutual exchange of love as constituting the sacrament of marriage, on married love as the source of the institution of marriage, on the need for growth in this love in order to bring the sacrament to its full realization, and on the need for the Church constantly to bring forth the witness value of this sacrament to the whole community of faith. As husband and wife are called to be faithful, generous, and gracious to each other in fulfillment of their marriage covenant, so is the whole Church called to be faithful to its covenant with God in Christ. "When Christian marriage flounders," Father John T. Finnegan, former President of the Canon Law Society of America has written, "the witness of fidelity in all Christian vocations flounders" ("Marriage/Pastoral Care," *Origins* 5/10, August 28, 1975, p. 152).

Fourth, the council emphasizes the necessity of a faith commitment for the sacrament of marriage (see *Constitution on the Sacred Liturgy*, n. 59). Marriage is not just a ceremony by which two people are legally bound together. As a sacrament, it is an act of worship, an expression of faith, a sign of the Church's unity, a mode of Christ's presence. The council uses the term *christifideles*. Marriage is not just a union between *baptized* Christians; it is a union between *faithful* Christians.

Fifth, the full consummation of marriage is more than a biological act. The old theology and the old canon law asserted that a marriage between two baptized Christians, once performed according to the rite of the Church (*ratum*) and once consummated by a single act of physical union (*consummatum*), can never be dissolved, not even by the pope. But according to the council, the expression of the mutual love which is at the heart of the sacrament consists of more than biological union. "It involves the good of the whole person. Therefore it can enrich the expressions of body and mind with a unique dignity, ennobling these expressions as special ingredients and signs of friendship distinctive of marriage. . . . Such love pervades the whole of [the spouses'] lives" (n. 49; see also Pope Paul VI's *Humanæ Vitæ*, 1968, nn. 8–9). Consummation without love is without meaning. It would be difficult to see, in light of the council's teaching, how such purely biological consummation could have a sacramental character.

Rather, the council speaks of the "intimate partnership of married life" (*Intima communitas vitæ et amoris coniugalis*, n. 48).

Finally, the broader ecclesial dimension of the sacrament is maintained. "Christian spouses, in virtue of the sacrament of matrimony, signify and share in the mystery of that union and fruitful love which exists between Christ and the Church (see Ephesians 5:32)" (*Dogmatic Constitution on the Church*, n. 11).

Post–Vatican II Teachings

Soon after the council Pope Paul VI issued his famous encyclical on birth control, *Humanæ Vitæ*, in 1968 (to which we shall return in chapter 27); in 1981, Pope John Paul II issued an apostolic exhortation on the family, *Consortium Socialis*. The latter document spoke of the family as a community of persons in the service of life, participating in the development of society and in the life and mission of the Church. Significantly, John Paul II does not follow the Tridentine preference for celibacy/virginity over marriage. For him they are "two ways of expressing and living the one mystery of the covenant of God with [us]. When marriage is not esteemed, neither can consecrated virginity or celibacy exist; when human sexuality is not regarded as a great value given by the creator, the renunciation of it for the sake of the kingdom of heaven loses its meaning" (n. 16).

The New Rite of Marriage

The council's theology of matrimony is carried over into the new Rite of Marriage. The "Introduction" to the rite speaks of the union of Christ and the Church (n. 1), of the covenantal nature of the marriage bond (n. 2), of the essential element of mutual affection in body and mind (n. 3), of the importance of the procreation and education of children without prejudice to the other purposes of marriage (n. 4), of the virtue of faith required ("for the sacrament of matrimony presupposes and demands faith," n. 7), and of the significance of the eucharistic setting for marriage (n. 6).

The rite itself begins with a greeting by the priest, followed by the couple's affirmation of their freedom, their willingness to have children, and their readiness to bring them up according to the law of

Christ and the Church. The couple then exchange their vows: "I, [name], take you, [name], to be my [wife/husband]. I promise to be true to you in good times and in bad, in sickness and in health. I will love you and honor you all the days of my life." (Episcopal conferences may allow variations on this form.) There follows the blessing and exchange of rings. A nuptial blessing for both parties is given during the Eucharist, after the Lord's Prayer.

Some Canonical Considerations

Indissolubility

Following Mark 10:2–9 and parallels and because of its understanding of marriage as a *covenant*, the Catholic Church teaches that a marriage that is both sacramental and consummated is *indissoluble* (canons 1056 and 1141). On the other hand, the Church's own pastoral practice over the years has tolerated certain limited measures of ecclesiastical reconciliation where the rigorous imposition of the full demands of Christian law would require moral heroism. Origen (d. 254) had proposed a formula that was widely quoted throughout the first thousand years of the Church's history: "The matter of divorce and remarriage was contrary to what has been handed down, but not entirely without reason." It was a kind of "lesser-of-two-evils" principle. At the beginning of the medieval period various church synods and penitential books permitted a second marriage even when the first partner was still alive. But the Western Church, via Gratian's Decree (mid-twelfth century), eventually established a stricter practice than was common in the East, moving from a "should not" to a "cannot" approach to the possibility of dissolution.

The Eastern Orthodox churches developed and continue to maintain the principle of *economy* (similar to the Catholic notion of *dispensation*), by which the unintended harshness of a given law is removed. Thus, the Orthodox churches have permitted remarriage after divorce. The teaching of the Council of Trent (Session XXIV, canon 7, 1563) on indissolubility was formulated against the Reformers, not against the Orthodox. While the official position of the Catholic Church is clear—i.e., that marriage is permanent—it does not absolutely exclude the kind of pastoral flexibility embodied in the principle of economy.

For example, Walter Kasper, a German theologian who later became a bishop, has proposed that the Church can admit divorced-and-remarried persons to the sacraments when they are sorry for any guilt they may have incurred in the breakdown of the first marriage, when everything humanly possible has been done to save the first marriage, and when the second marriage has become "a morally binding union that cannot be dissolved without causing fresh injustice" (*Theology of Christian Marriage*, p. 70).

Canonical Form

The Catholic Church requires that all Catholics normally marry in the presence of three persons: the local bishop, the pastor, or a priest or deacon delegated by either one, and two witnesses (canon 1108). This is known as the requirement of "canonical form," as distinguished from "liturgical form," i.e., the rites and ceremonies accompanying the exchange of consent. Before 1966 there were serious penalties incurred by Catholics who married "outside the Church" and before a Protestant minister. Between 1966 and 1970 Pope Paul VI retroactively lifted and abolished all such penalties. Catholics are now permitted to marry in a Protestant church before a Protestant minister with permission from the local bishop (called the dispensation from canonical form). Protestants and Orthodox may also act as official witnesses (bridesmaid or best man) at a Catholic marriage, and Catholics may serve in the same capacity at a marriage which is properly celebrated between separated brethren (*Ecumenical Directory*, May 14, 1967, n. 58).

Mixed Marriage

A "mixed marriage" is one between a Catholic and a non-Catholic. In the strict sense, it is a marriage between a Catholic and a baptized non-Catholic. To receive the dispensation to marry a non-Catholic, the Catholic party must make the following affirmation: "I reaffirm my faith in Jesus Christ and, with God's help, intend to continue living that faith in the Catholic Church. I promise to do all in my power to share with our children the faith I have received by having them baptized and brought up as Catholics" (*Statement of the United States Catholic Bishops,* January 1, 1971; see also canon 1125). This promise can be made orally or in writing by the Catholic party. The other party must be informed of the fact and content of this promise.

Pauline Privilege

The "Pauline Privilege" is a historical elaboration of 1 Corinthians 7:10–16, where Paul states that, in the case of the marriage of two unbaptized, one of whom later becomes a Christian without the consent of the other, the convert is no longer bound to remain with the non-Christian. "It is to peace that God has called you" (v. 15). This principle became part of the Church's canonical legislation in 1199, was used frequently during the missionary expansion of the Church from the sixteenth through the nineteenth centuries, and is still employed today (canon 1143).

Petrine Privilege

The "Petrine Privilege" is also known as the "Privilege of the Faith." It is not found in the Code of Canon Law but developed as a pastoral practice in the United States after the promulgation of the Code of Canon Law in 1917. The "Petrine Privilege" allows the pope to dissolve a marriage between a Christian and a non-Christian which, by the very nature of the bond, was not sacramental in the first place (no marriage can be sacramental unless both parties are Christians). There has to be a good reason for such papal action: One of the parties to the first marriage (presumably severed in divorce) wishes to marry a Catholic in a second ceremony, or the non-Christian party wants to become a Catholic and remarry.

Annulment

The Catholic Church does not grant divorces, only annulments. An annulment is an official declaration that a canonically valid marriage never existed between the two parties. An annulment does *not* say that a *relationship,* even a loving relationship, never existed, or that a *marriage* never existed, or that the children born of the canonically invalid marriage are *illegitimate* (see canon 1137). The traditional grounds for nullity so carefully listed in the 1917 Code of Canon Law include the twelve impediments listed in the 1983 Code (canons 1083–94) and various consensual defects (canons 1095–1103).

Pastoral Care of the Divorced and Remarried

The Marriage Tribunal (or court) of a diocese or of the Holy See is referred to as the "external forum." Its proceedings are public. Decisions are rendered in the open. However, it is not always possible to find adequate public reasons justifying an annulment decree. In some such difficult cases, the Church is committed to a caring and compassionate ministry toward those who are in stable and responsible second marriages. When a public annulment process is impossible, a Catholic who, after prayerful consultation, has decided to remarry or to remain in the present second marriage may, according to some theological opinion and pastoral practice, be readmitted to the Church's sacramental life, assuming that no grave scandal is involved (see again Bishop Walter Kasper above). This is the so-called "internal forum" solution. In either case, the party must honor his or her moral or legal obligations remaining from the prior marriage.

Ecumenical Reflections

There is agreement between the Catholic Church, on the one hand, and the Orthodox and Anglican churches, on the other, regarding the sacramentality of marriage. The *Orthodox–Roman Catholic* "Agreed Statement on the Sanctity of Marriage" (*Origins* 8/28, December 28, 1978, pp. 446–47) notes that "marriage [is] the fundamental relationship in which a man and woman, by total sharing with each other, seek their own growth in holiness and that of their children, and thus show forth the presence on earth of God's kingdom" (I, par. 2). Although marriage involves a permanent commitment, the statement acknowledges that the Orthodox Church, "out of consideration of the human realities, permits divorce . . . and tolerates remarriages in order to avoid further human tragedies" (II, par. 2).

An *Anglican–Roman Catholic* Commission on the Theology of Marriage and Its Application to Mixed Marriages concluded that there is "no fundamental difference of doctrine between the two Churches, as regards what marriage of its nature is or the ends which it is ordained to serve" (*Final Report,* June 27, 1975, Washington, D.C.: United States Catholic Conference, 1976, p. 20). The report refers favorably to the teaching of Vatican II on the covenantal character of marriage, and to marriage's relationship to the covenantal union of Christ and the Church.

Jesus, the Church, and Matrimony

When seen as a covenantal rather than contractual bond, Christian marriage is a sacrament of the union between Christ and Church (Ephesians 5:22–32). The sacrament of Matrimony is also a decisive moment when the *Church* reveals itself as the bride of Christ, as the sign that God is irrevocably committed to the human community in and through Christ. The new community signified and effected by marriage is also a sign of what the Church is, a community of love brought about by the Holy Spirit. The Church comes into being at various levels of Christian community. The *family* is its most basic level. Indeed, the family has been called "the domestic Church" (Vatican II, *Dogmatic Constitution on the Church,* n. 11; Paul VI, *Evangelii Nuntiandi* [1975], n. 71; John Paul II, *Consortium Socialis* [1981], n. 21). "This means that there should be found in every Christian family the various aspects of the entire Church" (Paul VI).

Jesus himself is revealed in this sacrament as one whose whole life and being are oriented toward the loving service of others for the sake of creating and sustaining a community of love. He calls upon us to love one another as he has loved us (John 15:1–17).

HOLY ORDER

It is important that the reader situate the following material in the larger context of the theology of *ministry* (treated in chapter 20). The episcopate, the presbyterate, and the diaconate are, first and foremost, ministries, not canonical states-in-life. The reader should also consult chapter 20 for a specific discussion of the question of women's ordination.

Terminology

The sacrament of Holy Order is exceedingly complicated in its origin and in the development of its terminology. Tertullian chose the word *ordo* ("order") to apply to the clergy as a whole, probably under the influence of Psalm 110:4 and Hebrews 5–7, which refer to the priesthood "according to the order of Melchizedek." This "order" was composed of various grades of ministers. The bishop, a modern term derived from the Latinization of *episcopos* ("overseer"), was commonly called *sacerdos* ("priest"). The priest (in the modern sense of the word) was called *presbyter*. The deacon was usually called *minister* ("servant"). In the course of history, the corporate or collegial sense of *ordo* gradually evaporated, only to be rediscovered at Vatican II. Because of these extreme variations in terminology, one must interpret ancient texts with great care, not reading back into them some medieval or modern understanding of the words.

History

Outlines of the history of the origins and evolution of the Church's ordained ministries have already been provided in chapters 16 and 20. What follows is supplemental.

Old Testament

As is explained in the Epistle to the Hebrews, Jesus' priesthood must be understood in light of the Old Testament. The patriarchs, as heads of families or tribal groups, performed priestly functions, such as offering sacrifice (Genesis 22:2; 31:54). Eventually, a specific office of priesthood evolved and a priestly professionalism developed, especially in the tribe of Levi (thus, the levitical priesthood). This professionalism involved certain skills and training. It also required sanctity (Leviticus 19:2; 21:8). Deuteronomy 33:8–10 suggests three basic priestly functions: the discernment of God's will through the casting of sacred lots (1 Samuel 14:41–42), teaching (Deuteronomy 33:10), and sacrifice and cultic offering (Deuteronomy 33:10). The priest, therefore, was an intermediary between God and humankind. (For an extensive synthesis, see John J. Castelot and Aelred Cody, "Religious Institutions of Israel," *The New Jerome Biblical Commentary* [1990], especially pp. 1254–59.)

New Testament

Nowhere in the New Testament is the Greek word for priest (*hiereus*) applied to someone who holds an office in the Church. Where it is used for an individual, as in the Epistle to the Hebrews, it is applied only to Christ. The term *is* applied to Christians *collectively* in 1 Peter 2:0; Revelation 1:6; 5:10; and 20:6. Only in the last quarter of the second century, after Christianity's separation from Judaism had become complete and definitive, did *hiereus* become a common designation for Christian officeholders. This occurred as recognition of the sacrificial nature of the Eucharist grew. The one who presided at the Eucharist was seen as exercising a priestly role.

The classic image of the Christian priest is really a fusion of several different roles: disciple, apostle, presbyter-bishop, and eucharistic presider. The first formal ministry in the Church was that of the Twelve, who were charismatic missionaries. Thereafter the original Jewish-Christian communities organized themselves according to the synagogue model with elders, prophets, and preachers. As the Church moved to culturally different communities through the ministry of the apostles, different models of ministry, with bishops and deacons, were adopted in and adapted to those places. We find an integration of these two kinds of ministry—missionary and residential—in the Pastoral Epistles, but even there the precise relationship between bishops and deacons on the one hand and presbyters on the other is not clear. Everything is marked by pluralism, diversity, and variety.

The elders (*presbyteroi*), deacons (*diakonoi*), and overseers (*episcopoi*) are of particular interest here because their offices, beginning with Ignatius of Antioch, came to be regarded by the Catholic Church as constituting the threefold division of the one sacrament of Holy

Order: diaconate, presbyterate, and episcopate—deacon, priest, and bishop.

Postapostolic Period

As the Apostles disappeared from the scene and false teachers emerged (1 Timothy 4:1–3; Titus 1:10–13; 2 Timothy 3:1–9; 4:3–4), there was a growing recognition of the need for church order. Presbyters (elders) were appointed in each town and were given an episcopal (supervisory) function: monitoring the religious and moral behavior of the faithful, caring for the needy out of the common goods, and ensuring sound doctrine. Those holding this office were to be people of good judgment, prudent and temperate, able to manage their own households, married no more than once, having well-behaved children, not recent converts, neither greedy nor given to violence. Deacons were also part of this structure, but it is not clear what deacons did that distinguished them from the presbyters.

As the older charismatic structure of apostles, prophets, and teachers gave way (1 Corinthians 12:28), the *Didache* urged Christians to appoint bishops and deacons (15:1–2). By the 90s itinerant prophets and apostles became a source of trouble and their credentials were unverifiable (11:1–2; see also Revelation 2:2,20), so the need for a more regulated and controllable structure intensified. Clement of Rome (d. 100) canonized the offices of presbyter/bishop and deacon by situating them in a clear line of authority: from God to Jesus Christ to the Apostles to the bishops and deacons and their successors (*1 Clem* 42; 44:1).

The awareness of a sacrificial Eucharist and of a separate Christian priesthood began to appear in Christian writings about this time, especially in the *Didache*, in the writings of Clement of Rome, in Ignatius of Antioch, and in the *Apostolic Tradition* of Hippolytus of Rome (d. c. 236).

It is not clear, however, that anyone in particular was commissioned to preside over the Eucharist in the beginning. Paul never mentions that he presided. In fact, he seems to have been little involved in the administration of sacraments (1 Corinthians 1:14–15). There is no explicit mention that any of the Apostles presided over the Eucharist. Indeed, there is no compelling evidence that they presided when they were present, or that a chain of ordination from Apostle to bishop to priest was required for presiding.

We simply do not know how a certain individual came to preside and whether it came to be a permanent or regular function for that person. The most that can be said is that those who presided did so with the consent of the local church and that this consent was tantamount, but not always equivalent, to ordination.

As the Church grew larger and became more complex in its organizational structure, the element of selection and consent came to be regularized. Presiding eventually became the exclusive privilege of bishops and presbyters. The *Didache* may have been written just at the turning point when the system was placed into effect. There is an instruction for bishops and deacons to render to the community the ministry (liturgy) of the prophets. By the year 96, Clement's *Epistle to the Corinthians* speaks of the sin of ejecting from office "men who have offered the sacrificial gifts of the episcopate worthily" (44:4). Fifteen years later the practice of episcopal and presbyteral presiding at the Eucharist is well established. Ignatius of Antioch makes it clear that only the bishop or his appointee is to preside at the Eucharist and to baptize (*Smyrnaeans* 8:1). The tripartite ministry of bishop, presbyter, and deacon also emerges in place of the twofold ministry of presbyter/bishop and deacon. By the end of the second century this threefold structure became universal in the Church.

Thus, by the turn of the second century or soon thereafter, two roles that were probably once separated are joined together: the role of the presbyter-bishop and the role of the presiding minister of the Eucharist. Significantly, not until the year 1208 is there an official declaration that priestly ordination is necessary to celebrate the Eucharist (Innocent III, *Profession of Faith Prescribed to the Waldensians*), and then, more solemnly, by the Council of Florence (1439) and the Council of Trent (1563).

It is also in the postapostolic period that we first find evidence for the so-called *monarchical episcopate*, i.e., a local church presided over by one bishop. The primary source is Ignatius of Antioch, and specifically his letters to the *Smyrnæans* (8:1; 9:1), the *Ephesians* (5:1,3), the *Trallians* (2:1), and the *Magnesians* (4:1; 7:1). Such respect as Ignatius recommended for bishops served as a weapon against disunity and heresy. But we must keep certain qualifications in mind: (1) The local

867

churches over which the bishop presided were not dioceses in the modern sense of the term. They were nothing more than one-parish towns. (2) We have no evidence that the monarchical episcopal structure was universal in the Church at this time. Indeed in Paul's day, some churches had presbyters and deacons, but no bishops (e.g., Philippi); others had only a charismatic structure (e.g., Corinth). Neither is there any mention of bishops in the *Didache,* one of the most ancient and authoritative documents of the Church. (3) On the contrary, in the mid-second century, when *The Shepherd of Hermas* was written, the Roman church still seems to have been ruled by a presbyterate, and Ignatius makes no mention of a bishop in his letter to the *Romans.* A slower acceptance of the monoepiscopate there would have been consistent with Rome's reluctance about innovations. (4) Presbyters also served as overseers (bishops) of churches (1 Peter 5:1–3). (5) Neither the presbyter-bishops nor the monarchical bishops can be considered "successors of the Apostles" in the sense that all were duly appointed and ordained by an Apostle, i.e., one of the Twelve. (6) Historians and theologians simply don't know how we arrived at Ignatius's monoepiscopal concept.

Third Through Fifth Centuries

The *Apostolic Tradition* of Hippolytus sketches a picture of the third-century Church. The *bishop* is the *sacerdos,* elected by the people, but he receives the imposition of hands from another bishop. According to the rite of ordination, the bishops' role is to proclaim God's word, forgive sins, preside over the Eucharist, and supervise the work of the presbyters and deacons.

The *presbyter,* or priest, is ordained by the bishop, with other priests joining in with the laying on of hands. According to the rite of ordination, presbyters were compared with the elders whom Moses had chosen (Numbers 11:17–25). They did not preside at the Eucharist, but formed a ring, or crown, around the bishop as he presided. With the bishop's permission a presbyter could replace a bishop as the presiding eucharistic minister.

The *deacon* is ordained by the bishop alone because the deacon is ordained to the service of the bishop. The deacon did not become a member of the college of presbyters, and the deacon's job description was determined entirely by the bishop.

Significantly, the rite of consecration of a bishop is clearly inspired by the New Testament, while the ordination of the priest is inspired by the Old Testament. This anomaly tends to confirm what was suggested above about the probable origins of the Christian priesthood. At first the Church seems to have had no intention of having a priesthood of its own, distinct from the Jewish priesthood. But when the concept of Christian priesthood took hold, the Church understandably drew upon the Old Testament for models, standards, and inspiration.

The Edict of Constantine in the early fourth century established Christianity as the state religion and conferred authority and privileges upon the clergy, thereby introducing a sharp division between clergy and laity and constituting the clergy as a special caste within the Church. This division would be accentuated in the Middle Ages with the development of the distinction between the *ordo clericorum* and the *ordo laicorum*, the former devoted to higher things of the spirit and the latter devoted to lower things of the flesh (see again chapter 20).

As the local churches grew, parishes were created outside the major Christian centers, and the presbyters were given pastoral care over them. Canon 6 of the Council of Chalcedon (451) would later decree that a priest always be ordained for a particular church. So strong was this canon that the ordination of anyone who was not called by a particular community was null and void. Anyone so ordained would not be paid by the state. His expenses would have to be borne by the bishop who presumed to ordain him. Later Isidore of Seville (d. 636) called those ordained in this way headless people, "neither man nor beast."

Sixth Through Twelfth Centuries

With the Germanization of Christianity in the early Middle Ages, the understanding and exercise of priesthood took another turn. Priestly and royal power were fused. Priests themselves were caught up into the feudal system and were ordained not only for the celebration of the Eucharist and the administration of sacraments, but also for certain tax-collecting chores. Their loyalty was to the feudal lords who selected them, not to the bishop. In the Frankish churches new rites of ordination were added. The bishop was anointed with holy chrism, the crozier (staff) and ring were given, and then he was enthroned. The priest was ordained with an anointing of the hands, the giving of bread and wine, and a second laying on of hands in view of the absolution of sins. These developments reflected Germanic customs which attached great importance to the transmission of the emblems of power, a "princely" power for bishops and a cultic power for priests. Toward the end of the tenth century this liturgy was merged with the Roman tradition in the *Romano-Germanic Pontifical* of Mainz.

A monastic model of priesthood also emerged in the early Middle Ages, pushing the priesthood toward even more of a castelike existence within the Church. This movement reached its apex with the imposition of *celibacy* in the twelfth century as a universal requirement for priests of the Latin rite.

It was also at this time that the unfortunate distinction between the power of orders and the power of jurisdiction was introduced, thereby separating the spiritual "powers" of the priesthood (especially the celebration of Mass) from the call to "minister" to a particular community. Thus, even if a man were ordained without the call from a community, he still received the power to "say Mass" and forgive sins, in direct violation of the longstanding rule laid down by Chalcedon in the fifth century. The priesthood became increasingly a state in life rather than a ministry.

Neoplatonism also exerted its influence through the delayed impact of the works of the sixth-century Syrian author who wrote under the pseudonym of Dionysius the Areopagite, the Athenian convert of Paul (Acts of the Apostles 17:34). Thought to be from the first century and therefore accorded great authority, the writings proposed a hierarchical view of the Church modeled on the author's conception of the divinely ordered structure of the universe. Just as there were three orders in the angelic hierarchy, so there were three orders in the clerical hierarchy—bishops, priests, and deacons—and three orders in the lay hierarchy—religious, laity, and catechumens. In this schema, higher orders always influenced lower. Laity were passive recipients of grace from the clergy. Thus was the stage set for the upheavals of the sixteenth century.

The Reformation and the Council of Trent

The increasing alienation of the clergy from the rest of the Church provoked a reaction. The Reformers insisted that there exists in the Church no ministerial power received through the sacrament of Holy Order. There is only a priesthood of all believers. All specialized ministry is delegated by the community. Furthermore, since the Eucharist is not a sacrifice (Calvary cannot, and need not, be repeated), there is no need for a cultic priesthood in the Church.

The *Council of Trent* rejected these views, declaring that the ordained priesthood, separate from and superior to the priesthood of all believers, is conferred through one of the seven sacraments, that the Mass is a true sacrifice, and that there is a true hierarchy in the Church consisting of bishops, priests, and deacons and that these ministers do not depend on the call of the community for their authority and powers (*Doctrine on the Sacrament of Order*, Session XXIII, 1563).

The Counter-Reformation to Vatican II

Under the impact of Trent, the Catholic Church launched a reform of the clergy. Seminaries for the education and training of future priests were established, and greater emphasis was placed on priestly spirituality. The reform of priestly formation and spirituality was supported by such apostolic figures as Charles Borromeo (d. 1584) and Francis de Sales (d. 1622), and by the new religious orders. But the spirituality was still individualistic, and the notion of priesthood on which it was based was still cultic and sacramental.

With the Baroque period (seventeenth and early eighteenth centuries), dominated by the Jesuits, priestly ministry becomes inseparable from the great drama of grace which is played out within the soul of the individual priest. Catholic romanticism (eighteenth century) reinforced the tendency to isolate the priest and to emphasize his personal and, in a sense, his private identification with the sacrifice of Christ.

Under the impact of the anticlericalist wave of the *French Revolution* in the late eighteenth century, the Church launched yet another spiritual renewal, this time sparked by principles enunciated earlier by Vincent de Paul (d. 1660), Jean-Jacques Olier (d. 1657), Pierre de Bérulle (d. 1629), and others. The so-called French school of priestly spirituality insisted that Christ's own priesthood is rooted in his divinity, not his humanity, and that through ordination priests share in a very mysterious, highly mystical power.

This view was consistent with the ecclesiology of the post-Reformation period when everything was seen in the Church as coming "from above." The Church became identified with the hierarchy. Bishops and priests were seen as "churchmen" with special spiritual powers and authority. "Ministry" became identified more and more with Protestantism.

Vatican II

With its stress on the Church as the whole People of God, the Second Vatican Council acknowledged that all the baptized participate in some way in the one priesthood of Christ and in the mission of the Church itself (*Dogmatic Constitution on the Church*, nn. 11, 30, 31). Although the priesthood of ordination and the priesthood of Baptism differ "in essence and not only in degree," they are nonetheless related to this one priesthood of Christ. The ministerial priesthood of ordination consists of three degrees or orders: episcopate, presbyterate, and diaconate (nn. 20–29). Each order is truly sacramental.

Taken as a body (*ordo*), bishops are the successors to the college of the Apostles in teaching authority and pastoral rule (n. 22). United with their head, the bishop of Rome, the bishops constitute a college and are the subjects of "supreme and full power over the universal Church." The union of bishops among themselves and with the bishop of Rome symbolizes the communion of churches which constitutes the whole Body of Christ (n. 23). At the same time, bishops "enjoy the fullness of the sacrament of orders," whereas priests and deacons are "dependent upon them in the exercise of authority" (*Decree on the Bishops' Pastoral Office in the Church*, n. 15).

The presbyterate is a specific participation in the priesthood of the episcopate (*Dogmatic Constitution on the Church*, n. 28). Priests,

872

"prudent fellow workers of the episcopal order," are united with their bishop in priestly dignity (*Decree on the Bishops' Pastoral Office in the Church*, n. 15). They are collaborators with the bishop and constitute a college with him.

Since the priesthood of Christ includes prophetic and shepherding as well as "priestly" or cultic functions, the ordained priesthood of the Church embraces more than sacramental and liturgical responsibilities (*Decree on the Ministry and Life of Priests*, nn. 2–6). The medieval distinction between the powers of orders and the power of jurisdiction is abandoned.

The diaconate is also a sacramental degree of Holy Order (*Dogmatic Constitution on the Church*, n. 29). Deacons are "ordained for service and ministry to the People of God in communion with the bishop and his presbytery" (*Decree on the Bishops' Pastoral Office in the Church*, n. 15). The council recommended the restoration of the *permanent* diaconate (as distinguished from reception of the diaconate as a *transitional* step on the way to priesthood).

The New Rites of Ordination

The rite of *episcopal ordination* is now modified to include the consecratory prayer from the *Apostolic Tradition* of Hippolytus of Rome, in order to bring out the apostolic succession of bishops and their various duties and functions beyond the purely cultic. The collegial character of the episcopate is also emphasized.

The rite, conducted by a principal consecrator and usually two other consecrating bishops, begins with a hymn (usually the *Veni, Creator Spiritus*), followed by the presentation of the bishop-elect, the reading of the apostolic letter from the Holy See, the consent of the people, a homily, an examination of the candidate, the litany of the saints, the laying on of hands, the placing of the Book of Gospels on the head of the new bishop, the prayer of consecration, the anointing of the new bishop's head, the presentation of the Book of the Gospels, the investiture with ring, miter, and pastoral staff, the seating of the bishop in the chair of authority, and the kiss of peace.

In *presbyteral ordination* the collaborative relationship between the priest and the bishop is more clearly drawn. Significantly, the Old Testament flavor is preserved in the consecratory prayer.

873

The rite begins with the calling and presentation of the candidate, the election by the bishop and the consent of the people, a homily, the examination of the candidate, the promise of obedience, the litany of the saints, the laying on of hands, the prayer of consecration, the investiture with stole and chasuble, the anointing of hands, the presentation of the gifts for Mass, and the kiss of peace.

Only minor changes have been made in the rite of *ordination to the diaconate* to take into account recent prescriptions concerning the diaconate as a proper and permanent grade of the hierarchy in the Latin Church and also for the sake of clarifying and simplifying the ceremony.

The rite begins with the calling and presentation of the candidate, the election by the bishop and the consent of the people, a homily, the commitment to celibacy, the examination of the candidate, the promise of obedience, the litany of the saints, the laying on of hands, the prayer of consecration, the investiture with stole and dalmatic, the presentation of the Book of the Gospels, and the kiss of peace.

Ecumenical Developments

Several of the ecumenical consultations in the United States and internationally have addressed themselves to the question of ordained ministry: for example, Lutheran-Catholic, Anglican–Roman Catholic, United Methodist–Roman Catholic, Orthodox–Roman Catholic, and Presbyterian-Reformed–Roman Catholic. The *Lutheran-Catholic* consultation issued an important statement, "Eucharist and Ministry," in 1970 (*Lutherans and Catholics in Dialogue*, vol. 4, Washington, D.C.: United States Catholic Conference, 1970, pp. 7–33). It distinguishes between the general ministry (lowercase) of the whole People of God and the ordained Ministry (uppercase), which is a particular form of service within and for the sake of the Church in its mission to the world. It is a ministry of proclaiming the Gospel, celebrating the sacraments, caring for the faithful, witnessing, and serving. It stands *with* the People of God under Christ, but also speaks in Christ's name *to* his People. The Catholic participants in this dialogue noted a "gratifying degree of agreement" with the Lutherans "as to the essentials of the sacred Ministry." They concluded that they "see no persuasive reason to deny the possibility of the Roman Catholic church recognizing the validity of this [Lutheran] Ministry," and they urged the Catholic authorities to do so.

Similar agreement was recorded by the *Anglican–Roman Catholic* consultation. In its twelve-year report of December 1977, the dialogue noted only a continuing difference or emphasis on the ministry of *episcope* (literally "oversight"). For Catholics, this ministry is centered in the Bishop of Rome; for Anglicans it is less centralized. But certain pastoral developments in the Catholic Church have brought the two churches closer together even on this matter. Collegiality and coresponsibility are now the order of the day: international synods of bishops, national episcopal conferences, national advisory boards, diocesan pastoral councils, parish council, priests' senates. And the ministry of the Bishop of Rome is increasingly perceived and exercised as one of service. (*Origins* 7/30, January 12, 1978, pp. 465, 467–73.)

The *Orthodox–Roman Catholic* joint statement of July 1976 on the pastoral office of "Bishops and Presbyters" lists several points of agreement: Ordained ministry is a commissioning by the Holy Spirit to build up the Church; the offices of bishop and presbyter are different realizations of the sacrament of Order; bishops exercise authority over a whole community, and presbyters share in that authority under the bishop; ordination is required for both offices because they are "an essential element of the sacramental reality of the church"; the pastoral officer is distinct but not separated from the rest of the community; on the other hand, he is not dependent on the community for the exercise of his service, since he receives the special bestowal of the Spirit in ordination (*Origins*, 6/9, August 12, 1976, pp. 142–43).

The *Presbyterian-Reformed–Roman Catholic* consultation offers a more congregational approach to the ordained ministry. It stresses, first, the call of all Christians to ministry, for the building up of the Church. Within this general ministry there are ministers who are "called and ordained to represent Christ to the community and the community before Christ. Through the proclamation of the Gospel and the celebration of the sacraments this ministry has endeavored to unite and order the Church for the ministry of the whole people of God." Its function is to see to it that "the Word of God is proclaimed,

875

the sacraments celebrated, individuals led to Christian maturity, and the Christian community built up" (*The Unity We Seek*, New York: Paulist Press, 1977, pp. 11–13).

The high point of the ecumenical discussions on ordained ministry is the *Baptism, Eucharist and Ministry* paper (also known as *BEM*) of the Faith and Order Commission of the World Council of Churches (Geneva: World Council of Churches, 1982) and the Vatican's critical response to it (*Origins*, 17/23 [November 19, 1987] 401, 403–16). *BEM* situated the ordained ministry within the context of "the calling of the whole people of God," spoke of "episcopal succession" as "a sign, though not a guarantee, of the continuity and unity of the church," and claimed that the "threefold ministry of bishop, presbyter and deacon may serve today as an expression of the unity we seek and also as a means for achieving it."

Contemporary Catholic Theology

Like Catholic ecclesiology itself, the Catholic theology of ordained ministry has been affected most profoundly by New Testament studies (and history in the broader sense) and by the Second Vatican Council. To the extent that there have been significant changes in our theological understanding of the episcopate and the presbyterate in particular, those changes have come about as theologians progressively assimilated and applied the work of biblical scholars and church historians, and the documents of the council.

There is a greater emphasis now on ordained ministry as *ministry* rather than as a spiritual and/or canonical state in life, and upon its pastoral *functions*, especially that of *leadership* (see, for example, the works of Yves Congar, Edward Schillebeeckx, and Thomas F. O'Meara). On the other hand, some theologians emphasize the ministry of the word (Karl Rahner and Joseph Ratzinger), others the representational aspect of priesthood (Avery Dulles), others the traditional ontological and cultic dimensions (Jean Galot). (For a survey of views, see Daniel Donovan, *What Are They Saying About the Ministerial Priesthood?*)

Jesus, the Church, and Holy Order

The *Church* is a sacrament. Through the exercise of this sacramental ministry of Holy Order the whole sacramental reality of the Church is expressed: The good news of the Reign of God is proclaimed, the Eucharist is celebrated, the death and resurrection of Christ are made real and effective for individuals in Baptism, sins are forgiven, the sick are ministered to and healed, human love is sanctified, the Holy Spirit is poured forth, and the mediating, priestly work of Christ is continued.

Jesus alone is our High Priest, the model of the Church's priesthood: building bridges between God and humankind, identifying with our weaknesses, saving those who approach him "with a true heart in full assurance of faith" (Hebrews 10:22). He came among us, this High Priest, "not to be served but to serve, and to give his life a ransom for many" (Mark 10:45).

SUMMARY

1. In *Matrimony* the Christian community is built up and manifested at its most natural, familial level. The union of Christ and his Church is symbolized. In *Holy Order* the Christian community is provided structure and direction for the exercise of its mission.

2. *Matrimony* is rooted in the Old Testament notions of *creation* and *covenant*. The ambivalence of the New Testament regarding marriage (i.e., that it is at once holy and to be avoided, if possible) may be explained by its sense of the imminence of the Kingdom of God. In later New Testament writings (Ephesians) this sense of the imminence of the Kingdom has waned, and so marriage is linked with the union of Christ and the Church.

3. The ambivalence carries through much of the Church's history. The largely negative attitude of *Augustine* toward marriage and sexuality is well known, but neither he nor the other early writers of the Church denied the basic sanctity of marriage. Its sacramentality was affirmed by the Councils of *Florence* and *Trent*.

4. *Vatican II* introduced a whole new perspective on marriage: (1) It is a covenant, not a contract; (2) mutual love is not "secondary" to the begetting of children; (3) mutual love is, in fact, what is sanctified by the sacrament; (4) its sacramentality is not automatic; it requires faith; (5) the consummation of marriage encompasses more than a single biological act; and (6) the sacrament incorporates one more fully into the mystery of the Church.

877

5. The Catholic Church has always taught that marriage is *indissoluble*. On the other hand, it has always tolerated certain modifications of this principle through *dispensations* (similar to the Eastern Orthodox application of the principle of *economy*) designed to remove the unintended harshness of the law.

6. Church law requires that Catholics marry before the local bishop, the pastor, or a priest or a deacon delegated by either one, and two witnesses (*canonical form*). Since Vatican II, however, exceptions have been granted frequently, given the many instances of mixed marriage.

7. A *mixed marriage* is one between a Catholic and a non-Catholic; it requires both a dispensation and a promise by the Catholic party to do all in his or her power to share the Catholic faith with any children of the union.

8. The *Pauline Privilege* permits a second marriage to one who converts to Christianity when the first partner does not. The *Petrine Privilege* allows the pope to dissolve a marriage between a Christian and a non-Christian when the Christian wishes to marry another Christian or when the non-Christian wishes to become a Catholic and remarry.

9. An *annulment* is an official declaration that a marriage was sacramentally invalid from the beginning. When an official declaration is impossible, some theological opinion and pastoral practice allow Catholics in a second marriage to be readmitted to the Church's sacramental life, assuming no grave scandal is present.

10. There is fundamental agreement between Catholics and Orthodox, on the one hand, and Catholics and Anglicans, on the other, on the *sacramentality* of marriage.

11. Through the sacrament of Matrimony the *Church* reveals itself as the bride of Christ, the sign of God's love for us in Christ, and as a community of love. *Jesus* is revealed as one whose whole life and ministry are an expression of love in the service of community.

12. The sacrament of *Holy Order* presents a very complicated history. There is an *Old Testament* priesthood identified with the tribe of Levi. In the *New Testament* Jesus is the only individual who is called a priest, although Christians collectively are also sometimes referred to as priests.

13. The classic image of the *Christian priest* is really a fusion of several different roles: disciple, apostle, presbyter-bishop, and eucharistic presider. The image does not emerge until after the definitive separation from Judaism and the gradual growth in a sacrificial understanding of the Eucharist.

14. Those who *presided* at the Eucharist did so with the consent of the community, but we don't know how and why certain figures presided at first. By the time of Ignatius of Antioch (turn of the second century), only the bishop and his appointees presided.

15. Ignatius is also the earliest witness to the development of a *monarchical episcopate*, which became universal by the end of the second century.

16. By the third century, *ordination* to the ministries of bishop, presbyter, and deacon are witnessed to in the *Apostolic Tradition* of Hippolytus.

17. Priestly and *royal power* were fused in the early Middle Ages as the Church was drawn into the *feudal system* of the time.

18. A *monastic* model of priesthood also developed, culminating in the imposition of *celibacy* on all priests of the Latin rite in the twelfth century. The distinction between the power of *orders* and the power of *jurisdiction* also emerged at this time, making the priesthood more a state in life than a ministry.

19. The issue of the priesthood of all believers and the priesthood of the ordained was joined at the *Reformation*, with the Council of *Trent* insisting on the latter.

20. In the *post-Tridentine* period emphasis was placed on the *personal* and *private* dimensions of the priesthood, and on the innate superiority of priests over the laity.

21. *Vatican II* restored the understanding of the Church as the whole People of God and stressed the participation of the laity in the priesthood of Christ, without prejudice to the special priesthood of the ordained. Emphasis was placed on the role of bishops in the Church and on their collegial union, one with another and with the Bishop of Rome, as a symbol of the collegial nature of the Church itself. The corporate or collegial nature of the presbyterate was also emphasized once again, and the permanent diaconate was restored.

22. Various *ecumenical* agreements and contemporary *Catholic theology* situate the ordained ministries within the context of the ministry of the whole People of God. The emphasis is on ministry to be done rather than on the spiritual or canonical status of the minister.

23. The whole sacramental reality of the *Church* is expressed in the sacrament of Holy Order, and through it *Jesus*, our High Priest, continues to minister on our behalf.

SUGGESTED READINGS

Brown, Raymond. *Priest and Bishop: Biblical Reflections*. New York: Paulist Press, 1970.

Cahill, Lisa Sowle. *Between the Sexes: Foundations for a Christian Ethics of Sexuality*. Philadelphia: Fortress Press, 1985.

Carmody, Denise Lardner. *Caring for Marriage: Feminist and Biblical Reflections*. New York: Paulist Press, 1985.

Donovan, Daniel. *What are they saying about the ministerial priesthood?* New York: Paulist Press, 1992.

Fransen, Piet. "Orders and Ordination." *Encyclopedia of Theology: The Concise Sacramentum Mundi.* New York: Seabury Press, 1975, pp. 1122–48.

Galot, Jean. *Theology of the Priesthood.* San Francisco: Ignatius Press, 1984.

John Paul II, Pope. *Pastores Dabo Vobis* (Apostolic Exhortation on the Formation of Priests). *Origins* 21/45 (April 16, 1992).

Kasper, Walter. *Theology of Christian Marriage.* New York: Seabury Press, 1980.

Lawler, Michael G. *Secular Marriage, Christian Marriage.* Mystic, Conn.: Twenty-Third Publications, 1985.

Mackin, Theodore. *The Marital Sacrament.* New York: Paulist Press, 1989.

Mitchell, Nathan. *Mission and Ministry: History and Theology in the Sacrament of Order.* Wilmington, Del.: Michael Glazier, 1982.

O'Meara, Thomas F. *Theology of Ministry.* New York: Paulist Press, 1983.

Orsy, Ladislas. *Marriage in Canon Law.* Wilmington, Del.: Michael Glazier, 1986.

Osborne, Kenan B. *Priesthood: A History of the Ordained Ministry in the Roman Catholic Church.* New York: Paulist Press, 1988.

Schillebeeckx, Edward. *The Church with a Human Face: A New and Expanded Theology of Ministry.* New York: Crossroad, 1985.

Whitehead, James, and Evelyn Whitehead. *Marrying Well: Stages on the Journey of Christian Marriage.* New York: Doubleday, 1984.

Christian Morality

C HRISTIAN faith expresses itself through love (Galatians 5:6). Indeed, such faith does not really exist unless there is a commitment to the Gospel of Jesus Christ. This commitment is initially made, shaped, and sustained within a sacramental community of faith, which is the Church.

We come in Part Six of the book to the question of *Christian morality*. What does it mean to be a disciple of Jesus Christ and a member of his Body, the Church? What kinds of decisions and behavior, at both the personal and social levels, are consistent with the preaching of Jesus and the faith of the Church?

In chapter 25, we ask: How did Jesus understand the nature and implications of discipleship? To what extent was his message in continuity with the faith of Israel, and to what extent was it a departure? How was the call to discipleship understood after the resurrection: within the New Testament churches, in the earliest centuries of the Church through the Middle Ages, and into the twentieth century?

In the light of this long and complex historical development, can we identify any distinguishing marks which set apart the moral vision of Christians in general and of Catholics in particular? What are the models of the Christian moral life? What kind of person is the Christian called to become? How is the Christian to act in the world? What virtues and what sort of character does the authentic Christian display? What are the defining relationships of the Christian life (chapter 26)?

How are the principles of Christian and Catholic morality applicable to specific dilemmas and conflict situations? For example, what is the Christian, and particularly the Catholic, to think of contraception, homosexuality, the intervention of the state in the economic order, and abortion—the last not simply as a moral issue but also as a public policy issue (chapter 27)?

Like the social teachings of the Church, this part of the book does not propose to offer specific and detailed answers to every major moral question. Rather, it provides a biblical, historical, and theological framework within which, it is hoped, the reader can better understand the nature and scope of Christian and Catholic morality.

XXV

Christian Morality: A Historical Perspective

MORAL THEOLOGY/CHRISTIAN ETHICS

The standard distinction between "dogmatic" and "moral" theology has been drawn on the basis of a perceived difference between *theory* and *practice*. In dogmatic theology we specify what we must believe; in moral theology we determine how we are to *live* and what we are required to *do* (or *not* do) because of those beliefs. And the traditional catechisms would thereafter introduce the sacraments as those God-given "aids" to correct belief and moral action.

These distinctions, however, are based on a faulty understanding of the theory-practice relationship. The two are in reality not separate but are united in the one notion of *praxis*. *Praxis* means more than "practice" alone. It is practice-plus-reflection, and it is reflection-in-practice. Truth is not only to be thought but also to be lived and done, and the living and doing of truth is a condition of grasping it. "But those who do what is true come to the light, so that it may be clearly seen that their deeds have been done in God" (John 3:21). Similarly, Paul insists that "the only thing that counts is faith working through love" (Galatians 5:6). Indeed, faith cannot exist, and does not exist, without commitment to the implementation of the Gospel. Systematic theology, therefore, must embrace both dogmatic (or doctrinal) *and* moral theology. This is how Thomas Aquinas understood their relationship in his *Summa Theologiæ*. The two disciplines were not formally separated until after the Council of Trent, as we shall see below.

On the other hand, reflection and practice do not collapse completely into one another. Although an *integral* understanding of the Gospel is not possible without a commitment to, and practice of, the Gospel, most people will always find themselves far short of the ideal. The relationship between theory and practice in the integrating notion of *praxis* is a *dialectical* relationship, not one of *identity*. It is possible, in other words, for a person to be a sincere believer in the Gospel of Jesus Christ and yet not fully practice what she or he believes and preaches. The Council of Trent declared: "If anyone says that with the loss of grace through sin faith is also always lost, or that the faith which remains is not true faith, granted that it is not a living faith; or that the [person] who has faith without charity is not a Christian, *anathema sit*" (*Decree on Justification*, canon 28, Session VI, 1547). For a *living* faith, there must be an expression of love. But faith itself can exist, at least for a time, without love. Thus, although systematic theology embraces both dogmatic (or doctrinal) and moral theology, the two are not the same, no more than faith and action are the same. The other common term to describe and encompass the theological reflections contained in these next three chapters is *Christian ethics*, a term more often used in Protestant circles.

Some *distinctions* are in order, however. A very important distinction exists between the discipline of moral theology or Christian ethics and *morality*. The distinction partakes of the more general differentiation between *ethics* and morality. To better understand this distinction one might ask the following question: Are ethicists the most moral people and the best decision makers in the world? The answer is obviously, "No."

The distinction between ethics and morality is similar to the distinction between psychiatry and human psychic behavior. Without depreciating an honorable profession, we readily recognize that psychiatrists are not necessarily the most mature, well-balanced people in the world. Psychiatry is a second-order discipline which studies human psychic behavior in a thematic, systematic, reflective manner. Many people who have never read Freud or Jung are very well balanced and lead truly healthy and satisfying psychic lives. However, when people are in trouble or seriously anxious about the direction of their lives, the second-order discipline of psychiatry can help them stand back and examine their lives in a more reflective and systematic way. In a similar manner, morality refers to how people live and act: *moral theology or Christian ethics is the thematic, systematic, reflective study of Christian morality.* The ethicist or moral theologian is concerned with such questions as coherency, adequacy, and how all aspects of the moral life fit together in a systematic way. Degrees of reflection and systematization exist so that whenever individuals stand back to examine their moral lives, they are moving into the area of second-order discourse and ethics.

One must recognize not only the role and the importance, but also the limitations of moral theology or Christian ethics. A Christian person can live a very good moral life and make very good decisions without ever having studied moral theology. Moral theology as a second-order discourse stands back to study Christian morality in a scientific and systematic way which can help understand better the moral life, but it is not absolutely necessary for living a good moral life.

There also have been recent discussions about what is *unique* or *distinctive* about Christian morality or Christian ethics. The above distinction is very important for addressing this question of uniqueness or distinctiveness.

Moral theology or Christian ethics is a branch of ethics. Ethics is generally divided into philosophical ethics and religious ethics. *Philosophical ethics* in its reflection and systematization uses only human sources such as reason and experience. *Religious ethics* uses the sources of a particular religion such as its scripture, tradition, and teaching authorities. Religious ethics can be Christian, Muslim, Hindu, or whatever. Christian ethics, because it has unique *sources*, thus differs from all other ethics. One of the present discussions in moral theology, for example, concerns how the Christian Scriptures should be used in the discipline.

The question of uniqueness on the level of *morality* is more keenly debated. Charles Curran holds that "others can and do arrive at the same ethical conclusions, dispositions, and attitudes as Christians" (*Toward an American Catholic Moral Theology*, Notre Dame, Ind.:

University of Notre Dame Press, 1987, p. 59). Christians are not the only ones who value forgiveness, mercy, care for the poor, justice, and love. This position coheres with the continuing emphasis in this book that there can be no dichotomy between grace and nature. The history of the world is the history of salvation. Authentic human progress in the struggle for justice, peace, freedom, and so forth, is an intrinsic part of the movement of, and toward, the final Reign of God. However, some other theologians may disagree with this approach.

Curran and many others maintain that Christian belief adds a unique *intentionality and motivation* to what Christians do, that is, to love as Jesus has loved us. Also, just as God calls by name and gives special gifts to different people, so Christians have unique vocations and gifts in the service of the Church.

HISTORY

The Moral Message of the Old Testament

Faithful *praxis* is linked in ancient Israel with the *Law* (*Tôrāh* = "instruction"), and that, in turn, with the *Covenant*. Although scholars do not completely agree, most seem to hold that the Israelites learned and developed their legal traditions from their more sophisticated Canaanite neighbors, after entering the Promised Land. It is also widely assumed that the *Covenant Code* (Exodus 20:22–23:33) belongs to the oldest part of Israelite history because it contains the greatest number of parallels to the pagan laws. Whether this is true, we cannot finally determine here. It is sufficient to note that the Code was inserted into the book of Exodus as part of the terms of the covenant of Sinai (where the Ten Commandments were promulgated). Consequently, the Covenant Code (or Code of the Covenant) is attributed to Moses and given the supreme authority which Israel attributed to all its laws.

Most of the Old Testament laws which have parallels in the ancient Near Eastern law collections are formulated in case form (the common way of teaching law even today); e.g., "If a man strikes his father they shall cut off his hand" (Hammurabi Laws, 195), and "When someone delivers to a neighbor money or goods for safekeeping, and they are stolen from the neighbor's house, then the thief, if caught, shall pay double. If the thief is not caught, the owner of the house shall be brought before God, to determine whether or not the owner had laid hands on the neighbor's goods" (Exodus 22:7–8). In the beginning, of course, such laws were unwritten. When a judge was puzzled about the law, he did not consult the law books but sought the help of a higher official in the capital (Deuteronomy 17:8–11).

Other codes of Israelite law were the "Yahwist ritual decalogue" dealing with the prohibition of images, festivals, and offerings (Exodus 34:17–27), the Deuteronomic Code (Deuteronomy 12–26), which prohibits the worship of gods other than Yahweh, the Holiness Code (Leviticus 17–26), which regulates such matters as diet, worship, hygiene, marriage, and sexual morality, the Priestly Code (scattered throughout the Pentateuch, the first five books of the Old Testament), whose cultic-ritual prescriptions often refer only to priests, and, finally, the Decalogue, or Ten Commandments (Exodus 20:2–17; Deuteronomy 5:6–21).

That ten words (*dābār* = "word") or commandments were given by God to Moses on Mount Sinai is an accepted part of ancient Hebrew tradition (Exodus 34:28; Deuteronomy 4:13; 10:4). But the enumeration of these ten commandments has taken at least three different forms in subsequent centuries. The best seems to be the one proposed by Philo (d. c. 50), Josephus (d. c. 100), the Greek Fathers, and the modern Greek church: (1) prohibition of false or foreign gods; (2) prohibition of images; (3) prohibition of the vain use of the divine name; (4) keeping holy the Sabbath; (5) honoring one's father and mother; (6) prohibition of murder; (7) prohibition of adultery; (8) prohibition of theft; (9) prohibition of false witness against one's neighbor; (10) prohibition against coveting a neighbor's house, wife, slaves, or possessions.

The first four commandments state one's duties toward God, and the last six refer to duties toward other human beings.

The enumeration followed in the modern Latin Church, with roots in Origen (d. c. 254), Clement of Alexandria (d. c. 215), and Augustine (d. 430), is as follows: (1) prohibition of false gods *and* images; (2) vain use of divine name; (3) Sabbath; (4) parents; (5) murder; (6) adultery; (7) theft; (8) false witness; (9) coveting of neighbor's wife; (10) coveting of neighbor's goods. Modern Jews put the introduction, "I am the Lord your God...," as (1) and then collapse (9) and (10) into (10). Everything else follows the same order as the Latin form.

One must keep in mind, however, that not even in Jesus' time had the Decalogue acquired the set form and importance as a charter of morality that it would acquire in later Christianity. The separate commandments are mentioned in the New Testament, but never as ten. When Jesus himself was asked by the young man how he could become perfect, Jesus cited some of the ten, but not in the usual order nor completely (Matthew 9:18–19; Mark 10:19; Luke 18:20).

Although the Ten Commandments bear some resemblance to other sources—e.g., the Code of Hammurabi—they are unique in the sense that they are regarded as the revealed will of God. Other Near Eastern collections were based on the conviction that the gods had authorized their formulation, but the laws themselves were the work of human hands alone. The conception of law as a sacred *covenant* obligation is indeed peculiar to Israel. It is important also to note that *the Decalogue was not intended as the ultimate norm of all morality.* On the contrary, it barely touches upon individual moral obligations. Its consistent focus is *the needs of the whole community,* and it prohibits those actions which might injure the community. What was important was the survival of the People of God. *Thus, the Ten Commandments were not so much an ethical document as a religious document, i.e., a testimony to the unbreakable bond between God and Israel.*

The Covenant, of course, is a basic and constant motif in the whole of the Old Testament. It is the motive for observing the Law (Deuteronomy 4:23), for Yahweh's punishments (Leviticus 26:15, 25), for Yahweh's coming to Israel's aid in times of distress (Leviticus 26:9), for Yahweh's mercy and forgiveness (Leviticus 26:42), and for the permanence both of Yahweh's mercy and of Israel's status as Yahweh's own people (Leviticus 26:45; Psalms 111:9; Isaiah 54:10; 59:21; 61:8; Jeremiah 32:40; Ezekiel 34:25; 37:26). It is never a bilateral contract between equals, but an agreement between a greater and a lesser party. The greater imposes its will upon the lesser, but the contract is also an act of grace and magnanimity. However, it is more than a mere contract. It establishes an artificial blood kinship between the parties that is second only to the bond of blood. The word used to signify covenant affection and loyalty (*ḥesed*) is also used to signify the affection and loyalty of kinsmen. The Covenant has its initial historical grounding in the covenant with *Abraham* (Genesis 15–17), but it was the covenant with *Moses* on Sinai that established Israel definitively as God's people (Exodus 19:1–8). The latter is summed up in the formula: "I will be your God and you shall be my people" (Jeremiah 7:23; see also 11:4; 24:7; Ezekiel 11:20; 14:11; Hosea 2:25).

The ancient Israelites had come to believe that a God who asked for righteousness and justice would also supply the means of instructing the people in the divine ways. Who in ancient Israel was competent to *interpret* the Covenant? Jeremiah 18:18 refers to three groups of leaders: the *priests*, who are the source of "instruction" (the root meaning of the word for Law, *Tôrāh*); the *prophets*, who convey the word of God; and *wise persons*, who offer counsel. These three classes of leaders were not mutually opposed to one another, nor indeed to the Law itself. On the contrary, Ezekiel was himself both prophet and priest, and the prophets were within the tradition of the Law. Nor was the teaching authority vested in any one group, not even in the priests.

The Moral Message of Jesus

The Reign, or Kingdom, of God

Although the idea of the Covenant is the axis around which the history of ancient Israel revolves, and although there was some expectation of a new covenant among the prophets (Jeremiah 31:31–34; Ezekiel 36:26–28), it was not central to the preaching of Jesus. As we have already noted in chapter 12 and will see again in chapter 31, the *Kingdom* (or *Reign*) *of God* was at the core of Jesus' proclamation and ministry, as it was, and must remain, at the heart of the Church's total mission. All else flows from that, including our understanding of Christian morality.

The whole of Jesus' preaching is summed up by Mark: "The time is fulfilled, and the kingdom of God has come near; repent, and believe in the good news" (1:15). Thus, his preaching is at once a proclamation and a warning, i.e., an announcement of a divine act and a demand for a response from men and women. Moral existence is always a response to a divine call. Nowhere in Jesus' preaching, nor in the New Testament at large, do we find an ethical system as such. On the other hand, neither do we find an existence devoid of obligation nor a faith divorced from action.

What Jesus announced was not only a renewal of the Covenant with the people of Israel. His message was even more comprehensive than that. It would embrace the whole world. Jesus returned to his hometown of Nazareth to begin his preaching in the synagogue with these words from Isaiah (61:1–2): "The spirit of the Lord is upon me, because the Lord has anointed me to bring good news to the poor. He has sent me to proclaim release to the captives and recovery of sight to the blind, to let the oppressed go free, to proclaim the year of the Lord's favor" (Luke 4:18–19). Then he said, "Today this Scripture passage has been fulfilled in your hearing." So obvious was his meaning that his fellow townspeople were filled with indignation and expelled him from Nazareth, attempting even to hurl him over the edge of a hill.

As also noted in chapter 12, Jesus' preaching of the reign of God was often couched in parables in which he often inverted his listeners' whole worldview. Thus, the parable of the Good Samaritan (Luke 10:30–37) is not simply an example of neighborliness. If that is all Jesus wanted to communicate, he would have made the Samaritan the injured party and the Israelite the one who comes along to aid him. As it is, no Jew would ever have expected hospitality from a Samaritan (see Luke 9:52–56). Thus, the parable challenges the listener to conceive the inconceivable: The despised Samaritan is "good." The listener is thereby required to reexamine his or her most basic attitudes and values. The parable is no longer merely instruction; it is proclamation itself.

For Jesus nothing is more precious than the Kingdom of God, i.e., the healing and renewing power and presence of God on our behalf. "Instead, strive for his kingdom, and these things will be given to you as well" (Luke 12:31). Like a person who finds a hidden treasure in a field, or a merchant who discovers a precious pearl, everyone must be prepared to give up everything else in order to possess the Kingdom (Matthew 13:44–46). But it is promised only to those with a certain outlook and way of life (see the Beatitudes in Matthew 5:3–12). One can inherit the Kingdom through love of one's neighbor (Matthew 5:38–48), and yet one must also accept it as a child (Mark 10:15). Jesus assured the Scribe who grasped the meaning of the chief of the commandments (love of God and love of neighbor), "You are not far from the kingdom of God" (12:34). He also insisted to his disciples that their commitment to the Kingdom would make strong demands upon them (Mark 10:1; Luke 9:57–62; Matthew 19:12).

The Call to Conversion and Repentance

Jesus' fundamental though not ultimate demand was that they should *repent*. The Greek word *metanoia* suggests a "change of mind." To the Semite it suggested someone's turning away from his or her former consciousness, now recognized as wrong, and striking out in a completely new direction. Therefore, *metanoia*, or conversion and repentance, is not just sorrow for sin but a fundamental reorientation of one's whole life. Jesus demanded that his listeners not only repent but also believe the Gospel of forgiveness that he preached (Mark 2:10,17). He drove home his point with various parables, especially those in Luke 15 and the parable of the Prodigal Son in particular. Jesus was so committed to the forgiveness of sins in the name of God that he made himself the friend of outcasts—e.g., publicans and sinners (Matthew 11:19)—and did not avoid their company (Mark 2:16). He rejoiced over their conversion (Luke 15:7–10; Matthew 18:13).

The antithesis of a repentant attitude is an attitude of self-righteousness and presumption. Jesus repudiates the proud Pharisee (Luke 18:10–14), the elder brother who resents his father's benevolent reaction to the prodigal son's return (Luke 15:25–30), and the discontented laborers in the vineyard (Matthew 20:1–15). To those who set themselves proudly above others, Jesus declared that publicans and harlots would enter the Kingdom before they would (Matthew 21:31–32). He condemned them for trying to shut the doors of the Kingdom (Matthew 23:13). All of us, he warned, are unprofitable servants (Luke 17:10), ever in God's debt (Matthew 6:12). God will exalt the humble and bring down the proud (Luke 14:11; 18:14). Each must pray that God forgives his or her trespasses. And whoever is without

891

sin should cast the first stone (John 8:7). Repentance, therefore, remains a major requirement of Christian existence.

The early Church would continue this message: "Repent, and be baptized..." (Acts of the Apostles 2:38).

The Demand for Faith

Jesus also demanded *faith*, which is the positive side of conversion (Mark 1:15). He says to the woman afflicted with a hemorrhage for a dozen years and who is cured by touching his clothing, "Daughter, your faith has made you well" (Mark 5:34). From there he went to the official's house where the man's daughter was reported as being already dead. Jesus disregarded the report and said to the official, "Do not fear, only believe" (5:36). It was the faith of the lame man's friends which called forth from Jesus the forgiveness of his sins and physical healing (2:5). Faith is central to the narrative of the cured boy (9:14–29). Jesus sighed over this unbelieving generation (9:19) and reminded the boy's father that all things are possible to those who believe (9:23). The great faith of the Syro-Phoenician woman moved Jesus to heal her daughter (7:30), and he drew attention to the faith of the pagan centurion who believed that a mere word from Jesus would heal his sick servant (Matthew 8:10; Luke 7:9). On the other hand, where Jesus encountered an obstinate lack of faith, he was not able to manifest the signs of salvation (Mark 6:5).

The Call to Discipleship

Jesus also gathered disciples around him, a point that is not unrelated to the question of Jesus' intentions regarding the "founding" of the Church (see chapter 16). He encouraged people to leave home, take up their cross, and become his disciples (Luke 14:26–27). He advised the rich young man to sell all that he had, give the money to the poor, and then come follow him (Mark 10:21). To become his disciples meant leaving everything else behind (Luke 5:11; 9:58; 14:26; Mark 2:14). But this was consistent with the traditional Jewish notion of discipleship. *What was not traditional was his sending of disciples to act in his name* (Matthew 10). "Let the dead bury their own dead," he chastised the man who wanted to bury his father first, "but as for you, go and proclaim the kingdom of God" (Luke 9:59–60). To do so was to share in Jesus' own destiny. "Where I am, there will my servant be" (John 12:26). There would be an identification of the disciple with the suffering of the master (Mark 8:34–35), but also a participation in his triumph (Luke 22:28–30). *The call to discipleship is a call to the imitation of Christ* (John 13:15). The disciple was to act as Jesus himself: with compassion, humility, generosity, and suffering service of others (Mark 9:33–50; 10:42–45). The disciple was always to be marked by love (John 13:34–35), in particular love for one another.

The Law

It was not Jesus' purpose simply to set aside the Law of the Old Testament. He was in the synagogue on the Sabbath (Mark 1:21; 6:2), went on pilgrimage during the festivals (Luke 2:41–52; John 2:13; 5:1; 7:14; 10:22; 12:12; Mark 11:1–11), taught in the synagogues and in the Temple (e.g., Mark 1:39; 14:49; John 6:59; 7:14; 8:20). He celebrated the paschal feast in the traditional way with his disciples (Mark 14:12–16; Luke 22:14–23), wore the prescribed tassels on his cloak (Mark 6:56; Luke 8:44), sent lepers to show themselves to the priests in accordance with the Law (Mark 1:44; Luke 17:14). He insisted that he had come not to destroy the Law but to fulfill it (Matthew 5:17).

On the other hand, Jesus also found himself at odds with some of the Jewish teachers of the Law. He insisted that the Sabbath was made for men and women, not men and women for the Sabbath (Mark 2:27). He defended his disciples when they had neglected to perform the ritual hand-washing (Mark 7:1–23; Matthew 15:1–20). He argued that the tradition to which the teachers appealed was a merely human institution (Mark 7:8), and he gave a concrete example of what he meant (7:9–13): They neglected the duty of supporting parents (the fourth commandment of the Decalogue) because they permitted so-called *korban* oaths, even to the detriment of their parents' rights. These oaths expressed a son's intention to give money to the Temple, and the money, in turn, was no longer part of the support given to one's parents, even if later on the son decided not to give it to the Temple. More fundamentally, Jesus attacked the traditional notion that every part of the Law was of equal importance and that the

893

external observance is what finally counted. For Jesus it is the inner disposition that determines an act's moral value (7:14–23).

But he did not ignore the external action itself (Luke 6:43–45). The final parable of the Sermon on the Mount, the house built on a rock (Matthew 7:24–27), is a call not only to listen to Jesus' words but to put them into action. "In everything do to others as you would have them do to you; for this is the law and the prophets" (7:12). And this must really be done, in deed and not only in word. "Not everyone who says to me, 'Lord, Lord,' will enter the kingdom of heaven, but only the one who does the will of my Father in heaven" (7:21). The same insistence on the connection between word and action is given in his indictment of the Scribes and Pharisees (23:1–36). He attacks them for straining at gnats and swallowing camels and for neglecting the weightier matters of the law: justice, mercy, and good faith (23:23). He is especially intolerant of their hypocrisy (23:4, 28). To return to the notion of *praxis* to which we referred at the beginning of this chapter: Jesus not only proclaimed the Kingdom of God; he practiced it, and he expected the same of others. God's will must be *done*.

The austere demands of Jesus are not to be explained away simply on the basis of his expectation of the coming of the Kingdom, but they are to be interpreted always in light of the coming Kingdom. Thus, it is clearly hyperbolic to say, as Jesus did, that it is easier for a camel to pass through the eye of a needle than for a rich man to enter into the Kingdom (Mark 10:25). The disciples expressed alarm: "Then who can be saved?" Jesus answered, "For mortals it is impossible, but not for God; for God all things are possible" (10:27). But as severe as his ethical teaching may have been, his readiness to forgive was even stronger. Thus, a repentant Peter is singled out as the shepherd of the sheep despite his denial of Christ (Luke 22:32; John 21:15–17). Admonition and mercy are found together.

The Commandment of Love

All of Jesus' moral teaching is concentrated in the one commandment of love: the love of God and the love of neighbor (Mark 12:28–34; Matthew 22:34–40; Luke 10:25–28). On them all the Law and the prophets depend (Matthew 22:40). Apart from the great commandment, Jesus

894

did not speak explicitly about loving God. He did say that we should not offer sacrifice to God unless and until we have been reconciled with our brother or sister (Matthew 5:23–24) and that we cannot ask forgiveness for our sins unless we are also ready to forgive those who sin against us (6:12). But it would be wrong to equate love for God entirely with love for neighbor. Religious acts, such as prayer, also belong to the love of God (Matthew 6:1–15; 7:7–11; Mark 14:38). On the other hand, "religious" access to God through prayer cannot finally be divorced from the principal sacramental encounter with God in one's neighbor. The great picture of the Last Judgment in the parable of the Sheep and the Goats (Matthew 25:31–46) offers one of the classic illustrations of this principle.

According to John, Jesus gave himself as an example of unselfish love for others. He humbled himself to wash the feet of the disciples (13:4–15). He insisted that he was in their midst as one who serves (Luke 22:27), who gives his life as a ransom for many (Mark 10:45), and who thereby leaves a new commandment: "Love one another. Just as I have loved you, you also should love one another. By this everyone will know that you are my disciples, if you have love for one another" (John 13:34–35). But such love is not to be reserved for one's friends. The disciple of Jesus is also commanded to love the enemy (Luke 6:27–28), to renounce revenge (6:29). We are to avoid judging and condemning others (6:37) and to be careful not to dwell on the speck in our neighbor's eye while missing the plank in our own (6:41–42). All of this is summed up in Paul's classic hymn to love: "And now faith, hope, and love abide, these three; and the greatest of these is love" (1 Corinthians 13:13).

Discipleship in the World

Jesus did not come to change the *political order*, but neither was he indifferent to it. What he preached was bound to affect the consciousness and behavior of those who heard and assimilated his words. The values he proclaimed would surely transform the world of those who shared them. But to make of him primarily a political figure is to put more into the New Testament than is there.

Jesus declared that he was sent to call sinners (Mark 2:17), to save the lost (Luke 19:10), to give his life for many (Mark 10:45). His kingdom was not of this world, he assured Pilate (John 18:36–37). He fled from the desire of his Galilean supporters to make him a political messianic king and national liberator (John 6:14–15). He rejected Peter's plea that he relinquish the path of suffering and death, just as he repelled the temptations of Satan to worldly power (Matthew 16:22–23). He maintained no contacts with the Zealot party. But all of this does not mean that Jesus' moral teaching had no bearing on political life.

He sent his disciples into the world (Matthew 10:16) and prayed, not that the Father would take his disciples out of the world, but that he would keep them safe in the world (John 17:15). He criticized contemporary institutions (Matthew 10). He saw what is dangerous and corrupting in political power as well as in riches: "You know that among the Gentiles those whom they recognize as their rulers lord it over them, and their great ones are tyrants over them. But it is not so among you" (Mark 10:42–43). When asked if he thought his fellow Jews should pay the tax to Caesar (Mark 12:13–37), he said they should, but he gave this answer only after asking about the image on the coin and pointing out to his interrogators that they already recognized Caesar's political authority over them by using his coinage. And then he added: "Give to the emperor the things that are the emperor's, and to God the things that are God's" (12:17). Always it is the Kingdom which is supreme.

Jesus, of course, was a carpenter's son, and he himself labored for a time as a carpenter (Mark 6:3). His parables reflect his sense of identification with the *poor* and the *workers:* on the farm (Mark 4:3–8), in the vineyard (Matthew 20:1–15), on the sea (Matthew 13:47–50), in the home (Matthew 13:33; Luke 12:37–39; 17:7–10). But others also appear in his parables, without his passing judgment on their occupations or professions: e.g., merchants, traders, builders, soldiers, kings, judges, physicians, stewards. He did not attack the notion of private property, nor did he demand a redistribution of worldly goods. "For you always have the poor with you," he declared (Mark 14:7). Although he directed his severest warnings against the *rich* (Luke 6:24), he accepted hospitality from them (Luke 7:36; 10:38–42; 14:1, John 11:1–3; 12:1–3) and support from women of property (Luke 8:3). He certainly did not intend to exclude from the Kingdom such wealthy men as Nicodemus, Joseph of Arimathea, Zacchæus the rich publican, and others like them (Luke 19:1–10).

The theme of *wealth and property* has an important place in the Gospel of Luke, so much so that some scholars have suggested that Luke deliberately intensified Jesus' sayings against the rich and riches. This may have been the case here and there (e.g., 5:11,28; 9:3; 10:4), but not as a general rule. As early as the Infancy Narrative Jesus' earthly origin is characterized as poverty-stricken (1:52–53; 2:7,24). The motif is sounded again in various discourses and parables (12:15–21; 14:12–14,33; 16). In Luke's version of the Beatitudes, Jesus first blesses the poor, for the reign of God is theirs (6:20)—not just the "poor" in the sense of the "poor in spirit" or the "just," but the economically poor. In the parable of the Rich Man and Lazarus (16:19–31), Lazarus, too, is literally poor. On the other hand, it is not poverty that entitles one to entrance into the Kingdom, but fidelity to the will of God (Matthew 7:21).

In comparing the presentation of the Beatitudes in Matthew (5:3–12) and Luke (6:20–26), however, it is clear that Matthew emphasizes the religious and moral attitude of those who are called blessed and to whom the Kingdom of God is promised, whereas Luke stresses their social and economic position. Luke makes the same kind of modification in the parables of the Unfaithful Steward (16:1–7) and of the Rich Fool (12:16–20) and also in Jesus' attack on the Pharisees because of their greed (20:47).

Why do we find such a spirit in Luke? The evangelist had close contacts with certain circles in the original Jerusalem community who were literally poor and may have called themselves "the poor" in the religious sense (see Romans 15:26; Galatians 2:10). He praises the practice of sharing goods within the community of the first Christians (Acts of the Apostles 2:44–45; 4:32; 5:1–11). This contact undoubtedly shaped his own personal theology and piety.

What is of major, if not of revolutionary, significance in all of this is the assertion that *the poor have any place at all in the divine scheme of things*. Not only Luke but Matthew, too, removes the curse on poverty. Poverty is not by any means an obstacle to the Kingdom, as some apparently thought. Although other New Testament writings pay little attention to the poor and to poverty (it must have been discussed intensely in the Hellenistic communities for which Luke wrote), *the Christian movement itself was unique in the Roman world as one springing from the poor and lower classes.*

Women, Marriage, and the Family

The linchpin of Jesus' attitude toward marriage and the family was his concern for the *dignity of women,* which went far beyond contemporary Jewish attitudes and customs. He spoke with a Samaritan woman at Jacob's Well, though it was frowned upon for a man and a rabbi to do so (John 4:27). He allowed himself to be touched by the woman with the hemorrhage, even though this made him ritually unclean (Mark 5:27–34). He broke the Sabbath to cure a "daughter of Abraham" (Luke 13:10–17). He healed an unusually large number of women—e.g., Peter's mother-in-law (Mark 1:29–31), Jairus's daughter (Mark 5:21–43), the daughter of the Syro-Phoenician woman (Mark 7:24–30), and Mary Magdalene (Luke 8:2). He praised the widow for contributing her mite to the Temple treasury (Mark 12:41–44) and defended Mary of Bethany for anointing his head and feet (Mark 14:3–8; John 12:1–8). He welcomed women among his disciples and received help from them (Luke 8:2–3). When he visited the family at Bethany, he wished both sisters to hear what he had to say (Luke 10:38). The risen Lord appeared first to Mary Magdalene, who brought the good news of the resurrection to the other disciples (John 20:11–18).

Of special importance was Jesus' insistence that *marriage* is permanent. Women are not to be cast aside at will, as was the custom. He spoke strongly against adultery and divorce (Mark 10:2–12; Matthew 19:3–9). His injunction "What God has joined together, let no one separate" is a clear allusion to Genesis, where women and men are assigned equal dignity, coming as they do from the same creative hand of God. (For a fuller consideration of the so-called exceptive clause in Matthew 5:32 and 19:9, see Joseph Fitzmyer, *To Advance the Gospel: New Testament Studies,* New York: Crossroad, 1981, pp. 79–111. See also the brief discussion in chapter 24.)

Jesus' high regard for *family life* is confirmed by the scene which immediately followed the discussion with the Pharisees on divorce. People brought their children to him to have him touch them, and his disciples began to scold them for it. Jesus became indignant and said, "Let the children come to me.... For it is to such as these that the kingdom of God belongs" (Mark 10:13–16). He also emphasized the fourth commandment, "Honor your father and mother," in his reply to the rich young man (10:19).

On the other hand, he spoke almost disdainfully of his family when they came to take him home (3:31–35), and he corrected a woman who blessed his mother (Luke 11:27). His mother, too, may have felt rejected at the marriage feast at Cana when she suggested he might produce more wine (John 2:4), although he did eventually honor her request. So, too, he seemed to belittle blood ties in his command to his disciples regarding their own families (Luke 9:60; 14:26), and he predicted dissensions within homes on his account (Matthew 10:34–36; Luke 12:51–53; Mark 13:12).

What emerges from these assorted sayings is the principle that when Jesus gathers his eschatological family around him, blood ties are of less importance than fidelity to the will of God and readiness for the Kingdom.

Reward and Punishment

The principal motive for living according to the Gospel is, of course, the Kingdom of God and its blessings (Matthew 5:3–11). But Jesus also speaks of both rewards and punishments, and they serve perhaps as secondary motives for Christian fidelity. The standard of measurement is often our attitude to the neighbor (25:31–46). On the other hand, Jesus explicitly warns against those who perform certain actions simply to gain a reward (6:2,5,16). The reward he promises is always the future Kingdom or one of its blessings, such as eternal life (Mark 10:30). The parable of the Laborers in the Vineyard (Matthew 20:1–16) is especially important because it shows that God's criteria and ours are not the same. What finally governs the divine judgment is God's own mercy. Thus, those who come to work in the vineyard at a late hour are rewarded on the same basis as those who come at the first hour. So, too, those who bury their talents are singled out for particular condemnation (25:30). The principle is: "From everyone to whom much has been given, much will be required; and from the one to whom much has been entrusted, even more will be demanded" (Luke 12:48).

In the end, we are called to imitate Jesus (Mark 10:45), to follow his example (John 13:15), to love one another as he has loved us (13:14). This is his first and greatest commandment.

The Moral Message of the Church of the New Testament

The reader is referred again to chapter 16 for an outline of the Church in the New Testament. It is a community radically shaped by its expectation of the coming of God's Kingdom and by the conviction that the first fruits of the Kingdom had already been given in the Holy Spirit (2 Corinthians 1:22; 5:5; Ephesians 1:14). It is the Spirit who is the driving force of Christian existence (Romans 8:12–17; Galatians 5:16–26), which begins at Baptism (Romans 6:4; 1 Corinthians 6:11). The Christian no longer lives according to the flesh but according to the Spirit. The Christian is a "new creature" in Christ (2 Corinthians 5:17).

There is an awareness, too, of being a new community in the Spirit, the new People of God. Christian existence, therefore, is corporate existence. We are called to a life of brotherly and sisterly love. We are all one in Christ, whether Jew or Greek, slave or free, male or female (Galatians 3:28). We are one body, the Body of Christ (1 Corinthians 12:13,27). The ethical significance of this is drawn out in Romans 12:4–8 and Colossians 3:11–17. We are to be clothed with mercy, kindness, humility, meekness, patience. We are to bear with one another and to forgive as the Lord has forgiven us. We are to put on love, which binds the rest and makes them perfect. Christ's peace must reign in our hearts. We are to be grateful people and to do everything in the name of the Lord Jesus. In short, we are "to lead a life worthy of the calling to which [we] have been called" (Ephesians 4:1).

As for the Law, it is summed up and fulfilled in this one saying: "You shall love your neighbor as yourself" (Galatians 5:14). The Gospel is a new Law, a perfect law of freedom (James 1:25), the law of love (2:8). Jesus himself is the new Law (John 1:17). "And this is his commandment, that we should believe in the name of his Son Jesus

Christ and love one another, just as he has commanded us" (1 John 3:23). If we do love one another, "God lives in us, and his love is perfected in us" (4:12). On the other hand, "Those who say, 'I love God,' and hate their brothers and sisters, are liars; for those who do not love a brother or sister whom they have seen, cannot love God whom they have not seen" (4:20). In any case, "perfect love casts out fear" (4:18).

(For a more complete discussion of the moral teaching of the New Testament Church, see Raymond F. Collins, *Christian Morality: Biblical Foundations*, 1986.)

Second Through Sixth Centuries

Of major concern to the early Church was the threat posed by pagan society and culture. There were prohibitions against pagan worship and the fashioning of idols by Christian craftsmen. Also discussed were the proper Christian attitude toward the theater, military service, martyrdom, flight from persecution, virginity, prayer. *Ignatius of Antioch* (d. c. 107) italicized the Pauline and Johannine teaching that Christian existence is life in and with Christ. The Christian is a temple of God and a bearer of Christ (Ephesians 9:1). The Eucharist is the source and center of the Christian life.

Clement of Alexandria (d. c. 215) made perhaps the first attempt at some modest systematization of moral theology. He strove to point out the connection between the positive values in pagan philosophy and those of the Gospel. Genuine Christian life is imitation of God in Christ. Christ is always our teacher. He is the *Logos*-made-flesh. Against the Gnostic hostility toward marriage, Clement defended the married state as a way of salvation. But he also refused to disparage virginity. What counts in the end is the good of the community of love and the things of the Lord (*Stromata*, III, 12).

Clement's successor in the catechetical school at Alexandria was *Origen* (d. c. 254), who was less open to the world than his predecessor but perhaps more realistic. He focused on the imitation of God in the contemplative as well as the active life, and reflected on free will, sin, virtues, and the restoration of all things in God. *Ambrose* (d. 397) provides the first case-approach to moral theology, laying down the various duties of his priests. He insists on the superiority of the Christian moral ideal over pagan philosophies.

One of the earliest to set Christian moral discourse in the context of sacramental initiation was *Cyril of Jerusalem* (d. 386). His moral instruction, in keeping with Eastern practice, was drawn principally from the liturgical texts. Christian existence is sacramental existence.

The first great figure in Christian moral theology, however, is Ambrose's disciple, *Augustine* (d. 430), who attended to such fundamental problems as the relationship of grace and freedom, faith and works, faith and love, Original Sin and the restoration of grace, grace and the law, natural law and revealed law, and divine love and the natural appetites. Christian morality is the way and means to eternal union with God. Morality, in turn, requires obedience to the divine law of love, but not merely through external observance. The moral disposition of the heart is decisive. And so we find a strongly psychological orientation in Augustine's writings (e.g., his own *Confessions*) which makes him a kind of forerunner of modern thought. Indeed, Bernard Häring has called him "one of the greatest, if not the very greatest, moral theologian of all time" (*The Law of Christ*, vol. 1, p. 8).

Seventh Through Twelfth Centuries

This is a significant period in the history of moral theology because moral theology became attached for the first time to the specific needs of *confessors*. Indeed, one modern historian of moral theology has concluded that "the single most influential factor in the development of the practice and of the discipline of moral theology is to be found in the growth and spread of 'confession' in the Church" (John Mahoney, *The Making of Moral Theology*, p. 1).

Under the influence of the Celtic monks, the sacrament of Penance, originally reserved for public sins and celebrated only once in a Christian's lifetime, was now received with some frequency. Appropriate penances had to be determined for particular sins that were being confessed. A new genre of theological literature developed, the so-called penitential books (*libri poenitentiales*), to assist the generally uneducated clergy.

These works did not focus on the ideals of Christian existence but only on varieties of sins. They led to the belief that Christian life is

902

essentially one of *avoiding sin;* the mere avoidance of sin, in turn, led some to conclude to their own *moral righteousness.* Absolution was not perceived as an act of forgiveness and mercy, but of *judgment.* And emphasis was placed increasingly on the nature of the *individual moral act,* apart from the larger context of one's whole existence.

Thirteenth Century

By now a new institution had come upon the scene in the West: the *university.* It was to change the character and course of moral theology. Systematization became the rule rather than the exception. There was a push to organize and to integrate, to produce *summæ,* or syntheses, of theology. The two great figures were Bonaventure (d. 1274) and Thomas Aquinas (d. 1274).

For *Bonaventure,* and the Franciscan school generally (e.g., Alexander of Hales, d. 1245), the *will,* not the intellect, was the primary faculty. The intellect was but the tool of the will, which was the instrument of decision. The purpose of theology is to "make us holy."

Thomas Aquinas, on the other hand, stressed the *intellectual* side of human existence. What Bonaventure played down, i.e., contemplation of the true, Thomas emphasized. Theology is for the sake of understanding. Therefore, there could be no separation of doctrinal from moral theology, because there is no separation of truth from behavior. Thomas's entire moral outlook is based on our relation to creation and the last end, on the fact that we are made in the image and likeness of God, and on the humanity of Christ as our way to God (see the prologues to the second and third parts of the *Summa Theologiæ*). The foundation for his whole theology is God, the Creator, and Christ, the Redeemer. We shall achieve beatitude or union with God through participation in God's own knowledge and love through the grace of Christ. Indeed, this *grace* is the heart of the new Law, i.e., "the grace of the Holy Spirit, which is given to those who believe in Christ" (I-II, q. 106, a. 1). The virtues, or God-given "powers" to do what is right and to avoid what is evil, are also explicitly treated: the theological virtues of faith, hope, and love, and the cardinal virtues of prudence, fortitude, temperance, and justice. Aquinas's moral teaching, therefore, centered not upon us and the rewards we seek, but upon God as the source of both created and eternal life. (The reader should not neglect to scan the table of contents of I-II and II-II of the *Summa Theologiæ* in order to appreciate the comprehensiveness and detailed character of Thomas's reflections on the Christian moral life.)

After Thomas's death several of his basic theological and philosophical positions were radically questioned almost immediately by members of the so-called Franciscan school. John Duns Scotus (d. 1308), for example, who was more attracted to Platonism and Augustinianism than to Aristotelianism, placed greater stress on the will and on love than on the intellect.

Fourteenth and Fifteenth Centuries

It was within this Franciscan school of thought that the English philosopher and theologian William of Ockham [Occam] (d. 1347) developed his own distinctively individualistic approach to moral issues. Where Thomas had emphasized *habits,* i.e., basic attitudes, the Nominalists like Ockham who followed him emphasized *individual acts.* Second, they defined *the good* as that which conforms with the *will* of the individual. And so a thoroughly individualistic and voluntaristic ethic emerges, one which underlines the unique situation of every person in the face of a moral decision. If society feels threatened by this individualism, it has one recourse: the exercise of power. Individual moral agents can be "collected together" and given some shape and direction by the imposition of law, which demands conformity. Thus, the Nominalist approach generates first an ethical *individualism* and then an ethical *legalism,* in which commands and obligations dominate.

Ockhamism and Nominalism spread rapidly throughout the European universities. Their influence throughout the fifteenth century and the next was to encourage "the fragmentation of theology and the proliferation of disparate casuistry as well as to inculcate an anti-rational, mystical, and pious fideism" (Mahoney, p. 184). At the same time, Nominalism *did* call attention to real, everyday moral problems, and casuistry (resolving moral problems on a case-by-case basis) *did* try to deal with those problems.

This was also a time of extraordinary economic expansion and complexification. Medieval feudalism was yielding to the new middle-class commerce. Such activities as the buying and selling of goods and the making of contracts were commonplace. One could no longer rely on relatively simple principles of charity. It became necessary to state precisely the demands of justice, which has to do with rights and duties. The other virtues, such as faith and love, became secondary to justice. A *moral minimalism* developed ("What am I absolutely required to do, as a bare moral minimum?").

It was against this state of affairs that Martin Luther (d. 1546) would react so vehemently. "The situation emphasized justice, and Luther was convinced that no one is just. The situation focused on minimums, and Luther felt driven to perfection. The situation cherished good works, and Luther placed his trust in faith" (Timothy O'Connell, *Principles for a Catholic Morality*, rev. ed., San Francisco: Harper & Row, 1990, p. 16).

This was also the period of the great medieval penitential books, in the tradition of the Irish penitential books of the early Middle Ages. They were not textbooks. They were more akin to reference books, such as a dictionary, presenting basic information on a wide range of topics arranged alphabetically. The most important was that of St. Antonine (d. 1459), which presents a sweeping picture of the moral life of the fifteenth century. It exercised profound influence on subsequent works.

Sixteenth Century

Although the first commentary on the *Summa* of Thomas Aquinas had been produced by Henry of Gorkum (d. 1431) in the fifteenth century, it was not until the beginning of the sixteenth century that the *Summa* was used as a textbook in the schools, thereby replacing Peter Lombard's *Book of Sentences*. This Thomistic revival had a pronounced impact on moral theology because Thomas, unlike Peter Lombard, had a relatively complete and well-integrated treatment of moral questions, especially of the virtues (*Summa* I-II and II-II). Conrad Koellin (d. 1536), a German Dominican, published the first complete commentary on the first part of the second part of the *Summa* (I-II), and there followed another major commentary by Thomas de Vio, Cardinal Cajetan (d. 1534), in Italy. The Thomistic revival also took hold in Spain at the school of Salamanca through the teachings and writings of Francis of Vitoria (d. 1546), Melchior Cano (d. 1560),

Dominic Soto (d. 1560), and Domingo Báñez (d. 1604)—all Dominicans, like Thomas Aquinas himself.

Concurrent with this Thomistic revival was the Catholic Church's broader struggle with Protestantism. This effort was focused in the work of the *Council of Trent*. Its *Decree on Justification* (Session VI, 1547) stressed the freedom of the person to assent to, and cooperate with, grace and thus to dispose himself or herself for justification. Free will was not destroyed by Original Sin. Furthermore, the council also took care to specify the nature and number of the seven sacraments and placed special emphasis on the necessary elements in the sacrament of Penance: contrition, confession, absolution, and satisfaction. It also decreed that Catholics were to receive the sacrament of Penance at least once a year, thereby intensifying the need to train confessors. The council established the Catholic seminary system for the education and training of priest-confessors.

The Society of Jesus (the Jesuits) was the center of this educational enterprise throughout the sixteenth and seventeenth centuries. Their *ratio studiorum* (order of studies) dictated that those professors who were charged with lecturing on the *Summa* of St. Thomas should limit their courses to the more basic principles of moral teaching. Some professors of moral doctrine, however, were assigned to deal with "cases of conscience" in order to determine the correct solution of problems. As a result, an independent and self-contained field of moral theology emerged. Always the concern was to discover if, in fact, a penitent has sinned. All the necessary sources, including canon law, were incorporated into these moral texts to aid in the solution of each problem. Indeed, some topics such as Matrimony and Penance were treated exclusively from a canonical point of view.

The first comprehensive manual of moral theology, whose basic form was followed until the Second Vatican Council, was the *Institutiones Morales*, by John Azor (d. 1603). General principles are followed in order by the commandments of God and the Church, the sacraments, censures, indulgences, and the particular obligations of the various states of life.

Seventeenth and Eighteenth Centuries

Moral theology was by now a separate division of theology, no longer flowing from doctrinal theology nor from the classic sources of doctrinal theology, i.e., Scripture and the early Christian writers. Moralists were expected primarily to answer the question "What morally may I do?" Two extremes developed. At one extreme the *Jansenists* rejected every kind of casuistry, insisting instead that the strictest standards must always be followed. We are radically corrupted by Original Sin, they argued. Only grace can overcome that corruption, and that grace is given to few. When it *is* given, however, it is irresistible. Jansenism was condemned in 1653 by Pope Innocent X's (d. 1655) Constitution *Cum Occasione*. There was also *Quietism*, which excluded all moral effort from the spiritual life. This was condemned by Pope Innocent XI (d. 1689) in his Constitution *Cælestis Pastor* in 1687. At the other extreme were the *laxists*, who were devoted exclusively to casuistry and who solved literally thousands of cases, usually in favor of liberty.

These debates led to the growth of a variety of moral systems, one of which was known as "probabilism." This was a method of solving difficult moral cases by allowing the Christian to follow the more lenient opinion, according to some, even if it was held by only one reputable theologian. Variations on "probabilism" developed: *equiprobabilism* required that the two conflicting opinions should have equal support among the experts; *probabiliorism* required that the more lenient opinion should also be the majority opinion.

The principal moderating force at this time was *Alphonsus Liguori* (d. 1787). He was regarded as a prudent and balanced theologian, one whose opinions could be relied upon. In an age when extreme views were the order of the day, Alphonsus injected a measure of reason and restraint into moral discourse. His methodological approach to moral theology also had a strong impact on subsequent theologies. He always identified and summarized all the opinions on a particular question, then tried to fashion a position somewhere in between the extremes. He counseled against *rigorism*, i.e., against imposing more on the penitent than was required by the law or by the Gospel, and against *laxism*, i.e., against disregarding the clear requirements of either law or Gospel, or both. His own position was one of equiprobabilism. On the one hand, a doubtful law does not oblige and one may follow a probable opinion, but, on the other hand, a law is really doubtful only when the opinions for and against are evenly balanced. Although some in France accused him of laxism, Alphonsus was beatified and later canonized soon after his death and was declared a Doctor of the Church in 1871 by Pope Pius IX (d. 1878). In 1950 Pope Pius XII (d. 1958) remarked that Alphonsus had not only dispelled the darkness of Jansenism but was also "most thoroughly approved" as a "safe norm" throughout the Church.

Nineteenth to Mid-Twentieth Century

A reaction set in at the German University of Tübingen with the work of Johann Michael Sailer (d. 1832), bishop of Regensburg, and Johann Baptist von Hirscher (d. 1865). Both attempted a reformulation of moral theology disengaged from its customary casuistry and legalism and reconnected with doctrinal theology. Both were also influenced by the renewal of biblical studies, and hence understandably called for a return to the central New Testament notions of conversion and discipleship. In his *Christian Moral Teaching as Realization of the Kingdom of God* (1834), J. B. Hirscher focused especially on the Kingdom of God as the basis of Christian morality.

An integrated, biblically and historically grounded theology was carried forward into the twentieth century, particularly in the works of Joseph Mausbach (d. 1931), Otto Schilling (d. 1956), Fritz Tillmann (d. 1953), and Theodore Steinbuechel (d. 1949). For them the law of love, the ethos of the Sermon on the Mount, is the heart and soul of moral theology. When two other German theologians, Joseph Fuchs, a Jesuit, and Bernard Häring, a Redemptorist, assumed teaching positions at the Gregorian University and the Alphonsianum in Rome respectively, a wider dissemination of this evolving German theology was assured. Its effects can be seen outside of Europe in the writings of Charles Curran, one of Häring's first American students, and of Richard A. McCormick, a Jesuit, who studied under Fuchs. Another major influence on recent Catholic moral thought was Gerard Gilleman, whose *The Primacy of Charity in Moral Theology* (Westminster, Md.: Newman Press, 1959) along with Häring's three-volume *The Law of Christ* (1961–1966), were among the most widely read books in Catholic seminaries in the years just before and during Vatican II.

In the first half of the twentieth century, especially in France, the neo-Thomist movement stressed an intrinsicist, intellectualistic, and realistic understanding of natural law as the basis for moral theology as distinguished from the extrinsicist, voluntaristic, and nominalistic method of the theology manuals. For the neo-Thomists the "good" is the primary ethical category. Something is commanded because it is *good*—in contrast to the view that something is good because it is *commanded*. In keeping with the approach of the *Summa*, the Thomists also placed great emphasis on the virtues.

But even into the 1950s, this broadly based development on the Continent notwithstanding, the manuals remained unchanged in content and in their *legalistic* approach, and seminary moral theology for the most part remained oriented toward the preparation of confessors (see John Mahoney, *The Making of Moral Theology*, chapter 1, "The Influence of Auricular Confession," pp. 1–36). The emphasis was on the individual act to determine whether or not it fell into the category of sin, and, if so, whether it was mortal or venial. Stress was still placed on obedience to law: divine law, natural law, human law. The "good" is what is commanded by law. Therefore, conformity with law is the fulfillment of the good. Short shrift was given to the theoretical aspects of moral theology.

Heavy emphasis was placed on the teaching of the hierarchy, especially papal teaching, and the reigning pope, Pius XII, produced an unprecedented amount of moral guidelines, especially in areas such as medical ethics. He also made clear the obligation of theologians to accept and adhere to that teaching, without quarrel or criticism. He wrote: "But if the Supreme Pontiffs in their official documents purposely pass judgment on a matter up to that time under dispute, it is obvious that the matter, according to the mind and will of the same Pontiffs, cannot be any longer considered a question open to discussion among theologians" (*Humani Generis* [1950], n. 29).

Vatican II

The legalistic orientation and tone of moral theology changed with Vatican II. In its *Decree on Priestly Formation* the council urged the renewal of moral theology: "Its scientific exposition should be more thoroughly nourished by scriptural teaching. It should show the nobility of the Christian vocation of the faithful, and their obligation to bring forth fruit in charity for the life of the world" (n. 16). In general, moral theology should be "renewed by livelier contact with the mystery of Christ and the history of salvation." Elsewhere in its two major constitutions, the *Dogmatic Constitution on the Church* and the *Pastoral Constitution on the Church in the Modern World*, the council proposes an ideal of Christian morality which goes well beyond the observance of law and of juridical norms.

Every member of the Church is part of the People of God, and insofar as the whole Church is called to be the sacrament of Christ, the whole Church is also called to holiness (*Dogmatic Constitution on the Church*, n. 40). This consists in the following of Christ (n. 41), which leads to the perfection of love (n. 42). This is at once a love of God and a love of neighbor. These two kinds of love cannot be separated (*Pastoral Constitution on the Church in the Modern World*, n. 24).

But the most significant aspect of the council's moral teaching is its advancement of the Church's social doctrine, to which we turn our attention at the end of the chapter.

Post–Vatican II Developments

Under the impact of the council, Catholic moral theology has continued to develop along new paths since 1965. Postconciliar developments that have helped to shape the content and orientation of Catholic moral theology include the following:

1. *The assimilation of modern biblical scholarship.* This has moved moral theology away from being a legalistic discipline principally oriented to the training of confessors to a *life-centered* discipline concerned with the challenge of Christian discipleship. The newer biblical approach is especially apparent in the work of Bernard Häring.

2. *The integration of moral theology into the whole of theology.* For example, the theological anthropology of Karl Rahner (summarized in chapters 4 and 5) has helped Catholic moral theology to overcome the dualism between the realm of the natural order and that of the supernatural; the development of Christologies "from below" and of liberation theology has helped to underscore the social and political dimensions of Christian discipleship; and advances in liturgical and sacramental theology have helped to integrate moral theology with liturgical and sacramental celebration and spirituality.

3. *The move away from classicism to historical consciousness.* Classicism stressed the universal, the essential, and the unchanging. It applied moral commandments and official teachings to specific cases by a process of deduction. Historical consciousness conceives the Christian moral life as one of personal responsibility within changing historical circumstances. Moral norms are important and binding, but they reflect the historical situation in which they were formulated and subsequently interpreted. Its method is more inductive than deductive, as it emphasizes the particular, the evolutionary, and the changeable. (Two official documents of the Catholic Church that reflect this historical emphasis are the Pontifical Biblical Commission's "Instruction on the Historical Truth of the Gospels" (1964) and the Congregation for the Doctrine of the Faith's *Mysterium Ecclesiæ* (1973). Excerpts from both are provided in the Appendix.)

4. *The new emphasis on the person not only as a moral agent but also as a subject.* This is especially, though not exclusively, reflected in theology's increased attention to the dynamics of human growth and development in the moral life. Accordingly, the works of Jean Piaget (d. 1980), Erik Erikson (d. 1994), Lawrence Kolhberg (d. 1987), Carol Gilligan, James Fowler, and others have been of great interest to contemporary moral theologians.

5. *Changes in the Church and in Catholic ecclesiology.* As the Catholic Church has moved away from an institutional, or hierarchical, model of the Church as the dominant ecclesial model and closer to a communal and collegial understanding of the Church, moral theologians have begun to interpret and apply official teachings more critically, though no less faithfully, and have developed a more nuanced understanding of the complementary relationship between their own scholarly work and the teaching responsibilities of the pastoral leadership.

6. *The change in the primary setting of moral theology from seminaries to colleges and universities.* Prior to the council, almost all of the Church's moral theologians taught in seminaries. Today many are members of college and university faculties, most in Catholic institutions but a significant number as well in private non-Catholic and state institutions. As moral theology moved from the more pastorally oriented seminary environment to the more academically oriented university environment, it also became more academically rigorous and more directly engaged in dialogue with other disciplines and with theologians and ethicists of other ecclesiastical and religious traditions.

7. *The impact of ecumenism.* Catholic and Protestant theologians not only read one another's work, they also often teach together in the same institutions and belong to the same professional associations (in the United States, for example, the Society of Christian Ethics). Major Protestant ethicists like James Gustafson have devoted considerable attention to Catholic moral theology and to methodological differences that continue to divide the two groups (see his *Protestant and Roman Catholic Ethics: Prospects for Rapprochement*). The traditional Catholic-Protestant differences in their respective approaches to the analogical and the dialectical are also apparent in the realm of morality and ethics (see again chapters 1 and 2). Gustafson is critical of much Catholic moral theology because it is too anthropocentric and too much based on the human. For the Catholic tradition, which is inclined to stress continuity over discontinuity, and similarity over dissimilarity, there is no need to choose between God and the human. The glory of God is the human person come alive. The glory of God is manifested in and through human fulfillment and happiness.

The Ongoing Development of Catholic Social Doctrine

Catholic social doctrine is to be distinguished from the social implications of the Gospel. Catholic social doctrine is a clearly discernible body of official teachings on the social order, in its economic and political dimensions. It is concerned, on the one hand, with the *dignity of the human person* as created in the image of God, and with human rights and duties which protect and enhance this dignity, and it is concerned, on the other hand, with the *common good*, that is, with the radically social nature of human existence, with the nature of society and of the state, with the relationship between society and state (balancing the principle of subsidiarity and the principle of socialization), and with voluntary associations, e.g., labor unions, which serve as a buffer and a bridge between state and society.

Catholic social doctrine did not begin to take formal shape until the end of the nineteenth century, which is not to say that the Catholic Church expressed no official interest in, or concern for, the world outside the sanctuary until Pope Leo XIII's encyclical, *Rerum Novarum* ("The Condition of Labor"), in 1891. But not until Leo XIII did the Catholic Church begin to articulate in its official hierarchical teaching in a consciously *systematic* manner a theology of *social justice* and all that this implies. (A fuller discussion of social justice will be presented in chapter 26.)

Catholic social doctrine is not a detailed blueprint for the reform of the world. It offers rather a broad theological and philosophical framework of social analysis. Thus far Catholic social doctrine has been developed in three stages:

Stage one consists of the Church's response to the problems posed by the *Industrial Revolution*. The key texts are Leo XIII's *Rerum Novarum* (1891) and Pius XI's *Quadragesimo Anno* ("Reconstructing the Social Order," 1931). The principal issues are the role of government in society and in the economy, the right of laborers to organize, the principle of a just wage, and a Christian critique of both capitalism and socialism.

Stage two emerges during the Second World War and continues to the present (overlapping with a third stage). It is the *international-ization* of Catholic social doctrine, confronting the growing material interdependence of the world and seeking to provide a moral frame-work for the political, economic, and strategic issues facing the human community. The key texts are those of Pope Pius XII (his Pentecost Message of 1941 and his Christmas Addresses of 1939–1957), John XXIII (*Mater et Magistra*, "Christianity and Social Prog-ress," 1961, and *Pacem in Terris*, "Peace on Earth," 1963), Paul VI (*Populorum Progressio*, "The Progress of Peoples," 1967), the Second

Vatican Council's *Pastoral Constitution on the Church in the Modern World* (*Gaudium et spes*, 1965), and the Synod of Bishops' *Justice in the World* (*Iustitia in mundo*, 1971). The principal issues are the political and juridical organization of the international community, the demands of international social justice in determining the rules and relationships of international economic policy, and the moral issues regarding warfare in a nuclear age.

Stage three is represented by Pope Paul VI's apostolic letter *Octagesima Adveniens* ("The Eightieth Year," 1971), reaffirmed to some extent in his apostolic exhortation *Evangelii Nuntiandi* ("On Evangelization in the Modern World," 1975), and Pope John Paul II's *Redemptor Hominis* ("Redeemer of Humankind," 1979), *Laborem Exercens* ("On Human Work," 1981), *Sollicitudo Rei Socialis* ("The Social Concern of the Church," 1988), and *Centesimus Annus* ("The Hundredth Year," 1991). The keynote is sounded in *Octagesima Adveniens* as it addresses "new social questions." It examines the issues faced in an acute way by postindustrial societies, which have been so transformed by *technology* and its effects, especially in the area of communications and mobility (see our discussion in chapter 3). On the other hand, the papal letter returns to the theme of how postindustrial and developing societies are related internationally. The document focuses on the forms of organization which compete for primacy in society and on the intellectual currents which seek to legitimate other kinds of social and political orders.

The *Second Vatican Council*, although still very much a part of stage two, prepared the way for the expansion of Catholic social doctrine to include the political dimension as well. Among the fundamental principles the council stresses, especially in its *Pastoral Constitution on the Church in the Modern World*, are the dignity of the human person created in the image of God (n. 12), the dignity of the moral conscience (n. 16), the excellence of freedom (n. 17), the social nature of human existence and of our destiny (n. 24), the interdependence of person and society (n. 26), the need to promote the common good for the sake of human dignity (n. 26), respect for persons (n. 27), their fundamental equality as the basis of social justice (n. 29), the value of all human activities because of the redemption (n. 34), the rightful autonomy of temporal realities (n. 36), and the missionary responsibility of the Church to attend to this constellation of values and

914

principles (the document as a whole, especially nn. 40–45). The same insistence on human freedom is sounded in the council's *Declaration on Religious Freedom*, a freedom that belongs not only to individuals but to groups (n. 4) and that is always subject to the common good (n. 7).

This broader political approach is carried forward in Pope John Paul II's encyclicals, which speak of our alienation from the products and byproducts of technology—e.g., environmental pollution and destruction, the arms race, the widening gap between rich and poor, increasingly sophisticated methods of torture and oppression, wasteful attitudes and practices, inflation, and modern methods of warfare. What is essential today is the right of citizens to share in the "political life of the community" in service of the common good, whether national or international, and in service of the human person, whose dignity in Christ is the foundation and linchpin of the whole social and political order. "Thus the principle of human rights is of profound concern to the area of social justice and is the measure by which it can be tested in the life of political bodies" (*Redemptor Hominis*, section 17, par. 7). "As far as the Church is concerned," he writes, "the social message of the Gospel must not be considered a theory, but above all else a basis and a motivation for action" (*Centesimus Annus*, n. 57).

A similar approach is taken by various national episcopal conferences. Two pastoral letters by the National Conference of Catholic Bishops in the United States are cases in point: "The Challenge of Peace" (1983) and "Economic Justice for All: Catholic Social Teaching and the U.S. Economy" (1986). There is a fuller discussion of the latter document in chapter 27.

Ever since the Second Vatican Council, the social mission of the Church has been seen as intimately connected with the Gospel. The social mission of the Church is even more explicitly articulated in the 1971 synodal document *Justice in the World:* "Action on behalf of justice and participation in the transformation of the world fully appear to us as a constitutive dimension of the preaching of the Gospel, or, in other words, of the Church's mission for the redemption of the human race and its liberation from every oppressive situation" (Introduction, par. 6). And later the same declaration applies the principle to the Church itself, for "anyone who ventures to speak to people about justice must first be just in their eyes" (III, par. 2). The Church, which is the sacrament of Christ, is called upon by missionary mandate to practice what it preaches about justice and rights.

SUMMARY

1. Just as faith and action are united in the one notion of *praxis,* so dogmatic and moral theology are united in one systematic theology. Truth is not only to be thought about but also to be lived and done, and the living and doing of truth is a condition of grasping it.

2. *Christian morality* has to do with the way Christians live and act; *moral theology* or *Christian ethics* is the thematic, systematic, and reflective study of Christian morality.

3. In its systematic reflection on morality, *philosophical ethics* uses only human sources, such as reason and experience. *Religious ethics* uses the sources of a particular religion, such as its scripture, tradition, and teaching authorities. *Moral theology* or Christian ethics is *unique* or *distinctive* because of its sources, and because it adds a unique intentionality and motivation to what Christians do.

4. Faithful *praxis* is linked in ancient Israel with the *Law* (especially the Ten Commandments) and that, in turn, with the *Covenant.* The latter was always the principal motive for obeying the former.

5. The moral message of *Jesus* was centered on the Kingdom of God. His preaching of the Kingdom was both a *proclamation* of good news and a call to *conversion, repentance, faith,* and *discipleship.*

6. Jesus attacked the traditional notion that every part of the *Law* was of equal importance and that the external observance is what finally counted. For Jesus it is the *inner disposition* that determines an act's moral value. He was especially intolerant of *hypocrisy.*

7. All of Jesus' teachings were concentrated in the one commandment of love: of God and of neighbor.

8. Jesus was concerned with *the world,* but he did not come to change the political order directly. He had a special regard for *the poor,* and he warned against the temptations of *wealth and power.*

9. Jesus' teaching on *marriage* and the *family* was founded on his concern for the *dignity of women,* far beyond the concern shown in contemporary Jewish attitudes and customs. He was in the company of women, healed women, and included them among his disciples. He insisted on the permanence of marriage, lest women be regarded as mere objects to be set aside at will.

10. Jesus was not silent about *rewards and punishments,* but he criticized those who acted morally only for the sake of rewards. He also reminded his listeners that God's standards are not our standards. Those who come into the vineyard at the eleventh hour can also be saved.

11. The *early Church's* moral teaching was shaped by the same focal concern for the coming Kingdom of God. Christian existence is existence in *community.* The Law is summed up in the call to love one another.

12. The earliest *postbiblical reflections* on Christian moral existence were influenced by the threat of paganism. Thus, moral questions were concerned with false worship and the use of pagan images.

13. The first great figure in moral theology was *Augustine,* who emphasized always the disposition of the heart.

14. Moral theology took a significant turn in the *sixth century,* when, under the influence of the Celtic monks, the sacrament of Penance began to be administered more than once in a lifetime. This led to the need for *penitential books* to aid the clergy in determining appropriate penances for a variety of confessed sins.

15. Christian moral life was now perceived primarily as a matter of *avoiding sin.* The focus of moral theology was on the *individual act,* apart from the wider context of one's whole existence.

16. With the emergence of *universities* in the high Middle Ages (thirteenth century), attention to moral questions became more systematic. *Aquinas* is the period's major figure, arguing that *grace* is the center of the whole Law.

17. *Nominalism* reintroduced an *individualistic* ethic and an ethical *legalism.* It promoted a *casuistic* approach to moral theology.

18. This was also the period of extraordinary *economic* expansion and complexification. Moral theology became preoccupied with such problems as contracts and the buying and selling of goods. A moral *minimalism* resulted, as people asked simply what they were absolutely required to do to avoid sin.

19. The *Council of Trent* decreed that all Catholics must confess at least once a year and it established a seminary system to train priest-confessors. *Manuals* of moral theology were focused on the sacrament of Penance, and moral questions were treated in isolation from wider doctrinal and biblical themes.

20. Extreme approaches to moral theology quickly developed: *Jansenism* followed a rigorist path and *laxists* followed a permissive path. Debates between the two sides led to the development of various moral systems: *Probabilism, Equiprobabilism,* and *Probabiliorism.* The principal mediating voice at the time was that of *St. Alphonsus Liguori.*

21. A reaction to legalism developed in the *nineteenth century* in Germany and in the twentieth century among neo-Thomists in France. Two major

German moralists, *Bernard Häring* and *Joseph Fuchs*, influenced countless other moral theologians through their teaching at Roman universities in the mid-twentieth century.

22. At the same time, the traditional *legalistic, hierarchically oriented* approach continued to be taught through the *manuals* in most seminaries around the world.

23. The *Second Vatican Council* called for a renewal of moral theology, stressing its biblical roots, the idea of Christian vocation, the primacy of charity, the mystery of Christ, and the history of salvation.

24. *Post–Vatican II moral theology* has been influenced by the following: modern biblical scholarship, wider developments in theology, the move away from classicism to historical consciousness, a developmental understanding of the human person, changes in the Church and in ecclesiology, moral theology's move from the seminary to the university, and ecumenism.

25. *Catholic social doctrine* began to take formal shape during the pontificate of *Leo XIII.* The Church's social teachings have been formulated in *three stages:* (1) the response to the *Industrial Revolution;* (2) the response to the growing *internationalization* of life; and (3) the response to *new social questions* posed by *technology.*

26. Catholic social doctrine is based upon two moral demands: the *dignity of the human person* and the *common good.*

27. The broader *social dimensions* of Christian moral existence are emphasized in Vatican II's *Pastoral Constitution on the Church in the Modern World,* the 1971 Synod of Bishops' *Justice in the World,* and the encyclicals and apostolic exhortations of John XXIII, Paul VI, and John Paul II.

SUGGESTED READINGS

Collins, Raymond F. *Christian Morality: Biblical Foundations.* Notre Dame, Ind.: University of Notre Dame Press, 1986.

Curran, Charles E., ed. *Moral Theology: Challenges for the Future.* New York: Paulist Press, 1990.

Gustafson, James M. *Protestant and Roman Catholic Ethics: Prospects for Rapprochement.* Chicago: University of Chicago Press, 1978.

Häring, Bernard. "Historical Survey of Moral Theology." *The Law of Christ.* Vol. 1. Westminster, Md.: Newman Press, 1965, pp. 3–33.

————. *Free and Faithful in Christ: Moral Theology for Clergy and Laity.* Vol. 1. New York: Seabury Press, 1978, chapters 1 and 2, pp. 7–58.

Mahoney, John. *The Making of Moral Theology: A Study of the Roman Catholic Tradition*. Oxford: Clarendon Press, 1987.

O'Brien, David J., and Thomas A. Shannon. *Catholic Social Thought: The Documentary Heritage*. Maryknoll, N.Y.: Orbis Books, 1992.

Schnackenburg, Rudolf. *The Moral Teaching of the New Testament*. New York: Herder & Herder, 1971.

XXVI

Foundations of Christian Morality

The material in this chapter is organized around three fundamental topics: (1) *models of the Christian moral life;* (2) *the kind of person the Christian is called to become;* and (3) *Christian action in the world.*

The formulation, interpretation, and application of Christian moral principles are always historically conditioned. Christian existence itself is always historical existence. One not only *is* a Christian; one is constantly *becoming* a Christian. Conversion to the Gospel is both an act and a process. Accordingly, Christian existence moves between the polarities of principle and process, of being and becoming, of essence and existence, of the universal and the particular, of conviction and risk, of substance and form. But these are not mutually opposed; the one requires and includes the other. Principles are at once *products* of experience and *shapers* of experience. Catholic moral theology is concerned with principles and process alike.

MODELS OF THE CHRISTIAN MORAL LIFE

Three different models of the Christian moral life have been proposed in the theological literature: the teleological, the deontological, and the relational.

The *teleological* model views the Christian moral life in terms of the goal or end (*telos*) to be achieved, namely, eternal union with God. Something is good if it leads to the achievement of the goal, and evil if it prevents one from achieving it. In the complexity of human, historical existence, however, one must distinguish the ultimate goal from intermediate and subordinate goals. Thomas Aquinas is a classic exponent of the teleological model of the Christian life. Modern utilitarians also fit under this heading.

The *deontological* model views the Christian moral life primarily in terms of duty (*deon*), law, or obligation. The categorical imperative of Immanuel Kant is an example of that approach ("Act as if the maxim from which you act were to become through your will a universal law"). Popular Christian piety, in effect, adopts this approach also when it makes the Ten Commandments the basis of the moral life. Although the traditional manuals of moral theology assumed they were in the tradition of Thomas Aquinas (whose approach was teleological), they were really operating within the deontological model, with their heavy emphasis on law as the objective norm of morality and on conscience as the subjective norm.

The *relational* model, developed especially in the writings of Bernard Häring, views the Christian moral life primarily in terms of the Christian's multiple relations with God, neighbor, world, and self. Although preferable to the teleological and deontological models, the relational model does not exclude some place for them in moral theology.

Why is the relational model primary? Contemporary biblical studies indicate that the primary ethical concept in the Old Testament is not law but covenant. Indeed, the Law is always to be understood in terms of the Covenant. In the New Testament love occupies the central place. The Scriptures often describe the moral life as our response to the gracious gift of God in Christ. Finally, the Trinity itself provides a paradigm of the relationality that is inherent in the Christian moral life (see again chapter 8 for a discussion of personhood in God).

The relational model avoids an excessive personalism only if it views the moral life in terms of the full spectrum of human relationships, including those with the neighbor and with the world. Consider, for example, the sacrament of Penance. In the context of a preconciliar deontological model, the sacrament was called *Confession* from the name of the primary act: the confession of sins according to number and kind. Today, because of Vatican II, the sacrament is called *Reconciliation*, a relational term which includes our multiple relationships with God, neighbor, world, and self. It is not only our relationship with God that is healed, because sin breaks or damages all of our relationships. (For a fuller development of the relational model, see Charles E. Curran, *Directions in Fundamental Moral Theology*, pp. 11–14; see also H. Richard Niebuhr, *The Responsible Self: An Essay in Christian Moral Philosophy*, New York: Harper & Row, 1963.)

What follows in this chapter is formulated within the framework of the relational model of the Christian moral life.

THE KIND OF PERSON THE CHRISTIAN IS CALLED TO BECOME

Conversion

A Christian is a person who has moved to a different level of human consciousness in response to the call of Jesus Christ. The Christian is one who accepts Jesus' call to discipleship and whose whole life is shaped by that call. The process (rather than a single once-and-for-all act) by which the human person moves to Christian discipleship is called *conversion*. More precisely, it is *Christian* conversion, since conversion to God is an invitation and a possibility for every human being.

In chapter 25 we touched upon the element of conversion in the preaching of Jesus (Mark 1:15) and of the early Church (Acts of the Apostles 2:38). It was a call to repentance and belief, to a change of mind and of heart, and to a new mode of behavior in keeping with that change, that is, to a life of discipleship. The New Testament, therefore, says that we are to live according to the demands of the Kingdom of God. We are to make God the center and source of our being. We are to allow ourselves to be transformed by the redemptive, healing presence of God and then to allow God to continue to work through us to redeem and heal others and the whole world, enemies as well as friends, the outcasts as well as the respectable, the poor as well as the rich, sinners as well as the righteous.

This, of course, is a broader and more profound understanding of conversion than was often proposed after the Council of Trent, with its necessary emphasis on the intellectual and objective character of faith. To be converted was to accept divine revelation as authoritatively presented by the Church. A "convert" was a non-Catholic who had become a Catholic. The determining feature of conversion, therefore, was ecclesiastical, not Christological or anthropological. It had to do, primarily, with one's new institutional relationship to the Catholic Church rather than with one's new personal relationship to God and to Jesus Christ.

Conversion in its more contemporary sense, therefore, refers to a change in one's basic orientation. To be converted to Christ is to adopt a whole new basic Christian orientation, what theologians like Josef Fuchs and Bernard Häring call the *fundamental option*. According to Häring, it is close to Erik Erickson's vision of the quest for personal identity and integrity (see Häring, *Free and Faithful in Christ*, vol. 1, pp. 168–77). Erikson views the individual person in a continuing development, but also faced with constantly threatening decay. He places great stress on personal relationships and the interdependence between individuals and their environment. This development unfolds, he says, through various stages or cycles of life. Each stage opens new horizons of creativity. And at each stage there are important moments or crises in which a decisive turn one way or the other is unavoidable. Such a crisis, in a developmental sense, calls for a fundamental option, or rather for its deepening (see, for example, *Young Man Luther*, New York: Norton, 1962; *Childhood and Society*, New York: Norton, 1963; and *Identity, Youth, and Crisis,* New York: Norton, 1968).

When there is a firm fundamental option for the good, the human heart is filled with the Holy Spirit (Ephesians 5:18). A moral theology that focuses on relationships and responsibilities, that is, the capacity to respond to God and to Jesus Christ with all of one's being and life, is of necessity an *ethics of the heart*. "A good decision and the right deed express morality in the full sense only when the act comes from one's heart where the fundamental option is for God and good, and reaches into that depth where one turns in the right direction" (Häring, p. 186). The call to conversion is accompanied by the divine promise of a new heart. "Change your heart," Augustine said, "and your work will be changed" (*Sermo* 72).

The very essence of conversion, therefore, is to assume the inner spirit of Christ. The new basic orientation of the disciple of Christ is made possible not merely by the disciple's conformity with the example of Christ but, above all, by the indwelling of Christ (Romans 8:10; Ephesians 4:17–24). The final test of religious conversion is whether or not it leads to and is continually manifested in *love for the neighbor*. "Those who do not love a brother or sister whom they have seen, cannot love God whom they have not seen. The commandment we have from him is this: those who love God must love their brothers and sisters also" (1 John 4:20–21). (For another view of conversion, as intellectual, moral, and religious, see Bernard Lonergan, *Method in Theology*, New York: Herder & Herder, 1972, pp. 237–44.)

Character

The Christian convert is called to become a person of *character*, that is, a person with the capacity for self-determination and for healthy, life-giving relationships. A person of character is one who takes responsibility for her or his actions. Those actions are not determined simply by rules or principles but by an intelligent and sometimes courageous response to a concrete situation and challenge, involving always relationships to God, to neighbor, to the world, and to the self. An ethics of character focuses our attention more on the person performing an act than on the acts performed by the person. The person does not set out to acquire and cultivate moral goodness. The actions a person performs not only shape a particular situation; they also *form* the person who does them. In other words, doing the act which the situation calls for will take care of shaping us into morally good persons. (See, for example, Stanley Hauerwas, *Character and the Christian Life: A Study in Theological Ethics*, San Antonio: Trinity University, 1975; *A Community of Character*, Notre Dame, Ind.: University of Notre Dame Press, 1981; and *The Peaceable Kingdom: A Primer in Christian Ethics*, Notre Dame, Ind.: University of Notre Dame Press, 1983.)

925

Catholic moral theology has traditionally stressed the concept of character, especially in treatises on the theological and moral virtues, because it is our character which gives orientation and direction to our lives. Indeed, there is an old maxim: "Plant an act, reap a habit; plant a habit, reap a virtue; plant a virtue, reap a character; plant a character, reap a destiny." *Habits* are regular patterns of activity. *Virtues* are good habits (and vices are bad habits). *Character* emerges from the network of virtues (or vices). Our final *destiny* depends upon the character we build in response to grace, within the context of a network of relationships forged through life, with God, the neighbor, the world, and the self.

Character, like conversion, can never be finished once and for all. Good or bad habits can be reversed or broken. A pattern of habits can be modified or uprooted. Sometimes this occurs gradually; at other times it may happen through a single decisive act (as in a profound conversion experience, or in mortal sin). By definition, we are open always to change as we respond to new experiences and influences in our lives. Our moral future is created cumulatively and relationally out of our present and our past. That moral future is fashioned not by a resolution to obey certain moral rules but by a resolution to become, in response to the offer of grace, a certain kind of person within a certain network of relationships.

Since character is so closely linked with personality, and since personality is always unique, rooted as it is in self-consciousness and self-determination, there is no one type of character which is normative for everyone. There are different modes of life, even within the Christian community. Through our beliefs, intentions, and actions we acquire a particular moral history befitting our nature as self-determining persons.

Virtue

A virtue is a "power" (*virtus*), in the literal sense of the word. It is the power (facility, disposition, attitude) to accomplish moral good, and especially to do it joyfully and perseveringly even against inner and outer obstacles and at the cost of sacrifice. (When that power is turned to evil, it is called a *vice*.) Virtues are powers rooted in the presence of God, in grace, that enable us to establish and nurture healthy and life-giving relationships with God, the neighbor, the world, and the self. They prompt us to act in such a way as to exclude extreme forms of action. Thus, the saying: *In medio stat virtus* ("In the middle stands virtue"). For example, a person may "hope" so strongly in his eventual salvation that he begins to take it for granted. He sins by *presumption*. On the other hand, someone else may be so despondent about her chances for salvation that she "hopes" too little, and falls into *despair*. The *virtue of hope* stands in the middle of these two extremes: It is confidence in the mercy and love of God, but it also accepts responsibility for cooperating with the saving grace that has been bestowed upon us both at birth and in the sacraments. Christ, of course, is the model of all virtue. Christian moral existence is not only based on the *imitation of Christ* (John 13:15), it is also life *in* Christ (Philippians 2:5).

Theology has traditionally distinguished between *natural* and *supernatural* virtues. But in light of our present understanding of the relationship between nature and grace (see chapter 5), this hard and fast distinction needs to be understood in a different way. Supernatural virtues are not something added to natural virtues. On the other hand, the distinction does remind us that virtue is rooted in the human, not divorced from it. Another distinction is between *acquired* and *infused* virtues. Seen from the point of view of its source and rootedness, a virtue is "infused" by God. A third distinction is between *theological* (faith, hope, and charity) and *moral*, or *cardinal*, virtues (prudence, justice, temperance, and fortitude). But given the *relational* model of the Christian moral life being employed here, the operative distinction of this presentation of the virtues is between *general* virtues that affect the totality of our relationships (with God, the neighbor, the world, and the self), and *particular* virtues that primarily affect specific relationships rather than the totality thereof. The theological virtues of faith, hope, and charity fall under the heading of *general* virtues because they affect the totality of relationships to one degree or another. Other virtues fall under the heading of *particular* virtues. For example, the virtue of temperance primarily affects the relationship with the self, while the virtue of justice primarily affects the relationship with the neighbor and the world.

The notion of virtue is not without its parallels in contemporary psychology. Erik Erikson, to whom we referred previously, sees the virtues as representing the strengths of the *ego* over against the animal instincts of the *id* and the imposing claims of the *superego*. "Ego strength" is equivalent to virtue. The *id* and the *superego* can rob the person of his or her freedom. In the one case, the person becomes the slave of passions, and in the other, the slave of "higher authorities." It is at the level of the *ego* that a person takes responsibility for his or her life, keeping the animal drives under some measure of control and maintaining a healthy attitude toward the pressures of an overweening conscience. (See William Meissner, *Foundations for a Psychology of Grace*, New York: Paulist Press, 1966, pp. 153–63.)

Similar parallels can be drawn from the writings of Abraham Maslow (d. 1970), especially in his notion of "self-actualization" as an unceasing trend toward unity and toward the integration of energy within the person. For example, the self-actualized person has an increased self-acceptance, acceptance of others, increased autonomy, less hostility, less need for honors and prestige. A person who has achieved these characteristics in the course of personal growth has established a life-pattern very similar to that of the traditional "virtuous person, or person of character." (See *Toward a Psychology of Being*, Princeton, N.J.: Van Nostrand, 1968, and *Motivation and Personality*, 2d ed., New York: Harper & Row, 1970.)

General Virtues Affecting the Totality of Relationships

The Theological Virtues

Faith

Certain important aspects of the virtue of faith have already been addressed in chapters 2, 6, and 7. In chapter 2 we described faith as the foundation of theology, doctrine, and especially discipleship. In chapter 6 we outlined the present crisis of faith and the challenge to belief. In chapter 7 we placed the problem of faith in the larger context of the theology of revelation. Here we shall only touch again upon some of the points in chapter 2 insofar as they directly relate to the shape and character of Christian existence.

Avery Dulles makes a useful schematization of faith as a theological virtue ("The Meaning of Faith Considered in Relationship to

Justice," *The Faith That Does Justice*, John C. Haughey, ed., New York: Paulist Press, 1977, pp. 10–46). Faith can be understood as *conviction*, as *trust*, and as *commitment*. The first is an *intellectualist* approach; the second, a *fiducial* approach; the third, a *performative* approach. In the classical tradition, Catholics have tended to emphasize the first, Protestants the second; today both increasingly support the third.

Faith As Conviction

The so-called intellectualist approach takes two forms. The "illuminist" school (Augustine, Thomas Aquinas, et al.) understands faith as an inner light or as the beginning of wisdom. Its modern exponents— e.g., Bernard Lonergan—regard faith as "the knowledge that is born of religious love," as the "eye of religious love." This is a view of faith, however, which does not regularly foster an intense human concern. Its primary focus is on the personal relationship between the individual and God in a contemplative union that could unwittingly encourage a spirit of indifference to the needs of others. Pressed too far, the illuminist notion of faith produces a split between faith and daily life.

The "body of doctrines" school, on the other hand, sees faith as a firm assent of the mind to what the Church authoritatively teaches in the name of God. It tends to equate faith with belief, to think of it as an act of intellectual submission and obedience. Although faith is always expressed in some form, its expressions are always historically conditioned. Furthermore, faith is not the acceptance of someone else's point of view on reality but is one's own interpretation of reality. The "body of doctrines" school also focuses believers' attention so strongly on what there is to believe that they tend to ignore the moral (social, political, economic as well as personal and interpersonal) implications of accepting the Gospel in faith.

Faith As Trust

This is usually called the "fiducial" approach. It underlines the elements of personal trust and stresses the personal relationship of the believer with God. God is less the revealer than the savior. This concept of faith is, of course, solidly biblical (as we saw in chapter 2). It was also the emphasis of the Protestant Reformers. The problem with it is the ease with which it can overlook the importance of human initiative and undermine the sense of human responsibility for the future of the world. Everything is left in the hands of God, who will save us in spite of our iniquity. Although the justified person will perform good works and evil works alike, the deeds themselves do not bring about salvation. Faith alone saves.

Ernst Troeltsch (d. 1923), the Protestant church historian, pointed out how the Lutheran doctrine of justification entails a lack of real interest in social reform (*The Social Teaching of the Christian Churches*, vol. 2, New York: Harper Torchbook, 1960, p. 540). The Protestant ethicist Reinhold Niebuhr (d. 1971) made a similar criticism of Luther's doctrine of the two kingdoms in his *The Nature and Destiny of Man*, vol. 2 (New York: Scribners, 1964, p. 195). If everything depends upon the grace of God and nothing finally depends on human effort, Christian commitment to social justice and peace is of no ultimate interest to the Kingdom of God.

Faith As Commitment

This is the so-called performative approach. Faith can never be a matter of disembodied words. It must be incarnate in *praxis* (faith-in-action). Faith is a transforming acceptance of the Word, which challenges us through the cries of the poor and oppressed. Only in liberating *praxis* can we give to the Word the "warm welcome" that constitutes faith. Faith is not a passive waiting upon God's decision to act; rather, it seizes the initiative and reshapes the world by its God-given power. Faith, therefore, is not a passive virtue. It does not protect us from the world; it remakes the world. It is active engagement in the service of the Kingdom of God. This is the understanding especially dominant in Latin American liberation theology today, and it has a stronger biblical basis than many may have heretofore acknowledged. Thus, "Those who do what is true come to the light" (John 3:21). The Gospel is the power of God revealing God's justice and leading to salvation (Romans 1:16–17). Faith works through love (Galatians 5:6). Our faith overcomes the world (1 John 5:4). But neither is this "performative" view by itself a sufficient understanding of faith.

Faith As Synthesis of Conviction, Trust, and Commitment

Each one of these approaches says something that is enduringly true about the virtue of faith. First, faith inevitably seeks understanding, and the understanding achieved is expressed theologically and sometimes doctrinally, as the "intellectualist" approach insists. Faith, therefore, has content; there are truths to be grasped and become convinced of. Faith is also an inner disposition, an illumination of consciousness by which we see and comprehend reality in a wholly new light. Second, faith is acceptance of the Word of God. It is trust in God's power to bestow new life, as the "fiducial" approach argues. Finally, faith is an act of self-surrender, demanding total commitment to the Kingdom of God, as the "performative" approach emphasizes. But that Kingdom is not an otherworldly reality alone. It is also a Kingdom of justice and peace here and now. God is present in history, calling us to collaboration in the coming of the Kingdom. To define faith only as conviction or only as trust is to undermine those principles which are so central to Catholicism: the principles of sacramentality, mediation, and communion. For it is in and through the neighbor whom we see that we respond to the God whom we do not see.

Faith Development

Faith is not only an act but also a process. Faith has always been understood as a virtue, and virtues are in the category of *habits*. Faith, then, can never be merely a once-and-for-all decision; it is a habitual disposition of the mind and heart toward God (in the case of religious faith in general) and toward Jesus Christ (in the case of Christian faith). Recent developments in the cognate disciplines of social and educational psychology have prompted even deeper probings into the processive or ongoing aspect of faith. Specifically, the work of Erik Erikson, Jean Piaget, and Lawrence Kohlberg, on the psychological and secular educational side, has influenced the work of Methodist theologian James Fowler and the many influenced, in turn, by him, on the theological and religious educational side. What is characteristic of all of these authors is the conviction that human persons grow and develop morally in *stages*.

931

Erikson's stages are easily adaptable to the process of Christian faith. The faith commitment can be viewed sequentially or developmentally as: trust in the Church as mother; a sense of personal autonomy in which self-expression and self-control are balanced; a sense of personal initiative, with the aggressive potential of self-growth balanced by the regulating force of authority; entrance into the give-and-take situation of life, and movement from the private society of the family into the larger, more demanding society of other persons; the experience of a certain disintegration catalyzed by doubt and the struggle for reintegration; interpersonal commitment calling for sacrifice; concern for others who are to follow in the next generation(s); and a heightened eschatological sense of reality. (See *Childhood and Society*, pp. 247–74.)

For Kohlberg, moral maturity does not consist simply in internalizing rules and norms but in developing one's ability to integrate one's conception of social interaction. Moral development is achieved by the stimulation of the natural development of the individual child's own moral judgment and capacities. This occurs either through discussing moral dilemmas which involve a conflict of interests between persons or through establishing "just communities" which offer many opportunities for engaging in social communication and interaction.

According to Kohlberg, an individual moves through the following stages of moral development: (1) Good is done or evil avoided on a reward-or-punishment basis. (2) Good is done or evil avoided as a result of self-centered use of other people. (3) Good is done or evil avoided as a result of a desire for peer approval. (4) Good is done or evil avoided as a result of devotion to a fixed order established by law, authority, and obligation. (5) Good is done or evil avoided as a result of a sense of equity and mutual obligation arising in a democratic view of the social order. (6) Good is done or evil avoided as a result of conscientious decisions made in the light of values which have been internalized. (See his "Stage and Sequence: The Cognitive-Developmental Approach to Socialization," in *Handbook of Socialization Theory and Research*, David Goslin, ed., Chicago: Rand McNally, 1969.)

James Fowler applies the Kohlberg schema of *moral* development to the development of *faith:*

932

1. *Intuitive-protective faith.* The imitative, fantasy-filled phase in which the child can be powerfully and permanently influenced by the examples, moods, actions, and language of the visible faith of primal adults.

2. *Mythic-literal faith.* Persons begin to take on for themselves the stories and beliefs and observances which symbolize belonging to their community. Beliefs are appropriated with literal interpretation, as are moral rules and attitudes.

3. *Synthetic-conventional faith.* The person's experience of the world goes beyond the family and primary social groups. Coherence and meaning are certified by either the authority of properly designated persons in each group or by the authority of consensus among "those who count."

4. *Individuating-reflexive faith.* Persons begin to take seriously the burden of responsibility for their own commitments, lifestyle, beliefs, and attitudes. This stage develops under the tutelage of ideologically powerful religions or of charismatic leadership. It both brings and requires a qualitatively new and different kind of self-awareness and responsibility for one's choices and rejections.

5. *Paradoxical-consolidative faith.* Persons recognize the integrity and truth in positions other than their own. They affirm and live out their own commitments and beliefs in such a way as to honor that which is true in the lives of others without denying the truth of their own. This kind of faith requires a regard for those who are different and who oppose one's own position.

6. *Universalizing faith.* Persons dwell in the world as transforming presences, but are not of the world. They discover that in being-for-others they are being most truly themselves. (See his *Life Maps: Conversations on the Journey of Faith,* with Sam Keen, Waco, Texas: Word Books, 1978.)

The National Catechetical Directory for Catholics of the United States, *Sharing the Light of Faith* (Washington, D.C.: United States Catholic Conference, 1979), basically accepts this developmental approach to faith and moral development. The life of faith is related to human development, and so passes through stages or levels. Furthermore, different people possess aspects of faith to different de-

933

grees. It is the task of catechesis to help at each stage of human development and to lead the person ultimately to full identification with Jesus (par. 174, p. 100). The Directory warns, however, against making any one scientific theory normative. There are different schools of psychology and sociology which do not agree in all respects, nor are all developmental theories of equal merit. Catechists should not assume that any one school or theory has all the answers. Furthermore, these scientific disciplines supply nothing of the doctrinal or moral content of catechetical programs (par. 175, pp. 100–101). The Directory seems finally to adopt, or perhaps *adapt*, Erikson's framework: infancy and early childhood (birth–age 5), childhood (ages 6–10), preadolescence and puberty (ages 10–13), adolescence (14–17), early adulthood (ages 18–35), middle adulthood, and later adulthood. (The Directory gives no specific ages for the last two categories.) There are specific recommendations for catechesis at every stage of development (see pp. 102–13). Although the *Catechism of the Catholic Church* (1992) acknowledges that there are stages of revelation, it does not acknowledge that there are stages of faith-development.

With regard to the Kohlberg-Fowler approach to moral and faith development, so popular in recent years among Catholic religious educators, criticisms have centered on the following points: (1) Kohlberg's assumption that morality is a matter of *rational* perception; (2) Kohlberg's focus on *justice alone*, which does not touch upon the human quest for intimacy, community, and friendship, nor on the other moral virtues (prudence, temperance, fortitude); (3) Fowler's distinctly and almost exclusively Tillichian notion of faith as a fundamental *attitude*, and his corresponding deemphasis of faith's *content* (*fides quæ creditur*, i.e., that which is believed, faith as "conviction") and its broader *social and political dimension* ("transformative" faith); and (4) the tendency of this approach's adherents to "typecast" their fellow Christians as if these stages were evaluative rather than descriptive and particular rather than general. However, the overall estimation of the value and usefulness of this approach has been largely positive.

Hope

The virtue of hope received little attention from the classical theologians who followed either a teleological or a deontological approach to the Christian moral life. Even Thomas Aquinas devoted only a few sections to it in his *Summa Theologiæ* (II-II, qq. 17–22). Where hope was discussed, it was viewed in an individualistic, nonrelational manner, i.e., as *my* hope for *my* salvation. It was understood as the elevation of the will, made possible by grace, by which we expect eternal life and the means to attain it, ever confident of the omnipotent aid of God. We sin against hope by despair (anticipated failure) and by presumption (anticipated success).

Since the mid–1960s, under the impact of such books as Protestant theologian Jürgen Moltmann's *Theology of Hope* (New York: Harper & Row, 1967), the virtue of hope has assumed a different meaning. It is that virtue by which we take responsibility for the *future*, not simply *our* individual future but the future of the *world*. Hope is oriented toward the Kingdom of God, not as heaven alone but as the renewal and re-creation of the whole world. God is not above us but ahead of us, summoning us to cocreate the future. The future holds the primacy. Indeed, in one sense all theology is eschatology. It is *hope* seeking understanding (*spes quærens intellectum*), and not simply *faith* seeking understanding (*fides quærens intellectum*), as Augustine, Anselm, Aquinas, and others insisted. Revelation is not information about another world but promise about this one. Christian existence is life within the horizon of *expectation:* expectation of the Kingdom of God. The *resurrection* of Jesus Christ is the first fruits of the Kingdom; it is God's "down payment" on the promise. Our future is the future of the risen Christ.

These same themes were assimilated into Catholic theology in the late 1960s and early 1970s by Johannes Metz in particular. Our understanding of the world, he insisted, is oriented toward the future. We are not so much contemplative as productive. We are called to build a new world (and not only to interpret it), to engage in "political theology," a theology which constantly critiques the "city" (*polis*) according to the standards of the Kingdom of God. Renunciation of the world is not escape from earthly responsibilities. It is simply the refusal to accept anything in the world as absolute, as

935

identical already with the Kingdom. Nothing is as yet the Kingdom. Everything, therefore, is subject to criticism, including even the Church. The Church, after all, is not the "nonworld" but that segment of the world which acknowledges the Lordship of Jesus and lives in light of that confession of faith. It is a community of hope, i.e., a relational community which lives always for the other, in love of neighbor (*Theology of the World*, New York: Herder & Herder, 1969, pp. 107–40). A similar although not identical approach was fashioned by Latin American liberation theology, but its emphasis was placed on the virtue of faith as *praxis* rather than on the virtue of hope.

Karl Rahner reminds us that death relativizes all of our grand designs. It italicizes the hardness and the darkness of human existence. Only in God do we have hope. It is hope that makes us free. Yet it is not, to paraphrase Dietrich Bonhoeffer, a "cheap hope." What we hope for we cannot present in advance, and what we enjoy here and now is not what we ultimately hope for. Hence the Christian will always be regarded as a utopian by the absolute pessimists (those who see no life beyond death and see *this* life as absurd) and also by the absolute optimists (those who find this life completely meaningful and worthwhile without any reference at all to a life beyond death). The Christian "is not a person who grasps for something tangible so that he [or she] can enjoy it until death comes, nor is he [or she] a person who takes the darkness of the world so seriously that he [or she] can no longer venture to believe in the eternal light beyond it" (*Foundations of Christian Faith*, New York: Seabury Press, 1978, p. 405).

Christian existence, of course, is always historical existence. We experience joy at one moment and tears at another. We experience the grandeur and the vitality of human life, and also taste illusions, disappointment, death. "But to be able to open oneself to the reality of life freely and unsystematically, and to do this without absolutizing either earthly life or death, this can be done only by someone who believes and hopes that the totality of the life which we can experience is encompassed by the holy mystery of eternal love" (p. 405).

This new emphasis on the virtue of hope and on the future has had a significant impact on Catholic moral theology. It helps us to see that ethical norms and obligations are always open-ended, imperfect, incomplete, never finished until the Kingdom comes in all its fullness. It helps us see, too, that humankind is itself in process and in

936

development toward a reality beyond itself: ahead and not above. It helps broaden the scope of moral vision because we hope not only in our own salvation but in the salvation of others and of the whole world. And, finally, it underlines the critical function of all moral reflection, analysis, pronouncement, and action within and by the Church, for hope measures everything against the standard of the coming Kingdom. It views reality, therefore, in terms of the totality of human relationships: with God, the neighbor, the world, and the self.

We have already seen in chapter 18 how and to what extent the Second Vatican Council also embraced this wider understanding of hope. Hope does not diminish the importance of our duties in this life but rather gives them special urgency (*Pastoral Constitution on the Church in the Modern World*, n. 21). Indeed, it is precisely in our recognition of Christ in our sisters and brothers and in our love of Christ in word and deed alike that we give witness to the truth and share with others the mystery of God's love. "As a consequence, people throughout the world will be aroused to a lively hope—the gift of the Holy Spirit—that they will finally be caught up in peace and utter happiness in that fatherland radiant with the splendor of the Lord" (n. 93). Christian existence, therefore, is existence *in* hope, but also existence which seeks to *give* hope to others.

Charity/Love

No virtue is more fully expressive of the relational model of the Christian moral life than charity, or love. We saw in chapter 25 that all of Jesus' moral teachings and those of the early Church have been concentrated in the one commandment of love: love of God and love of neighbor (Mark 12:28–34; Matthew 22:34–40; Luke 10:25–37; Galatians 5:14; 1 John 3:23; 1 Corinthians 13). "And now faith, hope, and love abide, these three; and the greatest of these is love" (1 Corinthians 13:13). It should be obvious by now that these three virtues are distinct but not separate. Love is a lived faith and a lived hope. The one virtue without the other two is radically incomplete, dead.

First, what does the word *love* mean? In English there is only the one word; in Greek there are four. *Epithemia* is desire, with the connotation of lust. This is sexual love. *Eros* is the drive toward union with others which brings self-fulfillment. *Philia* is affectionate love such as that among brothers, sisters, and friends. *Agape* is total dedication and devotion to the welfare of the other, regardless of sacrifice and personal cost. Many experiences of authentic love by human beings will entail a proportionate blending of these four elements.

Christian love consists in an intimate participation in the life of God who *is* Love (1 John 4:8,16). It is a gift from God that is mediated by Christ and activated by the Spirit. It calls us to share in the paschal mystery by which Christ handed himself over to death and therefore was raised from the dead and exalted by the Father (Philippians 2:5–11). Christian love is rooted in the whole life, death, and resurrection of Christ. He is its model through his life of service (Mark 10:45), through his complete self-giving on the cross, and through his passing over to the Father. Christian love is the same self-giving, even to the point of crucifixion. "No one has greater love than this, to lay down one's life for one's friends" (John 15:13).

Modern psychologists (Erich Fromm, Rollo May, et al.) insist that a person's capacity to love depends on his or her *personal maturity*. Love requires self-knowledge, effort, conviction, courage, generosity, respect, a sense of responsibility, sensitivity, patience, and a fundamental acceptance of oneself with all of one's strengths and limitations. Thus, modern psychology often agrees with the basic Christian principle that we are called to love our neighbor as we love ourselves (Mark 12:31). If, however, individuals have not resolved the inevitable crises of human development, they may not attain sufficient human maturity for Christian love. The child starts out by being attached to his or her mother as the "ground of being." The child feels helpless and needs the all-enveloping love of a mother. The child then turns to the father as a guiding principle for thought and action. The child is motivated by the need to acquire the father's praise and avoid his displeasure. At full maturity, the child frees himself or herself from the person of both father and mother as protecting and commanding powers. The adult becomes "his or her own father and mother." Love of God passes through similar stages: love of God in helpless attachment; love of God in obedient attachment; and love of God as personal incorporation of the principles of love and justice into oneself.

If we are really to love as Christ intends, we have to overcome our own narcissism. We must strive for objectivity in every situation and become sensitive to the situations where objectivity eludes us. We must see the difference between our picture of another and the other's behavior, on the one hand, and, on the other hand, the way the other really is, apart from our own interests, needs, fears, and "hang-ups." Christian loving also means readiness to take risks, to accept pain and disappointment. It means using one's human powers productively. Loving demands a state of intensity and commitment. Christian love cannot coexist with indifference. Indeed, the opposite of love is not hate but *apathy*, a lack of concern, a suspension of commitment (literally, *apathy* means to be "without pain").

Love is also closely related to the *will*. Will without love becomes manipulation; love without will becomes sentimentality. We are afraid, in the latter case, that if we choose one person rather than another, we will lose something, and we are too insecure to take that chance. And so we hold back, remaining cool and aloof. But the same fear of commitment can be expressed in a flurry of seemingly interpersonal activity, especially of a sexual kind. Sensuality then smothers sensitivity. Sex becomes an instrument to express one's anxieties, about death in particular. We try to prove to ourselves that we are still young and can "perform."

If love is the soul of Christian existence, it must be at the heart of every other Christian virtue. Thus, for example, *justice* without love is legalism; *faith* without love is ideology; *hope* without love is self-centeredness; *forgiveness* without love is self-abasement; *fortitude* without love is recklessness; *generosity* without love is extravagance; *care* without love is mere duty; *fidelity* without love is servitude. Every virtue is an expression of love. No virtue is really a virtue unless it is permeated, or informed, by love (1 Corinthians 13).

"Every benefit which the People of God during its earthly pilgrimage can offer to the human family stems from the fact that the Church is 'the universal sacrament of salvation,' simultaneously manifesting and exercising the mystery of God's love for humankind" (Vatican II, *Pastoral Constitution on the Church in the Modern World*, n. 45). It is the cross of Christ which is "the sign of God's all-embracing love and ... the fountain from which every grace flows" (*Declaration on the Relationship of the Church to Non-Christian Religions*, n. 4).

Creative Freedom and Fidelity

Bernard Häring employs two general virtues as the integrating elements of his major three-volume work, *Free and Faithful in Christ* (1978–1981): creative freedom and fidelity. They, in turn, are linked by the virtue of responsibility. The general virtues of creative freedom (the capacity or disposition to move beyond settled patterns of thinking and action) and fidelity (the disposition to maintain continuity in moral consciousness and behavior) situate the Christian in relationship to God, the neighbor, the world, and the self. "Only one who understands his or her self in a relationship of response and dialogue with God and fellowmen can reach that selfhood that is truly free to love and to be faithful in a creative way" (vol. 1, p. 85). But Christ remains at the center of these relationships. "The liberty for which Christ has freed us cannot reveal its responsive and creative dynamics without an equally creative fidelity to the Lord of history" (p. 3). But in Christ there is no ultimate incompatibility between being both free and faithful. (For a full exposition of the virtues of creative freedom and fidelity, in the context of responsibility, see vol. 1, pp. 59–163.)

Particular Virtues Primarily Affecting Specific Relationships

The Relationship with God

Humility

God's call to communion and eternal life and God's offer of grace invite a response from the disciple. This requires openness on the part of the disciple to hear and to respond to the call. The particular virtue by which we are disposed to be open to the call and invitation of God is called humility. From the time of Abraham and Sarah the great believers were those who were ready to hear the call of God and were willing to leave everything else behind in order to respond to it. Jesus himself is the model of humility. "My Father," he said in the garden of Gethsemane, "if it is possible, let this cup pass from me; yet not what I want but what you want" (Matthew 26:39). Mary, in turn, is the model of humility for all disciples. In response to the call of God given through the angel, she said: "Here am I, the servant of the Lord; let it be with me according to your word" (Luke 1:38).

The virtue of humility, or of openness to God's call, is the antithesis of self-centeredness and closed-mindedness. One who is consumed with self-interest, with advancing one's own goals and ambitions, is not likely to hear the call of God. The true disciple is always alert and vigilant, ever open to God's call when it is least expected, like the five wise bridesmaids in the parable of the bridegroom and the ten bridesmaids. "Keep awake therefore, for you know neither the day nor the hour" (Matthew 25:13). Disciples must seize the *kairos*, the special time of opportunity. They must read the "signs of the times" and respond to them (*Pastoral Constitution on the Church in the Modern World*, n. 4).

Gratitude

A second particular virtue that characterizes the Christian's relationship with God is gratitude, or thankfulness. Christians not only respond to the call of God by accepting it and living in fidelity to it, but also by giving thanks for it, particularly in worship, and, more particularly still, in the Eucharist (literally, "thanksgiving"). Liturgy, therefore, is a constitutive dimension of the Christian moral life. Ingratitude, or obliviousness to the divine origin of the gifts and talents we have, is the antithesis of the particular virtue of gratitude.

The Relationship with the Neighbor

Mercy and Concern for the Poor

The particular virtue of mercy is rooted in, and evoked by, the mercy of God, and all Christian mercy is rooted in the example of Christ himself (Acts of the Apostles 10:38; John 13:15). Human mercy, however, does not give of its own but of what God has bestowed (Romans 11:30–32; Ephesians 2:4). We see the distress of others as our own distress. Mercy is an act which testifies to our solidarity in sin and our common need for redemption and healing.

It is not ritual that the Lord desires, but love, which is the soul of mercy (Hosea 6:6; Hebrews 10:5–8). "Is not this the fasting that I choose: to loose the bonds of injustice, to undo the thongs of the yoke, to let the oppressed go free, and to break every yoke? Is it not to share your bread with the hungry, and bring the homeless poor into your house; when you see the naked, to cover them, and not hide yourself from your own kin? Then your light shall break forth like the dawn, and your healing shall spring up quickly;..." (Isaiah 58:6–8). In the parable of the Sheep and the Goats (Matthew 25:31–46) the Lord proclaims that we will be judged by our response to the hungry, the thirsty, the stranger, the naked, the prisoner. "Truly I tell you, just as you did it to one of these who are members of my family, you did it to me" (25:40).

These works of mercy traditionally have been divided into *corporal* works (concerned with needs of the body) and *spiritual* works (concerned with needs of the soul). Such a dichotomy is no longer appropriate in light of our understanding of the integrity of the human person as at once bodily and spiritual, but the listings provide a useful reminder of the kind of life that the Christian is called to lead. Thus, the *corporal works of mercy* are the following: feeding the hungry, giving drink to the thirsty, clothing the naked, sheltering the homeless, visiting the sick, ransoming the captive, and burying the dead (the last was added out of respect for the sanctity of the body as a temple of the Holy Spirit; see 1 Corinthians 3:16). The *spiritual works of mercy* are these: instructing the ignorant, counseling the doubtful, admonishing the sinner, bearing wrongs patiently, forgiving offenses, comforting the afflicted, and praying for the living and the dead.

Although most of these works have to do with a Christian's obligations to the neighbor in need, they also have broader social and political implications today and are to be linked in many cases with the overriding demands of *social justice* (see below). But the dimension of mercy reminds Christians that their obligations go beyond even those required by social justice. Perhaps the bridge between social justice and mercy today is the "preferential option for the poor," now enshrined in Catholic social teachings (for example, Pope John Paul II, *Centesimus Annus* [1991], n. 11).

Forgiveness

Like mercy and concern for the poor, the particular virtue of forgiveness is rooted in the fact that God has first forgiven us. "Forgive us our trespasses," Jesus taught us to pray, "as we forgive those who trespass against us." Indeed, our sins will be forgiven only to the extent that we are prepared to forgive others (Matthew 6:15; see also the parable of the unforgiving slave, Matthew 18:23–35). And there is no limit on the Christian's call to forgive others. Peter asked Jesus how many times he would have to forgive a member of the Church who sinned against him: "As many as seven times?" Jesus replied: "Not seven times, but, I tell you, seventy-seven times" (Matthew 18:21–22).

Justice

Insofar as the particular virtue of justice is rooted in Sacred Scripture, it is linked with the idea of *righteousness* (Hebrew, ṣedeq, and Greek, *dikaiosynē*). It is intimately connected with the Covenant, i.e., with the obligations of the Israelite to the community of Israel. A person is righteous insofar as he or she is conformed and faithful to the Covenant. According to Paul, Christian righteousness is the state of vindication and deliverance achieved through the death of Christ (2 Corinthians 5:21; Romans 5:16). The Kingdom of God is "righteousness and peace and joy in the Holy Spirit" (Romans 14:17). Accordingly, perfect and complete righteousness is still an object of hope to be achieved beyond history (Galatians 5:5). Christian righteousness requires that Christians themselves live in a way that is consistent with the death and resurrection of Christ and with the new life in the Spirit that flows from Christ's saving work. This righteousness cannot be achieved by the observance of the Law. It is a free gift of God which reaches its fullness in the Kingdom (Romans 3:30; 1 Corinthians 6:11).

Justice is derived from the Latin word *ius*, which means "right." Justice is concerned with *rights* and with *duties* which correspond to those rights. One's duty to respect another's bodily integrity flows from the other's right to life in all its fullness. A right, therefore, is a power that we have to do things which are necessary for achieving

943

the end or purpose for which we are destined as rational and free persons. A right is a person's moral claim upon other persons or society in general to the means of reaching an end that is his or hers, and that he or she is responsible for reaching. In that sense, rights flow from duties.

Among the principal human rights, as enumerated, for example, in Pope John XXIII's *Pacem in Terris* (1963) are the following: the right to life and a worthy manner of living; the right to respect for one's person regardless of sex, race, religion, or national origin; the right to freedom in the pursuit of truth and in its expression and communication; the right to be informed truthfully about matters of concern; the right to a basic education; the right to worship God freely; the right to choose one's state in life; the right to gainful employment, to decent working conditions, to a proper compensation, to private property, to organize; the right of meeting and association; the right to freedom of movement (emigration and immigration); the right to participate in public affairs and to contribute to the common good (see pars. 11–45). There is, however, a *hierarchy* of rights not only in terms of their relationship to the last end, but also in terms of their relationship to the rights of others.

It has been said that justice would not be possible unless we were, in fact, separate from one another. Justice regulates relationships between strangers. Where there is perfect love and communion, the question of rights and duties becomes moot. They are completely fulfilled. Justice, therefore, mediates between the otherness which arises from our exteriority and the oneness which arises from our interiority.

But even if unselfish love among all persons were achieved, the virtue of *social justice* would still be required. In the larger community, beyond the small family units or the bonds of love and friendship, there is "a dynamic interpenetration of all those fundamental human rights upon which the aspirations of individuals and nations are based" (*Justice in the World*, Synod of Bishops, 1971). Persons develop fully only in a societal context, since by definition we are fundamentally and radically social. The quality of life in society, the justice of its mode of organization, the orientation of its structures and systems (e.g., political, legal, economic, social, educational, religious) will either enhance or retard the full human development of the person.

As the Protestant social ethicist Reinhold Niebuhr argued, it is not enough to present Christian ethics as a love ethic. Given the sinful condition of the world, it is impossible to envisage a society of pure love. Christian ethics must come to terms with the reality of inevitable conflicts and with the demands for their harmonization, often on the basis of arrangements that are far from the Christian idea of disinterested love. Christian realism tells us that interests must be balanced and claims recognized. To conceive of a world of love without the imperfect harmonies established by justice is to create an illusion. A simple Christian moralism, Niebuhr insisted, will counsel men and women to be simply unselfish. A profound Christian faith must encourage them to create systems of justice which will save society from its own selfishness. Indeed, if that portion of society that benefits from social inequality attempts to counsel only love, forgiveness, and patience to the discontented and disenfranchised instead of working for justice, it will convict itself of hypocrisy. (See, for example, *Moral Man and Immoral Society*, New York: Scribners, 1932.)

A correct understanding of social justice demands, furthermore, a correct understanding of the distinction between society and the state. *Society* is constituted by the total network of social, political, economic, cultural, and religious relationships which are necessary for full human development. The *state* is the center of coercive power in society. It is the civil authority by which the purposes of society are procured and preserved. The distinction between society and the state is presumed in John XXIII's *Pacem in Terris* and in the Second Vatican Council's *Declaration on Religious Freedom*.

The extent to which the state should intervene in the life of its citizens is attended to in the *principle of subsidiarity*, first enunciated by Pope Pius XI in *Quadragesimo Anno* (1931). This principle seeks to establish and maintain a balance between individual initiative and governmental assistance and direction. The principle holds that the presumption is always in favor of individual or small-group action over against governmental intervention. The state should intervene only when lesser bodies cannot fulfill a given task required by the common good. In broader terms, the principle of subsidiarity means that nothing should be done at a higher level that can be done as well or better at a lower level.

The principle has to be balanced off, however, by the *process of socialization*, first referred to by John XXIII in *Mater et Magistra* (1961) as "the growing interdependence of citizens in society giving rise to various patterns of group life and activity and in many instances to social institutions established on a juridical basis" (par. 59). Given the increased complexity of modern economic and political life, more intervention is required, without prejudice to the principle of subsidiarity. The two—subsidiarity and socialization—must be kept in creative tension.

The virtue of justice, therefore, is divided as follows: *commutative justice*, which relates to contractual obligations between individuals involving a strict right and the obligation of restitution (e.g., one person lends another person a sum of money; the second person is obliged in conscience to return that money according to the agreement); *distributive justice*, which relates to the obligation of a government toward its citizens, by which the government regulates the burdens and benefits of societal life (e.g., a government is to tax its citizens fairly and according to their ability to pay, and to distribute those tax monies according to need, especially in the areas of housing, food, health care, and education); *legal justice*, which relates to the citizen's obligation toward the government or society, without prejudice to the right of conscientious objection or even civil disobedience (e.g., citizens must pay their fair share of the taxes; the greater the wealth, the greater the burden); and *social justice*, which relates to the obligation of all parties to apply the Gospel to the structures, systems, and institutions of society which are the framework in which all human relationships take place (e.g., an individual and/or groups must take an active interest in necessary social and economic reform).

These four kinds of justice are interrelated and mutually limiting. All four are attempts to express the demands of Christian love (*agape*). All four have to do with rights and duties. Such a notion of justice does not provide immediate answers to the complex problems of social existence, but it does provide *principles of discernment and specific guides for judgment*. If the movement of history is toward the Kingdom of God—a Kingdom of "justice, love, and peace" (*Pastoral Constitution on the Church in the Modern World*, n. 39)—the pursuit of justice is itself part of this movement. If we are called in the meantime to participate

946

in the death and resurrection of Christ, justice helps us to specify the terms and demands of that participation. Conversely, efforts toward the fulfillment of human needs, the protection of human rights, and the realization of structures of genuine mutuality are consequences of faith in the saving power of Christ's death and resurrection.

Truthfulness

In the history of moral theology, truthfulness is considered only from a negative point of view. Thus, Augustine wrote no treatise on truthfulness, but he did write two on lying (*De Mendacio* and *Contra Mendacium*). Thomas Aquinas subsumed truthfulness under the virtue of justice. One must tell the truth to another who has a *right* to it. That laid the foundation for a casuistry regarding truthfulness that became specially evident during the Counter-Reformation—a morality employing a whole catalog of distinctions regarding mental reservations. This morality allowed almost every possible equivocation and dissimulation, provided one found the right distinction. The concern for truthfulness as such declined, and was replaced by the question: How can I achieve my goal without telling a formal lie? While all sins against the sixth commandment were regarded always as mortal, sins against the eighth commandment (concerning the bearing of false witness) were regarded as venial, unless special circumstances and consequences made them more serious.

Jesus calls his disciples to a much higher standard. He inveighs against the hypocrisy of the religious establishment of his day (Matthew 23). He reminds us that he came into the world "to testify to the truth" (John 18:37). Grace and truth came through him (1:17); the knowledge of the truth is promised to those who believe in him (8:32); the word that he brings is truth (17:17); and he is himself the truth (14:6). The Spirit leads us into the truth (16:3), a truth that sets us free (8:32).

The New Testament condemns almost no other sin as vehemently as hypocrisy (besides Matthew 23, see Matthew 6:1–17; 15:7–11; Acts of the Apostles 5:1–11; 1 Timothy 4:1–2). Indeed, Paul opposed Peter "to his face" for his "hypocrisy" because he stopped eating with Gentiles under pressure from the ultraconservative Jews known as the "circumcision faction." Paul accused Peter, Barnabas, and others in their company of "not acting consistently with the truth of the gospel" (Galatians 2:11–14). (See Hans Küng, *Truthfulness: The Future of the Church*, New York: Sheed & Ward, 1968; and also Walter Kasper, "The Church as the Place of Truth," in *Theology and Church*, New York: Crossroad, 1989, pp. 129–47.)

When applied to the self, truthfulness becomes the particular virtue of *integrity*, marked by a capacity for self-criticism.

The Relationship with the World

Stewardship

Because the world comes from the creative hand of God, the Christian recognizes that the goods of creation exist to serve the needs of all. No one has the right to arrogate to oneself an excessive amount of those goods at the expense of the legitimate needs of others nor does anyone have the right to be destructive or wasteful of those goods, in disregard or contempt of the generations to follow (see Pope John Paul II, *Sollicitudo Rei Socialis* [1988], n. 39).

"The right to private property," John Paul II points out, "is valid and necessary, but it does not nullify the value of this principle [that "the goods of the world are originally meant for all"]. Private property, in fact, is under a 'social mortgage,' which means that it has an intrinsically social function, based and justified precisely by the principle of the universal destination of good" (n. 42). He refers in a subsequent encyclical, *Centesimus Annus* (1991), to the "senseless destruction of the natural environment," rooted in the erroneous belief that we "can make arbitrary use of the earth, subjecting it without restraint to [our] will as though it did not have its own requisites and a prior God-given purpose, which humankind can indeed develop but must not betray" (n. 37).

The pope reflects Catholicism's essentially sacramental vision when he deplores the human desire "to possess things" and our concomitant lack of an "aesthetic attitude that is born of wonder in the presence of being and of the beauty which enables one to see in visible things the message of the invisible God who created them. In this regard, humanity today must be conscious of its duties and obligations toward future generations" (n. 37).

948

Some have criticized Christianity's emphasis on stewardship as being too anthropocentric, thus giving human beings too much dominion over the created world and contributing to our ecological problems. However, if one takes proper account of the Christian's relationship to the world and creation, stewardship should not have this negative impact.

The Relationship to Self

Temperance

One very important dimension of our being human is rooted in what the traditional theology called the "concupiscible appetites," i.e., our desire to achieve the good through food, drink, or sex. The virtue which enables us to achieve some *balance* in these areas while still living in a state of legitimate self-interest is temperance. It is a virtue which has attracted the attention of philosophers from the earliest centuries. The ancient Greeks viewed it as a way of ensuring "good hygiene." Plato regarded these sensuous cravings as "an ugly brute of a horse" which had to be curbed by the "charioteer" which is the human mind. The Stoics, too, looked upon these appetites as having to be brought under the complete control of reason.

The early Christian writers saw this particular virtue as part of the "grace-full" life, as a way of participating in the death and resurrection of Christ. Death to self leads to greater life in the Spirit. Thomas Aquinas insisted, however, that the virtue is not the *repression* of the desire for sensual pleasure but rather its *tempering* in the service of human growth. Temperance, therefore, is positive, not negative. It is a virtue which humanizes the pleasures of food, drink, and sex. Aquinas referred to three "subjective parts" or divisions of the virtue: *abstinence*, which humanizes our desires for food and other pleasure-producing elements such as tobacco and drugs; *sobriety*, which humanizes our desires for intoxicating drink; and *chastity*, which humanizes our desires for sexual pleasure in accordance with our state in life. Each of these appetites, when properly satisfied, contributes to the preservation of the individual and of the human species. Intemperance makes them ends in themselves.

949

Moderation of the sensual appetites through the virtue of temperance is closely allied with Christian *asceticism*. The word *askesis* itself means "exercise." Asceticism is concerned with those exercises which help us regulate the conflict between the spirit and the flesh. It involves a painful struggle, self-denial, and renunciation. The medieval and postmedieval notion of asceticism was not unmixed with rationalism, Stoicism, and Pelagianism—all emphasizing the innate power of the human person to live according to a certain pattern *without grace.* This traditional concept of asceticism was also often founded on a dualistic understanding of human existence, as if the bodily aspects of the human person were unholy, even sinful. Indeed, the traditional moral theology textbooks referred to certain organs of the body as *partes inhonestæ* ("dishonorable parts").

In light not only of modern psychology but also of contemporary theology, we understand asceticism as the free and faithful acceptance of one's self, of one's painful limitations, weaknesses, inadequacies, of one's sorrows, disappointments, and frustrations, and, finally, of death itself. One is ascetical in not trying to escape the facticity of human existence by immersing oneself in, or distracting oneself by, purely material pleasures. There is nothing wrong with food, drink, or sexual expression. On the contrary. But they can become crutches or escapes from one's human and Christian responsibilities. At the very least, their misuse is symptomatic of a fundamental disorder. Thus, those who are excessively heavy do not simply have healthier appetites than others. Those who are frequently intoxicated to the point where they cannot function are not simply people who like the taste of liquor. Those who move from one sexual liaison to another with commitment to none are not simply people with uncontainable, overflowing love.

The Christian must pattern her or his life on that of Christ, who did not flee suffering and death but who became obedient even unto death (Mark 10:45; Philippians 2:5–11). Christian asceticism is an asceticism of the cross, a readiness to face death in the service of others and ultimately in the service of the Kingdom of God. Asceticism is an affirmation of the cross as the path to resurrection. The ascetic is one who is patient (literally, "one who suffers"), prepared for the coming of the Lord, ever vigilant, looking toward the Kingdom. It is life on pilgrimage.

How can one tell if his or her asceticism is genuinely Christian or if it is distorted? First, is it an expression of self-acceptance, or of self-loathing? Does one deny oneself because self-denial frees one for greater service to others and makes one a more effective sign of Christ to the world, or does one regard the appetites in question as base and unworthy of a Christian? Second, is the asceticism oriented to dedicated Christian service, or is it finally a way of avoiding commitment, especially the commitment implied in interpersonal intimacy? Third, is the ascetic freer to love, more creative, or is the ascetic an isolated figure, closed-minded, difficult to be with?

Fortitude

Whereas temperance balances our concupiscible appetites, fortitude moderates our *irascible* appetites. It strengthens them against the passion of *fear*, on the one hand, and on the other restrains their immoderate tendencies toward *audacity* and *rashness.* Fortitude enables a person to face serious challenges, even death, with some measure of calm. It gives the strength to endure suffering for a just cause. It is the virtue of *courage,* by which one overcomes an instinctive fear in order to pursue the good. Fortitude, therefore, has an active and a passive side. Its active side has to do with taking bold action for the sake of the Kingdom of God; its passive side has to do with enduring some pain, suffering, or even death for the sake of the Kingdom. But not even endurance is merely passive. Martin Luther King, Jr. (d. 1968) always insisted that nonviolent resistance was still *resistance*, requiring much courage and commitment.

Biblically, courage and strength are linked (2 Samuel 10:12; Deuteronomy 31:7). The prophets were evidently courageous figures. But every form of true courage and every manifestation of real strength is rooted in God (1 Samuel 17:37; Psalms 27:14; 31:25). In the New Testament this *andreia*, or courage, is commended to us by Paul (1 Corinthians 16:13; 2 Corinthians 5:6–7; 10:1–2) and by the Lord himself (Matthew 9:2; 14:27; John 16:33). The early Church looked to Jesus as the model of courage (Hebrews 12:2). Indeed, the whole eleventh chapter of the Epistle to the Hebrews is a tribute to Christian faith and courage. The martyrs followed in Jesus' path—e.g., Stephen (Acts of the Apostles 7) and others (Revelation 7:14).

951

Fortitude must always be in the service of justice. It marks a path between the extremes of temerity (rashness) and timidity. Without fortitude, growth is impossible. Nietzsche once said that whatever does not destroy us makes us stronger. We can grow in and through adversity. We can be ennobled by suffering—not that we ever seek it or embrace it for its own sake. Fortitude, then, is our affirmative answer to the inevitable shocks of human existence. It is the ability to dare and to endure.

The virtue of fortitude is missing in persons who are always fearful of displeasing others, who remain silent in the face of injustice, who shun conflict at all costs, who avoid "rocking the boat," and who, therefore, do only whatever they think is "expected" or "safe."

Sin

Deepening the relationships with God, the neighbor, the world, and the self as well as the virtues which direct these relationships constitutes the growth and ongoing conversion of the Christian. Breaking or damaging those same relationships with God, neighbor, world, and self constitutes sin. We can see this already in the first chapters of Genesis. After Adam and Eve sinned, they hid from God (Genesis 3:8) and were subsequently expelled from the Garden of Eden (3:23–24) because their relationship with *God* had been broken. Adam blamed Eve for the fall (3:12), and one of their children, Cain, subsequently slew another of their children, Abel (4:8). Sin had disrupted the relationship with the *neighbor*. Because of their sin, Adam learned what it was to earn his living off the earth by "the sweat of [his] face" (3:19), and Eve knew what it was to bring forth children "in pain" (3:16). Sin had disrupted the relationship with the *world*. Finally, when they recognized themselves to be naked, they were ashamed and hid (3:10). Sin had disrupted the relationship with the *self*.

Biblical Notions

A first understanding of the word *sin* in the Bible is "to miss the mark." To sin is to fail to achieve one's goal or to fail to measure up to one's highest standards. In the *Old Testament*, with its emphasis on the Covenant, sin is *infidelity to the covenantal relationship* between God and ourselves. It is our failure to live up to the terms of the agreement. It is a missing of the mark. Sin is also a form of idolatry. It is a substituting of human concerns and interests for God's sovereign will (Exodus 32:1–6; Deuteronomy 9:7–21). We sin against the God whom we do not see by violating the rights of our neighbor whom we do see (Leviticus 19:9–18; Isaiah 1:23–25). Rejection of the neighbor is rejection of God (Ezekiel 18:3–32).

The same relationships are present in the *New Testament*. Love of God and love of neighbor are inextricably linked (Matthew 22:34–40; Mark 12:28–31; Luke 10:25–37). It is striking that where the word for sin appears in the *Synoptics*, it almost always is used in connection with the *forgiveness of sins*. Jesus himself associates with sinners and calls them to repentance (Matthew 9:10,13; 11:19; Luke 7:34; 15:1–2; 19:7). For Jesus sin comes only from the heart, and only insofar as it does is the human person defiled (Matthew 15:18–19; Mark 7:20–22). But the sinner need only ask for forgiveness (Luke 18:13–14). There is joy in heaven over the sinner's return (Luke 15:7,10).

The malice of sin is more explicit in John: It is lawlessness (1 John 3:4), wrongdoing (5:17), lust and pride (2:16), darkness (3:9–11). But Jesus is also the conqueror of sin (John 8:46; 1 John 3:5). He is the lamb who takes away the sin of the world (John 1:29). The fullest theology of sin in the New Testament appears in the writings of Paul, and in the first part of the Epistle to the Romans in particular. It is not observance of the Law which brings us victory over sin, he writes. The Law only makes us aware of our sin. In Christ we die to sin. Our old sinful self is crucified with him "so that the body of sin might be destroyed, and we might no longer be enslaved to sin" (Romans 6:6). Therefore, we are now all "alive to God in Christ Jesus" (6:11). But if we are indeed new creatures in Christ, freed of sin, we must act in accordance with our status. And yet we do in fact sin. We act against who we are and against the God who is within us: "For I do not do the good I want, but the evil I do not want is what I do" (7:19). Our inner selves want to follow the way of the spirit, but our outer selves are still pulled by the flesh. The Spirit has already been given to us as "first fruits" of the new creation, of the redemption of our bodies (8:23). The Spirit helps us in our weakness and makes intercession for us (8:26). "If God is for us, who is against us?" (8:31).

Therefore, Paul is not conceding here the inevitability of sin, only the permanent state of conflict which characterizes human existence: conflict between the spirit and the flesh. We need not be defeated. We can achieve victory in Christ. His Spirit has taken possession of us.

Philosophical and Theological Reflections

Freedom and Responsibility

The spirit-flesh conflict raises the larger theological question of freedom and responsibility, to which we referred above under "general virtues." It is important to note, first, what freedom is *not*. It is not a faculty alongside other faculties (e.g., intellect, will) by which a person decides to do this or that. Freedom enters into the very definition of what it means to be human. To be free is to be present to oneself, to be in possession of oneself, to be conscious of oneself as a distinct, responsible being. Freedom does not so much allow us to *do something* as to *be someone,* in relation to God, neighbor, world, and self.

Such freedom, however, is not absolute. Only God is absolutely free, i.e., fully and perfecting self-possessive and responsible. Human freedom is *limited* from without and from within. *From without* our self-possession is qualified by our situatedness in history. Since the world is "mediated by meaning" (Lonergan), our very self-understanding and, therefore, our very freedom are shaped by the meanings which are mediated through our experience (e.g., what our parents tell us we are, what our friends and relatives and neighbors tell us, what society tells us, how our institutions, including the Church, define us, what our economic and social status disclose to us). Our freedom is also limited from without by various natural and physical realities and events—i.e., by the sheer facticity of worldly existence. *From within* our freedom is qualified by the fact that we can never be fully present to ourselves. There is a psychic universe, a portion of which Freud and others have only recently discovered, which remains hidden from our consciousness and yet influences profoundly our awareness, our vision, and our sense of personal responsibility.

Freedom, therefore, is *the relatively limited capacity to decide who we shall be.* It is not something that is active only from time to time, such as at the moment of a choice or decision. Freedom is permanently operative. It governs our whole being all the time. Such freedom is not an immediate datum of our experience. We cannot see it or readily identify it by testing. Nor is freedom (to use Karl Rahner's analogy) like a knife which always remains the same in its capacity for cutting, and in cutting always remains the same knife. Freedom is not simply an instrument for meeting specific needs of choice. It is that fundamental capacity for making a final and irrevocable choice to *be* someone, to be a particular kind of human being. In that sense, freedom is the capacity for the eternal, for God. It is that which allows us to orient ourselves beyond ourselves, to recognize who we are ultimately and to shape our entire life (not just this or that individual act) according to that new self-consciousness of who we are in the presence of God.

And this is precisely what contemporary Catholic moral theologians such as Joseph Fuchs and others mean by the *"fundamental option,"* to which we referred at the beginning of the chapter. In being truly converted to the Kingdom of God, everything we do assumes its direction, purpose, and meaning in light of the Kingdom, i.e., in light of God's saving and transforming will. This does not rule out the possibility, indeed the probability, that we shall occasionally act against this fundamental choice for God. But only a fundamental reversal of that choice (what the traditional textbooks called *aversio a Deo,* a "turning away from God") is sufficient to cancel out the original decision to understand oneself in relation to God and to orient one's whole life in view of that new self-understanding. In other words, no single (*categorical*) act by itself is sufficient to merit eternal punishment in hell unless that act is of sufficient depth and magnitude to constitute a fundamental repeal of the (*transcendental*) conversion experience. (Pope John Paul II's 1993 encyclical *Veritatis Splendor* [The Splendor of Truth] is insistent on the point that an individual act can change the fundamental option [n. 65]. Catholic moral theologians agree with him.)

Only a *mortal sin,* Thomas Aquinas wrote, truly deserves the name *sin* (*Summa Theologiæ* I-II, q. 88, a. 1). So rare an occurrence should that be in the case of one who is sincerely oriented to God that for the first several centuries the Church expected its members to have recourse to the sacrament of Penance no more than once in their entire lifetimes, if that often! (See chapter 23 on the sacrament of Penance.)

Freedom, then, is a *transcendental* capacity (see chapters 4 and 5 on Transcendental Thomism's understanding of human existence). It is a capacity which allows persons to go beyond themselves, to become something other than they are, and not simply to do this or avoid that *categorical* act. But because it *is* a transcendental capacity, we can never be directly conscious of it. We acknowledged earlier (in chapter 5) that it is impossible for us to answer completely the question "Who are we?" because we are at one and the same time the questioners and the ones questioned. Only God has a view of human existence which is objective and comprehensive. Indeed, as soon as we begin reflecting on our freedom, we are already exercising it. We experience ourselves as free, but there is no scientific way of verifying our freedom as we verify, for example, the existence of the lungs or the kidneys. We argue to freedom not only on the basis of our experience, which in any case can be distorted by external and internal forces, but on the basis of the implications of its denial. *If we are not free, we are not responsible.* And if we are not responsible, human existence is reduced to mechanical existence. Without freedom and responsibility there is no love, no faith, no hope, no trust, no compassion, no friendship, no justice. Everything is calculated, predetermined, subject only to accident and/or *mis*calculation. (For Pope John Paul II's reflections on freedom, see *Veritatis Splendor*, nn. 31–41.)

In summary, in our original, transcendental experience of ourselves as *subjects,* i.e., as distinct, conscious, interrelating, free persons, we know who we are. But we can never objectify with absolute certainty what we know. We know more of ourselves than we can say. No statement, no formulation can ever capture fully what we experience of ourselves as selves, no more than we can adequately report to another the beauty of a symphony, the powerful impact of a speaker, or the horror of an accident. We are at once present to ourselves and distant from ourselves. We are *present* to ourselves in that we are who we are and in that we alone are directly conscious of who we are. But we are also *distant* from ourselves in that even our self-knowledge is impaired by factors and forces outside and inside ourselves.

The Capacity for Sin

Freedom is the capacity to say either "Yes" or "No" to God, i.e., to see ourselves either as having ultimate worth because we are alive by a principle which transcends us, or, on the other hand, to see ourselves as merely a constellation and network of biological responses and of psychological and sociological conditioning. Evidence (not overwhelming proof) of our capacity to say "Yes" to God appears in various acts of heroism and of extraordinary generosity where self-interest is clearly subordinated to the interests of others. One need only reflect on the obscenity of Auschwitz and Buchenwald, and other more recent horrible examples of inhumanity, to find similar evidence of our radical capacity to say "No" to God.

On the other hand, we can almost never point to a particular moment or act in our lives and say that precisely here and not somewhere else we made a fundamental and irrevocable choice for or against God. Whether our lives are oriented toward God or away from God must be judged on the basis of the totality of our lives, not on the basis of a totaling up of virtuous acts and sinful acts and then figuring the difference. Nor are we saying that the possibility of a "No" to God is about the same as that of a "Yes." *Although the Church has always taught that we have the capacity to reject God fundamentally (mortal sin), it has never taught that there are, in fact, persons in hell.* Insofar as Sacred Scripture describes the miseries of eternal punishment, it presents them as possibilities of human life and as instructions about the absolute seriousness of our moral decisions.

Furthermore, *we can never be certain that we have finally and fully said "No" to God, even in an act which appears on the surface to be of such a kind.* We cannot say with certitude to what extent outside and inside forces manipulated us, because that is never obvious to superficial examination. "We can never know with ultimate certainty whether we are sinners. But although it can be suppressed, we do know with ultimate certainty that we really *can* be sinners, even when our bourgeois everyday life and our own reflexive manipulation of our motives appear to give us very good grades" (Karl Rahner, *Foundations of Christian Faith*, p. 104).

What is to be said, finally, of *God's sovereignty?* If we have the capacity to say a final and definitive "No" to God, does not that limit God's power over us? It is God who created us as free beings and who willed and established our freedom. Subjectivity, therefore, must exist without limiting the sovereignty of God. If that seems too simple, consider the alternatives: (a) we are not free, and, therefore, not really human; or (b) God is essentially limited, and, therefore, not really God.

Mortal, Serious, and Venial Sins

Our discussion up to now has generally concentrated on *mortal sin,* the breaking of our fundamental option and the rupturing of our relationship with God, neighbor, world, and self. As we reflect on our own lives and on the lives of others (the latter is usually the easier task), we recognize that those lives are marked by ambiguity and inconsistency. No one is perfectly good all the time, nor absolutely evil all the time. There is good and bad in everyone, it would appear. This indicates, first, that our fundamental option does not ensure uniformity of behavior. It also indicates, second, that there are forces which impede our intended course of action. Why this should be so, we can never say. *That* this is so, we know all too well. This condition derives from what we know as *Original Sin* (see again chapter 5).

Venial sin is a human act which is not fully consistent with our fundamental orientation toward God. In venial sin there is a genuine decision to do this or that *action* (the *categorical* dimension), but there is no decision to become this or that sort of *person* (the *transcendental* dimension). In venial sin a person chooses to do a particular deed, but he or she also wants even more deeply to be the kind of person who stands opposed to the deed. In every venial sin, therefore, there is a contradiction between the *act* and the *person* doing the act.

Venial sin admits of *degrees* of seriousness. Some actions are objectively more serious violations of the Gospel than others. Some sinful motives are more clearly defined than others. Some circumstances make an attitude or a deed more *serious* than others.

958

Serious sin, therefore, is even more inconsistent with the Gospel than is venial sin. But serious sin is not the same as mortal sin. Missing Mass on Sunday, without a good reason, is an example of a serious sin. *Mortal sin* is an act which fully engages the person. The person chooses not only the act (the *categorical* dimension) but also the kind of person he or she wants to be or become in and through the act (the *transcendental* dimension). An older view in moral theology assumed that the commission of every objectively serious act involved or engaged the fundamental option; the categorical was collapsed into the transcendental. In other words, every *serious* sin is a *mortal* sin. That is, if (1) an act was seriously sinful, and (2) a person knew it was seriously sinful, and (3) freely consented to it nonetheless, it was a mortal sin.

The insights of both psychology and sociology have compelled contemporary Catholic moral theology to revise that assumption. If these actions were always mortally sinful under these three conditions, and if those who committed them had frequent recourse to the sacrament of Penance throughout their lives, then we are left with the conclusion that many people are constantly changing their very self-definition. But is it really conceivable that a person could define himself or herself as someone oriented toward God, then repudiate that definition one Sunday morning by deciding against attending Mass in order to watch a sports event, and then reassert that definition in the sacrament of Penance a few hours or a few days later? To suggest this, many moral theologians are saying, is to undermine our human dignity and to cheapen us as persons.

CHRISTIAN ACTION IN THE WORLD

Natural Law

Its Meaning and Grounding

From where do the Church and individual Christians derive their moral wisdom and knowledge? Is it from revelation alone, and specifically the revelation of God in Jesus Christ? The Catholic tradition says "No." It insists that *human reason*, reflecting on human nature and human experience, can also arrive at a true moral wisdom and knowledge that holds not only for Christians but for all people. This methodological approach, called *natural law*, is consistent with, and expressive of, Catholicism's three identifying principles: sacramentality, mediation, and communion. The presence and will of God are available in all created realities, because these realities come from the creative hand of God and have been redeemed by the Word-made-flesh (the *sacramental* principle); the presence and will of God are *mediated* through the use of human reason (the principle of *mediation*); and, finally, they are the source of moral wisdom and knowledge for the whole human community and for the sake of its present and future unity (the principle of *communion*).

The natural-law approach, Catholics contend, is biblically grounded in the testimony of St. Paul: "When Gentiles, who do not possess the law, do instinctively what the law requires, these, though not having the law, are a law to themselves. They show that what the law requires is written on their hearts, to which their own conscience also bears witness; and their conflicting thoughts will accuse them or perhaps excuse them on the day when, according to my gospel, God, through Jesus Christ, will judge the secret thoughts of all" (Romans 2:14–16). The Second Vatican Council cites this text as a basis for its teaching on the binding force of natural law (*Pastoral Constitution on the Church in the Modern World*, n. 16, footnote), and Thomas Aquinas used the text to settle the question whether or not there is a natural law (*Summa Theologiæ*, I-II, q. 91, a. 2, *sed contra*).

It must be said at the outset, however, that the term *natural law* is interpreted very differently as one moves across disciplinary lines: from theology, to philosophy, to jurisprudence. Some have proposed that, since the words *law* and *natural* are both fraught with such ambiguity, the term *natural law* ought not to be used at all.

The Thomistic Notion

Thomas Aquinas's theory of natural law has strongly influenced the Catholic tradition, philosophically, theologically, and doctrinally. He understands natural law as the participation of the rational creature in the eternal law. Unlike nonrational creatures, human beings can understand in some measure the divine plan of providence and, in the light of that understanding, provide moral guidance for themselves and others (*Summa*, I-II, q. 91, a. 2). Citing Psalm 4, Aquinas refers to natural reason as a "light" reflected upon us from the face of God. But what the natural law reveals is not something that is transcendent to human reason, but something immanent to it, namely, the natural inclination of human beings to their appropriate actions and end. The principles of natural law are those basic aspects of human perfection toward which persons have natural inclinations (q. 94, a. 2).

Thus, the natural law is a special kind of knowledge, not about God, but about human beings and human nature. Through human reason reflecting on human nature, human beings can determine what is for their own good and at the same time what God requires. Natural law does not disclose divine commands, but the providential plan of final end and of intermediate ends within which human beings are to realize their perfection. Such a morality, therefore, is intrinsic, not extrinsic. *Something is commanded because it is good; it is not good because it is commanded.*

Nature in the Thomistic tradition describes the principle of operation in every living thing. Human nature has built-in inclinations toward its end or goods. Human morality and human fulfillment consist in achieving these goods and ends. The three basic inclinations of human nature are those we share with all substances (the preservation and conservation of our being); those which are common to human beings and to animals (procreation and education/ training of offspring); and those which are proper to rational beings (to know the truth about God and to live in human community).

Human reason, or the *gnoseological* aspect of natural law, can discover these built-in inclinations and from them derive other general principles of action (like the Ten Commandments) and then apply those principles to particular actions. Most followers of Aquinas understand reason to operate in a deductive manner, using the syllogism (major premise, minor premise, conclusion). However, Jacques Maritain (d. 1973) and other neo-Thomists of the twentieth century understood Aquinas to refer to knowledge by inclination and connaturality, not based on deduction and the syllogism. But the hierarchical magisterium throughout much of the twentieth century followed the deductive and syllogistic approach.

Vatican II

According to the *Pastoral Constitution on the Church in the Modern World,* we discover the natural law in the depths of our conscience. It is a law which we do not impose upon ourselves, and yet it holds us to obedience. It summons us to love the good and avoid what is evil, to do this and not do that. The natural law is written in the human heart by God. "To obey it is the very dignity of the human person; according to it the human person will be judged" (n. 16; see also the *Declaration on Religious Freedom,* nn. 2, 3, 14). At the same time, the council insists throughout its teachings that faith, grace, and the Gospel must also decisively affect and shape our daily lives, and not only what comes from the realm of the natural and from human reason. Discussion continues since the council about how all these various aspects relate to one another, but one continues to recognize the heavy Catholic emphasis on the human and on human reason.

Post–Vatican II Developments

Most discussions since the council have centered on the philosophical approach to natural law. The hierarchical magisterium, however, has continued to employ the philosophical approach of the preconciliar manuals of moral theology, especially in its teaching in the area of sexual and medical ethics (see Pope John Paul II, *Veritatis Splendor,* nn. 42–53). Pope Paul VI made specific appeal to this understanding of natural law in his encyclical on birth control, *Humanæ Vitæ* (1968), to which we shall return in chapter 27.

Catholic revisionists, as they are often called, have criticized three aspects of the preconciliar manual approach to natural law, as employed by the hierarchical magisterium, especially in sexual and biomedical issues (by contrast with a more revisionist method in the Church's social teachings). They argue, first, that a more historically conscious method is needed in order to give greater attention to historical change and development, and in order to move away from an uncritical concept of an eternally immutable human nature. A historically conscious approach to natural law is less deductive in its moral reasoning and more tentative in its specific judgments about complex issues. Second, revisionists criticize the present teaching of *physicalism,* in which the human moral act is identified with the physical structure of the act. Thus, the physical act of sexual intercourse can never be interfered with either to avoid procreation (artificial contraception) or to promote procreation (artificial insemination). The Catholic moral tradition, by contrast, has recognized a distinction between the physical act (killing) and the moral act (murder). Third, the revisionists argue, the accepted natural law theory gives too much emphasis to faculties, powers, and natures and not enough to persons. At times the good of the person can justify interference with the sexual power or faculty.

Other Catholic moralists (usually philosophers rather than theologians) also disagree with some aspects of the preconciliar textbook understanding of natural law (its emphasis, for example, on the nature of the faculty) and they insist on certain fundamental human goods necessary for human development, which human beings can never directly go against. On the other hand, these moralists (especially John Finnis and Germain Grisez) strongly support the teaching of the hierarchical magisterium on sexual and medical issues. (See John Finnis, *Natural Law and Natural Rights,* Oxford: Oxford University Press, 1980, and Germain Grisez, *The Way of the Lord Jesus, Volume 1: Christian Moral Principles,* Chicago: Franciscan Herald Press, 1983.)

Values and Norms

How precisely does the Church and the individual Christian determine what the Gospel demands in a particular situation, where there are special circumstances and conflicting claims? They do so by the application of *values* and *norms.*

Definitions and Distinctions

Values are of two kinds: premoral and moral. *Premoral values* are those concrete good things that ought to be done, to the extent possible. They have to do with the real world of such things as life and death, knowledge and ignorance, health and sickness, friendship and alienation, beauty and ugliness, wealth and poverty. Insofar as anything exists, it has value. It participates in *being.* If it is antithetical to human growth, however, it is a *disvalue*. The attainment of premoral values may or may not contribute to one's moral growth. Thus, one might preserve the value of life in a prison camp by killing a fellow prisoner in one's own place—clearly a disvalue.

Moral values, on the other hand, are those which are essential to proper human living. They are not merely things that we should attend to (as premoral values are), but are things we must possess if we are to be fully human. Thus, one need not be physically attractive to be fully human, but one must be loving. Moral values include such virtues as honesty, justice, chastity, fortitude, temperance. They are not only a matter of *doing* just deeds or courageous acts, but of *being* just and courageous.

Norms are also of two kinds: material and formal. *Material norms* tell us what we should *do*. They point out premoral values which we are to pursue, or premoral evils which we are to avoid. Some examples of material norms are, Do not kill. Do not take what belongs to another. Tell the truth. Pay your debts.

Concrete material norms are not absolute. There are times when one may have to withhold the truth or even kill. Thus, although material norms are concrete, informational, and instructive, they are also debatable, often tentative, and open to exceptions. These norms do not provide final answers to specific problems. They point to values and illuminate situations. They provide the moral agent with at least some of the factors that must be taken into account in reaching a final judgment.

Formal norms point to moral values which must be pursued. They indicate attitudes which we should acquire. They tell us the "form" our conduct should take. They indicate what is the right thing *to be*. Formal norms do not tell us to "do what is good" but to "do what is right." They are vague and almost totally without specific content. They proclaim goals rather than tactics, strategies, or policies. Examples of formal norms are, Be honest. Respect life. Do not murder. Do not steal.

Formal norms challenge us to be responsible, to be faithful Christians. They remind us of what it means to accept the Gospel of Jesus Christ, particularly in those moments and situations where we may be tempted to act against that Gospel. *Only formal norms are absolute, universal, and exceptionless.* Thus, it is not always wrong to kill (a

964

material norm), but it *is* always wrong to commit murder (a *formal* norm). The same contrast could be made between taking what belongs to another (material) and stealing (formal), or between telling the truth (material) and being honest (formal).

As human persons and as Christians, we are called to be moral. We must know what we should *be* (formal norms tell us this) and what we should *do* (material norms tell us this). Formal norms point to moral values, i.e., to those things which the moral person must *be*. Material norms point to premoral values, i.e., to those things which the moral person must *do* in the here and now if he or she is to maximize the good and minimize the evil. To be moral, therefore, it is not enough to be sincere (adhering to material norms); one must also be correct and right (adhering to formal norms as well).

Material norms give us information and direction; formal norms give us motivation and encouragement. Both kinds of norms exist because moral theology goes on at two levels simultaneously. Moral theology not only helps us to determine what we must *do* if we are to live faithfully to Christ, but also the kind of person we should *be* if we are to be perceived by God, by others, and by ourselves as faithful Christians.

In the final accounting, there is no authoritative guidebook by which Christians can determine in almost every conceivable circumstance what is consistent with the Gospel and what is not. The Christian lives in a world of premoral and moral values and of material and formal norms which express those values. But those norms have to be applied in each case, and no case is exactly like another. The challenge of moral education, therefore, is not the teaching of moral rules but the development of Christian character. The rudder of that course toward authentic character is the virtue of *prudence* (to which we shall refer below). It is the ability to *discern*, the capacity to make wise and responsible decisions and to act on them.

Formulation of Norms and Evaluation of Acts

The Three-Source Theory

In the formulation of norms and judgments about the morality of individual actions, Catholic moral theology since medieval times has insisted on the evaluation of three sources: the *object*, the *end*, and the *circumstances*. What is the object? For example, killing. What is the end? For example, preventing a person from killing another. What are the circumstances? For example, a deranged person has started shooting a gun in a crowded street and there is no other way to stop the harm. In the light of the *intention* and the *circumstances*, the killing in this case is justified. The three-source theory strongly opposes *utilitarianism* which claims that if the end results in a greater good, it can justify any act or means (e.g., dropping a nuclear bomb on civilian populations in order to end a war).

However, the traditional approach claims that some objects (e.g., contraception, but not killing) are intrinsically evil and can never be justified no matter what the end and circumstances. Catholic revisionist theologians today have difficulty with this concept of intrinsically evil objects or acts, while at the same time opposing utilitarianism. Many of these theologians propose a theory called *proportionalism*.

Proportionalism

Proportionalism is a type of analysis for determining the objective moral rightness or wrongness of human actions in conflict situations, as well as a procedure for establishing exceptions to behavioral norms. It is called proportionalism because it uses what it calls "proportionate reason" to determine concretely and objectively the rightness or wrongness of acts and the various exceptions to the norms. This method of moral analysis began in the mid–1960s as a revision of both the principle of the double-effect and the doctrine on intrinsic moral evil. (The *principle of the double-effect* is engaged when two effects follow, one good and one evil, from an essentially good or at least morally neutral act. If the evil effect is unintended and not a direct result of the act, and if the good effect is proportionate to the evil effect, the act itself is morally legitimate.)

Proportionalists argue that no moral judgment can be made without consideration of all the circumstances. Because the human act is a structural unity, all aspects of the act have to be considered together, not in isolation from the others. That means taking into account the person's intention, the foreseeable consequences, and the proportion between the premoral values and disvalues as previously defined. Proportionalists use the distinction between premoral values and disvalues in their application of the principle of proportionate reason.

Thus, a proper relation must exist between the premoral disvalue(s) contained in, or caused by, the act and the end of the act, or between the end and the premoral disvalue(s) in the consequences of the act. In making exceptions to negative behavioral norms, proportionate reason is used to discern if the premoral disvalue(s) contained in, or caused by, the means stands in proper proportion to the premoral value in the act itself. For example, there is a negative behavioral norm which says, "Thou shalt not kill." But killing another person (a premoral disvalue) may be justified because it is an act of self-defense (a premoral value). Therefore, exceptions to behavioral norms that prohibit premoral evil are made on the basis of the presence of a proportionate reason.

Common to all proportionalist analyses is "the insistence that causing certain disvalues (ontic, nonmoral, premoral evils) in our conduct does not ipso facto make the action morally wrong. The action becomes morally wrong when, all things considered, there is no proportionate reason justifying it. Thus just as not every killing is murder, not every falsehood a lie, so not every artificial intervention preventing (or promoting) conception is necessarily an unchaste act. Not every termination of a pregnancy is necessarily an abortion in the moral sense" (Richard A. McCormick, *The Critical Calling*, p. 134.).

Proportionalism is rejected both by those who espouse the older understanding and by moralists, such as Germain Grisez and John Finnis, who maintain that there are certain basic human goods which one can never directly go against, no matter what the circumstances or the end. Pope John Paul II is also critical of proportionalism (*Verita-*

tis Splendor, nn. 75–76), but proportionalists themselves insist that they do not hold the position that is criticized.

Conscience

One must keep in mind here, as elsewhere in Part Six, the three models by which the Christian moral life is understood: deontological, teleological, and relational. According to the deontological model (employed in the pre–Vatican manuals of moral theology), conscience keeps before us the demands of God's law. According to the teleological model (employed by Thomas Aquinas), conscience keeps before us our ultimate end. According to the relational model, conscience keeps before us our relationships to God, neighbor, world, and self.

What Conscience Is Not

Conscience is not a *feeling*, whether good or bad. It is not to be equated, therefore, with the *superego*, our psychic police officer. The fact that we feel that something is right or wrong or that we feel very guilty about some action does not mean that our conscience is telling us something. Someone who is trying to lose ten pounds in time for the summer swimming season may feel terribly "guilty" about having broken his or her diet one day. But that does not make it a matter of conscience. Another person knows that it is not a mortal sin to miss Mass when one is sick but wishes to confess the "sin" anyway because he or she does not "feel right" about it. A third person feels "guilty" about going on her or his scheduled vacation before finishing a project in the office. In themselves such feelings are morally neutral. They indicate nothing at all about the moral character of the actions in question. They have nothing to do with conscience. Similar examples could be drawn from the other side of the line. For example, the fact that many people do not feel guilty about discrimination based on race or gender does not make such discrimination right. Here again, feelings are not indicative of moral rectitude or deficiency.

What Conscience Is

Only when one *decides* to do this or that, or not to do this or that, is one acting out of conscience. Conscience is the *radical experience of ourselves as moral agents. Christian* conscience is the radical experience of ourselves as *new creatures in Christ, enlivened by the Holy Spirit.* But since we never know ourselves completely (self-knowledge is some-thing one works at; it is not ready-made), decisions of conscience are necessarily incomplete and partial. And because our own circum-stances are always historically, socially, and culturally defined, deci-sions of conscience are necessarily fallible and subject to correction and change. Catholic moral theologians, therefore, are in complete agreement with Pope John Paul II when he insists that conscience is not infallible (*Veritatis Splendor,* n. 32).

Biblical Notions

There is no Hebrew word for *conscience* in the Old Testament. The Greek word *syneidesis* occurs only once, in Wisdom of Solomon 17:11. The closest word to it is *heart.* "Oh, that today you would listen to his voice: 'Do not harden your hearts...'" (Psalm 95:7–8). God is spoken of frequently as probing the heart (Jeremiah 11:20; 17:10; Proverbs 21:2; Psalm 26:2). The "pangs of conscience" are described in Genesis 3. Job insists: "My heart does not reproach me for any of my days" (Job 27:6). Fidelity to conscience is a central theme in the whole book of Job, as it is in the call of the prophets to fidelity to the Covenant and to the Law (Ezekiel 11:14–21; Jeremiah 31:31–34).

Although there are references to the inner disposition of the person in the Gospels (Luke 11:33; 14:28–32; 16:8; Matthew 5:8,28; 6:21–22; Mark 7:21), the word for conscience is absent. The word occurs twenty-five times in the Pauline writings, including Hebrews, three times in 1 Peter, and twice in the Acts of the Apostles, both times uttered by Paul. For him conscience is the fundamental aware-ness of the difference between moral good and evil. The law is written in our hearts (Romans 2:15). Paul appeals to his own clear conscience (2 Corinthians 1:12; Romans 9:1; Acts of the Apostles 23:1, 24:16). Conscience is a principle of freedom (1 Corinthians 10:29), but such freedom is conditioned by our obligations to our neighbor

(10:23). We must commend ourselves to every person's conscience before God (2 Corinthians 4:2; 5:11). Conscience itself can be weak and even erroneous (1 Corinthians 8:10–12), but obedience to such a conscience can still lead to salvation (8:11). Love proceeds from a pure heart and a good conscience and genuine faith (1 Timothy 1:5). The sacrificial ritual of the Law cannot purify the conscience (Hebrews 9:9; 10:2), but Christ purifies the conscience (10:22). Those who finally reject a good conscience can make a shipwreck of their faith (1 Timothy 1:19).

Postbiblical Reflections

In spite of individual references to conscience in some of the early Christian writers—e.g., Tertullian, Origen, Chrysostom, and Augustine—we find no systematic treatment of it until the Middle Ages. The occasion was a dispute over the meaning of a text of St. Jerome, the *Commentary on Ezekiel,* which distinguished between the terms *synderesis* and *syneidesis.* Bonaventure and the Franciscans explained the distinction in one way; Thomas Aquinas and the Dominicans explained it in another way. The Thomistic explanation would influence Catholic moral theology for the next several centuries.

Aquinas distinguished between conscience as a permanent natural habit (*synderesis*) and conscience as an act of moral judgment (*syneidesis*). The process of moral judgment is essentially rational. The human will affirms and carries out what is affirmed by right reason. It would seem, however, that the whole distinction was based on an error. In preparing the first Latin text of the Bible, Jerome was working from a Greek manuscript that was not entirely legible. Recent scholarship concludes that Jerome was wrong in finding two different Greek words for conscience. We may still make a distinction, as Bonaventure and Thomas did, between conscience as a habit and as an act of moral judgment but that distinction cannot be attributed to the Bible.

Vatican II

The tradition is summed up at Vatican II in its *Pastoral Constitution on the Church in the Modern World.* Conscience is what summons us to

970

love good and avoid evil, to do this and shun that. "To obey it is the very dignity of the human person; according to it the person will be judged. Conscience is the most secret core and sanctuary of a person. There the person is alone with God, whose voice echoes in the depths of the person." But conscience is no infallible guide. It frequently errs from invincible ignorance (i.e., an ignorance for which we are not morally responsible). Christians search for truth and for the genuine solution of problems in collaboration with others and in fidelity to conscience (n. 16).

A Contemporary View

Timothy O'Connell suggests that we abandon the language of *synderesis* and *syneidesis* and speak instead of three different levels of meaning of the word *conscience*. At the first and most general level, conscience is a fundamental sense of value and of personal responsibility. The human capacity for self-direction and self-determination implies a human responsibility for right direction and correct determination. Human beings may disagree about what in particular is right or wrong, but there is a general awareness that there *is* a difference between right and wrong. In this meaning of the word, conscience belongs to the whole human community and is part of the definition of what it means to be human. In our experience of ourselves as subjects, as human persons, we have an innate sense of the difference between good and evil.

O'Connell suggests a second level of conscience, which is more exactly an *act* of conscience and not conscience itself. This is the judgment that something is morally good or bad. This judgment is subject to error. There are differences of opinion. Thus, some believe that gambling in itself is evil; others insist that it is morally neutral at worst. When individuals try to make up their minds about what they should do, they have to have as much information about their available options as they can get. Accordingly, they will consult their own experience, their parents, their friends, their colleagues, the findings of various scientific disciplines such as psychology. If they are Christians, they will also consult the opinions of theologians and the testimony of Sacred Scripture. And if they are Catholics, they will

971

also pay attention to the official teachings of the Church. This is known as the process of conscience-formation.

A third level, according to O'Connell, is reached with the decision itself. "I may be wrong, but I am convinced that I should do this." This is the final norm by which a person's act must be guided. It is not that it guarantees correctness of judgment, but only that it allows us to be true to ourselves. And we are judged finally by God on the basis of what is in our hearts, not on what we actually did or did not do. "Everyone, of course, must ultimately follow his conscience; this means he must do right as he sees the right with desire and effort to find and do what is right" (Bernard Häring, *The Law of Christ*, vol. 1, Westminster, Md.: Newman Press, 1961, p. 151). So strongly rooted is this principle of the primacy of conscience over both external act and external authority that Thomas Aquinas himself argued that "anyone upon whom the ecclesiastical authority, in ignorance of true facts, imposes a demand that offends against his clear conscience, should perish in excommunication rather than violate his conscience" (*IV Sentences*, dist. 38, q. 2, a. 4). This principle is now taken for granted in Catholic theology, even though the opposite would have been thought to be the case a few decades ago.

In the final analysis, how does one know that she or he has made a good decision of conscience? One classic sign is *peace of mind*. You have no more pertinent questions to ask.

Conscience and Authority, Civil and Religious

The Second Vatican Council's *Declaration on Religious Freedom* declares that we are bound to follow our conscience faithfully in all our activity, and that no one is "to be forced to act in a manner contrary to one's conscience. Nor, on the other hand, is one to be restrained from acting in accordance with one's conscience, especially in matters religious" (n. 3). This principle applies as well to children (see *Declaration on Christian Education*, n. 1). But what is to be done in situations where others oppose our conscientious decision? What does the Church or the civil authority do if they sincerely believe that another's conscientious act will be harmful to themselves, to others, to the common good?

972

As a general rule, a person should not be prevented from following even an erroneous conscience, unless the action is seriously injurious to himself/herself, to others, or to the common good. Thus, a person should be prevented from committing suicide, if possible, or from killing his family as an act of "reparation" for his sins. A businessperson may be required by law to provide a just wage, fringe benefits, and working conditions even if he or she is a conscientious *laissez-faire* entrepreneur. On the other hand, there are instances where the civil or ecclesiastical authority clearly may not interfere with another's conscience. For example, the government cannot force a conscientious objector to engage in military combat (*Pastoral Constitution on the Church in the Modern World*, n. 79). These general rules do not prohibit the authority from trying to reason with others in order to make them change their judgment about a proposed moral action.

Given the inviolable character of conscience and the individual's right to follow conscience, even when it is erroneous, what are members of the Church to do in the face of moral teachings with which they disagree? Are they bound to obey all official moral teachings of the Church and to assume, almost as a matter of course, that their consciences are necessarily erroneous and not to be followed if they are in conflict with those teachings? The following principles must be taken into account:

1. It is taken for granted that the Church's moral teaching is normally a source for positive illumination for Christians in forming their consciences. If, however, after appropriate study, reflection, and prayer, a person is convinced that his or her conscience is correct, in spite of a conflict with the moral teachings of the Church, the person not only may but *must* follow the dictates of conscience rather than the teachings of the Church.

2. The Church has never explicitly claimed to speak infallibly on a moral question, so there is probably no instance as yet of a conflict between an individual's fallible decision in conscience and a teaching of the Church which is immune from error.

3. No teaching of the Church can hope to account for every moral situation and circumstance. Every teaching still has to be applied in particular cases. One is not necessarily repudiating the values af-

firmed in the teaching if one decides that the teaching does not bind or apply in a particular instance.

4. The teachings themselves are historically conditioned. What may have been perceived as morally wrong in one set of circumstances—e.g., charging interest on a loan in the Middle Ages—would be regarded as morally justifiable in another situation—e.g., charging interest on a loan today, in the context of modern commercial life.

On the other hand:

5. No individual or group of individuals can hope to identify and grasp moral truth by relying entirely on their own resources. We are all finite and sinful. We all need assistance and correction. We all rely on the moral vision of others as well as our own. The Church, as the Temple of the Holy Spirit and as a universal community, is a major resource of such moral direction and leadership. It is the product of centuries of experience, crossing cultural, national, and continental lines. Catholics in Latin America, for example, have challenged Catholics in more economically developed countries to respond to the global demands of justice. Catholics in the United States have helped Catholics in other parts of the world to be more aware of the dignity and the equality of women in the Church and in society alike.

While Catholics give antecedent attention and respect to official teachings, they must also take account of other sources of moral reflection and counsel—e.g., their associates, the findings of scientific disciplines, the Bible, the writings of theologians. Thus, the *Declaration on Religious Freedom* of the Second Vatican Council asserts: "In the formation of their consciences, the Christian faithful ought carefully to attend to the sacred and certain doctrine of the Church. The Church is, by the will of Christ, the teacher of truth. It is its duty to give utterance to, and authoritatively to teach, that truth which is Christ himself, and also to declare and confirm by its authority those principles of the moral order which have their origin in human nature itself" (n. 14). One is not a faithful Catholic who deliberately and systematically excludes all references to official church teachings in making moral decisions. At the same time, "the authority of the Church, when she pronounces on moral questions, in no way undermines the freedom of conscience of Christians" (Pope John Paul II, *Veritatis Splendor*, n. 64).

Prudence/Discernment

If it is not already clear from the preceding, it is surely clear from our own life experience that conscience poses a dilemma for all of us. On the one hand, we have to follow our conscience; on the other hand, our conscience may be wrong. In the latter case, we may be responsible for the erroneous conscience (in which instance our error is *vincible*) or our error may be beyond our control (*invincible* error). The former is the product of our *sinfulness*, the latter of our *finitude*.

The exercise of conscience, however, is always guided by the cardinal virtue of prudence. Prudence is essentially the capacity for *discernment*. It is not to be equated with an attitude of caution, restraint, timidity, or conservatism. Rather, the prudent person is one who can make decisions. Prudence formulates and imposes the correct dictates of reason upon the human person (*recta ratio agibilium*, as Thomas Aquinas put it). Prudence does not answer the question: "What is the best way *in principle* to do the right thing?" Rather: "What is the best way for me, *in this situation* (i.e., in the light of these relationships and responsibilities), to do the right thing?" The prudent person, therefore, must investigate the situation and take counsel from others. A judgment must be formulated in light of this inquiry and advice, and a decision must be made. The prudent person is in the moral order what a creative artist is in the intellectual and aesthetic orders. The novelist, for example, is constantly faced with the problem of deciding what to write and how to write it.

Prudence presupposes the following qualities: knowledge of moral principles, experience *and* the ability to profit by it, an ability to learn from others, an ability to make rational inferences, a certain inventiveness or creativity, vision or foresight, an ability to see and weigh circumstances, an ability to anticipate obstacles and plan to surmount them, and finally an ability to decide in light of all the preceding.

The virtue of prudence is closely allied with the *discernment of spirits* and with *spiritual direction*. To be a Christian is to live in

975

communion with the Spirit of God. It is to be open to that Spirit and receptive to the specific promptings of the Spirit. But the promptings of the Spirit are never unequivocally and unmistakably clear. If "no one has ever seen God" (John 1:18), neither has anyone seen the Spirit. One *infers* the Spirit's presence from what we do see, experience, and feel. The last reminds us of the importance of "reasons of the heart." This *discernment* is at once individual and corporate. Community discernment both derives from and leads to individual discernment. Community discernment presupposes prayer, but it also requires community discussion, the free exchange of opinions in a climate of truthfulness and mutual respect.

It is never easy to discern the Spirit. First, the Spirit itself is invisible and transcendent. Second, we are prone to rationalize in our own favor—i.e., to highlight those elements which support our predisposition toward one or another course of action and to ignore those elements which work against that predisposition. Third, many issues are complicated and do not admit ready solutions.

Although we can never be absolutely certain that we are indeed responding to the Spirit, there are certain *negative criteria* by which obviously false responses can be exposed: (1) If the discernment process does not issue forth in the classic "fruits" of the Spirit—love, joy, peace, patient endurance, kindness, generosity, faith, mildness, and chastity (Galatians 5:22–23)—it is probably not "of the Spirit." (2) If the discernment process leads to doctrinal or moral positions which are clearly inconsistent with the doctrinal tradition of the Church and/or with recognized norms of biblical and theological scholarship, it is probably not "of the Spirit." (3) If the discernment process intensifies the isolation and even spiritual eccentricities of those involved in it rather than enhancing the life of the whole Body of Christ (Ephesians 4:15–16), it is probably not "of the Spirit." (4) If the discernment process ignores pertinent information, rejects the counsel of others who have knowledge and experience in the matter at hand, and formulates its judgments by imposition rather than by corporate reflection, it is probably not "of the Spirit." (See also William C. Spohn, "The Reasoning Heart: An American Approach to Christian Discernment," in *Introduction to Christian Ethics: A Reader*, pp. 563–82; the article originally appeared in *Theological Studies* 44 [March 1983], pp. 30–52.)

976

The Christian moral life is, from beginning to end, a life "in the Spirit."

SUMMARY

1. There are three different *models* of the Christian moral life: the *deontological* (concerned with laws and obligations), the *teleological* (concerned with ends), and the *relational* (concerned with relationships with God, neighbor, world, and self).

2. The process by which the human person moves to Christian discipleship is called *conversion*.

3. Conversion in its more contemporary sense refers to a change in one's basic orientation, what theologians call the *fundamental option*.

4. The final test of conversion is whether or not it leads to and is continually manifested in *love for the neighbor*.

5. The Christian convert is called to become a person of *character*, that is, a person with the capacity for self-determination and for healthy, life-giving relationships.

6. A *virtue* is the facility, disposition, or attitude that moves one to accomplish moral good, and especially to do it joyfully and perseveringly even against inner and outer obstacles and at the cost of sacrifice.

7. There is a distinction between *general* virtues that affect the totality of our relationships (with God, neighbor, world, and self), and *particular* virtues that primarily affect specific relationships rather than the totality thereof.

8. The *theological virtues* of faith, hope, and charity affect the totality of our relationships. *Faith* is at once conviction, trust, and commitment. The first is intellectualist, the second is fiducial, and the third is performative.

9. Faith is not only an act but a *process*. Faith passes through stages of development. It is the task of catechesis to help at each stage of faith and moral development and to lead the person ultimately to full identification with Jesus Christ.

10. *Hope* is that virtue by which we take responsibility for the *future*, not simply *our* individual future but the future of the *world*. Hope is oriented toward the Kingdom of God, not as heaven alone but as the renewal and re-creation of the whole world.

11. No virtue is more fully expressive of the relational model of the Christian moral life than charity, or *love*. It is the heart of every other virtue and of the Christian life itself.

977

12. *Creative freedom* is the capacity or disposition to move beyond settled patterns of thinking and action, and *fidelity* is the disposition to maintain continuity in moral consciousness and behavior.

13. *Humility* is the particular virtue by which we are disposed to be open to the call and invitation of *God*.

14. *Gratitude,* or thankfulness, is the virtue by which Christians give thanks for the call and gifts of *God,* particularly through worship, and, more particularly still, in the Eucharist.

15. The particular virtue of *mercy* and *concern for the poor* is rooted in, and evoked by, the mercy and concern of God as manifested in the example of Christ himself. The virtue relates us to *neighbor.*

16. The particular virtue of *forgiveness,* also relating us to *neighbor,* is rooted in the fact that God has first forgiven us.

17. *Justice* is concerned with rights and with duties which correspond to those rights. Relating us also to *neighbor,* it is divided into *social, distributive, legal,* and *commutative* justice.

18. *Truthfulness* is the particular virtue directly opposed to hypocrisy. Although it primarily relates us to *neighbor,* it can also be applied to the *self,* in which case it becomes the particular virtue of *integrity.*

19. *Stewardship* is the particular virtue by which we care for the things of the *world* as goods entrusted to us by God for our sake and for the sake of future generations.

20. *Temperance* is the virtue which humanizes and moderates the pleasures of food, drink, and sex (the *concupiscible appetites*). It is closely allied with *asceticism.* Both are concerned primarily with the *self.*

21. *Fortitude,* also concerned primarily with the *self,* moderates our *irascible* appetites. It strengthens them against the passion of *fear,* on the one hand, and on the other restrains their immoderate tendencies toward *audacity* and *rashness.*

22. *Sin* is the breaking or damaging of our relationships with God, neighbor, world, and self.

23. In the Bible sin means "to miss the mark." In the *Old Testament* it is infidelity to the Covenant. In the New Testament it is a violation of the law of love, that is, acting against who we have become in Christ.

24. *Freedom* is the relatively limited capacity to decide who we shall be. It is that fundamental capacity for making a final and irrevocable choice to *be* someone, to be a particular kind of human being. We call that choice the "*fundamental option.*"

25. We can never be certain that we have finally and fully said "No" to God, even in an act which appears on the surface to be of such a kind.

26. In *venial sin* there is a genuine decision to do this or that *action* (the *categorical* dimension), but there is no decision to become this or that sort of *person* (the *transcendental* dimension).

27. *Mortal sin* is an act which fully engages the person. The person chooses not only the act but also the kind of person he or she wants to be or become in and through the act.

28. Thomas Aquinas understands *natural law* as the participation of the rational creature in the eternal law.

29. Natural law does not disclose divine commands, but the providential plan of final end and of intermediate ends within which human beings are to realize their perfection. Such a morality, therefore, is intrinsic, not extrinsic. *Something is commanded because it is good; it is not good because it is commanded.*

30. *Premoral values* are those concrete good things that ought to be done, to the extent possible. *Moral values* are those which are essential to proper human living.

31. *Material norms* tell us what we should *do*. *Formal norms* point to moral values which must be pursued. They indicate what is the right thing *to be*. Material norms give us information and direction; formal norms give us motivation and encouragement.

32. Medieval and post-Tridentine moral theology insisted that every moral act has to be evaluated in terms of *object, end,* and *circumstances*. This is known as the *three-source theory*, which stands in opposition to *utilitarianism* (the end justifies the act or the means).

33. *Proportionalism* is a type of analysis for determining the objective moral rightness or wrongness of human actions in conflict situations, as well as a procedure for establishing exceptions to behavioral norms. It is called pro-portionalism because it uses what it calls "proportionate reason" to deter-mine concretely and objectively the rightness or wrongness of acts and the various exceptions to the norms.

34. *Conscience* is the radical experience of ourselves as moral agents. *Christian* conscience is the radical experience of ourselves as new creatures in Christ, enlivened by the Holy Spirit.

35. The *dilemma* that we face is that we are required to follow our conscience, but, because of our sinfulness and finitude, our conscience can be wrong.

36. As a general rule, a person should not be prevented from following even an *erroneous* conscience, unless the action is seriously injurious to himself/herself, to others, or to the common good.

37. It is possible for a Catholic to *differ* with an official moral teaching of the Church. However, the Catholic should give antecedent attention and respect to such teachings and should ordinarily expect to be illumined by them.

38. The exercise of conscience, however, is always guided by the cardinal virtue of *prudence.* Prudence is essentially the capacity for *discernment.* Since it is never easy to discern the Spirit, one must consult various positive and negative criteria by which to judge one's discerning process.

SUGGESTED READINGS

Conn, Walter E., ed. *Conversion: Perspectives on Personal and Social Transformation.* New York: Alba House, 1978.

Curran, Charles E. *Directions in Fundamental Moral Theology.* Notre Dame, Ind.: University of Notre Dame Press, 1985.

———. *Toward an American Catholic Moral Theology.* Notre Dame, Ind.: University of Notre Dame Press, 1987.

———, ed. *Moral Theology: Challenges for the Future: Essays in Honor of Richard A. McCormick, S.J.* New York: Paulist Press, 1990.

Fuchs, Josef. *Human Values and Christian Morality.* Dublin: Gill and Macmillan, 1970.

Grisez, Germain, and Russell Shaw. *Fulfillment in Christ: A Summary of Christan Moral Principles.* Notre Dame, Ind.: University of Notre Dame Press, 1991.

Gula, Richard J. *Reason Informed by Faith: Foundations of Catholic Morality.* New York: Paulist Press, 1989.

Hamel, Ronald P., and Kenneth R. Himes, eds. *Introduction to Christian Ethics: A Reader.* New York: Paulist Press, 1989.

Happel, Stephen, and James J. Walter. *Conversion and Discipleship: A Christian Foundation for Ethics and Doctrine.* Philadelphia: Fortress Press, 1986.

Häring, Bernard. *Free and Faithful in Christ: Moral Theology for Clergy and Laity,* 3 vols. New York: Seabury Press, 1978–1981.

John Paul II, Pope. *Veritatis Splendor.* Origins 23/18 (October 14, 1993), pp. 297, 299–334.

McCormick, Richard A. *The Critical Calling: Reflections on Moral Dilemmas Since Vatican II.* Washington, D.C.: Georgetown University Press, 1989.

O'Connell, Timothy E. *Principles for a Catholic Morality,* rev. ed. San Francisco: Harper & Row, 1990.

XXVII

Christian Morality: Special Questions

This chapter seeks to clarify the meaning of the foundational principles described and explained in chapter 26 by showing how they are
variously applied to *selected* contemporary moral questions. Four
such questions are addressed in this chapter, two having to do with
interpersonal ethics and two having to do with *social ethics*. To be sure,
the distinction is not entirely satisfactory, because the interpersonal
also has a social and even political dimension.

The two issues of an interpersonal nature treated here are *birth
control* and *homosexuality*. Both do clearly have a public and political
dimension as well. The two socioethical issues are the *intervention of
the state* in the economic order and *abortion*, a public policy issue that
illustrates the relationship between moral law and civil law. The
emphasis in the chapter will always be on method, not solutions. It
engages in analysis, not advocacy.

Section One:
Interpersonal Ethics

BIRTH CONTROL

An Overview

The birth control question, once a sharply divisive issue in the Catholic Church, is no longer a matter of intense discussion among theologians. But it retains its importance as a paradigm of the twentieth-century debates concerning the nature of Catholic morality and the limits of Catholic teaching authority on moral issues.

There are two sides to the birth control question in Catholic moral theology. Neither side, however, rejects birth control totally and absolutely. The traditional position (reflected also in the official teaching of the Church) acknowledges, for example, that a married couple may deliberately employ the techniques of natural family planning (what used to be known as the rhythm method) by which sexual union is restricted to those days when the woman is biologically incapable of conceiving a child. That is clearly a form of birth control. What is really at issue here, therefore, is not birth control in this generic sense, but *contraception*, i.e., the intentional placing of a material obstacle to the conception of a child: e.g., a contraceptive pill, an intrauterine device, contraceptive foam, a condom.

One side argues that contraception by such artificial means is always wrong. (That remains the official teaching of the Church today.) The other side argues that contraception may be not only legitimate under certain circumstances but even mandatory. This side speaks in terms of "responsible parenthood." The two sides differ on three major counts: (1) their respective understandings of natural law; (2) their respective understandings of the binding force of official church teachings; and (3) their respective understandings of the development of doctrine.

The argument was joined in 1968 with the publication of Pope Paul VI's encyclical *Humanæ Vitæ* (*On the Regulation of Birth*). The pope had before him the majority and minority reports of a special papal commission established by his predecessor Pope John XXIII and continued in existence by himself. The majority proposed a change in the Catholic Church's traditional teaching by which contraception was condemned; the minority urged the pope to hold fast to that teaching, and raised the question of the impact of a change of view on the credibility of the papal magisterium. Pope Paul VI decided in favor of the minority view, and the rest is history. Theologians and even some episcopal conferences voiced opposition to the encyclical or at least took positions that were less than enthusiastic in their support. Surveys in the United States, for example, have indicated that the overwhelming majority (more than 80%) of Catholics of childbearing ages do not, in fact, observe the encyclical's teaching.

Official Teaching Prior to
Humanæ Vitæ

Pope Pius XI (d. 1939), in his encyclical *Casti Connubii* (1930), declared: "Since the conjugal act is destined primarily by nature for the begetting of children, those who in exercising it deliberately frustrate its natural power and purpose sin against nature and commit a deed which is shameful and intrinsically vicious.... Any use whatsoever of matrimony exercised in such a way that the act is deliberately frustrated in its natural power to generate life is an offense against the law of God and of nature and those who indulge in such are branded with the guilt of grave sin...."

Pope Pius XII (d. 1958) in his Allocution to Midwives (1951), reaffirmed this teaching: "Our predecessor ... solemnly restated the basic law of the conjugal act and conjugal relations: every attempt on the part of the married couple during the conjugal act ... to deprive it of its inherent power and to hinder the procreation of new life is immoral: no indication or need can change an action that is intrinsically immoral into an action that is moral and lawful. This prescription holds good today just as much as it did yesterday. It will hold tomorrow and always, for it is not a mere precept of human right but the expression of a natural and divine law."

On June 23, 1964, Pope Paul VI (d. 1978), after much discussion at the Second Vatican Council, promised a thorough review of the subject in the light of new knowledge but asked that the traditional teaching be observed in the meantime. He also reserved to himself the final decision on the matter. After much debate within the drafting committee, the council's *Pastoral Constitution on the Church in the Modern World* formulated its view in 1965 in this way: "Therefore, when there is question of harmonizing conjugal love with the responsible transmission of life, the moral aspect of any procedure does not depend solely on sincere intentions or on an evaluation of motives. It must be determined by objective standards. These, based on the nature of the human person and his or her acts, preserve the full sense of mutual self-giving and human procreation in the context of true love. Such a goal cannot be achieved unless the virtue of conjugal chastity is sincerely practiced. Relying on these principles, [members] of the Church may not undertake methods of regulating procreation which are found blameworthy by the teaching authority of the Church in its unfolding of the divine law" (n. 51).

On October 29, 1966, Paul VI stated that the official magisterium was in a state of "reflection" on the issue but not in a state of "doubt." On July 25, 1968, the matter was officially settled with the publication of the encyclical *Humanæ Vitæ* (literally, "Of Human Life").

Arguments in Support of the Traditional Teaching

The *first* argument given in the minority report of the Papal Commission for the Study of Population, the Family, and Birth (1966) is the "constant and perennial" teaching of the Church. The authors (John Ford, S.J., of the United States; Jan Visser, C.SS.R., of the Netherlands; Marcellino Zalba, S.J., of Rome; and Stanley de Lestapis, S.J., of France) cite those sources already referred to in the previous section of this chapter as well as several other assorted addresses of Pope Pius XII, the encyclical *Mater et Magistra* (1961) of Pope John XXIII, statements of various bishops, and the consistent answers given by the Holy See to questions on the subject from around the Catholic world.

"If the Church could err [on this issue], the authority of the ordinary magisterium in moral matters would be thrown into question. The faithful could not put their trust in the magisterium's presentation of moral teaching, especially in sexual matters." The question is not whether this teaching on birth control is "infallible" (i.e., immune from error) according to the traditional criteria of infallibility. "For if this doctrine is not substantially true, the magisterium itself will seem to be empty and useless in any moral matter." The assumption here seems to be that if the Church, or any comparable moral agency, can be found to be in error on this important matter, its judgment on *all* matters is automatically suspect.

The *second* major argument in favor of the traditional teaching is based on an analysis of the conjugal act itself. The minority theologians acknowledge, in what is perhaps the most remarkable statement in their entire report, that "if we could bring forward arguments which are clear and cogent based on reason alone, it would not be necessary for our commission to exist, nor would the present state of affairs exist in the Church as it is." What the conservative theologians bring forward, therefore, is a suggestion of a line of argument based on natural law, but not of such a character that it can equal the argument from authority in either clarity or force. Thus, "the Fathers, theologians, and the Church itself have always taught that certain acts and the generative processes are in some way specially inviolable precisely because they are generative. This inviolability is always attributed to the act and to the process, which are biological; not inasmuch as they are biological, but inasmuch as they are human, namely inasmuch as they are the object of *human acts* and are destined by their nature to the good of the human species." Contraception is evil, the minority report maintains, because it changes an act which is naturally oriented to procreation into an act which is oriented to the mutual benefit of the spouses.

But the minority report returns immediately to its first argument. The case does not depend finally on the strength of philosophical or even theological points. "It depends on the nature of human life and human sexuality, *as understood theologically by the Church*" (my italics). Indeed, in such a matter we "need the help of the teaching Church, explained and applied under the leadership of the magisterium, so that [we] can with certitude and security embrace the way, the truth, and the life."

Arguments Against the Official Teaching

According to the majority opinion, the argument in favor of the traditional teaching based on authority fails to recognize the *evolutionary* character of that teaching. The early Christian writers held that the use of sex in marriage was justified *only* for procreation. Later it was admitted that a sterile woman might marry and enjoy full conjugal relations. Eventually intercourse during the so-called safe period was approved. The next step would be to admit that the procreative value of the conjugal act is not bound up with every individual act of intercourse. Moreover, the official Church has changed its teachings in other matters—e.g., religious liberty and usury. One need only compare the teachings of Pope Pius IX and even of Leo XIII with Vatican II's *Declaration on Religious Freedom* (see chapter 18).

Catholic legal and ethical scholar John Noonan has argued that the condemnation of usury, or lending money at interest, was far more authoritative in terms of the biblical, patristic, conciliar, and theological sources adduced in support of the condemnation than was the condemnation of contraception (see his *Contraception: A History of Its Treatment by the Catholic Theologians and Canonists*, Cambridge, Mass.: Harvard University Press, 1965). And yet the teaching on usury changed because certain theologians in the sixteenth century concluded that economic conditions had changed, making the old condemnations obsolete, and that the experience of lay Christians had to be listened to. Thus, Navarrus (d. 1586), a professor at Salamanca in Spain and author of a *Manual for Confessors*, argued that an "infinite number of decent Christians" were engaged in exchange-banking, and he objected to any analysis which would "damn the whole world." Three papal bulls promulgated over a seventeen-year period (1569–1586) had unequivocally denounced and condemned usury. In a similarly short space of time, thirty years, the bulls were deprived of force to influence anyone's behavior. Theologians refused to support the teachings, and the laity continued about their business as if the teachings did not exist (see John Noonan, "The Amendment of Papal Teaching by Theologians," in *Contraception: Authority and Dissent*, Charles E. Curran, ed., New York: Herder & Herder, 1969, pp. 41–75).

Furthermore, a change in the traditional teaching would not necessarily undermine the moral teaching authority of the Church. According to the majority theologians on the birth control commission (Josef Fuchs, S.J., of Rome, Philippe Delhaye of Belgium, and Raymond Sigmond of Rome), "such a change is to be seen rather as a step toward a more mature comprehension of the whole doctrine of the Church. For doubt and reconsideration are quite reasonable when proper reasons for doubt and reconsideration occur with regard to some specific question. This is part and parcel of the accepted teaching of fundamental theology."

This majority view also rejects the natural-law theory of those who support the traditional teaching. It is a concept of nature as something so mysterious and sacred, they maintain, that any human intervention tends to destroy rather than perfect this very nature. Because of this mentality many advances in medical science were prohibited for a time, and the same was true of other areas of scientific experimentation. The dignity of the human person consists in this: "that God wished human beings to share in [the divine] dominion.... In the course of human life [human beings] must attain [their] perfection in difficult and adverse conditions, [they] must accept the consequences of [their] responsibility, etc. Therefore, the dominion of God is exercised through [human beings], who can use nature for [their] own perfection according to the dictates of right reason." It follows that we must use our skill to "intervene in the biological processes of nature so that [we] can achieve the ends of the institution of matrimony in the conditions of actual life, [rather] than [to] abandon [ourselves] to chance."

Indeed, the majority report argues, the conjugal act itself must be viewed not as an isolated reality but in the larger context of human love, family life, education, etc. (the *principle of totality*). Sexuality is not ordered only to procreation. Sacred Scripture says not only "Be fruitful and multiply" (Genesis 1:28), but also "they become one flesh" (2:24), portraying the partner as another helpful self (2:18). "In some cases intercourse can be required as a manifestation of self-giving love, directed to the good of the other person or of the community, while at the same time a new life cannot be received. This is neither egocentricity nor hedonism but a legitimate communication of persons through gestures proper to beings composed of body and soul with sexual powers."

Vatican II insisted that the decision to have children must take into account the welfare of the spouses and of their children, the material and spiritual conditions of the times, their state in life, the interests of the family group, of society, and of the Church. "The parents themselves should ultimately make this judgment in the sight of God" (*Pastoral Constitution on the Church in the Modern World*, n. 50). And Paul VI, in his encyclical *Populorum Progressio* (1967), acknowledged that "the population explosion adds to the difficulties of development.... Parents themselves must decide how many children to have. Parents themselves must consider their responsibilities before God and before each other, before their present children and before the community. Parents themselves must follow their consciences, formed by the law of God" (par. 37).

The final report of the Papal Birth Control Commission (June, 1966) followed this same line of argument, appealing to the *Pastoral Constitution on the Church in the Modern World*. The regulation of conception now appears "necessary for many couples who wish to achieve a responsible, open and reasonable parenthood in today's circumstances." The morality of sexual acts between married people "does not depend upon the direct fecundity of each and every particular act.... In a word, the morality of sexual actions is thus to be judged by the true exigencies of the nature of human sexuality, whose meaning is maintained and promoted especially by conjugal chastity...." On the other hand, the final report condemns what it calls a truly "contraceptive" mentality which egotistically and irrationally opposes all fruitfulness in marriage. But the "true opposition is not to be sought between some material conformity to the physiological processes of nature and some artificial intervention. For it is natural to the human person to use his [or her] skill in order to put under human control what is given by physical nature. The opposition is really to be sought between one way of acting which is contraceptive and opposed to a prudent and generous fruitfulness, and another way which is in an ordered relationship to responsible fruitfulness and which has a concern for education and all the essential human and Christian values."

With regard to the contraceptive method to be used, the report of the Papal Birth Control Commission suggested four criteria: (1) it must be consistent with the humanity of the persons and with the love the conjugal act is intended to express; (2) it must be effective; (3) it must exclude as many negative factors as possible—e.g., threats to health or hygiene; and (4) it must inevitably depend on what happens to be available in a certain region at a certain time for a certain couple, and this may depend on the economic situation. In any event, "condemnation of a couple to a long and often heroic abstinence as the means to regulate conception cannot be founded on the truth."

Humanæ Vitæ

The central teaching of Pope Paul VI's encyclical on the regulation of births is contained in its eleventh paragraph: "the Church calling human beings back to the observance of the norms of the natural law, as interpreted by constant doctrine, teaches that each and every marriage act must remain open to the transmission of life." The foundation for that teaching is a particular understanding of natural law as it applies to the conjugal act, namely, that there is an "inseparable connection, willed by God and unable to be broken by the human person on his [or her] own initiative, between the two meanings of the conjugal act: the unitive meaning and the procreative meaning" (n. 12). It is "unitive" in that it brings husband and wife together, and it is "procreative" in that it "capacitates them for the generation of new lives." The *principle of totality*, according to which contraception could be considered morally legitimate in the context of the totality of a fruitful married life, is declared erroneous (n. 14).

The encyclical's particular understanding of natural law clearly emerges in its defense of the rhythm method, or the restriction of marital relations to sterile periods of the month (now called natural family planning). In this case, the couple makes "legitimate use of a natural disposition; in the [other case], they impede the development of natural processes" (n. 16). The encyclical, therefore, rests its argument on the physiological structure of the act, while some contemporary theologians insist that the basic criterion for the meaning of human actions is the total person and not some isolated aspect of the person (see again chapter 26).

Indeed, even theologians who accept in principle an inseparable connection between the procreative and unitive elements of sexuality regard the explanation given in the encyclical as too strongly biological. Vatican II allowed for a wider basis for evaluating the morality of such a human act, namely, "the full sense of mutual self-giving and human procreation in the context of true love" (*Pastoral Constitution on the Church in the Modern World*, n. 51).

The encyclical also argues against contraception on the grounds that it leads to certain negative consequences: conjugal infidelity, a general lowering of morality, easy corruption of youth, loss of respect for women (n. 17).

Reaction to *Humanæ Vitæ*

The negative reaction of many theologians, moralists and nonmoralists alike, was vigorous and widespread. These can be sampled in such books as *Contraception: Authority and Dissent* (cited previously), *Human Sexuality: New Directions in American Catholic Thought: A Study Commissioned by the Catholic Theological Society of America* (New York: Paulist Press, 1977), pp. 114–28, and Joseph Komonchak's "*Humanæ Vitæ* and Its Reception: Ecclesiological Reflections," *Theological Studies* 39/2 (June 1978), pp. 221–57. A proencyclical view is presented in the same issue of *Theological Studies* by John C. Ford (one of the authors of the Papal Birth Control Commission's minority report) and Germain Grisez, "Contraception and the Infallibility of the Ordinary Magisterium," pp. 258–312.

Bishops' conferences around the world accepted the encyclical as authoritative teaching. However, some of these conferences drew attention, for example, to the primacy of conscience, the need to be understanding and forgiving, and the judgment that Catholics who sincerely cannot follow the encyclical's teaching are not thereby separated from the love of God. Such themes were sounded by the bishops of Belgium, Germany, the Netherlands, France, Canada, and the Scandinavian countries.

Catholics who cannot follow the encyclical's teaching "should not consider that because of this they are separated from God's love" (Belgian bishops). "Pastors must respect the responsible decisions of conscience made by the faithful" (German bishops). Although Catholics must show "respect to the authority and pronouncements of the pope," there are "many factors which determine one's personal conscience regarding marriage rules, for examples mutual love, the relations in a family, and social circumstances" (Dutch bishops). Contraception is always a disorder, "but this disorder is not always culpable." Thus, "when one faces a choice of duties, where one cannot avoid an evil whatever be the decision taken, traditional wisdom requires that one seek before God to find which is the greater duty. The spouses will decide after joint reflection" (French bishops). "No one, including the Church, can absolve anyone from the obligation to follow his [or her] conscience.... If someone for weighty and well-considered reasons cannot become convinced by the argumentation of the encyclical, it has always been conceded that he [or she] is allowed to have a different view from that presented in a non-infallible statement of the Church. No one should be considered a bad Catholic because he [or she] is of such a dissenting opinion" (Scandinavian bishops). All of these themes recur in the statement of the Canadian bishops: Such couples "may be safely assured that whoever honestly chooses that course which seems right to him [or her] does so in good conscience."

A similar, although more conservative, approach was taken by the Sacred Congregation for the Clergy (April 26, 1971) over the signature of its prefect, Cardinal John Wright (d. 1979), in response to a dispute between certain priests of the archdiocese of Washington, D.C., and their archbishop, Cardinal Patrick O'Boyle (d. 1987). Without equivocating on the clear meaning of *Humanæ Vitæ*, the Congregation acknowledged that "conscience is inviolable and no person is to be forced to act in a manner contrary to his [or her] conscience, as the moral tradition of the Church attests." Thus, in pastoral practice priests must not be too quick to assume either complete innocence or moral guilt in the persons they counsel. One must recognize persons who are "honestly trying to lead a good Christian life." There must be confidence "in the mercy of God and the forgiving power of Christ...."

Declaration on Certain Questions
Concerning Sexual Ethics

On December 29, 1975, the Congregation for the Doctrine of the Faith issued a declaration on sexual ethics which reaffirms the teaching of *Humanæ Vitæ* as well as that encyclical's particular understanding of natural law. But the declaration fixed its attention primarily on three particular issues: premarital sexual intercourse, homosexuality, and masturbation. It is particularly skeptical about the arguments of contemporary Catholic moral theologians regarding the difficulty of committing a real mortal sin, i.e., an act that involves the rejection of one's fundamental option toward God (n. 10). It is true, the Congregation acknowledged, that sins of the sexual order more frequently than other sins may lack full and free consent of the will, but "it in no way follows that one can hold the view that in the sexual field mortal sins are not committed" (n. 10).

Christian Values Underlying This Issue

In making moral decisions on this issue, there are certain undoubted principles which Catholics have to take into account:

1. The goodness of procreation, as an expression of mutual love and for the welfare of the human community at large.

2. The sanctity of human life.

3. The personal dignity and welfare of the spouses, their children, and their potential children.

4. The inviolability of conscience.

5. The responsibility to act on an informed conscience.

6. The right and responsibility of the Church to teach on matters pertaining to sexual morality. Clearly, the teaching of the Church involves that of pope and bishops, but other qualified teachers have a contribution to make as well.

7. The duty of Catholics to take such teaching seriously into account in the process of forming their consciences.

HOMOSEXUALITY

The Biblical Data

Wherever homosexuality is mentioned in the Bible it is condemned. It is a crime worthy of death (Leviticus 18:22; 20:13), a sin against nature (Romans 1:27), which excludes one from the Kingdom of God (1 Corinthians 6:9–10). God is said to have visited a terrible punishment upon Sodom for this sin (Genesis 19:1–29). One must remember, however, that various forms of sexual intercourse, including homosexuality, were considered a necessary part of worship by contemporary pagan groups. The severity of the Old Testament's judgment against homosexuality must be seen in that context. The Israelite would be imitating pagan cultic practices and would thereby defile himself or herself (Leviticus 18:3,20,24,30). The worship of Yahweh was to be unconditionally exclusive. No trace of pagan influence was to be countenanced. Such would be idolatrous and an abomination (e.g., Leviticus 18:26,29–30; Deuteronomy 12:31; 13:14; 17:4; 18:9; 2 Kings 16:3; 21:2,11; 2 Chronicles 33:2; Ezekiel 5:9,11). In a world where worship permeated every aspect of life, anything suggestive of pagan cultic practice—e.g., the fertility rites of the Canaanites—would be for the Israelite tantamount to infidelity to Yahweh.

Even after the danger of ritual intercourse had passed, the prohibition against homosexual activity was retained just as various dietary prescriptions had been maintained. The Talmud extended the prohibition, but not the death penalty, to women as well. The Levitical teaching, of course, had considerable influence on the Church, affecting Paul's estimation of the sexual practices of first-century Greeks. The Genesis story of Sodom and Gomorrah (Genesis 19) was even more influential on Christian thought. The early Christian writers would automatically assume that the sin for which Sodom was punished was the homosexual practice of sodomy. A parallel story speaks of the wickedness of the people of Gibeah (Judges 19:22–30) who seize a concubine and abuse her "all night until the following dawn, when they let her go."

What is common to the two stories—the one involving the male visitors of Sodom and the other, the female concubine of Gibeah—is rape. If sexuality is involved in the condemnations of both towns, it is less important than the issues of hospitality and justice. Indeed, there is no uniform tradition regarding Sodom's offense: for Isaiah it was injustice (1:10; 3:9); for Jeremiah, adultery, lying, and unrepentance (23:14); for Ezekiel, pride, gluttony, too much comfort, indifference to the poor and needy (16:49); for the Wisdom literature, folly, insolence, and inhospitality (Wisdom 10:8; 19:14; Sirach 16:8). Jesus refers to Sodom but makes no mention of its specific sin (Matthew 10:14–15, 11:23–24; Luke 10:12; 17:29). Not until late in the New Testament is an explicit link made between Sodom and sexuality (Jude 6–7; 2 Peter 2:4,6–10).

Sodom was to become for the early Christians a symbol of the depravity of Greek society. This, in turn, provides some background for the isolated references made to homosexual practices in the New Testament. Jesus says nothing about it. The Epistles mention it three times: in two instances as an item on a list of vices prevalent in first-century Rome (1 Corinthians 6:9–10; 1 Timothy 1:9–10), and in another, extended reference (Romans 1:18,22–28) to those who deliberately choose homosexual over heterosexual relations. There was, of course, no distinction between deliberate perversion and indeliberate homosexual orientation rooted in a particular personality with a particular psychological history and constitution.

Postbiblical Tradition

The early Christian writers were consistent in their denunciation of homosexuality: Augustine, John Chrysostom, et al. The sixth-century Code of Justinian added to pre-Christian laws protecting minors from homosexual violation the prohibition of all sodomistic practices under penalty of death by fire. This legal document had influence on both ecclesiastical and civil laws even into the Middle Ages, and perhaps indirectly into our own time in the West. Thomas Aquinas treated homosexual acts in connection with sins against temperance, specifically lust, and listed sodomy along with masturbation and bestiality as "unnatural vices" (*Summa Theologiæ* II-II, q. 154). Catholic moral theology, until very recently, made no discernible changes in Aquinas's approach. Although there were very few references to the sin in the Church's official teachings, the manuals regularly numbered homosexual acts alongside masturbation and bestiality as against nature and always gravely sinful. The appeal to Scripture is to the Sodom story.

Contemporary Authoritative Statements

Thus, from the time of Paul, through Thomas Aquinas, down to the statement of the Vatican's Congregation for the Doctrine of the Faith, "Observations Regarding Legislative Proposals Concerned With Discrimination Toward Homosexual Persons" (1992), official Catholic teaching has consistently judged all homosexual acts as at once unnatural and gravely sinful (*Origins* 22/10 [August 6, 1992], pp. 173, 175–77). The Congregation's 1986 pastoral letter to the world's bishops, "The Pastoral Care of Homosexual Persons," called not only the homosexual act "an intrinsic moral evil," but even the "inclination itself must be seen as an objective disorder" (n. 3; *Origins* 16/22 [November 13, 1986] 377, 379–82).

The hierarchical magisterium's argument is based on the principle of finality which, according to the Vatican's "Declaration on Sexual Ethics" in 1975, "states that the use of the sexual function has its true meaning and moral rectitude only in true marriage." The Declaration does not go into further detail regarding the norms of sexual life within marriage, but these norms are clearly taught in the encyclical letters *Casti Connubii* and *Humanæ Vitæ*. The 1975 Vatican document does make a distinction "between homosexuals whose tendency comes from a false education, from a lack of sexual development, from habit, from bad example, or from other similar causes, and is transitory or at least not incurable; and homosexuals who are definitively such because of some kind of innate instinct or a pathological constitution judged to be incurable." This second category of homosexuals "must certainly be treated with understanding and sustained in the hope of overcoming their personal difficulties and their inability to fit into society." But there is no basis for morally justifying their actions. "For according to the objective moral order, homosexual relations are acts which lack an essential and indispensable finality.... Homosexual acts are intrinsically disordered and can in no case be approved of."

Three Approaches

Notwithstanding the clear and unequivocal teaching of the hierarchical magisterium on this important moral issue, new questions are arising in light of new developments and scientific research in medicine, psychiatry, and psychology. In attempting to uphold the basic tradition and to respond to the contemporary findings, theologians have reacted in different ways to the question at hand. For purposes of illustration, we list and summarize three theological approaches here: (1) that homosexual acts are always sinful in themselves; (2) that they are neutral; and (3) that they are essentially imperfect, neither always wrong nor an ideal.

Homosexual Acts Are Always Sinful in Themselves

This position follows the approach of Thomas Aquinas. The order of nature requires that a male should join with a female so that procreation will occur and the human species will continue in existence. Sexual union between persons of the same sex is "unnatural" because procreation is impossible, whereas the act itself is ordered for that purpose alone. A leading defender of this view is Catholic theologian John F. Harvey, O.S.F.S. Harvey argues that, while a homosexual is not responsible for his orientation, he or she *is* responsible for controlling actions which spring from that orientation. Since all sexual acts outside of marriage are objectively immoral, homosexuals, like all other unmarried people, are called to a life without overt sexual activity (see "Homosexuality," *New Catholic Encyclopedia*, VII, New York: McGraw-Hill, 1967, pp. 117–19; and "Contemporary Theological Views," in *Counseling the Homosexual*, John R. Cavanaugh, ed., Huntington, Ind.: Our Sunday Visitor Press, 1977, pp. 235–37). Edward A. Malloy, C.S.C., also insists that the homosexual way of life, centered on the pursuit of unrestricted sexual pleasure, is irreconcilable with the Christian way of life because it is opposed to the three basic values of chastity, love, and faithfulness (*Homosexuality and the Christian Way of Life*, Washington, D.C.: University Press of America, 1981). However, in the final pastoral section at the end of his book, he provides some limited acceptance of homosexual couples committed to a permanent and exclusive relationship, without prejudice to the Christian ideal of celibacy (pp. 359–60).

The teaching of the official magisterium is unmistakably clear. The 1975 *Declaration on Sexual Ethics* from the Sacred Congregation for the Doctrine of the Faith insists that "homosexual acts are intrinsically disordered and can in no case be approved of" (n. 8), a position reaffirmed in the 1986 pastoral letter of the same Congregation and extended even to the "inclination" itself (n. 3). And the National Conference of Catholic Bishops of the United States adopted the same approach in its *Principles to Guide Confessors in Questions of Homosexuality* (Washington, D.C.: NCCB, 1973): genital sexual expression may take place only in marriage; each such act must be open in principle to procreation and must as well be an expression of mutual love between a husband and a wife. Although homosexual acts are "a grave transgression of the goals of human sexuality and of human personality, and are consequently contrary to the will of God" (p. 3), the confessor must avoid "both harshness and permissiveness. . . . But, generally, [the homosexual] is responsible for his [or her] actions, and the worst thing that a confessor can say is that the homosexual is not responsible for his [or her] actions" (pp. 8–9). Overt homosexuals are not to be encouraged to receive the Eucharist (pp. 14–15). Finally, while the *Catechism of the Catholic Church* (1992) also reaffirms the teaching that homosexual acts are "intrinsically disordered," it does not lay blame on the homosexual for the orientation or condition. On the contrary, it explicitly asserts that they "do not choose their homosexual condition," and insists that they "must be accepted with respect, compassion and sensitivity" and are not to be subject to "unjust discrimination."

Homosexual Acts Are Morally Neutral

This position argues that the morality of the sexual act depends upon the quality of the relationship. The moral determination does not rest on whether the act is heterosexual or homosexual, but rather on the quality of the relationship of the persons. Accordingly, "It is the task of homosexuals to acknowledge themselves as such before God, accept their sexual inclination as their calling, and explore the meaning of this inclination for the Christian life" (Gregory Baum, "Catholic Homosexuals," *Commonweal* 99 [February 15, 1974], p. 481).

Another exponent of the neutrality view is John J. McNeill, a former Jesuit priest. In his book, *The Church and the Homosexual* (New York: Pocket Books, 1978), he argues that the basic moral norm for sexuality, whether for heterosexuals or homosexuals, is love, and that sexual relations can be justified morally if they are a true expression of human love. Among the conditions for a genuine intrapersonal love relationship are mutuality, fidelity, and unselfishness (see pp. 111–17, 207–8). The nature of the love relationship, not its procreative aspect, is the norm for sexual expression.

This view is at variance not only with the official teaching of the Church, but also with the views even of so-called revisionist Catholic theologians. "It would seem," such theologians have argued against this "neutral" approach, "that the elements of mutual love, fidelity, and caring need more detailed and specific explanation if this approach is to provide a suitable pastoral norm for counseling homosexuals" (*Human Sexuality: New Directions in American Catholic Thought*, Anthony Kosnik, et al. New York: Paulist Press, 1976, p. 206). Charles E. Curran is critical of McNeill's heavy emphasis on freedom, without recognizing its limitation by our multiple relationships with others, the world, and ourselves, and he is also critical of McNeill's contention that male-female differences and complementarity do not enter into the meaning of human sexuality (see "Moral Theology and Homosexuality," in *Critical Concerns in Moral Theology*, pp. 87–88).

Homosexual Acts Are Essentially Imperfect

A third position has been described by one of its principal advocates, Charles E. Curran, as a mediating one, that is, between those who hold the traditionally accepted approach and those who hold for a more radical position (op. cit., p. 93). His position is that "for an irreversible, constitutional, or genuine homosexual, homosexual acts in the context of a loving relationship striving for permanency are objectively morally good. On the other hand, the ideal meaning of human sexual relationships is in terms of male and female" (pp. 92–93).

He fits this position into a broader theory, which he himself calls a "theology of compromise." According to this theory, because of the presence of the sin of the world, "Christians are justified in doing certain acts which would not be justified without the presence of such sin of the world." By "sin of the world," he means the "objective condition... existing independently of one's own responsibility or guilt." This objective condition is not a good; it is an evil. But it is not a *moral* evil. "Christians are called, in general, to struggle against such evil, but it is not always possible to overcome it" (p. 93).

Philip S. Keane, S.S., takes a similar position in his *Sexual Morality: A Catholic Perspective* (New York: Paulist Press, 1977). He calls it an "ontic but not necessarily moral evil" approach to homosexual acts. He accords "a priority or normativity to heterosexual acts and relationships," and holds that homosexual acts "always involve a significant degree of ontic evil because of their lack of openness to procreation and to the man/woman relationship as it functions in marriage." At the same time, "there are cases in which the ontic evil in homosexual acts does not become an objective moral evil because in the circumstances germane to these cases it is truly proportionate for the homosexual acts to be posited." Such cases are those where the homosexual "is not free to be otherwise or to be perfectly chaste" and is "achieving responsible relationships and personal growth in his or her homosexual acts..." (p. 87).

For another rendering of this third position from a more deliberately pastoral point of view, see Richard A. McCormick, *The Critical Calling*, pp. 289–314.

Christian Values Underlying This Issue

In making moral decisions on this issue, there are certain undoubted principles which Catholics have to take into account.

1. The goodness of procreation, as an expression of mutual love and for the welfare of the human community at large.

2. The personal dignity of every human being, regardless of his or her sexual orientation, and the existence of natural and civil rights which flow from that dignity.

3. The need of every person for love, friendship, even intimacy, although not necessarily of a genitally sexual nature.

4. The inviolability of conscience.

5. The responsibility to act on an informed conscience.

6. The existence of many internal and external impediments to full human freedom.

7. The right and responsibility of the Church to teach on matters pertaining to sexual morality. Clearly, the teaching of the Church involves that of pope and bishops, but other qualified teachers have a contribution to make as well.

8. The duty of Catholics to take such teaching seriously into account in the process of forming their consciences.

Section Two:
Social Ethics

THE INTERVENTION OF THE STATE IN THE ECONOMIC ORDER

Subsidiarity and Socialization

This issue illustrates the thrust of Catholic teaching on questions of social justice, and shows the nature of the Church as a community of moral discourse. It is "a gathering of people with the explicit intention to survey and critically discuss their personal and social responsibilities in the light of moral convictions about which there is some consensus and to which there is some loyalty" (James Gustafson, *The Church as Moral Decision-Maker*, Philadelphia: Pilgrim Press, 1970, p. 84). The Church does not pretend, and should not be expected, to have precise answers to complex social and political questions. Rather it attempts only to elaborate a framework of values, principles, and responsibilities within which a discussion of such issues can be carried on, the formation of a Christian conscience can be promoted, and decisions fundamentally consistent with the Christian tradition can be made. This is also the position taken by Pope John Paul II in *Sollicitudo Rei Socialis* (n. 41) and *Centesimus Annus* (nn. 43 and 47).

The question of the right and duty of the state to intervene in the economic order highlights the relationship between two important elements of Catholic social doctrine: the *principle of subsidiarity* and the *process of socialization*. Both are expressed in the social encyclicals of Pope John XXIII, *Mater et Magistra* (1961) and *Pacem in Terris* (1963), and elsewhere in the social teachings of Paul VI and John Paul II. The *principle of subsidiarity*, according to which nothing is to be done at a higher level which can be done as well or better at a lower level, places the burden of proof for intervention always on the higher body, principally the state. This is a conservative principle; it leans against state intervention. The *socialization process* reminds us of our growing interdependence and the benefits that can be produced when there is planned interventionist action on the part of the state. It is not just that a lower group cannot do something as well or better than the state, but that there are simply too many groups, institutions, structures, and political factors for any one group or level apart from the state to meet a problem common to all of these diverse social elements. To the extent that socialization can also be considered a principle, it is a liberal principle; it encourages state intervention.

These two principles are to be understood as dialectically related, in creative tension one with another. "The thrust of subsidiarity is to preserve a sphere of freedom, while recognizing the need for a certain degree of centralization and control. The counterthrust of socialization is to highlight the need for coordination and direction of complex social systems if they are to benefit the citizens for whom they exist" (J. Bryan Hehir, "Church and State: Basic Concepts for Analysis," *Origins* 8/24, November 30, 1978, p. 381). In deciding for or against state intervention, and also regarding the degree and type of intervention, both values have to be taken into account.

Recent Catholic Teaching

Papal Teaching: Leo XIII to John Paul II

The *principle of subsidiarity* was first formally articulated by *Pope Pius XI* in his encyclical *Quadragesimo Anno* (1931): "It is a fundamental principle of social philosophy, fixed and unchangeable, that one should not withdraw from individuals and commit to the community what they can accomplish by their own enterprise and industry. So, too, it is an injustice and at the same time a grave evil and a disturbance of right order, to transfer to the larger and higher collectivity functions which can be performed and provided for by lesser and subordinate bodies" (cited also by Pope John XXIII's *Mater et Magistra*, 1961, par. 53). Although this is a conservative principle, it does not justify a laissez-faire approach by which the state allows the economic order to run by its own power and according to its own designs. The encyclical *Quadragesimo Anno* clearly placed the Church on the side of those arguing that economic activity should be regulated for the sake of the common good.

Pope Pius XII and *Pope John XXIII* carried this principle of subsidiarity forward to meet the growing complexity of the economic order (so, too, has Pope John Paul II, in *Centesimus Annus*, n. 48, as we shall see later). Although Pius XII's contributions never took the form of an encyclical letter, they were nevertheless incorporated into the explicit social teachings of John XXIII. Pius XII is cited in 34 of the 73 footnotes in John XXIII's *Pacem in Terris*. In *Mater et Magistra* John XXIII moved the discussion of state intervention to a new level of clarity and development. First, he reasserted the validity of the principle of subsidiarity as a norm of social policy. Second, he called attention to the substantially changed social and political context in which that principle has to function today. And, third, he introduced the notion of socialization as a complement to that of subsidiarity.

John XXIII argued that the role of the state in society had to be understood in light of three contemporary elements: (1) the impact of technological change, (2) the rise of the welfare state, and (3) the growing aspirations of people to participate in the political process (pars. 46–50). From the confluence of these three elements, John XXIII proposed his notion of *socialization* (par. 59; see also Vatican II, *Pastoral Constitution on the Church in the Modern World*, n. 25). This process, he argued, is at once the result and cause of increasing state intervention in the socioeconomic order. The need to intervene follows from such basic needs as health care, education, housing. Such intervention has both positive and negative effects. On balance, John XXIII finds the benefits outweighing the liabilities.

Also at the heart of Catholic social doctrine and centrally related to the policy judgment the state has to make about intervention is the teaching on *rights and duties*. The clearest statement of which rights are necessary to preserve the human dignity of each person in society is found in John XXIII's *Pacem in Terris* (pars. 8–35). The concept of *right* implies a *moral claim* by a person to some good of the physical or spiritual order which is necessary for proper human development and dignity. When such a right is established, a correlative duty is also established to recognize the right and to see to it that it is fulfilled either through private action or through governmental action.

It is one of government's principal responsibilities to balance rights and duties of members and groups within society. The state must recognize and reinforce those rights which protect the individual or groups from undue intrusion by public authority. It must also determine when and in what way the state can be used to promote the socioeconomic rights of people, especially those in need and/or the politically weak. *Pacem in Terris* refers specifically to those rights: "the right to life, to bodily integrity, and to the means which are necessary and suitable for proper development of life; these are primarily food, clothing, shelter, rest, medical care, and finally the necessary social services. Therefore a human being also has the right to security in case of sickness, inability to work, widowhood, old age, unemployment or in any other case in which he [or she] is deprived of the means of subsistence through no fault of his [or her] own" (par. 11).

Pope Paul VI brought Catholic social doctrine yet another step beyond John XXIII when, in *Octagesima Adveniens* (1971), he emphasized the responsibility of the political sector in the task of assuring justice for people in society. The ultimate decision in the social and economic field, both national and international, rests with political power (par. 46). The document does not provide solutions to complex policy questions, but it locates the ultimate arena where such questions are decided, and it thereby calls attention to the role of the state as the final agency of justice if other means fail to provide minimum economic justice for people. Thus, state intervention in some cases may be not only legitimate but even imperative.

In his address to the 34th General Assembly of the United Nations Organization (October 1979), Pope John Paul II argued that "it is a question of the highest importance that in internal social life, as well as in international life, all human beings in every nation and country should be able to enjoy effectively their full rights under any political regime or system" (n. 19).

Pope John Paul II advanced Catholic social doctrine substantially with his three major social encyclicals, *Laborem Exercens* (1981), *Sollicitudo Rei Socialis* (1988), and *Centesimus Annus* (1991). "One of the greatest injustices in the contemporary world," he wrote in *Sollicitudo Rei Socialis*, "consists precisely in this: that the ones who possess much are relatively few and those who possess almost nothing are many. It is the injustice of the poor distribution of the goods and services originally intended for all" (n. 28). He applied this principle to the international order as well, pointing out that "the stronger and richer nations must have a sense of moral responsibility for the other nations" (n. 39; see also *Centesimus Annus*, n. 35).

But Pope John Paul II's most explicit statements about the role and responsibility of government are to be found in *Centesimus Annus*. Invoking the name and authority of Pope Leo XIII, whose pioneering social encyclical *Rerum Novarum* (1891) John Paul's own encyclical was commemorating, he declared that "the more that individuals are defenseless within a given society, the more they require the care and concern of others, and in particular the intervention of governmental authority" (n. 10). He also appealed to Leo in criticizing the view that "completely excludes the economic sector from the state's range of interest and action" (n. 15; see also n. 48).

John Paul II spoke of the economic rights of workers that are to be guaranteed by the state: social security, pensions, health insurance and compensation in the case of accidents, unemployment insurance, a safe working environment, the right to form labor unions (nn. 15, 34). In a society which upholds "the absolute predominance of capital," justice demands that "the market be appropriately controlled by the forces of society and by the state so as to guarantee that the basic needs of the whole of society are satisfied" (n. 35). The state also has a specific right and duty to intervene to protect the common goods of all, especially the environment (n. 40).

He cited additional purposes for governmental intervention in the economic order: the sustaining of business activities to ensure job opportunities, the regulation of monopolies, exercising a "substitute function when social sectors or business systems are too weak or are just getting under way and are not equal to the task at hand" (n. 48). The range of such interventions in recent years, he pointed out, has created a new type of state, known as the "welfare state." The pope acknowledged its positive and negative aspects, and invoked the principle of subsidiarity to help curb the latter (n. 48)

Love for others and "in the first place" love for the poor is "made concrete in the promotion of justice." For societies, for individual governments, and for the world political community it is "not merely a matter of 'giving from one's surplus,' but of helping entire peoples which are presently excluded or marginalized to enter into the sphere of economic and human development. For this to happen, it is not enough to draw on the surplus goods which in fact our world abundantly produces; it requires, above all else a change of lifestyles, of models of production and consumption, and of the established structures of power which today govern societies" (n. 58).

Many of these teachings have been recapitulated in the *Catechism of the Catholic Church* (1992) in its discussion of the Seventh Commandment.

Vatican II

The Second Vatican Council's *Pastoral Constitution on the Church in the Modern World* adopted the same basic position as the recent popes. In principle, government has the right and the duty to intervene in the economic order to ensure and promote justice, to defend the interests of the weak against the strong, and to see to it that the material goods which belong in principle to all are fairly distributed to all. "Because of the increased complexity of modern circumstances," the council declared, "government is more often required to intervene in social and economic affairs, by way of bringing about conditions more likely to help citizens and groups freely attain human fulfillment with greater effect" (n. 75). This is the case because "God intended the earth and all that it contains for the use of every human being and people." Therefore, according to the ability of each, "let all individuals and governments undertake a genuine sharing of their goods. Let them use these goods especially to provide individuals and nations with the means for helping and developing themselves" (n. 69).

U.S. Catholic Bishops

Although it represents the teaching of only one episcopal conference, albeit one of the world's largest, the U.S. Catholic Bishops' pastoral letter, "Economic Justice for All: Catholic Social Teaching and the U.S. Economy" (1986), contains perhaps the most explicit and detailed moral justification for the intervention of government in the economic order. *Social justice* requires that people be assured a minimum level of participation in the economy (nn. 15 and 71). *Distributive justice* requires that the economic benefits and burdens of society be distributed fairly and that the rights of the poor have a special priority (nn. 16 and 70). *Commutative justice,* regulating agreements and exchanges between individuals and private groups (n. 69) must always be balanced against the two preceding forms of justice. The emphasis throughout the letter is on the *common good* (n. 21).

For the bishops, government's primary obligation is to the poor (n. 86). Indeed, "*government has a moral function: protecting human rights and securing basic justice for all members of the commonwealth*" (n. 122; italics in original). Moreover, the "way society responds to the needs of the poor through its public policies is the litmus test of its justice or injustice." Government, therefore, must empower the poor, the disadvantaged, the disabled, and the unemployed; it must generate employment, establish fair labor practices, maintain the economy's infrastructure (bridges, harbors, public transportation), regulate trade and commerce, and impose a fair tax system based on the ability to pay (n. 123).

Government action, to be sure, must be guided and restrained by the principle of subsidiarity, but this does not mean that "the government that governs least governs best" (n. 124). The precise form of governmental intervention cannot be determined in the abstract. It will depend upon an assessment of the specific needs and of the most effective ways to meet those needs. The pastoral letter itself addresses four specific subjects: employment (nn. 136–69), poverty (nn. 170–215), food and agriculture (nn. 216–50), and the U.S. role in the global economy (nn. 251–94). There are exceedingly detailed analyses and policy recommendations under each heading.

Perhaps the most significant portion of the whole pastoral letter is its application of its moral principles to the Church itself: "*All the moral principles that govern the just operation of any economic endeavor apply to the church and its agencies and institutions; indeed the church should be exemplary"* (n. 347; italics in original). Although the pastoral letter does not appeal explicitly to the principle of sacramentality, it is that principle that theologically undergirds its position. This means that the Church must put into practice what it urges upon government, business, labor, and other economic actors in society. Thus, if business is bound in justice to provide adequate salaries and benefits, so too is the Church. If business must recognize the rights of workers to unionize, so too must the Church (see nn. 351–58).

Christian Values Underlying This Issue

In making moral decisions on this issue, there are certain undoubted principles which Catholics have to take into account.

1. The universal destiny of the goods of the earth.

2. The moral priority of the common good over one's own individual good.

3. The duty of government to guarantee fairness and the enforcement of rights in the economic order, especially on behalf of the poor.

4. The limitations on that duty imposed by the principle of subsidiarity.

5. The right and responsibility of the Church to articulate a moral vision on matters of social and economic policy. Clearly, the teaching of the Church involves that of pope and bishops, but other qualified teachers have a contribution to make as well.

6. The duty of Catholics to take such teaching and such a moral framework seriously into account in the process not only of forming their consciences but of expressing their views in the socioeconomic and political orders.

7. The obligation of the Church to practice what it preaches.

ABORTION

If the preceding issue raises the question of the proper role of the state in the economic order, the abortion issue raises the question of the proper role of religious bodies (including the Church) in the public order. More broadly, it raises the question of the relationship between the moral law and the civil law.

Although the abortion issue, since the *Roe v. Wade* decision of the U.S. Supreme Court in 1973, has had its primary political impact in the United States, it has also been the subject of much national tension and debate in other countries like Ireland and Poland. However, the broader issue—the relationship between the moral law and the civil law—continues to be played out not only in countries where there is a significant Catholic presence, but also in countries with a significant Islamic presence.

The morality of abortion is not at issue here. The official teaching of the Church, as an interpretation of the natural law, is taken as a given in the discussion that follows.

Moral Law Versus Civil Law

Whether abortion is defined as a civil rights issue (the pregnant woman's right to choose, or the right to privacy) or as a human rights issue (the fetus' right to life), it is always reducible to a question of *law*. Should the law allow abortions or not? Should the law authorize the use of tax monies to pay for abortions or not? More broadly, should the civil law mirror the moral law, and, if so, whose version of the moral law?

The orders of moral and civil law are frequently confused. Either morality is thought to be determinative of law, or law is thought to be determinative of morality. According to the first view, whatever is good should be enforced by law and whatever is evil should be prohibited by law. According to the second view, whatever is legal is by that fact moral, and whatever is not against the law is thereby morally acceptable. "From the foolish position that all sins ought to be made crimes," the late Jesuit theologian John Courtney Murray (d. 1967) once wrote, "it is only a step to the knavish position that since certain acts... are obviously not crimes, they are not even sins" (*We Hold These Truths: Reflections on the American Proposition*, New York: Sheed & Ward, 1960, p. 158).

Neither view respects the *difference* between the moral law and the civil law. The former "governs the entire order of human conduct,

personal and social; it extends even to motivations and interior acts."
The latter "looks only to the public order of human society; it touches
only external acts, and regards only values that are formally social"
(ibid., p. 166). Thus, the scope of civil law is limited, and its moral
aspirations are minimal. To have made the *moral* argument against
abortion is not necessarily to have made the *legal* argument.

Murray's view is entirely consistent with the Catholic tradition,
as expressed particularly in Thomas Aquinas. Although civil law is
concerned with leading everyone to virtue, he wrote, it does so
gradually, not suddenly. "Therefore it does not lay upon the multitude of imperfect people the burdens of those who are already virtuous, namely, that they should abstain from all evil. Otherwise these
imperfect ones, being unable to bear such precepts, would break out
into yet greater evils.... Therefore, human law does not prohibit
everything that is forbidden by the natural law" (*Summa Theologiæ*,
I-II, q. 96, a. 2). Conversely, civil law does not codify all virtues. Since
human law is always and only ordered to the common good, it
prohibits vices and prescribes virtues only to the extent that one or
the other "can be ordered to the common good" (a. 3). The making of
such laws "belongs either to the whole people or to a public personage who has care of the whole people" (I-II, q. 90, a. 3). In the case of a
democracy, it is the whole people, directly or through their elected
representatives, who alone can decide what laws they will live by for
the sake of justice and peace.

In the Catholic tradition, a good law must be *enforceable*. Otherwise, it will be disregarded and contempt for all law is risked. But a
law is only enforceable to the extent that it is based on a *consensus*. In a
pluralistic society, however, winning consent for a law, necessary for
its enforcement, is very difficult. What are we to do in that case?

Murray offers four guidelines: (1) Each group within society
retains the right to demand conformity from its members, regardless
of the civil law. (Thus, Catholics are still forbidden by the moral law to
have abortions even if the civil law permits them. At the same time,
the civil law cannot command them to have an abortion.) (2) No
group in a pluralistic society has the right to expect a government to
impose or prohibit some act of behavior when there is no support for
such action in society at large. (3) Any group has the right to work
toward building the necessary consensus through persuasion and

pacific argument. (4) No group has the right to impose its own religious or moral views on others through force, coercion, or violence.

It is evident, however, that the Church has failed thus far to convince even its own members not to have abortions. Catholic women have abortions today with the same frequency as non-Catholic women.

Vatican II

"It is highly important, especially in pluralistic societies," Vatican II's *Pastoral Constitution on the Church in the Modern World* declared, "that a proper view exist of the relation between the political community and the Church. Thus the faithful will be able to make a clear distinction between what a Christian conscience leads them to do in their own name as citizens, whether as individuals or in association, and what they do in the name of the Church and in union with its shepherds."

The council specifically cautions the Church against a too close identification with any political system. Its proper role is not to become one political agent among others or to enter into formal or informal alliance with one or another political party or force, but to preach the truth of the Gospel and shed light on all areas of human activity through its teaching and through the example of its members. At the same time, the Church must show "respect for the political freedom and responsibility of citizens" and it must foster those values. In speaking on behalf of justice and human dignity, the Church seeks no special privileges from the civil authority, and it must be prepared to renounce those privileges already acquired "if it becomes clear that their use raises doubts about the sincerity of its witness and that new conditions of life demand some other arrangement" (n. 76).

Concluding Reflections

Should abortion be made illegal? Yes, but only in those societies where there is a consensus to make such a law enforceable. If it is not possible to legislate a total ban on abortion, is it permissible to support laws that place restrictions on it but otherwise allow it? Yes again, because laws can only go so far as the consensus in society will allow them to go. Otherwise, they are not enforceable.

The answer to the first question, "Should abortion be made illegal?" would have been "No" if abortion were a perfectly moral or at least morally neutral act. Those who believe that it is one or the other generally oppose all legal restrictions on a woman's right to an abortion. Their position is eminently logical. Those who regard every abortion as the termination of innocent human life, at one or another stage of development, are equally convinced that such an act needs to be restricted or prohibited by law. In a pluralistic society, where consensus on such an issue does not exist, only the path of political compromise is possible. St. Thomas Aquinas said as much over seven hundred years ago.

Christian Values Underlying This Issue

In making moral decisions on this issue, there are certain undoubted principles which Catholics have to take into account:

1. The dignity of human life at every stage of development.

2. The difference between the moral law and the civil law.

3. The right and duty of Catholics to work to change a consensus that is in opposition to the moral law.

4. The limitations on that duty imposed by life in a pluralistic society.

5. The right and responsibility of the Church to articulate a moral vision on matters of public policy. Clearly, the teaching of the Church involves that of pope and bishops, but other qualified teachers have a contribution to make as well.

6. The duty of Catholics to take such teaching seriously into account not only in forming their consciences but in participating in the political process.

SUMMARY

1. The *traditional teaching* against *birth control,* or contraception, is based on a structural analysis of the conjugal act itself as naturally oriented toward

procreation and on an appeal to previous authoritative teachings of the Church.

2. The argument *against* the traditional teaching emphasizes the evolutionary character of the Church's traditional teaching on sexual morality, on a nonphysicalist understanding of natural law, and on the principle of totality, according to which the conjugal act is to be viewed in relation to such values as human love, family life, education.

3. *Humanæ Vitæ* reaffirmed the traditional teaching: "Each and every marriage act must remain open to the transmission of life."

4. The reaction to *Humanæ Vitæ* was diverse: all the way from unequivocal acceptance to outright rejection.

5. There are certain *Christian values* underlying the issue of birth control which must always be taken into account, including the goodness of procreation, personal dignity and human welfare, the inviolability of conscience and the responsibility to act on an informed conscience, the right and responsibility of the Church to teach on such matters, and the duty of Catholics to take such teaching seriously into account.

6. The Catholic tradition has consistently judged all *homosexual* acts as at once unnatural and gravely sinful.

7. There are three principal theological approaches to the question today: (1) Homosexual acts are *always sinful* in themselves because they are unnatural; (2) homosexual acts are morally *neutral;* and (3) homosexual acts are *essentially imperfect.*

8. There are certain *Christian values* underlying this issue of homosexuality which must always be taken into account, including the goodness of procreation, the personal dignity of every human being, the need of every person for love, friendship, even intimacy, the inviolability of conscience and the responsibility to act on an informed conscience, the existence of many internal and external impediments to full human freedom, the right and responsibility of the Church to teach on matters of this sort, and the duty of the Catholic to take such teaching seriously into account.

9. Catholic teaching on the *intervention of government in the economic order* is based on the principle of subsidiarity and the process of socialization.

10. The *principle of subsidiarity* holds that nothing is to be done at a higher level which can be done as well or better at a lower level. The *process of socialization* highlights the need for coordination and direction of complex social systems in order to benefit the citizens for whom they exist.

11. *Vatican II* and the *popes,* from Leo XIII to John Paul II, have consistently affirmed the right and duty of the state to intervene in the economic order for

the sake of social and distributive justice. Recent popes in particular have stressed the "preferential option for the poor."

12. The *U.S. Bishops' 1986 pastoral letter on the economy* offered highly detailed proposals to implement Catholic social principles in the economic order. Significantly, the letter also applied those principles to the Church itself.

13. Among the *Christian values* underlying this issue of *governmental intervention in the economic order* are the universal destiny of the goods of the earth, the moral priority of the common good over one's own individual good, the duty of government to guarantee fairness and the enforcement of rights in the economic order, especially on behalf of the poor, the right and duty of the Church to teach on this question, the duty of Catholics to take such teaching seriously into account, and the obligation of the Church to practice what it preaches.

14. *Abortion* is not only a moral issue in its own right, but a public policy issue as well. It raises the question of the difference between the *moral* law and the *civil* law.

15. The *moral law* governs the entire order of human conduct, personal and social; it extends even to motivations and interior acts. The *civil law* looks only to the public order of human society; it touches only external acts, and regards only values that are formally social. To have made the *moral* argument against abortion is not necessarily to have made the *legal* argument.

16. Good law must be *enforceable*. But it cannot be enforced without a *consensus* in society to support its enforcement. Those who wish to translate moral law into civil law in a pluralistic society need to build the necessary consensus.

17. Among the *Christian values* underlying this issue of *abortion* are the dignity of human life, the right and duty of the Church to articulate a moral vision on matters of public policy, and the duty of Catholics to take such teaching seriously into account, not only in forming their consciences but in participating in the political process.

SUGGESTED READINGS

Bernardin, Joseph Cardinal, et al. *Consistent Ethic of Life.* Kansas City, Mo.: Sheed & Ward, 1988.

Cahill, Lisa Sowle. *Women and Sexuality.* New York: Paulist Press, 1992.

Coleman, John A., ed. *One Hundred Years of Catholic Social Thought: Celebration and Challenge.* Maryknoll, N.Y.: Orbis Books, 1991.

Curran, Charles E. *Moral Theology: A Continuing Journey.* Notre Dame, Ind.: University of Notre Dame Press, 1982.

———. *Critical Concerns in Moral Theology.* Notre Dame, Ind.: University of Notre Dame Press, 1984.

———. *Directions in Fundamental Moral Theology.* Notre Dame, Ind.: University of Notre Dame Press, 1985.

———. *The Living Tradition of Catholic Moral Theology.* Notre Dame, Ind.: University of Notre Dame Press, 1992.

Haughey, John C., ed. *The Faith That Does Justice: Examining the Christian Sources for Social Change.* New York: Paulist Press, 1977.

Himes, Michael J., and Kenneth R. Himes. *Fullness of Faith: The Public Significance of Theology.* New York: Paulist Press, 1993.

Hollenbach, David. *Justice, Peace, and Human Rights: American Catholic Social Ethics in a Pluralistic World.* New York: Crossroad, 1988.

McBrien, Richard P. *Cæsar's Coin: Religion and Politics in America.* New York: Macmillan, 1987.

McCormick, Richard A. *The Critical Calling: Reflections on Moral Dilemmas Since Vatican II.* Washington, D.C.: Georgetown University Press, 1989.

Rosenblatt, Roger. *Life Itself: Abortion in the American Mind.* New York: Random House, 1992.

PART SEVEN

Christian Spirituality

S PIRITUALITY is one of the most widely misunderstood and misinterpreted words in the Christian tradition. For many Christians it has meant something marginal and even exotic, as if spirituality were the special preserve of clergy and religious and a tiny minority of intensely "pious" lay people. But Christianity is not simply a system of *beliefs* (about God, grace, Christ, redemption, the Church, and salvation), but also a *life to be lived*: a life of *worship*, shaped by the Eucharist and the other sacraments, and a life of *moral commitment and behavior*, shaped by distinctively Christian moral values and norms that are rooted in the teaching and example of Jesus. In a word, the Christian is called to a life of *discipleship*.

But the disciple cannot truly be conformed to Christ—in faith, in worship, and in moral behavior—without the gift of the Holy Spirit. Indeed, the Holy Spirit is *the* gift of Christ to his disciples (Acts of the Apostles 2:38; 8:20; 10:45; 11:17; Hebrews 6:4), and it is given to the whole community of disciples (Acts of the Apostles 1:15; 2:1–3). The gift of the Spirit enables the disciples to "live according to the Spirit" (Romans 8:5).

Spirituality, therefore, is a comprehensive term, pertaining to *our way of being Christian,* in response to the call of God, issued through Jesus Christ in the power of the Holy Spirit. It is life in the Holy Spirit who incorporates the Christian into the Body of Jesus Christ, through whom the Christian has access to God the Creator in a life of faith, hope, love, and service.

Christian spirituality is comprehensive because it is trinitarian, Christological, ecclesiological, pneumatological, and eschatological. It is rooted in the life of the triune God, centered on Jesus Christ, situated in the Church, ever responsive to the Holy Spirit, and oriented always to the coming of God's Reign in all its fullness at the end of human history.

In this seventh and final part of the book, therefore, we are attempting to bring together all the major theological, doctrinal, sacramental, liturgical, and moral themes that constitute the present and historic reality of Catholicism and of Christian discipleship.

Chapter 28 offers a comprehensive review of the historical development of the Christian and Catholic understanding of spirituality, from the Bible to the final years of the twentieth century and the Second Christian Millennium. Chapter 29 addresses the specific question of Christian worship: the Church's liturgical life, its prayer life, and its devotional life. Chapter 30 focuses on some of the distinctively Catholic components of the Church's liturgical and devotional life: Mary and the saints. Chapter 31 presents the substance of Christian hope in eternal life, the ultimate outcome of our faithful response to Jesus' call to discipleship. This next-to-last chapter of the book could just as easily have been placed at the beginning as at the end. Eschatology is not only about the "last things" in a chronological sense, but about the "last things" as the finally important things: the Reign of God, which has already "come near" (Mark 1:15) in the life, death, and resurrection of Jesus Christ and which has been given to us as a "pledge of our inheritance" in the outpouring of the Holy Spirit (Ephesians 1:14).

XXVIII

Christian Spirituality

WHAT IS "SPIRITUALITY"?

The previous three chapters were concerned with principles of Christian and Catholic morality and their application to Christian discipleship. This chapter addresses itself not so much to the moral requirements of discipleship as to its spiritual manner and modality, given by the indwelling of the Spirit of Jesus Christ. "For those who live according to the flesh," Paul wrote, "set their minds on the things of the flesh, but those who live according to the Spirit, set their minds on the things of the Spirit" (Romans 8:5).

To live according to the spirit is to enjoy "life and peace." The Spirit of God dwells in such a one as the principle of life (8:6,8,11). *Spirituality*, therefore, has to do with *our way of being religious*. We are not only alive by a principle which transcends us (see chapter 5 on nature and grace); we are, in our own personalities, consciously aware of, in touch with, and motivated by, that principle of life.

To be *spiritual* means to know, and to live according to the knowledge, that there is more to life than meets the eye. To be *spiritual* means, beyond that, to know, and to live according to the knowledge, that God is present to us in grace as the principle of personal, interpersonal, social, and even cosmic transformation. To be *open to the Spirit* is to accept explicitly who we are and who we are called always to become, and to direct our lives accordingly, in response to God's grace within us.

Since God is not present to Christians alone, spirituality is not exclusively Christian. There are, for example, various Buddhist and Hindu spiritualities. What, then, is *Christian* spirituality? Christian spirituality has to do with *our way of being Christian,* in response to the call of God, issued through Jesus Christ in the power of the Holy Spirit. It is *life in the Holy Spirit who incorporates the Christian into the Body of Jesus Christ, through whom the Christian has access to God the Creator in a life of faith, hope, love, and service.*

Christian spirituality, therefore, is *trinitarian, Christological, ecclesiological, pneumatological,* and *eschatological.* It is rooted in the life of the triune God, centered on Jesus Christ, situated in the Church, ever responsive to the Holy Spirit, and oriented always to the coming of God's Reign in all its fullness at the end of human history.

Christian spirituality is also visionary, sacramental, relational, and transformational. Christian spirituality is *visionary* in that it involves a new way of seeing reality and of seeing through things to their spiritual core, of thus "interpreting spiritual things to those who are spiritual" (1 Corinthians 2:13). In that sense, Christian spiritual vision is inevitably *sacramental.* Every created reality is imbued, to one degree or another, with the hidden presence of God. Christian spirituality is also *relational.* Neither Christian life nor human life itself is ever isolated existence. We are, by definition, relational beings: beings in relation to God, neighbor, world, and self. To be human is to live in community. To be Christian is also to live in community, i.e., the Church. To be spiritually Christian is to live always in relation with others: with our brothers and sisters in the Body of Christ and in the human community at large. Christian spirituality demands sensitivity to the presence, the needs, and the gifts of others, as well as to the created goods of the earth. Finally, Christian spirituality is *transformational.* The spiritual Christian is consciously in touch with the presence of the Spirit as the power which heals, reconciles, renews, gives life, bestows peace, sustains hope, brings joy, and creates unity. Christian spirituality requires that the Spirit be allowed to work so that through the instrumentality of the individual and of the Church the transformation of the world into the Reign of God might continue to occur.

Contemporary Christian spirituality also takes into explicit account the experience of *women,* the *poor* and *socially marginalized,* the *global* outreach of spiritual experience (ecumenical, interfaith, and transcultural), its *prophetic* dimension (justice and peace), its *ecological* dimension (rooted in creation), and its *incarnational* character (integrated with the *body*).

There is not, and never has been, a single Christian spirituality, nor a single Catholic spirituality. The following historical account should make that unmistakably clear.

HISTORY

Biblical Origins

Although *Christian* spirituality as such did not begin to take shape until Jesus' proclamation of the Kingdom of God and the gathering of the first disciples around him, its foundations were already laid in the *covenantal relationship* between Yahweh and Israel. The Israelites were convinced of the nearness and even the presence of their God, as the Psalms clearly indicate. Jesus, too, proclaimed that the Father had drawn near to us in a dramatically and definitively new way. The Kingdom of God has "come near" (Mark 1:15). Jesus suggests that he has a unique relationship with the Father (Matthew 11:25–27). The power of God breaks through in Jesus' words (Mark 4:14; Luke 12:32) and in his healing works (Luke 11:20; Matthew 12:28). To be "in Christ" is to be a "new creation" (2 Corinthians 5:17). It is to be brought to life with Christ "when we were dead through our trespasses" (Ephesians 2:5). It is to have God living in us because God lives in Christ (John 17:23). The love of God for Christ lives in us, because Christ lives in us (17:26).

It is through the death and resurrection of Jesus that we are liberated from sin and for new life (Romans 6:3–11). Jesus was raised from the dead "in order that we may bear fruit for God" (7:4). Indeed, the Spirit cannot be given until the resurrection and glorification of Jesus (John 7:39; 16:7), and the first thing the Lord does when he appears to the disciples afterward is to breathe the Holy Spirit upon them (20:19–23). Our very bodies are given life through the Spirit which now possesses us (Romans 8:11). And the Father will raise us just as Jesus was raised (2 Corinthians 4:14). Christian life and spirituality is knowing that truth, having hope in what we know, and living according to that hope so that our life would not make sense if it were not for such a hope. It is life in possession of "the light of life" (John 8:12). It is a life of discipleship, lived within "the community of the disciples" (Acts of the Apostles 6:2).

Second Through Seventh Centuries

If spirituality has to do essentially with our union with God in Christ through the Holy Spirit, *martyrdom* provided in the earliest centuries of the Church an ideal means to such union. Martyrdom's importance was rooted in its close connection with Christ's own death and resurrection. To be put to death for the faith, that is, to be martyred (literally, to become a "witness"), was to experience ahead of schedule the final eschatological event.

After the Roman persecutions had ended, Christians wondered if the complete union with God in Christ offered by martyrdom was accessible in any other way. Origen (d. c. 254) suggested that a life of complete self-sacrifice was a kind of unbloody martyrdom, and Clement of Alexandria (d. c. 215) noted that every death is a true martyrdom provided one approaches it with the proper dispositions.

The first "spiritual" heresy in the Church was Gnosticism, which looked upon matter as evil. Salvation comes only in the rejection of the material world for the world of the spirit. *Irenæus* (d. 200) led the counterattack, insisting on the incarnation as a principle of recapitulation of all things, material and spiritual, in Christ. But the Gnostic stress on knowledge, so characteristic of contemporary Greek philosophy, penetrated even orthodox Christian theology and spirituality. The emphasis, however, was much less esoteric and more fully oriented to Christian life. Thus, for *Clement of Alexandria*, the summit of Christian consciousness is the knowledge of the God of love by loving as God loves. This assimilation to God occurred through *apatheia*, i.e., the domination through grace of everything opposed to Christian love (*agape*). Such a state was itself a kind of anticipation of eternal life. Platonist influence was strong in *Origen*, who taught that the soul must struggle to uproot itself from the world in which it is buried by selfish desires. The struggle is won by imitation of Christ and a sharing in his life. The approach carried over into Origen's notion of prayer. For him, prayer is the contemplation of God rather than a means of achieving material benefits. It involves the withdrawal into an inner chamber, which means shutting the doors of the faculties of sense. He even suggested that one should avoid praying near the marital bed since it is inappropriate to pray in a place where even legitimate sexual intercourse occurs. However, Origen's fundamental concern was to show how prayer, which involves the action of all three Persons of the Trinity within us, should pervade the entire life of the Christian. (For Origen's understanding of prayer, see Joseph Wilson Trigg, *Origen: The Bible and Philosophy in the Third-Century Church*, Atlanta: John Knox Press, 1983, especially pp. 156–63.)

Monasticism had its roots in the New Testament where some early Christians embraced celibacy "for the sake of the kingdom" (Matthew 19:12) and in postapostolic Syria, where ascetics, inspired by Luke's Gospel (9:60), sought to imitate the poor, homeless, and celibate Jesus. The more conventional rendering locates its beginnings in Egypt, where it developed first as flight from persecution and later as a rejection of the Constantinian embrace of the Church in 312. Under the leadership of *Antony of Egypt* (d. 356) and others, individual Christians went into the desert (*eremia*, thus the word "hermit") to confront the devil, to come to terms with all the dark forces that war against the spirit, and to find simplicity of life in order to focus more sharply on the demands of the Gospel. Some forms of asceticism were severe. In Syria, for example, various hermits used iron chains to punish themselves; others exposed themselves heedlessly to the elements. Gradually the hermits were joined by others, and a transition was made from the solitary form of monastic existence (*anchoritism*) to a modified community existence (*cenobitism*). Almost from the beginning, therefore, monastic life was looked upon as a continuation of apostolic life: perseverance together in prayer, in the community of goods, and in the breaking of the bread (Acts of the Apostles 2:42). The practice of consecrating virgins also developed at this time as yet another way of achieving fuller union with Christ.

Two or three generations passed before a spiritual theology emerged from the new monastic movement. According to the Neoplatonic schema of *Pseudo-Dionysius* (d. c. 500)—probably a Syrian monk who identified himself with Dionysius the Areopagite, mentioned in Acts of the Apostles 17:34—the soul finds union with God only in going beyond itself, by rejecting all particular knowledge and allowing itself to be absorbed totally in the knowledge of God, whose intra-Trinitarian life of love overflows in a stream of self-communicating goodness in creation. Thus, the spiritual life is divided into three stages: purification (the *purgative* way), meditation on the word of God (the *illuminative* way), and union with God (the *unitive* way).

Augustine (d. 430) was himself dependent upon this monastic spirituality as developed and practiced in the East. But he subtly revised it in a more psychological and critical direction. Spiritual discernment does not bring us knowledge of God in Christ so much as *self-knowledge* in the light of Christ, the interior teacher of wisdom. On the other hand, it was also Augustine who wrote in the *City of God* that "no man must be so committed to contemplation as, in his contemplation, to give no thought to his neighbor's needs, nor so absorbed in action as to dispense with the contemplation of God" (Book XIX, chapter 19). It was *John Cassian* (d. 435), however, who translated the purer form of Eastern monasticism to the West. The monk is not to seek anything beyond the Kingdom of God, and only purity of heart will open the mystery of the Kingdom to him. Christian life is one of constant prayer wholly inspired by the Gospel.

One of the greatest spiritual authorities in the entire history of Church, is *Benedict of Nursia* (d. c. 550), generally regarded as the patriarch of Western monasticism and author of the famous Rule of Benedict. The latter was composed for the monks of Monte Cassino, and was drawn freely from earlier monastic rules, both for individual, anchoritic spirituality and for communal, cenobitic, spirituality. Augustine, Basil, and Pachomius were among his sources. Marked by prudence and humanity, the Rule leads by observance and obedience to the perfect following of Christ. It speaks of the divine presence as "everywhere and... in every place," but especially in the monastic liturgy of the Divine Office (19:1–2). The basic asceticism is in the common life. Everything is centered on the needs of others (34), and much attention is paid to interpersonal relations. The person in whom Benedict most concentrates the divine presence, however, is the superior of the monastery, the abbot, through whom the will of God is mediated. He insists, at the same time, that God is to be met in the least likely circumstances and in the most unprepossessing persons (53:21).

Another key spiritual leader and writer of the time was *Pope Gregory the Great* (d. 604), an adept popularizer of doctrine and an influential author on matters of faith and piety. His works are the first major sources of material on the lives of the saints, including Benedict, whose rule he observed and whose cult he promoted. One of Gregory's books, *Regula Pastoralis* ("Pastoral Norms"), had almost as much impact on the Church well into the Middle Ages as did Augustine's *City of God*. It was a practical treatise on the spirituality and ministerial skills required of bishops and of all who have the care of souls. The social disruptions created by the so-called barbarian invasions disclosed the fragile character of much of the Christianization that had occurred thus far. Gregory's simple, straightforward style was particularly appealing because it was reassuring, and the monastic type of life which his work advocated and celebrated proved to be one of the mainstays of the Church and of society generally for the next several centuries.

The Middle Ages: Eighth Through Fourteenth Centuries

From the time of Gregory the Great until the middle of the eighth century, monks generally maintained the ascetical ideal and gave an example of Christian life for all: laity, clergy, and bishops alike. Under the new Germanic influence, however, a certain externalism inserted itself into Christian spirituality: devotions to the cross, relics, and tombs of the saints; various forms of penances; the encouragement of confession of sins, etc. But Carolingian piety was also marked by a deep reverence for the Bible and a love of the liturgy—both abiding preoccupations of Christian monks.

By the tenth and eleventh centuries various monasteries began to develop loose federations, and these gave rise to congregations of monasteries and eventually to religious orders. The monastic ideal was spread ever more widely throughout the Christian world. Austerity characterized penitential practice even among the laity. Long pilgrimages and self-flagellation were common means of making reparation for sin or for curbing one's unruly appetites. Contemplative prayer, too, was presented as the standard which all Christians should meet. *John of Fécamp* (d. 1079), one of the most widely read spiritual writers of the time, recommended quiet, meditative reading to induce unimpeded and undistracted thoughts about God.

The new Cistercian Order, founded in 1098 as observant, renewed followers of the Rule of Benedict, accentuated the *mystical* element in Christian spirituality. Its principal proponents, *Bernard of Clairvaux* (d. 1153) and *William of St. Thierry* (d. 1148), regarded the soul as being the image of God because of the gift of free will. But sin marred that image. Only by a contemplative life that conforms oneself to the Word of God can the individual soul be restored to its intended perfection, for Christ is the interior Lover who pursues and embraces the soul in a union of intimate love.

The stress on the contemplative life over dialectics (i.e., critical theology) continued into the twelfth century in the Parisian monastery of St. Victor, whose members, known as the *Victorines*, included some of the best-known writers of the period: *Hugh of St. Victor* (d. 1141), *Richard of St. Victor* (d. 1173), and others. Richard's work would later be simplified by the English Augustinian *Walter Hilton* (d. 1396) and Hilton's, in turn, carried forward by *Julian of Norwich* (d. 1442), an anchoress who lived outside the walls of St. Julian's Church in Norwich, England.

But there also appeared at this time another, more idealistic spiritual movement urging radical poverty and an end to all formalism and legalism. Accordingly, by the end of the thirteenth century many lay persons were criticizing the existing social conditions, especially in the new urban centers of Europe, as well as the lives of the clergy and hierarchy. Extreme forms of this new purist tendency were to be found in Waldensianism and Albigensianism. But there were also more mainstream attempts to confront the same social conditions, abuses, and pastoral problems. The rise of the mendicant orders in the thirteenth century—Franciscans and Dominicans—built on the many groups seeking the *vita apostolica* and popular preaching in the twelfth century. The new orders brought a more realistic, but no less serious, approach to poverty and service, because they were closer to the lives of ordinary people than were the monastic orders.

Dominic (d. 1221) provided his new Order of Preachers with an ideal that combined the best of monasticism with the best of the apostolic life. One of his spiritual sons, *Thomas Aquinas* (d. 1274), would produce an oft-cited formula on the interrelationship between

1026

the two: neither contemplation alone nor action alone is the highest form of Christian life, but contemplation in action (a concept not far removed from the modern notion of *praxis*), that is, a sharing with others the fruits of the contemplative life. Like other medieval theologians, Thomas's spirituality was one with his speculative theology.

Francis of Assisi (d. 1226), on the other hand, stressed imitation of the life of Christ in all its simplicity and poverty. God is reflected in the sun, the moon, and stars, and indeed in all of the things of creation (the principle of *sacramentality* again). As with the Dominicans, it took another great theologian to systematize, and thereby give wider circulation to, Francis's basic insight. *Bonaventure* (d. 1274), who saw the whole of creation as a mirror reflecting the power, wisdom, and goodness of God, identified three elements in the Franciscan way of life: (1) following Christ through the evangelical counsels, especially poverty (the other counsels are chastity and obedience); (2) laboring for the salvation of souls by preaching and hearing confessions; and (3) contemplation.

Another alternative to the traditional structures of monastic life was provided by the Beguines (and their male counterparts, the Beghards) who emerged toward the end of the twelfth century in Germany, the Low Countries, and France. They began as single women living with parents or separately in tenements, with no rule of life. Their main apostolic purpose was service of the sick and needy. Their social views and sympathies led to a perception among church authorities that they were allied with the Spiritual Franciscans, and so they came under scrutiny and censure.

At the beginning of the fourteenth century a new current of spirituality took root in the Rhineland and the Low Countries, and in England. A century earlier the works of Pseudo-Dionysius had been translated into the vernacular and made the subject of an extended commentary. Because the author was commonly associated in people's minds with Paul's convert, the Areopagite mentioned in Acts of the Apostles 17:34, his newly translated writings were accorded a quasiapostolic authority throughout the Middle Ages. (They had already been translated into Latin in the ninth century by Duns Scotus Erigena.) The writings had particular influence on *Meister Eckhart* (d. 1327), *John Tauler* (d. 1361), and *Henry Suso* (d. 1366), three German Dominican mystics, and on *Jan van Ruysbroeck* (d. 1381), a

Flemish canon regular of St. Augustine. Their common concern was the soul's union with God, which reached its zenith in contemplation. Such union is impossible, however, apart from complete abandonment of, and detachment from, all creatures and worldly realities. This orientation was most pronounced in *The Cloud of Unknowing*, composed by an anonymous English author. The same stress on the interior life was to be found in *Hildegard* (d. 1179) and *Hedwig* (d. 1243), and it is to be found again today in the "centering prayer" approach (see the later discussion of *The Cloud of Unknowing*, under the treatment of post–Vatican II spirituality).

Other spiritual writers, firmly committed to a life of prayer and penance, saw more clearly the pastoral implications and effects of their contemplative life. *Catherine of Siena* (d. 1380) was exceedingly concerned with the reform of the Church but insisted that her prayers and penances did more for the Church than her public acts did. Yet she advocated theological study, reformed religious life, and worked against papal corruption and endemic warfare.

The same concern for ecclesiastical renewal in the Low Countries stimulated the formation of a lay group, the Brethren of the Common Life, founded by *Gerard Groote* (d. 1384). The movement's spirituality was known as the *Devotio Moderna*. Its one great product, written probably by Groote or by *Thomas à Kempis* (d. 1471), was *The Imitation of Christ*, which laid great stress on the inner life of the individual and encouraged methodical meditation, especially on the life and passion of Christ.

There was, however, a lack of intellectual and theological substance in much popular piety of the time, and it brought with it many serious problems: superstition (e.g., the belief that one could be saved from blindness by gazing on the Communion host), ignorance of the Bible, fascination with reports of visions, exaggeration of the value of relics, emotionalism, inordinate fears of the afterlife and of God's judgment, and devotional excesses unrelated to the central mysteries of Christian faith.

The Postmedieval Period

Although Protestantism rejected contemporary medieval spirituality's emotionalism, superstition, and inordinate reverence for such material objects as relics, it did not at the same time reject its *individualism*. Martin Luther (d. 1546) stressed the uniqueness of the Christian believer's relationship with God and the realm of personal conscience (*sola fides*, "faith alone"). His recourse to the Word of God in Sacred Scripture (*sola Scriptura*, "Scripture alone") only underlined his concern for finding a direct approach to Christ, one in which the individual is illumined by the interior witness of the Holy Spirit (*sola gratia*, "grace alone"). Although it was not always obvious in the midst of medieval excesses, it *is* a matter of Catholic principle that the believer's relationship with God is a *mediated* relationship; mediated not only, nor even primarily, through the biblical Word, but in and through the community of faith in which that Word is proclaimed. "Thus Protestantism tends to produce a spirituality which springs entirely from the co-presence and mutual relationship between the Person of God revealed in the Christ of the Gospels and the individual person of the believer. But, for Catholicism, there is no fully authentic Christian spirituality without the realization of an equal co-presence of our fellow-believers with Christ and ourselves, the Church" (Louis Bouyer, *Introduction to Spirituality*, New York: Desclée Co., 1961, p. 11).

Although various Christian humanists were sympathetic toward the contemporary emphasis on mysticism, they were strongly committed to the general restoration of Christian life itself, so much corrupted then by the worst of the Renaissance spirit. Love for classical antiquity and an optimistic view of human nature were characteristic of this so-called devout humanism, and the spiritual writings of *Erasmus* (d. 1536) are representative of it. In spite of his clashes with Luther on free will and his fidelity to the Catholic Church, he was subjected to censure and censorship, before and after his death.

The same emphasis on the unity of prayer and action is found in one of the classics of Christian spirituality, the *Spiritual Exercises* of *Ignatius Loyola* (d. 1556), a work that reflected the Baroque period's emphasis on personal conversion and method in prayer. Ignatian spirituality was marked by dialectical parallels: between the medieval concepts of *contemplation* and *action*, on the one hand, and between *flight from the world* and *acceptance of the world*, on the other. Contemplation is adherence to the God who transcends this world. Action is the fulfillment of one's duty within the world, consistent with one's own individuality. Hence the Ignatian formula which originated with the first circle of his followers: *"in actione contemplativus"* (contemplative in action). Ignatius's affirmation of the world, therefore, is not a naive optimism. It springs rather from a true grasp of the cross: at once a judgment upon sin and a proclamation of our liberation from it. On the other hand, his profoundly positive evaluation of the contingencies of history puts him at the head of a whole new spiritual tradition—so much so, in fact, that Karl Rahner is convinced that the Holy Spirit raised up in Ignatius an original, creative reinterpretation of the Christian life.

"Work as if everything depended upon you, but pray as if everything depended upon God," another well-known Ignatian formula has it. Although this is not the exact wording, it is close enough to the sense of the original, which says, in effect, that we should trust in God in such a way that we never forget to cooperate with God, and yet at the same time we should cooperate with God in such a way as to remain always aware that it is God alone who is at work. We are always at a *distance*, therefore, from God and even from our own deeds. We are at a distance *from God*, who is never revealed except in works carried out with the cooperation of secondary causes (i.e., free human beings); and we are at a distance *from our deeds*, which must never be taken as something of final value in themselves. The Christian must look to Christ, in whom alone the divine-human interaction is fully realized, and seek to imitate him. This is the core of Ignatian spirituality. (For the original Ignatian text in Latin and a brief commentary on it, see Hugo Rahner, *Ignatius the Theologian*, New York: Herder & Herder, 1968, pp. 25–27; see also Karl Rahner, "The Logic of Concrete Individual Knowledge in Ignatius Loyola," *The Dynamic Element in the Church*, London: Burns & Oates, 1964, pp. 84–170.)

The four hundred years from 1560 to 1960, the eve of Vatican II, were to form broadly one major period in Catholic history. After the shock of the Reformation, the Catholic Church underwent a major renewal, propelled by the Council of Trent and inspired by saints like Ignatius Loyola. Spirituality, joined by art, affirmed and defended everything the Protestants attacked: devotion to Mary and the saints, images, sacraments. This was especially the case with the *Baroque period*, in which individuals and groups proclaimed ways in which Jesus' incarnation was extended into people's lives and cultures. The period's art dramatically, and even emotionally, depicted the life of Christ, and of Mary and Joseph. The emotional element was also prominent in the biographies of saints, in sermons, in pastoral work at the parish level and in foreign missions. The Christian life becomes manifest no longer in ordinary but in extraordinary events: dramatic conversions, visions, stigmata, and ecstasies.

The authentically mystical way, present in Ignatius, continued to flourish, however, especially in *Spain*. For *Teresa of Ávila* (d. 1582) prayer consisted essentially in an exchange of love with God, but in the context of life in the Church. From our side, the signs of our love for God are manifested in the practice of the virtues, especially in love of neighbor, leaving to God the communication of ·grace whenever and however God wishes (see her *Autobiography*, New York: Doubleday-Image, 1960; and *The Way of Perfection*, New York: Doubleday-Image, 1964). *John of the Cross* (d. 1591), one of Teresa's companions in her work of reform within the Carmelite Order, is regarded by many as the greatest of the mystical writers (see *The Collected Works of St. John of the Cross*, Washington, D.C.: Institute of Carmelite Studies Publications, 1991). His writings were at once poetic and speculative, drawing not only upon personal spiritual experience but upon Sacred Scripture and the classical authors as well. They detail the processes of spiritual purification, through trials and temptations and through deliberate detachment from external things, and they try to explain the life of union with God—a union brought about through the prayer of gifted contemplation. These great Carmelites employed not only an autobiographical method but also a kind of developmental psychology, pointing out that we move progressively in life to even higher stages of prayer.

Although Spanish spirituality after John of the Cross became increasingly theoretical and scientific, *Italian* spirituality was more practical. Reform of the Church, renewal of the interior life, and the improvement of priestly ministry were matters of immediate interest. These priorities are reflected in the works of *Catherine of Genoa* (d. 1510), *Charles Borromeo* (d. 1584), and *Philip Neri* (d. 1595).

In *France* developments in spirituality were centered on the life of Christ and the saints, especially mystics and missionaries, who were not only models for life but also objects of liturgy and celebration. Great directors of the spiritual life, like *Francis de Sales* (see below),

Madame Acarie (d. 1618), and *Pierre de Bérulle* (d. 1629) developed personal approaches to the life of prayer. Among the other great figures of this period were *Jean Eudes* (d. 1680), an Oratorian priest, who developed a theology of the hearts of Jesus and Mary, perhaps in response to the coldness of Jansenism. He chose the heart as a symbol of the overflowing love of God, most fully expressed in the Incarnation. Devotion to the Sacred Heart of Jesus received new impetus from *Margaret Mary Alacoque* (d. 1690), who reported having had visions of Jesus in which he revealed to her his human and divine love through the image of a heart resting on a throne of flames and surrounded by a crown of thorns. Encountering skepticism from the other sisters in her community, she found support from her Jesuit confessor *Claude de la Colombière* (d.1682).

This was also the time in France of theological controversy surrounding the whole issue of nature and grace. Some argued that human nature was so powerless that we can do absolutely nothing to advance our salvation (the *Quietism* of Madame Guyon, d. 1717). Others insisted on the evil of the flesh and of all human desires and pleasures, urging a life of total abnegation, self-denial, and even repression (*Jansenism*). Against the Quietists, *Jacques Bossuet* (d. 1704) taught that abandonment of the soul to God should actually induce the soul to apply itself more deliberately to its religious exercises and to other Christian duties. Meanwhile, *Francis de Sales* (d. 1622) and *Jane Frances de Chantal* (d. 1641) sought to bring Christian piety out of the monasteries and the convents into the world of the average lay person by showing the connection between Christian life and everyday occupations, and by emphasizing the joy of Christian existence (see Francis's *Introduction to the Devout Life*, New York: Doubleday-Image, 1972). A similar orientation appears in Italy in the writings of *Alphonsus Liguori* (d. 1787).

The spirit of the French school of spirituality, shorn of its excesses, is perhaps best expressed by *Jean Jacques Olier* (d. 1657), founder of the Sulpicians: "Christianity consists in these three points... to look upon Jesus, to unite oneself to Jesus, and to act in Jesus. The first leads us to respect and to religion; the second to union and to identification with Him; the third, to an activity no longer solitary, but joined to the virtue of Jesus Christ, which we have drawn upon ourselves by prayer. The first is called adoration; the

1032

second, communion; the third, cooperation" (cited by E. A. Walsh, "Spirituality, French School of," *New Catholic Encyclopedia*, vol. 13, New York: McGraw-Hill, 1967, p. 605).

In the early eighteenth century the devotion to the Sacred Heart spread rapidly through France and to other countries like Poland. Although Pope Clement XIII (d. 1769) approved the devotion in 1765, its great success came in the nineteenth century, when Margaret Mary was beatified (1864) and Pope Pius IX extended the liturgy and feast of the Sacred Heart to the universal Church (after 1856) and dedicated the universal Church to the Sacred Heart (1875). Various religious communities dedicated to the Sacred Heart were also founded in the late eighteenth and early nineteenth centuries.

Nineteenth Century

Catholic spirituality had been negatively affected by the suppression of religious orders, monasteries, and other religious institutions (orphanages, hospitals, libraries) during the French Revolution and by Napoleon's program of secularization, as well as by the eighteenth-century Enlightenment's hostility to the supernatural. After 1830 new orders and congregations appeared, old ones reappeared, monastic life was revived, amd various lay movements were initiated. But under pressure from secular states and the restrictive pontificates of Gregory XVI (1831–46) and Pius IX (1846–78), spirituality in the second half of the century tended to become introspective and popular piety turned increasingly to supernaturalism: apparitions of the Blessed Virgin (especially at Lourdes in 1858), miracles, visions, and stigmata. Individualism and even regimented piety (e.g., institutionalized devotions to the Sacred Heart, the Blessed Virgin, the Sacred Wounds, the Eucharist) flourished, and reactionary theological ideas were encouraged, and sometimes endorsed, by magisterial interventions of a highly conservative nature.

Those negative developments notwithstanding, the nineteenth century provides a bridge between medieval and modern spirituality, because the forces of renewal were also at work: the renewal of theology, of liturgy, of historical studies, and of social ministry. And so, too, were the forces of innovation: e.g., scientific and technological advances, developments in psychology and sociology. Together these forces of renewal and innovation would have a profound impact on Christian spirituality in the twentieth century. A number of apostolic congregations of women were also founded at this time, drawing their inspiration mainly from Ignatian spirituality.

Although the main currents of spiritual renewal were on the Continent, this incipient renewal of Christian spirituality was also evident in *England* and particularly in the Oxford Movement, whose driving force was *John Henry Newman* (d. 1890). His spiritual orientation was primarily interior, a life lived in intimate union with God under the guidance of the Holy Spirit. But it was also a Christocentric spirituality, stressing the incarnation as the basis for an active Christian life in the world. As in Ignatius, therefore, there was a blending of the contemplative and the practical. Newman, however, was not to exert very much influence as a spiritual writer. More influential was *Frederick William Faber* (d. 1863), who drew his own inspiration from the Italian and French styles of spiritual writing, especially that of Alphonsus Liguori and Cardinal Bérulle (d. 1629). Faber, too, was Christocentric (one of his works was entitled *All for Jesus*), but he was also highly emotional and florid. On the other hand, his emphasis on the psychology of the individual, his openness to all people, even non-Catholics and non-Christians, and his encouragement of the frequent reception of the sacraments, all anticipated by a century certain developments that would characterize modern Catholic spirituality.

Unfortunately, Catholic spirituality after 1860 and until the Second Vatican Council was hampered by its separation from theology and from the ordinary world of the lay person. The presumption was that spirituality is not for everyone, only for priests and religious.

Twentieth Century

1900 to 1950

What the history of Christian and Catholic spirituality makes clear is its *pluralistic* character. At the beginning of the twentieth century pluralism was taken for granted. There were spiritualities, not *a* spirituality. And those spiritualities were identified both with *charismatic individuals*, like Teresa of Ávila, John of the Cross, Thomas à

Kempis, John Vianney (the Curé d'Ars), and with *schools* which, in turn, were identified with religious orders. For example, there was Dominican spirituality (Dominic, Aquinas, Catherine of Siena; the priority of truth, or knowledge, that leads to love), Jesuit, or Ignatian, spirituality (Ignatius Loyola; finding God in all things), Franciscan spirituality (Francis of Assisi, Clare of Assisi, Bonaventure; a life of poverty, modeled on Jesus, in service of the poor), Benedictine spirituality (Benedict, Marmion; prayer—liturgy and the reading of Scripture—and work), Carmelite spirituality (Teresa of Ávila, John of the Cross, Thérèse of Lisieux; solitude and contemplative prayer), Carthusian spirituality (Bruno; solitude and prayer), Cistercian spirituality (Bernard of Clairvaux, Thomas Merton; solitude and contemplative prayer), and Sulpician spirituality (Olier, Tanquerey; the disciplining of the lower appetites by the higher faculties, especially the intellect). The last has had a profound impact on the formation of future priests, given the Sulpicians' primary commitment to seminary education.

Catholic spiritual writings during the first half of the twentieth century reflected the ambivalent character of Catholic theology itself. On the one hand, traditional neoscholastic theology was firmly in place in seminaries, in college religion courses, in catechisms, in sermons, and especially in official magisterial pronouncements. The manuals of spiritual theology were similar—e.g., Adolfe Tanquerey's *The Spiritual Life* and Reginald Garrigou-Lagrange's *The Three Ages of the Interior Life*. On the other hand, the liturgical movement, spurred by the renewal of historical and biblical studies, guided spirituality in a more Christocentric direction through the writings of such Benedictines as Abbot *Columba Marmion* (d. 1923) of Belgium, and, in a very different way, in the life and works of *Charles de Foucauld* (d. 1916).

Tanquerey (d. 1932), by his own account, showed "a certain preference for the spirituality of the French School of the seventeenth century" (*The Spiritual Life*, New York: Desclée, 1930, pp. vii–viii). He was himself a Sulpician priest, a community of priests founded by Olier, one of the leaders of seventeenth-century French spirituality. Certain elements of Tanquerey's system also remarkably anticipate some of the major theological and pastoral developments of the period of Vatican II: (1) the grounding of spirituality in Sacred Scripture and doctrine; (2) an understanding of human existence as spirituality's starting point; (3) the mystery of the Trinity as its primary theological context; (4) the centrality of Jesus Christ and of our union with Christ in the Church, his Mystical Body; and (5) the call of the whole Church, including the laity, to a life of Christian perfection. On the other hand, Tanquerey's use of biblical and doctrinal sources reflects the limitations of neoscholastic methodology; the ascetical almost totally overshadows the mystical; the human person is conceived as lacking something originally intended by God (which is the more traditional notion of Original Sin and of the relationship between nature and grace); and human existence is portrayed as a process of struggle between higher faculties (especially the intellect) and the lower appetites (including "a lust for freedom and independence"). It is this theological anthropology that appears most inconsistent with the main lines of Catholic theology and of Catholic spirituality today, as we shall see below.

Garrigou-Lagrange (d. 1964), a Dominican professor at the Angelicum (the University of St. Thomas) in Rome for many years, also presents an individualistic approach to the spiritual life, but with an emphasis on supernatural grace. All are called to sanctity, or a life in union with God. Christian life consists of intimate conversation with God in prayer, achieved through a threefold process: passing through the purgative, illuminative, and unitive ways successively. Discipline in life and prayer removes the obstacles and purges the senses, and so the soul moves to a second stage of Christian existence, in which the soul is progressively illumined by the gifts of the Holy Spirit and finds it increasingly easy to contemplate the mystery of God. And then there is entrance into a state of perfect mystical union with God in which the theological and moral virtues are practiced to a heroic degree (*The Three Ages of the Interior Life,* 2 vols., St. Louis: B. Herder Book Co., 1947–1948).

The same individualistic emphasis is carried forward in Dietrich von Hildebrand's *Transformation in Christ* (St. Paul, Minn.: Helicon Press, 1948; New York: Image Books, 1963), which describes Christian spirituality in terms of surrender, detachment from self, subordination and abnegation of self, a submerging of oneself in the adoration of God, and always in an I/Thou relationship. *Von Hildebrand,* a philosopher, rejected various contemporary pastoral developments which underlined the importance of community. He characterized the liturgical movement, for example, as antipersonal-ist (p. 394). "Our abandonment of self is an indispensable condition of the full unfolding in us of supernatural life" (p. 400). In its highest form, "being possessed" is a state of mystic ecstasy wherein "the mind tends to be aware of nothing besides God" (p. 401). But such an experience of God gives us a clearer perception of all creaturely reality. We see things as they really are in the sight of God (p. 402).

Although she had died at the end of the nineteenth century, *Thérèse of Lisieux* (d. 1897), a young French Carmelite nun, had a profound impact on pre–Vatican II Catholic spirituality. At the command of her superiors she wrote her autobiography, which was revised and circulated to all Carmelite houses. Her popular name, "The Little Flower," is taken from the subtitle. Miracles of healing and prophecy were soon reported and by 1910 proceedings were initiated for her beatification, which occurred in 1923. Two years later she was canonized as "St. Teresa of the Child Jesus and the Holy Face." The popularity of her cult was largely due to the simplicity of her spirituality and its practicality. Sanctity is not achieved through extreme mortification, but through continual renunciation in small matters.

A much less individualistic, more liturgically oriented, more fully Christocentric and more anthropologically positive approach was taken by Abbot *Columba Marmion* (d. 1923). It is the last characteristic that is the most significant. Although both Tanquerey and Garrigou-Lagrange assert the importance of the redemptive work of Jesus Christ, they also continue to speak of human existence as if the redemption is, for all practical purposes, a juridical event (i.e., God now "declares" us just) that has not really transformed and renewed the whole human person. For Marmion, however, the Holy Spirit is given to us in Baptism and Confirmation, filling us with peace and filial confidence in God. The Spirit makes us understand that we have everything in Jesus Christ, who is not only holy in himself but has been given to us to be *our* holiness (*Union with God*, St. Louis: B. Herder Book Co., 1949, p. 40).

For Marmion, the Lord is not our distant judge but the source of love, affection, and sympathy, for he is truly human himself. It is above all in the Eucharist that Christ's action in the soul becomes effective and fruitful for us. We are similarly impelled to the love of one another, for we have become one in Christ. This is what *Commun-*

ion implies and requires, for "to give oneself to Jesus Christ is to give oneself to others for love of Him, or rather to give oneself to Him in the person of our neighbour" (pp. 164–65). "We are neither spirits nor ghosts," he insists, "but human beings" (p. 166). Therefore, we are to love God humanly, that is with all our heart, soul, strength, and mind, and to love our neighbor in the same way. (See also his *Christ the Life of the Soul*, St. Louis: B. Herder Book Co., 1925.)

A creative move away from the mechanistic spirituality of the neoscholastics of the early twentieth century was taken by *Charles de Foucauld* (d. 1916), founder of the Little Brothers of the Sacred Heart of Jesus. Foucauld was in the tradition of French rather than Benedictine spirituality, and so his focus on Jesus was less liturgical and less socially oriented than Marmion's. To be a Christian is to follow Jesus in the way of poverty and humility. To take the lowest place among humankind is to be close to Jesus. Foucauld left the Trappist life to establish a small community whose purpose would be to live as nearly as possible the way Jesus lived, following to the letter all the evangelical counsels, possessing nothing, giving to whoever asks (see his *Spiritual Autobiography*, New York: P. J. Kenedy, 1964). The great Catholic philosopher *Jacques Maritain* (d. 1973) spent his own last days living in community with the Little Brothers of Charles de Foucauld (see his *The Peasant of the Garonne*, New York: Holt, Rinehart and Winston, 1968).

1950 to Vatican II

The turn to a spirituality oriented to the world did not begin in the twentieth century, under the impact of the liturgical and biblical movements, but the understanding of human existence as *historical* existence *is* a modern development. No Christian spiritual writer contributed more substantially to that new emphasis than the Jesuit paleontologist *Teilhard de Chardin* (d. 1955). The more intensely he came to know and experience the world, the closer God was to him. The entire universe is one "divine milieu" (see *The Divine Milieu*, New York: Harper & Brothers, 1960). We attain an experience of God not, as the traditional ascetical manualists argued, exclusively through purgation, contemplation, and mystical union, or a kind of "meditation with closed eyes." Rather we encounter God by turning toward the things of the earth in love and reverence. The natural delight we take in life and in all that exists is the first dawn of divine illumination.

The great mystery of Christianity is not that God appears (*epiphany*) but that God shines through the universe (*diaphany*). Our prayer, therefore, is not that we might see God "as He is in Himself" but that we might see God in all things. Here again we have an echo of the basic Ignatian vision, so characteristically Catholic in its sacramental orientation. It is not merely coincidental that Teilhard himself was a member of Ignatius's company, the Society of Jesus. And yet there is also a trace of Franciscan spirituality in his sense of the presence of God in the physical universe and in his sense of the activating energy of Christ, as the Omega of evolution, across the entire cosmos.

In spite of Teilhard's insistence that spirituality is not for the religiously professed alone, monks continued to exercise profound influence on Catholic spirituality in the years immediately preceding the Second Vatican Council. For Dom *Hubert Van Zeller* spiritual life is a life in search of truth. But the search for truth is not distinct from the quest for love, for the object of both is God, who is at once Truth and Love. Apart from God there is no end to our search, and Christ is the embodiment of God's truth and love.

For the Christian, therefore, the purpose of life is union with Christ, and the Christian's aim is always to live to the fullest possible extent the life outlined in the Gospel. This is no distant ideal proposed only to saints and mystics, but to every baptized person. All are called to a life based on the Christian love ethic, in the individual and the social orders alike. But our search is a prolonged one, involving progressive discovery. We experience frustration and loneliness on the way. "We look for Christ in darkness, and in darkness He reveals Himself. We flounder in unsatisfied longing, and in our floundering we discover love. We think we have lost faith and hope, when in our seeming faithlessness and hopelessness we discover true faith and hope.... We discover that the only thing in life which is worth doing is to search. The man in the Gospel who went digging for his buried treasure had already found it" (*The Inner Search*, New York: Sheed & Ward, 1957, pp. 7, 9). One finds a similar sensitivity to the human dimension of Christian spirituality, but with a more explicitly Thomistic orientation, in the works of *Gerald Vann*, O.P. (d. 1963): for example, *The Heart of Man*, Garden City, N.Y.: Image Books, 1960, and *The Divine Pity*, Image Books, 1962.

The change from a negative to a positive attitude toward the world is also apparent in the extraordinarily popular writings of the Trappist monk *Thomas Merton* (d. 1968). There is a discernible shift from his perception of the world as wicked in his *The Seven Storey Mountain* (New York: Harcourt, Brace, 1948) to *Conjectures of a Guilty Bystander* (New York: Doubleday, 1966), where he reports how, on a downtown corner in Louisville, Kentucky, he was suddenly overwhelmed with the realization that he loved all those people and that human beings cannot be alien to one another even though they are total strangers. The whole illusion of a separate holy existence is a dream, he insisted.

In his *Life and Holiness* (New York: Image Books, 1964) he declares that "a Christianity that despises [the] fundamental needs of man is not truly worthy of the name.... There is no genuine holiness without this dimension of human and social concern" (p. 100). Spiritual perfection is available not to those with superhuman powers but to those who, though weak and defective in themselves, trust perfectly in the love of God, who abandon themselves with confident joy to the apparent madness of the cross (p. 119). Perfection means "simple fidelity" to the will of God in every circumstance of our ordinary life. To be a saint means to be oneself, to be what God intended one to be. We are, in fact, called to share with God "the work of *creating* the truth of our identity" (*New Seeds of Contemplation*, New York: New Directions Books, 1961, p. 32).

"Finding God," therefore, "means much more than just abandoning all things that are not God, and emptying oneself of images and desires" (p. 39). Rather, "God discovers Himself in us." To find God, one must find herself or himself. But one cannot find oneself in isolation from the rest of humankind. We must give ourselves to others in the purity of selfless love. "For it is precisely in the recovery of our union with our brothers in Christ that we discover God and know Him, for then His life begins to penetrate our souls and His love possesses our faculties and we are able to find out Who He is from the experience of His mercy, liberating us from the prison of self-concern" (p. 78).

Eugene Boylan (d. 1964) was another Cistercian spiritual writer whose works enjoyed wide circulation: *Difficulties in Mental Prayer* (Westminster, Md.: Newman Press, 1946) and *This Tremendous Lover* (Westminster, Md.: Newman Press, 1947; reissued in 1961).

The erudite and voluminous writings of *Romano Guardini* (d. 1968) attempted to relate a Franciscan spirituality to twentieth-century culture. Ordained a diocesan priest in the midst of the Modernist crisis, he stayed clear of controversies posed by neoscholastic theology and wrote on such great literary figures as Dante and Dostoyevsky. He stressed the doctrine of creation, revelation as God's word addressed to us, and the symbolic and the liturgical. His widely read works included *The Spirit of the Liturgy* (London: Sheed & Ward, 1930), *The Lord* (Chicago: Regnery, 1954), *Meditations Before Mass* (Westminster, Md.: Newman Press, 1955), *The Life of Faith* (Glen Rock, N.J.: Paulist Press, 1963), and *Prayer in Practice* (Garden City, N.Y.: Image Books, 1963).

One of the few theologians who attempted a systematic description and definition of Catholic spirituality in the years immediately preceding Vatican II was the French Oratorian *Louis Bouyer*, perhaps best known for his book *The Spirit and Forms of Protestantism* (Westminster, Md.: Newman Press, 1956). Bouyer acknowledged that spirituality is available to, and practiced by, non-Christians as well as Christians, Protestants as well as Catholics. Spirituality is engaged wherever there is a personal relationship with God. *Christian* spirituality is engaged where that personal relationship is grounded in God's self-revelation in Jesus Christ. *Catholic* spirituality is more deliberately ecclesial. The Word-made-flesh is proclaimed and encountered in the Church. It is not only the content of the Word that one finds in the Church, but the Word itself.

"It is, therefore, into the Church, the true body of Christ, that we must be incorporated in order to participate in the Spirit of Christ, and, as a consequence, to receive His words, not as a mere dead letter, but as words which remain always living, always uttered by the very Word of God" (*Introduction to Spirituality*, p. 13). Catholic spirituality, for Bouyer, is "Christian spirituality in its fullness" (p. 14). We are called to love as God loves. The Church, which is built up around Christ, is "an extension, an opening out to all mankind of the society of the divine Persons, the Trinity of the *agape*" (p. 17).

Few preconciliar formulae provide as clear an introduction to post–Vatican II spirituality, however, as the title of *Josef Goldbrunner's* essay "Holiness Is Wholeness" (*Holiness is Wholeness and Other Essays*, Notre Dame, Ind.: University of Notre Dame Press, 1964). God, the All-Holy, he argues, is whole. There is "no blemish of disease ..., no poison of death.... The more we seek the perfection that makes man like God, that makes him holy, the more we should become healthy in body and soul, for holiness is health" (p. 1). This is not to say that the way to God is free of suffering and even death. "Only a slow advance in the spiritual life gives the body time to adapt itself, to expel, as it were, the poison of death which it has come to absorb" (p. 2). But there are also many "illegitimate illnesses" which have come to be associated with the spiritual life: sufferings and risks to health that are embraced for their own sake, assaults upon the laws of nature, and the like. The modern Christian should be ready to tread the way of the cross that leads to holiness, but he or she must rebel when "holiness appears in a guise contrary to nature" (p. 3).

Dualism is to be rejected: There is no warring between soul and body as if the two were separate components, the one higher and the other lower and base. The incarnation teaches us that there is a wholeness to human life, which comprehends the bodily as well as the spiritual. But there is more to it even than that. There is as well the universe of the unconscious with which each must get in touch. To live a spiritually healthy life one must find one's own truth; i.e., "one must consciously come to terms with the irrational forces within oneself, incorporating them into the total life of the soul but never allowing them a perfectly free rein" (p. 14). Not every soul is the same. Each has "a certain measure of energy." If the religious life claims a great deal of energy, it must inevitably be subtracted from other spheres of the spirit. It is clear, therefore, that there are limits to our conscious striving for union with God.

It was the French philosopher-poet *Charles Péguy* (d. 1914) who exposed the self-deception of those who believe that the way to God is the way of repression of all desires for intimacy and interpersonal warmth. "Because they love no one," he wrote, "they imagine they love God." This is not to say, of course, that the spiritual life is without paradox. How is one to be wholly worldly and wholly devoted to God? "Through the cross of Christ, holiness and health become one" (Goldbrunner, p. 34; for a post-Vatican II development of this approach, see Wilkie Au, *By Way of the Heart: Toward a Holistic Spirituality*, New York: Paulist Press, 1989).

Preconciliar spirituality was also identified with lay movements like the Catholic Worker Movement in the United States (and its charismatic leader, *Dorothy Day*), the Young Christian Workers (Jocists) in Belgium and France, the Legion of Mary in Ireland, the Grail Movement in Holland, the Cursillo movement in Spain and Latin America, and the Christian Family Movement, also in the United States.

Vatican II

The Second Vatican Council laid to rest, once and for all, the assumption that spirituality is for priests and nuns alone. The fifth chapter of its keynote *Dogmatic Constitution on the Church* is entitled "The Call of the Whole Church to Holiness." The Lord addressed all of his disciples when he said: "Be perfect, therefore, as your heavenly Father is perfect" (Matthew 5:48). We are already holy by reason of the Spirit's indwelling within us. Christian spirituality is a matter of living in accordance with who we have become in the Spirit, of manifesting the fruits of the Spirit's presence: mercy, kindness, humility, meekness, patience (Colossians 3:12; Galatians 5:22; Romans 6:22). "Thus it is evident to everyone," the council declares, "that all the faithful of Christ of whatever rank or status are called to the fullness of the Christian life and to the perfection of charity" (n. 40).

The next sentence is almost as significant: "By this holiness a more human way of life is promoted even in this earthly society." Holiness, therefore, is not only for everyone; it also comprehends far more than the individual soul's relationship with God. Furthermore, there is no single mode or style of spirituality for Christians. Each must adapt the call to perfection to his or her own situation. What will always be common to all is love of God and of neighbor. "For charity, as the bond of perfection and the fulfillment of the law (cf. Colossians 3:14; Romans 13:10), rules over all the means of attaining holiness, gives life to them, and makes them work. Hence it is the love of God and of neighbor which points out the true disciple of Christ" (n. 42).

Elsewhere the council reaffirms or elaborates upon these basic principles of Christian spirituality. The call to holiness is a call issued to laity as well as to clergy and religious. The spiritual life of all Christians will be rooted in the mysteries of creation and redemption, in the presence of the Holy Spirit, and in the mission of Christ and the Church (*Decree on the Apostolate of the Laity*, n. 29; see also n. 4). The Christian enters upon the spiritual life in response to the Word of God (*Dogmatic Constitution on Divine Revelation*, n. 21), and the Word of God, in turn, is proclaimed and celebrated in the liturgy of the Church, which is the "summit" and the "fountain" of the whole Christian life. "From the liturgy, therefore, and especially from the Eucharist, as from a fountain, grace is channeled into us; and the sanctification of persons in Christ and the glorification of God, to which all other activities of the Church are directed as toward their goal, are most powerfully achieved" (n. 10).

And what the council teaches about Catholic spirituality applies to the whole Body of Christ, for there can be "no ecumenism worthy of the name without a change of heart.... Let all Christ's faithful remember that the more purely they strive to live according to the gospel, the more they are fostering and even practicing Christian unity. For they can achieve depth and ease in strengthening mutual solidarity to the degree that they enjoy profound communion with the Father, the Word, and the Spirit" (*Decree on Ecumenism*, n. 7). The council insists that this is "the soul of the whole ecumenical movement, and can rightly be called 'spiritual ecumenism.'"

Post–Vatican II

The postconciliar period has been marked by a full-scale liturgical renewal (liturgy in the vernacular, diversified worship, active participation), by a stronger sense of the ecumenical and global breadth of the Church, by a more pronounced concern for social justice and the liberating mission of the Church, by a heightened sense of responsibility for the environment, by a deepening reverence for Sacred Scripture, by an increased striving for a personal experience of the Holy Spirit, and by a growing consciousness of the equality of women in the Church and in society at large. All of these developments— many of which are outgrowths of movements already at work in the nineteenth century and actively promoted in the pre–Vatican II period—shape contemporary Christian spirituality. Illustrative of the explosion of interest in spirituality since Vatican II are the Charismatic Renewal, the Cursillo movement, Marriage Encounter, directed retreats according to the original Ignatian mode, weekend youth retreats, the expansion of opportunities for spiritual direction, the resurgence of contemplative prayer, the establishment of many new centers and institutes for spiritual life, as well as the renewal and reform of religious congregations.

Individual spiritual writers, of course, continue to influence the style of Christian life. Dom *Aelred Graham* moves beyond the traditional ecumenical boundaries between Catholic and Protestant into the wider dialogue between East and West, in his *Contemplative Christianity: An Approach to the Realities of Religion* (New York: Seabury Press, 1974). What East and West have in common is the conviction that there are three paths to God: the path of self-forgetting adoration, expressed in both private worship and in the Church's liturgy; the path of selfless service of others, which finds expression in compassionate activity for the benefit both of the individual and of society as a whole; and the path of truth-realizing experience, through contemplative meditation (p. 65). Not all three paths have to be traveled. We will be inclined to one or another by temperament. But any one of these paths, selflessly pursued, can lead to union with God. They are not mutually exclusive, and each can be abused. The first can degenerate into mindless piety or an obsessive, even superstitious, preoccupation with rites and ceremonies. The second can be impractical and unrealistic. The third can become an "ego trip" with little regard for the needs of other people. In the end, the spiritual quest is a risk, but a risk that has to be taken in faith. And faith ultimately is "an awareness beyond sense-perception that the power behind the universe is not neutral, but gracious and beneficent, the unshakable confidence that 'all shall be well and all manner of thing shall be well'" (p. 68).

To be spiritual is to have achieved "God-realization," i.e., "to be in a state of awareness such that God is consciously *real*" (p. 74). It means seeing God everywhere and in everything and everyone. Christian spirituality, therefore, is incarnational. It welcomes what is fully human, including the physical, the down-to-earth, the concrete.

Any yet it is not simply materialistic. There is more to reality than meets the eye. God is present to the world as the power of love which is to be shared with others. It is an insight one finds among such Catholic authors as Ignatius, Teilhard de Chardin, and Karl Rahner, all of whom happen also to be Jesuit. But the insight is not exclusively Catholic. One finds it in such Protestant writers as Dietrich Bonhoeffer. The insight is not even exclusively Christian. One also finds it outside of Christianity—e.g., in Mahayana Buddhism's "man for others" embodied in the Bodhhisattva ideal, succinctly formulated by Shantideva: "Whoever wishes quickly to rescue himself and another, should practice the supreme mystery: the exchanging of himself and the other" (cited by Graham, p. 94).

The writings of *William Johnston* have a similarly global, and particularly Eastern, orientation: for example, *Christian Zen* (San Francisco: Harper & Row, 1979), *Christian Mysticism Today* (San Francisco: Harper & Row, 1984), and *Being in Love: the Practice of Christian Prayer* (San Francisco: Harper & Row, 1989).

Some other post–Vatican II spiritual writings fall to one or another side of Dom Aelred's comprehensive approach. On the one side is *Adrian van Kaam*, whose earlier writings reflected some preconciliar methodological assumptions about the nature of theology, revelation, doctrine, and Sacred Scripture, but who acknowledged, more than Garrigou-Lagrange, Tanquerey, and others, the close relationship between personality development and spirituality (see his *In Search of Spiritual Identity*, Denville, N.J.: Dimension Books, 1975; and especially his five-volume *Formative Spirituality*, New York: Crossroad, 1983–1992).

And the anonymously produced *Cloud of Unknowing* is a principal guide for the "centering prayer" movement. The term is inspired by Thomas Merton, who stressed in his earlier writings that the only way to come into contact with the living God is to go to one's center and from that point to pass into God. It is a spirituality of *interiority*, of going deeply into oneself in order to get in touch with the divine reality present there. As soon as we become aware of any thoughts, we must disavow them and return to God again. In the spirit of the *Cloud of Unknowing*, everything is to be abandoned except God. Far from removing us from others, this prayer should make us more conscious of our oneness with them. One spiritual writer in this

1046

tradition, Jesuit theologian *Thomas Clarke*, is more insistent upon this than some others appear to be. "The quality and intensity of contemplation is in direct, not in inverse, proportion to the quality and intensity of our action on behalf of justice and peace, and vice versa" ("Finding Grace at the Center," in *Finding Grace at the Center*, Thomas Keating, et al., Still River, Mass.: St. Bede Publications, 1978, p. 59. The name of *M. Basil Pennington*, a Trappist monk, is especially linked with the increasing popularity of centering prayer.).

Another individually oriented spirituality, but with a Russian flavoring, is offered by *Catherine de Hueck Doherty*, foundress of Madonna House in Ontario, Canada. Her approach is developed in a trilogy: *Poustinia* ("Desert"), *Sobornost* ("Unity"), and *Strannik* ("Pilgrimage") (Notre Dame, Ind.: Ave Maria Press, 1975, 1977, and 1978 respectively). We were created to be *one* with God in paradise. That unity was restored by the incarnation. Christ himself is the total pilgrim, on his way from the bosom of his Father to the hearts of men and women. He invites us to pilgrimage with him, to know God as Adam and Eve once knew God. One goes out to the desert to contemplate the unity God offers us in Christ. Meanwhile, our pilgrimage continues until we meet God again at the Second Coming (see *Strannik: The Call to Pilgrimage for Western Man*, pp. 9–16).

On the other side are more activist-oriented spiritualities. German theologian Johannes Metz, in his *Followers of Christ: Perspectives on the Religious Life* (New York: Paulist Press, 1978), argues that religious congregations are called in a special way to be a shock force in the Church, giving witness not only to the world but to the Church itself of how the Gospel is to be lived in an uncompromising fashion. Metz's reflections on the evangelical counsels, however, have applicability beyond the concerns of religious orders. *Poverty*, he suggests, is "a protest against the tyranny of having, of possessing and of pure self-assertion. It impels those practicing it into practical solidarity with those poor whose poverty is not a matter of virtue but is their condition of life and the situation exacted of them by society" (p. 49). *Celibacy* is "the expression of an uncompromising concentration of longing for the day of the Lord, a concentration that is not afraid of any temptation of loneliness.... It impels towards solidarity with those unmarried people whose celibacy (that is to say, loneliness; that is to say, not having anyone) is not a virtue but their social destiny, and towards those who are shut up in lack of expectation and in resignation" (p. 60). *Obedience*, finally, is "the radical and uncalculated surrender of one's life to God the Father who raises up and liberates. It impels one to stand close to those for whom obedience is not a matter of virtue but the sign of oppression and of being placed in tutelage, and to do this in a practical way" (p. 67). For Metz, then, there is a growing proportion between the mystical and the political aspects of Christian discipleship, with the balance apparently tilted in the political direction. It is also a life that is increasingly eschatological, i.e., governed by the expectation of the imminent coming of the Kingdom of God. Since the Lord is close at hand, there is no time for postponement. We must serve the least of the brethren now (p. 79).

Closer to the middle are the writings of Catholic pastoral theologian *Henri Nouwen*. Christian spirituality, he suggests, moves through three polarities. The first polarity deals with our relationship to ourselves: the polarity between loneliness and solitude. The second is at the root of our relationship to others: the polarity between hostility and hospitality. And the third, and most important, has to do with our relationship with God: the polarity between illusion and prayer. To live a spiritual life "means first of all to come to the awareness of the inner polarities between which we are held in tension" (*Reaching Out: The Three Movements of the Spiritual Life*, New York: Doubleday, 1975, p. 12). To be Christian we do not have to deny our loneliness, our hostilities, and our illusions. We have to have the courage to allow them to come to our full attention, to understand them, to confess them, and then to convert them into solitude, hospitality, and prayer. (See also *Seeds of Hope: A Henri Nouwen Reader*, Robert Durback, ed., New York: Bantam Books, 1989.)

Appealing also to a wide popular audience is former Dominican *Matthew Fox*. The titles of his early trilogy of spiritual books tended to veer somewhat from the conventional: *On Becoming a Musical Mystical Bear: Spirituality American Style* (New York: Paulist Press, 1972); *Whee! We, Wee All the Way Home: A Guide to the New Sensual Spirituality* (Wilmington, N.C.: Consortium Books, 1976); and *A Spirituality Named Compassion and the Healing of the Global Village, Humpty Dumpty and Us* (Minneapolis: Winston Press, 1979). The first book concentrates on the meaning of the word *prayer* and its relationship to the personal and the psychological (i.e., prayer as "mysticism") as well as to the social (i.e., prayer as "prophecy"). There is a necessary dialectic between the mystical and the prophetic. The second book deals with the recovery of what Fox calls a nonelitist understanding of spiritual experience, especially the experience of ecstasy. Such a spirituality leads, he argues, to a reexamination of the role of body and body politic, of pleasure and the sharing of pleasures that make up the spiritual journey. The third book moves from passion to compassion, which he defines as "a passionate way of living born of an awareness of the interconnectedness of all creatures by reason of their common Creator" (p. 34). Fox, referring his thought to Meister Eckhart, concludes: "You may call God love; you may call God goodness; but the best name for God is Compassion."

The Humpty Dumpty image reminds us that the egg of our world is cracked. It is the price we have paid for our aggressive, materialistic mode of life. Humpty Dumpty teaches us that the primary issue in spirituality is not redemption of the soul but redemption of the world. We are in the world, and the world is in us. To heal one is to heal the other. The world is only a projection of our inner selves. "It is because we worship upness inside that we build skyscrapers outside. It is because we prefer aggression to gentleness inside that we invest so mightily in armaments and so punily in artists on the outside. Humpty teaches us how the inside is the outside and the outside is the inside. For better or for worse ... until death do us part" (p. 268).

Fox has developed these themes in later works which stress reverence for the created world and a positive estimation of the human and particularly the bodily: *Original Blessing* (Santa Fe, N.M.: Bear, 1983), *The Coming of the Cosmic Christ: The Healing of Mother Earth and the Birth of a Global Renaissance* (San Francisco: HarperCollins, 1988), and *Creation Spirituality: Liberating Gifts for the Peoples of the Earth* (San Francisco: HarperCollins, 1991). His approach to spirituality is now identified with the title of the most recent book, "creation-centered spirituality."

A quest for balance is evident in the writings of Cardinal *Léon Joseph Suenens* of Belgium, whose *A New Pentecost?* (New York: Seabury Press, 1974) emphasizes both the charismatic and institutional elements of Christian community and the individual and social dimensions of Christian existence. To be spiritual is to be always ready to expect the unexpected from God, for God is even now creating anew. We are not prisoners of determinism or of sociological prognostications. The Holy Spirit is at work in the Church and in the rest of the world, even when unrecognized and unnamed. To those who welcome the Spirit there is liberty, joy, and trust. The Spirit has raised up prophets and saints who, in times of darkness, have discovered "a spring of grace and shed beams of light on our path" (p. xiii). John XXIII and Vatican II were such surprises. Who would dare to say, therefore, that the love and imagination of God are exhausted? "To hope is not to dream, but to turn dreams into reality. Happy are those who dream dreams and are ready to pay the price to make them come true." Pentecost continues.

One of the most significant postconciliar developments has been that of *feminist spirituality*. "It is the spirituality," Anne Carr writes, "of those who have experienced feminist consciousness raising and so have critical questions about inherited patterns and assumptions about gender differences and the implications of these for social and ecclesial roles and behavior" (*Transforming Grace,* p. 206). Carr makes clear that feminist spirituality, unlike women's spirituality, is for men as well as women. It is for anyone who is deeply aware of the historical and cultural restrictions placed upon women in the Church and in society at large.

Rooted in women's experience of friendship and solidarity and in their search for autonomy and freedom, feminist spirituality not only affirms and recognizes the realities of feminist sisterhood but also of the broader solidarity of humankind. "A Christian feminist spirituality calls everyone to wider visions of human mutuality, reciprocity, and interdependence before God who seeks the unity and community of all" (p. 208). Because of its sense of universal solidarity, feminist spirituality stands against all forms of human oppression, including racism, classism, sexism, and elitism; it is global in its compassion, and as such stands also against militarism and the exploitation of the environment.

Feminist writers suggest that God occasionally be imagined and worshipped as mother and sister, and that the Risen Christ be thought of, in a nonandrocentric way, as bearing the feminine qualities of the biblical Wisdom or Sophia as well as the masculine features of the Jesus of history and the *Logos*. The Church, therefore, is a community of equal discipleship, and Mary is the witness of both the strength of autonomy and the compassion of relatedness that human and Christian development implies. Christian virtue, in turn, is both active and passive strength in the solidarity of human community with God that is given in Christ and that is continually energized by the Spirit (pp. 213–14; see also the writings of Elisabeth Schüssler Fiorenza, Elizabeth Johnson, Sandra Schneiders, Rosemary Haughton, and others).

Liberation spirituality (also reflected in feminist spirituality) represents the spiritual turn in Latin American liberation theology, as represented, for example, in Gustavo Gutiérrez's *We Drink from Our Own Wells: The Spiritual Journey of a People* (Maryknoll, N.Y.: Orbis Books, 1984), *On Job: God-talk and the Suffering of the Innocent* (Orbis Books, 1987), and *The God of Life* (Orbis Books, 1991). Leonardo Boff explicitly links liberation and feminist concerns in *The Maternal Face of God: The Feminine and its Religious Expressions* (San Francisco: Harper & Row, 1987).

A *global* (ecumenical, interfaith, and transcultural) spirituality that is at once thoroughly Christian and Catholic has been fashioned by *Donald Nicholl*, an English philosopher whose book *Holiness*, originally published in 1981, has established itself as a modern classic (New York: Paulist Press, 1987). Drawing upon an extraordinarily wide range of classical and modern writers, he situates our "place" in creation while reflecting upon the role of solitude and stillness, spiritual companions, suffering, and daily life as an exercise in self-sacrifice and the service of others. He shows why solitude and communion (*koinonia*) are not incompatible: "because the principle that unites persons in the most intimate *koinonia* is the unique, incommunicable relationship with God which each person shares with every other person."

As in the pre–Vatican II period, postconciliar spirituality is also identified with movements as diverse as the Charismatic Renewal movement, Marriage Encounter, Bread for the World, Zen Buddhism, New Age (creation-centered), Opus Dei, and Communion and Liberation (*Comunione e Liberazione*).

MYSTICISM

Mysticism is not given a separate category here because it is something radically different from spirituality, or indeed from the Christian life itself. On the contrary, Christian mysticism is rooted in the
baptismal call of all Christians to enter into the divine mystery
through the Scriptures, the liturgy, and the sacraments. It is a gift
rather than the product of individual effort. In its most general sense,
therefore, mysticism is potentially the spiritual dimension of every
Christian's life. Yet some Christians do have more intense experiences of the divine mystery, and so mysticism serves also as a distinct
category of theology and spirituality.

Mysticism, in this stricter sense, is *the graced transformation of
consciousness that follows upon a direct or immediate experience of the
presence of God leading to deeper union with God.* That union, however,
does not isolate the individual from others or from the world. The
deep union achieved by Bernard of Clairvaux, Francis of Assisi, and
Catherine of Siena, for example, led them into greater apostolic activity and into service of others. Neither is mysticism confined to the
Church. *Christian* mysticism roots the experience of God in Jesus
Christ, an experience brought about by the Holy Spirit. All spirituality, and certainly all Christian spirituality, therefore, is oriented toward the experience of God. Individualistic spiritualities assume that
we can experience God only to the extent that we *exclude* experiencing
everyone else and everything else. Socially activist spiritualities assume that we experience God *only* in the other and in the social and
political movements of history. Balanced spiritualities insist on a
connection between the two: the experience of God as the presence
within, and the experience of God as the presence *in others* and in the
"signs of the times."

Historically, the use of the word *mystical* to describe a special
religious experience is peculiar to Christianity. And even at that its
use developed only gradually. It was first employed to designate the
deepest meaning of Sacred Scripture, a meaning accessible only to
faith. For Clement of Alexandria and for Origen, it was equivalent to
the Pauline notion of "mystery"—namely, Jesus Christ crucified (1
Corinthians 2:2). The mystery, hidden for ages but now revealed to
the saints, is "Christ in you" (Colossians 1:26–27). Christ, in whom

are hidden all the treasures of wisdom and knowledge, is the divine mystery (2:2–3).

Because mysticism is always particular and contextual, one can speak of various types. The most common ones usually involve some variation on the basic twofold distinction given in the treatise *The Mystical Theology*, by Denys the Areopagite, known as Pseudo-Dionysius, a Syrian monk of the late fifth and early sixth centuries. There is the way of imagelessness, stillness, and wordlessness (the *via negativa*, or "apophatic" way), and the way of imaging God by the use of the human imagination or in words (the *via affirmativa*, or "kataphatic" way). Thus, Meister Eckhart and the author of *The Cloud of Unknowing* would be in the first category, and Julian of Norwich and Francis of Assisi would be in the second. There is, of course, no real basis in theology for an absolute distinction between the two ways, because God is revealed in and through images and words and other visible realities and yet is always beyond them. Thus do the principles of *sacramentality* and *mediation* apply to mysticism. And since mysticism is always oriented to union with God issuing in service to others, so, too, is the principle of *communion* engaged herein.

GLOSSOLALIA: SPEAKING IN TONGUES

The New Testament refers several times to speaking "in new tongues" (Mark 16:17; Acts of the Apostles 2:4–11; 10:46; 19:6; 1 Corinthians 14). It is a speech that is unintelligible to the listeners, except in Acts of the Apostles 2:4–11. It is the work of the Holy Spirit, given particularly at Baptism (Acts of the Apostles 10:46; 19:6), and it becomes so routine a part of the life of some churches that the gift has to be regulated (1 Corinthians 14). Furthermore, it is addressed to God, not to people (14:2), and it edifies the speaker rather than those who hear the speaker (14:4). Accordingly, what is spoken "in tongues" must be interpreted (14:5–19,27).

It should be noted that one of the effects of religious ecstasy in contemporary Hellenistic and Oriental circles was the utterance of unintelligible speech. The appearance of unintelligible· "tongues" (Greek, *glossa*) in some of the early Christian communities, therefore, may have provided a bridge between the Hellenistic-Oriental world and the emerging world of Christian faith. As the cultural context changed, the gift of tongues gradually disappeared.

Paul, of course, acknowledged that this gift, even in its period of frequent use, was the least important in the hierarchy of gifts (1 Corinthians 12:1–11). It was only occasionally mentioned in subsequent centuries, entering the modern period via small marginal Protestant groups known as Pentecostals. Just after Vatican II, interest in and expression of the gift of tongues surfaced with vigor even in Catholicism. The phenomenon developed in connection with the emergence of the Catholic Charismatic Renewal, whose origin is usually placed at Duquesne University in Pittsburgh, Pennsylvania, in 1967, from where it spread quickly to the University of Michigan at Ann Arbor and the University of Notre Dame in Indiana.

Seen in its most positive light, the gift of tongues is a form of nondiscursive prayer, not unlike the protracted "A" sound at the end of the chanted "Alleluia" or the spontaneous but unstructured communications of a child who has not yet learned to speak. Others have compared it to the gift of tears, i.e., a religious experience by which a person is moved to a profound sense of sorrow for sin, repentance, adoration, or gratitude before God. Such tears are no different from any others, but their religious significance goes far beyond the merely physical. So, too, does that of the gift of tongues.

"In psychological terms, we could say that it is the voice of the subconscious rising to God, finding a manner of praying which is analogous to other expressions of our subconscious in dreams, laughter, tears, painting, or dance," Cardinal Suenens observes. "This prayer within the depths of our being heals at a profound yet often perceptible level hidden psychological wounds that impede the full development of our interior life" (*A New Pentecost?* p. 103).

On the other hand, the common approach of the great mystics has been to ignore such phenomena, even if they are God-given, since God's work has already been accomplished in Christ (John of the Cross, *The Ascent of Mount Carmel*, Part II, chapter 8). One should preserve, in any case, the Pauline principle that in the worship assembly no one should speak in tongues unless an interpreter can explain the meaning to the community, for every gift is, in the final accounting, always for the sake of the Church and ultimately for the sake of the Kingdom of God (1 Corinthians 14:28).

SPIRITUALITY AND SPIRITUALITIES:
THEOLOGICAL CRITERIA

We return to the Thomistic philosophical principle: "Whatever is received is received according to the mode of the receiver." Although God is one, the experience of God is individually, socially, historically, even economically conditioned. Thus, there is one God, but there are many religions. There is one Body of Christ but many churches. There is one faith and yet many theologies. And there is one Spirit and yet many spiritualities.

Indeed, as Paul reminded us, "Now there are a varieties of gifts, but the same Spirit; and there are varieties of services, but the same Lord; and there are varieties of activities, but it is the same God who activates all of them in everyone. To each is given the manifestation of the Spirit for the common good.... All of these are activated by one and the same Spirit, who allots to each one individually just as the Spirit chooses" (1 Corinthians 12:4–7,11). According to Thomas Aquinas, the "first cause of this diversity is to be sought on the part of God, who disposes [the divine] gifts of grace variously in order that the beauty and perfection of the Church may result from these various degrees" (*Summa Theologiæ*, I-II, q. 112, a. 4).

But to say that there are inevitably many spiritualities is not to say that all spiritualities are equally good or equally deficient, no more than one could say that all religions, or all theologies, or even all churches are of equal value and are equally faithful expressions of the divine reality. On what basis can one evaluate the worth of spiritualities? What *theological criteria*, consistent with the Catholic tradition, can one apply to the variety of spiritualities?

1. We are neither purely bodily creatures nor purely spiritual; nor are we primarily bodily or primarily spiritual. *We are body-spirits* (for this and the next five principles, see chapter 5). Accordingly, no Christian spirituality can be predicated on a *dualistic* understanding of human existence, as if the flesh (considered separately from the soul) were always at war with the spirit (considered separately from the flesh). The spirit-flesh opposition in Paul is between the *whole person* as oriented toward the Kingdom of God, and the *whole person* as oriented away from God in the pursuit of selfish interests.

2. *We are radically social beings.* Accordingly, no Christian spirituality can attend exclusively nor in an exaggerated fashion to the individual's personal relationship with God, as if other persons and the wider created order did not enter intrinsically into that relationship.

3. *We are individual human persons.* Accordingly, no Christian spirituality can allow the individual to be absorbed into some impersonal collective, as if the experience of God is only corporate or horizontal, never individual or vertical.

4. *We are also subjects,* i.e., distinct centers of consciousness and freedom. Accordingly, there is no single way of experiencing God or of expressing the experience of God. No Christian spirituality can impose itself as the *only* spirituality for *all*.

5. *We are graced.* The presence of God enters into the very definition of what it means to be human. The doctrines of creation and of redemption make it impossible for a Christian to reject the material, the fleshly, the bodily, the natural, the tangible, the visible, the concrete. Accordingly, no Christian spirituality can counsel a repression of the human nor dismiss whole components of human existence as if they were somehow dishonorable and bestial (e.g., the passions, or so-called lower appetites).

6. To be graced is to be alive by a principle that transcends us— namely, the presence of God. For the Christian, *God is always triune* (see chapter 8). Accordingly, Christian spirituality is trinitarian spirituality. We are created, called, and sustained by the Father; re-created in the Son and given new access to the Father through the Son; and renewed and empowered to live a fully human life by the Holy Spirit.

7. Since the triune God is present everywhere, *all reality has a sacramental, or mysterious, character.* The invisible is embodied in, and mediated by, the visible. Accordingly, the horizon of Christian spirituality will be as wide as the created order itself. It will be as worldly and as ecological as it is personal; i.e., it will strive always to see God in all things.

8. *Human existence and Christian existence alike are destined for, and therefore oriented toward, the Kingdom of God.* But the Kingdom is a kingdom of justice and peace as well as of holiness and grace (*Pastoral*

Constitution on the Church in the Modern World, n. 39). Accordingly, Christian spirituality will always be sensitive to the demands of justice, of peace, of human rights, and will never be closed off from, or indifferent to, the needs and the cries of the poor and the oppressed.

9. *We are also sinners.* Accordingly, there can be no authentic Christian spirituality apart from the cross. It is a spirituality always marked by sacrifice, by denial of selfish interests, even by contradictions. It will be attentive to the impact of Original Sin: to pride, to apathy, to temerity, to lust, to hypocrisy, to sloth, to envy.

10. *We are ecclesial persons.* Christian faith is given, received, nourished, sustained, and brought to fulfillment in the context of the Church. Accordingly, there is no authentic Christian spirituality that is not at the same time ecclesial spirituality, rooted not only in the primitive, foundational proclamation of the Word in and through Sacred Scripture, but also in the Word's constant reproclamation and celebration in the Church's liturgy and across the whole range of its sacramental and para-sacramental life.

11. As ecclesial persons, members of the Body of Christ, *we are called to Christian discipleship in relation to God, neighbor, world, and self.* Accordingly, Christian spirituality will be an expression of the virtues that relate us at once to God, neighbor, world, and self (faith, hope, charity, and creative freedom and responsibility), to God in particular (humility and gratitude), to the neighbor in particular (mercy and concern for the poor, forgiveness, justice, and truthfulness), to the world (stewardship), and to self (temperance and fortitude) [see chapter 26]. The center will always be charity: love of God and love of neighbor.

12. *The call to Christian holiness is a universal call* (*Dogmatic Constitution on the Church*, chapter 5). There is no "higher" spirituality for the ordained and the religiously professed than for the laity. Accordingly, Christian spirituality will never be hierarchical or elitist, nor patriarchal and androcentric. There will always be different spiritualities, but the differences will not necessarily imply superiority or inferiority in relation to one another, nor on the basis of ecclesiastical "states of life" or gender.

SUMMARY

1. *Spirituality* has to do with our experiencing of God and with the transformation of our consciousness and our lives as outcomes of that experience. Since God is available in principle to everyone, spirituality is not exclusively Christian.

2. *Christian spirituality* is life in the Holy Spirit who incorporates the Christian into the Body of Jesus Christ, through whom the Christian has access to God the Creator in a life of faith, hope, love, and service. It is *visionary, sacramental, relational,* and *transformational.*

3. The *foundations* of Christian spirituality were already laid in the *covenantal relationship* between Yahweh and Israel in the Old Testament. Through *Jesus' death and resurrection,* the Spirit of God comes to dwell within us anew, as the source of light, wisdom, hope, peace.

4. In the time of the persecutions *martyrdom* was regarded as the ideal way of achieving union with God. Later, a life of total self-sacrifice was regarded as a kind of martyrdom.

5. *Monasticism* began as a solitary form of existence (anchoritism) and later developed a communal form (cenobitism). The *consecration of virgins* was also introduced at this time.

6. A Christian *spiritual theology* developed only gradually from the new monastic movement. The monastic style of spirituality (especially that of *Benedict*) was given wider currency among the laity through the popular writings of *Pope Gregory the Great.* In the tenth and eleventh centuries, as federations of monasteries were established, the monastic ideal was spread even more widely throughout the Christian world.

7. Under *Germanic influence,* Christian spirituality became more externalized: devotions, relics, pilgrimages, penances, confession of sins, etc.

8. Emphasis on *contemplation,* as immediate experience of God, was made popular by the new Cistercian Order, especially by *Bernard of Clairvaux* and *William of St. Thierry,* and by members of the Parisian monastery of St. Victor (the "Victorines").

9. With the decline of social life and of Christian morals even in the Church, various lay movements developed, urging radical poverty and an end to all formalism and legalism. The rise of the *mendicant orders*—Franciscans and Dominicans—brought the monastic spirit into the apostolic life.

10. But the stress on contemplation continued with the increasing popularity of *Pseudo-Dionysius,* whose works were newly translated in the thirteenth century. Christian spirituality was described in terms of the

soul's union with God through abandonment of, and detachment from, all creatures and worldly realities.

11. Although *Protestantism* rejected the excesses of medieval spirituality (superstitions and near idolatries), it did not reject its individualism. For Protestantism, access to God is direct and unmediated, guided by the interior illumination of the Holy Spirit.

12. A reaction to contemplative excesses in Catholic spirituality was mounted by such Christian humanists as *Erasmus* and by such Christian activists as *Ignatius Loyola*. They insisted on the fundamental connection between prayer and the apostolate.

13. *Mysticism* continued to flourish especially in *Spain* (Teresa of Ávila and John of the Cross). *Italian* spirituality was more oriented toward the renewal of priestly life (Philip Neri, Charles Borromeo, and Catherine of Genoa). *French* spirituality was centered on devotion to the Sacred Heart (John Eudes, Margaret Mary Alacoque), a piety more accessible to the average lay person (Francis de Sales, Jane Frances de Chantal), and devotion centered on Jesus (Jean Jacques Olier).

14. In the *nineteenth century* individualism and regimented piety continue (e.g., new devotions) but the forces of renewal are already at work: in theology, liturgy, historical studies, and the social apostolate, as well as in the world of science and technology.

15. At the *beginning of the twentieth century* there were spiritualities based largely on neoscholastic presuppositions (Tanquerey, Garrigou-Lagrange) and a broader, Christocentric piety was being developed by such writers as Abbot Marmion.

16. By the *middle of the twentieth century* spiritualities begin to emerge which are more world-centered (Teilhard de Chardin), neighbor-oriented (Hubert Van Zeller), justice-concerned (Thomas Merton), and person-integrating (Josef Goldbrunner).

17. The *Second Vatican Council* taught that holiness is for everyone and that it comprehends more than the soul's individual relationship with God. Spirituality is shaped by one's situation in life. It is rooted in the mysteries of creation and redemption, in the presence of the Holy Spirit, and in the mission of Christ and the Church. The liturgy is its summit and fountain.

18. *Post–Vatican II* spirituality has been marked by a full-scale liturgical renewal, ecumenism, a more pronounced commitment to liberation and social justice, the environmental movement, a new emphasis on creation, a deepening reverence for Sacred Scripture, an increased striving for a personal experience of the Holy Spirit, feminist consciousness, and by various lay movements all across the theological spectrum.

1059

19. *Mysticism* is the graced transformation of consciousness that follows upon a direct or immediate experience of the presence of God leading to deeper union with God.

20. Within mysticism there is a traditional distinction between the way of imagelessness, stillness, and wordlessness (the *via negativa*, or "apophatic" way), and the way of imaging God by the use of the human imagination or in words (the *via affirmativa*, or "kataphatic" way).

21. *Speaking in tongues* is a form of ecstatic prayer. Like all gifts, it is for the good of the community.

22. Although there is only one Spirit, there are *many different spiritualities*, even within the Church itself. Some *theological criteria* for evaluating the various spiritualities are:

1. We are body-spirits.

2. We are social beings.

3. We are individual human persons.

4. We are subjects, i.e., distinct centers of consciousness and freedom.

5. We are graced.

6. God is triune.

7. The triune God is present to all reality.

8. Everything is destined for, and oriented toward, the Kingdom of God, a kingdom of justice and peace as well as of holiness and grace.

9. We are sinners.

10. We are ecclesial persons.

11. We are called to Christian discipleship.

12. All are called to holiness.

SUGGESTED READINGS

Aumann, Jordan. *Christian Spirituality in the Catholic Tradition.* San Francisco: Ignatius Press, 1985.

Bouyer, Louis, et al. *A History of Christian Spirituality.* 4 vols. New York: Desclée, 1963.

The Classics of Western Spirituality. New York: Paulist Press, 1978—.

Downey, Michael, ed. *The New Dictionary of Christian Spirituality.* Collegeville, Minn.: Liturgical Press, 1993.

Dupré, Louis, Donald Saliers, and John Meyendorff, eds. *Christian Spirituality: Post-Reformation and Modern,* World Spirituality, vol. 18. New York: Crossroad, 1989.

Dupré, Louis, and James Wiseman, eds. *Light from Light: An Anthology of Christian Mysticism*. New York: Paulist Press, 1988.

Egan, Harvey. *What are they saying about mysticism?* New York: Paulist Press, 1982.

Fischer, Kathleen. *Women at the Well*. New York: Paulist Press, 1988.

Jones, Cheslyn, Geoffrey Wainwright, and Edward Yarnold, eds. *The Study of Spirituality*. New York: Oxford University Press, 1986.

Lossky, Vladimir. *The Mystical Theology of the Eastern Church*. London: James Clarke, 1957.

Madigan, Shawn. *Spirituality Rooted in Liturgy*. Washington, D.C.: The Pastoral Press, 1988.

McGinn, Bernard. *The Foundations of Mysticism: Origins to the Fifth Century*. New York: Crossroad, 1991.

_____. and John Meyendorff, eds. *Christian Spirituality: Origins to the Twelfth Century*, World Spirituality, vol. 16. New York: Crossroad, 1985.

Raitt, Jill, ed. *Christian Spirituality: High Middle Ages and Reformation*, World Spirituality, vol. 17. New York: Crossroad, 1987.

Sheldrake, Philip. *Spirituality and History: Questions of Interpretation and Method*. New York: Crossroad, 1992.

XXIX

Worship: Liturgy, Prayer, Devotions

INTRODUCTION

Worship

At the center of the life of the Christian disciple and of the community of disciples (the Church) and at the heart of Christian and Catholic spirituality is *worship,* a comprehensive and complex term that encompasses liturgical and nonliturgical prayer. Worship is variously defined. It is understood here as an act of reverence and honor shown to God. Worship ("worth"–"ship") gives God what God is due, or "worth." It may be expressed in formal prayer (liturgical and nonliturgical, communal and private), or in the ordinary deeds of everyday human life that flow from an inner attitude of reverence and honor for God.

Christian worship is rooted in Jesus Christ, who alone gives God the fullness of reverence and honor. The highest expression of Christian worship is the Eucharist.

Liturgy

Liturgy is a form of worship. More precisely, liturgy is the *official public worship of the Church.* It is "the public worship which our

Redeemer as Head of the Church renders to the Father as well as the worship which the community of the faithful renders to its Founder, and through Him to the Heavenly Father. It is, in short, the worship rendered by the Mystical Body of Christ in the entirety of its Head and members" (Pope Pius XII, *Mediator Dei* [1947], n. 20; see also Vatican II's *Constitution on the Sacred Liturgy*, n. 7).

The Second Vatican Council points out that "the liturgy is the summit toward which the activity of the Church is directed; at the same time it is the fountain from which all of its power flows" (*Constitution on the Sacred Liturgy*, n. 10). It is "the outstanding means whereby the faithful may express in their lives and manifest to others the mystery of Christ and the real nature of the true Church" (n. 2). Therefore, each Christian "must share frequently in the sacraments, the Eucharist especially, and in liturgical rites. Each must apply himself [or herself] constantly to prayer, self-denial, active service of others, and the exercise of all the virtues" (*Dogmatic Constitution on the Church*, n. 42).

The word *liturgy* is derived from the Greek, *leitourgia*, a "public work" performed according to a prescribed ritual. The Septuagint uses the term to mean public religious service offered to God by priestly officials with the participation of others. The New Testament uses the term in more varied senses. In general, it refers to specific rites, such as baptism and the breaking of the bread. The *Didache* (n. 14) applies it to Eucharist specifically, a usage that generally continues in the East. In the West, *liturgy has come to include not only the Eucharist, but also the other sacraments and the Liturgy of the Hours* (the Divine Office). Some would also include funerals, the rites for religious profession, the blessing of abbots and abbesses, the consecration of virgins and of churches, and similar rites.

Liturgy is always situated in seasonal and festal contexts. "Within the cycle of a year... [the Church] unfolds the whole mystery of Christ, not only from his incarnation and birth until His ascension, but also as reflected in the day of Pentecost, and the expectation of a blessed, hoped-for return of the Lord" (*Constitution on the Sacred Liturgy*, n. 102). Through the liturgical year, therefore, the Church focuses its attention on the past, the present, and the future together. Thus, the liturgy and the liturgical year commemorate what God has already done for us in Christ and through the

Spirit; they draw us here and now into the mystery of God's saving activity; and they orient us toward, and offer us a foretaste of, the heavenly banquet at the end of history. At the center of the liturgical year always is the celebration of Easter, which is at the heart and core of Christian faith and hope, and the celebration of the Easter Triduum in particular (Holy Thursday, Good Friday, and the Easter Vigil).

Prayer

The traditional definition of *prayer* is the raising of the mind and the heart to God. It is the act by which one enters into conscious, loving communion with God. The word is derived from the Latin verb *precari*, "to entreat" or "to beg." In the Old Testament prayer is for the sake of the praise of God and the needs of human beings. The greatest collection of prayers in the Old Testament is the Book of Psalms, which served as the hymnal for worship in the Temple of Jerusalem. At the beginning of his public ministry, when he was baptized by John, "Jesus... was praying" (Luke 3:21–22). Then he was led by the Spirit into the desert where he spent forty days in fasting and prayer, in preparation for his public ministry (Luke 4:1–13). When he was practically overcome by the large crowds because of his preaching and healing, he "withdrew to deserted places to pray" (Luke 5:16). The longest prayer in the New Testament is the priestly prayer of Jesus at the Last Supper (John 17:1–26). The best known prayer is the Lord's Prayer (Matthew 6:9–13; Luke 11:2–4). But all the references to Jesus' praying are too numerous to cite here.

Prayer may be differentiated by reason of its *purpose.* Thus, there is the prayer of *adoration,* whose immediate end is the praise and glory of God; the prayer of *thanksgiving,* which gives gratitude to God for blessings received (the Eucharist is the prayer of thanksgiving *par excellence*); the prayer of *contrition,* which expresses sorrow for sin; and the prayer of *intercession,* or *petition,* which asks God for blessings upon oneself or others.

Prayer may also be differentiated by reason of its *context. Communal* prayer is offered to God by a group of persons together. It may be liturgical (the Eucharist) or nonliturgical (a wake-service). *Private* prayer is offered by an individual alone (the Rosary). By definition it is nonliturgical prayer.

Prayer may also be differentiated by reason of *method*. *Mental* prayer may or may not use words, but if it does use words, they do not follow a preset formula. *Vocal* prayer does use a given formula that may be spoken or sung. There is also the prayer of *bodily gesture*, such as expressed in dance.

There is another methodological distinction between *discursive* and *affective* prayer. In discursive prayer reason, or thinking, dominates. In affective prayer the feelings dominate (trust, surrender, gratitude, love). The normal development in the life of prayer is from discursive to affective prayer.

Meditation, which is a form of mental prayer, involves an extended reflection on the presence and activity of God. When the awareness of God's presence is not apprehended by thought but by love, it is called *contemplation*. (For an exposition on prayer as contemplative, that is, as the progressive appropriation of the joy and beauty of revelation, of infinity and of truth, of the majesty and the love of God, see Hans Urs von Balthasar's classic, *Prayer*.)

Meditation (sometimes called "active meditation" to distinguish it more clearly from contemplation) is generally understood to involve discursive reasoning, while contemplation is affective. It is simple awareness of, and focus upon, the presence of God. It is important to note that contemplation is not a method of prayer to be chosen at will, like meditation. It is a gift into which one is drawn. Its most intense form is attained when there is ecstatic union between the pray-er and God so that the human senses can no longer communicate with the outside world. This is sometimes known as absorption, or rapture.

Kataphatic ("affirmative") prayer uses words and images, while *apophatic* ("negative") prayer is simply silent in the presence of God. Apophatic prayer is a kind of contemplation.

Centering prayer is a special method of contemplation in which the person simply attends to the presence of God within, that is, at the center of one's being. A mantra or short phrase is sometimes repeated to keep one's attention centered.

Mystical prayer is also a form of contemplation in which the mind and heart are directly and powerfully influenced by God to operate in a way that is beyond the capacity of human effort, unaided by grace. This method of prayer has many forms and stages. *Glossolalia* is a speaking in tongues (see chapter 28).

Lectio divina, originally a monastic term, refers to the prayerful reading of, and meditative reflection upon, Sacred Scripture, the Christian classics, or other types of spiritual writing.

A final distinction may be made between *intensive* and *extensive* prayer. The former occurs at particular periods and is done either communally or privately. The latter permeates one's whole day; indeed, one's whole life. One lives in the presence of God (extensive prayer), but one's direct attention is focused on God only at particular moments and under particular circumstances (intensive).

All Christian prayer is trinitarian, Christocentric, ecclesial, pneumatological, and eschatological. It seeks union with the triune God, is centered on Jesus Christ, occurs within and by the Church, is empowered by the Spirit, and is oriented to final and complete union with God at the end of human history.

Devotions

Devotions (also called *popular devotions*, because of their appeal to the general populace of the Church) are forms of *affective* prayer. They appeal to religious feelings. The cultivation of popular devotions as a distinct form of prayer has its origins in the Counter-Reformation as a response to the spiritual needs of people who did not understand or feel fully at home in the Church's increasingly elaborate and complex liturgical celebrations.

Among the more traditional popular devotions of the twentieth century, especially before Vatican II, were the Rosary, the Way (or Stations) of the Cross, Benediction (now called Eucharistic Devotion), novenas (prayers with a specific intention, offered on nine consecutive days), the Nine First Fridays (Mass and Communion on the first Fridays of nine consecutive months), and Forty Hours (adoration, procession, and benediction of the Blessed Sacrament to commemorate the forty hours Jesus was entombed).

Because the liturgy itself has been so significantly reformed, bringing it closer to the ordinary experiences of people, many such devotions have declined in popularity since the council. However, the need for affective, nonliturgical, communal prayer remains. It is met in various ways, from communal penance services to Marian devotions. The Second Vatican Council "warmly commended" devotions, but cautioned that they "should be so drawn up that they harmonize with the liturgical seasons, accord with the sacred liturgy, are in some fashion derived from it, and lead the people to it..." (*Constitution on the Sacred Liturgy*, n. 13).

LITURGY

Eucharist

(Note to the reader: this section does not repeat, but presupposes, material already presented in chapter 22.)

The Eucharist is the "source of the Church's life and the pledge of future glory" (*Decree on Ecumenism*, n. 15). "No Christian community can be built up unless it has its basis and center in the celebration of the most Holy Eucharist" (*Decree on the Ministry and Life of Priests*, n. 6).It is the "summit" and the "fountain" of the whole Christian life (*Constitution on the Sacred Liturgy*, n. 10).

For the Catholic tradition, the Eucharist is a liturgical event in the ritual form of a commemorative, sacramental, sacrificial, and eschatological meal, in which the Church remembers, reenacts, celebrates, and proclaims Jesus' sacrificial life, death, and resurrection, and anticipates the heavenly banquet that awaits us. At the heart of the event is the offering and receiving of the body and blood of Jesus Christ, truly present in the sacrament of consecrated bread and wine.

"Day by day the liturgy builds up those within the Church into the Lord's holy temple, into a spiritual dwelling for God—an enterprise which will continue until Christ's full stature is achieved" (*Constitution on the Sacred Liturgy*, n. 2). The Eucharist is, therefore, a source of personal life and identity for every member of the Church, as well as "the source and apex of the whole work of preaching the Gospel" (*Decree on the Ministry and Life of Priests*, n. 5).

But more even than that, the Eucharist is the center, the summit, and the source of the whole Christian life. Everything converges on it and intersects with it; everything flows from it. No Catholic spirituality and no form of Catholic prayer and devotion can be regarded as

1068

authentically Catholic if it is not at the same time thoroughly and fundamentally eucharistic in substance and orientation.

The Other Sacraments

The pivotal statement of the *Constitution on the Sacred Liturgy* (n. 10) regarding the centrality of the liturgy, and the Eucharist in particular, is inclusive of the other sacraments of the Church. At the same time, the council did not intend to make the Eucharist and the other sacraments the sole nourishment of the spiritual life. It allows a role for popular devotions and spiritual exercises (nn. 12, 13).

With the renewal and revision of the sacramental rites following the council, the Church reminds us, for example, that the sacraments of initiation bring the faithful to the "full stature of Christ" and prepare them for engagement in the mission of the Church. The new Rite of Christian Initiation is based on a model of conversion, and so, too, is the new rite of Penance. The rite of Anointing focuses on the sick Christian's participation in Christ's passion, death, and resurrection, and the introduction to the new liturgy of marriage emphasizes its ecclesial dimension.

By contrast the Tridentine and post-Tridentine catechesis and spirituality tended to focus more on the sacraments as means of grace, on the obligation and necessity to receive them, and on the norms by which and by whom they were to be administered (matter and form, the authority and intention of the minister). That is one of the reasons why popular devotions (as we shall see again below) have had such wide appeal, especially between Trent and the renewal of Vatican II. The spiritual dimension of the sacramental life of the Church tended to be hidden from the ordinary Catholic's personal range of vision. As the model of Church shifted from institution to sacrament (see again chapter 19), so too did the understanding and celebration of the sacraments within the life of the Church. And that shift is reflected in the new rites and in their introductions (see *The Rites of the Catholic Church*, 2 vols.)

At the core of the conciliar reforms of the sacramental rites is their paschal orientation. The sacraments sanctify "almost every event in [our] daily lives," and through them we are "given access to the stream of divine grace which flows from the paschal mystery of the passion, death, and resurrection of Christ..." (n. 61). The paschal mystery is at the heart of Christian spirituality.

Liturgy of the Hours

The *Constitution on the Sacred Liturgy* declares that Christ continues "His priestly work through the agency of His Church . . . not only by celebrating the Eucharist, but also in other ways, especially by praying the divine Office" (n. 83). Before Vatican II the Divine Office (known as the Breviary) was recited as a daily obligation, under pain of mortal sin, by all clerics who had been ordained to the subdiaconate. With the reforms of Vatican II, the Office, now known as the Liturgy of the Hours, is seen as a prayer of the whole Church, especially the chief Hours of Morning Prayer and Evening Prayer (n. 100).

The Liturgy of the Hours consists of a pattern (that varies from Hour to Hour) of Scriptural and biblically inspired prayer that includes hymns, psalms and Scriptural canticles, Scripture readings and responses, non-Scriptural readings and responses, the Canticles of Zechariah and Mary, intercessions, the Lord's Prayer, collects, and final blessing and dismissal. The principal Hours of Morning and Evening Prayer, however, are essentially composed of psalmody and intercessory prayers.

The Hours are divided into the Office of Readings (formerly Matins), with the character of a night Office; Morning Prayer (formerly Lauds); Midmorning, Midday, Midafternoon Prayer (formerly Terce, Sext, and None), now subsumed under the name Daytime Prayer; Evening Prayer (formerly Vespers); and Night Prayer (formerly Compline). Morning and Evening Prayer are considered "the two hinges on which the daily Office turns; hence they are to be considered as the chief hours" (n. 89). At Morning Prayer the central themes include Christ's resurrection, praise for creation and redemption, and the dedication of the new day to the Lord's service. At Evening Prayer the themes include thanksgiving for Christ our light, reflection on his passion and burial, thanksgiving for the day's events, and an appeal for forgiveness for the day's misdeeds.

The Liturgy of the Hours offers the praying Church opportunities to "sanctify time," to become more sensitive to the needs of the whole Church and to the demands of nature and of the whole world, and to "pray without ceasing." It is a prayer rooted in ordinary daily life, using the Scriptures as its fundamental inspiration. In speaking of the Liturgy of the Hours as sanctifying time, the Church does not mean that secular time needs to be made sacred before it can be considered good. Rather, the Hours illuminate critical moments of the day, evening and morning, as revealing various aspects of the paschal mystery which is the center and foundation of the whole Christian life. Thus, those who pray the Hours are encouraged to see all moments of a day as sacramental expressions of that mystery.

Ideally, the Liturgy of the Hours is prayed in community to better express its ecclesial and public character. Even when recited alone, however, the Liturgy of the Hours is as fully liturgical prayer as the Eucharist and the other sacraments. It is public worship.

NONLITURGICAL PRAYERS AND DEVOTIONS

Communal Prayers and Devotions

The same faith that is expressed is the Church's public worship—the Eucharist, the other sacraments, and the Liturgy of the Hours—also can be expressed and, more often than not, *is* expressed in prayers and devotions outside of the liturgy. Even when those prayers and devotions *are* outside of the liturgy, they are often connected with it. This is especially the case with eucharistic devotions, such as Corpus Christi processions in which the Blessed Sacrament is carried publically in procession, Forty Hours adoration, what was once known as Benediction, the Nine First Fridays, the Five First Saturdays (in honor of the Blessed Virgin), various novenas, communal penance services, and the like. It is also the case with the Rosary, whose 150 Hail Marys are a kind of substitute for the 150 Psalms, and with the vesper services that were developed for use in parish churches as modifications of the liturgical hour of Vespers. They almost always concluded with Benediction.

As suggested above, the real impetus for popular devotions in the Catholic Church came with the reforms of the Council of Trent, following the Protestant Reformation. As a result of the codification of the Roman liturgy, the process of liturgical evolution and

1071

adaptation came to an end. In time explicit authorization came to be regarded as a necessary, even constitutive, element of Catholic liturgy. Popular devotions were regarded as second class, nonliturgical prayer, and so were left to develop for themselves, unimpeded by liturgical legislation. This made it possible for local needs and local cultures to put their stamp on them.

After the Reformation, for example, in countries where the vernacular tongue was not a Romance language, metrical hymns were composed to popular melodies for congregational singing in the native language. The hymns would be sung during the Mass while the priest and his servers recited the words of the liturgy quietly.

Perhaps no popular devotion, linked with the Eucharist, proved so popular and so spiritually formative as did Benediction of the Blessed Sacrament. Although a highly ceremonious ritual, it was easy to understand. Those present had a clear sense of the benevolent presence of Jesus, and at the same time they could adore him openly and directly. "It is probable," one scholar has suggested, "that the eucharistic and ecclesial piety of Roman Catholics during this period [mid-nineteenth century] and well into the present century was formed and expressed more by the experience of Blessed Sacrament devotions than by attendance at mass and reception of communion" (Carl Dehne, "Devotion and Devotions," *The New Dictionary of Theology*, Joseph A. Komonchak, et al., eds., Wilmington, Del.: Michael Glazier, 1987, p. 286).

With changes in theological understanding and pastoral practice, but also, and perhaps more fundamentally, in culture, popular devotions have declined since Vatican II. The language, style, and music of some of the nineteenth-century devotions no longer appeal. The afternoon celebration of Mass has taken over the time once reserved for afternoon devotions. Individual private devotion to the Blessed Sacrament continues, but the reception of Communion in the hand and the widespread use of lay eucharistic ministers has rendered the ceremonious exposition and benediction of the Blessed Sacrament "somehow incongruous" (Dehne, p. 287).

Now that the public worship has been reformed by the council, the elements that once attracted people to popular devotions are to be found in the liturgy itself: vernacular language, familiar expressions, light music, a friendly, communal atmosphere. One of the most popular communal devotions to have survived the conciliar changes is the prayer before meals, which is frequently spontaneous and sometimes elaborate.

Private Prayers and Devotions

Traditional private prayers and devotions include the following: Acts of Faith, Hope, and Charity; the Jesus Prayer; the Morning Offering; prayers before and after meals (which are also on the communal list); prayer before a crucifix; the Rosary (which can also be recited communally); prayers during visits to the Blessed Sacrament; Stations of the Cross (which can also be communal, especially during Lent); and special prayers to Mary and the saints. (For texts and/or more information on these and other prayers and devotions, see *The Catholic Source Book* [1990].)

CHRISTIAN FEMINISM AND WORSHIP

According to Rosemary Ruether, one important aspect of the emerging feminist spirituality is its recognition of the need for intentional communities of faith and worship. It is not enough, she points out, to hold an ideology of criticism and social analysis, nor to participate in protest and action groups that press for change in the Church. "One needs communities of nurture to guide one through death to the old symbolic order of patriarchy to rebirth into a new community of being and living... one also needs deep symbols and symbolic actions to guide and interpret the actual experience of the journey from sexism to liberated humanity" (*Women-Church,* p. 3).

The final section of her book presents both new versions of traditional sacramental and liturgical forms and also proposes new forms of ritual that will sacramentalize women's rites of passage that have been ignored or downplayed in the past: the onset of menstruation, the break from parent's home to autonomous living, marriage, divorce, coming out as a lesbian, embarking on new stages of life, menopause, sickness, and death. There are rituals for the healing of raped women, for battered and sexually abused women, for women who have had miscarriages, and so forth. Each of these situations was

1073

traditionally covered with shame, as if women themselves were at fault or as if the body was somehow dishonorable. Ruether's work assumes, in the end, that "the creation of liturgy is properly a function of local communities who are engaged in a collective project woven from the fabric of many concrete stories that make up the lives of each member of that body" (p. 7). (See also Miriam Therese Winter's *WomanPrayer, WomanSong*, 1987.)

It is a development still very much in process.

SUMMARY

1. *Worship* is an act of reverence and honor shown to God, expressed in formal prayer or in the ordinary deeds of everyday human life. *Christian worship* is rooted in Jesus Christ and reaches its highest expression in the Eucharist.

2. *Liturgy* is the official public worship of the Church. It includes the Eucharist, the other sacraments, and the Liturgy of the Hours.

3. *Prayer* is the act by which one enters into conscious, loving communion with God. It is differentiated by reason of its purpose (adoration, thanksgiving, contrition, petition), its context (communal or private), its method (mental or vocal; discursive or affective).

4. *Meditation* is a form of mental prayer, involving an extended reflection on the presence and activity of God. *Contemplation*, on the other hand, is the simple awareness of, and focus upon, the presence of God. It is not a method of prayer, but a gift from God.

5. *Mystical prayer* is a form of contemplation in which the mind and heart are directly and powerfully influenced by God.

6. *Devotions* are forms of *affective* prayer. They appeal to religious feelings. Vatican II insisted that devotions should be closely linked with the liturgy.

7. Just as the *Eucharist* is the summit and the source of the whole Christian life, so it is the center of Catholic spirituality.

8. The new rites of the *other sacraments* highlight their ecclesial dimension, the need for personal conversion, and their rooting in the paschal mystery of Christ.

9. The *Liturgy of the Hours* is an integral part of the public worship of the Church. Once regarded as the prayer only of monks and clerics, it is now recommended for the whole Church, especially Morning and Evening Prayer, which is composed of psalmody and intercessory prayers.

10. The most *popular devotions* before Vatican II were related to the Eucharist, e.g., Benediction of the Blessed Sacrament. Popular devotions declined after Vatican II because the reformed liturgy made them less necessary than before.

11. *Feminist spirituality* has liturgical and devotional outcomes, as women seek to develop communities of nurture, new symbolic actions, and new rituals that are expressive of the actual experience of women.

SUGGESTED READINGS

Balthasar, Hans Urs von. *Prayer*. San Francisco: Ignatius Press, 1986.

Brueggemann, Walter. *Praying the Psalms*. Winona, Minn.: St. Mary's Press, 1982.

Collins, Mary. *Contemplative Participation: Sacrosanctum Concilium, Twenty-five Years Later*. Collegeville, Minn.: Liturgical Press, 1990.

Cunningham, Lawrence S. *Catholic Prayer*. New York: Crossroad, 1989.

Downey, Michael, ed. *The New Dictionary of Catholic Spirituality*. Collegeville, Minn.: Liturgical Press, 1993.

Fink, Peter E., ed. *The New Dictionary of Sacramental Worship*. Collegeville, Minn.: Liturgical Press, 1990.

Foster, Richard J. *Prayer: Finding the Heart's True Home*. San Francisco: HarperCollins, 1992.

Klein, Peter, ed. *The Catholic Source Book*. Dubuque, Iowa: Brown Publishing–ROA Media, 1990.

Madigan, Shawn. *Liturgy: Source of Spirituality*. Washington, D.C.: The Pastoral Press, 1989.

Ostdiek, Gilbert. *Catechesis for Liturgy: A Program for Parish Involvement*. Washington, D.C.: The Pastoral Press, 1986.

The Rites of the Catholic Church as Revised by the Second Vatican Ecumenical Council. 2 vols. New York: Pueblo Publishing Co., 1976, 1980.

Ruether, Rosemary Radford. *Women-Church: Theology and Practice of Feminist Liturgical Communities*. San Francisco: Harper & Row, 1985.

Searle, Mark. *Liturgy Made Simple*. Collegeville, Minn.: Liturgical Press, 1981.

Weil, Louis. *Gathered to Pray: Understanding Liturgical Prayer*. Cambridge, Mass.: Cowley, 1986.

Winter, Miriam Therese. *WomanPrayer, WomanSong: Resources for Ritual*. Oak Park, Ill.: Meyer Stone Books, 1987.

_____. *WomanWord: A Feminist Lectionary and Psalter: Women of the New Testament*. New York: Crossroad, 1990.

Wright, John H. *A Theology of Christian Prayer*. 2d ed. New York: Pueblo Publishing Co., 1988.

XXX

Mary and the Saints

INTRODUCTION

No theological and doctrinal presentation of Catholicism could claim to be at once comprehensive and complete, i.e., "catholic," if it were to leave out the Blessed Virgin Mary and the other saints. But where does the discussion belong? As an appendix to Christology, where Thomas Aquinas situated his reflections on Mary? Or as part of the mystery of the Church, where the Second Vatican Council placed its teachings on Mary and the saints? Or here, in this final part on spirituality, within the theology of the Holy Spirit (pneumatology) and proximate to the theology of the final things (eschatology)?

There is no single correct answer. Mary and the saints could just as properly be considered within the mystery of God, since it is the holiness of God that is the gift they receive, by which they are transformed, and which they reflect as the moon reflects the rays of the sun. Or within the discussion of nature and grace (theological anthropology), since the drama of sin and grace is played out in their lives and, in Mary's case, the triumph of grace is definitive and complete. Or within the next chapter on eschatology, since the saints personify the fulfillment to which we are all called and are signs of hope in the promises of God.

This presentation on Mary and the saints has been reserved for this final part of the book because, in the everyday reality of Catholic life, Mary and the saints are more immediately objects of prayer and devotion than of theological and doctrinal reflection.

Finally, a word about the chapter title. A more theologically precise rendering of it would be "Mary and the Other Saints," since Mary is herself a saint, albeit the greatest of saints and the preeminent member of the Communion of Saints. Or something even more precise than that, but hopelessly cumbersome: "The Saints, With Special Attention to Mary." Because Mary holds so unique a place among the saints, the least precise, but simplest, title has been chosen.

THE BLESSED VIRGIN MARY

History

New Testament

Although God is mentioned in every book of the New Testament and also Jesus (Christ), except for 3 John, Mary is named only in the Synoptic Gospels and Acts of the Apostles. In the Johannine Gospel she is referred to as "the mother of Jesus" or "his mother" (2:1,3,5,12; 1:25–26). The only reference to Mary in the *Pauline* writings is in Galatians 4:4: "God sent his Son, born of a woman...." The theological interest of that statement is Christological, pointing to the true humanity of Jesus. The designation "born of a woman" is found in the Old Testament, at Qumran, and in non-Pauline New Testament passages simply as the designation of a human being. There is no other meaning of it in Paul that one can find. Nor is there any other Pauline text referring to Jesus' origin which assigns any unusual part to Mary in Jesus' birth.

The Infancy Narrative of *Matthew* says little about Mary apart from the virginal conception (see our discussion of the virginal conception in chapter 15). In the Gospel of *Luke*, however, the evangelist's estimation of Mary is found principally in his Infancy Narrative. She is hailed by Gabriel as one favored by God (1:28,30); her response shows her to be an obedient handmaid of the Lord (1:38); Elizabeth calls her "the mother of my Lord" (1:43) and declares her blessed because of what God has done for Mary (1:42) and because of Mary's faith "that there would be a fulfillment of what was spoken to her by

the Lord" (1:45). In her own canticle, the *Magnificat,* Mary acknowledges that "the Mighty One has done great things for me" (1:49).
Luke, therefore, depicts Mary as the spokeswoman and representative of the *anawim,* the poor of Israel. She is a faithful hearer of the
word, obedient to it and to the God who utters it.

On the other hand, Luke mentions Mary only once in the *Acts of
the Apostles* (1:14). It is after the ascension of Jesus into heaven that the
disciples return to Jerusalem, go to the upstairs room, and devote
themselves to constant prayer, "together with certain women, including Mary the mother of Jesus, as well as his brothers." Although
it is not possible to establish the time when Mary's own belief in her
Son's messianic significance began, or even the cause of it, it is clear
that she shared the faith in Jesus of the earliest Christian community
(see again chapter 12). She was from the first a member of the
post-Easter community.

We find a somewhat negative portrait of Mary in the Gospel of
Mark (3:20–35). It is just after Jesus' selection of the Twelve (3:13–19).
He is in a house with them and a great crowd gathers outside. His
own family concludes that "He has gone out of his mind" (3:21).
When his mother and his brothers arrive, they send word for him to
come out. Jesus is given the message. "Who are my mother and my
brothers?" he asks. Then he looks at his disciples gathered in the
circle: "Here are my mother and my brothers. Whoever does the will
of God is my brother and sister and mother" (3:33–35). The negative
view is strengthened in 6:4, which reports Jesus' return to his home in
Nazareth and the skeptical reaction of his neighbors, friends, and
relatives. Jesus complains: "Prophets are not without honor, except
in their hometown, and among their own kin, and in their own
house."

The Matthæn and Lucan parallels to Mark 3:20–25 (Matthew
12:24–50; Luke 8:19–21) present a different picture. Both drop the
harsh introduction in Mark 3:20–21. *Luke* goes further and eliminates
Jesus' question, "Who are my mother and my brothers?" Neither
Gospel excludes Mary from the spiritual, or eschatological, family of
Jesus. In Luke especially she is the obedient handmaid of the Lord
from the beginning. Later in 11:27–28 Jesus responds to a woman
who declares his mother blessed by saying that those are blessed
who hear the word of God and keep it. In light of Luke's positive

description of Mary in 8:19–21, it is likely that Jesus is emphasizing here that Mary's chief blessedness lies in her being one who obediently hears the word of God rather than in being his biological mother. Consistently with this interpretation, Luke's version of the rejection of Jesus at Nazareth speaks only of a prophet's being unacceptable "in the prophet's hometown" (4:24). There is no reference to "their own kin," as in Mark. Matthew, on the other hand, retains the phrase "in their own house" (13:57).

Thus, in the *Synoptic* depiction of Mary during Jesus' ministry there is a development from the negative estimation of Mark to the positive one of Luke, with Matthew representing the middle ground.

In the Gospel of *John*, which has no Infancy Narrative and which never names Mary, Jesus has an ambiguous exchange with his mother. He seems to dismiss her request to do something about the lack of wine (2:4), and yet he fulfills it in the end. In any case, the Cana story places Mary in a less negative light than in Mark, although still not so positive a light as in Luke. More important than the Cana story in John is the account of the crucifixion and of Mary's place at the foot of the cross. In giving the "disciple whom he loved" (John) to Mary as her son, and Mary to the disciple as his mother (19:25–27), Jesus brought into existence a new community of believing disciples, the same spiritual, or eschatological, family which appears in the Synoptics. The brothers of Jesus have no part in this family. They are unbelievers. But Mary is now associated with that Johannine Christianity which differs in some respects from the Christianity derived from the witness of Peter and the rest of the Twelve. In John's own symbolic treatment of Jesus' mother, an opening is made for the process of further Marian symbolizing within the Church. Indeed, she becomes a symbol for other Christians.

The Book of *Revelation*, chapter 12, tells of "a woman clothed with the sun, with the moon under her feet, and on her head a crown of twelve stars" (v. 1) who gives birth to a son "who is to rule all the nations" (v. 5). A huge dragon appears in hopes of devouring the child. When he fails in that, he pursues the woman. But he fails there, too, and goes off "to make war on the rest of her children, those who keep the commandments of God and hold the testimony of Jesus" (v. 17). Pious commentaries notwithstanding, the "woman" here is not Mary. Interpretations differ about the primary reference: the heavenly Jerusalem, personified wisdom, or the People of God, both Israel, which brings forth the Messiah, and the Church, which relives the experience of Israel and brings forth other children in the image of Christ. A *secondary* reference to Mary remains possible but uncertain. What is more certain is that the author's symbol of the woman who is the mother of the Messiah might well lend itself to Marian interpretation once Marian interest developed in the later Christian community. Eventually, when the Book of Revelation was placed in the same canon of Scripture with the Gospel of Luke and the Gospel of John, the various images of the virgin, the woman at the cross, and the woman who gave birth to the Messiah would reinforce each other.

Before we leave the New Testament, some more explicit mention should be made of Mary's *virginity*. Attention was given this topic in chapter 15, and the reader should review that material in connection with the present discussion. As noted in that chapter, the New Testament provides evidence only of a *belief* in the *ante partum* ("before birth") virginity of Mary, i.e., in the *virginal conception* of Jesus. The New Testament says nothing at all about Mary's virginity *in partu* ("in the act of giving birth"), i.e., that Jesus was born miraculously, without the normal biological disruptions, nor about her virginity *post partum* ("after birth"), i.e., that she had no normal sexual relationships after the birth of Jesus. On the contrary, the New Testament speaks of the brothers and sisters of Jesus. This does not constitute an insuperable barrier to the belief that Mary remained a virgin after the birth of Jesus, but neither is there any convincing argument from the New Testament alone against the literal meaning of the words *brother* and *sister* when they are used of Jesus' relatives.

(The preceding biblical discussion has been largely dependent upon two recent ecumenical investigations into the place of Mary in the New Testament: *Mary in the New Testament*, Raymond E. Brown, et al., eds., 1978; and *The One Mediator, the Saints and Mary*, H. George Anderson, et al., eds., 1992.)

Second Century

The literature of the second century is an important link between the emerging canon of the New Testament writings and the broader life-situation of the early Christian writers. We do not find here a fully developed interest in Mary. When she appears at all, it is on the margin of more central Christological discussions. The source material, too, is limited. Even in the literature that we do have, Marian references are extremely rare before the year 150 and are difficult to interpret in works written between 150 and 200.

The texts come from two principal groups of writings: the *apocrypha* (nonbiblical gospels, epistles, apocalypses) and the *patristic writings*. The former are so called because they were not accorded canonical authority (i.e., they were not included in the canon of Sacred Scripture) and/or were rejected as products of heretical or dissident groups. Among these, the most important source for Marian material is the *Protevangelium of James* (its oldest title was *Birth of Mary: Revelation of James*). It was probably composed around the year 150 or so. The author posed as James, the brother of Jesus. It contains much detail about the early family life of Mary, her birth, her betrothal to Joseph, the annunciation, the birth of Jesus, the coming of the Magi, etc. Despite its condemnation in official documents (for example, the so-called *Gelasian Decree* of the late fourth century), it dominated the development of the Marian legend for centuries. Neither in this document nor in any of the other material is there any clear evidence of a reliable historical tradition about Mary unrelated to what was said of her in the canonical Gospels. Some of the literature, in fact, is frankly Docetic. Thus, the Synoptic passage about Jesus' true family (Mark 3:31–35) is taken in this literature as a denial of his humanity.

The picture is the same when we look at the so-called patristic writings. Most do not even mention Mary. The principal exceptions are *Ignatius of Antioch, Justin,* and *Irenæus.* Ignatius gives an early witness to the belief in Jesus' virginal conception (*Smyrnæans* 1:1; *Ephesians* 7:2; 18:2; 19:1). Justin's interest in Mary serves a Christological and soteriological purpose. Jesus' birth from a virgin is proof of his messiahship and a sign of a new time (see his *Apology*, especially 32:9–35:1). Justin also draws a parallel between the virgin Eve and the virgin Mary. Eve believed and obeyed the serpent; Mary believed and obeyed the angel. Thus, Eve became the mother of sin through her disobedience, and Mary became the mother of the one who destroyed the works of the serpent through her obedience. Irenæus, finally, spells out the basis of this Eve-Mary typology by showing its parallel to Paul's Adam-Christ typology (*Adversus Hæreses* III, 21:10). Mary is the new Eve, the mother of the new humanity in whom God made a new beginning. These last two witnesses, Justin and Irenæus, in combination with the *Protevangelium of James*, accelerated the growth of Marian symbolism by the end of the second century. The Mary-Eve parallelism continued in the writings of the Syrian poet Ephrem (d. 373), the Cappodocian Gregory of Nyssa (d. 394), and the Latin Father, Ambrose (d. 397).

The Marian theme with which the second-century literature was mainly concerned is the *virginal conception*. The majority of references are affirmative, but there is also a significant amount of dissent. There is, however, no second-century evidence of belief in Mary's remaining a virgin after the birth of Jesus (*post partum*), apart from the implications of the *Protevangelium*. The later development coincided with a newly positive assessment of virginity. The evidence for belief in Mary's virginity during the birth of Jesus (*in partu*), while slight, is more abundant than for belief in her perpetual virginity. Indeed, we do not know the exact origin of the belief in Mary's perpetual virginity. We do know that the idea was actively resisted in the early Church by such writers as *Tertullian*, lest the Church yield ground to the Docetists and the Gnostics. The tradition of the miraculous birth, on the other hand, clearly originated in the second century. But it created a paradoxical situation for the Church. On the one hand, the Church wanted to uphold the reality of Jesus' birth over against the Docetists and the Gnostics (both of whom denied the humanity of Christ), but the Church fostered at the same time the glorification of the Virgin Mary for ascetical reasons, which allowed an interpretation of the birth in terms of her inviolate virginity and thus introduced a new danger of Docetic trends. And that very danger explains again Tertullian's resistance to the *in partu* and *post partum* notions.

Third Century to the Middle Ages

Mary's perpetual virginity, however, came to be almost universally accepted from the third century on. By now consecrated virgins had been established as a special state in the Church, and Mary was presented to them as their model. Both Latin and Greek writers saw in her the model of all virtues, in fact. The outstanding exception was

John Chrysostom (d. 407) who, as if in anticipation of modern biblical scholarship, acknowledged the negative flavor of Mark's estimation of Mary, and in his *Homilies on St. John's Gospel,* declared that "she did not cease to think little of [Jesus]... but herself she thought everywhere worthy of the first place, because she was his mother." At Cana, Mary told Jesus there was no more wine only because "she wanted to confer a favor on the others, and render herself more illustrious through her Son." Even at the annunciation she was at fault. The angel had to calm her down lest she kill herself in despair over the news that she was to have a son. Never before had a Christian preacher spoken in such derogatory terms of Mary, and never again for a thousand years would such be heard.

It was the *Nestorian controversy* which indirectly promoted Mariology in the fifth century. The Nestorians had so emphasized the distinction of the two natures in Christ, and the integrity of the human nature in particular, that they concluded to two persons as well. The crisis broke out when Nestorius publicly denied to Mary the title "Mother of God" (*theotokos*). According to him, she was only the mother of Christ (*Christotokos*), to whom the Person of the Word of God had united himself. We have already summarized the events surrounding the Council of Ephesus (431) in chapter 13. The council ruled against the Nestorian position and in favor of the term *theotokos*. Mary is indeed the "Mother of God" for there is only one Person in Jesus Christ, not two, and that Person is the very Word of God. The definition, one must remember, was not a Marian definition, but a Christological one. It was intended to safeguard not the motherhood of Mary but the true unity of Christ in one divine Person.

The decision at Ephesus gave a major impetus to Marian devotion. Popular interest in the apocryphal writings increased, especially in the *Protevangelium of James.* It is the source of the belief in her virginity *in partu* (during childbirth), and of the story of her presentation in the Temple (which, in turn, is the source of the liturgical feast of the Presentation). *St. Jerome* (d. 420), the pioneer Scripture scholar, would have none of this "delirious nonsense." But it caught on nonetheless and was mentioned by the Council of the Lateran (649) as it formulated its opposition to Monothelitism (one will in Christ).

Before the Council of Ephesus there had been one liturgical feast of Mary, the feast of the Purification, and that was celebrated only in certain parts of the Eastern Church. But after Ephesus the feasts began to multiply. From the beginning of the sixth century various churches celebrated Mary's bodily assumption into heaven. The belief originated not from biblical evidence nor even patristic testimony, but as the conclusion of a so-called argument from convenience or fittingness. It was "fitting" that Jesus should have rescued his mother from the corruption of the flesh, and so he "must have" taken her bodily into heaven. By the middle of the seventh century four separate Marian feasts were observed in Rome: the Annunciation, the Purification, the Assumption, and the Nativity of Mary. At the end of this century the feast of the Conception of Mary began in the East, but it remained unknown in the West until the eleventh century. *Andrew of Crete* (d. 740) wrote a hymn to Mary, calling her "alone wholly without stain." To Western ears this meant conceived without sin (the Immaculate Conception), but to Eastern ears, which had a different understanding of Original Sin, it meant only freedom from mortality and general human weakness.

Faith in Mary's power of intercession with God received a strong push from the growing belief in her assumption. Germanus (d. 733), patriarch of Constantinople, popularized the view that she had a maternal influence over God, that she could turn away God's anger and vengeance. She is our mediatrix with God. Thus, by the beginning of the eighth century, Mary's intercession and her importance for salvation had become well-established truths, especially in the East, both through popular literature and through preaching. The main contribution of the West at this time, as worked out by Ambrose and Augustine, was the close association of Mary with the Church. But compared with Eastern doctrine and devotion, the West's approach was sober and restrained. It was not yet in touch with the East's Theophilus legend which would so profoundly influence Mariology in the Middle Ages.

The Middle Ages

The idea that Mary appeases the wrath of God, the stern Judge, had been expressed by Germanus in the eighth century. It became one of the most popular themes of medieval Marian piety and devotion. Her power to save us was proclaimed even more dramatically by *the legend of Theophilus,* which was translated into Latin by Paul the Deacon (d. c. 799), a monk of Monte Cassino who had spent four years at the court of Charlemagne. Paul's version familiarized Western Christians with the story of the man who, like Dr. Faustus, gives his soul to the devil in order to get a desired post. Afterward he repents and asks Mary to obtain forgiveness for his terrible sin. She does, and the devil is forced to yield control. Mary is seen in the West now, as in the East, as the redemptrix of captives, as refuge of sinners, as mediatrix between God and humankind. The legend was reproduced even by serious theologians and made the subject of a play in which Christ is portrayed as a menacing Judge whose heart is softened only by the pleas of his mother. She also became known as "Star of the Sea" who guides us safely into heaven's port, and as the "Mother of Mercy."

By now theology in the West had become increasingly divorced from the Bible. A rational, deductive kind of argumentation prevailed. One form, to which we referred above, was known as the argument from convenience. Its structure was simple: God (or Christ) *could* do something; it was *fitting* that he should; therefore, he *did* it. *Potuit, decuit, fecit.* This principle would play a large role in the development of medieval Mariology.

One of the most influential of all medieval theologians on the development of Mariology was *Bernard of Clairvaux* (d. 1153). His sermons "In Praise of the Virgin Mary" were as persuasive as the legend of Theophilus in confirming the medieval Christian in his or her childlike trust in the all-powerful help of Mary. He influenced not only popular devotion but theology as well. It was Bernard's view that Mary had an intimate role in the redemption. She was the aqueduct that leads the waters of divine grace down to earth. God willed us to have "everything through Mary," a saying that became a principle of Mariology, to be repeated again and again by popes, theologians, and spiritual writers down to Pope Pius XII in the middle of the twentieth century.

Bernard did not deny that Christ was the one true Mediator, but felt that men and women might be afraid of him because he is also their God and their Judge. Hence we need "a mediator with that Mediator, and there is no one more efficacious than Mary." If Bernard used the image of the aqueduct, others used the image of the neck.

Mary is the neck which joins the Head with the rest of the Body of Christ, which is the Church.

Despite his intense devotion to Mary, Bernard was a strong opponent of the doctrine of the Immaculate Conception, and his whole Order followed his lead. Anselm of Canterbury also opposed the belief as well as the feast. When the feast began making headway in the West, Bernard addressed himself vehemently to the issue. He called the belief a "superstition." It was enough, he insisted, that Mary was sanctified in the womb and remained sinless throughout her life. The doctrine was successfully resisted, because of Bernard and Peter Lombard's *Sentences*, until the beginning of the fourteenth century, at which time two English Franciscans opened a wedge in the opposition: *William of Ware* (d. early 1300s) and *Duns Scotus* (d. 1308).

William insisted that he would rather err in giving the Blessed Virgin too much than too little. To that end he employed the medieval formula: *potuit, decuit, fecit*. He also repeated the legend current in England that St. Bernard appeared to a lay brother soon after death in a radiant white garment, on which there was one small stain: his error in the matter of the Immaculate Conception. Scotus's argument was more sophisticated. Christ, he said, was primarily a Redeemer. He came to redeem us not only from actual sin, but from Original Sin. As our most perfect Redeemer, it is to be expected that he would have exercised his power to overcome even Original Sin at least once; and so it was, in the case of his mother. Scotus's approach effectively silenced those who sought to protect the universality of the redemption, and who objected that the Immaculate Conception would leave Mary without any indebtedness to Christ. On the contrary, she owed him more than any other creature because he preserved her alone from sin. The chief opponents were the Dominicans, who followed the lead of their greatest doctor, *Thomas Aquinas.*

Thomas based his opposition to the Immaculate Conception on the grounds that it would detract from the universality of Christ's redemptive work. Mary was sanctified in the womb and, as such, was the greatest of all the saints of history. Furthermore, her dignity is in some sense infinite because the infinite God took flesh from her. On the other hand, Thomas confined her mediating role to the fact that she gave birth to Christ, the author of grace. He had nothing to say about her connection with the redemptive work on the cross. *Bonaventure*, contemporary and friend of Thomas, similarly opposed the doctrine, quoting from Bernard. But Bonaventure also ascribed to her some role in the redemptive act of the cross, when she consented to the sacrifice of her Son and paid the price of her compassion. This view led eventually to belief in Mary as Co-Redemptrix of the human race, even though Bonaventure himself insisted on the uniqueness of Christ's redemptive act. One of his sermons, which became widely popular, suggested that Christ reserved to himself the realm of justice while ceding to his mother the realm of mercy.

With this growing reliance on Mary's protection, devotional forms continued to proliferate. "The Little Office of Our Lady" was recommended for use by the laity. The "Hail Mary" became one of the basic prayers to be learned by all the faithful, along with the Lord's Prayer and the Apostles' Creed. Saturday was dedicated to Mary, as Sunday was to Christ. Marian antiphons were composed between the eleventh and twelfth centuries: *Alma Redemptoris Mater* ("Sweet Mother of the Redeemer"), *Ave Regina Cælorum* ("Hail, Queen of Heaven"), *Regina Cæli* ("Queen of Heaven"), and *Salve Regina* ("Hail, [Holy] Queen"). Marian litanies also originated at this time, one of which (the Litany of Loreto) had as many as 73 invocations. By the early twelfth century the Rosary was in general use. It began as a substitute for the Psalter (a book of 150 psalms). The Hail Marys were divided into three groups of fifty and were called *rosarium* after Mary's title *rosa mystica* ("mystical rose"). They were eventually counted on beads which had come into use about this time for counting the "Our Fathers" given as a penance. The beginnings of the *Angelus* also appeared: the recitation of Hail Marys and prayers to Mary three times a day, at the ringing of the Angelus bells. The devotion became especially popular when the danger of Turkish invasion in the latter part of the fifteenth century led people to have recourse to the protection of the Blessed Mother.

Marian visions and special revelations, although reported from the earliest centuries, now increased and became more elaborate. *St. Bridget of Sweden* (d. 1373) claimed that Mary herself confirmed the doctrine of the Immaculate Conception in a private apparition to her. Images of Mary were thought to have miraculous powers, and in the fourteenth century the Holy House of Loreto was believed to have been transported through the air from Nazareth. It became one of the most popular places of pilgrimage. The *Divine Comedy* of Dante Alighieri (d. 1321) sums up the Mariology of the Middle Ages by depicting her as having influence throughout the entire universe: earth, purgatory, heaven, and even hell. Thus, on the eve of the Reformation, the central and unique role of Christ in our redemption had become obscured.

The Reformation to the Mid-Nineteenth Century

All of the great Reformers were brought up as Catholics and shared some measure of contemporary Catholic spirituality—especially *Luther*, who pointed to Mary as an example of faith and of the goodness of God. But we should ask neither her nor any of the saints for anything. Everything comes from the hand of God alone. The others, *Calvin* and *Zwingli* in particular, retained even less of contemporary Catholic spirituality, but they too attested to the purity of Mary. They objected, however, to the tendency to ascribe qualities to her which apply only to God—e.g., "our life, our sweetness, and our hope." At first, some of the Marian feasts were retained by the Protestants, but in due course they disappeared from their liturgical calendars.

Defense of Marian devotion and of her important role in our redemption was mounted by the *Council of Trent* and by various Counter-Reformation theologians: *Peter Canisius* (d. 1597), *Francisco de Suarez* (d. 1617), *Robert Bellarmine* (d. 1621). Apologists and church leaders encouraged veneration of Mary and the saints, along with emphasis on the papacy and the Blessed Sacrament, as badges of Catholic identity and as bulwarks against the disruptive forces unleashed by the Reformers. Canisius, for example, composed a major treatise on Mary, *De Maria Virgine incomparabili*, which ran through four editions in eight years. In 1563 the first Sodality of Our Lady was established, and by 1576 this new lay movement had over thirty thousand members. In 1573 Pope Pius VI instituted the Feast of the Holy Rosary.

Marian spirituality took another turn with the appearance of the French School: *Cardinal Pierre de Bérulle* (d. 1629), *Jean-Jacques Olier* (d.

1657), *Jean Eudes* (d. 1680), and *Louis Grignion de Montfort* (d. 1716). The last had the most enduring influence, having initiated the so-called true devotion to the Blessed Virgin, requiring absolute surrender to Mary as mystics had surrendered themselves to Christ. This, he argued, was the only effective way to Christ. If we presented ourselves directly to him, he would see our self-love, but to present ourselves through Mary is to get by his weak side.

With the rise of rationalism in the eighteenth century, Catholic theology assumed a more skeptical posture—e.g., in the works of Cardinal Prosper Lambertini, the future Pope Benedict XIV (d. 1758), who laid down rules for the treatment of miracles and mystical phenomena. Benedict protected *Ludovico Muratori* (d. 1750), who had written a treatise on *Moderation in Matters of Religion*, in which he opposed the so-called bloody vow to defend the doctrine of the Immaculate Conception even to the shedding of blood. Muratori also attacked other exaggerations of Marian piety—e.g., that Mary could give orders in heaven. In the second half of the eighteenth century, under the impact of the Enlightenment, mild skepticism turned to strong opposition, and the liturgy was stripped of most Marian feasts. Theologians were no longer interested in Mariology, and popular devotions were confined now to Italy, Spain, and a few other places untouched by the general European currents of thought.

In Italy Marian devotion was kept alive through the work of the Redemptorists, and especially of *St. Alphonsus Liguori* (d. 1787), whose book *The Glories of Mary* defended two beliefs: the Immaculate Conception and Mary's universal mediation of grace. He repeated the medieval idea that Christ is the king of justice, while Mary is the mother of mercy. She alone knows how to appease an angry God by her prayers. Alphonsus supported his teaching by a large number of quotations from medieval authors, including the revelations of St. Bridget. He also reproduced, without critical comment, a wealth of legends and miracles. His book was warmly received in southern Europe and in France, and it remained popular throughout the nineteenth century. Indeed, it has appeared in close to a thousand editions since first published in 1750.

The Romanticism of the early nineteenth century brought with it a new wave of enthusiasm for medieval practices and a corresponding distaste for the rationalism of the Enlightenment. Marian piety was propelled and intensified by a series of reported apparitions, beginning with the visions of Catherine Labouré in Paris in 1830 (see section following). In 1846 Mary was also reported to have been seen by a young boy and a young girl at La Salette in the French Alps. She appeared sitting on a stone, her face in her hands, weeping over the sins of desecration of Sunday and of blasphemy. After much controversy the apparition was approved, a shrine was erected in 1852, and a missionary congregation, the Missionaries of La Salette, was founded.

Devotion to Mary spread to the English-speaking world with the help of two prominent converts to Catholicism: *Frederick William Faber* (d. 1863) and *John Henry Newman* (d. 1890). Although Faber tried to popularize Marian devotions in a radical, Italian baroque style, Newman presented a clearly Christocentric view of the *theotokos*, reemphasized the patristic image of Mary as the new Eve, and insisted in a letter to the Reverend E. B. Pusey that Mary "is nothing more than Advocate, not a source of mercy" (cited by *The One Mediator, The Saints and Mary*, p. 103).

One of the first modern efforts to integrate Mariology into the total system of Catholic dogmatics came from the German theologian *Matthias Joseph Scheeben* (d. 1888). His final masterwork, *Handbuch der katholischen Dogmatik*, situated the theology of Mary between the treatises on Christ and the Church and singled out, as the fundamental principle of Mariology, the divine motherhood, understood not simply as her physical maternity of Jesus but as her spiritual maternity of all the redeemed.

From the Dogma of the Immaculate Conception (1854) to the Dogma of the Assumption (1950)

The dogma of the Immaculate Conception holds that Mary, the Mother of Jesus, was free from Original Sin from the very moment of her conception. The Immaculate Conception of Mary is often confused with the virginal conception of Jesus. The former was described as a "pious doctrine" by the Council of Basle in its thirty-sixth session (1439), but by that time the council was no longer in communion with the pope and, therefore, its decrees were not regarded as binding. Ten years later, however, all members of the University of Paris were required to take an oath to defend it, and other universities followed suit. In 1476 the feast of the Immaculate Conception was approved by Pope Sixtus IV (d. 1484), and the Council of Trent in the next century explicitly excluded Mary from its decree on the universality of Original Sin (*Decree on Original Sin*, Session V, 1546). In 1661 Pope Alexander VII (d. 1667) forbade any attacks on the doctrine, so that even the Dominicans, who had originally opposed it, began to change sides, taking pains to establish that perhaps St. Thomas had not really been opposed to it in the first place.

Interest in the doctrine waned until early in the nineteenth century when on December 17, 1830, St. Catherine Labouré claimed to have had a vision of the Immaculate Conception, standing on a globe, rays of light emanating from her hands spread out toward the earth. The vision was surrounded by an oval frame on which appeared the words: "O Mary, conceived without sin, pray for us who have recourse to thee." A voice commanded Catherine to have a medal struck depicting the vision. The medal was named *miraculous* because miracles were attributed to it, and it stimulated renewed interest in the doctrine and in demands for its definition.

Pope Gregory XVI (d. 1846) did not accede to these demands, perhaps in deference to objections of liberal Catholics in Europe, especially in Germany, France, and England. The situation changed with the succession of *Pope Pius IX* (d. 1878) to the chair of Peter. He immediately initiated proceedings leading to a definition. There was a consultation with some 603 bishops, 56 of whom, including the archbishop of Paris, opposed the definition. In a papal bull of December 8, 1854, entitled *Ineffabilis Deus* ("Ineffable God"), Pius IX solemnly decreed that "the most Blessed Virgin Mary was, from the first moment of her conception, by the singular grace and privilege of almighty God and in view of the merits of Christ Jesus the Savior of the human race, preserved immune from all stain of original sin, [that this] is revealed by God and, therefore, firmly and constantly to be believed by all the faithful." Thus, the dogma followed the line taken by Duns Scotus, overcoming the difficulty posed by Thomas Aquinas that the Immaculate Conception would infringe upon the universality of Christ's redemptive work.

The dogma was positively received by most Catholics, but it created a storm of protest from Protestants and Orthodox alike. Protestants rejected the view that Mary was unlike the rest of the human race, and the Orthodox dissented from the dogma's underlying notion of Original Sin. For the Orthodox, sin is human infirmity with which every person is afflicted.

After the definition, other Marian apparitions were reported. In 1858 a series of appearances occurred near Lourdes, in France, to Bernadette Soubirous, a simple girl of 14. She was ordered by the Blessed Mother to drink from a previously invisible fountain which sprang up as Bernadette scratched the ground. After much consternation and debate, officials asked Bernadette to seek the lady's name. "I am the Immaculate Conception" was the reply. An increasing number of pilgrims came to the site, which was officially recognized in 1862. By the turn of the century a large church had been built and the place became, and remains, a center of devotional interest, with many physical cures attributed to the spring water.

Still another famous apparition was reported in Fatima, a small Portuguese town, in 1917. Again there were small children involved: a 10-year-old girl and two of her younger cousins, all tending sheep at the time. The apparition revealed herself as "the Lady of the Rosary" and urged everyone to pray for peace. A shrine was built and in 1931 permission was given for devotion to Our Lady of Fatima. Other major Marian shrines are located at Guadalupe in Mexico, Knock in Ireland, Czestochowa in Poland, and Montserrat in Spain.

Although various popes since Pius IX have mentioned Mary in their official pronouncements, no pope did more to emphasize the importance of Marian devotion than *Pope Pius XII* (d. 1958), who was particularly devoted to Our Lady of Fatima. He consecrated the entire world to the Immaculate Heart of Mary in 1942, and on the occasion spoke in Portuguese as if to underline the connection between this act of consecration and the events at Fatima. His major contribution, however, was the definition of yet another Marian dogma, that of the bodily assumption of Mary into heaven. It was her "crowning glory ... to be preserved from the corruption of the tomb," he wrote in his Apostolic Constitution *Munificentissimus Deus* (1950), "and, like her Son before her, to conquer death and to be raised body and soul to the glory of heaven, to shine refulgently as Queen at the right hand of her Son, the immortal King of ages."

There were, however, many in the Catholic Church who questioned the opportuneness of such a definition. It seemed to them unnecessarily provocative at a time when ecumenical relations among the churches were just gaining strength. On the other hand, it was argued that the human race had just witnessed two world wars and the horrors of concentration camps, and that this was an appropriate moment to reaffirm the dignity of the human body and to rekindle faith in the resurrection of the body. Many, therefore, welcomed the definition.

The terms of the definition, however, are open to legitimate difference of interpretation. It is not clear whether the pope intended to teach that Mary died at all, and nothing is said about the manner or time of her assumption. Protestant reaction was negative, but this time the Orthodox were more positive, since this was a doctrine they also had held for centuries.

Three years later Pope Pius XII declared a Marian year (December 8, 1953–December 8, 1954) in honor of the centenary of the dogma of the Immaculate Conception. He urged frequent sermons on Mary and encouraged visits to her shrines, especially Lourdes. Marian congresses were held, and thousands of books and articles were published. At the end of the year the pope established yet another Marian feast, her Queenship, on May 31, at which time the consecration of the world to the Immaculate Heart of Mary was to be renewed.

Just before the opening of Vatican II, several influential Catholic theologians prepared the way for a new turn in Marian teaching—more biblical, more Christocentric, more ecclesial, and more ecumenical. They situated Mary's role in the context of the mystery of salvation in Christ and the mystery of the Church, just as the council would do: René Laurentin, Otto Semmelroth, Karl Rahner, Edward Schillebeeckx, and Yves Congar. This was true also of Cardinal Léon Joseph Suenens, one of the most important figures at Vatican II (see his *Mary the Mother of God*, 1959).

Vatican II

In the Second Vatican Council's *Dogmatic Constitution on the Church*, an entire chapter (chapter 8) is devoted to "The Role of the Blessed Virgin Mary, Mother of God, in the Mystery of Christ and the Church." The preface notes that Mary, who is "acknowledged and honored as being truly the Mother of God and Mother of the Redeemer" and who "surpasses all other creatures," at the same time "belongs to the offspring of Adam [and] is one with all human beings in their need for salvation" (n. 53). She is also the Mother of the Church since, according to St. Augustine, "she cooperated out of love so that there might be born in the Church the faithful, who are members of Christ their Head." Accordingly, she is "a preeminent and altogether singular member of the Church, and... the Church's model and excellent exemplar, in faith and charity. Taught by the Holy Spirit, the Catholic Church honors her with filial affection and piety as a most beloved mother" (n. 53). The council comes very close here to calling Mary "Mother of the Church," but it was left to Pope Paul VI to do so explicitly in his closing speech at the end of the third session, November 21, 1964.

The rest of the eighth chapter is divided into three parts: Mary's role in the economy of salvation, her relationship with the Church, and Marian devotions. Her cooperation in the work of salvation is foreshadowed in the Old Testament (n. 55) and is rooted fundamentally in her assent to become the Mother of God (n. 56). Throughout this section, however, the council consistently follows the most benign interpretation of her role in Jesus' ministry. Thus, the negative tone of Mark 3:31–35 is passed over, and the document simply reads: "He declared blessed (cf. Mark 3:35 and parallels; Luke 11:27–28) those who heard and kept the Word of God, as she was faithfully doing (cf. Luke 2:19,51)" (n. 58).

Mary's role continues in the life of the Church, but without any obscuring or diminution of the "unique mediation of Christ" (n. 60). None of the titles given to her, e.g., Advocate, Auxiliatrix, Adjutrix, Mediatrix, adds to, nor subtracts from, "the dignity and efficacy of Christ the one Mediator" (n. 62). On the other hand, the unique mediation of Christ "does not exclude but rather gives rise among creatures to manifold cooperation which is but a sharing in this unique source. The Church does not hesitate to profess this subordinate role of Mary" (n. 62).

With St. Ambrose the council affirms that Mary is a model of the Church "in the matter of faith, charity, and perfect union with Christ" (n. 63). The Church, too, acts as a mother by accepting God's word in faith and by bringing forth children by Baptism to a new and everlasting life. The Church is also a virgin "who keeps whole and pure the fidelity she has pledged to her Spouse" (n. 64). Although Mary has already reached perfection, the Church continues on pilgrimage (n. 65).

From the most ancient times Mary has been revered as the "God-bearer" (*Deipara*), and this is the foundation of the special devotion, or cult, that is directed toward her. But this cult differs "essentially" from the cult of adoration which is offered to the incarnate Word, as well as to the Father and the Holy Spirit. Thus, although the Church has endorsed many forms of Marian piety, the Church always insisted that they be "within the limits of sound and orthodox doctrine. These forms have varied according to the circumstances of time and place and have reflected the diversity of native characteristics and temperament among the faithful" (n. 66). Furthermore, theologians and preachers should "carefully and equally avoid the falsity of exaggeration on the one hand, and the excess of narrow-mindedness on the other.... Let them painstakingly guard against any word or deed which could lead separated brethren or anyone else into error regarding the true doctrine of the Church. Let the faithful remember moreover that true devotion consists neither in fruitless and passing emotion, nor in a certain vain credulity" (n. 67).

Postconciliar Papal Teachings

Marialis Cultus

Pope Paul VI's 1974 apostolic exhortation *Marialis Cultus* ("For the Right Ordering and Development of Devotion to the Blessed Virgin Mary") points out in its Introduction that although Mary remains "a most excellent exemplar of the Church in the order of faith, charity and perfect union with Christ," the world and the Church have changed dramatically since many of our traditional Marian devotions were first developed. "Certain practices of piety that not long ago seemed suitable for expressing the religious sentiment of individuals and of Christian communities seem today inadequate or unsuitable because they are linked with social and cultural patterns of the past."

Consequently, the apostolic exhortation offers four guidelines "for the right ordering and development" of Marian devotion, drawn from Scripture, liturgy, ecumenism, and anthropology.

1. Every form of worship, including Marian devotions, should have a biblical imprint. The texts of prayers and songs should draw their inspiration and their wording from the Bible and above all they should be "imbued with the great themes of the Christian message" (n. 30).

2. Marian devotions should always harmonize with the liturgy, not be mixed in some hybrid form. Specifically, novenas and similar practices of piety are not to be inserted into the very celebration of the Eucharist. "This creates the danger," he writes, "that the Lord's Memorial Rite, instead of being the culmination of the meeting of the Christian community, becomes the occasion, as it were, for devotional practices" (n. 31). The pope includes the Rosary in his admonition, making it clear that "it is a mistake to recite the rosary during the celebration of the liturgy, though unfortunately this practice still persists here and there" (n. 48).

3. Because of our new appreciation of the wider ecumenical scope of the Church and our eagerness to reestablish Christian unity, "every care should be taken," the pope continues, "to avoid any exaggeration which could mislead other Christian brethren about the true doctrine of the Catholic Church" (n. 32). Specifically, our non-Catholic brothers and sisters should never have any reason to doubt that, in our Catholic devotions to Mary, Christ always remains our "sole Mediator" with God.

4. "Devotion to the Blessed Virgin," finally, "must also pay close attention to certain findings of the human sciences.... The picture of the Blessed Virgin presented in a certain type of devotional literature cannot easily be reconciled with today's life style, especially with the way women live today. In the home, women's equality and coresponsibility with men in the running of the family are being justly recognized by laws and the evolution of customs. In the sphere of politics women have in many countries gained a position in public life equal to that of men. In the social field women are at work in a whole range of different employments, getting further away every day from the restricted surroundings of the home. In the cultural field new possibilities are opening up for women in scientific and intellectual activities" (n. 34).

Mary was a true disciple. When she heard the Word of God, she acted upon it. She was "far from being a timidly submissive women or one whose piety was repellent to others." On the contrary, "she was a woman who did not hesitate to proclaim that God vindicates the humble and the oppressed, and removes the powerful people of this world from their privileged positions (cf. Luke 1:51–53)" (n. 37).

Redemptoris Mater

John Paul II's 1987 encyclical *Redemptoris Mater* ("The Mother of the Redeemer"), written to herald the opening of a Marian year (1987–1988), concentrates on Mary's life as a pilgrimage of faith in which she faithfully preserved her twofold bond with Christ and with the Church. Although more devotional in tone than *Marialis Cultus, Redemptoris Mater* underscores the ecumenical dimensions of a true understanding of Mary as one "obedient of faith" and he applauds the progress that has already been made by various ecumenical dialogues on Christian beliefs relating to Mary. He makes special mention, however, of the Orthodox and Oriental churches, with whom the Catholic Church's Marian doctrines, theology, and piety have so much in common. His reference to Mary's *Magnificat* incorporates the Church's "preference for the poor" (n. 37), and his reflection on her discipleship stresses the Church's call to the service to others.

Postconciliar Theology

Since the council Mary has become an object of distinctive interest in Latin American liberation theology and in feminist theology. Regarding the latter, Karl Rahner has written that "Mariology today and in [the] future still has a great deal to do if it wants to have an image of

1098

Mary that will really be true also for the religious existence of woman as such. It is an image that can perhaps be produced authentically today only by women, by women theologians" ("Mary and the Christian Image of Woman," *Theological Investigations*, vol. 19, New York: Crossroad, 1983, p. 217).

Liberation theology and feminist theology, of course, share much in common. They both arise out of a situation of oppression and marginalization. While both theologies have had significant development since Vatican II, Mariological concerns surfaced at a later stage. *Liberation theology* has given particular attention to the "*Magnificat*," where Mary is seen as one who speaks on behalf of the poor and the oppressed. *Leonardo Boff* devotes a chapter of his *Maternal Face of God* (New York: Harper & Row, 1987) to "Mary, Prophetic Woman of Liberation." *Ivone Gebara* and *Maria Bingemer* portray Mary as "the image of God who through the power of God's Spirit brings to birth men and women committed to justice, living out their relationship to God in a loving relationship to other human beings" (*Mary: Mother of God, Mother of the Poor*, p. 73). The 1979 Puebla document of the Third General Conference of the Latin American Bishops develops similar themes, employing also the powerful Latin American image of Mary as Our Lady of Guadalupe.

Feminist theology, like Vatican II and the early Christian writers, sees Mary as a type of the Church. It sees her relationship with Jesus predicated on more than her motherhood. She is also a *disciple* who heard the word of God and was faithful to it. As a disciple, unlike as a mother, Mary is a model for *all* Christians.

"Both liberation and feminist Mariologies see Mary as a potent symbol of their call to take human historical experience seriously," *Mary E. Hines* writes. "Mary calls us today particularly to listen to the voices of those traditionally marginalized by Church and society, women and the poor" ("Mary," *The New Dictionary of Catholic Spirituality*, Michael Downey, ed. Collegeville, Minn.: Liturgical Press, 1993, p. 645).

THE MARIAN DOGMAS

The Immaculate Conception

How one finally understands and explains the dogma of the Immaculate Conception will depend in very large measure on how one understands and explains the doctrine of Original Sin (see chapter 5). If Original Sin means being conceived and born with a stain on the soul, or being conceived and born without grace, then the dogma of the Immaculate Conception means that Mary alone was born in the state of grace.

If, on the other hand, one understands Original Sin as the *sinful condition* in which every human being is born, i.e., the corporate *alienation* of the whole human race from God, then we have to propose a different explanation for the Immaculate Conception. It is not that Mary alone was conceived and born in grace, but that, in view of her role in the redemption, God exempted her from this condition of alienation and was fully present to her in grace from the beginning. This is not to be understood in any quantitative sense. Grace is divine life. To be in the "state of grace" is to be in union with God: God in us, and we in God. By reason of Mary's unique call to be the Mother of the incarnate Word (which is the primary basis for the dogma), she was from the very beginning of her existence united with God in the most intimate of ways. And this union was, in turn, grounded in the yet-to-be-accomplished redemptive work of the Son she was to bear.

This does not mean that Mary was exempt also from the "consequences" of Original Sin: sickness, suffering, even death. These, too, are part of the human condition, and they are part of the mystery of sin. We do not know why we are subject to physical deterioration; we only know *that* we are. Paul attributed this condition to sin, just as those before him in the Old Testament consistently linked sin and human suffering. But we no longer accept that connection, nor are we required to do so by the doctrine of the Church. Suffering is a part of the human condition, but we do not know why. Sin is also part of the human condition, and we do not know ultimately why either. We *do* know that we freely sin in individual instances, and that this is a reflection of the sinful situation in which we are all born.

The dogma of the Immaculate Conception teaches that Mary was exempt in a unique and exceptional way from the normal and the usual impact of sin, or, more positively, that she was given a greater degree of grace (i.e., God was more intensely present to her than to others) in view of her role as the "God-bearer." So profound is her union with God in grace, in anticipation of her maternal function and in virtue of the redemptive grace of Christ, that she alone remains faithful to God's will throughout her entire life. *She is truly redeemed, but in an exceptional and unique manner.* The Immaculate Conception shows that God can be, and is, utterly gracious toward us, not by reason of our merits but by reason of divine love and mercy alone.

The Assumption

The dogma of the Assumption complements the dogma of the Immaculate Conception in the same way that the resurrection of Christ complements his crucifixion and life of sacrificial service to others. Just as the Immaculate Conception was not merely a personal privilege conferred upon Mary but a reality bestowed in view of her role in the economy of salvation, so the Assumption is not merely a personal privilege unrelated to the wider mission of her life. Her union with God in Christ was unique from the beginning. Her call to final union with God in Christ, in the totality of her human existence (body and soul), was also unique in the end. The dogma of the Assumption asserts something about human existence in asserting something about Mary: that human existence is bodily existence, and that we are destined for glory not only in the realm of the spiritual but in the realm of the material as well.

> In the midst of the anguish and distress of this generation, the Church, so readily accused of being political and attached to earthly power, of liking to install herself far too positively in this world, of being insufficiently eschatological, raises her head and by proclaiming this doctrine of the faith, gazes towards the only hope in which she really trusts, the future of God, who is so far advanced with his Kingdom, that he has already begun to be wholly present. The Church looks on high and greets in Mary her own type and model, her own future in the resurrection of the body. (Karl Rahner, *Mary Mother of the Lord,* pp. 91–92; see

also Avery Dulles, "The Dogma of the Assumption," in *The One Mediator, the Saints and Mary*, pp. 279–94.)

Binding Force

(What follows in this brief section is not intended to challenge or to raise doubts about the two dogmas, but simply to acknowledge and deal directly with the questions and concerns that many—Catholics and non-Catholics alike—have had about them. The material is drawn directly from the statement prepared by the Catholic representatives to the Lutheran–Catholic dialogue in the United States, in *Theological Studies* 40 [March 1979], pp. 138–57, especially pp. 152–55.)

In defining the dogma of the Immaculate Conception, Pope Pius IX warned all those who might be tempted to reject his teaching: "If, therefore, any persons shall dare to think—which God forbid—otherwise than has been defined by us, let them clearly know that they stand condemned by their own judgment, that they have made shipwreck of their faith and fallen from the unity of the Church." Pope Pius XII issued a similarly severe warning in connection with the definition of the dogma of the Assumption: "Wherefore, if anyone—which God forbid—should willfully dare to deny or call in doubt what has been defined by us, let [that person] know that he [or she] certainly has abandoned the divine and catholic faith."

What is to be said, however, of the binding force of these dogmas of faith? (1) Is it possible to deny them and at the same time remain in the Church? (2) Is it possible to deny them and remain in the *Catholic* Church?

Concerning the first, Catholics do not hold that membership in Christ's Church is restricted to persons who formally and explicitly accept these two Marian dogmas. There is "an order or 'hierarchy' of truths, since they vary in their relationship to the foundation of the Christian faith" (*Decree on Ecumenism*, n. 11). No one could reasonably hold that the dogmas of the Immaculate Conception and the Assumption are so central to Christian faith that the faith itself would disintegrate without either or both. Such would be the case, on the other hand, if one were to deny the divinity of Jesus Christ or the redemptive value of his life, death, and resurrection.

Furthermore, the Second Vatican Council permitted limited eucharistic sharing between Catholics and Orthodox, even though the Orthodox do not accept both of these dogmas (*Decree on Eastern Catholic Churches*, nn. 26–29). The presumption must be that, in spite of differences on these two dogmas, the unity of Christian faith that *is* present between Catholics and Orthodox is sufficient for eucharistic sharing. The same kind of reasoning could conceivably be extended to the cases of other Christian communities, such as Anglicans and Lutherans.

Concerning the second question (Is membership in the *Catholic* Church contingent upon acceptance of these dogmas?), the problem arises because each of these two dogmatic definitions is accompanied by an anathema or its equivalent. According to the 1917 Code of Canon Law, an anathema involves an excommunication (canon 2257, 2), but that consequence follows only when the rejection of the dogma is culpable, obstinate, and externally manifested. (The canon is not part of the revised 1983 Code.)

What of those Catholics who wish to belong to the Catholic Church, who confess the Lordship of Jesus, who assemble for the Eucharist in faith, who take the Word of God to heart, and who bear witness to the Gospel in their love of and service to their neighbor? Should the questioning or even denial of these dogmas be regarded today as presumptive evidence of a lapse from Catholic faith? It could be that in their questioning or denial of these dogmas, some Catholics are reacting not against the Word of God to which these dogmas propose to bear witness, but against the inadequacy, incompleteness, limited expressive power, and historically conditioned character of these definitions. If such Catholics are otherwise faithful to their Catholic heritage and to the practice of their Catholic faith, would it not be possible to presume the opposite—namely, that they are sincere in their questioning and even denial of these dogmas (i.e., not culpable or obstinate) and that their rejection implies no correlative rejection of the major truths of faith with which these dogmas are related, e.g., the redemptive significance of Christ's life, death, and resurrection; our hope in the resurrection of the body; the power of God's grace to overcome completely the impact of sin?

It is possible, of course, that a Catholic's rejection of either or both of these Marian dogmas would be a sign that one has separated himself or herself from the Catholic tradition and faith, and therefore from communion with the Catholic Church, just as Popes Pius IX and Pius XII warned. A person might, for example, reject these definitions precisely because they are papal actions. That person might believe that the Petrine office has no necessary place in the life and mission of the Church for the benefit of the Church universal. A person might also reject any place for Mary in the Christian dispensation and the Catholic tradition. Such views would effectively disengage one from the Catholic tradition and the community which embodies it. This is not to say, on the other hand, that a faithful and committed Catholic could not question the *process* by which these dogmas were formulated.

MARIAN DEVOTIONS: THEOLOGICAL CRITERIA

There are *two extremes* to be avoided in one's attitude toward devotion to Mary. *First,* there is a temptation to so exaggerate the *divine* role in salvation that the value and importance of *human cooperation* is lost (see the discussion of nature and grace in chapter 5). In this view, human cooperation plays no role at all in our salvation. Therefore, no fellow creature, Mary included, is ever worthy of veneration, because such attention inevitably detracts from the glory owed to God alone and to Jesus Christ in whom and through whom God acted on our behalf for the forgiveness of sins. The consequence of this first extreme is Marian *minimalism,* or "mariophobia."

The *second* temptation is to exaggerate the *human* role in salvation at the expense of the divine and correspondingly to deemphasize the effectiveness of the *mediating work of Christ,* who is perceived as more divine than human. And if he is more divine than human, he is not so much our bridge to God as he is the God from whom we have been alienated by sin. We need access, therefore, not only to the Father but the Son as well. According to this view, we need other ways of reaching God, and these ways must be adapted to our own limited human condition. Consequently, we turn to our fellow human beings who have already won the crown of glory and who have obviously found much favor in the sight of God. But in that regard Mary is in a spiritual class by herself, for she alone is "full of grace" and she alone is *Theotokos.* Therefore, there is no limit to the help she can give us, nor is there any limit to the veneration we can show her in virtue of her standing before God. The consequence of this second extreme is Marian *maximalism,* or "mariocentricism."

Marian minimalism in effect denies (or at least narrowly applies) the principle of secondary or *instrumental causality,* i.e., that God works through finite agents to achieve infinite ends. It also denies (or narrowly applies) the principle of *sacramentality,* i.e., that God is present to us, is disclosed, and works on our behalf in and through visible, material realities: persons, events, nature, objects, the cosmos. (It is not always clear if the Marian minimalist understands that the humanity of Jesus Christ is also an instrumental cause and sacrament of salvation.) And it denies, finally, that the Church is a *communion of saints,* i.e., that our relationship with God and with Christ is both vertical and horizontal, and that our relationship is always *mediated.*

Marian maximalism in effect exaggerates the secondary or *instrumental causality* of Mary and the other saints and demeans the instrumental causality of the humanity of Christ. It also misunderstands the *sacramental principle.* Sacramentality means that God works *in* and *through* some visible, material reality. It is always the inner transforming presence of God that ultimately counts, and not the sign and instrument of that presence. Therefore, it is not because Mary and the saints have the power of influence with God that they are objects of veneration and devotion. Rather it is because the grace of God has triumphed *in them.* They have been transformed by, and have become effective images of, Christ (*Dogmatic Constitution on the Church,* n. 50). It is Christ's, not Mary's, achievement that we celebrate. Finally, Marian maximalism misunderstands the nature of the *communion of saints.* The Church is not just an institution of salvation, with Mary and the saints as "successful graduates" who have some measure of influence with "the administration." It is not comparable to a filling station, where automobiles replenish their supply of fuel. The Church is the People of God, the Body of Christ, and the Temple of the Holy Spirit. It is, first and foremost, a community (*communio, koinonia*), but not just any community. It is a community of those who have been transformed by Christ and the Holy Spirit and who have explicitly and thankfully acknowledged the source of that transformation. Since transformation is a process, to be completed when the

Kingdom of God is fully realized at the end of history, our bond in Christ and the Spirit is not broken by death.

Mary is the preeminent member of this communion of saints. Our link with her is an expression of our link with the whole Church. It is a bond, however, not just of advocates and supplicants, but of brothers and sisters in the Lord, the very Body of Christ on the way to achieving "the fullness of God" (Ephesians 3:19).

Between these two extremes of Marian minimalism and Marian maximalism there is wide spectrum of legitimate devotional options. One should be careful not to categorize pejoratively those forms of spirituality with which one is not personally comfortable or from which one feels culturally alienated. The following *theological criteria* might be helpful in evaluating various expressions of Marian devotion:

1. Devotion to Mary, and to all of the saints, is ultimately devotion to Christ, whose grace has triumphed in Mary and the saints.

2. Jesus Christ in his humanity and divinity alike is the one Mediator between God and humankind. In him we are forgiven our sins, for he is full of mercy and compassion toward us.

3. On the other hand, just as God worked through the instrumentality of Jesus' humanity for our salvation, so divine grace is symbolized and mediated through other visible, material, bodily realities, including those fellow creatures who have shown themselves striking examples of the transforming power of this grace.

4. Since God saves us not just as individuals but as members of a people, we are joined one with another in a community of saints, i.e., of "holy ones" sharing in the holiness [the life] of God. "You shall be holy, for I the Lord your God am holy" (Leviticus 19:2).

5. Mary is, by reason of her faith and obedience to the Word of God, a model of the Church and is its preeminent member. She is a disciple *par excellence.*

6. Insofar as Mary is truly the mother of Jesus Christ, she can be called the "God-bearer." Again, she is a model for the Church in that the Church, too, is a "reality imbued with the hidden presence of God" (Pope Paul VI). Just as the hidden presence of God is the basis of all that we believe about the Church in faith, so it is also the basis of all that we believe about Mary in faith.

7. And yet just as the Church is not itself the Kingdom of God, even though the Church can be called "the initial budding forth" of the Kingdom (*Dogmatic Constitution on the Church*, n. 5), so Mary is not herself the mediator or the redeemer, even though she is the mother of Jesus and bears the incarnate Word within her.

8. On the contrary, Mary is, before all else, one of the redeemed. Exemption from Original Sin does not mean that she was herself in no need of the redemptive work of Christ. She was full of grace from the beginning precisely because of the redemptive work of Christ on her behalf.

9. While a Catholic will normally accept the Marian dogmas without reservation, it is less important *that* one affirms or denies them than *why* one affirms it or denies them. Thus, on a relative scale at least, one is actually more "orthodox" in *denying* the Immaculate Conception because it might detract from the universality of the redemption (as Thomas Aquinas feared) than in affirming the Immaculate Conception on the grounds that Mary's closeness to God made the redemptive work of Christ unnecessary in her own unique case.

10. Apparitions, visions, and other unusual occurrences attributed directly or indirectly to Mary may or may not be believed. None of them can ever be regarded as essential to Christian faith, whether they are approved by the official Church or not. If these phenomena do have any final authority, they are authoritative only for those who directly and immediately experience them. No one but the recipient(s) can be bound in conscience by whatever is communicated.

11. In any case, the "contents" (messages, directives, etc.) of such events can never be placed on par with the Gospel itself, neither in terms of their authority nor in terms of the attention they elicit and/or demand. Those "contents," in turn, must always be measured against the totality of the Christian faith and must not contradict or contravene any essential component of that faith.

MARY AND THE CHURCH

"Neither the Gospel nor past Christian tradition have been able to separate Mary and the Church," the Protestant monk and theologian of Taizé, Max Thurian, has written. "To speak of Mary is to speak of the Church. The two are united in one fundamental vocation—maternity" (*Mary, Mother of the Lord, Figure of the Church*, p. 9).

There is, of course, more to the relationship between Mary and the Church than maternity, although that is certainly foundational. The Church is a mother in several senses. It brings forth new creatures in Christ out of the womb of the baptismal font. It nourishes the Christian family at the table of the Eucharist. It is the source of encouragement, of forgiveness, of order, of healing, of love. Each of these maternal activities is linked with one or another of the Church's seven sacraments.

Mary, too, is the mother of all Christians insofar as she is, first of all, the mother of Jesus Christ. She gives birth to Jesus and so makes it possible for Jesus to give birth to us anew in the Holy Spirit. As a model, or type, or figure, or image of the Church, Mary is preeminently a person of faith, of hope, of love, of obedience to the Word of God. She is a disciple *par excellence* in a community of disciples.

She is conceived without sin and in the fullness of grace, as the Church was. She is a faithful and undefiled virgin, as the Church is called to be. She is redeemed by Christ, as the Church is. She is the sign of God's presence among us, as the Church is. She is transformed and renewed by the presence of God within her, as the Church is. She shared fully in the resurrection of Christ, body and soul, as the Church is destined to share in it. And she intercedes for us before the throne of God, as the Church does.

Devotion to Mary is a characteristically Catholic phenomenon in that it expresses three fundamental principles of Catholic theology and practice: the principle of *mediation*, the principle of *sacramentality*, and the principle of *communion*.

The universe of grace is a *mediated* reality: mediated principally by Christ, and secondarily by the Church and other signs and instruments of salvation beyond the Church. The Catholic understands the role of Mary in salvation and accepts it because the Catholic already understands and accepts the principle of mediation as applied in the incarnation and in the life and mission of the Church (a point made so effectively by Yves Congar in his *Christ, Our Lady, and the Church*, 1957).

The Catholic also understands that the invisible, spiritual God is present and available to us through the visible and the material, and that these, in turn, are made holy by reason of that divine presence. The Catholic therefore, readily engages in the veneration of Mary, not because Mary is confused with some ancient goddess or super-creature or rival of the Lord himself, but because Mary is herself a symbol or image of God. It is the God who is present within her and who fills her whole being that the Catholic grasps in the act of venerating yet another *"sacrament"* of the divine.

Finally, the Catholic perceives the Church as itself a *communion* of saints (see below) in its visible as well as its invisible dimensions. It is an institutionalized, structured reality in which and through which the grace of the Holy Spirit is disclosed, celebrated, and released for the renewal and reconciliation of the whole world. Our relationship with God and with Christ is not only bilateral but multilateral, which is to say communal. The Church *as* Church enters directly into that saving relationship with God and with Christ. It is not simply the place where one hears the Word of God and testifies to her or his faith in the Word. The Church is itself the very Body of Christ. To be *in* the Church is to be *in* Christ and one *with* Christ.

So, too, devotion to Mary is consequent upon the fact that we are united with her, as with one another, in and with Christ. She is the preeminent member of the community of saints by reason of her unique relationship with Christ, but she is a member nonetheless, and the most exalted one at that. Our unity with her is an expression of our unity in and with Christ.

"In Mary," Otto Semmelroth writes, "the Church affirms her own holy, co-redemptive and redeemed essence.... Thus, the veneration of Mary is the Church's testimony to herself... [to her] own essence and to her task of imparting salvation" (*Mary, Archetype of the Church*, p. 174).

THE SAINTS

"Hardly any practice," Avery Dulles writes, "is so distinctively Catholic as the cult of the saints" (*The Catholicity of the Church*, Oxford: Clarendon Press, 1985, p. 85). There are at least four different meanings of the word *saints*: (1) all those who have been justified by the grace of Christ, whether they be living or dead; (2) those who, having been justified by Christ on earth, have entered into eternal life; (3)

particular figures, especially biblical personages, who are examples of holiness; (4) those whom the Church, either through custom or formal canonization, has singled out as members of the Church triumphant so that they may be commemorated in public worship. In the Catholic tradition, all four levels of meaning apply to the term *saints*. In this discussion, however, we are focusing on the fourth level, namely, saints formally recognized as such by the Catholic Church.

History

New Testament

The term *holy* (*hagios*) was applied to Christian disciples during their earthly life. 1 Peter 1:15–16 explicitly quotes Leviticus 11:44–45 or 19:2 and applies it to Christians. For Paul *saints* becomes the common designation of Christians to whom he writes (Romans 1:7; 15:25; 1 Corinthians 1:2; 2 Corinthians 1:1; Philippians 1:1). The term is later extended even to those who had died and were raised at the time of Jesus' death and who appeared in Jerusalem after his resurrection (Matthew 27:52–53). The Epistle to the Hebrews speaks of various Old Testament figures as "a cloud of witnesses" that surround us (12:1). The Book of Revelation blesses the dead "who from now on die in the Lord" (14:13). The later Pauline letters, however, reflect an ambiguity in the veneration of the holy ones, especially when it is meant as the "worship of angels" (Colossians 2:18).

It is Jesus' own resurrection that is the starting point for the development of teachings regarding life after death. The development is accelerated with the early martyrdoms of his disciples (1 Thessalonians 4:14,16–17; 1 Corinthians 15:20–21).

Second Century to the Reformation

It had become already a common Christian conviction that a martyr's reward was immediate transition to eternal life with Christ. Early in the second century *Ignatius of Antioch* expresses the hope that he will be killed by wild beasts quickly so that he may "belong to Jesus Christ" (*Romans* 1:2; 5:3). The earliest mention of a memorial cult at the resting place of the bones of a Christian martyr is in the *Martyrdom of Polycarp* (18:1–3), written in the mid-second century. Veneration of the burial sites, pilgrimages to places where the martyrs had lived or died, adoption of a saint as patron of a church or town, belief in the power of the saints to perform miracles on behalf of the living—all these practices developed very early in the Church's history. From the fourth century on, the cult was also extended to confessors, i.e., those who suffered for the faith, short of being executed for it; ascetics, especially those who lived a life of celibacy; wise teachers and prudent church leaders; and those who cared for the poor.

Augustine warned the faithful that they must "worship God alone," but he also exhorted them to "honor the saints," and specifically the martyrs (*Sermo* 273.9). Although he was critical of excesses and superstition, he clearly encouraged the cult of the saints, including their invocation. They are models for us to imitate as well as intercessors who pray to God for the faithful. An elaborate martyrs' cult, including the regular invocation of the saints, was a common feature of worship and devotional life in Africa at his time.

Pope Gregory the Great (d. 604) took special interest in the fate of the human soul after death. Book IV of his *Dialogues* is rich in detailed speculation about the condition of the saints in heaven and about their lively interactions with the Church on earth. By the end of the so-called patristic era, it was "a constant challenge for church leaders, theologians, and the laity to keep all affirmations about the honor and veneration of the angels, the saints, and the Virgin Mary under the judgment of the christological affirmations established by the early church" (*The One Mediator, the Saints and Mary*, p. 91). Thus, the Second Council of Nicea in 787 taught that God alone is worshipped and adored (*latria*), while the saints are given simple respect and veneration (*dulia*). (Mary, alone among the saints, is worthy of *hyperdulia*.)

Compared with the East where the cult of Mary and the saints was strong, the West provided much less fertile ground. But the works of Gregory the Great and of numerous monastic writers, as well as the preaching of the Irish monks on the Continent, nourished a keen interest in the afterlife, in the benefits of penitential discipline, and in Western saints and their miracles. The cult of relics which had been endorsed by the *Libri Carolini* (based on a manifesto issued in 790 by Frankish bishops and later expanded and published in this form) was an important part of feudal society. Relics were sold, traded, and stolen. Pilgrimages to the shrines of particular saints were matters of local pride and profit. Monastic piety gave prominence to saints as founders, patrons, and protectors, and this served as a model for popular devotion. The sanctoral cycle in the liturgy grew rapidly. The elaborate liturgies popularized by the monastery at Cluny gave the saints a prominent place.

As the veneration of certain saints spread beyond the limits of a given diocese or country and beyond the control of the local hierarchy, concerns were increasingly expressed about the need to curtail abuses and install some measure of regulation. The papacy eventually intervened. The first historically attested canonization is that of Ulrich of Augsburg by Pope John XV in 993. About 1170 Alexander III, in a letter to the king of Sweden, asserted that no one should be venerated as a saint without the authority of the Church of Rome. When this letter was included in the *Decretals* of Gregory IX in 1234, it became part of the general law of the Church in the West.

As the ordinary faithful became more and more obsessed with the question of life after death, Pope Benedict XII issued a constitution *Benedictus Deus* in 1336 in which he taught that the saints see the divine essence "in an intuitive vision face to face" (the Beatific Vision). The Council of Florence reaffirmed the teaching in 1439. By the eve of the Reformation the notion of a "treasury of merits" had taken hold. The Church, it was believed, had at its disposal a wealth of merits from the saints and Mary as well as from Christ for the relief of temporal and purgatorial punishments. It was a time when shrines, feasts, and pilgrimages proliferated.

The Reformation to Vatican II

As pointed out earlier in the section on Mary, the cult of the saints was emphasized following the Reformation as one of the badges of Catholic identity. In the Baroque period of the sixteenth and seventeenth centuries, as the liturgy became increasingly ornate and complex, the people turned to extraliturgical devotions that they could understand and in which they could comfortably participate. Novenas in honor of the saints, pilgrimages, and prayers to the saints became a dominant part of Catholic life. Canonization of new saints increased significantly. The Romanticism of the eighteenth century brought with it a new wave of enthusiasm for medieval practices, as noted earlier, and a general disdain for the rationalism of the Enlightenment. Devotion to the saints (and especially to Mary), as sources of spiritual and material benefits, became even more widespread.

It remained an integral part of Catholic piety right up to the Second Vatican Council.

Vatican II

The council situates its teaching on the saints (and Mary) in its keynote *Dogmatic Constitution on the Church* (nn. 50–51). When we look at their lives, "we are looking for the city that is to come (Hebrews 13:14; 11:10). At the same time we are shown a most safe path by which... we will be able to arrive at perfect union with Christ, that is, holiness."

The principle of sacramentality is central: "In the lives of those who shared in our humanity and yet were transformed into especially successful images of Christ (cf. 2 Corinthians 3:18), God vividly manifests to us the divine presence and face. [God] speaks to us in them, and gives us a sign of [the] kingdom, to which we are powerfully drawn, surrounded as we are by so many witnesses (cf. Hebrews 12:1), and having such an argument for the truth of the gospel."

But we do not simply cherish the memory of the saints for the sake of their example. "We do so still more in order that the union of the whole Church may be strengthened in the Spirit by the practice of communal charity (cf. Ephesians 4:1–6)" (n. 50).

While it reaffirms the teachings of earlier councils on the legitimacy of venerating the saints, Vatican II warns of "abuses, excesses, or defects which may have crept in here and there" and urges that the cult of saints be subordinated always "to a more ample praise of Christ and of God."

"Let the faithful be taught, therefore, that the authentic cult of the saints consists not so much in the multiplying of external acts, but rather in the intensity of our active love." What the saints offer us is an "example in their way of life, fellowship in their communion, and aid by their intercession" (n. 51).

Finally, when the Church celebrates the feasts of saints, it does so not to draw attention away from Christ who is the one mediator between ourselves and God, but rather to "proclaim the wonderful works of Christ in his servants, and display to the faithful fitting examples for their imitation" (*Constitution on the Sacred Liturgy*, n. 111). And always the paschal mystery is central. The saints have suffered and been glorified with Christ. We, like the saints who preceded us, are to "pass over" with Christ through death to new life (n. 104).

What the council has done is to change the model by which we understand the relationship between the saints and the living. It is no longer that of supplicant and benefactor, but one of communion and solidarity. Saints are fellow disciples. They are not situated between us and Jesus Christ, but are with us, *in* Christ, as sisters and brothers with whom we share a common humanity and a common faith.

Post–Vatican II Theological Developments

Karl Rahner situates his understanding of the saints in the context of a theology of grace and ecclesiology. When the Church canonizes a saint, it affirms that God really has redeemed, really has poured out the Spirit, really has done mighty things for sinners, and really has let the divine light shine in the darkness. "Because the Church must praise *God's grace*, she must also profess herself to be the holy Church" ("The Church of the Saints," *Theological Investigations*, vol. 3, Baltimore: Helicon Press, 1967, p. 94). By proclaiming the victory of God's grace in particular individuals, the Church affirms that grace is more than a possibility and a challenge. It is a reality. Without saints, the Church would not be what it is and what it is called to be: a *holy* people, a "historically tangible" expression of "the victory of God's grace" (p. 97). The saints are "living embodiments of the gospel and archetypical instances of its transforming power" (Avery Dulles, op. cit., p. 85).

The Church's veneration of saints is a necessary part of its life and work. Otherwise, there would be a danger of looking upon sanctity as an abstraction. The saints help us to see how the Gospel can be incarnated and lived in many different ways and under many different social and historical circumstances. The basic mystery of

1114

Christianity, after all, is not that God has created a world different from God and in which God must be served and glorified, but rather that grace, which is identical with God, has "permeated the world with God's own presence" ("Why and How Can We Venerate the Saints?" in *Theological Investigations*, vol. 8, New York: Seabury Press, 1977, p. 23; the essay is a reflection on the conciliar teaching summarized earlier).

Latin American liberation theologians have been critical of the present list of canonized saints, most of whom are white, European, and upper- and middle-class. The poor and the oppressed are not represented. Theologians like *Leonardo Boff* have employed the liberation motif as a prism through which to reread the life of Francis of Assisi, finding in him a powerful witness to God's love for the poor and the need to speak and act on their behalf (*Saint Francis: A Model for Human Liberation*, New York: Crossroad, 1982). He and others writing from a Latin American perspective also point to Mary, singing the song of justice in her *Magnificat*, as a herald of liberation: a poor village woman, living under an occupying power, forced to flee with her newborn child from the wrath of a murderous ruler, the bereaved mother of a son unjustly executed.

Feminist theology, too, calls for a reexamination of the theology of the saints, pointing out that over 70 percent of the saints on the liturgical calendar are men and that, of the saints canonized in this century to the end of Paul VI's pontificate (1978), 79 percent are clergy, 21 percent lay, and a smaller percentage, women. (See, for example, Joann Wolski Conn's feminist interpretation of St. Thérèse of Lisieux's life and spirituality in *Women's Spirituality: Resources for Christian Development*, New York: Paulist Press, 1986, pp. 317–25.)

Post–Vatican II Devotional Developments

For many reasons (some of which were mentioned in chapter 29), the cult of the saints and of Mary has declined in the Western Catholic world since Vatican II. It may be, as some have speculated, a direct (and essentially positive) result of the biblical, eucharistic, and Christocentric spirituality to which the council gave impetus. But it is probably also a result of the individualism and growing secularization of Western culture where God is only experienced now as "silent mystery" (Karl Rahner). In other regions of the world, however, the situation is different. Popular devotions and, in particular, the cult of the saints and of Mary continue to flourish. This is the case in much of Latin America, Eastern Europe, and the Mediterranean countries. In some countries (one thinks of Poland under the former Communist regime), these devotions have been closely linked with national aspirations and identity. In Africa, on the other hand, Catholics are drawing upon the genius of the African tradition with its sense of the vital relationship that exists between the living and the "living dead," of the unseen presence of ancestors as integral elements in current social and moral life (see John Mbiti, *New Testament Eschatology in an African Background,* Oxford: Oxford University Press, 1971).

There are more than Western ways of understanding the meaning of the Communion of Saints.

THE COMMUNION OF SAINTS

The article on the "communion of saints" was first found in the Apostles' Creed at the end of the fifth century and was used much earlier in the East, though not as a part of the Creed. It was understood as our participation in the blessings of salvation and in the fellowship of God's holy people. Although this community of salvation encompassed the whole Church, the term *communion of saints* only gradually came to apply principally to the communion between the heavenly Church and the earthly Church. More recently still, the term came to apply principally to the exchange of graces and blessings between individuals here on earth and the saints in heaven and the souls in purgatory (the Church militant, triumphant, and suffering).

Its fundamental biblical and theological meaning, however, remains locked in the noun *communion* (*koinonia*). The Church is, first and foremost, a communion, a fellowship called by the Father, in Christ, through the power of the Spirit (Hebrews 2:14–17; Romans 5:8–10; 8:3,32–35; John 1:14; and especially 2 Corinthians 13:13). The "Communion of Saints" means that *the Church is a communion of disciples who have been transformed by the grace of Christ.* This communion is not broken by death.

1116

The doctrine is explicitly affirmed in the Second Vatican Council's *Dogmatic Constitution on the Church* (and reaffirmed in Pope Paul VI's "Credo of the People of God" and the 1992 *Catechism of the Catholic Church*): "For all who belong to Christ, having his Spirit, form one Church and cleave together in him (see Ephesians 4:16). Therefore the union of the pilgrims with the brothers and sisters who have gone to sleep in the peace of Christ is not in the least interrupted." Those in heaven, because of their close union with Christ, "establish the whole Church more firmly in holiness, lend nobility to the worship which the Church offers on earth to God, and in many ways contribute to its great upbuilding (see 1 Corinthians 12:12–27)" (n. 49). Such persons intercede for those of us on earth and place their merits at our disposal.

The council's vision is eschatologically wide-ranging. When Christ appears at the end and the glorious resurrection of the dead occurs, "the splendor of God will brighten the heavenly city and the Lamb will be the lamp thereof (see Revelation 21:24)" (n. 51). At that supreme moment, the charity of the whole Church will be manifested in adoration of God and of the Lamb who was slain, and all will proclaim with one voice: "To the One seated on the throne and to the Lamb be blessing and honor and glory and might forever and ever!" (Revelation 5:13).

SUMMARY

1. There is relatively little about Mary in the *New Testament*. *Mark*'s portrait is somewhat negative (3:20–35), while *Luke* presents her as the obedient handmaid of the Lord from the beginning and as the spokeswoman for the poor of Israel. *John* reports that Jesus, on the cross, included her in his eschatological family. *Matthew* takes a middle position between Mark and Luke.

2. The New Testament says nothing about Mary's virginity *in partu*, nor does it say she was a virgin *post partum*. On the contrary, it speaks of brothers and sisters of Jesus.

3. *Second-century* literature on Mary is thin. Among the *apocrypha* (noncanonical writings) the most important was the *Protevangelium of James*, for centuries the source of many legends about Mary and the life of the Holy Family. Among the *patristic sources* are *Ignatius of Antioch*, *Justin*, and *Irenæus*, who witness to the virginal conception of Jesus and who first develop the Eve-Mary parallel.

4. Discussions of Mary's *perpetual virginity* were complicated by the fact that, on the one hand, the Gnostics and Docetists denied the humanity of Jesus, and, on the other, by the fact that virginity was being emphasized within the Church at this time for ascetical reasons, and Mary presented a persuasive model for Christian women. It came to be almost universally accepted from the third century on.

5. The *Council of Ephesus* (431) defined, against the Nestorians, that Mary is truly the Mother of God (*theotokos*) and not only the mother of Christ.

6. Following Ephesus, *Marian devotion* increased. The apocryphal literature became popular again, and liturgical feasts were multiplied.

7. From the eighth century on, faith in Mary's *intercessory power* received a strong push from growing belief in her assumption, especially in the East.

8. As popular Eastern legends (e.g., the story of Theophilus) were translated and circulated in the West, and as theology in the West became increasingly divorced from the Bible and the early Christian writers, excesses in Marian piety increased.

9. *Bernard of Clairvaux* stressed Mary's role in the channeling of saving grace ("everything through Mary"). He did not deny that Christ was the one Mediator, but pointed out that he is also our God and Judge. Mary provides the component of mercy.

10. Two centuries later controversy developed on the *Immaculate Conception*. Aquinas and others argued that such a doctrine would contradict the universality of redemption; Scotus replied that Mary, too, was redeemed, but that she alone was preserved from Original Sin in view of her relationship with Christ and as a sign of Christ's power over Original Sin as well as over actual sins.

11. Marian prayers, hymns, devotions, feasts, and reports of apparitions proliferated between the eleventh and fourteenth centuries.

12. The *Reformers* resisted the underlying assumptions of much of this Marian devotion. The *Council of Trent* and various Counter-Reformation theologians defended Marian devotion and Mary's role in our redemption.

13. In the seventeenth and eighteenth centuries, especially in France, newer *excesses* developed, e.g., "True Devotion," involving absolute surrender to Mary in order to get by Christ's "weak" side. The rise of *rationalism* and the coming of the *Enlightenment* tempered this spirituality, at least in northern Europe, but Marian interest was kept alive in Italy and elsewhere through the popular works of Alphonsus Ligouri.

14. Concern for the doctrine of the *Immaculate Conception* was rejuvenated in 1830 with a reported apparition of Mary to Catherine Labouré. In 1854 Pope

Pius IX solemnly defined the Immaculate Conception as a *dogma of faith,* endorsing the approach taken by Scotus against Thomas.

15. Other reported visions and apparitions (e.g., Lourdes, Fatima) along with other factors led in 1950 to a second Marian definition: the *Assumption.*

16. Unlike these earlier devotional currents, the *Second Vatican Council* emphasized Mary's role in the economy of salvation, her relationship with the Church, and the subordination of all Marian devotions to the unique mediation of Christ. The council also warned against devotional exaggerations and excesses.

17. Two postconciliar papal teachings include Paul VI's *Marialis Cultus* (1974) which offered guidelines for Marian devotion and warned against excesses, and John Paul II's *Redemptoris Mater* (1987), a more devotional document.

18. The dogma of the *Immaculate Conception* means that God was fully present to Mary in grace from the beginning, in view of her divine motherhood. She, too, is truly redeemed, but in an exceptional and unique manner.

19. The dogma of the *Assumption* complements the Immaculate Conception. The intimate union with God from the beginning of her existence is fulfilled at the end of her earthly life. The dogma also attests to the fact our human existence is bodily existence and that we are destined for glory in the totality of that existence.

20. Two extremes are to be avoided in Marian devotion: a *minimalism* which withholds any and all veneration from Mary, and a *maximalism* which assumes there are practically no limits to such veneration.

21. *Criteria* for evaluating Marian devotions include the following: (1) Is Christ at the center? (2) Is he always a merciful and compassionate Christ? (3) Is there room for human cooperation with Christ? (4) Is there a sense of the Church as a communion of saints? (5) Is Mary's discipleship highlighted? (6) Is her sacramentality ("God-bearer") properly emphasized, and is it linked with the sacramentality of the Church? (7) Is Mary's role always properly subordinate to Christ's in the work of redemption? (8) Is it clear that she, too, is one of the redeemed? (9) If there are denials *or* affirmations of dogma, are the *reasons* orthodox? (10) The fact of apparitions is always an open question; no one is bound to accept them in faith except those to whom they are originally given. Who has received them? (11) The *content* of apparitions is always to be measured against the totality of Christian faith. Is the content consistent with that faith?

22. *Devotion to Mary* is a characteristically Catholic phenomenon in that it expresses three fundamental principles of Catholic theology and practice: (1) grace is a *mediated* reality; (2) the invisible God is present to us *sacramentally,* uniquely through Christ, but also in Mary and the saints; and (3) we belong to a *communion* of saints of which Mary is the preeminent member.

1119

23. In the strict sense, *the saints* are those whom the Church, either through custom or formal canonization, has singled out as members of the Church triumphant so that they may be commemorated in public worship.

24. The *New Testament* spoke of all disciples as "saints." Later the term was applied to *martyrs,* and eventually to *confessors, ascetics,* and other outstanding deceased members of the Church.

25. As concern with the afterlife and penitential discipline increased (especially by the seventh century), so, too, did the *cult of the saints.* Excesses and abuses developed. Canonization was reserved to the pope by the twelfth and thirteenth centuries.

26. In spite of the reservations of the Reformers, the cult of the saints (with its excesses and abuses) became more widespread in the *late medieval, Baroque, and Romanticist periods,* until Vatican II.

27. *Vatican II* changed the model of the relationship between the saints and the living from one of benefactor and supplicant to one of *communion* and *solidarity.*

28. *Post–Vatican II theology* situated the cult of the saints in the context of the Church as a *communion of saints* (Karl Rahner), while others highlighted critical principles of interpretation: the saints as advocates of the poor and the oppressed (liberation theology) and as liberated women (feminist theology).

29. The *Communion of Saints* means that the Church is a communion of disciples who have been transformed by the grace of Christ. This communion is not broken by death.

SUGGESTED READINGS

Anderson, H. George, et al., eds. *The One Mediator, the Saints and Mary: Lutherans and Catholics in Dialogue VIII.* Minneapolis: Augsburg Fortress Press, 1992.

Brown, Peter. *The Cult of the Saints: Its Rise and Function in Latin Christianity.* London: SCM Press, 1981.

Brown, Raymond E., et al., eds. *Mary in the New Testament: A Collaborative Assessment by Protestant and Roman Catholic Scholars.* Philadelphia: Fortress Press, and New York: Paulist Press, 1978.

Congar, Yves. *Christ, Our Lady, and the Church.* Westminster, Md.: Newman Press, 1957.

Cunningham, Lawrence S. *The Meaning of Saints.* New York: Harper & Row, 1980.

Donnelly, Doris, ed. *Mary, Woman of Nazareth: Biblical and Theological Perspectives.* New York: Paulist Press, 1989.

Gebara, Ivone, and Maria Clara Bingemer. *Mary: Mother of God, Mother of the Poor*. Maryknoll, N.Y.: Orbis Books, 1989.

Græf, Hilda. *Mary: A History of Doctrine and Devotion*. 2 vols. New York: Sheed & Ward, 1963; reprint, Westminster, Md.: Christian Classics, 1985.

Greeley, Andrew. *The Mary Myth: On the Femininity of God*. New York: Seabury Press, 1977.

Johnson, Elizabeth A. "Saints and Mary," in *Systematic Theology: Roman Catholic Perspectives*, vol. 2. Minneapolis: Fortress Press, 1991, pp. 143–77.

Rahner, Karl. *Mary, Mother of the Lord: Theological Meditations*. New York: Herder & Herder, 1963.

Semmelroth, Otto. *Mary, Archetype of the Church*. New York: Sheed & Ward, 1963.

Suenens, Léon Joseph. *Mary the Mother of God*. New York: Hawthorn Books, 1959.

Thompson, William M. *Fire and Light: The Saints and Theology*. Mahwah, N.J.: Paulist Press, 1987.

Thurian, Max. *Mary, Mother of the Lord, Figure of the Church*. London: Faith Press, 1963.

Woodward, Kenneth L. *Making Saints: How the Catholic Church Determines Who Becomes a Saint, Who Doesn't, and Why*. New York: Simon and Schuster, 1990.

XXXI

The Last Things

ESCHATOLOGY

Eschatology, in the traditional sense of the word, is that area of theology which is directly concerned with the "study of the last thing(s)." The "last thing" (*eschaton*) is God, or, more precisely, the Kingdom, or Reign, of God, i.e., the final manifestation of the reconciling, renewing, and unifying love of God. The "last things" (*eschata*) are various moments or stages in the final manifestation process: death, particular judgment, heaven, hell, purgatory, Second Coming of Christ, resurrection of the body, general judgment, consummation of all things in the perfection of the Kingdom of God. The final destiny of Christians is not different from the final destiny of all human beings, nor is it different from the destiny of the world itself or of its history. *There is only one beginning and one end of all created reality: God.*

Eschatology is about the Kingdom, or Reign, of God, i.e., *the redemptive presence of God actualized through the power of God's reconciling Spirit.* God is the active, incarnate power of love by which we ourselves, our sisters and brothers, our world, and our history are healed, renewed, and brought to the fullness of perfection. And this is precisely what the Kingdom of God is all about.

To reflect on the meaning of the Kingdom of God in relation to us, our world, and our history is to "do eschatology." But to do eschatology is to do what is central to theology: It is to explore the reality of the active, incarnate, redeeming, loving God as that God is

1123

known and accepted in faith. Eschatology, however, is not simply coextensive with all of theology, which addresses the mystery of God in its fullness. Eschatology centers its attention on that aspect of God by which God is the destiny and consummation of all reality. To do eschatology is to do theology itself, from the point of view of our *absolute future*. If theology is *faith* seeking understanding, in a sense eschatology is *hope* seeking understanding.

This is not to say that eschatology is concerned only with the future. On the contrary, the future is being realized even now, in the *present*, with the continued outpouring of the Holy Spirit, and has begun to be realized already in the *past*, with the death and resurrection of Jesus Christ. Therefore, the placement of this chapter near the end of the book should not mislead the reader. Eschatology could just as properly be placed at the *beginning* as at the end. In fact, eschatological themes have run all the way through the book, wherever there has been a discussion of the saving activity of the triune God, proclaimed in Jesus' preaching of the Kingdom of God and centered in his death and resurrection.

We are already redeemed in grace, in faith, in hope, in love (John 5:24; 12:31; 16:8). The Spirit has already been given (Philippians 1:19; Romans 8:23). Our resurrection has already taken place in the Spirit (John 5:25,28). Our *death*, therefore, is, or should be, a participation in the redemptive death and resurrection of Jesus Christ, which have already taken place. Our *particular judgment* will be the visible manifestation of the judgment of acquittal already rendered in Jesus Christ (e.g., John 12:31–32; Romans 8:3; Galatians 3:13). The final, *general judgment* will only make clear what is already true—namely, that history is the work of God, that its center is Jesus Christ, and that its moving force is the Holy Spirit. This is, at the same time, the *consummation of all things*, the disclosure of God's acceptance of the world in the incarnation. The Second Coming of Christ (*Parousia*) is simply the final stage of the one coming of Christ (Matthew 12:40). Christ's *return* is really the *arrival* of all things at their final destination in Christ. It is the definitive revelation of God's all-embracing love for the world (Matthew 24:36; 25:31–46; 1 Thessalonians 5:2; 2 Thessalonians 2:1–8; Revelation 20:11–15; 22:12,20).

The *anticipation* of these final events occurs not only in faith, in hope, and in the active love of one another in charity, but also sacramentally in the *Eucharist*, where we eat and drink of the Lord's body and blood "until he comes" (1 Corinthians 11:26), and in the *Church* itself, which is the eschatological community, the Temple of the Holy Spirit, the carrier even now of the divine glory (Ephesians 5:27).

This is not to say that history's movement toward the Kingdom of God is smooth and unimpeded. There are powers at work in the world which are hostile to God (e.g., Ezekiel 38–39; Daniel 2:20–45; 7:7–8; Psalm 2) and which are directed immediately against Christ (Revelation 12:1–5) and the Church (12:17), growing in intensity as the end draws near. All of these evil forces are focused in the one known as *Satan* (the Hebrew word *sātān* means "adversary," and it was translated into Greek as *diabolos*, the word which passed into various European languages). He is regarded as the prince of the angels who fell away from God before the creation of the world and who were thrust out of heaven. He becomes in the New Testament the evil one (Matthew 13:19), the enemy (Luke 10:19), the ruler of this world (John 12:31), the father of lies (John 8:44), the evil force behind the passion of Jesus (Luke 22:3,31; John 13:27). But the passion is also the source of victory over Satan (1 Corinthians 2:8; John 12:31; Acts of the Apostles 12:7–11), who is himself destined to be cast finally into hell (Revelation 20:8,10).

We believe, therefore, that the outcome of history is already decided by Christ, even though that outcome is still hidden and can be grasped only in faith, in hope, and in love.

THE KINGDOM OF GOD: THE FINAL DESTINY OF CREATION AND HUMANITY

Although the chapter is organized according to the traditional distinction between general and individual eschatology (the final destiny of creation and all humanity, on the one hand, and of individuals, on the other), it is important to remember that the two are radically inseparable. There is only one Kingdom, and it is the final destiny of all.

1125

Old Testament

The Old Testament never uses the expression *Kingdom of God* except in Wisdom 10:10. Nevertheless, the notion of the kingship of Yahweh permeates its pages. The God of Israel is Lord of all creation and has chosen Israel and made a covenant with her. As divine sovereign, Yahweh is just and the administrator of ultimate justice. Those whom Yahweh has chosen must serve Yahweh, not primarily by sacrificial cult or poetic hymns but by a corresponding justice. "Justice, and only justice, you shall pursue" (Deuteronomy 16:20). In early apocalyptic literature this divine sovereignty is handed over to the Son of Man to bring down and to establish on earth (Daniel 7:13,14), a vision that would be decisive for Jesus.

Israel experienced the kingship of Yahweh in Yahweh's action in history. But that kingship was also beyond history. On the one hand, David becomes aware that his own kingdom was instituted by God and established by God's grace forever (2 Samuel 7:12–16). On the other hand, Gideon, the judge, can declare: "I will not rule over you, and my son will not rule over you; the Lord will rule over you" (Judges 8:23).

Furthermore, the Kingdom is at once localized and universal. Thus, God is said to be in royal residence in the ark of the covenant (Exodus 25:8; 40:34–38; Numbers 14:10), but Yahweh's throne is also in heaven itself, and "The whole earth is full of his glory" (Isaiah 6:3). Yahweh's rule, therefore, is not over Israel alone, but over all people (Amos 9:7; Jeremiah 10:7,10–12; Psalm 22:29–30; Isaiah 44:24–28; 45:1–6). Indeed, the whole of creation, and not merely the Gentiles, is destined to share in the Kingdom of God's peace (Hosea 2:20; Isaiah 35:1–10). Everything will be brought together at the end in a divine banquet (Isaiah 25:6–8).

The *liturgical life* of Israel disclosed yet another dialectical aspect of the Kingdom: It is at once present and future. God even now reigns over and guides the people of Israel, all nations, and the whole created order. But in times of severe affliction Yahweh's rule is perceived to be withdrawn temporarily, and Israel prays in hope that one day Yahweh will powerfully restore the Kingdom and destroy Israel's oppressors. Thus, after the fall of the monarchy the so-called royal Psalms (2, 18, 20, 21, 72, 101, 110, 132, 144:1–11) are "spiritualized," and the king is now identified with the messianic king who is to come.

This hope in a future, this-worldly liberation is particularly emphasized in the *prophetic literature*. All peoples will drink of the cup of God's wrath (Jeremiah 25:15–29). Yahweh will deliver the wicked to the sword (25:30–38). The godless armies will be annihilated (Ezekiel 39:1–7), and all nations will see the glory of God and the divine judgment (39:21). A similarly cosmic vision is sketched by Isaiah (24–27) and in Daniel (2 and 7). Jerusalem is identified as the focal point of God's new reign over Israel (Micah 4:7), and the return of the Israelites shall be like a second Exodus (7:14–15). It is to the mountain of God (Zion) in Jerusalem that all nations will stream (Micah 4:1–4; Isaiah 2:2–4), and the glory of God will be manifested there (Jeremiah 16:19; Isaiah 56:7; 60; 66:19–21; Zechariah 2:14–17; 8:20–22; 14:16).

This universal kingship will bear fruit in a whole new moral order where the will of God is operative. As a result, peace will be achieved among the peoples of the earth (Isaiah 2:4; Zechariah 9:9–10) through the Messiah who is the prince of peace, and God will be revealed again as a shepherd (Isaiah 40:11), but a kingly one (43:15; 44:6). The Lord comes, not to punish and to judge, but to bring peace, goodness, and salvation: "How beautiful upon the mountains are the feet of the messenger who announces peace, who brings good news, who announces salvation, who says to Zion, 'Your God reigns!' " (52:7). Jesus begins his own ministry in the same spirit (Mark 1:14; compare also Isaiah 61:1 with Luke 4:18 and Matthew 11:5). And so it is *Deutero-Isaiah* (or Second Isaiah, chapters 40–55) which most directly anticipates Jesus' own conception of the Kingdom.

In *later Judaism*, however, a more *nationalistic* orientation develops, and this too persists into the New Testament and creates a problem for Jesus. The two sons of Zebedee, for example, vie for the first places in the messianic kingdom of Jesus (Mark 10:37), and Peter himself tries to deter the Lord from the way of suffering (8:32). In direct contrast to this nationalistic eschatology, which focused on Palestine and the earthly Jerusalem, *apocalyptic* (from the Hebrew *gālāh* and the Greek *apocalypsis,* meaning "revelation") literature directed its vision rather to the heavenly Jerusalem and to paradise as the abode of the elect and the blessed. The book of Daniel provides the original pattern for this literature. The heavenly origin and character of the Kingdom emerges in the vision of the four beasts and the one who is like the Son of Man, who appears in the clouds of heaven after judgment is rendered on the beasts (7:9–12). The whole scene takes place in heaven. "However we interpret the 'Son of man', he is in no sense an earthly savior who wages war in God's name and exercises justice. He is a heavenly and pre-existent being" (Rudolf Schnackenburg, *God's Rule and Kingdom*, p. 65).

The apocalypses, therefore, place the strongest possible emphasis on God's sovereign action and final intervention without any cooperation at all on our part. They sometimes think they can determine the moment of the divine intervention and recognize the signs that will precede it. Accordingly, they divide the history of the world into periods, on the lines of the four world empires (Daniel 2:37–45), or according to weeks of years and jubilees, seven times seven, or after the seventy shepherds of the people, etc. They inquire how much of the course of world history has already elapsed and then work out the conclusion. And, finally, they look for signs and portents such as earthquakes, plagues, confusion, fighting, the fall of rulers and princes (Daniel 12:1). They dwell upon the fantastic and the fearsome and boast of special apocalyptic knowledge, concealed from the common person. There appear a spirit of revenge and a perverted joy in the annihilation of the wicked. However noble the apocalyptic conception of the Kingdom, much of this literature is marred by pettiness, narrowness, and self-righteousness. It is also characterized by an individualism that weakens the community's commitment to the abiding struggle for justice and peace and the transformation of all creation that had been voiced so powerfully by the prophets.

The Preaching of Jesus

Although Jesus repeatedly referred to the Kingdom of God in his preaching—indeed he began his whole ministry with the announcement that the Kingdom of God had "come near" (Mark 1:15)—there is no biblical evidence that he ever defined it or was asked to do so by his hearers. (Paul comes closest to defining it in Romans 14:17: "For the kingdom of God is not food and drink but righteousness and peace and joy in the Holy Spirit.") Nevertheless, Jesus used the term, especially in parables, with the apparent assurance that his listeners knew what he meant. And they did. The Kingdom of God was an integral part of contemporary Jewish vocabulary. It was something they all understood and longed for. As we already noted (in chapters 12 and 25), the notion of the Kingdom received a radically new interpretation from Jesus, but the interpretation did not break the line of continuity reaching far back into the history of Israel and the pages of the Old Testament.

What caught Jesus' contemporaries by surprise was his proclamation that the Kingdom of God had "come near" (Mark 1:15) and is "among you" (Luke 17:21). Thus, he called for conversion and repentance (Luke 10:13–15; Matthew 11:20–24; Luke 13:1–5; 19:41–44) and underlined the importance of watching and being ready for the Kingdom (Luke 12:35–40; Matthew 25:1–13). In the final accounting, however, the Kingdom comes from divine power and grace (Mark 4:26–29). God gives it (Luke 12:32) or assigns it (22:29–30). It is especially for *sinners*. (Mark 2:16–17; Luke 7:34 = Matthew 11:19; Luke 15:7,10,24,32; 18:10–14; 19:7; Matthew 21:31). The scandal aroused by Jesus' associating with publicans and prostitutes (Mark 2:15–17; Luke 7:34,36–50; 19:7) showed how unexpected his proclamation and interpretation of the Kingdom had been. Jesus emphasizes always the mercy of God (Matthew 18:23–35), and, unlike the prophets, he presupposes in his call for repentance that God's redemptive activity on our behalf has already begun (Mark 1:15). In the beatitudes in the Sermon on the Mount, he insists that God shows special favor toward *the poor, the oppressed, the despised, the persecuted* (Matthew 5:1–12). In fact, entrance into the Kingdom will be determined in large measure by our response to the neighbor in need (Matthew 25:31–46).

Jesus also excluded a *political* interpretation of the Kingdom; not that the values of the Kingdom have no political consequences, but that its coming is not dependent upon any one political order. He did not accept the widespread Jewish hope for a political kingdom, nor did he cooperate with the Zealots in their own activities against Roman rule. Why else did he conceal the messianic character of his work, as is evident especially in Mark's Gospel? Indeed, he reminds the Sadducees that after the resurrection from the dead there will be no marrying in heaven (Mark 12:24–25).

But Jesus also excluded an *elitist* understanding of the Kingdom. He carried his ministry to the whole of Israel, just and sinners alike, even the outcasts and the despised. He leaves the separation of the good from the bad to the final judgment (Matthew 13:24–30,47–50) and tolerates failures even within his own circle of followers (Mark 14:27,30; Luke 22:31–34). The doors to the Kingdom are open to all, including those from East and West. Some of the children of the Kingdom will be found unworthy and will be cast out into the exterior darkness (Matthew 8:11–23; Luke 13:24–28). What will be decisive is not membership in Israel but the fulfillment of the call to conversion (Matthew 21:43; Mark 12:1–9). To be converted is to seek first the Kingdom of God (Matthew 6:25–33). The Kingdom will come when the will of God is done (6:9–13).

Doing the will of God involves *discipleship* (Luke 9:57–60 = Matthew 8:19–22; Luke 9:61–62; Mark 10:21; Mark 9:38 = Luke 9:49), which makes absolute demands upon each disciple (Luke 14:33). He calls for a renunciation of earthly goods when these become an obstacle to entry into the Kingdom (Mark 10:24–27). He takes under his influence those who have made themselves eunuchs for the Kingdom (Matthew 19:12) but does not impose celibacy on all.

Jesus' works give substance to his preaching. His healings and exorcisms are *signs* that the Kingdom has drawn near in him: "But if it is by the finger of God that I cast out the demons, then the kingdom of God has come to you" (Luke 11:20). When the disciples of John the Baptist come out into the desert to inquire whether or not Jesus is the Messiah, he tells them to go back to John and report what they themselves have seen and heard: "The blind receive their sight, the lame walk, the lepers are cleansed, the deaf hear, the dead are raised, and the poor have good news brought to them" (Matthew 11:4–5).

Although Jesus had a unique relationship to God (Matthew 11:25–27), it is not his Kingdom but *the Father's* (Luke 12:32; 22:29–30), who alone knows the hour of its final coming (Matthew 24:36). In the meantime, we can pray for it (Matthew 6:10; Luke 11:2). But because it *is* the Father's work and because the manifestation of the Father's love cannot be understood in this world's terms, Jesus made no attempt to describe the Kingdom, much less define it, except in parables (Mark 4:33–34). (See again chapters 12 and 25.)

Early Christianity

With the death and resurrection of Jesus there is a remarkable shift from the proclamation of the Kingdom of God to the proclamation of the Lordship of Jesus (Romans 10:9; 1 John 5:1; John 20:31). The historical details of this transition are probably lost to us forever. But this is not to say that the early Church corrupted the original message of Jesus. On the contrary, the Kingdom of God was still at the core of the primitive proclamation (Acts of the Apostles 1:3; 13:16–41; 28:23,31). Furthermore, insofar as Jesus identified himself so closely with his message that he can be regarded as the very incarnation of the Kingdom of God, the early Church's proclamation of Jesus as the Christ represents no fundamental departure from Jesus' own preaching. Jesus' Gospel about the Kingdom of God thereby became the Church's Gospel about Jesus, the Christ of God.

The early Church recognized not only that the Kingdom of God had broken into history in a new and definitive way in Jesus Christ but also that it continued to grow and develop in the course of postresurrection history. This is particularly characteristic of the *Lucan* writings (the third Gospel and the Acts of the Apostles). We are living now between-the-times: between the decisive inbreaking of the Kingdom in Jesus Christ and the fulfillment of the Kingdom at the Second Coming of Christ when history is brought to perfection.

Although *Paul* speaks only rarely of the Kingdom of God (1 Corinthians 6:10; 15:50; Galatians 5:21; and the text cited above, Romans 14:17), his eschatology is explicitly Christ-centered, beginning with 1 Thessalonians, which emphasizes the resurrection and Second Coming of Christ. For Paul, Christ is "the fullness of time" (Galatians 4:4; Ephesians 1:10), so that "if anyone is in Christ, there is a new creation: everything old has passed away; see, everything has become new" (2 Corinthians 5:17). We are even now living in "the ends of the ages" (1 Corinthians 10:11).

The Kingdom is realized in the Lordship of Christ (1 Corinthians 15:24; Colossians 1:13) and is present to the faithful (Colossians 3:1–4) in the Church (1:18,24). The exalted Christ continues to exercise his sovereignty over the world through the Church (Ephesians 1:21–23; 3:10; 4:8–10), and that Lordship will be brought to completion at the

Second Coming, when God will be all in all (1 Corinthians 15:24–28). Christ's rule, therefore, extends beyond the Church.

Except for one text (John 3:5) the term Kingdom of God does not occur in the *Johannine* writings. At times there are glimpses into the future: resurrection of the body, judgment, and eternal life (5:28–29; 12:25). History is the battlefield where the powers of Satan war against the reign of God in Christ (Revelation 11:15; 20:4).

The *early Church*, consequently, is always conscious that the Kingdom of God under Christ is still on the way, and that the Church itself is a pilgrim people, strangers and sojourners in this world (1 Peter). Christ's rule is hidden now, but it will be manifested fully in the end, when the Kingdom of God will be realized in all its perfection. And nowhere is the orientation of the Church toward the Kingdom more explicitly revealed than in its Eucharist, which anticipates the eating and drinking at the Lord's table in the Kingdom (Luke 22:30).

Postbiblical Development

There are four main currents of interpretation of the Kingdom of God in the history of the Church from the close of the New Testament canon to about the year 1000, and even down to the present. The first is the *eschatological* current, which is a continuation of the New Testament tradition as summarized above. The greatest representative of this current is *Irenæus*. The second current is *spiritual-mystical*. The Kingdom is identified with some present spiritual good in the soul of the believer, e.g., knowledge, spiritual illumination. Or it may be equated with heaven. A major representative of this current is *Origen*. The third current is *political*. The Kingdom of God on earth is identified with some political structure or program, e.g., the Christian Empire of Constantine in the East (Byzantium) or the Holy Roman Empire of Charlemagne in the West. One major exponent of this view is *Eusebius of Cæsarea*. The fourth current is *ecclesial*. The Kingdom of God on earth is identified with the Church, sometimes called the Kingdom of Christ to differentiate it from the Kingdom of God in heaven. This current was especially strong in Catholicism until the Second Vatican Council. Its major proponent was *Augustine*. (The schema is derived from Benedict T. Viviano, *The Kingdom of God in History*, pp. 30–31.)

Second Century to High Middle Ages

Early patristic theology (the *first* current) was influenced by the notion of the Lordship of Jesus and the imminence of his Second Coming (e.g., Ignatius of Antioch, *Letter to the Ephesians*, 11; and Irenæus of Lyons, *Adversus Hæreses* 5.33.3). There were also some apocalyptic elements—e.g., the notion of the thousand-year reign in Justin's *Trypho* (80–81) and Tertullian's *Against Marcion* (3, 24). The reign of God in Clement of Alexandria and in Origen tends to be *spiritualized* (the *second* current). Prayer for the coming of the Kingdom is a petition for wisdom and knowledge (Origen, *On Prayer*, 13). This strongly interiorized concept of the Kingdom prevailed in the East, especially under the philosophical influence of neo-Platonism. Eusebius of Cæsarea (d. ca. 340), however, offered a kind of *political* theology of the Kingdom by referring to the earthly Roman empire, with its enforcement of peace, as the image of the Kingdom (the *third* current).

In the West, the *Church* became increasingly identified with the Kingdom of God (the *fourth* current). This is especially evident in Augustine: "It follows that the Church even now is the kingdom of Christ and the kingdom of heaven" (*City of God*, book XX, chapter 9). It is important to remember that Augustine's identification of the Church with the Kingdom of God on earth remained the dominant Catholic understanding of the Kingdom of God until the middle of the twentieth century, when modern critical biblical scholarship brought about a fresh reexamination of the question.

Even more significant than his ecclesial interpretation of the Kingdom of God, however, is Augustine's notion of the two cities: the city of God and the earthly city. It would seem that the city of God is closely connected, if not simply identified, with the Kingdom of God. The city of God, he says, is "on pilgrimage in this world, and it is by regeneration that it is brought to another world, whose children neither generate nor are generated" (XV, 20). In any case, Augustine introduces a distinction here which probably laid the foundation for Martin Luther's distinctive doctrine of the two kingdoms; and this, in turn, was at the root of so much of the indifference to social and political questions within Christianity between the Reformation and the nineteenth century. The Kingdom of God is God's work alone. We can do absolutely nothing to bring it about. The kingdom of humankind, on the other hand, is destined to pass away without a trace. Therefore, what point is there in striving to alter the face of this earth, since it will not survive? Only God's work will endure.

For Augustine the earthly city is created by self-love and with contempt for God, whereas the city of God, or heavenly city, is created by the love of God and has contempt for self. The earthly city glories in itself; the heavenly city glories in the Lord. The earthly city lusts for domination; the heavenly city seeks to serve others. The earthly city operates according to human standards; the heavenly city fulfills the will of God. The earthly city is destined for eternal punishment; the heavenly city is destined to reign with God for all eternity. The earthly city is begotten from Cain; the heavenly city, from Abel. The earthly city is born of nature, like Ishmæl; the heavenly city is born of promise, like Isaac. And the earthly city is divided against itself; the heavenly city enjoys eternal and perfect peace (*City of God*, XIV, 28–XV, 1–5).

This is not to say that the parallels are always clear and consistent. Thus, Augustine sometimes writes of the earthly city as if it had two aspects itself, one good and one evil: "One part of the earthly city has been made into an image of the Heavenly City, by symbolizing something other than itself, namely that other City; and for that reason it is a servant. For it was established not for its own sake but in order to symbolize another City..." (XC, 2). The evil part, in turn, is divided against itself as were Remus and Romulus, "for this is how Rome was founded, when Remus, as Roman history witnesses, was slain by his brother Romulus. The difference from the primal crime was that both brothers were citizens of the earthly city" (XV, 5).

An even more pronounced identification of the Kingdom of God and the Church is found in the succeeding centuries in such writings as those of Pope Gregory the Great, who interpreted Luke 9:27 ("But truly I tell you, there are some standing here who will not taste death before they see the kingdom of God") to apply to the Church, which is opposed to the "power and glory" of the world.

1134

Once the Franks came to power in the West, this ecclesiastical interpretation of the Kingdom of God was fully *politicized*. Charlemagne was the new David who had taken over the reins of royal lordship in the Church, allowing the pope the role of Moses at prayer (see his *Letter to Leo III*), while remaining himself the sovereign who shared in the reign of Christ and of God. This same notion was one of the inspirations of the Crusades and was used to justify the investiture of bishops by kings.

High Middle Ages

Apocalyptic notions were then added to the political. The kingdom of the Franks along with that of the Romans was regarded as the "third kingdom" mentioned in the seventh chapter of Daniel, following the kingdoms of the Greeks and the Persians. Thus, the world awaited a last ruler to restore the empire to its glory and lay down his crown in Jerusalem, before the coming of the Antichrist. The most direct opposition to this imperial notion of the Kingdom of God was formulated by Pope Boniface VIII's bull, *Unam Sanctam* (1303), in which he declared that the pope alone has supreme authority over the whole world.

Joachim of Fiore (d. 1202) was the principal source of yet another interpretation which set the terms of the theological discussion of the Kingdom of God in the medieval period. He divided history into three great periods: (1) the age of the Father (the time of the Old Testament when the human community lived under the Law); (2) the age of the Son (the time of the New Testament and for forty-two generations of about thirty years each, or until the year 1260, during which the human community lived under grace); and (3) the age of the Spirit, in which there would be new religious orders leading to the conversion of the world and the establishment of a spiritual church. Some carried Joachim's vision to extremes—e.g., the Spiritual Franciscans, who saw Francis of Assisi as the "angel with the sign of the living God" ushering in the age of the Spirit, and the Fraticelli, who regarded themselves as the new order of spiritual men foretold by Joachim. Although strongly resisted by Thomas Aquinas, this view of the Kingdom persisted well into the Middle Ages and would influence some of the Protestant sects at the margin of the Reformation movement—e.g., Bohemian Brethren and the Anabaptists.

Dominican *mysticism*—e.g., Meister Eckhart, Tauler, Suso—saw the Kingdom of God as "God himself with all his riches" in the depths of the soul, but this notion coexisted with the more ecclesiastical and political interpretations put forth later by Martin Bucer (d. 1551), Tommaso Campanella (d. 1639), and Thomas More (d. 1535) in his *Utopia* (1516).

Reformation to the Nineteenth Century

Luther's doctrine of the two kingdoms rejected both the sectarian interpretations as well as the grand theocratic understanding of the Kingdom as proposed by some Catholics. God's reign is essentially invisible and spiritual. The law is the affair of the secular powers. The Church is concerned only with the preaching of the Gospel. Salvation is through faith, not works. The two kingdoms "must be sharply distinguished," he wrote ("Secular Authority: To What Extent It Should Be Obeyed," in *Martin Luther: Selections From His Writings,* New York: Doubleday Anchor, 1961, p. 371). The one kingdom produces piety; the other brings about external peace and prevents evil deeds. Each needs the other. Without piety, there is only hypocrisy. Without law, however, evil is given free reign. (For an understanding of Protestant thought on this question as it developed in the United States from its beginnings, see H. Richard Niebuhr, *The Kingdom of God in America,* New York: Harper & Row, 1937.)

By the eighteenth century, and particularly under the impact of the *Enlightenment,* the Kingdom of God was once again perceived not only as an earthly reality but even as the product of human initiative and effort. It comes about through the establishment of human society according to moral principles. *Immanuel Kant* defined the Kingdom as an "ethical commonwealth" (*Religion Within the Limits of Pure Reason Alone*). Other philosophical interpretations were placed upon it. Hegel, for example, saw it as the final manifestation of the spirit in which it becomes fully conscious of itself. It is the completion and perfection of history.

The same evolutionary and historical understanding shaped the thinking of *Karl Marx* and then, in the twentieth century, of the

Marxist philosopher *Ernst Bloch* (d. 1977) who inspired much of the "theology of hope" movement in Europe in the 1960s. The future now becomes decisive. *Praxis* replaces reflection, or theory. We are called to participate in the struggle to bring the future kingdom into the present, to narrow the gap between justice and injustice, freedom and oppression. But in none of these views is the sovereignty of God the "incalculable and impenetrable irruption of grace in love" (Peter Hünermann, "Reign of God," *The Concise Sacramentum Mundi*, New York: Seabury Press, 1975, p. 1356). The Kingdom of God becomes equivalently the kingdom of humankind. It was against this Liberal (i.e., antitranscendental) interpretation that modern biblical scholarship reacted, as we shall see in the next section (on twentieth-century biblical theology).

At the same time, other interpretations of the Kingdom of God from within the churches adhered to a less historical, more *"spiritual"* line. Thus, for *Blaise Pascal* (d. 1662) the Kingdom was the order of charity which takes us out of ourselves, and the realm where we experience the forgiveness of sins and the friendship of God. With the rise of the Tübingen School in Germany, the Kingdom of God becomes "the idea of Christianity which contains and produces all others" (e.g., J. S. Drey, *Introduction to the Study of Theology*). J. B. Hirscher took it to be the "basic idea" for Christian moral theology. Entrance is gained by conversion, and the Kingdom itself is the rule of God in every realm of life.

Twentieth-Century Biblical Theology

There is a sense in which it can be said that modern New Testament scholarship begins with the debate about the eschatological question. The following survey focuses almost entirely on Protestant biblical theologians and exegetes, because Catholic biblical scholarship was "under wraps" for most of the first half of the twentieth century, beginning with the anti-Modernist instructions from the Pontifical Biblical Commission during the pontificate of Pope Pius X (1903–1914). Not until Pope Pius XII's encyclical *Divino Afflante Spiritu* (1943), known as the "Magna Carta" of modern Catholic biblical scholarship, were Catholic biblical scholars encouraged to engage in a historically and scientifically critical study of the Bible. In the absence

of such critical correction, twentieth-century Catholic theology, catechesis, and preaching had continued, until the middle of the century,
to take for granted the identification of the Church with the Kingdom
of God on earth.

Futurist Eschatology: The Kingdom as Future

Over against the dominant nineteenth-century Liberal Protestant
view that the Kingdom of God is an earthly reality produced by
human hands (Albrecht Ritschl, d. 1889), New Testament exegetes
like *Albert Schweitzer* (d. 1965) and *Johannes Weiss* (d. 1914) argued that
the disciples were to pray for the coming of the Kingdom but that
neither they nor we could do anything to establish it. Not even Jesus
could do that. When the Kingdom comes, God will destroy this old
order which is ruled and spoiled by the devil and will create a
completely new world (see Johannes Weiss, *Jesus' Proclamation of the
Kingdom of God*, Philadelphia: Fortress Press, 1971; originally published in 1892). A more recent expression of this school of thought,
known as *futurist* (or consequent, consistent, or thorough-going)
eschatology, is offered by *Martin Werner*. The irruption of the Kingdom, he argues, signified for Jesus the end of the present natural
world. The Kingdom, therefore, was in no sense a present reality. It is
always in the future, but imminent (*The Formation of Christian Dogma*,
Boston: Beacon Press, 1965).

Realized Eschatology: The Kingdom As Past

Selecting a different set of New Testament passages, the British
scholar *Charles H. Dodd* (d. 1973) argued that "in the earliest tradition
Jesus was understood to have proclaimed that the Kingdom of God,
the hope of many generations, had at last come. It is not merely
imminent; it is here.... The *eschaton* has moved from the future to the
present, from the sphere of expectation into that of realized experience" (*The Parables of the Kingdom*, London: Collins/Fontana, 1963, pp.
40–41; originally published in 1935). For Dodd, however, the challenge of the Kingdom is a challenge for individuals and for the
immediate situation, for "Jesus passed directly from the immediate

1138

situation to the eternal order lying beyond all history" (p. 154). History moves by crisis, not by evolution. The Church proclaims the Gospel of the Kingdom that each might experience the "hour of decision" that Jesus brought (p. 152). The school of "realized eschatology" assumes, therefore, that "history in the individual life is of the same stuff as history at large; that is, it is significant in so far as it serves to bring men face to face with God in his Kingdom, power and glory." (See also Joachim Jeremias, *The Parables of Jesus*, New York: Scribners, 1955.)

Existentialist Eschatology: The Kingdom As Present

For *Rudolf Bultmann* (d. 1976) the Kingdom of God is a new mode of existential existence, for "the question of God and the question of myself are identical" (*Jesus Christ and Mythology*, London: SCM Press, 1958, p. 53). The living God encounters us here and now in the Word, i.e., in the preaching instituted by Jesus Christ. "The idea of the omnipresent and almighty God becomes real in my personal existence only by His Word spoken here and now" (p. 79). The decisive significance of Jesus Christ is that he—in his person, his coming, his passion, and his glorification—is the eschatological event. That event happens here and now in the preaching of the Word regardless of whether this Word is accepted or rejected (p. 81). "It is only in the light of the proclaimed word that what has happened or is happening here or there assumes the character of God's action for the believer" (p. 85). Our relation to the world remains paradoxical. It is our world, but it is really God's. We must live as if it is not ours at all.

This highly existential, present-oriented, and antipolitical understanding of the Kingdom is even more explicitly developed in *Jesus and the Word* (London: Collins/Fontana, 1958; originally published in 1934). The Kingdom of God is "no ideal social order" (p. 78). Jesus paid no apparent attention to the social and economic conditions of his time. "*No programme for world-reformation is derived from the will of God*" (p. 79, sic). Instead, every person stands under the judgment of God at this moment. The decision is against the world and for God. Every claim of one's own is to be silenced. "The *real* future stands before man in decision, not the false future over which he already has control, but the future which will give him a character which he does not yet have" (p. 96).

Salvation-History Eschatology:
The Kingdom As Past, Present, and Future

Directly opposed to Bultmann's existentialist interpretation is *Oscar Cullmann's* notion of salvation history. The Kingdom of God has its beginning at creation, reaches its zenith or midpoint in Jesus Christ, and will be brought to completion at the *Parousia*, or Second Coming. We live now "between-the-times," i.e., between the first and second comings of Christ. This is also "church-time." The mission of the Church is to recall what God has already accomplished in Christ, to focus the attention of the world on the events to come, and to make possible, here and now, a meeting with the Lord through the preaching of the Word and the celebration of the sacraments. What finally distinguishes Christian faith, therefore, from other views of reality is the Christian's conviction that history itself is salvific and that it moves with purpose and direction. Everything leads up to, and flows from, the central Christ-event (see *Christ and Time,* Philadelphia: Westminster Press, 1947).

In a later work he acknowledged the bitter dispute with Bultmann evoked by *Christ and Time.* Cullmann insists in his *Salvation in History* (New York: Harper & Row, 1967) that he agrees with Bultmann that the call to decision is essential to the New Testament faith. Where they disagree, he points out, is over Bultmann's exclusion of salvation history as if it were simply opposed to Christian existence as portrayed in the New Testament. Rather, we find both elements there: the call to decision and salvation history. "By our decision in faith we align ourselves with this very special history, salvation history... comprehending past, present, and future..." (p. 21).

Other contemporary biblical scholars who recognize the three-fold temporal dimension of the Kingdom include Rudolf Schnackenburg (*God's Rule and Kingdom,* 1963), Werner G. Kümmel (*Promise and Fulfillment: The Eschatological Message of Jesus,* London: SCM Press, 1956), and Norman Perrin (*Jesus and the Language of the Kingdom,* Philadelphia: Fortress Press, 1976). The book by Schnackenburg, the only Catholic name in the preceding survey, was described by

Norman Perrin as "probably the best discussion of the subject" (op. cit., p. 210).

Feminist Interpretation

Feminist biblical scholarship underscores the *universality* and *inclusiveness* of the Kingdom of God in the preaching and *praxis* of Jesus. According to *Elisabeth Schüssler Fiorenza,* Jesus used the central image of a festive meal to describe the hoped-for *basilea*. But unlike the Pharisees who sought to realize Israel's calling as a "nation of priests" by carefully observing the ritual purity of the "holy table" and by eating their meals "like priests," Jesus and his disciples did not observe these purity regulations and even shared their meals with "sinners." No one is excluded. Everyone is invited: women as well as men, prostitutes as well as Pharisees, the poor as well as the rich, and even tax-collectors. The *basilea* is also revealed in Jesus' healings and exorcisms—healings of women as well as of men, of the poor as well as the rich (see *In Memory of Her,* New York: Crossroad, 1983, pp. 118–30).

Twentieth-Century Catholic Theology

Karl Rahner

For Karl Rahner, the Church is the sacrament of the Kingdom in the "eschatological phase of sacred history which began with Christ, the phase which brings about the kingdom of God" ("Church and World," *The Concise Sacramentum Mundi,* p. 239). The Kingdom will not be definitively present until history ends with the Second Coming of Christ and the last judgment. On the other hand, the Kingdom is not something totally in the future. It is already coming to be in the history of the world, wherever obedience to God occurs in grace as the acceptance of God's self-communication. But this does not take place solely in the Church nor solely in the personal inwardness of conscience, but in the concrete fulfillment of an earthly task, of active love of others, even of collective love of others.

All of this follows from basic Catholic principles: (1) that grace and justification are to be found also outside the Church; (2) that there is an inseparable unity between material and formal morality, between action and intention; and (3) that there is a fundamental unity between love of God and love of neighbor. This Kingdom is manifested in the "unity, activity, fraternity, etc., of the *world*" (p. 240).

Is the Kingdom the work of God, or the product of human effort? Rahner argues that this question can be answered only dialectically, i.e., by holding in balance two apparently opposed principles: (1) the Kingdom of God will come about at the end of history as an action of God; and (2) human history enters somehow into that endpoint. Thus, human history has ultimate validity, and yet it will undergo radical transformation. These two propositions remain unresolved and so must remain dialectically related in order to keep the future open (God will give the Kingdom when God wills) and to allow the present to keep its basic importance (human effort somehow enters into God's final act). What is permanent in history is the concrete work of love.

Why can it be said that history enters into God's own fullness? "Because the Word of God has himself both made and endured history" ("Christianity and the new earth," *Theology Digest*, 15, Winter 1967, p. 281). Rahner's notion of the Kingdom, therefore, is rooted in the basic Catholic principle of sacramentality, centered in the incarnation.

Edward Schillebeeckx

Edward Schillebeeckx notes that one of the first changes effected by the Second Vatican Council was its abandoning of the earlier tendency to identify the Church too easily with the Kingdom of God. The council also acknowledged the presence of saving grace outside the Church. For Schillebeeckx the Church and the world are on the way to the Kingdom, but are not yet the Kingdom. The powers of the Kingdom, however, are already actively present in the Church and in the world at large. It is, in fact, our common hope in the radically new and final Kingdom that stimulates us never to rest satisfied with what has already been achieved in this world (see *Church: The Human Story of God*, New York: Crossroad, 1990, pp. 154–57).

Historically, we can never say that *this* is the promised future. The Gospel message calls us always to overcome the limitations of the present. It contains a permanent criticism of the present: institutions, structures, mentalities. It urges constant improvement. "Eschatological hope makes the commitment to the temporal order *radical* and by the same token declares any already existing temporal order to be only relative. Thus the Christian's social and political commitment, rooted in his care for mankind, is the hermeneutic of what in Revelation the Kingdom of God's promise implies" (*God the Future of Man*, New York: Sheed & Ward, 1968, p. 161).

For Schillebeeckx, the Kingdom of God is "the divine power itself in its saving activity within our history, but at the same time the final, eschatological state of affairs that brings to an end the evil world, dominated by the forces of calamity and woe, and initiates the new world in which God 'appears to full advantage'; 'your kingdom come' (Matthew 6:10)" (*Jesus: An Experiment in Christology*, New York: Seabury Press, 1979, p. 141). Thus, present and future are essentially interrelated.

God's Lordship is God's mode of being God. God is shown as a loving and caring God who is mindful of humanity (Titus 3:4). The Kingdom of God is our well-being. To surrender to the Lordship of God is to love the other, to work for the other's well-being. "Man's caring for his fellow-men is the visible form and aspect in which the coming of God's kingdom is manifested; it is the way God's Lordship takes" (p. 153). In its fullness, therefore, Jesus' message of the Kingdom is that we must love one another as God loves us, and he (Jesus) discloses this in and through his own mode of conduct, i.e., his *praxis* of the Kingdom. Jesus brings the message that God says "No" to the continuing course of human suffering, to all forms of hunger and poverty, and that the purpose of life and history is "peace, laughter, total satisfaction: the 'final good' of salvation and happiness.... Showing mercy is, despite everything, the deepest purpose that God intends to fulfill in history" (p. 177).

Jesus is the sacrament of God's universal love for us. He is "God translated" for us. Jesus shows us a "most human God" (*Deus humanissimus*). "The cause of God as the cause of man is personified in the very person of Jesus Christ.... He is the firstborn and 'the leader' of a new mankind in that he has lived out proleptically in his own experience, the praxis of the kingdom of God and because that praxis has been endorsed by God" (p. 670).

The Church "bears symbolic witness to that kingdom through its word and sacrament, and in its praxis...." It thereby "effectively anticipates that kingdom. It does so by doing for men and women here and now, in new situations (different from those in Jesus' time), what Jesus did in his time: raising them up for the coming of the kingdom of God, opening up communication among them, caring for the poor and outcast, establishing communal ties within the household of faith and serving all men and women in solidarity" (*Church*, p. 157).

Hans Küng

In the light of modern (German) exegesis, Hans Küng asserts, it is impossible to speak of the Church as the Kingdom of God on earth, nor does the Church build up the Kingdom. The Kingdom is *God's* Kingdom. "Man's part is the way of readiness and openness, obedience and watchfulness, faith and repentance" (*The Church*, New York: Sheed & Ward, 1968, p. 92). The Church is the work of humanity; the Kingdom is the work of God. It is not the Church but the Kingdom which is the goal of creation. To belong to the Church is no guarantee of entrance into the Kingdom. The Church is the anticipatory sign of the Kingdom. The Church moves always toward the Kingdom as its goal. It does not bring the Kingdom; it announces it. God alone brings about the Kingdom; the Church is devoted entirely to its service.

Thus, the Kingdom is not merely God's continuing rule, existing from the moment of creation, but is that which is promised for the future. It is not a religio-political theocracy or democracy, but the immediate, unrestricted rule of God over the world, to be awaited without recourse to violence. It is not for an elite but is the glad tidings of God's infinite goodness and unconditional grace, particularly for the abandoned and the destitute. It is not constructed by human effort but is an act of God. It will, therefore, be a Kingdom of "absolute righteousness, of unsurpassable freedom, of dauntless love, of universal reconciliation, of everlasting peace" (*On Being a Christian*, New York: Doubleday, 1976, p. 215). Just as a false interiorizing of the Kingdom once had to be avoided, so a false secularizing of the Kingdom now is to be avoided. In language close to Bultmann's, Küng insists that our situation is critical. We are "pressed to make a final decision, to accept the offer to commit [ourselves] *to the reality of God*, which is ahead. . . . It is a decision in which everything is at stake: an either-or, for or against God" (p. 225).

Walter Kasper

A similar approach is taken by Walter Kasper. The Kingdom of God is "totally and exclusively God's doing. It cannot be earned by religious or moral effort, imposed by political struggle, or projected in calculation. We cannot plan for it, organize it, make it or build it, we cannot invent or imagine it. It is given (Matthew 21:43, Luke 12:32), 'appointed' (Luke 22:29). We can only inherit it (Matthew 25:34)" (*Jesus the Christ*, New York: Paulist Press, 1976, p. 81). This is not to say that we can do nothing at all in relation to the Kingdom. We are not condemned to Quietism or pure passivity. "What is demanded of us is repentance and faith (Mark 1:15 and parallels)." It means ceasing to rely on one's own capabilities, admitting human powerlessness. It means expecting nothing from oneself and everything from God.

Kasper insists that God's divinity consists in God's self-giving, or God's entering into the other without losing "himself." Indeed, "he is himself precisely when he enters into that which is other than himself. It is by surrendering himself that he shows his divinity. Concealment is therefore the way in which God's glory is revealed in the world" (p. 83). Jesus' message announces that the "ultimate source and meaning of all reality is now becoming a reality in a new and final form. The final decision about the meaning of reality is now being made. With the entry of the Kingdom of God the world enters into salvation."

Johannes Metz

If Küng and Kasper emphasize the role of God in the coming of the Kingdom, Johannes Metz stresses the role of human effort in the political realm. Christian theology, Metz argues, veered too far in an existentialist, personalist, indeed *privatized* direction under the influence of Rudolf Bultmann. The future dimension was all but lost, and

1145

so, too, the critical function of theology. The modern person no longer experiences the world as an imposed fate, but rather as raw material which has to be shaped and directed into something greater. Christian faith is guided by hope, a "crucified hope for the world." Such a hope is "an initiative for the passionate innovating and changing of the world toward the Kingdom of God" (*Theology of the World*, New York: Herder & Herder, 1969, p. 93).

The Church exists within that world as that part of the world which calls the world in question when it takes itself with ultimate seriousness. "The eschatological City of God is *now* coming into existence, for our hopeful approach *builds* this city. We are workers building this future, and not just interpreters of this future.... The Christian is a 'co-worker' in bringing the promised universal era of peace and justice. The orthodoxy of a Christian's faith must constantly *make itself* true in the 'orthopraxy' of his actions orientated toward the final future, because the promised *truth* is a truth which must be *made* (see John 3:21ff.)" (pp. 94–95).

Metz rejects, therefore, an eschatology like Bultmann's which focuses on the "making present" of the Kingdom in the moment of personal decision, and also the eschatology of Weiss, Werner, and others, which makes life in this world a time of waiting until God brings about the Kingdom. Metz's eschatology is the basis of a *political theology*, a theology of the emerging social and political order. Political theology, therefore, is "a positive attempt to formulate the eschatological message under the conditions of our present society" (p. 107). It is theology which attends always to the relation between theory and practice, between understanding the faith and social practice.

But that political theology is sharpened even more by a focus on *discipleship* as the fundamental category of Christian existence. The Church is a community of disciples living in "imminent expectation" of the coming Kingdom of God, by contrast with most of the Church which lives under an "evolutionistically softened eschatology" that pushes the coming of the Kingdom safely into the distant future. Radical discipleship, he insists, "is de facto not livable 'if the time is not shortened' and the 'Lord does not soon return.' Discipleship and imminent expectation belong inseparably together" ("For a Renewed Church Before a New Council: A Concept in Four Theses," in *Toward*

Vatican III: The Work That Needs to Be Done, David Tracy, ed., New York: Seabury Press, 1978, p. 143).

Gustavo Gutiérrez

A similarly strong emphasis on the social and political dimension of the Kingdom is given in Latin American liberation theology. Gustavo Gutiérrez warns against a spiritualizing of the reality of the Kingdom. It is "inevitably historical, temporal, earthly, social, and material" (*A Theology of Liberation,* Maryknoll, N.Y.: Orbis Books, 1973, p. 167). The prophets announced a kingdom of peace, but peace presupposes justice. It presupposes the defense of the rights of the poor, punishment of the oppressors, liberation from oppression. The struggle for justice *is* the struggle for the Kingdom of God (p. 168). On the other hand, the Kingdom of God "must not be confused with the establishment of a just society" (p. 231).

The proclamation of the Kingdom, Gutiérrez writes, opens up new horizons and leads us to see unsuspected dimensions and to pursue unexplored paths. Only within a commitment to liberation and in solidarity with the oppressed can we understand the meaning of the Kingdom and the implications of the Gospel message (p. 269). The alleviation of poverty and oppression is not identical with the Kingdom, but poverty and oppression are certainly incompatible with the Kingdom of love and justice (p. 295).

And this was the vision of Jesus as well. Misery and social injustice reveal a "sinful situation," a disintegration of community. By freeing us from sin, Jesus attacks the roots of an unjust social order. "Far from showing no interest in... liberation, Jesus rather placed it on a deeper level, with far reaching consequences" (p. 231). Jesus' announcement of the Kingdom is subversive because it heralds the end of domination of human beings over human beings. In preaching the universal love of the Father, Jesus inevitably preached against all injustice, privilege, oppression, and narrow nationalism (p. 232).

Dermot Lane

Irish theologian Dermot Lane points out that, in light of the many changes that have occurred both inside and outside theology (especially in modern science), eschatology now requires a whole new framework to overcome the individualism and dualisms of much classical eschatology. Such a framework, he writes, is "at present struggling to come to birth through the confluence of many impulses from different areas of life: feminism (A. Carr, R. R. Ruether) focuses on the interconnectedness of the whole of life; ecology (J. Conn, C. Birch) encourages a new relationship between the individual and nature; the new physics (F. Capra, D. Bohm) points toward the dynamic character of all reality; process philosophy (A. N. Whitehead, C. Hartshorne) highlights the permanency of becoming within being. These emphases are beginning to add up to a new vision of life which is described, for want of a better name, as a Post-Modern view of the world (D. Griffin). Within this emerging vision, it is impossible to understand the part in isolation from the whole. An organic unity obtains between the one and the many." ("Eschatology," in *The New Dictionary of Theology*, J. Komonchak, M. Collins, and D. Lane, eds., Wilmington, Del.: Michael Glazier, 1987, p. 340).

Twentieth-Century Protestant Theology

Paul Tillich

The entire fifth part of Paul Tillich's (d. 1965) *Systematic Theology* is devoted to the Kingdom of God and its relation to history. For Tillich, the Kingdom is the answer to the ambiguities of history. It has both an inner-historical and transhistorical side. "As inner-historical, it participates in the dynamics of history; as transhistorical, it answers the questions implied in the ambiguities of the dynamics of history" (vol. 3, Chicago: University of Chicago Press, 1963, p. 357).

The first connotation of the Kingdom symbol is *political*, in that it is a manifestation of the power of God. The second characteristic is *social*, since there is no holiness without justice. The third element is *personal*, in that the Kingdom gives eternal meaning to the individual person. And the fourth characteristic is its *universality*, in that it is the fulfillment of all life and not only of human life.

The appearance of Jesus as the Christ is the historical event in which history becomes aware of itself and of its meaning. This is the central manifestation of the Kingdom (pp. 368–69). The churches represent the Kingdom of God but are not themselves identical with it (pp. 376–77). As for individuals, "one cannot reach the transcendent Kingdom of God without participating in the struggle of the inner-historical Kingdom of God" (p. 392). The Kingdom is already present. We stand now in the face of the eternal. But we do so looking ahead toward the end of history and the end of all that is temporal in the eternal (p. 396).

Reinhold Niebuhr

It was Reinhold Niebuhr (d. 1971) more than any other Protestant theologian who challenged both the Liberal equation of Kingdom and "secular city" and the progressive view of history upon which the equation was often based. It is not that history is static or that we have no tasks and obligations within it. Niebuhr insists, however, that grace is related to nature partly as fulfillment and partly as negation. "If the contradiction between 'nature' and 'grace' is not recognized, and the continued power of 'nature' in the realm of 'grace' is not conceded, new sins are brought into history by the pretension that sin has been progressively eliminated" (*The Nature and Destiny of Man*, vol. 2, New York: Scribners, 1943, pp. 245–46).

"Nature" here represents "the historical possibilities of justice," and "grace" represents the "ideal possibility of perfect love.... [in] the complete obedience of all wills to the will of God" (p. 246). Thus, the relation between historical justice and the love of the Kingdom of God is dialectical. "Love is both the fulfillment and the negation of all achievements of justice in history. Or expressed from the opposite standpoint, the achievements of justice in history may rise in indeterminate degrees to find their fulfillment in a more perfect love and brotherhood; but each new level of fulfillment also contains elements which stand in contradiction to perfect love." We are bound to bring about justice in indeterminate degrees, but we can never achieve the perfection of justice within history. "Sanctification in the realm of social relations demands recognition of the impossibility of perfect sanctification" (p. 247).

The Kingdom, or sovereignty, of God, therefore, has the same two relations as eternity has to time. "It is on the one hand the authority of the source of life over all life at any moment. It is on the other hand a sovereignty which is finally vindicated in 'the end' " (p. 300, n. 1). History after Christ is an "interim between the disclosure of its true meaning and the fulfillment of that meaning.... Sin is overcome in principle but not in fact. Love must continue to be suffering love rather than triumphant love. The distinction," he argues, "becomes a basic category of interpreting history in all profound versions of the Christian faith..." (p. 49).

The spirit of Niebuhr influenced such activist Christians as Martin Luther King, Jr. (d. 1968), who acknowledged that Niebuhr helped him to "recognize the complexity of man's social involvement and the glaring reality of collective evil" as well as "the illusions of a superficial optimism concerning human nature and the dangers of false idealism" (*Stride Toward Freedom*, New York: Harper & Row, 1958, p. 81).

Jürgen Moltmann

The Kingdom of God is a symbol for the "comprehensive Christian horizon of life" (*The Church in the Power of the Spirit*, New York: Harper & Row, 1977, p. 134). It requires conversion to the God of the future, and it brings liberation from the godless and inhuman relationships of this world. The Kingdom of God, therefore, is the "eschatological fulfillment of the liberating lordship of God in history" (p. 190). It is both the actual rule of God in the world and the universal goal of that divine rule. It is thus at once present and future. As present, it is relevant to our earthly concerns. As future, it cannot be identified with anything in history. It draws us into history and beyond history.

Through his own mission and resurrection Jesus has brought the Kingdom into history. It has become the power of the future which determines the present. We can already live in the light of the "new era" in the circumstances of the "old" one. "Since the eschatological becomes historical in this way, the historical also becomes eschatological" (p. 192). Moltmann calls this "messianic mediation." The Lordship of Christ points beyond itself to the Kingdom of God.

The presence of the Holy Spirit puts the new creation into force. Past, present, and future are brought together: "Just as the messianic era stands under the token of the 'not yet', so it also stands under the sign of 'no longer' and therefore under the sign of 'already'.... The dreams of hope lead to the pains of love" (p. 193). The Kingdom of God is the goal of history in the midst of history (p. 196).

The Church in the Power of the Spirit, in effect, broadens the horizon of Moltmann's earlier, and better known, *Theology of Hope* (New York: Harper & Row, 1967, pp. 325–338). Since the Kingdom has not yet come, everything is to be called into question which already identifies itself with the Kingdom. The Church is called to engage in the historic transformation of life into the Kingdom of righteousness, peace, freedom, and humanity. Its mission is shaped by its expectation of the coming Kingdom. To disclose to the world "the horizon of the future of the crucified Christ is the task of the Christian Church" (p. 338). (See also *The Trinity and the Kingdom: The Doctrine of God,* San Francisco: Harper & Row, 1981.)

Wolfhart Pannenberg

Wolfhart Pannenberg defines the Kingdom of God variously as "that perfect society of men which is to be realized in history by God himself," as "the utterly concrete reality of justice and love," and as "the destiny of present society" (*Theology and the Kingdom of God,* Philadelphia: Westminster Press, 1969, pp. 76, 79, and 84). It is the rule, or sovereignty, of God; its principal effect is unity among humankind. That is why Jesus explained the will of God by the commandment of love. But it is not a purely interpersonal love. There is no dualism of religion and society, of love and justice. "Subjective behavior is related always to social institutions.... Obviously, then, the Kingdom of God is pointedly political" (pp. 79–80). Our present world, with its wars, injustices, and brutalities, demonstrates the gap between itself and the Kingdom of God. God's Kingdom has not yet come in all its fullness. No present form of life or society is ultimate. But this situation need not lead to political paralysis. "The future of the Kingdom releases a dynamic in the present that again and again kindles the vision of man and gives meaning to his fervent quest for the political forms of justice and love" (p. 80).

Twentieth-Century Anglican Theology

John A. T. Robinson

John A. T. Robinson (d. 1983) is best known for his controversial *Honest to God* (1963). In an earlier and much less heralded piece in *The Historic Episcopate in the Fullness of the Church* (Kenneth M. Carey, ed., London: Dacre Press, 1960), Robinson argued that the Kingdom of God is "the controlling category of biblical theology for both Old and New Testaments" (p. 15). The whole constitution of the universe has been transformed through Christ, although the transformation still remains to be acknowledged and fulfilled in obedience. To see all reality, including the Church, always in subordination to the Kingdom is to view everything as situated between the two great moments of Christ's sovereignty over the world: the finished work of Calvary and the Second Coming in glory.

Eschatology, therefore, is not just the teaching about the "last things" but rather the teaching about the relation of all things to the "last things," or about the finality of things. The Christian lives not *at* the end of time but rather *from* the end and *in* the end. Everything is seen from an eschatological perspective, and every moment is, in turn, an eschatological moment. "What the Christian faith provides is not a blue-print for the future of man.... Its assurance rests in the fact that the whole of life is *response*, that the initiative—whether in the Beginning or the End—does not lie with us. It speaks of an evocation, a trust, an endurance, by which, in freedom, men find themselves impelled and drawn on. It points to those whose whole way of life betokens a 'beyond' that will not let them rest..." (*In the End God*, New York: Harper & Row, 1968, p. 139).

John Macquarrie

The Kingdom of God is "the full manifestation of the holiness of Being" (*Principles of Christian Theology*, 2d ed., New York: Scribners, 1977, p. 369). It will issue forth in "a commonwealth of free beings, united in Being and with each other through love...." The Kingdom, although not to be identified with the Church, is already present in history. Macquarrie rejects both the extremes of a Liberalism which

1152

exaggerates human effort in the coming of the Kingdom, and of an apocalypticism which makes the Kingdom totally otherworldly. But his concern is directed perhaps more strongly against the former: "It is God who is the author of the kingdom, and it is his grace that is realizing it, albeit with the free cooperation of human beings. And while the eschatological interpretation may seem to become other-worldly in placing the kingdom beyond history, it is only being realistic. It is utopian and foolish to suppose that the kingdom could be realized on earth, though on the other hand it is not foolish to strive toward its increasing realization..." (p. 370). He returns to this point: "The eschatological consummation of the kingdom of God is a mystery to be realized by the movement of Being, not by creaturely striving, even if this makes an indispensable contribution. We delude ourselves if we think that some ideal state of affairs is attainable on earth, or that the main business of Christianity is to establish a super welfare state" (p. 519).

Norman Pittenger

Norman Pittenger, a theologian of the process school of thought, suggests that God is present to history as a "lure" (Whitehead's term), not as a coercive force. For the Christian, Christ is the disclosure of what God is up to in the world. Talk about the "last things" is not talk about something that will happen only in the future, after death; rather, it is talk about us as we now live, in this world and with this world's responsibilities as well as its privileges.

Our purpose in life is to be the personalized instruments of cosmic Love. Everything we are and do has to be understood in light of that purpose. Thus, death reminds us that we are mortal and have only a relatively short time to contribute to humankind. Judgment means that we are what our decisions have made us. They cannot be undone. Heaven is the sheer joy of relationship with God and with one another. Hell is the absence of God. It is always and only a possibility—a possibility of rejecting God in freedom. But God's action surrounds us with love, and we respond in love. "The Lord came from God precisely in order to love, in order to be the humanly visible instrument of the divine charity. Christian theology ... is nothing other than the explication and application of what that statement *means"* (*"The Last Things" in a Process Perspective*, London: Epworth Press, 1970, p. 105).

Twentieth-Century Orthodox Theology

John Meyendorff

The Kingdom of God is not one of the major categories of Orthodox theology (see the index of John Meyendorff's [d. 1992] *Byzantine Theology: Historical Trends and Doctrinal Themes*, New York: Fordham University Press, 1974). Where it is mentioned, it is linked always with the Holy Spirit, which is its "content" (p. 169). The prayer "Thy Kingdom come" is understood as "May Thy Holy Spirit come upon us and cleanse us." The Byzantine liturgical tradition addresses the Holy Spirit as "Heavenly King." The Spirit is the first fruits of the eschatological transfiguration of creation. If salvation is understood essentially in terms of *participation* in, and *communion* with, the deified humanity of the incarnate Logos, it is the Spirit who makes this possible (p. 171). On the other hand, nowhere except in the *sacraments* can we achieve the "truly liberating divine life.... The Kingdom to come is already realized in the sacraments, but each individual Christian is called to grow into it, by exercising his own efforts and by using his own God-given freedom with the cooperation of the Spirit" (p. 176). But those efforts are not of a political or even ethical nature. They are part of the process toward "perfection" and "holiness."

Eschatology, however, qualifies the whole of Orthodox theology (p. 218). Everything is viewed in relation to the end, to our destiny in God. But that future reality is also a present experience, accessible in Christ through the gifts of the Spirit. Orthodox eschatology is a realized eschatology. The movement of humankind toward its goal is a mystical movement, not a historical movement (p. 219). We are moving "from glory to glory," i.e., to the moment when we will be restored to our original stature, which has been corrupted by sin and death. This will be the resurrection of the flesh.

Significantly, the last things (Second Coming, cosmic transfiguration, resurrection, and judgment) "are not subjects of detailed speculation by Byzantine theologians; yet they stand at the very center of Byzantine liturgical experience" (p. 220).

Official Teachings of the Church

Nowhere has the Kingdom of God been defined by the official magisterium, nor has any official position been taken regarding the precise relationship between the divine and the human, the transcendental and the immanent, the spiritual and the political in the Kingdom of God. One has to infer a doctrinal position from the explicit teachings on grace, Original Sin, and Jesus Christ (see chapters 4, 5, and 13).

Second Vatican Council

The most explicit conciliar declaration on the meaning of the Kingdom was given by the Second Vatican Council (1965) in its *Pastoral Constitution on the Church in the Modern World.* It describes the Kingdom variously as "the consummation of the earth and of humanity," "a new dwelling place and a new earth where justice will abide, and whose blessedness will answer and surpass all the longings for peace which spring up in the human heart," a "new age," and as a reality "of truth and life, of holiness and grace, of justice, love, and peace" (n. 39). That Kingdom is already growing on this earth, but it is present only in mystery, i.e., sacramentally.

What are some of the signs of God's growing rule? The nurturing on earth of the values of "human dignity, solidarity and freedom, and indeed all the good fruits of our nature and enterprise," which we shall find again at the end, "but freed of stain, burnished and transfigured." To what extent is human effort incorporated into, or necessary for, the Kingdom of God? Although the Kingdom will be given in the end by God, "the expectation of a new earth must not weaken but rather stimulate our concern for cultivating this one. For here grows the body of a new human family, a body which even now is able to give some kind of foreshadowing of the new age." Accordingly, "earthly progress must be carefully distinguished from the growth of Christ's kingdom. Nevertheless, to the extent that the former can contribute to the better ordering of human society, it is of vital concern to the Kingdom of God."

This same Kingdom was at the center of Jesus' own proclamation, and he revealed it to humankind in his word, his works, and his presence (*Dogmatic Constitution on the Church*, n. 5). Although the council describes the Church as the "initial budding forth" of the Kingdom, the Church nonetheless must strain toward the consummation of the Kingdom at history's end. The whole of human history meanwhile is moving toward the same final goal, which it will reach "in the Holy City, whose light shall be the glory of God, when the nations will walk in his light" (*Declaration on the Relationship of the Church to Non-Christian Religions*, n. 1). Human solidarity and all human activity will attain their final destiny therein (*Pastoral Constitution*, nn. 32, 39). For Christ is both the beginning and the end of all creation (n. 45). And so the "final stage of time has already come upon us (see 1 Corinthians 10:11). The renewal of the world is irrevocably determined and, in some real manner, it is anticipated in the present era..." (*Dogmatic Constitution on the Church*, n. 48).

The teaching of the council is significant because it overcomes the separation between general and individual eschatology, links the present and the future, and establishes a fundamental unity between the earthly and the heavenly.

Evangelii Nuntiandi

Pope Paul VI's 1975 apostolic exhortation, *Evangelii Nuntiandi* ("On Evangelization in the Modern World") acknowledges at the outset that the whole mission of Jesus is summed up in his own declaration that he was sent to proclaim the good news of the Kingdom of God (Luke 4:43), and in a particular way to the poor (Luke 4:18; Isaiah 61:1). Jesus' evangelizing activities, however, were not restricted to verbal proclamation. Christ also proclaimed the Kingdom by "innumerable signs...: the sick are cured, water is changed into wine, bread is multiplied, the dead come back to life. And among these signs there is the one to which he attached great importance: the humble and the poor are evangelized..." (n. 12). Evangelization, therefore, consists also of "liberation from everything that oppresses [us] but... is above all liberation from sin and the Evil One..." (n. 9). However closely linked it is with human liberation, the Kingdom of God is not simply identical with it (n. 35). Some notions of liberation are, in fact, incompatible with the Gospel, and the Kingdom itself will not come about even through proper expressions of liberation, well-being, and human development alone.

This Kingdom, of course, is available to every human being "as grace and mercy," and yet each individual gains entrance "through a total interior renewal which the Gospel calls *metanoia*; it is radical conversion, a profound change of mind and heart" (n. 10; see also n. 36). The Church itself comes into being as a community gathered in Jesus' name "in order to seek together the Kingdom, build it up and live it" (n. 13). This means that the Church's call to evangelization, i.e., to the proclamation of the good news of the Kingdom of God, is directed to its total mission. It is a proclamation in word, in sacrament, in witness, and in service.

Catechism of the Catholic Church

The 1992 *Catechism of the Catholic Church* treats the Kingdom of God within the context of the Lord's Prayer: "In the New Testament, the same word *basilea* can be translated by royalty (abstract noun), kingdom (concrete noun), or reign (action noun). God's kingdom is ahead of us. It is brought near by the Word incarnate, it is proclaimed throughout the whole Gospel, and it comes in Christ's death and resurrection. Since the Last Supper God's kingdom has come in the Eucharist and is made present among us. The kingdom comes in glory when Christ hands it over to the Father."

The petition in the Lord's Prayer refers primarily to the coming of God's Kingdom through Christ's return. "Instead of distracting the Church from its mission in the world, this desire commits it all the more strongly to this mission. . . . Our vocation to eternal life does not lessen but reinforces our duty to serve justice and peace in this world with all the powers and skills the Creator has given us."

THE LAST THINGS: THE DESTINY OF INDIVIDUALS

The Destiny of Each Individual:
Death and Judgment

Death

Old Testament

Because of the ancient Hebrew concept of the human person as an *animated body* rather than as an incarnated spirit, death was perceived as a state in which the spirit had departed from the body. The deceased continued to exist in *Sheol* (the underworld, or the abode of the dead), but completely shorn of their human powers (Psalms 6:6; 30:10; 88:11; 115:17; Isaiah 38:11,18). Ideally, death comes in the fullness of age to a person of undiminished powers (Genesis 25:8; Job 21:23–24; 29:18–20). Such a one dies easily and quickly and goes immediately down to *Sheol* (Job 21:13). Death is the natural end of the human person (2 Samuel 14:14), but it is the consequence of sin (Genesis 2–3). On occasion, there is an expression of hope that death is not terminal. In Psalm 16:10 the poet rejoices that Yahweh will not abandon him to *Sheol* ("the nether world") nor permit him to "undergo corruption." In Psalm 49:16 the poet is assured that God will redeem him from *Sheol*. Psalm 73:23–28 is even clearer. If Yahweh's promises and loving kindness are everlasting, then there must be some way in which the faithful Israelite will experience them. Only gradually, however, did this subordinate line of thought emerge as a more dominant force in the Israelite theology of death. Thus, there is no trace of a clear belief in the resurrection of the dead before the second century B.C., in Daniel (12:2). To be sure, the Book of Wisdom (written probably in the last half of the first century B.C.) testifies to a trend in late postexilic Jewish thought that looked forward to life after death (1:1–6:21).

New Testament

The New Testament is explicit and unequivocal about the origin of death: It is the consequence of sin and a punishment for it (Romans 5:12–14). Likewise in 1 Corinthians 15:22, Paul asserts that we all die in Adam, but rise to life in Christ. Indeed, Jesus overcame death by his own death (15:25–26). He has deprived death of its power (2 Timothy 1:10), rendering the devil, the lord of death, impotent (Hebrews 2:14). Death no longer has power over Christ (Romans 6:9), and so he rules over the living and the dead (14:9). The Christian experiences Jesus' victory over death by sharing in his death (6:2–11). To die with Christ is to live with him (6:8). We overcome death by being baptized into Christ (6:4) and by partaking of the Eucharist (John 6:50–51).

On the other hand, death is at once final and unique. There is no question of *reincarnation:* "Those who might want to pass from here to you cannot do so, and no one can cross from there to us" (Luke 16:26; see also John 9:4; 2 Corinthians 5:10; Galatians 6:10).

Early Christian Writers

One of the most interesting developments within patristic eschatology concerns its understanding of death. Rather than seen as a punishment for sin, several of the early Christian writers suggested that God invented death as a kind of remedy for sin. Without death, sin could become immortal. With death, sin can be removed once and for all. Some of the writers compared death to the melting down of a flawed piece of art so that it can be restored to perfection. Thus, the breakdown of the individual in death becomes the basis of the breakthrough in resurrection.

Official Teachings of the Church

At first the Church's eschatological vision centered on the Second Coming of Christ and the entrance of the whole Church into the final Kingdom. The individual received much less attention. The Middle Ages brought about a shift from the communal to the individual. Theologians focused on the moment of death as the key point at which individual destiny was to be decided.

Church documents on the subject of death and the afterlife are comparatively few in number. Since they belong for the most part to the Middle Ages, they also reflect an individual rather than a communal or ecclesial perspective. They deal primarily with the beatific vision and the resurrection of the individual body (as we shall see later). Not until the Second Vatican Council is there once again a fuller, more comprehensive statement on the reality of death and its universal significance.

Council of Trent

Adam's sin not only involved a loss of holiness and justice but also brought death with it as a punishment. This punishment was applied not only to Adam but to all of his offspring. The council cites Romans 5:12 (*Decree on Original Sin*, Session V, 1546).

Second Vatican Council

"It is in the face of death that the riddle of human existence becomes most acute.... All the endeavors of technology, though useful in the extreme, cannot calm [the individual's] anxiety" (*Pastoral Constitution on the Church in the Modern World*, n. 18). Only faith can overcome this anxiety. We have been "created by God for a blissful purpose beyond the reach of earthly misery." We are all called to an "endless sharing of a divine life beyond all corruption," and this was won for us by the death and resurrection of Christ. "Through Christ and in Christ, the riddles of sorrow and death grow meaningful. Apart from his gospel, they overwhelm us" (n. 22).

Congregation for the Doctrine of the Faith

In its "Letter on Certain Questions Concerning Eschatology" (May 1979), the Congregation for the Doctrine of the Faith reaffirms the Church's traditional belief in the resurrection of the dead, the resurrection of the whole person, survival of the human self after death, the meaningfulness of prayers for the dead, the Second Coming and general judgment, the assumption of the Blessed Virgin Mary, and heaven, hell, and purgatory. The document also warns, however, against "arbitrary imaginative representations" of life after death and calls such excesses "a major cause of the difficulties that Christian faith often encounters." At the same time, the document encourages continued theological exploration of these issues.

Catechism of the Catholic Church

The 1992 *Catechism of the Catholic Church* affirms that "Death is the end of our earthly pilgrimage, of the time of grace and mercy God offers us so that we may work out our ultimate destiny by lives led in keeping with his plan.... There is no reincarnation after death."

Theological Reflections

All romantic, idealized versions of human life are brought low by the reality of death. More than anything else, death forces us to acknowledge the radical finitude of our existence. But this is not to say that death nullifies everything, rendering all life absurd and meaningless. On the contrary, death projects an ambiguous character. In spite of the certainty of death, we go on living with a deeply rooted conviction that life does make sense, or at least can make sense. Death itself can be an affirmative, even courageous act. An individual's life—not to say a nation's or a world's—can assume extraordinary significance by the manner in which death is faced. A person dies that another might live, as in the case of Maximilian Kolbe (d. 1941), the Polish priest who went to his death at Auschwitz to spare the life of a family man marked out for execution by the Nazis. The circumstances of a person's death, too, can be understood as in some way redeeming the blameworthy actions of his or her life, as in the case of Sydney Carton in Charles Dickens' *A Tale of Two Cities*.

Although theologians such as Karl Rahner and Ladislas Boros and scientists such as Elisabeth Kubler-Ross attempted to illuminate the darkness surrounding this perennial mystery of death (see E. Kubler-Ross, *On Death and Dying*, New York: Macmillan, 1969; K. Rahner, *On the Theology of Death*, New York: Herder & Herder, 1961; and L. Boros, *The Mystery of Death*, New York: Herder & Herder, 1965), perhaps no one has substantially improved upon the fundamental insights of the existentialist philosopher Martin Heidegger (d. 1976). Death is the horizon that closes off the future. All human possibilities are seen in the context of death, because it brings into existence a responsibility and a seriousness that it could scarcely have had otherwise. Death, therefore, not only destroys; it brings some degree of unity and coherence and purpose into one's life. We shape and direct our lives with the certainty of future death in mind. We do not have unlimited time at our disposal. We have a certain amount of time, and everything has to be arranged in relation to that "deadline." Moreover, death exposes the superficiality and triviality of much of what we count as important and to which we dedicate so much of our resources and energies. In the face of death, things get put into perspective (see *Being and Time*, New York: Harper & Row, 1962, pp. 279–311).

For the Christian, of course, the death of Jesus is the model and norm of every human death. He accepted death in freedom. He could have escaped but did not. Moreover, only in death was he able to accomplish what he had proclaimed in life. In dying he made possible the release of the Holy Spirit as the first fruits of the final Kingdom. Only in death did he reveal to others the ultimate seriousness of the claims of God. His whole existence was oriented toward his death, for he knew that a final conflict between the powers of this world and the Word of God was inevitable, and that this conflict would be played out in the conflict between the contemporary religious establishment and himself. Such a death brought a wholeness (integrity) to his life, and so it can to the lives of others.

Judgment

Old Testament

Judgment is both *defense* and *vindication* of Israel by Yahweh (Isaiah 1:27; 30:18) and also *punishment* (Ezekiel 5:7–15; 7:3–27; 16:38; 11:10; 24:13–14). Yahweh is also judge of the whole world (Psalms 7:8; 9:9–10; 96:13; 110:6; Genesis 18:25; 1 Samuel 2:10). The idea of the judgment of all nations is characteristic of apocalyptic literature (Joel 4:9–12; Daniel 7:9–11).

New Testament

In the Synoptics, judgment is often condemnation of sinners (e.g., Matthew 5:22; 23:33; Luke 12:58). In Paul such judgment is not only in the future (Romans 2:1–3,16; 3:5–6) but also in the past (Romans 5:16,18) and in the present (1 Corinthians 11:29,32). In any event, the judgment of God is unsearchable (Romans 11:33). In John the judgment is always in the present (3:18; 5:24; 12:31; 16:11). Hebrews looks to the resurrection of the dead and eternal judgment (6:2). It will not go well with those who were unfaithful (10:27; 13:4). Those who break the law, according to James, will be judged mercilessly (2:12–13), and so, too, will unfaithful teachers (3:1). On the other hand, we should be careful not to judge others (4:12; see also Matthew 7:1; Luke 6:37). God will judge the living and the dead (1 Peter 4:5), and that process will begin with the Church (4:17). In 2 Peter and Jude the judgment has an apocalyptic tone, comparable to the judgment of Sodom and Gomorrah (2 Peter 2:6,9; 3:7). This is even more explicit in Revelation, where judgment is the downfall of a world power (17:1–19:2). All will be judged in the end (11:18; 10:12–13).

Biblical belief, therefore, is that the judgment of God is final, that it is outside and beyond history, and that it is *the act by which evil is overcome once and for all.* On the other hand, the judgment also occurs even now in our acceptance or rejection of Christ and the Gospel (Matthew 25:31–46). In faith and hope the future judgment and salvation are already a reality (John 5:24; 12:31; 16:8). The Spirit is already given (Philippians 1:19; Romans 8:23), and the resurrection has already taken place (John 5:25,28; 2 Timothy 2:18).

Official Teachings of the Church

The *fact* of the final judgment is attested to throughout the history of the Church: In the *Apostles' Creed* ("He shall come again to judge the living and the dead"); the *Nicene Creed* (325) ("He ascended to the heavens and shall come again to judge the living and the dead"); the *Nicene-Constantinopolitan Creed* (381) from the Council of Constantinople ("He shall come again in glory to judge the living and the dead"); the so-called *Athanasian Creed* (end of the fifth century) ("He shall come to judge the living and the dead"); the *Fourth Lateran Council* (1215), which added the words: "and to render to each one according to his works, to the reprobate as well as to the elect"; the *Second Council of Lyons* (1274), which said essentially the same thing as Lateran IV; the Constitution *Benedictus Deus* (1336) of Pope Benedict XII (d. 1342); and the *Council of Florence* (1439). The *Second Vatican Council* simply presumes this line of teaching (see the *Pastoral Constitution on the Church in the Modern World,* nn. 17 and 45).

1163

Theological Reflections

One must distinguish always between the general judgment and the particular judgment. The *general judgment* applies to the consummation of the whole world and of history itself. It is connected with the Second Coming, or *Parousia*, of Christ. Because it affects all it is called the "general" judgment. Because it is the act which terminates history it is also called the "last" judgment. Everything in the first part of this chapter, on the Kingdom of God, is applicable to this general or last judgment.

The *particular judgment*, which is also the subject of the preceding biblical texts and of the official teachings of the Church, underscores the uniqueness and particularity of every human person before God. We are not simply part of some larger, impersonal collective reality. Just as it is erroneous to exaggerate the destiny of the individual and to forget the cosmic and communal destiny which is the Kingdom of God, so it is wrong to deny the hope that burns in each individual heart that his or her own life has final meaning and purpose. Correspondingly, we are to be judged not simply on the basis of our community's activity but on the basis of our own as well.

If everything were to return to a kind of undifferentiated unity, then creation itself would have been pointless in the first place. What we look forward to in the end is a community of free and responsible persons united in love. But such a community is impossible unless the persons within it are preserved in some kind of individual identity. It is hardly "good news" to hear that we are worth something on this earth while we are still alive but that we are not worth anything thereafter, for eternity.

The Destiny of the Faithful: Beatific Vision, Purgatory, Resurrection of the Body

Beatific Vision/Heaven/Eternal Life

New Testament

The vision of God after death, known as the *beatific vision*, is rarely referred to in the New Testament and not at all in the Old Testament.

The Old Testament's belief in the invisibility of God generally persists into the New Testament (1 John 3:6; 4:12,20; John 1:18: 1 Timothy 1:17; 6:16). The promise of the vision of God, however, is found in Matthew 5:8: "Blessed are the pure of heart, for they shall see God." Given the background of Jewish thought, it is remarkable that the promise is uttered without any refinement or explanation. The vision of God which is promised to the peacemakers is the full of love in 1 Corinthians 13:12. Paul contrasts the vision of God after death with the dim view seen in a mirror. He chooses the expression *face to face*, which echoes the traditions of Moses; a veil concealed the glory of God reflected in the face of Moses. Paul insists that the Christian will behold the glory of the Lord without such a veil (2 Corinthians 3:12–18). In 1 John 3:2 we are assured that we shall see God and that the vision will transform us into God's likeness.

Such a vision inaugurates us into a new life, "eternal life." God gives eternal life to those who are faithful (Romans 2:7; 6:23). It comes through faith (1 Timothy 1:16; John 3:15,36; 20:31) and is assured by hope (Titus 1:2; 3:7). It becomes a present reality by Baptism (Romans 6:4). Jesus has the words of eternal life (John 6:68). His followers retain life by loving one another (12:50). Thus, death is never final (6:39,44,54). Those who partake of the Son will have eternal life (1 John 5:11–12). It consists of the knowledge of the one true God and of Jesus, whom God has sent (John 17:3).

Official Teachings of the Church

The principal texts are the Constitution *Benedictus Deus* (1336) of Pope Benedict XII and the Council of Florence's *Decree for the Greeks* (1439). Both insist that the souls of the faithful, provided they are in no need of purification, will immediately see "the divine essence with an intuitive vision and even face to face, without the mediation of any creature by way of object of vision; rather the divine essence immediately manifests itself to them, plainly, clearly and openly, and in this vision they enjoy the divine essence" (*Benedictus Deus*). Such faithful will "see clearly God, one and three, as God is, though some more perfectly than others, according to the diversity of merits" (Council of Florence). It is made possible by the *lumen gloriæ* ("light of glory"). The traditional teaching is reaffirmed by Pope Paul VI (d. 1978) in his

Credo of the People of God (1968) and by the Congregation for the Doctrine of the Faith, "Letter on Certain Questions Concerning Eschatology" (May 1979).

Theological Reflections

The beatific vision is *the full union of the human person with God*. It is that toward which every person strives. It is that which transcends the person on this earth and draws the person beyond herself or himself to become something other than she or he is at present. It is the goal of every human inquiry, search, and gesture toward the other. It is the completion of all that we are as human beings. "Our hearts are restless," Augustine cried out to God, "until they rest in Thee."

We thereby become fully like God. No trace of selfishness remains. We are fully open to other. We cling to nothing of our own. We pour out our own being as God poured out the divine Being in Christ. This is why the early Church believed that the martyrs went directly to heaven without purification. The martyrs completely transcended selfish being and attained a likeness to Christ, and so to God. Heaven for them is not a reward for being good. Rather, "It is the reward of having been delivered from any seeking for rewards" (John Macquarrie, *Principles of Christian Theology*, p. 366). The only reward for such self-giving love is an increased capacity for it. Heaven, therefore, is neither mythological nor simply the satisfaction of all egocentric human longings. It is the goal of human existence as such.

Purgatory

Biblical Foundations

There is, for all practical purposes, no biblical basis for the doctrine of purgatory. This is not to say that there is no basis at all for the doctrine, but only that there is no clear *biblical* basis for it. On the other hand, there is no contradictory evidence in either Old or New Testaments. The classic text is 2 Maccabees 12:38–46: "For if he were not expecting the fallen to rise again, it would have been useless and foolish to pray for them in death.... Thus he made atonement for the dead that they might be freed from this sin" (12:44,46). The New Testament was insistent on the fact that the Kingdom of God had already come in Jesus Christ, and the Christian's attention was drawn to the immediate and imminent consummation and to the decision required of everyone in the face of the Kingdom's drawing near. The real testing of faith and its works is expected in the "fire" of "the Day" (when the Lord returns) (1 Corinthians 3:12–15) and in "the age to come" (Matthew 12:32). It is clear that notions of *Sheol* are still operative (Luke 16:19–31).

Postbiblical Development

In the *patristic period*, Justin and Tertullian shared this Lucan perspective and taught that the dead are waiting "in the grave" for the consummation. Origen argued that everyone will be saved but that there is a particular purification for each individual. The purification occurs, however, at the moment of judgment and not as some intermediate state between the particular judgment and the final passage into the sight of God. The Origenist belief in universal salvation (*apokatastasis*) was condemned by the provincial council of Constantinople in 543, a judgment approved by all the Eastern patriarchs and confirmed by Pope Vigilius (d. 555).

Augustine emphasized that all the just, not only the martyrs, enter immediately into heaven. But gradually the fire of judgment referred to in 1 Corinthians 3:12–15 becomes after Augustine the purgatorial fire and appears as an intermediate realm after death. The very fact of not yet being totally with God constitutes a punishment, according to Pope Gregory the Great. It was not until the twelfth century, however, that the existence of purgatory as a place came into prominence.

The Western theology of the *Middle Ages* emphasized the penal and expiatory character of purgatory. The Christian East, however, rejected this highly juridical approach and stressed instead the more mystical nature of purgatory, as a process of maturation and spiritual growth. The Orientals also denied that the beatific vision was available to anyone, including the just, before the general resurrection and the final judgment.

Official Teachings

The traditional doctrine is enunciated by the Second Council of Lyons (1274), Benedict XII's *Benedictus Deus* (1336), and especially in the Council of Florence's *Decree for the Greeks* (1439), which tried to strike a careful balance between the Western concept of satisfaction and expiation and the Eastern emphasis on purification. Out of consideration for the Orientals, the council deliberately omitted all reference to fire (which the Orientals considered an echo of Origen's notion that all are saved by the one purifying fire) and avoided any language that would lead to a concept of purgatory as a place.

The *Reformation*, however, called into question what until now no one had questioned, either in the East or the West—namely, the appropriateness of prayers for the dead. From 1530 onward, Luther and Melanchthon joined Calvin and Zwingli in rejecting this doctrine, consistently with their teaching that salvation is by grace alone. In reply the *Council of Trent* defined the existence of purgatory, insisted that the souls detained there are helped by acts of intercession of the faithful, and especially by the sacrifice of the Mass. On the other hand, the council explicitly warned against any dwelling upon "the more difficult and subtle questions which do not make for edification and, for the most part, are not conducive to an increase of piety." These should not be included in popular sermons to uneducated people. Likewise, doubtful theological views should not be given wide circulation, and whatever belongs to the realm of "curiosity or superstition" or smacks of "dishonorable gain" should be forbidden as "scandalous and injurious to the faithful" (*Decree on Purgatory*, Session XXV, 1563).

The doctrine is reaffirmed in Pope Paul VI's *Credo of the People of God* (1968) and by the Congregation for the Doctrine of the Faith's "Letter on Certain Questions Concerning Eschatology" (1979) and is assumed by the Second Vatican Council's *Dogmatic Constitution on the Church*, n. 51. It is, of course, reaffirmed in the 1992 *Catechism of the Catholic Church*.

Theological Reflections

Purgatory is best understood as *a process by which we are purged of our residual selfishness so that we can really become one with the God who is totally oriented to others, i.e., the self-giving God.* It is also part of that larger process by which we are called out of nothingness into existence, from existence to selfhood, or responsible human existence, from responsible human existence to Christian existence, and from Christian existence to full and final incorporation into God. The kind of suffering associated with purgatory, therefore, is not suffering inflicted upon us from the outside as a punishment for sin, as the late medieval theology of the West understood it, but *the intrinsic pain that we all feel when we are asked to surrender our ego-centered self so that the God-centered loving self may take its place.* It is part of the process by which we are called to die and rise with Christ.

A Note on Indulgences

The 1983 Code of Canon Law defines an indulgence as "a remission before God of the temporal punishment for sin the guilt of which is already forgiven..." (canon 992).

From the earliest days the Church imposed penances upon those who had sinned after Baptism (see chapter 23). It was not enough to be sorry for one's sins; that only removed the *guilt* of sin. One also had to pay the *penalty* of sin. Since sin always involved some violation of the Church which is called to be a holy community and the sacrament of Christ's presence in the world, the Church is also involved in the process by which the sinner is reconciled to God. Not only did the Church decide when the penitent was ready to be restored to communion, but the Church also prayed with the penitent as he or she pursued the path of repentance. At times, the Church drew upon its own spiritual treasury of grace and merit to cancel out some (*partial indulgence*) or all (*plenary indulgence*) of the punishment still due to an individual's sin.

The first actual indulgences appeared in France in the eleventh century. They were at once a remission of some penance and a remission of the temporal punishment due to sin. Even into the thirteenth century, however, indulgences were regarded as concessions to the imperfect, which more faithful Christians should not claim. (They are not to be confused with redemptions and commutations, which came out of the Germanic period. These applied only to imposed penances and not to punishment due to sin.) At first, some theologians contested the bishop's right to grant indulgences, but as the actual practice became more widespread, theological opposition diminished.

On the other hand, the practice itself changed. Where previously the Church only *prayed for* the remission of temporal punishment due to sin and had excused a canonical penance on that account, now the Church definitively declared that such temporal punishment was canceled on the basis of the Church's control over the treasury of grace and merit. By the middle of the thirteenth century, the granting of indulgences became increasingly divorced from the sacrament of Penance, and more and more an act of the pope. The number of indulgences multiplied, and the need for doing some penitential work declined. Any reasonable cause was now regarded as sufficient grounds for granting an indulgence (Aquinas, *Summa Theologiæ*, Supplement, q. 25, a. 2).

Plenary indulgences, i.e., the remission of all temporal punishment due to sin, had come into prominence during the Crusades in the eleventh century when the crusaders were promised complete remission of punishment in return for their military service (Pope Urban II, d. 1099). Indulgences for the dead began to be granted from the middle of the fifteenth century. Their connection with almsgiving was established as early as the eleventh century. In the later Middle Ages, however, they became a convenient source of income for the Church and, as such, were multiplied to scandalous proportions. Simony (i.e., buying and selling spiritual goods) was not unknown. Some preached indulgences in a theologically unsound and exaggerated way. The Council of Trent condemned such practices in its *Decree on Indulgences* (1563), but perhaps too late, since those very abuses were among the proximate causes of the Reformation.

The most recent and fullest official exposition of the meaning of indulgences is contained in Pope Paul VI's Apostolic Constitution *Indulgentiarum Doctrina* (1967). The pope linked the doctrine of indulgences with the doctrine of the Communion of Saints. The Church on earth is united with the Church in heaven and in purgatory. The "treasury of the Church" is not "akin to a hoard of material wealth accumulated over the centuries" but is the "infinite and inexhaustible value which the expiation and merits of Christ have in the sight of God. . . ." An indulgence, he declares, is "the remission in the sight of

God of the temporal punishment due to sins which have already been blotted out as far as guilt is concerned." They are either plenary or partial, and they can be applied to the dead. Henceforth, however, partial indulgences will be described without reference to numbers of days and years. (The medieval approach had been to specify the precise amount of time subtracted from one's purgatorial "sentence.") It is, of course, always required that an individual be truly contrite, be a member of the Church in good standing, perform the work attached to the indulgence, and at least have the general intention of gaining the indulgence.

The doctrine of indulgences is best understood in the context of the whole mystery of Christian existence. We are all members of the Body of Christ. As such, we are beneficiaries of Christ's saving work on our behalf. Death is not the end of life, nor, therefore, is it the end of our relationships with our loved ones or with our sisters and brothers in the Church. Our obligations of concern and mutual assistance do not lapse with their death. Accordingly, decline of interest in indulgences is inconsistent with Catholic principles if that decline reflects a growing indifference to the Communion of Saints and/or to our abiding spiritual responsibility toward our dead relatives and friends. On the other hand, a calculating, egocentric approach to Christian destiny, where an individual is concerned primarily with the accumulation of spiritual "credits," is so antithetical to sound theological and doctrinal principles that the disappearance of that sort of interest in indulgences can only be welcomed.

Resurrection of the Body

Old Testament

The Hebrew concept of the human person as an animated body made it impossible for any idea of the afterlife to arise which did not involve a restoration of life to the body. This came, as we have already seen, very late in the Old Testament (Daniel 12:2;2 Maccabees 7:9,11,23; 14:46). Isaiah 26:19 mentions the resurrection of the dead, but it may refer, as Ezekiel 37:1–14 does, to the restoration of Israel. By the time of the New Testament, resurrection was affirmed by the Pharisees

1171

but not by the Sadducees (Matthew 22:23; Mark 12:18; Luke 20:27; Acts of the Apostles 23:8).

New Testament

In his discussion with Sadducees (Mark 12:16–27), Jesus refutes their denial of the resurrection by an appeal to the Torah and above all to the power of God. But he also corrects the Pharisees' doctrine that the resurrection meant a return to the conditions of earthly life (12:25). In the Synoptics no mention is made of the resurrection of the sinner, although it might be implied in what is said about God's judgment upon every person at the end. The reward granted in the resurrection of the just (Luke 14:14) reflects a Jewish rather than a Christian approach.

A resurrection to life is mentioned in John 5:28–29 (see also 6:39–40; 11:25–26) in terms very close to Daniel 12:2, and the same conception is contained in 2 Corinthians 5:10 (see also Philippians 3:21). But it is especially pronounced, and most powerfully presented, in 1 Corinthians 15:12–58. Hebrews 6:2 counts it among the basic doctrines of Christian faith. The Book of Revelation alone speaks of a double resurrection, the second being the general resurrection of all the dead at the last judgment (20:11–15); the first is reserved to the martyrs who will then rule with Christ for one thousand years (20:4–6).

Most of the references to the resurrection in the New Testament, however, are references not to the resurrection of the body after death but to the Christian's *present* resurrection with Christ by being baptized into his death and rising with him unto new life (e.g., Romans 6:4–11). Other texts look to the *future* (e.g., 2 Corinthians 4:14; Philippians 3:11; John 11:25; 6:39–44,54), but they are not explicit about the *bodily* character of this resurrection.

In fact, whenever the New Testament speaks about the resurrection, it speaks of the resurrection of the dead, never of the resurrection of the body, which is not found until Clement of Rome and Justin's *Dialogue* (80, 5). Resurrection of the body, in the sense of resurrection of the flesh (*sarx*), would not have been consistent with Paul's distinction between *sarx* and *soma* ("body"). The latter embraces the whole person, whereas the former is something weak, perishable, and even sinful. The flesh (*sarx*) cannot rise, because "flesh and blood cannot inherit the kingdom of God; nor does the perishable inherit the imperishable" (1 Corinthians 15:50).

Some Protestant scholars like Oscar Cullmann have interpreted such texts to mean that death does not consist in the soul's being separated from the body and continuing to live on its own in some intermediate state, awaiting the resurrection of the body, but rather that death is the destruction of the whole person. Only at the general resurrection will there be a completely new creation. We live on between death and resurrection in the mind of God alone. Such a position has to reconcile itself with such texts as Philippians 1:21; 2 Corinthians 5:6–8; Luke 23:42–43; and Revelation 6:9; 20:4.

Official Teachings of the Church

The resurrection of the body is attested to in the *Apostles' Creed* ("I believe in ... the resurrection of the body..."); the *Nicene-Constantinopolitan Creed* (381); the so-called *Athanasian Creed* (late fifth century); the Fourth Lateran Council (1215); the Second Council of Lyons (1274); and in the Constitution *Benedictus Deus* of Pope Benedict XII (1336). Usually the belief was simply included with other essential elements of Christian faith. Sometimes, however, the doctrine was deliberately and specifically formulated over against a heretical tendency to deny the radical goodness of the body, as in Lateran IV's rejection of Catharism, Albigensianism, and the Manichæism upon which they were based. More recently, the belief is reaffirmed by the Second Vatican Council in its *Dogmatic Constitution on the Church* (n. 51) and in its *Pastoral Constitution on the Church in the Modern World* (n. 39), and also by the aforementioned Vatican "Letter on Certain Questions Concerning Eschatology" (1979). These teachings are reaffirmed in the 1992 *Catechism of the Catholic Church*.

Theological Reflections

We must reassert here what has already been presented in chapter 5—namely, that the human person is not simply an embodied spirit, in the sense that the body is base, inhuman, and without intrinsic worth. "Holiness is wholeness" (Goldbrunner) because the human person is bodily as well as spiritual, or, in biblical terms, is an animated body (*soma*). Our hope is not simply the salvation of our soul but the salvation of our whole being. Our immortality is not something required by philosophical speculation (namely, because the soul is spiritual, it is indestructible) but is grounded on God's promise of eternal life and the conferral of new life in the resurrection of Jesus Christ himself. And it is not life for part of us, i.e., the soul, but for all that we are, i.e., animated body.

Nor is our resurrection at the end the resurrection only of so many individuals. Our bodiliness also is the natural basis of our solidarity with others and with God. We are human insofar as we are oriented toward others. And our orientation toward others is made possible and necessary by our bodiliness. The doctrine of the resurrection of the *body* is a foundation for the doctrine of the Communion of Saints. Thus, life after death is also communal life. And thus, too, the resurrection of the body cannot be achieved until the consummation of history itself.

The Destiny of the Unfaithful: Hell

Old Testament

The word *hell* is not used in the Old Testament. Its counterpart is *Gehenna*, which is an abbreviation of "valley of the son of Hinnom." Gehenna was an actual place on the boundary between the tribes of Judah and Benjamin (Joshua 15:8; 18:16); it was regarded as unholy because it was the site of a shrine where human sacrifices were offered to the Canaanite gods Molech and Baal (2 Kings 23:10; 2 Chronicles 28:3; 33:6; Jeremiah 7:31; 19:2–5; 32:35). It was considered, therefore, to be the place where the dead bodies of those who rebelled against Yahweh would lie (Isaiah 66:24). The term is frequently used in extrabiblical Jewish writings and applies there to a fiery abyss, a place of darkness, chains, etc.

New Testament

Gehenna is mentioned seven times in Matthew, three times in Mark, once in Luke, and once in James. It is a place of unquenchable fire

1174

(Mark 9:43; Matthew 5:22; 18:9; James 3:6), a pit into which people are cast (Matthew 5:29–30; 18:9; Mark 9:45,47; Luke 12:5). The wicked are destroyed there (Matthew 10:28). The place is described, although not named, elsewhere (e.g., Matthew 3:10,12; 7:19; Luke 3:9,17). It is the final destination of the wicked (Revelation 19:20; 20:9–15; 21:8). It is a place of weeping and gnashing of teeth (Matthew 8:12; 13:42,50; 22:13; 24:51; 25:30), where the worm does not die (Mark 9:48); it is shrouded in darkness (Matthew 8:12; 22:13; 25:30).

Elsewhere in the New Testament the language is less concrete. Paul speaks of a day of wrath (Romans 2:5) and of death as the wages of sin (6:23). Sinners will have no share in the Kingdom of God (1 Corinthians 6:10; Galatians 5:19–21). The enemies of the cross of Christ are doomed to destruction, and so are all the impious (Philippians 3:19; 2 Thessalonians 1:9). It is a terrible and fearful thing to fall into the hands of the living God (Hebrews 10:26–31).

Official Teachings of the Church

The existence of hell as a condition of eternal punishment for sin is attested to in the *Athanasian Creed* (end of fifth century); the Fourth Lateran Council (1215), which speaks of "perpetual punishment with the devil"; the Second Council of Lyons (1274), which taught that not only those who die in mortal sin but also those who die with Original Sin only "go down immediately to hell, to be punished however with different punishments"—a teaching which differed from an earlier letter of Pope Innocent III to Humbert, the Archbishop of Arles, in 1201, in which the pope made a distinction between those who commit mortal sin and merit the "torture of hell" and those who are not yet baptized and suffer instead the "loss of the beatific vision" (see the discussion of limbo below); and in Benedict XII's Constitution *Benedictus Deus* (1336). Significantly, hell is not explicitly mentioned in the Second Vatican Council nor even in Pope Paul VI's otherwise very complete *Credo of the People of God* (1968). There *is* reference to "eternal punishment for the sinner" in the Congregation for the Doctrine of the Faith's "Letter on Certain Questions Concerning Eschatology" (1979). The 1992 *Catechism of the Catholic Church*, however, accords a relatively prominent place for the doctrine of hell in its treatment of article 12 of the Apostles' Creed ("I Believe in Life

Everlasting"). "To die in mortal sin without repenting and accepting God's merciful love is to remain separated from him forever by our own free choice. This state of final self-exclusion from communion with God and his blessed ones is called 'hell'." The "chief punishment" of hell is "eternal separation from God."

Theological Reflections

The word *hell* is derived from the German *hel* ("realm of the dead"). The New Testament really assumes rather than affirms its existence when it simply takes over the notions and imagery of later Judaism. What the New Testament says about hell is to be interpreted according to the same principles which govern our interpretation of apocalyptic literature. Apocalypticism is too individualistic, too much oriented to worlds beyond this one, too elitist or Gnostic in its approach to revelation and salvation, and too fascinated with the esoteric and the ominous. Hence what the New Testament says about hell is not to be taken literally.

When Jesus used this imagery, he did so not to describe a particular place but to dramatize the urgency of his proclamation of the Kingdom and the seriousness of our decisions for or against the Kingdom. The stakes are as high as they can be. Our personal integrity and destiny are at issue. To turn our backs on God is to be finally and fully alienated and estranged from God. It is to choose inauthentic existence. It is to reject community with God and with others. It is to opt for isolation and separation.

Neither Jesus, nor the Church after him, ever stated that persons actually go to hell or are there now. He—as does the Church—restricts himself to the *possibility*. *If* someone really and deliberately rejected God, *this* is what he or she would be choosing instead of God: a totally isolated existence. Even in this sense, hell is not the product of divine vindictiveness. Rather, *it is God's yielding to our freedom*. To reject God is to reject life in community. Conversely, it is to choose life in isolation. Hell is absolute isolation. The radical sinner *chooses* that. God does not impose it as a punishment.

Some have argued that if an individual really chooses hell, i.e., a totally isolated existence, that individual is choosing self-annihilation, for one cannot even exist that way. To reject God completely and absolutely is to reject Being itself. It is to opt for nonbeing, for nothingness. Hell, in this conception, is not a place or a state but simply the condition of nonbeing.

Jesus' own "descent into hell," to which the Apostles' Creed attests, is the underworld (*Sheol*) rather than the place of fire. By dying Jesus entered the company of those who had died before him and thereby shared with them what he had achieved. The words "he descended into hell," therefore, mean simply that he died and that he remained dead, at least for a short time.

A Note on Demonology

In the *Old Testament*, belief in demons was generally excluded by the severe prohibitions against magic in Hebrew law. This is not to say that Israel knew no superstition at all. There is evidence of it here and there (1 Samuel 28:13; Psalm 106:37; Isaiah 13:21; 34:14). The situation changes, however, in the intertestamental and early New Testament periods. The belief in evil forces that was prevalent in Mesopotamian culture was assimilated almost whole, without change. The apocryphal literature traces the origin of demons to the fallen angels, the sons of God who married the daughters of men (Genesis 6:1–4).

The mention of demons is less frequent in the *New Testament* than in later Judaism. The victims of heathen sacrifices are offered to demons (1 Corinthians 10:20–21). Deceiving spirits are behind false teachings (1 Timothy 4:1). The spirits of demons perform wonders (Revelation 16:14), and the ruins of Babylon are haunted by demons (18:2). The demons are called the angels of Satan, for whom eternal fire is prepared (Matthew 25:41). They are the "principalities" who separate Christians from the love of God (Romans 8:38), but they are disarmed by the crucifixion of Christ (Colossians 2:15). There are, of course, many other references to diabolical possession and to exorcisms (Matthew 8:16; Mark 1:34; Luke 7:21; Acts of the Apostles 5:16).

Demons do not occupy a significant place in the *official teachings of the Church*. The Council of Braga (561), in Portugal, rejected the teachings of Priscillian (d. 385), founder of a Manichæan sect in Spain. The council denied the radical dualism of matter and spirit. All that exists is from God and is under the authority and power of God. Thus, even the devil was created by God and was in the beginning a good angel. The existence of demons is simply presupposed by the provincial council of Constantinople (543) and by the *Decree on Original Sin* of the Council of Trent (1546).

The Church has taught, therefore, that there is evil in the world which transcends the particular evil that human beings do (see chapter 9). But no clear theology of demons emerged until the Middle Ages, when it appeared as part of the discussions of creation. Insofar as a theology of demons has any relevance today, it is more appropriately an element of the theology of sin. Demonology is "an expression of the personal basis of our guilt and mortality which is not within our power to control or reach by any human action in history. It is also an expression of the fact that, as a human situation, evil in the world has a certain depth which is not simply attributable to man and the history which is subject to his autonomous control, but is something that can only be overcome by God's eschatological act in Christ in fulfillment of his promise" (Karl Rahner, "Demonology," *The Concise Sacramentum Mundi,* p. 334).

Beyond that, who really knows, or can know?

The Destiny of the Unbaptized: Limbo

The word *limbo* is derived from the Latin *limbus* ("border"). It is the *state or place,* according to some, *reserved for the dead who deserved neither the beatific vision nor eternal punishment.* The *limbus patrum* ("limbo of the fathers"), containing the pre-Christian just who had to await the opening of heaven by Christ (Luke 16:22; 1 Peter 3:18–22), was distinguished from the *limbus puerorum,* containing unbaptized infants and children, who therefore remained in Original Sin without ever incurring any actual sins. The concept of *limbus patrum* was probably a Christian adaptation of the Hebrew notion of *Sheol* (Luke 16:19–31). The concept of *limbus puerorum* was originated by the Pelagians, whose theology of Original Sin envisioned no guilt in unbaptized children. Consequently, they could not be consigned to hell.

Over against the Pelagians, Augustine (d. 430) had argued that such children were condemned to real, though diminished, pains of hell (*Enchiridion,* 93). Anselm of Canterbury (d. 1109) and the Scholastics after him (especially Aquinas) held to the Augustinian belief that such individuals were forever excluded from eternal happiness, but they allowed them a place of natural happiness, i.e., limbo. The belief was maintained throughout the Middle Ages and into the twentieth century, although the official magisterium has never taken a position on it. With the Second Vatican Council and the theological climate it reflected and sanctioned, however, the idea of limbo has seemed less and less tenable in light of the universal offer of grace from the very beginning of each person's existence. Indeed, Karl Rahner points out that the council "tacitly buried the doctrine of 'limbo' for children dying before baptism [and] boldly postulated a revelation properly so called, and consequently a real opportunity of faith even where the Christian message had not been proclaimed" (*Concern for the Church*, New York: Crossroad, 1981, p. 101).

Nevertheless, the Catholic Church continues to endorse, indeed mandate, the practice of immediately baptizing infants in danger of death. There is no indication in the new rites of Baptism, however, that the practice is based on a belief in limbo. Rather, the texts speak of the Church's desire to associate the child with the death and resurrection of Christ, to become a member of Christ's Church, and to share in the glory of the Kingdom of God.

Communion of Saints

With the doctrine of the Communion of Saints (see chapter 30), cosmic, or general, eschatology and individual eschatology converge. Our hope in the Kingdom of God for all humankind and for the world is at one with our hope in our own personal entrance into that Kingdom, that we might share with others and with the whole cosmos the fruits of the saving work which God has accomplished in Jesus Christ, by the power of the Holy Spirit.

SUMMARY

1. *Eschatology* is about the Kingdom, or Reign, of God, i.e., the redemptive presence of God actualized through the power of God's reconciling Spirit. As such, eschatology is concerned with the past, the present, and the future alike.
2. The *Kingdom of God* in the *Old Testament* referred to the provident and protective kingship of God over the chosen people, *in* history and *beyond* history.

3. There is a *prophetic* eschatology that focuses on justice, peace, and concern for the poor; a *nationalistic* eschatology that focused on the nation itself; and an *apocalyptic* eschatology which focused entirely on the heavenly Jerusalem.

4. *Jesus* proclaimed the Kingdom as having "come near." He called for conversion, repentance, watchfulness, and discipleship.

5. Jesus' preaching of the Kingdom brought into balance the *present* and the *future*, the *prophetic* and the *apocalyptic*. But he rejected *political, elitist,* and *nonuniversal* interpretations of it.

6. Jesus not only preached the Kingdom; he *put it into practice* through healings, exorcisms, eating with outcasts, etc.

7. The *early Church* proclaimed Jesus as the personification of the Kingdom. Christ's rule is hidden now, but it will be manifested fully in the end. In the meantime, it is anticipated in the Eucharist.

8. There are four main currents of interpretation of the Kingdom of God from the close of the New Testament canon to about the year 1000: *eschatological, spiritual-mystical, political,* and *ecclesial*.

9. *Augustine* was one of the most important interpreters of the Kingdom of God. He tended to identify it with the Church. He also distinguished between the heavenly city and the earthly city.

10. *Joachim of Fiore* divided history into three great periods: (1) the age of the Father (Old Testament existence under the Law); (2) the age of the Son (from the New Testament until about 1260); and (3) the age of the Spirit, in which there would be new religious orders leading to the conversion of the world and the establishment of a spiritual church. Joachim's views dominated the medieval discussion.

11. With the *Enlightenment* of the eighteenth century, the Kingdom was once again perceived not only as an earthly reality but as the product of human initiative and effort.

12. *Twentieth-century New Testament scholarship* begins as a reaction against the Liberal Protestant views of the Kingdom. Among the various approaches are: *futurist eschatology* (the Kingdom is in the future and is imminent), *realized eschatology* (the Kingdom is already realized in the past), *existentialist eschatology* (the Kingdom is present; we are called to choose authentic or inauthentic existence), *salvation-history eschatology* (the Kingdom is past, present, and future).

13. Twentieth-century *Catholic systematic theology* insists that the Church and Kingdom of God are not the same, that the Kingdom is the product of divine initiative and human collaboration alike, that it has social and political dimensions, and that it is both present and future.

1180

14. The Catholic Church has never *officially* defined the meaning of the Kingdom of God. The *Second Vatican Council* overcomes the separation between general and individual eschatology, links the present and the future, and establishes a fundamental unity between the earthly and the heavenly.

15. The *last things* pertain to the destiny of *individuals* as well as the whole of humanity and the world. *The destiny of each individual* includes *death* and *judgment*.

16. *Death* was perceived in the *Old Testament* as a state in which the spirit had departed from the body to dwell in *Sheol,* the underground or abode of the dead. For the *New Testament* we overcome death by sharing in Christ's victory over it.

17. The *postbiblical Church* at first emphasized the Second Coming and the destiny of the Church, but in the *Middle Ages* there was a shift to the death of individuals and to life after death for the individual. *Vatican II* restored the fuller, more comprehensive view.

18. *Judgment* is both vindication and punishment in the *Old Testament.* For the *New Testament* the judgment of God occurs even now in our acceptance or rejection of Christ and the Gospel and in the giving of the Spirit. But it is also to take place outside and beyond history, and it will be the act by which evil is finally overcome.

19. The *general judgment* pertains to the consummation of the whole world, and the *particular judgment* to the fulfillment of the individual's personal life.

20. The *destiny of the faithful* includes the *beatific vision* (heaven, eternal life), *purgatory,* and the *resurrection of the body.*

21. The *beatific vision* is the full union of the human person with God, and so with one another in God. The reality of the beatific vision is affirmed by *Benedictus Deus* of Pope Benedict XII (1336) and the *Council of Florence* (1439).

22. *Purgatory* is without clear *biblical* foundation. The classic text that is cited for the belief is 2 Maccabees 12:38–46.

23. *Origen's* notion of the universal salvation (*apokatastasis*) was condemned by the provincial council of Constantinople (543). *Augustine* insisted that the just enter heaven immediately. Only gradually, by the time of the Middle Ages, did the idea of a penal and expiatory state develop in the West. The *East* did not reject purgatory, only its juridical character. Rather, purgatory is a process of maturation and spiritual growth after death. The Western and Eastern traditions were blended in the Council of Florence's *Decree for the Greeks* (1439).

24. The *Reformers* rejected purgatory on the principle that grace alone saves. Prayers for the dead are useless. The *Council of Trent* defined its existence and

defended prayers for the dead, especially the Mass. But it also warned against superstition and other spiritual excesses.

25. *Indulgences* are the remission of punishment still due to sins which, however, have already been forgiven. If the indulgences remit all punishment, they are *plenary*. Otherwise, they are *partial*.

26. At first indulgences were linked with the sacrament of Penance, but gradually, in the *Middle Ages,* became an act of the pope. They were applied to the dead, beginning in the fifteenth century. In the later Middle Ages they became a convenient source of income. Abuses followed, and so, too, did the Protestant Reformation.

27. In the Bible the *resurrection of the body* is always the resurrection of the whole person (*soma*) and not of the flesh alone (*sarx*), since the Bible knew no sharp distinction between body and soul. The New Testament speaks rather of the resurrection of the *dead*. Our resurrection has already begun by our baptism into Christ's death and resurrection (Paul).

28. The *official Church* taught the resurrection of the body against those who denied the goodness of the body; see especially *Lateran IV, Lyons II,* and *Benedictus Deus* of Pope Benedict XII. It is also an integral part of the traditional *creeds* of the Church.

29. The *destiny of the unfaithful* is *hell*. In the *Old Testament* it is called *Gehenna.* In later Judaism it is understood as a fiery abyss, a place of darkness and chains. When *Jesus* used such imagery, he did so not to describe a place but to dramatize the urgency of his proclamation of the Kingdom and the seriousness of our decision for or against God.

30. *Hell* is attested to in the Athanasian Creed, Lateran IV, Lyons II, and *Benedictus Deus* of Pope Benedict XII.

31. The Church has never defined that anyone is actually *in* hell, only that it exists as a *possibility* for those who totally and deliberately reject God. Hell is not a punishment by God, but it is God's yielding to our freedom to reject the Kingdom.

32. *Demonology* was prevalent in Mesopotamian culture, but the *Old Testament* generally rejected it because of Israel's severe prohibitions against magic. Later Judaism, however, tended to assimilate such beliefs. There are some few references to demons in the *New Testament*.

33. *Demons* do not occupy a significant place in the official teachings of the Church, except where the Church wanted to insist that whatever exists, including evil spirits, exists by the creative act of God and is under the authority of God (Council of Braga, 561).

34. The *destiny of the unbaptized* is *limbo*. There is the limbo of the *pre-Christian just,* and the limbo of *unbaptized infants* and young children. The belief was

maintained throughout the Middle Ages and into the twentieth century, but has practically disappeared since Vatican II.

35. Cosmic and individual eschatology converge in the doctrine of the *Communion of Saints*.

SUGGESTED READINGS

Bright, John. *The Kingdom of God: The Biblical Concept and Its Meaning for the Church.* Nashville: Abingdon Press, 1953.

Fischer, Kathleen. *Winter Grace.* New York: Paulist Press, 1985.

Guardini, Romano. *The Last Things.* New York: Pantheon Books, 1954.

Hayes, Zachary. *What are they saying about the end of the world?* New York: Paulist Press, 1983.

_____. *Visions of a Future: A Study of Christian Eschatology.* Wilmington, Del.: Michael Glazier, 1989.

Küng, Hans. *Eternal Life? Life After Death as a Medical, Philosophical, and Theological Problem.* Garden City, N.Y.: Doubleday, 1984.

Papin, Joseph, ed. *The Eschaton: A Community of Love.* Villanova, Penna.: Villanova University Press, 1971.

Rahner, Karl. *On the Theology of Death.* 2d ed. New York: Herder & Herder, 1965.

Ratzinger, Joseph. *Eschatology, Death and Eternal Life.* Washington, D.C.: The Catholic University of America Press, 1988.

Schnackenburg, Rudolf. *God's Rule and Kingdom.* London: Nelson, 1963.

Viviano, Benedict T. *The Kingdom of God in History.* Wilmington, Del.: Michael Glazier, 1988.

Conclusion

XXXII

Catholicism: A Synthesis

CATHOLICISM IN CONTEXT

As we pointed out in chapter 1, Catholicism is not a reality that stands by itself. The word *Catholic* is a qualification of *Christian*, and *Christian* is a qualification of *religious*, and *religious* is a qualification of *human*. Thus, the Catholic Church is a community of persons (the human dimension) who believe in God and shape their lives according to that belief (the religious dimension); who believe in God as triune and in Jesus Christ as the Son of God and the redeemer of humankind, and who shape their lives according to that belief (the Christian dimension); who ritually express and celebrate that belief especially in the Eucharist, and who, in the words of the Second Vatican Council (*Lumen gentium*, n. 23), recognize the Bishop of Rome to be "the perpetual and visible source and foundation of the unity of the bishops and of the multitude of the faithful" (the ecclesial dimension). To be Catholic, therefore, is to be a kind of human being, a kind of religious person, and a kind of Christian disciple belonging to a specific eucharistic community of disciples within the worldwide, or ecumenical, Body of Christ.

After examining the foundations of Catholicism in chapters 1 and 2, we explored in sequence its *human* dimension (chapters 3–5 on nature, grace, and Original Sin), its *theo-logical* dimension (chapters 6–10 on the triune God), its *Christological* dimension (chapters 11–15 on Jesus Christ and our redemption), its *ecclesiological* dimension

1187

(chapters 16–20 on the nature, mission, and structure of the Church), its *sacramental* and especially *eucharistic* dimension (chapters 21–24 on the seven sacraments), its *moral* dimension (chapters 25–27 on Christian values and norms), and, finally, its *spiritual* and *eschatological* dimension (chapters 28–31 on Christian life as rooted in the death and resurrection of Jesus Christ, transformed by the Holy Spirit, and destined for the final Kingdom of God).

To what extent, however, is the understanding of human existence, of God, of Christ, of the Church, of the sacraments, of the moral life, of spirituality, and of hope in eternal life distinctively Catholic? If Catholicism is distinguishable within the Body of Christ from Protestantism, Anglicanism, and Eastern Orthodoxy, it must be on the basis of some belief(s) or characteristic(s) which Catholicism alone possesses. One belief that is obviously distinctive is Catholicism's commitment to the Petrine office, more specifically, the papacy. At this point in the history of the Church, the Catholic Church alone affirms that the Petrine ministry as exercised by the Bishop of Rome is an integral institutional element in the Body of Christ, and that without the papal office the Church universal lacks something essential to its wholeness. It is the one issue which still finally divides the Catholic Church from all other Christian churches and traditions, notwithstanding various other differences regarding liturgy, spirituality, morality, polity, and doctrinal formulations. When all else is stripped away, the official Catholic position on the Petrine ministry and office is different from every other official and/or representative position of every other formal Christian church. This is not to suggest that it must always be so, however, and therein lies the difficulty in linking Catholic distinctiveness with the papacy alone.

The Lutheran–Roman Catholic consultation in the United States, for example, has already achieved a remarkable measure of consensus on the question of papal primacy (see chapter 20), giving promise of even greater breakthroughs. It is conceivable, in other words, that Catholicism's affirmations about the Petrine ministry will, at some later date, no longer be Catholicism's affirmations alone. They may be shared by Lutherans, Anglicans, the Orthodox, Presbyterians, Methodists, and others. Will all of Christianity at that point be identified simply with Catholicism? Will Lutheranism, Calvinism, Anglicanism, and Orthodox Christianity fade from the scene once and for all? Will there be, then, one theology, one spirituality, one liturgy, one canon law, one vehicle of doctrinal formulation? If so, it would be the first time in the entire history of the Church, not excluding the New Testament period itself (see, for example, Raymond E. Brown's *The Community of the Beloved Disciple*, New York: Paulist Press, 1979; see also chapter 17 of this book).

We have suggested from the beginning that a more fruitful, and more theologically and historically nuanced, approach to the question of Catholic distinctiveness would lie in the direction of identifying and describing various *characteristics* of Catholicism, each of which (apart from the commitment to the papacy) Catholicism shares with one or another Christian church or tradition. But how can one distinguish Catholicism from other theological, doctrinal, spiritual, liturgical, moral, and institutional expressions of Christianity on the basis of characteristics which Catholicism presumably *shares* with one or another Christian church? It is true: There is no one characteristic, apart from the Petrine doctrine, which sets the Catholic Church apart from *all other* churches. On the other hand, a case can be made that nowhere else except in the Catholic Church are *all* of Catholicism's characteristics present in the precise *configuration* in which they are found within Catholicism.

The point is crucial to the central thesis of the first and now the last chapter of this book. An example may help to illustrate it. The flag of the United States of America has individual characteristics which it shares with the flags of other nations of the world. (1) It is *tricolored*. But so, too, are the flags, for example, of Australia, Belgium, Cameroon, Colombia, the United Kingdom, France, Ireland, Italy, Lithuania, and Germany. (2) Its three colors are *red, white, and blue*. But so, too, are the flags, for example, of Chile, Cuba, the Dominican Republic, France, Iceland, the Netherlands, Panama, Russia, the United Kingdom, and New Zealand. (3) It has *stars* in its basic design. But so, too, do the flags, for example, of Australia, China, Honduras, Iraq, New Zealand, and Venezuela.

Despite these common characteristics, no flag in the entire community of nations is identical with the flag of the United States, a reasonably close similarity to the flag of the African nation of Liberia notwithstanding. What is *distinctive* about the United States' flag is not any one of its several *characteristics* but the precise *configuration* of those characteristics. So, too, with the Catholic Church in relation to all of the other churches and traditions within the Body of Christ.

GENERAL CHARACTERISTICS OF CATHOLICISM

As its very name suggests, Catholicism is characterized by a *radical openness to all truth and to every authentic value.* It is *comprehensive* and *all-embracing* toward the totality of Christian experience and tradition, in all the theological, doctrinal, spiritual, liturgical, moral, canonical, institutional, and social richness and diversity of that experience and tradition. Catholicism is not a postbiblical phenomenon. It does not emerge from some historical moment and from particular historical (i.e., national, cultural, political) circumstances that are removed in time from Jesus' proclamation of the Kingdom, his gathering of disciples, and the formation of the Church in the period encompassed by the New Testament. Catholicism does not begin as a distinctive expression of Christian faith in the sixteenth century, nor are its basic lines already fixed by the fourteenth. It is not itself a sect or a schismatic entity, although sectarianism and schism are not unknown to it. Nor is it inextricably linked with the culture of a particular nation or region of the world. Catholicism is, in principle, as Asian as it is European, as Slavic as it is Latin, as Mexican or Nigerian as it is Irish or Polish.

There is no list of "Catholic Fathers" or "Catholic Mothers" which does not include the great theological and spiritual writers of the period *before* as well as after the division of East and West and the divisions within the West. Nor are there *schools of theology* which Catholicism excludes. Nor *spiritualities.* Nor *doctrinal* currents.

Catholicism is a comprehensive, all-embracing, *catholic* tradition, characterized by a *both/and* rather than an *either/or* approach. It is not nature *or* grace, but graced nature; not reason *or* faith, but reason illumined by faith; not law *or* Gospel, but law inspired by the Gospel; not Scripture *or* tradition, but normative tradition within Scripture; not faith *or* works, but faith issuing in works and works as expressions of faith; not authority *or* freedom, but authority in the service of freedom.

There have been many moments in the history of the Catholic Church when these delicate balances were disrupted, often through events beyond anyone's control and at other times through narrow-mindedness, blindness, stubbornness, and malice. But the Church is at once holy and sinful, not in the sense that sin exists *alongside* grace, but in the sense that even graced existence is ambiguous, fragile, and subject to disintegration. The record is always mixed. The Kingdom of God is neither coextensive with the Church nor totally divorced from the Church.

One person looks at a glass and sees that it is half empty; another looks at the same glass and declares it half full. One person looks at the story of the Church and sees only the Church's complicity in the feudal system, the Crusades, the pretentious claims of Innocent III and Boniface VIII, its blindness to the gathering storm clouds of the Reformation, its insensitivities to the East, its arid neoscholasticism of the post-Reformation period, its handling of the Galileo affair, its declaration of war against modernity in the nineteenth century, its suppression of theological freedom under Pope Pius X, its diplomatic hesitancies in the face of Nazism, its authoritarianism, its patriarchalism, and its sexism.

Another looks at the same Church and notes the extraordinary, and finally inexplicable, manner in which it drew unity out of seeming chaos in the Christological controversies of the fourth and fifth centuries. Still another marvels at how the Church can be the Church of John and Paul, of Luke and Timothy, of the martyrs and apologists, of Gregory of Nyssa and Augustine of Hippo, of Gregory the Great and Anselm of Canterbury, of Francis of Assisi and Thomas Aquinas, of Hildegard of Bingen and Julian of Norwich, of John of the Cross and Teresa of Ávila, of monasticism and religious orders, of heroic reformers like Catherine of Siena, of contemporary saints like John XXIII and Dorothy Day, of Cesar Chavez and Mother Teresa, of Archbishop Oscar Romero and of the women martyrs of El Salvador.

But perhaps more than anything or anyone else, one must marvel at the Church of *Vatican II*: a *pluralistic* Church open to pluralism, a *modern* Church open to modernity, an *ecumenical* Church open to the whole wide world (the literal meaning of *ecumenical*), a *living* Church open to new life and to the change it brings and requires, a *catholic* Church open in principle to all truth and to every value.

For Lutheran church historian Martin Marty, of the University of Chicago, "Catholicism is a family of apostolic churches, rich in regional, national, ethnic diversity; it is a faith that teaches me that because you have a *core* or center, you can make room for a variety of apparently competitive and interactive elements" ("Something Real and Lumpy," *U.S. Catholic,* vol. 44, May 1979, p. 24).

Like the flag of the United States of America, there are colors here that others share; there are patterns here that others display; there are symbols here that others use. But no other church or tradition within the Body of Christ puts them all together in quite this way. It is in their special configuration that the distinctiveness of Catholicism is disclosed and expressed. It is expressed in its systematic theology, in its body of doctrines, in its liturgical life, especially its Eucharist, in its variety of spiritualities, in its religious congregations and lay apostolates, in its social teachings and commitments to justice, peace, and human rights, in its exercise of collegiality, and in its Petrine ministry.

THE PHILOSOPHICAL FOCUS OF CATHOLICISM: CHRISTIAN REALISM

Catholicism is not bound to any one school of theology, although there is something distinctively Catholic in the way the pluralism of theologies is integrated, systematized, and applied within the Catholic tradition. If the Catholic Church is not linked exclusively to a particular theology, much less is it linked to a particular philosophy: existentialist, process, phenomenological, even Thomistic. And yet there is a distinctively Catholic way of integrating the pluralism of philosophies underlying its various theological and doctrinal orientations. For want of a better term, that distinctively Catholic philosophical focus is *Christian realism*, as outlined, for example, by Bernard J. F. Lonergan (see his "The Origins of Christian Realism" in *A Second Collection*, Philadelphia: Westminster Press, 1974, pp. 239–61).

Lonergan reminds us that infants, in contrast to adults, do not speak. They live, therefore, in a world of immediacy: of sights and sounds, of tastes and smells, of touching and feeling, of pleasure and pain. But as infants learn to speak, they gradually move into a larger world, a world mediated by meaning. That world includes the past and the future as well as the present, the possible and the probable as well as the actual, rights and duties as well as the facts.

The criteria of reality in the infant's world of immediacy are given in immediate experience. They are simply the occurrence of seeing, hearing, tasting, smelling, touching, pleasure, and pain. But the criteria of reality in the world mediated by meaning are far more complex. They include immediate experience but also go beyond it.

"For the world mediated by meaning is not just given," Lonergan insists. "Over and above what is given there is the universe that is intended by questions, that is organized by intelligence, that is described by language, that is enriched by tradition. It is an enormous world far beyond the comprehension of the nursery. But it is also an insecure world, for besides fact there is fiction, besides truth there is error, besides science there is myth, besides honesty there is deceit" (p. 241).

Now this insecurity and ambiguity does not really bother too many people. But it does trouble philosophers and those whose sciences, like theology, depend in some significant measure on correct philosophical presuppositions. Philosophical answers to the question of reality differ. First, there is *naive realism*, which insists that knowing is simply a matter of taking a good look; objectivity is a matter of seeing what is there to be seen; reality is whatever is given in immediate experience. The offspring of naive realism is *empiricism*. The empiricist takes naive realism seriously. The only reality that counts is the reality that one can determine by quantitative measurement. Empiricism, in turn, begets its philosophical opposite, *critical idealism* (Kant), in which the categories of understanding of themselves are empty and refer to objects only insofar as the categories are applied to the data of the senses. This is the world of *phenomena*. We cannot know things in themselves, the *noumena*.

"Insofar as Christianity is a reality, it is involved in the problems of realism," Lonergan suggests. First, Christianity itself is mediated by meaning. "It is mediated by meaning in its communicative function inasmuch as it is preached. It is mediated by meaning in its cognitive function inasmuch as it is believed. It is mediated by meaning in its constitutive function inasmuch as it is a way of life that is lived. It is mediated by meaning in its effective function inasmuch as its precepts are put into practice" (p. 244).

But there is ambiguity within the Christian's world, as there is in human life itself. For the Christian world is not *exclusively* a world mediated by meaning. There is also the immediacy of God's grace creating the new creature in Christ by the power of the Holy Spirit. The grace of God is not produced by the preacher, nor is it the result of believing the Gospel, nor does it come as a reward for good works. The offer of grace is present to the individual person, as we have seen in chapter 5, from the very beginning of the person's existence. In the order of salvation (which is the only *real* order we have), grace enters into the definition of what it means to be human.

Thus, the real is not only what we can see and touch, as naive realism suggests. Nor is the real just an idea in the mind, as idealism insists. The real is what we judge to be real. The reality of the world mediated by meaning is known not by experience alone, nor by ideas alone, but by judgments and beliefs.

It is this commitment to *critical* realism that has moved the Catholic Church, first at Nicea (325) and again and again in its official teachings, to deliberate, to issue decrees, to condemn, to explain, to defend, to make distinctions, to use technical terms, to engage in the most acute rational reflection. Indeed, it is this commitment to critical realism that is at the foundation of the medieval effort toward systematization and of our own contemporary systematic enterprises as well.

What does all this mean? It means that the Catholic tradition philosophically rejects both naive realism and idealism as adequate bases for Catholicism's theological vision. One contemporary form of naive realism is *fundamentalism,* of both a biblical and a doctrinal kind. For the *biblical fundamentalist,* the meaning of the Word of God is obvious. "Just take a look," the biblicist seems to say. "The requirements of Christian existence are clear. The answers are readily available in the pages of Sacred Scripture." For the *doctrinal fundamentalist,* the meaning of the Church's official teachings is also obvious. There is no need to take into account their original historical settings, the controversies that provoked them, the precise views that were condemned, the language and concepts in which the doctrines were couched. *Moralism* is another contemporary form of naive realism. "Just consult your gut feelings, or use your common sense," the moralist insists. "Of course, violence is against the Gospel of Jesus Christ." Or: "Of course, violence can be justified to counteract oppressive violence." But moralism provides no arguments, no warrants, no reasons. It is assumed that the convictions are self-evidently true and their intrinsic power compelling.

Idealism, on the other hand, makes of Christianity a system of principles and ideas, but without clear or meaningful connection with the pastoral situation or the human condition at large. One need not worry about the effectiveness of preaching and teaching, for example, if one is convinced that the ideas to be preached and taught are plainly, even though not infallibly, true. One need not engage in time-consuming and ultimately diverting moral speculation about what it is one must do in such-and-such a conflict-situation when there is a clear statement of moral principle already "on the books." The contemporary forms of idealism are *dogmatism* and *legalism.* Dogmatism assumes that salvation is linked primarily to "right belief" (orthodoxy) and that the rightness of beliefs is clear and almost self-evident. Legalism assumes that salvation is linked primarily to "right practice," i.e., of obedience to church laws. There is never any serious doubt about what the law demands, so specific and so detailed is it.

Critical realism, or what Lonergan calls *Christian realism,* insists that experience itself is not enough. One can "take a look," but one cannot be sure that what one sees corresponds entirely to what is real. "Appearances can be deceiving," the old saying has it. Christian realism also rejects the notion that clear and distinct ideas (doctrines, dogmas, canonical directives) are equivalent to the real itself. Ideas are never formulated except in relation to other ideas, to events, to one's associates, to the problems and resources at hand, to the historical circumstances, to social, economic, and political conditions, to one's own background, age, sex, nationality, occupation, income level, social status, and the like. Just as Christian realism rejects biblicism and moralism in favor of a critical and systematic approach to reality, so Christian realism rejects dogmatism and legalism in favor of a critical and systematic approach to reality, an approach that goes beyond what seems to be there and that takes historicity into account in the use and interpretation of ideas and principles.

This critical realism carries over into everything the Church does. Thus, the Church's moral vision and its approach to the demands of Christian existence are qualified always by its confidence in the power of grace and by its readiness to expect and understand the weaknesses and failures rooted in Original Sin. And so Catholicism is a moral universe of laws but also of dispensations, of rules but also of exceptions, of respect for authority but also for freedom of conscience, of high ideals but also of minimal requirements, of penalties but also of indulgences, of censures and excommunications but also of absolution and reconciliation.

THE THEOLOGICAL FOCI OF CATHOLICISM: SACRAMENTALITY, MEDIATION, COMMUNION

As we have seen throughout this book, no theological principle or focus is more characteristic of Catholicism or more central to its identity than the principle of *sacramentality*. The Catholic vision sees God in and through all things: other people, communities, movements, events, places, objects, the world at large, the whole cosmos. The visible, the tangible, the finite, the historical—all these are actual or potential carriers of the divine presence. Consequently, the Catholic sees all material reality ("nature") as essentially good ("graced nature"). It comes from the creative hand of God, has been redeemed by Jesus Christ, continues to be renewed by the Holy Spirit, and is destined to become part of "a new heaven and a new earth" (Revelation 21:1). Grace, not sin, is the driving force of history.

Indeed, it is only in and through visible, material realities that we encounter the invisible, spiritual God. The primordial sacrament of our encounter with God and of God's encounter with us is Jesus Christ. The Church, in turn, is the fundamental sacrament of our encounter with Christ and of Christ's with us, and the sacraments, in turn, are the signs and instruments by which that ecclesial encounter with Christ is expressed, celebrated, and made effective for the glory of God and the salvation of women and men.

A corollary of the principle of sacramentality is the principle of *mediation*. A sacrament not only signifies; it also causes what it signifies. Thus, created realities not only contain, reflect, or embody the presence of God, they also make that presence effective for those who avail themselves of these realities. Just as we noted in the previous section that the world is mediated by meaning, so the universe of grace is a mediated reality: mediated principally by Christ, and secondarily by the Church and by other signs and instruments of salvation outside and beyond the Church.

Catholicism rejects naive realism, which holds to the immediacy of the experience of God as the normal or exclusive kind of encounter with the divine presence. Catholicism also rejects idealism, which holds that the encounter with God occurs solely in the inwardness of conscience and the inner recesses of consciousness. Catholicism holds, on the contrary, that the encounter with God is a mediated experience but a *real* experience, rooted in the historical and affirmed as real by the critical and systematic judgment that God is truly present and active here or there, in this event or that, in this person or that, in this object or that.

Consequently, for Catholic social doctrine human effort on behalf of the common good and the transformation of the world can and does make a significant difference to history. We are personally and corporately responsible (with God) for the welfare of all and for the care and well-being of the created world itself.

Finally, Catholicism affirms the principle of *communion:* that our way to God and God's way to us is not only a mediated way but a communal way. And even when the divine-human encounter is most personal and individual, it is still communal in that the encounter is made possible by the mediation of the community. Thus, there is *not* simply an individual personal relationship with God or Jesus Christ that is established and sustained by meditative reflection on Sacred Scripture, for the Bible itself is the Church's book and is the testimony of the Church's original faith. The mystics (even in the narrowest sense of the word) rely on language, ideas, concepts, presuppositions when they reflect upon and share with others their intimate experience of God. We are radically social, i.e., *relational,* beings; our use of language and our sexuality are clear evidence of that. There is no relationship with God, however intense, profound, and unique, that dispenses entirely with the communal context of *every* human relationship with God. Indeed, we are defined by our relationships: with God, with neighbor, with the world, and even with ourselves.

And this is why, for Catholicism, the mystery of the Church has so significant a place in theology, doctrine, pastoral practice, moral vision and commitment, and spirituality. Catholics have always emphasized the place of the Church as both the *sacrament* of Christ, *mediating* salvation through sacraments, ministries, and other institutional elements and forms, and as the *communion of disciples*, the preview or foretaste, as it were, of the perfect communion to which the whole of humankind is destined in the final Kingdom of God.

And so it is with the *mystery of the Church* that we come at last to the point at which the distinctively Catholic understanding and practice of Christian faith most clearly emerges. For here we find the convergence of those principles which have always been so characteristic of Catholicism: sacramentality, mediation, and communion. They are principles grasped and interpreted according to the mode of critical realism rather than of naive realism or idealism.

These principles, at once philosophical and theological, have shaped, and continue to shape, Catholicism's Christology, ecclesiology, sacramental theology, canon law, spirituality, Mariology, theological anthropology, moral theology, liturgy, social doctrine, and the whole realm of art and aesthetics. The last item is a particular case in point. In contrast, Protestantism, as a religion of the word, has had a "mixed" record when it comes to the arts. It has been "uneasy about objectification of the divine drama in images which might themselves draw the devotion of the supplicant from the invisible God beyond the gods. It has often and maybe even usually been uneasy about unrestricted bodily attention, and has rather consistently feared the ecstasy of the dance through most of the years of its history" (Martin Marty, *Protestantism*, p. 228; for a broader view of Catholicism's aesthetical impact, see Kenneth Clark's *Civilisation*, New York: Harper & Row, 1969, pp. 167–92).

Baptist theologian Langdon Gilkey saw many of the same characteristics when he probed the reality of Catholicism in search of its distinctive identity. First, he concluded, there is Catholicism's "sense of reality, importance, and 'weight' of tradition and history in the formation of this people and so of her religious truths, religious experience, and human wisdom."

Second, there is, "especially to a Protestant, a remarkable sense of humanity and grace in the communal life of Catholics.... Consequently the love of life, the appreciation of the body and the senses, of joy and celebration, the tolerance of the sinner, these natural, worldly and 'human' virtues are far more clearly and universally embodied in Catholics and in Catholic life than in Protestants and in Protestantism."

Third, there is Catholicism's "continuing experience, unequalled in other forms of Western Christianity, of the presence of God and of grace mediated through symbols to the entire course of ordinary human life." For Gilkey, a symbol points to and communicates the reality of God which lies beyond it. A symbol can be viewed and appropriated "as *relative,* as a 'symbol' and not God, without sacrificing this relation to the *absoluteness* that makes it a vehicle of the sacred." The experience of the symbol can unite "sensual, aesthetic, and intellectual experience more readily than the experiences of proclamation or of an ecstatic spiritual presence." The Catholic principle of symbol or sacramentality, according to Gilkey, "may provide the best entrance into a new synthesis of the Christian tradition with the vitalities as well as the relativities of contemporary existence."

Finally, there has been "throughout Catholic history a drive toward rationality, the insistence that the divine mystery manifest in tradition and sacramental presence be insofar as possible penetrated, defended, and explicated by the most acute rational reflection" (*Catholicism Confronts Modernity: A Protestant View,* pp. 17–18, 20–22).

CONCLUSION

It is not a question here in this chapter, or indeed in this book, of arguing that the Catholic Church and the Catholic tradition are necessarily superior to all of the other churches and traditions on this point or that, but that there is within Catholicism a configuration of values which enjoy a normative character in discerning the Christian tradition as a whole.

These values include Catholicism's sense of *sacramentality* (God is present everywhere, the invisible in the visible, within us and within the whole created order); its principle of *mediation* (the divine is available to us as a transforming, healing, renewing power through the ordinary things of life: persons, communities, events, places, institutions, natural objects, etc.); its sense of *communion,* or of peoplehood (we are radically social and so, too, is our relationship with God and God's with us); its drive toward *rationality* and its *critical realism* (reality is neither self-evident nor confined to the realm of ideas); its corresponding respect for *history*, for *tradition*, and for *continuity* (we are products of our past as well as shapers of our present and our future); its *analogical imagination* (the divine and the human are more alike than unalike); its conviction that we can have as radical a notion of *sin* as we like so long as our understanding and appreciation of *grace* is even more radical; its high regard for *authority* and *order* as well as for *conscience* and *freedom;* indeed its *fundamental openness to all truth and to every value*—in a word, its *catholicity.*

SUMMARY

1. Catholicism is not a reality that stands by itself. The word *Catholic* is a qualification of *Christian,* and *Christian* is a qualification of *religious,* and *religious* is a qualification of *human.*

2. The Catholic Church alone affirms that the *Petrine ministry,* or papacy, is an integral institutional element in the Body of Christ. It is the one issue which finally divides the Catholic from all other Christians.

3. The *distinctiveness* of Catholicism, however, lies not simply in its affirmation of the Petrine office but in the unique *configuration of characteristics* which Catholicism possesses and manifests as a Church and as a tradition within the Body of Christ and Christianity at large.

4. *In general,* Catholicism is characterized by a *radical openness to all truth and to every value.* Catholicism does not emerge from a particular time after the foundational period of the New Testament, nor is it tied to a particular nation or culture. It endorses no one school of theology or spirituality and no single interpretation of doctrine.

5. Catholicism is characterized by a *both/and* rather than an either/or approach to nature and grace, reason and faith, law and Gospel, Scripture and tradition, faith and works, authority and freedom.

6. The *historical record* of Catholicism is mixed: There are, e.g., the triumphalism and even the decadence of the medieval papacy and the simplicity and sanctity of Francis of Assisi, the condemnatory spirit of Pius IX and the openness of John XXIII.

7. Nowhere is the *catholicity* of the Church more evident, however, than at *Vatican II:* A Church at once *pluralistic* and open to pluralism, *modern* and open to modernity, *ecumenical* and open to the whole wide world, *alive* and open to new life, and *catholic* and open in principle to all truth and every value.

1200

8. Catholicism's *philosophical focus* is *critical*, or *Christian, realism*. It sees the world as mediated by meaning, rather than a world of immediate experience alone (naive realism, empiricism) or of ideas alone (idealism).

9. Christian realism is opposed to *naive realism* in its various forms: *fundamentalism*, of both a biblical and a doctrinal kind, and *moralism*. It is also opposed to *idealism* in its various forms: *dogmatism* and *legalism*.

10. This *critical realism* carries over into everything the Church does. In the realm of moral demands, for example, Catholicism is a religion of laws but also of dispensations, of censures but also of absolutions.

11. The *theological foci* of Catholicism include the principles of *sacramentality, mediation,* and *communion.*

12. The principle of *sacramentality* means that God is present and operative in and through the visible, the concrete, the tangible, the finite, the historical: persons, communities, places, events, natural objects, the whole created order. *Christ* is the primordial sacrament; the *Church* is the fundamental sacrament.

13. The principle of *mediation* is a corollary of the principle of sacramentality. God uses signs and instruments to communicate grace.

14. The principle of *communion* means that our way to God and God's way to us is mediated through community: the human community at large and the Church in particular. The *communion of disciples* is the preview or foretaste of the perfect communion to which the whole of humankind is destined in the final Kingdom of God.

15. *Langdon Gilkey* identifies the following as characteristic of Catholicism: its sense of tradition and history, its sense of peoplehood and community, its sense of symbol and sacrament, and its drive toward rationality and rational reflection.

16. It was not the purpose of this chapter or of this book to establish the *superiority* of Catholicism but to identify its *distinctiveness* by calling attention to the *configuration of values* which one finds nowhere else in the Body of Christ or in Christianity at large: sacramentality, mediation, communion, rationality, continuity, the triumph of grace over sin, the regard for authority and order as well as conscience and freedom, and its fundamental openness to all truth and to every value. In a word, its *catholicity.*

SUGGESTED READINGS

Cunningham, Lawrence S. *The Catholic Heritage.* New York: Crossroad, 1983.
_____. *The Catholic Experience.* New York: Crossroad, 1985.

Gilkey, Langdon. *Catholicism Confronts Modernity: A Protestant View*. New York: Seabury Press, 1975.

Lossky, Vladimir, *The Mystical Theology of the Eastern Church*. London: Clarke, 1957.

Marty, Martin E. *Protestantism*. New York: Holt, Rinehart and Winston, 1972.

Rausch, Thomas P. *The Roots of the Catholic Tradition*. Wilmington, Del.: Michael Glazier, 1986.

APPENDIX

The Nicene-Constantinopolitan Creed

(The Council of Constantinople was convened to reaffirm the faith of the council of Nicea, of 325. Though not itself promulgated by the Council of Constantinople, this creed soon acquired greater authority than even the Nicene Creed. Since the seventh century it has been known by its present name.)

> We believe in one God,
> the Father, the Almighty,
> maker of heaven and earth,
> of all that is seen and unseen.
> We believe in one Lord, Jesus Christ,
> the only Son of God,
> eternally begotten of the Father,
> God from God, Light from Light,
> true God from true God,
> begotten, not made, one in Being with the Father.
> Through him all things were made.
> For us and for our salvation
> he came down from heaven:
> by the power of the Holy Spirit
> he was born of the Virgin Mary, and became man.
> For our sake he was crucified under Pontius Pilate;
> he suffered, died, and was buried.
> On the third day he rose again
> in fulfillment of the Scriptures;
> he ascended into heaven
> and is seated at the right hand of the Father.

He will come again in glory to judge the living and the dead,
and his kingdom will have no end.
We believe in the Holy Spirit, the Lord, the giver of life,
who proceeds from the Father and the Son.
With the Father and the Son he is worshiped and glorified.
He has spoken through the Prophets.
We believe in one holy catholic and apostolic Church.
We acknowledge one baptism for the forgiveness of sins.
We look for the resurrection of the dead,
and the life of the world to come. Amen.

Instruction on the Historical Truth of the Gospels, Pontifical Biblical Commission, April 21, 1964. (Excerpt. Full text in the *Catholic Biblical Quarterly*, vol. 26, July 1964, pp. 305–12.)

1. The Catholic exegete, under the guidance of the Church, must turn to account all the resources for the understanding of the sacred text which have been put at his disposal by previous interpreters, especially the holy Fathers and Doctors of the Church, whose labors it is for him to take up and to carry on. In order to bring out with fullest clarity the enduring truth and authority of the Gospels he must, whilst carefully observing the rules of rational and of Catholic hermeneutics, make skillful use of the new aids to exegesis, especially those which the historical method, taken in its widest sense, has provided; that method, namely, which minutely investigates sources, determining their nature and bearing, and availing itself of the findings of textual criticism, literary criticism, and linguistic studies. The interpreter must be alert to the reminder given him by Pope Pius XII of happy memory when he charged him "to make judicious inquiry as to how far the form of expression or the type of literature adopted by the sacred writer may help towards the true and genuine interpretation, and to remain convinced that this part of his task cannot be neglected without great detriment to Catholic exegesis."[5] In this reminder Pius XII of happy memory is laying down a general rule of hermeneutics, one by whose help the books both of the Old Testament and of the New are to be explained, since the sacred writers when composing them followed the way of thinking and of writing current amongst their contemporaries. In a word, the exegete must make use of every means which will help him to reach a deeper understanding of the character of the gospel testimony, of the religious life of the first churches, and of the significance and force of the apostolic tradition.

In appropriate cases the interpreter is free to seek out what sound elements there are in "the Method of Form-history," and these he can duly make use of to gain a fuller understanding of the Gospels. He must be circumspect in doing so, however, because the method in question is often found alloyed with principles of a philosophical or theological nature which are quite inadmissible, and which not infrequently vitiate both the method itself and the conclusions arrived at regarding literary questions. For certain exponents of this method, led astray by rationalistic prejudices, refuse to admit that there exists a supernatural order, or that a personal God intervenes in the world by revelation properly so called, or that miracles and prophecies are possible and have actually occurred. There are others who have as their starting-point a wrong notion of faith, taking it that faith is indifferent to historical truth, and is indeed incompatible with it. Others practically deny *a priori* the historical value and character of the documents of revelation. Others finally there are who on the one hand underestimate the authority which the Apostles had as witnesses of Christ, and the office and influence which they wielded in the primitive community, whilst on the other hand they overestimate the creative capacity of the community itself. All these aberrations are not only opposed to Catholic doctrine, but are also devoid of any scientific foundation, and are foreign to the genuine principles of the historical method.

2. In order to determine correctly the trustworthiness of what is transmitted in the Gospels, the interpreter must take careful note of the three stages of tradition by which the teaching and the life of Jesus have come down to us.

Christ our Lord attached to Himself certain chosen disciples[6] who had followed Him from the beginning,[7] who had seen His works and had heard His words, and thus were qualified to become witnesses of His life and teaching.[8] Our Lord, when expounding His teaching by word of mouth, observed the methods of reasoning and of exposition which were in common use at the time; in this way He accommodated Himself to the mentality of His hearers, and ensured that His teachings would be deeply impressed on their minds and would be easily retained in memory by His disciples. These latter grasped correctly the idea that the miracles and other events of the life of Jesus were things purposely performed or arranged by Him in such a way that men would thereby be led to believe in Christ and to accept by faith the doctrine of salvation.

The Apostles, bearing testimony to Jesus,[9] proclaimed first and foremost the death and resurrection of the Lord, faithfully recounting His life and words[10] and, as regards the manner of their preaching, taking into account the circumstances of their hearers.[11] After Jesus had risen from the dead, and when His divinity was clearly perceived,[12] the faith of the disciples, far from blotting out the remembrance of the events that had happened, rather consolidated it, since their faith was based on what Jesus had done and taught.[13] Nor was Jesus transformed into a "mythical" personage, and His teaching distorted, by reason of the worship which the disciples now paid Him, revering Him as Lord and Son of God. Yet it need not be denied that the Apostles, when handing on to their hearers the things which in actual fact the Lord had said and done, did so in the light of that fuller understanding which they enjoyed as a result of being schooled by the glorious things accomplished in Christ,[14] and of being illumined by the Spirit of Truth.[15] Thus it came about that, just as Jesus Himself after His resurrection had "interpreted to them"[16] both the words of the Old Testament and the words which He Himself had spoken,[17] so now they in their turn interpreted His words and deeds according to the needs of their hearers. "Devoting [themselves] to the ministry of the word,"[18] they made use, as they preached, of such various forms of speech as were adapted to their own purposes and to the mentality of their hearers; for it was "to Greek and barbarian, to learned and simple,"[19] that they had a duty to discharge.[20] These varied ways of speaking which the heralds of Christ made use of in proclaiming Him must be distinguished one from the other and carefully appraised: catecheses, narratives, testimonies, hymns, doxologies, prayers and any other such literary forms as were customarily employed in Sacred Scripture and by people of that time.

The sacred authors, for the benefit of the churches, took this earliest body of instruction, which had been handed on orally at first and then in writing—for many soon set their hands to "drawing up a narrative"[21] of matters concerning the Lord Jesus—and set it down in the four Gospels. In doing this each of them followed a method suitable to the special purpose which he had in view. They selected certain things out of the many which had been handed on; some they synthesized, some they explained with an eye to the situation of the churches, painstakingly using every means of bringing home to their readers the solid truth of the things in which they had been instructed.[22] For, out of the material which they had received, the sacred authors selected especially those items which were adapted to the varied circumstances of the faithful as well as to the end which they themselves wished to attain; these they recounted in a manner consonant with those circumstances and with that end. And since the meaning of a statement depends, amongst other things, on the place which it has in a given sequence, the Evangelists, in handing on the words or the deeds of our Savior, explained them for the advantage of their readers by respectively setting them, one Evangelist in one context, another in another. For this reason the exegete must ask himself what the Evangelist intended by recounting a saying or a fact in a certain way, or by placing it in a certain context. For the truth of the narrative is not affected in the slightest by the fact that the Evangelists report the sayings or the doings of our Lord in a different order,[23] and that they use different words to express what He said, not keeping to the very letter, but nevertheless preserving the sense.[24] For, as St. Augustine says: "Where it is a question only of those matters whose order in the narrative may be indifferently this or that without in any way taking from the truth and authority of the Gospel, it is probable enough that each Evangelist believed he should narrate them in that same order in which God was pleased to suggest them to his recollection. The Holy Spirit distributes His gifts to each one according as He wills;[25] therefore, too, for the sake of those Books which were to be set so high at the very summit of authority, He undoubtedly guided and controlled the minds of the holy writers in their recollection of what they were to write; but as to why, in doing so, He should have permitted them, one to follow this order in his narrative, another to follow that—that is a question whose answer may possibly be found with God's help, if one seeks it out with reverent care."[26]

Unless the exegete, then, pays attention to all those factors which have a bearing on the origin and the composition of the Gospels, and makes due use of the acceptable findings of modern research, he will fail in his duty of ascertaining what the intentions of the sacred writers were, and what it is that they have actually said. The results of recent study have made it clear that the teachings and the life of Jesus were not simply recounted for the mere purpose of being kept in remembrance, but were "preached" in such a way as to furnish the Church with the foundation on which to build up faith and morals. It follows that the interpreter who subjects the testimony of the Evangelists to perserving scrutiny will be in a position to shed further light on the enduring theological value of the Gospels, and to throw into clearest relief the vital importance of the Church's interpretation.

5. *Divino afflante Spiritu; EB* 560.
6. Cf. *Mc.* 3,14; *Lc.* 6,13.
7. Cf. *Lc.* 1,2; *Act.* 1,21–22.
8. Cf. *Lc.* 24,48; *Jn.* 15,27; *Act.* 1,8; 10,39; 13,31.
9. Cf. *Lc.* 24,44–48; *Act.* 2,32; 3,15; 5,30–32.
10. Cf. *Act.* 10,36–41.
11. Cf. *Act.* 13,16–41 with *Act.* 17,22–31.
12. *Act.* 2,36; *Jn.* 20,28.
13. *Act.* 2,22; 10,37–39.
14. *Jn.* 2,22; 12,16; 11,51–52; cf. 14,26; 16,12–13; 7,39.
15. Cf. *Jn.* 14,26; 16,13.
16. *Lc.* 24,27.
17. Cf. *Lc.* 24,44–45; *Act.* 1,3.
18. *Act.* 6,4.
19. *Rom.* 1,14.
20. *1 Cor.* 9,19–23.
21. Cf. *Lc.* 1,1.
22. Cf. *Lc.* 1,4.
23. Cf. St. John Chrys., *In Mat. Hom.* I,3; *PG.* 57,16,17.
24. Cf. St August., *De consensu Evang.* 2,12,28; *PL* 34, 1090–1091.
25. *1 Cor.* 12,11.
26. *De consensu Evang.* 2,21,51 s.; *PL* 34,1102.

Declaration in Defense of the Catholic Doctrine on the Church Against Certain Errors of the Present Day (Mysterium Ecclesiæ), Congregation for the Doctrine of the Faith, June 24, 1973. (Excerpt. Full text in *Origins: NC Documentary Service*, vol. 3, July 19, 1973, pp. 97, 99, 100.)

The transmission of divine Revelation by the Church encounters difficulties of various kinds. These arise from the fact that the hidden mysteries of God 'by their nature so far transcend the human intellect that even if they are revealed to us and accepted by faith, they remain concealed by the veil of faith itself and are as it were wrapped in darkness.' Difficulties arise also from the historical condition that affects the expression of Revelation.

With regard to this historical condition, it must first be observed that the meaning of the pronouncements of faith depend partly upon the expressive power of the language used at a certain point in time and in particular circumstances. Moreover, it sometimes happens that some dogmatic truth is first expressed incompletely (but not falsely), and at a later date, when considered in a broader context of faith or human knowledge, it receives a fuller and more perfect expression. In addition, when the Church makes new pronouncements she intends to confirm or clarify what is in some way contained in Sacred Scripture or in previous expressions of Tradition; but at the same time she usually has the intention of solving certain questions or removing certain errors. All these things have to be taken into account in order that these pronouncements may be properly interpreted. Finally, even though the truths which the Church intends to teach through her dogmatic formulas are distinct from the changeable conceptions of a given epoch and can be expressed without them, nevertheless it can sometimes happen that these truths may be enunciated by the Sacred Magisterium in terms that bear traces of such conceptions.

In view of the above, it must be stated that the dogmatic formulas of the Church's Magisterium were from the very beginning suitable for communicating revealed truth, and that as they are they remain for ever suitable for communicating this truth to those who interpret them correctly. It does not however follow that every one of these formulas has always been or will always be so to the same extent. For this reason theologians seek to define exactly the intention of teaching proper to the various formulas, and in carrying out this work they are of considerable assistance to the living Magisterium of the Church, to which they remain subordinated. For this reason also it often happens that ancient dogmatic formulas and others closely connected with them remain living and fruitful in the habitual usage of the Church, but with suitable expository and explanatory additions that maintain and clarify their original meaning. In addition, it has sometimes happened that in this habitual usage of the Church certain of these formulas gave way to new expressions which, proposed and approved by the Sacred Magisterium, presented more clearly or more completely the same meaning.

As for the meaning of dogmatic formulas, this remains ever true and constant in the Church, even when it is expressed with greater clarity or [is] more developed. The faithful therefore must shun the opinion, first, that dogmatic formulas (or some category of them) cannot signify truth in a determinate way, but can only offer changeable approximations to it, which to a certain extent distort or alter it; secondly, that these formulas signify the truth only in an indeterminate way, this truth being like a goal that is constantly being sought by means of such approximations. Those who hold such an opinion do not avoid dogmatic relativism and they corrupt the concept of the Church's infallibility relative to the truth to be taught or held in a determinate way.

"A Courageous Worldwide Theology," an address by Karl Rahner, S.J., at John Carroll University, Cleveland, Ohio, April 6, 1979, on the occasion of receiving an honorary degree marking his seventy-fifth birthday. (Excerpt. Full text in *National Jesuit News*, vol. 8, June 1979, p. 10.)

It is my preference that both the tribute and my thanks be directed toward the contemporary theology in its entirety—that theology shaped in the last 30 years and recognized somewhat officially by the Second Vatican Council.

Of course, I have in mind an orthodox Catholic theology. That goes without saying. A theology which would not be obedient and docile under the word of God as it is proclaimed in the Church would not be Catholic theology. But I am envisaging a Catholic theology that is courageous and does not shun relative and restricted conflicts with Church authorities. I am thinking of a theology which can no longer be uniform in a neoscholastic approach.

I call that time of uniformity the "Pius epoch," but that era of the Popes who bore the name "Pius" has after all come to an end. I envisage a theology which is in dialogue with its time and lives courageously with it and in it.

This is all the more possible because it is characteristic of this time to be at a critical distance from itself, something *God makes possible*. It is a special grace to this age to be able now to have a critical distance from ourselves given us from the Cross of Christ.

From this more critical distance, I envisage a theology which in the Church at large must be the theology of a worldwide Church. That means a theology which does not only recite its own medieval history, but one that can listen to the wisdom of the East, to the longing for freedom in Latin America, and also to the sound of African drums.

I envisage a systematic theology that is an inner unity and what Trinitarian theologians call *perichoresis* (literally a dancing around together) of fundamental and dogmatic theology. I envisage a theology that enables human beings of our time to have a real grasp on the message of freedom and redemption, a theology that courageously abandons external stanchions of seemingly self-evident truths and things, something which does not stem necessarily from what is Christian, but rather from the changing historical situation structured by its intellectual and social elements.

I envisage a theology that does not only move along the numbers in our familiar friend "Denzinger" interpreting old ecclesiastical pronouncements, but a theology which breaks new ground for *new* pronouncements of the Church.

It would be a theology which takes seriously the hierarchy of truths, a theology which lives by the ecumenical hope that baptized Christians should be able to communicate in that which they all live in their faith. Such a communication should be possible without losing sight of the multiplicity of charisms of life and thought.

I envisage a theology which comprehends itself as an interpretation of the reality which through grace is present in every human being; a reality which is not only given to man by external indoctrination.

It would be a theology through which this reality would find itself, and which would not pride itself upon its clear concepts but would force them to open over and over again into the incomprehensibility of God. Such a theology would not secretly seek to understand itself as *the* theoretical underpinning of a life of middle-class ethics supervised by God.

One could continue in this vein for long. But my purpose is not to degrade the old theology, whose grateful children we are and remain. It has been rather to hint from afar that our time calls also us theologians sleeping under the broom tree of orthodoxy like Elijah in old days: *Surge, grandis tibi restat via*–Arise, a long journey lies ahead of you.

DISCUSSION QUESTIONS

I What Is Catholicism? (3)

1. What element(s) did you once think distinguished Catholicism from every other Christian church and tradition? What is your estimate of that (those) distinguishing characteristic(s) now?

2. Do you think the distinctiveness of Catholicism—its openness in principle to all truth and to every value, for example—is reflected in (a) the homilies you hear, (b) the official pronouncements you receive from the pope and bishops of the Church, (c) the catechisms and textbooks you read, or (d) the attitudes of your children, parents, relatives, and friends? If not, wherein lies the discrepancy, and what needs to be emphasized to close the gap?

3. Before reading this chapter, did you equate all Catholics with *Roman* Catholics? Do you see now why that isn't correct? Were you aware that some Anglicans, Protestants, and Orthodox also regard themselves as Catholic? What do you make of their claim?

4. A project: Visit various churches (Protestant, Anglican, Orthodox, Catholic) and note how, if at all, the distinctiveness of their respective traditions is reflected in architecture, sculpture, paintings, images, music, prayer books, and the like.

5. Outline an essay, chapter, or full-length book entitled "Why I Am a Catholic."

II Faith and Its Outcomes: Theology, Doctrine, Discipleship (19)

1. If you think that reason, evidence, and argument play little or no part in the process of *Christian* faith, how do you explain the faith of so many exceedingly insightful, intelligent, and logical people? If you think, on the other hand, that the evidence for *Christian* faith is fairly clear and convincing, how do you explain (a) its lack of persuasive force for other insightful, intelligent, and logical people who choose to remain outside the Church and (b) the continued alienation of insightful, intelligent, and logical people from the Church of their Baptism?

2. Apply these same questions now to *Catholic* faith. Why do so many extraordinarily gifted people remain Catholics? Why are other gifted people still outside the Catholic Church (first, non-Christians, and, second, Protestants, Anglicans, and Orthodox)? Why do you think many gifted Catholics are leaving the Church today?

3. Is it possible to have faith without belonging to a particular religion? Explain. Is it possible to have Christian or Catholic faith without belonging to the Church? Explain.

4. What is a theologian? Does the Church really need theologians?

5. Can you think of any traditions (lowercase *t*) which some Catholics confuse with Tradition (uppercase *T*)? To what effect? Can you think of any elements of Tradition which are taken too lightly, as if they were a matter only of tradition? To what effect?

6. How effectively does the liturgy as presently structured convey the substance of faith to the Church? Can you think of anything in liturgy (whether prayer formulae, rituals, distribution of roles, or other elements) that reflects an unsatisfactory understanding of faith? If you had the chance to change anything in today's liturgy, what would you change, and why?

7. Apply the same kinds of questions to Christian education. Do our catechisms, textbooks, and religious education programs reflect good theology, or defective theology? Explain. If you had a chance to change anything in the field of Christian education today, what would it be, and why?

8. Have you associated the Christian life with "discipleship" before now? How have you understood the term in the past? How do you understand it today? Are you satisfied that the contemporary Catholic Church is truly a community of disciples? Explain.

III *The Human Condition Today* (77)

1. How do you explain the fact that, within a century or so, the Catholic Church officially condemned and then officially welcomed, if not fully endorsed, the modernization of the world?

2. If dialogue and the experience of human interdependence are characteristic of modern life, to what extent is the Church embodying those characteristics in its own structures and institutions and missionary work, and to what extent is it resisting or ignoring them?

3. Do you think fundamentalism in the interpretation of the Bible and the teachings of the Church is a problem in the Church today? Among which groups and/or on which issues? In your opinion, what is the most effective way to deal with such fundamentalists?

IV Understandings of Human Existence (99)

1. Which do you think poses the greater threat to human existence today: the trend in the direction of greater freedom (leading in some cases to extreme permissiveness and license), or the trend in the direction of greater controls over human behavior (whether through behavior modification, advertising, censorship, or other forms of political coercion)?

2. Select your own sampling of current novels, films, and music, and explore the notion of human existence presented in them. Do you think modern artistic trends are in the direction of a spiritually oriented understanding of the human person, or in the direction of a materialistic understanding? Why do you think this is so?

3. In general, do you think that the official teachings of the Church are consistent with, or at odds with, other contemporary approaches to the meaning of human existence? To what extent are the teachings consistent or inconsistent?

V A Theology of Human Existence: Nature, Grace, Original Sin (157)

1. List some traditional Catholic devotional practices which you, or at least your parents, have experienced over the years (e.g., giving up candy and films for Lent, making novenas, reciting prayers as a penance following Confession), or which you have seen other members of the Church, especially priests and sisters, practice in their own lives (e.g., celibacy, periods of silence, the wearing of special dress). How do such practices reflect an understanding of human existence, again with specific reference to nature, grace, and Original Sin? Do actual or recommended changes in such practices necessarily imply a compromise with the world or a weakening of standards? Explain.

2. Modern theologians like Karl Rahner suggest that God's original offer of grace affects us in the very depths of our being, so that we are transformed from within and oriented toward God even before we become conscious and free. If this were not the case, how can we explain the persistence of some fundamental belief in God among people across the whole spectrum of intellectual, ethnic, racial, cultural, and historical differences? In other words, do you think there is something within the human heart that makes us all seekers after God?

3. Do you think Catholicism's understanding of the relationship between nature and grace has, or should have, any real impact on our ordinary, everyday lives? Explain. Do you think that non-Catholics have a fundamentally different understanding of nature and grace? If so, how do those differences manifest themselves?

4. How did you understand and explain Original Sin before reading this chapter? To what extent, if any, has your understanding changed? What questions remain in your mind? How would you at least begin to answer them?

5. It has been said that the Orthodox make too little of Original Sin and the Protestants make too much of it. After struggling with this question, are you more sympathetic with the Orthodox or the Protestants? Or are you generally content with the Catholic approach?

VI Belief and Unbelief: The Search for God
(205)

1. Do you know people who say they do *not* believe in God? Have you ever discussed the matter with them? What reasons do they have for their unbelief? What kinds of responses have you given in the past? In the light of your reading of this book thus far and the discussions provoked by the book, how, if at all, would you modify your responses today?

2. Do you agree with the Second Vatican Council that it is not enough to communicate our beliefs more effectively, but that we must chiefly live up to what we believe and teach? Why do you think that, for many people, example *is* more important than forcefulness of argument?

3. Do you think that education necessarily undermines belief in God? If so, how do you explain the faith of so many intellectually gifted and educationally sophisticated people? If not, how do you explain the data presented by sociologists and historians, and perhaps even by your own experience?

VII Revelation: God's Self-Disclosure to Us
(227)

1. What was your own working definition of *revelation* before reading this chapter? How would you revise that definition now, if at all?

2. If you had been alive at the time of Christ, do you think it would have been easier, or harder, to believe him to be the Son of God?

1216

3. What were your views on prophecy before reading this chapter? Has there been any change in those views? Explain.

4. Do you understand the assertion that the principle of sacramentality is one of the distinguishing characteristics of Catholic theology and of the Catholic tradition generally? Explain it in your own words, giving your own examples. What other principles, if any, would you regard as equally characteristic of Catholic faith and practice?

5. In what sense is it true to say that revelation has been closed? In what sense is it true to say that revelation is a continuing reality? What do you make of the possibility of private revelation? Are there any private revelations you find credible? Why? Are there any you find particularly unpalatable? Why? What are your criteria for judging, one way or the other?

VIII The Triune God (275)

1. What has been your own theological and spiritual stance with regard to the mystery and doctrine of the Trinity? Have you regarded it as something practical or only theoretical? If the doctrine of the Trinity were declared null and void by the Church tomorrow, would it really make any difference to you? If so, why? If not, why not?

2. Do you think other religions are poorer for not having a trinitarian understanding of God? Explain.

3. If you were preparing a class lecture on the Trinity, how would you present it: (a) to a group of Catholic adults, of reasonably good educational background; (b) to a group of high school students; (c) to grammar school students (pick the grade); (d) to children preparing for First Holy Communion; or (e) to a group of Jewish adults?

IX God: Special Questions (333)

1. Do you believe in miracles: the miracles of Jesus, first of all, and then other, more modern miracles (Lourdes cures, for example)? Is your attitude toward miracles challenged in any way by the principles summarized in this chapter?

2. How do you explain the mystery of evil? If it is difficult to reconcile evil with a merciful God, would it be any easier to explain heroic charity if there were no God? What would (or do) you say to console a parent whose young son or daughter has just been killed in an auto accident? How, if at all, would your comment be different if the child had been murdered? Had taken his or her own life? Had died of cancer?

3. Do you think that the constant references to God as "he" distort our understanding not only of God but of human existence, specifically of the relationship between women and men? On the other hand, do you believe we should completely eliminate all reference to the Fatherhood of God? How can we "fix" the problem of androcentric and patriarchal thinking and language without harm to our biblical, liturgical, and doctrinal traditions?

4. Why do you pray? Do you think your prayer is consistent with the theology outlined in this chapter? If not, what theology is implied in the way you pray and in your intentions at prayer?

X Religion and Its Varieties (359)

1. Did you ever catch yourself saying, "She [He] is a very religious person"? What did you mean by *religious?* How would you now distinguish a religious person from a non-religious person?

2. Have you ever spoken to any non-Christians about their religion? What have you found most attractive about their religion? Least attractive? Why? Do you think you individually, and the Church collectively, really have anything substantial to learn from non-Christian religions? If so, what specifically? If not, how do you explain the teaching of Vatican II?

3. What do you make of the balance between the charismatic and institutional elements of Catholicism today? Do you think the one dominates the other? If so, to what effect? Give examples.

4. Have you ever met persons who use the argument that they have no need for religion, that they have a personal relationship with God wherever they happen to be? How have you answered them in the past? How would you answer them today?

5. Most Christians know relatively little about non-Christian religions. In the light of the brief review offered in this chapter, were you more surprised by the similarities, or by the differences, between Christianity and the non-Christian religious? Explain.

XI Christ and Contemporary Culture (399)

1. Do you agree that people, even within the Church, have different notions of Jesus Christ? How many different ideas about Christ are you aware of among your friends, in your parish, school, or elsewhere? Which ideas seem to predominate? Why do you think so? What practical effect, if any, do these ideas about Christ have on the life of the Church?

2. Do you think young people take Christ seriously today? If so, what is their principal understanding of Christ? If not, why not? What practical suggestions would you urge upon the Church to help it do a better job of reaching young people? What, if any, are the Church's major failings in this regard at present?

3. Are you generally comfortable with people who criticize the Church? If not, why not? If so, which people do you think are genuinely prophetic in the Church today? Is there any evidence that the Church has changed for the better because of them? Be specific.

4. If you passed a car bearing the bumper sticker, "Honk If You Love Jesus," would you honk your horn? If so, why? If not, why not? If you had to design a bumper sticker of your own, what wording would you use to get your own message across concerning Christ?

5. We hear a lot these days about the necessity of the Church being "countercultural." What do you think people mean by that? How would you explain the countercultural role of the Church?

XII *The Christ of the New Testament* (415)

1. Before reading this chapter, what was your own understanding of the historical character of the New Testament? Did you regard the gospels as biographies of Jesus? If not, to what do you attribute your more nuanced understanding?

2. Is there anything in this chapter regarding the resurrection that especially surprised (or even disturbed) you? Explain.

3. What has been your understanding of the purpose of Jesus' death? Are you troubled by the explanation of vicarious atonement suggested in this chapter, or reassured? Why?

4. Do you usually think of Jesus as a Jew? If not, why not? Do you think your view is the usual view of other Catholics or of other Christians? If not, why not?

5. Why is it important that we understand correctly how the Jews at the time of Jesus were involved in his being handed over to the Romans for judgment? Do you think our understanding has anything to do with our attitude to Jews today?

6. If you had been asked before reading this book—and certainly before reading this chapter—what was at the heart of Jesus' whole message, how would you have answered the question? How would you answer it now? If your present answer is different, indicate some of its practical implications for Christian faith.

7. What place does the Kingdom of God occupy in the Church's preaching and teaching today? Does it make a difference one way or the other? Explain.

8. Does the use of the term *Kingdom of God* pose a problem for you? Would you prefer *Reign of God*, or some other term? Explain.

XIII The Christ of Postbiblical Theology and Doctrine (461)

1. Which do you think had been most in danger of being undermined in the early centuries of the Church: the divinity of Christ, or his humanity? What about the situation in the Church today? Explain.

2. Does this historical survey make it any easier to understand why we cannot simply quote texts from one ecumenical council or another in order to "prove" a particular theological argument? Explain.

3. In your own catechetical and/or theological education, was the resurrection presented as an integral part of Christ's redemptive work, or was it seen principally as a reward for Christ and a proof of his divinity? Again, what difference does it make one way or the other in the life of the Church and in your own spiritual life?

XIV The Christ of Contemporary Theology (491)

1. If you asked a random sample of churchgoers, "What was the heart of Jesus' preaching and teaching?" what kind of answer(s) would you expect to receive? How would you yourself answer the question?

2. What is the operative Christology of the so-called evangelical, or pentecostal, or charismatic Christians? In what ways is it consistent with the principles outlined in this chapter and in the two previous chapters? In what ways is charismatic Christology inattentive to these Christological principles?

3. How would you answer a person who says, "I don't care whether Jesus was divine or not, whether he rose from the dead or not, or anything like that. What matters for me is that Jesus is a symbol of what it means to be human, and by following his example I, too, can be fully human"?

4. How would you answer a person who says, "I don't like all this talk about liberation and politics in reference to Our Lord. He wasn't a political person. He was the Son of God, interested not in changing the world but in saving our souls"?

XV Special Questions in Christology (539)

1. Before reading this chapter, what was your general understanding of the virginal conception of Jesus? Did you think it an important truth of Christian faith? If so, why? If not, why not?

2. What did you understand about the sinlessness of Jesus before doing this chapter? Do you find the distinction between *impeccantia* and *impeccabilitas* important and helpful—namely, that Jesus did not sin, but that this does not mean he was absolutely incapable of sinning?

3. Were you surprised to learn that some scholars and theologians are ready to concede that Jesus was ignorant about certain things, and even occasionally was in error? How did you understand the knowledge of Jesus before reading this chapter? Do you see how Jesus' freedom as a human being would have been compromised if he knew precisely what the future had in store for him? If not, why not?

4. Does it shake your faith at all to contemplate the possibility that Jesus may have had sexual desires? What if it were historically verified that Jesus was married? Would that undermine his message and the Church's faith in him as the unique Son of God? Explain.

5. Are you generally satisfied with the way sexuality has been discussed and taught by the Church—for example, in the Church's art, spirituality, catechisms, sermons, retreats, and counseling sessions? If not, why not? If so, how do you explain the fact that so many people have complained about the effect of the Church's attitude on their own psychic health?

XVI The Church of the New Testament (571)

1. The relationship between local churches and the universal Church is important, but it is sometimes misunderstood. Give examples of instances where the universality of the Church has been exaggerated at the expense of its local character, and examples of where its local character has been stressed to the point of neglecting its universality. Do you think the relationship between the two is properly understood and operative in the Catholic Church today?

2. On the basis of the New Testament, how would you answer someone who says, "I don't need a Church. My faith is in the person of Jesus."

3. In the New Testament, the Church assumed a different character and structure as it took root in different communities (Jewish, Hellenistic, or combinations of the two). Can you think of anything comparable in the Church of today? What does this adaptation say about the need for unity rather than uniformity?

4. Are the common elements (summarized in point 12 of the Summary) still the common elements present in all of the local churches today? If not, which are missing? Why? To what effect? Are there additional common elements? If so, which are they?

5. All offices and ministries are for the sake of service, not domination. Do you think that New Testament ideal has been adhered to in today's Church? Explain.

6. The term *People of God* has been used frequently since the Second Vatican Council. Do you think it adequately expresses the nature of the Church? Explain.

7. Do you think the image of the Body of Christ makes much difference? What practical effect *should* that image have on our life as Christians and on the activity of the Church today?

8. Answer the same questions in relation to the image of the Temple of the Holy Spirit.

XVII *The Church in History (607)*

1. Would the abolition of obligatory celibacy for priests of the Latin rite be comparable to the exemption from circumcision? What about the ordination of women to the priesthood?

2. Does it necessarily follow that when the Church is persecuted it must be doing something right? Does it necessarily follow that the Church will always be a more committed Church when under persecution? Discuss these questions in relation to the history of the Church.

3. Do you think the Edict of Constantine was, in the long run, a positive factor in the subsequent history of the Church, or a negative one?

4. The Gregorian Reform of the twelfth century was not an unmixed blessing. Some evils were rooted out, but the papacy itself accrued too much power to itself. Does this say anything about the nature of reform? Does it say anything about where reform should be initiated, and by whom?

5. In the light of history, discuss the significance of Pope John Paul I's decision in 1978 not to be crowned with the papal tiara, a decision which broke a nine-hundred-year tradition.

6. In view of the recent history of the Church, was the Second Vatican Council a leap into the future, or the product of some organic development? Explain.

7. In general, do you think Christians (and Catholics in particular) know much, little, or no church history? Comment on the implications of your answer.

XVIII The Church of the Second Vatican Council (655)

1. Were you aware of the two currents of theology in existence *before* Vatican II? If not, how did you think Vatican II happened? Were you under the impression it was a natural evolution, or a break with the immediate past? Do you still see any evidence of these two currents of theology in the Church today?

2. Did you know anything about Pope John XXIII before reading this chapter? If so, what opinion did you have of him? Do you remember him while he was alive? What were your impressions then, and now? If you do not personally remember him, what were you first told about him? How does that information compare with your present appreciation? Compare him with other popes you are familiar with, either in early history, in the recent past, or in the present.

3. From your knowledge of the council documents, would you add or subtract any principles on the list of ten principles in the last section of the chapter? Give reasons.

4. On balance, do you think the Second Vatican Council was a plus or a minus for the Catholic Church? Explain.

XIX The Church in Contemporary Theology and Doctrine (691)

1. Do you think the post–Vatican II ecclesiology, as summarized in this chapter, is reflected in (a) homilies, (b) religious education programs, (c) official statements from your local bishop, (d) university, college, and seminary courses, (e) catechisms and other textbooks, (f) church laws and regulations, (g) the thinking of your fellow parishioners and/or students, (h) the thinking of your closest friends? Do you think there are discrepancies between the post–Vatican II ecclesiology and any or all of these categories? If so, what are some of these discrepancies?

2. Which of the three models, or perspectives (institution, community, servant), is dominant in (a) your parish, (b) your school, (c) your religious education program, (d) your community (religious or geographical), (e) your home and among your closest friends, (f) the rules and regulations of the Church? If all three are integrated at each of these levels, how do you explain that? If they are not integrated, how do you explain *that*? How can any imbalance best be corrected?

3. Suggest some ways in which the Church could be more effective than it is in the mission of (a) proclamation (give special attention to teaching, preaching, worship, and prophecy), (b) signification (give special attention to lifestyles and institutional changes), and (c) service (indicate problems in the world, the nation, your area, or your parish which the Church could help solve).

4. Do you think the word *Catholic* applies only to members of the Catholic Church? Do you know some non-Catholics who are Catholic in spirit? Explain. Do you know some Catholics who are *not* Catholic in spirit? Explain.

XX *Special Questions in Ecclesiology* (739)

1. Give an example of ecclesiastical authority which is exercised today in a manner consistent with the model of Jesus and the principles of the New Testament. Give an example of the opposite.

2. In the early Church, bishops were assumed to have special gifts of the Holy Spirit, and they were selected bishops for that reason. What qualities would you look for in a prospective bishop if this ancient principle were to be adhered to?

3. On the basis of the historical evidence (including the New Testament), do you think it possible for a Catholic to dismiss the Petrine ministry as essentially unimportant to the life and mission of the Church? If so, why? If not, why do you think so many Catholics today do discount the significance of the Bishop of Rome?

4. What was your own operative definition of ministry before reading this chapter? Would you change it in light of the chapter? Explain.

5. Were you surprised that women were so much (or so little) involved in the life of the early Church? Explain.

6. What do you think of the arguments for and against the ordination of women to the priesthood? Which side would most of your friends be on, and why? What about the majority of your fellow parishioners? Do you think the Catholic Church will ever ordain women? Why? Why not?

XXI *The Sacraments in General* (787)

1. Can you think of any "secular sacraments," i.e., ways in which people apart from the Church express their relationship with God through the things of this world? Do you think the Church's seven sacraments have any "secular" equivalents? In other words, are there "secular" forms of initiation, of expressing solidarity with others, of reconciliation, of healing, and so on?

2. Do you think there is a balance today in our understanding of sacraments as both signs of faith and causes of grace? If not, where do you find an imbalance? Why do you think it exists? What can be done about it?

3. Do you think most people recognize the liturgical dimension of every sacrament—that every sacrament is an act of worship? How would you explain that dimension to someone who does not understand it?

4. Have you ever had the experience (referred to by Vatican II) whereby "the very act of celebrating" a sacrament actually produced the proper disposition in your heart and mind? Has the opposite ever happened to you, where a poorly celebrated sacrament actually undermined a good disposition?

5. Did you think that each of the seven sacraments was directly, immediately, and explicitly instituted by Christ? If not, how did you link the sacraments with Christ? How would you explain this question of "institution by Christ" to someone who thinks that Christ did indeed arrange for each rite?

XXII The Sacraments of Initiation: Baptism, Confirmation, and Eucharist (805)

1. Is there a catechumenate program in your parish? Do you see the point in restoring the catechumenate today? If not, why not? If so, how can a good catechumenate program affect the life of the whole parish?

2. Have you been to a Confirmation recently? What did the bishop say during his homily? What do you think is the common understanding of your friends and/or fellow parishioners regarding Confirmation? Do you think most are aware of the historical development of the separate rite of Confirmation? Were you aware of it? Suppose you were the bishop. What points would you make in a Confirmation sermon?

3. If you are old enough, do you remember much of the traditional Latin Mass? Compare it with the present Eucharist in the light of the historical development. Regardless of your age, do you think the liturgical changes mandated by Vatican II are an improvement, a regression, or of no consequence one way or the other? What do you think are the most significant changes in the celebration of the Eucharist?

XXIII The Sacraments of Healing: Penance and Anointing of the Sick (835)

1. If you have "received" and/or administered the sacrament of Penance in both the "old way" (confession in a darkened confessional box) and the "new way" (face-to-face exchange in a reconciliation room, with Scripture readings and varied penances), compare them in the light of the principles outlined in this chapter. Do you think the Church should return to the ancient practice of once-in-a-lifetime Penance? Why? How else would the forgiveness of sins be carried out if the sacrament of Penance were not regularly available as it is today?

2. Have you ever been anointed, or seen anyone anointed, in the "old way" and/or according to the new rite? If so, how did either or both act(s) of celebration reflect the historical facts and theological principles outlined in this chapter?

3. What would you say to a person who expressed fear of receiving the sacrament of the Anointing of the Sick?

4. Can you think of situations where it might be more appropriate for someone who is not a priest to administer these sacraments? Even under the present law of the Catholic Church (restricting their administration to a priest), what can a lay person or religious or deacon do that would help communicate the grace of these sacraments?

5. Do you think the recent emphasis on healings in certain Christian circles is consistent with the New Testament concern for healing and the forgiveness of sins? Do you think many people still regard sickness as a punishment for sin? To what effect?

XXIV The Sacraments of Vocation and Commitment: Matrimony and Holy Order (851)

1. Before reading this chapter, did you realize how significant the teaching of Vatican II was regarding the sacrament of Matrimony? Do you find the council's broadened perspective reflected in (a) your own attitude, (b) the attitude of your friends, (c) the attitude of priests, or (d) the attitude of society at large? How do those attitudes differ from Vatican II, if at all?

2. Do you think the Catholic Church is still too strict about divorce and remarriage? If so, why? Do you think the Church has become too permissive about remarriage? If so, why? If you were giving advice to an engaged couple and you heard one or both of them say, "Oh, well, if it doesn't work out, we can try again with someone else," what response would you make?

3. What is your reaction to the complexity of the New Testament record on the sacrament of Holy Order? Does the biblical evidence tend to undermine your faith in the authority of bishops and priests?

4. Apart from present laws limiting priesthood in the Latin rite to celibate males, would you like to serve the Church as a priest? Why? Why not? A bishop? Why? Why not?

XXV Christian Morality: A Historical Perspective (883)

1. When some complain today that the Church does not put enough emphasis on the Ten Commandments, are they concerned about the loss of a sense of our covenantal relationship with God, or do they seem to be regarding the Decalogue principally as a charter of Christian morality? In any case, how would you respond to this complaint?

2. Are you surprised that there was no single teaching authority in the Old Testament? Is this consistent, or inconsistent, with what we saw about teaching authority in the New Testament? How important do you think teaching authority is in relation to the actual observance of God's will? If very important, what room do you leave for personal responsibility? If unimportant, what role, if any, do extrinsic or objective norms have in moral decision-making?

3. What do you make of the connection between Christian faith and poverty? For example, is it always better to be poor than to be rich? Does God speak primarily through the poor? Does God speak at all through those who are not poor? If the Church is called to live according to the spirit of poverty, what does that mean?

4. There has been a strongly antisexual bias in Catholic moral theology from time to time. Do you know of Catholics who have left the Church because of this bias? Do you know of other Catholics who are upset because the Church seems too permissive these days about matters of sexual morality? What is your own impression of the present state of Catholic moral teaching on this question: too negative about sexuality, too liberal, or just about right?

5. In general, do you think the Church (Catholic or other) has become too much interested in social, economic, and political issues today, or is it not interested enough? How would you answer those who complain that the Church is losing its spiritual and religious significance, that its principal task is somehow to link time and eternity?

XXVI Foundations of Christian Morality (921)

1. When some Catholics and other Christians complain that nowadays we do not seem to be paying sufficient attention to sin, what do you think they mean? How would you respond to their concern?

2. Do you think all, most, many, some, a few, or no Christians have truly been converted to Christ and the Kingdom of God? Explain. In that connection, what do you make of the recent emphasis of some evangelical Christians on the need to be "reborn" in Christ?

1227

3. Does the principle of subsidiarity apply to such cases as the ordination of women, obligatory celibacy for priests, standards of seminary education and religious formation, the election of bishops? Is the principle faithfully observed, or violated, in the Church today? Explain.

4. Are there particular people you admire for their courage (fortitude)? Who are they, and what evidence of courage do you see in them? To what extent was Jesus courageous?

5. Do you think the institutionalization of charity today has diminished the need or the opportunity for works of mercy? How can the works of mercy be carried out in highly technological societies that have strong central governments?

6. In light of this chapter, what meaning does the principle "Let your conscience be your guide" have?

XXVII Christian Morality: Special Questions (981)

1. Can you think of any other arguments in favor of the traditional teaching against contraception? Can you think of any additional arguments against the traditional teaching? Do you think *Humanæ Vitæ*'s case looks stronger, or weaker, in light of developments since 1968?

2. Why do you think the overwhelming majority of Catholics of childbearing age do not follow the moral directives of *Humanæ Vitæ?* What is your own view and (where applicable) practice? Do you think Catholics who do not follow the teaching of *Humanæ Vitæ* are unworthy Catholics?

3. Which position regarding the morality of homosexuality do you most readily identify with: always sinful, neutral, or essentially imperfect? Would you prefer a fourth position? How do you reconcile your position (if it is not the first one) with the biblical record and the teaching of the Catholic Church? How do you reconcile your position (if it *is* the first one) with recent developments in psychology and moral theology?

4. Do you think homosexuality is an appropriate topic for this chapter? Do you think it provides a good exercise in moral analysis to face such a controversial issue head-on? If not, why not?

5. Do you think Catholics, or Christians generally, take either the principle of subsidiarity or the process of socialization into account when making up their political minds? Do you think Catholic social doctrine makes any significant difference to Catholic and/or Christian political opinions and behavior? If so, why do you think so? If not, why not?

6. Select an economic issue like health care and analyze it according to the moral principles and values given in this chapter.

7. What do you think about abortion? Is it always wrong, no matter what the circumstances? If not, under what circumstances is it morally permissible?

8. Is it possible to be antiabortion on moral grounds but prochoice on legal or political grounds? Do you think that all of God's moral laws should be enforced by civil law? How do you understand the relationship between moral law and civil law? Apply your answer to both the abortion issue and the birth control issue.

XXVIII Christian Spirituality (1019)

1. Have you ever referred to another person or persons as "very spiritual"? What did you mean by that? What do you look for in such a person's character and behavior? Do you think that many people who have been regarded as "unspiritual" were really more "spiritual" than their detractors thought? If so, give some examples.

2. Do you think Christian spirituality is still too much influenced by the concerns of monks, priests, and religious? If so, give examples. What points would you like to see incorporated into and emphasized in a genuinely "lay" spirituality?

3. How important to Christian spirituality are popular devotions (e.g., Sacred Heart, Marian)? Do you have any such devotional practices in your own life? If so, why are they important to you? If not, why do you think they are so unimportant to your Christian life?

4. Do you think the basic principles of the Second Vatican Council regarding the spiritual life have been assimilated into the Catholic Church today? Indicate where they have and where they have not.

5. Have you had any contact with some of the modern movements mentioned in this chapter—e.g., Marriage Encounter, Cursillo, Charismatic Renewal, retreats? If so, what has been your reaction? If not, do you at least know of people who have been involved with these movements? What impression do these people make on you?

6. When you hear church officials and others saying that we need a renewal of spirituality today, what do you think they really mean? What would you mean if you made the same kind of statement? Would you make such a statement? If not, why not?

XXIX Worship: Liturgy, Prayer, Devotions (1063)

1. The ancient axiom "The rule of prayer is the rule of belief" brings out the intimate connection between faith and its various ritual expressions. What happens when we do not believe what we "act out"? What happens when we do not "act out" what we believe? Give examples drawn from political and cultural life as well as from religious life.

2. The Second Vatican Council said that the liturgy (especially the Eucharist) is at the heart of the whole Christian life and is the source from which all else flows. Do you think the liturgy actually functions in that way in your parish or religious community? If not, how would you change the way it is done?

3. How essential do you think prayer is to the Christian life? Is it possible to be a good Christian and never pray? How specifically do you understand the word *prayer*. Do you know of any "prayerful" people who are really odd rather than holy? Do you know of any "prayerful" people who are models of Christian life? How do you explain the difference?

4. Why do you think devotions have declined in recent years? Which, if any, traditional devotions do you think are still important to the life of the Church? If you could create a new devotion, more in keeping with the culture, the times, and the life of the Church, what would it be like?

XXX Mary and the Saints (1077)

1. Are you surprised by the New Testament data on Mary? Did you expect more, or less, about her? Were you aware of the diversity of attitudes toward Mary—e.g., those of Mark and Luke? If not, why do you think this was never mentioned in sermons, in catechism classes, and so on?

2. What do you make of the reported apparitions of Mary at places such as Lourdes and Fatima? Do you believe in them? If so, do they make any difference in your life? Do they enhance your understanding of Christian faith? If you do not believe in them, why not?

3. Secure a copy, or copies, of some Marian devotional literature and analyze it theologically, in light of the teachings of the Second Vatican Council. Is it consistent, or inconsistent, with Vatican II?

4. In your parish and/or within the circle of your own friends and colleagues, is there a stronger tendency toward minimalism, or toward maximalism, in Marian devotion? Explain.

5. What do you think of the suggestion that devotion to Mary is important to highlight the femininity of God? What role, if any, has Marian devotion played in the way the Church has understood and depicted women? Do you think Mary has anything at all to "say" to the feminist movement today, whether positively or negatively?

6. Do you pray to Mary and the saints? If so, which saints and why? If not, why not?

7. Why do you think so many canonized saints are priests and nuns? If you were in charge of making saints today, which contemporary Christians—living or dead—would you regard as good candidates? Explain.

XXXI *The Last Things* (1123)

1. What is your own experience and/or impressions of the way eschatology is presented in homilies, catechisms, religious education, and even formal theology courses and programs today? Is the emphasis more on the destiny of all humankind and all creation, or on the individual? Is there any future dimension at all? Is it only future-oriented?

2. How important is the Kingdom of God in Christian belief and practice? How can it best be explained to people today?

3. A young man or woman has just been killed in an auto accident. What do you say to the parents? Would your words or gestures be any different if the young person had died after a long illness?

4. How can we "see" God "face to face" if God is spirit? What do you say to a child who asks, "What is heaven like?" What do you say to a skeptical friend who asks, "Do you still believe in that heaven stuff?"

5. Had you assumed that the doctrine of purgatory was "out"? Does anyone you know talk about it at all? What do you make of the present attitude toward purgatory? Do you believe in it? Explain.

6. What do you believe about hell? Is it a place? If so, how do you imagine it? Do you think anyone is there? Is it a state? If so, what do you mean by that? Is it nothing at all? If so, why has the Church taught about it so long?

7. Do you believe in demons, or evil spirits? Apparently, many of our contemporaries do, to judge by films, television shows, and books. How do you explain this fascination with evil spirits in a world so scientifically and technologically advanced as ours?

8. Do you believe in limbo? Do you know anyone who does? Do you think, on the whole, the doctrine of limbo has been helpful, or unhelpful, to parents who have lost a child at birth or in infancy (before Baptism)?

9. Do you believe in the Second Coming of Christ? If not, why not? If so, what difference does that belief make in your understanding and practice of Christian faith?

10. On what basis do you think God will judge you after your death? Do you think that some members of the Church would be harsher on you than God? Explain.

XXXII Catholicism: A Synthesis (1187)

1. Now that you have read and discussed this entire book, how would you put in your own words the meaning and value of Catholicism?

2. Do you think the explanation of Catholicism given in this book is the common understanding of Catholicism among non-Catholics today? If not, what are the differences? Do you think the explanation given in this book is the common understanding that Catholics themselves have of their own tradition? If not, what are the differences?

3. Do you think the Catholic Church today faithfully embodies the best of the Catholic tradition? If not, where are the discrepancies? What needs to be done to close the gap?

4. If someone approached you today and said, "I'm thinking about becoming a Catholic," would you encourage or discourage the person? Explain. If the person asked you, "Are you happy being a Catholic?" how would you answer the question?

GLOSSARY

(The purpose of this glossary is *not* to provide new information or greater precision. Each term has already been explained, and in most cases defined, in the text itself. The reader should consult the Index of Subjects for such references. The glossary is provided instead as a convenience to the reader, as a quick memory-refresher and time-saver.)

ADOPTIONISM General term for views which look upon Jesus Christ as the purely human, "adopted" son of God.

AGNOSTICISM The suspension of belief regarding the reality of God.

ALEXANDRIA, SCHOOL OF Theological and catechetical center in Egypt, from the end of the second century, which emphasized the divinity of Christ.

ANALOGICAL IMAGINATION Pertains to a typically Catholic way of thinking about God and of understanding the divine-human encounter that seeks always to find "similarity-in-difference."

ANATHEMA An official condemnation by the Church of a doctrinal or moral position.

ANNULMENT An official declaration that a canonically valid marriage never existed between the two parties.

ANOINTING OF THE SICK The new name for the sacrament of Extreme Unction, which is for those seriously sick and/or in danger of death.

ANTHROPOLOGY, THEOLOGICAL The interpretation of human existence in the light of Christian faith. Includes the theology of *grace* (see below).

ANTICHRIST The personification of all historical forces hostile to God.

ANTINOMIANISM A disregard or contempt for law.

ANTIOCH, SCHOOL OF Theological and catechetical center in Syria, from the end of the second century, which emphasized the humanity of Jesus.

APOCALYPTICISM A comprehensive name for a style of thought and writing from about 200 B.C. to A.D. 100, emphasizing visions, signs, and predictions of future events beyond history brought about by divine power.

APOCRYPHA Old Testament books written in Greek that are included in the Catholic Bible but often omitted in Protestant Bibles (e.g., Judith, 1 and 2 Maccabees, Sirach, Tobit, Wisdom).

APOKATASTASIS The belief, associated with Origen, that every human being (and even angels and demons) will ultimately be saved.

APOLLINARIANISM The fourth-century heresy that denied the existence of a rational soul in Christ.

APOLOGETICS That part of theology which tries to show the reasonableness of Christian faith and to refute objections against it.

APOSTASY The deliberate and complete abandonment of the faith by a baptized Christian.

APOSTLE Literally, "one who is sent." A missionary of the Church in the New Testament period. The term is not co-extensive with *the Twelve* (see below).

APOSTOLIC FATHERS The name for the oldest, nonbiblical, and orthodox Christian writings, e.g., the *Didache*, Clement of Rome, Ignatius of Antioch, the *Shepherd of Hermas*, Polycarp of Smyrna.

APOSTOLICITY A mark of the Church identifying its faith and practice with those of the Apostles.

APOSTOLIC SUCCESSION In the wider sense, the process by which the whole Church continues, and is faithful to, the word, the witness, and the service of the Apostles. In the stricter sense, the legitimation of the bishops' office and authority by their valid derivation from the Apostles.

ARIANISM The heresy, condemned by the council of Nicea (325), which made the Son of God the highest of creatures, greater than us but less than God.

ASCENSION The risen Christ's "going up" into heaven to enter into his final glory at "the right hand of the Father."

ASCETICISM Exercises undertaken to live the Gospel more faithfully, especially in light of the cross of Christ and the sacrificial nature of his whole life.

ASSUMPTION Dogma defined in 1950 by Pope Pius XII that the body of the Blessed Virgin Mary was taken directly to heaven after her life on earth had ended.

ATHEISM The denial of the reality of God.

ATONEMENT The act of healing the breach between God and humankind opened by sin. Although usually associated with the crucifixion of Christ, it applies to the whole Paschal Mystery.

AUTHENTICITY OF CHURCH TEACH-INGS A quality of teachings which have authority because they are issued by persons holding a canonically recognized teaching office in the Church.

AUTHENTICITY OF SACRED SCRIP-TURE A quality of the various books of the Bible by which they are recognized to have been produced by the individuals or communities with whom the Church associates these writings.

BAPTISM The sacrament of rebirth by which one becomes a member of the Church and a new creature in Christ.

BAPTISM OF BLOOD The martyrdom of an unbaptized person.

BAPTISM OF DESIRE The process by which individuals are said to merit eternal life because of their good will, even though, through no fault of their own, they have not been baptized with water.

BEATIFIC VISION The final union with God in heaven, when the saved see God "face to face."

BIBLE The collection of sacred writings accepted by the Church as inspired by God and normative for Christian faith.

BISHOP Literally, an "overseer." A priest of the third order. If he heads a diocese, he is called the Ordinary or local bishop.

BODY OF CHRIST A term which designates the human body of Christ, his risen body, his eucharistic body, and the Church.

CANON A list which serves as a "rule" or "measuring rod."

CANON LAW, CODE OF Body of church laws. For the Roman Catholic Church, promulgated in 1983 (and superseding that of 1917); for the Eastern Catholic churches, promulgated in 1990.

CANONICAL FORM The requirement that Roman Catholics normally marry in the presence of three persons: the local bishop, the pastor, or a priest or deacon delegated by either one, and two witnesses (canon 1108).

CANON OF SCRIPTURE The official list of inspired books of the Bible, solemnly defined by the Council of Trent (1546).

CANON OF THE MASS The Eucharistic Prayer, or Anaphora.

CAPPADOCIAN FATHERS Basil of Cæsarea, his brother Gregory of Nyssa, and Gregory of Nazianzus, well known for their writings about the Trinity and Christology.

CARDINAL VIRTUES Prudence, justice, temperance, and fortitude.

CASUISTRY The science of applying moral principles to specific "cases."

CATECHESIS The process of "echoing" the Gospel, of introducing young people or adult converts to the main elements of the Christian faith.

CATECHUMEN An unbaptized person who is undergoing catechesis in preparation for entrance into the Church.

CATECHUMENATE The formal stage of preparation for entrance into the Church.

CATHOLIC CHURCH The Catholic communion of churches (Roman and Eastern-rite alike) which are in full communion with the Bishop of Rome.

CATHOLICITY Mark of the Church that emphasizes its universality, its inclusiveness, and its openness to truth and value wherever they might be found.

CHALCEDON The city in Asia Minor where in 451 the fourth ecumenical council was held, in which it was defined that Jesus Christ is true God and true man, and that his divine and human natures are united in one divine person, without confusion, change, division, or separation.

CHARACTER, MORAL That which gives orientation, direction, and shape to our lives. The cluster of virtues which makes a person what he or she is.

CHARACTER, SACRAMENTAL The permanent effect of three sacraments: Baptism, Confirmation, and Holy Order. (Hence, these sacraments are never conferred more than once.)

CHARISM A gift of the Holy Spirit.

CHARITY Theological virtue of love —of God and of neighbor.

CHASTITY That virtue, associated with the cardinal virtue of temperance, by which the sexual appetite is healthily integrated into the whole of one's personality.

CHRISTOLOGY The theological study of Jesus Christ: natures, person, ministry, consciousness, etc. Christology "from above" begins with the Word of God (*Logos*) in heaven and tends to emphasize the divinity of Christ. Christology "from below" begins with the Jesus of history and tends to emphasize his humanity.

CHURCH The worldwide body of Christians known as the community of disciples, the Body of Christ, the People of God, the Temple of the Holy Spirit. See also *Communion of Saints* (below).

CIRCUMINCESSION The reciprocal presence, or indwelling, of the three divine Persons in one another. Also known as *perichoresis*.

CLASSICISM The philosophical worldview which holds that reality (truth) is essentially static, unchanging, and unaffected by history or culture.

COLLEGIALITY The principle that the Church is a communion (college) of local churches which together constitute the Church universal. In practice, collegiality introduces a mode of decision-making in the Church which emphasizes coresponsibility among the bishops expressed in ecumenical councils, synods, and episcopal conferences.

COMMUNICATIO IDIOMATUM The "communication [interchange] of properties" between the divine and human natures of Jesus Christ because both natures are united in one divine Person, without confusion. The properties of both natures can and must be applied to, or predicated of, the one divine person; e.g., "The Son of God was crucified," and "The Son of Mary created the world."

COMMUNICATIO IN SACRIS Literally, "communication in sacred things." Participation in the liturgy of a church other than one's own, especially through eucharistic sharing.

COMMUNION OF SAINTS The spiritual union of the whole community of believers in Christ, living and dead. Those on earth are called the *Church Militant*. Those in purgatory are the *Church Suffering*. Those in heaven are the *Church Triumphant*.

CONCILIARISM The medieval movement which viewed an ecumenical council as superior in authority to the pope.

CONCUPISCENCE Natural "desires," impulses, or instincts of human persons which move them toward something morally good or morally evil even before they have begun any moral reflection about it.

CONFIRMATION The second sacrament of initiation, known in the East as chrismation, by which the recipient is sealed with the gifts of the Holy Spirit.

CONSCIENCE The experience of ourselves as moral agents, as persons responsible for our actions.

CONSTANTINOPLE Seat of the Byzantine Empire where a council, held in 381, defined the divinity of the Holy Spirit.

CONSUBSTANTIATION The Reformation view that the bread and wine remain along with the body and blood of Christ after the eucharistic consecration. To be distinguished from *transubstantiation* (see below).

CONTEMPLATION Conscious attention to, and focus upon, the presence of God.

CONVENIENCE, ARGUMENT FROM A method of reaching theological conclusions on the basis of their seeming appropriateness. Especially applicable to *Mariology* (see below).

CONVERSION The fundamental change of heart (*metanoia*) by which a person turns away from a former mode of life and accepts Jesus as the Christ and orients her or his whole life around Christ and the Kingdom of God.

COREDEMPTRIX A title sometimes given to the Blessed Virgin Mary to emphasize her cooperative role in the redemption of the human race by her Son.

COUNCIL An official church assembly. It may be *ecumenical* (the "whole wide world"), *regional*, or *local* (one or several local churches).

COUNTER-REFORMATION The Catholic response to the Protestant Reformation of the sixteenth century. At the center was the Council of Trent and its reform of doctrine, liturgy, and law.

COVENANT The bond, contract, or "testament" between God and Israel in the Old Testament, and between God and the whole human community in the New Testament, established by the blood of Christ.

CREATION The original and ongoing act of God by which reality is produced and sustained from nothingness.

CREATURE Whatever is not God and depends on God for its existence.

CREED An official profession of faith, usually promulgated by a council of the Church and used in the Church's liturgy. Also known as a *symbol* (see below).

CRITICISM, FORM A method of biblical study employed to uncover the second layer of tradition in the composition of the Gospels, namely, the oral proclamation of the Apostles and the disciples (catechesis, narratives, hymns, prayers, etc.).

CRITICISM, HISTORICAL A method of biblical study employed to uncover the first layer of tradition in the composition of the Gospels, namely, the original words and deeds of Jesus.

CRITICISM, REDACTION A method of biblical study employed to uncover the third layer of tradition in the composition of the Gospels, namely, the writings themselves.

DAMNATION The fate of those who die in the state of unrepented mortal sin.

DECALOGUE The Ten Commandments.

DEISM A view of God which looks upon God as a divine "watchmaker." Once the world has been created, God no longer takes an active part in its course. Rejected by Vatican I (1869).

DEMYTHOLOGIZATION A method of New Testament interpretation originated by Rudolf Bultmann. It seeks to get back to the original message of Jesus by stripping away all irrelevant stories (myths) about Jesus' divine powers and his comings and goings between heaven and earth.

DENZINGER A collection of excerpts from church documents, first published by Heinrich Joseph Denzinger in 1854.

DEONTOLOGICAL Pertaining to a way of doing moral theology which emphasizes duty and obligation in relation to law.

DEPOSIT OF FAITH The "content" of Christian faith given by Christ and the Apostles and preserved as a treasury by the Church ever since.

DESCENT INTO HELL The item in the Apostles' Creed which refers to the time between the crucifixion and the resurrection when Jesus was "among the dead." It does not refer to hell as a state of eternal punishment for sin, but rather to *Sheol* (see below).

DEVIL The name used for Lucifer or Satan, chief of the fallen angels.

DEVOTIONS Nonliturgical prayers and practices.

DIACONATE The ministry of a deacon of the Church, i.e., an ordained assistant to the *bishop* or the *presbyter* (see below).

DIALECTICAL Pertains to a typically Protestant way of thinking that emphasizes always what is unique in God and, therefore, the radical dissimilarities that exist between the divine and the human.

DIDACHE Late first-century work that presents important "teaching" on Baptism, fasting, prayer, prophets, and the Eucharist.

DISCERNMENT The process, associated with the virtue of prudence, by which we try to decide what God wills us to do in particular circumstances and for the future.

DISCIPLE A follower of Christ.

DISPENSATION An action of the official Church by which an individual or individuals are exempted from an ecclesiastical law, temporarily or permanently.

DISVALUE That which is antithetical to human growth.

DIVINE LAW An unchangeable decree of God regarding a structural practice or form.

DOCETISM An early heresy which held that Christ only "seemed" to have a human body.

DOCTRINE An official teaching of the Church.

DOCTRINE, DEVELOPMENT OF The process by which official teachings are revised in accordance with changes in historical circumstances and understanding.

DOGMA A doctrine which is promulgated with the highest authority and solemnity. Its denial is a *heresy* (see below).

DOGMATIC THEOLOGY Systematic reflection on the whole of Christian faith. Roughly equivalent to *systematic theology* (see below).

DONATISM A North African movement of the fourth century which held that Baptism had to be administered a second time to those who had left the Church and then returned.

DOUBLE EFFECT, PRINCIPLE OF The principle which holds that an evil effect can be permitted so long as it is not directly intended, is not the means of achieving a good effect, and is not out of proportion to the good effect.

DUALISM The general theological view that all reality is composed of, and arises from, distinct, absolutely independent, antagonistic, and coequal principles: Good and Evil.

DULIA Reverence and devotion given to the saints.

EBIONITES A first- and second-century ascetic group of Jewish Christians who considered Jesus to be the son of Mary and Joseph, not of God.

ECCLESIAL Pertaining to the Church as a mystery, the Body of Christ, and the People of God, as distinguished from *ecclesiastical,* which pertains to the Church as a structured institution.

ECCLESIOLOGY The theological study of the Church.

ECONOMY, DIVINE God's saving plan for humankind revealed through creation and the redemption. In Eastern theology, *economy* refers to the Church's concessions to human weaknesses in the fulfillment of laws and obligations.

ECUMENISM The movement which seeks to achieve unity of Christians within the Church and ultimately of all humankind throughout the "whole wide world" (the literal meaning of the word).

ENCYCLICAL A letter written by the pope and "circulated" throughout the whole Church and (more recently) beyond.

ENLIGHTENMENT The eighteenth-century philosophical movement which exalted intellectual freedom and moral autonomy.

EPHESUS A city in Asia Minor where the third ecumenical council was held in 431. It condemned *Nestorianism* (see below) and held that Mary is truly the Mother of God (*theotokos*).

EPISCOPACY The highest level of the sacrament of Holy Order. Those who are ordained to the episcopacy are called "bishops." The word is derived from *episkopos,* meaning "overseer."

ESCHATOLOGY Literally, "the study of the last things." That area of theology which focuses on the Kingdom of God, judgment, heaven, hell, purgatory, the resurrection of the body, and the Second Coming of Christ.

ETHICS, CHRISTIAN Another name for moral theology, historically more popular with Protestants than with Catholics.

EUCHARIST Literally, a "thanksgiving." The common name for the Mass, or Lord's Supper. Also, the third sacrament in the process of Christian initiation.

EUNOMIANISM An extreme form of Arianism, holding that the Son is created by the Father, and the Holy Spirit is created by the Son.

EVANGELIZATION The proclamation of the Gospel.

EX CATHEDRA Literally, "from the chair." Refers to infallible, or definitive, teachings of the pope as earthly head of the Church.

EXCOMMUNICATION The expulsion of an individual from the Church, more particularly from the Eucharist.

EXEGESIS, BIBLICAL The scientific interpretation of the texts of Sacred Scripture.

EX OPERE OPERANTIS "From the work of the worker." A phrase explaining how a *sacramental* (see below) achieves its effect: not only by the prayer of the Church but also, and necessarily, by the faith and disposition of the recipient and minister.

EX OPERE OPERATO "From the work done." A phrase explaining how a sacrament achieves its effect: not because of the faith of the recipient and/or the worthiness of the minister but because of the power of Christ who acts within and through it.

EXPIATION See *Atonement*.

EXTRA ECCLESIAM NULLA SALUS "Outside the Church no salvation." The belief that unless one is somehow related to the Church, that person cannot be saved. Vatican II used a more positive formula: "universal sacrament of salvation."

EXTREME UNCTION The former name for the sacrament of the Anointing of the Sick.

FAITH The gift of God by which we freely accept God's self-communication in Christ. One of the theological virtues.

FAITH DEVELOPMENT A growth in the living and understanding of faith that follows the stages of human maturation.

FATHERS OF THE CHURCH Writers of Christian antiquity who had a major impact on the doctrinal tradition of the Church. The period of the Fathers is said to have ended in the West in the mid-seventh century and in the East in the mid-eighth century.

FEMINIST THEOLOGY Positively, a theology that reflects on Christian faith and its traditions in the light of the experiences of women. Negatively, a way of doing theology that rejects its traditional androcentric and patriarchal presuppositions.

FIDEISM The nineteenth-century view that faith is without rational content or support.

FIDES FIDUCIALIS Luther's notion of faith as "trust," without objective content.

FILIOQUE Literally, "and [from] the Son." This word was added to the Nicene-Constantinopolitan Creed at the end of the seventh century, contending that the Holy Spirit proceeds from the Father and the Son as from a single principle. It was opposed by the Greek Church, which preferred the term *per Filium* to emphasize the primacy of God the Father in the work of salvation.

FLORENCE An Italian city where in 1439 the seventeenth ecumenical council attempted unsuccessfully to heal the East-West schism. It also defined the seven sacraments.

FORMAL NORM Points to moral values that *must* be pursued, e.g., "Be honest," "Do not commit murder." See *Material Norm* (below).

FORTITUDE A cardinal virtue by which we moderate our irascible appetites, steering us between fear and rashness.

FUNDAMENTAL OPTION The radical orientation of one's whole life toward or away from God. Akin to conversion. This moral concept is directly opposed to *legalism* (see below), which focuses on the morality of individual acts.

FUNDAMENTAL THEOLOGY That area of theology which deals with the most basic introductory questions: e.g., revelation, faith, authority, the ways of knowing God, the nature and task of theology itself.

FUNDAMENTALISM An interpretation of the Bible and church doctrine in a literal and nonhistorical manner.

GALLICANISM A form of national *conciliarism* (see above) peculiar to France (Gaul), and implicitly rejected by the First Vatican Council.

GAUDIUM ET SPES Vatican II's *Pastoral Constitution on the Church in the Modern World.*

GNOSTICISM The earliest of Christian heresies which denied the reality of the incarnation. Besides stressing the role of saving knowledge, it also denied the goodness of creation and of the material order.

GOSPEL The "good news" proclaimed by Jesus Christ and thereafter by the Apostles and the Church. The Gospel is interpreted and recorded in the four Gospels of Matthew, Mark, Luke, and John.

GRACE Literally, "a favor." The self-communication, or presence, of God.

GRACE, ACTUAL The presence of God given as a power to guide particular human actions.

GRACE, CREATED The presence of God in particular persons, manifested in virtues, in gifts of the Holy Spirit, etc.

GRACE, EFFICACIOUS A grace that is offered by God and accepted.

GRACE, MERELY SUFFICIENT Grace that is offered but not accepted.

GRACE, SANCTIFYING The abiding presence of God in the human person. Also called "habitual."

GRACE, UNCREATED The self-communication of God.

HEART The center and innermost place of a person's knowledge, feelings, and decisions.

HEART, SACRED The wounded heart of Jesus seen as a symbol of his self-sacrificing love for all. A devotion begun in the seventeenth century to counteract *Jansenism* (see below).

HEAVEN The dwelling place of God and the saints.

HELL The state of permanent separation from God.

HERESY Literally, a "choice." It is the denial of a *dogma* (see above).

HERMENEUTICS The science of interpretation; the body of principles which governs the interpretation of any statement or text.

HIERARCHY Literally, "rule by priests." It is the body of ordained ministers in the Church: pope, bishops, priests, and deacons.

HIERARCHY OF TRUTHS Pertains to the degrees of importance accorded to church teachings by reason of their relative proximity to the core of Christian faith (*Decree on Ecumenism*, n. 11).

HISTORICAL CONSCIOUSNESS A theological and philosophical mentality which is attentive to the impact of history on human thought and action and which, therefore, takes into account the concrete and the changeable. Distinguished from *classicism* (see above).

HISTORICITY That fundamental human condition by which we are set in time and shaped by the movement of history.

HISTORY The movement of the world toward the final Kingdom of God under the impact of God's grace and the shaping influence of human freedom.

HOLINESS Mark of the Church indicating that it is a community being transformed by the indwelling of the Holy Spirit.

HOLY ORDER[S] A sacrament by which members of the Church are ordained for the ministerial service of the Church as bishops, presbyters, and deacons.

HOLY SPIRIT The third Person of the Trinity, one in nature and equal in divine dignity to the Father and the Son. The principle of sanctification.

HOMOOUSIOS Literally, "of the *same* substance." Used in the teaching of the early Christological councils, especially Nicea (325), to affirm that the Father and the *Logos* (see below) are of the same substance, or divine nature.

HOPE A theological virtue by which we trust in the promises of God regarding eternal life, and we seek to hasten the coming of the Kingdom by working even now for the transformation of the world.

HYLOMORPHISM A medieval Scholastic notion which regarded all reality as composed of matter and form. The notion was applied to the theology of the Eucharist, grace, the human person, and the sacraments in general; e.g., the *matter* of a sacrament is what is used (water in Baptism), the *form* of a sacrament is the words and gestures (pouring the water and saying the baptismal formula); or, the body is the *matter* of the human person, the soul is the *form*.

HYPERDULIA The special reverence and devotion accorded to Mary as the Mother of God.

HYPOSTATIC UNION The permanent union of divine and human natures in the one divine Person (*hypostasis*) of the Word (*Logos*) in Jesus Christ (see *Chalcedon* above).

ICONOCLASM Literally, "the destroying of images." The negative attitude toward images (*icons*) and their veneration. An iconoclastic controversy raged in the East during the eighth and ninth centuries.

IDEALISM The philosophical attitude which identifies reality with ideas. It is distinguished from *realism* (see below).

IDOLATRY The worship of idols. The term applies to any tendency to equate something finite with the infinite (God).

IMMACULATE CONCEPTION The dogma defined by Pope Pius IX in 1854 which holds that the Blessed Virgin

Mary was free from sin from the very first moment of her existence. This is not to be confused with the *virginal conception* (see below).

IMPECCABILITAS The attribute of Jesus Christ by which he is incapable of sinning.

IMPECCANTIA The *de facto* sinlessness of Jesus.

INCARNATION The process by which the Word of God became flesh. (See also *Hypostatic Union*.)

INCULTURATION The process of adapting (without compromise) the Gospel and the Christian life to an individual culture. Negatively, it means that Christianity cannot be identified with any one culture.

INDEFECTIBILITY Pertains to the promise of Christ that the Church will last until the end of time without fundamental corruption of its faith and teaching. Not to be confused with *infallibility* (see below).

INDIFFERENTISM A theological attitude which holds that one religion is as good, or as bad, as another.

INDISSOLUBILITY The quality of permanence (literally "unbreakability") which applies to marriage.

INDULGENCE The partial or full remission of the temporal punishments still due to sins which have already been forgiven.

INERRANCY The immunity of Sacred Scripture from fundamental error about God and the things of God. Rooted in *inspiration* (see below).

INFALLIBILITY Literally, "immunity from error." The charism by which the Church is protected from fundamental error in formulating a specific teaching regarding a matter of faith or morals. It can be exercised by the pope and by an ecumenical council. Not to be confused with *indefectibility* (see above).

INFRALAPSARIAN Pertaining to the period of history after the "fall" of Adam.

INITIATION, CHRISTIAN The total liturgical and catechetical process of becoming a Christian through Baptism, Confirmation, and Eucharist.

INITIUM FIDEI Literally, the "beginning of faith." The grace of God is necessary for the whole process of faith, from beginning to end.

INSPIRATION, BIBLICAL The guidance of the Holy Spirit in the writing of Sacred Scripture, so that it can be called the Word of God.

INTEGRALISM A theological attitude, prevalent especially in France in the nineteenth and twentieth centuries, which insists that nothing is "whole" (integral) unless and until it is brought within the orbit of the Church.

INTERCOMMUNION See *Communicatio in Sacris* (above).

INTERNAL FORUM The realm of conscience and/or of the sacrament of Penance. A decision reached in the "internal forum" is known only to God, the individual, and the confessor or spiritual director.

IRENICISM A "peaceful" approach to problems of church unity which may try to water down existing differences in order to achieve reunion.

JANSENISM A seventeenth- and eighteenth-century movement in Europe, especially France, which stressed moral austerity, the evil of the human body and of human desires, a restrictive concept of grace, and a scrupulous approach to the reception of the sacraments.

JESUS OF HISTORY/CHRIST OF FAITH Refers to the distinction between Jesus as he actually was (and whom we can never fully know on the basis of historical evidence) and Jesus as he was understood and interpreted by the Church after the resurrection (namely, as the Christ).

JURIDICAL Pertains to a mentality that views the Christian life and the work of the Church primarily in terms of laws, obligations, and the duty to obey authority.

JUSTICE A cardinal virtue that is concerned with rights and duties in relationship to others, not only one-on-one (*commutative* justice) but also societally (*social* justice) and governmentally (*distributive* and *legal* justice).

JUSTIFICATION The event by which God, acting in Jesus Christ, makes us holy (just). The immediate effect of justification is *sanctification* (see below). The ultimate effect is *salvation* (see below). The foundation of justification is the *redemption* (see below).

KENOSIS A biblical term which refers to the "self-emptying" of Christ. He did not cling to his divinity but became obedient even unto death.

KERYGMA The "message" of the Gospel. That which was originally proclaimed.

KERYGMATIC THEOLOGY A theology which adheres closely to the literal meaning and emphasis of the biblical message.

KINGDOM OF GOD The reign, or rule, of God. It is the transforming presence of God in the heart, in groups, in the world at large, renewing and reconciling all things. It is both a process and the reality toward which the process is moving. Thus, it is "already" and "not yet."

KOINONIA Community, or fellowship, produced by the Holy Spirit.

LAITY Literally, "people." The People of God. Those who have been incorporated into the Church through Baptism, Confirmation, and Eucharist, but who have not been ordained or religiously professed.

LAST THINGS Death, judgment, heaven, hell, purgatory, Second Coming of Christ, resurrection of the body, and the fulfillment of the Kingdom of God.

LATERAN Refers to the Lateran Palace adjoining the church of St. John Lateran, the pope's cathedral church in Rome. The site of various synods and five ecumenical councils, the most important of which was the fourth (1215).

LATRIA The adoration due only to God.

LAW In the Old Testament: the Ten Commandments, the Torah, and other norms of conduct, founded in the *Covenant* (see above). In the New Testament: the law of the Gospel, fulfilled in the commandment of love of God and love of neighbor.

LAXISM A moral attitude which tries to find ways of getting around Christian obligations and which always resolves the doubt in favor of exemption, even when good reasons are not present.

LEGALISM A moral attitude which identifies morality with the literal observance of laws, even if the spirit of the law requires something more or different.

LEX ORANDI, LEX CREDENDI "The law of praying is the law of believing." Christian faith is expressed in Christian worship. Christian worship is, in turn, a norm of faith.

LIBERATION THEOLOGY A type of theology which emphasizes the motif of liberation (from poverty and oppression) in both Old and New Testaments and which reinterprets all doctrines in terms of that motif. Especially prominent in Latin America.

LIMBO The supposed permanent dwelling place of unbaptized infants who die in the state of Original Sin.

LITURGY The official public worship of the Church: the Eucharist, the other six sacraments, and the Liturgy of the Hours (Divine Office).

LOGOS The Word of God, the Second Person of the Trinity, who became flesh in the *incarnation* (see above).

LOGOS-ANTHROPOS CHRISTOLOGY "Word-man." A Christology "from below," emphasizing the humanity of Jesus. Characteristic of the School of Antioch.

LOGOS-SARX CHRISTOLOGY "Word-flesh." A Christology "from above," emphasizing the divinity of Christ. Characteristic of the School of Alexandria.

LUMEN GENTIUM Vatican II's *Dogmatic Constitution on the Church.*

LUMEN GLORIÆ "The light of glory." That power by which we are enabled to "see God face to face" in heaven. (See also *Beatific Vision.*)

MACEDONIANISM A fourth-century heresy which denied the divinity of the Holy Spirit. Condemned by the Council of Constantinople (381).

MAGISTERIUM The teaching authority of the Church, which belongs to some by reason of office (pope and bishops). Others contribute to the teaching mission by scholarly competence (e.g., theologians).

MANICHÆISM A blend of *dualism* and *Gnosticism* (see above for both), which began in the mid-third century and did not finally die out until the fourteenth century.

MANUALS Neoscholastic, Latin textbooks of dogmatic and moral theology in common use in Catholic seminaries before Vatican II.

MARCIONISM A second-century movement that rejected the Old Testament because of its alleged incompatibility with the God of love and the preaching of Jesus.

MARIOLOGY The theological study of the Blessed Virgin Mary in terms of her role in the Church and in our redemption.

MARKS OF THE CHURCH The essential qualities, or "notes," by which the Church is known: unity, holiness, catholicity, and apostolicity.

MARRIAGE The sacrament by which a man and a woman are united for life in a covenantal relationship modeled on the union of Christ and the Church.

MARTYR Literally, a "witness." One who is put to death because of his or her faith in Jesus Christ.

MASS The Eucharist, or Lord's Supper.

MATERIAL NORM Tells us what we should do, e.g., "Do not kill." Unlike a *formal norm* (see above), it is debatable and subject to exceptions.

MEDIATION The theological principle that God is available to us and acts upon us through secondary causes: persons, places, events, things, nature, history, and decisively in the humanity of Jesus Christ.

MEDIEVAL Pertaining to the period known as the Middle Ages, the beginning of which some place as early as the seventh century and the end as late as the sixteenth. The high Middle Ages (twelfth and thirteenth centuries) are sometimes mistakenly identified with the origins of Catholicism itself.

MERIT Spiritual "reward" earned from God for having performed some good action.

METANOIA See *Conversion.*

MINISTRY Literally, a "service." Any service rendered in the Church to assist in the fulfillment of its mission.

MIRACLE A special manifestation, or sign, of the presence and power of God in human history.

MISSION OF THE CHURCH That for which the Church has been "sent"; i.e., its purpose: to proclaim the Gospel in word, in sacrament, in witness, and in service.

MIXED MARRIAGE A marriage between a Catholic and one who is not a Catholic.

MODALISM A general theological approach to the Trinity which sees the three Persons as three different modes of the one God's operations, but not as three distinct Persons.

MODERNISM A generic early-twentieth-century movement in Catholicism condemned by Pope Pius X because it seemed to deny the permanence of dogmas and tended to reduce all doctrines to their rational or humanistic components.

MONARCHIANISM An early heretical belief that so stressed the unity of God that it denied the distinctly divine personhood of the Son.

MONASTICISM A style of Christian life that emphasizes life-in-community, common worship, poverty, celibacy, silence, and contemplation.

MONOGENISM The view that the whole human race is descended from a single couple, Adam and Eve. It is distinguished from *polygenism* (see below).

MONOPHYSITISM The teaching, condemned by the Council of Chalcedon (451), that the human nature of Christ was totally absorbed by the divine nature.

MONOTHEISM The belief in one God. It is distinguished from *polytheism* (see below).

MONOTHELITISM The view, rejected by the Third Council of Constantinople (681), that there is only one will in Christ, the divine will. Known in a variant form as *Monenergism*.

MONTANISM A second-century charismatic belief which stressed the imminent end of the world and imposed an austere morality in preparation for the event.

MORAL THEOLOGY That branch of theology which attends to the individual and social implications of the Gospel, and which draws normative inferences for the conduct of the Church and its members.

MORAL VALUES Those concrete good things which are essential to proper human living, e.g., the capacity for love. See also *Premoral Values* (below).

MORTAL SIN So fundamental a rejection of the Gospel and/or the will of God that, without contrition, it merits eternal punishment.

MYSTERY A reality imbued with the hidden presence of God. The term is most akin to *sacrament* (see below). It also refers to the plan of God for our salvation, as disclosed historically in Christ.

MYSTICISM The graced transformation of consciousness that follows upon a direct or immediate experience of the presence of God leading to deeper union with God.

NATURAL LAW The universal moral law given by God for all creatures, and knowable by reason alone.

NATURE The human condition apart from grace, but with the radical capacity to receive grace. ("Pure" nature, i.e., without the capacity for grace, does not exist.)

NEOORTHODOXY The early-twentieth-century movement within Protestantism (especially Karl Barth) which sought to return to the basic principles of Reformation theology, especially the primacy of the Word of God.

NEOPLATONISM The final stage of ancient Greek philosophy (third to sixth centuries) which strongly influenced certain Christian thinkers, especially Origen and Augustine. Everything emanates in a kind of hierarchical arrangement from the One and is destined to return to the One through a process of purification.

NEOSCHOLASTICISM A revival of medieval Scholastic theology and philosophy, with a heavy emphasis on nonhistorical orthodoxy, that shaped the content and tone of theology textbooks from the sixteenth century to Vatican II.

NEO-THOMISM A twentieth-century retrieval of Thomism, centered especially in France.

NESTORIANISM The teaching, condemned by the Council of Ephesus (431), that posited two separate persons in Jesus Christ, the one human and the other divine.

NICEA The city in Asia Minor where in 325 the first ecumenical council was held to condemn *Arianism* (see above).

NICENE-CONSTANTINOPOLITAN CREED Associated with the Council of Constantinople (381) but presupposing the creed of Nicea (325), this creed is widely used during the Eucharist and at Baptism.

NOMINALISM A medieval philosophical view which denied the reality of universal principles. Every substance is irreducibly individual.

ORDINATION A sacramental act, with a laying on of hands by a bishop, through which an individual is admitted to the diaconate, the presbyterate (priesthood), or the episcopate.

ORIGENISM A tendency in Eastern theology of the third through fifth centuries which emphasized the necessity and eternity of the world and of souls and which looked upon matter as a consequence of sin.

ORIGINAL JUSTICE The state in which the first human beings were thought to have existed before Original Sin.

ORIGINAL SIN The state of alienation from God in which all human beings are born.

ORTHODOXY Literally, "right praise." Consistency with the faith of the Church as embodied in Sacred Scripture, the early Christian writers, official teaching, and the liturgy.

ORTHOPRAXY Literally, "right practice." Doing the truth in justice and love.

PAPACY See *Petrine ministry.*

PARABLE A story which makes a theological point through the use of metaphors.

PARENESIS Literally, "exhortation." Preaching that is aimed at building up the community by practical recommendations or warnings.

PAROUSIA The Second Coming of Christ at the end of history.

PASCHAL MYSTERY The whole redemptive "passing over" of Christ through his life, death, resurrection, ascension, and exaltation, in which Christians participate through Baptism, the Eucharist, and the other sacraments.

PASTORAL Pertaining to the actual life of the Church, especially at the parish and diocesan levels.

PATRIPASSIANISM An early heresy that held that the Father suffered and died on the cross.

PATRISTIC Pertaining to the *Fathers of the Church* (see above).

PAULINE PRIVILEGE Based on 1 Corinthians 7:10–16, the principle which allows a convert to the Church to remarry if his or her unbaptized spouse does not also become a Christian.

PELAGIANISM A heresy with roots in the fifth century which declared that salvation is possible through human effort alone, without grace.

PENANCE The sacrament of Reconciliation by which the penitent is reconciled with God and the Church through the forgiveness of sins.

PENTATEUCH The first five books of the Old Testament: Genesis, Exodus, Leviticus, Numbers, and Deuteronomy. Also known as the *Torah*, or the *Law* (see above).

PERICHORESIS See *Circumincession*.

PERSON An existing being with the capacity for consciousness, freedom, and especially relationships. In the Trinity, the word *person* is used analogically; there are not three separate Gods, only different relationships in God.

PETRINE MINISTRY The service of unity and the strengthening of faith rendered to the universal Church by the Bishop of Rome. Also known as the papacy.

PETRINE PRIVILEGE Also known as the "Privilege of the Faith." It allows the pope to dissolve a marriage between a Christian and a non-Christian when the Christian wishes to marry another Christian or the non-Christian wishes to become a Catholic and remarry.

PHILOSOPHY The intellectual discipline concerned with the ultimate meaning of reality, but without assuming responsibility (as *theology* does) for articulating that meaning in terms of particular religious traditions.

PIETISTIC Pertaining to a spiritual or moral attitude which stresses personal devotion, often at the expense of sound biblical, theological, and doctrinal principles.

PLURALISM The inevitable variety of human experiences and cultural expressions. The opposite of *uniformity*.

PNEUMATOMACHIANS A late fourth-century sect that denied the full divinity of the Holy Spirit. Also called *Macedonians*.

PNEUMATOLOGICAL Pertaining to the Holy Spirit.

POLITICAL THEOLOGY A type of theology which stresses the relationship between Christian faith and the socio-political order or, more generally, between theory and practice.

POLYGENISM The view that the human race is descended not from a single pair of ancestors, but from many.

POLYTHEISM Belief in many gods.

POPE Literally, "father." A title accorded to various bishops and priests in the early Church, but reserved to the Bishop of Rome since the eleventh century.

POSITIVE THEOLOGY A branch of theology which deals with historical data. Also known as *historical theology*.

POTENTIA OBEDIENTIALIS The fundamental human capacity for grace.

PRAXIS Reflective action. Reflection which is the fruit of one's concrete experience and situation, and action which is the expression of such reflection.

PREAMBLES OF FAITH Those presuppositions of Christian faith that show its reasonableness, e.g., the existence of God.

PREDESTINATION The eternal decree of God regarding the destination, or final goal, of all reality and especially of humankind.

PREDESTINATIONISM The Calvinist doctrine that God decides, independently of a person's exercise of freedom and manifestation of good will, who will be saved and who will be damned. The latter decree is also known as *antecedent negative reprobation*.

PREEVANGELIZATION Those pastoral activities that are performed in order to prepare people for the preaching of the Gospel.

PREMORAL VALUES Those concrete good things that ought to be done or achieved, to the extent possible, e.g., physical health. See *Moral Values* (above).

PRESBYTER An "elder" of the early Church. A priest of the second order, i.e., less than a bishop but more than a deacon.

PRESBYTERATE The body of priests in a local church, or diocese.

PRIMACY The authority which the pope has over the whole Church as its leading bishop, or primate.

PRISCILLIANISM A fourth-century heresy which regarded the three Persons of the Trinity as three modes or facets of one divine Being.

PROBABILISM The moral system which holds that one can safely follow a theological opinion if it is proposed by someone having sufficient theological authority and standing. *Equiprobabilism* requires that the more lenient opinion be at least as strong as the stricter opinion. *Probabiliorism* requires that the more lenient opinion be stronger than the stricter opinion.

PROCESSIONS A theological term for the way in which the Son and the Holy Spirit originate from the Father. The derivation of the Son from the Father is called *generation* or *filiation*. That of the Holy Spirit from the Father and the Son is called *spiration*.

PROCESS THEOLOGY A type of theology which emphasizes the movement, dynamism, changeability, and relativity of God, of history, and of all reality.

PROPHECY Literally, a "speaking [or acting] on behalf [of God]." More specifically, the critical interpretation of past and present events against the standard of the future Kingdom of God.

PROPORTIONALISM A theory of moral analysis which holds that an action becomes morally wrong when, all things considered, there is no proportionate reason justifying it.

PROSELYTISM The active effort to persuade people by whatever means to abandon their present religious community and join another.

PROTOLOGY The "study of the first things" (creation, Original Justice, Original Sin).

PROVIDENCE God's abiding guidance of the whole created order toward the final Kingdom.

PRUDENCE A cardinal virtue, known also as the "rudder virtue," because without it there is no direction or stability in one's moral life. It has to do without choosing the right course in our moral actions.

PURGATORY The state of purification and/or maturation which one may need to enter after death and before the *beatific vision* (see above).

QUIETISM A seventeenth-century movement in France which held that we can do nothing at all for our salvation and that the way of Christian spirituality is a way of inwardness, of resignation, and of complete passivity.

RATIONALISM A system of thought that accords reason a privileged role in the pursuit of truth, even religious truth.

REALISM A philosophical view which emphasizes the objectivity of things, apart from the person thinking about them.

REAL PRESENCE The sacramental presence of Christ in the Eucharist.

RECEPTION The process by which official teachings and disciplinary decrees are accepted, assimilated, and interpreted by the whole Church.

RECONCILIATION See *Penance.*

REDEMPTION The act by which we are literally "bought back" from the bondage of sin into the grace of God by the work of Jesus Christ. See also *Soteriology.*

REIGN OF GOD The more active, or dynamic, expression for the *Kingdom of God* (see above). It is the Kingdom in process.

RELATIONS, DIVINE The ordering of the three Persons in the Trinity among themselves in a way that constitutes them as three distinct Persons in one God. There are four relations: paternity, filiation, active, and passive spiration.

RELIGION The external, social, institutionalized expression of our faith in God.

RELIGIOUS CONGREGATION/ORDER An organized group of Christians who have taken vows to live in community and to observe the evangelical counsels of poverty, chastity, and obedience.

RELIGIOUS EDUCATION That field which comes into existence at the point of intersection between theology and education. It is concerned with interpreting and directing human experience in light of Christian faith.

RES ET SACRAMENTUM Literally, "the reality and the sign." In sacramental theology, it refers to the lasting effect of a sacrament—e.g., the Real Presence of Christ in the Eucharist.

RES TANTUM Literally, "the reality alone." In sacramental theology, it refers to the immediate effect of a sacrament, namely, grace.

RESURRECTION The passage of Jesus from death to new life. The heart of the Paschal Mystery and of our redemption, and the basis of our hope in the resurrection of the body.

REVELATION God's self-disclosure (literally, "unveiling") to humankind through creation, events, persons, and especially Jesus Christ.

REVIVISCENCE The revival of grace, through subsequent contrition, from a *character* sacrament that had been received in *mortal sin* (see above for both).

RIGHT A power that we have to do things which are necessary for achieving the end or purpose for which we are destined as rational and free persons.

RIGHTEOUSNESS The state of being just in the sight of God.

RIGORISM A moral system that always resolves the doubt in favor of law over liberty. It is the opposite of *laxism* (see above).

RITE The order of service for celebrating a particular sacrament or series of sacraments (as in the Rite of Christian Initiation of Adults). It also designates the worship of a particular church, e.g., the Roman Rite.

ROMAN CATHOLICISM That tradition within the Catholic communion of churches which follows the Roman Rite.

ROME The Italian city which was the seat of the Roman Empire and later of the Catholic Church in the West. Oftentimes used generically for "the Vatican."

SABELLIANISM A third- and fourth-century heresy which held that God is three only in relation to the world. A form of *Modalism* (see above).

SACRAMENT In general, any visible sign of God's invisible presence. Specifically, a sign through which the Church manifests and celebrates its faith and communicates the saving grace of God. In Catholic doctrine there are seven: Baptism, Confirmation, Eucharist, Penance, Marriage, Holy Order, and the Anointing of the Sick.

SACRAMENTAL A grace-bearing sign, e.g., holy water, a crucifix, which does not so fully express the nature of the Church as a sacrament does and which, according to Catholic doctrine, does not carry the guarantee of grace associated with the seven sacraments.

SACRAMENTALITY, PRINCIPLE OF The fundamentally Catholic notion that all reality is potentially and in fact the bearer of God's presence and the instrument of divine action on our behalf. Closely related to the principle of *mediation* (see above).

SACRAMENTUM TANTUM Literally, "the sign alone." In sacramental theology, it is a rite or sacred action—e.g., the pouring of the water and the recitation of the formula "I baptize you...."

SAINTS Those who have been transformed fully by the grace of Christ and are with God in the heavenly kingdom.

SALVATION From the Latin word *salus,* meaning "health." It is the goal and end-product of creation, the incarnation, the redemption, conversion, justification, and sanctification. To be saved is to be "made whole" and eternally united with God and with one another in God.

SALVATION-HISTORY History perceived as the arena in which God progressively brings humankind toward the Kingdom, beginning with creation, ending with the Second Coming of Christ, with its midpoint in Jesus Christ.

SANCTIFICATION The state of holiness by reason of the presence of God within oneself. It is not to be confused with *justification* (see above). Eastern Christians prefer to speak of *deification.*

SATAN Literally, "the opponent." The personification of evil. The one in whom all evil is focused.

SCHISM A breach of church unity which occurs when a whole group or community separates itself from the rest of the Body of Christ. In Catholic theology, this happens when communion with the pope is broken.

SCHOLASTICISM A theological and philosophical movement in the Middle Ages attached to certain "schools" (thus, the term *scholastic*) and emphasizing the systematic interpretation of texts, especially of other theologians and philosophers rather than of the Bible and the early Christian writers.

SCRIPTURE The Bible understood and read as the Word of God.

SECTARIANISM An understanding of the Church as a relatively small, morally pure group of Christians living in a hostile world from which they must insulate and protect their faith.

SECULARISM A system of thought that denies the reality of the spiritual and/or supernatural order. Its belief is limited to this "world" (*sæculum*).

SEMI-PELAGIANISM The heresy, condemned by the Second Council of Orange (527), which held that the beginning of faith (*initium fidei*) is made independently of God's grace but that thereafter the grace of God is necessary for salvation.

SENSUS FIDELIUM Literally, "the sense of the faithful." It is one of the norms of theological truth, namely, the actual belief of Christians down through the centuries.

SEXISM A system of thought, speech, and behavior which demeans women and the experience of women because it views reality as essentially androcentric and patriarchal.

SHEOL The Old Testament name for the "underworld" inhabited by all the dead. Not to be confused with hell, which is a state of eternal alienation from God because of sin.

SIMUL JUSTUS ET PECCATOR Literally, "at the same time just and a sinner." A formula made famous by Martin Luther to make the point that even though we have been declared just by God because of Christ, we are still as corrupt as ever inside. Catholic doctrine insists that *justification* leads to *sanctification* (see above).

SIN Any deliberate infidelity to the will of God. It can be individual or social and systemic. Sins which reverse our *fundamental option* (see above) for God, are *mortal sins*. Sins which reflect poorly on our commitment to God but which do not reverse our course toward God are *serious sins*. Less serious sins are *venial sins*. Below those in gravity are *imperfections*.

SOCIAL DOCTRINE The body of official teachings, developed since Pope Leo XIII in 1891, which identify the implications of the Gospel in matters pertaining to social justice, peace, and human rights.

SOLA FIDE Literally, "by faith alone." The Protestant principle that we are saved by faith alone, not by good works. Catholic doctrine insists that faith must issue in good works and that good works are saving insofar as they are expressions of faith.

SOLA GRATIA Literally, "by grace alone." The Protestant principle that we are saved by grace alone, i.e., by

God's action and not at all by our own. Catholic doctrine insists that God requires our free cooperation although it is God alone who makes that cooperation possible.

SOLA SCRIPTURA Literally, "by Scripture alone." The Protestant principle that the Word of God is given to us in the Bible alone and not in the official teachings of the Church. Catholic doctrine insists that the Bible itself is the Church's book—i.e., that the authority of the Church has determined which books are inspired and, therefore, *canonical*. Furthermore, all official teachings are subject to the authority of the Word of God as contained in the Bible.

SOPHIA Literally, "wisdom." Personified as God's agent in creation and a prophetess who invites to her feast those who are not yet wise (Proverbs 8:1–36; 9:1–6). Christ, too, is personified as wisdom, a female principle.

SOTERIOLOGY Literally, "the study of salvation." It is that area of theology which focuses on the passion, death, resurrection, and exaltation of Christ insofar as they bring about our salvation.

SOUL The spiritual principle of human beings which survives after death.

SPIRATION Literally, "breathing." A technical term that describes the way the Spirit proceeds from the Father and the Son.

SPIRITUALITY, CHRISTIAN Life in the Holy Spirit who incorporates the Christian into the Body of Jesus Christ, through whom the Christian has access to God the Creator in a life of faith, hope, love, and service.

SUBJECT The human *person* (see above) insofar as the person is conscious, interrelates with others, and freely determines who and what he or she will become.

SUBORDINATIONISM A second- and third-century heresy which held that the Son and the Holy Spirit are less than the Father because they proceed from the Father. Therefore, the Son and the Spirit are not fully divine.

SUBSIDIARITY A principle in Catholic social doctrine which holds that nothing should be done by a higher agency which can be done as well, or better, by a lower agency.

SUMMA THEOLOGIÆ Literally, a "summary of theology." The major work of systematic theology done by Thomas Aquinas.

SUPERNATURAL Pertaining to that which exceeds the power and capacity of human nature apart from the grace of God.

SUPERNATURAL EXISTENTIAL A term coined by Karl Rahner, meaning our radical capacity for God. It is the permanent modification of the human person, in the depths of one's being, by which the person is transformed from within and oriented toward God. It is not grace itself, but God's offer of grace.

SYMBOL A sign of some other reality. In religious usage, it is close to the meaning of *sacrament* (see above), i.e., a visible expression of an invisible reality. The word may also mean a creed or a basic belief, as in "symbol of faith."

SYNOD An official assembly of the Church at the international, national, regional, provincial, or diocesan levels.

SYNOPTICS The first three Gospels, Matthew, Mark, and Luke, so called because when they are read side by side (synoptically), certain parallels in structure and content readily emerge.

SYSTEMATIC THEOLOGY That theology which tries to see the Christian tradition as a whole, by understanding the whole in terms of the interrelationships among all its parts, and each part in terms of its relationship to other parts and to the whole.

TELEOLOGICAL Pertaining to a way of doing moral theology which emphasizes the end (*telos*), or purpose, of human existence.

TEMPERANCE A cardinal virtue by which we humanize and moderate our concupiscible appetites and passions.

THEODICY The discipline that deals with the knowledge of God available through reason alone. Also known as *natural theology.*

THEOLOGOUMENON A nondoctrinal theological interpretation that cannot be verified or refuted on the basis of historical evidence, but that can be affirmed because of its close connection with some defined doctrine about God.

THEOLOGY The ordered effort to understand, interpret, and systematize our experience of God and of Christian faith. It is "faith seeking understanding" (Anselm).

THEOTOKOS Literally, "the bearer of God." The title given to Mary at the Council of Ephesus (431), to establish that Mary is truly the "Mother of God" and not only the mother of the human Jesus.

THOMISM An approach to theology and philosophy derived from Thomas Aquinas.

TRADITION Both the process of "handing on" the faith and that which has been handed on. Tradition (uppercase) includes Scripture, the essential doctrines of the Church, the Eucharist and the other sacraments, and so forth. Tradition (lowercase) includes changeable customs, institutions, teachings, and practices.

TRADITIONALISM The nineteenth-century opinion, rejected by Vatican I, that reason can know nothing at all about religious truth because such knowledge comes only through the revelation that has been "handed down" to us. As a modern term, it refers to the attitude of Catholics radically opposed to the reforms of Vatican II.

TRANSCENDENTAL Pertaining to that which is above and beyond the ordinary, the concrete, the tangible—i.e., to God.

TRANSCENDENTAL THOMISM That twentieth-century approach to theology which is rooted in the principle that God is already present to life as a principle that renders all life open to becoming something more than it is already.

TRANSUBSTANTIATION The official Catholic teaching, given by the Council of Trent, that the substance of the bread and the wine are changed into the substance of Christ's body and blood at the Eucharist, so that nothing of the bread and wine remains except what is accidental. To be distinguished from *consubstantiation* (see above).

TRENT The Italian city in which the nineteenth ecumenical council was held from 1545 to 1563, and hence the council itself. This council was the Catholic Church's principal response to the Protestant Reformation. It defined the canon of Sacred Scripture, Original Sin, grace, justification, the seven sacraments, etc. The primary influence on Catholic life until the pontificate of John XXIII (1958–1963).

TRIDENTINE Pertaining to a mentality that favors a more conservative, legalistic approach to Catholic doctrine and life.

TRINITY, ECONOMIC The exterior activity of the Trinity in history.

TRINITY, IMMANENT The so-called inner life of the Trinity.

TRITHEISM Belief in three gods. A distortion of the doctrine of the Trinity.

TUTIORISM The moral system whereby one always chooses the "safer" course.

TWELVE, THE The twelve men, symbolizing the twelve tribes of Israel, called and "sent" by Jesus to carry his message of the Kingdom of God to the world.

TYPE A person in whom the qualities of a greater or later reality are somehow "typified" or anticipated—e.g., Mary as a "type" of the Church, and Moses as a "type" of Christ.

ULTRAMONTANISM Literally, "beyond the mountains" (the Alps). It is a form of rigid *traditionalism* (see above) developed in France, distrustful of theological reflection, and militantly loyal to the Holy See.

UNITY A mark of the Church whereby the unifying presence of the Holy Spirit is manifested.

UTILITARIANISM A moral system which judges the morality of human acts in terms of the happiness or good that they bring about.

VATICAN The city-state surrounded by Rome and under the jurisdiction of the papacy. The site of the twentieth and twenty-first ecumenical councils. *Vatican I* addressed itself to questions of reason and faith, and papal primacy and papal infallibility. *Vatican II* reformed the liturgy and broadened the Church's understanding of its mission in the world, the role of the laity, and ecumenism.

VENIAL SIN A less serious infidelity to the will of God, sufficient to diminish one's Christian character but not to reverse one's fundamental orientation toward God.

VIATICUM Literally, "food for the journey." The last sacrament, i.e., the final reception of Holy Communion before death.

VICAR OF CHRIST A traditional title for a bishop. Now applied exclusively to the Bishop of Rome.

VICAR OF PETER The most traditional title designating the function of the Bishop of Rome.

VIRGINAL CONCEPTION The belief that Jesus was conceived in the womb of Mary without the cooperation of a human father. Not to be confused with the *Immaculate Conception* (see above).

VIRTUE The facility, disposition, or attitude that moves one to accomplish moral good and to do it joyfully and perseveringly even against obstacles and at the cost of sacrifice.

VOLUNTARISM A theological and philosophical view which exaggerates the place and function of the human will in the attainment of truth as well as moral good. It is the opposite of *rationalism* (see above).

VULGATE The name given since the thirteenth century to the Latin translation of the Bible done by St. Jerome.

WORLD The totality of created reality. Insofar as it is shaped and directed by human consciousness and human freedom under the grace of God, the world is identical with *history* (see above).

WORSHIP Adoration of God expressed publically and officially (*liturgy*) or through various prayers and devotions.

YAHWEH The Old Testament name for God.

INDEX OF SUBJECTS

This index should be used in conjunction with the Table of Contents, Index of Personal Names, and Glossary.

Catholic social doctrine, 10–11, 912–16, 1001–7
Catholic Worker Movement, 1043
Catholicism: philosophical focus of, 1192–96
Catholicity, 698, 717
Celibacy, 63, 560, 563, 609, 623, 838, 858, 870
Cenobitism, 1023
Centesimus Annus, 715, 914, 915, 942, 948, 1001, 1002, 1004
Chalcedon, Council of, 45, 464, 465, 468, 474–77, 480, 493, 509–10, 531, 547, 548, 625, 637, 869, 870
Challenge of Peace, The, 717–18, 915
Character (moral), 925–26
Character (sacramental), 795–96
Charismatic renewal, 1045, 1051, 1054
Charisms, 173, 366–67
Charity. *See* Love
Chastity, 949. *See also* Evangelical counsels
Christian ethics, *See* Moral theology
Christian Family Movement, 1043
Christianity: and Hellenistic culture, 448; and Judaism, 384–85; as one, true religion, 363, 389, 614; and other religions, 379–85; and the poor, 448; uniqueness of, 280–81
Christifideles Laici, 776
Christology, 397–98, 455, 464–65, 491–533; "from above," 493–95, 500, 506, 513–17, 527, 799; "from below," 493–513, 517, 799, 911; cosmic, 497; and ecclesiology, 522, 571–73; Orthodox, 526–29; Protestant, 517–26; and soteriology, 503; and world religions, 515–16
Christomonism, 278, 530
Church, the: and authority, 685, 739–50; as Body of Christ, 600–601, 609; as Bride of Christ, 706; call to holiness, 1043–44; Catholicity of, 698; as communion, 580, 709, 720–22, 756, 758; as communion of churches, 684; as communion of saints, 705–6; as community of

disciples, 68, 698, 714, 718, 724, 1116, 1146; and culture, 673, 678; definition of, 723–24; and dialogue, 699–700, 713; in diaspora, 660–61; "domestic," 863; etymology of, 579–82; founding of, 577–79, 799; Germanization of, 618–19, 869–70; in history, 607–49; and the Holy Spirit, 582–83, 597, 601–2, 702, 704, 709; "house church," 597; as institution, 719–20; and Judaism, 596, 598–99, 608, 611–12, 677; justice in, 711–12, 718, 915–16, 1006; and the Kingdom of God, 586–87, 658, 670, 673, 685–86, 692, 694, 699, 708, 709, 724–25, 726, 727, 728, 730, 1132–33, 1138, 1156; and laity, 671, 678, 747; and liberation, 701–3; local church, 709, 723–24; and Mary, 671; 1107–9; and ministry, 767–72; mission of, 591–92, 660, 672–73, 683–84, 685, 692–94, 699, 701–3, 705, 707, 708, 710, 711–12, 715–16, 724–29, 915–16; and missions, 642, 677; models of, 692–98, 718–23; as monarchical, 658, 670, 755–56; as mother, 683; as mystery, 610, 669, 1197–98; necessity of, 659, 729–33; and non-Christian religions, 389, 676–77; notes of, 659; as one, true Church, 684, 733; and other churches, 670, 684, 685; origins of, 572–602, 611–13; as People of God, 598–99, 609, 670, 671, 675, 683; and the political order, 673, 722, 729, 1010; as prophet, 726; as sacrament, 661–62, 669–70, 674, 683, 692, 702, 708, 916; and the sacraments, 587, 815–16, 819, 830, 842–43, 848, 863, 877; as sacrament of universal salvation, 673, 800, 836; and salvation, 694; as servant, 88, 722–23, 728–29; social teachings of, 912–16, 1001–7; and state, 614–15, 619–20, 627–29; 662–63; structure of, 593–94, 670–71; as

INDEX OF PERSONAL NAMES

ABOUT THE AUTHOR

Richard P. McBrien, a priest of the Archdiocese of Hartford, has authored fifteen books on theology. He is the Crowley-O'Brien-Walter professor of theology and former chairman of the department of theology at the University of Notre Dame. Until 1980 he was professor of theology at Boston College and director of its Institute of Religious Education and Pastoral Ministry. He is past president of the Catholic Theological Society of America, and in 1976 he received the Society's John Courtney Murray Award "for distinguished achievement in theology." Father McBrien received a 1980 Christopher Award for *Catholicism*, and in 1981 *Catholicism* received the Annual Book Award from the College Theology Society.

Richard McBrien has taught and lectured at many colleges and universities throughout the nation—among them, Harvard University, Yale University, Cornell University, Purdue University, the University of Wisconsin, Stanford University, the University of Minnesota, Andover Newton Theological School, and the Weston School of Theology in Cambridge, Massachusetts. He has published many articles and reviews in professional and popular journals, and his syndicated weekly theology column has won several awards from the Catholic Press Association as the best column in its field.

His ecumenical activities have included the chairmanship of the Joint Graduate Program of Boston College and Andover Newton Theological School, two terms as a trustee of the Boston Theological Institute (the largest ecumenical consortium in the United States), and the chairmanship of the Catholic Theological Society of America's special committee to evaluate the bilateral consultations.

Many will recognize Father McBrien as an on-air commentator on Catholic events for network television.